5, 6, 7 Years

Aardema, Verna. *Borreguita and the Coyote*, illustrated by Petra Mathers. Knopf, 1991.

Ahlberg, Janet and Allan Ahlberg. *The Jolly Postman*. Little, Brown, 1986.

Anno, Mitsumasa. *Anno's Counting Book*. Crowell, 1977.

Cleary, Beverly. *Ramona the Brave*, illustrated by Alan Tiegreen. Morrow, 1975.

Cooney, Barbara. *Miss Rumphius*. Viking, 1982.

de Paola, Tomie. *Strega Nona*. Prentice-Hall, 1975.

Huck, Charlotte. *Princess Furball*, illustrated by Anita Lobel. Greenwillow, 1989.

Hutchins, Pat. *The Doorbell Rang*. Greenwillow, 1986.

Hyman, Trina Schart. *Little Red Riding Hood*. Holiday, 1983.

Lobel, Arnold. *Frog and Toad Are Friends*. Harper, 1970.

Prelutsky, Jack, ed. *The Random House Book of Poetry for Children*, illustrated by Arnold Lobel. Random, 1983.

Rylant, Cynthia. *Henry and Mudge Take the Big Test*, illustrated by Sucie Stevenson. Bradbury, 1991.

Sendak, Maurice. *Where the Wild Things Are*. Harper, 1963.

Steig, William. *Doctor De Soto*. Farrar, Straus, 1982.

Steptoe, John. *Mufaro's Beautiful Daughters: An African Tale*. Lothrop, 1987.

Wilder, Laura Ingalls. *Little House in the Big Woods*, illustrated by Garth Williams. Harper, 1953.

Williams, Vera B. *A Chair for My Mother*. Greenwillow, 1982.

Yolen, Jane. *Owl Moon*, illustrated by John Schoenherr. Philomel, 1987.

7, 8, 9 Years

Burnett, Francis Hodgson. *The Secret Garden*, illustrated by Graham Rust. David R. Godine, 1987 (1911).

Cameron, Ann. *The Most Beautiful Place in the World*, illustrated by Thomas B. Allen. Knopf, 1988.

Cleary, Beverly. *Ramona Quimby, Age 8*, illustrated by Alan Tiegreen. Morrow, 1981.

Cole, Joanna. *The Magic School Bus Inside the Human Body*, illustrated by Bruce Degen. Scholastic, 1989.

de Regniers, Beatrice Schenk, ed. *Sing a Song of Popcorn*. Scholastic, 1988.

Fleischman, Sid. *The Whipping Boy*, illustrated by Peter Sis. Greenwillow, 1986.

Fritz, Jean. *Where Do You Think You're Going, Christopher Columbus?*, illustrated by Margot Tomes. Putnam, 1980.

Gollenbeck, Peter. *Teammates*, illustrated by Paul Bacon. Harcourt, 1991.

Greenfield, Eloise. *Honey, I Love and Other Love Poems*, illustrated by Leo and Diane Dillon. Crowell, 1978.

Grimm, Jacob and Wilhelm Grimm. *Snow White and the Seven Dwarfs*, illustrated by Nancy Ekholm Burkert. Farrar, Straus, 1972.

L'Engle, Madeleine. *A Wrinkle in Time*. Farrar, Straus, 1962.

Lester, Julius. *The Tales of Uncle Remus: The Adventures of Brer Rabbit*, illustrated by Jerry Pinkney. Dial, 1987.

Lewis, C. S. *The Lion, the Witch, and the Wardrobe*, illustrated by Pauline Baynes. Macmillan, 1961.

MacLachlan, Patricia. *Sarah, Plain and Tall*. Harper, 1985.

Osborne, Mary Pope. *American Tall Tales*, illustrated by Michael McCurdy. Knopf, 1990.

Stanley, Fay. *The Last Princess: The Story of Princess Ka'iulani of Hawai'i*, illustrated by Diane Stanley. Four Winds, 1991.

Wiesner, David. *Tuesday*. Clarion, 1991.

Williams, Karen Lynn. *Galimoto*, illustrated by Catherine Stock. Lothrop, 1990.

Yagawa, Sumiko. *The Crane Wife*, translated by Katherine Paterson, illustrated by Suekichi Akaba. Morrow, 1981.

(continued)

Children's Literature
in the
Elementary School

FIFTH
EDITION

Children's Literature in the Elementary School

FIFTH EDITION

CHARLOTTE S. HUCK
THE OHIO STATE UNIVERSITY

SUSAN HEPLER

JANET HICKMAN
THE OHIO STATE UNIVERSITY

HARCOURT BRACE COLLEGE PUBLISHERS

FORT WORTH   PHILADELPHIA   SAN DIEGO   NEW YORK   ORLANDO   AUSTIN

SAN ANTONIO   TORONTO   MONTREAL   LONDON   SYDNEY   TOKYO

Editor in Chief	Ted Buchholz
Acquisitions Editor	Jo-Anne Weaver
Developmental Editor	Karee Galloway
Project Editor	Angela Williams
Senior Production Manager	Kenneth A. Dunaway
Senior Book Designer	Serena Barnett Manning/ Vicki McAlindon Horton
Photo/Permissions Editor	Sandra Lord
Cover/Part-Opening Photos	Skeeter Hagler
Illustrations	Candice Swanson

Address for Editorial Correspondence
Harcourt Brace College Publishers, 301 Commerce Street, Suite 3700, Forth Worth, TX 76102

Address for Orders
Harcourt Brace & Company, 6277 Sea Harbor Drive, Orlando, FL 32887
1-800-782-4479, or 1-800-433-0001 (in Florida)

Credits and acknowledgments begin on page 855.

ISBN: 0–03–047528-7

Library of Congress Catalogue Number: 92–70635

Printed in the United States of America
4 5 6 7 8 9 0 1   036   9 8 7 6 5 4 3

*To all those students and teachers whom we have taught
and from whom we have learned . . .*

Preface

The fifth edition of *Children's Literature in the Elementary School* is written for all adults with an interest in providing good literature for children. It also provides a rationale and suggestions to teachers for planning and evaluating a literature-based curriculum. The text is designed for classes in children's literature at the pre-service and graduate levels in education or English departments and in library schools in colleges and universities. It may also be used for in-service courses and as a useful resource for the school professional library.

PURPOSES

Our primary purpose in writing this textbook is the same as in the previous four editions and updates—to share our knowledge and enthusiasm for the literature of childhood with students, teachers, and librarians in the hope that they, in turn, will communicate their excitement about books to the children they teach. As a nation, we have become so concerned with teaching the skills of reading that we have often neglected to help children discover the joys of reading. We believe that children become readers only by reading many books of their own choosing and by hearing high-quality literature read aloud with obvious delight and enthusiasm. It is our hope that the students, teachers, and librarians who read this book will be able to create in children a love of good books and a joy in reading them. We emphasize the development of lifetime readers in all teaching suggestions and in Part Three of this text.

The growth of the field of children's literature has been phenomenal with the number of books published annually increasing fivefold since the first edition of this text was published in 1961. With more than 73,000 children's books in print, prospective or in-service teachers and librarians need a guide for selecting the best ones, based on a knowledge of book selection criteria and an understanding of children's responses to literature. Chapter 1 and each genre chapter provide guidelines for evaluating books, while Chapter 2 presents current research on children's responses to books.

Educators have finally realized the importance of story and real books in developing readers who not only know *how* to read but who *do* read. Increasingly, teachers are using children's books both in the reading program and throughout the curriculum. Superb informational books and biographies can enhance every subject taught in the curriculum by providing readers with the most up-to-date information and facts. Chapters on developing early literacy, evaluating informational books and biography, and planning and evaluating the literature program all speak to the development of readers.

ORGANIZATION

The three-part organization of *Children's Literature in the Elementary School* emphasizes the triple focus of this text: the reader, the book, and teaching. Part One emphasizes the values and criteria for choosing and using literature with children at various stages in their development. It also includes a historical overview of the ways in which children's literature has changed over the years. Part Two provides an in-depth look at the various genres of children's literature and establishes evaluative criteria for each one. Part Three focuses on teaching children, structuring learning in classrooms, using literature across the curriculum, and evaluating literature-based reading programs.

NEW TO THIS EDITION

Twelve new *Teaching Features* have been included, one in each chapter with the exception of Chapter 1. These authentic teaching examples, which include actual children's work and pictures from real classrooms, show exciting literature-based programs in action.

We have also given increased attention to literature that reflects varied cultures. Rather than devote a single chapter to multicultural and cross-cultural literature, however, we maintain that such literature should be integrated into all areas of the curriculum. In this textbook, we have discussed multicultural literature as a part of each genre or subject area. Students are introduced to picture storybooks, poetry, novels, and information and biographies about people of all races and all cultural backgrounds. This point of view assures that the literature and accomplishments of all groups will be a part of every subject taught. Guidelines for evaluating multicultural literature appear in Chapter 9 in the section "Living in a Diverse World." *Teaching Features* in Chapters 9 and 13 also focus on multicultural literature, while the opening anecdote in Chapter 13 describes an all-school thematic study of Africa.

The boxed *Resources for Teaching* include new charts on "Mother Goose Books," "Books that Introduce Aspects of Fantasy Novels," "Some Native-American Folktales by Region," "Fooling with Traditional Literature," "Books that Serve as Writing Models," "Author Autobiographies," and "Books about Quilts and Stitchery." The many other features, charts, and annotated bibliographies have been updated and reformatted. In Chapter 12, "Guiding In-Depth Study of Books" has been expanded with a special section on "Making and Using Guides." A model based on a picture storybook is featured here to give teachers an easy and useful format for writing their own curricula from a single book. Two new themes have been added to the curriculum webs that conclude Chapter 12: "Studying an Author: Pat Hutchins" and "Stewards of the Earth: Ecology Web."

Other sections that reflect new or expanded coverage include "Trends in Informational Books," "Critical Thinking," "Talk About Books,"
"Literature in the Writing Program," "Readers Theater," and "Evaluation and Assessment." In addition, the Ages and Stages chart in Chapter 2 now extends through the middle school. Each chapter has been rewritten to include the latest research and the newest titles. More than half of the poetry selections are new to this edition. New color pictures have been used throughout the text.

From endpaper to endpaper, we have hoped to produce a practical textbook that will serve as a reference both for students who are just beginning their teaching and for teachers and librarians already in the field. We believe teachers and librarians are professional people who want a book of substance, documented with pertinent research and based on real practice in the classroom. This is the kind of book we have tried to write.

SPECIAL FEATURES

- ◆ *Teaching Features* focus on ways teachers have actually used literature as the heart of curriculum.
- ◆ *Guidelines for Evaluation* provide criteria for evaluating books within each genre, as well as suggestions and criteria for evaluating children's responses to literature and literature-based programs.
- ◆ *Resources for Teaching* present a wide variety of useful information regarding children, book titles, and curriculum concerns in a compact, easily accessible format.
- ◆ *Related Readings* at the end of each chapter present a comprehensive annotated selection of books, articles, and research relevant to the chapter discussion.
- ◆ *Suggested Learning Experiences* at the end of each chapter serve as a built-in study guide for sharing and comparing books with elementary-age children or university students.
- ◆ *Appendixes* include "Children's Book Awards," "Book Selection Aids," "Publishers' Addresses" and Book Club addresses.
- ◆ *Endpapers* serve as an introductory core to the field of children's literature by providing an updated list of 110 books to read aloud to six overlapping age groups.

INSTRUCTOR'S MANUAL

Skillfully prepared by Mary Lou White of Wright State University, the instructor's manual is a valuable resource for teaching and evaluating students' understanding of children's literature.

Teaching suggestions focus on both lectures and participatory activities. Recommendations for poetry and brief readings to stimulate class discussions accompany each lecture topic. Guidelines and recommendations for using audiovisual material are listed at the end of each chapter.

A special section in the instructor's manual is devoted to helping professors assist students in reading and studying a textbook of this type. Guided reading, key terms, and chapter summaries help students determine which sections of each chapter should be read in-depth and which ones can be skimmed and used for reference.

Appendixes include materials that can be duplicated for distribution and a list of "Book Cart Books," an annotated bibliography of books designed to motivate students to explore further particular topics.

In addition to traditional true-false, multiple-choice, and essay test questions, the instructor's manual includes many suggestions for qualitative evaluation.

Acknowledgments

No one writes a book of this magnitude without the help of friends. We are deeply indebted to many people: the teachers, librarians, and children in the schools where we have always been welcomed; our students at The Ohio State University and elsewhere, both undergraduates and graduates, who have shared with us their insights into children's responses and interpretations of literature; and those teachers who have sent pictures of and allowed us to take pictures in their classrooms. We thank them all and hope they continue to share their classroom experiences and enthusiasm for children's literature.

Specifically, we wish to express our appreciation to the following teachers and schools who shared their children's work and classroom photos with us: Marlene Harbert and other faculty members at Barrington Road School, Upper Arlington, Ohio; Diane Driessen, librarian, and Jean Sperling, Peggy Harrison, and Peg Reed at Wickliffe Alternative School, Upper Arlington, Ohio; Kristen Kerstetter and the staff at Highland Park School, Grove City, Ohio; Marilyn Parker at Columbus School for Girls; Arleen Stuck, Richard Roth, and Melissa Wilson at Columbus Public Schools; Lisa Dapoz and Joan Fusco at Emerson Elementary School, Westerville, Ohio; Linda Woolard at Miller Elementary School, Newark, Ohio; Rebecca Thomas, Shaker Heights Public Schools, Ohio; Barbara Friedberg and other faculty members at the Martin Luther King Jr. Laboratory School, Evanston Public Schools, Illinois; Joan Manzione, librarian, Susan Steinberg, Marci El-Baba and other staff members at George Mason Elementary School, Alexandria City Public Schools, Virginia; Shirley Bealor at Fairfax County Public Schools, Virginia; Nancy Anderson and Joan Schleicher at Mission School, Redlands Public Schools, California; Sharon Schmidt and other faculty members at Idyllwild Elementary School, Idyllwild, California; Janine Batzle at Esther L. Watson School, Anaheim, California; Joan Nassam and other faculty members at Mt. Eden Normal School in Auckland, New Zealand; Colleen Fleming at Mangere Bridge School, Auckland, New Zealand; Leanna Traill from Auckland, New Zealand; and Roy Wilson formerly at Dhahran Hills Elementary School, Dhahran, Saudi Arabia.

We also wish to thank Sally Oddi and her staff at Cover to Cover Bookstore in Columbus, Ohio; Katherine Thomerson at The Frugal Frigate Bookstore in Redlands, California; and Marilyn Dugan, Sheilah Egan and their staff at A Likely Story Bookstore in Alexandria, Virginia for their counsel and gracious help in obtaining and loaning us hard-to-find books. We are grateful to The Ohio State University Photography Department and to Larry Rose, photographer, Redlands, California, for their careful work in photographing many of the pictures for this edition. We also wish to thank Connie Compton and Regina Weilbacher for special photographs.

We are indebted to Barbara Chatton at the University of Wyoming for preparing Appendix B, "Book Selection Aids"; to Roy Wilson for obtaining the poetry permissions; to Roy and Thelma Wilson for careful help in preparing the Index; to Barbara Peterson for help in securing photographs; to Mary Lou White at Wright State

University for preparing the Instructor's Manual; and to Barbara Fincher, a faithful friend who has helped with almost every edition of this book and who skillfully typed a part of this one.

We express gratitude to the following reviewers of this edition whose comments and suggestions were most helpful: Amy L. Cohn, Children's Literature Specialist; Maryann Eeds, Arizona State University; Carol J. Fisher, The University of Georgia; Barbara Z. Kiefer, Teachers College, Columbia University; Linda Leonard Lamme, University of Florida; Susan Lehr, Skidmore College; Jill P. May, Purdue University; Amy McClure, Ohio Wesleyan University; Joy Moss, University of Rochester.

We give special thanks to our friends at Harcourt Brace Jovanovich including Jo-Anne Weaver, acquisitions editor, for her persistence in obtaining permission for color pictures throughout the text; to Karee Galloway, developmental editor, for her careful attention to detail; to Angela Williams, our remarkable project editor who knows when to use *which* and *that* correctly; and to Sandra Lord who cheerfully obtained all picture permissions.

Finally, we want to thank our families for their patience, tolerance, and sheer endurance. There is no adequate way to thank friends and family except to wonder at the glory of having had their company and support in creating this text.

Charlotte S. Huck
Susan Hepler
Janet Hickman

Contents

Children's Literature in the Elementary School

FIFTH
EDITION

Children's Literature in the Elementary School

FIFTH EDITION

Part One

Learning About Books and Children

Chapter One

Valuing Literature for Children

Was there ever a baby who didn't giggle with delight when her toes were touched to the accompaniment of "This little pig went to market"? Children's introduction to literature comes in the crib as babies listen to Mother Goose rhymes and nursery songs. It continues with the toddler's discovery of *Where's Spot?* by Eric Hill or Eric Carle's *The Very Hungry Caterpillar.* Later, children beg to hear Margaret Wise Brown's *Goodnight Moon* or Beatrix Potter's *The Tale of Peter Rabbit* just one more time.

If he is fortunate in his teachers the primary child will hear stories two and three times a day. He will see his own reaction to a new baby in the family mirrored in *Julius, the Baby of the World* by Kevin Henkes or *Peter's Chair* by Ezra Jack Keats. He will identify with the feelings of Max, who when scolded takes off in his imagination to *Where the Wild Things Are* in the book by Maurice Sendak. And somewhere in those early years he will discover that he can read, and the magical world of literature will open before him.

The growing child experiences loneliness and fear as she imagines what it would be like to survive alone on an island for eighteen years as Karana did in *Island of the Blue Dolphins* by Scott O'Dell. She encounters personal toughness and resiliency as she lives the life of Katherine Paterson's *The Great Gilly Hopkins,* a foster child of today. She can taste the bitterness of racial prejudice in Mildred Taylor's *Roll of Thunder, Hear My Cry,* and she can share in the courage and determination of young people who helped others escape the Holocaust in *Number the Stars* by Lois Lowry.

A vast treasure of thoughts, deeds, and dreams lies waiting to be discovered in books. Literature begins with Mother Goose. It includes Sendak as well as Shakespeare, Milne as much as Milton, and Carroll before Camus. Children's literature is a part of the mainstream of all literature, whose source is life itself.

KNOWING CHILDREN'S LITERATURE

Literature Defined

In the introduction to his book *The Call of Stories*, noted child psychiatrist Robert Coles tells how, during his childhood, his mother and father would read aloud to each other every evening. They were convinced that the great novels of Dickens, Tolstoy, and others held "reservoirs of wisdom." "'Your mother and I feel rescued by these books,'" his father told him. "'We read them gratefully.'"[1]

What is it about literature that can inspire such passionate attention? What *is* literature? And, with more than 73,000 titles for boys and girls now in print, how can we choose those books that will bring the full rewards and pleasures of literature to children?

There are many ways of defining literature. Our ideas about what should be included have changed through history; definitions vary a bit from culture to culture, from critic to critic, and from reader to reader. In this book we think of literature as the imaginative shaping of life and thought into the forms and structures of language. Where appropriate, we consider pictures as well as words, asking how both sets of symbols work to produce an aesthetic experience. How do they help the reader perceive pattern, relationships, and feelings that produce an inner experience of art? This aesthetic experience may be a vivid reconstruction of past experience, an extension of experience, or creation of a new experience.

> We all have, in our experience, memories of certain books which changed us in some way—by disturbing us, or by a glorious affirmation of some emotion we knew but could never shape in words, or by some revelation of human nature. Virginia Woolf calls such times "moments of being," and James Joyce titles them "epiphanies."[2]

[1]Robert Coles, *The Call of Stories: Teaching and the Moral Imagination* (Boston: Houghton Mifflin, 1989), p. xii.
[2]Frances Clarke Sayers, *Summoned by Books* (New York: Viking, 1965), p. 16.

The province of literature is the human condition. Literature illuminates life by shaping our insights. W. H. Auden differentiated between first-rate literature and second-rate literature, writing that the reader responds to second-rate literature by saying:

> "That's just the way I always felt." But first-rate literature makes one say: "Until now, I never knew how I felt. Thanks to this experience, I shall never feel the same way again."[3]

The experience of literature always involves both the book and the reader. Try as we might to set objective criteria, judgments about the quality of literature must always be tempered by an awareness of its audience. Some critics consider Lewis Carroll's *Alice in Wonderland* the greatest book ever written for children. However, if the child has no background in fantasy, cannot com-

[3]W. H. Auden, as quoted by Robert B. Heilman in "Literature and Growing Up," *English Journal*, vol. 45 (September 1956), p. 307.

One way to define literature for children is to describe the books that children continue to read and enjoy.

Martin Luther King, Jr., Laboratory School, Evanston, Illinois, Public Schools. Photo by James Ballard.

❦ ❦ ❦

prehend the complexity of the plot, nor tolerate the logic of its illogic, *Alice in Wonderland* will not be the greatest book for that child.

WHAT IS CHILDREN'S LITERATURE?

It might be said that a child's book is a book a child is reading, and an adult book is a book occupying the attention of an adult. Before the nineteenth century only a few books were written for the specific readership of children. Children read books written for adults, taking from them what they could understand. Today, children continue to read some books intended for adults; for example, the work of Stephen King and *All Creatures Great and Small* by James Herriot. And yet some books first written for children—such as Margery Williams's *The Velveteen Rabbit,* A. A. Milne's *Winnie the Pooh,* and J. R. R. Tolkien's *The Hobbit*—have been claimed as their own by college students.

Books *about* children may not necessarily be *for* them. Richard Hughes's adult classic *A High Wind in Jamaica* shows the "innocent" depravity of children in contrast to the group of pirates who had captured them. Yet in Harper Lee's novel *To Kill a Mockingbird,* also written for adults, 8-year-old Scout Finch reveals a more finely developed conscience than the small southern town in which she is raised. The presence of a child protagonist, then, does not assure that the book is for children. Obviously, the line between children's literature and adult literature is blurred.

Children today appear more sophisticated and knowledgeable about certain life experiences than those of any previous generation. They spend a great deal of time within view of an operating television. According to the *Nielsen 1990 Report on Television,* actual watching time for children ages 6 to 11 averages almost 24 hours per week. Preschoolers watch more, approximately 27 hours per week.[4] The evening news has shown them actual views of war while they ate their dinners. They have witnessed air strikes, assassinations, and starvation. While the modern child is

separated from first-hand knowledge of birth, death, and senility, the mass media bring vicarious and daily experiences of crime, poverty, war, death, and depravity into the living rooms of virtually all American homes. This generation is exposed to more violence in the name of entertainment than any other generation in the past.

Such exposure has forced adults to reconsider what seems appropriate for children's literature. It seems unbelievable that only a generation ago Madeleine L'Engle's *Meet the Austins* was rejected by several publishers because it began with a death; or that some reviewers were shocked by a mild "damn" in *Harriet the Spy* by Louise Fitzhugh. Such publishing taboos have long since moderated. While children's books are generally less frank than adult books, contemporary children's literature does reflect the problems of today, the ones children read about in the newspapers, see on television and in the movies, and experience at home.

However, the content of children's literature is limited by the experience and understanding of children. Certain emotional and psychological responses seem outside the realm of childhood. For example, the feeling of nostalgia is an adult emotion that is foreign to most boys and girls. Children seldom look back on their childhood, but always forward. Stories that portray children as "sweet" or that romanticize childhood, like the Holly Hobbie books that go with cards and gift products, have more appeal for adults than for children. Likewise, a sentimental book like *Love You Forever* by Robert Munsch, despite its popularity with teachers, is really not for children. Its themes of the passing of childhood and the assumption of responsibility for an aging parent both reflect adult experiences. The late Dr. Seuss (Theodor S. Geisel) also took an adult perspective in books such as *Oh, the Places You'll Go.* His enduring place in children's literature rests on earlier titles such as *And to Think That I Saw It on Mulberry Street* and *The Cat in the Hat,* books that are filled with childlike imagination and joyful exuberance.

Cynicism and despair are not childlike emotions and should not figure prominently in a child's book. While children are quick to pick up

[4]Reported by the now disbanded lobby group, Action for Children's Television.

a veneer of sophistication, of disillusionment with adults and authority, they still expect good things to happen in life. And although many children do live in desperate circumstances, few react with real despair. They may have endured pain, sorrow, or horror; they may be in what we would consider hopeless situations, but they are not without hope. The truth of the Russian folktale by Becky Reyher, *My Mother Is the Most Beautiful Woman in the World*, shines clear. Children see beauty where there is ugliness; they are hopeful when adults have given up. This is not to suggest that all stories for children must have happy endings; many today do not. It is only to say that when you close the door on hope, you have left the realm of childhood. The only limitations, then, that seem binding on literature for children are those that appropriately reflect the emotions and experiences of children today. Children's books are books that have the child's eye at the center.

WRITING FOR CHILDREN

Editor William Zinsser says:

> No kind of writing lodges itself so deeply in our memory, echoing there for the rest of our lives, as the books that we met in our childhood, . . . To enter and hold the mind of a child or a young person is one of the hardest of all writers' tasks.[5]

The skilled author does not write differently or less carefully for children just because he thinks they will not be aware of style or language. E. B. White asserts:

> Anyone who writes *down* to children is simply wasting his time. You have to write up, not down. . . . Some writers for children deliberately avoid using words they think a child doesn't know. This emasculates the prose and . . . bores the reader. . . . Children love words that give them a hard time,

provided they are in a context that absorbs their attention.[6]

Authors of children's literature and those who write for adults should receive equal approbation. C. S. Lewis[7] maintained that he wrote a children's story because a children's story was the best art form for what he had to say. Lewis wrote both for adults and children, as have Rumer Godden, Madeleine L'Engle, Paula Fox, E. B. White, Isaac Bashevis Singer, Penelope Lively, and many other well-known authors.

The uniqueness of children's literature, then, lies in the audience that it addresses. Authors of children's books are circumscribed only by the experiences of childhood, but these are vast and complex. Children think and feel; they wonder and they dream. Much is known, but little is explained.

Children are curious about life and adult activities. They live in the midst of tensions, of balances of love and hate within the family and the neighborhood. The author who can bring these experiences imagination and insight, give them literary shape and structure, and communicate them to children is writing children's literature.

Valuing Literature for Children

PERSONAL VALUES

Literature should be valued in our homes and schools for the enrichment it gives to the personal lives of children, as well as for its proven educational contributions. We consider these affective values of literature before we discuss the more obvious educational ones.

Provides Enjoyment

First and foremost, literature provides delight and enjoyment. Much of what is taught in school is

[5]William Zinsser, ed., *Worlds of Childhood: The Art and Craft of Writing for Children* (Boston: Houghton Mifflin, 1990), p. 3.

[6]E. B. White, "On Writing for Children," quoted in Virginia Haviland, ed. *Children and Literature: Views and Reviews* (Glenview, Ill.: Scott, Foresman, 1973), p. 140.
[7]C. S. Lewis, "On Three Ways of Writing for Children," *The Horn Book Magazine*, vol. 39 (October 1963), p. 460.

not particularly enjoyable. Our Puritan backgrounds have made literature somewhat suspect. If children enjoy it, we reason, it can't be very good for them. Yet literature can educate at the same time it entertains.

Children need to discover delight in books before they are asked to master the skills of reading. Then learning to read makes as much sense as learning to ride a bike; they know that eventually it will be fun. Four- and 5-year-olds who have laughed out loud at Judi Barrett's funny book, *Animals Should Definitely Not Wear Clothing,* can hardly wait to read it themselves. After hearing the ugly troll's cry of "Who's that tripping over my bridge?" children are eager to take parts in playing out *The Three Billy Goats Gruff* by P. C. Asbjørnsen and Jorgen Moe. They respond to the distinctive rhythm of the poem "Deer Mouse" by Marilyn Singer as the tiny creature goes scurrying for food; or the sound of David McCord's "The Pickety Fence." Six- and 7-year-olds giggle at the silly antics of Arnold Lobel's Frog and Toad books, and they laugh uproariously when Beverly Cleary's *Ramona Quimby, Age 8* mistakenly cracks a raw egg on her head thinking it is hard-boiled. Later they empathize with her when she overhears her teacher calling her a nuisance and a showoff.

Bingo Brown, a funny and genuine preadolescent first brought to life by Betsy Byars in *The Burning Questions of Bingo Brown,* is popular with middle graders. This age group also identifies with Lois Lowry's *Anastasia Krupnik,* a fourth grader who is horrified that her parents are having another baby. A warm, loving family relationship helps her to change her mind in this very funny yet touching novel. Sad books also bring a kind of enjoyment, as the children who have read *Bridge to Terabithia* by Katherine Paterson or *Stone Fox* by John Gardiner will tell you. Most children love being frightened by a story. Watch 6- and 7-year-olds respond to a scary sharing of Joanna Galdone's *The Tailypo* and you will have no doubt of their shivery delight. Many older children revel in tales of suspense such as *Something Upstairs* by Avi or the haunting *Balyet* by Patricia Wrightson.

The list of books that children enjoy can go on and on. There are so many fine ones—and so many that children won't find unless teachers, librarians, and parents share them with children. A love of reading and a taste for literature are the finest gifts we can give to our children, for we will have started them on the path of a lifetime of pleasure with books.

Reinforces Narrative as a Way of Thinking

Storytelling is as old as human history and as new as today's gossip. Ask any of your friends about their weekends or last vacations and they will organize their remarks in narratives about when their car stalled in the middle of a freeway or their child broke his leg or the marvelous place they stayed at the ocean. Barbara Hardy of the University of London suggests that all our constructs of reality are in fact stories that we tell ourselves about how the world works. She maintains that the narrative is the most common and effective form of ordering our world today:

> We dream in narrative, day-dream in narrative, remember, anticipate, hope, despair, believe, doubt, plan, revise, criticize, construct, gossip, learn, hate, love by narrative. In order really to live, we make up stories about ourselves and others, about the personal as well as the social past and future.[8]

Susanne Langer underscores the importance of narrative as a way of thinking with the dramatic statement that "Life is incoherent unless we give it form." She adds,

> Usually the process of formulating our own situations and our own biography . . . follows the same pattern—we 'just put it into words,' tell it to ourselves, compose it in terms of 'scenes,' so that our minds can enact all its important moments. The basis for this imaginative work is the poetic art we have known, from the earliest nursery rhymes to the most profound, or sophisticated, or breath-taking drama and fiction.[9]

[8]Barbara Hardy, "Narrative as a Primary Act of the Mind," in *The Cool Web: The Pattern of Children's Reading* by Margaret Meek, Aidan Warlow, Griselda Barton (New York: Atheneum, 1978), p. 13.
[9]Susanne K. Langer, *Feeling and Form* (New York: Scribner's, 1953), p. 400.

Illustrations can ignite the imagination just as narrative or poetry can. This symbolic dream flower was created by Leo and Diane Dillon for *The Big Book for Peace* edited by Ann Durell and Marilyn Sachs.

🙶 🙶 🙶

If thinking in narrative form is characteristic of adult thought, it is even more typical of children's thinking. Watch young children and observe all the stories that they are playing out in their lives. When they are naughty and sent to their rooms, they tell themselves a story about how they will run away—and then won't their parents be sorry? Does this plot sound familiar? Of course, for it is the basis for Maurice Sendak's modern classic *Where the Wild Things Are*. Part of this book's tremendous popularity no doubt rests on the fact that it taps the wellsprings of the stories children have been telling themselves for years. Because it is literature, however, this story brings order and structure to the imagined events. Max returns to

his room after his fantastic dream "where he finds his supper waiting for him—and it was still hot."[10] Ask 5- or 6-year olds who brought Max his supper and they will reply "His mother." Then ask them what this ending means, and they will answer "that she's not mad at him anymore." Critics will call the hot meal a symbol of love and reconciliation, but children are simply satisfied that all is well. The book narrative has provided a reassuring ending for the inner story that they have told themselves.

Develops the Imagination

Literature develops children's imagination and helps them to consider nature, people, experiences, or ideas in new ways. Tana Hoban's exciting photographic puzzle, *Look Again!*, gives children a rich visual experience and helps them to see a sunflower or a snail or a zebra from a new perspective. Children love to discover secrets hidden in certain illustrations: the little secondary story of the mouse in the informational book *"Charlie Needs a Cloak"* by Tomie de Paola; the fairy-tale characters and those from Sesame Street in *Anno's Journey* by Mitsumasa Anno; or the shipwreck seen through the window of Sendak's *Outside Over There*.

Good writing may pique the child's curiosity just as much as intriguing art. Literature helps children to entertain ideas they never considered before—"to dwell in possibility," as one of Emily Dickinson's poems suggests. Literature frequently provides answers to the child's "what if?" questions. *The Indian in the Cupboard* by Lynne Banks answers the question: what if I could bring my plastic toys to life? Then it asks another of Omri, the protagonist: what responsibility do I have for a live 2-inch Indian? Madeleine L'Engle explores the idea of changing the past in *A Swiftly Tilting Planet*. What if we could enter history? Could we change certain major decisions? Charles Wallace has to find that out and so does the reader. Literature explores possibility.

Some books invite children to use their imaginations to solve real problems, including the need

[10]Maurice Sendak, *Where the Wild Things Are* (New York: Harper & Row, 1963), unpaged.

to envision a better future for the world. *The Big Book for Peace,* edited by Ann Durell and Marilyn Sachs, offers the work of nearly three dozen authors and illustrators. In stories, poems, and pictures, this volume presents many perspectives on living in harmony with nature and our neighbors.

One of the values of fairy tales and myths is the way in which they stretch the child's imagination. How many children would imagine creating a coach out of a pumpkin, horses from mice, and coachmen from lizards? Yet they readily accept it all in the well-loved tale of Cinderella. Bettelheim maintains: "Fairy tales have unequaled value, because they offer new dimensions to the child's imagination which would be impossible for him to discover as truly on his own."[11]

Today television has made everything so explicit that children are not developing their power to visualize. Teachers need to help them see with their inner eye to develop a country of the mind. Mollie Hunter paints the landscape of a Shetland Island fishing village in her exciting story, *A Stranger Came Ashore.* We can see and feel the night of the wild storm and shipwreck with its sudden appearance of the stranger; or the magic night of the ancient celebration of Up Helly Aa as the skuddler and the guisers dance under the northern lights and Robbie tries to save his sister from the dark powers of the stranger. All of Mollie Hunter's books have this power to create the visual image in the mind of the reader and to stretch the imagination. She herself says that the whole reward of reading is:

> . . . to have one's imagination carried soaring on the wings of another's imagination, to be made more aware of the possibilities of one's mind, . . . ; to be thrilled, amazed, amused, awed, enchanted in worlds unknown until discovered through the medium of language, and to find in those worlds one's own petty horizons growing ever wider, ever higher.[12]

---

[11]Bruno Bettelheim, *The Uses of Enchantment: The Meaning and Importance of Fairy Tales* (New York: Knopf, 1976), p. 7.
[12]Mollie Hunter, *The Pied Piper Syndrome* (New York: HarperCollins, 1992), p. 92.

Offers Vicarious Experiences

The experiences children have with literature give them new perspectives on the world. Good writing can transport the reader to other places and other times and expand his life space. The reader feels connected to the lives of others as he enters an imagined situation with his emotions tuned to those of the story. One 10-year-old boy, sharing his love of Jean George's survival story *My Side of the Mountain,* said, "You know, I've always secretly felt I could do it myself." This boy had vicariously shared Sam Gribley's adventure of "living off the land" in his tree home in the Catskill Mountains. Sam's experiment in self-sufficiency had strengthened the conviction of a 10-year-old that he, too, could take care of himself. James Britton points out that ". . . we never cease to long for more lives than the one we have . . . [a reader can] participate in an infinite number."[13]

How better can we feel and experience history than through a well-told story of the lives of its people and times? Readers of Lois Lowry's *Number the Stars* hold their breath as Nazi soldiers ask questions about 10-year-old Annemarie's dark-haired "sister." The girl is really Annemarie's Jewish friend Ellen, whose Star-of-David necklace is at that moment hidden in Annemarie's hand. Fear and courage become very real to the reader in this story of the Danish Resistance in World War II. The young reader does not need to be told that slavery is wrong in Paula Fox's *The Slave Dancer;* instead, the author shows him the devastation that it wreaks on slave and master. A history textbook tells; a quality piece of imaginative writing has the power to make the reader feel, to transport him to the deck of a slave ship and force him into the hold until he chokes on the very horror of it.

Literature provides vicarious experiences of adventure, excitement, and sometimes of struggle. In fantasy, Will Stanton, seventh son of a seventh son, must do battle against the forces of evil,

---

[13]James Britton, *The Dartmouth Seminar Papers: Response to Literature,* edited by James R. Squire (Champaign, Ill.: National Council of Teachers of English, 1968), p. 10.

the power of the dark, and the unbelievably intense cold before he can complete his quest. The strength of this fantasy, *The Dark Is Rising* by Susan Cooper, is the degree to which the author involves the reader in Will's struggle. Both words and pictures in *The Whales' Song* by Dyan Sheldon and Gary Blythe create a dreamlike oceanside setting and the quiet adventure of being there, first with anticipation and then with awe as the enormous whales leap in the moonlight.

Whether reading takes them to another place, another time, or an imaginary world, young readers will return home enriched. Reading gets us out of our own time and place, out of ourselves; but in the end it will return us to ourselves, a little different, a little changed by this experience.

Develops Insight into Human Behavior

Literature reflects life, yet no book can contain all of living. By its very organizing properties literature has the power to shape and give coherence to human experience. It may focus on one aspect of life, one period of time in an individual's life, and so enable a reader to see and understand relationships that he had never considered. In *Dicey's Song* by Cynthia Voigt a 13-year-old girl learns to release her brothers and sisters to the care of her independent, feisty grandmother. Only as she grows into loving and respecting this eccentric mother of her own mentally ill mother does Dicey begin to understand her grandmother's advice to reach out and let go. Gradually Dicey realizes how hard it is for Gram, whose own three children are lost to her, to reach out to this new family, to let herself love again. As Dicey sands down the rough places on the old derelict boat she has found, she symbolically smooths out her own rough life and readies herself for her independent voyage into maturity.

So much of what we teach in school is concerned with facts. Literature is concerned with feelings, the quality of life. It can educate the heart as well as the mind. Chukovsky, the Russian poet, says:

> The goal of every storyteller consists of fostering in the child, at whatever cost, compassion and humanness, this miraculous ability of man to be disturbed by another being's misfortune, to feel joy about another being's happiness, to experience another's fate as your own.[14]

Good Night, Mr. Tom by Michelle Magorian is a long, powerful novel of an 8-year-old boy who is evacuated from London during World War II to a tiny village in the English countryside. An abused child of a single deranged mother, Willie is placed with a kindly but gruff widower who has almost become a recluse since the death of his wife and infant son. Though violent in parts, this is a deeply moving story in which a boy and a lonely old man nurture each other through mutual love. Others in the village are portrayed as real persons who also show compassion and understanding for both Will and Tom. It is a novel that educates the heart as well as the mind.

Literature can show children how others have lived and "become," no matter what the time or place. As children gain increased awareness of the lives of others, as they vicariously try out other roles, they may develop a better understanding of themselves and those around them. Through wide reading as well as living, the child acquires his perceptions of literature and life.

Presents the Universality of Experience

Literature continues to ask universal questions about the meaning of life and our relationships with nature and other people. Every story provides a point of comparison for our own lives. Are we as courageous as William Steig's *Brave Irene?* As troubled as Nam Huong in Diana Kidd's *Onion Tears?* Do we grieve for opportunity lost as Mandy does in *Borrowed Children* by George Ella Lyon?

We also learn to understand the common bonds of humanity by comparing one story with another. Children who read *Stevie* by John Steptoe and *Thy Friend, Obadiah* by Brinton Turkle can discover the universal truth that we seldom know how much we like a person (or even a pet gull) until we've lost him. Pride of accomplishment is

---

[14]Kornei Chukovsky, *From Two to Five*, translated by Miriam Morton (Berkeley: University of California Press, 1963), p. 138.

strong for Ahmed when he learns to write his name in *The Day of Ahmed's Secret* by Florence Parry Heide and Judith Heide Gilliland and no less so for Kondi, who makes his own toy car from discarded wire in *Galimoto* by Karen Williams.

The story of Max leaving home to go to the island of *Where the Wild Things Are* follows the ancient pattern of Homer's *Iliad* and *Odyssey*. This pattern is repeated again and again in myth and legend and seen in such widely divergent stories as *Call It Courage* by Armstrong Sperry, *A Wrinkle in Time* by Madeleine L'Engle, and *Park's Quest* by Katherine Paterson. These are all stories of a journey through trials and hardship and the eventual return home. The pattern reflects everyone's journey through life.

War stories frequently portray acts of compassion in the midst of inhumanity. *The Upstairs Room* by Johanna Reiss and *Rose Blanche* by Christophe Gallaz and Roberto Innocenti both tell of the uncommon bravery of common people to do what they can to right a wrong. Children's literature is replete with stories of true friendships, as seen in Katherine Paterson's *Bridge to Terabithia*, E. B. White's *Charlotte's Web*, and picture books such as *Ernest and Celestine* by Gabrielle Vincent or *Willy and Hugh* by Anthony Browne. Other stories reflect the terrible renunciation of friendship such as found in *Friedrich* by Hans Richter or *The Friendship* by Mildred Taylor. Literature illumines all of life; it casts its light on all that is good, but it may also spotlight what is dark and debasing in the human experience. Literature enables us to live many lives, good and bad, and to begin to see the universality of human experience.

EDUCATIONAL VALUES

The intrinsic values of literature should be sufficient to give it a major place in the curriculum. Unfortunately, our society assigns a low priority to such aesthetic experiences. Only when literature is shown to be basic to the development of measurable skills does it receive attention in the elementary schools. Fortunately, research has proven the essential value of literature in helping children learn to read and write.

Language Development

Characteristic of the development of all children is the phenomenal growth of language during the preschool years. Kornei Chukovsky, the Russian poet, refers to the tremendous "speech-giftedness of the pre-school child" and maintains that "beginning with the age of two, every child becomes for a short period of time a linguistic genius."[15]

While there are different points of view concerning how children acquire language, most language theorists would subscribe to the importance of providing a rich language environment for the young child. While it is not our purpose to give a detailed description of language acquisition, it is appropriate to discuss the role literature plays in developing the language power of children.

An early study by O. C. Irwin indicates that the systematic reading of stories to infants over an 18-month period will increase the spontaneous vocalizations of 2 1/2-year-old children. Mothers of the experimental group spent 15 to 20 minutes daily reading and talking about the story and pictures with the child. After the first four months, the experimental group began to vocalize significantly more than the control.[16]

Courtney Cazden[17] contrasted two methods of providing young children with adult language input. One treatment was to expand the child's short telegraphic utterance into a complete sentence. For example, when he said "Dog bark," the mother replied, "Yes, the dog is barking." The other treatment focused less on sentence form and more on meaning. The adult picked up the child's ideas and extended them in conversation and in reading stories. A third group of children in the experiment received no treatment. Contrary to Cazden's expectations that the direct expansion of the child's language would be the

---

[15]Kornei Chukovsky, *From Two to Five*, pp. 7, 9.
[16]O. C. Irwin, "Infant Speech: Effect of Systematic Reading of Stories," *Journal of Speech and Hearing Research*, vol. 3 (June 1960), pp. 187–190.
[17]Courtney B. Cazden, "Environmental Assistance to the Child's Acquisition of Grammar" (unpublished Ph.D. dissertation, Harvard University, 1965).

more effective, it was the second treatment, which focused on extending meaning through talk and through stories, that produced the greater gain on all six measures of language development. Later research has supported Cazden's idea that reading to a child stimulates language growth because it encourages conversation about the pictures, to which both adult and child are paying attention.

Ninio and Bruner[18] found that one of the first language patterns or frames to be developed occurred as a turn-taking routine when a parent shared a picture book with a child from the time she was 8 months to 1 1/2 years old. The parent

[18]A. Ninio and J. Bruner, "The Achievement and Antecedents of Labelling," *Journal of Child Language*, vol. 5 (1973), pp. 1–15.

Reading aloud to older children gives the teacher a chance to introduce and discuss more complex stories than the ones they choose themselves.
Martin Luther King, Jr., Laboratory School, Evanston, Illinois, Public Schools. Barbara Friedberg, teacher. Photo by James Ballard.

supported the child's dialogue, adjusting her comments as the child gradually could participate more. This the researchers referred to as "scaffolding" or supporting the child's language growth (see Chapter 4, page 223).

Henrietta Dombey has described an extension of this kind of support in a study of 3-year-old Anna and her mother. Their discussion of a story shows how the mother uses stress and intonation as she reads and speaks to familiarize Anna with new syntactic forms. She also encourages Anna to take an active language role, to ask questions and test her own predictions.[19]

The effects of these early contacts with books carry over into the elementary school years. Carol Chomsky[20] measured the language acquisition of thirty-six children between the ages of 5 and 10 and found a high positive correlation between their linguistic stages of development and their previous exposure to literature, as measured by a simple inventory of their literary backgrounds. She concluded that a valid relation between reading exposure and linguistic stages exists.

A group of researchers[21] from New York University studied 500 African-American children from kindergarten through third grade in four New York City schools. The experimental group participated in a literature-based oral language program which included a daily read-aloud story followed by creative dramatics, role playing, storytelling, puppetry, or discussion. The control groups participated in the literature program, but not in the language activities. The researchers found that the experiences with literature did expand the language skills of both groups significantly, but the experimental group made greater advances in their ability to use standard English

dialect. Also, the greatest gain was evident among the kindergarten group, suggesting that such a program should start at as early an age as possible.

Victoria Purcell-Gates[22] asked kindergartners who had heard many stories at home to pretend to read a wordless picture book. She found that as they "read," they were able to use language features like direct quotes and adjectives placed before the noun, features common in written language but not in everyday speech. In other words, they had learned to use "book language" in their storytelling.

Vocabulary, too, seems to grow as children spend time with literature. One research report[23] indicates that children in third grade and above learn the meanings of about 3,000 new words each year. Since teachers could not possibly devote enough time to direct vocabulary instruction to account for this result, the researchers assume that many of these new words are acquired by children in the context of their reading. These and other studies confirm that reading aloud to children, discussing literature with children, and children's independent reading are all positive influences on child language development.

Literature and Reading

READING ALOUD AND LEARNING TO READ
Many studies have sought to determine the reasons some children learn to read early and easily, without formal teaching at school. All of them report the significance of having been read to at an early age. In Dolores Durkin's studies[24] of children who learned to read before entering school, family respect for reading was found to be a significant factor. All her early readers had been read to from the age of 3 or before. Margaret Clark's

[19]Henrietta Dombey, "Learning the Language of Books," in Margaret Meek, ed., *Opening Moves: Work in Progress in the Study of Children's Language Development.* Bedford Way Papers 17. (Portsmouth, N.H.: Heinemann, 1985), pp. 26–43.
[20]Carol Chomsky, "Stages in Language Development and Reading Exposure," *Harvard Educational Review*, vol. 42 (February 1972), pp. 1–33.
[21]Bernice E. Cullinan, Angela Jaggar, and Dorothy Strickland, "Language Expansion for Black Children in the Primary Grades: A Research Report," *Young Children*, vol. 29 (January 1974), pp. 98–112.

[22]Victoria Purcell-Gates, "Lexical and Syntactic Knowledge of Written Narrative Held by Well-Read-to Kindergartners and Second Graders," *Research in the Teaching of English*, vol. 22 (May 1988), pp. 128–160.
[23]William Nagy, Patricia Hermann, and Richard Anderson, "Learning Words from Context," *Reading Research Quarterly*, vol. 20 (1985), pp. 233–253.
[24]Dolores Durkin, *Children Who Read Early* (New York: Columbia Teachers College Press, 1966).

study[25] of *Young Fluent Readers* in Scotland confirmed the value of being read aloud to at an early age. Not all of the children in her study came from wealthy homes, but they all came from homes that valued books. The families made good use of the local library and one father was a superb storyteller, telling his family fairy tales every night. Thorndike's study[26] of reading in fifteen different countries also found that books in the home and reading aloud were potent factors in children's learning to read.

Dorothy Butler[27] has recorded the powerful influence that reading aloud had on a multiply handicapped child in her moving book, *Cushla and Her Books*. Doctors predicted a future of severe retardation for this little girl, who confounded them completely by learning to read at a level well beyond her actual age. Cushla was read to from the time she was 4 months of age and literally discovered the world through books.

An important longitudinal study by Gordon Wells[28] showed that hearing many stories in the preschool years can have lasting benefit. The amount of experience that 5-year-old children in this study had had with books was directly related to their reading comprehension at age 7 and even later, at age 11.

A long-term effect of reading to children was also determined by Judith Sostarich,[29] who compared sixth-grade "active readers" with nonactive readers in the same class. In every instance the active readers had been read to from the time they were 3 years old, and, in some cases, families were still sharing books aloud.

Libraries and schools can provide rich literature experiences for those children deprived of books in the home, or where parents and children are watching television rather than reading. Dorothy Cohen[30] sought to determine if reading aloud to 7-year-olds who had not previously been exposed to literature would make a difference in their ability to read. Books were read aloud to children in ten experimental classrooms in New York City on a daily basis for a period of one year. Following the 20-minute story time, the children were asked to do something with the book to make it memorable. For example, they might act out the story, draw a picture of their favorite characters, or compare it with a similar story—something to make them think about the story and revisit the book several times. At the end of the year, Cohen found the experimental group was significantly ahead of the control group on reading vocabulary and reading comprehension. Evidently, reading *to* children and giving them a chance to work with real books had helped them learn to read.

In the past 10 years many teachers have written articles for professional journals about their successes with using children's trade books in the reading program. These reports confirm the research that links literature with success in learning to read. They also stress that increased enjoyment and interest in reading are important outcomes of regularly reading aloud to children.

DEVELOPING A SENSE OF STORY   Hearing stories read aloud is a powerful motivation for the child to begin to learn to read. Children learn that reading provides enjoyment and they want to learn themselves. They also see someone important in their lives valuing books. Too frequently we tell children that reading is important, but we show by our actions that we really value other activities more.

Early exposure to stories also provides a rich input of literary language. Frank Smith maintains:

> Children need to become acquainted with the
> language of books; it is not the language they hear

[25]Margaret Clark, *Young Fluent Readers* (London: Heinemann Educational Books, 1976), p. 102.
[26]Robert Ladd Thorndike, *Reading Comprehension, Education in 15 Countries: An Empirical Study*, vol. 3, International Studies in Education (New York: Holstead Wiley, 1973).
[27]Dorothy Butler, *Cushla and Her Books* (Boston: Horn Book, 1980).
[28]Gordon Wells, *The Meaning Makers* (Portsmouth, N.H.: Heinemann, 1986).
[29]Judith Sostarich, "A Study of the Reading Behavior of Sixth Graders: Comparisons of Active and Other Readers" (unpublished Ph.D. dissertation, Ohio State University, 1974).
[30]Dorothy Cohen, "The Effect of Literature on Vocabulary and Reading Achievement," *Elementary English*, vol. 45 (February 1968), pp. 209–213, 217.

spoken around them in their daily life, and it is unrealistic to expect them to learn this unfamiliar style at the same time they learn to read.[31]

Listening to stories introduces children to patterns of language and extends vocabulary and meaning. Young children love to repeat such refrains as "Not by the hair on my chinny chin chin" from Paul Galdone's *Three Little Pigs* or the well-loved rhyme from Wanda Gág's *Millions of Cats:*

> Cats here, cats there,
> Cats and kittens everywhere,
> Hundreds of cats,
> Thousands of cats,
> Millions and billions and trillions of cats.[32]

They delight in new words such as "humiliated" in Lynd Ward's *The Biggest Bear* or the line from Beatrix Potter's *The Tale of Peter Rabbit* in which the friendly sparrows "implored him to exert himself" when Peter was caught in the gooseberry net. A first-grade teacher read to her class Charlotte Zolotow's *Say It!*, in which a mother and her little girl go for a walk on a beautiful autumn day—"a splendiferous day," the mother calls it. Later on, a child asked her to reread the "splendiferous book." Children love the sounds of words and enjoy repeating them over and over.

Knowing the structure of a story and being able to anticipate what a particular character will do helps the young child predict the action and determine the meaning of the story he is reading. For example, children quickly learn the rule of three which prevails in most folktales. They know that if the first Billy Goat Gruff goes trip-trapping over the bridge, the second Billy Goat Gruff will go trip-trapping after him, and so will the third. In reading or listening to the story of the Gingerbread Boy, the child who has had a rich exposure to literature can anticipate the ending on the basis of what he knows about the character of foxes in stories. As one little boy said, "Foxes are clever. He won't be able to get away from him!"

The more experience with literature, the greater the child's ability to grasp the meaning of the story and understand the way the author tells it. Carol Fox[33] reported on the stories told over a period of time by two 5-year-olds. "Jack" and "Jill" had both heard a great many stories read aloud, and their mothers were able to identify several of the books that had influenced the content, the language style, and the more complex story devices used by the children. Fox suggests that young children often have greater ability to use and understand complex narratives than school reading programs give them credit for.

DEVELOPING FLUENCY   Wide reading of many books is essential to the development of fluency in reading. This was the kind of reading, even rereading, of favorite stories that Margaret Clark found to be characteristic of her avid readers.[34] Such reading is characteristic of middle-grade students who get "hooked" on a particular author or series of books. Frequently, a sign of a good reader is the child who rereads favorite books.

In a year-long study of children's reading behavior in a literature-based program in a fifth and sixth grade class, Susan Hepler found these children read an average of 45 books per child for the year, with the range being 25 to 122 books.[35] Compare this record with the usual two basal texts read in a year by children in the typical basal reading programs. Only such wide reading will develop fluency. Children used to do this at home, but the advent of television and video games has drastically curtailed the amount of children's home reading.

When the National Assessment of Educational Progress asked third-grade students how much independent reading they did in school, 75 percent of the most successful readers reported read-

---

[31]Frank Smith, *Reading Without Nonsense* (New York: Teachers College, Columbia University, 1979), p. 136.
[32]Wanda Gág, *Millions of Cats* (New York: Coward McCann, 1928), unpaged.

[33]Carol Fox, "Talking Like a Book," in Meek ed., *Opening Moves*, pp. 12–25.
[34]Margaret Clark, *Young Fluent Readers*, p. 103.
[35]Susan Hepler, "Patterns of Response to Literature: A One-Year Study of a Fifth- and Sixth-Grade Classroom" (unpublished Ph.D. dissertation, Ohio State University, 1982).

ing every day. Only 57 percent of the least successful readers gave that answer.[36] Teachers at every grade level from preschool on up need to make time for children to spend with books every day. If children do not have the opportunity to read widely at school, they will not become fluent readers.

Literature and Writing

Teachers have always believed that there was a relationship between reading and writing—the good writers were avid readers, and good readers often seemed to be the best writers. Now we have research that validates those observations and explores how reading and writing develop together.

Walter Loban conducted one of the most extensive studies of the relationship between reading achievement as measured by reading scores and the ratings of writing quality. He discovered a high correlation, particularly in the upper elementary grades, and concluded: "Those who read well also write well; those who read poorly also write poorly."[37]

Glenda Bissex[38] studied the evolution of her own child's writing and published the results in a book titled after the sign 5-year-old Paul posted over his workbench: "DO NAT DSTRB GNYS AT WRK." This "genius" learned to write and read at the same time. Reading appeared to have a broad influence on the forms of writing Paul did. He first demonstrated his awareness of print by making signs, labels, and advertisements. He then went on to write shopping lists, little stories, notes, newspapers, and a science-fiction book. Books at all times served as models for Paul's increasing sense of form.

If reading provides models for children's writing, then the kinds of reading children are exposed to become even more important. Exposure to much good literature appears to make a difference in children's writing abilities, just as it does in their linguistic abilities. Fox and Allen maintain: "The language children use in writing is unlikely to be more sophisticated in either vocabulary or syntax than the language they read or have had someone else read to them."[39]

Barbara Eckhoff's[40] research clearly shows that the writing of children reflects the features and style of their reading texts. Comparing children who read from the typical simplified text of most basal readers with those who read from one whose text more nearly matched the style and complexity of literary prose, she found that the children's writing closely resembled the style of writing used in their texts. One group wrote more complex sentences; the basal group copied the style and format of their reader, writing simple sentences, one sentence per line.

Diane DeFord's[41] study of children's writing in three first grades taught by different methods (i.e., phonics, skills and a whole-language model using children's literature) shows the influence of both method and texts on children's writing. The first two groups created repetitious drill-type texts, whereas the children's literature group produced a wider variety of literary forms, including stories, informational prose, songs, poetry, and newspaper reports. This same group was also more competent at retelling stories. Simplified stories produced simplified stories, both written and oral.

The content of children's stories also reflects the literature they have heard. Whether consciously or unconsciously, children pick up words,

[36]Arthur Applebee, Judith Langer, and Ina Mullis, *Who Reads Best? Factors Related to Reading Achievement in Grades 3, 7, and 11* (Report No. 17-R-01), National Assessment of Educational Progress (Princeton, N.J.: Educational Testing Service, 1988).
[37]Walter Loban, *The Language of Elementary School Children*, Research Report No. 1 (Urbana, Ill.: National Council of Teachers of English, 1963), p. 75.
[38]Glenda Bissex, *GNYS AT WRK: A Child Learns to Write and Read* (Cambridge, Mass.: Harvard University Press, 1980), p. 197.

[39]Sharon Fox and Virginia Allen, *The Language Arts: An Integrated Approach* (New York: Holt, Rinehart and Winston, 1983), p. 206.
[40]Barbara Eckhoff, "How Reading Affects Children's Writing," *Language Arts*, vol. 60 (May 1983), pp. 607–616.
[41]Diane DeFord, "Literacy: Reading, Writing, and Other Essentials," *Language Arts*, vol. 58 (September 1981), pp. 652–658.

phrases, parts of plots, even the intonation pattern of dialogue from books they know. A second grader wrote the following when a researcher asked him to "Write a story." No other directions were given. Notice the number of stories that he "borrows" from in telling his own. The titles of his probable sources are given at right.

THE LONESOME EGG

Once there lived a Lonesome Egg	*The Golden Egg Book* (Brown)
And nobody liked him because he was ugly. And there was an Ugly duck too but they didn't know each other.	*The Ugly Duckling* (Andersen)
One day while the Lonesome Egg was walking, he met the Ugly duck. And the Egg said to the Duck,	
"Will you be my friend?" "Well, O.K." "Oh, thank you."	*Do You Want to Be My Friend?* (Carle)
"Now let's go to your house, Duck"	
"No, let's go to your house"	Dialogue from the
"No, we'll go to your house first and my house too."	*Frog and Toad* series (Lobel)
"O.K."	
And while they were walking they met a Panda Bear and they picked it up and took it to Duck's house. And then the baby Panda Bear said: "I'm tired of walking." So they rested.	
And soon came a tiger. And the tiger ate them up except for Duck. And right as he saw that he ran as fast as he could until he saw a	*The Fat Cat* (Kent)
woodcutter and he told the woodcutter to come very quickly. And when they got there the tiger was asleep. So the woodcutter cut open the	*Gingerbread Boy* (Galdone) *Little Red Riding Hood* (Grimm)

tiger and out came Egg and Baby Panda Bear. And they ate the tiger and lived happily ever after.[42]

Not only the content of this writing, but also certain conventions of the text reflect previous exposure to literature. The conventional beginning, "once there lived," and the traditional ending, "lived happily ever after," are obvious examples. Phrases such as "and soon came a tiger" and "out came Egg and Baby Panda Bear" have a literary ring to them. Discussion of whose house they will go to echoes the many conversations in the *Frog and Toad* series by Arnold Lobel. There can be little doubt about the influence of other stories on the shape and content of this 7-year-old's writing.

Older children become more consciously aware of the way they use literature to create stories of their own. In Australia, Trevor Cairney[43] asked 80 sixth graders if they ever thought of stories they had read when they were writing a story. Ninety percent were able to tell him about specific instances they remembered. A few high-ability students could describe writing a story based on several other stories. More common responses were related to using specific ideas from a story, using an established character as a model, borrowing a plot to use with a different character or setting, and using a genre such as legend for a model. He concluded that writing is influenced by reading in many different ways.

The role of literature, then, is significant to the development of writing. For ". . . the development of composition in writing cannot reside in writing alone, but requires reading and being read to. Only from the written language of others can children observe and understand convention and idea together."[44]

[42]Collected for NIE Research Project, "Study of Cohesion Elements on Three Modes of Discourse," Martha L. King and Victor Rentel, co-researchers, Ohio State University, 1983.
[43]Trevor Cairney, "Intertextuality: Infectious Echoes from the Past," *The Reading Teacher*, vol. 43 (March 1990), pp. 478–484.
[44]Frank Smith, *Writing and the Writer* (New York: Holt, Rinehart and Winston), 1982.

Literature and Critical Thinking

Recent calls for reform in education have stressed the need for children to become better critical thinkers and problem solvers. Many schools have set goals for developing these abilities, which has resulted in the publication of special practice materials and packaged programs as well as tests to measure specific skills. One of the benefits of using literature in the elementary school is that it encourages critical and creative thinking in a more natural way than worksheet exercises in logic.

Comparing, summarizing, and finding the main idea are generally recognized as components of critical thinking. These are also built-in features of good book discussions and other literature activities. As children compare many variants of the Cinderella story, for instance, they will identify similarities and differences and weigh the comparative merits of each. Talking about the moral of a fable, or the theme of a story, such as what lesson the animals learned in the tale of "The Little Red Hen," is a way of exploring its main idea. Children might also consider which of two biographies of Christopher Columbus presents the more balanced view of the famous explorer or which of several books about the Civil War presents the most complete picture of the issues behind the conflict. Because of its variety in content and the availability of many books on one topic, literature provides great opportunity for thinking critically and making judgments.

Literature Across the Curriculum

The widely read person is usually the well-informed person. The content of literature educates while it entertains. Fiction includes a great deal of information about the real world, present and past.

A 10-year-old reading *The Cry of the Crow* by Jean George learns much that is authentic and true about crow behavior. Written by a naturalist who has studied animal behavior and owned several pet crows, this story includes such concepts as crow communication, imprinting, and dispersal. More important than the factual information, however, is the story's theme of the significance of choice and growing up.

My Brother Sam Is Dead by the Colliers gives authentic information about one part of the American Revolution while it contrasts different points of view held by the various characters toward the war itself. This story helps the reader to imagine what it was like to live in a family torn apart by divided loyalties. And it raises the larger political question concerning the role of neutrality in a revolution.

Picture books, too, can add information and human perspective to the curriculum. Patricia MacLachlan's story about a dog called *Three Names* offers pertinent historical detail about going to school in a one-room schoolhouse on the prairie during the early 1900s. Anita Lobel's lovely alphabet book *Alison's Zinnia* or Lois Ehlert's *Growing Vegetable Soup* can help young children learn the names of flowers and vegetables. The story of *The Doorbell Rang* by Pat Hutchins incorporates a math problem about sharing Grandma's cookies that children will want to solve.

All areas of the curriculum may be enriched through literature. Children may start with a story and research the facts; or they may start with the facts and find the true meanings in the stories surrounding those facts. Literature has the power to educate both the heart and the mind.

Introducing Our Literary Heritage

In general, the educational values of literature described here center on learning *through* literature. We must never forget, however, that as children have experiences with books, they are also learning *about* literature. As they enjoy nursery rhymes, traditional literature, and well-loved classics, they build a background for understanding genre, story structure, and many literary allusions.

Through in-depth discussions of such books as *The Whipping Boy* by Sid Fleischman, *Julie of the Wolves* by Jean George, or *Tuck Everlasting* by Natalie Babbitt, children become aware of what constitutes fine writing. While children will usually focus on plot or story, teachers can help them see the changes in Prince Brat's character under the influence of the whipping boy, or ask them why they think Jean George began her book when Julie was lost on the vast tundra rather than starting with the beginning of her story. Children can be led to discover the recurring references to the wheel, the toad, and the music box in *Tuck Everlasting* as a way of shedding light on their understanding of this lovely fantasy. Children's appreciation for literature and knowledge of their literary heritage should be developed gradually in the elementary school as a way to add to the enjoyment of literature rather than as an end in itself.

Evaluating Children's Books

What makes a good children's book? Who will read it? Why? Whose purposes will it serve? All these are important considerations to be taken up in later sections of this chapter and throughout the book. The primary concern of evaluation, however, is a book's literary and aesthetic qualities. Children show what they think of books through their responses, but they are not born critics in the conventional sense. Teachers and librarians need to value children's own interpretations and judgments. At the same time, they need to help children discover what practiced readers look for in a well-written book.

The traditional criteria by which we evaluate a work of fiction look at such elements as plot, setting, theme, characterization, style, point of view, and format. Special criteria need to be applied to different types of literature, such as picture storybooks, biographies, and informational books. Additional criteria are also needed to evaluate certain forms of fiction. For example, modern fantasy has to establish believability in a way that realistic fiction does not. Historical fiction requires added criteria for authenticity of setting. Perhaps the most important task for critics of any age is to identify the kind of book they are reading in order to apply the appropriate criteria for evaluation. In general, though, the following elements are crucial.

PLOT

Of prime importance in any work of fiction for children is the plot. Children ask first, "What happens? Is it a good story?" The plot is the plan of action; it tells what the characters do and what happens to them. It is the thread that holds the fabric of the story together and makes the reader want to continue reading.

A well-constructed plot is organic and interrelated. It grows logically and naturally from the actions and the decisions of the characters in given situations. The plot should be credible and ring true rather than depend on coincidence and contrivance. It should be original and fresh rather than trite, tired, and predictable.

In books that have substance, obstacles are not quickly overcome, and choices are not always clear-cut. In *Cracker Jackson* by Betsy Byars, 12-year-old Jackson struggles to find a way to help his ex-babysitter Alma, who he feels sure is being abused by her husband. He doesn't know who to tell or what to do. The problem is not easily solved, even though he goes so far as to "borrow" his mother's car to drive Alma to a shelter in a nearby town. This book is serious and funny at the same time, with a plot that seems true to the life of the characters.

Plot is the chief element of appeal in stories of mystery and suspense. In series mysteries, the action is frequently predictable; Nancy Drew never fails, and the Hardy Boys move smoothly from one major feat to the next. The action is usually beyond the capabilities of the characters and becomes contrived and sensational. In contrast, Avi's *The True Confessions of Charlotte Doyle* is a tautly constructed story of suspense. In this nineteenth-century shipboard murder mystery, events become increasingly surprising although the author makes them seem inevitable. The action begins sedately but moves at breakneck speed to the climax. As in other well-plotted books, the climax develops naturally from the interaction of characters and events. Children prefer a swift conclusion following the climax. The purpose of this brief denouement is to knit together the loose ends of the story.

Most plots in children's literature are presented in a linear fashion. Frequently children find it confusing to follow several plot lines or to deal with flashbacks in time and place. However, several excellent books for middle graders do make use of these devices. In the Newbery award book *Mrs. Frisby and the Rats of NIMH* by Robert O'Brien, the mouse's story is interrupted by a long flashback in which Nicodemus relates the strange tale of the escape of the intelligent rats from the national laboratory. The flashback

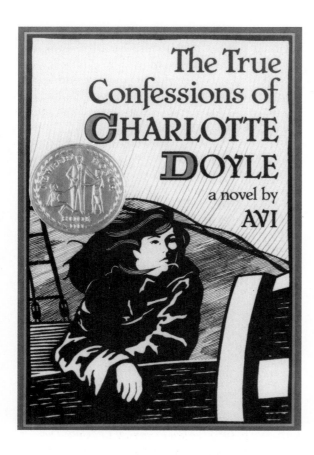

The jacket art for Avi's book provides a storm and a rolling sea to suggest the tumultuous action of the plot.

Illustration by Ruth E. Murray.

reveals the debt the rats owe to Mrs. Frisby's deceased husband and creates suspense as the reader is left worrying about the fate of Mrs. Frisby's very ill son, Timothy.

In *Cousins*, Virginia Hamilton dramatically portrays the grief and guilt young Cammy feels when her cousin, spoiled Patty Ann, is drowned on a day camp excursion. Although the book is a short one, it has multiple plot lines. The reader's attention is also drawn to Cammy's concern over the time her brother spends with troublesome cousin Richie and to her own attempts to brighten the life of Gram Tut, who is in the Care Home. The author uses remembered and imagined events, making part of the "action" take place in

Cammy's head. This gives the story a wonderfully rich texture but makes it more challenging. The effectiveness of structure in stories like these depends on the clarity of the author's presentation and the child's ability to comprehend complexity.

Plot is but one element of good writing. If a book does not have a substantial plot, it will not hold children's interest long. But well-loved books are memorable for more than plot alone.

SETTING

The structure of a story includes both the construction of the plot and its setting. The setting may be in the past, the present, or the future. The story may take place in a specific locale, or the setting may be deliberately vague to convey the universal feeling of all suburbs, all large cities, or all rural communities.

The setting for the haunting tale of *Sounder* by William Armstrong is the rural South sometime near the turn of the century. The story portrays the injustices and cruelties inflicted on a black sharecropper because he had stolen a ham for his hungry family. While the story has a specific setting in time and place, for many it represents the plight of all blacks in the rural South before Selma. The filmed version of *Sounder* changed the locale from Virginia to Louisiana and the time from the early 1900s to the depression year of 1933, with little loss in the impact of the story. Such a change suggests the universality of this story and its setting.

Both the time and place of the story should affect the action, the characters, and the theme. Place, time, and people are inextricably bound in Pam Conrad's *Prairie Songs*. Although Louisa's family see the huge Nebraska prairie with its endless skies as home, their new neighbor Mrs. Berryman is driven mad by its isolation and hardships. The setting that the author constructs includes geography, weather, the news of the day, and the details of everyday life. Pam Conrad drew on the work of a pioneer photographer in supplying these elements for *Prairie Songs*. Readers can compare their mental images of sod houses and prairie grass with the actual photographs in Conrad's nonfiction book, *Prairie Visions: The Life and Times of Solomon Butcher*.

Stories of the present often seem to occur in

homogenized settings that have little impact on character and action. There are notable exceptions, of course. When Brian's plane crashes at the edge of a wilderness lake in Gary Paulsen's *Hatchet*, the rigors of that setting dictate the terms of the tense survival story which follows. Jamal and Tito in *Scorpions* by Walter Dean Myers lead lives circumscribed by their urban ghetto environment. Marty's struggle to rescue his neighbor's mistreated hunting dog is perfectly at home in the rural West Virginia community created by Phyllis Reynolds Naylor in *Shiloh*. Books that provide a unique sense of place are more memorable than those which do not.

The imaginary settings of fantasy must be carefully detailed in order to create a believable story. In *Charlotte's Web*, E. B. White has made us see and smell Wilbur's barnyard home so clearly that it takes little stretch of the imagination to listen in on the animals' conversations. In *A Wizard of Earthsea*, a more serious fantasy by Ursula Le Guin, the tale of wizards, dragons, and shadows is played out in an archipelago of imagined islands. Ruth Robbins has provided a map of Earthsea, for its geography is as exact as the laws and limits of magic used by the wizards of the isles. The Yorkshire setting of *The Secret Garden* by Frances Hodgson Burnett looms large in the memories of generations of children who have loved this mysterious tale. In the mind's eye, the reader can see the many-roomed Misselthwaite Manor with its long corridors and tapestry-covered doors and hear the faint sound of the far-off crying of Colin mixed with the mournful wind from the moor. By contrast, the walled garden that Mary discovers is still and quiet, holding the promise of spring and restored health for both the lonely forgotten children.

The setting of a story, then, is important in creating mood, authenticity, and credibility. The accident of place and time in a person's life may be as significant as the accident of birth, for places may have tremendous significance in our life story.

THEME

A third point in the evaluation of any story is its overarching theme or themes, the larger meanings that lie beneath the story's surface. Most well-written books may be read for several layers of meaning—plot, theme, or metaphor. On one level the story of *Charlotte's Web* by E. B. White is simply an absurd but amusing tale of how a spider saves the life of a pig; on another level, it reveals the meaning of loneliness and the obligations of friendship. A third layer of significance can be seen in the acceptance of death as a natural part of the cycle of life. Finally, E. B. White himself wrote that it was ". . . an *appreciative* story. . . . It celebrates life, the seasons, the goodness of the barn, the beauty of the world, the glory of everything."[45]

The theme of a book reveals something of the author's purpose in writing the story. Katherine Paterson eloquently states how authors and readers are partners in calling up true meaning:

> We are trying to communicate that which lies in our deepest heart, which has no words, which can only be hinted at through the means of a story. And somehow, miraculously, a story that comes from deep in my heart calls from a reader that which is deepest in his or her heart, and together from our secret hidden selves we create a story that neither of us could have told alone.[46]

Theme provides a dimension to the story that goes beyond the action of the plot. The theme of a book might be the acceptance of self or others, growing up, the overcoming of fear or prejudice. This theme should be worth imparting to young people and be based on justice and integrity. Sound moral and ethical principles should prevail. However, one danger in writing books for children particularly is that the theme will override the plot. Authors may be so intent on conveying a message that story or characterization may be neglected. Didacticism is still alive and well in the twentieth century. It may hide behind the facade of ecology, drug abuse, or alienation, but it destroys fine writing.

Some well-written stories do make their themes fairly explicit, however. In Natalie Babbitt's *Tuck Everlasting*, three motifs provide

---

[45]Dorothy L. Guth, ed., *Letters of E. B. White* (New York: Harper & Row, 1976), p. 613.
[46]Katherine Paterson, "Hearts in Hiding," in William Zinsser, ed., *Worlds of Childhood: The Art and Craft of Writing for Children* (Boston: Houghton Mifflin, 1990), p. 153.

meaningful threads that reappear again and again: a toad, a music box, and the concept of a wheel. The wheel is the one that represents the theme of this gentle fantasy, the cycle of life and death that the Tuck family can never experience because they have drunk by accident from a spring that has frozen them in time, to live forever. As Angus Tuck tries to persuade young Winnie Foster not to drink from this water, he uses the example of a wheel to carry his message about life:

> It's a wheel, Winnie. Everything is a wheel, turning and turning, never stopping. The frog is part of it, and the bugs, and the fish and the wood thrush, too. And people. But never the same ones. Always coming in new, always growing and changing, and always moving on. That's the way it's supposed to be. That's the way it *is*.[47]

Children in the middle grades can also comprehend symbolic meaning and recurring motifs. Literary symbols are the fusion of some concrete object with an abstract concept or meaning. Eight- and 9-year olds, for example, were able to understand the significance of Jean Fritz's title *The Cabin Faced West* with the brothers' admonition that no one was to mention their former home on the eastern side of the mountain. Children as young as 7 and 8 realized the symbolic meaning of the cloak Sarah Noble's mother had given her to wear when she went into the wilderness with her father in the story of *The Courage of Sarah Noble* by Alice Dalgliesh.

CHARACTERIZATION

True characterization is another hallmark of fine writing. The people portrayed in children's books should be as convincingly real and lifelike as our next-door neighbors. Many of the animal characters in modern fantasy have human personalities, also. The credibility of characters depends on the author's ability to show their true natures, their strengths, and their weaknesses.

Just as it takes time to know a new friend in all his various dimensions, so, too, does an author try to present many facets of a character bit by bit. In revealing character an author may tell about the person through narration, record the character's conversation with others, describe the thoughts of the character, show the thoughts of others about the character, or show the character in action. A character that is revealed in only one way is apt to lack depth. If a single dimension of character is presented, or one trait overemphasized, the result is likely to be stereotyped and wooden. One-dimensional characters are the norm in folk and fairy tales, where witches are prototypes of evil and youngest children are deserving and good. However, modern fiction requires multi-dimen-

From *Frog and Toad Are Friends* by Arnold Lobel.

[47]Natalie Babbitt, *Tuck Everlasting* (New York: Farrar, Straus and Giroux, 1975), p. 62.

From *Winnie the Pooh* by A. A. Milne. Illustration by E. H. Shepard.

❦ ❦ ❦

sional characters whose actions and feelings grow out of the circumstances of the story. Books are usually more satisfying when readers feel they are discovering the character through the story rather than relying on authors' labels, like jealous, troublesome, or shy. Children do not need to be told that Gus overcomes his fear of the dark in *The Stone-Faced Boy* by Paula Fox; he shows his bravery by rescuing a dog for his sister in the middle of the night.

In addition to depth in characterization, there should be consistency in character portrayal. Everything characters do, think, and say should seem natural and inevitable. We can expect them to act and speak in accordance with their age, culture, and educational background. In *Tales of Belva Jean Copenhagen* by Sandra Dutton, Belva Jean tells stories of her experiences in "country language." In her words, "I could have told you these stories in Standard English, but I'm not on

TV, and this ain't a formal occasion."[48] Belva Jean's way of speaking is an important part of herself that ties her to her family but separates her from classmates in her new school. In *Mirandy and Brother Wind* by Patricia McKissack, all the characters use a dialect appropriate to African-American culture in the rural South in the earliest years of the twentieth century. Grandmama Beasley, the oldest character, uses the most pronounced version of this dialect: "'Can't nobody put shackles on Brother Wind, chile. He be special. He be free.'"[49]

Another aspect of sound characterization is growth and development. Do the characters change in the course of the story, or are they untouched by the events in which they have a part? In picture books and short tales, we might expect characters to be fully described but not to

From *Ramona and Her Father* by Beverly Cleary. Illustration by Alan Tiegreen.

❦ ❦ ❦

[48]Sandra Dutton, *Tales of Belva Jean Copenhagen* (New York: Atheneum, 1989), p. 74.
[49]Patricia C. McKissack, *Mirandy and Brother Wind* (New York: Knopf, 1988), unpaged.

From *Little House in the Big Woods* by Laura Ingalls Wilder. Illustration by Garth Williams.

change much. In longer fiction, however, characters have time to learn and grow. Many characters are best remembered for the turnarounds they have made or the way they have matured. Readers do not quickly forget the struggle of headstrong, self-centered Jo of Louisa May Alcott's *Little Women* in taming her rebellious ways. Marguerite de Angeli has created a vivid character study of Robin in her outstanding book, *The Door in the Wall.* Robin, crippled son of a great lord, must learn to accept his infirmity and find a useful place in life. The gradual development of his character is made clear as he solves these problems. Another character who grows before the reader's eyes in a gradual and convincing manner is *Lyddie* in Katherine Paterson's book of the same title. A nineteenth-century New England girl who becomes a mill worker in an effort to save the family farm, Lyddie is courageous and determined throughout the story. The change comes in her ability to see the options of her life realistically and in her growing sense of the possibilities of her future as she sets off to attend the first women's college in the nation.

Not all characters change, though. A character may be well developed, multidimensional, and interesting and yet seem to remain frozen in that

particular time of his or her life. Such characters are common in humorous stories. In Robert McCloskey's *Homer Price* and Astrid Lindgren's *Pippi Longstocking,* the title characters remain consistent to their natures in all their adventures. Some stories, then, may be notable for character delineation rather than character development.

Long after we have forgotten their stories, we can recall some of the personalities of children's literature. We recognize them as they turn the corner of our memories, and we are glad for their friendship. The line is long; it includes animals and people. It is hard to tell where it begins, and we are happy there is no end. In our mind's eye we see the three loyal friends, Mole, Toad, and Rat, returning from their adventures on the open road; Mary Poppins flies by holding tightly to her large black umbrella with one hand and carrying her carpetbag in the other; she passes right over those comic friends, Frog and Toad, who are out looking for the corner that spring is just around; while Georgie hops down the road announcing "New folks coming" and nearly interrupts Pooh and Piglet in their search for a Woozle. In the barnyard Wilbur has just discovered a wonderful new friend, Charlotte A. Cavatica, much to the amusement of the wise geese and the sly rat, Templeton. If we look closely, we can see tiny Arrietty and Pod, out for a Borrower's holiday; Stuart Little paddles his souvenir canoe along the drainage ditch; and our favorite Hobbit, Bilbo Baggins, outwits the terrifying Gollum. Gathered in the schoolyard are the Great Gilly Hopkins and her tag-along friend, Agnes Stokes; while Meg Murry is consulting with the principal, Mr. Jenkins, about her little brother, Charles Wallace. Ramona comes by wearing the crown of burrs she had made so she can star in a TV commercial; Harriet with flashlight and notebook is just beginning her spy route, and Jeffrey "Maniac" Magee comes loping along with his sneaker soles slapping.

The line is long in this procession of real personages in children's literature. It reaches back in our memories to include Beth, Jo, Amy, and Meg; it stands outside a Secret Garden and listens to the laughing voices of Mary, Colin, and Dickon; and, with Laura, it delights in the warm coziness of the fire and the sound of Pa's fiddling in *Little*

House in the Big Woods. We know all these characters well because their authors created them and blew the breath of life into each one of them. They have come alive in the pages of books; and they will live forever in our memories.

STYLE

An author's style of writing is simply selection and arrangement of words in presenting the story. Good writing style is appropriate to the plot, theme, and characters, both creating and reflecting the mood of the story. Although some authors develop a style so distinctive that it is easily recognizable, their work may show variation from book to book. Gary Paulsen's *Hatchet* is a survival story told as a continuous record of the thoughts and actions of Brian, the survivor. The brief sentences arranged as individual paragraphs are choppy, breathless, tense:

🐛 I was flying to visit my father and the plane crashed and sank in a lake.

There, keep it that way. Short thoughts.

I do not know where I am.

Which doesn't mean much. More to the point, *they* do not know where I am. . . .[50]

Paulsen's *The Winter Room* is a more lyrical story that takes as its backdrop the changing seasons of a northern Minnesota farm. Carefully placed sentence fragments punctuate this narrative also, but here they are contrasted to long chains of sensory details. The following is only a part of a sentence:

🐛 . . . [when] Rex moves into the barn to sleep and Father drains all the water out of all the radiators in the tractors and the old town truck and sometimes you suck a quick breath in the early morning that is so cold it makes your front teeth ache; when the chickens are walking around all fluffed up like white balls and the pigs burrow into the straw to sleep in the corner of their pen, and Mother goes to

Hemings for the quilting bee they do each year that lasts a full day—when all that happens, fall is over.

But it still isn't winter.[51]

Most children do not enjoy a story that is too descriptive, but they can appreciate figurative language, especially when the comparisons are within their background of understanding. Katherine Paterson's island setting for *Jacob Have I Loved* is so vividly described that the reader can almost smell the saltwater marsh and the fisherman's catch of the day. In the introduction, Louise is returning to the island after having been away for many years. She strains to see the first sight of it, calling up island images as she imagines how it will look.

🐛 The ferry will be almost there before I can see Rass, lying low as a terrapin on the faded olive water of the Chesapeake. Suddenly, though, the steeple of the Methodist Church will leap from the Bay, dragging up a cluster of white board houses.[52]

Another example of style that mirrors the setting of the story and the background of its characters is *Sarah, Plain and Tall* by Patricia MacLachlan. The writing reflects the prairie setting and the straightforward manner of Sarah, a mail-order bride from Maine. The tension of the story lies in its themes of longing and belonging—Sarah's understated longing for the sea and the children's longing for a mother. The beauty of the sea is contrasted with that of the prairie; the light after a prairie storm reminds Sarah of a sea squall. At the end of the story, when Sarah has decided to stay, the child-narrator, Anna, reflects on the future:

🐛 Autumn will come, then winter, cold with a wind that blows like the wind off the sea in Maine. . . . There will be Sarah's sea, blue and gray and green, hanging on the wall. And songs old and new. And Seal with yellow eyes. And there will be Sarah, plain and tall.[53]

[51]Gary Paulsen, *The Winter Room* (New York: Orchard Books, 1989) p. 62.
[52]Katherine Paterson, *Jacob Have I Loved* (New York: Crowell, 1980), p. 1.
[53]Patricia MacLachlan, *Sarah, Plain and Tall* (New York: Harper & Row, 1985), p. 58.

[50]Gary Paulsen, *Hatchet* (New York: Bradbury Press, 1987), p. 47.

The repeated phrases in this passage have a rhythm like music, a cadence that is very satisfying, especially when the book is read aloud.

There is no one style or set of language patterns that is more appropriate than others for a children's book. Yet the tastes of children do place some demands on the writer. Since young readers tend to prefer action over description or introspection, those elements must be handled with special skill. Like readers of all ages, children crave dialogue. They feel as Alice in Wonderland did when she looked into her sister's book and said, "What's the use of a book without pictures or conversation?" Masters at writing dialogue that sounds natural and amusing are Rosemary Wells in her picture books such as *Max's Dragon Shirt*, Cynthia Rylant in *Henry and Mudge Take the Big Test*, and Ann Cameron in *Julian, Dream Doctor*. Writing the dialogue for a book of contemporary realistic fiction is particularly difficult because slang and popular expressions are quickly dated. Betsy Byars is one writer who skillfully captures the sound of today's idiom in her stories. Lois Lowry makes talk sound real in her books about *Anastasia Krupnik*, and Walter Dean Myers captures the sound of urban street language in books like *The Mouse Rap*.

The best test of an author's style is probably oral reading. Does the story read smoothly? Does the conversation flow naturally? Does the author provide variety in sentence patterns, vocabulary, and use of stylistic devices?

Although it is difficult for children to analyze a particular author's style, they do react to it. Children are quick to detect the patronizing air of an author who talks down to them in little asides, for example. They dislike a story that is too sentimental; and they see through the disguise of the too moralistic tales of the past. Adults are more responsive than children to the clever, the slyly written, and the sarcastic. Frequently, children are better able to identify what they dislike about an author's style than to identify what they like. Obviously, the matter of style is important when adults evaluate books for children.

POINT OF VIEW

The term *point of view* is often used to indicate the author's choice of narrator(s) and the way the narrator reveals the story. Whose story is it? Who tells it? In folk and fairy tales, for instance, the storyteller tells the tale, and the storyteller knows the thoughts and actions of all the characters. The storyteller's voice is also used in modern fiction, for books in which the author reports the comings and goings, the conversations, and the feelings of all the characters, villains as well as heroes. We say that such stories have an omniscient, or all-knowing, narrator. C. S. Lewis presents his Narnia series in this way. In *The Lion, the Witch and the Wardrobe*, we are sometimes with Lucy, sometimes with Edmund, sometimes with all four of the adventuring children, and occasionally in places where they can never go. With the use of the third person, the omniscient point of view allows the author complete freedom to crawl inside the skins of each of the characters, thinking their thoughts, speaking their words, and observing the action of the story. It also allows the author to speak directly to the reader, if he or she chooses, just as a storyteller would in a face-to-face situation. C. S. Lewis comments to his readers in parentheses, a practice that some children and adults find detracts from their enjoyment of the story.

Many children's books take a point of view that also uses the third person but gives the author less freedom. This limited-omniscient, or concealed narrator view does, however, provide closer identification with a single character. The author chooses to stand behind one character, so to speak, and tell the story from over his or her shoulder. The story is then limited to what that character can see, hear, believe, feel, and understand. Katherine Paterson has told the story of *The Great Gilly Hopkins* from this perspective. Gilly is "on stage" throughout and we see the world as Gilly sees it. We know what others think about her through their reactions to her and her interpretations of their thoughts. For example, Gilly is having her first dinner at the home of Trotter, her latest foster mother:

The meal proceeded without incident. Gilly was hungry but thought it better not to seem to enjoy her supper too much. William Ernest ate silently and steadily with only an occasional glance at Gilly. She could tell that the child was scared silly of her.

It was about the only thing in the last two hours that had given her any real satisfaction. Power over the boy was sure to be power over Trotter in the long run.[54]

The more direct narrative voice of the first person, once considered unusual in children's books, is quite common today. In contemporary realism it is almost the norm. Judy Blume helped to popularize this kind of storytelling with books such as *Are You There God? It's Me, Margaret* and *Blubber*. Blume's stories are not known for strong characterization, but they do reveal the author's ability to recreate the everyday language of children. Consider this bit of background from *Blubber*, in which a fifth grader describes where some of her classmates live:

🖐 Linda lives in Hidden Valley.... It's called hidden valley because there are a million trees and in the summer you can't see any of the houses. Nobody told me this. It's something I figured out by myself.

My stop is next. Me and Tracy are the only ones who get off there.[55]

The advantage of this sort of writing is that it makes for easy reading. It attempts to invite its audience by taking a stance that says, "Look—we speak the same language." The disadvantages, however, may outweigh the advantage of accessibility. This sort of writing does not stretch the reader's vocabulary or imagination. The short, choppy sentences simply reflect a 10-year-old's idioms and grammatical errors. Mollie Hunter warns that the first-person point of view can be restricting:

The result of this device may be a story to which a reader can relate in very direct terms; but simply because of the narrator's limited vocabulary, there is no scope for adventure in language which allows the reader's mind to soar.[56]

[54]Katherine Paterson, *The Great Gilly Hopkins* (New York: Harper & Row, 1978), p. 14.
[55]Judy Blume, *Blubber* (New York: Bradbury Press, 1974), p. 10–11.
[56]Mollie Hunter, *Talent Is Not Enough* (New York: Harper & Row, 1976), p. 23.

A child's perspective on the world is limited by lack of experience, just as vocabulary is. This is an added challenge for an author writing in the first person; for although it may be easy to present the narrator's thoughts and feelings in an appealing way, it will be more difficult to show that the narrator's view may be narrow, misguided, or simply immature when seen from a broader perspective. Stories told by older characters, or those who are especially intelligent or sensitive, usually do a better job of dealing with complex issues. Katherine Paterson's *Jacob Have I Loved* is written in the voice of Louise, who feels strongly that her family favors her talented sister. This beautifully written book is not limited in vocabulary, and it contains ample clues that Louise's version of life is not the only possible interpretation of the events that she reports. Still, the first-person account is so intense and so compelling that it takes a practiced reader to discover that the narrator's view might be flawed.

One of the ways that authors counter the limitations of a single point of view is to alternate the presentation of several views within the same story. Even picture books may present two sides of a situation in this way. *Two Terrible Frights* by Jim Aylesworth intertwines the stories of a little girl and a little mouse who are both looking for a midnight snack but find each other instead. Betsy Duffey's easy chapter book, *A Boy in the Doghouse*, tells how young George feels about the problems of training his new puppy, Lucky; alternate chapters provide Lucky's own amusing views about the difficulties of getting people to take proper care of dogs. In *A Chance Child*, Jill Paton Walsh extends a search through time, alternating the action and point of view to focus first on Christopher in England today and then on his horribly neglected half-brother, Creep, who has slipped down the canal into the time of the Industrial Revolution. Yet another way of manipulating viewpoint is to tell a well-known story in a totally new voice, as Jon Scieszka has done in *The True Story of the 3 Little Pigs as Told by A. Wolf*.

The author's choice of point of view (or points of view) necessarily influences style, structure, and revelation of character. In evaluating books we need to ask not just who is telling the story, but how it influences the story. What perspective does the narrator bring to events, and what vision of the world does that offer to children?

ILLUSTRATION

Today we have so many picture storybooks and so much beautifully illustrated nonfiction, poetry, and other genres that any attempt to evaluate children's literature without considering the role of illustration would be incomplete. The first task is to decide what function the art in a book is intended to have. Are the pictures meant to be decorations? Were they designed to complement or clarify the text? Are they so much a part of the story that you cannot imagine the book without them?

Most novels for older readers have no illustrations, although some include decorative designs to mark chapter breaks or an occasional drawing. Shorter chapter books for younger readers generally do have pictures. For instance, Beverly Cleary's *Ramona and Her Father* has black and white drawings by Alan Tiegreen that give emphasis to the family warmth and situational humor so prominent in the story. These pictures enrich the story but are not essential to the telling as they would be in a picture storybook. In picture storybooks, the words and the illustrations share the job of storytelling, of communicating the mood and message. In a wordless picture book the illustrations must do the job by themselves. In every case we would look for art that is aesthetically pleasing and carefully crafted. Naturally, we need to give more attention to illustrations in books where the pictures play a more important role.

Just as there are elements of writing like plot, theme, and characterization, so too are there elements of design like line, space, and color that help describe an artist's work. An artist may choose to use strong vertical lines or graceful curving ones, to apply light colors or dark colors, to leave quite a bit of space empty on the page or cover every inch. The artist selects the content of the picture, which may show its subject up close or far away, from below, above, beside, or head on. The artist's medium could be watercolor wash, pen and ink, woodcut, fabric collage, or acrylic paint, to name just a few possibilities. None of these choices is inherently better than another, but each produces an effect. It is up to those who evaluate books to determine if that effect is a good one for the story and its audience.

Leo and Diane Dillon use strong black lines and accents against shaded colors to picture *The Tale of the Mandarin Ducks*, a Japanese folktale retold by Katherine Paterson. These handsome illustrations give dimension to the characters by showing facial expressions and gestures; they also reflect the Japanese setting through their content and by borrowing the style of eighteenth-century Japanese woodcuts. Ken Robbins chose to use hand-tinted photographs for his concept book, *Bridges*. The pictures look more like paintings than photographs, which emphasizes the aesthetic as well as the functional nature of his subject. Margaret Wild's picture book, *Let the Celebrations Begin!* is based on a report that Polish prisoners at the Belsen concentration camp managed to make stuffed toys to give the children of the camp when they were liberated. Julie Vivas has taken the challenge of bringing such a grim setting to a young audience by almost eliminating background detail and dressing the characters in soft colors, even though their garments are rags. Though the figures are gaunt and their nearly bald heads and huge eyes are haunting, the rounded shapes of their clothing and their closeness to one another do convey a sense of warmth and a celebration of the human spirit. Critics may have differing opinions about the appropriateness of the artist's interpretation in relation to the topic and to the age level.

In considering illustration, then, we need to look at its purpose in a particular book. Are the pictures consistent with the story or intended as a deliberate counterpoint to it? Do they present a unique, aesthetically satisfying vision of the world of the story? See Chapter 5 for more about evaluating the art of picture storybooks.

FORMAT

The format of a book includes its size, shape, the design of pages, illustrations, typography, quality of paper, and binding. Frequently, some small aspect of the format, such as the book jacket, will be an important factor in a child's decision to read a story.

The total format of Marguerite de Angeli's

novel *The Door in the Wall* complements the medieval background of this well-written historical fiction. Her many black-and-white pictures realistically portray the castle, churches, and people of that period. The three full-color illustrations are as rich in detail as an original illuminated manuscript. The design of the title and dedication pages reminds the reader that fine books can be works of artistic as well as literary merit.

All types of books—novels, picture books, poetry, biography, informational books—should be well designed and well made. Many factors other than illustration are important. The type should be large enough for easy reading by the age level for which the book is intended. At the same time, if the type is too large, children may see the book as "babyish." Space between the lines (leading) should be sufficient to make the text clear. The paper should be of high quality, heavy enough to prevent any penetration of ink. Off-white with a dull finish prevents glare, although other surfaces are used for special purposes. The binding should be durable and practical, able to withstand hard use. Publishers produce many books in alternate bindings, one for the trade (bookstore sales) and an extra-sturdy version for library use. However, a book should never be selected on the basis of format alone. No book is better than its content.

The books we think of as truly excellent have significant content, and, if illustrated, fine illustrations. Their total design, from the front cover to the final endpaper, creates a unified look that seems in character with the content and invites the reader to proceed. One such book is Karla Kuskin's *Jerusalem, Shining Still* with woodcuts by David Frampton. This is an unusual nonfiction treatment of the history of the city of Jerusalem, done in picture book format. The text begins with a lyrical introduction about the passage of time and goes on to describe cataclysmic events in rhythmic prose. Repeated refrains in verse emphasize the rebuilding and endurance of the city from century to century. The typeface, the generous margins, the use of symbolic forms such as arrows, arches, and stars in the illustrations, the choice of gold and red and bronze as predominant colors—all contribute to the book's unified sense of place and of permanence in the face of change.

Desert colors, an emphasis on architecture, and sturdy lettering make a title page that effectively introduces the story of an enduring city in *Jerusalem, Shining Still* by Karla Kuskin.

Illustration by David Frampton.

COMPARISON TO OTHERS

A book should not be considered in isolation but as a part of the larger body of literature. Individual books need to be compared with others on the same subject or theme. Is this just another horse story, or does it make a distinctive contribution? Every teacher and librarian should know some books well enough to develop a personal list of books of excellence that can serve as models for comparison. How does this adventure story compare with Armstrong Sperry's *Call It Courage*, this fantasy with *A Wrinkle in Time* by Madeleine L'Engle, or this historical fiction with Elizabeth George Speare's *The Sign of the Beaver?*

These reference points of outstanding books help to sharpen evaluations.

An author's new book should be compared with his or her previous works. Contributions by the same author may be uneven and inconsistent in quality. What is the best book Jean George has written? Is *On the Far Side of the Mountain* as good as *My Side of the Mountain?* How does *Water-Sky* compare with *Julie of the Wolves?* Too frequently, books are evaluated on the basis of the author's reputation rather than for their inherent worth.

Many informational and biographical series are written by different authors. The quality of the book varies with the ability of the writer, despite similarities in approach and format. Rather than condemning or approving an entire series, evaluate a book on its own merits.

A book needs to be compared with outstanding prototypes, with other books written by the same author, and with other books in the same series. What have reputable reviewers said about this book? Where have they placed it in relation to others of its type? A comparison of reviews of one book usually reveals more similarities than differences, although reviewers have personal preferences just as other readers do.

In summary, the basic considerations for the evaluation of fiction for children are a well-constructed plot that moves, a significant theme, authentic setting, a credible point of view, convincing characterization, appropriate style, and attractive format. Not all books achieve excellence in each of these areas. Some books are remembered for their fine characterizations, others for their exciting plots, and others for the evocation of the setting. The "Guidelines: Evaluating Children's Literature" on pages 34–35 may help the reader look at a book more carefully. However, not all questions will be appropriate for each book.

Classics in Children's Literature

Knowledge of children's classics, those books that have stood the test of time, may provide further guidance for evaluating children's books. What makes a book endure from one generation to another? Alice Jordan states: "Until a book has weathered at least one generation and is accepted

in the next, it can hardly be given the rank of a classic. . . ."[57]

Many books and poems have achieved an honored position in children's literature through a combination of adult adoration, parent perpetuation, and teacher assignments. Most adults remember with nostalgia the books they read as children. They tend to think that what they read was best and ignore the possiblity of the production of any better books. It is easy to forget that every "classic" was once a new book; that some of today's new books will be the classics of tomorrow. Teachers and librarians should begin with modern children and their interests, not adults' interests when *they* were children.

Certain books became classics when there were very few books from which children could choose. In fact, many classics were not children's books at all, but were written for adults. In their desire to read, children claimed these adult books, struggled through the difficult parts, and disregarded what they did not understand. They had no other choice. Today's child is not so persevering because he sees no reason for it. The introductory sentence of *Robinson Crusoe* runs the length of the entire first page and contains difficult vocabulary and syntax. Defoe wrote the story in 1719 for adult readers, but children quickly discovered this story of shipwreck and adventure and plunged into it. However, they can find the same tingling excitement and more readable prose in modern survival stories such as Avi's *The True Confessions of Charlotte Doyle* or *From the Mixed-Up Files of Mrs. Basil E. Frankweiler* by E. L. Konigsburg.

The classics should not be exempted from reevaluation by virtue of their past veneration. They should be able to compete favorably with contemporary books. Unimpressed by vintage or lineage, children seldom read a book because they think they should. They read more for enjoyment than edification. Some books have been kept alive from one generation to the next by the common consent of critics and children; these are the true classics of children's literature.

---

[57]Alice M. Jordan, *Children's Classics* (Boston: Horn Book, 1947), p. 4.

No teacher or parent has to cajole a child into reading them. These books can hold their own amid the ever-increasing number of new and beautiful books of today.

What is the continuing appeal of these well-loved books for the contemporary child? Primarily, they are magnificent stories. There are adventure and suspense in Robert Louis Stevenson's *Treasure Island* and *The Adventures of Tom Sawyer* and *The Adventures of Huckleberry Finn*, both by Mark Twain. Mystery and excitement fill the stories *Hans Brinker, Or the Silver Skates* by Mary Mapes Dodge and *The Secret Garden* by Frances Hodgson Burnett. The characterization in most of the classics is outstanding. There is very little plot in the story of *Little Women*, but what reader can forget the March sisters? They could have been your next-door neighbors. In A. A. Milne's *Winnie the Pooh*, the animal personalities of Christopher Robin's stuffed toys are unmistakable. Even adults have known a gloomy Eeyore! And anyone, young or old, can admire the enduring loyalty of Ratty and Mole for the rich conceited Toad who drags them away from their beloved riverbank on wild escapades in *The Wind in the Willows* by Kenneth Grahame.

The appeal of many of the classics is based on the type of story they represent. Family chronicles such as *Little Women* by Louisa May Alcott and "The Little House" books by Laura Ingalls Wilder give the reader a sense of warmth and security. A feeling of place and atmosphere is skillfully developed in Johanna Spyri's well-loved *Heidi*. Animal stories are represented by *Black Beauty*, *The Jungle Book*, and *Bambi*. *Black Beauty* is a sentimental tale filled with short essays on the prevention of cruelty to animals. The theme was timely in 1877 when Anna Sewell wrote this story. However, the genuine emotion in *Black Beauty* appears to be timeless, for it remains popular despite its Victorian airs. Boys and girls still enjoy Rudyard Kipling's *The Jungle Book*, the beautifully written story of Mowgli, who was adopted by the wolf pack when he was a baby and taught the law of the jungle by Bagheera, the panther, and Baloo, the bear. Most children also like Felix Salten's sensitively written, if somewhat sentimental, *Bambi*, the life story of a deer of the Danube forest.

Many classics are fantasies. Children's reactions to fantasy are similar to those of many adults, who thoroughly enjoy or completely reject the fantastic. For some people, *Alice in Wonderland* by Lewis Carroll, *Peter Pan* by J. M. Barrie, A. A. Milne's *Winnie the Pooh*, Kenneth Grahame's *The Wind in the Willows*, and *The Wizard of Oz* by L. Frank Baum have never been surpassed in the field of children's literature. Others actively dislike these books. Many readers do not "discover" these fantasies until they are adults, and then they applaud them as excellent fare for children! True classics appeal to both children and adults.

The Award Books [58]

Teachers and librarians will find it helpful to be familiar with books that have won awards. These awards, which have been established for various purposes, provide criteria for what experts consider to be the best in children's literature. Such awards have helped to counteract the judgment of the marketplace by focusing attention on beautiful and worthwhile books. In an age of mass production, they have stimulated artists, authors, and publishers to produce books of distinction and have helped children's literature achieve a worthy status.

The award books are not always popular with children. However, most of the awards are not based on popularity but on recognized excellence. They were never intended to rubber-stamp the tastes of children, but to raise them. Children's reactions to books are significant, and many awards, particularly state awards, are voted on by children. However, popularity of a book, whether for children or for adults, is not necessarily a mark of distinctive writing or artistic achievement. How many bestsellers win the Pulitzer Prize for literature? Because there are now so many awards in so many categories of children's literature, only the best known ones will be discussed here.

[58]See Appendix A for various children's book awards, criteria, and winners. For a complete listing of awards for children's books, consult *Children's Books: Awards and Prizes* published by the Children's Book Council. Information also appears in *Children's Books in Print*, New York: R. R. Bowker.

GUIDELINES

Evaluating Children's Literature

♦ Before reading:
What kind of book is this?
What does the reader anticipate from the:
> Title?
> Dust jacket illustration?
> Size of print?
> Illustrations?
> Chapter headings?
> Opening page?

For what age range is this book intended?

♦ Plot:
Does the book tell a good story?
Will children enjoy it?
Is there action? Does the story move?
Is the plot original and fresh?
Is it plausible and credible?
> Is there preparation for the events?
> Is there a logical series of happenings?
> Is there a basis of cause and effect in the happenings?

Is there an identifiable climax?
How do events build to a climax?
Is the plot well constructed?

♦ Setting:
Where does the story take place?
How does the author indicate the time?
How does the setting affect the action, characters, or theme?
Does the story transcend the setting and have universal implications?

♦ Theme:
Does the story have a theme?
Is the theme worth imparting to children?
Does the theme emerge naturally from the story, or is it stated too obviously?

Does the theme overpower the story?
Does it avoid moralizing?
How does the author use motifs or symbols to intensify meaning?

♦ Characterization:
How does the author reveal characters?
> Through narration?
> In conversation?
> By thoughts of others?
> By thoughts of the character?
> Through action?

Are the characters convincing and credible?
Do we see their strengths and their weaknesses?
Does the author avoid stereotyping?
Is the behavior of the characters consistent with their ages and background?
Is there any character development or growth?
Has the author shown the causes of character behavior or development?

♦ Style:
Is the style of writing appropriate to the subject?
Is the style straightforward or figurative?
Is the dialogue natural and suited to the characters?
How did the author create a mood? Is the overall impression one of mystery, gloom, evil, joy, security?

♦ Point of view:
Is the point of view from which the story is told appropriate to the purpose of the book?

NEWBERY AND CALDECOTT AWARDS

Two of the most coveted awards in children's literature are the Newbery and Caldecott Medals. Winners are chosen every year by two committees of the Association for Library Service to Children, a division of the American Library Association. A candidate for either of the awards must be a citizen or resident of the United States.

The John Newbery Medal, established in 1922, is the oldest award for children's books. It is named for John Newbery, a British publisher and bookseller of the eighteenth century. Appropriately called the "father of children's literature," he was the first to publish books expressly for children. The Newbery Medal is awarded to the author of the most distinguished contribution to American literature for children published the preceding year. Although the award is occasionally given to a book with outstanding illustrations, such as *A Visit to William Blake's Inn* by Nancy Willard, with pictures by Alice and Martin Provensen, the Newbery Medal honors the quality of the writing. Many age ranges are represented, but most of the Newbery books are for able, mature readers. Frequently, these books have to be read aloud and discussed with an adult before children develop a taste for their excellence.

The Randolph J. Caldecott Medal is named in honor of the great English illustrator of the nineteenth century, Randolph Caldecott. Caldecott was well known for his sprightly picture books depicting the country life of England. The Caldecott Medal, established in 1938, is awarded to the most distinguished American picture book for children chosen from those first published in the United States during the previous year. The text should be worthy of the illustrations, but the award is made primarily for the artwork.

Students of children's literature would do well to acquaint themselves with some of these award-winning books and their authors and illustrators. The Honor Books for each award are also worth knowing. Since the selection for the awards must be limited to books published in one year, the quality of the award books varies, for certain years produce a richer harvest than others. In the majority of cases the years have shown the choices were wise ones, but there have been a few surprises. In 1953, for instance, the highly praised *Charlotte's Web* was a Newbery Honor Book, edged out in the competition by Ann Nolan Clark's *Secret of the Andes,* a beautifully written but far less popular story. Books by Laura Ingalls Wilder were in the Honor category five different years, but never received the award. Final restitution was made, perhaps, by the establishment of the Laura Ingalls Wilder Award, which serves a different purpose.

The list of Caldecott Medal winners shows great variety as to type of artwork, media used, age appeal, and subject matter. The range of artwork includes the lovely winterscapes by John Schoenherr for Jane Yolen's *Owl Moon,* the comic, almost cartoon, style of William Steig's *Sylvester and the Magic Pebble,* the stylized patterns in *Drummer Hoff* by Ed Emberley, the surrealism of Chris Van Allsburg's *The Polar Express* or David Wiesner's *Tuesday,* and the expressionistic *Lon Po Po* of Ed Young. Various media are represented among the winners, including collage, woodcut, watercolor, opaque paint, and various combinations of pen and ink and paint. Marcia Brown has won the Caldecott award three times; Chris Van Allsburg, Robert McCloskey, Nonny Hogrogian, Leo and Diane Dillon, and Barbara Cooney have been honored twice. Joseph Krumgold, Elizabeth Speare, and Katherine Paterson have each received two Newbery awards; Robert Lawson continues to be the only person who has won both the Newbery and Caldecott awards.

INTERNATIONAL BOOK AWARDS

The Hans Christian Andersen Medal was established in 1956 as the first international children's book award. It is given by the International Board on Books for Young People every two years to a living author and an illustrator (since 1966) in recognition of his or her entire body of work. Meindert DeJong, Maurice Sendak, Scott O'Dell, Paula Fox, and Virginia Hamilton are the only Americans to have received a medal so far.

The Mildred L. Batchelder Award was established to honor the U.S. publication of the year's most outstanding translated book for children. Like the Newbery and Caldecott, the award is given by the Association for Library Service to Children of the American Library Association. Appropriately, it is always presented on International Children's Book Day, April 2, which was Hans Christian Andersen's birthday.

LIFETIME CONTRIBUTIONS

The Laura Ingalls Wilder Award honors an author or illustrator for a substantial and lasting contribution to children's literature. It was established in 1954 by the Association for Library Service to Children and was presented first to Laura Ingalls Wilder herself, for her "Little House" books. First presented every five years, and now every three, the award makes no requirement concerning the number of books that must be produced, but a body of work is implied and the books must be published in the United States. The recipients of the award, including Beverly Cleary, Theodor S. Geisel (Dr. Seuss), Maurice Sendak, Jean Fritz, and Marcia Brown, are all creators who have made an indelible mark on American children's literature.

Some of the other awards presented for a body of work are the Catholic Library Association's Regina Medal and the University of Mississippi's Children's Collection Medallion. The Kerlan Award, which honors "singular attainments" in children's literature, also recognizes the donation of original manuscripts as resource material in the Kerlan Collection at the University of Minnesota.

There was no major award for children's poetry until 1977, when the National Council of Teachers of English established the Award for Excellence in Poetry for Children, to be given to a living American poet. This award recognizes the writer's entire body of work. Octogenarian David McCord was the first recipient; others have included Aileen Fisher, Karla Kuskin, Myra Cohn Livingston, Eve Merriam, John Ciardi, Lilian Moore, Arnold Adoff, and Valerie Worth.

Several other awards, like the Scott O'Dell Award for Historical Fiction and the Edgar Allen Poe Award of the Mystery Writers of America, honor particular kinds of writing. These prizes are given for individual books rather than for a body of work, however.

No one but the most interested follower of children's literature would want to remember all the awards that are given for children's books. And certainly no one should assume that the award winners are the only children's books worth reading. Like the coveted Oscars of the motion picture industry and the Emmys of television, the awards in children's literature focus attention not only on the winners of the year but also on the entire field of endeavor. They recognize and honor excellence and also point the way

In this Caldecott Medal–winning book, the father loads up his ox-cart with the many things his family has been making and growing all year long to take to market. Barbara Cooney's paintings accurately reflect the New England landscapes and early American primitive art.

From *Ox-Cart Man* by Donald Hall.

to improved writing, illustrating, and producing of worthwhile and attractive books for children.

GUIDELINES FOR SELECTION OF MATERIALS

The Need for Selection

Evaluation of a single book involves knowledge of literary criticism. Evaluation of a particular book for a particular child involves an understanding of both literature and the background and development of the child as a reader. Evaluation of many books, films, videos, discs, tapes, and other media for many children who will use them for a variety of purposes involves many considerations and requires the establishment of criteria for selection.

While the subject of this text is primarily children's books, we do support the concept of a school library media center for each school that offers a variety of materials in addition to books. With more than 73,000 children's titles in print, it becomes almost impossible for one text to include adequate discussion of both books and media. Thorough criteria for the evaluation of films, filmstrips, tapes, and computer software require another text.

Since the subject matter of contemporary children's books is changing, the need for written criteria of selection has increased. Realism in children's books and young adult novels reflects the same range of topics that can be seen on TV, at the movies, and in current bestsellers. It makes no sense to "protect" children from well-written or well-presented materials on such controversial subjects as abortion, narcotics, or sexual preferences, when they see stories on the same subjects on TV. Increased sensitivity to sexism, racism, and bias in books and nonbook materials is another area of recent concern that points up the need for a clear statement on selection policies.

Our children are growing up faster today than twenty years ago. In the limited time children have to be children, we want to give them the very best books available. The adage of "the right book at the right time" still holds true. Most children's books have to be read at the appropriate age and stage in the development of a child or they will *never be read.* The 8-year-old does not read *The Tale of Peter Rabbit;* the 12-year-old doesn't want to be seen reading *Ramona Quimby, Age 8;* and the 16-year-old has outgrown *Sign of the Beaver.* Introduced at the right time, each of these books would have provided a rich, satisfying experience of literature.

The number of books that any one child can read is limited, also. Assuming that a child reads one book every two weeks from the time he is 7 (when independent reading may begin) until he is 13 or 14 (when many young people start reading adult books), he will read about 25 books a year, or some 200 books. Given the number and variety of children's books in print, it is possible that a child may read widely, *yet never read a significant book.* Under these circumstances, the need for good book selection becomes even more imperative.

Principles of Selection

With the increase of both numbers of books published and objections to the selection of certain books, it is essential that schools develop a selection policy. All library groups strongly recommend that each school district develop such a written statement that governs its selection of material. This policy statement should be approved by the school board and subsequently supported by its members if challenged. Factors to be considered in such a policy would include the following: who selects the materials, the quality of material, appropriate content, needs and interests of special children, school curriculum needs, providing for balance in the collection, and procedures to follow for censorship and challenged material.

Who Selects The Materials?

Teachers, students, and parents may recommend particular titles, but the final selection of materials for the school library should be determined by professionally trained personnel. Larger school systems frequently have book selection meetings of all their librarians. At these meetings individual librarians review publishers' advance copies or books that have been ordered on approval. They give their own evaluations but usually say how they agree or disagree with reviews of the book in professional journals. Some librarians from smaller school systems or communities must select the books from reviews without seeing the books themselves. Reliable reviews of children's books play an important part, then, in the selection of books. Four well-known review journals are *Booklist, The Bulletin of the Center for Children's Books, The Horn Book Magazine,* and *School Library Journal.* Other sources for reviews are listed in Appendix B.

Quality Of Material

Criteria for evaluation and selection of all types of instructional materials should be established. Such criteria should be available in written form. Books for the collection should meet the criteria of fine writing described earlier in this chapter.

More detailed criteria for each genre are given in the chapters in Part II.

Decisions have to be made concerning the conflict between popular demand and quality literature. Librarians have agonized over whether to buy such popular formula books as the Nancy Drew mysteries, the Baby-Sitters Club books or the Pee Wee Scouts series. Some have voted in favor of including them in their libraries on the basis that they "hook children on books." Others have held the line for better written stories, maintaining that it is possible to find the same kind of excitement and satisfaction in better written books. This is a decision that must be made by individual librarians, based on their knowledge of the reading ability and interests of the children they serve and their own basic philosophy of book selection.

Arguments for and against rewritten classics have followed the same line of reasoning. If a child can't read Mark Twain's *Tom Sawyer*, shouldn't we provide an edition that she can read? But immediately we realize that it is the *original* book that has become a classic. When it is rewritten, though it may retain the original plot line, it is likely to lose the qualities that made it a classic in the first place.

Any book that Walt Disney adapts for a film immediately becomes Walt Disney's . . . , as in *Disney's Beauty and the Beast*, for example. The quality and language of these stories are drastically changed, and yet these are the books that children know and ask for. Many children seeing the film about Mrs. Brisby and "The Secret of NIMH" do not even know O'Brien's Newbery award winner, *Mrs. Frisby and the Rats of NIMH*, on which it was based. Do we give them the book based on the film and let them compare it to the original, or do we give them just the award winner? These are difficult decisions, but they must be made when selecting books. A written policy statement of the criteria to be used when purchasing books will help solve this dilemma.

APPROPRIATE CONTENT

The content of the materials to be selected should be evaluated in terms of the quality of the writing or presentation. Almost any subject can be written about for children depending on the honesty and sensitivity of its treatment by the author. In order to be specific, two examples are given. The first book is recommended; the second is not.

In *The Goats* by Brock Cole, a boy and girl are the victims of a cruel camp prank, stripped of their clothing and marooned together on tiny Goat Island for the night. Desperately embarrassed, they manage to escape. Rather than return to the camp, they "just disappear" into the countryside, where they resort to lies and petty thievery in order to survive. During their brief adventure, Howie and Laura, almost adolescents, develop a deep friendship and a new sense of their own strength as individuals. The opening incident, which forces the protagonists to think about their own and each other's bodies, sets the entire plot in motion. It also gives meaning to the story as an exploration of childhood confronted by an adult culture focused on sexuality and governed by rules that do not always respond to real needs. The author shows great sensitivity in his portrayal of these two young people and their seemingly hostile world.

A brief encounter with sexuality is also part of the story of *Gone and Back* by Nathaniel Benchley. Obadiah, a 13-year-old boy, and his family join the race for new lands in the West. During their trek Obadiah meets Lennie, a girl about his age. Talking in a barn one day Lennie asks Obadiah if he knows what it is to mate and if he would like to learn. He does; he would; so they do. And that's the end of the scene. It could be removed from the story and never missed in much the same way as the obligatory sex scenes of some adult fiction. Such writing may have shock value, but it does not constitute high quality literature.

Controversy about the inappropriateness of violence in books for young children has long been a subject for discussion. After protests by some psychologists, fairy tales were rewritten to temper the grim details that were once included. However, folktales represent the plight of the human condition and are symbolic of good and evil. The horror may serve as catharsis for fears and anxieties that may be larger than those depicted in the stories. In Grimm's story of *The Seven Ravens* the little girl must cut off her finger in order to enter the crystal palace and save her brothers. Neither pain nor blood is described. In the broad context of the story the action represents the sacrifice of the girl who was partially responsible for the original curse placed on her brothers. The rewards of the fairy tale are not easily won, and something must be given for each favor received. The monsters in *Where the Wild Things Are* by Sendak have been criticized for being too grotesque and frightening for young children. Yet children do not seem frightened of them at all. And the important theme of that story is that Max does return home where he finds the reality of warmth and love.

In some instances, books may be the very instruments by which children first encounter tragedy. Countless children have wept over the death of Beth in *Little Women* and the end of a loyal spider in *Charlotte's Web*. We hope that no children will ever again know the horror of a nuclear attack. *Hiroshima No Pika* by Toshi Maruki, with its starkly vivid writing and expressionistic pictures, helps children see the tragic events in the lives of one family. Seven-year-old Mii survives the first atomic bomb, but she never grows in mind or body after "the flash." Her mother saves her father, only to have him die later of radiation sickness. The book clearly shows that Americans caused "the flash." The author wrote it for children in the hope that never again would one nation inflict such horror on another. This may not be a book all children are fortified to withstand, yet our very survival may depend on today's children understanding the facts surrounding Hiroshima. This simple account of one family's survival particularizes their suffering in a way that social studies texts fail to do.

We should not deliberately shock or frighten a child until such time as he or she may have developed the maturity and inner strength to face the tragedies of life. However, literature is one way to experience life, if only vicariously. In the process, a reader can be fortified and educated.

Needs And Interests Of Children

Materials should always be purchased in terms of the children who will be using them. Chapter 2 emphasizes the needs and interests of all children in terms of their response to literature. As more and more schools mainstream children with special needs, libraries should be certain to include materials for them. Partially sighted children require books with large type; blind children, books in Braille or on tape. Children who come from nonreading homes (and increasingly television has made the climate in many homes today nonreading) may need more easy-reading books. At the same time our sophisticated culture has pushed the child into growing up faster and faster. As a result middle graders are clamoring for young adult books. All children, regardless of their background, should have access to a wide diversity of multicultural books to choose from. African-American children should have many books that reflect their experience, just as Hispanics and Asian Americans should have an opportunity to see themselves in books. In a pluralistic society, all children should have an opportunity to read about children of different racial, religious, and ethnic backgrounds. Children need books that will give them insight into their own lives, but they should also have books to take them out of those lives to help them see the world in its many dimensions. Suburban children need to read of life in the ghetto—it may be their only contact with it. And slum children must be introduced to the best literature we have. We cannot tolerate the notion that somehow it is all right to give poor children poor books. Regardless of a child's background, a good selection policy should provide a wide range of quality books and diversity of materials for all children.

School Curriculum Needs

Librarians consider the particular needs of the school curriculum when ordering materials. Particular units in social studies—such as "The Role of Women in History," a science unit on ecology, or a study of African folklore in literature—may require special books, films, videos, or artifacts. Intensive study of the local region will require additional copies of books about the particular state, industries, and people of the region. Children may want equipment for videotaping interviews of persons in the neighborhood or filming sites of local interest. With the increase of literature-based reading programs, teachers need large classroom collections of paperbacks. They also need sets of the same title for group readings. These are best ordered and kept in a central location, where teachers can select from them. Such arrangements must be made jointly with the personnel of the center and the rest of the faculty. The function of the school library media center is to provide a wide range of materials specially chosen to meet the demands of the school curriculum.

BALANCE IN THE COLLECTION

Every school library needs to maintain a balanced collection. Keeping in mind the total needs of the school, the librarian should consider the following balances: book and nonbook material (including videotapes, tapes, records, films, discs, filmstrips, and other materials), hardback and paperback books, reference books, and trade books, fiction and nonfiction, poetry and prose, classics (both old and "new"), realistic and fanciful stories, books for younger and older children, books for poor and superior readers at each grade level, books for teachers to read to students and use for enrichment purposes, and professional books for teachers and parents.

The librarian must always select materials in terms of the present library collection. What are the voids and needs in the collection now? What replacements should be considered? How many duplicate copies of a particularly popular book should be ordered? Every book added to a collection should make some distinct contribution to it. Just because children are interested in magnets does not mean that all new books on magnets should be ordered. What is unique about a particular book? Perhaps it presents new information; perhaps the experiments are more clearly written than in similar books; or it may be for a different age group than the one already in the library. Only the person who knows the total collection can make these book-buying decisions.

SELECTION VS. CENSORSHIP

There is a fine line between careful selection of books for children and censorship. The goal of selection is to *include* a book on the basis of its quality of writing and total impact; the goal of censorship is to *exclude* a book in which the content (or even one part) is considered objectionable. Selection policies recommend a balanced collection representative of the various beliefs held by a pluralistic society; censors would impose their privately held beliefs on all.

The National Council of Teachers of English has published a statement contrasting the characteristics of censorship with those of professional guidelines set up to provide criteria for selection of materials (p. 42).

The American Library Association has issued a "Library Bill of Rights," adopted in 1948 and amended in 1967, 1969, and 1980. This statement contains six policies relating to censorship of books and the right of free access to the library for all individuals or groups. This statement has been endorsed by the American Association of School Librarians, also. (See p. 44.)

Almost every school and each children's librarian in a public library has faced some criticism of the books in the children's collection. Criticism is not necessarily censorship, however. Parents, other faculty members, or citizens have a right to discuss the reasons for the selection of a particular book and to make their own feelings known. Only when they seek to have the book banned, removed from the shelves, restricted in use, or altered are they assuming the role of censors.

In the 1980s, censorship increased dramatically throughout the country. Individuals and groups from both the right and left, like the Moral Majority, religious fundamentalists, members of the feminist movement, and The Council on Interracial Books for Children, have all demanded the removal of certain children's books from libraries for various reasons. Targets of the censor generally include profanity of any kind; sex, sexuality, nudity, obscenity; the "isms," including sexism, racism, ageism; and the portrayal of witchcraft, religion, and drugs.

Award books are objects of censorship as readily as other books. The Caldecott award–winning book, *Sylvester and the Magic Pebble* by William Steig, was objected to by law enforcement groups because it portrays police as pigs. It made no difference that all the characters in the book are animals, that Sylvester and his family are donkeys, and that other characters besides police are also

RESOURCES FOR TEACHING

CENSORSHIP DISTINGUISHED FROM
PROFESSIONAL GUIDELINES: EXAMPLES[59]

EXAMPLES OF CENSORSHIP	EXAMPLES OF PROFESSIONAL GUIDELINES
1. EXCLUDE SPECIFIC MATERIALS OR METHODS *Example:* Eliminate books with unhappy endings.	1. INCLUDE SPECIFIC MATERIALS OR METHODS *Example:* Include some books with unhappy endings to give a varied view of life.
2. ARE ESSENTIALLY NEGATIVE *Example:* Review your classroom library and eliminate books that include stereotypes.	2. ARE ESSENTIALLY AFFIRMATIVE *Example:* Review your classroom library. If necessary, add books that portray groups in non-stereotypical ways.
3. INTEND TO CONTROL *Example:* Do not accept *policeman.* Insist that students say and write *police officer.*	3. INTEND TO ADVISE *Example:* Encourage such nonlimiting alternatives for *policeman* as *police officer, officer of the law,* or *law enforcer.*
4. SEEK TO INDOCTRINATE, TO LIMIT ACCESS TO IDEAS AND INFORMATION *Example:* Drug abuse is a menace to students. Eliminate all books that portray drug abuse.	4. SEEK TO EDUCATE, TO INCREASE ACCESS TO IDEAS AND INFORMATION *Example:* Include at appropriate grade levels books that will help students understand the personal and social consequences of drug abuse.
5. LOOK AT PARTS OF A WORK IN ISOLATION *Example:* Remove this book. The language includes profanity.	5. SEE THE RELATIONSHIP OF PARTS TO EACH OTHER AND TO A WORK AS A WHOLE *Example:* Determine whether the profanity is integral to portrayal of character and development of theme in the book.

[59]*Statement of Censorship and Professional Guidelines*, approved by the Board of Directors of the National Council of Teachers of English, 1982. Reproduced with permission.

shown as pigs. Steig obviously enjoys telling about and drawing pigs; his first book for children was *Roland the Minstrel Pig*, and the main character in *The Amazing Bone* is Pearl, an attractive and exceptional pig.

Madeleine L'Engle's Newbery award book, *A Wrinkle in Time*, has been attacked as being non-Christian because of its references to the Happy Medium and Mrs. Who, Mrs. Whatsit, and Mrs. Which, supernatural beings that some have labeled witches. Madeleine L'Engle is well known for her adult writings on Christianity; ironically, religious literalists have paid no attention to the total message of good overcoming evil in this well-written fantasy, but have seen only "witches." *The Great Gilly Hopkins*, a National Book Award winner written by Katherine Paterson, a minister's wife and twice the winner of the Newbery award for excellence in writing, was criticized because Gilly uses an occasional "damn." Yet surely a foster child who has been in three homes in three years is not likely to be a model of refinement. What is noteworthy about this book is the gradual and believable *change* in Gilly's behavior and character. In Jean Fritz's well-received picture-book biography *And Then What Happened, Paul Revere?*, an English Redcoat swears as he apprehends Paul Revere riding to rouse Concord. Fritz was criticized for using "damn," even though it is a matter of historical record.

Contemporary fiction for older children has come under increasing attack as these books have begun to show the influence of the new freedom allowed in books and films for adults. Such titles as Isabelle Holland's *The Man Without a Face*, which deals sensitively with a homosexual relationship, Alvin Schwartz's *Scary Stories to Tell in*

the Dark, which recounts tales of horror well-known in folklore, or Judy Blume's *Deenie*, which includes several references to masturbation, have all been targets of criticism and censorship attempts. Criteria for these books are thoroughly discussed in Chapter 9.

A more subtle and frightening kind of censorship is the kind practiced voluntarily by librarians and teachers. If a book has come under negative scrutiny in a nearby town, it is carefully placed under the librarian's desk until the controversy dies down. Or, perhaps the librarians and the teachers just do not order controversial books. "Why stir up trouble when there are so many other good books available?" they falsely reason. Some librarians have even defaced books in their misguided efforts to avoid controversy. More than one librarian censored Maurice Sendak's *In the*

RESOURCES FOR TEACHING

LIBRARY BILL OF RIGHTS[60]

The American Library Association affirms that all libraries are forums for information and ideas, and that the following basic policies should guide their services.

1. Books and other library resources should be provided for the interest, information, and enlightenment of all people of the community the library serves. Materials should not be excluded because of the origin, background, or views of those contributing to their creation.

2. Libraries should provide materials and information presenting all points of view on current and historical issues. Materials should not be proscribed or removed because of partisan or doctrinal disapproval.

3. Libraries should challenge censorship in the fulfillment of their responsibility to provide information and enlightenment.

4. Libraries should cooperate with all persons and groups concerned with resisting abridgment of free expression and free access to ideas.

5. A person's right to use a library should not be denied or abridged because of origin, age, background, or views.

6. Libraries which make exhibit spaces and meeting rooms available to the public they serve should make such facilities available on an equitable basis, regardless of the beliefs or affiliations of individuals or groups requesting their use.

[60]*Information Power: Guidelines for School Library Media Programs* (Chicago: American Library Association, 1988), Appendix D.

Night Kitchen by painting black tempera diapers on the naked hero, Mickey! In-house censorship or closet censorship is difficult to identify. Selection is a positive process; books are added to a collection for their excellence, to meet a curriculum need, to bring balance to the curriculum. Censorship is negative. Whenever books are rejected for nonliterary reasons, for fear of outside criticism, for example, librarians and teachers need to ask themselves if they are practicing selection or censorship.

DEALING WITH CENSORSHIP

If there is a demand for censorship, how should it be handled? The first rule is to recognize that anyone has the right to question specific selections. The second rule is to be prepared—have an accepted response process. The written selection policy statement should contain a standardized procedure to follow when materials are challenged. The following guidelines may be useful:

1. Do not discuss the issue until you can be prepared. Give the person a form for "reconsideration of a book" and make an appointment to discuss the book.

2. Write out a rationale for choosing and using this book with children if you have not already done so.

3. Make copies of reviews of the questioned book from professional reviewing journals.

4. Notify your principal of the expressed concern. Give him or her copies of the reviews and of your rationale.

5. At your conference explain the school's selection policy and present copies of the reviews of the book and the rationale explaining your reason for selecting it.

6. Listen to the stated concern as objectively as possible.

7. Inform the person that the material will be reconsidered by the selection committee if he or she wishes it to be.

8. Submit the reconsideration form to the book selection committee of librarians, teachers, and parent representatives for their discussion and decision.

In Mickey's dream he falls out of his clothes and into the fanciful world of the "night kitchen." More than one librarian censored Mickey's nudity by painting black tempera diapers on him.

From *In the Night Kitchen* by Maurice Sendak.

9. Inform the person expressing the concern what the committee decided and why.

Several forms for Reconsideration of Materials are available upon request. The National Council of Teachers of English provides one in their booklet *The Students' Right to Know*.[61] The American Library Association suggests two questions: (1) What brought this title to your attention? (2) Please comment on the resource as a whole, as well as being specific about those matters that concern you.[62] The major consideration, then, is to have a form available when you need it and to make it specific to the book itself and simple enough to fill out.

[61]*The Students' Right to Know* (Urbana, Ill.: National Council of Teachers of English, 1982).
[62]"Statement of Concern About Library/Media Center Resources" in *Intellectual Freedom Manual* (Chicago: American Library Association, 1983), p. 167.

Generally, if parents or other citizens feel their voices have been heard and that they have been dealt with fairly, they will abide by the decision of the book selection committee. If, however, they represent a group that is determined to impose its values on the schools, they will continue their pressure. This is why it is essential that every library have a Library Selection Policy supported by the board and administration. Librarians and teachers also need to be aware of the support they can obtain from such organiza-

tions as the Office for Intellectual Freedom of the American Library Association, Freedom to Read Foundation of ALA, The National Council of Teachers of English, the International Reading Association, American Civil Liberties Union, and People for the American Way.

Any challenge to a book is a matter to be taken seriously. Ultimately, what is involved is the freedom to learn and freedom of information, both essential to American rights based on our democratic heritage and principles.

SUGGESTED LEARNING EXPERIENCES

1. Write your reading autobiography. What memories do you have of your early reading? Did either of your parents read to you? Do you recall any of the books they read? Did any teachers or librarians read aloud to you? What books did you own as a child? What were some of your favorites? Do you recall any that you did not like? Do you know why?

2. Can you think of any one book that you read and reread as a child? What particular qualities of the story appealed to you? Reread it and evaluate it according to the criteria established in this chapter. Would you still recommend it for children?

3. Interview two or three classmates, colleagues, or family members about the influence of literature in their lives. In what way(s) have books been important to them? What titles are most memorable? Why?

4. Read one of the series books: the Baby-Sitters Club, Sweet Valley High, The Boxcar Children, or the Nancy Drew series. Look closely at the literary craftsmanship of the book. How many contrived incidents can you find? Do the characters have real strengths *and* weaknesses? If you read this book aloud, how would it sound?

5. Form a mock Newbery award committee and review the winners and Honor Books for one year. Do you agree with the opinions of the actual judges? Be prepared to state your reasons why or why not.

6. Read a recently published children's book and write a brief reaction to it. Then find reviews from two or more published sources. List the criteria that seem important to the reviewers. How are their criteria like or different from yours?

7. Using at least three of the selection aids described in Appendix B, make a list of appropriate poems, books, and materials that you would want to use to explore a particular topic with a selected age grouping. You might choose "mice," "night," or "friends" for primary grades; "the role of women," or "journeys" might be topics for older children. Be prepared to explain and defend your choices.

8. Interview a librarian and ask to see the current Policy for Selection. Ask if the library has had censorship problems and what was done about them.

RELATED READINGS

1. Butler, Dorothy. *Cushla and Her Books*, Boston: Horn Book, 1980.
   A moving account of the power of books in the life of a little girl with multiple handicaps. Charts at the end of the report show all of Cushla's interactions with books for one typical day; another one lists the books shared with her for the first four years of her life.

2. Coles, Robert. *The Call of Stories: Teaching and the Moral Imagination*. Boston: Houghton Mifflin, 1989.
    A noted child psychiatrist describes the influence of literature in his own life and its impact on the young adults he has taught at Harvard University and elsewhere.
3. Egoff, Shelia, G. T. Stubbs, and L. F. Ashley. *Only Connect: Readings on Children's Literature*, 2nd ed. Toronto: Oxford University Press, 1980.
    An excellent collection of essays on children's literature encompassing literary criticism, standards, changing tastes, children's responses to books, and writing and illustrating books. Many well-known contributors, including Rumer Godden, Nat Hentoff, C. S. Lewis, John Rowe Townsend, and others.
4. Hearne, Betsy. *Choosing Books for Children: A Commonsense Guide*. New York: Delacorte, 1990.
    This guide for parents features top quality selections and graceful style.
5. Hunt, Peter. *Criticism, Theory, & Children's Literature*. Cambridge, Mass.: Basil Blackwell, 1991.
    A fresh examination of important questions and issues such as what is children's literature, the nature of reading, and the role of style and narrative in children's books. Much attention goes to the underlying assumptions of critics and other adults regarding children and their reading, with emphasis on the relationship of ideology and literature. These complex ideas in generally readable terms will spark discussion and debate.
6. Kemp, Betty, ed. *School Library and Media Center Acquisition Policies and Procedures*, 2nd ed. Phoenix, Ariz.: Oryx Press, 1986.
    Provides sample policies, procedures, and forms from a variety of city, suburban, and county library systems.
7. Kingman, Lee, ed. *Newbery and Caldecott Medal Books 1976–1985*. Boston: Horn Book, 1985.
    The acceptance speeches of the award winners are included, along with biographical sketches, photographs, and illustrations or quotes from their work. In addition there are critical essays by Barbara Bader, Ethel Heins, and Zena Sutherland. Speeches of recent award winners are published each year in the July/August issue of *The Horn Book Magazine*.
8. Landsberg, Michele. *Reading for the Love of It: Best Books for Young Readers*. New York: Prentice Hall, 1987.
    Lively writing and strong convictions make this guide to choosing children's books exceptionally readable for parents as well as professionals. Landsberg does not hesitate to give low marks to popular authors like Judy Blume or to make clear her distinction between good books and bad books. Ten chapters organized around elements of reader interest are followed by an annotated "treasury" of 400 titles.
9. Reichman, Henry. *Censorship and Selection: Issues and Answers for Schools*. Chicago: American Library Association and Arlington, Va.: American Association of School Administrators, 1988.
    This indispensable book examines censorship issues with a rational, low-key approach that respects differences in belief. It suggests specific procedures for establishing selection policies and for dealing with censorship. Appendixes provide documents on intellectual freedom, sample letters, selection policy guidelines, and other helpful reference material for school librarians, administrators, and teachers.
10. Trelease, Jim. *The New Read-Aloud Handbook*, 2nd rev. ed. New York: Penguin Books, 1989.
    Written for a popular audience by a father who discovered what fun it was to share books with his family, this is a delight to read and a good gift for parents. The selection is highly personal.
11. Vandergrift, Kay E. *Child and Story: The Literary Connection*. New York: Neal-Schuman, 1986.
    Literary form, critical theory, and elements of story are some of the topics explored in this discussion of the aesthetics of children's literature. One of the book's strengths is that the author sustains her critical perspective without losing sight of contemporary children.
12. West, Mark I. *Trust Your Children: Voices Against Censorship in Children's Literature*. New York: Neal-Schuman, 1988.
    The case against censorship is presented in a series of interviews with authors, publishers, and anti-censorship activists. The book is unique in its focus on the censorship of children's literature and in the number of individual voices that are heard.
13. Zinsser, William, ed. *Worlds of Childhood: The Art and Craft of Writing for Children*. Boston: Houghton Mifflin, 1990.
    Essays by six gifted writers for children—Jean Fritz, Jill Krementz, Maurice Sendak, Jack Prelutsky, Rosemary Wells, and Katherine Paterson—reveal individual personality and a common concern for the needs of their audience. A special bibliography lists books that were childhood favorites of each author or ones that have influenced his or her adult life and work.

REFERENCES[63]

Alcott, Louisa May. *Little Women*. Dell Yearling, 1987 (1868).

Andersen, Hans Christian. *The Ugly Duckling*, retold and illustrated by Troy Howell. Putnam, 1990.

Anno, Mitsumasa. *Anno's Journey*. Philomel, 1978.

Armstrong, William. *Sounder*. Harper, 1969.

Asbjørnsen, P. C. and Jorgen E. Moe. *The Three Billy Goats Gruff*, illustrated by Marcia Brown. Harcourt, 1957.

Avi. *Something Upstairs: A Tale of Ghosts*. Orchard, 1988.

_____. *The True Confessions of Charlotte Doyle*. Orchard, 1990.

Aylesworth, Jim. *Two Terrible Frights*, illustrated by Eileen Christelow. Atheneum, 1987.

Babbitt, Natalie. *Tuck Everlasting*. Farrar, 1985.

Banks, Lynne Reid. *The Indian in the Cupboard*. Doubleday, 1981.

Barrett, Judi. *Animals Should Definitely Not Wear Clothing*, illustrated by Ron Barrett. Atheneum, 1970.

Barrie, J. M. *Peter Pan*, illustrated by Scott Gustafson, Viking, 1991 (1906).

Baum, L. Frank. *The Wizard of Oz*, illustrated by Michael Hague. Holt, 1982 (1900).

Benchley, Nathaniel. *Gone and Back*. Harper, 1971.

Blume, Judy. *Are You There, God? It's Me, Margaret*. Bradbury, 1970.

_____. *Blubber*. Bradbury, 1974.

_____. *Deenie*. Bradbury, 1973.

Brown, Margaret Wise. *The Golden Egg Book*, illustrated by Leonard Weisgard. Golden Press, 1976.

_____. *Goodnight Moon*, illustrated by Clement Hurd. Harper, 1947.

Browne, Anthony. *Willy and Hugh*. Knopf, 1991.

Burnett, Frances Hodgson. *The Secret Garden*, illustrated by Shirley Hughes. Viking, 1989 (1910).

Byars, Betsy. *The Burning Questions of Bingo Brown*. Viking, 1988.

_____. *Cracker Jackson*. Viking, 1985.

Cameron, Ann. *Julian, Dream Doctor*, illustrated by Ann Strugnell. McKay, 1990.

Carle, Eric. *Do You Want to Be My Friend?* Crowell, 1971.

_____. *The Very Hungry Caterpillar*. Philomel, 1969.

Carroll, Lewis. *Alice's Adventures in Wonderland* and *Through the Looking Glass*, illustrated by John Tenniel. Macmillan, 1963 (first published separately, 1866 and 1872).

Clark, Ann Nolan. *Secret of the Andes*, illustrated by Jean Charlot. Viking, 1952.

Cleary, Beverly. *Ramona and Her Father*, illustrated by Alan Tiegreen. Morrow, 1977.

_____. *Ramona Quimby, Age 8*, illustrated by Alan Tiegreen. Morrow, 1977.

Cole, Brock. *The Goats*. Farrar, 1987.

Collier, James Lincoln, and Christopher Collier. *My Brother Sam Is Dead*. Four Winds, 1974.

Conrad, Pam. *Prairie Songs*, illustrated by Darryl Zudeck. Harper, 1985.

Cooper, Susan. *The Dark Is Rising*, illustrated by Alan Cober. Macmillan, 1973.

Dalgliesh, Alice. *The Courage of Sarah Noble*, illustrated by Leonard Weisgard. Scribner's, 1954.

de Angeli, Marguerite. *The Door in the Wall*, Doubleday, 1949.

Defoe, Daniel. *Robinson Crusoe*. Houghton Mifflin, 1972 (1719).

de Paola, Tomie. *"Charlie Needs a Cloak."* Prentice-Hall, 1974.

Disney's Beauty and the Beast, illustrated by Don Williams. Disney Press, 1992.

Dodge, Mary Mapes. *Hans Brinker, Or, The Silver Skates*, Scholastic, 1988 (1865).

Duffey, Betsy. *A Boy in the Doghouse*, illustrated by Leslie Morrill. Simon & Schuster, 1991.

[63]Books listed at the end of each chapter are recommended, subject to qualifications noted in the text. See Appendix for publishers' complete addresses. In the case of new editions, the original publication date appears in parentheses.

Durell, Ann, and Marilyn Sachs, eds. *The Big Book for Peace.* Dutton, 1990.

Dutton, Sandra. *Tales of Belva Jean Copenhagen.* Atheneum, 1989.

Ehlert, Lois. *Growing Vegetable Soup.* Harcourt, 1990.

Emberley, Barbara. *Drummer Hoff,* illustrated by Ed Emberley. Simon & Schuster, 1974.

Fitzhugh, Louise. *Harriet the Spy.* Harper, 1964.

Fleischman, Sid. *The Whipping Boy,* illustrated by Peter Sis. Greenwillow, 1986.

Fox, Paula. *The Slave Dancer,* illustrated by Eros Keith. Bradbury, 1973.

————. *The Stone-Faced Boy,* illustrated by Donald A. Mackay. Bradbury, 1968.

Fritz, Jean. *And Then What Happened, Paul Revere?,* illustrated by Margot Tomes. Putnam, 1973.

————. *The Cabin Faced West,* illustrated by Feodor Rojankovsky. Putnam, 1958.

Gág, Wanda. *Millions of Cats.* Putnam, 1977 (1928).

Gallaz, Christophe, and Roberto Innocenti. *Rose Blanche.* Creative Education, 1985.

Galdone, Joanna. *The Tailypo.* Clarion, 1984.

Galdone, Paul. *The Gingerbread Boy.* Clarion, 1983.

————. *The Three Little Pigs.* Clarion, 1979.

Gardiner, John. *Stone Fox,* illustrated by Marcia Sewall. Crowell, 1980.

George, Jean. *Cry of the Crow.* Harper, 1980.

————. *Julie of the Wolves,* illustrated by John Schoenherr. Harper, 1972.

————. *My Side of the Mountain.* Dutton, 1988 (1959).

————. *On the Far Side of the Mountain.* Dutton, 1990.

————. *Water-Sky.* Harper, 1987.

Grahame, Kenneth. *The Wind in the Willows,* illustrated by John Burningham. Penguin, 1984 (1908).

Grimm, Jacob, and Wilhelm Grimm. *Little Red Riding Hood,* illustrated by Trina Schart Hyman. Holiday, 1983.

————. *The Seven Ravens,* illustrated by Lisbeth Zwerger. Picture Book Studio, 1989.

Hamilton, Virginia. *Cousins.* Philomel, 1990.

Heide, Florence Parry, and Judith Heide Gilliland. *The Day of Ahmed's Secret,* illustrated by Ted Lewin. Lothrop, 1990.

Henkes, Kevin. *Julius, the Baby of the World.* Greenwillow, 1990.

Herriot, James. *All Creatures Great and Small.* St. Martin's, 1972.

Hill, Eric. *Where's Spot?* Putnam, 1980.

Hoban, Tana. *Look Again!* Macmillan, 1971.

Holland, Isabelle. *The Man Without a Face.* Lippincott, 1987.

Hunter, Mollie. *A Stranger Came Ashore.* Harper, 1974.

Hutchins, Pat. *The Doorbell Rang.* Greenwillow, 1986.

Keats, Ezra Jack. *Peter's Chair.* Harper, 1967.

Kent, Jack. *The Fat Cat: A Danish Folktale.* Parents, 1971.

Kidd, Diana. *Onion Tears,* illustrated by Lucy Montgomery. Orchard, 1991.

Kipling, Rudyard. *The Jungle Book,* illustrated by Fritz Eichenberg. Grosset & Dunlap, 1950 (1894).

Konigsburg, E. L. *From the Mixed-up Files of Mrs. Basil E. Frankweiler.* Atheneum, 1967.

Kuskin, Karla. *Jerusalem, Shining Still,* illustrated by David Frampton. Harper, 1987.

Le Guin, Ursula. *A Wizard of Earthsea,* illustrated by Ruth Robbins. Parnassus, 1968.

L'Engle, Madeleine. *Meet the Austins.* Vanguard, 1960.

————. *A Swiftly Tilting Planet.* Farrar, 1978.

————. *A Wrinkle in Time.* Farrar, 1962.

Lewis, C. S. *The Lion, the Witch, and the Wardrobe,* illustrated by Pauline Baynes. Macmillan, 1986 (1961).

Lindgren, Astrid. *Pippi Longstocking,* translated by Florence Lamborn, illustrated by Louis Glanzman. Viking Penguin, 1950.

Lobel, Anita. *Alison's Zinnia.* Greenwillow, 1990.

Lobel, Arnold. *Days with Frog and Toad.* Harper, 1979.

————. *Frog and Toad All Year.* Harper, 1976.

————. *Frog and Toad Are Friends.* Harper, 1970.

————. *Frog and Toad Together.* Harper, 1972.

Lowry, Lois. *Anastasia Krupnik.* Houghton Mifflin, 1979.

————. *Number the Stars.* Houghton Mifflin, 1989.

Lyon, George Ella. *Borrowed Children.* Orchard, 1988.

McCloskey, Robert. *Homer Price.* Viking, 1943.

————. *Time of Wonder.* Viking, 1957.

McCord, David. "The Pickety Fence" in *Every Time I Climb a Tree,* illustrated by Marc Simont. Little, 1985.

McKissack, Patricia. *Mirandy and Brother Wind,* illustrated by Jerry Pinkney. Knopf, 1988.

MacLachlan, Patricia. *Sarah, Plain and Tall.* Harper, 1985.

_____. *Three Names,* illustrated by Alexander Pertzoff. Harper, 1991.

Magorian, Michelle. *Good Night, Mr. Tom.* Harper, 1982.

Maruki, Toshi. *Hiroshima No Pika.* Lothrop, 1982.

Milne, A. A. *Winnie the Pooh,* illustrated by Ernest H. Shepard. Dutton, 1988 (1926).

Munsch, Robert. *Love You Forever,* illustrated by Sheila McGraw. Firefly Books, 1986.

Myers, Walter Dean. *The Mouse Rap.* Harper, 1990.

_____. *Scorpions.* Harper, 1988.

Naylor, Phyllis Reynolds. *Shiloh,* Atheneum, 1991.

O'Brien, Robert. *Mrs. Frisby and the Rats of NIMH,* illustrated by Zena Bernstein. Atheneum, 1971.

O'Dell, Scott. *Island of the Blue Dolphins,* illustrated by Ted Lewin. Houghton Mifflin, 1990 (1960).

Paterson, Katherine. *Bridge to Terabithia,* illustrated by Donna Diamond. Crowell, 1977.

_____. *The Great Gilly Hopkins.* Crowell, 1978.

_____. *Jacob Have I Loved.* Crowell, 1980.

_____. *Lyddie.* Lodestar, 1991.

_____. *Park's Quest.* Lodestar, 1988.

_____. *The Tale of the Mandarin Ducks,* illustrated by Leo and Diane Dillon. Lodestar, 1990.

Paulsen, Gary. *Hatchet.* Bradbury, 1987.

_____. *The Winter Room.* Orchard, 1989.

Potter, Beatrix. *The Tale of Peter Rabbit.* Warne, 1902.

Reiss, Johanna. *The Upstairs Room.* Crowell, 1972.

Reyher, Becky. *My Mother Is the Most Beautiful Woman in the World,* illustrated by Ruth Gannett. Lothrop, 1945.

Richter, Hans Peter. *Friedrich.* Penguin, 1987.

Robbins, Ken. *Bridges.* Dial, 1991.

Rylant, Cynthia. *Henry and Mudge Take the Big Test,* illustrated by Suçie Stevenson. Bradbury, 1991.

Salten, Felix. *Bambi.* Buccaneer Books, 1981 (1929).

Schwartz, Alvin. *Scary Stories to Tell in the Dark,* illustrated by Stephen Gammell. Harper, 1981.

Scieszka, Jon. *The True Story of the 3 Little Pigs as Told by A. Wolf,* illustrated by Lane Smith. Viking, 1989.

Sendak, Maurice. *In the Night Kitchen.* Harper, 1970.

_____. *Outside Over There.* Harper, 1981.

_____. *Where the Wild Things Are.* Harper, 1988 (1963).

Seuss, Dr. (Theodor S. Geisel) *And to Think I Saw It on Mulberry Street.* Random, 1989 (1937).

_____. *The Cat in the Hat.* Random, 1966 (1957).

_____. *Oh, the Places You'll Go!* Random, 1990.

Sewell, Anna. *Black Beauty.* Grosset & Dunlap, 1945 (1877).

Sheldon, Dyan. *The Whales' Song,* illustrated by Gary Blythe. Dial, 1977.

Singer, Marilyn. "Deer Mouse" in *Turtle in July,* illustrated by Jerry Pinkney. Macmillan, 1989.

Speare, Elizabeth George. *The Sign of the Beaver.* Houghton Mifflin, 1983.

Sperry, Armstrong. *Call It Courage.* Macmillan, 1940.

Spyri, Johanna. *Heidi,* illustrated by Troy Howell. Messner, 1982 (1884).

Steig, William. *The Amazing Bone.* Farrar, 1976.

_____. *Brave Irene.* Farrar, 1986.

_____. *Roland the Minstrel Pig.* Harper, 1968.

_____. *Sylvester and the Magic Pebble.* Simon & Schuster, 1969.

Steptoe, John. *Stevie.* Harper, 1969.

Stevenson, Robert Louis. *Treasure Island,* illustrated by N. C. Wyeth. Scribner, 1981 (1883).

Taylor, Mildred. *The Friendship,* illustrated by Max Ginsburg. Dial, 1987.

_____. *Roll of Thunder, Hear My Cry,* illustrated by Jerry Pinkney. Dial, 1976.

Tolkien, J. R. R. *The Hobbit,* Houghton Mifflin, 1938.

Turkle, Brinton. *Thy Friend, Obadiah.* Viking, 1969.

Twain, Mark. (Samuel Clemens). *The Adventures of Huckleberry Finn.* Scholastic, 1982 (1884).

_____. *The Adventures of Tom Sawyer,* illustrated by Barry Moser. Morrow, 1989 (1876).

Van Allsburg, Chris. *The Polar Express.* Houghton Mifflin, 1985.

Vincent, Gabrielle. *Ernest and Celestine.* Morrow, 1986.

Voigt, Cynthia. *Dicey's Song.* Atheneum, 1982.

Walsh, Jill Paton. *A Chance Child.* Farrar, 1978.

Wells, Rosemary. *Max's Dragon Shirt.* Dial, 1991.

White, E. B. *Charlotte's Web*, illustrated by Garth Williams. Harper, 1952.
Wiesner, David. *Tuesday*. Clarion, 1991.
Wild, Margaret. *Let the Celebrations Begin!*, illustrated by Julie Vivas. Orchard, 1991.
Wilder, Laura Ingalls. *Little House in the Big Woods*, illustrated by Garth Williams. Harper, 1953 (1932).
Willard, Nancy. *A Visit to William Blake's Inn*, illustrated by Alice and Martin Provensen. Harcourt, 1981.
Williams, Karen. *Galimoto*, illustrated by Catherine Stock. Lothrop, 1990.
Williams, Margery. *The Velveteen Rabbit*, illustrated by William Nicholson. Doubleday, 1969 (1922).
Wrightson, Patricia. *Balyet*. Atheneum, 1989.
Yolen, June. *Owl Moon*, illustrated by John Schoenherr. Philomel, 1987.
Young, Ed. *Lon Po Po: A Red Riding Hood Story from China*. Philomel, 1989.
Zolotow, Charlotte. *Say It!*, illustrated by James Stevenson. Greenwillow, 1980.

Chapter Two

Understanding Children's Response to Literature

Five-year-old Michael hurried to the block corner from the story circle, where his teacher had just read *Little Red Riding Hood*. He whispered parts of the story under his breath as he worked to build a low enclosure around himself. When an aide walked by, Michael stood and made a growling noise. "I'm the big bad wolf!" he announced.

One rainy noon hour Sean and Dan, both 7, found a quiet corner by the bookcase and read to each other from Shel Silverstein's book of verse, *Where the Sidewalk Ends*. "Listen to this one!" (Giggles) "I can read this one!" (More giggles) Two other children discovered the fun and joined them. All four were soon arguing heatedly about which poem was "the best one."

A small group of 9- and 10-year-olds searched the well-stocked library corner of their own classroom for something to read at sustained silent-reading time. Jason picked a book, glanced at the cover, and quickly reshelved it. "Who would want to read a book like *that?*" he muttered. Emily whispered to Julie that she had found another Lois Lowry book about Anastasia Krupnik. "I get it next," the friend said, and went on looking for a book about horses.

At regular silent-reading time, 10-year-old Evie curled up in her class's reading-and-rocking chair to finish Katherine Paterson's book, *The Great Gilly Hopkins*. "The way it ended wasn't fair," Evie later protested to her teacher. "Gilly should have gone back to Trotter. This way just isn't right!"

A teacher asked her sixth graders to explain why they thought Jean George had written *Cry of the Crow*. Katie wrote: "I think what the author was trying to tell you is that once something has lived in the wild, it should stay there even if it's just like your brother or sister. . . . When you catch a bird and try to make it do something, it is like being in prison for the bird."

These glimpses of children responding to literature show some of the many different ways in which they may express their preferences, thoughts, and feelings. Although each of these responses is personal and unique, each one also reflects the child's age and experience. Young children like Michael are often so totally involved in a story that they relive it through dramatic play. Those like Dan and Sean, who are developing independent reading skills, seem particularly eager to demonstrate that ability and to share newly discovered favorites. Middle graders choosing books, like Jason, Emily, and Julie show definite preferences. In Evie's case, both the expectation of a happy ending and her concern with injustice in a character's life are typical of middle childhood. Katie's success in generalizing a theme about all wild things from the story of one crow and her fluency in discussing the author's purpose are representative of older children's growing ability to deal with abstract ideas about a story.

In order to have a successful literature program, teachers and librarians must know books well, but that is only half the task. It is also necessary to understand children and the changing patterns of their response to literature.

READING INTERESTS AND PREFERENCES

The term *response to literature* is used in a variety of ways. Theoretically, *response* refers to what happens in the mind of the reader or listener as a story or poem unfolds. In this sense, response is personal and private, hidden from the world. In another sense, a *response* also refers to any outward sign of that inner activity, something said or done that reveals a reader's thoughts and feelings about literature. A 6-year-old's drawing of a favorite character and a book review in the *New York Times* are both responses in this sense. Teachers or librarians who predict that a book will bring "a good response" use the term in a different way, focusing on the likelihood that children will find a book appealing and will be eager to read and talk about it.

Most of the early research on children and literature focused on this third area of response to discover what reading material children liked or disliked. Children's interests and preferences are still a major concern for teachers, librarians, parents, publishers, and booksellers. Everyone who selects children's books can make better choices by knowing which books are likely to have immediate appeal for many children and which ones may require introduction or encouragement along the way.

Studies of reading interests over the years have consistently identified certain topics and elements of content that have wide appeal.[1] *Animals* and *humor,* for instance, are generally popular across age levels. Among other elements that are frequently mentioned for reader appeal are *action, suspense,* and *surprise.* A study by Greenlaw and Wielan[2] looked at the comments of more than a thousand Georgia schoolchildren who were reviewing and "grading" new books in a program called Children's Choices, sponsored by the Children's Book Council and the International Reading Association. They found that most student comments referred to traditionally popular topics and elements of appeal, with humor, riddles and jokes, adventure, how-to, and animals among the most mentioned themes.

Even though we can identify commonly chosen topics and story features that have wide general appeal, it is still impossible to concoct a formula for books that would have unfailing popularity with *all* children. Teachers and librarians need to be sensitive to children's individual tastes, which are often unique and very particular. Nevertheless, the variations in interests among different

[1] Angela M. Broening, "Factors Influencing Pupils' Reading of Library Books," *Elementary English Review*, vol. 11 (1934), pp. 155–158; Fannie Wyche Dunn, *Interest Factors in Reading Materials* (New York: Teachers College, Columbia University, 1921); Jeanie Goodhope, "Into the Eighties: BAYA's Fourth Reading Interest Survey," *School Library Journal*, vol. 29 (December 1982), p. 33; S. A. Graham, "Assessing Reading Preferences: A New Approach," *New England Reading Association Journal*, vol. 21 (Winter 1986), pp. 8–11; George W. Norvell, *What Boys and Girls Like to Read* (Morristown, N.J.: Silver Burdett, 1958).

[2] M. Jean Greenlaw and O. Paul Wielan, "Reading Interests Revisited," *Language Arts*, vol. 56 (April 1979), pp. 432–434.

groups of children seem to be linked to age, gender, and certain other influences.

Age and Gender Differences

The most obvious change in children's interest patterns occurs with age as they take on more complex material and new areas of concern. Good book choices for first and sixth graders seldom overlap, even when the general topic is the same. Robert McCloskey's picture book *Make Way for Ducklings* is a favorite animal story among 4- and 5-year-olds; 12-year-olds prefer their animal characters to be part of something more dramatic, like Wilson Rawls's story about two coon dogs, *Where the Red Fern Grows*. Seven-year-olds laugh at Peggy Parish's *Amelia Bedelia* and her literal interpretation of instructions like "Draw the drapes" and "Dress the chicken." Eleven-year-olds like "funny" books, too, but prefer a different brand

of humor, such as the puns and wisecracking dialogue of *Borgel* by Daniel Manus Pinkwater or the comic situations in Barbara Park's *Skinnybones*.

Some of the broader shifts in preference that have been reported for elementary school children are summarized in the extensive review of research by Alan Purves and Richard Beach.[3] For instance, most children move away from a preference for fairy tales toward more interest in realistic subject matter. According to these studies, adventure becomes more important through the middle grades. Research continues to confirm older children's liking for adventure, mystery, and contemporary realistic stories. All of these

[3]Alan Purves and Richard Beach, *Literature and the Reader: Research in Response to Literature, Reading Interests, and the Teaching of Literature* (Urbana, Ill.: National Council of Teachers of English, 1972), pp. 69–71.

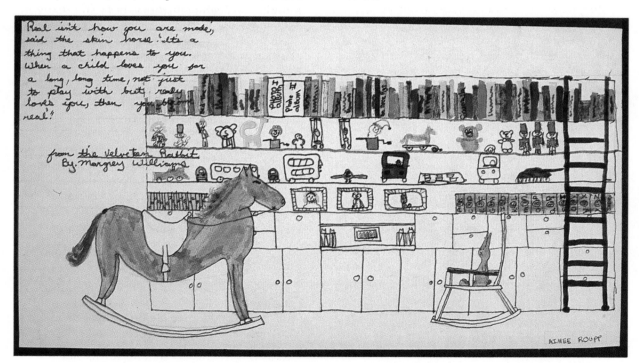

Choosing favorites and interpreting them are both a part of response to literature. Notice how the details of the modern playroom setting in this child's illustration for *The Velveteen Rabbit* provide a glimpse of her unique personal perspective on the book.

Martin Luther King, Jr., Laboratory School, Evanston, Illinois, Public Schools.

studies also show that upper-grade students begin to show marked content preferences according to their sex.[4]

The influence of gender differences on reading interests is not entirely clear. Most studies do report that interests vary with gender as well as age level. In the 1960s, Helen Huus reviewed twenty years of interest research and listed seven conclusions about age and gender differences in children's preferences for books:

♦ Interests of children vary according to age and grade level.

♦ Few differences between the interests of boys and girls are apparent before age 9.

♦ Notable differences in the interests of boys and girls appear between ages 10 and 13.

♦ Girls read more than boys, but boys have a wider interest range and read a greater variety.

♦ Girls show an earlier interest in adult fiction of a romantic type than do boys.

♦ Boys like chiefly adventure and girls like fiction, but mystery stories appeal to both.

♦ Boys seldom show preference for a "girl's" book, but girls will read "boys'" books to a greater degree.[5]

These statements still hold true for most children today, with one exception. Differences in boys' and girls' book choices, especially those related to the choice between fiction and nonfiction, are now evident long before age 9. Glenda Childress[6] found that in the library children of kindergarten age already had strong recreational reading interests, with boys picking nonfiction most of the time and girls picking fiction. Library circulation figures for more than 200 children in grades two through four studied by Pamela Jordan[7] showed that 53 percent of the boys' choices were nonfiction compared to 35 percent of the girls' choices. The difference became more pronounced in grades five through eight, where the boys chose 65 percent nonfiction and the girls only 28 percent.

What we do not know about gender differences in children's choices is whether they reflect a "natural" interest or conformity to cultural expectations. We might suspect that boys' increasing demand for informational books is in part a learned preference. In school and home settings where traditional sexual stereotypes are downplayed, boys and girls share enthusiasm for many common favorites. Elizabeth Segel writes that "the still prevalent tendency of boys to shun books with a female protagonist probably testifies more to the power of peer pressure than to any difficulty of cross-gender identification."[8] Segel stresses that it is important to keep the options for book choice open so that boys and girls can have a chance to explore each other's perspectives. It is just as unfortunate for girls to miss the excellent nonfiction being published today as it is for boys to turn away from fine fiction that offers insight into human relationships.

Other Determinants of Interest

Many factors other than age and gender have been investigated in relation to children's reading interests. At one time the influence of mental age as measured by standardized tests received considerable attention. A generation ago, David Russell came to three major conclusions after comparing the studies of reading interests and intelligence:

♦ Bright children like books that less able children two to three years older like.

♦ Bright children read three or four times as many books as average children and do not taper off in reading at 13 as most children do.

[4]B. A. Bundy, *The Development of a Survey to Ascertain the Reading Preferences of Fourth, Fifth, and Sixth Graders,* Dissertation Abstracts 44 (1983), University Microfilms No. DA 8312392; J. W. Coomer and K. M. Tessmer, "1986 Books for Young Adults Poll" *English Journal* vol. 75 (November 1986) pp. 58–66.
[5]Helen Huus, "Interpreting Research in Children's Literature" in *Children, Books and Reading* (Newark, Del.: The International Association, 1964), p. 125.
[6]Glenda Childress, "Gender Gap in the Library: Different Choices for Boys and Girls," *Top of the News,* vol. 42 (Fall 1985), pp. 69–73.

[7]Pamela Jordan, "Gender Differences in Library Circulation of Fiction and Nonfiction Titles by Grade Level," unpublished research paper, Ohio State University, 1991.
[8]Elizabeth Segel, "Choices `For Girls'/`For Boys': Keeping Options Open," *School Library Journal,* vol. 28 (March 1982), p. 106.

Although reading preferences are influenced by age, gender, and many other factors, children often make specific choices based on the book itself—its length, format, cover, or the appeal of a sample paragraph.

Martin Luther King, Jr., Laboratory School, Evanston, Illinois, Public Schools. Photo by James Ballard.

♦ There is little variation in the reading interests of bright, average, and less able children, except bright children have a wider range of interests.[9]

Children of varying academic abilities still are more alike than different in the character of their reading interests, but the quantity of books involved and the rate at which interests develop may vary widely.

[9]David Russell, *Children Learn to Read* (Boston: Ginn, 1961), pp. 394–395.

Illustrations, color, format, length, and type of print are all features of the books themselves that may influence children's choices. In one study of 2,500 kindergarten children, Dan Cappa[10] found that illustrations were the most important source of appeal, edging out story content. When Carol Brown[11] compared fifth graders' choices based on actual handling of books with choices made from annotations alone, she found that seeing the cover and illustrations did make a difference. G. Fenwick's[12] study of school library circulation among junior high school pupils revealed high popularity for books with a high percentage of illustrations. The editor[13] of one series of informational books has reported that when market research was undertaken to find what format the intended audience would prefer, middle-grade children resoundingly chose a 70/30 picture-text ratio over a 50/50 one. Conventional beliefs about children's color and style preferences were underscored in a formal study by Jerry Watson,[14] who found younger children drawn to bright, opaque colors, and all ages showing most interest in a realistic style of illustration.

It is tempting to oversimplify the effect of pictures on children's book choices, especially since so much of the research is done outside the context of normal reading and choosing situations. Barbara Kiefer[15] studied primary children choosing and using books in their own classroom set-

[10]Dan Cappa, "Sources of Appeal in Kindergarten Books," *Elementary English*, vol. 34 (April 1957), p. 259.

[11]Carol Lynch Brown, "A Study of Procedures for Determining Fifth Grade Children's Book Choices" (unpublished Ph.D. dissertation, Ohio State University, Columbus, 1971).

[12]G. Fenwick, "Junior School Pupils' Rejection of School Library Books," *Educational Research*, vol. 17 (February 1975), pp. 143–149.

[13]Pat Robbins, ed., *National Geographic Books for World Explorers*, in a talk before the Children's Literature Assembly, Washington D.C., November 22, 1982.

[14]Jerry Watson, "A Comparison of Picture Book Illustrations Preferred by Teachers and Children," *The Bulletin of the Children's Literature Assembly*, vol. 6 (Autumn 1980), pp. 13–15.

[15]Barbara Kiefer, "The Responses of Children in a Combination First/Second Grade Classroom to Picture Books in a Variety of Artistic Styles," *Journal of Research and Development in Education*, vol. 16 (Spring 1983), pp. 14–20.

ting and found their reactions to pictures and picture books were more complex than controlled
experiments or surveys could reveal. A child in
Kiefer's study commented about one of Lloyd
Bloom's illustrations for *We Be Warm Till
Springtime Comes* by Lillie Chaffin that it made
her feel "like I'm on my Mommy's lap."
Realizing that a black-and-white picture can give
such strong feelings of satisfaction helps us see
generalizations about children's preference for
color in a new perspective. Since books are in
increasing competition with media as a source for
both entertainment and information, it is surprising that there have not been more studies of their
visual impact.

Social and environmental influences also affect
children's book choices and reading interests.
Many teachers and librarians feel that cultural and
ethnic factors are related to reading interests. One
of the arguments for providing culturally authentic picture books and novels about Asian,
Hispanic, African-American, and Native-
American children is that readers from a particular
culture will find material drawn from their own
culture more interesting. The relationship
between interests and culture does not seem to
be simple, however, and unfortunately there is
not yet much research to clarify this point.

While interests do not seem to vary greatly
according to geographical location, the impact of
the immediate environment—particularly the
availability and accessibility of reading materials
in the home, classroom, and public and school
libraries—can be very strong. Children in classrooms where books are regularly discussed,
enjoyed, and given high value tend to show liveli-
er interest in a wider range of literature than children from situations where books are given less
attention. It is hard to tell how much of this effect
is due to contact with the books and how much is
social. Teachers' favorite books are often mentioned by children as their own favorites, perhaps
because these are the stories closest to hand, or
perhaps because of positive associations with the
teacher.

Children frequently influence each other in
their choice of books. In the culture of the classroom, a title or an author or a topic may rise to
celebrity status for a time. Shel Silverstein's *A

Light in the Attic may be "the book" to read in one
group of third graders, or children may make their
own sign-up sheets to read the classroom's only
copy of Judy Blume's *Fudge-a-Mania*. Younger
children may spend time on a theme study of
bears and long afterward point out "bear stories"
to each other. Media presentations like the
prime-time TV dramatization of Patricia
MacLachlan's *Sarah, Plain and Tall*, the
"Reading Rainbow" series, or "Wonderworks"
from the Public Broadcasting System create
demand for specific books.

Peer recommendations are especially important
to middle graders in choosing what to read. Some
fifth and sixth graders are very candid:

"Everyone else in the class read it, so I figured I
ought to, too." . . . "I usually read what Tammy
reads." ". . . most of my friends just like the same
type of book I like. So, if they find a book, I'll
believe them and I'll try it."[16]

Explaining Children's Choices

How can children influence each other's book
choices so readily? Part of the answer may be simply that age-mates are likely to enjoy the same
kinds of stories because they share many developmental characteristics. As children grow and
learn, their levels of understanding change, and
so do their favorites in literature. A few thought-
provoking studies have suggested that children
like best those stories which best represent their
own way of looking at the world.

André Favat[17] has argued that children reach
the peak of their liking for fairy tales between 6
and 8 years old because the reasoning and belief
systems in the tales are compatible with the
child's thinking pattern. Favat analyzed well-
known fairy tales and then compared characteristics of the stories to characteristics of young
children's thinking as described by noted psy-

[16]Susan I. Hepler and Janet Hickman, "'The Book
Was Okay. I Love You'—Social Aspects of Response
to Literature," *Theory into Practice*, vol. 21 (Autumn
1982), p. 279.
[17]André Favat, *Child and Tale: The Origins of Interest*
(Urbana, Ill.: National Council of Teachers of
English, 1977).

TEACHING FEATURE

Helping Kindergarten Children Respond to Fairy Tales

Taking advantage of 5- and 6-year-olds' interest in fairy tales, the kindergarten teachers in the Martin Luther King, Jr., Laboratory School in the public schools of Evanston, Illinois, have a folk and fairy tale unit toward the end of the school year. Each child selects a favorite fairy tale to share with the class, either telling it or reading it depending on his or her capabilities and the difficulty of the tale.

On the date of presentation, the child may choose to dress as one of the characters and/or bring food appropriate to the story. Each child also brings some artifact to place in the changing exhibit of the Fairy Tale Museum. The "museum" consists of a large bulletin board with tables in front of it. The child curators of the museum see that each object is appropriately labeled before it is put on permanent display.

Molly brought goat cheese and parsley when she told the "Three Billy Goats Gruff." Bashamba contributed an "original" brick from the little pig's house; Morton created a pipe cleaner replica of the stove used by the witch in "Hansel and Gretel." Asher brought the pea from "The Princess and the Pea" and Eric put in the stone from "Stone Soup," after he had served soup to his classmates.

Parents, of course, were alerted to the purpose of the fairy tale unit and told how the children would share the tales. They were asked to become involved in helping the children select the tale and ways to symbolize it with costume and artifact. The parents often came to school to be supportive and take pictures on their child's special day to tell the story. As one parent remarked, "I've had so much fun! It made me remember my favorite fairy tales." Another parent became very involved in helping her daughter select a story in which the female character was a strong heroine.

By the time all the children had shared their favorite tales, the rest of the class had heard new versions and discovered unfamiliar stories. They also found there were many ways to represent the same story. Well after the last story had been told, children still brought in artifacts to add to the museum.

Esther Weiss
Lynne Gilbert
Tatiana Simonaites
Martin Luther King, Jr. Laboratory School

chologist Jean Piaget. Favat found several similarities. For example, young children seem to believe that unrelated objects or actions can have magical influence on each other, just as in the fairy tales the kiss of the prince magically wakens Sleeping Beauty. Young children also tend to think that inanimate objects have human characteristics and that questions of right and wrong can be settled by swift punishment. Both of these situations are common in fairy tales. Although most 6- to 8-year-olds are growing beyond this way of thinking, Favat maintained that children find comfort in stepping back, through the story, into old familiar patterns of belief.

Norma Schlager's[18] study of literature choices in middle childhood reaches a similar conclusion; books with main characters who reflect the emotional and psychological aspects of the reader are the ones that gain a wide readership. Schlager compiled behavioral characteristics of 7- to 12-year-olds based on the developmental theories of Piaget and Erikson. Then she analyzed Newbery award–winning books that showed the highest and lowest circulations in a large library system. She found that the most popular books portray the world of childhood much the same as children see it, according to the child development experts, while the least popular books show a different view.

The analysis of Scott O'Dell's *Island of the Blue Dolphins*, the most widely circulated book in Schlager's study, shows that Karana, the story's main character, displays many of the mental attributes common in 7- to 12-year-olds. Karana lives virtually alone on her island off the California coast for eighteen years and must learn to survive without adult help. Children in the middle grades are also concerned with testing their own self-sufficiency, although the circumstances are usually much less dramatic. Karana's success is due to her ability to plan ahead, think logically, and work to make the things she needs. Schlager points out that children in the 7- to 12-age range are also developing the power of syllogistic reasoning, which allows preplanning and

[18]Norma Marian Schlager, "Developmental Factors Influencing Children's Responses to Literature" (Ph.D. dissertation, Claremont Graduate School, 1974).

problem solving, and that they too are task-oriented, with newfound abilities in craftsmanship. Schlager suggests that middle-grade readers showed little interest in the least circulated book (*Dobry* by Monica Shannon) because it does not include the characteristic behavior and thinking of their age level.

The argument that children's favorite types of stories reflect their intellectual and psychological development has also been applied to preschoolers and young teens. Nicholas Tucker[19] has provided a thorough discussion of the characteristics of children and their favorite literature up to age 14. For example, for children up to age 3, nursery rhymes fit the child's perspective by making the adult world seem more childlike and by representing the young child's sketchy understanding of cause and effect. Three- to 7-year-olds are better able to pick out a pattern of events, not just disconnected episodes, and so can really enjoy

[19]Nicholas Tucker, *The Child and the Book: A Psychological and Literary Exploration* (Cambridge: Cambridge University Press, 1981).

Children's interests and reading habits change as they grow. Still, many books bring shared delight across grade levels as these "reading buddies" show.

Mission School, Redlands Public Schools, Redlands, California. Photo by Larry Rose.

carefully structured stories like *Rosie's Walk* by Pat Hutchins. Many popular books for 7- to 11-year-olds reveal a changing relationship with parents, and children's hope of proving themselves to be as capable as adults. In the 11-to-14 range, Tucker points out that stories often echo young people's complex intellectual and emotional processes, with characters who are more analytic and introspective.

There are many other things to consider, however, in explaining children's book choices. One of the most important is prior experiences with literature. Some children have heard many stories read aloud at home or have been introduced by their teachers to many different authors and genres. These children are likely to have tastes and preferences that seem advanced compared to children their age who have had less exposure to books. Children's personal experiences influence their interests in ways that teachers and librarians may never be able to discover. And sometimes, apparent interests are only the product of which books are available and which are not.

We must be careful not to oversimplify any explanation of children's book choices. Even so, it is important not to underestimate a developmental perspective that takes into account both experience and growth. This is a powerful tool for predicting reading interests and for understanding other ways in which children respond.

GROWTH PATTERNS THAT INFLUENCE RESPONSE

The child development point of view begins with recognizing and accepting the uniqueness of childhood. Children are not miniature adults but individuals with their own needs, interests, and capabilities—all of which change over time and at varying rates.

In the early decades of child study, emphasis was placed on discovery of so-called normal behavior patterns for each age. Growth studies revealed similarities in patterns of physical, mental, and emotional growth. More recently, longitudinal studies have shown wide variations in individual rates of growth. One child's growth may be uneven, and a spurt in one aspect of development may precede a spurt in another. Age trends continue to be useful in understanding the child, but recent research has also been concerned with the interaction of biological, cultural, and life experience forces. We know, for example, that development is not simply the result of the maturation of neural cells but evolves as new experience reshapes existing structures. Experience affects the age at which development may appear.

Studies in children's cognitive and language growth as well as in other areas of human development have direct application for the choice of appropriate books and the understanding of children's responses. While this text can highlight only a few recent findings, it can serve to alert the student of children's literature to the importance of such information.

As we begin it seems worthwhile to offer a word of caution about graded school organization, which falsely appears to provide homogeneous classroom groups. Not only may there be a two-to-three-year chronological age range within one class, but children of the same age will reflect wide and varied levels of individual development. Many of our schools have developed multi-age units or family groupings which further increase diversity of interest and ability. In order to provide appropriate literature experiences for these children, the teacher needs to know each of them as individuals—their level of development, their rate of development, and their varying interests. To meet their needs, the school must provide an extensive collection of books and media covering a wide range of topics at various interest and reading levels.

Physical Development

Children's experiences with literature can begin at a very early age. Studies of infant perception show that even tiny babies hear and see better than was thought possible a few decades ago. For instance, newborns show more response to patterned, rhythmic sounds than to continuous tones. They also show preferences for the sound frequencies of the human voice.[20] This supports

[20]Aidan Macfarlane, *The Psychology of Childbirth* (Cambridge, Mass.: Harvard University Press, 1977).

the intuition of parents who chant nursery rhymes or sing lullabies that the sound of songs and rhymes provides satisfaction even for the youngest.

Infants gain visual perception very rapidly within their range of focus. According to Leslie Cohen's[21] summary of research, babies in their first 2 months of life see lines, angles, and adjacent areas of high contrast. They progress to seeing simple dimensions such as forms or colors, and before 6 months are perceiving more complex patterns (faces or colored shapes) as whole units. Books designed for babies and toddlers like Tana Hoban's *Red, Blue, Yellow Shoe* often acknowledge this developmental pattern by featuring simple, clearly defined pictures with firm outlines, uncluttered backgrounds, and bright colors.

As visual perception develops, children begin to show fascination with details and often enjoy searching for specific objects in illustrations. One 18-month-old boy spotted a clock in Margaret Wise Brown's *Goodnight Moon* and subsequently pointed out clocks in other books when he discovered them. Older preschoolers make a game of finding "hidden" things in pictures, like the apple in each scene of Clyde and Wendy Watson's *Applebet* or the Mother Goose and fairy tale characters tucked into each illustration of Janet and Allan Ahlberg's *Each Peach Pear Plum*.

Children's attention spans generally increase with age as well as interest. In their first school experiences some young children have trouble sitting quietly for even a 20-minute story. It is better to have several short story times for these children than to demand their attention for longer periods and so lose their interest. Some kindergarten and primary teachers provide many opportunities for children to listen to stories in small groups of two or three by using the listening center or asking parent aides or student teachers to read to as few as one or two children.

Physical development influences children's interests as well as their attention span. Growth in size, muscularity, and coordination is often reflected in children's choice of a book in which characters share their own newly acquired traits or abilities. *Whistle for Willie* by Ezra Jack Keats, for example, seems most rewarding for young children who have just learned to whistle. The demand for sports books increases as boys and girls gain the skills necessary for successful participation.

American children are growing up faster, both physically and psychologically, than they ever have before.[22] Girls reach puberty, on the average, two years earlier than boys, often while they are still in elementary school or just beginning middle school. The age of onset of puberty figures prominently in early adolescents' self-concept and influences book choices. Girls are still reading Judy Blume's *Are You There God? It's Me, Margaret* (1970) because it reflects their own concerns about menstruation. Margaret has frequent chats with God, which include such pleas as: "Are you there God? It's me, Margaret. I just told my mother I want a bra. Please help me grow God. You know where. . . ."[23]

Both physical maturity and social forces have led to younger heterosexual interests. Sophisticated 7-year-olds are teased about their "boyfriends" or "girlfriends," and one report indicates that 6 percent of young females beginning junior high school are already sexually active.[24] It is somehow as if childhood were something to be transcended rather than enjoyed. One result of this shortened childhood is a decrease in the length of time in which boys and girls are interested in reading children's literature. Many of them turn to reading teenage novels or adult fiction before they have read such fine books as *A Solitary Blue* by Cynthia Voigt or *Lyddie* by Katherine Paterson, both well-written complex stories about young adolescents.

[21]Leslie B. Cohen, "Our Developing Knowledge of Infant Perception and Cognition," *American Psychologist*, vol. 34 (1979), pp. 894–899.

[22]For hypotheses to explain this change, see Marie Winn, *Children Without Childhood* (New York: Pantheon, 1983), chapter 10.

[23]Judy Blume, *Are You There God? It's Me, Margaret* (Englewood Cliffs, N.J.: Bradbury Press, 1970), p. 37.

[24]Cullen Murphy, "Kids Today," *The Wilson Quarterly*, vol. 6 (Autumn 1982), p. 80.

Cognitive Development

The work of the great Swiss psychologist Jean Piaget[25] has had a great influence on educators' understanding of children's intellectual development. Piaget proposed that intelligence develops as a result of the interaction of environment and the maturation of the child. In his view children are active participants in their own learning.

Piaget's experiments led him to conclude that there are distinct stages in the development of logical thinking. According to his theory, all children go through these stages in the same progression, but not necessarily at the same age. He identified these stages as the *sensory-motor period*, from infancy to about 2 years of age; *the preoperational period*, from approximately 2 to 7 years; the *concrete operational period*, from about 7 to 11; and a two-phase development of *formal operations*, which begins around age 11 and continues throughout adult life. It will be useful for us to look at some of the characteristics of children's thinking described by Piaget and consider how these are related to the books children like and to their responses to literature.

During the sensory-motor period, infants and toddlers learn through coordinating sensory perceptions and motor activity. By the end of their first year, most children enjoy the action or game rhymes of Mother Goose. They delight in the rhythm of "Pat-a-Cake, Pat-a-Cake," and anticipate the pinching and patting that accompanies the rhyme. Tactile books such as *Pat the Bunny* by Dorothy Kunhardt or *Misty's Mischief* by Rod Campbell appeal to their sensory perceptions by encouraging them to touch special materials pasted on the page. Such an introduction to books incorporates what the young child responds to best—sensory-motor play and participation with a loving adult.

Preschool and kindergarten children fall into Piaget's category of preoperational thinking, during which children learn to represent the world symbolically through language, play, and drawing. Thinking is based on direct experience and perception of the present moment. Many of the particular features ascribed to this stage of thought seem to be reflected in young children's response to literature. For instance, preoperational children are not yet able to "conserve." That is, they are unable to hold an idea or image constant in their mind as it changes in shape or form. (If they pour one cup of water into a tall, slim container and another cup into a short, stout container, they are still likely to report there is more water in the tall container.) This model may explain why young children so enjoy cumulative stories like "The Gingerbread Boy" or *Mr. Gumpy's Outing* by John Burningham. Built-in repetition in these stories carries the sequence of the action along from page to page. Children who have learned to conserve can remember the events without aid and often say that the repetitious language is boring.

Egocentrism is another characteristic of the thinking of children during the preoperational period. Egocentrism, in this sense, does not imply selfishness or putting one's own desires ahead of others. It simply means that the young child is not capable of assuming another person's point of view. Piaget maintained that preschoolers cannot figure out, in the literal sense, what objects will be seen from vantage points different from their own. However, work by Margaret Donaldson[26] and others suggests that children as young as 3 or 4 *can* demonstrate this ability when the situation is concrete and has meaning for them.

Still, in the figurative sense, young children are likely to see things from a personal perspective. A story that clearly demonstrates this kind of egocentrism is *Fish Is Fish* by Leo Lionni. In this picture storybook, a tadpole becomes a frog and crawls out of the pond to discover the wonders of a new world. He splashes back into the water and describes these extraordinary things to his old

[25]Barbel Inhelder and Jean Piaget, *The Growth of Logical Thinking* (New York: Basic Books, 1962); John Flavell, *The Developmental Psychology of Jean Piaget* (Princeton, N.J.: Van Nostrand, 1963); Hans G. Furth, *Piaget for Teachers* (Englewood Cliffs, N.J.: Prentice-Hall, 1970).

[26]Margaret Donaldson, *Children's Minds* (New York: Norton, 1979), chapter 2.

The fish's conception of birds as fish with wings in Leo Lionni's *Fish Is Fish* is like the young child's egocentric, personalized view of the world.

friend the fish. As he tells of birds with wings and legs, the fish imagines large feathered fish with wings. He sees a cow as a "fish cow," people as "fish people." In fact, he sees everything from his own fishy point of view.

This book also makes a point about concept formation, another area of tremendous activity during the preoperational period. Lionni's fish illustrates what Piaget calls the *assimilation* process, in which a child accepts new ideas and information into an already existing set of schema. In the companion process, *accommodation*, the new information finally transforms the child's underlying ideas. Literature gives rise to this accommodation process as readers of any age come to see themselves or their world in a new light. When new insights are developed, the child is accommodating.

Most children of elementary school age would be described as concrete operational thinkers in Piaget's model. Classifying and arranging objects in series are important abilities within children's command during this period, making them more systematic and orderly thinkers. Their thought also becomes flexible and reversible, allowing them to unravel and rearrange a sequence of events. It is no surprise, then, that elementary children begin to like mysteries and to understand stories with more complex plot features such as flashbacks or a story within a story. Shifting from an egocentric pattern of thought, children in the concrete operational period also seem to identify more spontaneously with different points of view. A book like *The True Story of the 3 Little Pigs* by Jon Scieszka and illustrated by Lane Smith suits this developmental level well because readers understand what the author has done with the structure of a familiar tale and can also begin to see the events through the eyes of a new narrator, in this case the wolf.

One interesting aspect of concrete-operational children's thinking is described by psychologist David Elkind[27] as "cognitive conceit." As children begin to have some success in reasoning and problem solving, they tend to get the idea that they must be as able as adults, or even smarter. They enjoy besting an older child, parent, or teacher. Although children's visions of superiority may seldom come true in real experience, books for middle graders often feature young protagonists on their own who manage just as well as, or better than, their elders. In E. L. Konigsburg's *From the Mixed-Up Files of Mrs. Basil E. Frankweiler,* for instance, young Claudia is clever enough to outwit adults by living undetected in New York's Metropolitan Museum of Art and shrewd enough to make an important discovery about one of the statues there.

The last stage of cognitive development described by Piaget is formal operations, which begins with a transitional period that corresponds roughly to the middle school years. Students begin to develop abstract theoretical thought; they are no longer dependent on concrete evidence but can reason from hypotheses to logical conclusions. This allows them to think of possibilities for their lives that are contrary to prior experience and enables them to see the future in new ways. Complex novels and science fiction in particular begin to have appeal for students at this level. Also, students gain understanding of the use of symbols for symbols, such as letters for numbers in algebra or symbolic meanings in literature. While they have understood the use of obvious symbols like the broom in *Hurry Home, Candy* by Meindert DeJong, they can now deal with the layers of meaning found in some poetry and complex stories like Alan Garner's *The Stone Book.*

This would appear to be the time, then, when literary criticism would be most appropriately introduced. While teachers at every grade level would have been steadily building some knowledge and appreciation of literature, detailed analysis of a work would probably not be undertaken before this period of intellectual development. Even then, teachers would want such a discussion to arise from the child's personal response to the book.

It is important to remember that not all young people entering middle schools or junior high schools have reached the level of formal operations.[28] At the same time, some young children demonstrate considerable analytical competence as they talk about books that are familiar and meaningful to them.

Educators today express many concerns such as these about the interpretation of Piaget's theory. The whole idea of stages, for instance, suggests a progression of development that may be far more orderly than what occurs in real life. Some feel that the theory fails to describe the intricacy and complexity of children's thinking and may lead teach-

[27]David Elkind, *Children and Adolescents* (New York: Oxford University Press, 1970).

[28]David Elkind, "Investigating Intelligence in Early Adolescence," in Mauritz Johnson and Kenneth J. Rehage, eds., *Toward Adolescence: The Middle School Years,* Seventy-ninth Yearbook of the National Society for the Study of Education (Chicago: University of Chicago Press, 1980), pp. 282–294.

ers to focus on what children are supposedly not able to do, thus falsely lowering expectations. We need to keep these cautions in mind if we look to Piagetian theory for guidance in selecting books for children and planning literature experiences.

Other views of cognitive development may help us broaden our base for understanding children and their response to literature. Russian psychologist Lev Semenovich Vygotsky,[29] for instance, stresses the ties between development of thought and language, the social aspect of learning, and the importance of adult-child interaction. One crucial idea is that children grow in their thinking abilities within a "zone of proximal development," an area in which they are asked to stretch their ability, but not too far. For example, if students can identify the similarities in two versions of a familiar folktale like "Little Red Riding Hood," they may also be able to see how these stories are related to Ed Young's *Lon Po Po: A Red Riding Hood Tale from China*. However, they may not yet be ready to connect these tales to the modern spoof *Ruby*, by Michael Emberly, which draws its humor from sly references to Red Riding Hood.

American psychologist Howard Gardner[30] has proposed that there is no single "intelligence," but a cluster of at least seven intellectual abilities, or "multiple intelligences": linguistic, musical, spatial, logical-mathematical, bodily, knowledge of self, and understanding of others. The stages of development he sees for each of these are different. Appreciation of literature falls into the category of "linguistic intelligence." Increasing sensitivity to balance, composition, style, and sound of language characterize growth within this domain. The idea of multiple intelligences would help to explain why some children breeze through math but blank out during discussions of literature and vice versa.

However we look at cognitive development, we need to remember that it is only one part of a much larger picture of growth patterns that influence interests and response.

Language Development

The pattern of early language learning moves from infant babbling and cooing to the use of single words, frequently ones that name familiar people or things, like "Mama" or "kitty." Next, somewhere around 2, children begin to use two words together. They develop the ability to change inflection, intonation, or word order to expand their range of meaning ("Daddy go?" "*Bad* kitty!"). Theorists disagree on just how children are able to acquire a functional command of such a complex system as language so early in life. There is strong evidence, however, that the child is more than just an imitator. Children seem to construct on their own the system for making themselves understood; M. A. K. Halliday calls this "learning how to mean."[31] To do so they must *use* language—talk as well as listen.

Verbal participation with an adult is an important element in sharing literature with young children. ABC or picture identification books like Tana Hoban's *Of Colors and Things* provide special opportunities if they are "talked through" rather than simply read as a string of nouns. Toddlers learn more than vocabulary from such encounters. Very early experiences with books encourage many aspects of language development. (See Chapters 1 and 4 for more on this point.)

Language development proceeds at a phenomenal pace during the preschool years. By the end of that time children will have learned to express their thoughts in longer sentences that combine ideas or embed one idea within another. In short, they will have gained access to the basic structure of grammar—all this by about age 4, and regardless of native language.[32]

Children improvise and explore words[33] as they learn, chanting and playing with language as they gain confidence. Rythmic rhymes and nonsense verses are natural choices for preschoolers

[29]L. S. Vygotsky, *Thought and Language* (Cambridge, Mass.: MIT Press, 1962); *Mind in Society: The Development of Higher Psychological Processes* (Cambridge, Mass.: Harvard University Press, 1978).
[30]Howard Gardner, *Frames of Mind* (New York: Basic Books, 1983).

[31]M. A. K. Halliday, *Explorations in the Functions of Language* (New York: Elsevier, 1974).
[32]Dan I. Slobin, "Children and Language: They Learn the Same Way All Around the World," in E. Mavis Hetherington and Ross D. Parke, eds., *Contemporary Readings in Child Psychology*, 2nd ed. (New York: McGraw-Hill, 1981), pp. 122–126.
[33]Ruth Weir, *Language in the Crib* (The Hague: Mouton and Co., 1970).

because they fit this pattern so well. However, children's fun in playing with language as various forms are mastered is not limited to the very young. Middle-grade children, with their wider range of language competence, are fascinated by the variety of jokes, riddles, tongue twisters, and folklore miscellany offered by Alvin Schwartz in collections like *Tomfoolery: Trickery and Foolery with Words*. They are also intrigued by ingenious uses of language in a story context, as in Norton Juster's *The Phantom Tollbooth*, Ellen Raskin's *The Westing Game*, or *The BFG* by Roald Dahl.

We know that children's language growth continues through the elementary grades and beyond, although the rate is never again as dramatic as during the preschool years. The average length and complexity of children's statements, both oral and written, increase as they progress through school.[34] We also know, however, that children's capacity to produce language consistently lags behind their ability to understand it. This suggests that we owe students of all ages the opportunity to read and hear good writing which is beyond the level of their own conversation. Seven-year-olds, for instance, cannot speak with the eloquence and humor that characterize William Steig's picture books, such as *Amos & Boris* or *Doctor De Soto*. Still, they can understand the language in its story context, and hearing it will add to their knowledge of how language sounds and works. Books by Virginia Hamilton or Natalie Babbitt might serve the same function for older students. Unlike novels that do little more than mirror contemporary speech, the work of these and other fine writers can give children a chance to consider the power of language used with precision and imagination.

Moral Development

Piaget's extensive studies of children included special attention to their developing ideas about fairness and justice. According to Piaget,[35] the difference between younger and older children's concepts is so pronounced that there are really "two moralities" in childhood. Lawrence Kohlberg's studies of moral development build on Piaget's work, providing a hierarchy of six stages reaching into adulthood.[36]

The general direction of elementary children's development described by both Piaget and Kohlberg indicates that, as they grow in intellect and experience, children move away from ideas of morality based on authority and adult constraint toward morality based on the influence of group cooperation and independent thinking. Carol Gilligan[37] adds a dimension based on gender to the later stages of this development. She suggests that as girls mature, their sense of self-identity is influenced by interconnections with others to a greater degree than boys. Consequently, their moral judgment develops along lines of an enhanced sense of responsibility and caring for others. Girls may seem less decisive than boys in discussing moral dilemmas because they are trying to take into account a whole network of people who may be affected by a choice. This concern for others is present in boys' thinking as well, but seldom takes precedence over their ideas about what is "fair."

Some of the contrasts between the moral judgment of younger and older children are as follows:

- ◆ Young children judge the goodness or badness of an act according to its likelihood of bringing punishment or reward from adults; in other words, they are constrained by the rules that adults have made. Older elementary children usually understand that there are group standards for judging what is good or bad and by then are very conscious of situations where they can make their own rules.
- ◆ In a young child's eyes, behavior is totally right or totally wrong, with no allowance for an alternate point of view. More mature children are willing to consider that

[34]Walter Loban, *Language Development: Kindergarten Through Grade Twelve* (Urbana, Ill.: National Council of Teachers of English, 1976).
[35]Jean Piaget, *The Moral Judgment of the Child*, translated by M. Gabain (New York: Free Press, 1965).

[36]Lawrence Kohlberg, "Development of Moral Character and Moral Ideology" in M. L. Hoffman and L. W. Hoffman, eds., *Review of Child Development Research* (New York: Russell Sage Foundation, 1964).
[37]Carol Gilligan, *In a Different Voice: Psychological Theory and Women's Development* (Cambridge, Mass.: Harvard University Press, 1982).

circumstances and situations make for legitimate differences of opinion.

♦ Young children tend to judge an act by its consequences, regardless of the actor's intent. By third or fourth grade, most children have switched to considering motivation rather than consequences alone in deciding what degree of guilt is appropriate.

♦ Young children believe that bad behavior and punishment go together; the more serious the deed, the more severe the punishment they would prescribe. Its form would not necessarily be related to the offense, but it would automatically erase the defender's guilt. Older children are not so quick to suggest all-purpose pain. They are more interested in finding a "fair" punishment, one that somehow fits the crime and will help bring the wrongdoer back within the rules of the group. Several children who had heard Taro Yashima's *Crow Boy* were asked what the teacher in the story would do about shy Chibi, who hid under the schoolhouse on the first day. Most of the first graders who were questioned said "Spank him!" Nine- and 10-year-olds suggested explaining to him that there was nothing to be afraid of or introducing him to classmates so he wouldn't be shy.

Stories for children present different levels of moral complexity. Fables are often used with young children because they are brief, have appealing animal characters, and appear to teach a moral lesson. However, in Arlene Pillar's[38] research on the response of second, fourth, and sixth graders to fables, few of the second graders could give explanations that indicated full understanding of important questions raised by the stories, such as why the shepherd boy cried "Wolf!" Significantly more sixth graders—but not all of them—were successful in explaining the fables,

grasped subtle aspects that younger children missed, and were able to generalize that the stories represented broader human qualities. All this suggests that most fables make their point more effectively with older readers.

Piggybook, a picture book by Anthony Browne, is sly but not subtle with its message about an overworked, underappreciated woman whose husband and sons act like (and appear to turn into) pigs. She leaves, they learn their lesson; she returns, they pitch in with the housework. The surprise in this story is the wide variation in response it brings depending on the reader's age, gender, sense of fair play, and expectations about the roles of men and women.

On My Honor by Marion Dane Bauer provides older elementary readers with a chance to discuss

In *Piggybook*, Anthony Browne uses humorous visual cues to show shifting power relationships between a woman and her family. It is a moment of poetic justice when she finally stands above them, but readers may interpret the "fairness" of this scene in different ways.

🐷 🐷 🐷

[38]Arlene M. Pillar, "Aspects of Moral Judgment in Response to Fables," *Journal of Research and Development in Education*, vol. 16 (Spring 1983), pp. 39–46.

the complexities of a tragic personal experience. If Joel had obeyed the spirit rather than the letter of his father's rules, would his friend Tony have been spared from drowning in the river? Was Joel wrong for making a dare, or Tony for taking it? Could it possibly have been Joel's father's fault for not saying "no" in the first place? Avi's *Nothing but the Truth* also poses many questions on values for middle school readers to discuss.

Working through dilemmas, the experts suggest, allows us to move from one level of moral judgment toward another. Literature provides a means by which children can rehearse and negotiate situations of conflict without risk, trying out alternative stances to problems as they step into the lives and thoughts of different characters.

Personality Development

Every aspect of a child's growth is intertwined with every other. All learning is a meshing of cognitive dimensions, affective or emotional responses, social relationships, and value orientation. This is the matrix in which personality develops. The process of "becoming" is a highly complex one indeed. To become a "fully functioning" person the child's basic needs must be met. He needs to feel he is loved and understood; he must feel he is a member of a group significant to him; he has to feel he is achieving and growing toward independence. Psychologist Abraham Maslow's research suggests that a person develops through a "hierarchy of needs" from basic animal-survival necessities to the "higher" needs that are more uniquely human and spiritual:

- ♦ Physiological needs
- ♦ Safety needs
- ♦ Love and affection, belongingness needs
- ♦ Esteem needs
- ♦ Self-actualization needs
- ♦ Needs to know and understand
- ♦ Aesthetic needs[39]

The search for self-actualization may take a lifetime, or it may never be achieved. But the concept that the individual is continually "becoming" is a more positive view than the notion that little change can take place in personality. Literature may provide opportunities for people of all ages to satisfy higher-level needs, but it is important to remember that books alone cannot meet children's basic needs.

Psychologist Erik Erikson[40] sees human emotional and social development as a passage through a series of stages. Each stage centers around the individual meeting a particular goal or concern associated with that stage. Erikson theorized that accomplishments at later stages depend on how well the individual was able to meet the goals of preceding stages. According to this theory, a sense of *trust* must be gained during the first year; a sense of *autonomy* should be realized by age 3; between 3 and 6 years the sense of *initiative* is developed; and a sense of duty and *accomplishment* or *industry* occupies the period of childhood from 6 to 12 years. In adolescence a sense of *identity* is built; while a sense of *intimacy*, a parental sense of *productivity*, and a sense of *integrity* are among the tasks of adulthood.

The elementary school audience for children's books falls into the categories *initiative, accomplishment,* and *identity.* Preschool and early primary children can be described as preoccupied with first ventures outside the circle of familiar authority. The majority of elementary children are caught up in the period of industry or "task orientation," proud of their ability to use skills and tools, to plan projects, and to work toward finished products. Middle-school students are more concerned with defining values and personal roles. Writers of children's books sometimes suggest a natural audience for their work by bringing one of these orientations into the foreground. In Beatrix Potter's *The Tale of Peter Rabbit*, Peter's adventures demonstrate a developing sense of initiative like that of the preschoolers listening to his story. *Germy Blew* The Bugle, by Rebecca Jones, focuses on the industriousness of its middle-childhood protagonist; Caroline MacDonald's *The Lake at the End of the World* speaks directly to the adolescent's struggle for identity.

---

[39]Abraham H. Maslow, *Motivation and Personality*, rev. ed. (New York: Harper & Row, 1970).

[40]Erik H. Erikson, *Childhood and Society*, rev. ed. (New York: Norton, 1964).

Some researchers interested in response to literature have found special value in the theory of personality developed by George Kelly.[41] His *theory of personal constructs* does not describe a particular pattern of development. Instead it provides a framework for understanding how the changing pattern of children's experience leads them to form and change ideas about their world, including the stories they read or hear. According to Kelly, each person's behavior is channeled by continuous prediction about the world based on the set of constructs the person holds at that time. Constructs are unique, personal patterns of perception that define the range of possibilities we see within a particular domain. "Bravery" and "cowardice," for instance, are likely to be construed differently by a fifth-grade gymnast and a test pilot. One of the applications of this idea for the classroom helps explain children's varying reactions to the same book. For instance, a child who has read stories of King Arthur and Lloyd Alexander's Prydain series will have a different understanding of what constitutes a hero in literature than someone who has not read beyond the Hardy Boys. Every child brings to literature a different lifetime of experiences and a set of constructs that is not quite the same as any other's. Whenever we consider the broad outlines of similarity that mark developmental levels, we have to remember that each reader is also one of a kind.

The Growing Concept of Story

The way a child's concept or sense of story grows and changes is a developmental pattern of crucial interest to teachers of reading and literature. The educational value of nurturing this development was outlined in Chapter 1. Technically, sense of story is a part of the construct system through which we see the world. It is what we *expect* a story to be, a frame of interwoven ideas about what will happen and how it will be told. This frame guides our interpretation of the story. Our concept of story is a product of all aspects of development interacting with the experience of narrative in our own culture.

One way to understand growth in concept of story is through longitudinal studies that focus on one or a few children, keeping track of a broad range of data. This might include contacts with literature, responses, and developing skills in reading and writing. One such study, *Books Before Five*,[42] is Dorothy White's diary account of her daughter Carol's experiences with books. It shows the beginnings of Carol's curiosity about authorship and the origin of stories, her concern about whether things represented in stories are "real" or "true," and other aspects of her changing ideas about literature. Hugh and Maureen Crago[43] have also published accounts of their young daughter's response to books during the preschool years, giving special attention to her understandings and expectations about the illustrations.

Glenda Bissex's study of her son Paul, *GNYS AT WRK*,[44] follows the development of his reading and writing abilities from ages 5 to 11. Although his early development in concept of story is not included, Bissex shows how his later expectations about literary form are influenced by his reading and brought to light through his spontaneous writing. For instance, at 10 years he wrote a sequel for the *Battlestar Galactica* novel he had read and also produced his own newspaper and magazine, demonstrating his knowledge of a variety of forms in writing.

The most comprehensive research on children's sense of story has been done by Arthur Applebee.[45] Since young children do not easily examine or explain their own ideas, Applebee drew inferences about their understanding of

---

[41]George A. Kelly, *A Theory of Personality* (New York: Norton, 1963).

[42]Dorothy White, *Books Before Five* (Portsmouth, N.H.: Heinemann Educational Books, 1954, 1984).

[43]Hugh Crago and Maureen Crago, "The Untrained Eye? A Preschool Child Explores Felix Hoffman's 'Rapunzel'," *Children's Literature in Education*, no. 22 (Autumn 1976), pp. 133–151; Maureen Crago, "Incompletely Shown Objects in Children's Books, One Child's Response," *Children's Literature in Education*, vol. 10 (Autumn 1979), pp. 151–157.

[44]Glenda L. Bissex, *GNYS AT WRK: A Child Learns to Write and Read* (Cambridge, Mass.: Harvard University Press, 1980).

[45]Arthur N. Applebee, *The Child's Concept of Story: Ages Two to Seventeen* (Chicago: University of Chicago Press, 1978).

He was the strongest king in the world. He could get anything he wanted.

He had the beautifulest castle and the beautifulest queen. He was the kindest king.

Children's expectations about stories are influenced by the stories they know. "Spot the King" was composed by first graders who combined their knowledge of fairy tales with a favorite character from the books of Eric Hill.

Dana Avenue Elementary School, Columbus, Ohio, Public Schools. Elizabeth Strong, research participant.

story structure from the patterns he found in stories told by 2- to 5-year-olds. These patterns reflect an increasing ability to chain events together and to develop at the same time a thematic center. The most commonly told pattern was the focused chain, the "continuing-adventures-of" type of story. This is a pattern that professional writers use, also; it can be found in many picture books. The more complex organizational forms really make reading simpler; stories become easier to understand and to remember because they are more predictable and make more sense.

Some of the other expectations that children develop about stories concern character roles and the distinction between the real world and the story world. Applebee interviewed 6- and 9-year-olds in London to find out what they thought certain characters were "usually like" in a story. The 9-year-olds were much more confident than the younger group about the stock roles that lions play (brave) and the fact that fairies should be good. Half the 6-year-olds expected witches to be wicked, but with 9-year-olds it was unanimous.[46] It is sometimes much later, however, before students begin to notice and expect multiple dimensions in characterization.

[46]Applebee, *The Child's Concept of Story,* chapter 3.

In order to find out what children knew of the relation of stories to real life, Applebee asked the question, "Where does Cinderella live?" Their answers indicated that "stories are astonishingly real even for 6-year-olds who have had a year in a school environment where they hear stories at least daily."[47] By 9, most children had given up thinking that Cinderella is far away over a river or "just a dolly" and could say that it's just a story or that it isn't true.

Like other areas of development, continued growth in concept of story depends on the interaction of new capabilities and experiences. All children are exposed to a variety of narrative forms through the media, but this will not guarantee their growth toward a fully developed sense of story. Children must be steadily nurtured with books that help them discover new possibilities and increasing complexity in literature.

Guides for Ages and Stages

Adults who are responsible for children's reading need to be aware of child development and learning theory and of children's interests. They must keep in mind characteristics and needs of children at different ages and stages of development. At the same time, it is important to remember that each child has a unique pattern of growth. The following charts summarize some characteristic growth patterns, suggest implications for selection and use of books, and provide examples of suitable books for a particular stage of development. Remember that the age levels indicated are only approximate. Also, books suggested as appropriate for one category may fit several other categories as well.

RESPONSE IN THE CLASSROOM

Understanding response to literature would be much easier if it were possible to peer inside a child's head. Then we might see firsthand what concept of story guides progress through a book or just what children are thinking as a story unfolds. Instead, teachers must be satisfied with

[47]Applebee, *The Child's Concept of Story*, p. 42.

secondary evidence. Children's perceptions and understandings are revealed in many different ways—as they choose and talk about books, as they write, paint, play, or take part in other classroom activities.

Classroom responses may be obvious and direct (primary children have been known to kiss a favorite book) or hidden within a situation that appears to have little to do with literature (block corner play). Many responses are verbal, many come without words. Some are spontaneous, bubbling up out of children too delighted to be still or shyly offered, in confidence. Other responses would not be expressed at all without the direct invitation of teachers who plan extension activities or discussions (see Chapters 12 and 13) to generate thoughtful reaction to literature. To understand any of these observed responses, it is helpful to be acquainted with a few basic theoretical perspectives.

Theories of Response

What really goes on between a reader and a story or poem is a complex question with many answers. Theories about reader response draw from many disciplines, including psychology, linguistics, aesthetics, and, of course, literature and education.

Some theories focus on what is read; others focus on the reader. For instance, some researchers have examined in careful detail the structure of stories, noting the precise arrangement of words and sequence of ideas. These patterns are called story grammars, and studies indicate that they can affect the way readers understand and recall a story.[48] Other theorists are more concerned with individual readers and how their personalities may influence their ideas about what they read.[49]

[48]Nancy L. Stein and Christine G. Glenn, "An Analysis of Story Comprehension in Elementary School Children," in Roy O. Freedle, ed., *New Dimensions in Discourse Processing* (Norwood, N.J.: Ablex, 1977); Bertram Bruce, "What Makes a Good Story?" *Language Arts*, vol. 55 (April 1978), pp. 460–466.

[49]Norman H. Holland, *Five Readers Reading* (New Haven, Conn.: Yale University Press, 1975).

RESOURCES FOR TEACHING

♦ BOOKS FOR AGES AND STAGES ♦
BEFORE SCHOOL—INFANCY, AGES 1 AND 2

Characteristics	Implications	Examples
Rapid development of senses. Responds to sound of human voice, especially rhythmic patterns. Vision stimulated by areas of color and sharp contrast; increasingly able to see detail.	Enjoys rhymes, songs, and lullabies. Likes simple, bright illustrations. Looks for familiar objects.	*Tomie de Paola's Mother Goose*, de Paola *Singing Bee!*, Hart *Hush, Little Baby*, Zemach *What Is It?*, Hoban, T. *Colors*, Reiss
Uses all senses to explore the world immediately at hand; learns through activity and participation.	Gets maximum use from sturdy books with washable pages. Needs to participate by touching, pointing, peeking, moving.	*Anno's Peekaboo*, Anno *Where's Spot?*, Hill *Pat the Bunny*, Kunhardt *Tickle, Tickle*, Oxenbury
Very limited attention span; averts eyes or turns away when bored.	Needs books that can be shared a few pages at a time or in a brief sitting; many short story times are better than one long one.	*Babies*, Isadora *Max's Ride*, Wells *Dear Zoo*, Campbell *1, 2, 3*, Hoban, T.
Building foundations of language; plays with sounds, learns basic vocabulary along with concepts, begins to learn implicit "rules" that govern speech and conversation.	Needs to hear many rhymes and simple stories. Needs encouragement to use language in labeling pictures and in sharing dialogue with adults as they read aloud.	*Crash! Bang! Boom!*, Spier *Catch Me and Kiss Me and Say It Again*, Watson *Sam Who Never Forgets*, Rice *Baby Says*, Steptoe
Building basic trust in human relationships.	Needs love and affection from care-givers, in stories as well as in life. Thrives on dependable routines and rituals such as bedtime stories.	*Goodnight Moon*, Brown *The Blanket*, Burningham *Tom & Pippo Books*, Oxenbury *"More. More. More." Said the Baby*, Williams
Limited mobility and experience; interests centered in self and the familiar.	Needs books that reflect self and people and activities in the immediate environment.	*The Baby's Catalogue*, Ahlberg *The Cupboard*, Burningham *Sam's Cookie*, Lindgren *Things to Play With*, Rockwell
Learning autonomy in basic self-help skills.	Enjoys stories of typical toddler accomplishments such as feeding self or getting dressed.	*Alfie's Feet*, Hughes *Mother's Helper*, Oxenbury *How Do I Put It On?* Watanabe *Going to the Potty*, Rogers

RESOURCES FOR TEACHING

♦ BOOKS FOR AGES AND STAGES (CONTINUED) ♦
PRESCHOOL AND KINDERGARTEN—AGES 3, 4, AND 5

Characteristics	Implications	Examples
Rapid development of language.	Interest in words, enjoyment of rhymes, nonsense, and repetition and cumulative tales. Enjoys retelling simple folktales and "reading" stories from books without words.	*Random House Book of Mother Goose*, Lobel *Is Your Mama a Llama?*, Guarino *Roll Over!*, Gerstein *Mr. Gumpy's Outing*, Burningham *Millions of Cats*, Gág *The Three Bears*, Rockwell *Sunshine*, Ormerod
Very active, short attention span.	Requires books that can be completed in one sitting. Enjoys participation such as naming, pointing, singing, and identifying hidden pictures. Should have a chance to hear stories several times each day.	*Eating the Alphabet*, Ehlert *The Very Hungry Caterpillar*, Carle *Each Peach Pear Plum*, Ahlberg *The Wheels on the Bus*, Zelinsky *Have You Seen My Duckling?*, Tafuri *Over in the Meadow*, Langstaff
Child is center of own world. Interest, behavior, and thinking are egocentric.	Likes characters that are easy to identify with. Normally sees only one point of view.	*Noisy Nora*, Wells *Fix-It*, McPhail *Where Is Ben?*, Russo *A Baby Sister for Frances*, Hoban, R.
Curious about own world.	Enjoys stories about everyday experiences, pets, playthings, home, people in the immediate environment.	*The Snowy Day*, Keats *Pancakes, Pancakes*, Carle *Jesse's Daycare*, Valens *Building a House*, Barton *Trucks*, Rockwell
Beginning interest in how things work and the wider world.	Books feed curiosity and introduce new topics.	*My Visit to the Dinosaurs*, Aliki *I Want to Be an Astronaut*, Barton *Is This a House for a Hermit Crab?*, McDonald *An Octopus Is Amazing*, Lauber
Building concepts through many firsthand experiences.	Books extend and reinforce child's developing concepts.	*Feathers for Lunch*, Ehlert *Freight Train*, Crews *I Read Signs*, Hoban, T. *Trucks*, Gibbons *26 Letters and 99 Cents*, Hoban, T.

RESOURCES FOR TEACHING

♦ BOOKS FOR AGES AND STAGES (CONTINUED) ♦

Characteristics	Implications	Examples
Child has little sense of time. Time is "before now," "now," and "not yet."	Books can help children begin to understand the sequence of time.	*When You Were a Baby*, Jonas *A Year of Beasts*, Wolff *The Little House*, Burton *Time To . . .* , McMillan
Child learns through imaginative play; make-believe world of talking animals and magic seems very real.	Enjoys stories that involve imaginative play. Likes personification of toys and animals.	*Martin's Hat*, Blos *May I Bring a Friend?*, DeRegniers *We're Going on a Bear Hunt*, Rosen *Corduroy*, Freeman
Seeks warmth and security in relationships with family and others.	Likes to hear stories that provide reassurance. Bedtime stories and other read-aloud rituals provide positive literature experiences.	*The Runaway Bunny*, Brown *Some Things Go Together*, Zolotow *Little Bear*, Minarik *Ten, Nine, Eight*, Bang *Julius, the Baby of the World*, Henkes
Beginning to assert independence. Takes delight in own accomplishments.	Books can reflect emotions. Enjoys stories where small characters show initiative.	*Will I Have a Friend?*, Cohen, M. *I Hate to Go to Bed*, Barrett *Alfie Gets in First*, Hughes *Titch*, Hutchins *Flap Your Wings and Try*, Pomerantz
Makes absolute judgments about right and wrong.	Expects bad behavior to be punished and good behavior rewarded. Requires poetic justice and happy endings.	*The Three Billy Goats Gruff*, Asbjørnsen and Moe *The Little Red Hen*, Galdone *The Tale of Peter Rabbit*, Potter *Maxi, the Hero*, Barracca *Babushka's Doll*, Polacco

PRIMARY—AGES 6 AND 7

Characteristics	Implications	Examples
Continued development and expansion of language.	Frequent story times during the day provide opportunity to hear the rich and varied language of literature. Wordless books and simple tales encourage storytelling.	*Sylvester and the Magic Pebble*, Steig *Rachel Fister's Blister*, MacDonald, A. *Strega Nona*, de Paola

RESOURCES FOR TEACHING

◆ BOOKS FOR AGES AND STAGES (CONTINUED) ◆

Characteristics	Implications	Examples
		Chicka Chicka Boom Boom, Martin and Archambault *The Little Old Lady Who Was Not Afraid of Anything*, Williams, L. *The Snowman*, Briggs
Attention span increasing.	Prefers short stories; may enjoy a continued story provided each chapter is a complete episode.	*Hard to Be Six*, Adoff *Frederick*, Lionni *Frog and Toad Together*, Lobel *The Courage of Sarah Noble*, Dalgliesh *The Stories Julian Tells*, Cameron *Ramona the Brave*, Cleary
Striving to accomplish skills expected by adults.	Proud of accomplishments in reading and writing. Needs reassurance that everyone progresses at own rate. First reading experiences should be enjoyable, using familiar or predictable stories.	*When Will I Read?*, Cohen, M. *Leo the Late Bloomer*, Kraus *The Day of Ahmed's Secret*, Heide and Gilliland *The Holiday Handwriting School*, Pulver *Brown Bear, Brown Bear*, Martin *The Napping House*, Wood *Cookie's Week*, Ward
Learning still based on immediate perception and direct experiences.	Uses information books to verify as well as extend experience. Much value in watching guinea pigs or tadpoles *before* using a book.	*Frog: See How They Grow*, Taylor, K. *My Puppy Is Born*, Cole *Look Again!*, Hoban, T. *Bugs*, Parker and Wright *Summer*, Hirschi
Continued interest in own world; more curious about a wider range of things. Still sees world from an egocentric point of view.	Needs wide variety of books. TV has expanded interests beyond home and neighborhood.	*Fish Is Fish*, Lionni *How My Parents Learned to Eat*, Friedman *What Happened to the Dinosaurs?*, Branley *Up Goes the Skyscraper!*, Gibbons *Sam Goes Trucking*, Horenstein
Vague concepts of time.	Needs to learn basics of telling time and the calendar. Simple biographies and historical fiction may give a feeling for	*The Grouchy Ladybug*, Carle *Ox-Cart Man*, Hall, D. *The House on Maple Street*, Pryor *Follow the Dream*, Sis

RESOURCES FOR TEACHING

♦ BOOKS FOR AGES AND STAGES (CONTINUED) ♦

Characteristics	Implications	Examples
	the past, but accurate understanding of chronology is beyond the age group.	*When I Was Young in the Mountains*, Rylant *Little House in the Big Woods*, Wilder *Diego*, Winter
More able to separate fantasy from reality; more aware of own imagination.	Enjoys fantasy. Likes to dramatize simple stories or use feltboard, puppets.	*Where the Wild Things Are*, Sendak *And to Think That I Saw It on Mulberry Street*, Seuss *Sam, Bangs, and Moonshine*, Ness *Abiyoyo*, Seeger *Uncle Wizzmo's New Used Car*, Greenblat *Heckedy Peg*, Wood
Beginning to develop empathy and understanding for others.	Adults can ask such questions as "What would you have done?" "How do you think Stevie felt about Robert?"	*Stevie*, Steptoe *Chester's Way*, Henkes *The Balancing Girl*, Rabe *When I Am Old with You*, Johnson *Crow Boy*, Yashima
Has a growing sense of justice. Demands application of rules, regardless of circumstances.	Expects poetic justice in books.	*Flossie and the Fox*, McKissack *Python's Party*, Wildsmith *Once a Mouse . . .*, Brown, Marcia *Baba Yaga*, Kimmel
Humor is developing.	Needs to hear many books read aloud for pure fun. Enjoys books and poems that have surprise endings, plays on words, incongruous situations, and slapstick comedy. Likes to be in on the joke.	*For Laughing Out Loud*, Prelutsky *Amelia Bedelia*, Parish *Big Goof and Little Goof*, Cole and Cole *The Stupids Have a Ball*, Allard *Alexander and the Terrible, Horrible, No Good, Very Bad Day*, Viorst *Tuesday*, Wiesner
Shows curiosity about gender differences and reproduction.	Teachers need to accept and be ready to answer children's questions about sex.	*How I Was Born*, Wabbes *The Story of Birth*, Abel-Prot *How You Were Born*, Cole, J.

RESOURCES FOR TEACHING

◆ BOOKS FOR AGES AND STAGES (CONTINUED) ◆

Characteristics	Implications	Examples
Physical contour of the body is changing; permanent teeth appear; learning to whistle and developing other fine motor skills.	Books can help the child accept physical changes in self and differences in others.	*You'll Soon Grow into Them, Titch*, Hutchins *One Morning in Maine*, McCloskey *Whistle for Willie*, Keats *Julian's Glorious Summer*, Cameron
Continues to seek independence from adults and to develop initiative.	Needs opportunities to self-select books and activities. Enjoys stories of responsibility and successful ventures.	*Galimoto*, Williams, K. *Ira Sleeps Over*, Waber *The Climb*, Carrick *By Myself*, Hopkins *Raymond's Best Summer*, Rogers, J. *Amazing Grace*, Hoffman
Continues to need warmth and security in family relationships.	Books may emphasize universal human characteristics in a variety of lifestyles.	*Willie's Not the Hugging Kind*, Barrett *A Chair for My Mother*, Williams, V. *The Relatives Came*, Rylant *Osa's Pride*, Grifalconi

MIDDLE ELEMENTARY—AGES 8 AND 9

Characteristics	Implications	Examples
Attaining independence in reading skill. May read with complete absorption; others may still be having difficulty learning to read. Wide variation in ability and interest.	Discovers reading as an enjoyable activity. Prefers an uninterrupted block of time for independent reading. During this period, many children become avid readers.	*Kids of Polk Street School* Series, Giff *Rats on the Roof*, Marshall *Sunken Treasure*, Gibbons *Ramona Quimby, Age 8*, Cleary *Staying Nine*, Conrad *Charlotte's Web*, White
Reading level may still be below appreciation level.	Essential to read aloud to children each day in order to extend interests, develop appreciation, and provide balance.	*Sing a Song of Popcorn*, DeRegniers *Dawn*, Bang *Sarah, Plain and Tall*, MacLachlan *Abel's Island*, Steig
Peer group acceptance becomes increasingly important.	Children need opportunities to recommend and discuss books. Sharing favorites builds sense	*Fudge-a-Mania*, Blume *A Light in the Attic*, Silverstein *Bunnicula*, Howe and Howe

◆ BOOKS FOR AGES AND STAGES (CONTINUED) ◆

Characteristics	Implications	Examples
	that reading is fun, has group approval. Popular books may provide status, be much in demand.	*It's Not Easy Being George*, Smith, J. *Class Clown*, Hurwitz
Developing standards of right and wrong. Begins to see viewpoints of others.	Books provide opportunities to relate to several points of view.	*Danny the Champion of the World*, Dahl *The Indian in the Cupboard*, Banks *Molly's Pilgrim*, Cohen, B.
Less egocentric, developing empathy for others. Questioning death.	Accepts some books with a less than happy ending. Discussion helps children explore their feelings for others.	*Blackberries in the Dark*, Jukes *Mustard*, Graeber *Stone Fox*, Gardiner *The War with Grandpa*, Smith, R. *Beyond the Ridge*, Goble
Time concepts and spatial relationships developing. This age level is characterized by thought that is flexible and reversible.	Interested in biographies, life in the past, in other lands, and the future. Prefers fast-moving, exciting stories.	*The Last Princess*, Stanley *What's the Big Idea, Ben Franklin?*, Fritz *The Secret Soldier*, McGovern *Trouble for Lucy*, Stevens *The Green Book*, Walsh
Enjoys tall tales, slapstick humor in everyday situations. Appreciates imaginary adventure.	Teachers need to recognize the importance of literature for laughter, releasing tension, and providing enjoyment.	*The Not-So-Jolly Roger*, Scieszka *Paul Bunyan*, Kellogg *The Celery Stalks at Midnight*, Howe *Skinnybones*, Park *American Tall Tales*, Osborne
Cognitive growth and language development increase capacity for problem solving and word play.	Likes the challenge of solving puzzles and mysteries. High interest in twists of plot, secret codes, riddles, and other language play.	*The Polar Express*, Van Allsburg *Anno's Math Games II*, Anno *Fun with Hieroglyphs*, Roehrig *A Basket Full of White Eggs*, Swann *The Dollhouse Murders*, Wright

RESOURCES FOR TEACHING

◆ BOOKS FOR AGES AND STAGES (CONTINUED) ◆

Characteristics	Implications	Examples
Improved coordination makes proficiency in sports and games possible and encourages interest in crafts and hobbies.	Interest in sports books; wants specific knowledge about sports. Enjoys how-to-do-it books.	*The Trading Game*, Slote *Soccer: A Heads-Up Guide to Super Soccer!*, Brenner *A Very Young Gymnast*, Krementz *The Paper Airplane Book*, Simon *Playing with Plasticine*, Reid *The Little House Cookbook*, Walker
Sees categories and classifications with new clarity; interest in collecting is high.	Likes to collect and trade paperback books. Begins to look for books of one author, series books. Enjoys books that collect facts, informational identification books.	*Meet Samantha (The American Girl Collection)*, Adler *Encyclopedia Brown's Book of Wacky Cars*, Sobol *Herbie Jones* and others, Kline *Ramona Forever* and others, Cleary *101 Questions and Answers About Dangerous Animals*, Simon
Seeks specific information to answer questions; may go to books beyond own reading ability to search out answers.	Requires guidance in locating information within a book and in using the library.	*The Magic Schoolbus Lost in the Solar System*, Cole *The Way Things Work*, Macaulay *Insect Zoo*, Meyers *Kenneth Lilly's Animals*, Pope *Dinosaurs Walked Here*, Lauber

LATER ELEMENTARY—AGES 10 AND 11

Characteristics	Implications	Examples
Rate of physical development varies widely. Rapid growth precedes beginning of puberty. Girls are about two years ahead of boys in development; both increasingly curious about all aspects of sex.	Guide understanding of growth process and help children meet personal problems. Continued differentiation in reading preferences of boys and girls.	*Asking About Sex and Growing Up*, Cole, J. *Are You There God? It's Me, Margaret*, Blume *Jenny Archer, Author*, Conford *My Buddy, the King*, Brittain *Car (Eyewitness Books)*, Sutton
Understanding of sex role is developing; boys and girls form ideas about their own and each other's identity.	Books may provide identification with gender roles and impetus for discussion of stereotypes.	*The Agony of Alice*, Naylor *The Burning Questions of Bingo Brown*, Byars *The Explorer of Barkham Street*, Stolz *Piggybook*, Browne

RESOURCES FOR TEACHING

◆ BOOKS FOR AGES AND STAGES (CONTINUED) ◆

Characteristics	Implications	Examples
Increased emphasis on peer group and sense of belonging.	Book choices often influenced by peer group; many requests for books about "kids like us."	*Libby on Wednesday*, Snyder *Risk N' Roses*, Slepian *Anything for a Friend*, Conford *The Real Me*, Miles *Choosing Sides*, Cooper, I. *The Mouse Rap*, Myers
Deliberate exclusion of others; some expressions of prejudice.	Books can emphasize unique contribution of all. Discussion can be used to clarify values.	*Alan and Naomi*, Levoy *Nobodies & Somebodies*, Orgel *Roll of Thunder, Hear My Cry*, Taylor
Family patterns changing; may challenge parents' authority. Highly critical of siblings.	Books may provide some insight into these changing relationships.	*Dear Mr. Henshaw*, Cleary *Anastasia Krupnik*, Lowry *Hating Alison Ashley*, Klein *Dicey's Song*, Voigt *The Outside Child*, Bawden *Cousins*, Hamilton
Begins to have models other than parents drawn from TV, movies, sports figures, books. Beginning interest in future vocation.	Biographies may provide models. Career books broaden interests and provide useful information.	*Franklin Delano Roosevelt*, Freedman *Martin Luther King, Jr.*, Patrick *Little by Little*, Little *Bo Jackson: Pro Sports Superstar*, Raber *Public Defender*, Hewett
Sustained, intense interest in specific activities.	Seeks book about hobbies and other interests.	*Once Upon a Horse*, Jurmain *Crazy About German Shepherds*, Ashabranner *Drawing from Nature*, Arnosky *Mountain Bikes*, Abramowski
A peak time for voluntary reading.	Avid readers welcome challenges, repeated contact with authors, genres.	*Other Bells for Us to Ring*, Cormier *Prairie Songs*, Conrad Prydain Series, Alexander Narnia Series, Lewis *Heroes and Monsters of Greek Myth*, Evslin *The Legend of King Arthur*, Lister

RESOURCES FOR TEACHING

◆ BOOKS FOR AGES AND STAGES (CONTINUED) ◆

Characteristics	Implications	Examples
Seeks to test own skills and abilities; looks ahead to a time of complete independence.	Enjoys stories of survival and "going it alone."	*Julie of the Wolves*, George *Hatchet*, Paulsen *The Sign of the Beaver*, Speare *Secret City, U.S.A.*, Holman *Monkey Island*, Fox *The Lake at the End of the World*, MacDonald, C.
Increased cognitive skill can be used to serve the imagination.	Tackles complex and puzzling plots in mysteries, science fiction, fantasy. Can appreciate more subtlety in humor.	*The Westing Game*, Raskin *The Haunting*, Mahy *The Dark Is Rising*, Cooper, S. *Dew Drop Dead*, Howe *Borgel*, Pinkwater
Increased understanding of the chronology of past events; developing sense of own place in time. Begins to see many dimensions of a problem	Literature provides opportunities to examine issues from different viewpoints. Guidance needed for recognizing biased presentations.	*The Night Journey*, Lasky *My Daniel*, Conrad *Homesick*, Fritz *Shades of Gray*, Reeder *The Boys' War*, Murphy *Now Is Your Time!*, Myers
Highly developed sense of justice and concern for others.	Willing to discuss many aspects of right and wrong; likes "sad stories," shows empathy for victims of suffering and injustice.	*Shiloh*, Naylor *On My Honor*, Bauer *Beat the Turtle Drum*, Greene *How It Feels to Fight for Your Life*, Krementz *The Long Way Home*, Cohen, B. *Journey to Jo'Burg*, Naidoo *Number the Stars*, Lowry
Searching for values; interested in problems of the world. Can deal with abstract relationships; becoming more analytical.	Valuable discussions may grow out of teacher's reading aloud prose and poetry to this age group. Questions may help students gain insight into both the content and literary structure of a book.	*Hiroshima No Pika*, Maruki *Tuck Everlasting*, Babbitt *Mrs. Frisby and the Rats of NIMH*, O'Brien *The Great Gilly Hopkins*, Paterson *This Delicious Day*, Janeczko

RESOURCES FOR TEACHING		

♦ BOOKS FOR AGES AND STAGES (CONTINUED) ♦
MIDDLE SCHOOL—AGES 12 AND 13

Characteristics	Implications	Examples
Wide variation in physical development; both boys and girls reach puberty by age 14. Developing sex drive; intense interest in sexuality and world of older teens.	Books provide insight into feelings, concerns. Guidance needed to balance students' desire for frank content with lack of life experience.	*What's Happening to Me?*, Mayle *The Goats*, Cole, B. *A Couple of Kooks*, Rylant *Hold On to Love*, Hunter *Bingo Brown, Gypsy Lover*, Byars
Self-concept continues to grow. Developing a sense of identity is important.	Books help students explore roles, rehearse journey to identity. Many stories based on myth of the hero.	*Bearstone*, Hobbs *Dogsong*, Paulsen *A Wizard of Earthsea*, Le Guin *Dragonsong*, McCaffery *Jason and the Argonauts*, Evslin *The Hero and the Crown*, McKinley
Peer group becomes increasingly influential; relationships with family are changing.	Concerns about friends and families reflected in books. School should provide chance to share books and responses with peer group.	*Scorpions*, Myers *Back to Class: Poems*, Glenn *Friends First*, McDonnell *The Moves Make the Man*, Brooks *Moonlight Man*, Fox *Baseball in April*, Soto *Maniac Magee*, Spinelli
New aspects of egocentrism lead to imagining self as center of others' attention and feeling one's own problems are unique.	Students begin to enjoy introspection; may identify with characters who are intense or self-absorbed.	*Jacob Have I Loved*, Paterson *Ring of Endless Light*, L'Engle *Borrowed Children*, Lyon *Everywhere*, Brooks
Cognitive abilities are increasingly abstract and flexible, but not consistently so. New capacity to reason from imaginary premises, manipulate symbolic language, and make hypothetical judgments.	Students read more complex stories, mysteries, and high fantasy that call for complex logic; enjoy science fiction and high adventure. Metaphor, symbols, and imagery are understood at a different level.	*Saturnalia*, Fleischman *The True Confessions of Charlotte Doyle*, Avi *The Outlaws of Sherwood*, McKinley *The Stonewalkers*, Alcock *A Swiftly Tilting Planet*, L'Engle *Merlin Dreams*, Dickinson *The Place My Words Are Looking For*, Janeczko

RESOURCES FOR TEACHING

♦ BOOKS FOR AGES AND STAGES (CONTINUED) ♦

Characteristics	Implications	Examples
Able to apply ideas of relativity to questions of values; girls may see moral issues differently from boys.	Students need discussion time to negotiate meanings in stories that pose moral dilemmas.	*Shabanu*, Staples *An Honorable Prison*, De Jenkins *Plague Year*, Tolan *Rice Without Rain*, Ho *The Devil's Arithmetic*, Yolen
Sensitive to great complexity in human feelings and relationships.	Students seek richer and more complex stories.	*The Borning Room*, Fleischman *The Road to Memphis*, Taylor *Goodnight, Mr. Tom*, Magorian *The Master Puppeteer*, Paterson *Sweet Whispers, Brother Rush*, Hamilton
Cumulative effects of development and life experience produce wide variation among individuals in abilities and interests.	Reading ability and interests in one class may range from early elementary to adult.	*Something Big Has Been Here*, Prelutsky *Animalia*, Base *The Ballad of Belle Dorcas*, Hooks *The Star-Fisher*, Yep *The Hobbit*, Tolkien *Lonesome Dove*, McMurtry

One important point on which scholars agree is that the process of reading and responding is active rather than passive. The words and ideas in the book are not transferred automatically from the page to the reader. Response is dynamic and open to continuous change as readers anticipate, infer, remember, reflect, interpret, and connect. The "meaning" and significance of a story like Patricia MacLachlan's *Journey* will vary from reader to reader, depending on age and personal experience as well as experience with literature. However, the response of a single reader will also change given time for reflection, discussion, or repeated readings.

Some scholars avoid the word "response" because they do not want to suggest the predetermined reaction of a behaviorist point of view (stimulus-response). Louise Rosenblatt uses the term "transaction," explaining:

The literary work exists in the live circuit set up between reader and text: the reader infuses intellectual and emotional meanings into the pattern of verbal symbols, and those symbols channel his thoughts and feelings.[50]

Teachers who focus on rigidly prescribed materials and questions with predetermined answers are narrowly interpreting what happens when a reader reads. Rosenblatt's dynamic theory of response, on the other hand, suggests that children will see many variations of meaning in a poem or story. Sensitive teachers can then begin to encourage a more conscious participation in predicting, reflecting, making inferences, and sharing ideas.

Reader response theory also points out that readers approach works of literature in special ways. James Britton[51] proposes that in all our uses

[50]Louise M. Rosenblatt, *Literature as Exploration*, 3rd ed. (New York: Noble and Noble, 1976), p. 25.
[51]James Britton, et al., *The Development of Writing Abilities (11–18)*, Schools Council Research Studies (London: Macmillan Education Limited, 1975).

of language we may be either *participants* or *spectators*. In the participant role we read in order to accomplish something in the real world, as in following a recipe. In the spectator role we focus on what the language says as an end in itself, attending to its forms and patterns, as we do in enjoying poetry.

Rosenblatt[52] suggests that reading usually involves two roles or stances and that we shift our emphasis from one to the other according to the material and our purposes for reading it. In the *efferent* stance we are most concerned with what information can be learned from the reading. In the *aesthetic* stance the reader's concern is for the experience of the reading itself, the feelings and images that come and go with the flow of the words. Most readers, of course, find themselves switching back and forth from one of these stances to the other as they read. One thing that teachers can do to help children share the world the author has created is to help them find an appropriate stance as they begin to read.

Recent research has described stances in greater detail and variation (as many as twenty-nine)[53] and with an emphasis on the process of making meaning. Judith Langer[54] writes about four major stances used by students as they make progressive "envisonments" of a work of literature: 1) Being Out and Stepping In, 2) Being In and Moving Through, 3) Being In and Stepping Out, and 4) Stepping Out and Objectifying the Experience. Teachers who study these theories will discover that they provide a basis for supporting children's growth in interpretation.

Types of Responses

The most common expressions of response to literature are statements, oral or written. In their most polished form such responses are known as literary criticism. One traditional line of research in literature involves measuring young people's statements against this standard of mature critical ability. Many years ago when I. A. Richards[55] was concerned that college English students were not making "correct" literary judgments, he categorized a sample of their written statements about poems according to what seemed to keep them from speaking like professional critics. For example, the students often failed to get the "plain sense" of the work, they had inappropriate preconceptions, they made stock responses, and they tended to be, at least in Richards's view, overly sentimental.

In a later study of verbal response,[56] James Squire interviewed ninth and tenth graders at various stopping points in the reading of short stories. One of his most interesting observations was a tendency he called *happiness binding,* the students' inclination to expect and interpret a happy ending regardless of contrary evidence in the story. This is the same phenomenon observed by the middle-grade teacher whose children predicted that Hop in Palmer Brown's *Hickory* would survive the cold winter—despite eloquent clues about the brevity of a grasshopper's life.

Verbal responses can be categorized in a number of ways. Many researchers begin with a system developed by Alan Purves[57] from the responses of 300 teenagers in four countries. All of the categories in this system have descriptive labels. They help teachers see what *kinds* of statements about literature are made by students without indicating whether the statements are "right" or "wrong."

Most early studies of response involved high school students or young adults rather than elementary or preschool children. Young children also talk about books and write about them, but

[52]Louise M. Rosenblatt, *The Reader, the Text, the Poem: The Transactional Theory of the Literary Work* (Carbondale, Ill.: Southern Illinois University Press, 1978).
[53]Patricia Enciso Edmiston, "The Nature of Engagement in Reading: Profiles of Three Fifth-Graders' Engagement Strategies and Stances." Ph.D. dissertation, Ohio State University, 1990. University Microfilms no. 9111696.
[54]Judith Langer, "Understanding Literature," *Language Arts*, vol. 67 (December 1990), pp. 812–816.

[55]I. A. Richards, *Practical Criticism* (New York: Harcourt Brace, 1929).
[56]James R. Squire, *The Responses of Adolescents While Reading Four Short Stories* (Urbana, Ill.: National Council of Teachers of English, 1964).
[57]Alan C. Purves with Victoria Rippere, *Elements of Writing About a Literary Work: A Study of Response to Literature* (Urbana, Ill.: National Council of Teachers of English, 1968).

Children's pictures or other classroom work may furnish important evidence about their understanding of literature.

Martin Luther King, Jr., Laboratory School, Evanston, Illinois, Public Schools. Ellen Esrick, teacher.

🙶 🙶 🙶

their responses have not yet received as much systematic attention. Arthur Applebee's study of children's statements about stories, the base for his work on concept of story discussed on pages 70–72 shows how characteristics of responses change as students gain in age and experience. Only recently have other researchers begun to look carefully at what elementary children have to say about literature, often collecting data from intensive interviews or long periods of observation.[58]

Susan Lehr[59] talked with children about the interpretation of story themes ("The Three Little Pigs," for instance) in kindergarten, second, and fourth grades. Although she noted some differences across age levels in the statements children

made, she found that previous high exposure to literature enabled them to make more sophisticated statements than might have been expected. She also noted that the content and structure of interview questions and the presence of the actual book during the discussion could make an important difference in the substance of their responses.

Where children are concerned, it is important to remember that direct comment is only one of many ways of revealing what goes on between the book and its audience. Language used in other ways—to tell or write stories based on other stories, for instance—often provides good clues about a child's feelings and understandings about the original. Parents and teachers of young children also recognize nonverbal behaviors as signs of response. For instance, young listeners almost always show their involvement, or lack of it, in body postures and facial expressions. Children's artwork, informal drama, and other book extension activities (see Chapter 13) also provide windows on response.

Interpreting Children's Responses

RECOGNIZING PATTERNS OF CHANGE

Teachers and researchers alike have observed that when children at different grade levels read and respond in ways that are comfortable for them, their responses will be alike in some ways and different in others. What might teachers expect to see in a fourth-grade classroom? What are typical first-grade responses? No one can answer these questions with exactness, for every child is a unique reader and every classroom represents a different composite of experiences with literature and with the world. Even so, it is helpful to know what researchers and practiced teachers have discovered about the responses of their students at various grade levels. This section outlines some of these findings[60] to provide information on the patterns of change in responses that usually take place as children have experiences with literature in the elementary school.

[58]Lee Galda, "Assuming the Spectator Stance: An Examination of the Responses of Three Young Readers," *Research in the Teaching of English*, vol. 16 (February 1982), pp. 1–20; Rudine Sims, "Strong Black Girls: A Ten Year Old Responds to Fiction About Afro-Americans," *Journal of Research and Development in Education*, vol. 16 (Spring 1983), pp. 21–28.

[59]Susan Lehr, *The Child's Developing Sense of Theme: Responses to Literature* (New York: Teachers College Press, 1991).

[60]These outlines are based on our observations with reference to Applebee, *The Child's Concept of Story*, pp. 123–125, and other researchers.

Although the outline is presented in an age-level sequence, keep in mind that any of these characteristics can be seen at other ages depending on the child, the situation, and the challenge presented by the material. Like the Ages and Stages chart (pp. 73–84), this guide is more useful for making predictions about a class than for an individual child.

Younger Children (Preschool–Primary)

♦ Are *motor-oriented*. As listeners they respond with their whole selves, chiming in on refrains or talking back to the story. They lean closer to the book, point at pictures, clap their hands. They use body movements to try out some of the story's action, "hammering" along with *John Henry* by Ezra Jack Keats or making wild faces to match the illustrations in Ruth Park's *When the Wind Changed*. Actions to demonstrate meaning ("like this") may be given as answer to a teacher's questions. These easily observable responses go under cover as children mature; older children reveal feelings through subtle changes of expression and posture.

♦ Spontaneously act out stories or bits of stories using actions, roles, and conventions of literature in their *dramatic play*. Witches, kings, "Wild Things," and other well-defined character types appear naturally, showing how well children have assimilated elements of favorite tales. Examples of story language ("We lived happily ever after") are sometimes incorporated. Spontaneous dramatic play disappears from the classroom early in the primary years (although it persists out of school with some children) and is replaced by more structured drama of various kinds. Older children are usually much more conscious of their own references to literature.

♦ Respond to stories piecemeal. Their responses deal with *parts rather than wholes*. A detail of text or illustration may prompt more comment than the story itself, as children make quick associations with their own experience: "I saw a bird like that once" or "My sister has bunk beds just like

those." This part-by-part organization can also be seen in very young children's art where the pictures show individual story items without any indication of relationship ("This is the baby bear's chair, and this is Goldilocks, and this is the house the bears lived in, and here is the bed. . ."). This is the same sort of itemization or catalog of characters, objects, and events that children sometimes use when asked to tell something about a story. Young children are more likely to respond to the story as a whole if they have heard it many times or if an adult provides that focus by asking good questions.

♦ Use *embedded language* in answering direct questions about stories. Because young children see the world in literal, concrete terms, their answers are likely to be couched in terms of the characters and events and objects found in the story. One first grader made a good attempt to generalize the lesson of "The Little Red Hen," but couldn't manage without some reference to the tale: "When someone already baked the cake and you haven't helped, they're probably just gonna say `no'!" A teacher or other adult who shares the child's context—who knows the story, has heard or read it with the child, and knows what other comments have been made—will understand the intent of such a statement more readily than a casual observer.

Children in Transition (Primary–Middle Grades)

♦ Develop from listeners to readers. They go through a period of focus on the *accomplishment of independent reading*. There are many comments about quantity—number of pages read, the length of a book, or the number of books read. Conventions of print and of bookmaking may draw attention. One third grader refused to read any of the poems from Shel Silverstein's *Where the Sidewalk Ends* without locating them in the index first; a classmate was fascinated with the book's variety of word and line arrangements for poetry. Another child studied the front matter of a picture book and pronounced it "a dedicated book." So-called independent reading may be more sociable than it sounds, since many children like to have a listener or reading partner and begin to rely on peers as sounding boards for their response.

♦ Become more adept at *summarizing* in place of straight retelling when asked to talk about stories. This is a skill that facilitates discussion and becomes more useful as it is developed. Summarizing is one of the techniques that undergirds critical commentary, but adults use it more deliberately and precisely than children do.

♦ Classify or *categorize* stories in some of the same ways that adults do. Middle graders who are asked to sort out a random pile of books use categories like "mysteries," "humorous books," "make believe," "fantasy." If you ask kindergartners to do the same, they are more likely to classify the books by their physical properties ("fat books," "books with pretty covers," "red books") than by content.

♦ *Attribute personal reactions to the story* itself. A book that bores an 8-year-old will be thought of as a "boring book," as if "boring" were as much a property of the story as its number of pages or its first-person point of view. Children judge a story on the basis of their response to it, regardless of its qualities as literature or its appeal to anyone else. This is a very persistent element in response; it affects the judgment of students of children's literature and of professional book reviewers as well as children in elementary school. Personal response can never be totally eliminated from critical evaluation; but with experience, readers can develop more objectivity in separating a book's literary characteristics from its personal appeal.

♦ *Use borrowed characters, events, themes, and patterns from literature in writing,* just as younger children do in dramatic play. In the earliest stages much of this is unconscious as well as spontaneous. One example is a 7-year-old who was convinced her story about a fish with paint-splashed insides was "made up out of my own head," even when reminded that the class had just heard Robert McCloskey's *Burt Dow, Deep Water Man.* A 9-year-old spontaneously combined a favorite character with a field-trip experience in his story "Paddington Bear Goes to Franklin Park Conservatory," but he was aware of his idea sources. Other children produce their own examples of patterns, forms, or genres. The direction of growth is toward more conscious realization of the uses of literature in writing (see Chapter 13 on "Extending Literature Through Writing").

Older Children (Middle Grades–Middle School)

♦ Express *stronger preferences*, especially for personal reading. Younger children seem to enjoy almost everything that is reasonably appropriate, but older ones do not hesitate to reject books they do not like. Some children show particular devotion to certain authors or genres or series at this time. Some children also become more intense and protective about some of their reactions, and they should not be pressed to share those feelings that demand privacy.

♦   Are more skillful with language and m able to deal with abstractions. They can *dis-embed ideas* from a story and put them in more generalized terms, as in stating a universal moral for a particular fable.

♦ Begin to *see* (but not consistently) *that their feelings about a book are related to identifiable aspects of the writing.* Responses like "I love this book because it's great" develop into "I love this book because the characters say such funny things" or "*Strider* [Cleary] is my favorite because Leigh is a lot like me."

♦ Go beyond categorizing stories *toward a more analytical perception* of why characters behave as they do, how the story is put together, or what the author is trying to say. They begin to test fiction against real life and understand it better through the comparison. They use some critical terminology, although their understanding of terms may be incomplete. In talk and writing, children who are encouraged to express ideas freely begin to stand back from their own involvement and take an evaluative look at literature. One sixth grader had this to say about *A Taste of Blackberries* by Doris Buchanan Smith:

I thought the author could have put more into it. I really didn't know much about the kid who died. I mean, it really happened fast in the book. It started out pretty soon and told about how sad he was and what they used to do. All the fun things they used to do together. I wished at the beginning they would have had all the things that he talked about and then have him thinking about what a good friend he is and then all of a sudden he dies—a little closer to the end. Because when he died, you didn't much care cause you didn't really know him. But I guess the author wanted to talk about how it would be, or how people feel, or maybe what happened to her— how it felt when one of her friends died like that.[61]

In general, children's responses move toward this sort of conscious comment. Young children sometimes make stunningly perceptive observations about stories, but they are not usually able to step back and see the importance of what they have said. Older children begin to know what they know, and can then take command of it. This allows them to layer mature appreciation on top of the beginner's natural delight.

However, older children's increasing capacity for abstraction, generalization, and analysis should *not* be interpreted as a need for programs of formal literary analysis or highly structured study procedures. Opportunities to read, hear, and talk about well-chosen books under the guidance of an interested and informed teacher will allow elementary school children to develop response to their full potential.

One way to demonstrate the differences in response that teachers may notice from one grade level to another is to compare what children at different ages have to say about a particular book. In one school small groups of children from different grades responded to *The Tub People*, a picture book by Pam Conrad and Richard Egielski,

after hearing it for the first time.[62] The tub people are seven wooden toys who stay in line on the tub's edge until bathtime. One night the Tub Child goes "down the drain without a sound." He is later rescued by someone with a big voice and a plumbing tool, and the tub people are happily reunited in the relative safety of a bedroom. One illustration that adults find very moving shows the mother of the tub child looking down through the grating where he has disappeared. The vantage point is from below, so that we seem to be looking up through the dark pipe to the mother's face far above. One kindergarten student looked at this picture and asked in a matter-of-fact tone why the tub child's parents didn't just go after him. A fifth grader looked at the same illustration and commented that she wouldn't have thought of drawing it from that point of view. The younger child focused on the action of the story as it unfolded, calling up his own expectation about parents. The fifth grader, who waited until the story was finished to comment, was taking a step back from the story and considering the creator's role, an indication of growth in perception and more flexible thinking. Adults are likely to bring strong feelings as parents or caregivers into their response to this part of the story. While children will be able to consider this perspective and talk about it if questioned, it is not the one that comes naturally to them.

Different age levels respond to a story on their own terms of understanding. It does little good (and can be destructive to enjoyment of literature) if younger children are pushed to try to formulate the abstractions achieved by more mature ones. However, James Britton[63] maintains that teachers may refine and develop the responses that children are already making by gradually exposing them to stories with increasingly complex patterns of events.

[61]Recorded in the classroom of Lois Monaghan, teacher, Barrington School, Upper Arlington, Ohio.

[62]Janet Hickman, "What Comes Naturally: Growth and Change in Children's Free Response to Literature" in *Stories and Readers: New Perspectives on Literature in the Elementary Classroom*, Charles Temple and Patrick Collins, eds. (Norwood, Mass.: Christopher Gordon, 1992), pp. 185–193.
[63]James Britton, in *Response to Literature*, James R. Squire, ed. (Champaign, Ill.: National Council of Teachers of English, 1968), p. 4.

LEARNING FROM LITERARY MISCUES

In one sense, it is impossible for any child to make a "wrong" response to literature. Each reader's own feelings and personal interpretations are valid because each reader is different. After all, everyone has a different correct answer for the question "What do *you* think?" But some responses that readers make, although they may reflect true feelings, contradict the evidence of the text.

In the teaching of reading, deviations from the text in oral reading are sometimes called *miscues*. According to Goodman and others[64] who have developed this idea, it is not very useful to see miscues as mistakes. It is more profitable to see them as clues that reveal what thinking process or cueing systems the child uses during reading. An example is the child who reads "Daddy" for "Father," cueing on the meaning but not paying attention to the form of the word. The whole notion of miscues focuses the teacher's attention on the kind of thinking children are doing, not just on the errors they make.

This positive point of view is just as important in considering childrens' efforts at making meaning from whole stories or episodes as it is at the level of words and phrases. We cannot say that a 6-year-old is wrong, for instance, in calling "The Three Little Pigs" a sad story, but the label does not really seem to fit a tale of diligence, cleverness, and success. If we take the attitude that this is a literary miscue and not simply a lack of understanding, we will go on to try to find out what kind of thinking led to that response. The child in this example explained to his teacher that he thought it would be terrible to fall into a pot of boiling water, and it was sad for the wolf. This helped the teacher to see that he was basing his judgment on a part of the story rather than the whole; other observations showed that this was often the strategy behind his responses.

Sometimes a response will seem so at odds with the original text that an adult may wonder if the child has read or heard an entirely different story. One 7-year-old girl, after several experiences with

Leo Lionni's *Little Blue and Little Yellow*, made a tissue-paper collage picture and wrote a caption which she read aloud as follows:

> I made a pretty picture of Little Yellow and Little Blue. They want to go home but they can't lead back home because the birds has eatened all the crumbs.

In the book, the paper-shape characters play together and then hug each other so tightly that they blend into one green shape. They do not get lost, but when they go home neither set of parents recognizes them until they literally dissolve in tears and regain their own shape and color. When asked about the trail of bread crumbs, this

Teachers need to listen carefully to children's responses to literature in order to discover their thinking strategies.

Mission School, Redlands Public Schools, Redlands, California. Joan Schleicher, teacher. Photo by Larry Rose.

🐞 🐞 🐞

[64]Yetta M. Goodman and Carolyn L. Burke, *Reading Miscue Inventory* (Chicago: Richard C. Owen, 1972).

student did not immediately remember any connection to "Hansel and Gretel," and she repeated that Little Blue and Little Yellow were lost and couldn't find their way home. To say that she confused two familiar stories only describes the surface of things. She cued in on an image that exists in both stories—that of separation from parents—and this seems to have linked them solidly in her perception. The teacher talked to her about both stories but wisely did not try to "correct" the writing, recognizing that only maturity and continued experience with stories could help her toward a clearer understanding.

Many other examples of response can be profitably interpreted as literary miscues. A group of third graders who were reading and discussing Laura Ingalls Wilder's *By the Shores of Silver Lake* misread the passage that describes the death of Jack, the Ingalls family's beloved dog:

🐾 . . . Pa was going to do the chores. He spoke to Jack, but Jack did not stir.

Only Jack's body, stiff and cold, lay curled there on the blanket.

They buried it on the low slope above the wheat field, by the path he used to run down so gaily when he was going with Laura to bring in the cows. Pa spaded the earth over the box and made the mound smooth. . . .

"Don't cry, Laura," Pa said, "He has gone to the Happy Hunting Grounds."

Perhaps, in the Happy Hunting Grounds, Jack was running gaily in the wind over some high prairie, as he used to run on the beautiful wild prairies of Indian Territory. Perhaps at last he was catching a jack rabbit.[65]

The children told their teacher that Jack was stiff and cold when he woke up because of the weather, and that later he was out chasing rabbits in the Happy Hunting Grounds. These students seem to have reacted to part of the clues in the text while blocking out others. Their concept of story included such a firm expectation that things in stories will work out all right ("happiness binding") that they didn't see the dog's death as a

possible meaning for the text at all. Children who make responses like this one are not so much slow to pick up meaning as they are quick to operate out of trust in what they already know. Their teacher's questioning acknowledged their competence but refocused their attention on other details that changed their perception of "stiff" and "cold."

This group of students also struggled with another passage in the same book that deals with Pa Ingalls receiving government land from "Uncle Sam." Laura's Aunt Docia is a prominent character in the same chapter, and some children identified Uncle Sam as Aunt Docia's husband. The logic was sound, but based on insufficient world knowledge. This type of literary miscue is common in the reading of historical fiction or other books with unfamiliar background context.

Recognizing the origin of children's interpretations is important because it suggests how teachers can intervene to help students clarify their thinking or adjust their expectations for certain types of stories. Sometimes, however, the evidence will suggest that more conventional interpretation is not within reach for a particular child or group at a particular time. Sensitive teachers accept this and do not press for signs of superficial understanding but go on to selections that may be more suitable.

Collecting Children's Responses

Finding out how children understand literature and which books they like is such basic information for elementary teachers and librarians that it should not be left to chance. Luckily there are good techniques for discovering responses that are simple and fit naturally into the ongoing business of classrooms and library media centers.

OBSERVING CHILDREN

Observation provides many clues to the reading interests and habits of children. Watching children as they select books will help adults determine what their interests in books are. Do they go directly to a specific book section? Do they know where to find science books, poetry, biography, or fiction? Do they look at the chapter headings or illustrations before selecting a book. Do

[65]Laura Ingalls Wilder, *By the Shores of Silver Lake* (New York: Harper & Row, 1953), pp. 12–13.

they ask for help in locating books? Do they seem to follow the lead of one or two others, selecting in accordance with the leader's choice? Are they really browsing and getting to know books, or are they engaged in aimless wandering? Do they select books that are too difficult to read in order to gain status?

Observing children as they begin to read reveals other helpful information. Do they begin quickly? Can you sense their appreciation of the illlustrations? Does body position reflect relaxation and interest in the book? How long is spent in actual reading? If children are truly absorbed in their books, they are not distracted by ordinary movements or sounds in the library or classroom.

Regardless of how much we know about the general characteristics and interest patterns of children at various age levels, it is only after studying individual children that we can begin to think: "David loved Madeleine L'Engle's *A Wrinkle in Time*. I must tell him about the sequel, *A Wind in the Door*. Beth enjoys ballet so much—I wonder if she has seen Mark Helprin's version of *Swan Lake* with the Chris Van Allsburg illustrations. Peter is somewhat slow in reading, but he enjoyed hearing the informational book on snakes we read during our science unit. Maybe he would feel successful with an easy book like *Snakey Riddles* by Katy Hall and Lisa Eisenberg."

And so the teacher plans for the extension of children's reading interests with care. This information can be shared with the school librarian, who is in a unique position to study the child over a period of years.

Understanding of the child and the accumulated effect of past experiences is gained through observation in many situations. The teacher or librarian observes the child studying or reading alone, reacting to others in work and play situations, and meeting problems. The teacher will note what the child does not do or say, as well as active behavioral responses. The teacher seeks to understand the child's perception of self, for this self-concept influences behavior and choices as well as achievement.

It is especially useful to watch and listen to children as they work at book extension activities such as the ones described in Chapter 13. For instance, making a gameboard that traces the adventures of the three animal companions in Sheila Burnford's *The Incredible Journey* requires deciding which events are important enough to represent and remembering their sequence—or referring back to the book to check. Watching the work in progress allows the teacher to see false starts and self-corrections as well as to note how the child uses the book for information. It is a bonus if two or three students are working together, for then the teacher may listen as they negotiate next steps. Sometimes the most revealing comments a child makes about literature are offered to another child in just such a setting.

Obviously teachers will not have time for daily, detailed observation of each individual child. One efficient primary teacher in a classroom busy with activities takes a moment as she moves from one group to another to stand back and focus on what just one child is doing. A teacher may single out certain children to watch when they seem to be having difficulties or when they are having special success. Some teachers find that a self-designed checklist is a useful tool. This gives some structure to the observation (Chooses fiction_____; chooses nonfiction_____; Reads alone_____; reads with a friend . . . , etc.) and makes it possible to share the task with classroom aides or parent volunteers. For other ideas about observing children, see Chapters 12 and 13.

ELICITING RESPONSES

Children do not always express their ideas about literature spontaneously, and even when they do, the teacher may not be there to see or hear them. There are many ways, however, of deliberately evoking children's responses.

Talking over a story that has just been read aloud or one that a child has just read independently is a natural and satisfying thing to do. Such discussions are a primary teaching tool in helping children build a framework for literature (see Chapter 12). Discussions with a slightly different tone are just as useful in helping teachers get a more complete picture of where the children are to start with. When the focus is on finding out what children are thinking, it is important to begin with general questions that invite talk and do not suggest their own answers: What do you like about the story? What do you notice about it?

How does it make you feel? What does this story make you think of? While many comments may not seem relevant from an adult perspective, the careful listener will find out what is in the foreground of the children's perception of the story. This is a time when it is especially important to be accepting, to offer encouraging comments, nods, and other signals of affirmation. Children who fear giving a "wrong" answer will say what they think the teacher wants to hear or perhaps not say much at all. It takes time for readers of any age to frame their thoughts about a book; a little reflection time between reading and discussion may make for a more productive session.

More directive questioning can also be used to explore a particular area of children's understanding. Again, however, the emphasis should be on discovering children's own ideas and not on reaching predetermined answers. To find out more about her children's perception of fantasy, one teacher asked, about Maurice Sendak's *Outside Over There*, "Just where *is* `outside over there'?" and encouraged them to explain their answers. Another, wanting clues to the same sense of moral judgment her second graders brought to stories, asked them why they thought Jack's mother in the Steven Kellogg version of *Jack and the Beanstalk*, which she had just read aloud, did not punish Jack for stealing from the giant.

Teachers can direct many extension activities to bring out certain aspects of response. One strategy is to ask children to translate meaning from a story through artwork using other characters, incidents, or settings to represent their understanding of the author's message. For instance, a picture-making activity could be used to determine students' understanding of *Fritz and the Mess Fairy* by Rosemany Wells. In this amusing story, Fritz, who is far behind on his cleaning chores, accidentally conjures up a mess fairy during a science experiment. Finally remorseful about the trouble she has caused, he gets rid of her and straightens up everything. Then, in a burst of affection for his family, he prepares breakfast in bed for everyone. "It's the new Fritz," he declares, but the final illustration shows the kitchen in a shambles! Ask children to sup-

pose that Fritz's problem was not making messes, but being noisy. How would that change the story? What would the illustration that shows the "new Fritz" be like? Children who show Fritz being quiet or doing a good deed for his family understand the story in one way. Those who show him making new kinds of noise despite his good intentions understand at a different level.

The pictures on pages 94–95 show two children's responses to the story, *The Biggest House in the World*, by Leo Lionni. After reading this book, the children were asked to choose any animal and grant it the same wish as the little snail had; namely, that it could change itself in any way. Julia, age 8, chose a bird, and she made his tail large, more elaborate, and more colorful. Rick, age 10, also drew a bird. He used the vocabulary of the story, saying: "The bird twitched his tongue in order to make his beak bigger so he could eat more." Finally, his beak becomes so heavy that he can't see over it or lift it up. The boy's comment was: "He'll have to get a derrick to lift it up now." This 10-year-old got the notion of the bird becoming the cause of his own self-destruction, as in the story of the snail, whereas the 8-year-old girl saw only the change of size and the elaboration of color. Both had translated the story into their own creative drawings, but one child appeared to have a fuller understanding of the meaning of the story.

A middle-school teacher whose students had heard *Tuck Everlasting* by Natalie Babbitt asked them to chart out, with words and pictures, the cycle of their own lives, including what they knew of their past and what they predicted for the future. Many of the children could not transfer the ideas about life and death from the book to their own speculations. They did not get beyond young adulthood in their plans, skipping directly from getting a job and getting married to death at an advanced age. Of those who revealed a deeper connection with the book, some portrayed the possibility that their lives might be troubled or brief; some represented life as a circle with themselves in the older generation giving way to the new. The teacher then used these charts to begin a discussion relating the book to the students' own lives.

When asked to replicate Leo Lionni's story of *The Biggest House in the World* using a new main character, these two children demonstrated different levels in their understanding of the theme. The 8-year-old (this picture) showed a bird growing more elaborate; the 10-year-old (right) portrayed a change leading to the bird's self-destruction.

Tremont Elementary School, Upper Arlington, Ohio, Public Schools. Jill Boyd, teacher.

Writing activities can easily be tailored to bring out personal responses. A letter of advice to a friend about what to read helps the teacher judge what kinds of books are important to the writer. Asking a middle grader to write an updated folktale or a story based on the information about medieval times in Sheila Sancha's *The Luttrell Village* will show something about the child's knowledge of genre as well as a more general concept of story. Children should never have to be subjected to formal testing to determine their response. The number of ways for inviting natural responses in the classroom is limited only by the teacher's ingenuity.

KEEPING TRACK

Observing and inviting children's responses have more value if the teacher can somehow keep track of what has been discovered. Because of the time demands that exist in all classrooms, it is wise to use the simplest methods. Many teachers take advantage of existing reading records (see Chapter 13) to jot down brief notes about children's responses. A teacher's journal or log, even one with brief entries, provides a good overview account of classroom responses. It can also be narrowed in focus to record children's changing attitudes and understandings during a theme of study or to collect information about interests and preferences.

Personal portfolios of children's writing and work samples are even easier than notes, although they require space. A real advantage of this sort of file is that it provides a history of growth in response that can be accessible to the child as well as the teacher. Children who have

this concrete evidence of how far they have come are helped in their progress toward self-awareness and are assured that their work is valued. Some of children's most interesting products may not fit in any file, but they can be photographed. Photos capture the setting of response or the larger context of an activity and serve as a reminder of what prompted this particular work or how it was tied to other concerns in the classroom. Portfolios can be collected with minimum effort if children share the responsibility for choosing and updating the contents.

Another valuable tool for keeping track of responses is the audiotape recorder. Taping read-aloud sessions and the talk that follows gives the teacher a chance to sort out patterns of comments that are not easy to catch while in the midst of leading the discussion. Young children or those struggling with the mechanics of writing may be more fluent in their comments on a story if they can dictate them directly into a tape recorder rather than writing them. Two or more children may record their private small-group discussion about a book with the idea that the teacher will hear it later. Or the teacher may tape book confer-

ences with one or two children to save for comparison with later responses.

Videotape equipment can be used to record drama experiences or other large-scale activities. While video can capture nonverbal responses beautifully, the apparatus is too intrusive (and expensive) to make this an everyday possibility for most classrooms. However, some teachers have had great success with getting children to watch tapes of their own activities or discussions and then to reflect on their own responses. This is a technique that helps students develop the ability to step back from a story and from their own experience of it.

Computers are especially useful in the library, where they are indispensable for many tasks. Teachers and children can also use a classroom computer to help keep track of many reading experiences. For instance, the class could keep a cumulative file of readers' comments about particular books on a disc for other students' reference. If children enter specific information about their free-reading choices into a database program, it will be possible to sort out the class's favorite authors and genres or differences in boys' and girls' reading patterns as well as other summaries.

As elementary school teachers become aware of the way they can tune in to children's responses to literature, they will see the value of examining the nature of children's thinking about it. While we all believe that literature is important for children, we do not truly know what difference it makes in a child's life, if any. An in-depth study of children's responses to books is just as important, if not more important, than the studies of children's interests in books. We should explore the developmental nature of response and conduct longitudinal studies of a child's responses over the years. As teachers and librarians, we need to be still and listen to what the children are telling us about their involvement with books and what it means to them.

SUGGESTED LEARNING EXPERIENCES

1. If there is a young child in your household, keep a log for four to five weeks of his or her interaction with literature. What do the child's choices, reactions, comments, and questions reveal about cognitive skills or moral judgment? Do you see any changes that reflect experiences with books?
2. Observe young children as a parent or teacher reads to them. Note as many behaviors (verbal, nonverbal, or artistic/creative) as you can. What clues do you get about the value of reading aloud and about means of effective presentation?
3. Ask three children of various ages (5, 7, 9) to retell the story of "Goldilocks and the Three Bears" from the point of view of Baby Bear. Who is able to begin the story as Baby Bear? Who can maintain the role change? What problems do 5-year-olds have with the language that 9-year-olds seem to solve easily?
4. Set up a play corner in a primary classroom, including props from stories such as a magic wand, a witch's hat, a cardboard crown. What happens over the course of time? What seem to be the sources for children's imaginative play?
5. Choose one of the book extension activities described in Chapter 13 and try it with two or more children. Pay careful attention to their working procedures and analyze the products. What variations or individual differences do you see? What similarities?
6. In a middle-grade classroom, assemble 20 to 30 books that are mostly familiar to the children. Ask a small group to categorize and label these for a tabletop display. Tape their comments as they work. What do you notice about their categories? About the process? If possible, repeat the activity with younger children and books that they have heard. What differences do you notice? Arrange to see the Weston Woods film, *What's a Good Book?* Discuss the categories suggested by children in contrast to those mentioned by the adult experts interviewed.
7. If you can meet with a class of children, ask them to submit the names of their ten favorite books. How do their choices seem to reflect their particular ages and stages of development?
8. Visit the children's room of a public or school library to watch children in the process of choosing books. Keep a list, if you can, of the books examined and rejected, as well as those finally chosen. What factors seem to influence the children's choices?
9. With a small group of fellow students or teachers, read and discuss an award-winning children's book. Working together, plan two sets of questions that could be used with children, one to discover children's initial response to the story, the other to direct their thinking toward the characters' motivations and decisions, the author's effective use of language, or other noteworthy features of the writing.
10. Arrange to talk with one or more readers in the 11 to 13 age range about a book that you and the child(ren) have read individually—for example, Jerry Spinelli's *Maniac Magee*. Plan questions and comments that will encourage the students to share their own interpretations of characters and events. How are their ideas about the book similar to or different from your own? How could you use this information in planning for teaching?

RELATED READINGS

1. Agee, Hugh, and Lee Galda, eds., *Journal of Research and Development in Education*, vol. 16, no. 3 (Spring 1983).

   An entire issue devoted to "Response to Literature: Empirical and Theoretical Studies." Ten diverse articles examine a variety of topics from classroom reponses to theoretical notions of the secondary world and the child as implied reader. It is unusual to find a collection of writings based on research that gives so much attention to elementary children.

2. Applebee, Arthur. *The Child's Concept of Story: Ages Two to Seventeen*. Chicago, Ill.: University of Chicago Press. 1978.

   A report of systematic research on children's developing perceptions of stories. Applebee provides fresh insight on the child's sense of story and response to literature. Among the contributions of this important work are a description of organization and complexity in the structure of stories children tell and a model of developmental stages in the formulation of children's response.

3. Carlsen, G. Robert, and Anne Sherrill. *Voices of Readers: How We Come to Love Books*. Urbana, Ill.: National Council of Teachers of English, 1988.

   Drawing on "reading autobiographies" collected over a 30-year period, the authors have synthesized and categorized more than a thousand reports of young people's reading experiences. Many excerpts preserve the individual "voices of readers" in a book that provides evidence of the paradoxical uniqueness and similarity of human response.

4. Elkind, David. *The Hurried Child: Growing Up Too Fast Too Soon*. Reading, Mass.: Addison-Wesley, 1981.

   In a book addressed mainly to parents, a noted psychologist argues that contemporary children are under too much pressure. They are rushed toward adulthood both at home and at school without regard for normal patterns of development or individual differences. Chapters 5 and 6 present a very readable overview of intellectual, emotional, and social development, with particular reference to Piaget. Chapter 4, which deals with the influence of books and media in "hurrying" children, provides good discussion material for adults considering selection policies.

5. Langerman, Deborah. "Books & Boys: Gender Preferences and Book Selection." *School Library Journal*, vol. 36 (March 1990) pp. 132–136.

   This brief but thought-provoking look at recent evidence on what boys and girls like to read considers several explanatory theories and raises many issues relevant to the classroom as well as the library.

6. Lehr, Susan. *The Child's Developing Sense of Theme: Responses to Literature*. New York: Teachers College Press, 1991.

   The author provides a background of discussion and research as well as a report of her own work in discovering the interpretations of story meaning held by preschool and elementary children. Her findings suggest that adults need to be very good listeners when talking to children about literature. Many examples of children's talk and an engaging, conversational tone make this scholarly work particularly readable.

7. Martinez, Miriam, and Nancy Roser, "Children's Responses to Literature." In James Flood, *et al.*, eds. *Handbook of Research on Teaching the English Language Arts*. New York: Macmillan, 1991.

   This comprehensive review of research since the 1960s is organized around three major categories of factors that affect children's response—characteristics of the reader, context factors, and the nature of the text. Included among the many other sections of this reference volume are an essay on adolescents' "Response to Literature" by Robert Probst, "Reading Preferences" by Dianne Monson and Sam Sebesta, and articles on child development in the preschool, elementary, and middle school years.

8. Purves, Alan C., Theresa Rogers, and Anna O. Soter. *How Porcupines Make Love II: Teaching a Response-Centered Literature Curriculum*. New York: Longman, 1990.

   This lively book for teachers is designed to explain the implications of reader-response theory for literature instruction. Although it deals with the adolescent years, teachers of older elementary students find that many of the ideas and principles discussed here are useful.

9. Rosenblatt, Louise M. *The Reader, the Text, the Poem: The Transactional Theory of the Literary Work*. Carbondale, Ill.: Southern Illinois University Press, 1978.

   A scholarly discussion of the reader's role in evoking a literary work from an author's text. The distinction between aesthetic and efferent reading stances is clearly explained. Although elementary children are seldom mentioned, the book gives a valuable basis for understanding the responses of readers at any age.

10. Tucker, Nicholas, *The Child and the Book: A Psychological and Literary Exploration*. Cambridge: Cambridge University Press, 1981.
    A British psychologist with wide knowledge of literature outlines the "changing imaginative and intellectual outlook" of children from infancy to age 14. Although his major concern is explaining why certain types of stories are popular at various ages, he also considers why some children show more general interest in reading than others.

REFERENCES

Abel-Prot, Viviane. *The Story of Birth*, illustrated by Rozier Gaudriault. Translated by Vicki Bogard. Young Discovery, 1991.

Abramowski, Dwain. *Mountain Bikes*. Watts, 1990.

Adler, Susan S. *Meet Samantha* (The American Girl Collection), illustrated by Nancy Niles. Pleasant Company, 1990.

Adoff, Arnold. *Hard to Be Six*, illustrated by Cheryl Hanna. Lothrop, 1990.

Ahlberg, Janet, and Allan Ahlberg. *The Baby's Catalogue*. Little, 1983.

_____. *Each Peach Pear Plum*. Viking, 1978.

Alcock, Vivien. *The Stonewalkers*. Delacorte, 1983.

Alexander, Lloyd. *The Black Cauldron* (The Chronicles of Prydain), Holt, 1965.

_____. *The Book of Three*. Holt, 1964.

_____. *The Castle of Llyr*. Holt, 1966.

_____. *The High King*. Holt, 1968.

_____. *Taran Wanderer*. Holt, 1967.

Aliki. *My Visit to the Dinosaurs*. 2nd ed. Harper, 1987.

Allard, Harry. *The Stupids Have a Ball*, illustrated by James Marshall. Houghton Mifflin, 1978.

Anno, Mitsumasa. *Anno's Peekaboo*. Philomel, 1988.

_____. *Anno's Math Games II*. Philomel, 1989.

Arnosky, Jim. *Drawing from Nature*. Lothrop, 1983.

Asbjørnsen, P. C., and Jorgen E. Moe. *The Three Billy Goats Gruff*, illustrated by Marcia Brown. Harcourt, 1957.

Ashabranner, Brent. *Crazy About German Shepherds*, photos by Jennifer Ashabranner. Cobblehill, 1991.

Avi. *Nothing but the Truth*. Orchard, 1991.

_____. *The True Confessions of Charlotte Doyle*. Orchard, 1990.

Babbitt, Natalie. *Tuck Everlasting*. Farrar, 1975.

Bang, Molly, *Dawn*. Morrow, 1983.

_____. *Ten, Nine, Eight*. Greenwillow, 1983.

Banks, Lynne Reid. *The Indian in the Cupboard*. Doubleday, 1981.

Barracca, Debra, and Sal Barracca. *Maxi, the Hero*, illustrated by Mark Buehner. Dial, 1991.

Barrett, Joyce D. *Willie's Not the Hugging Kind*, illustrated by Pat Cummings. Harper, 1989.

Barrett, Judi. *I Hate to Go to Bed*, illustrated by Ray Cruz. Four Winds, 1977.

Barton, Byron. *Building a House*. Greenwillow, 1981.

_____. *I Want to Be an Astronaut*. Crowell, 1988.

Base, Graeme. *Animalia*. Abrams, 1987.

Bauer, Marion Dane. *On My Honor*. Clarion, 1986.

Bawden, Nina. *The Outside Child*. Lothrop, 1989.

Blos, Joan. *Martin's Hats*, illustrated by Marc Simont. Morrow, 1984.

Blume, Judy. *Are You There, God? It's Me, Margaret*. Bradbury, 1970.
_____. *Fudge-a-Mania*. Dutton, 1990.
Branley, Franklyn. *What Happened to the Dinosaurs?*, illustrated by Marc Simont. Crowell, 1989.
Brenner, Fred. *Soccer: A Heads-Up Guide to Super Soccer!* Sports Illustrated, 1990.
Briggs, Raymond. *The Snowman*. Random, 1978.
Brittain, Bill, *My Buddy, the King*. Harper, 1989.
Brooks, Bruce. *The Moves Make the Man*. Harper, 1984.
_____. *Everywhere*. Harper, 1990.
Brown, Marcia. *Once a Mouse*. Scribners, 1961.
Brown, Margaret Wise. *Goodnight Moon*, illustrated by Clement Hurd. Harper, 1947.
_____. *The Runaway Bunny*, illustrated by Clement Hurd. Harper, 1942.
Brown, Palmer. *Hickory*. Harper, 1978.
Browne, Anthony. *Piggybook*. Knopf, 1986.
Burnford, Sheila. *The Incredible Journey*, illustrated by Carl Burger. Bantam, 1990.
Burningham, John. *The Blanket*. Crowell, 1976.
_____. *The Cupboard*. Crowell, 1975.
_____. *Mr. Gumpy's Outing*. Holt, 1971.
Burton, Virginia Lee. *The Little House*. Houghton Mifflin, 1942.
Byars, Betsy. *Bingo Brown, Gypsy Lover*. Viking, 1990.
_____. *The Burning Questions of Bingo Brown*. Viking, 1988.
Cameron, Ann. *Julian's Glorious Summer*, illustrated by Doris Leder. Random, 1989.
_____. *The Stories Julian Tells*, illustrated by Ann Strugnell. Knopf, 1987.
Campbell, Rod. *Dear Zoo*. Four Winds, 1983.
_____. *Misty's Mischief*. Viking, 1985.
Carle, Eric. *The Grouchy Ladybug*. Crowell, 1977.
_____. *Pancakes, Pancakes*. Picture Book Studio, 1990.
_____. *The Very Hungry Caterpillar*. Philomel, 1969.
Carrick, Carol. *The Climb*, illustrated by Donald Carrick. Clarion, 1980.
Chaffin, Lillie D. *We Be Warm Till Springtime Comes*, illustrated by Lloyd Bloom. Macmillan, 1980.
Cleary, Beverly. *Dear Mr. Henshaw*, illustrated by Paul O. Zelinsky. Morrow, 1983.
_____. *Ramona Forever*. Morrow, 1984.
_____. *Ramona Quimby, Age 8*, illustrated by Alan Tiegreen. Morrow, 1981.
_____. *Ramona the Brave*, illustrated by Alan Tiegreen. Morrow, 1975.
_____. *Strider*, illustrated by Paul O. Zelinsky. Morrow, 1991.
Cohen, Barbara. *The Long Way Home*. Lothrop, 1990.
_____. *Molly's Pilgrim*, illustrated by Michael Deraney. Lothrop, 1983.
Cohen, Miriam. *When Will I Read?*, illustrated by Lillian Hoban. Greenwillow, 1977.
_____. *Will I Have a Friend?*, illustrated by Lillian Hoban. Macmillan, 1971.
Cole, Brock. *The Goats*. Farrar, 1987.
Cole, Joanna. *Asking About Sex and Growing Up: A Question and Answer Book for Boys and Girls*, illustrated by Alan Tiegreen. Morrow, 1988.
_____. *How You Were Born*. Morrow, 1984.
_____. *The Magic Schoolbus Lost in the Solar System*, illustrated by Bruce Degen. Scholastic, 1990.
_____. *My Puppy Is Born*, photos by Margeret Miller. Morrow, 1990.
Cole, Joanna, and Philip Cole. *Big Goof and Little Goof*, illustrated by M. K. Brown. Scholastic, 1989.
Conford, Ellen. *Anything for a Friend*. Little, 1979.
_____. *Jenny Archer, Author*, illustrated by Diane Palmisciano. Little, 1989.
Conrad, Pam. *My Daniel*. Harper, 1989.
_____. *Prairie Songs*, illustrated by Darryl Zudeck. Harper, 1985.
_____. *Staying Nine*, illustrated by Mike Wimmer. Harper, 1988.
_____. *The Tub People*, illustrated by Richard Egielski. Harper, 1990.
Cooper, Susan. *The Dark Is Rising*, illustrated by Alan Cober. Atheneum, 1973.
Cooper, Ilene. *Choosing Sides*. Greenwillow, 1990.
Cormier, Robert. *Other Bells for Us to Ring*, illustrated by Deborah Kogan Ray. Delacorte, 1990.
Crews, Donald. *Freight Train*. Greenwillow, 1978.
Dahl, Roald. *The BFG*, illustrated by Quentin Blake. Farrar, 1982.
_____. *Danny the Champion of the World*, illustrated by Jill Bennett. Knopf, 1975.
Dalgliesh, Alice. *The Courage of Sarah Noble*, illustrated by Leonard Weisgard. Scribner's, 1954.
De Jenkins, Lyll B. *The Honorable Prison*. Lodestar, 1988.

DeJong, Meindert. *Hurry Home, Candy*, illustrated by Maurice Sendak. Harper, 1953.
de Paola, Tomie. *Strega Nona*. Prentice-Hall, 1975.
_____. *Tomie de Paola's Mother Goose*. Holiday House, 1984.
DeRegniers, Beatrice Schenk. *May I Bring a Friend?*, illustrated by Beni Montresor. Atheneum, 1964.
_____. ed. *Sing a Song of Popcorn: Every Child's Book of Poems*, illustrated by Caldecott-Medal winning artists. Scholastic, 1988.
Dickinson, Peter. *Merlin Dreams*, illustrated by Alan Lee. Delacorte, 1988.
Ehlert, Lois. *Eating the Alphabet*. Harper, 1989.
_____. *Feathers for Lunch*. Harcourt, 1990.
Emberley, Michael. *Ruby*. Little, 1990.
Evslin, Bernard. *Heroes and Monsters of Greek Myth*, illustrated by William Hunter. Scholastic, 1988.
_____. *Jason and the Argonauts*, illustrated by Bert Dodson. Morrow, 1986.
Fleischman, Paul. *The Borning Room*. Harper, 1991.
_____. *Saturnalia*. Harper, 1990.
Fox, Paula. *Monkey Island*. Orchard, 1991.
_____. *The Moonlight Man*. Bradbury, 1986.
Freedman, Russell. *Franklin Delano Roosevelt*. Clarion, 1990.
Freeman, Don. *Corduroy*. Viking, 1968.
Friedman, Ina. *How My Parents Learned to Eat*, illustrated by Allen Say. Houghton Mifflin, 1984.
Fritz, Jean. *Homesick: My Own Story*, illustrated by Margot Tomes. Putnam, 1982.
_____. *What's the Big Idea, Ben Franklin?*, illustrated by Margot Tomes. Coward, 1976.
Gág, Wanda. *Millions of Cats*. Coward, 1956 (1928).
Galdone, Paul. *The Gingerbread Boy*. Clarion, 1975.
_____. *The Little Red Hen*. Clarion, 1973.
Gardiner, John. *Stone Fox*, illustrated by Marcia Sewall. Harper, 1980.
Garner, Alan. *The Stone Book*, illustrated by Michael Foreman. Philomel, 1978.
George, Jean. *Cry of the Crow*. Harper, 1980.
_____. *Julie of the Wolves*, illustrated by John Schoenherr. Harper, 1972.
Gerstein, Mordicai. *Roll Over!* Crown, 1984.
Gibbons, Gail. *Sunken Treasure*. Harper, 1990.
_____. *Trucks*. Crowell, 1981.
_____. *Up Goes the Skyscraper!* Macmillan, 1990.
Giff, Patricia Reilly. *Kids of Polk Street School* (Series). Dell, 1988.
Glenn, Mel. *Back to Class: Poems*, photos by Michael J. Bernstein. Clarion, 1988.
Goble, Paul. *Beyond the Ridge*. Bradbury, 1989.
Graeber, Charlotte. *Mustard*, illustrated by Donna Diamond. Macmillan, 1982.
Greenblat, Rodney A. *Uncle Wizzmo's New Used Car*. Harper, 1990.
Greene, Constance C. *Beat the Turtle Drum*, illustrated by Donna Diamond. Viking, 1976.
Grifalconi, Ann. *Osa's Pride*. Little, 1990.
Guarino, Deborah. *Is Your Mama a Llama?*, illustrated by Steven Kellogg. Scholastic, 1990.
Hall, Donald. *Ox-Cart Man*, illustrated by Barbara Cooney. Viking, 1979.
Hall, Katy, and Lisa Eisenberg. *Snakey Riddles*. Dial, 1990.
Hamilton, Virginia. *Cousins*. Philomel, 1990.
_____. *Sweet Whispers, Brother Rush*. Philomel, 1982.
Hart, Jane. *Singing Bee! A Collection of Favorite Songs*, illustrated by Anita Lobel. Lothrop, 1982.
Heide, Florence Parry, and Judith Heide Gilliland. *The Day of Ahmed's Secret*, illustrated by Ted Lewin. Lothrop, 1990.
Helprin, Mark. *Swan Lake*, illustrated by Chris Van Allsburg. Houghton Mifflin, 1989.
Henkes, Kevin. *Chester's Way*. Greenwillow, 1988.
_____. *Julius, the Baby of the World*. Greenwillow, 1990.
Hewett, Joan. *Public Defender: Lawyer of the People*, photos by Richard Hewett. Lodestar, 1991.
Hill, Eric. *Where's Spot?* Putnam, 1980.
Hirschi, Ron. *Summer*, photos by Thomas D. Mangelson. Cobblehill, 1991.
Ho, Minfong. *Rice Without Rain*. Lothrop, 1990.
Hoban, Russell. *A Baby Sister for Frances*, illustrated by Lillian Hoban. Harper, 1964.
Hoban, Tana. *I Read Signs*. Greenwillow, 1983.
_____. *Look Again!* Macmillan, 1971.
_____. *Of Colors and Things*. Greenwillow, 1989.
_____. *1, 2, 3*. Greenwillow, 1985.

_____. *Red, Blue, Yellow Shoe*. Greenwillow, 1986.

_____. *26 Letters and 99 Cents*. Greenwillow, 1987.

_____. *What Is It?* Greenwillow, 1985.

Hobbs, Will. *Bearstone*. Atheneum, 1989.

Hoffman, Mary, *Amazing Grace*, illustrated by Caroline Binch. Dial, 1991.

Holman, Felice. *Secret City, U.S.A.* Scribner's, 1990.

Hooks, William. *The Ballad of Belle Dorcas*, illustrated by Brian Pinkney. Knopf, 1990.

Hopkins, Lee Bennett. *By Myself*, illustrated by Glo Coalson. Crowell, 1980.

Horenstein, Henry. *Sam Goes Trucking*. Houghton Mifflin, 1990.

Howe, James. *The Celery Stalks at Midnight*, illustrated by Leslie Morrill. Atheneum, 1983.

_____. *Dew Drop Dead*. Atheneum, 1990.

Howe, James, and Deborah Howe. *Bunnicula*, illustrated by Alan Daniel. Atheneum, 1979.

Hughes, Shirley. *Alfie Gets in First*. Lothrop, 1981.

_____. *Alfie's Feet*. Lothrop, 1983.

Hunter, Mollie. *Hold On to Love*. Harper, 1984.

Hurwitz, Johanna. *Class Clown*, illustrated by Sheila Hamanaka. Morrow, 1987.

Hutchins, Pat. *Rosie's Walk*. Macmillan, 1968.

_____. *Titch*. Macmillan, 1971.

_____. *You'll Soon Grow into Them, Titch*. Greenwillow, 1983.

Isadora, Rachel. *Babies*. Greenwillow, 1990.

Janeczko, Paul. *The Place My Words Are Looking For: What Poets Say About and Through Their Work*. Bradbury, 1990.

_____. *This Delicious Day: Sixty-Five Poems*. Orchard, 1987.

Johnson, Angela. *When I Am Old with You*, illustrated by David Soman. Orchard, 1990.

Jonas, Ann. *When You Were a Baby*. Greenwillow, 1982.

Jones, Rebecca. *Germy Blew* The Bugle. Arcade, 1990.

Jukes, Mavis. *Blackberries in the Dark*, illustrated by Thomas B. Allen. Knopf, 1985.

Jurmain, Suzanne. *Once Upon a Horse: A History of Horses and How They Shaped Our History*. Lothrop, 1989.

Juster, Norton. *The Phantom Tollbooth*. Random, 1961.

Keats, Ezra Jack. *John Henry: An American Legend*. Pantheon, 1965.

_____. *The Snowy Day*. Viking, 1962.

_____. *Whistle for Willie*. Viking, 1964.

Kellogg, Steven, *Jack and the Beanstalk*. Morrow, 1991.

_____. *Paul Bunyan*. Morrow, 1984.

Kimmel, Eric A., reteller. *Baba Yaga: A Russian Folktale*, illustrated by Megan Lloyd. Holiday, 1991.

Klein, Robin. *Hating Alison Ashley*. Viking, 1987.

Kline, Suzy, *Herbie Jones*, illustrated by Richard Williams. Putnam, 1985.

Konigsburg, E. L. *From the Mixed-Up Files of Mrs. Basil E. Frankweiler*. Atheneum, 1967.

Kraus, Robert. *Leo the Late Bloomer*, illustrated by Jose Aruego. Windmill, 1971.

Krementz, Jill. *How It Feels to Fight for Your Life*. Knopf, 1990.

_____. *A Very Young Gymnast*. Knopf, 1978.

Kunhardt, Dorothy. *Pat the Bunny*. Golden Press, 1962 (1940).

Langstaff, John. *Over in the Meadow*, illustrated by Feodor Rojankovsky. Harcourt, 1957.

Lasky, Kathryn. *The Night Journey*, illustrated by Trina Schart Hyman. Scribner's, 1981.

Lauber, Patricia. *Dinosaurs Walked Here and Other Stories Fossils Tell*. Bradbury, 1987.

_____. *An Octopus Is Amazing*, illustrated by Holly Keller. Harper, 1990.

Le Guin, Ursula. *A Wizard of Earthsea*, illustrated by Ruth Robbins. Parnassus, 1968.

L'Engle, Madeleine. *A Ring of Endless Light*. Farrar, 1980.

_____. *A Swiftly Tilting Planet*. Farrar, 1978.

_____. *A Wind in the Door*. Farrar, 1973.

_____. *A Wrinkle in Time*. Farrar, 1962.

Levoy, Myron. *Alan and Naomi*. Harper, 1978.

Lewis, C. S. (The Chronicles of Narnia) *The Horse and His Boy*, illustrated by Pauline Baynes. Macmillan, 1962.

_____. *The Last Battle*, illustrated by Pauline Baynes. Macmillan, 1964.

_____. *The Lion, the Witch, and the Wardrobe*, illustrated by Pauline Baynes. Macmillan, 1961.

_____. *The Magician's Nephew*, illustrated by Pauline Baynes. Macmillan, 1964.

_____. *Prince Caspian*, illustrated by Pauline Baynes. Macmillan, 1964.

_____. *The Silver Chair*, illustrated by Pauline Baynes. Macmillan, 1962.

_____. *The Voyage of the "Dawn Treader,"* illustrated by Pauline Baynes. Macmillan, 1962.

Lindgren, Barbro. *Sam's Cookie,* illustrated by Eva Eriksson. Morrow, 1982.

Lionni, Leo. *The Biggest House in the World.* Pantheon, 1968.

_____. *Fish Is Fish.* Pantheon, 1970.

_____. *Frederick.* Pantheon, 1966.

_____. *Little Blue and Little Yellow.* Astor-Honor, 1959.

Lister, Robin. *The Legend of King Arthur,* illustrated by Alan Baker. Doubleday, 1990.

Little, Jean. *Little by Little: A Writer's Education.* Viking, 1987.

Lobel, Arnold. *Frog and Toad Together.* Harper, 1972.

_____. *The Random House Book of Mother Goose.* Random, 1986.

Lowry, Lois. *Anastasia Krupnik.* Houghton Mifflin, 1979.

_____. *Number the Stars.* Houghton Mifflin, 1989.

Lyon, George Ella. *Borrowed Children.* Orchard, 1988.

Macaulay, David. *The Way Things Work.* Houghton Mifflin, 1988.

McCaffrey, Anne. *Dragonsong,* illustrated by Laura Lydecker. Atheneum, 1976.

McCloskey, Robert. *Burt Dow, Deep Water Man.* Viking, 1963.

_____. *Make Way for Ducklings.* Viking, 1941.

_____. *One Morning in Maine.* Viking, 1952.

MacDonald, Amy. *Rachel Fister's Blister,* illustrated by Marjorie Priceman. Houghton Mifflin, 1990.

MacDonald, Caroline. *The Lake at the End of the World.* Dial, 1989.

McDonald, Megan. *Is This a House for a Hermit Crab?,* illustrated by S. D. Schindler. Orchard, 1990.

McDonnell, Christine. *Friends First.* Viking, 1990.

McGovern, Ann. *The Secret Soldier: The Story of Deborah Sampson,* illustrated by Ann Grifalconi. Four Winds, 1975.

McKinley, Robin. *The Hero and the Crown.* Greenwillow, 1984.

_____. *The Outlaws of Sherwood.* Greenwillow, 1988.

McKissack, Patricia C. *Flossie and the Fox,* illustrated by Rachel Isadora. Dial, 1986.

MacLachlan, Patricia. *Journey.* Delacorte, 1991.

_____. *Sarah, Plain and Tall.* Harper, 1985.

McMillan, Bruce. *Time To...* Lothrop, 1989.

McMurtry, Larry. *Lonesome Dove.* Simon & Schuster, 1985.

McPhail, David. *Fix-It.* Dutton, 1984.

Magorian, Michelle. *Goodnight, Mr. Tom.* Harper, 1981.

Mahy, Margaret. *The Haunting.* Atheneum, 1982.

Marshall, James. *Rats on the Roof.* Dial, 1991.

Martin, Bill, Jr. *Brown Bear, Brown Bear, What Do You See?,* illustrated by Eric Carle. Holt, 1983.

Martin, Bill, Jr., and John Archambault. *Chicka Chicka Boom Boom,* illustrated by Lois Ehlert. Simon & Schuster, 1989.

Maruki, Toshi. *Hiroshima No Pika.* Lothrop, 1980.

Mayle, Peter. *What's Happening to Me?,* illustrated by Paul Walter and Arthur Robbins. Carol Publishing, 1975.

Meyers, Susan. *Insect Zoo,* photos by Richard Hewett. Lodestar, 1991.

Miles, Betty. *The Real Me.* Knopf, 1974.

Minarik, Else Holmelund. *Little Bear,* illustrated by Maurice Sendak. Harper, 1957.

Murphy, Jim. *The Boys' War: Confederate and Union Soldiers Talk About the Civil War.* Clarion, 1990.

Myers, Walter Dean. *The Mouse Rap.* Harper, 1990.

_____. *Now Is Your Time! The African-American Struggle for Freedom.* HarperCollins, 1991.

_____. *Scorpions.* Harper, 1988.

Naidoo, Beverley. *Journey to Jo'Burg: A South African Story,* illustrated by Eric Velasquez. Lippincott, 1986.

Naylor, Phyllis Reynolds. *The Agony of Alice.* Atheneum, 1985.

_____. *Shiloh.* Atheneum, 1991.

Ness, Evaline. *Sam, Bangs, and Moonshine.* Holt, 1966.

O'Brien, Robert. *Mrs. Frisby and the Rats of NIMH,* illustrated by Zena Bernstein. Atheneum, 1971.

O'Dell, Scott. *Island of the Blue Dolphins.* Houghton Mifflin, 1990 (1960).

Orgel, Doris. *Nobodies & Somebodies.* Viking, 1991.

Ormerod, Jan. *Sunshine.* Lothrop, 1981.

Osborne, Mary Pope. *American Tall Tales,* illustrated by Michael McCurdy. Knopf, 1991.

Oxenbury, Helen. *Mother's Helper.* Dial, 1982.

_____. *Tickle, Tickle*. Macmillan, 1988.

_____. *Tom & Pippo's Day*. Macmillan, 1989.

Parish, Peggy. *Amelia Bedelia*, illustrated by Fritz Siebel. Harper, 1963.

Park, Barbara. *Skinnybones*. Knopf, 1982.

Park, Ruth. *When the Wind Changed*, illustrated by Deborah Niland. Coward, 1981.

Parker, Nancy Winslow, and Joan R. Wright. *Bugs*, illustrated by Nancy Winslow Parker. Morrow, 1988.

Paterson, Katherine. *The Great Gilly Hopkins*. Crowell, 1978.

_____. *Jacob Have I Loved*. Crowell, 1980.

_____. *Lyddie*. Lodestar, 1991.

_____. *The Master Puppeteer*, illustrated by Haru Wells. Crowell, 1976.

Patrick, Diane. *Martin Luther King, Jr.* Watts, 1990.

Paulsen, Gary. *Dogsong*. Bradbury, 1985.

_____. *Hatchet*. Bradbury, 1987.

Pinkwater, Daniel. *Borgel*. Macmillan, 1990.

Polacco, Patricia. *Babushka's Doll*. Simon & Schuster, 1990.

Pomerantz, Charlotte. *Flap Your Wings and Try*, illustrated by Nancy Tafuri. Greenwillow, 1989.

Pope, Joyce. *Kenneth Lilly's Animals*, illustrated by Kenneth Lilly. Lothrop, 1988.

Potter, Beatrix. *The Tale of Peter Rabbit*. Warne, 1902.

Prelutsky, Jack. *Something Big Has Been Here*, illustrated by James Stevenson. Greenwillow, 1990.

_____, ed. *For Laughing Out Loud*, illustrated by Marjorie Priceman. Knopf, 1991.

Pryor, Bonnie. *The House on Maple Street*, illustrated by Beth Peck. Morrow, 1987.

Pulver, Robin. *The Holiday Handwriting School*, illustrated by G. Brian Karas. Macmillan, 1991.

Rabe, Berniece. *The Balancing Girl*, illustrated by Lillian Hoban. Dutton, 1981.

Raber, Rom. *Bo Jackson: Pro Sports Superstar*. Lerner, 1990.

Raskin, Ellen. *The Westing Game*. Dutton, 1978.

Rawls, Wilson. *Where the Red Fern Grows*. Doubleday, 1961.

Reeder, Carolyn. *Shades of Gray*. Macmillan, 1989.

Reid, Barbara. *Playing with Plasticine*. Morrow, 1989.

Reiss, John J. *Colors*. Bradbury, 1969.

Rice, Eve. *Sam Who Never Forgets*. Greenwillow, 1977.

Rockwell, Anne. *Things to Play With*. Dutton, 1988.

_____. *The Three Bears and 15 Other Stories*. Crowell, 1975.

_____. *Trucks*. Dutton, 1984.

Roehrig, Catherine. *Fun with Hieroglyphs: From the Metropolitan Museum of Art*. Viking, 1990.

Rogers, Fred. *Going to the Potty*, illustrated by Jim Judkis. Putnam 1986.

Rogers, Jean. *Raymond's Best Summer*, illustrated by Marilyn Hafner. Greenwillow, 1990.

Rosen, Michael. *We're Going on a Bear Hunt*, illustrated by Helen Oxenbury. McElderry, 1989.

Russo, Marisabina. *Where is Ben?* Greenwillow, 1990.

Rylant, Cynthia. *A Couple of Kooks and Other Stories About Love*. Orchard, 1990.

_____. *The Relatives Came*, illustrated by Stephen Gammell. Bradbury, 1985.

_____. *When I Was Young in the Mountains*, illustrated by Diane Goode. Dutton, 1982.

Sancha, Sheila. *The Luttrell Village: Country Life in the Middle Ages*. Crowell, 1982.

Schwartz, Alvin. *Tomfoolery: Trickery and Foolery with Words*, illustrated by Glen Rounds. Harper, 1973.

Scieszka, Jon. *The Not-So-Jolly Roger*, illustrated by Lane Smith. Viking, 1991.

_____. *The True Story of the 3 Little Pigs as Told by A. Wolf*, illustrated by Lane Smith. Viking, 1989.

Seeger, Pete. *Abiyoyo*, illustrated by Michael Hays. Macmillan, 1986.

Sendak, Maurice. *Outside Over There*. Harper, 1981.

_____. *Where the Wild Things Are*. Harper, 1963.

Seuss, Dr. (Theodor S. Geisel). *And to Think That I Saw It on Mulberry Street*. Vanguard, 1937.

Shannon, Monica. *Dobry*, illustrated by Atanas Katchamakoff. Viking, 1934.

Silverstein, Shel. *A Light in the Attic*. Harper, 1981.

_____. *Where the Sidewalk Ends*. Harper, 1963.

Simon, Seymour. *101 Questions and Answers About Dangerous Animals*, illustrated by Ellen Friedman. Macmillan, 1985.

_____. *The Paper Airplane Book*, illustrated by Byron Barton. Viking, 1971.

Sis, Peter. *Follow the Dream*. Knopf, 1991.

Slepian, Jan. *Risk 'N Roses*. Philomel, 1990.

Slote, Alfred. *The Trading Game*. Lippincott, 1990.

Smith, Doris Buchanan. *A Taste of Blackberries*, illustrated by Charles Robinson. Crowell, 1973.

Smith, Janice. *It's Not Easy Being George,* Illustrated by Dick Gackenbach. Harper, 1989.

Smith, Robert. *The War with Grandpa*, illustrated by Richard Lauter. Delacorte, 1984.

Snyder, Zilpha. *Libby on Wednesday*. Doubleday, 1990.

Sobol, Donald J. *Encyclopedia Brown's Book of Wacky Cars*, illustrated by Ted Enik. Morrow, 1987.

Soto, Gary. *Baseball in April and Other Stories*. Harcourt, 1990.

Speare, Elizabeth George. *The Sign of the Beaver*. Houghton Mifflin, 1983.

Spier, Peter. *Crash! Bang! Boom!* Doubleday, 1972.

Spinelli, Jerry. *Maniac Magee*. Little, 1990.

Stanley, Fay. *The Last Princess: The Story of Princess Ka'iulani of Hawai'i*, illustrated by Diane Stanley. Four Winds, 1991.

Staples, Suzanne. *Shabanu: Daughter of the Wind*. Knopf, 1989.

Steig, William. *Abel's Island*. Farrar, 1976.

_____. *Amos & Boris*. Farrar, 1971.

_____. *Doctor De Soto*. Farrar, 1982.

_____. *Sylvester and the Magic Pebble*. Windmill, 1969.

Steptoe, John. *Baby Says*. Lothrop, 1988.

_____. *Stevie*. Harper, 1969.

Stevens, Carla. *Trouble for Lucy*, illustrated by Ronald Himler. Clarion, 1979.

Stolz, Mary. *The Explorer of Barkham Street*, illustrated by Emily McCully. Harper, 1985.

Sutton, Richard. *Car* (Eyewitness Books). Knopf, 1990.

Swann, Brian. *A Basket Full of White Eggs: Riddle-Poems*, illustrated by Ponder Goembel. Orchard, 1988.

Tafuri, Nancy. *Have You Seen My Duckling?* Greenwillow, 1984.

Taylor, Kim. *Frog* (See How They Grow Series). Lodestar, 1991.

Taylor, Mildred D. *The Road to Memphis*. Dial, 1990.

_____. *Roll of Thunder, Hear My Cry*. Dial, 1976.

Tolan, Stephanie. *Plague Year*. Morrow, 1990.

Tolkien, J. R. R. *The Hobbit*, illustrated by Michael Hague. Houghton Mifflin, 1989 (1938).

Valens, Amy. *Jesse's Daycare*. Houghton Mifflin, 1990.

Van Allsburg, Chris. *The Polar Express*. Houghton Mifflin, 1985.

Viorst, Judith. *Alexander and the Terrible, Horrible, No Good, Very Bad Day*, illustrated by Ray Cruz. Atheneum, 1972.

Voigt, Cynthia. *Dicey's Song*. Atheneum, 1982.

_____. *A Solitary Blue*. Atheneum, 1983.

Wabbes, Marie. *How I was Born*. Tambourine, 1991.

Waber, Bernard. *Ira Sleeps Over*. Houghton Mifflin, 1973.

Walker, Barbara. *The Little House Cookbook: Frontier Foods from Laura Ingalls Wilder's Classic Stories*, illustrated by Garth Williams. Harper, 1979.

Walsh, Jill Paton. *The Green Book*, illustrated by Lloyd Bloom. Farrar, 1982.

Ward, Cindy. *Cookie's Week*, illustrated by Tomie de Paola. Putnam, 1988.

Watanabe, Shigeo, *How Do I Put It On?*, illustrated by Yasuo Ohtomo. Philomel, 1979.

Watson, Clyde. *Catch Me and Kiss Me and Say It Again*, illustrated by Wendy Watson. Philomel, 1978.

Watson, Clyde, and Wendy Watson. *Applebet: An ABC*, illustrated by Wendy Watson. Farrar, 1982.

Wells, Rosemary. *Fritz and the Mess Fairy*. Dial, 1991.

_____. *Max's Ride*. Dial, 1979.

_____. *Noisy Nora*. Dial, 1973.

White, E. B. *Charlotte's Web*, illustrated by Garth Williams. Harper, 1953.

Wiesner, David. *Tuesday*. Clarion, 1991.

Wilder, Laura Ingalls. *By the Shores of Silver Lake*, illustrated by Garth Williams. Harper, 1953 (1939).

_____. *Little House in the Big Woods*, illustrated by Garth Williams. Harper, 1953 (1932).

Wildsmith, Brian. *Python's Party*. Watts, 1975.

Williams, Karen. *Galimoto*, illustrated by Catherine Stock. Lothrop, 1990.

Williams, Linda. *The Little Old Lady Who Was Not Afraid of Anything*, illustrated by Megan Lloyd. Crowell, 1986.

Williams, Vera B. *A Chair for My Mother*. Greenwillow, 1982.

_____. *"More. More. More." Said the Baby*. Greenwillow, 1990.

Winter, Jonah. *Diego*, illustrated by Jeanette Winter. (In English and Spanish; translated from the English by Amy Prince). Knopf, 1991.

Wolff, Ashley. *A Year of Beasts*. Dutton, 1986.

Wood, Audrey. *Heckedy Peg*, illustrated by Don Wood. Harcourt, 1987.

————. *The Napping House*, illustrated by Don Wood. Harcourt, 1984.

Wright, Betty Ren. *The Dollhouse Murders*. Holiday, 1983.

Yashima, Taro. *Crow Boy*. Viking, 1955.

Yep, Laurence. *The Star-Fisher*. Morrow, 1991.

Yolen, Jane. *The Devil's Arithmetic*. Penguin, 1988.

Young, Ed. *Lon Po Po: A Red Riding Hood Story from China*. Philomel, 1989.

Zelinsky, Paul O. *The Wheels on the Bus*. Dutton, 1990.

Zemach, Margot. *Hush, Little Baby*. Dutton, 1976.

Zolotow, Charlotte. *Some Things Go Together*, illustrated by Karen Gundersheimer. Crowell, 1983.

Chapter Three

The Changing World of Children's Books

CRUEL BOYS

"O, what a shame!" a kind child may be ready to say on looking at this picture. You see these boys, little as they are, have hard and cruel hearts. They have been robbing a happy little bird family of one of the young ones; and now they will so hurt it that it will die, or they will let it starve to death. And they have robbed another pair of birds of their nest and eggs. How unhappy must all these birds now be! and how wicked it is to give such needless pain to any of God's creatures! No kind child can think of hurting a dear, innocent little bird. But those who delight in such sport will very likely grow up to be capable of injuring their fellowmen in the various ways of which we so often hear and read. Let us be kind to every thing that lives.

And this isn't the whole story about these wicked boys. Don't you see they are in a *quarrel*, how they shall divide what they have so cruelly stolen from the birds? Ah, that is the way in doing wrong—one wrong step leads on to another; and robbing birds' nests does not usually go alone—a quarrel, or some other wickedness, usually follows it. Beware, then of the *beginnings* of cruelty and wickedness.[1]

CRUEL BOYS.

"Cruel Boys" from *Sunnybank Stories: My Teacher's Gem*. Boston, Mass.: Lee and Shepard, 1863.

❦ ❦ ❦

[1] Asa Bullard, *Sunnybank Stories: My Teacher's Gem* (Boston: Lee and Shepard, 1863), pp. 22–24.

EXCERPT FROM *LET'S BE ENEMIES*

James used to be my friend.
But today he is my enemy.
James always wants to be the boss.
James carries the flag.
James takes all the crayons.
He grabs the best digging spoon
and he throws sand. . . .
I'm going right over to James' house and tell him. . . .
"Hullo, James."
"Hullo, John."
"I came to tell you that I'm not your friend any more."
"Well then, I'm not *your* friend either."
"We're enemies."
"All right!"
"GOOD-BYE!"
"GOOD-BYE!"
"Hey, James!"
"What?"
"Let's roller skate."
"O.K. Have a pretzel, John."
"Thank you, James."[2]

"GOOD-BYE!"
"GOOD-BYE!"

From *Let's Be Enemies* by Janice May Udry. Illustration by Maurice Sendak. New York: Harper & Row, 1961.

❦ ❦ ❦

Compare the language, the content, and the illustrations in these two stories—the ways in which society has changed its cultural values and its attitude toward children are strikingly apparent. "Cruel Boys" is taken from *My Teacher's Gem*, a collection of moralistic stories printed in 1863. Its purpose was to instruct the young by first describing a horrible example of misbehavior and then warning of the dire consequences of, in this instance, stealing. It is told in the third person from the point of view of an adult admonishing all children. The moral of the story is explicitly stated.

The story of "Cruel Boys" contains only one black and white print, the one pictured here. This same illustration was used in many different books at that time. The "pirating" of pictures and stories from other books was a common practice.

Let's Be Enemies (1961), on the other hand, captures the experience, the feelings, and the language of the young child. The story is told in the first person from the point of view of the child protagonist, which makes it easier for the reader to identify with the growing anger of John. But 5-year-olds' quarrels are as fleeting as the brief showers that Sendak includes in his childlike illustrations. The sun soon comes out; and true to the nature of young children, John and James are fast friends by the end of the story.

The contrast between these stories mirrors the changes in literature for children. In *Let's Be Enemies*, children are allowed their childhood; they can be their 5-year-old selves. Their private feelings, thoughts, and language are considered worthy of attention. As much care has gone into conveying the meaning of the story through the pictures as through the text. It has taken a very long time for books to move from the didactic and moralistic to books that delight and entertain.

The literature intended for children always reflects the changing attitude of society toward childhood and the family. As Philippe Ariès[3] contends, the idea of

[3]Philippe Ariès, *Centuries of Childhood: A Social History of Family Life,* translated from the French by Robert Baldick (New York: Knopf, 1962).

childhood itself was a seventeenth-century invention that has been transformed and reconstituted in every subsequent historical period. Books for children provide a fascinating record of society and the values it has wished to inculcate in its youth.

Children's literature has a brief history when seen in relationship to the history of the world. Nevertheless, it has evolved from a rich and interesting background. Literature reflects not only the values of society but also the books that have preceded it—literature of one generation builds on literature of the past generation. An understanding of family stories of today is enriched by acquaintance with the family stories of the past. How, for example, do the Beverly Cleary stories of the Quimby family (*Ramona and Her Father*, 1977, etc.) or Cynthia Voigt's descriptions of the Tuckermans in *Homecoming* (1981) compare with *The Moffats* (1940) by Eleanor Estes or Edith Nesbit's Bastable children in *The Story of the Treasure-Seekers* (1899) or even that earliest of well-loved family stories, *Little Women* (1868), by Louisa May Alcott?

One danger in evaluating stories of the past is the tendency to use contemporary criteria, rather than to recognize the prevailing values of the period in which a book was published. Some modern-day critics see *Little Women* as being antifeminist, but at the time of its publication in 1868, its main character was considered much too independent and tomboyish. Obvious as it may seem, books for children are a product of their times. They need to be evaluated in relationship to the other books of the day and against the social and political values of the period. Only then is it possible to identify the books that were real breakthroughs in the changing literature of childhood.

EARLY BEGINNINGS—THE MIDDLE AGES

The Oral Tradition

Before there were books, there were stories. In the medieval days—from the fifth to the fifteenth century—stories were told around the fires in cottages or sung in the great halls of castles. Young and old alike listened, with no distinction made between stories for children and stories for adults, just as there was little difference in the work they did, the food they ate, or the clothes they wore. All gathered to listen, to be entertained after a hard day's labor. A comparison can be made between this time of the oral tradition and today, when an entire family gathers to view a television show. True, there are children's programs, but many surveys show children watch what adults watch. All are exposed to the same stories.

In the Middle Ages, there were differences in the kinds of stories told in the cottages and the castles and in the way they were told. In the castles and great manor houses wandering minstrels or bards told the heroic tales of Beowulf or King Arthur or the ballad of Fair Isabella, whose stepmother had her cooked and served in a pie. Often these tales were sung, accompanied by harp or lyre. By contrast, the tales told around the peat fires in the cottages or at the medieval fairs were about simple folk: farmers, woodcutters, and millers or beast tales about wolves, foxes, and hens. Frequently, the stories portrayed the poor peasant outwitting the lord of the manor or winning the hand of the princess by a daring deed. These tales were told over and over for generations until they were finally collected by scholars and thus passed into recorded literature.

It is important to remember that the oral tradition did not cease with the invention of the printing press. Most common folk could not read or afford to buy books. And the first books were not intended for entertainment; they were for religious or instructional purposes—frequently both. It was the told tale that continued to delight far into the nineteenth century. Today the storyteller is still a welcome visitor in the classroom, library, or home. The increased number of storytelling festivals today signals a revival of interest in this art.

The Earliest Manuscripts

Before the invention of movable type, the first books available for children were lesson books handwritten in Latin by monks. Mostly religious or instructional, these were intended only for the wealthy or for use by teachers in monastery schools. Such handwritten books were extremely valuable; houses and lands were often exchanged for a single volume.[4]

Most early lesson books followed one of two forms, which continued in popularity up to the early twentieth century: (1) a dialogue between the pupil and teacher, usually in the form of questions and answers, or (2) rhymed couplets, which made for easy memorization. Aldhelm, Abbot of Malmesbury during the seventh century, is credited with introducing the question-and-answer approach. Also during this century, the Venerable Bede translated and wrote some forty-five books for his students at the monastery at Jarrow in England.

Another type of book, the *Elucidarium*, or book of general information for young students, was developed by Anselm, Archbishop of Canterbury during the twelfth century. This type of book, a forerunner of the encyclopedia, treated such topics as manners, children's duties, the properties of animals and plants, and religious precepts.

Early lesson books are only important to the history of children's literature in that they represent some concession to developing specific books for the *instruction* of children. Another six centuries would pass before John Newbery would add the word "amusement" to the word "instruction."

The Gesta Romanorum (Deeds of the Romans), compiled in Latin about 1290, served as a source book of stories for the clergy for instruction and for enlivening sermons. This compilation of stories included many myths, fables, and tales from as far away as the Orient. Both Chaucer and Shakespeare drew incidents and stories from the Gesta. For example, it contained anecdotes of the three caskets and the pound of flesh found in *The Merchant of Venice* and a synopsis of the medieval romance *Guy of Warwick*. These tales were often dressed up with suitable morals and then told to children.

Only one well-known work remains from these early manuscripts, Chaucer's *Canterbury Tales*.

Although written for adults in 1387, the tales are full of legendary stories and folktales that were known to children as well as adults of the period.

Caxton Begins English Printing

Some historians maintain that printing first began in Holland sometime between 1380 and 1420.[5] However, in the 1450s, Gutenberg in Germany devised a practical method for using movable metal type, producing a quality far superior to printing from the early Dutch type. William Caxton, an English businessman, went to Cologne, Germany, to learn the printing trade. Returning to England, he set up a printing press in Westminster about 1476. Among the first books that he published were *A Book of Curteseye* (1477), *The Historye of Reynart the Foxe* (1481), and *Aesop's Fables* (1484). Malory's *Le Morte d'Arthur* first appeared in printed form in 1485. Caxton is credited with publishing some 106 books, including traditional romance literature, ballads, texts, and religious books. His books were of high quality and expensive, which made them available only to wealthy adults, not children. The impact of the printing press can be seen, however, in the number of books owned by some individuals. Before its invention in the 1450s, even scholars and physicians possessed only a few books. A century later, to give one example, Columbus of Seville (the son of Christopher Columbus) owned a library of more than 15,000 titles.

Hornbooks, ABCs, and Primers

The first children's books to be influenced by the invention of printing were then the only children's books: lesson books or textbooks. Young children learned to read from "hornbooks." A hornbook was really not a book at all but a little wooden paddle to which was pasted a sheet of parchment printed with the alphabet, the vowels, and the Lord's Prayer. A thin sheet of transparent protective horn bound with strips of brass covered the text. Most hornbooks were tiny, measur-

[4]Louise Frances Story Field (Mrs. E. M. Field), *The Child and His Book*, 2nd ed. (London: Wells Gardner, 1892; reprint: Detroit: Singing Tree Press, 1968), p. 13.

[5]Elva S. Smith, *Elva S. Smith's History of Children's Literature*, revised by Margaret Hodges and Susan Steinfirst (Chicago: American Library Association, 1980), p. 38.

ranne in to the foreſt / And whanne the wyld beſtes ſawe
hym come/they were ſo ferdfull that they alle beganne to flee/
For they wend/ that it had be the lyon/ And the mayſter of
the aſſe ſercked and ſought his aſſe in every place al aboute
And as he had ſought longe/he thought that he wold go in
to the foreſt for to ſee yf his aſſe were there/ And as ſoone as

Woodcut and type for Caxton's version of *Aesop's Fables* in 1484.

❦ ❦ ❦

ing 2 3/4 by 5 inches. Sometimes a hole in the handle made it possible for the child to carry the book on a cord around his or her neck or waist. What made these little "books" unique was that now the child could handle them and see the print close up, rather than merely look at a manuscript held by the teacher. Hornbooks were also made of leather, silver, copper, ivory, and sometimes gingerbread! First appearing in the 1440s, they served for over 200 years as tools of instruction for young children. Brought to this country, they were used by the Puritans and in the Colonial Dame Schools.

Children advanced from the hornbooks to ABC books and primers. These had more text than the hornbooks but were still of a religious nature. The first primers developed from the books of hours intended as private devotionals for laypeople, with prayers for each hour. In 1514 an alphabet was added to a book of hours for use by children. When Henry VIII came to the throne he authorized printing a set of English primers for children that presented his religious beliefs. These little books, appropriately called King Henry's Primers, appeared about 1548.

Johann Amos Comenius, a Moravian bishop, planned a book for schools that has been called the first picture book. Titled *Orbis Pictus* (The World Illustrated), the book was translated into English in 1658 and published with many woodcuts illustrating everyday objects.

Lasting Contributions of the Period

Children were not much better off after the invention of printing than before. They still derived their enjoyment from the told story.

During the fifteenth and sixteenth centuries, hornbooks were often the child's first introduction to literature.

This facsimile of a colonial hornbook was ordered from The Horn Book, Inc., 14 Beacon Street, Boston, MA 02108.

True, some concession had been made to their youth in devising special books of instruction for them. But only crudely written and printed chapbooks, (inexpensive booklets sold by peddlers or chapmen) provided a kind of underground literature of enjoyment for both adults and children. The two lasting books of this period are Chaucer's *Canterbury Tales* and Thomas Malory's collection of Arthurian legends, later published in 1485 by Caxton under the title *Le Morte d'Arthur*. Neither of these books was written for children, but children probably knew the stories from hearing them told by bards and minstrels.

What strikes a twentieth-century reader as remarkable about this period is how few books there were and how long they stayed in print. Many of the books published by Caxton in the 1440s were still in print in the late 1600s, more than 200 years later. This seems almost unbelievable when compared with today's publishing world where some books go out of print in less than a year.

CHILDREN'S BOOKS: SEVENTEENTH AND EIGHTEENTH CENTURIES

The "Goodly Godly" Books of the Puritans

Books of the seventeenth century were dominated by the stern spiritual beliefs of Puritanism. As William Sloane has put it, "Nothing in our own diffuse civilization holds quite the pivotal position, the centrality, which religion held in seventeenth-century England and America. To man's relationship with God all the other circumstances of his life were peripheral."[6]

Children were considered to be miniature adults by the Puritans, and they were thus equally subject to sin and eternal damnation. Concern for the salvation of their souls became the central goal of their parents and teachers. Given the high mortality rate of infants and young children (more than half did not live to reach the age of 10), instruction in the fear of God began early.

Children were expected to memorize John Cotton's catechism, *Spiritual Milk for Boston Babes in Either England, Drawn from the Breasts of Both Testaments for Their Souls' Nourishment*. Originally published in England in 1646, it was revised for American children in 1656, the first book written and printed for children in the American colonies. Later books followed its question-and-answer approach. For example, there was the question, "How did God make you?" The child had to memorize the accompanying answer, "I was conceived in sin and born in iniquity." Even alphabet rhymes for the youngest emphasized the sinful nature of humans. *The New England Primer*, first advertised in 1683, includes "In Adam's fall/We sinned all." This primer also provided a catechism, the Ten Commandments, verses about death, and a woodcut of the burning at the stake of the Martyr John Foxe, watched by his wife and nine children. This primer was in print for more than a century and sold about three million copies.

In England in 1671, James Janeway published his book of gloomy joy titled *A Token for Children, Being an Exact Account of the Conversions, Holy and Exemplary Lives and Joyful Deaths of Several Young Children*. In his preface to Part I, he reminds his readers that they are "by Nature, Children of Wrath." Cotton Mather added the life histories of several New England children and published an American edition of Janeway's book in Boston in 1700 under the title *A Token for Children of New England, or Some Examples of Children in Whom the Fear of God Was Remarkably Budding Before They Died*. Virginia Haviland describes the American edition: "An account of youthful piety, in tune with the doctrine of original sin, this is the first of the few narratives that were available to 18th century children in America and undoubtedly the most widely read children's book in the Puritan age."[7]

Religious leaders also could give approval to the moral and spiritual instruction in John Bunyan's

[6]William Sloane, *Children's Books in England and America in the 17th Century* (New York: King's Press, Columbia University Press, 1955), p. 12.

[7]Virginia Haviland and Margaret N. Coughlan, *Yankee Doodle's Literary Sampler of Prose, Poetry and Pictures* (New York: Crowell, 1974), p. 11.

Pilgrim's Progress, first printed in 1678. No doubt children skipped the long theological dialogues as they found adventure by traveling with the clearly defined characters. Another book by John Bunyan, evidently written *for* children, was first published in 1686 under the title *A Book for Boys and Girls or Country Rhymes for Children*. In a later illustrated edition the title was changed to *Divine Emblems or Temporal Things Spiritualized*. In this strange little book, Bunyan would describe a common object in verse and then draw a lesson from the so-called "emblem." His choice of subjects included "Meditations on an Egg" and "A Bee," which provided the following lesson:

> This bee an Emblem truly is of Sin,
> Whose Sweet unto many a Death hath been.
> Now would'st have sweet from Sin, and yet not die,
> Do thou it in the first place mortify.

F. J. Harvey Darton[8] states that this particular emblem book was popular with both children and ignorant folk throughout the eighteenth century and remained in common use until at least the middle of the nineteenth century.

Chapbooks: Forerunners of Comics

Luckily, there was some relief from the doom and gloom of the religious-oriented books of the Puritans. Chapbooks, small inexpensive folded paper booklets sold by peddlers or chapmen, first appeared in the late 1500s, but achieved real popularity in the seventeenth and eighteenth centuries. Sold for a few pennies, these crudely printed little books brought excitement and pleasure into the lives of both children and adults with tales about Dick Whittington, Sir Guy of Warwick, Robin Hood, and other heroes. A ballad of a "most strange wedding of the froggee and the mouse" was licensed as early as 1580. "The Death and Burial of Cock Robin" was another early chapbook that children must have enjoyed. One of the most popular was about Tom Hickathrift, a giant-sized man who accomplished

Paul Bunyan–like feats like pulling up trees and felling four highwaymen with a single blow. By contrast, a 1630 story of the tiny Tom Thumb shows him disappearing into a bowl of pudding when he was young and later bravely riding into battle astride a mighty warhorse. The earliest known edition of "Jack the Giant Killer" seems to have been in a chapbook of 1711. Other chapbooks gave accounts of crimes and executions, descriptions of the art of making love, and riddles.

This woodcut from a seventeenth-century chapbook has two episodes, "Tom Thumb running a tilt" and "how Tom Thumb did take his sickness, and of his death and burial." c. 1650–1660.

The Walter Havighurst Special Collections, Miami University Libraries, Oxford, Ohio.

[8]F. J. Harvey Darton, *Children's Books in England*, 3rd ed., revised by Brian Alderson (Cambridge, England: Cambridge University Press, 1932, 1982), p. 64.

While these books were decried by the Puritans, they were read and reread by the common people of England and America. Their popularity with children is said to have influenced John Newbery's decision to publish a book solely for children. The chapbooks' greatly abbreviated texts and crude woodcut illustrations suggest that they were forerunners of today's comic strips, still read by both adults and children.

Nursery Rhymes or Mother Goose

No one knows for sure the exact origin of nursery rhymes. Apparently, the rhymes we know as Mother Goose, including counting-out rhymes, finger plays, and alphabet verses, originated in the spoken language of both common folk and royalty. Some have been traced as far back as the pre-Christian era. A few writers theorize that "Jack and Jill" refers to the waxing and waning of the moon. It is believed that many of the verses were written as political satires or told of tragedy. "Mary, Mary, Quite Contrary," for example, has been said to date back to the turbulent reign of Mary Queen of Scots. "Ring Around the Rosie" may have referred to the pink ringlike rash that marked the early signs of bubonic plague. People carried "posies" of herbs for protection, and "we all fall down," of course, refers to the final demise of the victims. Katherine Thomas cites the account of a deed in the possession of a Horner family signed by Henry VIII that was a "plum" pulled out of the pie—the King's collection of deeds.[9] However, other scholars have found little evidence of these relationships.[10]

Shakespeare evidently knew these nursery rhymes, for they are referred to in *King Lear* and other plays of his. Yet the oldest *surviving* nursery-rhyme book was published by Mary Cooper in 1744 in two or perhaps three little volumes under the title *Tommy Thumb's Pretty Song Book;* a single copy of Volume II is a treasured possession of the British Museum. This second volume includes such favorite verses as "Sing a Song of

Sixpence," "There Was an Old Woman," "Hickere, Dickere, Dock," and "London Bridge Is Broken Down." John Newbery is supposed to have published *Mother Goose's Melody or Sonnets for the Cradle* about 1765, although the book was not advertised until 1780, which is the more likely date of its publication. No copy of this edition exists. However, Isaiah Thomas of Worcester, Massachusetts, produced a second edition of *Mother Goose's Melody* in 1794. Since many of his books were pirated from Newbery, it is assumed that his first edition of about 1786 was a copy of the lost Newbery one.

The legend that Dame Goose is buried in Boston is kept alive for tourists and children who visit the Boston burying grounds, but it has created confusion regarding the origin of the verses. Even the publication of *Songs for the Nursery; or Mother Goose's Melodies* by the son-in-law of Dame Goose is itself a legend. According to the story, Thomas Fleet tired of the good woman's frequent renditions of the ditties as she cared for his children, so he decided to collect and publish them in 1719. No actual evidence of this edition has been found.

Other verses and rhymes were later added to Mother Goose after their publication as small separate books. *The Comic Adventures of Old Mother Hubbard and her Dog* by Sarah Martin first appeared in 1805. During the same year *Songs from the Nursery Collected by the Most Renowned Poets* was published. For the first time, "Little Miss Muffett" and "One, Two, Buckle My Shoe" were included in a Mother Goose book. *The History of Sixteen Wonderful Old Women*, issued by J. Harris and Son in 1820, contains the earliest examples of what we now call the limerick.

Uncertain of her origin as the historians are, they do recognize that the venerable Mother Goose became a welcome part of the nursery on both sides of the Atlantic during the eighteenth century. Since then she has never left her post.

Fairy Tales and Adventure

Another source of enjoyment for children came in the form of fairy tales, the first printed in France in 1697 by Charles Perrault. Titled *Histoires ou Contes du temps passé; avec des Moralités* (Stories or Tales of Times Past, with Morals), the collection

[9]Katherine Elwes Thomas, *The Real Personages of Mother Goose* (New York: Lothrop, 1930).
[10]Iona and Peter Opie, *The Oxford Nursery Rhyme Book* (London: Oxford University Press, 1952). William S. Baring-Gould and Ceil Baring-Gould, *The Annotated Mother Goose* (New York: Charles N. Potter, 1962).

included "The Sleeping Beauty," "Cinderella or the Glass Slipper," "Red Riding Hood," "Puss-in-Boots," and "Blue Beard," among others. These tales were in fashion at the French Court of the Sun King, Louis XIV, where they were told to adults. The frontispiece of Perrault's book, however, showed an old woman spinning and telling stories to children. The caption read *Contes de ma Mère l'Oye* (Tales of Mother Goose), which was the first reference to Mother Goose in children's literature. Translated into English in 1729, these fairy tales have remained France's gift to the children of the world.

Following the success of Perrault, other French authors, including Mme. d'Aulnoy, created original fairy tales. Only one remains well-known today and that is "Beauty and the Beast," rewritten from a longer version by Mme. de Beaumont.

The Arabian Nights is a collection of old tales from India, Persia, and North Africa. Galland published these tales in French in 1558, but not until about 1706 were they available in English. Intended for adults, such stories as "Aladdin," "Ali Baba," and "Sinbad the Sailor" were appropriated by children. Ridley also published a series of tales modeled after the Arabian Nights under the title *The Tales of the Genii* (1766).

Defoe did not write his account of the eighteenth-century hero Robinson Crusoe for children, but they made his story part of their literature. *The Life and Strange and Surprising Adventures of Robinson Crusoe* (1719) was later printed in an abridged and pocket-sized volume that became a "classic" of children's literature. This book was so popular that it spawned many imitations—so many, in fact, that a word, "Robinsonades," was coined for them.

While children no doubt did not understand the scathing satire of high society in Swift's *Gulliver's Travels*, they did find enjoyment in the hero's adventures with the huge and tiny folk and the talking horses. Thus young and old alike enjoyed this tale of adventure, first published in 1726.

Newbery Publishes for Children

The concept of a literature for children usually dates from 1744, the year the English publisher John Newbery printed *A Little Pretty Pocket-Book.* The title page is shown here. Newbery included Locke's advice that children should enjoy reading. The book itself attempted to teach the alphabet "by Way of Diversion," including games, fables, and little rhymes about the letters of the alphabet. What was significant about the book was that Newbery deliberately and openly set out to provide amusement for children, something no other publisher had had the courage or insight to do.

No documentary evidence is available to determine whether John Newbery or Oliver Goldsmith wrote *The History of Little Goody Two Shoes*, published by Newbery in 1765. London records do show that Newbery gave Goldsmith lodging above his shop called "The Bible and the

A Little Pretty
POCKET-BOOK,
Intended for the
INSTRUCTION and AMUSEMENT
OF
LITTLE MASTER *TOMMY*,
AND
PRETTY MISS *POLLY*.
With Two Letters from
JACK the GIANT-KILLER;
AS ALSO
A BALL and PINCUSHION;
The Use of which will infallibly make *Tommy* a good Boy, and *Polly* a good Girl.

To which is added,
A LITTLE SONG-BOOK,
BEING
A *New Attempt* to teach Children the Use of the *English Alphabet*, by Way of Diversion.

LONDON:
Printed for J. NEWBERY, at the *Bible and Sun* in St. *Paul's Church-Yard*. 1767.
[Price Six-pence bound.]

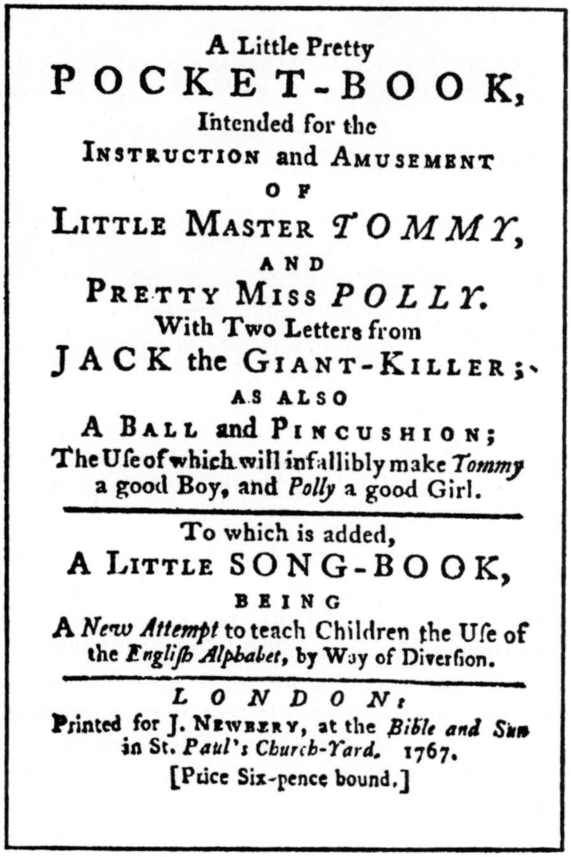

Title page of *A Little Pretty Pocket-Book* published by John Newbery in 1744.

Little Goody Two Shoes points to her two shoes in a facsimile reprint of John Newbery's best known publication.

❦ ❦ ❦

Sun." It is probable that Goldsmith was the author of some of the 200 books published by Newbery. In the story of *Goody Two Shoes*, Margery Meanwell and her brother are turned out of their home after the death of her parents, for "Her father had succumbed to a fever, in a place where Dr. James' Powder was not to be had." (Newbery also sold Dr. James' Powder and other medicines in his store.) At first the children are taken in by a kind parson, who properly clothes Tommy and sends him off to sea and provides Margery with two shoes instead of the poor one

left to her after their eviction. This kind man hopes to take her into his family, but the evil Graspall threatens to reduce his tithe if he does. Eventually, Margery becomes a tutor who moralizes as she teaches her young pupils to read. She marries a wealthy squire and continues to carry on her good works. *Goody Two Shoes* was read for well over a century. A modern eight-page version of it was sold to be read in air-raid shelters in England in the 1940s.

Newbery was obviously impressed with the advice given by the famous English philosopher John Locke in his *Thoughts Concerning Education* (1693). Locke maintained that as soon as the child knew his alphabet he should be led to read for pleasure. He advocated the use of pictures in books and deplored the lack of easy, pleasant books for children to read, except for *Aesop's Fables* and *Reynard the Fox*, both dating back to Caxton's times.

Newbery's books were all illustrated with pictures based on the text, rather than just any woodcuts available, as was the custom of other printers of the day. Many of his books were bound with Dutch gilt paper covers, which made for a gay appearance. While moral lessons were clearly there for young readers, his stories did emphasize love and play rather than the wrath and punishment of God. Except for *Goody Two Shoes*, none of his work has lasted, but we honor the man who was the first to recognize that children deserve a literature of their own.

Didactic Tales

During the last half of the eighteenth century, women writers entered the field of juvenile literature determined to influence the moral development of children. Mrs. Sarah Fielding published *The Governess* in 1749, which included character-building stories about Mrs. Teachum's School for Girls. *Easy Lessons for Children*, published in 1760 by Mrs. Barbauld, contained moral stories supposedly written for children as young as 2 to 3 years. Mrs. Sarah Trimmer thought of herself as the true *Guardian of Education*, the title she later gave to a magazine she published that contained articles on moral subjects and book reviews. Mrs. Trimmer did not approve of fairy tales or Mother

Goose. "All Mother Goose tales . . . were only fit to fill the heads of children with confused notions of wonderful and supernatural events brought about by the agency of imaginary beings."[11] She saw no inconsistency, however, in writing a story in which a family of robins could talk about day-to-day problems in their lives. First titled *Fabulous Histories* (1786), it was published for many years afterward under the title *The Robins*. The conversation between the parent robins and their offspring (called Flapsy, Pecksy, Dicky, and Robin) is stilted and lofty, indeed. Robin, the eldest, is portrayed as a conceited young bird who will take no advice. His parents discuss his behavior in this way:

> "You have been absent a long time, my love," said her mate, "but I perceive that you were indulging your tenderness towards that disobedient nestling, who has rendered himself unworthy of it; however, I do not condemn you for giving him assistance, for had not you undertaken the task, I would myself have flown to him instead of returning home; how is he, likely to live and reward your kindness?"
>
> "Yes," said she, "he will, I flatter myself, soon perfectly recover, for his hurt is not very considerable, and I have the pleasure to tell you he is extremely sensible of his late folly, and I dare say will endeavour to repair his fault with future good behaviour."[12]

Poor Mrs. Trimmer justified the use of this anthropomorphized bird family by calling the stories "fables" and stating that she was following the advice of John Locke, who had advocated the use of *Aesop's Fables* with children. No wonder Beatrix Potter[13] recalled hating this book and refusing to learn to read from it. Some memory of it must have lingered with her, however, for there is a strong resemblance in the sound of names of the young robins to her famous rabbit family, Flopsy, Mopsy, Cottontail, and Peter.

Other didactic writers of this period maintained they followed Rousseau's theory of education by accompanying the child in his natural search for knowledge. These stories frequently contained lengthy "conversations" that tried to conceal moral lessons in the guise of an exciting adventure.

Thomas Day utilized this conversational approach in *The History of Sandford and Merton*, a didactic tale that appeared in three sections (1783, 1786, 1789). Harry Sandford and Tommy Merton were 6-year-old boys who were tutored together, although Harry was the son of a farmer. It was Harry who exemplified the just and righteous for the spoiled Tommy Merton. Day after day, lecture after lecture, the tutor presented long lessons that interrupted the narrative. These priggish children served as models of behavior for nearly a hundred years.

Marie Edgeworth knew Thomas Day, and she also tried to follow the educational principles of Rousseau. Her approach was the classical narrative one in which the child learns through bitter experience. Her best-known story is "The Purple Jar," which first appeared in *The Parents' Assistant: or Stories for Children* (1796). In this story, Rosamund, who longed for a purple jar that she saw in an apothecary's window, chose it over the pair of new shoes she needed. Poor Rosamund learns to her great sorrow that the clear glass bottle is only filled with a foul-smelling liquid. Rosamund acknowledges the folly of her choice, saying:

> "Oh Mamma . . . how I wish I had chosen the shoes. They would have been of so much more use to me than that jar; however, I am sure—no, not quite sure—but I hope, I shall be wiser another time."[14]

Poetry

In this period poetry for children also emphasized religion and instruction. Although Isaac Watts spent most of his time writing hymns, he did write some poetry for children. In the preface to

[11]Darton, *Children's Books in England*, p. 97.
[12]Mrs. Trimmer, *The Robins: Or Domestic Life Among the Birds*, a revised edition (New York: C. S. Francis & Co., 1851), p. 93.
[13]Jane Crowell Morse, ed. *Beatrix Potter's Americans: Selected Letters* (Boston: Horn Book) 1982).

[14]Quoted by Darton, *Children's Books in England*, p. 141.

Divine and Moral Songs Attempted in Easy Language for Use of Children (1715), Watts wrote that his songs were to be memorized, which was how children were to be given "a relish for virtue and religion." Though written by a Puritan, these hymns were kind and loving, and the collection made up a real child's book. Altogether Watts wrote about 700 hymns, some of which are still sung today, notably "Joy to the World," "O God Our Help in Ages Past," and the lovely "Cradle Hymn" which begins "Hush, my dear, lie still and slumber." Charles Wesley was also a prolific hymn writer. His *Hymns for Children* (1763) included "Gentle Jesus, Meek and Mild."

John Newbery printed *Pretty Poems for Children Three Feet High* and added the inscription: "To all those who are good this book is dedicated by their best friend."

The engraver and artist William Blake wrote poetry that children enjoyed, but the poems comprising *Songs of Innocence* (1789) were not specifi-

cally written for children. Blake's poetry was filled with imagination and joy and made the reader aware of beauty without preaching. Children still respond to his happy poem that begins "Piping down the valleys wild,/Piping songs of pleasant glee." His desire to open the "doors of perception" is reflected in his well-known poem "To see a World in a Grain of Sand."

One British artist, Thomas Bewick, emerged during this period as an illustrator of books for boys and girls. He perfected the white-line method of engraving on the end grain of a block of wood to achieve a delicacy of line not found in usual carved woodblock designs. Bewick's *The New Lottery Book of Birds and Beasts* (1771) was one of the first instances of a master illustrator putting his name on a book for children. Among his other works were *A Pretty Book of Pictures for Little Masters and Misses; or Tommy Trip's History of Beasts and Birds* (1779), which was a variation of one of Newbery's titles of the early 1760s, and several books of fables, including his own *Fables of Aesop and Others* (1818).

As the century came near its end, most of the stories for children were about how to live the "good life." Information about the natural world was peddled in didactic lectures sugar-coated with conversational style. Little prigs were models for young people to follow. However, there was now a literature for children. Authors and publishers were aware of a new market for books. Parents and teachers were beginning to recognize the importance of literature for children.

CHILDREN'S LITERATURE: THE NINETEENTH CENTURY

Books of Instruction and Information

During the period immediately following the American Revolution, there was a rush to publish textbooks that reflected the changing social purposes and interests of the new nation. A picture of George Washington was substituted for the woodcut of George III in *The New England Primer*. The alphabet no longer intoned "In Adam's fall/We sinned all" but started with a less pious

SELECT FABLES.

THE FOX AND THE CROW.

A white-line woodcut of "The Fox and the Crow" from *Select Fables,* designed and engraved by Thomas and John Bewick, c. 1784.

The Walter Havighurst Special Collections, Miami University Libraries, Oxford, Ohio.

rhyme: "A was an Angler and fished with a hook./B was a Blockhead and ne'er learned his book."

Noah Webster's *Blue Backed Speller, Simplified and Standardized*, first published in 1783, was widely used. Revised many times, the third part of the series contained stories and became America's first secular reader. It sold more than 80 million copies during the nineteenth century.

Reading for patriotism, good citizenship, and industry was the purpose of the well-loved *Eclectic Readers* by William H. McGuffey. They were used so widely from 1834 to 1900 one could almost say these readers comprised the elementary curriculum in literature. A glance at the *Fifth Reader* reflects the type of material included in these readers: speeches by Daniel Webster, essays by Washington Irving, selections from Shakespeare (although the play is often not identified), narrative, sentimental, and patriotic poetry, and many didactic essays with such titles as "Advantages of a Well-educated Mind," "Impeachment of Warren Hastings" as reported in the *Edinburgh Review*, and "Eulogy on Candlelight."

Although compulsory education was being extended and the publicly supported common school was being established, parents were also expected to teach children at home. The parent's role was established through stories in which mothers embroidered, sipped tea, and dispensed information to *sweet* children. The following conversation was in *A Key to Knowledge*, published in 1822:

Louisa—By the By, when I come to think of it, what a dirty thing honey is; first swallowed by bees, and then by us.

Mother—Your description is certainly not very inviting. Suppose rather that we should call the honey, the syrup of flowers, drawn from the opened buds by the trunk, or proboscis, of the industrious bee.

Louisa—Now I like honey again. . . .[15]

[15]"19th Century Juvenilia," *Times Educational Supplement*, 2262:1412 (September 26, 1958).

In the early nineteenth century Samuel Goodrich was responsible for eliminating the British background in books for American children. Influenced by both the English and American Sunday School movement, which produced moral tales for the uneducated masses of children who could attend school only on Sunday, Goodrich wrote more than a hundred books for children. He created the venerable Peter Parley, an elderly gentleman who told stories to children based on his travels and personal experiences. History, geography, and science were included in his *Tales of Peter Parley About America* (1827). Nearly a million copies of *Peter Parley's Method of Telling About Geography to Children* (1829) were published. This series became so popular that Goodrich employed a writing staff to help him, which included Nathaniel Hawthorne and his sister, Elizabeth. Sales of Peter Parley's books totaled over 7 million copies, and they were frequently pirated and issued abroad.

The *Little Rollo* series by Jacob Abbott became as popular as the Peter Parley books. Abbott wrote about Little Rollo learning to talk, Rollo learning to read, and of Rollo's travels to Europe. In the first books of the series, published in 1834, Rollo was a natural little boy, but as he became older and traveled about the world he became another little prig.

The Bodley Family, conceived by Horace Scudder, explored New England, Holland, and other countries in a series of eight books beginning with *Doings of the Bodley Family in Town and Country* (1875). In *Seven Little Sisters Who Live on the Big Round Ball That Floats in the Air* (1861), Jane Andrews told of little girls who lived in the far north, in the desert, in China, and in Switzerland. Without talking down to children or lecturing them, Andrews presented truthful and interesting descriptions of the way foreign children lived. This book was followed in 1885 by *Ten Boys Who Lived on the Road from Long Ago Till Now*.

Only a few writers and publishers seemed to realize that children want to learn about their world. Children had to plod through pages of tiresome conversations with moralistic overtones to gain the information they sought. It was not until much later that informational books on almost every subject were placed on bookshelves for boys and girls.

Folktale Collections

Early in the nineteenth century two German brothers went about asking servants and peasants to recall stories they had heard. In 1812 Jacob and Wilhelm Grimm published the first volume of *Kinder und Hausmärchen* (Household Stories). These serious scholars tried to preserve the form as well as the content of the old tales that were translated and published in England by Edgar Taylor from 1823 to 1826. "The Elves and the Shoemaker," "Rumplestiltskin," and "Snow White," in addition to many others, became part of the literature of childhood.

In America, Washington Irving included "Rip Van Winkle" and "The Legend of Sleepy Hollow" in his 1819 *Sketch Book.* These tales, written mainly for adults, were also enjoyed by older children.

The origin of the story of "The Three Bears" has been questioned by various authorities. It was first credited to the poet Robert Southey, who published it in *The Doctor* (1837). Later, Edgar Osborne, the famous English collector of children's books, found the story handwritten in verse by Eleanor Mure in 1831. Both these early versions portray a wicked old woman who comes to visit the bears, which are described as wee, middle-sized, and huge. Through various retellings, the story has been changed to the more familiar fair-haired Goldilocks visiting a *family* of bears.

In 1846 Mary Howitt translated Hans Christian Andersen's fairy tales under the title of *Wonderful Stories for Children.* Now both English and American children could enjoy "The Princess and the Pea," "Thumbelina," and "The Emperor's New Clothes." In these stories, inanimate objects and animals like the heroic "Tin Soldier" and "The Ugly Duckling" come to life. The values and foibles of human life are presented in the stories with action and rich language.

Not until the last half of the nineteenth century were folktales and fairy tales completely accepted for children. John Ruskin was influenced by the Grimm tales as he wrote his *King of the Golden River* (1851). Charles Dickens' *The Magic Fishbone* appeared first as a serial in 1868. *The Wonder Book for Boys and Girls* was published by Nathaniel Hawthorne in 1852, followed by *Tanglewood Tales* in 1853. Now children had the Greek myths written especially for them. Sir George Dasent translated *Popular Tales from the North* in 1859, making it possible for children to enjoy more tales from Scandinavia. *The Nürnberg Stove* was another favorite, first published by Louise de la Ramee in a collection of children's stories in 1882. Joel Chandler Harris collected stories from the South for *Uncle Remus, His Songs and Sayings* (1883).

Andrew Lang's famous series of collections of folktales began with *The Blue Fairy Book.* The *Red, Green,* and *Yellow* fairy books followed the 1889 publication of the first volume of folklore. Joseph Jacobs was also interested in retelling folktales especially for children. *English Fairy Tales* was published in two volumes between 1890 and 1894; *Celtic Fairy Tales,* also in two volumes, appeared in 1892 and 1894; *Indian Fairy Tales* was written in 1892. All these tales were important contributions to the realm of folklore. As the merits of folklore were recognized everywhere, there was increasing interest in such volumes as Howard Pyle's collection of stories titled *Pepper and Salt* (1886) and *The Wonder Clock* (1888).

Family Stories

In the first half of the nineteenth century the didactic school of writing continued to flourish as women writers wielded influential pens. They still condemned fairy stories and relentlessly dispensed information in lengthy dialogues between parent and child. Mrs. Martha Sherwood, a prolific writer, produced over 350 moralizing books and religious tracts. While living in India, she wrote *Little Henry and His Bearer* (1814). This story illustrates her missionary theme by telling how little Henry converted his Indian servant to Christianity. However, she is remembered best for a series of stories about *The Fairchild Family,* the first part published in 1818, the third and last in 1847. Considered one of the first "family" stories, it contained some frighteningly realistic passages. In one scene Lucy, Emily, and Henry (all names in Mrs. Sherwood's own family) quarrel over a doll and say they do not love each other. Mr. Fairchild overhears them and whips their hands with a rod. After dinner he then takes them to Blackwood to see something "very dreadful, . . . a gibbet on which the decomposed body of a man still hangs in irons. The face of the corpse was so shocking the children could not look at it." It seems the man was a murderer who first hated and then killed his brother. Later revisions of this story omitted the grim scene. However, even without this passage, *The Fairchild Family* was a dramatic vital story. It was known on both sides of the Atlantic.

In contrast to the religious severity of *The Fairchild Family*, Charlotte Yonge described the milder Victorian experiences of the eleven motherless children of the May family in *The Daisy Chain* (1856). Women were always portrayed in the Victorian novel as inferior to men. This attitude is reflected in *The Daisy Chain* when Ethel May is advised not to try to keep up with her brother Norman in his university studies since "a woman cannot hope to equal a man in scholarship." In *The Clever Woman of the Family* (1865) Yonge devotes nearly the whole book to making the heroine "realize how much better and deeper were her husband's ideas than her own."[16] Yonge had an ear for dialogue and frequently recorded her friends' conversations. She was a superb storyteller and wrote over 120 books.

American children wept pools of tears over the pious sentimental story of *Elsie Dinsmore*. Writing under her maiden name, Martha Farquharson, Martha Farquharson Finley initiated the Elsie Dinsmore series in 1867. The best known scene is the one in which Elsie's father demands that she play the piano and sing for a group of his friends. Because it is the Sabbath, Elsie refuses. Her father will not have his authority questioned and makes her sit on the piano stool for hours until she finally faints and cuts her head in the fall. Filled with remorse, he gently carries her upstairs only to have her insist that she be allowed to pray before going to bed. Elsie at all

times is righteous and good. Her favorite book is the Bible, which she knows by heart and quotes regularly. The series contains eighteen books published from 1867 to 1905 that follow Elsie from girlhood through motherhood, widowhood, and into grandmotherhood. Unbelievable as the stories seem to us today, the Elsie Dinsmore books were tremendously popular.

The next year saw the publication of *Little Women* (1868) by Louisa May Alcott. This story must have blown like a fresh breeze through the stifling atmosphere of pious religiosity created by books like *Elsie Dinsmore*. As described by the

The first edition of *Little Women* (published as a single book in 1869) was illustrated by May Alcott, the author's sister.

The Walter Havighurst Special Collections, Miami University Libraries, Oxford, Ohio.

🍒 🍒 🍒

[16]Cornelia Meigs, et al., *A Critical History of Children's Literature*, rev. ed. (New York: Macmillan, 1969), p. 158.

Jessie Wilcox Smith pictured slightly older *Little Women* for the eight full-color illustrations she painted in oils for the popular 1915 edition.

🌿 🌿 🌿

irrepressible Jo (who was Louisa May Alcott herself), the March family were real people who faced genteel poverty with humor and fortitude. Louisa May Alcott didn't preach moral platitudes, but described the joys, the trials, and the fun of growing up in a loving family. Jo, one of the first tomboys in children's literature, hates the false Victorian standards of the day. When her older sister Meg tells her that she should remember she is a young lady, this follows:

🌿 "I'm not! and if turning up my hair makes me one, I'll wear it in two tails till I'm twenty," cried Jo, pulling off her net and shaking down a chestnut mane. "I hate to think I've got to grow up and be Miss March, and wear long gowns and look prim as

a China-aster. It's bad enough to be a girl, anyway, when I like boys' games and work and manners!"[17]

Little Women was not an immediate success with the critics of the time. One of the first reviewers wrote: "They [*Little Women* was originally two books] are not religious books, should not be read on Sunday, and are not appropriate for the Sunday School. This is the character of the book before us. It is lively, entertaining, and not harmful."[18]

Children loved it and have read it every day including Sundays since its publication. The first edition of Volume I of *Little Women* (it ended before Beth's death) was sold out within two months of printing. The publisher asked for a second volume which was ready the next year. Later the two books were combined into one.

Little Men and *Jo's Boys* were sequels to this American family classic. Still loved today, *Little Women* has been translated into many languages including Russian, Arabic, Bengali, and Urdu. Fortunately Thomas Niles, Alcott's Boston publisher, persuaded her to take a royalty on her books rather than the usual lump sum for the copyright. Within two years of publication of *Little Women*, Louisa May Alcott had paid off all the family debts, some of which were twenty-five years old. Never again would her family have to endure "genteel poverty."

Another vivacious heroine appeared in the celebrated Katy stories written by Susan Coolidge (pseudonym of Sarah Chauncey Woolsey). This series included such titles as *What Katy Did* (1872), *What Katy Did at School* (1873), and *What Katy Did Next* (1886). Susan Coolidge also wrote many other stories. Harriet Lathrop, under the pseudonym Margaret Sidney, presented a lively family story about a widowed mother and her *Five Little Peppers* in a series starting in 1881 and concluding in 1916 with *Our Davie Pepper*.

Other authors wrote dramatic family stories with foreign settings. In *Hans Brinker, Or the Silver Skates*, Mary Mapes Dodge gave accurate

[17]Louisa May Alcott, *Little Women* (Boston: Little Brown, 1868; 1922), p. 3.
[18]Lavinia Russ, "Not to Be Read on Sunday," Centenary of *Little Women*, 1868–1968. *The Horn Book Magazine*, vol. 44 (October 1968), pp. 521–526.

glimpses of Dutch life in 1865. The skating race is actually less important than the daring brain surgery performed on Father Brinker, who had been nearly an idiot for several years after an accident. The bravery and courage of Hans and his sister in facing poverty, scorn, and their father's illness provided further examples for child behavior.

Johanna Spyri's well-loved *Heidi* was translated from the German by Louise Brooks and published in this country in 1884. Not only did readers share the joys and sorrows of Heidi's life with her grandfather, they "breathed" the clear mountain air and "lived" in Switzerland.

Frances Hodgson Burnett described family conflict within the English aristocracy in *Little Lord Fauntleroy* (1886). Although born in England, Mrs. Burnett was an American citizen. The well-known English historian of children's literature F. J. Harvey Darton said in 1932, "It [*Little Lord Fauntleroy*] ran through England like a sickly fever. Nine editions were published in as many months, and the odious little prig in the lace collar is not dead yet."[19] Burnett's second book, *Sara Crewe* (1888), told of the pitiful plight of a wealthy pupil who is orphaned and reduced to servitude in a boarding school. Its Cinderella ending delights children and adults, and it was made into a very successful play. Mrs. Burnett then expanded the play into a longer novel under the title *The Little Princess* (1905). A new edition of *Sara Crewe* was published as recently as 1981, illustrated with appropriate Dickensian pictures by Margot Tomes. Mrs. Burnett's best written and most popular book is *The Secret Garden* (1910), which presents an exciting plot in a mysterious setting. This story depicts the gradual change wrought in two lonely and selfish children by a hidden garden and the wholesome influence of the boy Dickon. It is still read and loved by children today.

Tales of Adventure

The rise of family stories and series books for girls prompted more attention to tales of adventures and the development of so-called boys'

series. The best known of the Robinsonades, *The Swiss Family Robinson*, was written by Johann David Wyss, a Swiss pastor, and translated into English in 1814. Inaccurate in its description of flora and fauna (almost everything grew on that tropical island), it still delighted children's imaginations. Sir Walter Scott's novels *Rob Roy* (1818) and *Ivanhoe* (1820), while intended for adults, were frequently appropriated by young people. James Fenimore Cooper's Leatherstocking novels of exciting tales of Indians and pioneers in North America were avidly read by young and old alike. The bloody incidents and tragedy of *The Last of the Mohicans* (1826) brought a sense of tingling adventure to all readers. Richard Henry Dana's *Two Years Before the Mast* (1840) describes the author's own adventures as a young seaman sailing around Cape Horn to California. Again written for adults, it provided adventure for children.

An Englishman, Captain Frederick Marryat, had written sea adventures for adults. In an attempt to correct the many errors in principles of navigation and geography that he found in *The Swiss Family Robinson*, he began a series of sea adventures with *The Naval Officer; or Frank Mildmay*, published in 1829. His juvenile adventures included *Masterman Ready* written in three volumes between 1841 and 1842. Unfortunately, he reverted to the lecture approach used by Thomas Day in *Sandford and Merton* as Masterman Ready instructed *Mr. Midshipman Easy* (1836) on the principles of seamanship. In 1856 another Englishman, Robert Ballantyne, began his series of nearly eighty books with an account of his fur-trading experiences in *The Young Fur Traders*. George A. Henty, an English news correspondent for many years, was determined that English boys should know the military history of the British Empire. *Under Drake's Flag* (1883) ends with the defeat of the Spanish Armada; *By Pike and Dyke* (1889) details the sieges of Holland and tells of William of Orange. His military history was accurate in the almost ninety books he wrote. However, his characters never changed, as if the same persons were experiencing the wars of all centuries.

These British writers, Marryat, Ballantyne, and Henty, were read with enthusiasm by American

[19]Darton, *Children's Books in England*, p. 232–233.

children. At the same time the American names Horatio Alger, Jr., Oliver Optic, and Harry Castlemon were well known to English readers. The emphasis in American series was more on achievement by the individual, usually against unbelievable odds. The stories by Horatio Alger epitomized this rags-to-riches theme. In fact, since his first successful novel *Ragged Dick* (1868) was based on this formula, he saw no reason to change it in the more than a hundred books that followed. The final paragraph of *Struggling Upwards* presents the theme that was the basis for most of his stories:

❧ So closes an eventful passage in the life of Luke Larkin. He has struggled upward from a boyhood of privation and self-denial into a youth and manhood of prosperity and honor. There has been some luck about it, I admit, but after all he is indebted for most of his good fortune to his own good qualities.[20]

Oliver Optic was the pen name of William Adams, a New England teacher and principal who wrote such series as *The Yacht-Club Series* (1854), *The Army and Navy Series* (1865), and *The Starry Flag Series* (1867). His stories were lively and well told, and his readers learned some science and geography as they traveled with his heroes through more than a hundred of his books.

Harry Castlemon (pseudonym of Charles Austin Fosdick) based his book *Frank on a Gunboat* (1864) on his own experiences in the Civil War. He wrote some fifty-eight more volumes in his Gunboat, Rocky Mountain, Sportsman Club, Boy Trapper, Rod and Gun, and Pony Express series. His stories were exciting, as incident followed incident. He is quoted as saying: "Boys don't like fine writing. What they want is adventure, and the more of it you can get into 250 pages of manuscript, the better fellow you are."[21]

Though most of these series books provided plenty of adventure, the characters and plots tended to be superficial and predictable. However, there was one superb adventure story written during the last half of the nineteenth cen-

tury that included not only a bloody, exciting, and tightly drawn plot but also well-depicted characters. Serialized in an English magazine called *Young Folks* in 1881 and 1882, Robert Louis Stevenson's *Treasure Island* was published in book form in 1883. For the first time adults were drawn to a children's book of adventure rather than children reading adults' books. *Treasure Island* was an immediate success. As Meigs has said,

It is no wonder this book made Stevenson a popular author. It appealed to boys and to the eternal boy in men; to the story-loving spirit which had treasured the chapbooks and perpetuated folk literature by word of mouth for generation after generation.[22]

Other books written for boys changed in their portrayal of childhood. Little prigs became real live boys. Thomas Bailey Aldrich's *The Story of a Bad Boy* (1870) was based on his own life in Portsmouth, New Hampshire. The tale of this Tom's pranks and good times paved the way for another story of a real boy's adventures in Hannibal, Missouri. *The Adventures of Tom Sawyer* was published in 1876 by Mark Twain (pseudonym of Samuel Clemens). This book was soon followed by an American classic, *The Adventures of Huckleberry Finn* (1884). Mark Twain combined realism, humor, and adventure in these realistic portrayals of growing up in a small town near the end of the nineteenth century. While *Huckleberry Finn* has won literary acclaim, children prefer *The Adventures of Tom Sawyer*. This seems only natural, since Tom's adventures involve children their age.

The beginnings of science-fiction adventure stories came to us from France in the translations of Jules Verne's *Journey to the Center of the Earth* (1864), *Twenty Thousand Leagues Under the Sea* (1869), and *Around the World in Eighty Days* (1872). Modern readers may be surprised to note the early dates of these books.

Animal Stories

In *A Dog of Flanders and Other Stories* (1872), Louise de la Ramee presented a collection of stories that included the sad tale of a Belgian work

[20]Horatio Alger, Jr., *Struggling Upwards; or Luke Larkin's Luck* (New York: Superior Printing, n.d.), p. 280.
[21]Jacob Blanck, compiler, *Harry Castlemon: Boys' Own Author* (New York: R. R. Bowker, 1941), pp. 5–6.

[22]Meigs, *A Critical History*, p. 306.

dog and his friend, a boy artist. It has been considered the first modern dog story. *Black Beauty* appeared in 1877 as a protest against cruel treatment of horses. Children skipped the lectures calling for more humane treatment of animals and read the compelling first-person story of the life of Black Beauty. Some children today continue to enjoy Anna Sewell's rather overdrawn and sentimental tale. Rudyard Kipling's *The Jungle Books* (1894–1895) were exciting animal stories. Many children today know the story of Mowgli, a child raised by a wolf family, a bear, and a panther. They may be more familiar with the animated movie than with the original book, however.

Ernest Thompson Seton's own drawings and sketches added much to children's enjoyment of *Wild Animals I Have Known* (1898). This book presented true and interesting information in the form of "personal" histories of eight animals and became the forerunner of the modern books written about one animal.

The Rise of Fantasy and Humor

Although many of the early titles of books for children included the word *amusing*, their main purpose was to instruct or moralize. Undoubtedly, children enjoyed the broad humor in some of the folktales and the nonsense in Mother Goose, but few books used humor or nonsense before the middle of the nineteenth century.

The first stirrings of modern fantasy may be seen in a tale written by an English clergyman and scientist in 1863. *The Water Babies* by Charles Kingsley is a strange mixture of the fanciful overladen with heavy doses of morality. It is a story of a chimney sweep who has become a water baby with gills. Hidden within this little tale was Kingsley's social concern for the plight of the chimney sweeps, plus his attempt to reconcile the new science (Darwin's *Origin of the Species* had been published in 1859) with his religious belief that salvation can be obtained through love and compassion as easily as through punishment. Children probably skipped over the following passage or created their own meanings for the lessons of Mrs. Doasyouwouldbedoneby:

🐚 . . . for you must know and believe that people's
souls make their bodies just as a snail makes its shell

Although many artists (including Lewis Carroll himself) have illustrated *Alice in Wonderland,* it is Tenniel who created the best known images of Alice and her many adventures in nonsense.

(I am not joking, my little man; I am in serious solemn earnest). And therefore, when Tom's soul grew all prickly with naughty tempers, his body could not help growing prickly too, so that nobody would cuddle him or play with him, or even like to look at him.[23]

On a summer day in 1862 an Oxford professor of mathematics, Charles Dodgson, told a story to three little girls on a picnic. According to Meigs, this "was the real beginning of modern literature for children."[24] For the tale that was told was about Alice, who followed a White Rabbit down a rabbit hole and found herself a part of a remarkable adventure. At the children's request, Dodgson wrote that story as *Alice's Adventures Underground* and presented it to his young friends as a Christmas gift in 1864. At the insistence of others, he decided to have it published. By 1865 the artist Tenniel had completed the drawings,

[23]Charles Kingsley, *The Water Babies* (New York: Platt and Munk, 1863; 1900), p. 149.
[24]Meigs, *A Critical History*, p. 194.

Anthony Browne's updated illustrations for *Alice in Wonderland* feature vibrant color and touches of modern madness while remaining faithful to the spirit of the story.

🍒   🍒   🍒

and *Alice's Adventures in Wonderland*, published under the pseudonym of Lewis Carroll, was ready for the host of readers to come. What made this story absolutely unique for its time was that it contained not a trace of a lesson or a moral. It was really made purely for enjoyment, and it has delighted both children and adults ever since. Allusions to this book and its companion title, *Through the Looking-Glass* (1871), have become a part of our everyday speech: "jam tomorrow and jam yesterday—but never jam today"; "curiouser and curiouser"; "much of a muchness"; "begin at the beginning, then go on until you've come to the end: then stop;" "I've believed as many as six

impossible things before breakfast"; "O frabjous day," and many more.

Other well-known fantasies were published near the end of the century. George MacDonald was a friend of Lewis Carroll's; in fact he was one of the persons who had urged the publication of *Alice*. However, his own "invented fairy-tale" *At the Back of the North Wind* (1871) has much more of the sad spiritual quality found in many of Hans Christian Andersen's fairy tales than the mad inconsistencies of the world of Lewis Carroll. MacDonald's other works include *The Princess and the Goblin* (1872) and *The Princess and Curdie* (1883). "The Light Princess" and "The Golden Key" are well-known stories from his other books.

The Adventures of Pinocchio by Carlo Collodi first appeared in a children's newspaper in Rome in 1881. Translated into many languages, it was issued in English in 1891 under the title *The Story of a Puppet*, but the title was soon changed back to the original *Pinocchio*. Children still enjoy this story of the mischievous puppet whose nose grew longer with each lie he told the Blue Fairy. Collodi's real name was Carlos Lorenzini.

The prototype for Mary Poppins, Amelia Bedelia, Miss Pickerell, and all the other eccentric women characters in children's literature may be found in the nonsensical antics of Mrs. Peterkin and her family. Published in 1880 by Lucretia Hale, *The Peterkin Papers* provided children with real humor. One of the most amusing stories, "The Lady Who Put Salt in Her Coffee," appeared in a juvenile magazine as early as 1868. Mrs. Peterkin mistakenly substitutes salt for sugar in her coffee. The whole family troops to the chemist and the herb lady to find out what to do. Finally "the lady from Philadelphia" provides the answer—make another cup of coffee! The antics of the Peterkin family were just as exaggerated and as much fun in 1880 as McCloskey's *Homer Price* was in the 1940s.

Also in the category of books for fun may be included the many books with movable parts. Harlequinades, or turn-ups, first appeared in 1766. They consisted of pages of pictures that could be raised or lowered to create other scenes. Later (from the 1840s through the 1890s) pictures were made like Venetian blinds to create another scene. Circular wheels could be turned to provide more action, and whole pop-up scenes created miniature stages. *The Children's Theatre,* for example, shows four scenes of Little Red Riding Hood, Hansel and Gretel, the Nativity scene, and one of a family around a Christmas tree. This book, created by Franz Bonn of Germany in 1878, was reissued by the Viking Press a hundred years later. Three books first published in England by Ernest Nister in the 1890s, *Revolving Pictures, Merry Magic Go Round* (first published under the title *Merry Surprises*), and *The Great Panorama Picture Book,* were all reissued in the 1980s. Children today are as intrigued with the format of these books as children were a hundred years ago.

Poetry

Poetry for children began to flourish in the nineteenth century. In the first part of the century, poetry, like prose, still reflected the influence of religion and moral didacticism. The Taylor sisters, Ann and Jane, emphasized polite behavior, morals, and death in the poetry for their first book, *Original Poems for Infant Minds* (1804). While Jane Taylor wrote the often parodied "Twinkle Twinkle Little Star" for this collection and Ann provided the lovely "Welcome, welcome little stranger, to this busy world of care," the book also included such a morbid poem as this example:

> You are not so healthy and gay
> So young, so active and bright,
> That death cannot snatch you away,
> Or some dread accident smite.
>
> Here lie both the young and the old,
> Confined in the coffin so small
> The earth covers over them cold,
> The grave-worms devour them all.

William Roscoe's *The Butterfly's Ball and the Grasshopper's Feast* (1807) provided pure nonsense, rhyme, and rhythm that delighted children. There were no moral lessons here, just an invitation: "Come take up your hats and away let us haste/To the Butterfly's Ball and the Grasshopper's Feast. . . ." The arrival of each guest was illustrated by copper engravings of a "snail person" or a "bumble bee child" by

There was an Old Man on whose nose, most birds of the air could repose; But they all flew away at the closing of day, Which relieved that Old Man and his nose.

Edward Lear's laughable limericks and humorous illustrations in *A Book of Nonsense* are over a hundred years old, but they are still enjoyed today.

William Mulready. Roscoe, a historian and botanist, wrote the book for the pleasure of his own child. It was so fresh and different that it generated many imitations.

Clement Moore, a professor who also wrote to please his own children, gave the world the Christmas classic, *A Visit from St. Nicholas.* One of the first American contributions to a joyous literature for children, it was published with this title in 1823, but is now known as *The Night Before Christmas.* Tasha Tudor, Michael Hague, and Tomie de Paola have all created beautifully illustrated editions of this well-loved poem for today's children. Tomie de Paola has also illustrated a new edition of *Mary Had a Little Lamb,* first written by Sarah Josepha Hale in 1830. In 1837 the poem was included in McGuffey's reader and has since been recited by generations of American schoolchildren.

Dr. Heinrich Hoffman's *Struwwelpeter* was translated from the German in about 1848. His subjects included "Shock-Headed Peter," who wouldn't comb his hair or cut his nails; Harriet, who played with fire; and Augustus, who would not eat his nasty soup until he became as "thin as a thread/and the fifth day was dead." These cautionary tales in verse were meant to frighten children into good behavior. Instead, children loved the pictures and gruesome verse. Surely these poems are the forerunners of some of the modern verse by Shel Silverstein and Jack Prelutsky.

The century's greatest contribution to lasting poetry was the nonsense verse of Edward Lear, a poet who, like Lewis Carroll, wrote only to entertain. Lear was by profession a landscape painter and illustrator. He wrote his first book, *A Book of Nonsense*, in 1846 for his child friends; *More Nonsense* (1872) appeared twenty-six years later. Generations have delighted in "The Pobble Who Has No Toes," "The Dong with the Luminous Nose," the elderly "Quangle Wangle," and "The Owl and the Pussycat." Lear did not invent the limerick, but he certainly became master of the form. His black-line illustrations are as clever as his poetry.

Most of Lewis Carroll's nonsense verse is included in *Alice's Adventures in Wonderland* and *Through the Looking-Glass*. Many of Carroll's poems were parodies of the popular poems of his time. "The Lobster Quadrille" mimics Mary Howitt's "The Spider and the Fly," "Father William" copies Southey's "The Old Man's Comforts," while "How Doth the Little Crocodile" parodies Watts's "How Doth the Busy Bee." Interest in the original poems has all but disappeared, but the parodies continue to delight. "Jabberwocky" is a "made language" of portmanteau words that combine the meaning and parts of two words to create a new one. "Slithy," for example, carries the combined meaning of lithe and slimy; "mimsy" is both flimsy and miserable. The sound and play of words must have fascinated Carroll, for his poems and books abound with puns, double meanings, coined words, and wonderful nonsense.

Some of Christina Rossetti's poetry is reminiscent of Mother Goose, such as the well-loved "Mix a pancake/Stir a pancake/Pop it in the pan;/Fry the pancake/Toss the pancake/Catch it if you can." Others such as "Who has seen the wind?" gave children vivid descriptions of the world around them. Many poems from her book *Sing Song* (1872) are found in anthologies today. Her long poem *Goblin Market* (1864) has appeared as a separately illustrated book.

William Allingham's name is always associated with the poem "The Fairies," which begins "Up the airy mountain,/Down the rushy glen,/We daren't go a hunting,/For fear of little men." It appeared in his book *In Fairyland* (1870), which was beautifully illustrated in colored pictures by Richard Doyle. Allingham's *Ballad Book*, published in 1865, contained "Fourscore of the best of the old ballads," as stated in his preface. John Greenleaf Whittier included some of his own poems in his anthology *Child Life, A Collection of Poems* (1871) as well as some by Blake, Shakespeare, Tennyson, Keats, Shelley, Browning, and Wordsworth. He thought children were capable of understanding poetry of literary merit.

The century ended with a unique volume of poetry that celebrated the everyday life and thought of the child. *A Child's Garden of Verses* (1885) by Robert Louis Stevenson was first published under the title *Penny Whistles*. Stevenson was a poet who could enter the child's imagining in such well-loved poems as "My Shadow," "Bed in Summer," "The Swing," "Windy Nights," and "My Bed Is a Boat." He was the first to discover joy in child's play.

Two notable American poets were writing for children at the close of the nineteenth century. Eugene Field's *Poems of Childhood* (1896) included "The Sugar Plum Tree" and "The Duel." James Whitcomb Riley employed dialect as he described local incidents and Indiana farm life. This Hoosier dialect has made most of his poems seem obsolete except "Little Orphant Annie" and "The Raggedy Man," which continue to give children pleasure.

Magazines

Magazines formed a significant part of the literature for children in the last half of the nineteenth century. The first magazines for English children, which grew out of the Sunday School movement, were pious in their outlook. *The Child's Companion* was one of these which continued into the twentieth century. The first true children's magazine for English children appeared in 1853 under the title of *Charm*. It was ahead of its time, however, stating that there would always be room for stories of the little people or fairies on its pages; it lasted only two years. Charlotte Yonge's own stories appeared in her magazine titled *The Monthly Packet*. Mrs. Gatty and her daughter, Julia Horatio Ewing, contributed to this magazine until Mrs. Gatty herself started *Aunt Judy's Magazine* in 1866. The whole Gatty family worked on this, with Dr. Gatty writing articles from time to time, their son setting some of the poems to music, and Mrs. Ewing serving as a regular contributor. This magazine began the policy of reviewing children's books, reporting enthusiastically on *Alice's Adventures in Wonderland* and Hans Christian Andersen's stories.

The first magazine planned for children in America, *The Juvenile Miscellany*, appeared under the editorship of Lydia Maria Child in 1826. Child was a former teacher who wanted to provide enjoyable material for children to read. The magazine was very successful until Child, an ardent abolitionist, spoke out against slavery. Sales dropped immediately, and the magazine stopped publication in 1834. Frank Leslie's *Chatterbox* advertised that its policy was "to improve the mind, diffuse knowledge." It lasted for only seven years, from 1879 to 1886. *Our Young Folks*, edited by Lucy Larcom in Boston, lasted only eight years. Her literary taste was excellent; Dickens's "The Magic Fishbone" appeared in it in 1868 and Thomas Bailey Aldrich's *The Story of a Bad Boy* was first serialized in it in 1869. *Our Young Folks* was sold to Scribner's and became part of the famous *St. Nicholas Magazine* in 1874. Horace Scudder edited *The Riverside Magazine* for only three years, from 1867 to 1870. However, he was a moving force for literature for children and wrote true criticism of books and articles on children's reading. *The Youth's Companion* survived the longest of all the children's magazines in America, beginning in 1827 and merging with *The American Boy* in 1929, which in turn ceased publication in 1941. It published such well-known writers as Kipling, Oliver Wendell Holmes, Jack London, Mark Twain, and Theodore Roosevelt, among others. *The Youth's Companion* had a definite editorial policy. It proposed to "exile death from its pages"; tobacco and alcohol were not to be mentioned, and love figured in some of the stories only after 1890. Part of the popularity of this magazine may be attributed to the inviting premiums that were offered each week.

In 1873 Mary Mapes Dodge, author of *Hans Brinker, Or the Silver Skates,* became editor of the most famous magazine for children, *St. Nicholas.* The publisher announced that in this magazine "there must be entertainment, no less than information; the spirit of laughter would be evoked; there would be 'no sermonizing, no wearisome spinning out of facts, no rattling of dry bones of

Arthur Rackham became known for his imaginative worlds of gnomes and anthropomorphized trees. His illustrations appeared in magazines as well as books.

From *Mother Goose.*

history,' while all priggishness was condemned."[25] A promising young writer, Frank Stockton, became Dodge's assistant, and together they published a magazine that would become known throughout the English-speaking world. They attracted such well-known artists and writers as Arthur Rackham, Reginald Birch, Howard Pyle, Frances Hodgson Burnett, Rudyard Kipling, Robert Louis Stevenson, and Louisa May Alcott, among others. Many of the novels that were first serialized in *St. Nicholas Magazine* were published as books and became classics of their day. These included Louisa May Alcott's *An Old Fashioned Girl* (1870), *Jo's Boys* (1873), Frances Hodgson Burnett's *Little Lord Fauntleroy* (1886) and *Sara Crewe* (1888), Rudyard Kipling's *The Jungle Book*, and many others. This magazine guided children's reading for over three-quarters of a century and set standards of excellence for the whole publishing field.

Illustrators of the Nineteenth Century

During the nineteenth century illustrators of children's books began to achieve as much recognition as the authors. In the early part of the century, crude woodcuts were still being used, illustrators were not identified, and pictures were frequently interchanged among books. Gradually, however, several outstanding artists emerged as illustrators of children's books. George Cruikshank was an engraver who illustrated the English edition of *Grimm's Fairy Tales* in 1823. His tiny detailed pictures portrayed much action and humor, real characters, and spritely elves and fairies. His interpretations were so appropriate and seemed so much a part of these tales that they were republished in Germany with the original text. In 1853–1854 he published four volumes of his *Fairy Library*, which contain some of his best artwork. Unfortunately, he altered some of the stories to conform to what he called certain "temperance truths." For example, after Cinderella's marriage contract is signed, her godmother begs the king not to serve wine at the celebration, saying: ". . . your Majesty is aware that

Walter Crane's decorative borders and fine sense of design are seen in this frontispiece for *The Baby's Own Aesop*.

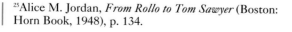

this same drink leads also to quarrels, brutal fights, and violent death."[26] Cruikshank was a friend of Dickens and his most famous illustrator, although they had a falling-out over Cruikshank's rewriting of these tales. Fortunately, he is remembered for his enchanting illustrations, not his rewritten texts.

The three best known illustrators of the nineteenth century are Walter Crane, Randolph Caldecott, and Kate Greenaway. All three were fortunate indeed to have Edmund Evans, the best color printer in England, as their engraver. Walter Crane, the son of a portrait painter, knew that Evans wanted to print some quality illustrated books for children, something that interested Crane also. Crane created beautifully designed pictures for four nursery-rhyme books, *Sing a Song of Sixpence*, *The House That Jack Built*, *Dame Trot and Her Comical Cat*, and *The History of Cock Robin and Jenny Wren*. Evans and Crane con-

[25]Alice M. Jordan, *From Rollo to Tom Sawyer* (Boston: Horn Book, 1948), p. 134.

[26]George Cruikshank, *George Cruikshank's Fairy Library; Cinderella and The Glass Slipper* (London: D. Bogue, 1853).

vinced Warne to publish these high-quality "Toy Books" during the years 1865–1866. They were very successful, and Crane went on to design some thirty-five other picture books, including two well-known nursery-rhyme collections with music and illustrations. These were titled *The Baby's Opera* (1877) and *The Baby's Bouquet* (1878). Crane had a strong sense of design and paid particular attention to the total format of the book, including the placement of the text, the quality of the paper, even the design at the beginning and end of chapters. He characteristically used flat colors with a firm black outline. His pages were usually decorated with elaborate borders. He made a point of studying the Victorian child's attitude toward art, saying: "Like the Ancient Egyptians, children appear to see most things in profile and like definite statements in design. They prefer well-defined forms and frank colour.

They don't want to bother about three dimensions."[27]

The picture books by Randolph Caldecott established new standards of illustration for children's books. His drawings were filled with action, joy of living, and good fun. His love of animals and the English countryside is reflected in the illustrations that seem to convey much meaning through a few lines. Although Caldecott, like Crane, illustrated many books, he is best remembered for his series of picture books. These included *The House That Jack Built* (1878), *The Diverting History of John Gilpin* (1878), *Sing a Song of Sixpence* (1880), and *Hey Diddle Diddle Picture*

[27]As quoted by Bryan Holme in his Preface to *An Alphabet of Old Friends and the Absurd ABC* by Walter Crane (New York: The Metropolitan Museum of Art, 1981), unpaged.

Randolph Caldecott was one of the first illustrators for children to show action in his pictures. The design for the Caldecott Medal is taken from this scene in *The Diverting History of John Gilpin*.

Without alerting Joan, the French had attacked the English bastion of Saint-Loup. The attack failed; the French were retreating in disorder. Joan rushed up, rallied them, and led them once more to the very foot of the bastion. The English, under their commander Talbot, fought back desperately for three hours, but despite their resistance the French overcame them and captured the bastion.

The extraordinary illustrations of Maurice Boutet de Monvel for the picture book *Joan of Arc* created in 1896 had a pervasive influence on the children's books that followed.

Book (1883). On the Caldecott medal for distinguished illustrations there is a reproduction of one of his pictures showing John Gilpin's ride, a reminder of this famous illustrator of the nineteenth century.

Kate Greenaway's name brings visions of English gardens; delicate, prim figures; and the special style of costume worn by her rather fragile children. Her art defined the fanciful world of Victorian sentimentality. After the publication of her first book, *Under the Window* (1878), it became the fashion to dress children in Greenaway cos-

tumes with large floppy hats. Greeting cards, wallpaper, and even china were made with designs copied after Greenaway. Her best known works include *Marigold Garden* (1885), *A Apple Pie* (1886), and *The Pied Piper of Hamelin* (1888). The Kate Greenaway Medal, similar to our Caldecott Medal, is given each year to the most distinguished British picture book.

From France came the remarkable work of Maurice Boutet de Monvel, best remembered for the superb pictures for *Jeanne d'Arc*, which he wrote and illustrated in 1896. The power of these paintings—the massed groupings of men and horses and the mob scenes in which every person is an individual, yet the focus is always on the Maid of Orleans—made this a distinctive book for young and old alike. It was translated into English in 1897. This book was reissued in 1980 by Viking Press in cooperation with the Pierpont Morgan Library.

In America, Howard Pyle was writing and illustrating his versions of *The Merry Adventures of Robin Hood of Great Renown* (1883), *Pepper and Salt* (1886), and *The Wonder Clock* (1888). He created *real* people in his illustrations for these collections of folktales and legends. His characters from the Middle Ages were strong; the life of the times was portrayed with interesting clear detail. In 1903, he published the first of four volumes of *The Story of King Arthur and His Knights,* reissued by Scribner's in 1984. Pyle also illustrated and wrote for *Scribner's Monthly Magazine* and *St. Nicholas.* Another of his important contributions was establishing classes for illustrators of children's books. Some of his students included N. C. Wyeth, Maxfield Parrish, and Jessie Wilcox Smith, all of whom became well-known illustrators in the twentieth century.

By the close of the nineteenth century, children's literature was alive and flourishing. Pious, moralistic, didactic books were no longer being written. Gone were the make-believe accounts of impossible children. In their place were real live persons living in fun-loving families. Pure nonsense and the fanciful were welcomed in both poetry and fantasy. The old folktales and the fairies were accepted once again. Children's books were more beautiful, with illustrations by recognized artists. A few magazines had given consideration to the place of literary criticism. Much would need to be done to bring books to all children in the next century, but a literature for children, designed to bring them joy and happiness, was now firmly in place.

CHILDREN'S LITERATURE: THE TWENTIETH CENTURY

If the nineteenth century saw the firm establishment of a literature for children, the twentieth may be characterized by the recognition of liter-

ary and artistic quality in children's books, the growth of children's book departments in publishing houses, and the expansion of both public and school library service to all children. Technological improvements made it possible to create beautifully illustrated, well-bound books for children and just as easy to mass-produce shoddy, cheap editions. The picture book as we know it today was created early in this century, as well as fine informational books for all ages.

Recognition of Children's Literature

Disturbed by the influence of the cheaply produced fifty-cent juvenile, Franklin K. Mathiews, Chief Scout Librarian, sought to raise the level of reading for children. His suggestion for establishing a Children's Book Week was promoted in 1919 by Frederick Melcher as a project of the American Booksellers Association. Schools, libraries, newspapers, and bookstores supported the event, which became a significant stimulant to the development of children's literature. In 1945 the Children's Book Council was established to promote Book Week and to distribute information on children's books throughout the year.

Melcher also promoted another event that has encouraged the development of children's literature. He proposed the presentation of an annual award for the most distinguished book for children. Initiated in 1922, the Newbery Medal was the first award in the world to be given for "distinguished contribution to literature for children." The Caldecott Medal for the most distinguished picture book of the year was first given in 1938. Both these awards have had great influence in raising the standards of writing and illustrating in children's books. They also gave prestige to the idea of creating books for children. An international award, The Hans Christian Andersen Award, was established in 1956 and is given every two years to a living author for his or her complete body of work. Starting in 1966, an artist was also recognized.

The addition of children's departments to publishing firms indicated the growing importance of literature for the young. In 1919 Macmillan made Louise Seaman its children's editor, and other companies were quick to follow this innovation.

May Massee became editor of children's books at Doubleday in 1922. The first critical reviews of children's books appeared in *The Bookman* in 1918. Anne Carroll Moore continued this influential work in her *New York Herald Tribune* column, "The Three Owls." *The Horn Book Magazine,* a publication solely devoted to children's literature, was first published in 1924 under the editorship of Bertha Mahony.

Public libraries instituted children's rooms and many elementary schools had libraries. By 1915 the American Library Association had established a School Library division. However, it was not until the enactment of the Elementary and Secondary Education Act of 1965 that the concept of school library media centers for *every* elementary school seemed a viable possibility.

The Junior Literary Guild was established in 1929 and was the first to send children selected books each month. In the late 1950s paperback book clubs made it possible for more children to own books and increased their enthusiasm for reading. Currently, many book clubs offer selections of children's literature.

The Rise of the Picture Storybook

One of the best loved stories for children is *The Tale of Peter Rabbit,* who appeared in Mr. MacGregor's garden at the turn of the century. After writing a short version of the tale in a letter to the ill son of a former governess, Beatrix Potter expanded the story and submitted it to Warne Publishers. When they rejected it, she had it published privately in 1901. Warne finally accepted and published *The Tale of Peter Rabbit* with the author's own watercolor illustrations in 1902. Potter later introduced stories of many other animals, such as Jemima Puddleduck, Benjamin Bunny, and Mrs. Tittlemouse, but the cottontail family is the best known and loved. Unfortunately, the books were not copyrighted in this country and so Peter Rabbit was pirated extensively and appeared with unattractive copied illustrations. A new edition of Potter's stories with illustrations by the English artist Allen Atkinson was published in 1983, but Beatrix Potter's own pictures are so right, so timeless, that it seems almost a travesty to try to reinterpret them today.

A trusting fowl listens to a "foxy-whiskered gentleman" in this scene from *Jemima Puddle-Duck.* Beatrix Potter created real personalities in both the text and pictures of her many books.

At the same time that Potter was writing and illustrating, Leslie Brooke was creating wonderfully humorous pictures for his nursery-rhyme picture books. No one could draw such expressive faces on pigs as Brooke did in *This Little Pig Went to Market,* which first appeared in *The Golden Goose Book* (1905). Brooke added whimsical details to his illustrations like a picture of "Home Sweet Home" hanging inside the pigs' house showing a mother pig and her little ones. Leslie Brooke's animals in the popular *Johnny Crow's Garden* (1903) were costumed and personified. They included the lion with a "green and yellow tie on" and the bear in his striped pants and tailcoat.

The other well-known English illustrator of this period was Arthur Rackham. He is recognized for the imaginative detail of his pictures, which frequently portrayed grotesque people and humanlike trees evoking an eerie atmosphere. His illustrations for *Mother Goose* (1913) show imaginative elves and gnomes hiding under mushrooms and in the roots of trees (see p. 129). He illustrated many other books, including Hans Christian Andersen's *Fairy Tales, Cinderella, Peter Pan in Kensington Gardens, Aesop's Fables,* and many more.

For many years these English books, along with those of Caldecott, Crane, and Greenaway, supplied the American picture-book market. There was much rejoicing, then, when in 1923 C. B. Falls's *ABC Book* with its boldly colored woodcuts was published in this country. Only a few persons knew that it was a rather poor copy of William Nicholson's *Alphabet* (1898) and his *Square Book of Animals,*[28] both published in England.

William Nicholson is credited with creating the first true picture book, *Clever Bill,* published in England in 1926 and in New York in 1927. Farrar, Straus reissued this book in 1972, including the following statement by Maurice Sendak on the jacket flap: "*Clever Bill,* I have long felt, is among the few perfect picture books ever created for children." At the most the text of this book is only two long run-on sentences. The illustrations carry the story of a little girl who goes to visit her aunt and leaves her favorite toy soldier at home. The toy runs after her and is "just in time to meet

her train at Dover. 'Clever Bill.'" Wanda Gág's delightful tale *Millions of Cats,* published in 1928, has been called the first American picture storybook. This is an outstanding example of how text and pictures work together. In the unfolding drama a very old man goes in search of the most beautiful cat in the world. The long horizontal format enabled Gág to spread the journey over both pages. Like a folktale with its repetition and refrain of "hundreds of cats, thousands of cats, millions and billions and trillions of cats," the story is still popular with children today. It opened the door to what was to become a treasure house of beauty and enjoyment for children, the modern picture storybook.

Progressive education and the growth of the nursery school movement made an impact on the development of books for the preschool child. Lucy Sprague Mitchell of the Bank Street School published her *Here and Now Story Book* in 1921. She pointed out the young child's preoccupation with self and interest in daily experiences. Her collection of stories provided simple little tales of the small child's everyday activities; none of them have lasted. However, she did conduct classes on writing for children, and Margaret Wise Brown attended these classes. When William Scott and his partner decided to start a new firm to publish books just for the very young child,

[28]See discussion and illustrations in Barbara Bader's *American Picturebooks from Noah's Ark to the Beast Within* (New York: Macmillan, 1976), p. 24.

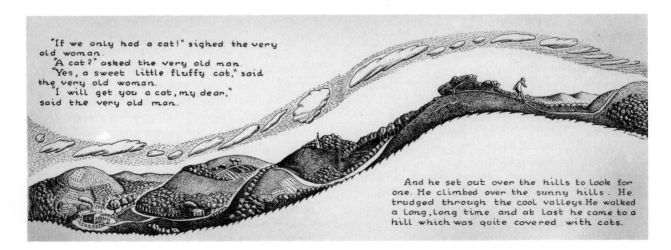

Wanda Gág's delightful tale *Millions of Cats,* published in 1928, has been called the first American picture storybook.

Mrs. Mitchell recommended that they contact Margaret Wise Brown. Their first success and breakthrough book for young children was *The Noisy Book* (1939). In this story a little dog has bandaged eyes and must guess at the noises he hears, as must the child listening to the story. These books (there are some seven in the series) invited participation by the child reader–listener.

Writing under her own name and three pseudonyms, Margaret Wise Brown created nearly a hundred books. Her most frequent illustrator was Leonard Weisgard, who won the Caldecott award for their book *The Little Island* (1946). Many of her books are still popular today, including *Goodnight Moon* (1947), the most favorite bedtime story of all, and *The Runaway Bunny* (1942) and *The Little Fur Family* (1946). After Brown's untimely death at 42, William Scott wrote: "All her books have an elusive quality that was Margaret Wise Brown. . . . [They have] simplicity, directness, humor, unexpectedness, respect for the reader and a sense of the importance of living."[29]

Other author-illustrators of this period include Marjorie Flack, who, like Margaret Wise Brown, knew how to tell a good story for preschoolers. Her *Angus and the Ducks* (1930) and *Ask Mr. Bear* (1952) are still shared with youngsters. Kurt Wiese illustrated her popular *The Story About Ping* (1933), the little runaway duck on the Yangtze River. Lois Lenski began creating her picture storybooks of *The Little Family* (1932) and *The Little Auto* (1934) at about this time. These pictured 5-year-olds as little adults doing what young children wished they could do, such as drive a car, sail a boat, or be a fireman.

Machines became popular characters in such books as Watty Piper's *The Little Engine That Could* (1929), Hardie Gramatky's *Little Toot* (1930), and Virginia Lee Burton's *Mike Mulligan and His Steam Shovel* (1939). Burton personified *The Little House* (1942), which was first built in the country, then engulfed by the city, and finally rescued and returned to the country again. This story, which won the Caldecott award, has been called a child's first sociology book.

[29]Louise Seaman Bechtel, "Margaret Wise Brown, 'Laureate of the Nursery,'" *The Horn Book Magazine*, vol. 24 (June 1958), p. 184.

Dr. Seuss wrote and illustrated the first of many hilarious rhymed stories for children, *To Think That I Saw It on Mulberry Street*, in 1937. That delightful daredevil, *Madeline*, appeared on the Paris streets in 1939. Though not Ludwig Bemelmans's first book, it is certainly his best known. Robert McCloskey's ducklings made their difficult journey across Boston streets in 1941. *Make Way for Ducklings* richly deserved the Caldecott award it received. In the same year H. A. Rey introduced the antics of everyone's favorite monkey, *Curious George*.

During the late 1930s and early 1940s the United States benefited from the influx of many fine European artists seeking political refuge in this country. These artists found a legitimate outlet for their creative talents in the field of children's literature. Picture storybooks were greatly enriched through their unique contributions. A glance at a roster of some of the names of well-known illustrators indicates the international flavor of their backgrounds: d'Aulaire, Duvoisin, Eichenberg, Mordvinoff, Petersham, Rojankovsky, Simont, Shulevitz, Slobodkin, and many more. (Some of their work is discussed in Chapter 5, "Picture Storybooks.") Certainly the variety of their national backgrounds has added a cosmopolitan flavor to our picture books that is unprecedented both in time and place. American children have become the beneficiaries of an inheritance from the whole artistic world.

Growth of Informational Books

Increased understanding of human development brought the recognition that the child was naturally curious and actively sought information. No longer did a discussion of nature have to be disguised as "an exciting walk with Uncle Fred," who lectured on the flowers and trees. Children enjoy facts, and they eagerly accept information given to them in a straightforward manner.

E. Boyd Smith created some of the earliest information picture books in *The Farm Book* (1910), *Chicken World* (1910), *The Seashore Book* (1912), and *The Railroad Book* (1913). The illustrations for these stories were large, colored double-page spreads filled with fascinating detail. His *Chicken World* tells the life story of a chick,

E. Boyd Smith was one of the first Americans to produce artistic and accurate informational picture books. *The Railroad Book* **was first published in 1913.**

🐦 🐦 🐦

ending with a roast bird on a platter! *The Railroad Book* helps its readers visualize all the details of a train trip, whether they had had that experience or not. Smith lived in France for a long period and some of his illustrations are reminiscent of Boutet de Monvel's work for *Joan of Arc*. Smith illustrated many other books including *The Story of Noah's Ark* (1909). His wonderful picture of the seasick animals stretched out on a rolling ark could compete with Peter Spier's more recent Caldecott award–winning *Noah's Ark* (1977).

From Sweden came a translation of *Pelle's New Suit* (1929) by Elsa Beskow. Large colored pictures illustrate the process of making clothes, beginning with the shearing of Pelle's lamb, card-ing the wool, spinning it, dyeing it, weaving the cloth, making the suit, and ending with a bright Sunday morning when Pelle wears his new suit. It is interesting for children to compare this book, which can still be found in libraries today, with Tomie de Paola's *"Charlie Needs a Cloak"* (1974). Maud and Miska Petersham used rich vivid colors on every page of their informational books, which frequently described processes. They published five storybooks, each composed of four parts that were also published as separate books. Thus *The Story Book of Things We Use* (1933), *The Story Book of Wheels, Trains, Aircraft* (1935), *The Story Book of Foods from the Field* (1936), and *The Story Book of Things We Wear* (1939) spawned some fifteen smaller books. These books were the predecessors of Holling C. Holling's beautifully illustrated story of the travels of a little carved canoe, *Paddle to the Sea* (1941), which gave rich geographical information on the Great Lakes Region, and *Tree in the Trail* (1942), which provided much that was of historical interest about the Southwest.

W. Maxwell Reed, a former professor at Harvard, started to answer his nephew's questions in a series of letters that resulted in two books, *The Earth for Sam* (1932) and the popular *Stars for Sam* (1931). These books exemplify the beginnings of accurate informational books written by recognized authorities in the field.

As a result of the preschool movement with its emphasis on the "here and now," young children also had their informational books. Mary Steichen Martin produced *The First Picture Book: Everyday Things for Babies* (1930), while her photographer father, Edward Steichen, took the pictures of such common objects as a cup of milk with a slice of bread and butter, a faucet with a bar of soap, a glass holding a toothbrush, and a brush and comb set. No text accompanied these pictures, which were clear enough to provoke recognition and discussion for the child. *The Second Picture Book* (1931) showed pictures of children using common objects. Neither one of these books was particularly popular, but they paved the way for other photographic information books. Lewis W. Hine published his *Men at Work* (1932), picturing train engineers, workers on a skyscraper, and cowboys. Lucy Sprague Mitchell created verses for the photos of Clara Lambert in their publication *Skyscraper* (1933). Harriet Huntington's book *Let's Go Outdoors* (1939) portrayed close-up pictures of bugs and flowers just as a child might discover them on a nature walk. Her style of contrasting a primary object in sharp focus against a blurred background is similar to the contemporary work of Tana Hoban. This book was followed by *Let's Go to the Seashore* (1941). Both books stayed in print well over twenty-five years. Henry Kane's fine close-ups of a mouse and frog in his *The Tale of the Whitefoot Mouse* (1940) and *The Tale of a Bullfrog* (1941) started the trend to create photographic stories of individual animals.

Since the 1940s, quantities of informational books have rolled from the presses to give children facts on almost every conceivable subject. Series books in the areas of science and social studies were important developments in this period. The *First Books, All About Books*, and the *True Books* series are examples of the trend. Many books of experiments by such authors as the Schneiders and Freemans stimulated children's interest in science. Developments in the fields of atomic energy and exploration of space have been reflected in books for children. In the 1950s factual books about rockets, satellites, and space almost seemed to be fantasy, but by the 1960s such books were an accepted fact of daily life.

New books for social studies included *America: Adventures in Eyewitness History* (1962) and *Africa: Adventures in Eyewitness History* (1963), both by Rhoda Hoff. These books, based on original sources, recognized children's ability to read complex materials and draw their own conclusions about history. Alex Bealer's *Only the Names Remain: The Cherokees and the Trail of Tears* (1972) was representative of a new emphasis on readable, carefully documented history. It also attempted to balance recorded history by presenting a Native American point of view.

Early in the twentieth century, historical fiction served as a source of information about the past. Laura Richards quoted from diaries and letters as she wrote *Abigail Adams and Her Times* (1909). *The Horsemen of the Plains* (1910) by Joseph Altsheler related exciting frontier stories of the Cheyenne War. The legendary approach to history was utilized by MacGregor in *Story of Greece* (1914). *When Knights Were Bold* brought another period of history to life when Tappan published this book in 1911. A historical overview was provided in Hendrik Van Loon's *The Story of Mankind* (1921), the first Newbery award winner.

Laura Ingalls Wilder's remarkable series of Little House books started with *Little House in the Big Woods* in 1932; Elizabeth Coatsworth began her *Away Goes Sally* series in 1934. Carol Ryrie Brink wrote of that vivacious tomboy *Caddie Woodlawn* the following year. Forty years later, most historical fiction was more concerned with social conscience than with personal issues. The Newbery award winner for 1974, *The Slave Dancer* by Paula Fox, realistically faced up to the wrongs of the past. Celebration of the Bicentennial spurred publication of many attractive and authentic books on eighteenth-century America.

Biographies appeared to satisfy children's interest in national heroes. Ingri and Edgar Parin d'Aulaire, who had lived in Norway and in many other parts of Europe, were fascinated with the heroes of the new world. They presented somewhat idealized images in their large picture-book biographies, *George Washington* (1930), *Abraham Lincoln* (1939), *Leif the Lucky* (1941), *Pocahontas* (1949), and many more. Since these stories were new to them, they were perhaps freer to interpret the lives afresh, seeing them as a child discovers them for the first time. James Daugherty portrayed many American pioneers with strong vibrant pictures and ringing epic prose. His *Daniel Boone* (1939) was awarded the Newbery Medal.

The *Childhood of Famous Americans* series initiated the trend of publishing biographies for boys and girls in series form. By the 1960s biographies gave less emphasis to the early years of great men and women. More biographies for young children became available, including such lively and authentic books as Jean Fritz's *And Then What Happened, Paul Revere?* (1973) and *Poor Richard in France* (1973) by F. N. Monjo. Biographies of civil rights leaders honored such well-known persons as Martin Luther King, Jr., and lesser known participants like Rosa Parks, the woman who refused to give up her seat on a bus in Montgomery, Alabama, in 1955. More concern was evidenced for publishing biographies about women, and Crowell began their series on Women in America.

There is no accurate accounting of the number of nonfiction children's titles that are published in contrast to fiction, but a survey of the new titles would suggest that a majority of the children's books published today could be classified as informational. Informational books are discussed in detail in Chapter 11; historical fiction and biography are presented in Chapter 10.

Proliferation of Series Books

The dime novel was initiated in the nineteenth century, and the series books of George Henty, Oliver Optic, and Horatio Alger introduced the repetitive incident plot and stereotyped characters. In the twentieth century "fiction factories" were developed by Edward Stratemeyer, who manufactured the plots for literally hundreds of books, including *The Rover Boys* (1899–1926), *The Bobbsey Twins* (1904–), the *Tom Swift* series (1910–1941), and *The Hardy Boys* (1927–), to name just a few. Using a variety of pseudonyms, Stratemeyer would give hack writers a three-page outline of characters and plot to complete. When he died in 1930, a millionaire, he had himself written or conceived for others to write more than 1,300 fifty-cent juveniles. His daughter, Harriet Stratemeyer Adams, continued his work, writing nearly 200 children's books, including the well-known *Nancy Drew* series (1930–), until her death at 89 in 1982. In all her books, Mrs. Adams portrayed an innocent, affluent, and secure world. The original Nancy Drew could be kidnapped, knocked unconscious, and locked in a room with no way to escape, but she always solved the crime and survived to spend another day chasing villains in her blue roadster. Although modern versions of the series books deal with nuclear war, space flights, and submarines, the plots and characters are much the same. The hero or heroine is always a child or adolescent acting with adult wisdom and triumphing over all obstacles—unaided, undaunted, undefeated. Despite bitter criticism from literary critics, these books have been translated into many languages and continue to be sold in our country and throughout the world.

Books that met with literary approval were also sold in series. The Lucy Fitch Perkins *Twins* series, beginning in 1911 with *The Dutch Twins*, provided authentic information on children of other lands in the form of an interesting realistic story. The series included books at various levels of difficulty; the story of *The Scotch Twins* (1919) was more complex, for example, than *The Dutch Twins*. The author also wrote stories of twins living in various historical periods, such as *The Puritan Twins* (1921), *The Pioneer Twins* (1927), and many more.

Folktales of the World

The publication of Grimm's *Household Tales* in the early part of the nineteenth century represented only the beginning of interest in recording the told tale. Not until the twentieth century would children have access to the folktales of almost the entire world. A famous storyteller, Gudrun Thorne-Thomsen, recorded stories from Norway in *East o' the Sun and West o' the Moon* in 1912. Kate Douglas Wiggin edited tales from the *Arabian Nights* in 1909, and Ellen Babbitt brought forth a collection of *Jataka Tales* from India in 1912. Constance Smedley provided children with stories from Africa and Asia in her *Tales from Timbuktu* (1923). The next year, Charles Finger published stories that he had collected from Indians in South America in his Newbery award–winning book *Tales from Silver Lands* (1924). Ruth Sawyer went to Spain in search of folktales like the Irish stories she already knew. *Picture Tales from Spain* (1936) came out of that trip, and other Spanish stories were eventually published in her *Way of the Storyteller* (1942) and *The Long Christmas* (1941). Mary Gould Davis collaborated with Ralph Steele Boggs in creating another collection of Spanish stories, *Three Golden Oranges* (1936).

Pura Belpré grew up in Puerto Rico in a family of storytellers. She later told these stories to American children in library story hours. Finally they were published in a collection called *The Tiger and the Rabbit* (1946). Philip Sherlock, vice principal of the University College of the West Indies in Jamaica, told stories of his homeland at a meeting of the American Library Association. A children's book editor heard him and persuaded him to publish *Anansi, The Spider Man* (1954). Harold Courlander, a folklorist and musicologist, gathered many fine collections of stories in West Africa, Ethiopia, Indonesia, Asia, and the islands of the Pacific. His first collection of tales for children was *Uncle Bouqui of Haiti* (1942). Courlander worked like the Grimm brothers, collecting his stories from the native storytellers of the country. Some of his best stories are contained in *The Cow-Tail Switch and Other West African Stories* (1947) and *The Hat-Shaking Dance and Other Tales from the Gold Coast* (1957). The tales in *The Terrapin's Pot of Sense* (1957) were collected from black storytellers in Alabama, New Jersey, and Michigan. Courlander related these stories to their origins in Africa in his interesting notes at the back of the book.

Lim Sian-Tek, a Chinese writer, spent ten years gathering many different Chinese myths, legends, and folktales from her country. These were introduced to American children in *Folk Tales from China* (1944). Frances Carpenter made "Grandmother" collections, such as her *Tales of a Chinese Grandmother* (1949). *The Dancing Kettle and Other Japanese Folk Tales* (1949) contains the favorite stories from Yoshiko Uchida's childhood. She also adapted old Japanese tales for American children in her popular *The Magic Listening Cap* (1955) and *The Sea of Gold* (1965, 1985). Alice Geer Kelsey introduced American children to the humorous tales of the Hodja of Turkey and the Mullah of Persia in *Once the Hodja* (1943) and *Once the Mullah* (1954).

Many other collections continue to be published each year, presenting American children with the folklore of the world. They also serve as source material for the many individual folktale picture storybooks that became so popular in the second half of the century.

Marcia Brown's portrayal of three soldiers clever enough to make soup from a stone helped start a trend toward illustrating single folktales as picture books.

From *Stone Soup.*

Marcia Brown developed this trend of illustrating single folktales in a picture-book format with her publication of the French tale of trickery *Stone Soup* (1947). Her *Cinderella* (1954) and *Once a Mouse* (1961) won Caldecott Medals; her other fairy tales, *Puss in Boots, Dick Whittington and His Cat*, and *The Steadfast Tin Soldier*, were Honor Books for the award. Other illustrators who have brought children richly illustrated picture-book fairy tales include Felix Hoffman, Adrienne Adams, Paul Galdone, Errol LeCain, Nonny Hogrogian, Margot Zemach, Steven Kellogg, and many others.

Greater emphasis was placed on individual African folktales, Jewish folktales, and legends of native Americans during the decades of the 1960s and 1970s. Gail Haley won the Caldecott award (1971) for *A Story, A Story*, an African tale of Anansi; *Anansi the Spider* by Gerald McDermott won the award in 1973. Leo and Diane Dillon were Caldecott winners for their illustrations for *Why Mosquitoes Buzz in People's Ears* (1975), an African tale retold by Verna Aardema. Two Jewish tales, *The Golem* (1976) by Beverly Brodsky McDermott and *It Could Always Be Worse* (1977) by Margot Zemach, were Honor Books. Folktales from around the world are not only an established part of children's literature but a frequently honored genre.

Fantasy

Fantasy for children in the first half of the twentieth century seemed to come mainly from the pens of English writers. Kipling stimulated the child's imagination in his *Just So Stories* (1902) with his humorous accounts of the origins of animal characteristics—how the elephant got his trunk or the camel his hump. Much of the delight of these stories is in Kipling's use of rich language like "great grey-green, greasy Limpopo River all set about with fever-trees" and "the bi-colored python rock snake" who could tie himself in "a double clothes-hitch" around a tree.

Also in 1902, Warne Brothers published Beatrix Potter's diminutive little book *The Tale of Peter Rabbit*, as we already noted. Another English storyteller, Kenneth Grahame, brought to life for his

son the adventures of a water rat, a mole, a toad, and a badger. *The Wind in the Willows* was published in 1908 with pictures by Ernest Shepard. This story of four loyal friends became a children's classic. It has been reissued in a variety of editions, including those illustrated by Arthur Rackham (1940), Michael Hague (1980), John Burningham (1983), and Alex Tsao (1989). Individual chapters have been published as picture books: *The River Bank*, illustrated by Adrienne Adams in 1973; *The Open Road* (1979), *Wayfarers All* (1981), and *Mole's Christmas* (1983), all illustrated by Beverly Gooding. Obviously *The Wind in the Willows* continues to delight new generations of children.

The boy who refused to grow up and lose the beauties of Never Never Land, Peter Pan, first appeared in a London play by J. M. Barrie in 1904. Later the play was made into a book titled *Peter Pan in Kensington Gardens* (1906), with elaborate illustrations by Arthur Rackham. Darton maintains that *Peter Pan*, though in the form of a play, "has influenced the spirit of children's books, and the grown-up view of them, more powerfully than any other work except the *Alices* and Andersen's *Fairy Tales*."[30]

The Wizard of Oz by L. Frank Baum has been called the first American fantasy. Published in 1900, this highly inventive story of the Cowardly Lion, the Tin Woodman, the Scarecrow, and Dorothy in the Land of Oz has been enjoyed by countless children. Several publishers felt *The Wizard of Oz* was too radical a departure from the literature of the day and refused to publish it. Baum and the illustrator W. W. Denslow finally agreed to pay all the expenses if one small Chicago firm would print it. Within two months of publication, the book had been reprinted twice. The first book of the series is the best and might well have sufficed, but Baum created some thirteen more titles; and after his death at least twenty-six others were added to the series by Ruth Plumly Thompson, John R. Neill, and others. The 1939 film version of *The Wizard of Oz*, starring Judy Garland, has helped to keep interest in this book alive.

[30]Darton, *Children's Books in England*, p. 309.

Talking animals have always appealed to children. Hugh Lofting created the eccentric Dr. Dolittle, who could talk to animals as well as understand their languages. In *The Story of Dr. Dolittle* (1920), Lofting describes the way Dolittle learns the animals' languages with the help of the parrot Polynesia and begins his animal therapy. There were ten books in this series; the second one, *The Voyages of Doctor Dolittle* (1922), won the Newbery Medal. Later readings would reveal racial stereotypes in these books, but readers in the 1920s were not alert to such flaws in writing.

Remembering her love of toys, Margery Williams wrote *The Velveteen Rabbit* (1922) while living in England. This story, with its moving description of what it means to be real, has delighted children and adults. It was first illustrated by William Nicholson. More recent editions display the work of Michael Hague (1983), David Jorgensen (1985), and Ilse Plume (1987).

One of the most delightful stories of well-loved toys was A. A. Milne's story of *Winnie the Pooh*, written for his son in 1926. Eeyore, Piglet, and Pooh may be stuffed animals, but they have real, believable personalities. Their many adventures in the "100 Aker Wood" with Christopher Robin have provided hours of amusement for both children and the parents and teachers fortunate enough to have shared these stories with boys and girls. Ernest Shepard created unsurpassed illustrations of these lovable toys.

Many American children found the books by Walter Brooks about Freddy the Pig highly entertaining. Starting with *To and Again* (1927), Brooks created some twenty-five novels about the high jinks that occurred on Mr. Bean's farm. Some of these books were reissued in 1986. Robert Lawson's *Rabbit Hill* (1944) and *The Tough Winter* (1954) captured the feelings and thoughts of the little wild animals that lived in the Connecticut meadows, farms, and woods near his house. Though the animals speak, each one remains an individual representative of his or her particular species.

All these stories paved the way for the most loved animal fantasy to be written by an American, E. B. White's *Charlotte's Web* (1952). This book, with its multiple themes of friendship, loyalty, and the celebration of life, is now delighting new generations of children.

Other significant fantasy appearing in the twentieth century certainly must include J. R. R. Tolkien's *The Hobbit* (1937), first discovered by college students and only recently shared with children, and *The Little Prince* by Antoine de Saint-Exupéry, which also appealed primarily to adults. Translated in 1943 from the French, this tale of a pilot's encounter with a Little Prince who lived alone on a tiny planet no larger than a house is really a story of the importance of uniqueness and love.

Fantasy in the third quarter of the century emphasized serious themes. C. S. Lewis's *The Lion, the Witch, and the Wardrobe* (1950) was the first of seven books about the imaginary kingdom of Narnia. These popular fantasy adventure tales reflect the author's background as a theologian and carry strong messages about right and wrong. The term *high fantasy* came into use during the 1960s to describe books that took as their themes the battle between good and evil and other cosmic issues. The most memorable works of high fantasy in the United States were written by Madeleine L'Engle, Lloyd Alexander, Susan Cooper, and Ursula Le Guin. (See Chapter 7 for further discussion of their work.)

Poetry

The turn of the century saw the publication of the first work by a rare children's poet, Walter de la Mare's *Songs of Childhood* (1902). This was a poet who understood the importance and meaning of early childhood experiences. Leonard Clark says of him: "Walter de la Mare wrote as if he were a child himself, as if he were *revealing* his own childhood, though with the mature gifts of the authentic poet. His children are true to childhood."[31] His poems can be mysterious, humorous, or delightfully realistic. De la Mare was also a master of lyric imagery; his often anthologized "Silver" paints a picture of the beauty of a moonlit night. In 1913 his *Peacock Pie* brought readers new melodies, nursery rhymes, and poems of enchantment.

---

[31]Leonard Clark, *Walter de la Mare* (New York: Henry Z. Walck, 1961), p. 44.

Eleanor Farjeon, also English, was writing merry imaginative verse for children at the same time Walter de la Mare was creating his poetry. Her first published work was *Nursery Rhymes of London Town* (1916). *Joan's Door* was published ten years later and *Over the Garden Wall* in 1933. Many of these poems later appeared in a collection titled *Eleanor Farjeon's Poems for Children* (1931, 1951, 1984). We remember her for such poems as "Mrs. Peck Pigeon," "Tippetty Witchet," and "The Night Will Never Stay."

Still another Englishman brought joy and fun into the nursery with *When We Were Very Young* (1924) and *Now We Are Six* (1927). A. A. Milne could tell a rollicking story, as in "Bold Sir Brian" or "The King's Breakfast" or "Sneezles," or he could capture a child's imaginative play, as in "Lines or Squares" and "Binker."

In this country Rachel Field, Dorothy Aldis, and Aileen Fisher were interpreting the delight of the child's everyday world. Frances Frost and Elizabeth Coatsworth were writing lyrical poems about nature. Many of Coatsworth's were contained within her historical series of books beginning with *Away Goes Sally* (1934). The transition in children's poetry from the didactic to the descriptive, from moralizing to poems of fun and nonsense, had at last been achieved. No longer were poems *about* children; they were *for* children.

The 1930s and 1940s saw many collections of poetry selected especially for children from the works of well-known contemporary poets. These included Edna St. Vincent Millay's *Poems Selected for Young People* (1917), Vachel Lindsay's *Johnny Appleseed and Other Poems* (1928), Carl Sandburg's *Early Moon* (1930), Sara Teasdale's *Stars Tonight* (1930), Emily Dickinson's *Poems for Youth* (1934), Robert Frost's *Come In and Other Poems* (1943) and later his *You Come Too* (1959), Countee Cullen's *The Lost Zoo* (1940), and many others.

Hildegarde Hoyt Swift gave a poetic interpretation of the African American in her book *North Star Shining* (1947), illustrated with powerful pictures by Lynd Ward. The Pulitzer Prize–winning black poet Gwendolyn Brooks presented the poignant poems of *Bronzeville Boys and Girls* in 1956. Each of these poems carries a child's name as the title and is written as the voice of that child. Selected works by noted black poet Langston Hughes were published for young readers in *The Dream Keeper* (1962).

Two fine poets for children emerged during the early 1950s, Harry Behn and David McCord. Harry Behn's first book, *The Little Hill* (1949), consisted of thirty-three poems written for his three children. His other books of poetry ranged from pure nonsense to childhood memories to lyrical poems of nature. Often he drew on his memories of growing up as a child when Arizona was still a territory. David McCord's poetry is more playful and humorous than Behn's. McCord's verse includes poems of nature and everyday experiences and an interest in language and the various forms of poetry. His first book of poetry was *Far and Few: Rhymes of Never Was and Always Is* (1952).

In the 1960s, the publication of several collections of poems written by children reflected new interest in poetry. Richard Lewis published his first volume of children's writing from around the world, *Miracles* (1966). The same year the poignant poetry and drawings of the children kept at the Theresienstadt concentration camp between 1942 and 1944 were published under the title *. . . I Never Saw Another Butterfly*. The strident voices of the protest of the 1960s were heard in *Young Voices* (1971), an anthology of poems written by fourth-, fifth-, and sixth-grade children in response to a 1969 poetry search by Schaeffer and Mellor. Nancy Larrick published a collection of poems written by American youth titled *I Heard a Scream in the Street* (1970).

Specialized collections of poetry celebrating the uniqueness of African Americans, Native Americans, Eskimos, and others were published in the 1960s and 1970s. Arnold Adoff published two such collections in 1970: *I Am the Darker Brother: An Anthology of Modern Poems by Negro Americans* and *Black Out Loud: An Anthology of Modern Poems by Black Americans*. Hettie Jones edited *The Trees Stand Shining* (1971), a collection of Papago Indian poems, and John Bierhorst presented a scholarly collection of poems, chants, and prayers from Indian cultures of both North and South America, *In the Trail of the Wind: American Indian Poems and Ritual Orations* (1971). Knud Rasmussen was the first to record the virile poetry of the Eskimo in his *Beyond the High Hills: A Book of Eskimo Poems* in 1961. James Houston edited and illustrated *Songs of the Dream People: Chants and Images from the Indians and Eskimos of North America* (1972). Two books about the uniqueness of girls marked a new awareness of feminist perspectives. *Girls Can Too* (1972) was edited by Lee Bennett Hopkins; *Amelia Mixed the Mustard and Other Poems* (1975) was selected and edited by Evaline Ness.

With such increased interest in poetry for children, it seems particularly fitting that the National Council of Teachers of English established the first award for Excellence in Poetry for Children in 1977.

RESOURCES FOR TEACHING

LANDMARKS IN THE DEVELOPMENT OF BOOKS FOR CHILDREN

◆ **Before 1700**

Oral stories told by minstrels—Beowulf, King Arthur, ballads, etc.

c. 700	Question-and-answer form of instruction—Aldhelm
c. 1200	*Elucidarium*, Anselm
c. 1290	*Gesta Romanorum*,
1387	*Canterbury Tales*, Geoffrey Chaucer
c. 1440	Hornbooks developed
1477	*A Book of Curteseye* published by Caxton
1481	*Historye of Reynart the Foxe* published by Caxton
1484	*The Fables of Aesop* published by Caxton
1485	*Le Morte d'Arthur*, Malory
1548	*King Henry's Primer*
c. 1580s	Beginnings of chapbooks

◆ **Seventeenth century**

1646	*Spiritual Milk for Boston Babes . . .*, John Cotton
1659	*Orbis Pictus*, Johann Amos Comenius
1678	*The Pilgrim's Progress*, John Bunyan
c. 1686	*The New England Primer*
1697	*Histoires ou Contes du Temps Passé*, Charles Perrault

◆ **Eighteenth century**

c. 1706	*The Arabian Nights* translated into English
1715	*Divine and Moral Songs*, Isaac Watts
1719	*Robinson Crusoe*, Daniel Defoe
1726	*Gulliver's Travels*, Jonathan Swift
1729	Perrault's *Fairy Tales* translated into English
1744	*A Little Pretty Pocket-Book*, John Newbery
1765	*The History of Little Goody Two Shoes*, John Newbery, publisher
1771	*The New Lottery Book of Birds and Beasts*, Thomas Bewick
c. 1780	*Mother Goose's Melody* (may have been Newbery)
c. 1786	*Mother Goose's Melodies*, Isaiah Thomas, American publisher
1789	*Songs of Innocence*, William Blake

◆ **Nineteenth century**

1804	*Original Poems for Infant Minds*, Ann and Jane Taylor

LANDMARKS IN THE DEVELOPMENT OF BOOKS FOR CHILDREN (continued)

1807	*The Butterfly's Ball,* William Roscoe
1823	*A Visit from St. Nicholas,* Clement C. Moore
1823	*Grimm's Popular Stories,* translated by Edgar Taylor, illustrated by George Cruikshank
1846	*Book of Nonsense,* Edward Lear
1846	*Fairy Tales of Hans Christian Andersen,* translated by Mary Howitt
1848	*Struwwelpeter,* Heinrich Hoffman (English translation)
1861	*Seven Little Sisters Who Live on the Big Round Ball That Floats in the Air,* Jane Andrews
1865	*The House That Jack Built, Sing a Song of Sixpence,* illustrated by Walter Crane
1865	*Alice's Adventures in Wonderland,* Lewis Carroll, illustrated by John Tenniel
1865	*Hans Brinker, Or the Silver Skates,* Mary Mapes Dodge
1868	*Little Women,* Louisa May Alcott
1869	*Twenty Thousand Leagues Under the Sea,* Jules Verne
1871	*At the Back of the North Wind,* George MacDonald
1872	*Sing-Song,* Christina Rossetti
1873	*St. Nicholas Magazine* begun, Mary Mapes Dodge, editor
1876	*The Adventures of Tom Sawyer,* Mark Twain
1878	*Under the Window,* Kate Greenaway
1878	*The Diverting History of John Gilpin,* illustrated by Randolph Caldecott
1880	*The Peterkin Papers,* Lucretia Hale
1881	*Adventures of Pinocchio,* Carlo Collodi
1883	*Merry Adventures of Robin Hood,* adapted and illustrated by Howard Pyle
1883	*Treasure Island,* Robert Louis Stevenson
1883	*Uncle Remus Stories,* Joel Chandler Harris
1884	*Heidi,* Johanna Spyri, translated by Louise Brooks
1884	*Adventures of Huckleberry Finn,* Mark Twain
1885	*A Child's Garden of Verses,* Robert Louis Stevenson
1889	*The Blue Fairy Book,* Andrew Lang
1894	*The Jungle Book,* Rudyard Kipling
1897	*Joan of Arc,* Maurice Boutet de Monvel (English translation)
1898	*Wild Animals I Have Known,* Ernest Thompson Seton

♦ First half of the twentieth century

1900	*The Wizard of Oz,* L. Frank Baum
1901	*The Tale of Peter Rabbit,* Beatrix Potter
1902	*Songs of Childhood,* Walter de la Mare
1902	*Just So Stories,* Rudyard Kipling
1903	*Johnny Crow's Garden,* L. Leslie Brooke
1903	*The Call of the Wild,* Jack London
1903	*Rebecca of Sunnybrook Farm,* Kate Douglas Wiggin
1906	*Peter Pan in Kensington Gardens,* J. M. Barrie, illustrated by Arthur Rackham
1908	*The Wind in the Willows,* Kenneth Grahame, illustrated by Ernest Shepard
1910	*The Secret Garden,* Frances Hodgson Burnett
1910	*The Farm Book* and *Chicken World,* E. Boyd Smith
1921	*Here and Now Story Book,* Lucy Sprague Mitchell
1922	*Rootabaga Stories,* Carl Sandburg

LANDMARKS IN THE DEVELOPMENT OF BOOKS FOR CHILDREN (continued)

1922   Newbery Medal for "most distinguished book for children" established
1924   *When We Were Very Young*, A. A. Milne, illustrated by Ernest H. Shepard
1926   *Smoky, the Cow-Horse*, Will James
1926   *Winnie the Pooh*, A. A. Milne, illustrated by Ernest H. Shepard
1926   *Clever Bill*, William Nicholson
1928   *Millions of Cats*, Wanda Gág
1929   *Pelle's New Suit*, Elsa Beskow (English translation)
1930   *The Earth for Sam*, W. Maxwell Reed
1932   *What Whiskers Did*, Ruth Carroll
1932   *Little House in the Big Woods*, Laura Ingalls Wilder
1934   *The Little Auto*, Lois Lenski
1934   *Mary Poppins*, Pamela Travers
1935   *Caddie Woodlawn*, Carol Ryrie Brink
1936   *The Story of Ferdinand*, Munro Leaf, illustrated by Robert Lawson
1936   *Roller Skates*, Ruth Sawyer
1937   *And to Think That I Saw It on Mulberry Street*, Dr. Seuss
1937   *The Hobbit*, J. R. R. Tolkien
1938   Caldecott Medal for "most distinguished picture book for children" established
1939   *Madeline*, Ludwig Bemelmans
1939   *The Noisy Book*, Margaret Wise Brown, illustrated by Roger Duvoisin
1939   *Mike Mulligan and His Steam Shovel*, Virginia Lee Burton
1940   *The Moffats*, Eleanor Estes
1940   *Blue Willow*, Doris Gates
1941   *Make Way for Ducklings*, Robert McCloskey
1941   *Paddle to the Sea*, Holling C. Holling
1941   *George Washington's World*, Genevieve Foster
1941   *In My Mother's House*, Ann Nolan Clark
1941   *Curious George*, H. A. Rey
1942   *The Little House*, Virginia Lee Burton
1943   *Johnny Tremain*, Esther Forbes
1943   *Homer Price*, Robert McCloskey
1944   *Rabbit Hill*, Robert Lawson
1944   *The Hundred Dresses*, Eleanor Estes, illustrated by Louis Slobodkin
1945   *Two Is a Team*, Lorraine and Jerrold Beim, illustrated by Ernest Crichlow
1945   *Call Me Charley*, Jesse Jackson
1946   *Bright April*, Marguerite de Angeli
1947   *Stone Soup*, Marcia Brown
1947   *White Snow, Bright Snow*, Alvin Tresselt, illustrated by Roger Duvoisin
1947   *Judy's Journey*, Lois Lenski
1947   *The Twenty-One Balloons*, William Péne du Bois
◆ Second half of the twentieth century
1952   *A Hole Is to Dig*, Ruth Krauss, illustrated by Maurice Sendak
1952   *Charlotte's Web*, E. B. White, illustrated by Garth Williams

RESOURCES FOR TEACHING

LANDMARKS IN THE DEVELOPMENT OF BOOKS FOR CHILDREN (continued)

1952	*Anne Frank: The Diary of a Young Girl*, Anne Frank
1956	*Bronzeville Boys and Girls*, Gwendolyn Brooks
1957	*The Cat in the Hat*, Dr. Seuss
1959	*Tom's Midnight Garden*, Philippa Pearce
1962	*A Wrinkle in Time*, Madeleine L'Engle
1962	*The Snowy Day*, Ezra Jack Keats
1963	*Where the Wild Things Are*, Maurice Sendak
1964	*Harriet the Spy*, Louise Fitzhugh
1965	*Dorp Dead*, Julia Cunningham
1966	Mildred L. Batchhelder Award established for most oustanding translated book
1969	Coretta Scott King Award established for best African-American children's literature.
1969	*Stevie*, John Steptoe
1969	*Where the Lilies Bloom*, Vera and Bill Cleaver
1970	*Are You There God? It's Me, Margaret*, Judy Blume
1970	*In the Night Kitchen*, Maurice Sendak
1971	*Journey to Topaz*, Yoshiko Uchida, illustrated by Donald Carrick
1974	*Where the Sidewalk Ends*, Shel Silverstein
1974	*My Brother Sam Is Dead*, James and Christopher Collier
1974	*The Blanket*, John Burningham
1975	*M. C. Higgins the Great*, Virginia Hamilton
1976	*Why Mosquitoes Buzz in People's Ears*, retold by Verna Aardema, illustrated by Leo and Diane Dillon
1977	Excellence in Poetry for Children Award established by National Council of Teachers of English
1980	*Hiroshima No Pika*, Toshi Maruki
1982	*A Visit to William Blake's Inn*, Nancy Willard, illustrated by Alice and Martin Provensen
1982	*Yeh-Shen: A Cinderella Story from China*, Ai-Ling Louie, illustrated by Ed Young
1985	*The Polar Express*, Chris Van Allsburg
1986	*The Magic School Bus at the Waterworks*, Joanna Cole, illustrated by Bruce Degan
1986	*Sarah, Plain and Tall*, Patricia MacLachlan
1987	*Lincoln: A Photobiography*, Russell Freedman
1987	*Mufaro's Beautiful Daughters: An African Tale*, John Steptoe
1988	*Stringbean's Trip to the Shining Sea*, Vera B. Williams, illustrated by Vera B. and Jennifer Williams
1990	*Baseball in April and Other Stories*, Gary Soto
1990	*Orbis Pictus* Award for outstanding children's nonfiction established by National Council of Teachers of English
1990	*Black and White*, David Macaulay
1991	*Maniac Magee*, Jerry Spinelli
1991	*The Wall*, Eve Bunting, illustrated by Ronald Himler
1992	*Encounter*, Jane Yolen, illustrated by David Shannon

Realistic Fiction

One characteristic of books in the past was how long they stayed in print and were read by generations of children. In the beginning of the twentieth century children continued to derive pleasure from *Little Women* (1868) and the other Alcott books, Dodge's *Hans Brinker, Or the Silver Skates* (1865), Spyri's *Heidi* (1884), all the Frances Hodgson Burnett books, including *Little Lord Fauntleroy* (1886), *The Little Princess* (1905), and *The Secret Garden* (1910). Many of these titles continue to bring pleasure to children today.

Perhaps the success of the orphaned Little Princess accounted for the number of stories about orphans. L. M. Montgomery wrote the very popular story *Anne of Green Gables* (1908) about a young orphan girl living on Prince Edward Island in Canada. Seven sequels covered Anne's growing up, her adulthood, and her children. Montgomery also wrote *Emily of New Moon* (1923), the story of an orphan who had to draw straws to see which of the family relations would take her. Books were never written in the first person at this time, but Emily's letters to her dead father and her journal allowed the reader to enter into her thoughts and feelings in a way that anticipated the many first-person stories of contemporary children's books. Jean Webster's story of *Daddy-Long-Legs* (1912) is also a story of an orphan and her benefactor. *Pollyanna* (1913) by Eleanor H. Porter was another popular story of an orphan who must learn to live with two disagreeable spinster aunts. Her unfailingly optimistic way of coping made her name last longer than her story. While Dorothy Canfield's *Understood Betsy* (1917) was not an orphan, she was a sickly city child sent to live with relatives on a Vermont farm in order to regain her health. Lucinda of *Roller Skates* (1936) was not an orphan either but was left with her teacher and sister while her father and mother went abroad for a year in the late 1890s. Lucinda had a gloriously free year to explore New York on her roller skates. She made friends with everyone she met—the fruit vendor, the policeman, the hansom cab driver, and Uncle Earle. Lucinda was an unforgettable character who loved life and people. Ruth Sawyer won the Newbery award for this book in 1937.

Kate Douglas Wiggin's *Rebecca of Sunnybrook Farm* (1903) epitomizes the happy family stories that were characteristic of the first half of the century. For younger children, Carolyn Haywood began her many Betsy and Eddie stories in 1939 with *B Is for Betsy;* these stories tell of simple everyday doings of children at school and home. In *Thimble Summer* (1938) Elizabeth Enright told an entertaining family story set on a Wisconsin farm. Enright's *The Saturdays* (1941) was the first of several stories capturing the joyous life of the four children of the Melendy family. In three books, *The Moffats* (1941), *The Middle Moffats* (1942), and *Rufus M* (1943), Eleanor Estes detailed the delights of growing up in West Haven, Connecticut. The four children, Jane, Rufus, Sylvie, and Joey, are clearly realized as individuals and grow up in ways consistent with their characters. Sydney Taylor's *All-of-a-Kind Family* (1955) and its sequels presented the adventures of five Jewish girls growing up on New York's Lower East Side.

Two humorous stories appeared at this time: Robert McCloskey's classic tale of *Homer Price* (1943) and his amusing adventures in Centerburg and Beverly Cleary's *Henry Huggins* (1950). Both centered around all-American boys growing up in small towns, and they have remained popular with children for half a century.

Not all realistic fiction told happy or humorous tales of growing up in mainstream America. Realistic fiction often reflected war, depression, and contemporary social problems. As adults became more aware of various ethnic and regional groups in our nation, children's books also reflected this interest. Lois Lenski pioneered in presenting authentic, detailed descriptions of life in specific regions of the United States. By living in the community, observing the customs of the people, and listening to their stories, she was able to produce a significant record of American life from the 1940s into the 1960s. Her first book, *Bayou Suzette* (1943), was set in the Louisiana bayou country; *Strawberry Girl* (1945), which won the Newbery Medal, told of life among the Florida Crackers. *Judy's Journey* (1947), her most forceful book, concerned the plight of the migratory workers. Doris Gates also dramatized the problems of the migratory worker in her classic

TEACHING FEATURE

STUDYING BOOKS OF THE PAST

Children in the fourth grade at the Martin Luther King, Jr., Laboratory School in Evanston, Illinois, were studying the past through the history of their families. Their teacher, Barbara Friedberg, shared books with them like *Miss Rumphius* by Barbara Cooney, *When I Was Young in the Mountains* by Cynthia Rylant, *Three Names* and *Sarah, Plain and Tall* both by Patricia MacLachlan, and *The Night Journey* by Kathryn Lasky.

Together the teacher and children developed questions they could ask their parents or grandparents in an interview or letter. Here are some of the questions they included on their lists:

What were their favorite foods as children?
What did they do on their birthdays or special days?
Where did they live as children?
What did they remember about their schools?
What were their favorite books to read?
What historic days do they remember?

The students made graphs and charts to depict what they found out. Some children, remembering the story of the samovar that the family saved in *The Night Journey*, asked their parents what was the oldest thing they had in their homes that had belonged to the family.

Frequently, the oldest things were books. Several children brought in the favorite children's books of both their parents and grandparents. They were excited to find out their grandparents had read and enjoyed *The Secret Garden* by Frances Hodgson Burnett and *Little Women* by Louisa May Alcott. The children made a display of the old editions compared with their new editions. They also exhibited some of the textbooks that were used for reading instruction including an old *McGuffey Reader* belonging to a great-grandparent, several *Elson Readers* that a grandmother had in her basement, and the "Dick and Jane" readers of their parents.

Dating and labeling these books for display helped the students see how books had changed over the years. They became aware of how many more books they had than their grandparents, for example. But probably the greatest value of this focus unit was the discussions that took place between family members recounting the traditions and excitement of the "olden days."

Barbara Friedberg
Martin Luther King, Jr. Laboratory School

story *Blue Willow* (1940), named after the family's one prized possession, a blue willow plate. Eleanor Estes was one of the first to write about poverty and children's interrelationships in their closed society. Her book *The Hundred Dresses* (1944) enabled teachers to undertake and guide frank discussions of the problem of being "different."

Until the 1950s and 1960s very few books portrayed African Americans or other racial minorities. Books that did portray blacks showed stereotypes—the bandana-wearing fat mammy and the kinky-haired, thick-lipped "funny" boy. This stereotype was epitomized in the Nicodemus series written by Inez Hogan in the late 1930s with such titles as *Nicodemus and the Gang* (1939). The jacket of this book quotes part of a *New York Herald Tribune* review that said: "A story that will get itself remembered when some longer and louder ones are forgotten." Fortunately, Nicodemus and his gang, with their stereotyped names and exaggerated black dialect, have been forgotten. African-American poet Arna Bontemps drew on authentic language patterns of the rural South in *You Can't Pet a Possum* (1934) and *Sad-Faced Boy* (1937). Unfortunately, his work has also been largely forgotten.[32]

The segregation of blacks was clearly shown in *Araminta* (1935) by Eva Knox Evans and the photographic essay *Tobe* (1939) by Stella Sharpe. It was nearly ten years later that blacks and whites were shown participating in activities together. The theme of *Two Is a Team* (1945) by the Beims is revealed in both the title and the action as a black and a white boy play together. Prejudice was openly discussed for the first time in Jesse Jackson's *Call Me Charley* (1945) and Marguerite de Angeli's *Bright April* (1946).

Mary Jane (1959) by Dorothy Sterling, *The Empty Schoolhouse* (1965) by Natalie Carlson, and *Patricia Crosses Town* (1965) by Betty Baum discussed the new social problems caused by school integration. By the mid-1960s, a few books showed black characters in the illustrations, but

did not mention race in the text. Examples included *The Snowy Day* (1962) by Ezra Jack Keats, *Mississippi Possum* (1965) by Miska Miles, and Louisa Shotwell's *Roosevelt Grady* (1963). In the 1970s such books were criticized for "whitewashing" blacks and attempting to make everyone the same. Books such as *Zeely* (1967) by Virginia Hamilton and *Stevie* (1969) by John Steptoe, both written by black authors, captured something of the special pride of the black experience in children's literature.

M. C. Higgins the Great by Virginia Hamilton, a black author, won the Newbery award for distinguished writing in 1975. Two years later, *Roll of Thunder, Hear My Cry* by Mildred D. Taylor, another fine black author, won the award. Books by and about African Americans had at long last received recognition. However, even today the

John Steptoe's *Stevie* was one of the first picture books to present an African-American family through an insider's eyes. It was published before this gifted author/illustrator was 20 years old.

❧ ❧ ❧

[32]See Violet J. Harris, "From Little Black Sambo to Popo and Fifina: Arna Bontemps and the Creation of African-American Children's Literature," *The Lion and the Unicorn*, vol. 14 (June 1990), pp. 108–127.

number of black authors is small when compared to the black population of this country.

The "new freedoms" of the 1960s were reflected in both adult and children's books. The so-called new realism in children's literature can probably be dated from the publication of *Harriet the Spy* (1964) by Louise Fitzhugh. Harriet is an 11-year-old antiheroine who keeps a notebook in which she records with brutal honesty her impressions of her family, friends, and New York neighborhood characters. Unlike Lucinda, who made friends with the people she met in *Roller Skates*, Harriet spies on them. Harriet's parents are psychologically absent, being too engrossed in their own affairs to be overly concerned about their daughter's activities. Children readily identified with Harriet, for she had the courage to think *and* say the things they didn't dare to say, including swearing. Following *Harriet*'s breakthrough, many long-standing taboos in children's literature came tumbling down.

Vera and Bill Cleaver wrote about death and suicide in *Where the Lilies Bloom* (1969) and *Grover* (1970); alcoholism and homosexuality are described in *I'll Get There, It Better Be Worth the Trip* (1969) by John Donovan; and *(George)* (1970) by E. L. Konigsburg includes divorced parents, a psychologically disturbed child, and LSD. In Judy Blume's popular novel *Are You There God? It's Me, Margaret* (1970), Margaret's vague interest in religion is overshadowed by the more immediate concern of when she will start menstruating. *Mom, the Wolfman and Me* (1972) by Norma Klein is the candid story of a young girl's fear that her single mother will get married. *Deenie* (1973) by Judy Blume is primarily the story of a beautiful girl who discovers she must wear a back brace for four years. This story contains several references to masturbation. Even picture books reflected the impact of this new freedom. Mickey falls out of bed and out of his clothes in Maurice Sendak's *In the Night Kitchen* (1970). In *My Special Best Words* (1974) by John Steptoe, bodily functions are discussed naturally, as a slightly older sister tries to toilet train her younger brother.

The literature published for the child's expanding world reflected the changes and challenges of life in the mid-twentieth century. Just as adult literature mirrored the disillusionment of depression, wars, and materialism by becoming more sordid, sensational, and psychological, children's literature became more frank and honest, portraying situations like war, drugs, divorce, abortion, sex, and homosexuality. No longer were children protected by stories of happy families. Rather it was felt that children would develop coping behaviors as they read about others who had survived similar problems.

All these problems are legitimate concerns of childhood. They have always existed, but only in the last twenty-five years have they been openly and honestly written about in books for children. Further discussion of realism in children's literature is in Chapter 9.

An International Literature for Children

An exciting development in children's literature was the rise of international interest in children's books during the years after World War II. This was indicated by an increased flow of children's books between countries. In 1950 *Pippi Longstocking* by the Swedish author Astrid Lindgren arrived in our country and was an immediate success. This was the beginning of many such exchanges.

The Mildred L. Batchelder Award for the most outstanding translated children's book originally published abroad and then published in the United States was established in 1966 by the Association for Library Service to Children of the American Library Association. It honored their retiring executive secretary, who had worked tirelessly for the exchange of books. This award has served as an impetus in promoting the translation of fine children's books from abroad. Such excellent books as *Don't Take Teddy* (1967) by the Norwegian writer Friis-Baastad; *Friedrich* (1970) by Hans Richter of Germany; and *Hiroshima No Pika* (1980) by Toshi Maruki of Japan have been the recipients of this award.

Another indicator of the growing internationalism of children's literature during the 1950s was the number of congresses, book fairs, and exhibitions of children's books that were held around the world. The first general assembly of the International Board on Books for Young People (IBBY) was held in 1953. Jella Lepman, founder of IBBY, maintained that the organization should serve as a world conscience for international children's books and call attention to the best in the field by awarding international prizes. Consequently, IBBY awarded its first Hans Christian Andersen Medal to Eleanor Farjeon in 1956. In 1966 IBBY decided to extend the award to include a medal for the most outstanding artist as well as author of children's books. Alois Carigiet was the first artist to receive this award. Then, in 1967, Jella Lepman created the annual International Children's Book Day, which was appropriately established on April 2, the birthday of Hans Christian Andersen. The IBBY congresses meet every other year.

In 1967 the Biennale of Illustrations in Bratislava, Czechoslovakia (BIB), held its first exhibition. It is now scheduled to meet in the odd-numbered years, alternating with the IBBY congress. Other international displays include the annual Frankfurt Book Fair in September of each year and the Bologna Children's Book Fair in April.

The 1950s and the 1960s, then, saw the formation of international organizations for the exchange and appreciation of children's books throughout the world. These developments paved the way for UNESCO to designate 1972 as International Book Year. Almost 250 years from the time Newbery first conceived of the idea of a literature especially for children's enjoyment, it had achieved worldwide recognition. Literature for children has indeed come of age.

RECENT TRENDS IN CHILDREN'S BOOKS

Children's Books: Big Business

At the present time the publication and distribution of juvenile books comprises a big business. Children's book sales quadrupled in a decade, skyrocketing to a billion dollars in 1990. The number of juveniles published in 1990 was approximately twenty times the number published in 1880. Enormous growth in children's book publishing occurred in the late 1980s.

These statistics show the increased rate of growth in publication of juveniles for over a century.

JUVENILES PUBLISHED[33]	
1880	270
1890	408
1900	527
1910	1,010
1920	477
1930	933
1940	984
1950	1,059
1960	1,725
1970	2,640
1980	2,895
1990	5,000

If paperback books are included in the count, more than 10,977 children's books were published in the United States in 1990. Paperback books account for an estimated one-third of sales. Recent years have seen a dramatic increase in both high-quality and inferior paperbacks for children. Individual publishing houses are selecting some of the best of their previously published titles for reissue in paperback form. Increasingly, publishers are bringing out new titles in hardcover and paperback simultaneously. Some have instituted new divisions devoted exclusively to paperbacks. In addition, many paperback houses have started commissioning their own original books to be published directly in paperback. Some of these originals qualify as imaginative writing, but many of them are written to formula. Reminiscent of the many series churned out by the Stratemeyer Syndicate beginning in 1885, these books promise to be almost as popular. Three years after the Baby-Sitter's Club series was launched, there were already some 11 million

[33]The Bowker Annual of Library and Book Trade Information (New York: Bowker, 1983, 1989). The 1990 figure was furnished by the Children's Book Council, with the caution that all such figures should be treated as approximate.

copies of these books in print, and by 1991 the series had sold over 41 million copies.[34]

Another factor hidden in the statistics is the large number of titles that go out of print each year. While it appears that many more books are being published, title turnover is far greater today. The life of a modern book is seldom more than 5 years in contrast to the 10- to 20-year life span of books in the mid-twentieth century, or in the case of the very early books, a 200-year life span. However, certain books do stay in print and continue to sell and sell. Judy Blume's publishers maintain that all her books have sold over 25 million copies. Shel Silverstein's poetry books have also sold over 25 million copies. The *Bowker Annual*[35] lists nearly fifty hardcover children's books that had sold over 750,000 copies by 1985. Heading the list is Beatrix Potter's *Tale of Peter Rabbit*, with 8 million copies; E. B. White's *Charlotte's Web* had sold over 1.5 million copies and *Where the Wild Things Are* by Maurice Sendak had sold 1 million hardback copies. Books by Dr. Seuss, Marguerite Henry, and Laura Ingalls Wilder are among other titles in this rarefied company.

The health of children's literature can also be seen by the increasing number of children's book stores and children's book fairs. Ten years ago the number of independent children's bookstores in the United States was less than a dozen or so; today the number is close to 400, not including the children's departments of larger bookstores and chains. Unfortunately, many large chain stores buy the cheaper books produced for mass marketing. This also applies to the jobbers whose entire business is supplying book fairs. Generally, book fairs sponsored by independent stores are more responsive to the schools' needs and provide better quality books.

Another trend in publishing is the increased number of mergers between publishing houses

and big business conglomerates. Few independently owned publishing companies are left today. A publishing company owned by a large conglomerate must show a profit; it is measured against the success of other companies in the corporation, most of which have nothing to do with publishing. Many of these changes began in the late 1970s when the cutback in federal assistance to education was felt in schools throughout the United States. In order to counteract the loss of school sales, publishers put more emphasis on the trade book market than ever before. In spite of the additional mergers and company changes needed to meet the economic pressures of the 1980s, children's book publishing became the strongest growth area in all of publishing by 1990.

New Books for New Markets

As publishers f the 1980s sought continued profits, they searched for new markets. As a result of the many research studies showing the value of reading aloud to young children and the interest of baby boomers in their new offspring, publishers discovered the infant market. Many companies are producing their own line of books for babies and toddlers. Helen Oxenbury's series of board books titled *Friends, Working, Playing, Dressing,* and *Family,* all published in 1981, were the first to portray the infant with his or her concerns and accomplishments. Her husband, John Burningham, had done the same thing for toddlers in his little books *The Blanket* and *The Cupboard,* first published in England in 1974. The creation of these new books for the very young, plus the publication of such popular titles as Jim Trelease's *The New Read-Aloud Handbook* (1989), contributed to a new awareness among conscientious parents of the value of reading aloud to youngsters.

Wordless books ("wordless" although many of them do contain some print in the introduction or afterword) first made their appearance in 1932 with *What Whiskers Did* by Ruth Carroll. This story of the adventures of a little Scottie dog was reprinted in 1965, when there was a greater emphasis on the importance of "reading pictures" in preparation for learning to read. The wordless

[34]N. R. Kleinfield, "Children's Books: Inside the Baby-Sitters Club," *New York Times Book Review* (June 11, 1989), p. 42; Ellen Creager, "A Black Mark for Children's Books," *Chicago Tribune* (May 15, 1991), pp. 1, 7.
[35]*The Bowker Annual of Library and Book Trade Information* (New York: Bowker, 1985).

books caught on, and the 1960s and 1970s saw a flood of them. Some of them, such as Mercer Mayer's *A Boy a Dog and a Frog* (1967) series, were amusing cartoon sequences; others reached a fine artistic level, such as *The Snowman* (1978) by Raymond Briggs. Wordless books are no longer only for beginning readers—watch adults and older children pore over *Anno's Journey* (1978) by Mitsumasa Anno, David Wiesner's Caldecott winner, *Tuesday* (1991), or *Window* (1991) by Jeannie Baker.

Some of today's "new" books are old books revisited. Toy books, including pop-up books and books with revolving pictures, were quite the vogue in the late Victorian era of the 1890s. First printed in Germany, they became too costly to be continued. Now cheaper to produce, reissues of books by Ernest Nister, such as *The Great Panorama Picture Book* (1895, 1982), and *The Animals' Picnic* (1988) are once again delighting children. Unlike the Victorian ones, modern pop-ups tell a continuous story like Brown's *Goodnight Moon Room* (1984) and Barbara Cooney's *Peter and the Wolf* (1986). Unless very well designed and sturdy, these manipulative books are more appropriate for the entertainment of one child than for library use.

In general, reissues and new editions of old favorites appeal to adult book buyers because they are familiar. Today's editions of classic stories often have the added attraction of appearing with fresh illustrations. Recently even a few criti-

Ernest Nister's bicycling bears are on their way to *The Animals' Picnic* in one of today's numerous reissues of Victorian pop-up books.

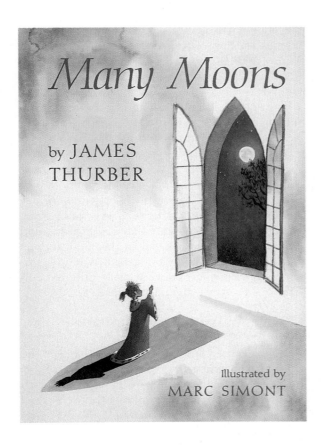

James Thurber's modern fairy tale, *Many Moons*, has been illustrated by two different winners of the Caldecott Medal. The lofty arch shapes on the cover of Marc Simont's new version emphasize the princess's yearning for the unattainable moon.

🦋 🦋 🦋

cally acclaimed picture books such as Alvin Tresselt's *Wake Up, City!* (1957, 1989) have been reillustrated. Although Louis Slobodkin won the Caldecott Medal for his pictures in James Thurber's *Many Moons* (1943), the 1990 version of this book is newly illustrated by Marc Simont, another Caldecott winner.

Another trend in the 1980s was the development of the "choose-your-own-ending" stories, which ask readers to help in creating plots by selecting various alternatives that then lead to different conclusions. The format meets the demands of today's children for quick action and participation. Written on many reading levels, there are choose-your-own mysteries, westerns,

and romances, with dozens of books in each series. Although the popularity of these books has diminished, other types of series books have multiplied and found an eager audience.

Walt Disney was the first to establish movie-related books, rewriting old classics to suit himself and titling them *Walt Disney's Cinderella*, for example. It is particularly unfortunate when this practice results in the distortion of a book noted for its literary merit. Robert O'Brien's *Mrs. Frisby and the Rats of NIMH* (1971), a Newbery winner, appeared on the screen and then in book form as *The Secret of NIMH*. The focus of the story is changed, and even "Mrs. Brisby's" attempt to save her son Timothy's life relies on magic rather than her own bravery, as in O'Brien's original book. A real concern is that children who read these spin-off books are under the impression that they have read the story as it was originally conceived—which is not true.

Another trend is the publication of the print book as a secondary form, a book based on a popular television show, film, or even video game. Frequently the result of this market-oriented approach to publishing is the packaging of cheaply produced books with other items such as stuffed animals, T-shirts, or greeting cards. Quality writing is seldom part of such a package.

Shifts in Publishing Emphases

One of the most notable trends in children's books today is the dominance of picture storybooks and picture-book formats. One survey showed that three picture-dependent categories—books for babies and toddlers, picture books, and books for young readers—accounted for nearly two-thirds of all purchases of children's books in bookstores.[36] Many publishers' catalogs show that a majority of their new titles are picture storybooks or profusely illustrated books. Also, editors report that it is typical to print many more copies of a new picture book than of a novel because picture storybooks are in far greater demand.

This emphasis on the visual is also evident in the tremendous increase in information books

[36]*Publishers' Weekly*, November 30, 1990.

published. It seems likely that the eye appeal of books like David Macaulay's *The Way Things Work* (1988) or the *Eyewitness* series has a lot to do with their success. Along with the increase in number of high-quality nonfiction books has come increased recognition of their place as literature. Russell Freedman's *Lincoln: A Photobiography* (1987) was a Newbery award winner, and many other nonfiction titles are earning critical acclaim.

The publication of poetry books also enjoyed a growth spurt in recent years. Like informational books, most of these new titles, both collections and single poems in book form, feature attractive illustrations that claim as much attention as the words. The production of new editions of folk and fairy tales, which rolled rapidly off the presses through the 1970s and early 1980s, has slowed somewhat. At the same time, myths, tall tales, and other lesser known forms of traditional literature seem to be gaining ground, with titles such as Leonard Everett Fisher's *Jason and the Golden Fleece* (1990), Steven Kellogg's *Johnny Appleseed* (1988), and Miriam Chaikin's *Exodus* (1987).

In books for middle-grade readers, recent years have seen greater emphasis on contemporary realistic fiction than on fantasy, historical fiction, or biography. While there are signs of revitalization in these genres, realism remains a clear favorite. The immensely popular series books such as The Baby-Sitters Club, Sweet Valley Twins, and even the Kids of Polk Street School and the Pee Wee Scouts for younger readers are marketed directly to their audiences through paperback book clubs and bookstores. Hardcover titles cater to this "more of the same" impulse in middle-grade readers by providing many sequels such as Betsy Byars's four books about Bingo Brown and James Howe's several Sebastian Barth mysteries. In general the content of realistic fiction has moved away from the narrowly focused "problem novel" of the 1960s and 1970s. The lighter fiction for elementary school readers today seems more innocent, and the serious fiction more realistically balanced, with characters less prone to despair than

the books of a decade or two ago.[37] Many sober themes remain, of course. Environmental issues were especially popular as the 1990s began, a trend seen in picture storybooks as well as longer fiction.

The return of many classic titles reflected the shift of the 1980s toward conservative values as well as a concern that children should not miss out on their literary heritage. It is a joy to have such books as *Treasure Island* and *Robinson Crusoe* back in print with their handsome N. C. Wyeth illustrations and to see new editions of *The Velveteen Rabbit* and others. At the same time, most of these books are available in libraries, and costly new editions may mean that new authors and artists are not being published. We can legitimately ask the question: How many different editions of *The Secret Garden* do we need?

Changes in Writing and Illustration

Although conservative trends have influenced the content of recent books, writers and illustrators today have great freedom to experiment with style and format. For years it was assumed that all books for children should be told in the third person, past tense; children were not supposed to like introspective first-person accounts. The recognition and popularity of such books as *Meet the Austins* (1960) by Madeleine L'Engle and Judy Blume's *Are You There God? It's Me, Margaret* (1970) certainly put an end to this myth. A first-person telling allows the author to reveal the thoughts and feelings of the main character, to give the reader a kind of "you are there" feeling. Even historical fiction and biography have assumed this point of view in such books as *My Brother Sam Is Dead* (1974) by the Colliers and the biography *I'm Deborah Sampson* (1977) by Patricia Clapp. First-person tellings are now used for picture storybooks, too, such as Riki Levinson's *I Go with My Family to Grandma's* (1986). Some authors have also begun to make greater use of the present tense. Patricia MacLachlan's *The Facts and Fictions of Minna Pratt* (1988) and Crescent Dragonwagon's *Winter Holding Spring* (1990) both demonstrate how this device gives a sense of immediacy and intimate participation in the character's experience.

[37]See Liz Rosenberg, "It's All Right to Be Innocent Again," *New York Times Book Review*, May 21, 1989, p. 46.

Another trend in writing may be seen in the books told from various points of view. Mary Stolz wrote two books about the same events but told from the different protagonists' points of view: *A Dog on Barkham Street* (1960, 1985) and *The Bully on Barkham Street* (1963, 1985). Betsy Byars used two different points of view to dramatize Clara's rescue at sea in *The Animal, the Vegetable & John D. Jones* (1982). *The True Story of the 3 Little Pigs as told by A. Wolf* (1989) by Jon Scieszka is a picture storybook that offers an unusual and very funny point of view. The use of shifting points of view, which can heighten the suspense of a story, serves the same purposes as flashbacks, cut-ins, and other devices on TV and in films. Avi's *Nothing but the Truth* (1991), a novel for older readers, uses this technique throughout.

Other experimentation in writing includes the telling of stories through letters and journals. Such an approach is not necessarily new. In *Little Women* (1868) Alcott included a copy of the "Pickwick Portfolio," a newspaper the four sisters created, a round-robin story they all composed, many letters, and a copy of Amy's "will." The Newbery award winner *A Gathering of Days* (1979) by Joan Blos consists of imaginary entries from a New England girl's diary for the years 1830–1832. Beverly Cleary won the Newbery award in 1984 for her story *Dear Mr. Henshaw*, which consists mostly of a boy's letters to his favorite author and later of entries in his own journal. Cleary uses this form with skill and imagination to tell the story of a child of divorce who is living with his mother but longing for his truck driver father. *Stringbean's Trip to the Shining Sea* (1988) by Vera Williams tells its story through the words and pictures on a sequence of postcards.

As authors tell stories in intriguing new ways, they may create books that are hard to classify according to traditional definitions of genre. For instance, several recent books have combined fantasy with historical fiction. In *A Chance Child* (1978) Jill Paton Walsh tells the story of Creep, an abused child of the twentieth century who drifts down a canal in an old rusty boat and passes from his time to that of England during the Industrial Revolution. *The Root Cellar* (1983) by Janet Lunn provides a mixture of modern-day living and the Civil War era. *The Devil's Arithmetic* (1988) by Jane

Even page layouts and the relationship of pictures to print may be unconventional in today's picture books, such as *The Magic School Bus Inside the Human Body*.

Illustration by Bruce Degen, text by Joanna Cole.

Yolen takes a contemporary Jewish girl bored with her family's emphasis on their heritage and thrusts her back in time into a Polish village during World War II. However, Hannah does not lose the knowledge of her own time and is able to anticipate her own fate as she relives the heroic story of her namesake. All these books use an element of fantasy to unite the past with the present and to capture contemporary children's interest in an earlier time.

Current books cross conventional genre lines in other ways as well. For instance, the boundaries between fact and fiction are crossed and recrossed by Joanna Cole and Bruce Degen in *The Magic School Bus Inside the Human Body* (1989). In this informational adventure, Ms. Frizzle takes her young students on a fantasy field trip through the circulatory system of one of their classmates and brings them home again to an everyday world of group projects and science reports. Blends of story and information for younger children are offered in Lois Ehlert's *Feathers for Lunch* (1990) and other concept books. Books such as this use a playful approach to draw readers into a content topic.

Illustrators have also departed from old notions about what is appropriate for a children's book.

Earlier in this century, for instance, experts advised against photography in children's books. Photos were not clear enough or appealing enough for a young audience. Now, thanks to improved quality of reproduction and rising standards of artistry, informational books like Ken Robbins's *A Flower Grows* (1990) offer photos that are clear and aesthetically satisfying. Technological advances have also lifted restrictions and encouraged experimentation with new tools for picture making. Daniel Pinkwater illustrated his story, *The Muffin Fiend* (1986), on his Macintosh computer. Alan Lee's illustrations for *The Mirrorstone* (1986) by Michael Palin make use of holography. Jeannie Baker is able to use textured materials from the natural environment in her collage pictures for books like *Where the Forest Meets the Sea* (1988) and *Window* (1991) because cameras, scanners, and other equipment which can now efficiently reproduce illustrations created in any medium, have replaced the laborious hand preparation of color separations for the printer.

Although new uses of media may be the most noticeable change in illustrations, artists have also established a more important role for the visual element in telling stories. In picture storybooks, some artists are creating more and more complex interactions between pictures and print, as David Macaulay does with the four intertwined, separately illustrated threads of story in his Caldecott winner, *Black and White* (1990). Other generously illustrated books of the past decade or so stretch our ideas about what constitutes a picture storybook. Shirley Hughes intersperses cartoon-fomat sequences in a chunky chapter book for young readers, *Chips and Jessie* (1986). Patricia Lauber's text for *Seeing Earth from Space* (1990) serves as captions for the stunning scientific photographs it accompanies. Although these books can be classified as realistic fiction and nonfiction, they are also picturebooks in their own ways.

Increased Use in Schools

A noteworthy trend of the past several years is the growing use of children's trade books in classrooms—for reading instruction, integrated language arts programs, and a variety of uses across the curriculum. The whole language movement and new understandings about children's literacy learning have brought the use of real literature to the classrooms of many schools. Unlike the 1960s this is not a trend nurtured by government funds (which are largely unavailable now), but by the grass-roots interest of teachers and the encouragement of professional associations.

A survey by the Association of American Publishers in 1989–1990 identified twenty states, including California, New York, and Texas, as being especially active in the use of trade books to teach elementary reading. In California with its well-publicized California Reading Initiative, using literature to teach reading has become an official mandate. Other state departments of education strongly support literature in the classroom. The actual extent of the use of children's books in instructional programs across the country is difficult to estimate, however, because many teachers use trade books on an individual basis rather than as part of a recognized program. Another complicating factor is that teachers and supervisors often use the same terminology to describe widely different practices.

The disturbing side of this trend is that some instructional programs use literature without regard for its imaginative and aesthetic characteristics. Some stories selected for "literature-based" basal texts are revised and adapted in ways that destroy their original merits.[38] In other instances, students read "real" books, but still use the same skill and drill activities that teachers were trying to avoid by switching from the basal textbooks. Uses of literature that ruin children's enjoyment of good books are a real disservice to children and to literature.

Children's books are now also part of many community literacy programs. During the 1980s, problems of illiteracy in the United States were widely acknowledged. Government agencies with an eye to tight budgets worked to involve corporations and private foundations in assisting community and school efforts, particularly among the poor. First Lady Barbara Bush made the encour-

---

[38]Kenneth S. Goodman, et al. *Report Card on the Basal Readers* (Katonah, N.Y., Richard C. Owen, 1988).

agement of family literacy a key project. Libraries, neighborhood groups, and businesses continue to sponsor a wide variety of reading-incentive programs like "Book It," which rewards children's reading accomplishments with free pizza from a nationwide chain.

Increased Censorship

It is impossible to speak of trends from the 1960s to the present without speaking of the increase in censorship of books in schools and libraries. The number of book challenges has increased every decade since the 1950s. Judith Krug, director of the American Library Association Office for Intellectual Freedom and executive director of the Freedom to Read Foundation, says that in 1980 and 1981 the number of censorship attempts reported to her office was three times greater than for the same period in the previous year—a jump from 300 to between 900 and 1,000.[39] According to research reported by ALA, about half of the censorship attempts in the United States succeed. It should be emphasized that censorship refers to an attempt to have a book removed from a library, not simply a complaint or challenge.

Most book challenges are directed at young adult books. However, as the new freedoms of the 1960s were reflected in children's books, censorship and book bannings became more common. Books can be objected to for almost any reason. In his book *Censors in the Classroom: The Mind Benders*,[40] Edward B. Jenkinson lists some 116 targets of the censors, including profanity, conflicts with parents, drug use and abuse, homosexuality, violence, depressing stories of the ghetto, realistic dialogue, secular humanism, values clarification—and the list goes on. Dictionaries, textbooks, trade books, and nursery rhymes have all come under attack.

As school use of children's literature increases, so does public scrutiny. Selections by C. S. Lewis, Nikki Giovanni, Maurice Sendak, and Martin Luther King, Jr., are among those included in *Impressions*, a literature-based elementary reading series that has been challenged in at least nine states. The charges range from endorsement of witchcraft to undermining respect for parental authority. While in most cases the censors have not been successful in removing the series from schools, they have influenced the publishers to exclude the most frequently questioned selections from the 1990 U.S. edition.[41]

Censorship attempts against books in the library are serious because they deal not with what children *must* read but with their free access to ideas and the full range of their literary heritage. A group of parents in Eagle Point, Oregon, asked the school board to remove *The Three Billy Goats Gruff* from the elementary school library because of its "violent content."[42] After a committee looked closely at the book and its use in the curriculum, the board unanimously decided to reject the challenge. Of all the children's authors who have come under attack, Judy Blume is cited most frequently. Her books have been challenged in Hanover, Pennsylvania, Peoria, Illinois, and Casper, Wyoming, to name just a few places. In some instances the books have been removed from the library; in other cases children have had to obtain parental consent to read them.[43] A survey in Ohio showed that even such Newbery award–winning books as Jean George's *Julie of the Wolves* and Madeleine L'Engle's *A Wrinkle in Time* have been objects of censorship.[44] Jack Prelutsky's poetry books, *Nightmares: Poems to Trouble Your Sleep* (1976) and *The Headless Horseman Rides Tonight* (1980) have also weathered attempts at censorship.

There is no doubt that censorship has been on the rise in American elementary schools during

[39]Joseph Deitch, "Portrait [of Judith Krug]," *Wilson Library Bulletin*, vol. 58 (May 1984), p. 656.
[40]Edward B. Jenkinson, *Censors in the Classroom: The Mind Benders* (New York: Avon, 1982).
[41]Millie Davis, "The *Impressions* Series: Reading or Witchcraft?", *Council-Grams*, vol. 54 (March/April 1991), pp. 1, 3.
[42]Judith F. Krug, ed., *Newsletter on Intellectual Freedom*, vol. 13 (September 1984), p. 155.
[43]Judith F. Krug, ed., *Newsletter on Intellectual Freedom*, vol. 14 (March 1985), pp. 1, 58.
[44]Amy McClure, "Censorship in Ohio: It *Is* Happening Here," *The Ohio Reading Teacher*, vol. 16 (April 1982), pp. 1–6.

the last thirty years. The censors represent both conservatives and liberals. Many of them are administrators, teachers, and librarians themselves![45] For a further discussion of censorship and what you can do about it, see Chapter 1, "Selection vs. Censorship" and "Dealing with Censorship."

Need for Multicultural Books

During the 1960s and early 1970s, federal support for children's libraries encouraged publishers to produce books about many ethnic groups. When these funds were drastically cut and bookstore sales began to play a bigger part in a book's success, publishers found that so-called ethnic books, which were selling poorly in the stores, were not profitable. Publication figures dropped. In the wake of the civil rights movement, the influential Council on Interracial Books for Children had encouraged minority authors to write about their own cultures, yet by the late 1970s, almost no new authors of color were being published. The availability of books that provide culturally authentic characters from African-American, Hispanic, Asian, and Native American groups remains shockingly low. Consider as an example the eligibility list for the Coretta Scott King Award. Every new publication by a black author or illustrator is automatically considered. In 1985 only 18 books were eligible, and in 1990 the award committee could pick from only 38 titles out of the well over 4,000 books published in 1989.[46]

Some changes for the better have begun along with the new decade. Predictions about the changing demographics of the school population and renewed demand by schools and libraries for multicultural books have led to more active recruitment of authors from a variety of ethnic backgrounds and to better recognition of high-quality titles. There is still a lack of cultural diversity among editors and other publishing professionals who make decisions about what books will be published and how they will be marketed. However, small presses such as Carolrhoda or Children's Book Press, with a commitment to multicultural publishing, have begun to make some impact, particularly in the realm of picture storybooks.

The recognition of need in the United States for literature that reflects cultural diversity extends to books from and about other countries. Global education is a curriculum concept that has made itself felt in the world of children's books. One result is a renewed interest in international literature, particularly in books like Beverley Naidoo's South African story, *Journey to Jo'burg* (1986) or Nina Ring Aamundsen's *Two Short and One Long* (1991), which explore the human side of political conflicts and questions of justice.

Development of a Multiliterate Society

Dire statements have been made about the death of the book as we know it today, statements that call this the postliterate society. Modern technology has certainly affected literature and the arts, with developments like interactive fiction, where the "reader" responds to and actually creates plot variations for the story that appears on her computer screen. Computers can be programmed to generate poetry, pictures, and music. Some of these works meet high standards of artistry and receive appropriate critical recognition. At this point, however, computer technology seems to have more to do with the production, marketing, and library circulation of children's books than with the way they are used by children.

Charles Suhor, deputy executive director of the National Council of Teachers of English, projects four possible scenarios for the role of print in the future, ranging from a technological takeover to books remaining the core of educational material. His most reasoned conclusion is that, "Ultimately, the new technologies will not be revolutionary, transforming, or pervasive in the schools. They will have a place, but that place will resemble at best a modified media center in

[45]Lee Burress, "Appendix B," *Battle of the Books* (Metuchen, N.J.: Scarecrow Press, 1989).
[46]Kathleen Horning and Clare Seguin, "The Search for Multiculturalism in Children's Books," *Rethinking Schools* (January/February 1991), p. 16.

which books, machinery, teachers, and students find more varied ways of relating to each other."[47]

It seems likely, then, that the youth of today will become multiliterate, using the new technologies for the rapid retrieval of information of all kinds, for writing and editing their thoughts, and for creating original programs of their own. But they will still need reading for a wide range of skills and books for pleasure. Just as many youth

[47]Charles Suhor, draft of unpublished paper, "The Role of Print as a Medium in Our Society," 41 pp., 1984.

today are multilingual, so the youth of the future will become multiliterate, reading a wide variety of formats.

As we move toward the close of the century, the future of the book is uncertain. Computers, videotapes, cassettes, films, cable TV—all have the potential to give us instant information in many forms. Will the book be as important in the twenty-first century as it is today? Those of us who love literature and have witnessed its positive influence on children's lives can only hope that it will be—that it will continue to live and flourish.

SUGGESTED LEARNING EXPERIENCES

1. Interview five adults of different ages and ask about their favorite childhood books and reading interests. How similar are their responses? How much overlapping of titles is there?
2. Conduct a survey of your literature class to find out how many students have read *Little Women, Alice in Wonderland, The Wind in the Willows, Charlotte's Web*, or one of Judy Blume's books. Make a chart of your findings.
3. Prepare a display of early children's books; note the printing and binding, the illustrations, the subject matter. Display a varied selection of recent books as well. What contrasts do you see, and what similarities?
4. Identify adult purposes in several recent books for children. Can you find any examples of didactic stories written in the last ten years? Be sure to look at several books dealing with current social problems and environmental concerns.
5. Read and compare two books of realistic fiction with African Americans as major characters—one published within the last five years, the other published before 1960. How does each book specifically reflect the time in which it was written?
6. If possible, read two books aloud to a group of children. Choose one old book and one new, but on a similar theme, such as the books about quarreling in the introduction to this chapter. Elicit the children's responses. What do they see as differences? Which book do they prefer?
7. Read one of the books listed as having been censored. Act out a meeting with a concerned person, letting him or her tell you of their reactions to the book. How will you treat this person? What will you say and do?
8. Read one of the new original paperbacks produced for a series. Compare it with a Nancy Drew book or a Sue Barton book. What similarities and differences do you see? Another person could compare it with a modern realistic story for children like those by Cynthia Voigt or Katherine Paterson. Again, how do they compare?
9. Plan a panel discussion on the role of the book in the future. What would you lose if you didn't have books?

RELATED READINGS

1. Ariès, Philippe. *Centuries of Childhood: A Social History of Family Life.* Translated from the French by Robert Baldick. New York: Knopf, 1962.
    A definitive study of the development of the concept of childhood. Ariès maintained that childhood was not discovered until the seventeenth century. While some have disputed this statement, Ariès's book has formed the basis of most historical studies of childhood.

2. Bader, Barbara. *American Picturebooks from Noah's Ark to the Beast Within.* New York: Macmillan, 1976.
    A comprehensive historical study of American picture books, including the influence of foreign artists, the impact of motion pictures and comic books, and the social scene. Over 700 illustrations, some in color, enable the author to discuss and show various styles of art. Emphasis is placed on books produced from the 1920s to the 1970s.

3. Bingham, Jane, and Grayce Scholt. *Fifteen Centuries of Children's Literature.* Westport, Conn.: Greenwood Press, 1980.
    An indispensable reference book for the historical scholar of children's literature. Provides an annotated chronology of both British and American books from A.D. 523 through 1945. The chronology is divided into six time segments, one for each chapter. Historical background, development of books, and the general atttitude toward children are presented for each time period. Includes information on series books as well as those that became classics.

4. Carpenter, Humphrey, and Mari Prichard. *The Oxford Companion to Children's Literature.* Oxford and New York: Oxford University Press, 1984.
    An excellent reference source on many aspects of children's literature including authors, illustrators, titles, and characters. The historical span stretches from early chapbooks through books published in the 1980s. Nearly 2,000 entries are included in this one-volume reference source to children's literature.

5. Darton, F. J. Harvey. *Children's Books in England: Five Centuries of Social Life,* 3rd ed., revised by Brian Alderson. Cambridge and New York: Cambridge University Press, 1982. (First published in 1932.)
    This updated version of a well-recognized text on the history of children's literature in England makes fascinating reading. Darton had great respect for children's books, seeing their relationship to the history of children, the socioeconomic situation of the times, the cultural-religious beliefs of the period, and the history of publishing. While Alderson added detailed notes to each chapter, he did not revise the text. Therefore the reader does need to remember that the "now" and "today" referred to in the text refers to Darton's time, 1932.

6. Jackson, Mary V. *Engines of Instruction, Mischief, and Magic: Children's Literature in England from Its Beginnings to 1839.* Lincoln: University of Nebraska Press, 1990.
    This readable scholarly work focuses on the economic, sociopolitical, and religious forces that helped to shape early children's books. Jackson's attention to issues of class distinction and debates about education provides a useful way to look at recent trends as well as titles of the eighteenth and nineteenth centuries.

7. Johnson, Diedre. *Stratemeyer Pseudonyms and Series Books.* Westport, Conn.: Greenwood Press, 1982.
    This book provides an annotated checklist of the Stratemeyer syndicated publications, plus historical information on the growth of the company. The bibliography is arranged alphabetically by authors and pseudonyms. Thus it is possible to see how many Laura Lee Hope books were published and note the various authors and publishers.

8. Lurie, Alison. *Don't Tell the Grown-ups: Subversive Children's Literature.* Boston: Little, Brown, 1990.
    In a collection of essays from the 1980s, this well-known scholar and novelist demonstrates that the enduring works of children's literature have been books that did not conform to the ideal values of their own time. She points to characters who are disobedient and who mock adult hypocrisy from folklore and fairy tales to the middle of the twentieth century.

9. Lystad, Mary. *From Dr. Mather to Dr. Seuss: 200 Years of American Books for Children.* Cambridge, Mass.: Schenkiman, 1980.
    Basing her conclusions on a content analysis of 1,000 books chosen from a random sample of the juveniles in the Rare Book Collection of the Library of Congress, Lystad determined the social values and social behavior reflected in American children's books over the last 200 years. The author traces the changes in literature for children from the religious admonitions of Dr. Mather to the nonsense of Dr. Seuss.

10. Meigs, Cornelia, et al. *A Critical History of Children's Literature*, rev. ed. New York: Macmillan, 1969.
    First published in 1953, this comprehensive history of children's literature was written and revised by four recognized authorities in the field: Cornelia Meigs, Anne Thaxter Eaton, Elizabeth Nesbitt, and Ruth Hill Viguers. The organization by four chronological periods emphasizes the social trends influencing children's literature in England and America from earliest times to 1967.
11. Smith, Elva S. *Elva S. Smith's The History of Children's Literature*. Revised by Margaret Hodges and Susan Steinfirst. Chicago: American Library Association, 1980.
    This very useful reference book on American and English children's books has been revised and enlarged by Hodges and Steinfirst. An introduction and outline for each period is given from Anglo-Saxon times to the close of the nineteenth century. Annotated references are provided for general works and individual writers of each period.
12. Townsend, John Rowe. *Written for Children: An Outline of English Children's Literature*, 4th ed., rev. New York: HarperCollins, 1990.
    Townsend supplies a readable overview of the development of children's books in England and America, with a brief nod at Canada and Australia. His critical comments add interest to the text and help to put the books in perspective. The survey begins with books before 1840 and carries them into the 1980s.

REFERENCES[48]

Aamundsen, Nina Ring. *Two Short and One Long*. Houghton Mifflin, 1990.
Aardema, Verna. *Why Mosquitoes Buzz in People's Ears*, illustrated by Leo and Diane Dillon. Dial, 1975.
Adoff, Arnold. *I Am the Darker Brother: An Anthology of Modern Poems by Negro Americans*. Macmillan, 1968.
Alcott, Louisa May. *Jo's Boys*. Penguin, 1984 (1873).
_____. *Little Men*. Scholastic, 1987.
_____. *Little Women*, illustrated by Jessie Wilcox Smith. Little, 1968 (1868).
_____. *An Old Fashioned Girl*. Dell Yearling, 1987 (1870).
Alger, Horatio, Jr. *Struggling Upward*. Galloway, 1971 (n.d.).
Anno, Mitsumasa. *Anno's Journey*. Putnam, 1981 (1978).
Avi. *Nothing but the Truth*. Orchard, 1991.
Baker, Jeannie. *Where the Forest Meets the Sea*. Greenwillow, 1988.
_____. *Window*. Greenwillow, 1991.
Barrie, J. M. *Peter Pan in Kensington Gardens*. Buccaneer Books, 1980 (1906).
Baum, L. Frank. *The Wizard of Oz*, illustrated by Michael Hague. Holt, 1982 (1900).
Bealer, Alex. *Only the Names Remain: The Cherokees and the Trail of Tears*, illustrated by William S. Bock. Little, 1972.
Bemelmans, Ludwig. *Madeline*. Viking Penguin, 1958 (1939).
Beskow, Elsa. *Pelle's New Suit*. Harper, 1929.
Blos, Joan. *A Gathering of Days*. Macmillan, 1979.
Blume, Judy. *Are You There God? It's Me, Margaret*. Bradbury Press, 1970.

[48]The references for this chapter are limited to books still in print as the decade of the 1990s began. The dates in parentheses refer to the original publication of the text portion of the book.

_____. *Deenie*. Bradbury Press, 1973.

Briggs, Raymond. *The Snowman*. Random, 1978.

Brink, Carol Ryrie. *Caddie Woodlawn*. Macmillan, 1970 (1935).

Brooke, Leslie. *Johnny Crow's Garden*. Warne, 1986 (1903).

Brooks, Gwendolyn. *Bronzeville Boys and Girls*, illustrated by Ronni Solbert. Harper, 1956.

Brown, Marcia. *Cinderella*. Macmillan, 1954.

_____. *Dick Whittington and His Cat*. Macmillan, 1988 (1950).

_____. *Once a Mouse*. Macmillan, 1961.

_____. *Stone Soup*. Macmillan, 1947.

Brown, Margaret Wise. *Goodnight Moon*, illustrated by Clement Hurd. Harper, 1947.

_____. *Goodnight Moon Room*, illustrated by Clement Hurd, Harper, 1984.

_____. *The Little Fur Family*. Harper, 1991 (1946).

Bunting, Eve. *The Wall*, illustrated by Ronald Himler. Clarion, 1991.

Burnett, Frances Hodgson. *Little Lord Fauntleroy*. Buccaneer, 1981 (1886).

_____. *A Little Princess*, illustrated by Tasha Tudor. Lippincott, 1963 (1905).

_____. *A Little Princess*, illustrated by Graham Rust. Godine, 1987.

_____. *The Secret Garden*, illustrated by Shirley Hughes. Viking, 1989 (1910).

Burningham, John. *The Blanket*. Harper, 1976.

_____. *The Cupboard*. Harper, 1976.

Burton, Virginia Lee. *The Little House*. Houghton Mifflin, 1978 (1942).

_____. *Mike Mulligan and His Steam Shovel*. Houghton Mifflin, 1939.

Byars, Betsy. *The Animal, the Vegetable, and John D. Jones*, illustrated by Ruth Sanderson. Dell, 1983.

Caldecott, Randolph. *Sing a Song of Sixpence*. Barron, 1988 (1880).

Canfield, Dorothy. *Understood Betsy*. Buccaneer, 1981 (1917).

Carlson, Natalie. *The Empty Schoolhouse*, illustrated by John Kaufman. Harper, 1965.

Carroll, Lewis (Charles Dodgson). *Alice's Adventures in Wonderland*, illustrated by Anthony Browne. Knopf, 1988 (1865, 1871).

Chaikin, Miriam. *Exodus*, illustrated by Charles Mikolaycak. Holiday, 1987.

Cleary, Beverly. *Dear Mr. Henshaw*, illustrated by Paul O. Zelinsky. Morrow, 1983.

_____. *Henry Huggins*, illustrated by Louis Darling. Morrow, 1957.

_____. *Ramona and her Father*, illustrated by Alan Tiegreen. Morrow, 1977.

Cleaver, Vera, and Bill Cleaver. *Where the Lilies Bloom*. Lippincott, 1969.

_____. *Grover*, illustrated by Frederic Marvin. Lippincott, 1970.

Cole, Joanna. *The Magic School Bus at the Waterworks*, illustrated by Bruce Degen. Scholastic, 1986.

_____. *The Magic School Bus Inside the Human Body*, illustrated by Bruce Degen. Scholastic, 1989.

Collier, James L., and Christopher Collier. *My Brother Sam Is Dead*. Macmillan, 1974.

Collodi, Carlo. *The Adventures of Pinocchio*, illustrated by Roberto Innocenti. Knopf, 1988 (1891).

Cooney, Barbara. *Miss Rumphius*. Viking, 1982.

Cooper, James Fenimore. *The Last of the Mohicans*, illustrated by N. C. Wyeth. Scribner's, 1986 (1826).

Cunningham, Julia. *Dorp Dead*, illustrated by James Spanfeller. Knopf, 1987 (1965).

Dana, Richard Henry. *Two Years Before the Mast*. Airmont, 1985 (1840).

d'Aulaire, Ingri, and Edgar Parin d'Aulaire. *Abraham Lincoln*. Doubleday, 1957 (1939).

de la Mare, Walter. *Peacock Pie*, illustrated by Edward Ardizzone. Faber and Faber, 1988 (1913).

_____. *Songs of Childhood*. Dover, n.d. (1902).

de Paola, Tomie. *"Charlie Needs a Cloak."* Simon & Schuster, 1974.

de Saint-Exupéry, Antoine. *The Little Prince*. Harcourt Brace, 1943.

Dickinson, Emily. *Poems for Youth*, illustrated by Doris Hauman and George Hauman. Little, 1934.

Dodge, Mary M. *Hans Brinker, Or the Silver Skates*. Scholastic, 1988 (1865).

Donovan, John. *I'll Get There, It Better Be Worth the Trip*. Harper, 1969.

Dragonwagon, Crescent. *Winter Holding Spring*, illustrated by Ronald Himler. Macmillan, 1990.

DuBois, William Pène. *The Twenty-One Balloons*. Viking, 1947.

Ehlert, Lois. *Feathers for Lunch*. Harcourt Brace, 1990.

Enright, Elizabeth. *The Saturdays*. Holt, 1988.

_____. *Thimble Summer*. Holt, 1938.

Estes, Eleanor. *The Hundred Dresses*, illustrated by Louis Slobodkin. Harcourt Brace, 1974 (1944).

_____. *The Middle Moffats*. Dell, 1989 (1942).

_____. *The Moffats*, illustrated by Louis Slobodkin. Harcourt Brace, 1941.

_____. *Rufus M*, illustrated by Louis Slobodkin. Harcourt Brace, 1943.

Farjeon, Eleanor. *Eleanor Farjeon's Poems for Children*. Harper, 1984 (1931, 1951).

Field, Eugene. *Poems of Childhood*. Airmont, 1969 (1896).

Finger, Charles. *Tales from Silver Lands*, illustrated by Paul Honore. Doubleday, 1965 (1924).

Fisher, Leonard Everett. *Jason and the Golden Fleece*. Holiday, 1990.

Fitzhugh, Louise. *Harriet the Spy*. Harper, 1964.

Flack, Marjorie. *Angus and the Ducks*. Macmillan, 1989 (1930).

_____. *Ask Mr. Bear*. Macmillan, 1986 (1932).

_____. *The Story About Ping*, illustrated by Kurt Wiese. Viking Penguin, 1933.

Forbes, Esther. *Johnny Tremain*, illustrated by Lynd Ward. Houghton, 1943.

Fox, Paula. *The Slave Dancer*, illustrated by Eros Keith. Bradbury Press, 1973.

Frank, Anne. *Anne Frank: The Diary of a Young Girl*, rev. ed. Doubleday, 1967 (1952).

Freedman, Russell. *Lincoln: A Photobiography*. Clarion, 1987.

Fritz, Jean. *And Then What Happened, Paul Revere?*, illustrated by Margot Tomes. Putnam, 1973.

Frost, Robert. *You Come Too*, illustrated by Thomas W. Nason. Holt, 1959.

Gág, Wanda. *Millions of Cats*. Putnam, 1928.

Gates, Doris. *Blue Willow*. Viking Penguin, 1940.

George, Jean. *Julie of the Wolves*, illustrated by John Schoenherr. Harper, 1972.

Grahame, Kenneth. *Mole's Christmas*, illustrated by Beverly Gooding. Prentice-Hall, 1986.

_____. *The Open Road*, illustrated by Beverly Gooding. Simon & Schuster, 1987.

_____. *The River Bank*. Simon & Schuster, 1987.

_____. *The Wind in the Willows*, illustrated by John Burningham. Viking, 1983 (1908).

_____. *The Wind in the Willows*, illustrated by Ernest H. Shepard. Scribner's, 1983 (1908).

_____. *The Wind in the Willows*, illustrated by Alex Tsao. Signet, 1989 (1908).

Gramatky, Hardie. *Little Toot*. Putnam, 1978 (1930).

Grimm, Jacob, and Wilhelm Grimm. *Grimm's Fairy Tales*, illustrated by George Cruikshank. Dover, n.d. (1823).

Hale, Lucretia P. *The Peterkin Papers*. Sharon, 1981 (1880).

Hale, Sarah Josepha. *Mary Had a Little Lamb*, illustrated by Tomie de Paola. Holiday, 1984 (1830).

Haley, Gail. *A Story, A Story*. Atheneum, 1970.

Hamilton, Virginia. *M.C. Higgins the Great*. Macmillan, 1974.

_____. *Zeely*, illustrated by Simeon Shimin. Macmillan, 1967.

Harris, Joel Chandler. *Uncle Remus*, illustrated by A. B. Frost. Schocken, 1987 (1881).

Hawthorne, Nathaniel. *Tanglewood Tales*. Sharon, 1981 (1853).

_____. *A Wonder Book for Boys and Girls*. White Rose, 1987 (1852).

Haywood, Carolyn. *B Is for Betsy*. Harcourt Brace, 1987 (1939).

Holling, Holling C. *Paddle to the Sea*. Houghton Mifflin, 1980 (1941).

_____. *Tree in the Trail*. Houghton Mifflin, 1990 (1942).

Hughes, Langston. *The Dream Keeper*, illustrated by Helen Sewell. Knopf, 1962.

Hughes, Shirley. *Chips and Jessie*. Lothrop, 1986.

Irving, Washington. *Sketch Book*. New American Library, 1961 (1819).

Jackson, Jesse. *Call Me Charley*, illustrated by Doris Spiegel. Harper, 1945.

Jacobs, Joseph, ed. *Celtic Fairy Tales*, illustrated by John D. Batten. Dover, 1968 (1892, 1894).

_____. *English Fairy Tales*, illustrated by John D. Batten. Dover, n.d. (1890–1894).

_____. *Indian Fairy Tales*, illustrated by John D. Batten. Roth, 1976 (1892).

James, Will. *Smoky the Cow Horse*. Scribner's, 1983 (1926).

Keats, Ezra Jack. *The Snowy Day*. Viking Penguin, 1962.

Kellogg, Steven. *Johnny Appleseed*. Morrow, 1988.

Kingsley, Charles. *The Water Babies*. Penguin, 1986 (1983).

Kipling, Rudyard. *The Jungle Books*, illustrated by Fritz Eichenberg. Grosset, 1950 (1894).

_____. *Just So Stories*, woodcuts by David Frampton. HarperCollins, 1991 (1902).

Klein, Norma. *Mom, the Wolfman and Me*. Pantheon, 1972.

Konigsburg, E. L. *George*. Dell, 1985 (1970).

Krauss, Ruth. *A Hole Is to Dig*, illustrated by Maurice Sendak. Harper, 1952.

Lang, Andrew, ed. *The Blue Fairy Book*. Airmont, 1969 (1889).

Lasky, Kathryn. *The Night Journey*, illustrated by Trina Schart Hyman. Viking, 1986.

Lauber, Patricia. *Seeing Earth from Space*. Orchard, 1990.

Lawson, Robert. *Rabbit Hill*. Viking Penguin, 1944.

_____. *The Tough Winter*. Viking Penguin, 1979 (1954).

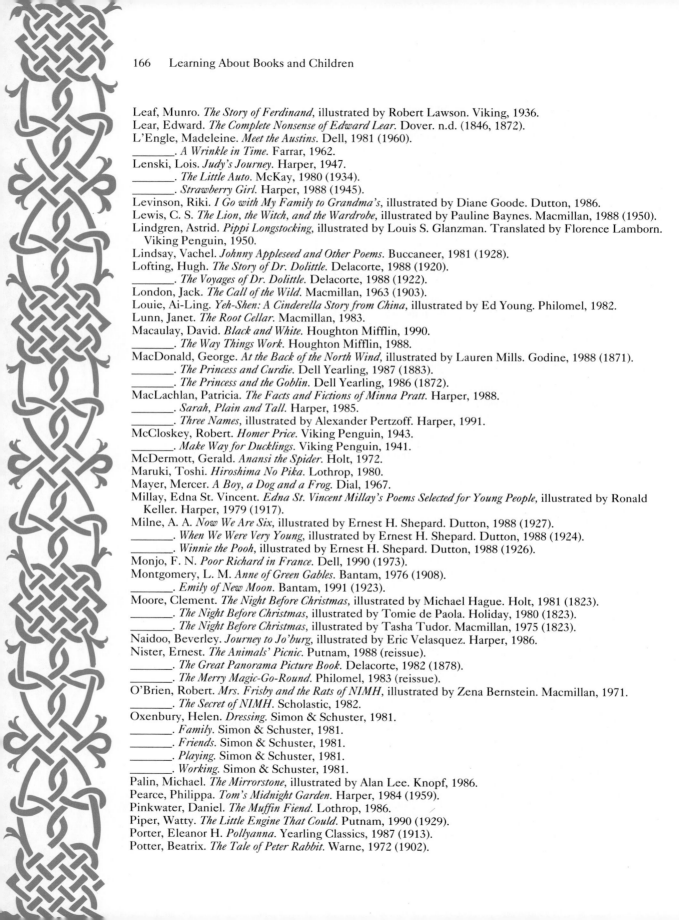

Leaf, Munro. *The Story of Ferdinand*, illustrated by Robert Lawson. Viking, 1936.

Lear, Edward. *The Complete Nonsense of Edward Lear*. Dover. n.d. (1846, 1872).

L'Engle, Madeleine. *Meet the Austins*. Dell, 1981 (1960).

_____. *A Wrinkle in Time*. Farrar, 1962.

Lenski, Lois. *Judy's Journey*. Harper, 1947.

_____. *The Little Auto*. McKay, 1980 (1934).

_____. *Strawberry Girl*. Harper, 1988 (1945).

Levinson, Riki. *I Go with My Family to Grandma's*, illustrated by Diane Goode. Dutton, 1986.

Lewis, C. S. *The Lion, the Witch, and the Wardrobe*, illustrated by Pauline Baynes. Macmillan, 1988 (1950).

Lindgren, Astrid. *Pippi Longstocking*, illustrated by Louis S. Glanzman. Translated by Florence Lamborn. Viking Penguin, 1950.

Lindsay, Vachel. *Johnny Appleseed and Other Poems*. Buccaneer, 1981 (1928).

Lofting, Hugh. *The Story of Dr. Dolittle*. Delacorte, 1988 (1920).

_____. *The Voyages of Dr. Dolittle*. Delacorte, 1988 (1922).

London, Jack. *The Call of the Wild*. Macmillan, 1963 (1903).

Louie, Ai-Ling. *Yeh-Shen: A Cinderella Story from China*, illustrated by Ed Young. Philomel, 1982.

Lunn, Janet. *The Root Cellar*. Macmillan, 1983.

Macaulay, David. *Black and White*. Houghton Mifflin, 1990.

_____. *The Way Things Work*. Houghton Mifflin, 1988.

MacDonald, George. *At the Back of the North Wind*, illustrated by Lauren Mills. Godine, 1988 (1871).

_____. *The Princess and Curdie*. Dell Yearling, 1987 (1883).

_____. *The Princess and the Goblin*. Dell Yearling, 1986 (1872).

MacLachlan, Patricia. *The Facts and Fictions of Minna Pratt*. Harper, 1988.

_____. *Sarah, Plain and Tall*. Harper, 1985.

_____. *Three Names*, illustrated by Alexander Pertzoff. Harper, 1991.

McCloskey, Robert. *Homer Price*. Viking Penguin, 1943.

_____. *Make Way for Ducklings*. Viking Penguin, 1941.

McDermott, Gerald. *Anansi the Spider*. Holt, 1972.

Maruki, Toshi. *Hiroshima No Pika*. Lothrop, 1980.

Mayer, Mercer. *A Boy, a Dog and a Frog*. Dial, 1967.

Millay, Edna St. Vincent. *Edna St. Vincent Millay's Poems Selected for Young People*, illustrated by Ronald Keller. Harper, 1979 (1917).

Milne, A. A. *Now We Are Six*, illustrated by Ernest H. Shepard. Dutton, 1988 (1927).

_____. *When We Were Very Young*, illustrated by Ernest H. Shepard. Dutton, 1988 (1924).

_____. *Winnie the Pooh*, illustrated by Ernest H. Shepard. Dutton, 1988 (1926).

Monjo, F. N. *Poor Richard in France*. Dell, 1990 (1973).

Montgomery, L. M. *Anne of Green Gables*. Bantam, 1976 (1908).

_____. *Emily of New Moon*. Bantam, 1991 (1923).

Moore, Clement. *The Night Before Christmas*, illustrated by Michael Hague. Holt, 1981 (1823).

_____. *The Night Before Christmas*, illustrated by Tomie de Paola. Holiday, 1980 (1823).

_____. *The Night Before Christmas*, illustrated by Tasha Tudor. Macmillan, 1975 (1823).

Naidoo, Beverley. *Journey to Jo'burg*, illustrated by Eric Velasquez. Harper, 1986.

Nister, Ernest. *The Animals' Picnic*. Putnam, 1988 (reissue).

_____. *The Great Panorama Picture Book*. Delacorte, 1982 (1878).

_____. *The Merry Magic-Go-Round*. Philomel, 1983 (reissue).

O'Brien, Robert. *Mrs. Frisby and the Rats of NIMH*, illustrated by Zena Bernstein. Macmillan, 1971.

_____. *The Secret of NIMH*. Scholastic, 1982.

Oxenbury, Helen. *Dressing*. Simon & Schuster, 1981.

_____. *Family*. Simon & Schuster, 1981.

_____. *Friends*. Simon & Schuster, 1981.

_____. *Playing*. Simon & Schuster, 1981.

_____. *Working*. Simon & Schuster, 1981.

Palin, Michael. *The Mirrorstone*, illustrated by Alan Lee. Knopf, 1986.

Pearce, Philippa. *Tom's Midnight Garden*. Harper, 1984 (1959).

Pinkwater, Daniel. *The Muffin Fiend*. Lothrop, 1986.

Piper, Watty. *The Little Engine That Could*. Putnam, 1990 (1929).

Porter, Eleanor H. *Pollyanna*. Yearling Classics, 1987 (1913).

Potter, Beatrix. *The Tale of Peter Rabbit*. Warne, 1972 (1902).

Prelutsky, Jack. *The Headless Horseman Rides Tonight*, illustrated by Arnold Lobel. Greenwillow, 1980.

_____. *Nightmares: Poems to Trouble Your Sleep*, illustrated by Arnold Lobel. Greenwillow, 1976.

Pyle, Howard. *The Merry Adventures of Robin Hood of Great Renown*. Dover, 1968 (1883).

_____. *The Story of King Arthur and His Knights*. Scribner's, 1984 (1903).

_____. *The Wonder Clock*. Dover, n.d. (1888).

Rey, H. A. *Curious George*. Houghton, 1973 (1941).

Richter, Hans. *Friedrich*. Penguin, 1987 (1970).

Robbins, Ken. *A Flower Grows*. Dial, 1990.

Rossetti, Christina. *Goblin Market*. Trafalgar Square/David & Charles, 1989 (1864).

_____. *Sing Song*, illustrated by Arthur Hughes. Dover, 1969 (1872).

Ruskin, John. *King of the Golden River*, illustrated by Richard Doyle. Dover, 1974 (1851).

Rylant, Cynthia. *When I Was Young in the Mountains*, illustrated by Diane Goode. Dutton, 1982.

Sandburg, Carl *Early Moon*, illustrated by James Daugherty. Harcourt, 1978 (1930).

_____. *Rootabaga Stories*, illustrated by Michael Hague. Harcourt, 1989 (1922).

Sawyer, Ruth. *Roller Skates*, illustrated by Valenti Angelo. Penguin, 1986 (1936).

Scieszka, Jon. *The True Story of the 3 Little Pigs by A. Wolf*, illustrated by Lane Smith. Viking, 1989.

Scott, Walter. *Ivanhoe*. Airmont, 1964 (1820).

Sendak, Maurice. *In The Night Kitchen*. Harper, 1970.

_____. *Where the Wild Things Are*. Harper, 1988 (1963).

Seton, Ernest Thompson. *Wild Animals I Have Known*. Creative Arts, 1987 (1898).

Seuss, Dr. (Theodor S. Geisel). *And to Think That I Saw It on Mulberry Street*. Random, 1989 (1937).

_____. *The Cat in the Hat*. Random, 1957.

Sewell, Anna. *Black Beauty*. Grosset, 1945 (1877).

Sherlock, Philip. *Anansi: The Spider Man*, illustrated by Marcia Brown. Harper, 1954.

Silverstein, Shel. *Where the Sidewalk Ends*. Harper, 1974.

Smith, E. Boyd. *The Farm Book*. Houghton Mifflin, 1990 (1910).

_____. *The Railroad Book*. Houghton Mifflin, 1983 (1913).

_____. *The Seashore Book*. Houghton Mifflin, 1985 (1912).

Soto, Gary. *Baseball in April and Other Stories*. Harcourt Brace, 1990.

Spier, Peter. *Noah's Ark*. Doubleday, 1977.

Spinelli, Jerry. *Maniac Magee*. Little, Brown, 1991.

Spyri, Johanna. *Heidi*, illustrated by Troy Howell. Messner, 1982.

Steptoe, John. *Mufaro's Beautiful Daughters: An African Tale*. Lothrop, Lee & Shepherd, 1987.

Steptoe, John. *Stevie*. Harper, 1969.

Stevenson, Robert Louis. *A Child's Garden of Verses*, illustrated by Michael Foreman. Delacorte, 1985 (1885).

_____. *Treasure Island*, illustrated by N. C. Wyeth. Scribner's, 1981 (1883).

Stolz, Mary. *The Bully of Barkham Street*, illustrated by Leonard Shortall. Harper, 1985 (1963).

_____. *A Dog on Barkham Street*, illustrated by Leonard Shortall. Harper, 1985 (1960).

Taylor, Mildred. *Roll of Thunder, Hear My Cry*, illustrated by Jerry Pinkney. Dell, 1976.

Taylor, Sydney. *All-of-a-Kind Family*, illustrated by John Helen. Dell, 1980 (1951).

Thurber, James. *Many Moons*, illustrated by L. Slobodkin. Harcourt Brace, 1943.

_____. *Many Moons*, illustrated by Marc Simont. Harcourt Brace, 1990 (1943).

Tolkien, J. R. R. *The Hobbit*, illustrated by Michael Hague. Houghton Mifflin, 1989 (1937).

Travers, P. L. *Mary Poppins*. Harcourt, 1934.

Tresselt, Alvin. *Wake Up, City!*, illustrated by Carolyn Ewing. Lothrop, 1989 (1947).

_____. *White Snow, Bright Snow*, illustrated by Roger Duvoisin. Lothrop, 1989 (1948).

Twain, Mark (Samuel Clemens). *The Adventures of Huckleberry Finn*. Scholastic, 1982 (1884).

_____. *The Adventures of Tom Sawyer*, illustrated by Barry Moser. Morrow, 1989 (1876).

Uchida, Yoshiko. *The Dancing Kettle and Other Japanese Folk Tales*. Creative Arts, 1986 (1949).

_____. *Journey to Topaz*, illustrated by Donald Carrick. Scribner, 1971.

_____. *The Magic Listening Cap*. Creative Arts, 1987 (1955).

Udry, Janice May. *Let's Be Enemies*, illustrated by Maurice Sendak, Harper, 1961.

Van Allsburg, Chris. *The Polar Express*. Houghton Mifflin, 1985.

Van Loon, Hendrik. *The Story of Mankind*. Updated in a new version for the 1980s. Liveright, 1985 (1921).

Verne, Jules. *Around the World in Eighty Days*, illustrated by Barry Moser. Morrow, 1988 (1872).

_____. *Journey to the Center of the Earth*. Penguin, 1986 (1864).

_____. *Twenty Thousand Leagues Under the Sea*. Airmont, 1964 (1869).

Voigt, Cynthia. *Homecoming.* Atheneum, 1981.

Walsh, Jill Paton. *A Chance Child.* Avon, 1978.

Webster, Jean. *Daddy-Long-Legs.* Dell Yearling, 1987 (1912).

White, E. B. *Charlotte's Web,* illustrated by Garth Williams. Harper, 1952.

Wiesner, David. *Tuesday.* Clarion, 1991.

Wiggin, Kate Douglas. *Rebecca of Sunnybrook Farm.* Penguin, 1986 (1903).

Wilder, Laura Ingalls. *Little House in the Big Woods,* illustrated by Garth Williams. Harper, 1953 (1932).

Williams, Margery. *The Velveteen Rabbit,* illustrated by Michael Hague. Holt, 1983 (1922).

_____. *The Velveteen Rabbit,* illustrated by David Jorgansen. Knopf, 1985 (1922).

_____. *The Velveteen Rabbit,* illustrated by William Nicholson. Doubleday, 1969 (1922).

_____. *The Velveteen Rabbit,* illustrated by Ilse Plume, Harcourt, 1987 (1922).

Williams, Vera B. *Stringbean's Trip to the Shining Sea,* illustrated by Jennifer Williams and Vera B. Williams. Greenwillow, 1988.

Willard, Nancy. *A Visit to William Blake's Inn,* illustrated by Alice and Martin Provensen. Harcourt, 1981.

Wyss, Johann. *Swiss Family Robinson.* Sharon, 1981 (1814).

Yolen, Jane. *The Devil's Arithmetic.* Viking, 1988.

_____. *Encounter,* illustrated by David Shannon. Harcourt Brace, 1992.

Zemach, Margot. *It Could Always Be Worse.* Farrar, 1990 (1977).

Part Two

Knowing Children's Literature

Chapter Four

Books to Begin On

One of our colleagues is a proud new grandfather. Everytime we meet him he regales us with tales of his granddaughter's progress in "reading"—Laura is 18 months old. However, her grandfather is determined that Laura will grow into reading as naturally as she is learning to speak. So he floods her house with books; he mixes books with her blocks so she will think of them as toys; he built her a special bookshelf for her books; he bought a miniature supermarket basket that he filled with books so she can have books available in every room in the house; he takes her to the library frequently. Of course, whenever he visits he is greeted with the welcome words, "Grandpapa, read!" And he always does. Laura's mother and father read to her also, so it is not unusual for Laura to hear six to ten stories a day.

Laura has favorite books, which she can readily find, and she asks to hear them over and over again. She relates books to her own life. For example, when she lost her teddy bear and finally found it, she went to her bookshelf and pulled out the story of *The Blanket* by John Burningham and laughed. In that story a little boy loses his blanket and the whole family searches for it. Laura had obviously connected it with her family's search for her bear. Each night when she hears *Goodnight Moon* by Margaret Wise Brown, she softly whispers, "Night night, chair, night night, Bear." Laura's grandfather is achieving his purpose; Laura is learning to love books and learning to read naturally in the process.

DEVELOPING INITIAL LITERACY

What a lot Laura already knows about books and reading at 18 months! First, she knows books are enjoyable and even has particular favorites. She also knows that adults hold the key to reading and can give meaning to the text. She herself knows how to hold a book and that it has to be right-side-up to read the print. She is beginning to relate books to her own life. If at 18 months she knows this much about how to read a book, think what she will know when she enters school.

At a year and a half, Laura already has entered the world of literature. Laura is learning to love books, as she has many opportunities to snuggle up close to her mother, father, and grandfather for story time. She is also increasing her vocabulary as she points to pictures and names them or hears new words used in the context of the story. The language development of children this age is phenomenal; preoccupation with words and sounds of language is characteristic of the very young child. Books help to fulfill this insatiable desire to hear and learn new words. Hearing literature of good quality helps the child to develop his or her full language potential.

Children cannot be introduced to books too soon. The human baby is first attuned to various sound patterns almost from the moment of birth. She will be startled by a cross voice or a loud noise, soothed by a gentle loving voice or a softly sung lullaby. Gradually the baby begins to develop comprehension skills as she attaches meaning to the sounds around her. Talk is essential at this time. In *A Language for Life*,[1] an educational report from England, parents are advised to "bathe the child with language." One parent read a best-selling novel to her infant son just so he could hear the sound of her voice. Primarily, however, the very young child listens for the "quack quack" of a duck in a picture book or the "rrroar" of a lion. Singing simple nursery rhymes or playing such finger rhymes as "This little pig went to market" will make the baby giggle with delight. Increasingly, publishers are producing books for babies' enjoyment, for in Dorothy Butler's words, "Babies need books."[2]

The young child who has the opportunity to hear and enjoy many stories is also beginning to learn to read. No one taught Laura how to hold a book or where to begin to read the text. Through constant exposure to stories, Laura is learning about book handling and developing some beginning concepts about print.[3] She is spontaneously learning some of the attitudes, concepts, and skills that Don Holdaway describes as a "literacy set," including a positive attitude toward books, an understanding about the sense-making aspect of stories, the stability of print to tell the same story each time, and the form and structure of written language itself. All of this learning occurs

Research suggests that one of the most important gifts a family can give to children is an early love of books.

Photo by Larry Rose.

at the prereading stage—what Holdaway refers to as the "emergent level of reading"—and seems to be essential for later success in reading.[4]

This certainly proved to be true in the longitudinal study that was conducted by Gordon Wells. Following thirty-two children for a full nine-year period, he studied the way differences in the preschool years affected children's later educational achievement. Of the many measures he recorded, he found early exposure to books to be the most significant:

> Of all the activities that had been considered as possibly helpful preparation for the acquisition of literacy, only one was significantly associated with the later test scores, and it was clearly associated with both of them. *That activity was listening to stories.*[5]

[1]*A Language for Life, The Bullock Report* (London: H.M.S.O., 1975).
[2]Dorothy Butler, *Babies Need Books* (New York: Atheneum, 1980).
[3]See Marie Clay, *The Early Detection of Reading Difficulties*, 3rd ed. (Portsmouth, N.H.: Heinemann Educational Books, 1985), for a description of her *Concepts About Print* test.

[4]Don Holdaway, *The Foundations of Literacy* (Sydney: Ashton Scholastic, 1979).
[5]Gordon Wells, *The Meaning Makers: Children Learning Language and Using Language to Learn.* (Portsmouth, N.H.: Heinemann Educational Books, 1986), p. 151 (emphasis added).

Researchers have also studied the way in which parents share books with young children. Ninio and Bruner[6] discovered that one of the first language patterns or frames that a parent and child develop is in relation to sharing a picture book. Parents appear to use a consistent language pattern when labeling objects in a picture book. For example, the mother (or father) will first get the child's attention by saying "Look" and point to the picture. Next, she will query the child, asking "What's that?" Third, she usually gives the picture a label and, finally, in response to the child's repeating the name she will smile and say "That's right." If, however, the child can provide the label first, she will fine-tune her response and give him immediate approval. The child and mother (or father) take turns in this dialogue and collaboratively make meaning out of the text. This book-reading context is unique because the attention of the participants is jointly focused on pictures and words that stay the same for each rereading. Thus the child can predict the story and build up vocabulary over numerous readings.

While the way parents share these books follows a distinctive pattern, the quality of the read-aloud time varies tremendously according to the parents' patience and ingenuity in holding the youngster's interest. Linda Lamme[7] videotaped parents sharing Carle's *The Very Hungry Caterpillar* and obtained a time variation of 1 minute 35 seconds to 16 minutes in reading the book. Evidently, some parents raced through this book; others progressed in a more leisurely fashion, taking time to talk about the story and let their children poke their fingers in the holes that the caterpillar makes as he "eats" his way through the pages.

Besides length of time given to reading aloud, the quality of that time is important. Two researchers studied the parent as a reader and developed a scale to measure read-aloud sessions. They discovered that a large percentage of the parents of very young children did not know how to use a book to maximize the child's learning and enjoyment. When looking at an identification book many of them gave the name of the object without waiting long enough to see if the child could name it by herself. Some parents, on the other hand, elaborated on the child's response so that when a little girl, on seeing a picture of popcorn, squealed "See the popcorn!" the mother responded by saying, "Yes, look at the popcorn. I wonder if it has butter on it." Only 22 percent of their sample of readers gave such feedback with expansion or repetition.[8] The quality of the read-aloud time for the young child is as important as the selection of the book and the length of time spent.

Early exposure to books with plenty of time for talk and enjoyment of the story appear, then, to be key factors in the child's acquisition of literacy. One father whose child has been exposed to books from infancy said, "You know, I haven't the slightest doubt that David will learn to read, any more than I was concerned that he would talk."

BABIES' FIRST BOOKS

First books for young children are frequently identification books or "naming books" that allow a child to point to one picture after another, demanding to know "wha dat?" It is probably this give-and-take of language between the adult and the child that makes sharing books at this age so important.

Recognizing the need for the young child to identify and name objects, publishers have produced many of these simple, sturdy "first books." The growth of good books for babies and toddlers was a publishing phenomenon of the 1980s. These books can be puffy books made of foam-filled cloth pages that are washable, or they may be constructed with heavy laminated cardboard or plastic pages that will withstand sticky fingers. Illustrations for these books need to be simple,

[6]A. Ninio and J. Bruner, "The Achievement and Antecedents of Labelling," *Journal of Child Language*, vol. 5 (1973), pp. 1–15.

[7]Linda Lamme and Pat Olmsted, "Family Reading Habits and Children's Progress in Reading." Paper presented at the Annual Meeting of IRA, Miami Beach, May 2–6, 1977. ERIC Document ED 138 963.

[8]Barry J. Guinagh and R. Emile Jester, "How Parents Read to Children," *Theory into Practice*, vol. XI, no. 3 (1972), pp. 171–177.

It's never too early to begin reading to children.

🐛 🐛 🐛

uncluttered, and easily identifiable, with little or no background to distract from the main object. Tana Hoban's *What Is It?* presents clear colored photographs of such familiar objects as a sock, a shoe, a bib, a cup, a spoon, and so on. Only one object is pictured on a page, shown against a plain white background, in this sturdy first book.

Nancy Tafuri's board books *Two New Sneakers* and *One Wet Jacket* are companion pieces. The first one details everything a boy puts on; the second shows everything a little girl takes off prior to climbing into her bath. Clear uncluttered pictures make these titles and others in her series of a small child's world excellent first books. The fun in sharing these books is in the naming and pointing to the familiar objects. The parent can say "Show me the boots," "Where are the socks?" or "Where do you put the ribbon?"

Helen Oxenbury has a series of "Baby Board Books" titled *Playing, Dressing, Working, Friends,* and *Family.* These books feature a delightfully droll round-headed infant doing what toddlers do, such as banging on pots, messily eating food, or sitting on the potty. A single noun such as "bowl," "potty," or "dog" represents the action on the page in much the same way that the young

child uses a single word to carry the force of a sentence. The simplicity of the illustrations is just right for the audience—plain white backgrounds, clearly outlined figures, single focused composition, attractive but not distracting color. Oxenbury continues the exploration of the toddler's world in her Baby Board Series with *I Can, I Hear, I See,* and *I Touch.* In *Tickle, Tickle; Clap Hands,* and *Say Goodnight,* this author/artist portrays wonderful babies of several races playing with each other. Slightly more background is represented in another set of first books by Oxenbury with such titles as *Mother's Helper, Beach Day,* and *Shopping Trip.* These show a toddler in a variety of amusing situations like "helping" mother by licking the cookie bowl and spilling water all over the kitchen while washing up. Though these are wordless books, the pictures portray little stories that nurture the narrative thinking of the child and at the same time entertain parents. Yet another series, the Pippo books, revolves around the daily activities of a 2- or 3-year-old boy named Tom and his favorite stuffed monkey called Pippo. Oxenbury provides

Delightful babies of different racial backgrounds play together happily in *Clap Hands* by Helen Oxenbury.

🐛 🐛 🐛

more text for these amusing incidents such as the trauma of Pippo's first bath in the washing machine. *Tom and Pippo Read a Story* could well serve as a parents' guide on how to read to your toddler. For Daddy *reads aloud* while Tom looks at the pictures, then his father *rereads* the story, and finally Tom *retells* the story to his stuffed monkey.

Jan Ormerod's "Baby Books" are unique in that they portray the special relationships between babies and fathers. The series includes *Dad's Back, Messy Baby, Reading,* and *Sleeping.* In *Reading,* for example, a bearded, handsome father attempts to read his book while a beguiling toddler crawls in and out of his legs, peeps over his book, and finally ends up resting in his arms, reading too.

A companion story to *Dad's Back* is *Mom's Home.* Others in the series include *Bend and Stretch, Making Friends,* and *This Little Nose.* While the texts are minimal in these books, clear pictures capture the love and humor required to communicate with a toddler. Ormerod also illustrates the popular "Gemma Series" by Sarah Hayes that depicts a delightful if determined black toddler and her slightly exasperated family in *Eat Up, Gemma* and *Happy Christmas, Gemma.*

John Steptoe also reflects this theme of learning to endure some of the antics of a new baby brother in his story *Baby Says.* Parents give this book a nod of recognition when the baby knocks down his big brother's blocks.

Babies by Rachel Isadora shows solitary children of different races eating, laughing, reading, playing, sleeping; *Friends* depicts multicultural pairs and groups of youngsters sharing typical activities such as drawing, building, or waving goodbye. Parents, preschool teachers, and librarians enjoy sharing these large lovely watercolors portraying joyful activities in the child's day.

Vera Williams's Caldecott Honor book *"More More More," Said the Baby* is aptly subtitled "Three Love Stories." Meet Little Guy, whose daddy has to run like anything to catch him up, toss him in the air, give his belly button a kiss, and then laugh as Little Guy squeals for "More. More. More." Three pairs of babies gleefully play with their grown-ups as the stories repeat the demand for "More. More. More." Williams repre-

Vera Williams's first book for babies is aptly subtitled "Three Love Stories." Here Little Pumpkin's grandmother runs to pick her up and swing her and hear her squeal *"More More More," Said the Baby.*

sents diversity within her three families. Little Guy and his father are white, Little Pumpkin is African American and her grandmother is white, and Little Bird and her mother are both Asian American. Yet the love they exhibit for their babies is universal.

Janet and Allan Ahlberg created *The Baby's Catalogue* when they noticed their own daughter's fascination with the mail-order catalogs that came to their house. Full of baby paraphernalia that toddlers will recognize, this book provides much to look at. It follows six babies (including a pair of twins) through their day. Instead of one dad, it portrays five fathers and five mothers of different economic and ethnic backgrounds. The Ahlbergs have also published *Peek-a-Boo!,* which pictures a toddler's day. Every other page has a cut-out round circle, which centers in on one part of the next picture and provides the recurring phrase "Peek-a-Boo." Turning the page, you then see the complete picture, which has many details to discuss.

Using cut paper colláge, Bettina Paterson creates animals that seem so real, children will want to touch them. *My First Wild Animals* presents one large animal to a page including a panda, elephant, and gorilla. This same format was used for more common animals in her *My First Animals*. These are handsome first books for the youngest to point to and label.

Slightly older toddlers delight in *Things I Like* by Anthony Browne. Here, an irresistible chimpanzee lists his favorite pleasures such as going to birthday parties, watching TV, and hearing a bedtime story. The same chimp describes the books he enjoys the most including "scary books" and books about monsters in *I Like Books*.

The bear in the "I Can Do It All By Myself" series, by the Japanese author Shigeo Watanabe and illustrator Yasuo Ohtomo, is a real character. Two-year-olds will giggle at his antics in *How Do I Put It On?* Pictures show the bear putting his pants on over his head, while the text asks "Do I put them on like this?" The child can join in on the resounding "no-o-o!" on the next page as the clever bear then puts them on correctly. After demonstrating the right and wrong way to get dressed, the bear finally does it "all by himself." An even messier bear shows children how not to eat in *What a Good Lunch!* Children love the warmth and humor portrayed in these books and they relish the feeling of knowing more than the bear, a feeling psychologists have called "cognitive conceit." Other books in this series about a confident bear include *I Can Ride It, I Can Build a House, I'm the King of the Castle, Get Set! Go!*, and *Where's My Daddy?* Other series by this talented pair include "I Love to Do Things with Daddy Books" and "I Love Special Days." *It's My Birthday* appears in this latest series and shows Baby Bear and his family looking at the pictures in the family album. As Bear responds to the photos, he cleverly echoes phrases Watanabe includes in the other books such as "Now I'm big enough to put my clothes on *all by myself.*"

Rosemary Wells's little board books about Max, a lovable rabbity creature, are described as "Very First Books." However, the humor is for slightly older toddlers. In *Max's First Word* his sister tries to get Max to talk. She names everything she shows him and Max always responds with "Bang." Giving him an apple, Ruby suggests he say "Yum, yum," but Max surprises her with "Delicious." *Max's Birthday* details Max's fear of the wind-up dinosaur that his sister gives him. By the end of the story he loves it, of course! *Max's Ride* emphasizes such directional terms as "down," "over," "out," "under" as Max careens down a hill in his baby buggy. *Max's Toys* becomes a counting story, but objects are grouped together too quickly in the book as a child is asked to find five balloons, six cars, seven trucks, and a beanbag octopus with eight legs all on one page. Other stories continue big sister Ruby's struggle to get Max to eat an egg for breakfast, take a bath, and go to bed. Max manages to outsmart her every move.

Young children love the lilt and rhyme of *Jesse Bear, What Will You Wear?* by Nancy Carlstrom. Jesse Bear not only wears his red shirt but he wears such unusual things as "the sun on his legs that run" or the three kisses and bear hug that his dad gives him at night. Exuberant paintings of Jesse Bear's day make this a very special book to share with preschoolers and kindergarten children. The two sequels are not as good as the first story.

Swedish author Barbro Lindgren has given us several stories about a funny toddler named Sam. In *Sam's Car* he definitely knows what he wants and fights with a playmate over a toy car until his mother comes to the rescue. In *Sam's Bath* all of his toys and his dog end up in the tub with him. Other titles in this amusing series include *Sam's Book, Sam's Potty*, and *Sam's Wagon*.

The Blanket, describing a whole family's frantic search for a lost blanket, is one of a series by the British artist-author John Burningham. Other titles include *The Rabbit, The Cupboard, The Baby, The Snow*, and *The School*. These squarish-shaped books have more text than those of Oxenbury or Watanabe, but they still portray the activities and interests of a 2- or 3-year-old. For example, in *The Cupboard* the little boy gets out all the pots and pans and then puts them back again. In *The Baby*, this same child details what the baby does at his house, such as eating, sleeping, going for a walk. It concludes with the candid statement that

"Sometimes I like the baby, and sometimes I don't." In these simple stories the young child is always at the center of the action, reflecting the ego-centered way of thinking that is characteristic of this age group. The plot line is not sequential; episodes could be interchanged at will. This is characteristic of the kind of stories the young children tell themselves.

TOY BOOKS

Young children actively respond to a book by pointing or labeling, but some books have a kind of "built-in participation" as part of their design. These books have flaps to lift up and peek under, soft flannel to touch, or holes to poke fingers through. Such books may serve as the transition between toys and real books. *Pat the Bunny* by Dorothy Kunhardt has been a bestseller for the very young child for more than 50 years. In this little book the child is invited to use senses other than sight and sound. A "pattable" bunny made of flannel is on one page, flowers that really smell on another, and Daddy's unshaven face, represented by rough sandpaper, is on still another. Young children literally wear out this "tactile" book.

An increasing number of sophisticated cut-out books and "lift the flap" stories are appearing on the market. In *Where Can It Be?* Ann Jonas uses cleverly designed half pages to open closets, cupboards, and refrigerator doors to further a little girl's search for her loved lost blanket. Just when she is about to give up, the blanket is returned by her friend. The half pages provide suspense; will the blanket be in the closet, under the tablecloth, in her bed?

Eric Hill's "lift the flap" stories about the dog Spot never fail to intrigue young children. In *Where's Spot?* Spot's mother Sally searches for her puppy behind a door, inside a clock, under the stairs, in the piano, and under the rug. As the child opens doors and lifts up flaps to join in the search, highly unlikely creatures such as monkeys, snakes, and lions answer "no" to the question "Is he in here?" Since "no" is one of 2-year-olds' favorite words, they love to chime in on the refrain. In *Spot's First Walk* the puppy meets all kinds of adventures behind fences, by chicken coops, and in the pond. These books are sturdily made, the pictures are bright and clear, and the stories are imaginative. Other titles in the series include *Spot's Birthday Party* and *Spot's First Christmas*. The titles are also available in Spanish editions.

Eric Carle's story of *The Very Hungry Caterpillar* is a favorite with children from 3 through 6. This imaginative tale describes the life cycle of a ravenous caterpillar who leaves behind a trail of holes in all the food that he eats. Children love to stick their fingers through the holes and count them. They particularly enjoy the caterpillar's menu for Saturday, which includes "one piece of chocolate cake, one ice cream cone, one pickle, one slice of Swiss cheese, one slice of salami, one lollipop, one piece of cherry pie, one sausage, one cupcake and one slice of watermelon." In Carle's multisensory story of *The Very Busy Spider*, children are invited to feel the pictures as well as see them. Brilliant collages depict familiar animals whose questions are never answered by the spider, who is too busy spinning her tactile web. No one can resist feeling these pictures in this story that emphasizes all the senses. Eric Carle's *The Very Quiet Cricket* tries and tries rubbing his legs together to make his cricket sound and nothing happens. He meets one insect after another including a humming bee, a whirring dragonfly, and a screeching cicada. Finally the little cricket meets a female cricket and responds with "the most beautiful sound she had ever heard." Turn the page and you hear the sound of the cricket coming from a computer chip imbedded in the pages of the book. Children are delightfully surprised by this multisensory book and ask to hear it over and over again. However, enjoyment of this book is limited by the life of the noisemaker.

Carle's story of *The Grouchy Ladybug* describes a nasty-tempered bug who quarrels with everyone she meets until she encounters a whale. Clever die-cut pages reinforce concepts of relative size and time of day. This book is more appropriate for children from ages 5 through 7.

Books that describe different kinds of sounds invite their own special kind of noisy participation. *Noisy* by Shirley Hughes pictures the noises a baby and a toddler can make, as well as the noises they hear. Realistic pictures show a frus-

GUIDELINES

Evaluating Books For The Very Young Child

The best books for babies and toddlers should meet these criteria:

♦ Relate to familiar life experiences.
♦ Provide clear uncluttered illustrations with little or no distracting background.
♦ Are well constructed with sturdy durable pages.
♦ Use clear, natural language.
♦ Have predictable stories.
♦ Provide some humor, especially so the child will feel superior.
♦ Offer opportunities for participation and interaction.
♦ Hold the attention of the child.

trated mother holding a bawling baby while the telephone rings and the stew boils over. Peter Spier's book of animal sounds is titled *Gobble Growl Grunt*, while in *Crash! Bang! Boom!* the reader may compare the quiet crunch of new boots in the snow with the police siren's commanding cry of "you, yo-u, y-o-u." *Pigs Say Oink* by Martha Alexander includes sounds of many animals, trains, children at a nursery school, and the quietest sound of all, when everyone is asleep. *Early Morning in the Barn* by Nancy Tafuri begins with a large double-page spread picturing a rooster waking the barnyard with his "cock-a-doodle-doo." A little chick responds with a "cheep," which awakens his brother and sister. All three run out of the henhouse into the barnyard, where they are greeted by an array of animals each making their familiar noise. Finally the story comes full circle as the chicks meet their mother hen. Lovely sunny pictures add to the fun of this noisy book.

If a book does not provide for participation, the adult reader can stimulate it by the kinds of questions he or she asks. For example, when sharing the old favorite *Caps for Sale* by Slobodkina, the parent might say to the child, "Find the monkey—not the one in the red hat, not the one in the blue hat, but the one in the green hat!" Such participation will help children develop visual discrimination, but, more importantly, it will add to the fun of the story time.

FINGER RHYMES AND NURSERY SONGS

Finger rhymes are one traditional way to provide for young children's participation as they play "Five Little Pigs" or sing "Where Is Thumbkin?" and the ever popular "Eensy, Weensy Spider." Finger plays date back to the time of Friedrich Froebel, the so-called father of the kindergarten movement, who went out in the German countryside and collected the finger plays and games that the peasant mothers were using with their children.

Sarah Hayes selected over twenty favorite finger rhymes to include in her book *Clap Your Hands*. Toni Gaffe provided the lively step-by-step illustrations to demonstrate the action of such rhymes as "Little Turtle . . . ," "Incey Wincey Spider . . . ," and "Ten Fat Sausages. . . ."

Marc Brown gives clear directions in his two books titled *Finger Rhymes* and *Hand Rhymes*. Each book inclues some fourteen popular rhymes such as "This is the church/This is the steeple" and "Five Little Goblins." *Finger Rhymes* is illustrated with amusing black-and-white pictures; *Hand Rhymes* is in full color.

Tom Glazer's *Eye Winker Tom Tinker Chin Chopper* provides the music and verbal directions for some fifty finger plays. His collection includes some for the youngest, such as "Eye Winker," "Pat-a-Cake," "Here Is the Church," and some longer cumulative songs for older children, such as "I Know an Old Lady Who Swallowed a Fly" and "There's a Hole in the Bottom of the Sea." Piano arrangements and guitar chords accompany each of these rhymes.

Babies and young toddlers often first respond to the sounds of music and singing. After Margot Zemach had sung the lullaby "Hush, Little Baby" to her daughter Rebecca every night for over a year, she decided to illustrate the song. Music is provided for the parents who might want to sing *Hush, Little Baby* and be delightfully entertained at the same time by the humorous visual images of each verse. Zemach's earthy pictures seem just right for this song and also for the cumulative Ozark song that her husband adapted for her pictures in *Mommy, Buy Me a China Doll*. Unfortunately, they did not include the music in this book, but Eliza Lou's ingenious suggestions of ways they can obtain money in order to buy her a doll make for an amusing tale without the music.

Another bit of authentic Americana is Aliki's spirited song *Go Tell Aunt Rhody*. Starting with brilliant endpapers of quilt blocks, this illustrated songbook tells the familiar tale of the death of the old gray goose. While the gander and the goslings mourn her death, Aunt Rhody is pleased indeed with her new feather bed.

Nadine Westcott creates a hilarious tale to accompany the old nursery song in *Skip to My Lou*. When his parents leave a young boy in charge of the farm, the animals take over and chaos ensues. But 15 minutes before his parents return, the boy ends the romp and the animals all help clean up the mess.

Children made up additional verses to the rollicking old folksong *Oh, A-Hunting We Will Go*, adapted by John Langstaff. Nancy Winslow Parker's childlike illustrations are carefully arranged so as not to give away the last lines of each verse. Once children have determined the pattern of the song, they can guess what will be seen in the next picture. They easily predict the goat will end up "in a boat," but they laugh at the bear who gets put "in underwear." Children may want to create their own additions to this song after they hear these verses.

Counting rhymes have also been made into individual songbooks. *Roll Over*, illustrated by Merle Peek, shows a little boy in bed with nine animals. Each time they roll over, one animal falls out of bed. As the number of animals in the bed dwindles, children can look to see where they have found resting places in the room. Finally, when only the boy is asleep in his bed, a lion in a picture in his room appears to be winking and all the other animals are seen on a wall frieze that rings the ceiling. The music accompanies this tale of a young child's imaginary game. Mordicai Gerstein's *Roll Over!* is a small-sized book featuring a fold-out flap on each page. As a little boy calls out "Roll over," the reader lifts the flap to discover which of his animal friends has fallen out of the huge bed. After the little boy is asleep alone in his bed, all the animals come creeping back.

Eileen Christelow illustrates another patterned rhyme in her amusing *Five Little Monkeys Jumping on the Bed*. Young children love to chant this story along with you. The surprise ending when Mama monkey jumps on her bed sends them into fits of laughter.

Ezra Jack Keats illustrated the old counting rhyme *Over in the Meadow* with collage pictures in jewel-like colors. The fine recording by Marvin Hayes for Scholastic increases children's enjoyment of the lilt and rhythm of this favorite nursery song. Paul Galdone's bright clear pictures for his version of this nursery rhyme emphasize the counting aspect of the story by including both the words for the numbers and the numerals themselves. Primary-grade children might compare these two different presentations of the traditional song with the illustrations by Feodor Rojankovsky for John Langstaff's version of this story of all the animals who lived in the sunny meadow by the cool pond. Rojankovsky received the Caldecott award for his amusing interpretation of an old Scottish ballad telling of the wedding festivities of Frog and Miss Mousie. Langstaff used the Southern Appalachian music for this tale of *Frog Went A-Courtin'*. Wendy Watson's version of this 400-year-old ballad depicts a miniature woodland world with tiny animal characters dressed in overalls, long skirts, and aprons. The tune at the end of the tale is the one the artist learned in childhood. By way of contrast, Chris Conover presents an elegant eighteenth-century small world complete with formal gardens and mouse statues in her version, *Froggie Went A-Courting*. A seafaring debonair frog woos a fashionably dressed Miss Mousie. Children could compare these three versions, contrasting both the art and the verses of this well-loved song.

Michael Rosen recounts the popular action rhyme *We're Going on a Bear Hunt* as an exciting adventure tale. Pictures by Helen Oxenbury portray a father and his four children (including the baby) crossing a field of waving grass ("Swishy, swashy"), wading in the mud ("Squelch, squerch"), and braving a snowstorm ("Hoooo woooo") until they reach a gloomy cave and see a

Helen Oxenbury portrays a father and his four children splashing through the deep cold river in Michael Rosen's retelling of *We're Going on a Bear Hunt*. The onomatopoetic text, lovely large watercolors, and surprise ending make this a favorite to read aloud.

bear! Oxenbury alternates black-and-white pictures with sweeping landscapes in full color. Children will relish the sound effects, the humor, and the drama of this tale.

Peter Spier's setting for the nursery rhyme song, *The Fox Went Out on a Chilly Night,* portrays the colorful autumn countryside outside of a New England village. Shimmering moonlit pictures won this book a Caldecott Honor Award. The complete text of the song is provided at the end of the book. Youngsters can sing along with a second sharing of the story or join in while viewing the excellent filmstrip from Weston Woods.

Children have their choice of many editions of *Old MacDonald Had a Farm.* Lorinda Cauley portrays a patient rotund farmer who does his best to get his chores done despite the interfering animals. By way of contrast, Glen Rounds uses bold primitive drawings to depict his bowlegged farmer and angular animals including a skunk! Cleverly designed die-cut pages add an animal each time you turn a page in Nancy Hellen's version of this cumulative song. And Carol Jones creates a peephole on each page of her engaging version. The first peephole view shows just a part of a chicken. Turn the page and you see the whole chicken in the hen house. While the number and kind of animals differ in these books, they all provide the words and the music except for Jones's version. Carol Jones created a similar format for a picture book of the traditional song *This Old Man.* Preschoolers and even toddlers love to join in with the chorus of this song:

With a nick nack Paddy whack
    give a dog a bone
This old man came rolling home.

The peephole on each page of this ingenious book allows the children to first guess what the old man and his young friend are doing; turn the page and you can see that they are involved in all kinds of activities from gardening to making a birdhouse.

Nadine Westcott illustrates the traditional version of the popular song *I Know an Old Lady Who Swallowed a Fly.* After using seven cans of bug spray to kill the fly she swallowed, the old lady reels from one epicurean delight to another. Devouring the horse, she dies of course! Colin and Jacqui Hawkins have the old lady sneeze after swallowing the horse and up come all the animals. By lifting up the old lady's apron, the reader can see all the animals in her stomach. This would make an excellent model for an enlarged old lady that children could then put their drawn animals into. A sealed sandwich bag stapled behind her apron would make a good imitation stomach. Open the bag and you could remove the animals. Also the speech balloons in the Hawkins's tale encourage children's own original writing.

One of primary children's favorite songs is *The Wheels on the Bus.* Maryann Kovalski provides a London setting for her picture story of Jenny and Joanna and their grandma who sing this song as they wait for their bus. They become so involved with their actions and singing, they miss their bus and have to take a taxi. Wonderful action-filled pictures illustrate each verse while the song within the context of a story creates more fun. Paul Zelinsky's interpretation of this song features paper engineering—wheels spin, the windshield wipers go "swish, swish, swish," and flaps and pullouts provide other items to manipulate. Well constructed, this movable version captivates children's attention.

Nancy Larrick compiled *Songs from Mother Goose* illustrated by Robin Spowart. Designed as a lap book, the book gives each verse its own illustration and traditional melody. Parents and teachers will find this collection very useful. Tom Glazer also collected some forty-four popular rhymes with their melodies in his *Mother Goose Songbook.* Large humorous illustrations by David McPhail extend each verse.

All children need to hear songs from the time they are babies right through school. Many emergent readers' first books are shared nursery rhymes and songs or chants. Children "read" the familiar words as they sing the songs. Just as families have favorite songs that they sing in the bath or in the car, classes should have favorite songs to start the day or to sing while they are waiting to go to lunch or outside to play. A class without favorite songs is as sad as a class without favorite books.

Two children practice reading the speech balloons in their nursery-rhyme mural.

Mission School, Redlands Public Schools, Redlands, California. Nancy Anderson, teacher. Photo by Larry Rose.

MOTHER GOOSE

For many children, Mother Goose is their first introduction to the world of literature. Even a 1-year-old child will respond with delight to the language games of "Pat-a-Cake! Pat-a-Cake!" or "This Little Pig Went to Market." Many of the Mother Goose rhymes and jingles continue to be favorites among the 4s and 5s. What is the attraction of Mother Goose that makes her so appealing to these young children? What accounts for her survival through these many years? Much of the language in these rhymes is obscure; for example, modern-day children have no idea what curds and whey are, yet they delight in Little Miss Muffet. Nothing in current literature has replaced the venerable Mother Goose for the nursery school age.

Appeal of Mother Goose

Much of the appeal of Mother Goose lies in the musical quality of the varied langauge patterns, the rhythm and rhyme of the verses, the alliteration of such lines as "Wee Willie Winkie runs through the town" or "Deedle, deedle, dumpling, my son John."

Three cognitive psychologists[9] from Oxford University have linked children's experience with nursery rhymes to developing a sensitivity to

[9]Morag Maclean, Peter Bryant, and Lynette Bradley, "Rhymes, Nursery Rhymes, and Reading in Early Childhood," *Merrill-Palmer Quarterly, Journal of Developmental Psychology*, vol. 33 (July 1987), pp. 255–281.

the sounds within words. Following preschool children for two years, they found that the ways in which the boys and girls could use rhyme and play with words that had the same beginning sounds was strongly related to their eventual success in reading. Singing and chanting nursery rhymes appears to contribute to children's emergent literacy development.

More importantly, however, children love the sound of the words, for they are experimenting with language in this period of their lives. The child learns new words every day; he likes to try them out, to chant them in his play. Mother Goose rhymes help the young child satisfy this preoccupation with language patterns and stimulate further language development.

Mother Goose rhymes also offer young children many opportunities for active participation and response. The young child loves to get bounced on Daddy's knee to the rhythm of "Ride a Cock Horse" or clap hands to the sound of "Pat-a-cake, pat-a-cake, baker's man." Some of the rhymes—such as "Pease Porridge Hot," "London Bridge," or "Ring a Ring o'Roses"—are games or involve direct action from the child. Other verses include counting rhymes—as in "1, 2, buckle my shoe, 3, 4, shut the door." Slightly older children enjoy answering the riddles in some of the Mother Goose verses or attempting to say their favorite tongue twisters. Every child likes to fool someone with the well-known riddle: "As I was going to St. Ives, I met a man with seven wives." And they never fail to delight in successful recitation of the entire verse of "Peter Piper picked a peck of pickled peppers."

Another attraction of many of the Mother Goose rhymes is their narrative quality; they tell a good story with quick action. In just six lines "Little Miss Muffet" proves to be an exciting tale with action, a climax, and a satisfying conclusion. This is also true of "Simple Simon," "Sing a Song of Sixpence," "The Old Woman in the Shoe," and "Three Blind Mice." Preschool and kindergarten children enjoy pantomiming or dramatizing these well-known verse stories.

Many of the characters in Mother Goose have interesting, likable personalities: Old King Cole *is* a merry old soul; Old Mother Hubbard not only

tries to find her poor dog a bone but she runs all over town at his special bidding; and although Tommy Lynn puts the pussy in the well, Johnny Stout pulls her out! Unpleasant but intriguing character traits are suggested by "Crosspatch," "Tom, the Piper's Son," and "Lazy Elsie Marley."

The content of the verses reflects the interests of young children. Many favorites are rhymes about animals—"The Three Little Kittens," "The Cat and the Fiddle," and the story of the mouse that ran up the clock in "Hickory Dickory Dock." Some of the verses are about simple everyday experiences and include such incidents as "Lucy Locket" losing her pocket, "The Three Little Kittens" losing their mittens, and "Little Bo Peep" losing her sheep. Children's pranks are enacted in "Ding, Dong, Bell!" and "Georgie Porgie." "Peter, Peter, Pumpkin-Eater" has a housing problem, as does the "Old Woman in the Shoe." There are many verses about seasons and the weather, a concern of both young and old. The pleading request of one child, "Rain, Rain, Go Away," reflects the universal feelings of all children.

A major appeal of Mother Goose is the varied humor. There is the jolly good fun of a ridiculous situation in:

One misty, moisty morning
When cloudy was the weather,
I chanced to meet an old man
Clothed all in leather;
He began to compliment
And I began to grin—
"How do you do" and "How do you do"
And "How do you do" again!

Two 6-year-olds interpreted this verse in action by pretending to pass each other; as one moved to the left, the other moved in the same direction. Their movements were perfect for this amusing and familiar situation.

The young child's rather primitive sense of humor, which delights in other persons' misfortune, is satisfied by the verses about "Jack and Jill" and "Dr. Foster":

Doctor Foster went to Gloucester
In a shower of rain;

He stepped in a puddle up to his middle
And never went there again.

The pure nonsense in Mother Goose tickles children's funny bones. Chukovsky,[10] a Russian poet, reminds us that there is sense in nonsense; a child has to know reality to appreciate the juxtaposition of the strawberries and the herrings in this verse:

🐦 The man in the wilderness asked me
How many strawberries grow in the sea.
I answered him as I thought good,
As many as red herrings grow in the wood.

Different Editions of Mother Goose

Today's children are fortunate in being able to choose among many beautifully illustrated Mother Goose editions. There is no *one* best Mother Goose book, for this is a matter for individual preference. Some Mother Goose books seem to stay in print indefinitely. Each generation may have its favorite edition, yet older versions remain popular. The children in every family deserve at least one of the better editions, however. Preschool and primary teachers will also want to have one that can be shared with small groups of children who may not have been fortunate enough ever to have seen a really beautiful Mother Goose.

COLLECTIONS

One of the most glorious nursery rhyme collections is *Tomie de Paola's Mother Goose*. Each of the over 200 verses is illustrated with brilliant jewel tones against a clear white background. Characters of many races are included quite naturally. Pictures are large enough to be shared with a large group of children. Several include a full-page spread; many show a sequence of action. Careful placement of the rhymes provides such interesting artistic contrasts as the jagged lines of the crooked man's house next to the rounded haystack of Little Boy Blue. The total format of this comprehensive Mother Goose is pleasing to the eye.

[10]Kornei Chukovsky, *From Two to Five*, translated by Miriam Morton (Berkeley: University of California Press, 1963), p. 95.

Tomie de Paola uses brilliant jewel-like tones to paint his traditional-appearing Mother Goose. Good humor abounds in both the illustrations and the verses selected from the authentic Iona and Peter Opie Collection.

From *Tomie de Paola's Mother Goose.*

Wendy Watson's Mother Goose incorporates over 200 traditional verses along with some well-known rhymes. Set in rural America, each verse is illustrated with small pictures of animal characters or round-figured rustic folk. A unique feature of this book is that the illustrations span the seasons of a year beginning with a frosty morning and ending with a chilly midnight New Year's Eve.

The Random House Book of Mother Goose should have been named for its editor/illustrator, Arnold Lobel, for it was one of the last books published before his death in 1987. Lobel illustrated over 300 rhymes in this lively collection. Large double-page spreads seem to swirl with energy as Wee Willie Winkie runs through a darkened town filled with houses with pointed roofs that look as

Peter, Peter, pumpkin eater,
Had a wife and couldn't keep her;
He put her in a pumpkin shell
And there he kept her very well.

Children will quickly spy the knife in Peter Peter's pumpkin and realize that despite what the rhyme says, he will not be able to keep his wife for very long. *James Marshall's Mother Goose* provides a humorous look at the venerable Old Goose.

frightened as little Willie. Jack and Jill wear paper crowns as they climb an enormous hill. Filled with fresh images and spontaneity, Lobel's Mother Goose book is a lasting contribution to children from this talented and well-loved illustrator. *Whiskers and Rhymes*, also by Lobel, is a lively collection of rhymes about cats. Although he only features several dozen rhymes, *James Marshall's Mother Goose* provides young children with a fresh and funny look at the venerable Old Goose. Most of the rhymes included in this collection are humorous, with hilarious illustrations to match. Children clever enough to spy the knife slipping through the pumpkin shell will realize that Peter Peter is not going to be able to keep his wife forever, despite the last line of the rhyme.

Sharing Marshall's funny parody on "Hey Diddle Diddle" might inspire older children to create their own original Mother Goose rhymes.

Adult readers will enjoy searching for such famous persons as Robert Frost, Princess Anne, Toscanini, Napoleon, and Hitler in Wallace Tripp's hilarious Mother Goose titled *Granfa' Grig Had a Pig*. Young children delight in the brightly colored pictures and the antics of the many funny animal characters; older children laugh at the frequent puns and comments included in the speech balloons of some of the verses. The crooked old man is really a "crook," portrayed with his accomplices, the crooked cat and mouse. This is a vibrant and modern Mother Goose book that will entertain all ages.

A recent collection by Zena Sutherland consists of some seventy-five verses under the title of *The Orchard Book of Nursery Rhymes*. Brilliant detailed illustrations by Faith Jaques depict an eighteenth-century setting of rural England, the source of many of these verses. A few, such as "How much wood would a woodchuck chuck," reveal their American origin. Adding to the authenticity of this edition are the carefully researched notes on the sources and variants of these verses by both author and illustrator.

Scholars of nursery rhymes are all indebted to Iona and Peter Opie for their definitive work, *The Oxford Dictionary of Nursery Rhymes*, in which they assembled almost everything known about these verses. In order to support the gift of their large children's literature collection to the Bodleian Library of Oxford, Iona Opie selected many previously unpublished rhymes for her book *Tail Feathers from Mother Goose: The Opie Rhyme Book*. Beginning with a cover by Maurice Sendak, each verse is illustrated by a different well-known artist. Some of these little known rhymes delight slightly older children. Sendak illustrated a new version of the Opies' first collection, *I Saw Esau*, which includes 170 rhymes, tongue twisters, jeers, and jump-rope rhymes. The many small pictures are just as sly and naughty as the children's rhymes. Only 7½ × 5 inches, this "Schoolchild's Pocket Book" is a superb example of fine bookmaking.

The Rooster Crows by Maud and Miska Petersham is sometimes called an American

Mother Goose for it includes many well-known American rhymes and jingles such as "A bear went over the mountain" and "How much wood would a woodchuck chuck . . ." Another bit of Americana is found in the highly original *Father Fox's Pennyrhymes*, written by Clyde Watson and illustrated by her sister, Wendy Watson. These nonsense rhymes and jingles have the lilt and rhythm of traditional verses of folklore. The little watercolor-and-ink illustrations detail the antics of Father Fox and his friends and relatives in old-fashioned pictures. The Watsons create more original rhymes in *Catch Me and Kiss Me and Say It Again*. Characterized by the sound of traditional

GUIDELINES

Evaluating Mother Goose Books

With so many editions of Mother Goose, what factors should be considered when evaluating them? The following points may be useful in studying various editions:

♦ *Coverage:* How many verses are included? Are they well-known rhymes, or are there some fresh and unusual ones?

♦ *Illustrations:* What medium has been used? What colors? Are the illustrations realistic, stylized, or varied? Are the illustrations consistent with the text? Do they elaborate the text? What is the mood of the illustrations (humorous, sedate, high-spirited)? Has the illustrator created a fresh original approach, avoiding cliché-ridden images?

♦ *Text:* Does the text read smoothly or have verses been altered? Is the text all on the same page, or fragmented by turning the page?

♦ *Setting:* What background is presented—rural or urban? Does the book take place in any particular country? Is the setting modern or in the past? What does the setting add to the collection?

♦ *Characters:* Do the characters come from a variety of ethnic backgrounds? Do the characters have distinct personalities? Are adults and children featured? Only children? How are animals presented—as humans or realistically?

♦ *Arrangement:* Is there a thematic arrangement of the verses? Is there a feeling of unity to the whole book, rather than just separate verses? Are pictures and verses well spaced or crowded? Is it clear which picture illustrates which verse?

♦ *Format:* What is the quality of the paper and the binding? Is the title page well designed? Is there an index or table of contents? Is there harmony among endpapers, cover, and jacket?

No matter what edition is selected, children should be exposed to the rhythm and rhyme of Mother Goose. It is part of their literary heritage and may serve as their first introduction to the realm of literature.

folklore, these little rhymes contain the loving humor captured in the title verse. Large watercolor pictures celebrate the daily games and activities of chubby, robust children. These include finger plays, piggyback rides, and rhymes for dressing, eating, cutting fingernails, watching thunderstorms, and sleeping.

With such a proliferation of nursery rhyme books, parents, teachers and librarians will want to examine a variety of collections before sharing them with their children. Even though you may have a favorite collection, try new ones with fresh images and unfamiliar rhymes after you have read the more traditional ones. Mother Goose should never be enjoyed only once, but read over and over again.

SINGLE-VERSE EDITIONS

A recent publishing trend has been the production of picture books portraying only one Mother Goose rhyme or a limited number of rhymes around a single theme.

Maurice Sendak was one of the first to extend the text of two single verses with illustrations in his *Hector Protector and As I Went over the Water*. The actual rhyme about Hector Protector is only five lines in length.

> ❦ Hector Protector was dressed all in green.
> Hector Protector was sent to the Queen.
> The Queen did not like him
> No more did the king
> So Hector Protector was sent back again.

Sendak provides many reasons why the queen did not like him: he has a young 5-year-old Hector arriving at the palace of Queen Victoria astride a lion and carrying a snake-wrapped sword. Some twenty-four action-filled pictures expand the story behind this five-line verse.

Colin and Jacqui Hawkins have created a clever lift-the-flap version of *Old Mother Hubbard*. In this humorous updated tale Mother Hubbard is a rounded, almost comic book, character. The first part of each rhyme appears on the left side of the page with a door on the right. Open the door and the reader discovers a very funny dog going through all kinds of capers, including brushing his teeth and writing a letter. The traditional verses of the supposed death of the dog and Mother Hubbard's trip to the undertaker have been eliminated. Tomie de Paola stages his version of *The Comic Adventures of Old Mother Hubbard and Her Dog*. Four box seats on the page facing the title page contain Bo-Peep and sheep, Humpty Dumpty, Mother Goose and friend, and a servant awaiting the arrival of the guests in the fourth box. On the next page, when the King and Queen of Hearts are in their places, the curtain rises on the story of Old Mother Hubbard and the antics of her dog. Children love to look for surprises in their books and Tomie de Paola seldom fails them. In this tale he incorporates some fifteen other nursery rhymes in four oval vignettes on the proscenium of the stage. A comparison of these Old Mother Hubbard books exposes young children to various art styles and helps them see how many different ways one nursery rhyme can be interpreted.

In his foreword to *Mary Had a Little Lamb*, Tomie de Paola reminds us that this well-loved verse was first written by Sarah Josepha Hale in

Clear color photographs of a young girl and her lamb give a brand-new look to the traditional rhyme of *Mary Had a Little Lamb*.

Photos by Bruce McMillan.

❦   ❦   ❦

1830 and then appeared in a McGuffey Reader. Since that time, however, it has been included in many collections of Mother Goose. In illustrating a single edition of this verse de Paola is faithful to the time and historical setting of the original poem. Bruce McMillan uses full-color photos of an African-American child who poses for a rural Mary in his artfully crafted version of Hale's verse. Equally faithful to the historical context of this verse, both books would be good choices for sharing with children.

In a succession of carefully selected nursery rhymes, Peter Spier tells the story of a farmer's day in New Castle, Delaware, during the early nineteenth century. Spier's detailed, colorful pictures begin before dawn as Mr. Marley (Lazy Elsie is asleep in the log farmhouse) prepares to go to market. In *To Market, to Market* a cohesive story is told with many nursery rhymes until the Marleys return to the farm on "silver Saturday," for "the morn's the resting day."

Two recent books make a kind of game based on children's knowledge of Mother Goose. The easiest one, Eric Hill's *Nursery Rhyme Peek-a-Book*, asks rhyming questions such as "Hickory, dickory, dock, what ran up the clock?" Lifting the flap covering the face of the clock, the child discovers not only a little mouse, but the text of the whole rhyme printed on the inside of the flap. Ten well-known rhymes such as "Old Mother Hubbard," "Sing a Song of Sixpence," "Humpty Dumpty," and "Little Miss Muffet" are included. If children don't know these verses, they will after hearing this book. Sturdily made with lively, clear pictures, it provides for much participation and learning.

Each Peach Pear Plum by the Ahlbergs pulls together characters from Mother Goose and traditional folktales in a kind of "I Spy" game. Starting with Little Tom Thumb, each successive picture hides a new character somewhere in its design. Thus the picture of Baby Bunting carries the text "Baby Bunting fast asleep, I spy Bo-Peep," while the next picture of Bo-Peep challenges the viewer to find Jack and Jill. Children delight in playing this game and they particularly love the ending, which pictures all of the characters together, eating plum pie, of course.

B. G. Hennessy creates a believable story about what happened to *The Missing Tarts*. All the

Mother Goose characters search diligently only to discover that the Knave of Hearts had given them to the children of "The Old Woman in The Shoe." Like *Each Peach Pear Plum* this story synthesizes children's knowledge of Mother Goose.

NURSERY RHYME COLLECTIONS OF OTHER LANDS

Nursery rhymes are difficult to translate because they are based on sound and nonsense. N. M. Bodecker's *It's Raining, Said John Twaining* is an enchanting translation of Danish nursery rhymes. Bodecker, a poet and artist, translated and adapted these rhymes into English so he could share his childhood favorites with his three sons. His pictures are as droll and humorous as some of the rhymes, particularly the title verse.

Barbara Cooney creates authentic settings for her pictures of Latin American rhymes collected from the Spanish community in America. Each rhyme in *Tortillitas Para Mama* by Margot Griego and others is written in both Spanish and English. The English verses do not rhyme but the Spanish

Barbara Cooney provides strong authentic paintings for this collection of Latin American nursery rhymes garnered from the Spanish community in the Americas by Margo Griego and others.

From *Tortillitas Para Mama*.

ones do. *Arroz Con Leche: Popular Songs and Rhymes from Latin America* collected by Lulu Delacre is another source of rhymes of Spanish origin.

Robert Wyndham's *Chinese Mother Goose Rhymes* has been reissued. Each page shows a rhyme in English and then the same rhyme is written in Chinese characters. Strikingly illustrated by Ed Young, this collection includes rhymes about dragons as well as counting out rhymes.

In *Dragons and Kites and Dragonflies,* Demi presents some twenty-two nursery rhymes illustrated with brilliant full-page watercolors. In this collection only the rhymed English versions are given. Students involved in a study of China could well begin with these rhymes about dragon boats, the Great Wall, and a Chinese wedding procession. All these rhymes reflect the culture of China as in

Little silk worms, if you please,
   Eat up all the mulberry leaves
   Make cocoons as white as milk
   And we'll have clothes of purest silk.[11]

Sharing rhymes from other countries lets children of many cultures tap into the memories of their parents to find rhymes in a variety of languages. The creation of nursery rhymes for the young child is a universal activity.

Young children enjoy all kinds of poetry besides nursery rhymes. See Chapter 8 for more about poetry.

[11]Demi, *Dragons and Kites and Dragonflies: A Collection of Chinese Nursery Rhymes* (New York: Harcourt Brace Jovanovich, 1986), unpaged.

RESOURCES FOR TEACHING

♦ MOTHER GOOSE BOOKS ♦

AUTHOR/ILLUSTRATOR	TITLE	UNIQUE FEATURES
TRADITIONAL COLLECTIONS		
Leslie Brooke	*Ring o' Roses*	Published in 1923, this was the first collection to include humorous animals.
Kate Greenaway	*Mother Goose, or the Old Nursery Rhymes*	This has been a treasured classic since 1901. Tiny format and precise old-fashioned pictures of proper children.
Arthur Rackham	*Mother Goose, or the Old Nursery Rhymes*	Contains small eerie pictures of pointed-eared elves and personified trees.
Feodor Rojankovsky	*The Tall Book of Mother Goose*	Pictures depict natural-looking children showing real emotions. Humpty Dumpty is portrayed as Hitler, appropriate to the time of this book's publication in 1942.
Blanche Fisher Wright	*The Real Mother Goose*	With pale flat traditional pictures, this book has been divided into four narrow-sized board books with checkered covers.

RESOURCES FOR TEACHING

♦ MOTHER GOOSE BOOKS (CONTINUED) ♦

AUTHOR/ILLUSTRATOR	TITLE	UNIQUE FEATURES
CONTEMPORARY COLLECTIONS		
Nicola Bayley	*The Nicola Bayley Book of Nursery Rhymes*	Jewel-like colors characterize the intricate illustrations by this well-known British illustrator.
Raymond Briggs	*The Mother Goose Treasury*	Contains over 400 rhymes and twice as many illustrations. A lively vibrant presentation by a British illustrator.
Marguerite de Angeli	*The Book of Nursery and Mother Goose Rhymes*	Some 250 soft watercolored illustrations portray the English countryside and show her love and knowledge of her children.
Tomie de Paola	*Tomie de Paola's Mother Goose*	See text.
Eric Hill	*The Nursery Rhyme Peek-a-Book*	See text.
Arnold Lobel	*The Random House Book of Mother Goose*	See text.
James Marshall	*James Marshall's Mother Goose*	See text.
Iona and Peter Opie, Maurice Sendak	*I Saw Esau*	See text.
Iona and Peter Opie	*Tail Feathers from Mother Goose*	See text.
Helen Oxenbury	*The Helen Oxenbury Nursery Rhyme Book*	Over fifty verses are illustrated with humorous, droll illustrations of common folk.
Maud and Miska Petersham	*The Rooster Crows*	See text.
Alice and Martin Provensen	*The Mother Goose Book*	By grouping rhymes around various subjects, the artists have made one large picture serve several verses. Victorian dress reflects the period and origin of Mother Goose.

RESOURCES FOR TEACHING		
◆ MOTHER GOOSE BOOKS (CONTINUED) ◆		
AUTHOR/ILLUSTRATOR	**TITLE**	**UNIQUE FEATURES**
Richard Scarry	*Richard Scarry's Best Mother Goose Ever*	Large brilliant-colored illustrations of animal characters make this a Mother Goose book that captures the attention of the youngest child.
Zena Sutherland, Faith Jaques	*The Orchard Book of Mother Goose*	See text.
Tasha Tudor	*Mother Goose*	Small soft pastel pictures are quaint and charmingly reminiscent of the work of Kate Greenaway.
Wallace Tripp	*Granfa' Grig Had a Pig*	See text.
Wendy Watson	*Wendy Watson's Mother Goose*	See text.
Brian Wildsmith	*Brian Wildsmith's Mother Goose*	Pictures are glowing watercolors with the typical Wildsmith trademarks seen in the harlequin designs on clothing and the frequency with which he portrays the backs of people.
SINGLE VERSE EDITIONS		
Lorinda Bryan Cauley	*The Three Little Kittens*	Appealing kittens would delight very young children.
Tomie de Paola	*The Comic Adventures of Old Mother Hubbard and Her Dog*	See text.
Susan Jeffers	*Three Jovial Huntsmen*	Three bumbling hunters search and search for their quarry and never see the many hidden animals watching them.
Paul Galdone	*The History of Simple Simon* *The House That Jack Built* *Old Mother Hubbard and Her Dog* *Three Little Kittens* *Tom, Tom, the Piper's Son*	Galdone's pictures for all these verses are large and clear with lively action, fine for sharing with groups.

RESOURCES FOR TEACHING

♦ MOTHER GOOSE BOOKS (CONTINUED) ♦

AUTHOR/ILLUSTRATOR	TITLE	UNIQUE FEATURES
Sarah Josepha Hale, Tomie de Paola	*Mary Had a Little Lamb*	See text.
Bruce McMillan	*Mary Had a Little Lamb*	See text.
Colin and Jacqui Hawkins	*Old Mother Hubbard*	See text.
Susan Ramsay Hoguet	*Solomon Grundy*	The life span of a nineteenth-century New England baker provides authentic period detail.
John W. Ivimey, Paul Galdone	*Three Blind Mice*	An expanded story with a happy ending. Illustrated in Galdone's usual lively style.
John W. Ivimey, Victoria Chess	*Three Blind Mice*	Same story as above with slightly more frightening pictures and sly wit by Victoria Chess. Fun to compare the two books.
Leonard Lubin	*Sing a Song of Sixpence*	Lubin captures the surprised expression of the seated royalty when the king cuts his famous pie. With historical note.
Tracey Campbell Pearson	*Sing a Song of Sixpence*	Children could compare this humorous version with Lubin's interpretation.
Rodney Peppe	*The House That Jack Built*	Splendid bold collage pictures illustrate this favorite cumulative rhyme.
Alice and Martin Provensen	*Old Mother Hubbard*	Old Mother Hubbard is illustrated with large colorful pictures.
Maurice Sendak	*Hector Protector and As I Went Over the Water*	See text.

RESOURCES FOR TEACHING		
◆ MOTHER GOOSE BOOKS (CONTINUED) ◆		
AUTHOR/ILLUSTRATOR	TITLE	UNIQUE FEATURES
Peter Spier	*London Bridge Is Falling Down*	Notes on the back page provide the history of London Bridge and the music.
Janet Stevens	*The House That Jack Built*	Bright red, yellow, and black pictures portray the characters as country bumpkins.
Ashley Wolff	*The Bells of London*	Full-color linoleum block prints tell a story of friendship and freedom and at the same time illustrate verses for the traditional "Bells of London."

ALPHABET BOOKS

In colonial days, children were first taught their ABCs from such cautionary rhymes as "In Adam's Fall/we sinned all," which combined early literacy and religion. Later, pictures of animals beginning with certain letters were added to Battledores and early primers for younger children. Alphabet books today may be equally deceptive. Many of them have moved beyond teaching children their alphabet to serving as a format to present detailed information about a particular subject for older boys and girls or to becoming a showcase for an art book, or to create complicated puzzles. Most of the alphabet books and criteria for their evaluation discussed in this chapter are directed at ABC books for the young child, however. Ages are given when an older audience is implied.

Besides learning the names and shapes of the letters, ABC books can also be used for identification or naming, as they provide the young child with large, bright pictures of animals or single objects to look at and talk about. One of the liveliest and jazziest alphabet books is Bill Martin, Jr., and John Archambault's *Chicka Chicka Boom Boom* illustrated with vibrant colors by Lois Ehlert. An alphabet chant, this book helps children memorize the letters and identify them. It does not provide an object or animal that goes with a beginning sound as most alphabet books do. But it does provide for much fun and merriment as children chant these active letters.

Certain factors need to be considered in selecting alphabet books. Objects should be clearly presented on a page, and these should be easily identifiable and meaningful for the intended age level. Only one or two objects should be shown for the very young child and it is best to avoid portraying anything that might have several correct names. For example, if a rabbit is presented for "R," the very young child might refer to it as a "bunny." Since text is necessarily limited, the pictures usually "carry" the story. For this reason they should be both clear and consistent with the text, reflecting and creating the mood of the book.

Alphabet books vary in both their texts and pictorial presentation from very simple to intricate levels of abstraction. Authors/illustrators use a variety of organizing structures to create ABC texts. Four types of ABC books are discussed here (some books incorporate several types): (1) word-picture formats; (2) simple narrative; (3) riddles or puzzles; (4) topical themes. Today there are so many alphabet books that only outstanding examples of each type are described. The table on pages 198–201 lists other titles with similar structure.

Striking pictures of realistic animals climb, poke through, or push large black block letters in *Animal Alphabet* by Bert Kitchen. A giraffe chins himself on the huge "G," while a small snail climbs up the "S." Each page contains only the letter and picture of the animal. Names of animals are given on a page at the end of this handsome book.

Suse MacDonald creates an original and imaginative book in *Alphabatics*. Each letter grows or tilts to become part of a beautifully clear graphic picture on the next page. For example, a "C" moves sideways, stretches, and becomes the smile on the clown's face. The "Y" moves off one page to become the head and horns of the yak on the other side. Children enjoy seeing the letters evolve and then finding them in the opposite picture.

In brilliant watercolor collages, Lois Ehlert introduces children to a wide variety of fruits and vegetables in her book *Eating the Alphabet*. Sometimes as many as four vegetables appear on a single page, but they are clearly depicted. Children might not know all the items presented, but it would extend their knowledge and be an excellent book to use prior to a trip to the grocery store.

At first glance Kate Duke's *The Guinea Pig ABC* looks like a one word-one picture identification book. A closer look reveals that the child must

Lois Ehlert cuts paper she has painted herself into a variety of fruit and vegetable shapes in her alphabet book titled *Eating the Alphabet*.

interpret the action and meaning of each small vignette on a page. Thus "M" stands for "mean" and shows one guinea pig about to pull a chair out from another. While the vignettes are clear and cleverly done, it is a more difficult task to interpret a story than to simply identify an object or animal.

Applebet by Clyde and Wendy Watson is a cheerful alphabet story told in rhymed verse of a farmer and her daughter Bet who take a cart full of apples to the country fair. The book portrays lovely rural scenes in the autumn and robust action at the fair. In keeping with the title, the binding is apple-green and the opening picture portrays a beautiful crisp red apple while the accompanying verse asks the child to find the apple hidden in each picture. Illustrations and verse celebrate a bit of rural Americana which will delight young children. The last page portrays an apple with several bites taken out as if reading *Applebet* has helped the reader digest a delicious apple experience.

Arnold and Anita Lobel combined their many talents to create a handsome and unique alphabet book. Starting with the picture of a small Victorian boy determinedly lacing up his high shoes, sailor hat ready to go and purse fat with change, we follow him on his journey to the title page, *On Market Street*. Then he proceeds on his way through all the shops from A to Z. He returns home in the evening exhausted, with an empty purse, but a gorgeous array of gifts, each purchased from a different shop. Rather than portray all the stores, Anita Lobel creates tradespeople and shopkeepers out of their own wares, making intriguing characters from *b*ooks, *c*locks, *e*ggs, *q*uilts, *t*oys, or *z*ippers.

Alpha and Betty decide to have a *Potluck*, so they call all of their friends. Action-filled pictures by Irene Trivas show children of various racial and ethnic backgrounds bringing a variety of delectable foods. The foods are not stereotyped as to the child's background. For example, Ben, an African-American child, brings bagels, but Hispanic triplets do turn up with tacos. Finally, they all sit down to a glorious feast eating everything from A to Z. This book by Anne Shelby invites classes to create their own potluck parties.

Anita Lobel's *Alison's Zinnia* is a brilliant alphabet book glowing with flower paintings. Listen to the carefully planned sentences in this book:

> 🍎 Alison acquired an Amaryllis for Beryl
> Beryl bought a Begonia for Crystal

and so it goes until

> 🍎 Yolanda yanked a Yucca for Zena
> Zena zeroed in on a Zinnia for Alison.

Older children might enjoy creating their own alphabet book based on a chosen subject using this one as a model.

Some alphabet books incorporate riddles or hidden puzzles in their formats. *Anno's Alphabet* by one of Japan's leading illustrators and designers, Mitsumasa Anno, is filled with quirky illu-

Anita Lobel shows her love for painting flowers in her brilliant alphabet bouquet of many varieties from *Alison's Zinnia*.

sions and puzzles. Each large letter looks three-dimensional, as if it had been carefully carved from wood. Suddenly, however, its perspective will appear to change and surprise you. The "M" is only half there as it disappears into its mirror image. Each letter is matched with a clear yet amusing picture and hidden in all of the borders are even more surprises. A glossary at the end provides clues to the hidden pictures in this visually exciting ABC book.

The Z Was Zapped by Chris Van Allsburg is a highly sophisticated alphabet drama presented in twenty-six acts. The large black and white picture of a letter on a stage appears before the sentence describing how it meets its sinister demise. For example, a pair of gloved hands picks up the "K"; turn the page to find "The K was quietly Kidnapped." Older children delight in guessing what happened to each letter and may want to create their own alphabet drama.

Topical themes are frequently used to tie the alphabet together. For example, Rachel Isadora brings the city to life with vibrant black and white street scenes for *City Seen from A to Z*. Her city is bustling with people—all ages, all races, all enjoy-ing their city, including the men playing *J*azz, a wonderfully graceful little girl dancing in her too big *T*utu and wearing new socks and sneakers, and a plump grandmother and her granddaughter licking *I*ce cream cones. Isadora captures action through body postures and storytelling vignettes in this city ABC. A fine example of a theme alphabet book is Mary Beth Owens's *A Caribou Alphabet*. From "A for Antlers" to "Z for Below Zero Weather," the author/illustrator portrays the world of the caribou. A compendium at the end gives even more information about this endangered species. Older students studying the Middle Ages will want to look at *Illuminations* by Peter Hunt. From alchemist to zither, Hunt depicts many aspects of life, architecture, and legends of these times in a format that reflects the illuminated manuscripts. This is an excellent sample of a theme alphabet book.

Another interesting alphabet book for older students is *ABC Americana* by Cynthia Rubin with illustrations of folk art from the National Gallery of Art. Such theme books suggest ways for older students to organize material they may be presenting for a particular study. Children could

RESOURCES FOR TEACHING

◆ ABC BOOKS ◆

AUTHOR/ ILLUSTRATOR	TITLE	AGE LEVEL	UNIQUE FEATURES
WORD/PICTURE IDENTIFICATION			
Dick Bruna	*B Is for Bear*	1, 2	Clear simple pictures of easily identifiable objects with some exceptions such as "igloo" and "Eskimo."
Bert Kitchen	*Animal Alphabet*	2–5	See text.
John Burningham	*John Burningham's ABC*	2–4	One clear picture for each letter. Unusual choices: "T" is for tractor; "V" shows a volcano.
Suse MacDonald	*Alphabatics*	3–6	See text.
Helen Oxenbury	*Helen Oxenbury's ABC of Things*	3–6	Provides a small vignette for each

	RESOURCES FOR TEACHING		
	♦ ABC BOOKS (CONTINUED) ♦		
AUTHOR/ ILLUSTRATOR	TITLE	AGE LEVEL	UNIQUE FEATURES
			letter. "H" is represented by a very funny picture of a *hare* and *hippopotamus* lying in bed in a *hospital*.
Marcia Brown	*All Butterflies*	4–7	Superb double-page woodcuts illustrate paired letters and words such as *C*ats *D*ance, *E*lephants *F*ly. A butterfly can be found on each page.
Tana Hoban	*A, B, See!*	5–7	Black-and-white photograms illustrate familiar objects. The page for "L" depicts a piece of *l*ace, a *l*ollipop, a *l*ock, and two *l*eaves.
	SIMPLE NARRATIVE		
Wanda Gág	*The ABC Bunny*	2–4	A little rabbit provides the story line for each letter. Beautifully designed woodcuts in black and white illustrate this classic ABC. Each letter is brilliant red, reminiscent of a child's block.
Kate Duke	*The Guinea Pig ABC*	4–6	See text.
Clyde Watson, Wendy Watson	*Applebet*	5–7	See text.
Anita Lobel, Arnold Lobel	*On Market Street*	5–7	See text.
Crescent Dragonwagon, Jose Aruego and Ariane Dewey	*Alligator Arrived with Apples*	6–10	A hilarious description of an animal potluck feast.
Anne Shelby, Irene Trivas	*Potluck*	6–10	See text.
	RIDDLES OR PUZZLES		
Mitsumasa Anno	*Anno's Alphabet*	5–10	See text.

RESOURCES FOR TEACHING

◆ ABC BOOKS (CONTINUED) ◆

AUTHOR/ ILLUSTRATOR	TITLE	AGE LEVEL	UNIQUE FEATURES
Jan Garten	*The Alphabet Tale*	5–7	Each letter is introduced on the preceding page by showing just the tail of an animal; turn the page and you see the whole animal. Children can predict the next animal by the rhyming verse, the picture of the tail, and the beginning letter.
Anne Rockwell	*Albert B. Cub and Zebra*	5–8	This wordless alphabet book is both a puzzle and a story. Albert B. Cub's beloved zebra is abducted. Albert's search for his friend takes him around the world and through the alphabet.
Chris Van Allsburg	*The Z Was Zapped*	7–12	See text.

TOPICAL THEMES

AUTHOR/ ILLUSTRATOR	TITLE	AGE LEVEL	UNIQUE FEATURES
Anita Lobel	*Alison's Zinnia*	3–7	See text.
Lois Ehlert	*Eating the Alphabet*	4–7	See text.
Rachel Isadora	*City Seen from A to Z*	6–9	See text.
Tasha Tudor	*A Is for Annabelle*	5–7	Delicate watercolors portray an old-fashioned doll with her different belongings representing different letters.
Mary Azarian	*A Farmer's Alphabet*	5–12	A handsome book that celebrates rural life in Vermont. Striking black-and-white woodcuts portray a *b*arn, *q*uilt, and wood *s*tove, for example.
Alice Provensen, Martin Provensen	*A Peaceable Kingdom: The Shaker ABECEDARIUS*	6–12	The Provensens illustrated this old 1882 alphabet verse of the Shakers in a way that depicts the rhyme of the animals but also provides much information about

RESOURCES FOR TEACHING

◆ ABC BOOKS (CONTINUED) ◆

AUTHOR/ ILLUSTRATOR	TITLE	AGE LEVEL	UNIQUE FEATURES
			the way the Shakers lived. Richard Barsan concludes the book with a note on Shaker history and education.
Muriel Feelings, Tom Feelings	*Jambo Means Hello*	6–12	Muriel Feelings gives children a simple lesson in Swahili while introducing some important aspects of the geography and culture of East Africa. Tom Feelings has produced soft, luminous gray, black, and white illustrations of the people and their villages.
Margaret Musgrove, Leo Dillon, Diane Dillon	*Ashanti to Zulu: African Traditions*	7–12	This is the only alphabet book to have won the Caldecott Medal. Musgrove describes many of the customs of some 26 African tribes; the Dillons create stunning illustrations picturing the people, their homes, an artifact and animal for each tribe. Pictures are framed and tied together at the corners with a design based on the Kano Knot, which symbolizes endless searching.
Ted Harrison	*A Northern Alphabet*	7–12	A striking book about northern Canada and Alaska, describes people, places, animals, and objects for each letter. Place names beginning with the appropriate letter form a frame around each picture. The flowing lines of the pictures recall Inuit art.
Cynthia Rubin	*ABC Americana*	7–12	See text.
Mary Beth Owens	*A Caribou Alphabet*	7–12	See text.
Peter Hunt	*Illuminations*	8–12	See text.

make their own ABC books of "Life at the Seashore," "Pioneer Life," or an ABC book of their favorite books.

COUNTING BOOKS

Ideally, boys and girls should learn to count by playing with real objects like blocks, boxes, bottle caps, or model cars. They can manipulate and group these as they wish, actually seeing what happens when you add one more block to nine or divide six blocks into two groups. Since time immemorial, however, we have been providing children with counting books, substituting pictures for real objects. The young child can make this transition from the concrete to its visual representation if he or she first experiences the real and the visual illustrations are clearly presented.

In evaluating counting books, then, we look to see if the objects to be counted stand out clearly on the page. Various groupings of objects should avoid a cluttered, confusing look. Illustrations and page design are most important in evaluating counting books. Accuracy is essential.

Counting books, too, vary from the very simple to the more complex. For the purposes of this text they are discussed under three categories: (1) one-to-one correspondence, (2) other simple mathematical concepts, and (3) number stories and puzzles. Examples of each category are given; the table on pages 205–8 lists other titles with similar structure.

Tana Hoban's *1, 2, 3* is a sturdy, well-designed first counting book which presents simple one-to-one correspondence. Colored photographs picture such well-known objects as two shoes, five small fingers, six eggs, seven animal crackers, and ten toes. Numbers and names of the numerals are given in this first board book for very young children. Such a beginning counting book may serve more for identification of the object than the actual counting. Certainly it requires a lower level of associative thinking for the very young child.

Hoban has also used clear black-and-white photographs to illustrate a counting book for

In *Anno's Counting Book,* Mitsumasa Anno's delicate watercolors portray a landscape changing with the various times of day, seasons, and year. The clock in the church steeple tells the time of day while sets of adults, children, and animals go about their daily activities. How many sets of nine can you discover on this page?

slightly older children, *Count and See*. Again she has photographed objects that are familiar and meaningful to the young child, such as three school buses, six candles on a birthday cake, nine firemen's hats, a dozen eggs in their carton, fifteen cookies, and amazingly, 100 peas in ten pea shells! Tana Hoban's *26 Letters and 99 Cents* is really two books in one. Clear magnetic letters are photographed with equally clear pictures of toys or objects beginning with that letter. Turn the book around and you have number concepts with photos of magnetic numbers and all the possible sets of coins to make up that number. Although the number section is far more difficult than the alphabet section, primary children who are learning to count lunch money would find it very useful.

Patricia MacCarthy creates beautiful batik paintings of patterned fish for her number book *Ocean Parade*. Every page swirls before your eyes as you look at three flat fish, twenty sea horses, and one hundred silverfish.

Brilliant colored graphics illustrate Lois Ehlert's book, *Fish Eyes: A Book You Can Count On*. A little black fish takes the reader on a journey of the ocean to discover "one green fish, two jumping fish, three smiling fish." Always the black fish adds himself to the group as the text reads "Three smiling fish plus me makes 4." Children delight in the spots and stripes of these gleaming fish with die-cut eyes.

Captivating language characterizes Olivier Dunrea's counting book *Deep Down Underground*. "Moudiewort" (pronounced moo-dee-wort) is a Scottish word for mole. In this cumulative story ten little creatures "deep down underground" hear the digging mole and "wriggle and wrangle" "burrow and scrape" "scrooch and scrunch" to get out of his way. Children will love to chant the verses while learning to count from one to ten and back again.

Ten Little Rabbits by Virginia Grossman portrays a variety of authentic Native-American traditions such as Navajo weaving and Pueblo Corn Dances. Appealing as the rabbit Indians are, real Native-American children would have seemed more appropriate for the amount of accurate research reflected in the pictures and afterword of this counting book.

Many mathematical concepts are developed in one of the most inventive and perfect counting books of recent years, *Anno's Counting Book*, by Mitsumasa Anno. Delicate watercolors portray a landscape changing with the various times of day, seasons, and year. The clock in the church steeple tells the time of day while adults, children, and animals go about their daily activities. As the buildings in the village increase, so do the groups and sets of children, adults, trees, trains, boats, and so on. This is one of the few counting books to begin with zero—a cold winter landscape showing only the river and the sky, no village. It ends with a picture of the twelfth month, a snowy Christmas scene and twelve reindeer in the sky. *Anno's Counting Book* requires real exploration to find the sets of children, adults, buildings, and animals, generating a higher level of thought and discussion about numerical concepts than a simple one-on-one counting book.

Pat Hutchins provides both a number story and a puzzle in her creative book *1 Hunter*. This is an account of a hunter's humorous walk through a jungle filled with hidden animals. The hunter determinedly stalks past two trees; turn the page and "the trees" are the legs of two elephants. The hunter continues on his way through a grove

Just at the crucial moment when it looks like there will be more children than cookies, Grandma arrives with a fresh batch of newly baked ones.

From *The Doorbell Rang* by Pat Hutchins.

of trees; the next page shows they were the legs of three giraffes. The hunter is oblivious to all he is missing until the very last page when the animals come out of hiding and the one hunter runs away! Children love finding hidden animals, and Hutchins reveals just enough of them so that the child reader can predict the next page.

Hutchin's well-loved story *The Doorbell Rang* could also be used for its math concepts. Victoria and Sam's mother makes them a dozen cookies just like Grandmother's to share (six each). The doorbell rings and two friends are welcomed in to share the cookies (three each). The doorbell rings twice more until there are a dozen children and a dozen cookies. The doorbell rings again. Should they answer it? They do, and it is their grandmother with an enormous tray of cookies!

Certainly there is no dearth of counting books and books that can be used for the development of math concepts. Since many of the criteria for evaluating counting books are similar to those for alphabet books, we have combined the criteria for both.

CONCEPT BOOKS

A concept book is one that describes various dimensions of an object, a class of objects, or an abstract idea. Concepts need to grow from first-hand experience as children gradually perceive common characteristics and relationships such as color, size, weight, or location. Some concepts like shape or color can be more easily presented in a book than such abstract concepts as growth, time, or distance. Certain concepts like love or

---

GUIDELINES

Evaluating ABC and Counting Books

ABC Books

♦ Objects or animals should be clearly presented on a page.
♦ For very young children, only one or two objects should be pictured.
♦ Common objects or animals that are easily identifiable are best for the young child.
♦ ABC books should avoid the use of objects that may be known by several names.
♦ The author/illustrator's purpose for the book should be clear.
♦ Illustrations should be consistent with text and reflect the mood of the book.
♦ The organizing principle of presentations should be clear.
♦ The intended age level should be considered in both pictures and text.

Counting Books

♦ Objects to be counted should stand out clearly.
♦ Accuracy is essential.
♦ Common objects that children know, such as fingers, toes, eggs, are usually best for the young child.
♦ Groupings or sets should be clearly differentiated.
♦ Number concepts should not be lost in the story.
♦ Level of thinking required should be challenging for appropriate ages.

RESOURCES FOR TEACHING

♦ COUNTING BOOKS ♦

AUTHOR/ ILLUSTRATOR	TITLE	AGE LEVEL	UNIQUE FEATURES
ONE-TO-ONE CORRESPONDENCE			
Tana Hoban	*1, 2, 3*	1–3	See text.
John J. Reiss	*Numbers*	3–5	Clear drawings of such common objects as shoes, kites, baseball players, etc., make this well within the young child's experience. The book ends with a picture representing 1,000 raindrops.
Eric Carle	*1, 2, 3 to the Zoo*	4–6	A circus train serves as the vehicle for this counting book as each passing car contains an increasing number of animals, such as two hippos and nine snakes.
Molly Bang	*Ten, Nine, Eight*	4–6	Starting with her ten toes, a father begins a countdown until his daughter is in bed. One of the few number books to portray a black father and daughter.
Helen Oxenbury	*Numbers of Things*	4–6	Delightfully amusing illustrations add to the fun of this number book. Fifty is represented by the appropriate number of ladybugs; the final page pictures an astronaut on the moon and asks "How many stars?"
Tana Hoban	*Count and See*	4–6	See text.
Bert Kitchen	*Animal Numbers*	5–9	A stunning counting book that begins with one baby kangaroo in its mother's pouch and ends with 100 baby tadpoles and frogs' eggs.

RESOURCES FOR TEACHING

◆ COUNTING BOOKS (CONTINUED) ◆

AUTHOR/ ILLUSTRATOR	TITLE	AGE LEVEL	UNIQUE FEATURES
Jim Aylesworth, Ruth Young	*One Crow, A Counting Rhyme*	5–7	The farm provides much to count, both in the summer and then again in the winter.
Peter Sis	*Waving, A Counting Book*	5–7	Mary's mother waved to a taxi. Two bicyclists waved back to her while three boys waved to the bicyclists. A city background provides even more to count.
Patricia MacCarthy	*Ocean Parade*	5–8	See text.
Ann Herbert Scott	*One Good Horse: A Cowpuncher's Counting Book*	5–9	From one good horse to 100 cattle, this book provides a unique territory for a counting book. The last double-page spread shows everything that has been counted on this western landscape.
Virginia Grossman, Sylvia Long	*Ten Little Rabbits*	6–12	See text.
Muriel Feelings, Tom Feelings	*Moja Means One*	7–12	This is more an informational book on East Africa and the Swahili language than a counting book. For example, the number six is represented by six persons in different kinds of dress, but only five kinds of clothing are identified.

OTHER SIMPLE MATHEMATICAL CONCEPTS

AUTHOR/ ILLUSTRATOR	TITLE	AGE LEVEL	UNIQUE FEATURES
Mitsumasa Anno	*Anno's Counting Book*	4–7	See text.
Mitsumasa Anno	*Anno's Counting House*	5–8	Ten little people living in a furnished house move to an empty house next door, taking their belongings with them. Concepts of addition and subtraction can be developed.

RESOURCES FOR TEACHING

♦ COUNTING BOOKS (CONTINUED) ♦

AUTHOR/ ILLUSTRATOR	TITLE	AGE LEVEL	UNIQUE FEATURES
			Die-cut windows pique the child's curiosity to see inside.
Paul Giganti, Jr., Donald Crews	*How Many Snails?*	4–8	A counting book that asks increasingly difficult questions. Not only how many snails, but how many snails with stripes, how many striped snails with their heads stuck out?
Olivier Dunrea	*Deep Down Underground*	5–8	See text.
Lois Ehlert	*Fish Eyes: A Book You Can Count On*	6–8	See text.
Peter Sis	*Going Up! A Color Counting Book*	5–8	In *Going Up*, ordinal numbers are presented as various costumed persons get on an elevator going up to a surprise party on the tenth floor.
Donald Crews	*Ten Black Dots*	4–8	A graphic counting book that shows what you can do with ten black dots. One can make a sun, two become fox's eyes, or eight the wheels of a train. Would make an interesting design assignment.
Tana Hoban	*26 Letters and 99 Cents*	6–8	See text.

NUMBER STORIES AND PUZZLES

AUTHOR/ ILLUSTRATOR	TITLE	AGE LEVEL	UNIQUE FEATURES
Shirley Hughes	*When We Went to the Park*	3–5	A little girl and her grandfather count all the things they see during their walk in the park. Detailed watercolors show "six runners running" and "ten birds swooping in the sky."
Eric Carle	*The Very Hungry Caterpillar*	5–7	A very hungry caterpillar eats through one apple, two pears, etc., until he becomes fat, spins a

RESOURCES FOR TEACHING			
◆ COUNTING BOOKS (CONTINUED) ◆			
AUTHOR/ ILLUSTRATOR	TITLE	AGE LEVEL	UNIQUE FEATURES
			cocoon, and emerges as a beautiful butterfly. Clever die-cut holes invite children to poke fingers through the various foods the caterpillar eats.
Maurice Sendak	One Was Johnny	5–7	Part of the small "Nutshell Library," this is the story of a small boy visited by many obnoxious animals. He threatens to eat them all if they are not gone by the time he counts down from ten.
Pat Hutchins	1 Hunter	5–7	See text.
Charlotte Pomerantz, Jose Aruego, Ariane Dewey	One Duck, Another Duck	5–7	A grandmother owl teaches her grandson to count to ten. Easy and entertaining story.
Sarah Hayes	Nine Ducks Nine	5–7	Nine ducks go for a walk, followed by a fox. One by one the ducks take off for the rickety bridge where Mr. Fox receives his comeuppance. A wonderful story that helps children count down.
Pat Hutchins	The Doorbell Rang	5–8	See text.

death develop gradually over years and may be best understood in the themes of storybooks or informational books for older children.

The books discussed in this chapter are those written for young children with the specific purpose of developing concepts. A concept book is really a young child's first informational book. It should stimulate much talk and help children develop their vocabularies while at the same time it helps sharpen their perceptions and enlarge their growing understanding of the world. Well-defined concepts are necessary for children's language and cognitive development.

Notice how the young child struggles to define his or her understanding of the concept "dog." At first "doggies" include all dogs and maybe even a few cats and squirrels. Later, after they have abstracted the essential qualities of "dogginess," young children can tell the difference. Still later, they can make finer differentiations—discriminate between the St. Bernard and the German shepherd, for example. Concept books help children to identify these essential elements of an object or a class of objects.

ABC books and counting books are really concept books. So, too, are the books that help children to identify and discriminate colors. John Reiss illustrates his book of *Colors* for very young children with clear, bright graphics showing several pages of familiar objects for each color; for example, the various shades of green are shown by green leaves, grass, a green snake, a frog, turtle, pickles, cucumbers, gooseberries, and peas. It is appropriate that a first book on colors should be as aesthetically pleasing to the eye as this one.

Tana Hoban's *Is It Red? Is It Yellow? Is It Blue?* is subtitled "An Adventure in Color." With clear close-up photographs, Hoban helps the child see the vivid colors in such common sights as fire hydrants, cars, a lollipop, oranges, apples, and balloons. Small circles of color below the pictures help the child to know what colors to look for on that page. With adult help, the child can explore other concepts like shape and size in these carefully planned pictures. Her *Of Colors and Things* again uses easily identifiable objects of clear bright color. Each page presents four objects, three the same color while the fourth includes that color with others. For example, the page on blue shows blue boots, a blue top, blue fork, knife and spoon, and a ball of many colors (including blue).

Color Dance by Ann Jonas shows what happens when you mix colors. Using four young dancers with colored scarves, the red dancer and yellow dancer unfurl their scarves to create orange. This is a joyous book of colors.

Hoban has written three books on shapes. The first, *Shapes and Things*, uses black-and-white photograms of real objects like scissors and a hammer to help children identify unique shapes. Each page shows sets of generic objects; thus shapes of tools are arranged on one page, and objects used in sewing are on the opposite page. *Circles, Triangles and Squares* uses photographs of familiar objects to present these particular concepts. Full-color photographs illustrate her third book, *Shapes, Shapes, Shapes*.

Color Zoo and *Color Farm* both by Lois Ehlert use sophisticated die-cut graphics to create the heads of stylized animals out of various shapes. A square, a triangle, and a circle produce a picture of a tiger's head. When you turn the page each shape is then clearly shown and identified. Primary and even older children might use shapes to make their own animals after looking at these brilliant pictures. (See photo on p. 731.)

Tana Hoban provides bright clear photographs of common objects that are blue with some slight exceptions. The young child can identify the picture that is not all blue and then enjoy naming the objects in this fine concept book titled *Of Colors and Things*.

Another fine photo concept book by Tana Hoban is one that looks at relative size in *Is It Larger? Is It Smaller?* Showing such familiar objects as three vases of flowers, or a large snow woman and a baby snowman, she presents the concept of size in a way children can easily understand. Her earlier book *Big Ones, Little Ones* shows relative size with fascinating black-and-white pictures of mother and baby animals. These creatures include zoo animals and domesticated ones. In *Exactly the Opposite*, Hoban uses a variety of situations to show open, shut; front, back; empty, full; far and near. Large colored photos capture children running up the stairs and the same children coming down the stairs. Children push a wagon, children pull a wagon. As always Hoban is inclusive of various races and avoids any gender stereotyping. A more complex book but one that children really enjoy is *Dig, Drill, Dump, Fill*. In this one Hoban turns her fine photographic lens on heavy machinery, including road rollers, trash trucks, street flushers, cranes with electric magnets, and dump trucks. Clear black-and-white pictures show these big machines in action; a glossary provides their names and functions. Hoban makes us look and see the beauty of *Shadows and Reflections* all around us. In full-color photos she shows reflections of sailboats in a harbor, reflections on a car, in dark glasses. The last picture is a reflection of the photographer herself as she snaps a picture in a window. Shadows are seen of a bike, children walking, and hands making a cat's cradle with string. This is a book that could be shared before taking a class on a neighborhood walk; how many reflections can they find, how many shadows? These concepts are more abstract than in her books on size or shape and would be more appropriate for older children. In her book *All About Where*, primary children could work in groups to see how many of the location words on the side of the pictures apply to each color shot. Since there is no one right answer, they would have much fun generating a variety of sentences. Again this would be too abstract for most preschoolers to try to do.

Margaret Miller explores professions and trades in two well-conceived concept books, *Whose Hat?* and *Who Uses This?* Clear colored pictures show just a chef's hat. Turn the page and there is a picture of a chef in his kitchen. The opposite page pictures white and African-American girls stirring a big pot, each wearing chef's hats. Nine professions are introduced by their hats. In *Who Uses This?* bakers, football players, and a conductor are identified by the tools of their trade.

Peter Spier's *Fast-Slow High-Low: A Book of Opposites* uses many little watercolor pictures to illustrate various aspects of opposites. "Smooth-Rough" includes a porcupine and a groundhog, a poodle and a dachshund, a slimy worm and a hairy caterpillar, a smooth highway and a bumpy road. Parents or teachers might have to help children find the two things being compared, but this book will help the child learn that a single concept can apply to many situations.

Bathwater's Hot is part of Shirley Hughes's Nursery Collection. Here a little girl discovers that many things have opposites, such as "Bathwater's hot, seawater's cold." Based on the everyday activities of youngsters, these opposites are shown in the context of the child's experiences. As usual, Hughes creates believable children in action-filled pictures.

In *All Shapes and Sizes*, Hughes pictures preschool children walking a *large* dog or holding a *small* mouse. They climb *up* a slide and slip

down it. Hughes's children represent many different races; they come in all sizes; some are fat, some are skinny, some wear glasses, others don't.

Charlotte Zolotow has written a loving book titled *Some Things Go Together* illustrated with cozy pictures by Karen Gundersheimer. Beginning with hearts and flowers for endpapers, the author rhymes all the things that seem to go together such as "franks with beans/kings with queens, sand with sea/and you with me." The illustrations for the refrain "you and me" always show a parent with a child as if emphasizing their love for each other.

In *My Dog* by Heidi Goennel, a little girl looks at all the characteristics of particular breeds of dogs, such as "a pug who has a nose as soft as silk" or "the long legs of a Great Dane." In the end she concludes she likes her dog best of all, "he's just a little brown dog but I love him so." The illustrations are as simple in composition as the loving message of the book.

Many of Donald Crews's books such as *Freight Train, Truck, School Bus*, and *Harbor* could be classified as concept books or easy informational books. Certainly all of them explore the various dimensions of their subjects. In the first one, Crews pictures an empty track, then each of the different cars; the red caboose, orange tank car, yellow hopper car, green cattle car, blue gondola, purple box car, and finally the black steam engine. The train goes faster and faster through the tunnels and over bridges until it becomes a rainbow of speeding colors and then fades out of sight. Both colors and specific names for the cars provide real information for young children. Using bold graphics, Crews swings a big red *Truck* across the country from east to west through cities, small towns, night and day, rain and shine. No text appears in this concept book except all the environmental print one naturally encounters on a trip, such as names of other trucks, traffic signs, highway exit signs, tunnels, and truck stops. In *School Bus* children again have an opportunity to see common signs and symbols: the green "walk" sign, the red "don't walk" sign, the school bus stop, and others. The yellow buses are large and small, but all pick up students and bring them home when school is over.

Other equally well-designed concept books by Crews include *Flying* and *Harbor*. While these books seem geared for young children, some of them contain hidden messages[12] that intrigue older children and adults. For example, *Harbor* is dedicated "to the women in my life and Malcolm." Each boat is named after a woman: his wife, his daughter, his editor, and so on. Malcolm is his nephew.

Another handsome concept book for primary children is *Feathers for Lunch* by Lois Ehlert. Written with a rhyming text, it tells about a little cat who would like to catch all the different birds that he sees, but luckily his bell frightens them away. The birds are pictured with life-sized brilliant collages. The birds, plants, and trees are labeled; a brief appendix gives information on each pictured bird.

Aliki's two informational concept books about *My Feet* and *My Hands* from the Let's-Read-and-Find-Out Science Book series seem just right for preschoolers. In simple words and with clear attractive pictures, Aliki explores all of the things hands do and feet do. As always, Aliki pictures children of different races and cuts across gender stereotypes. For example, the title page of *My Hands* shows a young boy doing cross-stitching. Another informational book that intrigues young children is Patricia Lauber's *An Octopus Is Amazing.*

Concept books are really children's first informational books. They help children see relationships between objects, develop awareness of similarities or differences, or grasp the various dimensions of an abstract idea. Often these books begin with the familiar and move to the unfamiliar or more complex. Many of them appear to be moving from the totally obvious concepts for younger children to more abstract and less obvious concepts for older children. Concepts for the younger child should be presented in a clear unconfusing manner, with one or more examples given. Where appropriate, functions of objects should be made clear. Concepts should be within the developmental scope of the child. Concept books can be used to enrich or reinforce an experience, not substitute for it. Young children enjoy hearing these beginning nonfiction books along

[12]See Susan Hepler. "Books in the Classroom," *The Horn Book Magazine*, vol 64, no. 5 (September/October, 1988), pp. 667–669.

A toddler shares his interest in *Machines at Work* by Byron Barton with his Raggedy Andy.
Photo by Susan Fertig.

with fictional stories, for the young child is curious and seeks information. He wants to know the *names* of things, *how* they work, and *why* this is so. Evaluative criteria for informational books are presented in Chapter 11.

WORDLESS BOOKS

Wordless books are picture books in which the story line is told entirely through pictures. They are increasingly popular with today's TV-oriented child. Many of them are laid out in the same sequential format as comic books and have wide appeal to different age levels.

Textless books are surprisingly helpful in developing some of the skills necessary for reading. Handling the book, turning the pages, beginning at the left-hand side and moving to the right are all skills that give the young child a sense of directionality and the experience of acting like a reader. These books are particularly useful in stimulating language development through encouraging children to take an active part in storytelling. As the child relates the story, she will become aware of beginnings, endings, the sequence of the story, the climax, the actions of the characters—all necessary for learning how a story works, for developing a sense of story. "Reading" a wordless book also requires specific comprehension of the illustrations. Teachers may want to record children's stories into language experience booklets. Older children might want to write their own creative stories to accompany the illustrations. In order to help the child tell the story, pictures must show action and sequence clearly so children will not be confused in their tellings. Also, children should be given an opportunity to examine the book and look through it completely before they try to tell the story orally. Otherwise, they will describe the action on each page but not understand the sequential relationship of the events.

In *Do You Want to Be My Friend?*, Eric Carle gives the child latitude to create his own story about a little mouse who in seeking a friend follows the lead of one tail after another, only to be very surprised at what is at the other end! The brilliant collage pictures will delight children and provide the opportunity to tell their own versions of this story.

Nancy Tafuri provides an exciting wordless adventure story in *Junglewalk*. A boy puts down his book, "Jungles of the World," and turns off his light just as his cat slips out the window. The tail of the cat becomes a tiger, and the boy is off on his dream adventure seeing monkeys, elephants, zebras, and many other creatures in this brilliant jungle. The tiger brings him home and the boy wakes from his dream just as his cat bounds into the window. In another wordless book, Tafuri uses exquisite large watercolors to show the explorations of a baby sea lion following a baby crab. But behind the baby sea lion is his mother carefully following him. When the crabs jump in the ocean, mother and child return to the herd. *Follow Me!* is a simple love story without words.

Alexandra Day tells a series of humorous stories about an almost human Rottweiler dog named Carl. In each wordless story when Carl is left to mind the baby, he gives the child a marvelous time and then manages to clean everything up before his humans return home. This is the plot of *Good Dog, Carl*. In *Carl Goes Shopping*, Carl takes care of the baby in the lobby of an elegant department store. In *Carl's Christmas*, Carl takes

the baby for a walk on a snowy Christmas Eve. They win a Christmas basket, join carolers, and return home just in time to greet Santa. It is hard to tell who is the most lovable, dependable Carl or the delightful baby.

A highly original wordless book is *Changes, Changes* by Pat Hutchins. Here, two wooden dolls arrange and rearrange wooden building blocks to tell a fast-paced circular story. When their block house catches fire, the resourceful couple dismantle it and build a fire engine, whose hose quickly douses the fire, thereby creating a flood! Undaunted, the wooden dolls then build a boat, which becomes a truck, which is changed to a train, until eventually they reconstruct their original block house. Hutchins has written and illustrated an even funnier story with the use of only one sentence. In this book Rosie—a very determined, flat-footed hen—goes for a walk, unmindful of the fact that she is being stalked by a hungry fox. At every turn of *Rosie's Walk*, the hen unwittingly foils the fox in his plans to catch her. The brightly colored comic illustrations help youngsters to tell Rosie's story. Primary children enjoy retelling this story from the point of view of the fox.

The first waking thought of a plump little lady is that this is the morning to have *Pancakes for Breakfast*. Tomie de Paola pictures her persistent efforts to make the pancakes despite the fact that she has to go to the hen house to gather the eggs, milk the cow, and churn the butter. Finally thinking she has all the ingredients, she discovers she must go and buy some maple syrup. She returns with a self-satisfied expression on her face only to discover that her dog and cat have tipped over the milk and flour and eaten the eggs. All is not lost, however, for from her neighbor's house comes the delicious aroma of pancakes. The recipe for the pancakes is given and asks to be tried out.

Two outstanding wordless books, *Sunshine* and *Moonlight* by Jan Ormerod, celebrate a small girl's joy with the simple pleasures of morning and nighttime rituals. In a series of watercolor vignettes, often several to a page, a lovable little girl "helps" her mother and father get up in the morning. The little girl wakens first, reads her book, and then gets dressed in a wonderful sequence of twelve narrow pictures across two pages. She looks at her clock and goes in to alert her parents that they have overslept. They both dash back and forth in various stages of getting dressed. Finally, her father kisses her goodbye, and the little girl goes off with her schoolbag and her mother. The sunshine of this story streams through the windows and the radiant love of this family. *Moonlight* concludes the day with dinner, bath, bedtime story, and stalling ploys familiar to all children and parents. Once again the illustrator captures the shining glow of moonlight with beautifully soft watercolors.

Through the ingenious use of half pages, John Goodall manages to add excitement and movement to his many wordless adventure stories. *Naughty Nancy Goes to School* is the tale of an irrepressible mouse's first day in school. Richly detailed watercolors depict just how naughty this mouse can be. *Creepy Castle* appeals to slightly older children as they "read" the mouse melodrama of the brave knight mouse who rescues his fair damsel mouse in distress. Goodall portrays *Little Red Riding Hood* as a mouse also. As she walks to her grandmother's she meets gracious neighbors who resemble Beatrix Potter's well-known animals. A duck reminds us of Mrs. Puddleduck, a squirrel of Squirrel Nutkin, and a courtly frog of Jeremy Fisher. The wolf is a very dapper but wicked fellow, and the woodcutter is a reassuring big brown bear. Children can tell this story easily based on their previous knowledge of Little Red Riding Hood and from the clear watercolors and half pages that advance the action.

It is interesting to see when children recognize that *Deep in the Forest* by Brinton Turkle is really a variant of "Goldilocks and the Three Bears," with the unique twist that a baby bear wreaks havoc in a pioneer cabin. Usually when the children see baby bear eating porridge from three different-sized bowls, they recall having "heard" something like this before.

Mercer Mayer was one of the first illustrators to create wordless books. His *A Boy, a Dog, and a Frog* series is very popular with children aged 5 and up. Simple line drawings in green and black portray the friendship between a boy, his dog, his frog, and a turtle. The stories are amusing and full of slapstick fun, particularly in *Frog Goes to Dinner*,

when frog hides in the boy's pocket and goes to the restaurant with the family. Jealousy is the theme of *One Frog Too Many* when the boy is given a new baby frog. These stories are humorous and easily told from their pictures.

Emily McCully tells delightful stories of a large mouse family and their seasonal fun in *Picnic*, *First Snow*, and *School*. In *Picnic* a little mouse falls out of the truck when they go down a bumpy road. Her loss is not discovered until all eight of her brothers and sisters are ready to eat. Then the whole family piles into the truck to go find her. In *First Snow*, the same little mouse hesitates to try sledding down the steep hill. After her first slide down, however, she loves it, and the whole family has to wait for her to take one last slide before the sun disappears over the snow-covered hill. In *School*, the little mouse runs off to join her eight brothers and sisters. When the teacher discovers her, she calls her mother only to have little mouse cry. But after she holds the pointer, passes out milk and cookies, and listens to the teacher share *Picnic*, little mouse is comforted and ready to go home with her mother. These books provide real narratives, with identifiable characters, exciting plots, and lush watercolors.

Peter Spier's Rain captures the delight of a brother and sister thoroughly enjoying playing in a rain-puddled day. It begins with just a few drops on the title page. The children's mother calls them into the house to get their macintoshes, rubber boots, and umbrella and then sensibly sends them outside to play. And play they do! A watery-blue double-page spread pictures the splashing raindrops and the children sloshing through the puddles. They see the shimmering beauty of drops of rain caught in a spider's web, with the spider safe and dry under the limb of the tree. They check on where other animals and birds hide in the rain and feed the ducks and geese and swans who are in their element as much as the children. Finally a strong wind comes up and they run for home where they enjoy all the cozy inside treats of a rainy day: cocoa and cookies, a hot bath, reading, and bed.

The story of *Noah's Ark* has been translated from the Dutch by Peter Spier and appears in verse form on the first page. What follows, however, is the virtually wordless story of all that transpires both inside and outside the ark for forty days and forty nights. Various-sized pictures portray Noah's many activities on the ark and capture his every mood, from deep concern to jubilant rejoicing over the dove's return with the olive branch. Mrs. Noah's washline of clothes contrasts sharply with the dirty, messy interior of the ark at the end of its long voyage. Humorous touches run throughout this book, including the number of rabbits that leave the ark and the slow final departure of the snails and tortoise. Each viewing of the book reveals more of Spier's wit and artistic talent. This book richly deserved the Caldecott Medal it received.

Another beautiful wordless book is Raymond Briggs's *The Snowman*. Using soft watercolors in a comic strip format, Briggs tells the story of a small boy and his snowman who comes to life one night. The boy invites the snowman inside to see the house but warns him away from the fireplace, the stove, and the hot water tap. The snowman has a childlike fascination for such simple things as an electric light switch, a skateboard, the father's false teeth in a glass, and the family car. The boy and the snowman share a meal and a fantastic predawn flight before returning to bed and the front lawn. In the morning the sun awakens the boy, and his first thought is for his snowman. He looks out the window—alas, his friend has melted. Children who look at this lovely picture book want to look at it over and over again. It is the kind of story that invites revisiting and discussing all the details which Briggs has included.

Free Fall by David Wiesner is also based on a dream. Intriguing in its visual storytelling, this book was first conceived as a frieze some 9 feet long. Later it was made into a dreamscape in which the boy's quilt becomes cultivated fields, then a chess board of five knights and queens who escort him into a castle with a magician and hidden dragon. Episodes flow into each other from the previous illustrations. The final picture shows the boy waking in bed surrounded by many of the objects in his dream. The age of the boy and his adventures would suggest that this wordless book is for older children.

David Wiesner's fascinating book, *Tuesday*, is the second almost wordless book to receive the Caldecott Award. On "Tuesday evening, around eight" all the frogs take off on their lily pads. Brilliant watercolors portray their joyous flight as they zoom through a house, chase birds and a dog, and return home at dawn. The next Tuesday evening—the pigs fly! Children could easily tell their own stories to accompany these action-filled pictures.

There appear to be fewer wordless books published today than five years ago. Increasingly, those being produced seemed geared to an older audience than preschool or even kindergarten children.

BOOKS ABOUT THE COMMON EXPERIENCES OF THE YOUNG CHILD

Increasingly, publishers are producing books that mirror the everyday common experiences and feelings of the preschooler. In these books for 2- through 5-year-olds the illustrations are simple and clear, but usually not of the same quality as the more expensive picture storybooks discussed in Chapter 5. The young child's activities and concerns are at the center of the action, but frequently the humor is directed at the parent reader.

Anne and Harlow Rockwell collaborated on producing the "My World" series including such titles as *I Love My Pets, Sick in Bed, I Play in My Room, Happy Birthday to Me,* and *Can I Help?* The text in these squarish books presents a straightforward first-person account of a child's response to these experiences. The Rockwells effectively cut across stereotyping; in *Sick in Bed,* the doctor is a woman, and when the child returns to nursery school her teacher is a man. A little girl helps her father polish the car in *Can I Help?,* but it is her mother who helps her fly a kite.

The "Betsy" series by Gunilla Wolde was first published in Sweden. In *Betsy and the Doctor,* Betsy falls off the climbing tree in nursery school and cuts her head. Robert, one of the nursery school teachers, takes her to the doctor for stitches. Back at school, Betsy becomes the center of attention. In *Betsy's Baby Brother,* Betsy's ambivalent feelings are described when her mother nurses her brother—that's the time she'd like to give him away to another lady! Betsy helps her mother take care of him, changes his dirty diapers, and talks to him until he goes to sleep—then he is "cuddly and sweet." Other titles in this frank series include *This Is Betsy* and *Betsy's First Day at Nursery School*.

As more and more mothers work, their children frequently experience child care outside their homes before they are old enough to attend school. In *Jesse's Daycare* by Amy Valens, Jesse is busy sharing toys and playing with Sara while his mom is busy working at her computer in a downtown office. The author describes Jesse's and Mom's parallel feelings and activities in a quiet reassuring way. Michelle Magorian gently explores a young boy's courage to stand on his own in her book *Who's Going to Take Care of Me?* When Eric and his big sister went to day care together, Karin taught him words to the songs and let him sit by her during story time. Now Karin is going to school and Eric feels small and wonders who will care for him, until he discovers a new child in his day care who needs his special care.

In *Alfie's Feet*, Shirley Hughes captures a young boy's delight in his new yellow boots but his puz-zlement at the way they feel. Finally, he realizes he has them on the wrong feet and switches them himself. In *Alfie Gets in First*, Alfie is so excited to be the first one home from a shopping trip that he races in the door as soon as his mother opens it and locks himself in. Hughes ingeniously uses the center gutter of the book as the door dividing the outside of the house from the inside. In this way the reader can see all the people who come to try to help open the door at the same time it is possible to see what Alfie is doing. Just at the moment when the window cleaner is about to climb up his ladder and go through a bathroom window, Alfie gets a chair, reaches the lock himself, and grandly opens the door. In *Alfie Gives a Hand*, Alfie worries about going to noisy Bernard's birthday party all by himself so he insists on taking his security blanket with him. Holding on to the blanket interferes with playing the games. When Bernard puts on a tiger mask, he frightens Min, who cries and clutches Alfie's hand. In order to join the circle games, Alfie puts down his blanket and holds Min's hand. Helping someone else gives Alfie all the security he needs. The *Big Alfie and Annie Rose Storybook* pro-

"Open the door, Alfie," said Mom.
But Alfie didn't know how to open the door from the inside. The catch was too high up. Mom looked into the mail slot.
"Try to reach the catch and turn it," she said. Alfie tried but he couldn't quite reach it.
"Can you put the key through the mail slot?" asked Mom. But Alfie couldn't reach the mail slot either.

Shirley Hughes ingeniously uses the gutter of the book to represent the door separating Alfie from his mom. Increasing frustration is shown on both sides of the door, until Alfie solves the problem himself.

From *Alfie Gets in First*.

Marisabina Russo captures a child's point of view in both her illustrations and story for *Why Do Grown-Ups Have All the Fun?* When Hannah can't sleep she imagines her parents are having a wonderful time playing with her blocks!

vides five delightful stories and three poems about Alfie and his younger sister, Annie Rose.

Marisabina Russo also has a talent for tapping into the way a young child feels. In *Where Is Ben?* a busy mother interrupts her baking of an apple pie to go and search for Ben when he calls, "Mama, come find me." Each time Ben's mother returns to the kitchen, he finds a new hiding place. Finally his patient mother reads him a story before his nap and promises him a piece of apple pie when he wakes up. *Waiting for Hannah* is a loving story in which a mother recounts to her daughter all the things she did during the long hot summer she was expecting her arrival. In *Why Do Grown-Ups Have All the Fun?*, Hannah lies in bed imagining the wonderful things her parents must be doing, like playing with her building blocks or Play-doh. She then slips downstairs only to discover her mother writing a letter and her father doing a crossword puzzle. So Hannah curls up on the couch with her parents and eventually falls asleep. Russo's bright childlike illustrations match the young child's naive perceptions of what her parents do for fun.

Eve Rice captures the feelings of a child whose birthday is almost a disaster. In *Benny Bakes a Cake*, Benny has a wonderful time helping his mother make his birthday cake. But when they go for a walk, Ralph, their dog, eats the cake. Benny is disconsolate until his father comes home with presents, birthday hats, *and* a beautiful birthday cake. A young child can easily follow the action of this story by looking at the large flat primary-colored pictures shown against a clear white background.

Learning to get along in the family is another developmental task of the young child. In *They Really Like Me!* Anna Hines tells the story of Joshua who is left home alone with his two older sisters. They won't let him watch television or share their popcorn, and when they play tricks on him Joshua isn't sure they like him. However, when Joshua outtricks them and they can't find him, he learns that they really do like him.

Sam, an African-American child and the youngest of his family, feels rejected by the members of his family—all are so engrossed in their own activities that they tell him to go somewhere else to play. Finally, completely frustrated, Sam begins to cry. Then all members of the family come together and realize the cumulative effect they have had on Sam. Consoled at last, Sam helps his mother make raspberry tarts. Symeon Shimin's illustrations portray the nuances of feelings in this fine book by Ann Herbert Scott.

The youngest child frequently feels left out, the tag end of the family. Pat Hutchins captures these feelings in her well-loved *Titch*. Titch is too small to ride a two-wheel bicycle or fly a kite or use a hammer. But he is not too small to plant a seed, and Titch's plant grows and grows. The ending of the story of Titch is a classic example of poetic justice for the youngest and smallest of a family. In *You'll Soon Grow into Them, Titch*, it is obvious that once again Titch as the youngest must wear the hand-me-downs. With the arrival of a new baby in the family it is at last Titch's turn to say, "You'll soon grow into them." Complementary stories of birth and growth are told only through the pictures of this ingenious tale. Mother's growing pregnancy coincides with a nesting robin seen outside the window. Buds on the tree and bulbs in the garden and in a pot in the house all bloom at the same time the baby robins hatch and the children greet the newest member of the family. *Tidy Titch* continues the story of this youngest child in the family. The classic story by Ruth Krauss titled *The Carrot Seed* has a similar theme as *Titch*. Here, the smallest in the family triumphs over all the doubts raised by his family. Little children need to feel big if only through their stories.

A family of birds give much encouragement to a baby seagull longing to fly. His mother tells him he will fly, his father says "by and by," and his sister tells him to *Flap Your Wings and Try*. Written by Charlotte Pomerantz and beautifully illustrated by Nancy Tafuri, the book has a dedication reading: "For All of Us Who Are Still Trying."

Young children also need much love and reassurance that they will always be needed and belong to their family. This is the theme of the favorite story *The Runaway Bunny* by Margaret Wise Brown. A little bunny announces that he is going to run away and his mother tells him that she will run after him. The little bunny thinks of all the things he will become—a fish in a stream, a crocus, a sailboat. His mother in turn says she will become a fisherman, a gardener, the wind, and come after him. The little rabbit decides just to stay and be her little bunny, after all. This story might seem suffocating for older children, but it is just what the preschool child wants to hear.

Bedtime stories provide the comfort and reassurance that children need to face the dark alone. No book for the very young child ever replaced Margaret Wise Brown's *Goodnight Moon*. First published in 1947, it was reissued in 1975 in paperback and made into a pop-up book, *The Goodnight Moon Room* in 1984. This gentle poetic story shows a little bunny going to bed while a grandmother bunny helps him whisper goodnight to everything in his room. Gradually the room darkens and only the light from the moon is seen when the little bunny is at last asleep. Children love to join in on the rhyme and look for the little mouse that is in each picture of the bedroom. Clement Hurd's gradually darkening pictures show each item mentioned in the room. Two- and 3-year-olds ask to hear this soothing book over and over again. Molly Bang has written and illus-

trated both a counting book and a loving bedtime story in *Ten, Nine, Eight*. Starting with his daughter's ten toes, a daddy counts backward until she is ready for bed. This is a warm reassuring story of an African-American father and his daughter.

In *Bedtime Story* Jim Erskine provides a story within a story as a mother tells her child all the things that are happening in the house and outside as he snuggles down to sleep and dreams of all she has told him. In *Close Your Eyes* by Jean Marzollo, Susan Jeffers's pictures show two stories going on simultaneously. Rhyming text suggests things a little girl can do in her dreams, such as play with "wooly lambs on a lazy day." Large close-up pictures show the wooly lambs; smaller ones show a harassed father getting his little one ready for bed. Despite the soothing visions of animals going to sleep, the little girl fights bedtime throughout the book. At last she does go to bed, with visions of all her father has told her as her dreams. Jeffers's large beautifully composed pictures will intrigue both children and their parents.

With glowing colors and verse, Gloria Kamen describes all that goes on from dawn until dusk in the lives of birds, animals, and a sleepy baby in her book, *"Paddle," Said the Swan*. She also provides some of the sounds of animals that always intrigue toddlers. As the sun sets, "Glow," said the fireflies, and Mother and baby prepare for bed. Lovely language and shimmering pictures make this a fine bedtime story. Repetition and soothing language characterize the story of *Where Does the Brown Bear Go?* by Nicki Weiss. When the lights go down on the city streets and the sun sinks behind the seas, all the animals are on their way home. Shown against a darkened sky, a cat, a monkey, a camel, and stray dog make their way home. In the last picture, all the animals are seen as stuffed ones surrounding a sleeping boy.

Stories that have no relationship to bedtime of course make fine reading at this time, too. So young children should see many of the appropriate picture storybooks described in Chapter 5 and hear the well-loved traditional tales of "The Three Bears," "The Three Billy Goats Gruff," and "The Gingerbread Man" discussed in Chapter 6. For although young children need books that mirror their own feelings and experiences, they also need books to take them beyond

Primary children need to hear many stories read several times a day by an enthusiastic teacher.

Highland Park Elementary School, South-Western City Schools, Grove City, Ohio. Kristen Kerstetter, teacher.

❦   ❦   ❦

those experiences and to help their imaginations soar.

BOOKS FOR THE BEGINNING READER

Learning to read begins at home with children hearing stories on their parents' laps and seeing loved persons in their lives valuing books. The child lucky enough to have had such a wide exposure to books will usually learn to read easily and fluently. The importance of reading aloud to young children for their success in learning to read has been consistently proven by researchers in this country and abroad (see Chapter 1: Clark 1976, Cohen 1968, Durkin 1966, Thorndike 1973, Wells 1986).

The books for the very young child, which have been discussed in this chapter, may be read again when children of 5 or 6 start to become readers. Increasingly, theories of reading emphasize the importance of reading for meaning and enjoyment from the very start of learning to read. Many preprimers and primers have stilted, unnatural language and pointless plots that cut across the child's spontaneous attempts to read; on the other hand, stories that children love and have heard over and over again have natural language and satisfying plots that encourage reading. Many of these books utilize repeated language and story patterns that help the child learn to read naturally as she or he joins in on the refrains or predicts the action of the story.

Jerome Bruner was the first to use the term *scaffold* to characterize adult assistance to children's language development.[13] It is also possible for a book to be an instructional scaffold or kind of temporary help in the child's first attempts to read. Such books include familiar texts like Mother Goose rhymes or songs that children know by heart and can easily "read" or they may be books with repetitive language or story patterns which help children remember or predict the story easily. Bridge and others[14] report a study with slower first graders that showed sight words were better learned in the context of predictable books and language experience stories than from preprimers.

Margaret Meek[15] points out in *How Texts Teach What Readers Learn* that as children explore a variety of texts, they learn how books work. She also emphasizes the importance of repeated readings, maintaining that each time a book is revisited new understandings are gained. See also research by Miriam Martinez and Nancy Roser in this country.[16]

[13]Identified by C. B. Cazden, "Adult Assistance to Language Development: Scaffolds, Models, and Direct Instruction," in R. P. Parker and F. A. Davis, *Developing Literacy: Young Children's Use of Language* (Newark, Del.: International Reading Association, 1983), pp. 3–18.

[14]Connie A. Bridge, et al., "Using Predictable Materials vs. Preprimers to Teach Beginning Sight Words," *The Reading Teacher*, vol. 36 (May 1983), pp. 884–891.

[15]Margaret Meek, *How Texts Teach What Readers Learn* (London: Thimble Press, 1988).

[16]Miriam Martinez and Nancy Roser, "Read It Again: The Value of Repeated Readings During Storytime," *The Reading Teacher*, vol. 38 (1985), pp. 782–786.

Kindergarten children enjoy reading their alternative version of *Goodnight Moon* by Margaret Wise Brown.
Mission School, Redlands Public School, Redlands, California. Nancy Anderson, teacher and photographer.

Predictable Books

Books that can help an emergent reader may be identified by such characteristics as repetitive language patterns or story patterns or the use of such familiar sequences as numbers, the days of the week, or hierarchical patterns. Frequently, texts combine several of these characteristics in a single story.

Many stories include repetitive phrases or questions that invite children to share in the reading. Eric Hill's *Where's Spot?* provides for active participation as the child helps search for the dog. Each time a flap is lifted to answer such a question as "Is he behind the door?" a hidden animal answers with an emphatic "No, No, No." Children quickly learn the language pattern of this very easy text.

Another well-liked patterned question-and-answer book is *Brown Bear, Brown Bear, What Do You See?* by Bill Martin, Jr. The question in the title is put to a large brown bear, who replies that he sees a redbird looking at him. The question is then directed at the redbird: "Redbird, redbird, what do you see?" He sees a yellow duck, who in turn sees a blue horse, and so on. Identification of animal and color in the picture allows the child to chime in on the answer for each page. The large, bold collage pictures by Eric Carle are a perfect match for the text and support the child's reading of the story. Author and illustrator have followed the same pattern of text in another story titled *Polar Bear, Polar Bear, What Do You Hear?*

Another excellent story similar to *Brown Bear, Brown Bear* is Sue Williams's, *I Went Walking.* A vivacious red-haired boy goes walking and sees a variety of animals. The phrase "I went walking" is always followed by the question "What did you see?" Looking closely, the reader can discover the next animal or bird partially hidden. Turn the page and you see the whole animal. Each animal joins the little boy, making the large pictures cumulative. A subplot reveals the little boy discarding his jacket, his sweater, and his shoes and socks as he continues on his walk. This story leads children into reading as easily as the animals follow the boy on his adventuresome walk.

Mirra Ginsburg's *The Chick and the Duckling* play a delightful game of follow-the-leader. Each thing the duckling does is copied by the chick, who echoes "Me too." When the duck decides to take a *second* swim, the chick has learned his lesson and says "Not me." Both the refrain and repeated action in the story make this a very predictable book. Other patterned language books may repeat certain words many times, as in *The Teeny Tiny Woman* by Paul Galdone.

Building on children's knowledge of numbers and the days of the week provides a kind of scaffold for reading. Clear pictures by Tomie de Paola illustrate the predictable book *Cookie's Week* by Cindy Ward. If a child knows the days of the week, she can easily read the description of everything a mischievous little black-and-white cat does each day. Much to children's delight it begins with "On Monday ... Cookie fell in the toilet." The next page sets the pattern of the book, "And there was water everywhere." Knowledge of the days of the week and numbers help children read *The Very Hungry Caterpillar* by Eric Carle. They particularly enjoy reciting the part where the caterpillar eats through *one* apple on *Monday*, *two* pears on *Tuesday*, *three* plums on *Wednesday*, until he has a huge feast on *Sunday*. In Maurice Sendak's rhyming *Chicken Soup with Rice*, each verse begins with the month and ends with doing something to the soup, such as blowing on it or sipping it. Some groups have made up their own verses for the months, using Sendak's pat-

I went walking.   What did you see?

A young boy goes for a walk and finds all the animals that he sees are following him in this story titled *I Went Walking* by Sue Williams. Julie Vivas's whimsical paintings add a story of their own to this predictable book.

Little Red Riding Hood is going to visit her grandmother.

Well-known folktales such as "Little Red Riding Hood" make easy reading for beginners. Here 6-year-olds have retold the story and illustrated it with tissue paper collage, paints, and crayons.

Mt. Eden Normal School, Auckland, New Zealand. Ava McGregor, teacher.

🐞 🐞 🐞

children recognize the story structure, they know that if the great big bear says, "Someone has been tasting my porridge," then the middle-sized bear and the baby bear will both say the same thing. A baby llama asks the repetitive question *"Is Your Mama a Llama?"* of each animal he

A kindergarten/first grade teacher honors all stories and interpretations of "Little Red Riding Hood" by cutting around the most important part of children's pictures and displaying them on this very tall mural.

Highland Park Elementary School, South-Western City Schools, Grove City, Ohio. Kristen Kerstetter, teacher.

🐞 🐞 🐞

tern and repeated phrases. Hierarchies based on size, such as those in the tales about the three bears and the three Billy Goats Gruff, help children to read these stories. With one reading, children easily discern the pattern of being the littlest in Pat Hutchins's story of *Titch*. They know that if his brother has a *great big* bike and his sister a *big bike*, then Titch will have a *tricycle*.

Repetitive story patterns also help the child predict the action in the plot. The easy folktales with their patterns of three, such as *The Three Billy Goats Gruff* by Marcia Brown and *The Three Little Pigs* and *The Three Bears*, both illustrated by Paul Galdone, support the child's reading. For once

meets. They in turn provide factual and rhyming clues that make it easy to guess the identity of their mothers. Children love these riddle rhymes by Deborah Guarino and the endearing pictures of baby animals by Steven Kellogg. Action and dialogue are repeated four times in the captivating story of *The Big Fat Worm* by Nancy Van Laan. Bold colorful pictures by Marisabina Russo make this circular story an easy one to retell and read.

Cumulative tales have repeated patterns and phrases that become longer and longer with each incident. Children love to read the story of *The Great Big Enormous Turnip* by Alexei Tolstoy, which tells of an attempt to pull up a turnip by a whole family including the Old Man, the Old Woman, the granddaughter, the black dog, the

house cat, and the little mouse, whose added strength is just what is needed. Rose Robart creates a rollicking cumulative tale in *The Cake That Mack Ate*. Even though every verse ends in the title phrase, it is only in the last few pictures that children discover the identity of Mack, a huge dog! Sarah Hayes uses rhyme to tell the cumulative adventure of a stuffed bear that falls into a garbage bin in *This Is the Bear*. Cartoon blurbs add to the humor of this story by providing the thoughts of boy, bear, and dog.

Some modern stories contain predictable plots, also. Certainly one of the easiest is Brian Wildsmith's *The Cat on the Mat*. In this simple yet beautifully illustrated book, one animal after another comes and sits on the mat until the cat

---

RESOURCES FOR TEACHING

◆ PREDICTABLE BOOKS ◆

LANGUAGE PATTERNS: REPETITIVE WORDS, PHRASES, QUESTIONS

Bennett, Jill. *Teeny Tiny*, illustrated by Tomie de Paola. Putnam, 1986.
Brown, Ruth. *A Dark Dark Tale*. Dial, 1981.
Burton, Marilee Robin. *Tail Toes Eyes Ears Nose*. Harper, 1989.
Campbell, Rod. *Dear Zoo*. Four Winds, 1983.
Carle, Eric. *Do You Want to Be My Friend?* Harper, 1971.
_____. *Have You Seen My Cat?* Picture Book, 1987.
_____. *The Very Busy Spider*. Philomel, 1984.
_____. *The Very Quiet Cricket*. Philomel, 1990.
Ginsburg, Mirra. *The Chick and the Duckling*, illustrated by Jose Aruego and Ariane Dewey. Macmillan, 1972.
_____. *Good Morning, Chick*, illustrated by Byron Barton. Greenwillow, 1980.
Hill, Eric. *Where's Spot?* Putnam, 1980.
Kraus, Robert. *Where Are You Going, Little Mouse?*, illustrated by Jose Aruego and Ariane Dewey. Greenwillow, 1986.
_____. *Whose Mouse Are You?*, illustrated by Jose Aruego and Ariane Dewey. Macmillan, 1970.
Martin, Bill, Jr. *Brown Bear, Brown Bear, What Do You See?*, illustrated by Eric Carle. Holt, 1983.
Shaw, Nancy. *Sheep in a Jeep*, illustrated by Margot Shaw. Houghton Mifflin, 1986.
Tafuri, Nancy. *Have You Seen My Duckling?* Greenwillow, 1984.
Williams, Sue. *I Went Walking*, illustrated by Julie Vivas. Harcourt, 1990.

FAMILIAR SEQUENCES: NUMBERS, DAYS OF WEEK, MONTHS, HIERARCHIES

Carle, Eric. *The Very Hungry Caterpillar*. Philomel, 1969.
Christelow, Eileen. *Five Little Monkeys Jumping on the Bed*. Clarion, 1989.
Galdone, Paul. *The Three Bears*. Clarion, 1985.
_____. *The Three Billy Goats Gruff*. Clarion, 1981.

RESOURCES FOR TEACHING

◆ PREDICTABLE BOOKS (CONTINUED) ◆

Hellen, Nancy. *The Bus Stop*. Orchard, 1988.
Hutchins, Pat. *Titch*. Macmillan, 1971.
Sendak, Maurice. *Chicken Soup with Rice*. Harper, 1962. (Big Book with same title, Scholastic, 1986.)
Shulevitz, Uri. *One Monday Morning*. Scribner's, 1967.
Ward, Cindy. *Cookie's Week*, illustrated by Tomie de Paola. Putnam, 1988.
Wolff, Ashley. *A Year of Beasts*. Dutton, 1986.
_____. *A Year of Birds*. Putnam, 1984.

REPETITIVE STORY PATTERNS

Barton, Byron, *Buzz Buzz Buzz*. Macmillan, 1973.
Brown, Marcia. *The Three Billy Goats Gruff*. Harcourt, 1957.
Brown, Margaret Wise. *Four Fur Feet*. Watermark, 1989.
Galdone, Paul. *The Three Bears*. Clarion, 1972.
_____. *The Little Red Hen*. Clarion, 1973.
_____. *The Three Little Pigs*. Clarion, 1970.
Guarino, Deborah. *Is Your Mama a Llama?*, illustrated by Steven Kellogg. Scholastic, 1989.
Krauss, Ruth. *The Carrot Seed*, illustrated by Crockett Johnson. Harper, 1945.
Lillegard, Dee. *Sitting in My Box*, illustrated by Jon Agee. Dutton, 1989.
Van Laan, Nancy. *The Big Fat Worm*, illustrated by Marisabina Russo. Knopf, 1987.

CUMULATIVE TALES

Duff, Maggie. *Rum, Pum, Pum*. Macmillan, 1978.
Emberley, Barbara. *Drummer Hoff*, illustrated by Ed Emberley. Prentice-Hall, 1967.
Galdone, Paul. *The Gingerbread Boy*. Seabury, 1975.
Hayes, Sarah. *This Is the Bear*, illustrated by Helen Craig. Lippincott, 1986.
Kent, Jack. *The Fat Cat*. Parents', 1971.
Robart, Rose. *The Cake That Mack Ate*, illustrated by Maryann Kovalski. Joy Street/Little, Brown, 1986.
Vipoint, Elfrida. *The Elephant and the Bad Baby*, illustrated by Raymond Briggs. Coward McCann, 1969.
Williams, Linda. *The Little Old Lady Who Was Not Afraid of Anything*, illustrated by Megan Lloyd. Harper, 1986.
Wood, Audrey. *The Napping House*, illustrated by Don Wood. Harcourt, 1984.

PREDICTABLE PLOTS

Brown, Margaret Wise. *Goodnight Moon*. Harper, 1947.
Burningham, John. *Mr. Gumpy's Outing*. Holt, 1971.
Hutchins, Pat. *Good-Night, Owl!* Macmillan (Penguin), 1982.
_____. *Happy Birthday, Sam*. Puffin/Penguin, 1981.
_____. *Rosie's Walk*. Macmillan, 1968.
_____. *You'll Soon Grow Into Them, Titch*. Greenwillow, 1983.
Rice, Eve. *Benny Bakes a Cake*. Greenwillow, 1981.
_____. *Sam Who Never Forgets*. Greenwillow, 1977.
Wildsmith, Brian. *The Cat Sat on the Mat*. Oxford, 1983.

◆ PREDICTABLE BOOKS (CONTINUED) ◆

FAMILIAR SONGS AND RHYMES

Aliki. *Go Tell Aunt Rhody*. Macmillan, 1986 (1974).
Hawkins, Colin, and Jacqui Hawkins. *Old Mother Hubbard*. Putnam, 1985.
_____. *I Know an Old Lady Who Swallowed a Fly*. Putnam, 1987.
Hill, Eric. *Nursery Rhyme Peek-a-Book*. Price, Stern, 1982.
Jones, Carol. *Old MacDonald Had a Farm*. Houghton Mifflin, 1989.
_____. *This Old Man*. Houghton Mifflin, 1990.
Peek, Merle, adapted and illustrated. *Mary Wore Her Red Dress and Henry Wore His Green Sneakers*. Clarion, 1985.
_____. *Roll Over! A Counting Song*. Clarion, 1981.
Raffi. *Down By the Bay: Songs to Read*, illustrated by Nadine Bernard Westcott. Crown, 1987.
_____. *Five Little Ducks*, illustrated by Jose Aruego and Ariane Dewey. Crown, 1989.
Westcott, Nadine Bernard. *Peanut Butter and Jelly: A Play Rhyme*. Dutton, 1987.
_____. *Skip to My Lou*. Joy Street/Little, Brown, 1989.

USE OF ENVIRONMENTAL PRINT

Crews, Donald. *Truck*. Greenwillow, 1980.
_____. *School Bus*. Greenwillow, 1984.
Goor, Ron, and Nancy Goor. *Signs*. Crowell, 1983.
Hoban, Tana. *I Read Signs*. Greenwillow, 1983.
_____. *I Read Symbols*. Greenwillow, 1983.
Preston, Edna Mitchell. *Where Did My Mother Go?*, illustrated by Chris Conover. Four Winds, 1978.

thinks there are too many. With one hiss he frightens them all away and once again he is left with complete ownership of the mat. *Rosie's Walk* by Hutchins is better for telling than reading, since the entire text is only one sentence long. However, children can learn how to predict what is going to happen to the fox by careful observation of where the unsuspecting hen takes her walk. The journey story *Three Ducks Went Wandering* by Ron Roy is filled with danger and narrow escapes from an angry bull, a hungry hawk, a family of foxes, and a snake. Children enjoy guessing how the ducks will survive each crisis. Another tale of a narrow escape, by Mirra Ginsburg, is the story of a hen and chicks who get *Across the Stream* and foil the hungry fox. These and other stories help children begin to develop an understanding of how the character of a fox will act in an animal tale. This developing sense of a story also begins to help them predict action.

Familiar Mother Goose rhymes such as "Little Miss Muffet" or "Old Mother Hubbard" or the popular song *Mary Wore Her Red Dress* by Merle Peek all enable the child to assume the role of a reader. Children can hold the books or point to a large chart and "read the words" because they know the verse or song. As they match sentences and phrase cards or point to individual words in the text, they begin to read the story. In the meantime, they are learning that those symbols stand for the words they already know. This enables them to behave like readers.

Some concept books like *Truck* by Donald Crews or *My Kitchen* by Harlow Rockwell give children an opportunity to read environmental print. Ron and Nancy Goor have produced a book based only on photographs of common *Signs*. Tana Hoban's books *I Read Signs* and *I Read Symbols* provide excellent photographs of the signs in their environmental context. These books help teachers see how aware of print their children are becoming. However, children may recognize a stop sign at the corner and not recognize it in a book. The proper context for reading is important.

As more and more primary teachers begin to use real books for teaching children to read, textbook publishers are beginning to produce made-to-order predictable books written to a formula. These so-called "little books" frequently lack the imaginative quality of true literature. They may use repetitive phrases or questions, but they have deadly dull plots and the unnatural language of primers. Look rather for imaginative trade books with natural language, a creative plot, and real child appeal. Look, too, for fine artwork such as that found in the books by Eric Carle, Pat Hutchins, Marisabina Russo, and many more outstanding author/illustrators.

The previously listed titles are all trade books that meet the criteria we have suggested. They help the emergent reader learn to read naturally and with real delight.

Big Books

As primary teachers begin to use real books to teach emergent readers, some of them put favorite stories and poems on large charts so that

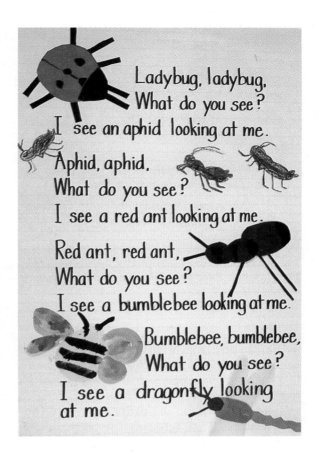

Using the structure of *Brown Bear, Brown Bear, What Do You See?*, first graders created their own story about insects.

Mission School, Redlands, California. Nancy Anderson, teacher. Photo by Larry Rose.

First graders show much interest in reading the Big Book they have created.

Idyllwild Elementary School, Idyllwild, California. Sharon Schmidt, teacher. Photo by Larry Rose.

everyone in the class can see them. During shared reading time, the children read them together as one of them points to the words. Frequently, children illustrate these homemade charts with their own drawings and then the teacher puts them together as a big book. Teachers may chat about the words and ask a child to point to a particular word that they are certain the child knows, or find all the words that begin the same as their name. At other times, children might create their own original version of a favorite story. (See the picture from "Spot the King" on p. 71.) One group transposed the popular tale of *Five Minutes' Peace*

The cover and one page from the story created by kindergarten and first graders about "Lady Bug Saves the Day." Notice their use of fingerpaint paper in their collage pictures, which they tried to do in the same way Eric Carle makes his.

Mission School, Redlands Public Schools, Redlands, California. Nancy Anderson, teacher. Photo by Larry Rose.

by Jill Murphy, which tells of a harassed mother elephant who could not get away from her family, to a schoolroom setting and a teacher's need for five minutes' peace.

Children love these alternative stories that they have a part in producing either by illustrating or by writing. They take ownership of them and read them to each other over and over again. In two trips we made to New Zealand to visit schools, these homemade big books were the only ones seen.

Since that time, publishers have recognized a need for commercial big books and predictable books and created their own. Commercial big books are necessarily expensive and do not provide the same sense of ownership that comes with the class-made books. This cost needs to be balanced against the number of trade books that can be purchased with the money. Some of the commercial big books use the same illustrations as the trade books; others have new illustrations. Almost all of the traditional tales such as "The Three Bears" are available in big books. Teachers need to ask if this is the version they want to share with their class, or if they would prefer a different one. Also, they must evaluate the text for ease of reading. Is this a version that helps students read the text? Does the placement of the text show the

repetitive phrases, for example? Do the illustrations help the children read the story? Big books need to be evaluated before their purchase. The best of the commercial ones are those that replicate good predictable trade books exactly. Examples would be *The Chick and the Duckling* by Mirra Ginsburg or *Rosie's Walk* by Pat Hutchins.

Controlled-Vocabulary Books

Most basal reading series control the number of words, the sounds of the words, and the length of the stories for beginning readers. Until the advent of books for babies and preschoolers, most picture storybooks were written to be read *to* children and thus were at a reading level of at least third grade. They were geared to the young child's interest and appreciation level, not reading ability level. That left very little for the beginning reader to read, except for preprimers and primers. This is no longer true with the number of easy predictable books available today.

A new genre of book was created when Dr. Seuss wrote *The Cat in the Hat* in 1957. This book was written with a controlled vocabulary (derived from the Dolch vocabulary list of 220 words) for the young child to read independently. In format, such books tend to look more like basal readers

CREATING BIG BOOKS WITH EMERGENT READERS

At the end of the year, Nancy Anderson's group of kindergarten/first graders at Mission School in Redlands, California, did a unit on insects. They read informational books on insects and all of Eric Carle's stories about insects including *The Very Hungry Caterpillar*, *The Very Busy Spider*, and *The Very Quiet Cricket*.

Using the structure of *Brown Bear, Brown Bear, What Do You See?* by Bill Martin, Jr., they wrote and illustrated their own big book with insects as their main characters. They read this together in shared reading time.

Later they decided to write their own story about a ladybug and illustrate it the way Eric Carle illustrated his stories. Using their fingerpaint pictures, they cut out butterflies, ladybugs, and bumblebees to illustrate their story titled:

Lady Bug Saves the Day

Once there was a red shiny spotted ladybug.
She lived in the forest. She kept busy eating
aphids off the flowers and bushes.

Along came a black and orange butterfly who
was being chased by a fierce mean bumblebee. The
ladybug heard a terrible buzzing sound. The butterfly
cried "Help Help!" The ladybug waved and whispered,
"Come over here, hide with me. Come in my house,
it's safe."

The butterfly followed the ladybug to her
house. She said, "Thank you for saving my life."

Both big books reflect what children learned about insects. The first one shows how a book helped to provide structure to their story; the second one gives them an opportunity to illustrate in the same way as Eric Carle, their favorite illustrator.

Nancy Anderson, teacher
Mission School
Redlands, California

Henry feels secure when his lovable 180-pound dog, Mudge, walks to school with him. This favorite easy-reading book, *Henry and Mudge,* is by Cynthia Rylant, illustrated by Suçie Stevenson.

❧ ❧ ❧

than picture storybooks, although they do have illustrations on every page. Some of these books, such as *Little Bear* by Else Minarik, illustrated by Sendak, and the superb "Frog and Toad series" by Arnold Lobel are easy-reading books that do not use controlled vocabulary. They can take their rightful place in children's literature. In fact, while *Frog and Toad Are Friends* was a Caldecott Honor Book, *Frog and Toad Together* was a Newbery Honor Book two years later, suggesting that quality writing can be achieved with a limited vocabulary. *Mouse Tales*, also by Lobel, consists of seven short bedtime stories that Papa Mouse tells, one for each of his seven mouse boys. The warmth, humor, and literary quality of these tales are complemented by Lobel's amusing illustrations of a tiny world of mouse people. Equally successful stories by Lobel include *Owl at Home* and *Uncle Elephant*.

Cynthia Rylant's *Henry and Mudge* series feature Henry and his lovable 180-pound dog, Mudge. Short episodes about these two inseparable friends are divided into chapters, just right for the newly independent readers who love them. While the language is simple, it almost has a poetic quality, particularly when the author contrasts Henry's life before and after acquiring Mudge. Before he had Mudge, he had to walk to school alone and he worried about "tornados, ghosts, biting dogs and bullies." But after he got Mudge, he'd think about "vanilla ice cream, rain, rocks and good dreams." Other well-loved Mudge stories include *Henry and Mudge and the Happy Cat* and *Henry and Mudge Take the Big Test*.

Today there are literally hundreds of these easy-reading books. Some are stories, some appeal to special interests such as sports, mysteries, science, or history. Not all achieve the literary excellence of The Little Bear series, Frog and Toad series, or Henry and Mudge series. Some appear contrived and restricted by the controlled vocabulary. Research has shown that the meaning of the story is far more important for ease of reading than limiting vocabulary. We should not accept a book just because it has a beginning-to-read label. Each book must be evaluated for literary qualities, child appeal, and difficulty of reading.

It is important to remember that no matter what we read, we are helping the child learn to read. Children need to hear many books. Frequently, they want to re-read a book. Sometimes children have a fascination with a long book in which they search for familiar words and teach themselves to read, so we need not limit the emergent reader's book exposure to just predictable books. One child, with whom one of the authors read in England, had taught himself to read with the Frances stories by Russell Hoban. He had learned to read *Bread and Jam for Frances* and was working on *A Baby Sister for Frances*. These are difficult books, but Gerald wanted to read them, and that is the key to helping children learn to read.

Today, with the number of fine trade books available, it is quite possible to find books that children want to read and find pleasure in learning to read them.

SUGGESTED LEARNING EXPERIENCES

1. Share several stories with a child under a year of age. What appears to capture his or her attention? How many different ways can you provide for the child's active participation in the story?
2. Learn several finger plays to try with young children. Can they do them? What is difficult for them? Teach these finger plays to your classmates.
3. Working in pairs and using the evaluative criteria established in this chapter, compare three different editions of Mother Goose, ABC, or counting books.
4. Select a wordless picture book to use with children of various ages. Record the retelling of the story by each child, noting differences in language development, sense of story, descriptive phrases, and complexity of plot. Be sure to let the child look through the book once before beginning to tell the story.
5. Assume you are going to compile a small Mother Goose book of twenty to twenty-five rhymes. Which ones would you choose? How would you arrange them in your book?
6. Find a concept book about one particular subject. *Before* you read it, list all the possible dimensions of that concept. Then compare your list with what the author/artist chose to include.
7. Read three or four bedtime stories to one child or several children. Which ones do they ask to hear repeated? Can you find any patterns among their favorites?
8. Select what you consider to be a predictable book. Share it with 5- and 6-year-olds, then reread it waiting for them to join in at various places. What did you learn about your selection?
9. Interview a nursery school teacher. How often does he or she read aloud to the group? How do the teachers select the books? Do they have any favorites? What are they? What recommendations for change could you make?
10. Compare several preprimers and primers with the books for the beginning reader described in this text. What do you notice as being different or significant for an emerging reader?

RELATED READINGS

1. Butler, Dorothy. *Babies Need Books*. New York: Atheneum, 1980.
   A firm believer in the importance of books for the young child, this New Zealander writes from her experience as a mother, grandmother, and a children's bookseller. She not only recommends books for ages 1 through 5, but she gives practical suggestions of when and how to read to wiggly children.
2. Cochran-Smith, Marilyn. *The Making of a Reader*. Norwood, N.J.: Ablex, 1984.
   This book focuses on how adults and children observed over an 18-month period in a preschool collaborate on building meaning in books. It emphasizes what the children know about books and ways they seem to be coming to know it. The observational charts will prove useful to other researchers.
3. Goelmann, Hillel, Antoinette Oberg, and Frank Smith, eds. *Awakening to Literacy*. Portsmouth, N.H.: Heinemann Educational Books, 1984.
   Based on a literacy symposium held at the University of Victoria, these fourteen papers provide a thorough review of the research on literacy before schooling. Articles by Yetta Goodman, Frank Smith, and Jerome Bruner are particularly significant. William H. Teale's paper on the importance of reading aloud to young children supports the point of view presented in this chapter.
4. Hill, Mary W. *Home: Where Reading and Writing Begin*. Portsmouth, N.H.: Heinemann Educational Books, 1989.

Written for parents, this book is filled with children's literature titles and helpful suggestions of ways to create literate environments in the home.

5. Hart-Hewins, Linda, and Jan Wells. *Real Books for Reading.* Portsmouth, N.H.: Heinemann Educational Books, 1990.

The subtitle of this book, "Learning to Read with Children's Literature," evolved from the extensive experience of two former teachers in Canada of using children's literature as the core of their classroom reading program. Practical suggestions for reading aloud, buddy reading, conferencing with children, and writing opportunities are all given. An extensive bibliography of books for children is also included.

6. McConaghy, June. *Children Learning Through Literature.* Portsmouth, N.H.: Heinemann Educational Books, 1990.

A Canadian describes her experience of teaching first graders to read by using literature. She emphasizes discussing children's responses to books rather than quizzing them with questions. She describes literature's influence on children's writing and gives examples of children's stories. She also provides samples from her own journal entries to show her growth as a teacher and researcher.

7. Short, Kathy Gnagey, and Kathryn Mitchell Pierce, eds. *Talking About Books: Creating Literate Communities.* Portsmouth, N.H.: Heinemann Educational Books, 1990.

Teachers and educators focus on the kinds of learning communities that support readers as they read and interact with others, particularly as they discuss literature. Emphasis is placed on collaborative learning from kindergarten through high school. Practical suggestions are provided about ways to organize the classroom to encourage talk about literature.

8. Strickland, Dorothy S., and Lesley Mandel Morrow, eds. *Emerging Literacy: Helping Young Children Learn to Read and Write.* Newark, Del.: International Reading Association, 1989.

Contains the text and the influential statement "Literacy Development and Prefirst Grade: A Joint Statement of Concerns About Present Practices in Prefirst Grade Reading Instruction and Recommendations for Improvement." Strickland's excellent chapter enlarges on this statement to provide a model for change in the curriculum.

9. Taylor, Denny, and Catherine Dorsey-Gaines. *Growing Up Literate: Learning from Inner-City Families.* Portsmouth, N.H.: Heinemann Educational Books, 1988.

Descriptions of growing up poor and black in an urban environment and still growing up literate. A devastating picture of the economic poverty and in many instances (see the chapter "Shanna's Day at School") the educational poverty of their lives. Yet despite it all, these children become literate. One needs to ask how.

10. Taylor, Denny, and Dorothy S. Strickland. *Family Storybook Reading.* Portsmouth, N.H.: Heinemann Educational Books, 1986.

These authors provide real-life experiences and photographs of the various ways parents share books in the home. Astute observers, the authors focus on the natural ways parents lead children to developing literacy.

11. Teale, William H., and Elizabeth Sulzby, eds. *Emergent Literacy: Writing and Reading.* Norwood, N.J.: Ablex, 1986.

A fine collection of articles about literacy by such well-known researchers as Emilia Ferreiro, Shirley Brice Heath, Catherine Snow, and Anat Ninio. Teale's last article sums up the research on children's home background and emergent literacy development.

12. Wells, Gordon. *The Meaning Makers: Children Learning Language and Using Language to Learn.* Portsmouth, N.H.: Heinemann Educational Books, 1986.

Wells reports on the importance of story and reading aloud to preschoolers for the later educational attainment of children. Based on fifteen years of longitudinal research, this is a significant book.

13. White, Dorothy. *Books Before Five.* Portsmouth, N.H.: Heinemann Educational Books, 1984 (1954).

A reissue of the first longitudinal study of a young child's response to books. Written by a young mother who was a former librarian, this book records how she and her daughter Carol explored books from the time Carol was 2 until she went to school. Long out of print, this new edition has a foreword by Marie Clay.

REFERENCES

Ahlberg, Janet, and Alan Ahlberg. *The Baby's Catalogue*. Little, Brown, 1982.
_____. *Each Peach Pear Plum*. Viking, 1979.
_____. *Peek-a-Boo!* Viking, 1981.
Alexander, Martha. *Pigs Say Oink*. Random, 1978.
Aliki (Brandenberg). *Go Tell Aunt Rhody*. Macmillan, 1986 (1974).
_____. *My Feet*. Crowell, 1990.
_____. *My Hands*. Crowell, 1990.
Anno, Mitsumasa. *Anno's Alphabet*. Crowell, 1975.
_____. *Anno's Counting Book*. Crowell, 1977.
_____. *Anno's Counting House*. Crowell, 1982.
Aylesworth, Jim. *One Crow, A Counting Rhyme*, illustrated by Ruth Young. Lippincott, 1988.
Azarian, Mary. *A Farmer's Alphabet*. Godine, 1981.
Bang, Molly. *Ten, Nine, Eight*. Greenwillow, 1983.
Barton, Byron. *Buzz Buzz Buzz*. Macmillan, 1973.
Bayley, Nicola. *The Nicola Bayley Book of Nursery Rhymes*. Knopf, 1975.
Bennett, Jill. *Teeny Tiny*, illustrated by Tomie de Paola. Putnam, 1986.
Bodecker, N. M. *It's Raining, Said John Twaining*. Atheneum, 1973.
Briggs, Raymond. *The Mother Goose Treasury*. Coward-McCann, 1966.
_____. *The Snowman*. Random, 1978.
Brooke, Leslie. *Ring O'Roses*. Warne, 1923.
Brown, Marc. *Finger Rhymes*. Dutton, 1980.
_____. *Hand Rhymes*. Dutton, 1985.
Brown, Marcia. *All Butterflies*. Scribner's, 1974.
_____. *The Three Billy Goats Gruff*. Harcourt, 1957.
Brown, Margaret Wise. *Four Fur Feet*. William R. Scott, 1961 (Hopscotch Books). Watermark, 1989.
_____. *Goodnight Moon*, illustrated by Clement Hurd. Harper, 1947.
_____. *The Goodnight Moon Room*, illustrated by Clement Hurd. Harper, 1984.
_____. *The Runaway Bunny*, illustrated by Clement Hurd. Harper, 1972 (1942).
Brown, Ruth. *A Dark Dark Tale*. Dial, 1981.
Browne, Anthony. *I Like Books*. Knopf, 1988.
_____. *Things I Like*. Knopf, 1989.
Bruna, Dick. *B Is for Bear*. Methuen, 1967.
Burningham, John. *The Baby*. Crowell, 1975.
_____. *The Blanket*. Crowell, 1976.
_____. *The Cupboard*. Crowell, 1976.
_____. *The Rabbit*. Crowell, 1975.
_____. *The School*. Crowell, 1975.
_____. *The Snow*. Crowell, 1975.
_____. *John Burningham's ABC*. Crown, 1986.
_____. *Mr. Gumpy's Outing*. Holt, 1971.
Burton, Marilee Robin. *Tail Toes Eyes Ears Nose*. Harper, 1989.
Campbell, Rod. *Dear Zoo*. Four Winds, 1983.
Carle, Eric. *Do You Want to Be My Friend?* Harper, 1971.
_____. *The Grouchy Ladybug*. Harper, 1977.
_____. *Have You Seen My Cat?* Picture Book Studio, 1987.
_____. *1, 2, 3, to the Zoo*. Philomel, 1968.
_____. *The Very Busy Spider*. Philomel, 1984.
_____. *The Very Hungry Caterpillar*. Philomel, 1969.
_____. *The Very Quiet Cricket*. Philomel, 1990.
Carlstrom, Nancy White. *Jesse Bear, What Will You Wear?*, illustrated by Bruce Degen. Macmillan, 1986.
Cauley, Lorinda Bryan. *Old MacDonald Had a Farm*. Putnam, 1989.
_____. *The Three Little Kittens*. Putnam, 1982.
Christelow, Eileen. *Five Little Monkeys Jumping on the Bed*. Clarion, 1989.
Conover, Chris. *Froggie Went A-Courting*. Farrar, 1986.
Crews, Donald. *Flying*. Greenwillow, 1986.
_____. *Freight Train*. Greenwillow, 1978.
_____. *Harbor*. Greenwillow, 1982.
_____. *School Bus*. Greenwillow, 1984.

_____. *Ten Block Dots*. Greenwillow, 1986 (1968).

_____. *Truck*. Greenwillow, 1980.

Day, Alexandra. *Carl's Christmas*. Farrar, 1990.

_____. *Carl Goes Shopping*. Farrar, 1989.

_____. *Good Boy, Carl*. Green Tiger Press, 1985.

de Angeli, Marguerite. *The Book of Nursery and Mother Goose Rhymes*. Doubleday, 1954.

Delacre, Lulu, ed. *Arroz Con Leche: Popular Songs and Rhymes from Latin America*. Scholastic, 1989.

Demi. *Dragons, and Kites and Dragonflies: A Collection of Chinese Nursery Rhymes*. Harcourt, 1986.

de Paola, Tomie. *The Comic Adventures of Old Mother Hubbard and Her Dog*. Harcourt, 1981.

_____. *Pancakes for Breakfast*. Harcourt, 1978.

_____. *Tomie de Paola's Mother Goose*. Putnam, 1985.

Dragonwagon, Crescent. *Alligator Arrived with Apples*, illustrated by Jose Aruego and Ariane Dewey. Macmillan, 1987.

Duff, Maggie. *Rum, Pum, Pum*. Macmillan, 1978.

Duke, Kate. *The Guinea Pig ABC*. Dutton, 1983.

Dunrea, Olivier. *Deep Down Underground*. Macmillan, 1989.

Ehlert, Lois. *Color Farm*. Lippincott, 1990.

_____. *Color Zoo*. Lippincott, 1990.

_____. *Eating the Alphabet*. Harcourt, 1989.

_____. *Feathers for Lunch*. Harcourt, 1990.

_____. *Fish Eyes: A Book You Can Count On*. Harcourt, 1990.

Emberley, Barbara. *Drummer Hoff*, illustrated by Ed Emberley. Prentice-Hall, 1967.

Erskine, Jim. *Bedtime Story*, illustrated by Ann Schweninger. Crown, 1982.

Feelings, Muriel. *Jambo Means Hello: Swahili Alphabet Book*, illustrated by Tom Feelings. Dial, 1974.

_____. *Moja Means One: Swahili Counting Book*, illustrated by Tom Feelings. Dial, 1971.

Gág, Wanda. *The ABC Bunny*. Coward-McCann, 1933.

Galdone, Paul. *The Gingerbread Boy*. Clarion, 1975.

_____. *The History of Simple Simon*. McGraw-Hill, 1966.

_____. *The House That Jack Built*. McGraw-Hill, 1961.

_____. *The Little Red Hen*. Clarion, 1973.

_____. *Old Mother Hubbard and Her Dog*. McGraw-Hill, 1960.

_____. *Over in the Meadow*. Prentice-Hall, 1986.

_____. *The Teeny Tiny Woman*. Clarion, 1984.

_____. *The Three Bears*. Clarion, 1972.

_____. *The Three Billy Goats Gruff*. Clarion, 1981.

_____. *Three Little Kittens*. Clarion, 1986.

_____. *The Three Little Pigs*. Clarion, 1970.

_____. *Tom, Tom, the Piper's Son*. McGraw-Hill, 1964.

Garten, Jan. *The Alphabet Tale*, illustrated by Muriel Batherman. Random, 1964.

Gerstein, Mordicai. *Roll Over!* Crown, 1984.

Giganti, Paul, Jr. *How Many Snails?*, illustrated by Donald Crews. Greenwillow, 1988.

Ginsburg, Mirra. *Across the Stream*, illustrated by Nancy Tafuri. Greenwillow, 1982.

_____. *The Chick and the Duckling*, illustrated by Jose and Ariane Aruego. Macmillan, 1972.

_____. *Good Morning, Chick*, illustrated by Byron Barton. Greenwillow, 1980.

Glazer, Tom. *Eye Winker Tom Tinker Chin Chopper*. Doubleday, 1973.

_____. *The Mother Goose Songbook*, illustrated by David McPhail. Doubleday, 1990.

Goennel, Heidi. *My Dog*. Orchard, 1989.

Goodall, John S. *Little Red Riding Hood*. McElderry, 1988.

_____. *Naughty Nancy Goes to School*. Atheneum, 1985.

Goor, Ron, and Nancy Goor. *Signs*. Crowell, 1983.

Greenaway, Kate. *Mother Goose, or The Old Nursery Rhymes*. Warne, n.d.

Griego, Margot C., et al. *Tortillitas Para Mama and Other Nursery Rhymes/Spanish and English*, illustrated by Barbara Cooney. Henry Holt, 1981.

Grossman, Virginia. *Ten Little Rabbits*, illustrated by Sylvia Long. Chronicle Books, 1991.

Guarino, Deborah. *Is Your Mama a Llama?*, illustrated by Steven Kellogg. Scholastic, 1989.

Hale, Sarah Josepha. *Mary Had a Little Lamb*, photo-illustrated by Bruce McMillan. Scholastic, 1990.

_____. *Mary Had a Little Lamb*, illustrated by Tomie de Paola. Holiday House, 1984.

Harrison, Ted. *A Northern Alphabet*. Tundra, 1982.

Hawkins, Colin, and Jacqui Hawkins. *I Know an Old Lady Who Swallowed a Fly*. Putnam, 1987.
_____. *Old Mother Hubbard*. Putnam, 1985.
Hayes, Sarah. *Clap Your Hands*, illustrated by Toni Gaffe. Lothrop, 1988.
_____. *Eat Up, Gemma*, illustrated by Jan Ormerod. Lothrop, 1988.
_____. *Happy Christmas, Gemma*, illustrated by Jan Ormerod. Lothrop, 1986.
_____. *Nine Ducks Nine*. Lothrop, 1990.
_____. *This Is the Bear*, illustrated by Helen Craig. Lippincott, 1986.
Hellen, Nancy. *The Bus Stop*. Orchard, 1988.
_____. *Old MacDonald Had a Farm*. Orchard, 1990.
Hennessy, B. G. *The Missing Tarts*, illustrated by Tracey Campbell Pearson. Viking Kestrel, 1989.
Hill, Eric. *Nursery Rhyme Peek-a-Book*. Price, Stern, 1982.
_____. *Spot's Birthday Party*. Putnam, 1982.
_____. *Spot's First Christmas*. Putnam, 1983.
_____. *Spot's First Walk*. Putnam, 1981.
_____. *Where's Spot?* Putnam, 1980.
Hines, Anna Grossnickle. *They Really Like Me!* Greenwillow, 1989.
Hoban, Tana. *A, B, See!* Greenwillow, 1982.
_____. *All About Where*. Greenwillow, 1991.
_____. *Big Ones, Little Ones*. Greenwillow, 1976.
_____. *Circles, Triangles and Squares*. Macmillan, 1974.
_____. *Count and See*. Macmillan, 1972.
_____. *Dig, Drill, Dump, Fill*. Greenwillow, 1975.
_____. *Exactly the Opposite*. Greenwillow, 1990.
_____. *I Read Signs*. Greenwillow, 1983.
_____. *I Read Symbols*. Greenwillow, 1983.
_____. *Is It Larger? Is It Smaller?* Greenwillow, 1985.
_____. *Is It Red? Is It Yellow? Is It Blue?* Greenwillow, 1978.
_____. *Of Colors and Things*. Greenwillow, 1989.
_____. *1, 2, 3*. Greenwillow, 1985.
_____. *Shadows and Reflections*. Greenwillow, 1990.
_____. *Shapes, Shapes, Shapes*. Greenwillow, 1986.
_____. *Shapes and Things*. Macmillan, 1970.
_____. *26 Letters and 99 Cents*. Greenwillow, 1987.
_____. *What Is It?* Greenwillow, 1985.
Hoban, Russell, *A Baby Sister for Frances*, illustrated by Lillian Hoban. Harper, 1964.
_____. *Bread and Jam for Frances*, illustrated by Lillian Hoban. Harper, 1964.
Hoguet, Susan Ramsay. *Solomon Grundy*. Dutton, 1986.
Hughes, Shirley. *Alfie's Feet*. Lothrop, 1983.
_____. *Alfie Gets in First*. Lothrop, 1982.
_____. *Alfie Gives a Hand*. Lothrop, 1983.
_____. *The Big Alfie and Annie Rose Storybook*. Lothrop, 1989.
_____. *All Shapes and Sizes*. Lothrop, 1986.
_____. "Nursery Collection." *Bathwater's Hot. Noisy. When We Went to the Park*. All Lothrop, 1985.
Hunt, Peter. *Illuminations*. Bradbury, 1989.
Hutchins, Pat. *Changes, Changes*. Macmillan, 1971.
_____. *The Doorbell Rang*. Greenwillow, 1986.
_____. *Good-Night, Owl!* Macmillan (Penguin), 1972.
_____. *1 Hunter*. Greenwillow, 1982.
_____. *Rosie's Walk*. Macmillan, 1968.
_____. *Tidy Titch*. Greenwillow, 1991.
_____. *Titch*. Macmillan, 1971.
_____. *What Game Shall We Play?* Greenwillow, 1990.
_____. *You'll Soon Grow into Them, Titch*. Greenwillow, 1983.
Isadora, Rachel. *Babies*. Greenwillow, 1990.
_____. *City Seen from A to Z*. Greenwillow, 1983.
_____. *Friends*. Greenwillow, 1990.
Ivemey, John W. *Three Blind Mice*, illustrated by Victoria Chess. Little, 1990.
_____. *Three Blind Mice*, illustrated by Paul Galdone. Clarion, 1987.

Jeffers, Susan. *Three Jovial Huntsmen*. Macmillan, 1989.

Jonas, Ann. *Where Can It Be?* Greenwillow, 1986.

————. *Color Dance*. Greenwillow, 1989.

Jones, Carol. *Old MacDonald Had a Farm*. Houghton Mifflin, 1989.

————. *This Old Man*. Houghton Mifflin, 1990.

Kamen, Gloria. *"Paddle," Said the Swan*. Atheneum, 1989.

Keats, Ezra Jack. *Over in the Meadow*. Four Winds, 1971.

Kent, Jack. *The Fat Cat*. Parents', 1971.

Kitchen, Bert. *Animal Alphabet*. Dial, 1984.

Kitchen, Bert. *Animal Numbers*. Dial, 1987.

Kovalski, Maryann. *The Wheels on the Bus*. Little, 1987.

Kraus, Robert. *Whose Mouse Are You?*, illustrated by Jose Aruego and Ariane Dewey. Macmillan, 1970.

————. *Where Are You Going, Little Mouse?*, illustrated by Jose Aruego and Ariane Dewey. Greenwillow, 1986.

Krauss, Ruth. *The Carrot Seed,* illustrated by Crockett Johnson. Harper, 1945.

Kunhardt, Dorothy. *Pat the Bunny*. Golden, 1962 (1940).

Langstaff, John. *Frog Went A-Courtin'*, illustrated by Feodor Rojankovsky. Harcourt, 1955.

————. *Oh, A-Hunting We Will Go*, illustrated by Nancy Winslow Parker. Atheneum, 1974.

————. *Over in the Meadow*, illustrated by Feodor Rojankovsky. Harcourt, 1967.

Larrick, Nancy. *Songs from Mother Goose*, illustrated by Robin Spowart. Harper, 1989.

Lauber, Patricia, *An Octopus Is Amazing*, illustrated by Holly Keller. Crowell, 1990.

Lillegard, Dee. *Sitting in My Box*, illustrated by Jon Agee. Dutton, 1989.

Lindgren, Barbro. *Sam's Ball*, 1983. *Sam's Bath*, 1983. *Sam's Book*, 1983. *Sam's Car*, 1982. *Sam's Cookie*, 1982. *Sam's Potty*, 1986. *Sam's Teddy Bear*, 1982. *Sam's Wagon*, 1986. All illustrated by Eva Erikson. All Morrow.

Lobel, Anita. *Alison's Zinnia*. Greenwillow, 1990.

Lobel, Arnold. "Frog and Toad Series." *Days with Frog and Toad*, 1979. *Frog and Toad All Year*, 1976. *Frog and Toad Are Friends*, 1970. *Frog and Toad Together*, 1972. All Harper.

————. *Mouse Tales*. Harper, 1972.

————. *On Market Street*, illustrated by Anita Lobel. Greenwillow, 1981.

————. *Owl at Home*. Harper, 1975.

————. *The Random House Book of Mother Goose*. Random House, 1986.

————. *Uncle Elephant*. Harper, 1981.

————. *Whiskers and Rhymes*. Greenwillow, 1985.

Lubin, Leonard. *Sing a Song of Sixpence*. Lothrop, 1987.

MacCarthy, Patricia. *Ocean Parade: A Counting Book*. Dial, 1990.

McCully, Emily Arnold. *First Snow*. Harper, 1985.

————. *Picnic*. Harper, 1984.

————. *School*. Harper, 1987.

MacDonald, Suse. *Alphabatics*. Bradbury, 1986.

Magorian, Michelle. *Who's Going to Take Care of Me?*, illustrated by James Graham Hale. Harper, 1990.

Marshall, James. *James Marshall's Mother Goose*. Farrar, 1979.

Martin, Bill, Jr. *Brown Bear, Brown Bear, What Do You See?*, illustrated by Eric Carle. Holt, 1983.

————. *Polar Bear, Polar Bear, What Do You Hear?*, illustrated by Eric Carle. Holt, 1991.

Martin, Bill, Jr., and John Archambault. *Chicka Chicka Boom Boom*, illustrated by Lois Ehlert. Simon & Schuster, 1989.

Marzollo, Jean. *Close Your Eyes*, illustrated by Susan Jeffers. Dial, 1978.

Mayer, Mercer. *A Boy, A Dog, and A Frog*. Dial, 1967.

————. *Frog Goes to Dinner*. Dial, 1974.

————. *One Frog Too Many*. Dial, 1975.

Miller, Margaret. *Whose Hat?* Greenwillow, 1988.

————. *Who Uses This?* Greenwillow, 1990.

Minarik, Else Holmelund. "Little Bear Series." *Father Bear Comes Home*, 1959. *A Kiss for Little Bear*, 1968. *Little Bear*, 1957. *Little Bear's Friend*, 1960. *Little Bear's Visit*, 1961. All illustrated by Maurice Sendak and published by Harper.

Murphy, Jill, *Five Minutes' Peace*. Putnam's, 1986.

Musgrove, Margaret. *Ashanti to Zulu: African Traditions*, illustrated by Leo and Diane Dillon. Dial, 1976.

Opie, Iona. *Tail Feathers from Mother Goose: The Opie Rhyme Book*. Little, 1988.

Opie, Iona, and Peter Opie. *I Saw Esau*, illustrated by Maurice Sendak. Candlewick Press, 1992.

_____. *The Oxford Dictionary of Nursery Rhymes*. Oxford, 1951.

Ormerod, Jan. "Jan Ormerod Baby Books." *Dad's Back. Messy Baby. Reading. Sleeping*. All Lothrop, 1985.

_____. "Jan Ormerod New Baby Books." *Bend and Stretch. Making Friends. Mom's Home. This Little Nose*. All Lothrop, 1987.

_____. *Moonlight*. Lothrop, 1982.

_____. *Sunshine*. Lothrop, 1981.

Owens, Mary Beth. *A Caribou Alphabet*. Brunswick, Me.: Dog Ear Press, 1988.

Oxenbury, Helen. "The Baby Board Books." *Dressing. Family. Friends. Playing. Working*. All Simon & Schuster, 1981.

_____. "Baby Board Books." *I Can. I Hear. I See. I Touch*. All Random House, 1986.

_____. *Clap Hands*. Macmillan, 1987.

_____. *Helen Oxenbury's ABC of Things*. Watts, 1972.

_____. *The Helen Oxenbury Nursery Rhyme Book*. Morrow, 1986.

_____. *Numbers of Things*. Watts, 1968.

_____. "The Pippo Series." *Tom and Pippo and the Dog*, 1989. *Tom and Pippo and the Washing Machine*, 1988. Tom and Pippo Go for a Walk, 1988. *Tom and Pippo Go Shopping*, 1989. *Tom and Pippo in the Garden*, 1989. *Tom and Pippo in the Snow*, 1989. *Tom and Pippo Make a Friend*, 1989. *Tom and Pippo Make a Mess*, 1988. *Tom and Pippo Read a Story*, 1988. *Tom and Pippo See the Moon*, 1989. *Tom and Pippo's Day*, 1989. All Aladdin Books, Macmillan.

_____. *Say Goodnight*. Macmillan, 1987.

_____. *Tickle Tickle*. Macmillan, 1988.

_____. "Very First Books." *Beach Day. Good Night, Good Morning. Monkey See, Monkey Do. Mother's Helper. Shopping Trip*. All Dial, 1982.

Paterson, Bettina. *My First Animals*. Crowell, 1990.

_____. *My First Wild Animals*. Crowell, 1991.

Pearson, Tracey Campbell. *Sing a Song of Sixpence*. Dial, 1988.

Peek, Merle. *Mary Wore Her Red Dress and Henry Wore His Green Sneakers*. Clarion, 1985.

_____. *Roll Over! A Counting Song*. Clarion, 1981.

Peppe, Rodney. *The House That Jack Built*. Delacorte, 1985.

Petersham, Maud, and Miska Petersham. *The Rooster Crows*. Macmillan, 1945.

Pomerantz, Charlotte. *Flap Your Wings and Try*, illustrated by Nancy Tafuri. Greenwillow, 1989.

_____. *One Duck, Another Duck*, illustrated by Jose Aruego and Ariane Dewey. Greenwillow, 1984.

Preston, Edna Mitchell. *Where Did My Mother Go?*, illustrated by Chris Conover. Four Winds, 1978.

Provensen, Alice, and Martin Provensen. *The Mother Goose Book*. Random, 1976.

_____. *A Peaceable Kingdom: The Shaker ABCEDARIUS*. Viking, 1978.

Rackham, Arthur. *Mother Goose, or the Old Nursery Rhymes*. Appleton, 1913.

Raffi. *Down By the Bay: Songs to Read*, illustrated by Nadine Bernard Westcott. Crown, 1987.

_____. *Five Little Ducks*, illustrated by Jose Aruego and Ariane Dewey. Crown, 1989.

Reiss, John J. *Colors*. Bradbury, 1969.

_____. *Numbers*. Bradbury, 1971.

Rice, Eve. *Benny Bakes a Cake*. Greenwillow, 1981.

_____. *Sam Who Never Forgets*. Greenwillow, 1977.

Robart, Rose. *The Cake That Mack Ate*, illustrated by Maryann Kovalski. Joy Street/Little, Brown, 1986.

Rockwell, Anne. *Albert B. Cub and Zebra: An Alphabet Storybook*. Crowell, 1977.

Rockwell, Anne, and Harlow Rockwell. "My World Series." *Can I Help?*, 1982. *Happy Birthday to Me*, 1981. *How My Garden Grew*, 1982. *I Play in My Room*, 1981. *I Love My Pets*, 1982. *Sick in Bed*, 1982. All published by Macmillan.

Rockwell, Harlow. *My Kitchen*. Greenwillow, 1980.

Rojankovsky, Feodor. *The Tall Book of Mother Goose*. Harper, 1942.

Rosen, Michael. *We're Going on a Bear Hunt*, illustrated by Helen Oxenbury. Macmillan, 1989.

Rounds, Glen. *Old MacDonald Had a Farm*. Holiday House, 1981.

Roy, Ron. *Three Ducks Went Wandering*, illustrated by Paul Galdone. Clarion, 1979.

Rubin, Cynthia, selected by. *ABC Americana from The National Gallery of Art*. Harcourt, 1989.

Russo, Marisabina. *Waiting for Hannah*. Greenwillow, 1989.

_____. *Where Is Ben?* Greenwillow, 1990.

_____. *Why Do Grown-Ups Have All the Fun?* Greenwillow, 1987.

Rylant, Cynthia. "Henry and Mudge Books." *Henry and Mudge*, 1987. *Henry and Mudge In Puddle Trouble*, 1987. *Henry and Mudge in the Green Time*, 1987. *Henry and Mudge Under the Yellow Moon*, 1987. *Henry and Mudge in the Sparkle Days*, 1988. *Henry and Mudge and the Forever Sea*, 1989. *Henry and Mudge Get the Cold Shivers*, 1989. *Henry and Mudge and the Happy Cat*, 1990. *Henry and Mudge Take the Big Test*. 1991. All illustrated by Suçie Stevenson and published by Bradbury Press.

Scarry, Richard. *Richard Scarry's Best Mother Goose Ever*. Golden Press, 1970.

Scott, Ann Herbert. *One Good Horse: A Cowpuncher's Counting Book*, illustrated by Lynn Sweat. Greenwillow, 1990.

_____. *Sam*, illustrated by Symeon Shimin. McGraw-Hill, 1992 (1967).

Sendak, Maurice. *Chicken Soup with Rice*. Harper, 1962.

_____. *Hector Protector and As I Went over the Water*. Harper, 1990 (1965).

_____. *One Was Johnny* (Nutshell Library, Vol. 3). Harper, 1962.

Seuss, Dr. (Theodor S. Geisel). *The Cat in the Hat*. Beginner Books, 1957.

Shaw, Nancy. *Sheep in a Jeep*, illustrated by Margot Shaw. Houghton Mifflin, 1986.

Shelby, Anne. *Potluck*, illustrated by Irene Trivas. Orchard, 1991.

Shulevitz, Uri. *One Monday Morning*. Scribner's, 1967.

Sis, Peter. *Going Up*. Greenwillow, 1989.

_____. *Waving*. Greenwillow, 1988.

Slobodkina, Esphyr. *Caps for Sale*. Addison, 1947.

Spier, Peter. *Crash! Bang! Boom!* Doubleday, 1972.

_____. *Gobble Growl Grunt*. Doubleday, 1971.

_____. *Fast-Slow High-Low*. Doubleday, 1972.

_____. *The Fox Went Out on a Chilly Night*. Doubleday, 1961.

_____. *London Bridge Is Falling Down*. Doubleday, 1967.

_____. *Noah's Ark*. Doubleday, 1977.

_____. *Peter Spier's Rain*. Doubleday, 1982.

_____. *To Market, to Market*. Doubleday, 1967.

Steptoe, John. *Baby Says*. Lothrop, 1988.

Stevens, Janet. *The House That Jack Built*. Holiday, 1985.

Sutherland, Zena. *The Orchard Book of Nursery Rhymes*, illustrated by Faith Jaques. Orchard, 1990.

Tafuri, Nancy. *Early Morning in the Barn*. Greenwillow, 1983.

_____. *Follow Me!* Greenwillow, 1990.

_____. *Have You Seen My Duckling?* Greenwillow, 1984.

_____. *Junglewalk*. Greenwillow, 1988.

_____. *One Wet Jacket*. Greenwillow, 1988.

_____. *Two New Sneakers*. Greenwillow, 1988.

Tolstoy, Alexei. *The Great Big Enormous Turnip*, illustrated by Helen Oxenbury. Watts, 1968.

Tripp, Wallace. *Granfa' Grig Had a Pig and Other Rhymes Without Reason*. Little, 1976.

Tudor, Tasha. *A Is for Annabelle*. Walck, 1954.

_____. *Mother Goose*. Walck, 1944.

Turkle, Brinton. *Deep in the Forest*. Dutton, 1976.

Valens, Amy. *Jesse's Daycare*, illustrated by Richard Brown. Houghton, 1990.

Van Allsburg, Chris. *The Z Was Zapped: A Play in Twenty-Six Acts*. Houghton, 1987.

_____. *A Mouse in My House*, illustrated by Marjorie Priceman. Knopf, 1990.

Van Laan, Nancy. *The Big Fat Worm*, illustrated by Marisabina Russo. Knopf, 1987.

Vipoint, Elfrida. *The Elephant and the Bad Baby*, illustrated by Raymond Briggs. Coward-McCann, 1969.

Ward, Cindy. *Cookie's Week*, illustrated by Tomie de Paola. Putnam, 1988.

Watanabe, Shigeo. "I Can Do It All By Myself Series," illustrated by Yasuo Ohtomo. *Get Set! Go!*, 1981. *How Do I Put It On?*, 1979. *I Can Build a House!*, 1983. *I Can Ride It!*, 1982. *I'm King of the Castle*, 1982. *What a Good Lunch!*, 1980. *Where's My Daddy?*, 1982. All Philomel.

_____. "I Love to Do Things with My Daddy Series." *Daddy Play with Me*, 1986. *Where's My Daddy?*, 1985. Both Philomel.

_____. "I Love Special Days" Series, illustrated by Yasuo Ohtomo. *It's My Birthday*. Philomel, 1988.

Watson, Clyde. *Applebet*, illustrated by Wendy Watson. Farrar, 1982.

_____. *Catch Me and Kiss Me and Say It Again*, illustrated by Wendy Watson. Philomel, 1978.

_____. *Father Fox's Pennyrhymes*, illustrated by Wendy Watson. Crowell, 1971.

Watson, Wendy. *Wendy Watson's Frog Went A-Courting*. Lothrop, 1990.

_____. *Wendy Watson's Mother Goose*. Dorothy Briley, ed. Lothrop, 1989.

Weiss, Nicki. *Where Does the Brown Bear Go?* Greenwillow, 1989.

Wells, Rosemary. "Very First Books." *Max's Bath*, 1985. *Max's Bedtime*, 1985. *Max's Birthday*, 1985. *Max's Breakfast*, 1985. *Max's First Word*, 1979. *Max's Ride*, 1979. *Max's Toys*, 1979. All Dial.

Westcott, Nadine Bernard. *I Know an Old Lady Who Swallowed a Fly*. Little, 1980.

_____. *Peanut Butter and Jelly: A Play Rhyme*. Dutton, 1987.

_____. *Skip to My Lou*. Joy Street/Little, Brown, 1989.

Wiesner, David. *Free Fall*. Lothrop, 1988.

_____. *Tuesday*. Clarion, 1991.

Wildsmith, Brian. *Brian Wildsmith's Mother Goose*. Watts, 1963.

_____. *The Cat on the Mat*. Oxford, 1983.

Williams, Linda. *The Little Old Lady Who Was Not Afraid of Anything*, illustrated by Megan Lloyd. Harper, 1986.

Williams, Sue. *I Went Walking*, illustrated by Julie Vivas. Harcourt, 1990.

Williams, Vera B. *"More More More," Said the Baby*. Greenwillow, 1990.

Wolde, Gunilla. "Betsy Books." *This Is Betsy*, 1975. *Betsy's Baby Brother*, 1975. *Betsy's First Day at Nursery School*, 1976. *Betsy and the Doctor*, 1978. All Random.

Wolff, Ashley. *The Bells of London*. Dodd, Mead, 1985.

_____. *A Year of Beasts*. Dutton, 1986.

_____. *A Year of Birds*. Putnam, 1984.

Wood, Audrey. *The Napping House*, illustrated by Don Wood. Harcourt, 1984.

Wright, Blanche Fisher. *The Real Mother Goose*. Rand McNally, 1965 (1916).

_____. *The Real Mother Goose: Green Husky Book*. Rand McNally, 1984.

_____. *The Real Mother Goose: Husky Book Four*. Rand McNally, 1983.

_____. *The Real Mother Goose: Yellow Husky Book*. Rand McNally, 1984.

Wyndham, Robert. *Chinese Mother Goose Rhymes*, illustrated by Ed Young. Philomel, 1968.

Zelinsky, Paul O. *The Wheels on the Bus*. Dutton, 1990.

Zemach, Harve. *Mommy, Buy Me a China Doll*, illustrated by Margot Zemach. Farrar, 1975.

Zemach, Margot. *Hush, Little Baby*. Dutton, 1987.

Zolotow, Charlotte. *Some Things Go Together*, illustrated by Karen Gundersheimer. Crowell, 1983 (1969).

Chapter Five

Picture Storybooks

One group of primary children in the Midwest were studying trees and autumn as a special unit. Their teacher[1] read them *Say It!* by Charlotte Zolotow, illustrated by James Stevenson. The children reviewed what the mother and the little girl had seen on their walk on that windy day. They talked about the words in the story they liked, particularly the word "splendiferous." Then *Say It!* was placed on the display table with the other books about autumn.

The next week the teacher shared the book again. The children then took clipboards, pencils, and paper and went outside. They each chose a favorite tree to sit under and to record what they saw, heard, smelled, thought, felt, or wished. They worked like this for about 15 minutes. Then they made a giant pile of leaves and jumped and played in them.

That afternoon the teacher read *Say It!* again to the children. They selected their favorite words and phrases to be listed on the board. These included "swirled," "wondrous," "dazzling," "zigzagging," "streaks of color," "scrunching," and so forth.

The following day they gave detailed attention to each of the illustrations, talking about the medium and the way James Stevenson had made the pictures. The children were given watercolors and an opportunity to paint what they had seen outside or a favorite part of the story. They were also asked to write about their paintings. Here are some of their comments:

> This is a pond of floating colors. The mother said it is a wonderful pond. (Ritchie)

> It was a golden splendiferous day in this town and the mommie and the girl walked down the road and saw lots of leaves. (Barbie)

> The little girl and her mother went on a walk. And on the walk they found a little floating cloud of seeds. (Valerie)

Obviously *Say It!* became one of their favorite books. It was read frequently and many of the children chose to share it with their "book buddies" in third grade.

---

[1]This description is based on a much longer article by Joetta M. Beaver, "*Say It!* Over and Over," Language Arts, vol. 59 (February 1982), pp. 143–148.

What a wonderful way this teacher related a book to life experiences and life experiences back to a book! Repeated readings heightened children's appreciation for the language and the art of the story. Their experiences with watercolors helped them see what they could do with that medium, and talking and writing about their own pictures enhanced and enlarged their vocabularies.

In the process of looking at one book in depth, children learned much about the way text and illustrations work together to create a story. A picture storybook had provided for the development of these students' visual, mental, and verbal imaginations.

THE PICTURE STORYBOOK DEFINED

This chapter is concerned with picture storybooks only. The picture storybook conveys its messages through two media, the art of illustrating and the art of writing. In a well-designed book in which the total format reflects the meaning of the story, both the illustrations and text must bear the burden of narration. Barbara Bader maintains that:

> As an art form it [the picture storybook] hinges on the interdependence of picture and words, on the simultaneous display of two facing pages, and on the drama of the turning of the page.[2]

In discussing the narrative art of children's picture storybooks, Perry Nodelman states:

> We perceive new experiences in terms of the experiences preceding them. . . . Each picture in a picture book establishes a context for the picture that follows—it becomes a schema that determines how we will perceive the next picture.[3]

Some persons differentiate between the picture book and the picture storybook; others maintain that any book with a picture-book format can be included under the umbrella term *picture book*.

[2]Barbara Bader *American Picturebooks from Noah's Ark to the Beast Within* (New York: Macmillan, 1976), Introduction.
[3]Perry Nodelman, *Words About Pictures* (Athens: University of Georgia Press, 1988), p. 176.

Yet a picture storybook places different demands on the artist than a picture book.

A picture book may be an alphabet book, a counting book, a first book, or a concept book (the books discussed in Chapter 4). In these the pictures must be accurate and synchronized with the text; however, it is not essential that they provide the continuity required by a story line. The illustrations for a concept book or an alphabet book may depict a different object or an animal on each page, providing for much variety in the pictures. Examples would be Bert Kitchen's *Animal Alphabet*, which shows large individual pictures for each letter, or Tana Hoban's *Shadows and Reflections*, which explores various dimensions of a concept with stunning photographs. In a picture storybook, pictures must help to tell the story, showing the action and expressions of the characters, the changing settings, and the development of the plot.

Uri Shulevitz chronicles the demise of a tiny small town post office in his picture storybook *Toddlecreek Post Office*. To the villagers of

Uri Shulevitz shows *Toddlecreek Post Office* suffused with a warm golden glow until the arrival of the postal inspector who decides to close this small community center. Now the glow is overshadowed with dark blue. Artists find many ways to create meaning in a story.

🦜 🦜 🦜

Toddlecreek, the post office was much more than a post office. It served as a special place for friends to gather and tell stories. It provided a warm safe haven for two old dogs to take their naps. And Vernon Stamps did much more than sell stamps. He repaired Mrs. Woolsox's broken lamp and sewed buttons on old Abner Flex's jacket. He provided a bulletin board for local announcements and a book exchange counter. The little post office was the center of a hub of activity until the day the inspector came and closed it forever. Expressive watercolors help tell this tale of the end of an era. Wreathed in golden light from the moment Mr. Stamps opens the door, the post office becomes suddenly dark and dim with the arrival of the postal inspector. In the end Vernon Stamps boards up the post office and walks forlornly away. Shulevitz's cubist illustrations capture a poignant moment in small town America. Unlike Virginia Lee Burton's classic story of *The Little House* that is encroached upon by the city, this tale has no happy ending. Pictures and story make their quiet statement about the loss of spirit that accompanies modern progress. While this book represents a real marriage between pictures and text, it also shows a trend in the content of picture storybooks, which increasingly tackle serious subjects in a way intended for older students.

The illustrated book is different from either a picture book or a picture storybook. In an illustrated book, no attempt is made to tell the whole story; only particular incidents may be illustrated to create interest. Chris Van Allsburg, noted for his fine picture storybooks, provided a dozen full-color plates for the illustrated edition of *Swan Lake* by Mark Helprin. This retelling of the classic ballet is a beautiful example of fine bookmaking with its cloth cover, gold imprinted title, endpapers with floating feathers, and two color borders. It is indeed a handsome illustrated edition, but it is not a picture storybook.

THE ART AND ARTISTS OF PICTURE STORYBOOKS

A picture storybook, then, must be a seamless whole conveying meaning in both the art and the text. An illustration does not merely reflect the action on that page but shares in moving the story forward. At every level of narration the pictures should convey and enhance the meaning behind the story. Artists do this in a variety of subtle and interesting ways.

Creating Meaning in Picture Storybooks

An outstanding example of a picture storybook that helps to move the plot is the classic *Blueberries for Sal* by Robert McCloskey. This is a story that children can tell by themselves just by looking at the clear blue-and-white pictures. The illustrations help the reader anticipate both the action and climax as Sal and her mother are seen going berry-picking up one side of Blueberry Hill, and Little Bear and his mother are seen coming up the other side. McCloskey uses a false climax, a good storytelling technique. Sal hears a noise and starts to peer behind an ominously dark rock; the reader expects her to meet the bears, but instead she sees a mother crow and her children. On the next page she calmly meets Mother Bear and tramps along behind her. A parallel plot gives Little Bear a similar experience, but Sal's mother is not so calm about meeting him! The human expressions of surprise, fear, and consternation on the faces of both mothers express emotion as well as action.

Narrative art may show mounting tension by increasing the size of the pictures. One of the best-known examples of this is seen in Maurice Sendak's fine story, *Where the Wild Things Are*. The pictures in this book become larger and larger as Max's dream becomes more and more fantastic. Following the climactic wild rumpus, which is portrayed on three full-sized spreads with no text whatsoever, Max returns home. The pictures decrease in size, although never down to their original size; just as, symbolically, Max will never be quite the same again after his dream experience.

Picture-book artists also provide clues to the future action of a story. A close look at the first and second pages of *Where the Wild Things Are* shows the mischievous Max dressed in his wild things suit and stringing up a homemade tent. A stuffed toy looking vaguely like a wild thing hangs near by. Later the tent and wild things appear in Max's dream trip to the far-off land of

Maurice Sendak's first picture in *Where the Wild Things Are* foreshadows later events in Max's dream journey. A stuffed toy looks vaguely like one of the wild things. Max is creating his own homemade tent, which later becomes a very elaborate one.

☙ ☙ ☙

the wild things. His drawing of a wild thing on page 2 shows his preoccupation with creating these creatures that later inhabit his dreams.

Some picture-book illustrations use visual metaphors in the same way poets add to the image-making qualities of their poems. In *Once a Mouse* Marcia Brown reinforces the drama of the little mouse who is about to be snatched up in the beak of a crow by making the shape of a hill in the background look like an open beak. Again, as she creates shadows of the animals, the reader can see the shadow of the tiger is that of a dog, his former self before the hermit transformed him.

Sendak's book *Outside Over There* is filled with visual metaphors and symbols. A comparison of the half title page and the last picture in the book reveals that the entire action of Ida's dream story happened in one moment of time, the time when her baby sister took one small step. The storm at sea and the shipwreck that the viewer can see outside the window accompany and intensify with Ida's fury over the goblin's stealing of her baby sister. Edmund Spenser used the same metaphor of a safe sea journey to accompany his telling of *Saint George and the Dragon*. Trina Schart

Hyman faithfully reproduced it in the borders of her superb illustrations for that story as retold by Margaret Hodges.

We have seen how the creative use of color in *Toddlecreek Post Office* signaled the climax of this story. Shulevitz also used increasing light and color to portray his quietly beautiful story of a man and his grandson rowing out on a lake to see the breaking of *Dawn*. Jamichael Henterly captures that special quality of light seen at dusk for W. Nickola-Lisa's poetic prose story *Night Is Coming*.

Pictures should not only reflect the action and climax of the plot, they should help to create the basic mood of the story. In a perfection of words and watercolors, Robert McCloskey captures the changing mood of the Maine coast in his *Time of Wonder*. Using soft grays and yellow, he conveys the warmth and mystery of the early morning fog in the woods. His ocean storm scene, on the other hand, is slashed with streaks of dark blues and emerald greens, highlighted by churning whites. The text is no longer quiet and poetic, but races along with "the sharp choppy waves and slamming rain." The storm subsides; the summer ends; and it is time to leave the island. The beauty of this book will not reach all children, but it will speak forever to young and old alike who have ever intensely loved a particular place on this earth.

Besides creating the basic mood of a story, illustrations also help portray convincing character delineation and development. The characterization in the pictures must correspond to that of the story. There is no mistaking the devilish quality of the incorrigible *Madeline* as she balances herself on the ledge of the Pont des Arts in Paris or says "pooh-pooh to the tiger in the zoo." Madeline is always her roguish self in the four other books that Ludwig Bemelmans wrote about her.

Expression and gesture can also reveal character and move the action forward. In *Just Plain Fancy*, Patricia Polacco tells the story of Naomi, an Amish girl, and her little sister who hatch a peacock from a fancy egg they find. Frightened that their bird is too fancy for Amish ways, they decide to hide it. The expression of awe and amazement on their faces when they first see

Patricia Polacco captures the expression of amazement and concern on the faces of the two young Amish girls when they see their peacock spread his tail feathers for the first time. The artist concentrates her attention on their expressions, and only when readers turn the page can they then see what the girls are looking at.

From *Just Plain Fancy* by Patricia Polacco.

Fancy raise his peacock feathers provides the emotional climax of this delightful story.

One of the few picture storybooks that portrays character development is the Japanese story of *Crow Boy* by Taro Yashima. In the very first picture of this wonderfully sensitive story, Chibi is shown hidden away in the dark space underneath the schoolhouse, afraid of the schoolmaster, afraid of the children. Once inside the school, the artist has pictured Chibi and his desk far removed from all the other children. His use of space helps to emphasize Chibi's isolation and intensifies his feelings of loneliness. In subsequent pictures he is always alone, while the other children come to school in twos and threes. With the arrival of the friendly schoolmaster and his discovery of Chibi's ability to imitate crows, Chibi grows in stature and courage.

In illustrating Paul Heins's version of the Grimm Brothers' *Snow White*, Trina Schart Hyman shows the gradual deterioration of the stepmother until in her last picture she has the stare of a mad woman standing in front of a mirror framed with skulls and jeering faces. Nancy Burkert, on the other hand, in her interpretation of *Snow White* by the Grimm Brothers never shows the face of the evil queen, only her back. But on her workbench is every conceivable symbol of evil and death including deadly nightshade, the thirteenth tarot card, a skull, spiders, bats, mushrooms, and an open book of formulas for poisonous concoctions. These symbols of evil are as eloquent as the face of the mad queen.

Another requirement of an excellent picture book is one of accuracy and consistency with the text. If the story states, as Ludwig Bemelmans does in *Madeline*, that "In an old house in Paris that was covered with vines lived twelve little girls in two straight lines," children are going to look for the vines; they are going to count the little girls; and they are going to check to see that the lines are straight. Bemelmans was painstakingly careful to include just eleven little girls in his picture after Madeline goes to the hospital. Six-year-olds are quick to point out his one failure in a small picture that shows twelve girls breaking their bread, even though Madeline was still hospitalized.

In an entertaining book on presidents of the United States titled *The Buck Stops Here*, Alice Provensen drew a picture of Gerald Ford writing with his right hand—Ford is left-handed. Filled with fascinating details of the presidents, pictures, symbols of their administrations, and mnemonic rhymes to remember their names, this is primarily an informational picture book. Accuracy is a requirement of both picture storybooks and informational picture books.

The Artist's Choice of Media

Children accept and enjoy a variety of media in the illustrations of their picture books. Many artists today are using the picture book as a vehicle for experimentation with new and interesting formats and media. (See also Chapter 13, "Exploring Literature Through Art and Media.") For example, David Macaulay's award-winning *Black and White* is really four stories, elements of which enter each story. Each story uses different media and colors including watercolors, torn paper, sepia, and pen and ink with paints. This highly inventive book is more like a game or a

Sometime in the early morning hours, the train comes to rest. All is quiet. Suddenly, the door of the compartment slides open. The conductor leans in, announces that something is blocking the tracks, and disappears. A few minutes later, an old woman enters the compartment and sits down opposite the boy. She says nothing.

The worst thing about Holstein cows is that if they ever get out of the field, they're almost impossible to find.

A double-page spread of David Macaulay's award-winning book, *Black and White,* shows four different stories done in four different media; or are there connections in this intriguing book?

puzzle. Middle graders are intrigued with it, however. Vera Williams and her niece Jennifer Williams must have had a wonderful time creating the story of *Stringbean's Trip to the Shining Sea,* for it is all told by way of postcards and pictures that Stringbean sends back home to his family in Kansas. The illustrators created the postcards using a variety of scenes and media. They even designed the stamps. The text causes the reader to fill in what Stringbean does not say, but implies in his notes to his parents back home. This requires a more sophisticated reading ability, whereas *Black and White* appeals to even older children capable of interpreting four stories at the same time. These two books represent the kind of creative experimentation that is taking place in picture storybooks today. The question of what medium the artist uses is not nearly as important as the appropriateness of the choice for the partic-

ular book and how effectively the artist used it. Nevertheless, teachers and children are fascinated with the how of illustrating and always ask what medium is used. This becomes increasingly difficult to answer as artists these days use a combination of media and printing techniques to achieve a particular effect. Some publishing houses provide information on the art techniques of some of their outstanding books. This may be found in a foreword, on the copyright page, or on a jacket flap. It is a service that teachers and librarians hope more companies will provide.

The following section gives a brief overview of some of the possibilities for the choice of media open to the artist.

WOODCUTS AND SIMILAR TECHNIQUES

In the beginning of printing, the woodcut was the only means of reproducing art. It is still used effectively today. In making a woodcut, the non-printing areas are cut away, leaving a raised surface which, when inked and pressed on paper, duplicates the original design. If color is to be used, the artist must prepare as many woodcuts as colors. Woodcut illustrations produce a bold simplicity and have a power not found in any other medium.

Marcia Brown uses woodcuts superbly in her fable of India, *Once a Mouse*, and her ABC book *All Butterflies*. Taking full advantage of her medium, she allows the texture or grain of the wood to show through, adding depth and interesting patterns to these dramatic illustrations. Striking color woodcuts by Keizaburo Tejima illustrate his fictionalized tales of animal and bird life in *Fox's Dream*, *Owl Lake*, and *Swan Sky*. Although Ed Emberley employs only three colors for woodcuts for *Drummer Hoff*, the book appears to explode with as much color as the powder of Drummer Hoff's cannon. This effect was created by careful overprinting of Emberley's very stylized designs.

Wood engravings are cut on the end grain of very hard wood (usually boxwood) rather than with the grain on the plank side of a soft wood. This process of wood engraving gives a delicate, finer line to the illustrations than the more crude woodcut. Not many modern picture books have been illustrated with wood engravings, although Arthur Geisert makes use of this medium for several of his books. His puzzle alphabet book *Pigs from A to Z* is illustrated with detailed sketches of seven little pigs constructing a tree house. Each picture shows five hidden forms of the letter and the seven pigs, and part of the fun of the book is to find them. The fine lines of these intricate wood engravings make superb hiding places for the letters. Geisert uses the same technique in his comic picture book for younger children simply titled *Oink!*

Linoleum block prints also give a finer line than woodcuts. Ashley Wolff's glowing linoleum block prints portray *A Year of Birds*. Birds and months are named, but the pictures extend these labels to show seasonal activities of humans—shoveling snow, swimming, going to school. The continuity of life is presented by a pregnant mother, a newborn baby, and the flight of the Canadian geese. Again the months of the year provide a similar framework for presenting *A Year*

Grosbeaks, purple finches, and black-capped chickadees in January

Ashley Wolff's glowing linoleum block prints portray *A Year of Birds*. Seasonal activities of humans such as shoveling snow, swimming, and going to school help young children relate the time of year to the kind of birds that can be seen.

of Beasts. The crisp black lines of the linoleum cuts seem to make the animals, birds, and people stand out in relief against brilliant skies and seasonal landscapes.

Scratchboard illustrations may be confused with wood engravings, since their appearance is similar. However, the process of making them is very different. In making scratchboard illustrations a very black ink is usually painted on the smooth white surface of a drawing board or scratchboard. When it is thoroughly dry, the picture is made by scratching through the black-inked surface with a sharp instrument. Color may be added with a transparent overlay, or it may be painted on the white scratchboard prior to applying the black ink. Scratchboard technique produces crisp black and white illustrations. Brian Pinkney, a young African-American artist, creates stunning scratchboard paintings for Burton Albert's lyrical text for *Where Does the Trail Lead?* The story simply recounts a young boy's explorations of Summertime Island—running down to the sea, discovering periwinkles in the tide pools, finding an old boat by the cattails. At the end of his circular trail, he returns to his family's beach fire and the smell of fresh-caught fish. Pinkney has also used scratchboard to illustrate William H. Hooks's retelling of one of the old Conjure tales from the Carolinas, *The Ballad of Belle Dorcas*. This is the tale of a free issue woman who mar-

...to a boat's bow of cattails at the edge of the sea.

Brian Pinkney, a young African-American artist, creates stunning scratchboard paintings for Burton Albert's lyrical text in *Where Does the Trail Lead?*

❦   ❦   ❦

ries a slave she loves. When he is sold, she saves him by turning him into a tree. Returning to life each evening, the two spend a long life together. Scratchboard illustrations seem most appropriate for this tale of sacrifice and transformation. Barbara Cooney has achieved an equally dramatic effect with this technique combined with brilliant color overlays for her award-winning book *Chanticleer and the Fox.*

COLLAGE

The use of collage for illustrating children's books has become very popular. The effect of this medium is simple and childlike, not unlike pictures children might make themselves. The word "collage," derived from the French verb *coller,* meaning "to paste," refers to the kind of picture that is made by cutting out a variety of different kinds of materials—newspaper clippings, patterned wallpaper, fabric, and the like, and assembling them

into a unified, harmonious illustration. Ezra Jack Keats proved himself a master of this technique with his award-winning *The Snowy Day.* Using patterned and textured papers and pen and ink, Keats captured young Peter's delight in a snowy day.

Leo Lionni used collage with patterned crayon shapes to create the grass, leaves, and birds in his highly original *Inch by Inch.* Circles of torn paper convey a satisfying story of the abstract families of *Little Blue and Little Yellow.* In his own version of the ant and grasshopper fable, Lionni has created a favorite character, *Frederick,* a mouse-poet torn from two shades of gray paper. In another simple yet important fable for our time titled *Six Crows,* Lionni emphasizes the importance of talking things over instead of fighting. Large-sized brightly colored collages portray the farmer, the owl, and the six crows. Lionni also uses his familiar collage techniques and brilliant colors to tell a

Ezra Jack Keats was one of the first authors to portray black children in his stories. Here he uses simple collage illustrations to capture a city child's delight in *The Snowy Day*.

🐛   🐛   🐛

fable of art, love, and the role of the imagination in seeing beauty in all things in the story of *Matthew's Dream*.

Eric Carle first paints many sheets of paper with various colors to achieve texture. Then he cuts them out and pastes them together to create such interesting characters as *The Very Hungry Caterpillar*, the animals in *The Very Busy Spider*, or insects for *The Very Quiet Cricket*. Mounted on clear white paper, the images are clearly seen or felt, as is the case with the tactile pictures in *The Very Busy Spider* or heard, as with the cricket chirp implanted in *The Very Quiet Cricket*. Children love these books with their bright large-sized collage images and their unique appeal to the senses. An Australian artist, Patricia Mullins, uses brilliant tissue paper collages to create the animals in Gail Jorgensen's foot-stomping *Crocodile Beat* and Mem Fox's whimsical tale of *Hattie and the Fox*.

Children will be intrigued by Barbara Reid's plasticine or modeling clay art for the tale of *Effie*, an ant with a loud voice. Effie's voice frightens the other insects away, but it is instrumental in preventing an elephant from stepping on all of them. The detail Reid can achieve with this mod-

eling clay material is quite amazing. Beverly Allinson is the author of this funny tale.

Jennie Baker makes what she calls "collage constructions" to illustrate her fine book *Where the Forest Meets the Sea*. Made from a multitude of materials including modeling clay, papers, textured materials, preserved grass, leaves, feathers, hair, and paints, these pictures stand out in relief. In this story of a visit to a tropical rain forest in North Queensland, Australia, a young boy imagines who else might have played there before him including the dinosaurs and later the aboriginal children. Baker also uses collage effectively for her environmental statement in her wordless book titled *Window*.

Molly Bang's folded paper sculpture, cut-out figures, and furniture seem just right for her modern folktale of *The Paper Crane*, which comes to life and restores the restaurant bypassed by a freeway. True to so many Chinese fairy tales, the owner of the restaurant receives his good reward as payment for his kindness to a gentle stranger. Children would love to learn to make their own paper cranes and create collage pictures after hearing this story.

Marcia Brown made sophisticated use of collage in her stunning interpretation of the French poet Blaise Cendrars's *Shadow*. Rich backgrounds of textured painted shapes have been cut out to form purple and orange mountains; the people and their shadows are done in black and tissue paper silhouettes. Some woodcuts printed in white represent the eerie spirits in this tale of Africa where shadows are both respected and feared. Other artists who make skillful use of collage include Elizabeth Cleaver, Lois Ehlert, Bettina Paterson, Susan Roth, and David Wisniewski.

PAINTS AND PEN AND INK

The vast majority of illustrations for children's books are done in paint, pen and ink, or combinations of these media. The creation of new materials, such as plastic paints or acrylics, and new techniques frequently make it very difficult to determine the medium used.

Generally, paint may be divided into two kinds: paint that is translucent and has a somewhat transparent quality, such as watercolor, and paint that is opaque and impenetrable to light, such as tempera, gouache, and oils.

We usually think of old-fashioned delicate pictures when we think of watercolor, but this is not necessarily the case. Edward Ardizzone, England's master of watercolor and pen-and-ink sketches, has produced full-color seascapes that have tremendous vitality and movement for his *Little Tim and the Brave Sea Captain*. The storm scenes in McCloskey's *Time of Wonder* have this same power, contrasted with the soft diffused light of the fog scene.

Ted Rand's dark ominous watercolors for *The Ghost-Eye Tree* by Bill Martin, Jr., and John Archambault create just the right spooky mood for this tale of two children's journey down a lonely road on a dark windy night. We can almost hear the huge black tree creak and groan as it bends in the wind. Bathed in eerie moonlight, the children's faces reflect their fear of the ghost-eye tree. Ronald Himler's understated bluish-gray watercolors beautifully reflect the somber moods of a little boy and his father as they visit *The Wall* to find the name of the boy's grandfather who was killed in the Vietnam War. Eve Bunting is the author of this moving story.

Watercolors can be warm and cozy too, as we see in Vera Williams's *A Chair for My Mother*. In this story of a family's struggle to recover from a household fire, we celebrate the day they have saved enough money to buy a big fat comfortable chair for the little girl's mother. Watercolors create the symbolic borders of these pictures and the velvet texture of the chairs in the furniture store.

Stephen Gammell captures the feel of sheets of rain and wind with colored pencil and watercolor for *Come a Tide* by George Ella Lyon. After it rains for four days and nights, Grandma warns her family that there will be a flood and she is so right. David Wiesner uses blue-and-green watercolors to create the remarkable *Tuesday* when all the frogs took off on their lily pads for a glorious flight. He helps the reader believe in this almost wordless book by using a photo-realistic style and giving the precise time of the flight.

Acrylics or plastic paints produce vibrant almost glowing colors. Barbara Cooney uses acrylic paints to create pictures for the well-loved *Miss Rumphius*. After her many travels throughout the

Bathed in eerie moonlight, the children's faces reflect their fear of *The Ghost-Eye Tree* by Bill Martin, Jr., and John Archambault. Ted Rand painted these wonderfully spooky pictures.

world, Miss Rumphius settles down in her little gray house in Maine beside a shimmering ocean. Crisp clear colors beautifully capture the Maine landscape, with its purple and blue blooming lupine.

The Painter and the Wild Swans is an exquisite book illustrated with acrylic paints by the French illustrator, Frédéric Clément. Claude Clément's (no relation to the illustrator) text was inspired by the beautiful pictures of Siberian swans taken by a Japanese photographer. The story tells of Teiji, a renowned Japanese painter who sees a flock of wild swans pass over his head. Their beauty is so breathtaking that he can no longer paint until he sees them again. He follows them to a treacherous ice-filled lake where his boat capsizes. After swimming to the island of the swans, Teiji freezes to death. Gradually he is transformed into a swan. The blue-gray paintings capture the Japanese setting, the feeling of the cold icy island, and the believable transformation of man to swan. The jacket painting shows black trees and hills against a backdrop of beautiful snowy mountains. A second look reveals that the tops of the snowcapped mountains are really resting swans.

Robert Blake used full-color oils to paint the vibrant seascapes and dramatic sea rescue by a golden retriever, appropriately named *Riptide*.

Written by Frances Weller.

❦ ❦ ❦

Opaque paint may give a brilliant sparkling look, such as Leonard Weisgard achieved in Golden MacDonald's *The Little Island*, or it may produce the rather somber colors of Leo Politi's *Song of the Swallows*. Maurice Sendak contrasted dark green and blue tempera with shades of purple to create Max's weird fantasy world in *Where the Wild Things Are*. Texture and shading are achieved with pen-and-ink cross-hatching strokes. The characters in Sendak's *In the Night Kitchen* are painted in bold flat colors that resemble a comic book world; details are reserved for the intricate labels and pictures that are on the cartons, bottles, and jars that make up the city of the night kitchen.

Gouache paint is the same as powder color or tempera, with the addition of white. Roger Duvoisin used this medium most effectively to create the fog-shrouded world of *Hide and Seek Fog* by Alvin Tresselt. The use of gouache is also characteristic of the many books illustrated by Alice and Martin Provensen, including their well-known *A Visit to William Blake's Inn* by Nancy Willard (see Chapter 8) and the Caldecott award-winner, *The Glorious Flight Across the Channel with Louis Blériot*.

Increasingly, we are seeing picture books illustrated with full-color oil paints. Robert Blake's vibrant seascapes portray the thrilling sea rescue of a young girl by a golden retriever named *Riptide* in a story by Frances Weller. Blake's bold expressive brushwork for these oil paintings captures the color, texture, and motion of a dog in the world he loved best.

Dramatic full-color oil paintings by Don Wood illustrate the modern fairy tale *Heckedy Peg* by Audrey Wood. Inspired by a sixteenth-century game still played today, this story tells of a witch's enchantment of seven children named after the days of the week. Only when their mother recalls what each asked her to buy can she break the spell and rescue her children. Wood's paintings of home and hearth sparkle with light and sharply contrast with the gloomy pictures of the interior of the witch's hut.

Thomas Locker, a well-known landscape artist, illustrates his picture books, *Where the River Begins*, *The Mare on the Hill*, and *Family Farm*, with majestic full-color oil paintings. Locker's rendering of light reminds us of the early landscape painters of the Hudson River School. Two other stories illustrated by Locker, *The Boy Who Held Back the Sea* by Lenny Hort and *The Young Artist*, reflect the influence of the early Dutch masters. Beautiful as these paintings are, they lack the narrative quality that we have come to appreciate in an integrated picture storybook.

CRAYON, CHALK, CHARCOAL AND PENCIL

Crayon and soft pencil illustrations are frequently employed for children's books. The subtle texture of crayon is easily discernible. In *Fish Is Fish*, Leo Lionni creates an underwater world with crayons, but he portrays the fish's conception of the frog's world with the brilliant colors of acrylics. The difference in color and media helps to separate the imagined world from the real one.

Pastels and charcoal are most appropriate media for Thomas Allen's rich illustrations for *In Coal Country* by Judith Hendershot. Told from a young girl's point of view, this is the evocative account of growing up in a small Ohio coal-mining town in the 1930s. The grayed pictures suggest the pervasive soot and smoke covering the town and their homes. Yet in the midst of poverty the children found joy in swimming and sledding. Despite the back-breaking work of heating water for the father's bath every day and scrubbing the clothes, the mother always had a jar of spring flowers on the table. Colored pastels shine through the gray paper and charcoal paintings like the love that surrounded this family.

Ann Grifalconi's brilliant chalk illustrations for *Osa's Pride* glow with the beauty of the African world and the nurturing love of the grandmother who helps Osa overcome her pride.

The soft grease pencil drawings of Stephen Gammell create a mystical mood for the legend of *Where the Buffaloes Begin* by Olaf Baker. The large full-page and double-page pictures capture the wide sweep of the prairie and the immensity of the buffalo. Yet the impressionistic indefinite shapes suggest the legendary nature of a story in which the buffalo arise from a misty lake and stampede an enemy tribe, thereby saving Little Wolf's people.

Using a conté pencil, a rather hard drawing pencil, Chris Van Allsburg creates a surrealistic world for the playing of the game *Jumanji*. In addition, he sandpapered the pencil and gathered the dust, which he applied with cotton balls. This gave his figures a sculptured three-dimensional

Seen from the floor level of a living room, two charging rhinoceroses look much more frightening than at the zoo. The sculpted three-dimensional effect of these animals against the background of an ordinary living room helps to create the surrealistic world of *Jumanji* by Chris Van Allsburg.

🌿 🌿 🌿

Ann Grifalconi's brilliant chalk illustrations for the cover of *Osa's Pride* glow with the beauty of the African world and the nurturing love of her grandmother.

🌿 🌿 🌿

effect that makes them appear very real against the bizarre background of a house suddenly inhabited by lions, pythons, and monkeys. His first book, *The Garden of Abdul Gasazi*, was also done in black-and-white, whereas *The Wreck of the Zephyr* uses glorious full-color pastels to create an equally astonishing story.

Increasingly artists are using combinations of many media. John Burningham creates the visual jokes in his book *Come Away from the Water, Shirley* by using crayons to depict Shirley's father and mother as they sit in their beach chairs giving frequent admonitions to Shirley. On the opposite page he employs rich paints, collage, and crayon to develop the wonderful pirate adventure story that Shirley creates in her imagination. The use of different media and color tones helps to create the humor of this juxtaposition of parents' and child's thinking. In *Time to Get Out of the Bath, Shirley* Burningham uses the same technique for Shirley's exciting adventures down the bath drain.

Elements of Design

Artists must also make choices about certain elements of design, particularly the use of line, space, and color as they decide what to illustrate in the story and how best to do it.

LINE

Line is so inherently a part of every illustration, we forget that it too can convey meaning. A horizontal line suggests repose and peace, a vertical line gives stability, and a diagonal line suggests action and movement. Uri Shulevitz has used diagonal rain lines superbly in the pictures and even endpapers of his book *Rain Rain Rivers*. Peter Parnall's many horizontal lines and rounded womblike shapes for Byrd Baylor's *Your Own Best Secret Place* and *The Way to Start a Day* suggest peace and a tapping of inner strength.

Even the size of a line may convey meaning. John Steptoe uses a heavy black outline for his figures to emphasize Robert's resentment of *Stevie*, the little boy his mother takes care of during the day. The clear fine lines of M. B. Goffstein for *Brookie and Her Lamb* and *My Noah's Ark* suggest the simplicity and universality of these quiet stories.

SPACE

The creative use of space, as we have seen in Taro Yashima's *Crow Boy*, can produce a feeling of isolation or the blurred line between reality and legend, as used by Stephen Gammell in *Where the Buffaloes Begin* (Olaf Baker). Shirley Hughes uses the gutter between pages to represent the door into the house in *Alfie Gets in First* (see picture, p. 215). In Burningham's *Granpa* when the little girl becomes angry at her grandfather, the artist places them on either edge of a large double-page spread with their backs to each other. Plain white in the middle emphasizes the distance between them. Lisbeth Zwerger uses pen and ink and soft watercolor wash to reduce her backgrounds to almost nothing, making the realistic wistful figures in Grimms's fairy tales stand out. In *The Seven Ravens*, she pictures the little girl who goes in search of her brothers as sitting on a little chair looking as if she were alone on the edge of the world.

Molly Bang makes use of negative space in her surrealistic wordless book, *The Grey Lady and the Strawberry Snatcher*. The grey lady appears to fade into the background of trees as she runs away from the strawberry snatcher. Part of the fun of David Macaulay's experimental book *Black and White* is his use of negative space to hide an escaping convict in a herd of Holstein cows.

The decision to use borders also involves the artist's use of space. The borders in Vera Williams's *A Chair for My Mother* or Trina Hyman's interpretation of *Little Red Riding Hood* provide a kind of coziness to these stories.

In inexpensive mass-marketed books that frequently must conform to one size for all, artists cannot afford the creative use of space. In a well-designed picture storybook, however, the illustrators may use space to enhance the meaning of the story.

USE OF COLOR

Many classic picture storybooks did not use color in the illustrations—the sepia pictures of Robert McCloskey's *Make Way for Ducklings*, the black-and-white humorous illustrations by Robert Lawson for the *The Story of Ferdinand* by Munro Leaf, and the well-loved black-and-white illustrations of *Millions of Cats* by Wanda Gág.

Illustrators today are successfully using black-and-white graphics to create exciting picture books. The unique story by Ann Jonas titled *Round Trip* describes a trip to the city past farms and silos, steel highway wires, and riding the subway; turn the book around and the reader returns in the dark. The farms and silos become factories, the highway poles support the freeway, and the subway becomes a parking garage. Black-and-white are the appropriate colors for this triumph of design. Chris Van Allsburg's black-and-white illustrations help to create an eerie otherworldly cast to *The Mysteries of Harris Burdick*.

The choice of color or colors depends on the theme of the book. Certainly, the choice of blue for both pictures and text in *Blueberries for Sal* by McCloskey was appropriate. Tawny yellow and black were the natural choices for Don Freeman's wonderfully funny story of the lion who suddenly decided to live up to the double meaning of his name, *Dandelion*. Quiet or nostalgic stories, such as Cynthia Rylant's *When I Was Young in the Mountains*, are appropriately illustrated with soft grays, browns, and blues. Diane Goode's gentle pictures for this story celebrate the love of an extended family and the beauty of a remote mountain region in Appalachia. M. B. Goffstein created pale watercolor paintings to capture the thoughts of *An Artist*. This tiny gem of a book is an ode to the artistic process. The small pictures reveal the love and reverence the artists feels for her vocation. By way of contrast, Rodney A. Greenblat uses brilliant electric colors for his zany story of *Uncle Wizzmo's New Used Car*. Weird cars that look like turtles, rabbits, and a bowl of fruit are on the showroom floor. Finally, Uncle Wizzmo chooses a brilliant blue one and off he zooms with his delighted niece and nephew. Choice of color, then, can set the mood of the story.

Certain artists have made effective use of color to show a change in mood for the story. In *Dawn* by Uri Shulevitz a grandfather takes his grandson camping by a lake. Early in the morning while it is still dark, they rise and row out to the center of the lake where they can see the beauty of the sunrise. Gradually, almost in a slowed down cinematic fashion, the pictures move from deep blues to subdued grays and finally to the blazing yellow green of the sun. Different perspectives show the boy and the old man moving farther and farther out into the lake until they almost appear to be swallowed up by the brilliance of the sun on the final page. Interest is created by changing the shapes of the pictures. One child, when asked why the artist chose to shape some of the pictures the way he did, noted that many were ovals, "like egg shapes because eggs are beginnings and this story is about a day's beginning."

Allen Say uses color most effectively in his picture-book biography of the very first Chinese matador. Titled *El Chino*, it is the account of a Chinese American who longs to be a great athlete. He is an ace basketball player in high school, but too short to compete in college. Following his graduation as an engineer, he goes on a vacation in Spain and falls in love with bullfighting. For the first half of the book, the pictures are in brownish-gray tones reminiscent of old photographs. However, after Billy Wong finds his true vocation, the pictures change to full color

symbolizing his joy at finding his life's work. In order to signify danger Marcia Brown has added red to her pictures for *Once a Mouse*. Starting with cool forest green, mustard yellow, and a trace of red, the red builds up in increasing amounts until the climax is reached and the tiger is changed back to a mouse. Only cool green and yellow are seen in the last picture as the hermit is once again "thinking about big—and little. . . ."

It is this rich use of many layers of color to create meaning that helps to distinguish the really fine picture storybooks. The splashy use of color for color's sake, so frequently seen in the grocery store or mass-produced books, does little to develop the artistic eye of children. It is the appropriate use of color that is significant.

POINT OF VIEW OR PERSPECTIVE

Just as an author decides what would be the best point of view from which to tell a story, so too does an artist think about perspective. One way to obtain action in what might otherwise be a static series of pictures is to change one's focus just as a movie camera changes perspective or shows close-ups and then moves back to pan the whole scene. In *The Napping House* by Audrey Wood, for example, the scene is always the bed where the granny, the dog, the cat, the mouse, and the flea are seen in various postures as they sleep during the quiet rain. Don Wood shows us a fish-eye view of the scene with the bed growing increasingly concave until its final collapse. His perspective is always looking down, but he moves it slowly until he is directly above the sleeping figures for the climax when the flea bites the cat and wakes them all up and the bed falls down.

Part of the perfection of the poetic Caldecott award-winning book *Owl Moon* by Jane Yolen is the way John Schoenherr uses shifting perspectives to provide the action. It is the quiet story of a child and her father who go out late one snowy night to look for owls. Starting with an owl's view of the farm bathed in moonlight, the artist shifts his focus showing the pair trudging through the snow from the side, the front, and finally looking up in awe at the huge owl landing on the tree.

The perspective in the surrealistic pictures for *Jumanji* changes from a worm's-eye point of view to a bird's-eye, adding to the constant shifts

Don Wood's perspective inches slightly higher with each picture until the viewer appears to be directly above the bed for the climax of this funny cumulative story of *The Napping House* by Audrey Wood.

between reality and fantasy in that story. Seen from the floor level of an ordinary living room, two charging rhinoceroses look much more frightening than in the zoo! Again in *The Polar Express*, Chris Van Allsburg shows dramatic shifts in perspective from the aerial views from Santa's sleigh to the floor-level view of the children opening their presents.

John Schoenherr uses shifting perspectives to provide action in Jane Yolen's quiet story of *Owl Moon*. Here we see the little girl and her father from the perspective of high up in a tree—perhaps the hidden owl's view.

Not all artists work with changing perspectives, but when they do, it is interesting to ask why and look to see how this adds to the meaning of the story.

The Matter of Style

Style is an elusive quality of an artist's work based on the arrangement of line, color, and mass into a visual image. The style of an illustrator will be influenced by his or her own skill as an artist and the vision of the story that is being interpreted. The primary decision for the artist to make is how to create a style that will harmonize and enhance the meaning of the text. The illustrator also needs to consider how the art might extend or add a new dimension to the message of the story.

Style can also refer to the particular artistic properties associated with an era or culture like Renaissance art or impressionism. Pictorial styles can be distinguished by certain constant elements or "umbrella conventions," which are widely accepted ways of depicting. Teachers may want to know these terms, just as they develop an understanding of literary terms for more careful evaluation of books for children. However, they are cautioned that it is more important to teach a child to look and really see how an illustrator creates meaning than it is to be glib with terms they may not understand. Also these terms were developed to describe the art of a single picture, not the cumulative effect of many images seen by turning the pages of a picture book.

REALISM OR REPRESENTATIONAL ART

While no designation of an art style can be precise because of the infinite variation within styles, realism is perhaps the easiest to recognize because it presents a picture of the world as we see it in real life. Of course the pictures still incorporate the artist's interpretation of the story, the choice of scenes to visualize, point of view, expressions, and so forth. Shirley Hughes, a British illustrator, is well known for her sketches of very real, even scruffy looking, children and their families. In *The Big Concrete Lorry*, she details a family's decision to add an extension onto their house on Trotter Street, a wonderful

It it obvious in this very realistic picture by Shirley Hughes that the Patterson family needs to build an addition to their house, and that is when the excitement begins.

From *The Concrete Lorry* by Shirley Hughes.

mixed neighborhood of people of various races, children, dogs and cats. Everything goes smoothly until the day the concrete lorry delivers quick-setting cement before the family is ready for it. The whole neighborhood comes to help in the crisis and when the extension is finally finished, they are all invited to a party. Hughes's line and color sketches capture expressions, gestures, and postures in a way that helps to tell this humorous story. Her interesting page layouts also move the action along.

By way of contrast, Barry Moser's realistic watercolor illustrations for Cynthia Rylant's *Appalachia: The Voices of Sleeping Birds* have the feeling of arrested motion almost like Depression-era photographs. The beauty of the countryside contrasts sharply with the harshness of the life as seen in the exhausted-looking face of the coal miner.

Donald Carrick illustrated his wife's real-life stories about children sleeping out in the woods for the first time, climbing mountains, and having a beloved dog run over. His brown and green natural watercolors realistically portray these experi-

ences in *Sleep Out, The Climb, The Accident,* and others. Carol and Donald Carrick's love of nature is reflected in these representational illustrations. Such illustrations have an immediacy about them and help readers to enter more fully into an experience they could actually have. Although Donald Carrick's work is generally representational, his last book *In the Moonlight, Waiting* seems almost impressionistic. This is because the art was photographed from his preliminary sketches for the book that he never had time to finish. The hazy first impressions add charm to the story of a little girl waking in the middle of the night and joining her parents to witness the birth of a lamb. It seems appropriate that at the time of Carrick's death, these illustrations reinforce the theme of birth and new life.

IMPRESSIONISM

Impressionism is associated with the French artists who worked in and around Paris in the latter part of the nineteenth century, including such well-known names as Monet, Sisley, Pissarro, and others.

James Stevenson's impressionistic watercolors create the illusion of a windy autumn day—"a splendiferous day" in *Say It!* by Charlotte Zolotow.

❦   ❦   ❦

Probably the best examples of impressionism in picture books are the Monet-like paintings by Maurice Sendak for *Mr. Rabbit and the Lovely Present*, written by Charlotte Zolotow. In luscious shades of blues and greens, he has created a dreamlike world where a very sophisticated rabbit and a little girl wander about the countryside looking for presents of red, yellow, green, and blue (her mother's favorite colors) for the little girl's mother. The dappled endpapers for this book are examples of impressionistic techniques in themselves.

Lloyd Bloom's oil paintings for the prose poem of *Yonder* by Tony Johnston seem most appropri-

ate for this nostalgic story of one family's history. In order to commemorate the births of his children, one nineteenth-century farmer always planted a plum tree. The plum trees grow and blossom pink with the arrival of more children and even grandchildren. Finally the grandfather who planted the first tree dies and the family remembers him by planting another tree. Bloom's impressionistic paintings capture the family's activities throughout the seasons. For example, one lovely picture shows the mother making a patchwork quilt; the one on the facing page shows the farmer plowing his patchwork fields. Always the plum trees "yonder way over yonder" define the passing seasons. Impressionistic paintings have a way of distancing viewers, placing them outside the action while at the same time their luminous beauty draws them in.

EXPRESSIONISM

Aspects of expressionistic art include shocking colors, figures slightly out of proportion, and rough rapid brushwork. The emphasis is on the artist's own self-expression rather than the reproduction of what he or she sees.

Vera Williams uses brilliant watercolors to paint slightly distorted body positions. These expressionistic paintings seem childlike and appropriate for the first-person telling of the search for *A Chair for My Mother*.

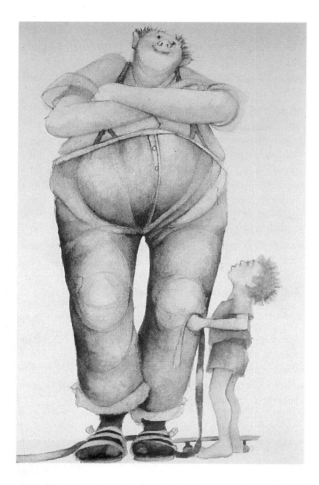

Julie Vivas paints larger-than-life expressionistic pictures for Mem Fox's story of *Wilfrid Gordon McDonald Partridge*. These pictures emphasize the small boy's determined search for Miss Nancy's memory as he asks each person in the rest home what a memory is.

In illustrations for children's books expressionism may take the form of brilliant blue horses or blue cats, as seen in some of Eric Carle's pictures for very young children. His endpapers for the unique picture book *The Very Busy Spider* are splashed with arresting bright colors, for example. The jewel-like but unusual colors for the four animals in Janina Domanska's interpretation of the Grimms' *The Bremen Town Musicians* are another fine example of expressionistic paintings. Here the striking colors and unusual angles shown in both animals and robbers help to create the excitement and action of this robust folktale. The well-known visual artist, Rodney A. Greenblat, creates vivid cars in unusual shapes for his story of *Uncle Wizzmo's New Used Car*. The brilliant colors and distorted body positions of the mother and grandmother as seen in *A Chair for My Mother* by Vera Williams reflect aspects of expressionism. At the same time, the decorative borders with their symbolic motifs give a feeling for naive style. The exuberant lively pictures of Julie Vivas for Mem Fox's *Wilfrid Gordon McDonald Partridge* are fine examples of expressionistic art. This is the story of a small red-haired boy who makes friends with the old folks who live next door in a home for the elderly. He likes them all, but his particular friend is 96-year-old Miss Nancy. When he hears his parents say she has lost her memory, he decides to help her find it. Vivas's unique characterizations are painted almost larger than life and seen from unusual perspectives. Vivas also illustrated Margaret Wild's book *The Very Best of Friends*, which describes the loving friendship between James and Jessie, and James and his cat William. Jessie doesn't like cats. When elderly James dies suddenly, Jessie locks the cat outside and herself inside. William becomes a mean lean cat and bites her one morning. That shocks Jessie into taming and feeding the cat and restoring her own life. Vivas's expressionistic illustrations show this life cycle superbly.

Surrealism

Surrealism is characterized more by subject matter than by technique, for the surrealist combines incongruous images in unnatural juxtapositions. In order to make the viewer believe in this unreal scene, the artwork will be meticulously detailed realism. Anthony Browne creates a surreal world in his picture storybooks *The Tunnel, Changes,* and *Piggybook.* Jack and his sister Rose do not get along. She wants to read fairy tales while he insists on exploring a tunnel. Finally, when he doesn't come back, Rose must go through the frightening tunnel and find him. Once on the other side she enters a dark forest of trees whose roots and branches form weird, threatening shapes. Finally, in a clearing she spies the figure of her brother Jack, turned to stone. Fearing she is too late, she throws her arms around him and he is slowly transformed back to his original self.

When his father left the house in the morning he told Joseph "things were going to change." Home alone, Joseph's world does begin to change. The shadow beneath the couch becomes an alligator, for example, in this surreal picture by Anthony Browne in *Changes*.

🐛 🐛 🐛

The transformation is also apparent in their friendship. This modern fairy tale becomes very real and frightening in this surrealistic setting.

In *Changes*, Anthony Browne shows the psychological effect on an older brother of the arrival of a new baby in the family. Before leaving for the hospital to pick up Joseph's mother, his father said, "Things were going to change," and they do. Home alone, Joseph sees everything in his world begin to change. The tea kettle changes into a cat, growing ears and a tail; the armchair becomes a gorilla and a shadow beneath the sofa forms an alligator. When his parents come home with the new baby, Joseph's surreal world disappears in light and love. This is hardly a model story to use in preparation for the arrival of a new baby. In fact, it is a frightening and disturbing story, but children ages 9 and up are fascinated with discovering all the things changing in Joseph's imagination. It is a fine example of surrealism in art.

Piggybook makes a feminist statement and is very funny. When an overworked mother returns home she finds the house a mess and her family watching TV. She calls them all pigs and storms out of the house. Suddenly they become pigs, with piggy wallpaper and pictures. A transformation back to real people also means a change in behavior. In expressing his choice of surrealism, Browne is quoted as saying:

> It's a part of not losing that visual openness that kids have . . . surrealism corresponds to a childlike view of the world, in that everything can be made new by putting unrelated objects together.[4]

Chris Van Allsburg's surrealistic worlds of *Jumanji* and *The Polar Express* are certainly well known, since both these stories won Caldecott awards. The plot for his book *The Stranger* is more surreal than the pictures of this enigmatic man who appears to have lost his memory but has some power over the change of seasons on the Baileys' farm. The fourteen pictures that make up *The Mysteries of Harris Burdick* are beautiful examples of surrealism. Here houses on Maple Street lift off, schooners magically appear, and a nun sits in a chair suspended thirty feet above the cathedral floor! While the pictures have no connecting narrative, they stimulate children to tell their stories. Van Allsburg is a master of juxtaposition of the real with the unreal.

NAIVE OR FOLK ART

One form of naive art is the style often found in such self-taught artists as Grandma Moses, Henri Rousseau, or the early American limners. It can be characterized by a lack of such conventions as perspective or so-called real appearances. Mattie Lou O'Kelley created thirteen vibrant paintings for Ruth Radin's nostalgic story *A Winter Place*. In lyrical prose she describes a special place in the hills where the children always went to skate. They walked past "the farm with the blue steel silos," through the town, and then took the path through the hills, skated, and returned home. In colors that sparkle as much as the new snow, O'Kelley creates naive paintings filled with stylized homes, trees, and mountains.

Barbara Cooney adapted her style to imitate that of the early American limners for *Ox-Cart Man* by Donald Hall. Tomie de Paola uses

[4]Douglas Martin, *The Telling Line* (New York: Delacorte Press, 1990), p. 283.

Frané Lessac's brilliantly colored naive paintings seem most appropriate for Charlotte Pomerantz's story of *The Chalk Doll*. In this story of a happy childhood in Jamaica, a mother tells her daughter of the small school she attended and her longing for a real chalk doll rather than a rag one.

❦   ❦   ❦

gouache paints reminiscent of the paintings on wood done by the early itinerant painters for *The Quilt Story* by Tony Johnston and the lively tale of *Tattie's River Journey* by Shirley Murphy. His illustrations for *Mary Had a Little Lamb* by Sarah Josepha Hale and the brightly colored illustrations for *Tomie de Paola's Mother Goose* all echo the early folk art style.

Kathy Jakobsen's folk art paintings for Reeve Lindbergh's narrative poem about *Johnny Appleseed* seem most appropriate for celebrating the life of one of America's legendary heroes. Brightly colored pictures show Johnny's journeys through the seasons; the poetry page is bordered with scenes of apple trees and blossoms tied together with the star quilt pattern in which an apple forms the center.

Frané Lessac's brilliantly colored paintings represent naive art and capture her love for her native islands in the West Indies. *Caribbean Canvas* portrays the people, places, sights, and sounds of the islands while illustrating West Indian proverbs and poetry. She also illustrated *The Chalk Doll* by Charlotte Pomerantz in which a mother tells her daughter stories of her happy childhood growing up in Jamaica. These detailed paintings are childlike and beautiful in their simplicity of style.

Many artists illustrating folktales or legends use the artform of their respective countries or cultures. Ted Harrison's illustrations for *Children of the Yukon* and *A Northern Alphabet* use bright flat colors for his stylized paintings of children's play and activities throughout the year in the lonely settlements of the Yukon. The simple lines of his illustrations suggest the art of the Inuit tribes. Paul Goble's use of Plains Indian designs in dress and on tepees for the well-known legend of *Star Boy* recall the hide paintings of these Native Americans. Gerald McDermott's use of geometric shapes in *Arrow to the Sun* reflects the symbolic artwork of the Pueblo Indians. Just as they made use of African motifs and art in Margaret Musgrove's *Ashanti to Zulu*, Leo and Diane Dillon have created vibrant powerful illustrations for

When the water reached the attic, we moved up to the roof."

James Stevenson uses cartoon blurbs in all Grandpa's exaggerated tales about his youth. In *We Hate Rain!* he recalls that it rained for a whole month when he and his brother Wainey were youngsters.

❦   ❦   ❦

Leontyne Price's retelling of the opera *Aïda* using borders and motifs from the one-dimensional Egyptian style of art. Deborah Nourse Lattimore always uses the style of art of the culture from which her tales come. For example, her Mayan tale *Why There Is No Arguing in Heaven* is illustrated with many bluish-gray figures that suggest the stone carvings of the ancient Mayas. In *The Sailor Who Captured the Sea*, she recreates the extraordinary art and design of the ancient Irish Book of Kells while telling its story.

CARTOON STYLE

Many children's books are illustrated in a cartoon style that depends on a lively line to create movement and humor. Certainly the gross exaggerations of the zany animals of Dr. Seuss are representative of this style. From the weird birds in *Scrambled Eggs Super* to the mess created by *The Cat in the Hat*, Seuss utilized cartoon art to tell his far-fetched stories. Sendak used cartoon style very effectively in some of his early art for *A Hole Is to Dig* and *A Very Special House*, both by Ruth

One can always recognize Roy Gerrard's style of painting little chunky people. In *Mik's Mammoth*, Mik and his tame mammoth rescue the tribe from attack. Good fun abounds in the rhymed text and the illustrations.

Krauss. The little boy who swings on doors and jumps on beds in *A Very Special House* is the only one painted in color, so the reader knows that all the other goings-on in this very special house are "root in the noodle" of his "head head head." Flat painted figures representative of cartoon art can be seen in the pictures for *In the Night Kitchen*.

Most of the work of Steven Kellogg reflects the influence of cartoon art. His wonderful large drawings of *The Mysterious Tadpole* who turns into the missing Loch Ness monster are fine examples of the expression and humor that can be achieved with this style of art. Kellogg's illustrations for Tom Paxton's *Engelbert the Elephant* are as hilarious as the story of this elephant who is invited to the queen's ball. Bursting with action and slapdash humor, Kellogg's illustrations fill in many of the details missing in the text, such as how the elephant happened to be invited in the first place.

William Steig creates his sophisticated dressed animals in line-and-wash drawings for *The Amazing Bone*, *Gorky Rises*, and *Doctor DeSoto*. Although Steig uses background in many of his pictures, the flat-looking characters and clever lines remind us of cartoon art. Certainly *Shrek!*, the green-headed ugliest creature in the swamp, comes straight from cartoon art.

James Stevenson, a fellow cartoonist at *The New Yorker*, has also created many books utilizing the cartoon style of art. His tall tale stories about Grandpa use cartoon balloons for speech and watercolor illustrations. All children enjoy Grandpa's story about *That Terrible Halloween Night* when as a child he went into a haunted house and was so frightened he came out an old man. Cartoon art requires skilled drawing and vivid imagination. It creates and extends much of the humor in children's books.

PERSONAL STYLES

Few picture-book artists use only one style of art; they adapt their work to meet the requirements of a particular story. At the same time, many of them do develop a recognizable personal style that may be identified by their preference for a particular pictorial style of art, use of medium, even choice of content. Thus we have come to associate the use of collage with Leo Lionni, Ezra Jack Keats, and Eric Carle, even though they each use it very differently. The delicate old-fashioned style of Tasha Tudor's watercolors is as easily recognizable as the flowing massive look of the watercolors of Warwick Hutton. Tomie de Paola's use of the symbols of folk art such as hearts, doves, and rabbits is another way of recognizing his work. The amusing animals in the stories by Pat Hutchins are frequently stylized with patterned fur and feathers. Her birds and animals in *What Game Shall We Play?* and that self-assured hen in *Rosie's Walk* are obviously vintage Hutchins. Frequently her illustrations are the first children can identify by the name of the artist. And yet Hutchins employs a very different style in *The Very Worst Monster* and *Where's the Baby?* Roy Gerrard always paints little chunky people as in his riotous spoof on westerns in *Rosie and the Rustlers* and his hero's tale of *Mik's Mammoth.* Word play and visual fun are characteristic of Gerrard's books.

Several artists are experimenting with both style and media and seem to gather strength with each new book. Maurice Sendak's pictures for *Mr. Rabbit and the Lovely Present, Where the Wild Things Are, In the Night Kitchen,* and *Outside Over There* vary, despite the fact that each has a moonlight setting. The impressionistic Monet-like pictures for *Mr. Rabbit and the Lovely Present* written by Charlotte Zolotow are easily identifiable. The trees and endpapers of *Where the Wild Things Are* have been compared to Henri Rousseau's French primitive paintings. However, Max, with his roguish smile, and the big ludicrous beasts with their "terrible eyes and terrible teeth" are very much Sendak. While the illustrations for *In the Night Kitchen* reflect the influence that Disney and the comics had on Sendak in his youth, they are very definitely Sendak's own creation. Max has now become Mickey, who sheds the last of his inhibitions in a dream in which he falls out of his clothes and into the night kitchen. Comic book characters have been refined to a work of art that captures the feelings and dream wishes of childhood. The lush watercolors in *Outside Over There* represent a new direction in Sendak's work. Here he is reaching the child at a deeper psychological level through symbolic art. His artistic metaphors call forth the same inner feelings that Ida is struggling with as she imagines in a momentary day-

dream what it would be like to be rid of the responsibility of her baby sister. Even though the art is very different in *Where the Wild Things Are, In the Night Kitchen,* and *Outside Over There,* Sendak refers to them as a trilogy, all united by the fact that they represent childhood dreams. Each new book of Sendak's represents a deeper involvement with his "child within."

His illustrations for *Dear Mili* are superbly drawn and more mature than any he has done before. The story of *Dear Mili* was preserved in a recently discovered letter Wilhelm Grimm wrote to a little girl in 1816. It is filled with religious connotations more appropriate for the children of the nineteenth century than for today's child. It tells of a mother who sends her daughter into the forest to save her from a terrible war. In the forest, the girl finds the hut of Saint Joseph who feeds her and gives her shelter for what she believes are three days when actually it is for thirty years. Returning home she meets her very old blind mother and that night the two of them die. The story suggests that the girl has been in heaven all this time and simply returns to earth to be with her mother at the time of her death. The illustrations are all filled with symbols that have personal meaning for the artist. Mili walks through a forest that can only be described as a valley of death as trees become skeletons and the outline of the Auschwitz railway station can be seen in the background while starved-looking people are herded over a bridge. Its theme is one of death, reunion, and hope, but today's child may not understand this nineteenth-century allegory.

Style, then, is an elusive quality. It includes the signature features of big hands and feet that Sendak always draws as well as the small chunky figures that are representative of Roy Gerrard's amusing illustrations. Style may be the use of characteristic media like the collages of Eric Carle or the patterned animals and birds of Pat Hutchins or the surrealism of Anthony Browne. Style is an elusive quality of the artist, which changes and varies over the years and with the particular demands of the work. Today there is more freedom to experiment in illustrating children's picture storybooks. Many of our artists are taking advantage of this new freedom and producing fresh and original art.

In *Dear Mili,* Maurice Sendak illustrates a story found in a letter Wilhelm Grimm wrote to a little girl in 1816. Filled with personal symbolism of death, reunion, and hope, it is a story that seems more appropriate for nineteenth-century children than for today's. This picture shows the big hands and feet characteristic of Sendak's illustrations.

Children who have been exposed to a variety of art styles through fine picture storybooks may develop more visual maturity and appreciation. Certainly there is no *one* style that is appropriate for children or preferred by children. The major consideration in evaluating style is how well it conveys and enhances *meaning.*

The Format of the Book

A picture storybook is not made up of single illustrated pictures but conveys its message through a *series* of sequential images. The impact of the total format of the book is what creates the art object known as the picture storybook.

Book size and shape are often decisions made jointly by the illustrator and the art director of the publishing house. They may search for a size that will enhance the theme of the story. *Owliver* by Robert Kraus is a large book, perhaps because illustrators José Aruego and Ariane Dewey saw the choice of a career and the problem of pleasing

or displeasing parents as "big" issues. The fact that José Aruego was a lawyer before he became a book illustrator might have influenced his feelings. *Noisy Nora* by Rosemary Wells is a very small book and certainly in keeping with the way middle sister Nora, a small mouse, felt about her left-out state. The size of Ellen Raskin's amusing story, *Nothing Ever Happens on My Block*, reflects the small narrow viewpoint of dull Chester, who misses the many exciting events that *are* occurring all around him.

The shape of some books suggests their content. The horizontal shape of Donald Hall's *Ox-Cart Man*, illustrated by Barbara Cooney, is very appropriate for portraying the long trek to the Portsmouth market to sell the family's produce in the early fall and the long walk home through leafless trees in late autumn after the father has sold everything, including the ox and his cart. *A Tree Is Nice* by Janice Udry, illustrated by Marc Simont, is tall and vertical in shape, much like the tree described in the text. The shape of *Fish Eyes* by Lois Ehlert is long and narrow like that of a fish or small aquarium.

Both the cloth cover and dust jacket of a book should receive careful attention. The primary purpose of the jacket is to call attention to the book. The jacket for the award-winning *Puss in Boots* illustrated by Fred Marcellino certainly calls attention to itself, for it features the huge head of a hat-bedecked puss in a ruffled collar that could only be the famous *Puss in Boots* by Charles Perrault. But the cover carries no title. Turn the book over and there is the title on the back. A dark brown cloth cover and golden brown endpapers harmonize well with the picture on the jacket. Sometimes the cloth cover has a design imprinted in it. Good cloth designs are usually small and symbolic of the content. For example, Vera Williams uses an imprint of a chair, heart-shaped to show the family's intense desire for a beautiful, comfortable [A] *Chair for My Mother.* Tomie de Paola's touching story of the relationship between a grandfather who has had a stroke and his grandson who helps him learn to walk again is described in *Now One Foot, Now the Other.* Bobby and his grandfather used to see how high they could build a tower of blocks, and it was always the elephant block that made it topple over. After his stroke, Grandfather didn't recognize any of them, but Bobby had faith that he would. The day he played the block game, Grandfather made an attempt to laugh when Bobby said, "Now, time for the elephant block." That was the turning point in Grandfather's recovery, so it is appropriate that de Paola placed the elephant block on the front cover of his story. A discussion with children of why de Paola made this choice would help them recognize the meaning of symbols.

The endpapers of a picture book may also add to its attractiveness. These are the first and last pages of the book, one of which is glued to the reverse of the cover, while the other is not pasted down. Endpapers are usually of stronger paper than printed pages. In picture books endpapers are usually of a color that harmonizes with the cover or other pictures in the book, and frequently these are illustrated. Fewer and fewer illustrators appear to be decorating the endpapers of picture storybooks. This is a loss, for endpapers can reflect the setting, the theme, or the content of the book. Well-designed ones serve as a special invitation into the book. Leo and Diane Dillon create stunning endpapers for the opera *Aïda*, retold by Leontyne Price. Stylized lotus blossoms and seedpods are placed against warm brown marbleized paper. Tomie de Paola made an Italian setting for *Strega Nona* by showing the arched piazza and tile roofs of Strega Nona's Calabrian town. Wonderful pigs frolic and dance on the front endpapers of *The Three Little Pigs* and three houses with a happy pig peering from each one grace the back endpapers of a version illustrated with batik by Edda Reinl. The endpapers of *Crow Boy* by Taro Yashima show a flower and butterfly alone against a dark background. They seem to symbolize the metamorphosis of Crow Boy's life from one of dark despair to brilliant hope.

Even the title page of a picture storybook can be beautiful and symbolic. Marcia Brown has created a striking title page for Cendrars's *Shadow*. She portrays a young boy in silhouette anxiously looking back at his long shadow that falls across a double-page spread, while the spirits of his ancestors, shown as white masks, look on. This primitive fear and respect for *Shadow* permeates the book. By way of contrast, William Steig emphasizes the friendship of a mouse and a whale at the same time he contrasts their size with his title page for *Amos & Boris*. The title page of *Just Plain Fancy* by Patricia Polacco provides the clue to the origin of the fancy peacock egg that Naomi and Ruth found in the tall grass by the drive. All aspects of a book can reinforce or extend the meaning of the story.

Attention should be given to the spacing of pictures and text so that they do not appear monotonously in the same position on each page. Full-sized pictures may be interspersed with smaller ones, or a page may show a sequence of four pictures. Beatriz Vidal's placement of pictures and use of shapes complement the rhythm of Verna Aardema's *Bringing the Rain to Kapiti Plain*. This African tale from the Nandi tribe is cumulative, reminiscent of the nursery rhyme "The House That Jack Built." First, Vidal shows a green verdant plain mostly on the right-hand page; then she switches to the left, while the third page rests the eye with a double-page spread showing a heavy cloud mass spreading over the entire plain. Then once again she places her masses on the right and then left page—readers anticipate this shift just as they anticipate the cumulative rhyme. It is not done throughout the book, however; it would be too monotonous. This is a beautiful example of how one image on a page blends into the next to create the total impact of the book.

The spacing of the text on the page, the choice of margins, and the white space within a book contribute to the making of a quality picture storybook. In Virginia Lee Burton's *The Little House* the text is arranged on the page in a way that suggests the curve of the road in the opposite picture. In the very funny story of the dog poet in *Max Makes a Million* by Maira Kalman, Max dreams of going to Paris. These longings are printed on the paper in the shape of the Eiffel Tower.

It is important also that the text can easily be read and not placed on dark paper. In Paul Goble's *The Girl Who Loved Wild Horses*, the text was changed to white when it was placed on the dark pages that represented night.

The appropriate choice of type design is also a matter for consideration. Type is the name given to all printed letters, and typeface refers to the more than 6,000 different styles available today.

These typefaces vary in legibility and the feeling they create. Some seem bold; others delicate and graceful; some crisp and businesslike. Nicolas Sidjakov describes the difficulty he and his editor had in finding a suitable typeface for Ruth Robbins's *Baboushka and the Three Kings*. When they did find one they liked, it was obsolete and not easily available. They finally located enough fonts to handset *Baboushka* a page at a time.[5] Aliki maintains that the illustrator must think of the text on the page as a part of the art itself. She hand-lettered the text for her book *Feelings* so that the appearance of the words would convey a more personal expression.[6]

Other factors in a picture book must be considered from a utilitarian standpoint. The paper should be dull so that it does not easily reflect light, opaque to prevent print showing through, and strong to withstand heavy usage. Side sewing in the binding of many picture books makes them more durable, but may distort double-page spreads, unless the artwork is prepared with the gutter separation in mind. Tall narrow books with side sewing will not lie flat when the book is open. Many librarians complain that the binding done today is of poor quality and will not last for the life of the book. These, then, are some of the practical considerations that may affect the beauty and the durability of a book.

In sum, no one single element creates an outstanding picture book; what does create one is the effective blending of all elements working together to create a cohesive whole that pleases the eye and delights the imagination.

THE LANGUAGE OF PICTURE STORYBOOKS

The words of picture storybooks are as important as the illustrations; they may help children develop an early sensitivity to the imaginative use of language. Since most of these books are read to children rather than by them, there is no reason to oversimplify or write down to today's knowledgeable and sophisticated child. Television does not talk down to children; neither should parents, teachers, or books. Beatrix Potter knew that given the context of *The Tale of Peter Rabbit* and the picture of Peter caught in the gooseberry net, most children would comprehend the sentence ". . . his sobs were overheard by some friendly sparrows, who flew to him in great excitement, and implored him to exert himself."[7]

Certainly one way to extend children's vocabulary and understanding of complex literary language is by reading aloud well-written books. *Amos & Boris* is a comical story by Steig of the friendship between two such unlikely mammals as a mouse and a whale. Amos, the mouse, delighted by all things nautical, builds himself a jaunty little boat named "Rodent." Admiring the starry skies one night, he rolls overboard and is saved by a huge whale who is amazed to find that the mouse is also a mammal. He gives him a ride to safety, and true to the lion and rat fable on which the story is based, Amos is able to reciprocate at a later time. Steig's luxuriant use of language and superb pictures make this an unusual picture storybook. The description of their trip home details their growing friendship:

> Swimming along, sometimes at great speed, sometimes slowly and leisurely, sometimes resting and exchanging ideas, sometimes stopping to sleep, it took them a week to reach Amos' home shore. During that time, they developed a deep admiration for one another. Boris admired the delicacy, the quivering daintiness, the light touch, the small voice, the gemlike radiance of the mouse. Amos admired the bulk, the grandeur, the power, the purpose, the rich voice, and the abounding friendliness of the whale.[8]

While these may seem difficult words to understand, children do make sense of the story, using the context of both the pictures and text. They sweep back and forth from one to the other,

[5]Nicolas Sidjakov, "Caldecott Award Acceptance" in *Newbery and Caldecott Medal Books: 1956–1965*, edited by Lee Kingman (Boston: Horn Book, 1965), pp. 223–225.
[6]In a speech given at the Children's Literature Conference at Ohio State University, Columbus, 1989.

[7]Beatrix Potter, *The Tale of Peter Rabbit* (London: Frederick Warne, 1902), p. 45.
[8]William Steig, *Amos & Boris* (New York: Farrar, Straus, 1971), unpaged.

TEACHING FEATURE

LEARNING ABOUT THE ART OF PICTURE STORYBOOKS

During Book Week in the fall, teachers in the Highland Park School in Grove City, Ohio, gave several minicourses on the making of books. One minicourse gave an overview of all the kinds of books a child might want to write. The teacher showed the children various kinds of ABC books and counting books. They looked at concept books for the young child, collections of poetry, and many informational books from Aliki's simple books on *My Feet* and *My Hands* to more complicated books such as Patricia Lauber's *The News About Dinosaurs*. Special books that are takeoffs on fairy tales such as *The Jolly Postman* by the Ahlbergs or *The Principal's New Clothes* by Stephanie Calmenson were discussed. Children then started to write their own stories in their classrooms.

Another minicourse emphasized the use of art media where children were introduced to the collage of Eric Carle, Ezra Jack Keats, and Jennie Baker. The teacher had cloth and newspapers available as they discussed the material Keats used in *The Snowy Day* or *Whistle for Willie*. They had fingerpaint paper to make large animals like those in Eric Carle's stories, and natural materials such as grasses, sponges, and mosses that Jennie Baker uses.

Another teacher had collected books with interesting endpapers such as those in *The Great White Man-Eating Shark* by Margaret Mahy, *At Grammy's House* by Eve Rice, or *Henny Penny* by Stephen Butler (see illustration p. 774). Then children used rubber stamps from inner tubing or vegetable stamps or cutout shapes from plastic foam meat trays were used to create their own endpapers. This same teacher had a collection of books with interesting title pages. In all instances, the teacher talked about the ways the artwork strengthened the theme of the book.

Another minicourse emphasized different ways of bookbinding with material or wallpaper covers.

At the end of the week, every child had created his or her own book. More importantly, the children had learned about the way text and art work together to create a unified impression. They had developed a greater appreciation for picture storybooks and the amount of work involved in creating a fine book. They looked at books differently after this experience.

Faculty of Highland Park School,
Kristen Kerstetter, project coordinator
Grove City, Ohio

obtaining the general feeling for this unusual friendship even if they do not know the exact meaning of every single word. This is the way that children increase their vocabularies—by hearing or reading words they do not know but in a context which provides the general sense of the meaning.

In contrast to Steig's exuberant use of words in *Amos & Boris*, the well-known New England poet Donald Hall portrays the journey of *Ox-Cart Man* in cadenced language that is as slow and deliberate as the pace of the ox on the 10-day journey to Portsmouth. When the father packs the family's products, which had taken them a whole year to make, the author describes them in a kind of litany of words:

> He packed a bag of wool
> he sheared from the sheep in April.
> He packed a shawl his wife wove on a loom
> from yarn spun at the spinning wheel
> from sheep sheared in April.
> He packed five pairs of mittens
> his daughter knit

The title page of *Amos & Boris* suggests the incongruous friendship of a monstrous whale and a tiny mouse.

from yarn spun at the spinning wheel
from sheep sheared in April.[9]

All children can appreciate figurative language, provided the comparisons are within the realm of their experiences. The vivid word pictures in Alvin Tresselt's *White Snow, Bright Snow* are thoroughly enjoyed by 5- and 6-year-olds and reflect a child's point of view:

❦ In the morning a clear blue sky was overhead and blue shadows hid in all the corners. Automobiles looked like big fat raisins buried in snow drifts.
    Houses crouched together, their windows peeking out from under great white eyebrows. Even the church steeple wore a pointed cap on its top.[10]

In Jane Yolen's prose poem for *Owl Moon* the little girl who goes owling with her father describes the cold:

❦ as if someone's icy hand
    was palm-down on my back.[11]

The dialogue of a story can be rich and believable, even in a controlled-vocabulary book like *Frog and Toad Are Friends*, or it can be dull and stilted, as in a Dick and Jane basal reader. Arnold Lobel was a master at creating understated humorous dialogue in his Frog and Toad Series. The two friends decide to go for a swim, and Toad admonishes Frog:

❦ "After I put on my bathing suit, you must not look at me until I get into the water."
    "Why not?" asked Frog.
    "Because I look funny in my bathing suit. That is why," said Toad.
    . . . When Toad came out from behind the rocks, . . . he was wearing his bathing suit. "Don't peek," he said.

All the animals come to watch Toad in swimming, and he is too embarrassed to get out. Finally he is freezing and has to. When they all laugh at his 1920 striped suit, Frog says:

"You *do* look funny in your bathing suit."
"Of course I do," said Toad.[12]

Similarly, part of the charm of the "Frances stories" by Russell Hoban is the natural-sounding dialogue of everyone's favorite badger, Frances. The expressive pictures are as humorous as the dialogue in both these well-written series.

In evaluating picture storybooks, it is good to remember that the story should be told quickly because the action must be contained within a thirty-two- to sixty-four-page book. Even within this limitation the criteria developed in Chapter 1 for all fiction apply equally well to picture storybooks. Both text and illustrations should be evaluated in a picture storybook. The artistry of the words should be equal to the beauty of the illustrations.

THE CONTENT OF PICTURE STORYBOOKS

Several recent changes can be noted in the content of picture storybooks; one is the increasing publication of books that are based on sharing memories of times past with children. Frequently these are told by grandparents much as they might have been told around the dinner table. Perhaps these books compensate for the lack of frequent contact with extended families in our fast-paced lives. These books seldom have a real plot but are based on what life was like when grandfather, or grandmother, or parents were children.

Another development in the content of picture storybooks is a tremendous increase in books that are geared to children in the middle grades. This seems appropriate for today's visually minded child. As the age range for picture storybooks increases, it becomes imperative to evaluate the appropriateness of the content for the age level of its intended audience. You do not want to share *Hiroshima No Pika* (The Flash of Hiroshima) by Toshi Maruki with young children any more than you would read *Goodnight Moon* by Margaret Wise Brown to older children.

[9]Donald Hall, *Ox-Cart Man*, illustrated by Barbara Cooney (Viking Press, 1979), unpaged.
[10]Alvin Tresselt, *White Snow, Bright Snow*, illustrated by Roger Duvoisin (New York: Lothrop, 1947, reissued 1988), p. 20.
[11]Jane Yolen *Owl Moon*, illustrated by John Schoenherr (New York: Philomel, 1987), unpaged.

[12]Arnold Lobel, *Frog and Toad Are Friends* (New York: Harper & Row, 1970), pp. 42, 52.

Other considerations regarding the content of picture storybooks need to be examined. For example, does the book avoid race, gender, or age stereotyping? Gender stereotyping begins early. Examples can be found in pictures as well as text. In the imaginative story *Can I Keep Him?* by Steven Kellogg, Albert asks his mother if he can keep one pet after another, ranging from real to imaginary to human. His distraught mother is always pictured attending to such household chores as scrubbing, ironing, and cleaning the toilet bowl. She explains in very literal terms why Albert cannot keep his pets; for example, a snake's scales could clog the vacuum. While the contrast between Albert's highly original ideas and his mother's mundane preoccupation with household duties is funny, it is also a devastating image of the traditional housewife.

An increasing number of books have been published that counteract gender stereotyping. *William's Doll* by Charlotte Zolotow is one of the best known of them. In this story, William is a little boy who desperately wants a doll. He has a basketball and a tiny train set that his father has given him, but he still wants a doll. His brother thinks he is a creep, and the boy next door calls him a sissy. Only his grandmother understands how he feels and so she brings him a baby doll "to hug . . . so that when he's a father . . . he'll know how to care for his baby. . . ."[13]

More and more books portray characters who are willing to step outside of traditional roles to fulfill their lives. In the story of *Max* by Rachel Isadora, a young baseball player walks his sister to her dancing class on his way to the park for his weekly game. One morning when Max is early he finds that he likes ballet dancing and decides that it is a super way to warm up for baseball. Soft gray pencil drawings show Max in his baseball uniform stretching at the barre and trying to do the split. His enjoyment increases until a jubilant Max does a high leap out the door and runs down to the park to hit a home run. The humor in the pictures and text save the story from appearing to be too contrived.

In *The Long Red Scarf* by Nette Hilton, Grandpa decides he would like to have a long scarf like his friend Jake. He takes his request to the female relatives in his family, but they either never learned to knit or are too busy. When he complains to his friend, he is surprised to learn that Jake made his own scarf. So Grandpa learns to knit and makes his own scarf.

In *Jeremy's Decision* by Ardyth Brott, Jeremy is constantly asked if he will be following his famous father's footsteps and become an orchestra conductor. In a surprise ending, Allegra, his sister, becomes the conductor, and Jeremy decides to become a paleontologist. Arnold Adoff, the well-known poet, cuts across several stereotypes in his story *Hard to Be Six*. He presents an affectionate view of sibling rivalry in a loving interracial family where the 6-year-old brother always kisses his sister goodnight, and his father does the cooking.

We have few picture books that portray modern Latinos and Native Americans. These groups have been maligned in print, television, and on commercial games as bloodthirsty warriors and

Written in both English and Spanish, *Family Pictures* does look like a family album showing all the special events in the author/illustrator's life while growing up in Kingsville, Texas.

By Carmen Lomos Garza.

GUIDELINES

Content:
- ♦ How appropriate is the content of the book for its intended age level?
- ♦ Is this a book that will appeal to children, or is it really written for adults?
- ♦ When and where does it take place? How has the artist portrayed this?
- ♦ Are the characters well delineated and developed?
- ♦ Are race, gender and other stereotypes avoided?
- ♦ What is the quality of the language of the text?
- ♦ How is the theme developed through text and illustrations?

Illustrations:
- ♦ In what ways do the illustrations help to create the meaning of the text?
- ♦ How are pictures made an integral part of the text?
- ♦ Do the illustrations extend the text in any way? Do they provide clues to the action of the story?
- ♦ Are the pictures accurate and consistent with the text?
- ♦ Where the setting calls for it, are the illustrations authentic in detail?

Medium and Style of Illustrations:
- ♦ What medium has the illustrator chosen to use? Is it appropriate for the mood of the story?
- ♦ How has the illustrator used line, shape, and color to extend the story?
- ♦ How would you describe the style of the illustrations? Is the style appropriate for the story?
- ♦ How has the illustrator varied the style and technique? What techniques seem to create rhythm and movement?
- ♦ How has the illustrator created balance in composition?

Format:
- ♦ Does the size of the book seem appropriate to the content?
- ♦ Does the jacket design express the theme of the book?
- ♦ Do the cover design and endpapers convey the spirit of the book?
- ♦ In what way does the title page anticipate the story to come?
- ♦ Is the type design well chosen for the theme and purpose of the book?
- ♦ What is the quality of the paper?
- ♦ How durable is the binding?

GUIDELINES

Comparison with Others:

♦ How is this work similar to or different from other works by this author and/or illustrator?

♦ How is this story similar to or different from other books with the same subject or theme?

♦ What comments have reviewers made about this book? Do you agree or disagree with them?

♦ What has the artist said about his or her work?

♦ Will this book make a contribution to the growing body of children's literature? How lasting do you think it will be?

* Note: These questions are listed to help the reader determine the strengths of the book. Not every question is appropriate for every book.

sleeping peons in sombreros. A few stories, such as *Annie and the Old One* by Miska Miles, portray the loving relationship between a Navaho girl and her grandmother. However, this story has been criticized by Native Americans for not being authentic in its representation of the Navaho lifestyle. The poetic story of life among the Pueblo Indians titled *In My Mother's House,* by Ann Nolan Clark, has been reissued with handsome black-and-white and colored illustrations by Velino Herrera. *This House Is Made of Mud,* by Ken Buchanan, celebrates the joy of living in a Navaho hogan. The desert is its yard, the mountains, its fence, and all the animals and birds are welcome visitors. Lovely clear watercolors by Libba Tracy add to the beauty of this simple story.

Marie Hall Ets and Aurora Labastida's *Nine Days to Christmas, a Story of Mexico* tells of a 5-year-old's excitement over having her own Christmas party and piñata game. Leo Politi's picture storybook *Pedro, the Angel of Olvera Street* also centers on the Posada celebration among the Mexican Americans in Los Angeles. *The Dream Stair* by Betsy James describes a Hispanic girl's goodnight and dream images. *Con Mi Hermano: With My Brother* by Eileen Roe relates the joyous times that a little boy spends with his older brother: playing ball, helping him deliver newspapers, and sharing picture books together. *Family Pictures: Cuadros de Familia* by Carmen Lomos Garza is like a family album of all the special events the author remembers from her childhood days of growing up in Kingsville, Texas. We need more such books written in both English and Spanish that celebrate our cultural diversity. Brilliant collage pictures by Elisa Kleven illustrate the imaginary trip Rosalba and her grandmother, her *Abuela,* take as they fly over Manhattan Island. Rosalba narrates their marvelous journey in a combination of English spiced with Spanish phrases that are easily understood in context. The author, Arthur Dorros, provides a glossary and pronunciation guide at the end. This book could be compared with another imaginary flight over New York in *Tar Beach* by Faith Ringgold.

While there are more books about the elderly than ever before, we can find stereotypes among these, too. One young-appearing grandfather came to a bookstore recently and said he wanted "a book about a grandfather in which the main character doesn't die." Many grandparents today in their 60s and 70s are vigorous and healthy; we might well ask if they are being portrayed this way.

Picture storybooks frequently give children their first impressions of various ethnic and racial groups. Only when our books portray characters of both sexes, all ages, all ethnic and racial groups in a wide range of occupations and from a great variety of socioeconomic backgrounds and settings will we have moved away from stereotyping to a more honest portrayal of the world for children.

THEMES AND SUBJECTS IN PICTURE STORYBOOKS

As teachers and librarians it is important that we know all the criteria by which to judge a quality picture book. Children, however, are most interested in one criterion—does it tell a good story? Story is all. Only gradually can they be interested in the art or the background of the authors and illustrators. For this reason, we discuss books by their themes for the benefit of those selecting particular books or preparing units for study.

Family Stories

Family stories today include single-parent families, divorced and remarried (blended) families, adoption and foster families, and the extended family. Children always beg to hear stories about when their parents were small. The little African-American girl in *Tell Me a Story, Mama* by Angela Johnson knows exactly what family stories she wants to hear, and she knows them so well that she can tell them herself with her mother adding just the right comment. This is the story of a tender parent-child relationship.

John Steptoe's *Daddy Is a Monster . . . Sometimes* depicts some of the difficulties of a single father raising his children. His prismatic pictures capture the feelings and tension in a household where fathers become monsters "when they have monster children."

Daddy by Jeannette Caines is a story of the warm loving relationship between an African-American little girl and her father. A child of divorced parents, she waits for him to come every Saturday. "Before Daddy comes to get me, I get wrinkles in my stomach. . . . Then on Saturday morning he rings one short and one long, and my

wrinkles go away."[14] The two of them go shopping, make chocolate pudding, and play hide-and-seek under the kitchen table and in the supermarket aisles. Paula, Daddy's wife, lets the little girl dress up in long fancy clothes. Ronald Himler's illustrations capture the joy and delight that both father and daughter feel for this magic day together.

Mama One and Mama Two by Patricia MacLachlan is an affectionate story of a child being reassured by her foster mother that she will be loved and cared for until her real mother recovers from her mental depression and the two of them can be together again. Pictures by Ruth Lercher Bornstein capture not only the warmth of the glad times the little girl remembers but also the dark, sad times. The story ends with the

[14]Jeannette Caines, *Daddy*, illustrated by Ronald Himler (New York: Harper & Row, 1977), pp. 30–31.

Lovely tender watercolors by James-Graham Hale illustrate the story of a little Asian child who flew *Through Moon and Stars and Night Skies* to reach his new adoptive family. Ann Turner tells his brave story of coming to a strange land.

🍃   🍃   🍃

hopeful promise of spring, the bluebird's return, and perhaps the return of the little girl's mother.

A warm loving story about adoption of a little Asian child from overseas is told by Ann Turner in *Through Moon and Stars and Night Skies*. Lovely tender, but not sentimental, watercolor pictures by James-Graham Hale illustrate this story of a brave little boy coming to a strange land.

Like Jake and Me by Mavis Jukes, longer than most picture storybooks, describes a sensitive boy's adjustment to his tough-appearing stepfather, who always wears Stetson hats and has real doubts about Alex's ability to help on the farm. Yet Alex and the reader are allowed to see Jake's softer side in his concern for his pregnant wife and his fear of spiders. When Alex calmly "saves" him from the wolf spider crawling down his neck, a bond of affection is forged between the two. Lloyd Bloom's bold illustrations capture the strong personalities in this well-written story.

Sibling rivalry over the anticipation of a new baby in the family is clearly expressed in the story and title of Martha Alexander's *When the New Baby Comes, I'm Moving Out*. When the new baby does arrive, Oliver is indignant at all the attention she receives so he puts her in his red wagon and tries to give her away in *Nobody Asked Me If I Wanted a Baby Sister*. The humorous pictures are just right for these childlike stories about real feelings.

Peter in *Peter's Chair* by Ezra Jack Keats doesn't give his sister away, but he decides to run away himself before all of his possessions are painted pink for his new baby sister. However, when he discovers that he no longer fits in his chair, he decides that maybe it would be fun to paint it pink himself. The collage pictures add greatly to this universally loved story. Sibling rivalry is also portrayed in *She Come Bringing Me That Little Baby Girl* by Eloise Greenfield. Kevin dislikes all the attention given to his new sister. Then his uncle tells him how he used to take care of his baby sister, and Kevin is surprised to learn that his mother was once a baby girl. Kevin gets over his resentment and goes to get his friends to show them his new sister. Illustrations by John Steptoe capture Kevin's changing emotions in this warm, loving story.

In Mildred Pitts Walter's story *My Mama Needs Me*, Jason is torn between wanting to play with his friends and his sense of responsibility to stay close to home to help his mother with his new baby sis-

ter. This story of an African-American older child's desire to be of help and yet his resentment at the changes in his life is a very real one.

Sibling conflict is portrayed more frequently in picture storybooks than are love and compassion. In Shirley Hughes's story of *Dogger*, a big sister, Bella, lovingly gives up the huge teddy bear which she had won at the fair in order to obtain her little brother's lost, much-loved stuffed dog. Hughes always portrays real, believable characters in messy confusing households in both her pictures and text. In this story Bella shows her love for Dave in her actions, whereas many family mood stories only talk about love.

In both *A Place for Ben* by Jeanne Titherington and the reissued *Evan's Corner* by Elizabeth Starr Hill, older brothers decide they need a place of their own. Ben finds his in the corner of the garage and Evan takes one of the eight corners in his black family's two-room apartment. But after they fix up their special places they find they need someone to visit them. Ben's baby brother comes and plays in his, and Evan begins to help his brother decorate a corner for himself. The themes of both these books emphasize the joy of sharing.

Aunts play a special role in several storybooks. Franz Brandenberg has written three books about remarkable Aunt Nina that Aliki has illustrated. In *Aunt Nina, Good Night*, this brave woman invites all six of her nieces and nephews to spend the night with her. Jeannette Caines tells of a niece's plans for a wonderful trip to North Carolina in Aunt Martha's new car in her book *Just Us Women*. Realistic illustrations by Pat Cummings detail the fun that these African-American women plan to have on their special trip together.

A warm jubilant picture storybook by Cynthia Rylant, illustrated by Stephen Gammell, describes the summer when all *The Relatives Came*. Driving up from Virginia in an old station wagon, some six or seven relatives arrive:

> Then it was hugging time. Talk about hugging! Those relatives just passed us all around their car, pulling us against their wrinkled Virginia clothes, crying sometimes. They hugged us for hours.[15]

[15]Cynthia Rylant, *The Relatives Came*, illustrated by Stephen Gammell (New York: Bradbury Press, 1985), unpaged.

The relatives stay for weeks and weeks, helping tend the garden and mend any broken things. They eat the strawberries and the melons and then they all pile in the station wagon and head back to Virginia. Stephen Gammell uses brightly colored pencil drawings for this award-winning book about a joyous family reunion.

Stories of Grandparents

There are an increasing number of stories about grandparents. Several themes may be discerned in these. One of them is the sharing of family stories frequently including the cultural feeling for the country from which the grandparents emigrated. Another theme is helping the child to overcome a fear or learn something new or just enjoyment in the relationship. The third type is learning to say goodbye and adjusting to the death of a grandparent.

In *Grandaddy's Place* by Helen Griffith, Janetta meets her grandaddy for the first time. She is apprehensive about staying at his house, which is way out in the country. Her grandfather understands her fears and helps her to make friends with all the animals on his place. A special closeness develops between the two of them. In *Georgia Music*, her grandaddy's health is failing and he has been brought to live with her family in the city. This time it is Janetta who helps him to learn to accept his new situation. James Stevenson's full-color watercolors create the settings for these two loving stories.

Two children visit their French grandmother every week for Sunday dinner at noon. Each week there are the same good things to eat and to make. Life on the farm seems always the same in this happy story of visiting *At Grammy's House* by Eve Rice. Nancy Winslow Parker's simple childlike illustrations seem just right for this cheerful book for younger children.

In *Storm in the Night* by Mary Stolz, a storm has cut off the electricity, so a grandfather and grandson sit together in the dark and enjoy the sounds and smells of the rain. The grandfather recounts the story of a stormy night from his childhood and how he overcame his fear of the dark. Pat Cummings's pictures show a loving relationship in an African-American family. Patricia Polacco

tells a memorable story of how a little girl is terrified of thunder until her Russian babushka teaches her to make a special *Thunder Cake*. As child and grandmother scurry around to get the ingredients for the Thunder Cake, the little girl doesn't have time to be frightened of the storm.

Amazing Grace is the story of a black child who loves stories of all kinds. Grace acts out every story she reads or her grandmother tells her. It is only natural then that she wants to try out for the lead in the class play *Peter Pan*. Other children tell her that she can't be Peter because she is a girl and black. Both her mother and grandmother tell her she can be anything she wants to be. Then her grandmother takes her to see a black ballerina who dances the role of Juliet in *Romeo and Juliet*. Grace practices and practices until she feels she can almost fly. On the day of the tryout, Grace is a glorious Peter and wins the part unanimously. The author of this fine self-esteem picture storybook is Mary Hoffman. Caroline Binch painted the remarkably expressive watercolors.

In *The Wednesday Surprise* by Eve Bunting, Anna teaches her grandmother to read by sharing books every Wednesday night when she comes to babysit. For Dad's birthday surprise, Anna gives the bag of books to Grandma, who proudly stands and reads them. Donald Carrick's full-color paintings capture the warmth and pride of this special moment.

Tomie de Paola has written two grandmother stories. In the first one Joey warns his friend as they go to visit his Italian grandmother to *Watch Out for the Chicken Feet in Your Soup*. The well-meaning grandmother feeds the two boys the entire time they are there. Eugene gets to help her make bread dolls (a recipe is provided in the text) and thoroughly enjoys his visit. The second story, *Nana Upstairs and Nana Downstairs*, is more serious, describing a boy's visits with his bedridden great-grandmother. After she dies, "Nana Downstairs" moves upstairs. *First One Step and Then the Other*, mentioned before, is de Paola's story of the little boy helping his grandfather recover from a stroke and learn to walk again.

Aliki's book *The Two of Them* depicts the loving relations between a grandfather and his granddaughter. The grandfather had made her a ring even before she was born. He made her a bed, a cradle for her dolls, and a bamboo flute. "And every year she loved him even more than the things he made for her." When he dies she is not ready, but knows she will always remember him. Lovely glowing pastel pictures capture the essence of their love for each other.

John Burningham's *Granpa* is a moving story showing the many experiences a little girl and her grandfather share, such as planting seeds, playing, building sand castles, and sledding. Alternating pages have simple line sketches that portray the grandfather's memories of his childhood. The parallel conversations are characteristic of the very young and very old, adding to the realism of this story. The grandfather becomes ill but can still sit in his favorite chair with his granddaugh-

Tanya loves to hear her African-American grandmother tell stories about the material she uses to make *The Patchwork Quilt*. This account of one family's history was written by Valerie Flournoy and illustrated with realistic pictures by Jerry Pinkney.

ter. The next scene pictures the girl alone and her grandfather's chair empty.

Through Grandpa's Eyes by Patricia MacLachlan is a longer story of a little boy who learns to "see" as his blind grandfather does. The two of them make music together, read, listen for the birds, do the dishes. In fact, there is little that this grandfather cannot do despite his handicap. This is a tender story in which the grandson realizes that his grandfather has many ways of seeing.

In *Happy Birthday, Grampie* by Susan Pearson, a little girl makes a very special birthday card that her grandfather can feel because he, too, is blind. Martha worries that he might not get her message, since he has gotten so old he only speaks in Swedish. Carefully, he traces her raised letters and then laughs out loud and says, "Martha, I love you, too." Lovely realistic pictures by Ronald Himler capture this moment of love and restored memory.

In Bill Martin, Jr., and John Archambault's story, *Knots on a Counting Rope*,[16] a young Native-American boy and his grandfather sit by the campfire and tell stories. The boy's favorite is the one about himself. The grandfather begins it, but the boy knows it so well he can almost tell it. It is the story of a birth of a small frail blind boy who is welcomed by his family and the great blue horses and named Boy-Strength-of-Blue-Horses. The story ends with his grandfather adding a knot to the counting rope that marks the number of times the boy has heard this story.

Every family makes its own history, creates its own mythology by retelling family stories many times over. Tanya loves to hear her black grandmother tell the stories of the material she is using to make *The Patchwork Quilt*. She helps her cut

[16]Native Americans have objected to the portrayal of tribal life in this book. They maintain that no Native-American child would interrupt his grandfather as the boy does in this story, since elders are always respected. Clothing and hairstyles are not authentic to any one nation, and the naming ceremony is incorrect. This points up the need for Native-American authors, or at least, consultation for authenticity. See "Book Reviews" in Beverly Slapin and Doris Seale, eds. *Books Without Bias: Through Indian Eyes* (Berkeley, Calif.: Oyate, 1988), pp. 273–278.

the squares and listens to her story of the quilt of memories. This story by Valerie Flournoy and realistic pictures by Jerry Pinkney capture a young girl's love for her treasured grandmother. In *Aunt Flossie's Hats (and Crab Cakes Later)*, Sarah and Susan hear the history of their Great-Great-Aunt Flossie's many hats including the time a dog retrieved her "favorite best Sunday hat" from the water. Sumptuous oil paintings by James Ransome capture the joy of the children's visit to their very special aunt. Elizabeth Fitzgerald Howard's own black 98-year-old aunt who never threw anything away was the inspiration for this delightful family story.

In *The Keeping Quilt* by Patricia Polacco, Great Gramma Anna, a Russian Jew who was an immigrant to this country, made a quilt to help the family always remember their homeland. Through four generations the quilt is a Sabbath tablecloth, a wedding canopy, and a blanket that welcomes babies warmly into the world. To this day, Patricia Polacco still treasures this family quilt.

The delightful story of *How My Parents Learned to Eat* by Ina Friedman tells of an American sailor who learned to eat with chopsticks in order to invite his future wife, a Japanese girl, out to dinner. She in turn learns how to use a fork and knife so he won't be embarrassed by her. Told by their daughter, this is a family story that explains why they sometimes eat with chopsticks and sometimes with knives and forks.

Riki Levinson has told a story within a story in her recounting of the immigrant experience in *Watch the Stars Come Out*. The story, which the small red-haired narrator inherited from her grandma's mama, describes the journey two young children made alone on a ship from Europe to America—a trip that took some twenty-three days in the late nineteenth century. They were met by their parents, taken to their new and strange home in America, and given a bath. Then they went to bed early and watched the stars come out just as the small red-haired narrator loved to do. Diane Goode's muted colored pictures help to distance the story, creating the feeling of looking through an old family album.

Barbara Cooney's *Island Boy* tells of four generations of a New England family who settled on Tibbett's Island. In the end, young Matthias replaces his grandfather who was the original young Matthias in the beginning of the story. Stunning pictures portray seascapes and the family members who make up this cycle of life. In *Hattie and the Wild Waves*, Cooney describes the affluent life of her mother growing up in Brooklyn and then Long Island while searching for her lifework. This story of a first-generation American captures a portrait of an American era.

Familiar Everyday Experiences

Everything is new to the young child the first time it happens—going to school, making friends, losing teeth, taking a trip, moving away, experiencing the death of a pet. Soon, however, children become accustomed to familiar experiences. Nevertheless, books may help children keep alive the wonder and the anticipation of such experiences. They may also alleviate some of their concerns and worries about the new and unknown. When Ira was invited to sleep overnight at Reggie's house he was very excited; he had never slept at a friend's house before. But then his sister asks him if he is going to take his teddy bear. First Ira decides he will, then he decides he won't. Luckily, Reggie lives right next door, so when he pulls his teddy bear out of a drawer, Ira can go home for his. While adults find this story, *Ira Sleeps Over* by Bernard Waber, very funny, 5- and 6-year-olds are serious about Ira's dilemma. An older Ira must learn to adjust to Reggie's moving away in *Ira Says Goodbye*.

Miriam Cohen writes believable reassuring stories about young children's concerns. On his first day of school Jim worriedly asks his father, *Will I Have a Friend?* He is equally apprehensive about *The New Teacher* and the skill of reading in *When Will I Read? Best Friends* details the way Jim and Paul cement their friendship by working together to solve the problem about the light in the classroom incubator. In another first-grade experience, Jim and some of his classmates become separated from their teacher in *Lost in the Museum*. In *It's George*, George becomes a hero and appears on TV, much to his and the class's delight. All these little books describe children's real fears and joys. Lillian Hoban's illustrations of a multicultural first-grade classroom in an old city school are as warm and reassuring as Jim's teachers and friendly classmates.

Jay, a young farm boy, loves the countryside and decides to take his pet cricket to school in Rebecca Caudill's sensitive story, *A Pocketful of Cricket*. An understanding teacher finds a way for him to keep his noisy cricket in the classroom and share it with others. Descriptive language and expressive pictures by Evaline Ness evoke the beauty of Jay's country walk. Another favorite picture book that seems particularly appropriate for 5- and 6-year-olds in the process of losing their teeth is *One Morning in Maine* by Robert McCloskey. Young Sal awakens one morning to find she has a loose tooth. She announces it to anyone who will listen, including her parents, a fish hawk, loon, seal, seagull, clam, and men at the general store. When she finally does lose it on the beach, she substitutes a gull's feather to put under her pillow.

For young children, birthdays are even more important than losing a tooth. In *Something Special for Me*, Vera Williams makes very real the decision that Rosa, the little girl in *A Chair for My Mother*, must make. Soon it will be her birthday, and this time she can have the money in the large money jar that contains her mother's waitressing tips to buy anything she wants. After much soul-searching, Rosa decides to spend the money on a used accordion. When her grandmother becomes ill and the money jar is empty from paying her bills, Rosa uses her birthday accordion to earn money in *Music, Music for Everyone*.

Samantha (everyone called her Sam) is the highly imaginative heroine in the Caldecott award winner *Sam, Bangs, and Moonshine* by Evaline Ness. Sam's fantasies are responsible for the near loss of her devoted friend, Thomas, when she sends him out to Blue Rock at high tide to see a mermaid. When Thomas is safely rescued, Sam decides to give him her pet gerbil named "Moonshine." Symbolically, Sam gives away her "moonshine" tendencies at the same time.

Ezra Jack Keats's stories about Peter begin with *The Snowy Day, Peter's Chair, Whistle for Willie,* and *A Letter to Amy.* As Peter grows up he is joined by his friend Archie in *Goggles, Hi Cat!,* and *Pet Show!* All these stories take place in the inner city and

have exciting story lines and convincing characterization. In *Goggles*, Peter, Archie, and Willie, Peter's dachshund, fool some big boys who want to take away the motorcycle goggles that the two friends have found. In *Hi Cat!* Peter is adopted by a crazy cat. In *Pet Show!* the crazy cat disappears just when Archie needs him for his entry. Being highly creative, Archie substitutes an empty bottle that contains his pet, a germ! He receives an award for the quietest pet. Keats has used bright acrylic paints for these well-loved stories of Peter and his friends.

John Steptoe has written a story of city children and their friendship in *Stevie*. At first Robert doesn't like *Stevie*, the little boy who comes and stays at their house every day while his mother goes to work. Robert tells how Stevie plays with his toys and breaks them, climbs all over his bed with his dirty shoes, and gets him into trouble. But then Stevie's mother and father come to take him away for good and Robert realizes that he misses him. The theme of this story of African-American children is universal; for we seldom learn to appreciate what we have until it is gone. A 9-year-old girl described Stevie as "a nice nuisance"—we have all experienced one!

In *I'll Fix Anthony* by Judith Viorst a younger brother dreams of revenge, planning all the different ways that he can think of to "fix Anthony," his older brother. The contrast between his plans and the ending provides much of the humor of this book. Everyone has a bad day occasionally, but few of us have experienced the kind of day that Viorst has written about in *Alexander and the Terrible, Horrible, No Good, Very Bad Day*. Alexander knew it was going to be a miserable day from the moment he woke up with gum in his hair. And he was right. It was a bad, bad day at school; he had lima beans for supper; and there was kissing on TV. When Alexander went to bed his bath was too hot and he got soap in his eyes; but the worst affront was the fact that he had to wear the railroad-train pajamas that he hated. He thought of moving to Australia, but "Mom says some days are like that. Even in Australia." Alexander has money problems in *Alexander, Who Used to Be Rich Last Sunday*. This is not quite as funny as the first Alexander story but the pictures by Ray Cruz are hilarious.

Viorst has written a quieter, more serious story about the death of a young boy's cat, *The Tenth Good Thing About Barney*. After Barney died, the little boy's mother told him to think about ten good things to say about Barney, and that they would have a funeral for him the next day. The little boy could only think of nine things, but later, while he was helping his father plant seeds, he thought of the tenth: Barney was in the ground helping the flowers to grow. The little black-and-white ink sketches by Erik Blegvad underscore the sincerity of this story of a boy's first experience with death.

Hans Wilhelm's tender story *I'll Always Love You* tells of a boy and his dog Elfie who grew up together, Elfie growing rounder while the boy grows taller. The story recalls their good times together, their play, Elfie's escapades, yet doesn't ignore the grief when Elfie dies. The whole family ". . . buried Elfie together." Soft delicate watercolors provide humor in detailing Elfie's plump lines and tenderness as a back view shows boy and dog sharing the boy's coat against an autumn wind. This story would encourage children to share stories of pets they will always love.

The Accident by Carol and Donald Carrick describes Christopher's dismay when his dog Bodger is run over by a truck and killed. In *The Foundling*, Christopher's dad takes him to the local animal shelter hoping that a dog there will attract his attention. However, Christopher feels it would be unfaithful to Bodger's memory and can't respond to any dog. Later, an abandoned pup that he thinks belongs next door starts waiting for him after school. When Christopher finds the pup doesn't belong to anyone, he decides to keep it. These stories are a part of a series of books about Christopher and his family. Donald Carrick's expressive watercolors authentically portray the people and settings of New England villages and the seacoast.

Picture Storybooks About Older People

For many years we believed that children only identified with stories about children their own age. More recently we have given them literature that includes persons of all ages. For example, young children delight in the adventures of Mr. Gumpy, the children's literature equivalent of Mr. Rogers on TV. In *Mr. Gumpy's Outing* by John Burningham, he takes two children and an assortment of animals in his boat, first giving such admonitions as not to squabble or hop about or flap or muck about. Of course, they do all these things and tip the boat over. But then kind, enduring Mr. Gumpy invites them home for tea. In *Mr. Gumpy's Motor Car*, the long-suffering Mr. Gumpy takes the whole gang for a ride in his old-fashioned car. When the rains come, the car gets stuck in the mud. In onomatopoetic language, Burningham describes them all pushing out the old car:

> They pushed and shoved and heaved and strained and gasped and slipped and slithered and squelched. . . . Slowly the car began to move.[17]

Rose lives all alone except for her big hulk of an English sheepdog named John Brown. One night Rose sees something move in the garden, a midnight cat. Each night when John Brown isn't looking she puts milk out for it, and each night when Rose isn't looking John Brown tips it over. One day Rose is sick and announces she is staying in bed indefinitely. John Brown asks Rose if the midnight cat will make her feel better. He lets her in and for the first time, Rose gets up and sits by the fire. The midnight cat sits on the arm of her chair and purrs. Jenny Wagner titled this amusing story of "sibling rivalry" *John Brown, Rose and the Midnight Cat*. Ron Brooks drew the expressive illustrations of a huge spoiled John Brown and a worried round little lady. Lovely landscapes place the story in Australia.

Mem Fox, also Australian, wrote the story of *Wilfrid Gordon McDonald Partridge*'s search for Miss Nancy's memory, which we discussed earlier. In *Night Noises* Lily Laceby who is nearly 90 drifts off to sleep by the fire dreaming of bygone days. Strange noises disturb Butch Aggie, her dog, but Lily sleeps on. Finally, the commotion grows louder and the old lady wakens and answers her door only to discover that her sons, daughters, grandchildren, and great-grandchildren have come to wish her happy birthday.

[17]John Burningham, *Mr. Gumpy's Motor Car* (New York: Harper & Row, 1976), unpaged.

Barbara Cooney illustrated two popular stories about older people, *Emma* and *Miss Rumphius*. *Emma*, written by Wendy Kesselman, is about a woman the author knew who didn't start painting until she was in her late 80s. In this story Barbara Cooney depicts her as a kind of Grandma Moses character who creates many primitive paintings based on her memories of her town. *Miss Rumphius* is a fine model of an independent older person. As a youngster she told her grandfather that she too wished to travel to faraway places as he had and live by the sea. He told her there was a third thing she must do—make the world more beautiful. And so years later she planted lupine all over her little seacoast village. Repetition of the story line is reflected as a very elderly Miss Rumphius passes along her grandfather's advice to her grandniece. The continuity of life is nicely portrayed by the many objects that we first saw in the grandfather's house, or on her travels, and which now comfortably reside in Miss Rumphius's home by the sea.

Another remarkable person who dreamed of going to faraway places was *My Great-Aunt Arizona*, a book by Gloria Houston. Born in a log cabin in the Blue Ridge mountains, Arizona never goes to those faraway places. Instead she stays at home and becomes one of those special teachers who each of us holds in our hearts. Great-Aunt Arizona dies on her ninety-third birthday but she goes to those faraway places with all of the students she taught. "She goes with us in our minds."

When *Old Henry* first rented the most dilapidated house in the town, people waited for him to fix it up. Henry had no such plans; he enjoyed reading and painting and ignored the mess. Finally the neighbors' complaints drive him out. Surprisingly, they miss him and Henry misses his tree, his house, and his yard. He writes to the mayor saying he will mend his ways, but he still wants to let his grass grow. Henry awaits the mayor's answer. Children love to write the mayor's reply to Old Henry. The theme of this story written in rhymed verse by Joan Blos is accepting those who are different. Stephen Gammell's soft pencil and wash illustrations create the perfect eccentric in *Old Henry*. Gammell is also the illustrator of the Caldecott award–

winning *Song and Dance Man* by Karen Ackerman that tells of an old soft-shoe vaudeville performer who dances for his grandchildren.

Blow Me a Kiss, Miss Lilly is a touching story by Nancy White Carlstrom of Sara's friendship with the very old lady who lives across the street from her. Miss Lilly tells Sara that you can be different when you are very old and even eat ice cream for breakfast. One day Miss Lilly doesn't feel well and Sara's father takes her to the hospital, where she dies. Sara takes in her cat, visits her garden, and always blows her a kiss the way she did when she was alive. Small precise illustrations by Amy Schwartz make this story particularly appealing.

The Child's World of Nature

Sometimes young children seem more attuned to the world about them than adults do. Watch children on the first day of snow, for example, and see the excitement in their eyes and their eagerness to go outside. Adults may complain about having to shovel the snow or getting the car stuck, but for children a snowstorm is pure joy. It is this very contrast between adults' and children's reactions to snow that formed the basis for Alvin Tresselt's well-loved book *White Snow, Bright Snow* illustrated with Roger Duvoisin's sparkling pictures. Repeating the same pattern in *Hide and Seek Fog*, Tresselt describes the children's joyous response to a fog that came and stayed for three days in a little seaside village on Cape Cod, while their parents grumbled about spending their vacations in the middle of a cloud. Duvoisin's hazy pearl-gray illustrations effectively convey the mystery of a fog-shrouded day.

In *Rain Rain Rivers* Uri Shulevitz has produced a strikingly well-designed book that expresses the mood of a rainy day in the city and the country. Indoors, a little girl watches, listens, and feels safe and cozy in her own small room. Outdoors it rains on the windowpanes, the rooftops; it rains on the fields, the hills, and the ponds. The streams, the brooks, the rivers, the seas, surge and swell, rage and roar. Watercolors in greens and blues are the appropriate medium and colors used for these lovely illustrations.

The various sounds the rain makes are explored in the poetic picture book *Rain Talk* by

Mary Serfozo. A young child hears the "first fat raindrops" fall on the summer dust of a country road. She smells the wet dust. Eventually she and her dog make their way home after enjoying their rainy day walk. Bright yellow and green illustrations by Keiko Narahashi portray the child's delight in this summer rain. In the well-known story *Umbrella* by Taro Yashima, a little Japanese-American girl is impatient for the rain so she can wear her new red rubber boots and carry her new umbrella to nursery school. At last the rain comes and Momo walks straight like a lady listening to the rhythmic patter of raindrops on her new umbrella.

Peter Spier's Rain by Peter Spier is a wordless book that has been described in Chapter 4. However, there is so much to be discerned by looking at this book that it deserves a second mention. All the dimensions of a rainstorm are included here—children's and animals' reactions, indoor and outdoor fun in the rain. No unit on weather would be complete without sharing it.

Hurricane by David Wiesner captures all of the excitement that two boys feel while waiting out a hurricane in their snug home. When a large elm tree blows down, it becomes a prop for their imaginary play in the days that follow the storm.

Rachel Carson tells us in the sensitive essay that she wrote about her grandnephew, Roger, just a few years before her death: "If a child is to keep alive his inborn sense of wonder. . . he needs the companionship of at least one adult who can share it, rediscovering with him the joy, excitement and mystery of the world we live in."[18]

A mother tells her daughter about all the things they will discover on the seashore *When the Tide Is Low* by Sheila Cole. Virginia Wright-Frierson has painted watery seascapes and accurate pictures of sea animals and shells for this quiet story of a mother and daughter's delightful day. A father shares a very special event in nature with his daughter Jenny in the story by Joanne Ryder *When the Woods Hum*. They watch the 17-year cicadas hatch and begin to fill the woods with their humming. Seventeen years later, Jenny and

[18]Rachel Carson, *The Sense of Wonder*, photographs by Charles Pratt and others (New York: Harper & Row, 1956, 1965), p. 45.

A boy and his Japanese-American father find more on their wilderness trip than just *The Lost Lake;* they find each other. Glowing watercolors by Allen Say portray their journey.

her son return to her father's home and the three of them walk the same path in the woods and listen to the sound of the cicadas. Catherine Stock's distinctive watercolors portray this family's love and respect for one of nature's most fascinating life cycles.

Glowing watercolors by Allen Say portray the wilderness trip that a Japanese-American father and his son take to *The Lost Lake*. The original lost lake that the father remembered had been found by too many people, so the two of them continue looking for another more private lake. At last after an arduous hike they find one. The boy and his father discover more than a lake on this trip; they come to a better understanding of each other, and of the necessity to preserve our natural environment.

Byrd Baylor's long narrative free verse reflects her love and appreciation for the western setting where she makes her home. The sweeping fluid lines of Peter Parnall's pen and ink and paints beautifully illustrate such titles as *Everybody Needs a Rock, Your Own Best Secret Place,* and *The Other Way to Listen*. In *The Way to Start a Day*, Baylor celebrates the way people all over the world have paid their respects to the wonder of each new sunrise. In her words: "You have to make a good day . . . you have to make a good world for the sun to live its one-day life in."[19]

Books are not a substitute for real experiences, but through the sharing of beautiful picture storybooks, teachers can enhance a real experience and keep the wonder of it alive with their own enthusiasm and appreciation for nature.

Animals as People

Ever since the day Peter Rabbit disobeyed his mother and squeezed through Mr. MacGregor's garden fence, children have enjoyed stories in which animals act like people, frequently like small children. In fact, many of these stories would be listed as family stories if you read just the text, since only in the pictures are the characters revealed as animals. Usually the animals are dressed and live in cozy furnished homes, hollow trees, or burrows and face the same problems as their child readers whose lives are mirrored in these stories.

Boys and girls can easily see their own behavior mirrored in *Bedtime for Frances* by Russell Hoban, the story of an engaging badger who finds as many excuses to avoid going to sleep as any 5-year-old child. In *A Baby Sister for Frances*, also by the Hobans, Frances decides that Gloria is receiving entirely too much attention, so she packs her knapsack, says goodbye to her parents, and runs away—under the dining room table. Frances continues to want to be the center of attention, even on Gloria's birthday. *A Birthday for Frances* is uproariously funny as the egocentric badger eats most of her present for her little sister! Frances outmaneuvers Albert and the rest of the boys in *Best Friends for Frances;* but Thelma nearly gets the best of her in an easy-reading book titled *A Bargain for Frances*. Frances is a funny, opinionated badger character that all primary-grade children should have the chance to meet.

The *Little Bear* series by Else Minarik also serves as a surrogate animal family. Maurice Sendak's illustrations are in perfect harmony with the tone of this book. He portrays a large Mother Bear whose Victorian dress and apron provide a very ample lap for Little Bear. When Little Bear decides to go to the moon, his mother joins in the fun of pretending that she is on the moon too, until Little Bear tells her to stop fooling:

🐾 "You are my Mother Bear and I am your Little Bear, and we are on Earth, and you know it. Now may I eat my lunch?"

"Yes," said Mother Bear, "and then you will have your nap. For you are my little bear, and I know it."[20]

Other stories about Little Bear include *Father Bear Comes Home, Little Bear's Friend, Little Bear's Visit,* and *A Kiss for Little Bear.*

Mem Fox's *Koala Lou* is a delightful Australian tale of a little koala bear. When she was first born she was very loved indeed. But then as time passes and more little brothers and sisters arrive, her mother becomes too busy to tell Koala Lou that she loves her. Koala Lou decides to enter the Bush Olympics and be a winner, and then her mother will have to notice her. She enters the tree climbing event and comes in second. When the dejected koala bear finally reaches home, her mother is waiting for her.

🐾 Before she could say a word, her mother had flung her arms around her neck and said, "Koala Lou, I DO love you! I always have, and I always will."[21]

Rosemary Wells creates many lovable animal characters that mirror the behavior of young children. As the middle sister in a mouse family, *Noisy Nora* has to find some unusual way to gain the attention of her parents—and this she does with a flourish. In simple verse and beguiling illustrations, Rosemary Wells has created a very lovable animal character who will gain the attention of every child lucky enough to hear this amusing story. *Shy Charles* is the amusing tale of a shy mouse who doesn't want to take ballet lessons or play football. He just wants to stay home and play by himself. However, in an emer-

[19]Byrd Baylor, *The Way to Start a Day*, illustrated by Peter Parnall (New York: Scribner's, 1978), unpaged.

[20]Else Holmelund Minarik, *Little Bear*, illustrated by Maurice Sendak (New York: Harper & Row, 1957), p. 48.
[21]Mem Fox, *Koala Lou*, illustrated by Pamela Lofts (San Diego: Harcourt Brace, 1988), unpaged.

Koala Lou receives a big hug from her mother when she comes in second in the tree climbing event, and that is all the lovable Australian bear wanted.

From *Koala Lou* by Mem Fox, illustrated by Pamela Lofts.

gency, Charles comes through as a real hero, but still a shy one. Wells is also the creator of *Stanley and Rhoda*, an older brother/sister combination in which Stanley shows he knows all the ploys of handling his toddler sister. Facial expressions and very funny dialogue make these books popular with 5-, 6-, and 7-year olds. Other animal personalities by Wells include child raccoons in *Benjamin and Tulip* and *Timothy Goes to School*.

Another demanding mouse-child is Celestine, who lives with a warm, understanding, avuncular bear named Ernest. In *Ernest and Celestine's Picnic*, a pouty Celestine refuses to be consoled when rain interferes with their planned picnic. The resourceful bear pretends the sun is shining and they have their picnic anyway. In *Feel Better, Ernest*, Celestine gives the bear excellent care and entertainment and he is soon well enough to celebrate his recovery—the two will have another picnic. Further adventures of these lovable two include *Ernest and Celestine; Merry Christmas,*

Ernest and Celestine; Smile, Ernest and Celestine; and others. Translated from the French, the stories derive much of their humor from the delicate expressive watercolors of the author-illustrator, Gabrielle Vincent.

Kevin Henkes is the creator of a remarkable mouse child named Lilly who was the very best until the arrival of her baby brother *Julius, the Baby of the World*. Lilly thinks he is disgusting and hopes he will go away; she hates Julius and the way her parents fawn over him. When no one is looking, Lilly pinches his tail, teaches him his numbers backward, and tells him, "If he was a number, he would be zero." Lilly spends a great deal of time in what her parents call "the uncooperative chair." But then Cousin Garland comes to visit and says Julius is disgusting. Suddenly Lilly has a complete change of heart. Lilly is a real character wearing her queen's crown and red cowboy boots. She was first introduced in *Chester's Way*, a story of the friendship between Chester and Wilson and, finally, Lilly. *Chrysanthemum* is another lively mouse character who thinks her name is "absolutely perfect" until she goes to school and is teased about her long flower name. Mrs. Twinkle, the music teacher, saves the day and restores Chrysanthemum's love for her name. These are real stories with genuinely humorous plots that appeal to adults as well as children. Henke's illustrations are as clever as the text in these wonderful mouse stories.

Jill Murphy created a hilarious story of a poor harried mother elephant named Mrs. Large, who tries to gain *Five Minutes' Peace* in the bathtub where she is joined by her three little ones. In *All in One Piece*, Mr. and Mrs. Large have a dreadful time trying to get ready for the office dinner dance. Finally they manage, but there is a surprise ending that only the children will see. In *A Piece of Cake*, Mrs. Murphy puts the whole elephant family on a fitness program including jogging and dieting. It doesn't work.

The series of stories about a young pig by David McPhail delights young children. In *Pig Pig Grows Up* a very overprotected pig refuses to grow up and act his age. His indulgent mother pushes him in a stroller and falls exhausted to the ground. When the stroller rolls downhill, Pig Pig acts swiftly and averts a crash into a baby buggy. Suddenly Pig Pig has grown up. In *Pig Pig Goes to*

A joyful *Chrysantheum* has her long name vindicated at last by the music teacher Mrs. Twinkle, Mrs. <u>Delphinium</u> Twinkle. Kevin Henkes's illustrations are as full of life as his wonderful stories.

🐛 🐛 🐛

Camp only the pictures reveal what camp is really like for Pig Pig. McPhail has also written a series of imaginative small books about a bear titled *The Bear's Toothache*, *Henry Bear's Park*, and *Stanley, Henry Bear's Friend*. These books have far more text than the Pig Pig series and appeal more to primary children. Stanley and Henry Bear are well worth knowing.

Almost all first graders love the stories of a silly goose, *Petunia*, who thinks she has acquired wisdom when she finds a book. She does not know that it is important to learn to read what is in the book, and as a result gives all kinds of poor advice to her unfortunate friends in the barnyard. Roger Duvoisin also illustrated his wife's many stories about that sophisticated French lion, *The Happy Lion* by Louise Fatio. Another sophisticated French "animality" is Tomi Ungerer's *Crictor*, a most affectionate boa constrictor pet of Madame Bodot, who teaches school in a peaceful French village—peaceful until a burglar breaks into her apartment only to meet Crictor!

Other favorite books about animal personalities include Jean de Brunhoff's *The Story of Babar*, a little elephant who runs away from the jungle and goes to live with an understanding lady in Paris. His cousins, Arthur and Celestine, come to visit and persuade him to return to Africa where his poise and elegant wardrobe are so impressive that he is made King of the Jungle. The Babar stories were continued by Jean de Brunhoff's son, Laurent. The *Curious George* stories by H. A. Rey are also children's favorites. This comical monkey has one escapade after another, but the man in the yellow hat always manages to save him from real danger. When the Primm family move into their apartment in *The House on East 88th Street*, they find Lyle, a performing crocodile, in the bathtub. They become fast friends and live happily together. Several other stories by Bernard Waber including *Lyle, Lyle Crocodile* continue the adventures of Lyle. The preposterous animals of Dr. Seuss need little introduction to children. They love the story of *Horton Hatches the Egg* that tells of the good-natured elephant who helps the ungrateful lazy bird, Mazie, to hatch her egg. The incongruity of a great big elephant sitting on a nest in a tree tickles the funny bone in all of us. Another lovable Seuss animal is *Thidwick, the Big-hearted Moose*, whose generosity nearly costs him his life. These earlier books by Dr. Seuss have more spontaneity and originality than many of his later ones, which were written with a controlled vocabulary and appeared to be following a formula of exaggeration.

First graders faced with the formidable (for some of them) task of learning to read can sympathize with *Leo the Late Bloomer* by Robert Kraus. Leo, a baby tiger, can't do anything right; he can't read, write, or draw; he is a sloppy eater and never talks. His mother assures his father that Leo is a late bloomer. And she is right. Eventually, and in his own good time, Leo blooms! Stunning pictures by José Aruego add much to the humor of this story. The same team has written and illustrated *Owliver* and *Milton the Early Riser*.

Good-Night, Owl! by Pat Hutchins is a brilliant, beautifully designed book. In this story poor owl tries to sleep during the day, but the bees buzz; the crows croak; the starlings chitter; the woodpecker taps his hollow nest—and sleep is impossible. Then, when night falls and there isn't a sound, owl screeches and screeches until everyone is wide awake! Young children will be intrigued by the onomatopoetic text that imitates the sounds of the birds and by the surprise ending.

A common theme for many fanciful animal stories is that of being true to one's own nature. *Dandelion* by Don Freeman is the story of a lion who becomes such a "dandy" in order to go to a party that his hostess does not recognize him and shuts the door in his face! The children do not recognize their own dog in the story of *Harry, the Dirty Dog* by Gene Zion. Harry, once a white dog with black spots, hides his scrub brush and so becomes a black dog with white spots! He digs up his scrub brush and when the children give him a bath, they finally recognize him. Waber's book, *"You Look Ridiculous," Said the Rhinoceros to the Hippopotamus*, is as funny as its title. Each animal the sensitive hippopotamus meets tells her that she looks ridiculous without the distinctive characteristic of his particular species. Even the hippopotamus thinks she looks ridiculous. When she looks at herself in the stream, she laughs so hard that she wakes herself up from her frightening dream and is delighted that she is still herself. Eric Carle's story for younger children, *The Mixed-Up Chameleon*, tells of a chameleon's many wishes when he sees all the animals in the zoo. He becomes so many different things that when a fly goes by, he can't catch it. Then he wants to be a chameleon again. Brilliant colored pictures and cut-out pages help the reader predict what the chameleon's next wish will be.

David McKee's story of *Elmer*, a patchwork-colored elephant who wanted to be gray like all the other elephants, is just the reverse of this theme. However, the other elephants missed the varied-colored clown who made them laugh. In brief, Elmer's true colors were patchwork. This reissued book is one youngsters have thoroughly enjoyed.

Modern Folktale Style

Perhaps Rudyard Kipling started the trend of writing modern folktales. The humor of his pourquoi tales, *Just-So Stories*, is based on his wonderful use of words and his tongue-in-cheek asides to the reader. A favorite with children is the story of the origin of *The Elephant's Child*'s trunk. Originally, his nose was no bigger than a bulgy boot. His "'satiable curtiosity" causes him all kinds of trouble and spankings. To find out what the crocodile has for dinner he departs for the "banks of the great grey-green, greasy Limpopo River, all set about with fever-trees. . . ." Here he meets the crocodile, who whispers in his ear that today he will start his meal with the elephant's child! Then, the crocodile grabs his nose and pulls and pulls. When the poor elephant is free, he has a trunk for a nose.

Some of these stories—such as *The Elephant's Child*, *How the Leopard Got His Spots*, and *How the Rhinoceros Got His Skin*—have been attractively illustrated in single picture-book editions by Lorinda Cauley, Jan Mogensen, and Quentin Blake. The language in these tales deserves to be heard read aloud by an enthusiastic teacher or librarian.

The foot-stomping rhythm of *Crocodile Beat* by Gail Jorgensen captures the sounds of the jungle animals at play down by the river—but then the crocodile wakes up. Brilliant tissue paper collages by Patricia Mullins provide close-ups of these unsuspecting animals.

Tricky Tortoise and *Lazy Lion* by Mwenye Hadithi have the sound and plot of the told tale. Tricky Tortoise, tired of being stepped on by the elephant, tells him his head (which the elephant can't see, of course) is "tiny and stupid." And then by enlisting his look-alike brother, he proves he can jump over the elephant's head. *The Lazy Lion* decides he needs a house for the rainy season, so he demands that the other animals and insects build him one. None of them suit him, so he still stands out on the plains in the sun and the rain. Adrienne Kennaway's stunning watercolors portray the African plains and jungles.

In *Possum Magic*, Grandma Poss makes bush magic. Her best trick is making Hush invisible to protect this little possum from a snake. Hush wants to become visible again and Grandma can't find the right magic. She knows it has something to do with food. So the two set off on what becomes a culinary visit of the cities of Australia to find the proper food. Mem Fox includes a map and glossary of Australian terms so readers will know what vegemite and pavlova are. Julie Vivas's watercolors of these two loving possums are irresistible.

Brian Wildsmith is a better illustrator than a storyteller. Some of his most successful stories, however, are those which have plots that sound like old folktales. *Python's Party* is a beautiful example of double trickery. All the animals are invited to perform tricks at a party. After the pelican shows how many of them he can take into his large bill, the python suggests he can swallow more than that. When he refuses to let the animals out, the elephant steps on his tail and out they all come, far wiser than when they accepted his invitation in the first place. Brilliant expressionistic pictures illustrate the story of *The Owl and the Woodpecker* by Wildsmith. In this tale of a grudge turned into a friendship, the troublesome woodpecker keeps the owl awake all day with his loud drumming, but saves him when Owl's tree blows down in a storm.

Leo Lionni frequently writes modern folktales. His story of *Alexander and the Wind-Up Mouse* includes a purple pebble, a magic lizard, and a transformation. Alexander envies a wind-up mouse, Willie, and wants to become one himself. However, fortunes change and in order to save his friend, Alexander asks the magic lizard to make Willie a real mouse, just like Alexander. In *Frederick* Lionni creates his own version of the fable of the "ant and the grasshopper," only this tale celebrates the contribution of Frederick, a mouse poet. The other mice bring in the harvest for the long winter, but Frederick does not work. He is gathering a harvest of sights and feelings. When the wind is cold and there is no food, Frederick shares his contribution of words and colors with his friends. He makes up poetry about the sun and the flowers and warms their souls. Lionni's statement about the role of an artist in society is direct and to the point.

Wit and humor abound in Arnold Lobel's collection of modern *Fables*, as in the pictures of a pirouetting camel in a tutu, an elephant reading "The Daily Trumpet," and a crocodile in bed admiring the perfect order of the flowers on the wallpaper in preference to the riotous growth of real flowers in the garden. Children love the stories and find the morals funny, too.

Many of William Steig's books use magic or transformations. He won the Caldecott award for his book *Sylvester and the Magic Pebble*. Sylvester is a young donkey who finds a magic red pebble that will grant his every wish. Hurrying home to show it to his family, he meets a lion and foolishly wishes to be a stone. The seasons pass but Sylvester remains a boulder. One day in May his mother and father have a picnic, and by chance use Sylvester's stone as their table! In trying to forget Sylvester, they remember him. Having just found the red pebble, they place it on the stone and Sylvester wishes he were his real self again— and he is!

The Amazing Bone by Steig is a remarkable talking bone that manages to save Pearl, a young pig, from robbers and a fox. In *Doctor DeSoto*, a mouse dentist and his wife use their ingenuity to outwit the fox who had decided to eat them following his dental treatment. Outfoxing a fox did require a special formula, however.

Brave Irene is the very epitome of the folktale heroine as she trudges through wind and snow and ice to deliver the duchess the gown her mother had made for her for the ball. The highly improbable ending just adds to the whole folktale quality of Irene's mission. *Shrek!* is Steig's funny wild version of the hero's quest by the ugliest character in the world. He finds the usual helpers along the way, a witch, a dragon, a dream, a donkey, and more. The text is a mixture of knightly talk, "you there, varlet . . . why so blithe?" and play on words, "Pheasant, peasant? What a pleasant present."[22] Shrek finally gains entrance to the ugly princess's castle and the two are married with the bride carrying a cactus bouquet. In all these tales the language and illustrations portray the tongue-in-cheek humor that we have come to expect from William Steig.

Rhythmic language is the source of the humor for Nancy Van Laan's rollicking tale of *Possum Come A-Knockin'* illustrated with George Booth's cartoon art. Indoors, all kinds of activities are

---

[22]William Steig, *Shrek!* (New York: Farrar, Straus and Giroux, 1990) unpaged.

They could guess what he was dreaming about. Mrs. De Soto handed her husband a pole to keep the fox's mouth open.

In *Doctor DeSoto* by William Steig, a mouse dentist and his wife outfox the fox with their very special treatment.

🐾   🐾   🐾

going on: "Pappy was a-whittlin', Granny was a-rockin', Ma cookin' taters, Sis tossin' Baby, Coon-dawg a-twitchin', Tom-cat a-sniffin'." While outside is just one little old possum having fun.

First told to Ken Kesey by his grandmother, *Little Tricker the Squirrel Meets Big Double the Bear* is a wonderful tall tale of how a sharp little squirrel bamboozles a "double-big-double-hungry grizzly bear." The language is soft and quiet before Big Double roars through the bottomlands:

🐾 It was a fine fall morning, early and cold and sweet as cider. . . . The night shifts and the day shifts were shifting very slow. The crickets hadn't put away their fiddles. The spiders hadn't shook the dew out of their webs yet. The birds hadn't quite woke up and the bats hadn't quite gone to sleep. Nothing

was a-move except one finger of sun slipping soft up the knobby trunk of the hazel.[23]

Tricker challenges the bear to a contest in running, jumping, climbing, *and* flying. And that is the end of Big Double. Moser's larger than life watercolors employ various perspectives and capture the humor of this modern folktale.

Certain contemporary stories provide a modern twist on a well-loved tale and require a previous knowledge of the folktales. Steven Kellogg's retelling and illustrations for *Chicken Little* are very funny indeed. The story starts out with Chicken Little's famous warning that "The sky is falling" after she has been hit on the head by an acorn. Foxy Loxy hears the animals cry for the police and quickly changes his "poultry" truck sign to read "poulice." Thinking his Thanksgiving dinner is safely locked in the truck, he shows the foolish fowls the harmless acorn and tosses it up in the air. It gets caught in Sergeant Hippo Hefty's helicopter, which crashes to the earth, landing on the truck and freeing all the birds while Sergeant Hefty "flattens the fleeing fox." Foxy Loxy is sent to prison and Chicken Little plants the acorn. It grows into a fine tall tree by the side of her house, where her grandchildren come to hear her retell her famous story. Action-packed illustrations accompany this hilarious retelling of the Chicken Little story.

Other books take known characters or the bones of a traditional tale and flesh them out in new and intriguing ways. A spin-off of "Jack and the Beanstalk" is *Jim and the Beanstalk* by Raymond Briggs. In this very funny reshaping of an old tale, the giant gains our sympathy when Jim discovers he needs a new wig, new glasses, and false teeth. After Jim supplies them all, the giant is so revitalized that Jim barely escapes, down the beanstalk, of course. Janet Stevens recasts Andersen's tales, such as *The Emperor's New Clothes*, with outlandishly costumed animals rather than the original human characters; Stephanie Calmenson changes the setting to a school in her funny version of *The Principal's New Clothes*. Children who know the story of the

[23]Ken Kesey, *Little Tricker the Squirrel Meets Big Double the Bear*, illustrated by Barry Moser (New York: Viking Press, 1990), pp. 2–3.

The Frog Prince and his wife are not happy despite the "they lived happily ever after" ending of their tale. The Princess can't stand the way he zaps flies and his croaking snore; he can't stand her nagging. So off he goes to find a witch to turn him back into a frog—she does, with still another surprising ending.

From *The Frog Prince Continued* by Jon Scieszka, illustrated by Steve Johnson.

🍎   🍎   🍎

"Three Little Pigs" are rightly suspicious of the babysitter, Mrs. Wolf, in *Mr. and Mrs. Pig's Evening Out* by Mary Rayner. Boys and girls anticipate the climax of this story way before Garth squeals for help and alerts all of his nine brothers and sisters. In *Garth Pig and the Ice Cream Lady*, Garth is abducted by the sinister Mrs. Wolf in her "Volfswagon" van. The van has engine trouble and Garth escapes just as his siblings cycle into view hot on his trail. In *Mrs. Pig's Bulk Buy* Rayner writes a very funny modern pourquoi story of why little pigs are pink instead of white.

Jon Scieszka's hilarious version of *The True Story of the Three Little Pigs* is told from the wolf's point of view. His explanation is that he just wanted to borrow a cup of sugar to bake a cake for his old granny, when he accidentally sneezed and blew the pigs' houses down. It seemed like a shame to leave a perfectly good warm dinner lying there in the straw. So he eats one pig, and the second one too. He blames the whole bad rap on the reporters and the fact that when the third pig insulted his granny he went berserk. Older students love this retelling, which easily invites them to write from a different point of view. *The Frog Prince Continued*, also by Scieszka, carries on from the traditional ending of "They lived happily ever after" to suggest that this was not so. Actually, they were miserable together. The Princess can't stand the Prince's froggy habits—the way he sticks out his tongue and zaps a fly and his horrible croaking snore. He, in turn, can't stand her nagging, so he goes to find a witch that will turn him back to a frog. On his journey he meets three witches and a fairy godmother. Both the Frog Prince and readers recognize them as coming from the tales of "The Sleeping Beauty," "Snow White," "Hansel and Gretel," and "Cinderella." Finally he returns home to the traditional ending of "They lived happily ever after," except for one minor change. Scieszka shows the intertextuality of stories in this imaginative roundup of well-known fairy tale characters. The pictures by Steve Johnson are a fascinating mix of old and new that will appeal to students ages 8 and up.

One of children's favorite modern retellings involves a roundup of fairy tale characters on the route of *The Jolly Postman* by Janet and Allan Ahlberg. In this rhymed tale, a postman delivers letters that readers may remove from real envelopes (which form the actual page), such as a letter of apology from Goldilocks to the Three Bears, a postcard from Jack to the Giant, and a business letter to the Wolf from The Three Pigs' lawyer representing the firm of Meany, Miny, Mo, and Company. This cleverly designed book synthesizes children's knowledge of folktales besides providing them a model for writing all kinds of letters and making them laugh in the process. (See Chapter 13, "Fooling with Folktales.")

Humorous Picture Storybooks

Young children's humor is simple and obvious. They laugh uproariously at the large comic pictures in *Animals Should Definitely Not Wear Clothing* by the Barretts. The broad humor of a moose tangled up in his trousers, a chicken trying to lay an egg in stretch pants, and opossums wearing their clothes upside down delights both adults and children. The sequel to this book, *Animals Should Definitely Not Act Like People*, while funny, doesn't seem quite as humorous as the first story.

Slapstick and nonsense are the order of the day at the royal party in *May I Bring a Friend?* by Beatrice Schenk de Regniers. A little boy is invited to tea by the king and queen and each time he goes he takes a friend: a giraffe, monkeys, lions, and hippos—not all of whom are very polite. The monkeys swing on the chandeliers; the hippopotamus puts his foot in the cake; the lions roar; and the seal plays "Long Live Apple Pie" on his bugle. Through it all their royal majesties retain their equanimity. The brilliant purple, pink, and yellow illustrations by Beni Montresor resemble stage sets for the passing parade of incongruities. Although Tom Paxton's *Englebert the Elephant* crashes the queen's party, he eventually takes the royal cake. Illustrations by Steven Kellogg are as uproarious as the antics of the guests. These two royal parties would be fun to compare.

Steven Kellogg is a master at drawing utter confusion and slapstick. A bored young girl gives her mother a deadpan account of the class trip to the farm in the hilarious story of *The Day Jimmy's Boa Ate the Wash* by Trinka Noble. The contrast between the girl's reporting of the events and the exuberant illustrations is extreme. The same approach is used in *Jimmy's Boa Bounces Back*, written and illustrated by the same team. The low-key narration is nicely balanced by the action-packed pictures. Kellogg has also produced many books of his own, which are equally funny. The tales of his own Great Dane in *Pinkerton, Behave!*, *A Rose for Pinkerton*, and *Prehistoric Pinkerton* provide the frame for his madcap pictures.

Children also enjoy books about funny weird characters who appear in a series of stories.

Seven- and 8-year-olds find the deadpan humor of Harry Allard's *The Stupids Die* very funny. When the lights go out, the Stupids decide that they have died. When the lights come back on, they think they are in heaven until Grandpa sets them right—"This isn't Heaven—This is Cleveland." Children love to look for the visual jokes in the Stupids' house; for example, the framed picture of beach balls is labeled "The Pyramids" and one of a dog is titled "Fish." *The Stupids Have a Ball* and *The Stupids Step Out* are other titles in this series. James Marshall's lumpy figures seem just right for the Stupid family. Marshall has created his own funny friends in his many stories about *George and Martha*, large hippopotamuses. Each book usually contains about five episodes, which gives the feeling of a chapter book for 6- and 7-year-olds. The two hippo friends continue their antics in *George and Martha Tons of Fun*, *George and Martha Round and Round*, and *George and Martha Back in Town*.

Marc Brown's Arthur stories are equally popular and include a variety of animal characters. Arthur bears the brunt of a good deal of teasing in *Arthur's Nose* and *Arthur's Eyes* (when he must wear glasses). Never very brave, Arthur is seen as very courageous when he goes into a large spooky house on Halloween to find his baby sister in *Arthur's Halloween*. A surprise ending to *Arthur's Valentine* delights children who have to guess the identity of his secret admirer. In *Arthur's April Fool* Arthur gets back at Binky Barnes, the class bully. All these Arthur books satisfy 6- and 7-year-olds' sense of humor and demand for poetic justice.

Another favorite character of children this age is Harry Allard's Miss Nelson, the lovely sweet teacher who cannot make the class behave. In *Miss Nelson Is Missing*, she is replaced by Miss Viola Swamp, who wears a dark black dress and is a witch, the children decide. After one week with Miss Swamp's rules and homework, the children are delighted to welcome Miss Nelson back. At home Miss Nelson takes off her coat and hangs it right next to an ugly black dress. Viola Swamp returns to coach the worst team in the state in *Miss Nelson Has a Field Day*. Readers will be delighted with the coach's ugly black sweatshirt, which reads "Coach and Don't You Forget It."

Children will have to solve the puzzle of how Miss Nelson and her alter ego can be in the same place at the same time.

John Burningham's book *Would You Rather . . .* gives children a choice of ridiculous situations, such as "Would you rather eat spider stew, slug dumplings, mashed worms or drink snail squash?" Other difficult choices include, would it be worse if your dad danced at school or your mom made a fuss in a café? After hearing this story, children enjoy creating their own "Would You Rather" books.

Young children are past masters at exaggeration, so they appreciate the humor of the tall tale. *Could Be Worse!*, Grandpa's laconic comment on anything that ever happened to anyone, is the title of a tale by James Stevenson. One day Grandpa hears Mary Ann asking Louie why Grandpa always says the same thing, and Louie says it is probably because nothing very interesting ever happened to him. The next morning Grandpa tells the children a tall tale that is unsurpassed, and their comment is most predictable: "Could be worse." Stevenson continues his grandpa's epic adventures, recounting what happened to him on *That Terrible Halloween Night* and his memories of all the scary things that could frighten children in *What's Under the Bed?* and the dreadful things that his baby brother did in *Worse Than Willy!* It is hard ever to get the best of Grandpa! Even when Mary Ann and Louie complain about their first day of school, it doesn't compare with his, *That Dreadful Day.* When they tell him how much *We Hate Rain*, he gives them a vivid description of the month it rained when he and his brother were young, or the time they planted *Grandpa's Too-Good Garden.* Stevenson's watercolor and cartoon style illustrations are as funny as his tales. For example, he always pictures young Grandpa and his baby brother Wainey with moustaches. Children can't seem to hear enough of Grandpa's tall tales.

Margaret Mahy writes a rib-tickling cautionary tale in *The Great White Man-Eating Shark.* Norvin has only two talents, acting and swimming. But since Norvin is not handsome the way most actors are, and in fact looks rather like a shark, he takes to swimming like a silver arrow in the bay. But too many people are there, so Norvin combines his two talents, straps a dorsal fin onto his back and has the whole bay to himself. This works very well until a female great white shark develops a special feeling for Norvin. Jonathan Allen's cartoonish pictures are perfect for this funny tale.

Fantasy in Picture Storybooks

The line is blurred between humorous picture stories for children and fanciful ones. Talking beasts and modern spin-offs on folktales are certainly fanciful stories, yet they can be very humorous. However, children appear to make a difference between the make-believe story and the funny one.

Leah Komaiko is the author of *My Perfect Neighborhood* in which a young girl describes her walk down the wackiest street in the world where a horse is out on roller skates, the grownups line up for recess, and all the dogs wave to the cats as they march by. The rhythmical trip and hopping rhymes are accompanied by Barbara Westman's vivid, snazzy street scenes. Children would describe this tale as slightly weird. *Max Makes a Million* by Maira Kalman also fits this description. Max is a dog, a poet, and a dreamer. He keeps dreaming of selling his poems and moving to Paris. But in the meantime, he delights in all the eccentricities he finds in New York such as Mrs. Hoogenschmidt wearing a fish on her head, or Mr. Van Tiegham playing drumsticks on garbage cans, or his good friend and fellow artist, Bruno, who paints invisible pictures. Kalman's New Wave art catches the Day-Glo colors of city life while her text beats out its rhythms. This wacky story, like its sequel, *Ooh La La, Max in Love*, seems more appropriate for New Yorkers and teenagers than for children, however.

John Burningham contrasts daydreams with reality in his two books *Come Away from the Water, Shirley* and *Time to Get Out of the Bath, Shirley.* The first book has been described in this chapter. In the second one, Shirley is taking a bath while her mother weighs herself, cleans the wash bowl, and generally picks up the bathroom, admonishing Shirley most of the time for being so messy. Meanwhile, Shirley in her imagination, shown in richly colored dream pictures, has ridden her duck down the drain and out onto a wider river.

The contrast between Shirley's vivid imagination and her mother's preoccupation with mundane matters is very funny indeed. The endpapers of this book also deserve mention as they combine pipes and sewers with all of Shirley's adventures. Burningham uses this same technique in his wonderful story of *John Patrick Norman McHennessy— The Boy Who Was Always Late*. Every day strange and improbable happenings occur to John to account for his being late, but his teacher never believes him. At the end of the tale when the tables are turned, a very strange and improbable thing happens to his schoolmaster. The pictures of John being attacked by a lion or carried off in a tidal wave are in full color while the school punishments are in black-and-white. This book is a natural to compare with the well-known *And To Think That I Saw It on Mulberry Street* by Dr. Seuss.

Rafe Martin and Stephen Gammell have produced an almost wordless book about *Will's Mammoth*. Will dreams about having a wonderful adventure riding his own mammoth until his mother's call for dinner interrupts his imaginative daydreaming. Wonderful action-filled pictures capture this joyous adventure.

Cassie Louise Lightfoot has a dream to be free, to go anywhere she wants. One night up on *Tar Beach*, the roof top of her family's Harlem apartment building, her dream comes true. Cassie can fly over the city. This magical story was originally written by Faith Ringgold for a story quilt of the same name.

In the story *George Shrinks* by William Joyce, George dreams he is small and wakes to find it is true. He discovers a note from his parents listing his chores. The words of the note become the text of the story; the illustrations show how George deals with each task. He uses a sponge to surf across the dishes as he cleans them. He takes the garbage out by hitching a little red wagon to his crawling baby brother, who is now much larger than George. He has a wonderful time flying in a model airplane until it is knocked down by the cat. Suddenly George is his own size again, with his parents at his side, but as in so many other fantasies, he has the damaged plane to remind him of the adventure and to make readers wonder if maybe it really did happen. The actual book of *George Shrinks* has shrunk and it is now available as a very small book.

Another popular book by Joyce is *Dinosaur Bob and His Adventures with the Family Lazardo*. Bob is discovered while the family is on a safari in Africa. They bring him home by boat and train. Bob can scare off burglars, dance, and play baseball. It is the latter talent that saves the day for the Pimlico Pirates and Bob. In Joyce's *A Day with Wilbur Robinson*, one weird thing after another happens, and they have little or no relationship to each other. Wilbur greets his friend at the door while an octopus takes his bag, Aunt Billie is playing with her life-sized train set, cousin Pete is walking the cats (which are tigers), and Uncle Gaton is sitting in the family cannon—and that's just the beginning. There is no plot, just strange incongruities that will intrigue some children.

Another form of fantasy of young children involves anthropomorphism, or the personification of inanimate objects, such as toys and machines. Most all children know and love Watty Piper's story of *The Little Engine That Could*, . . . and did get the toys over the mountain and Hardie Gramatky's story of *Little Toot*. Most of the books written by Virginia Lee Burton contain personification: *Katie and the Big Snow*, *The Little House*, and *Mike Mulligan and His Steam Shovel*. The modern problem of obsolescence is solved easily in the story of Mike and his beloved steam shovel, Mary Ann. After proving that Mary Ann could dig a basement for the new town hall in a day, Mike is forced to convert her into a furnace, since he has neglected to plan a way for Mary Ann to get out of the excavation. Katie is a snowplow who saves the day by plowing out a whole village. The encroachment of the city on the country is portrayed in Burton's classic story of *The Little House* that stood on the hill and watched day and night and the seasons pass. Gradually, a road is built, cars come, and soon the city grows up around the little house. Elevated cars speed by her; subway trains speed under her; and people rush to and fro in front of her. One day the great-great-granddaughter of the original owner sees the little house, buys her, and has her moved back to the country where she can once again see the stars.

Several picture books personify toys and dolls. All primary children love the story of the little wistful teddy bear named *Corduroy* for his green corduroy overalls. Corduroy waits patiently in the department store for someone to buy him. A little African-American girl, Lisa, sees him and wants him but her mother discourages her by pointing out that he doesn't look new and that one of the buttons on his shoulder straps is missing. Corduroy has many exciting adventures in the store as he goes in search of a new button. He doesn't find one, but the next morning he does find what he has wanted most—a home and a friend, for Lisa returns with the contents of her piggy bank and buys him. This book by Don Freeman is a completely satisfying story containing pathos, love, and excitement. The sequel to this story is *A Pocket for Corduroy*.

Pam Conrad tells the story of seven wooden toys, *The Tub People*, including a father, mother, grandmother, boy, dog, doctor, and policeman. Perhaps more than any other picture book, this shows the helplessness of dolls. For one day the little boy is sucked down the drain and the tub people no longer smile or wink at each other. When the plumber finally finds him, the tub people are all removed to a shelf in a bedroom. They line up the same way they always had on the edge of the tub, but each morning the little boy person is found between his parents, their sides barely touching. Richard Egielski's detailed watercolors show the tub people as rounded wooden dolls with the same expressions—or are they? While the separation and loss theme may be disturbing to very young children, 7- and 8-year olds see it as an adventure.

There are many editions of Margery Williams's sentimental classic tale of *The Velveteen Rabbit or How Toys Become Real*. The most attractive ones are those by Michael Hague, Ilse Plume, or David Jorgensen. Any child who has loved a stuffed animal of his own will understand the conversation between the old skin horse and the velveteen rabbit on the subject of becoming real. The skin horse tells the rabbit, "Real isn't how you are inside . . . It's a thing that happens to you when a child loves you for a long long while." When the rabbit asks how it happens, he replies. "It doesn't happen all at once . . . you become. It takes a long while."[24]

Today there are more stories about monsters than there are about toys and dolls. Baby monsters can be very lovable if *Clyde Monster* by Robert Crowe is an example. In a reversal of roles, Clyde is afraid to go to bed because people might be hiding in his cave to get him. His parents assure him that people and monsters came to an agreement years ago not to scare each other. Clyde is not completely convinced, for as he goes to bed he asks that they leave "the rock open just a little." In Mercer Mayer's well-loved story, *There's a Nightmare in My Closet*, a small boy ends up by comforting a monster who has a nightmare. In fact, the ugly yet lovable creature climbs into bed with him.

Sibling rivalry is the theme of *The Very Worst Monster* by Pat Hutchins. When Billy monster was born, his father said he would grow up to be "the very worst monster in the world." But Billy's sister Hazel intended to do that. Every time Billy did something awful, Hazel did something even more monstrous—but no one noticed. Then Hazel did something that did catch their attention—she gave her baby brother away, thereby achieving her goal. In *Where's the Baby?*, mother monster, grandmother monster, and Hazel, his sister monster, all search for the baby. All they can find are clues of where he had been by the monstrous messes he left. At last they find him safe in bed—but not for long. Grandmother's delight in all his naughty doings is very funny. Hutchins's green-colored monsters live in very cozy well-furnished houses.

In *Do Not Open*, Brinton Turkle bottled up one of the biggest, nastiest monsters in the world. Miss Moody read the label but she heard a small child's voice inside begging to be let out. The monster tried to scare her by getting bigger and bigger. She then informed him she was only frightened of mice and so of course he became a mouse, which her cat ate. This is an old folktale trick, but Turkle has made it seem new again in this surprising picture book.

Tog the Ribber; or Granny's Tale by Paul Coltman is deliciously spooky. The text is a long narrative poem by a British poet who uses nonsense words similar to those in Lewis Carroll's "Jabberwocky." His daughter has transformed it into a picture book with eerie yet beautiful full-color pictures. In the story Granny explains "Why her

[24]Margery Williams, *The Velveteen Rabbit*, illustrated by William Nicholson (New York: Doubleday, 1922), p. 17.

By placing the viewer above Santa and his reindeer, Chris Van Allsburg creates a feeling of enormous depth and distance in his well-loved book *The Polar Express*.

🐞   🐞   🐞

hair is white/And . . . why she don't speak right" by recounting an episode from her childhood. One night as she was coming home alone she was pursued by the ghostly bones of Tog the Ribber:

> 🐞 . . . Tog hobbed clitter clotter after.
> And still he come. I heard his snork.
> He snorked green breath upon my nick.[25]

The illustrations are filled with menacing shapes of insects, worms, spiders, snakes, owls, bones, disembodied faces all spilling out of the misty pages. It is with great relief that Granny ends her nightmarish tale safe in her "cosly bed." This is a story that begs to be read aloud or told.

Chris Van Allsburg is certainly the best known creator of fantasy in children's picture storybooks. *Jumanji* has been discussed previously. *The Garden of Abdul Gasazi* was Van Allsburg's first book. Children are intrigued with the stark black-and-white pictures portraying the strange garden and huge house of the magician. The puzzling ending of the story gives them much to discuss. *Two Bad Ants* provides a useful perspective on another

point of view. The ending for *The Wreck of the Zephyr* is another of Van Allsburg's puzzles. Superb full-color pictures illustrate this fantasy of the one time a boat could fly. The identity of *The Stranger* (who may be a relative of Jack Frost) is never fully revealed in this mysterious tale; *The Polar Express* by Van Allsburg is a haunting Christmas story for all children and for those who remain children at heart. It is the tale of a boy who on Christmas Eve boards a mysterious train filled with children, bound for the North Pole. When he arrives a large imposing Santa Claus offers him any gift he wants. The boy modestly chooses to ask for one of the silver bells from the reindeer's harness. On the way home he loses the bell; yet on Christmas morning there it is in a small box under the tree. The boy and his sister can each hear its sound but his parents cannot. Years later the boy, now a grown man, can still hear its silver tone. Changing perspectives from inside the train to outside the train, from floor level to an aerial view from Santa's sleigh create movement and add to the breathtaking quality of these pictures. The interplay of light and dark in these full-color pictures helps to create the memory of a child's dream of a snow-shrouded world. Yet the sound of the bell remains for those who

[25]Paul Coltman, *Tog the Ribber*, illustrated by Gillian McClure (New York: Farrar, Straus and Giroux, 1985), unpaged.

truly believe in Christmas. This picture storybook richly deserved the Caldecott award it received. In *Just a Dream* Van Allsburg predicts the kind of future we are going to have if we keep polluting the earth. Unfortunately, his message becomes too heavy-handed. However, children working on a unit on the environment might discuss Van Allsburg's vision of the future. *The Wretched Stone* is another message book that suggests the evils of watching television. Sailors find a glowing stone, which mesmerizes them. They refuse to work and, when the captain goes to the hold, he finds that they have all become monkeys. A storm at sea blacks out the stone at the same time the boat loses both mast and rudder. While awaiting rescue, the captain reads to his crew and they gradually become human beings again. This book could lead to a lively discussion of the seductive influence of television or computer games.

Appreciating Cultural Diversity

American children of the twenty-first century need to develop a worldview that appreciates the

Ted Lewin's photo-realistic pictures of the sights and sounds of Cairo provide the setting for the poignant story of *The Day of Ahmed's Secret,* the day this boy of about 10 or 11 first writes his name.

Written by Florence Parry Heide and Judith Heide Gilliland.

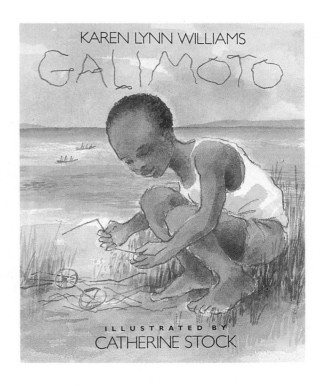

Karen Williams tells the story of Kondi, a resourceful 7-year-old from Malawi, Africa, who is determined to make his own *Galimoto,* a toy made of wire. Vibrant watercolors by Catherine Stock reflect the artist's weeks spent sketching in Malawi.

richness of other cultures at the same time that we preserve and celebrate our uniqueness. In this text we have integrated multi-racial and ethnic stories throughout chapters just as we would hope they would be used. A global view requires books about other cultures and countries that children may not be able to visit. Fortunately, we have an increasing number of titles of both nonfiction and fiction that will introduce children to others who share this earth.

Galimoto is a name of a popular toy car that boys in Malawi, Africa, make out of scraps of wire. In Karen Williams's story, Kondi, a resourceful 7-year-old boy, is determined to make one. He persists in finding enough wire and finally constructs what looks like a pickup truck from scraps and bits he has scavenged from various places. Vibrant watercolors by Catherine Stock portray this ingenious young boy and reflect her weeks spent sketching in Malawi.

In Cairo, Egypt, Ahmed, a young *butagaz* boy, must deliver his bottles of cooking fuel all over the city. As he makes his daily rounds through sun-bleached streets and daily market stalls, Ahmed hugs a special secret to his heart. Home, at last, he can finally show his newly acquired skill to his family: Ahmed has learned how to write his name. Ted Lewin's photo-realistic watercolors capture the sounds and sights of the mixture of ancient and modern city that is Cairo. Florence Parry Heide and Judith Heide Gilliland wrote this story of *The Day of Ahmed's Secret*.

Ann Grifalconi wrote and illustrated the tale of *Osa's Pride* with brilliant pastels on variously colored papers. Osa is proud, just a little too proud, to make friends with the rest of the children in her Cameroon village. Her grandmother tells her a story about another proud girl using her storytelling cloth. As her grandmother unrolls the scenes, Osa learns as much about herself as the girl in the story. In *Darkness and the Butterfly*, the Wise Woman helps Osa learn to overcome her fear of the dark. Grifalconi is also the author-illustrator of the well-known story of *The Village of Round and Square Houses*. Her illustrations glow with the beauty of the African world and the affection of a nurturing family.

A mother shares stories of her growing up in Jamaica with her little daughter, Rose, in *The Chalk Doll* by Charlotte Pomerantz. She describes the wonderful fun she had playing with the things she made such as her rag doll, high heels made from dipping dried mango pits into sticky tar, and the day she made a cake. Rose in her rich American environment feels deprived, because while she has had many chalk dolls, she has never had a rag doll. And so together they make one. Frané Lessac's brightly colored primitive paintings show the contrast between Rose's childhood and her mother's.

In *Sayonara, Mrs. Kackleman* Maira Kalman perfectly captures the way a child might see Japan. As Lulu and her younger brother make their madcap journey to Japan they do observe many things such as the politeness of people on the clean subway trains or the speed of the bullet train that "gets you back before you left." This fast-paced travelogue is told from a child's point of view, which makes it much fun. Kalman also wrote the equally irreverent but delightful *Hey Willy, See the Pyramids*. Kalman's New Wave art imaginatively reflects the childlike point of view of her stories.

Riki Levinson has told a more serious story of the families who live on the boats in Hong Kong harbor in *Our Home Is the Sea*. The boy journeys from his school through the bustling city down to his family's houseboat. He can't wait for the day when he too will be a fisherman. Dennis Luzak's handsome oil paintings portray the huge gray city of Hong Kong and the boat the boy calls home. Eve Bunting has written a moving story of the flight of a Cuban family to America in their very small boat. These people are pilgrims in their search for freedom so Bunting titled her story *How Many Days to America? A Thanksgiving Story*.

Chicken Man by Michelle Edwards describes the rotation of work that is characteristic of some of the kibbutzim in Israel. The chicken man, Rody, is so happy doing his work that everyone wants his job. But then Rody is cheerful about ironing and gardening. Finally when the chickens stop laying, Rody is assigned to work permanently in the chicken house and he couldn't be happier. A map of Kibbutz Hanan gives children a picture of the size of this community and the way the kibbutzniks live. The joy the chicken man takes in all his jobs is worthy of discussion.

In the *Very Last First Time*, Jan Andrews gives us a picture of life in the Inuit village of Ungava Bay in northern Canada. This is a special day for Eva Padlyat, for she is going to go alone below the sea ice and gather mussels. Eva is so intrigued with all she sees that she nearly doesn't make it back up before the tide comes in again. When she is at last safe with her mother, she says, "That was my very last *first* time for walking alone on the bottom of the sea." Ian Wallace's full-color illustrations picture an Inuit family in their modern-day kitchen but still gathering food in the traditional manner.

Rachel Isadora tells of a joyful reunion in *At the Crossroads*. A young boy tells how he, his brother and sister, and friends wait all day and all night for their fathers to come home after 10 months of working in the mines in South Africa. Underneath their anticipation and joy is the terrible injustice of apartheid that keeps families separated for such a long period of time. Glowing double-page watercolors contrast the swirling colors of the children's clothing and the red of the sun with the somber grayness of the corrugated iron shacks that the children call home. These impressionistic pictures vividly portray the landscapes and people of South Africa as Rachel Isadora saw them on her visit there. This simple story of joy reveals the cruelty of prejudice in a way that could be discussed with children of all ages.

Nigel Gray contrasts the story of two children, one black, one white, who wake, sleep, play, eat, and share in family life on opposite sides of the globe. The fascinating contrast between an African boy in his village and a Western child in his suburb is made clear by Phillippe Dupasquier's detailed illustrations for *A Country Far Away*. This story could lead to much discussion of the contrast between wealthy Western countries and those of the third world. Children need to develop a world vision at an early age.

Social and Environmental Concerns

As more and more picture storybooks are written for older children, more are dealing with major social and environmental concerns.

Eve Bunting's moving story of *Fly Away Home* tells of a homeless boy and his father who live in a large airport moving from terminal to terminal and trying never to be noticed. A trapped bird who finally manages to fly free becomes the boy's metaphor for hope. Ronald Himler's watercolors are as understated and honest as this story. In *Uncle Willie and the Soup Kitchen* by DyAnne DiSalvo-Ryan, a young boy goes with his uncle who volunteers at a soup kitchen. They stop and pick up chickens at the butcher shop; then the boy meets the other volunteers and helps set tables for "the guests" as Uncle Willie calls them. They serve 121 people for lunch. Uncle Willie is a wonderful model as he stands at the door and greets them, kids the other workers, and shares his zest for living. This warm sensitive story and pictures were inspired by the author's own experience as a soup kitchen volunteer.

Todd's grandfather has to sell his farm at *The Auction*, a story by Jan Andrews. Both of them recall happier days when his grandmother was living and the farm was thriving. Remembering the different kind of scarecrows she used to make, they cheer themselves up by making straw people for the combine and rocking chair. Yet both are dreading the inevitable auction the next day.

Alice and Martin Provensen describe the people and the shacks they lived in alongside *Shaker Lane*. Yet these people formed a community of their own until the new reservoir was built and flooded it forever. What was left of Shaker Lane became Reservoir Road with beautiful suburban homes and swimming pools. The Provensens have provided a sharply observed commentary on changing American society. Ann Turner's *Heron Street* provides a tale of so-called progress from wilderness to the arrival of settlers, the Revolutionary War, coming of houses, gaslights, cars, trolleys, and airplanes. One night a heron circles a house and flies higher and higher, "its legs like a long, thin good-bye." Lisa Desimini's jewel-like paintings perfectly complement this progression of change. Jennie Baker's collage pictures for *Where the Forest Meets the Sea* combine both the past and the future. As the young boy explores the forest, shadows of dinosaurs can be seen in the trees; and on the last page, shadows of a future Star Hotel, skyscrapers, homes, and swimming pools are superimposed on the picture of the beach and bay. *Window*, also by Jennie Baker, is a wordless book that depicts the view from a boy's window changing from wilderness, to country, to small town, to city. The boy, now 25 and with a baby of his own, looks through a window in his new house in the country and sees an ominous sign advertising "House blocks for sale," suggesting the whole destructive cycle will continue. Other books previously discussed, such as Van Allsburg's *Just a Dream* and Allen Say's *The Lost Lake*, also have an environmental theme.

War and Its Aftermath

My Hiroshima by Junko Morimoto describes Junko's life before the war and immediately after the atomic bomb fell. She was the youngest in a family of four children. Miraculously they all escaped being killed. Pictures and photographs of the events in which 70,000 persons died instantly and another 70,000 by the end of the first year are devastating. This story is not as moving, however, as that told by Toshi Maruki in *Hiroshima No Pika*, which means the flash of Hiroshima. Seven-year-old Mii and her family are calmly eating their breakfast of sweet potatoes on August 6, 1945, at 8:15 A.M. when the flash occurs. Mii's mother carries her wounded father to the river. There they all sleep for four days. Mii's father recovers, only to die later from radiation exposure. Mii herself never grows in mind or body beyond her seven years. The expressionistic pictures of the fires, the thunder and lightning, and the wounded and dying all create the horror of an atomic attack. Yet the book was written in the hope it would never happen again. In the afterword of this picture book the author-illustrator writes:

> I am now past seventy years old. I have neither children nor grandchildren. But I have written this book for grandchildren everywhere. It took me a very long time to complete it. It is very difficult to tell young people about something very bad that happened, in the hope that their knowing will help keep it from happening again.[26]

This, of course, is the reason teachers should share this book. For somehow when pain is particularized for a specific family it becomes more real and immediate than when it is depersonalized into mass numbers who were killed that day.

The kindness of one child who cared and provided food for children in a concentration camp is told in the moving story of *Rose Blanche* by Christophe Gallaz and Roberto Innocenti. Illustrated with paintings of almost photographic clarity, this picture book is certainly for older children. The courage of Rose Blanche and all persons who in their small ways try to maintain humanity in the midst of inhumanity is something that needs to be discussed with older children.

A little boy and his father visit the Vietnam Memorial in Washington, D.C., and find the name of his grandfather on *The Wall*. Eve Bunting tells this poignant story while Ronald Himler creates stark watercolor pictures for it. The pain the boy's father feels is contrasted with the young

[26]Toshi Maruki, *Hiroshima No Pika* (New York: Lothrop, Lee and Shepard, 1980), unpaged.

child's comments. His father tells him he is proud that his grandfather's name is on this wall. The boy replies:

> "I am, too."
> I am.
>   But I'd rather have my grandpa here,
> taking me to the river, telling me to button
> up my jacket because it's cold.
>   I'd rather have him here.[27]

Picture storybooks are for all ages and they can be about all subjects. They can enlarge children's lives, stretch their imaginations, increase their sensitivity, and enhance their living. The phenomenal growth of beautiful picture storybooks for children of all ages is an outstanding accomplishment of the past fifty years of publishing. Children do not always recognize the beauty of these books, but early impressions do exert an influence on the development of permanent tastes for children growing up.

[27]Eve Bunting, *The Wall*, illustrated by Ronald Himler (New York: Clarion Books, 1990), unpaged.

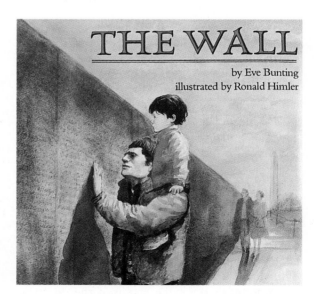

Eve Bunting tells the poignant story of a little boy and his father visiting the Vietnam Memorial to find his grandfather's name. Ronald Himler's stark blue-gray watercolors perfectly complement this moving story.

From *The Wall* by Eve Bunting.

SUGGESTED LEARNING EXPERIENCES

1. Look closely at three or more picture storybooks to discover how the illustrations carry the storys' meaning beyond the words. Note the effect of the artist's choice of medium, style, and color; look for content details present in the pictures but not in the text.
2. Study the work of one Caldecott award-winning illustrator. What medium does this artist use? What terms would you use to describe the style? How do earlier books compare to the most recent ones? Read his or her acceptance speech for the Caldecott. How has the illustrator's style been influenced by his or her concepts of childhood?
3. Form a mock Caldecott award committee and review the Honor Books and award-winning book for one specific year. Would you have made the same decision as the ALA committee? Why or why not?
4. Find three or four books that are examples of the use of one medium—such as scratchboard or collage. Experiment with the materials used in this medium to make a picture of your own.
5. Find examples of picture storybooks that you think might increase children's sensitivity to well-used language. Look for vivid descriptions, repetition of unusual words or phrases, figures of speech within the child's experience.
6. Select a group of stories based on a single subject or theme, such as stories about grandparents, "Be yourself" themes, or environmental concerns. Discuss which ones you would use to introduce a unit, which you would read aloud as a teacher, which would be appropriate for children's reading.
7. Collect stories written by one author such as Mem Fox, Eve Bunting, or Cynthia Rylant, but illustrated by different artists. How does the artist's vision affect the mood of the story?
8. If possible read several stories to a group of children over a period of weeks. Select different kinds of stories: humorous, folktale style, or nostalgic stories recalling the past. What are children's responses to these books? What do they single out to comment on? Record their comments and share with your children's literature class. What conclusions can you draw?

RELATED READINGS

1. Brown, Marcia, *Lotus Seeds: Children's Pictures and Books*. New York: Scribner's, 1986.
   A noted illustrator writes eloquently on picture books, the hero within, publishing, and her own work. Her three Caldecott acceptance speeches are included among these thought-provoking essays.
2. Cianciolo, Patricia. *Picture Books for Children*, 3rd ed. Chicago: American Library Association, 1990.
   A thorough discussion of the art of picture books with an annotated listing of all kinds of picture books for children. Particular attention is given to the media and style of illustrating for each entry as well as ethnic and racial background of the characters in the stories.
3. Kiefer, Barbara. "The Responses of Children in a Combination First/Second Grade Classroom to Picture Books in a Variety of Artistic Styles," *Journal of Research and Development in Education*, vol. 16, no. 3, 1983, pp. 14–20.
   A report on a 10-week study in the classroom of 7- and 8-year-olds' responses to picture books. Emphasis was placed on how the children's responses to books changed over time and the importance of the classroom context in fostering response.
4. Lacy, Lyn Ellen. *Art and Design in Children's Picture Books: An Analysis of Caldecott Award Winning Illustrations*. Chicago: American Library Association, 1986.
   An intelligent review of the art of over four dozen illustrators who have won the Caldecott Medal. The author also provides real help in ways to understand pictures and the way they create meaning.
5. Kingman, Lee, ed. *Newbery and Caldecott Medal Books: 1956–1965*. Boston: Horn Book, 1965.
   _____. *Newbery and Caldecott Medal Books 1966–1975*. Boston: Horn Book, 1975.
   _____. *Newbery and Caldecott Medal Books: 1976–1985*. Boston: Horn Book, 1985.

These volumes contain the acceptance speeches and biographies of the Newbery and Caldecott winners reprinted from the August issue of *The Horn Book Magazine*. In the most recent volume, Barbara Bader gives a very critical review of the committee's choices. She far prefers some of the Honor Books over the award winners and tells you why.

6. Martin, Douglas. *The Telling Line*. New York: Delacorte Press, 1989.

    Contains thoughtful essays on fifteen contemporary British illustrators. Based on interviews the author had with all of them, he quotes them regularly. Illustrated in color and black-and-white, this text makes a fine contribution to the story of twentieth-century illustration.

7. Nodelman, Perry. *Words About Pictures: The Narrative Art of Children's Picture Books*. Athens: University of Georgia Press, 1988.

    Nodelman explores the various means by which pictures tell stories. These elements include design, style, code, tension, action, irony, and rhythm. Nodelman draws on a number of aesthetic and literary theorists in his discussions. A significant book, unfortunately it contains few pictures.

8. Schwarcz, Joseph H., and Chava Schwarcz. *The Picture Book Comes of Age*. Chicago: American Library Association, 1991.

    A remarkable book that reveals knowledge of the creative process, children, artistic and literary expertise, and books from several different countries. A professor at the University of Haifa, Joseph Schwarcz taught children's literature for many years before his death in 1988.

REFERENCES

Aardema, Verna. *Bringing The Rain to Kapiti Plain*, illustrated by Beatriz Vidal. Dial, 1981.

Ackerman, Karen. *Song and Dance Man*, illustrated by Stephen Gammell. Knopf, 1988.

Adoff, Arnold. *Hard to Be Six*, illustrated by Cheryl Hanna. Lothrop, 1991.

Ahlberg, Janet, and Allan Ahlberg. *The Jolly Postman*. Little, 1986.

Albert, Burton, *Where Does the Trail Lead?*, illustrated by Brian Pinkney. Simon & Schuster, 1991.

Alexander, Martha. *Nobody Asked Me if I Wanted a Baby Sister*. Dial, 1971.

_____. *When the New Baby Comes, I'm Moving Out*. Dial, 1979.

Aliki, pseud. (Aliki Brandenberg). *Feelings*. Greenwillow, 1984.

_____. *My Feet*. Crowell, 1990.

_____. *My Hands*. Crowell, 1990.

_____. *The Two of Them*. Greenwillow, 1979.

Allard, Harry, and James Marshall. *Miss Nelson Has a Field Day*, illustrated by James Marshall. Houghton Mifflin, 1985.

_____. *Miss Nelson Is Missing*, illustrated by James Marshall. Houghton Mifflin, 1977.

_____. *The Stupids Die*, illustrated by James Marshall. Houghton Mifflin, 1981.

_____. *The Stupids Have a Ball*, illustrated by James Marshall. Houghton Mifflin, 1977.

_____. *The Stupids Step Out*, illustrated by James Marshall. Houghton Mifflin, 1978.

Allinson, Beverly, *Effie*, illustrated by Barbara Reid. Scholastic, 1991.

Andrews, Jan. *The Auction*, illustrated by Karen Reczuch. Macmillian, 1991.

_____. *Very Last First Time*, illustrated by Ian Wallace. McElderry, 1985.

Ardizzone, Edward. *Little Tim and the Brave Sea Captain*. Penguin, 1983.

Baker, Jennie. *Where the Forest Meets the Sea*. Greenwillow, 1987.

_____. *Window*. Greenwillow, 1991.

Baker, Olaf. *Where the Buffaloes Begin*, illustrated by Stephen Gammell. Warne, 1981.

Bang, Molly. *The Grey Lady and the Strawberry Snatcher*. Four Winds, 1980.

_____. *The Paper Crane*. Greenwillow, 1985.

Barrett, Judi. *Animals Should Definitely Not Act Like People*, illustrated by Ron Barrett. Atheneum, 1980.

_____. *Animals Should Definitely Not Wear Clothing*, illustrated by Ron Barrett. Atheneum, 1970.

Baylor, Byrd. *Everybody Needs a Rock*, illustrated by Peter Parnall. Scribner's, 1974.

_____. *The Other Way to Listen*, illustrated by Peter Parnall. Scribner's, 1978.

_____. *The Way to Start a Day*, illustrated by Peter Parnall. Scribner's, 1978.

_____. *Your Own Best Secret Place*, illustrated by Peter Parnall. Scribner's, 1979.

Bemelmans, Ludwig. *Madeline*. Viking, 1962 (1939).

Blos, Joan. *Old Henry*, illustrated by Stephen Gammell. Morrow, 1987.

Brandenberg, Franz. *Aunt Nina, Good Night*, illustrated by Aliki. Greenwillow, 1989.

Briggs, Raymond. *Jim and the Beanstalk*. Coward-McCann, 1970.

Brott, Ardyth. *Jeremy's Decision*, illustrated by Michael Martchenko. Kane/Miller, 1990.

Brown, Marc. *Arthur's April Fool*. Little, 1983.

_____. *Arthur's Eyes*. Little, 1979.

_____. *Arthur's Halloween*. Little, 1983.

_____. *Arthur's Nose*. Little, 1976.

_____. *Arthur's Valentine*. Little, 1980.

Brown, Marcia. *All Butterflies*. Scribner's, 1974.

_____. *Once a Mouse*. Scribner's, 1961.

Brown, Margaret Wise. *Goodnight Moon*, illustrated by Clement Hurd, Harper, 1975 (1947).

Browne, Anthony. *Changes*. Knopf, 1991.

_____. *The Piggybook*. Knopf, 1986.

_____. *The Tunnel*. Knopf, 1990.

Buchanan, Ken. *This House Is Made of Mud*, illustrated by Libba Tracy. Northland, 1991.

Bunting, Eve. *Fly Away Home*, illustrated by Ronald Himler. Clarion, 1991.

_____. *How Many Days to America? A Thanksgiving Story*, illustrated by Beth Peck. Houghton Mifflin, 1988.

_____. *The Wall*, illustrated by Ronald Himler. Clarion, 1990.

_____. *The Wednesday Surprise*, illustrated by Donald Carrick. Clarion, 1989.

Burningham, John. *Come Away from the Water, Shirley*. Harper, 1977.

_____. *Granpa*. Crown, 1985.

_____. *John Patrick Norman McHennessy—The Boy Who Was Always Late*. Crown, 1987.

_____. *Mr. Gumpy's Motor Car*. Harper, 1976.

_____. *Mr. Gumpy's Outing*. Holt, 1971.

_____. *Time to Get Out of the Bath, Shirley*. Harper, 1978.

_____. *Would You Rather* . . . Harper, 1978.

Burton, Virginia Lee. *Katie and the Big Snow*. Houghton Mifflin, 1943.

_____. *The Little House*. Houghton Mifflin, 1942

_____. *Mike Mulligan and His Steam Shovel*. Houghton Mifflin, 1939.

Butler, Stephen. *Henny Penny*. Tambourine, 1991.

Caines, Jeanette. *Daddy*, illustrated by Ronald Himler. Harper, 1977.

_____. *Just Us Women*, illustrated by Pat Cummings. Harper, 1982.

Calmenson, Stephanie. *The Principal's New Clothes*, illustrated by Denise Brunkus. Scholastic, 1989.

Carle, Eric. *The Mixed-Up Chameleon*, 2nd ed. Harper, 1984.

_____. *The Very Busy Spider*. Philomel, 1984.

_____. *The Very Hungry Caterpillar*. World, 1968.

_____. *The Very Quiet Cricket*. Philomel, 1990.

Carlstrom, Nancy White. *Blow Me a Kiss, Miss Lily*, illustrated by Amy Schwartz. Harper, 1990.

Carrick, Carol. *The Accident*, illustrated by Donald Carrick. Clarion, 1976.

_____. *The Foundling*, illustrated by Donald Carrick. Clarion, 1977.

_____. *In the Moonlight, Waiting*, illustrated by Donald Carrick. Clarion, 1990.

Caudill, Rebecca. *A Pocketful of Cricket*, illustrated by Evaline Ness. Holt, 1964.

Cendrars, Blaise. *Shadow*, illustrated by Marcia Brown. Scribner's, 1982.

Clark, Ann Nolan. *In My Mother's House*, illustrated by Velino Herrera. Viking, 1991 (1941).

Clément, Claude. *The Painter and the Wild Swans*, illustrated by Frédéric Clément. Dial, 1986.

Cohen, Miriam. *Best Friends*, illustrated by Lillian Hoban. Macmillan, 1971.

_____. *It's George!*, illustrated by Lillian Hoban. Greenwillow, 1988.

_____. *Lost in the Museum*, illustrated by Lillian Hoban. Greenwillow. 1979.

_____. *The New Teacher*, illustrated by Lillian Hoban. Macmillan, 1972.
_____. *When Will I Read?*, illustrated by Lillian Hoban. Greenwillow, 1977.
_____. *Will I Have a Friend?*, illustrated by Lillian Hoban. Macmillan, 1967.
Cole, Sheila. *When the Tide Is Low*, illustrated by Virginia Wright-Frierson. Lothrop, 1985.
Coltman, Paul. *Tog the Ribber; or Granny's Tale*, illustrated by Gillian McClure. Farrar, Straus, 1985.
Conrad, Pam. *The Tub People*, illustrated by Richard Egielski. Harper, 1989.
Cooney, Barbara. *Chanticleer and the Fox*. Crowell, 1958.
_____. *Hattie and the Wild Waves*. Viking, 1990.
_____. *Island Boy*. Viking, 1988.
_____. *Miss Rumphius*. Viking, 1982.
Crowe, Robert. *Clyde Monster*, illustrated by Kay Chorao. Dutton, 1976.
de Brunhoff, Jean. *The Story of Babar*. Random House, 1960.
de Paola, Tomie. *Nana Upstairs, Nana Downstairs*. Penguin, 1978.
_____. *Now One Foot, Now the Other*. Putnam, 1981.
_____. *Strega Nona*. Prentice-Hall, 1975.
_____. *Tomie de Paola's Mother Goose*. Putnam, 1985.
_____. *Watch Out for the Chicken Feet in Your Soup*. Prentice-Hall, 1974.
de Regniers, Beatrice Schenk. *May I Bring a Friend?*, illustrated by Beni Montresor. Atheneum, 1964.
DiSalvo-Ryan, DyAnne. *Uncle Willie and the Soup Kitchen*. Morrow, 1991.
Dorros, Arthur. *Abuela*, illustrated by Elisa Kleven. Dutton, 1991.
Duvoisin, Roger. *Petunia*. Knopf, 1950.
Edwards, Michelle. *Chicken Man*. Lothrop, 1991.
Ehlert, Lois. *Fish Eyes*. Harcourt, 1990.
Emberly, Barbara. *Drummer Hoff*, illustrated by Ed Emberley. Prentice-Hall, 1967.
Ets, Marie Hall, and Aurora Labastida. *Nine Days to Christmas*, illustrated by Marie Hall Ets. Viking, 1959.
Fatio, Louise. *The Happy Lion*, illustrated by Roger Duvoisin. McGraw-Hill, 1954.
Flournoy, Valerie. *The Patchwork Quilt*, illustrated by Jerry Pinkney. Dial, 1985.
Fox, Mem. *Hattie and the Fox*, illustrated by Patricia Mullins. Bradbury, 1988.
_____. *Koala Lou*, illustrated by Pamela Lofts. Harcourt, 1989.
_____. *Night Noises*, illustrated by Terry Denton. Harcourt, 1989.
_____. *Possum Magic*, illustrated by Julie Vivas. Harcourt, 1990.
_____. *Wilfrid Gordon McDonald Partridge*, illustrated by Julie Vivas. Kane Miller, 1985.
Freeman, Don. *Corduroy*. Viking, 1968.
_____. *Dandelion*. Viking, 1964.
_____. *A Pocket for Corduroy*. Viking, 1978.
Friedman, Ina. *How My Parents Learned to Eat*, illustrated by Allen Say. Houghton Mifflin, 1984.
Gág, Wanda. *Millions of Cats*. Coward-McCann, 1928.
Gallaz, Christophe, and Roberto Innocenti. *Rose Blanche*, illustrated by Roberto Innocenti. Creative Education, 1985.
Garza, Carmen Lomas. *Family Pictures: Cuadros de Familia*. Children's Book Press, 1990.
Geisert, Arthur. *Oink!* Houghton Mifflin, 1991.
_____. *Pigs from A to Z*. Houghton Mifflin, 1986.
Gerrard, Roy. *Mik's Mammoth*. Farrar, 1990.
_____. *Rosie and the Rustlers*. Farrar, 1989.
Goble, Paul. *The Girl Who Loved Wild Horses*. Bradbury, 1978.
_____. *Star Boy*. Bradbury, 1983.
Goffstein, M. B. *An Artist*. Harper, 1980.
_____. *Brookie and Her Lamb*, rev. ed. Farrar, Straus, 1981.
_____. *My Noah's Ark*. Harper, 1978.
Gramatky, Hardie. *Little Toot*. Putnam, 1939.
Gray, Nigel. *A Country Far Away*, illustrated by Philippe Dupasquier. Orchard, 1989.
Greenblat, Rodney A. *Uncle Wizzmo's New Used Car*. Harper, 1990.
Greenfield, Eloise. *She Come Bringing Me That Little Baby Girl*, illustrated by John Steptoe. Lippincott, 1974.
Grifalconi, Ann. *Darkness and the Butterfly*. Little, 1987.
_____. *Osa's Pride*. Little, 1990.
_____. *The Village of Round and Square Houses*. Little, 1986.
Griffith, Helen. *Georgia Music*, illustrated by James Stevenson. Greenwillow, 1986.

_____. *Grandaddy's Place*, illustrated by James Stevenson. Greenwillow, 1987.

Grimm Brothers. *The Bremen Town Musicians*, translated by Elizabeth Shub, illustrated by Janina Domanska. Greenwillow, 1980.

_____. *The Seven Ravens*, translated by Elizabeth D. Crawford, illustrated by Lisbeth Zwerger. Morrow, 1981.

_____. *Snow White*, translated by Paul Heins, illustrated by Trina Schart Hyman. Little, 1974.

_____. *Snow White*, translated by Randall Jarrell, illustrated by Nancy Ekholm Burkert. Farrar, Straus, 1972.

Grimm, Wilheim. *Dear Mili*, translated by Ralph Manheim, illustrated by Maurice Sendak. Farrar, Straus, 1988.

Hadithi, Mwenye. *Lazy Lion*, illustrated by Adrienne Kennaway. Little, 1990.

_____. *Tricky Tortoise*, illustrated by Adrienne Kennaway. Little, 1988.

Hale, Sarah Josepha. *Mary Had a Little Lamb*, illustrated by Tomie de Paola. Holiday, 1984.

Hall, Donald. *Ox-Cart Man*, illustrated by Barbara Cooney. Viking, 1979.

Harrison, Ted. *Children of the Yukon*. Tundra, 1977.

_____. *A Northern Alphabet*. Tundra, 1989.

Heide, Florence Parry, and Judith Heide Gilliland. *The Day of Ahmed's Secret*, illustrated by Ted Lewin. Lothrop, 1990.

Hendershot, Judith. *In Coal Country*, illustrated by Thomas B. Allen. Knopf, 1987.

Henkes, Kevin. *Chester's Way*. Greenwillow, 1988.

_____. *Chrysanthemum*. Greenwillow, 1991.

_____. *Julius, the Baby of the World*. Greenwillow, 1990.

Helprin, Mark. *Swan Lake*, illustrated by Chris Van Allsburg. Houghton Mifflin, 1989.

Hill, Elizabeth Starr. *Evan's Corner*, illustrated by Sandra Speidel. Viking, 1991 (1967).

Hilton, Nette. *The Long Red Scarf*, illustrated by Margaret Power. Carolrhoda, 1990.

Hoban, Russell. *A Baby Sister for Frances*, illustrated by Lillian Hoban. Harper, 1964.

_____. *A Bargain for Frances*, illustrated by Lillian Hoban. Harper, 1970.

_____. *Bedtime for Frances*, illustrated by Garth Williams. Harper, 1960.

_____. *Best Friends for Frances*, illustrated by Lillian Hoban. Harper, 1969.

_____. *A Birthday for Frances*, illustrated by Lillian Hoban. Harper, 1968.

Hoban, Tana. *Shadows and Reflections*. Greenwillow, 1990.

Hodges, Margaret. *Saint George and the Dragon*, illustrated by Trina Schart Hyman. Little, 1984.

Hoffman, Mary. *Amazing Grace*, illustrated by Caroline Binch. Dial, 1991.

Hooks, William H. *The Ballad of Belle Dorcas*, illustrated by Brian Pinkney. Knopf, 1990.

Hort, Lenny. *The Boy Who Held Back the Sea*, illustrated by Thomas Locker. Dial, 1986.

Houston, Gloria. *My Great-Aunt Arizona*, illustrated by Susan Condie Lamb. HarperCollins, 1992.

Howard, Elizabeth Fitzgerald. *Aunt Flossie's Hats (and Crab Cakes Later)*, illustrated by James Ransome. Houghton Mifflin, 1991.

Hughes, Shirley, *Alfie Gets in First*. Lothrop, 1981.

_____. *The Big Concrete Lorry*. Lothrop, 1990.

_____. *Dogger*. Lothrop, 1988.

Hutchins, Pat. *Good-Night, Owl!* Macmillan, 1972.

_____. *Rosie's Walk*. Macmillan, 1968.

_____. *The Very Worst Monster*. Greenwillow, 1985.

_____. *What Game Shall We Play?* Greenwillow, 1990.

_____. *Where's the Baby?* Greenwillow, 1988.

Hyman, Trina Schart. *Little Red Riding Hood*. Holiday, 1983.

Isadora, Rachel. *At the Crossroads*. Greenwillow, 1991.

_____. *Max*. Macmillan, 1976.

James, Betsy. *The Dream Stair*, illustrated by Richard J. Watson. Harper, 1990.

Johnson, Angela. *Tell Me a Story, Mama*, illustrated by David Soman. Orchard, 1989.

Johnston, Tony. *The Quilt Story*, illustrated by Tomie de Paola. Putnam, 1985.

_____. *Yonder*, illustrated by Lloyd Bloom. Dial, 1988.

Jonas, Ann. *Round Trip*. Greenwillow, 1983.

Jorgensen, Gail. *Crocodile Beat*, illustrated by Patricia Mullins. Bradbury, 1989.

Joyce, William. *A Day with Wilbur Robinson*. Harper, 1990.

_____. *Dinosaur Bob and His Adventures with the Family Lazardo*. Harper, 1988.

_____. *George Shrinks*. Harper, 1985; minature edition, 1991.

Jukes, Mavis. *Like Jake and Me*, illustrated by Lloyd Bloom. Knopf, 1984.
Kalman, Maira. *Hey Willy, See the Pyramids*. Viking, 1988.
_____. *Max Makes a Million*. Viking, 1990.
_____. *Ooh La La, Max in Love*. Viking, 1991.
_____. *Sayonara, Mrs. Kackleman*. Viking, 1989.
Keats, Ezra Jack. *Goggles*. Macmillan, 1969.
_____. *Hi Cat!* Macmillan, 1970.
_____. *A Letter to Amy*. Harper, 1968.
_____. *Peter's Chair*. Harper, 1967.
_____. *Pet Show!* Macmillan, 1972.
_____. *The Snowy Day*. Viking, 1962.
_____. *Whistle for Willie*. Viking, 1964.
Kellogg, Steven. *Can I Keep Him?* Dial, 1971.
_____. *Chicken Little*. Morrow, 1985.
_____. *The Mysterious Tadpole*. Dial, 1977.
_____. *Pinkerton, Behave!* Dial, 1979.
_____. *Prehistoric Pinkerton*. Dial, 1987.
_____. *A Rose for Pinkerton*. Dial, 1981.
Kesey, Ken. *Little Tricker the Squirrel Meets Big Double the Bear*, illustrated by Barry Moser. Viking, 1990.
Kesselman, Wendy. *Emma*, illustrated by Barbara Cooney. Doubleday, 1980.
Kipling, Rudyard. *The Elephant's Child*, illustrated by Lorinda B. Cauley. Harcourt, 1983.
_____. *The Elephant's Child*, illustrated by Jan Mogensen. Crocodile Books, Interlink, 1989.
_____. *How the Camel Got Its Hump*, illustrated by Quentin Blake. Bedrick, 1985.
_____. *How the Camel Got Its Hump*, illustrated by Krystyna Turska. Warne, 1988.
_____. *How the Leopard Got His Spots*, illustrated by Caroline Ebborn. Bedrick, 1986.
Kitchen, Bert. *Animal Alphabet*. Dial, 1984.
Komaiko, Leah. *My Perfect Neighborhood*, illustrated by Barbara Westman. Harper, 1990.
Kraus, Robert. *Leo the Late Bloomer*, illustrated by José Aruego. Crowell, 1971.
_____. *Milton the Early Riser*, illustrated by José Aruego and Ariane Aruego. Windmill, 1972.
_____. *Owliver*, illustrated by José Aruego and Ariane Dewey. Windmill, 1974.
Krauss, Ruth. *A Hole Is to Dig*, illustrated by Maurice Sendak. Harper, 1952.
_____. *A Very Special House*, illustrated by Maurice Sendak. Harper, 1953.
Lattimore, Deborah Nourse. *The Sailor Who Captured the Sea*. Harper, 1991.
_____. *Why There Is No Arguing in Heaven*. Harper, 1989.
Leaf, Munro. *The Story of Ferdinand*, illustrated by Robert Lawson. Viking, 1936.
Lessac, Frané. *Caribbean Canvas*. Lippincott, 1989.
Levinson, Riki. *Watch the Stars Come Out*, illustrated by Diane Goode. Dutton, 1985.
_____. *Our Home Is the Sea*, illustrated by Dennis Luzak. Dutton, 1988.
Lindbergh, Reeve. *Johnny Appleseed*, illustrated by Kathy Jakobsen. Little, 1990.
Lionni, Leo. *Alexander and the Wind-up Mouse*. Pantheon, 1969.
_____. *Fish Is Fish*. Pantheon, 1970.
_____. *Frederick*. Pantheon, 1967.
_____. *Inch by Inch*. Astor-Honor, 1962.
_____. *Little Blue and Little Yellow*. Astor-Honor, 1959.
_____. *Matthew's Dream*. Knopf, 1991.
_____. *Six Crows*. Knopf, 1988.
_____. *Swimmy*. Pantheon, 1963.
Locker, Thomas. *Family Farm*. Dial, 1988.
_____. *The Mare on the Hill*. Dial, 1985.
_____. *Where the River Begins*. Dial, 1984.
_____. *The Young Artist*. Dial, 1989.
Lobel, Arnold. *Days with Frog and Toad*. Harper, 1979.
_____. *Fables*. Harper, 1980.
_____. *Frog and Toad All Year*. Harper, 1976.
_____. *Frog and Toad are Friends*. Harper, 1970.
_____. *Frog and Toad Together*. Harper, 1972.
Lyon, George Ella. *Come a Tide*, illustrated by Stephen Gammell. Orchard, 1990.
Macaulay, David. *Black and White*. Houghton Mifflin, 1990.

McCloskey, Robert. *Blueberries for Sal*. Viking, 1963.
_____. *Make Way for Ducklings*. Viking, 1941.
_____. *One Morning in Maine*. Viking, 1952.
_____. *Time of Wonder*. Viking, 1957.
McDermott, Gerald. *Arrow to the Sun: A Pueblo Indian Tale*. Viking, 1974.
MacDonald, Golden, pseud. (Margaret Wise Brown). *The Little Island*, illustrated by Leonard Weisgard. Doubleday, 1946.
MacLachlan, Patricia. *Mama One, Mama Two*, illustrated by Ruth Lercher Bornstein. Harper, 1982.
_____. *Through Grandpa's Eyes*, illustrated by Deborah Ray. Harper, 1979.
McKee, David. *Elmer*. Lothrop, 1989 (1968).
McPhail, David. *The Bear's Toothache*. Little, 1972.
_____. *Henry Bear's Park*. Little, 1976.
_____. *Pig Pig Goes to Camp*. Dutton, 1983.
_____. *Pig Pig Grows Up*. Dutton, 1980.
_____. *Pig Pig Rides*. Dutton, 1982.
_____. *Stanley, Henry Bear's Friend*. Little, 1979.
Mahy, Margaret. *The Great White Man-Eating Shark*, illustrated by Jonathan Allen. Dial, 1990.
Marshall, James. *George and Martha*. Houghton Mifflin, 1972.
_____. *George and Martha Back in Town*. Houghton Mifflin, 1984.
_____. *George and Martha Round and Round*. Houghton Mifflin, 1988.
_____. *George and Martha Tons of Fun*. Houghton Mifflin, 1972.
Martin, Bill, Jr., and John Archambault. *The Ghost-Eye Tree*, illustrated by Ted Rand. Henry Holt, 1985.
_____. *Knots on a Counting Rope*, illustrated by Ted Rand. Henry Holt, 1987.
Martin, Rafe. *Will's Mammoth*, illustrated by Stephen Gammell. Putnam, 1989.
Maruki, Toshi. *Hiroshima No Pika*. Lothrop, 1980.
Mayer, Mercer. *There's a Nightmare in My Closet*. Dial, 1968.
Miles, Miska. *Annie and the Old One*, illustrated by Peter Parnall. Little, 1971.
Minarik, Else. *Father Bear Comes Home*, illustrated by Maurice Sendak. Harper, 1959.
_____. *A Kiss for Little Bear*, illustrated by Maurice Sendak. Harper, 1968.
_____. *Little Bear*, illustrated by Maruice Sendak. Harper, 1957.
_____. *Little Bear's Friend*, illustrated by Maurice Sendak. Harper, 1960.
_____. *Little Bear's Visit*, illustrated by Maurice Sendak. Harper, 1961.
Morimoto, Junko. *My Hiroshima*. Viking, 1987.
Murphy, Jill. *All in One Piece*. Putnam, 1987.
_____. *Five Minutes' Peace*. Putnam, 1986.
_____. *A Piece of Cake*. Putnam, 1989.
Murphy, Shirley Rousseau. *Tattie's River Journey*, illustrated by Tomie de Paola. Dial, 1983.
Musgrove, Margaret. *Ashanti to Zulu: African Traditions*, illustrated by Leo and Diane Dillon. Dial, 1976.
Ness, Evaline. *Sam, Bangs, and Moonshine*. Holt, 1966.
Nikola-Lisa, W. *Night Is Coming*, illustrated by Jamichael Henterly. Dutton, 1991.
Noble, Trinka H. *The Day Jimmy's Boa Ate the Wash*, illustrated by Steven Kellogg. Dial, 1980.
_____. *Jimmy's Boa Bounces Back*, illustrated by Steven Kellogg. Dial, 1984.
Paxton, Tom. *Engelbert the Elephant*, illustrated by Steven Kellogg. Morrow, 1990.
Pearson, Susan. *Happy Birthday, Grampie*, illustrated by Ronald Himler. Dial, 1987.
Perrault, Charles. *Puss in Boots*, illustrated by Fred Marcellino. Farrar, 1990.
Piper, Watty. *The Little Engine That Could*, illustrated by George Hauman and Doris Hauman. Platt and Munk, 1954 (1930).
Polacco, Patricia. *The Keeping Quilt*. Simon & Schuster, 1988.
_____. *Just Plain Fancy*. Bantam/Doubleday, 1990.
_____. *Thunder Cake*. Philomel, 1990.
Politi, Leo. *Pedro, the Angel of Olvera Street*. Scribner's, 1946.
_____. *Song of the Swallows*. Scribner's, 1949.
Pomerantz, Charlotte. *The Chalk Doll*, illustrated by Frané Lessac. Lippincott, 1989.
Potter, Beatrix. *The Tale of Peter Rabbit*. Warne, 1902.
Price, Leontyne. *Aïda*, illustrated by Leo and Diane Dillon. Harcourt, 1990.
Provensen, Alice. *The Buck Stops Here*. Harper, 1990.
Provensen, Alice, and Martin Provensen. *The Glorious Flight: Across the Channel with Louis Blériot*. Viking, 1983.

_____. *Shaker Lane*. Viking, 1987.

Radin, Ruth Yaffe. *A Winter Place*, illustrated by Mattie Lou O'Kelley. Little, 1982.

Raskin, Ellen. *Nothing Ever Happens on My Block*. Macmillan, 1989 (1966).

Rayner, Mary. *Garth Pig and the Ice Cream Lady*. Atheneum, 1977.

_____. *Mr. and Mrs. Pig's Evening Out*. Atheneum, 1976.

_____. *Mrs. Pig's Bulk Buy*. Atheneum, 1981.

Reinl, Edda. *The Three Little Pigs*. Picture Book Studio, 1983.

Rey, H. A. *Curious George*. Houghton Mifflin, 1941.

Rice, Eve. *At Grammy's House*, illustrated by Nancy Winslow Parker. Greenwillow, 1990.

Ringgold, Faith. *Tar Beach*. Crown, 1991.

Robbins, Ruth. *Baboushka and the Three Kings*, illustrated by Nicolas Sidjakov. Parnassus, 1960.

Roe, Eileen. *Con Mi Hermano: With My Brother*, illustrated by Robert Casilla. Bradbury, 1991.

Ryder, Joanne. *When the Woods Hum*, illustrated by Catherine Stock. Morrow, 1991.

Rylant, Cynthia. *Appalachia: The Voices of Sleeping Birds*, illustrated by Barry Moser. Harcourt, 1991.

_____. *The Relatives Came*, illustrated by Stephen Gammell. Bradbury, 1985.

_____. *When I Was Young in the Mountains*, illustrated by Diane Goode. Dutton, 1982.

Say, Allen. *El Chino*. Houghton Mifflin, 1990.

_____. *The Lost Lake*. Houghton Mifflin, 1989.

Scieszka, Jon. *The Frog Prince Continued*, illustrated by Steve Johnson. Viking, 1991.

_____. *The True Story of the Three Little Pigs*, illustrated by Lane Smith. Viking, 1989.

Sendak, Maurice. *In the Night Kitchen*. Harper, 1970.

_____. *Outside Over There*. Harper, 1981.

_____. *Where the Wild Things Are*. Harper, 1963.

Serfozo, Mary. *Rain Talk*, illustrated by Keiko Narahashi. McElderry Books: Macmillan, 1990.

Seuss, Dr., pseud. (Theodor S. Geisel). *And to Think That I Saw It on Mulberry Street*. Vanguard, 1937.

_____. *The Cat in the Hat*. Random, 1957.

_____. *Horton Hatches the Egg*. Random, 1940.

_____. *Scrambed Eggs Super*. Random, 1953.

_____. *Thidwick the Big-hearted Moose*. Random, 1948.

Shulevitz, Uri. *Dawn*. Farrar, Straus, 1974.

_____. *Rain Rain Rivers*. Farrar, Straus, 1969.

_____. *Toddlecreek Post Office*. Farrar, Straus, 1990.

Spier, Peter. *Peter Spier's Rain*. Doubleday, 1982.

Steig, William. *The Amazing Bone*. Farrar, Straus, 1976.

_____. *Amos & Boris*. Farrar, Straus, 1971.

_____. *Brave Irene*. Farrar, Straus, 1986.

_____. *Doctor DeSoto*. Farrar, Straus, 1982.

_____. *Gorky Rises*. Farrar, Straus, 1980.

_____. *Shrek!* Farrar, Straus, 1990.

_____. *Sylvester and the Magic Pebble*. Windmill, 1979.

Steptoe, John. *Daddy is a Monster . . . Sometimes*. Lippincott, 1980.

_____. *Stevie*. Harper, 1969.

Stevens, Janet. *The Emperor's New Clothes*. Holiday, 1985.

Stevenson, James. *Could Be Worse!* Greenwillow, 1977.

_____. *Grandpa's Too-Good Garden*. Greenwillow, 1988.

_____. *The Dreadful Day*. Greenwillow, 1985.

_____. *That Terrible Halloween Night*. Greenwillow, 1980.

_____. *We Hate Rain*. Greenwillow, 1989.

_____. *What's Under My Bed?* Greenwillow, 1983.

_____. *Worse Than Willy!* Greenwillow, 1984.

Stolz, Mary. *Storm in the Night*, illustrated by Pat Cummings. Harper, 1988.

Tejima, Keizaburo. *Fox's Dream*. Philomel, 1987.

_____. *Owl Lake*. Philomel, 1987.

_____. *Swan Sky*. Philomel, 1988.

Titherington, Jeanne. *A Place for Ben*. Greenwillow, 1987.

Turkle, Brinton. *Do Not Open*. Dutton, 1981.

Turner, Ann. *Heron Street*, illustrated by Lisa Desimini. Harper, 1989.

_____. *Through Moon and Stars and Night Skies*, illustrated by James-Graham Hale. Harper, 1990.

Tresselt, Alvin. *Hide and Seek Fog,* illustrated by Roger Duvoisin. Lothrop, 1988 (1965).
_____. *White Snow, Bright Snow,* illustrated by Roger Duvoisin. Lothrop, 1988 (1947).
Udry, Janice May. *A Tree Is Nice,* illustrated by Marc Simont. Harper, 1956.
Ungerer, Tomi. *Crictor.* Harper, 1958.
Van Allsburg, Chris. *The Garden of Abdul Gasazi.* Houghton Mifflin, 1979.
_____. *Jumanji.* Houghton Mifflin, 1981.
_____. *Just a Dream.* Houghton Mifflin, 1990.
_____. *The Mysteries of Harris Burdick.* Houghton Mifflin, 1984.
_____. *The Polar Express.* Houghton Mifflin, 1985.
_____. *Two Bad Ants.* Houghton Mifflin, 1988.
_____. *The Stranger.* Houghton Mifflin, 1986.
_____. *The Wreck of the Zephyr.* Houghton Mifflin, 1983.
_____. *The Wretched Stone.* Houghton Mifflin, 1991.
Van Laan, Nancy. *Possum Come A-Knockin',* illustrated by George Booth. Knopf, 1990.
Vincent, Gabriella. *Ernest and Celestine.* Greenwillow, 1982.
_____. *Ernest and Celestine's Picnic.* Greenwillow, 1982.
_____. *Feel Better, Ernest!* Greenwillow, 1988.
_____. *Merry Christmas, Ernest and Celestine.* Greenwillow, 1984.
_____. *Smile, Ernest and Celestine.* Greenwillow, 1982.
Viorst, Judith. *Alexander and the Terrible, Horrible, No Good, Very Bad Day,* illustrated by Ray Cruz. Atheneum, 1972.
_____. *Alexander Who Used to Be Rich Last Sunday,* illustrated by Ray Cruz. Atheneum, 1978.
_____. *I'll Fix Anthony,* illustrated by Arnold Lobel. Harper, 1969.
_____. *The Tenth Good Thing About Barney,* illustrated by Erik Blegvad. Atheneum, 1971.
Waber, Bernard. *The House on East 88th Street.* Houghton Mifflin, 1962.
_____. *Ira Says Goodbye.* Houghton Mifflin, 1988.
_____. *Ira Sleeps Over.* Houghton Mifflin, 1972.
_____. *Lyle, Lyle Crocodile.* Houghton Mifflin, 1965.
_____. *"You Look Ridiculous," Said the Rhineroceros to the Hippopotamus.* Houghton Mifflin, 1966.
Wagner, Jenny. *John Brown, Rose, and the Midnight Cat,* illustrated by Ron Brooks. Bradbury, 1978.
Walter, Mildred Pitts. *My Mama Needs Me,* illustrated by Pat Cummings. Lothrop, 1983.
Weller, Frances. *Riptide,* illustrated by Robert Blake. Philomel, 1990.
Wells, Rosemary. *Benjamin and Tulip.* Doubleday, 1973.
_____. *Shy Charles.* Dial, 1988.
_____. *Stanley and Rhoda.* Dial, 1978.
_____. *Timothy Goes to School.* Dial, 1983.
_____. *Noisy Nora.* Dial, 1973.
Wiesner, David. *Hurricane.* Clarion, 1990.
_____. *Tuesday.* Clarion, 1991.
Wild, Margaret. *The Very Best of Friends,* illustrated by Julie Vivas. Harcourt, 1990.
Wildsmith, Brian. *The Owl and the Woodpecker.* Watts, 1972.
_____. *Python's Party.* Oxford, 1974.
Wilhelm, Hans. *I'll Always Love You.* Crown, 1985.
Willard, Nancy. *A Visit to William Blake's Inn,* illustrated by Alice and Martin Provensen. Harcourt, 1981.
Williams, Karen Lynn. *Galimoto,* illustrated by Catherine Stock. Lothrop, 1990.
Williams, Margery. *The Velveteen Rabbit,* illustrated by William Nicholson. Doubleday, 1958 (1922).
_____. *The Velveteen Rabbit,* illustrated by Michael Hague. Henry Holt, 1983.
_____. *The Velveteen Rabbit,* illustrated by David Jorgensen. Knopf, 1985.
_____. *The Velveteen Rabbit,* illustrated by Ilse Plume. Harcourt, 1987.
Williams, Vera B. *A Chair for My Mother.* Greenwillow, 1982.
_____. *Music, Music for Everyone.* Greenwillow, 1984.
_____. *Something Special for Me.* Greenwillow, 1983.
Williams, Vera B., and Jennifer Williams. *Stringbean's Trip to the Shining Sea.* Greenwillow, 1988.
Wolff, Ashley. *A Year of Beasts.* Dutton, 1989.
_____. *A Year of Birds.* Dutton, 1984.
Wood, Audrey. *Heckedy Peg,* illustrated by Don Wood. Harcourt, 1987.
_____. *The Napping House,* illustrated by Don Wood, Harcourt, 1984.
Yashima, Taro, pseud. (Jun Iwamatsu). *Crow Boy.* Viking, 1955.

_____. *Umbrella*. Viking Penguin, 1958.

Yolen, Jane. *Owl Moon*, illustrated by John Schoenherr. Philomel, 1987.

Zion, Gene. *Harry, The Dirty Dog*, illustrated by Margaret Bloy Graham. Harper, 1956.

Zolotow, Charlotte. *Mr. Rabbit and the Lovely Present*, illustrated by Maurice Sendak. Harper, 1962.

_____. *Say It!*, illustrated by James Stevenson. Greenwillow, 1980.

_____. *William's Doll*, illustrated by William Pène du Bois. Harper, 1972.

Chapter Six
Traditional Literature

Ever since human beings realized they were unique among animals in that they could think and talk, they have tried to explain themselves and their world. Who were the first humans? How did they come to be? What made the sun and the moon and the stars? Why were the animals made the way they were? What caused night and day, the seasons, the cycle of life itself? Why were some people greedy and some unselfish, some ugly and some handsome, some dull and some clever? As people pondered these questions and many more, they created stories that helped explain the world to their primitive minds. The storytellers told these tales again and again around the fires of the early tribes, by the hearths of humble cottages, before the great fire in the king's hall; they told them as they sat in the grass huts of the jungle, the hogans of the Navajo, and the igloos of the Eskimo. Their children told them, and their children's children, until the stories were as smooth and polished as the roundest stones in the stream. And so people created their myths and their folktales, their legends and epics: the literature of the fireside, the poetry of the people, and the memory of humankind.

A PERSPECTIVE ON TRADITIONAL LITERATURE

Origin of Folk Literature

We have no one word that encompasses all of the stories that are born of the oral tradition. They are most often grouped under the heading of folklore, folk literature, or mythology. Generally, we say that myths are about gods and the creation of things; legends are about heroes and their mighty deeds before the time of recorded history; and folktales, fairy tales, and fables are simple stories about talking beasts, woodcutters, and princesses who reveal human behavior and beliefs while playing out their roles in a world of wonder and magic.

Children sometimes identify these stories as "make-believe," as contrasted with "true" or "stories that could really happen." Unfortunately, the word *myth* has sometimes been defined as an "imagined event" or a "pagan falsehood," as opposed to "historical fact" or "Christian truth." In literary study, however, *myth* does not mean "untrue"; rather, the term refers to a generalized meaning or a universal idea, a significant truth about humans and their lives. A single *myth* is a narrative that tells of origins,[1] explains natural or social phenomena, or suggests the destiny of humans through the interaction of people and supernatural beings. A *mythology* is a group of myths of a particular culture. Myth making[2] is continuous and in process today. Usually myth is

[1] X. J. Kennedy, *Literature: An Introduction to Fiction, Poetry and Drama* (Boston: Little, Brown, 1983), p. 610.
[2] Joseph Campbell with Bill Moyers, *The Power of Myth* (New York: Doubleday, 1988).

a product of a society rather than of a single author.

The origin of the myths has fascinated and puzzled folklorists, anthropologists, and psychologists. How, they wonder, can we account for the similarities among these stories that grew out of ancient cultures widely separated from each other? The Greek myth of *The Arrow and the Lamp: The Story of Psyche* (372)[3] is very much like the Norwegian tale of *East o' the Sun and West o' the Moon* (14). The Chinese "Cinderella" story, *Yeh-Shen* (200), is similar to the French *Cinderella* (239), except that a fish acts on the poor girl's behalf. And the story of "Cinderella" is found throughout the world, with nearly 500 variants in Europe alone.

In trying to explain this phenomenon, one group of early mythologists proposed the notion of *monogenesis*, or inheritance from a single culture. The Grimm brothers, who were among the first of the nineteenth-century scholars of folklore, theorized that all folktales originated from one prehistoric group called Aryans, later identified as Indo-Europeans by modern linguists. As this group migrated to other countries the scholars reasoned that they took their folklore with them, which led to the theory of *diffusion*.

Another approach to folklore involves the theory of *polygenesis*, or multiple origins. It is argued that each story could have been an independent invention growing out of universal desires and needs of humankind. Early anthropologists viewed myth as the religion of the people derived from rituals that were recounted in drama and narratives. They identified recurrent themes in myths of different cultures. Clyde Kluckhohn's study[4] of the myths of fifty cultures revealed such recurring themes as the flood, slaying of monsters, incest, sibling rivalry, and castration. He also found several patterns repeated in the myth of

the hero. Sir James Frazer's twelve-volume analysis of ritual, taboos, and myths, *The Golden Bough*[5], was of major importance. This anthropological study gave sexual symbolic meaning to primitive myths and greatly influenced modern literature.

Sigmund Freud's analysis[6] of myth as dream, or disguised wish fulfillment, was the beginning of psychological literary criticism. Freud held the view that all myths expressed the Oedipus theme with its incest motive, guilt, and punishment. Another psychological viewpoint was that of Carl Jung, a contemporary of Freud, who thought that a "collective unconscious" is "inherited in the structure of the brain."[7] These unconscious, recurring images created the primitive mythic heroes and still exist as individual fantasies for the civilized person as a kind of "race memory," according to Jung. The folklorist, however, may disagree with such psychological interpretations. Richard Dorson notes that "folk literature cannot all be prettily channeled into the universal monomyth," and "the folklorist looks with jaundiced eye at the excessive straining of mythologists to extort symbols from folk tales."[8]

Folktales are also of special interest to scholars of narrative theory. Because of the way the tales are honed by many generations of telling, only the most important elements of the story survive. Close study of the patterns of action and character relationships show how language shapes a form we recognize as a story. Vladimir Propp, for instance, analyzed Russian tales and identified a set sequence of thirty-one "functions" that might occur in a tale, such as the hero leaves home (departure); one member of a family lacks or desires something (lack); or, a villain attempts to deceive his victim (trickery).[9] Other researchers

---

[3]The number in parentheses following the title of a folktale or myth indicates the number of a reference in the bibliography at the end of this chapter. This reference lists the book in which the tale may be found.
[4]Clyde Kluckhohn, "Recurrent Themes in Myth and Mythmaking," in *The Making of Myth*, Richard M. Ohrmann, ed. (New York: Putnam, 1962), pp. 52–65.

[5]Sir James Frazer, *The Golden Bough*, 3rd ed. (London: Macmillan, 1911–1915).
[6]Stanley E. Hyman, *The Armed Vision*, rev. ed. (New York: Vintage, 1955).
[7]Carl C. Jung, "On the Relation of Analytic Psychology to Poetic Art," in O. B. Hardison, Jr., ed., *Modern Continental Literary Criticism* (New York: Appleton, 1962), pp. 267–288.
[8]Richard Dorson, "Theories of Myth and the Folklorist," in Ohrmann, *The Making of Myth*, p. 45.
[9]Vladimir Propp, *The Morphology of the Folktale* (Austin: University of Texas Press, 1968).

have used simplified folktale structures to develop models of children's story comprehension. Although looking at tales in such a technical way is definitely an adult perspective, children who have heard and enjoyed many traditional stories begin to discover for themselves that folktales seem to follow certain structural rules. One 10-year-old girl who wrote instructions for "Making a Fairy Story" summed up by saying ". . . fairy tales have to have a sort of pattern or they would just be regular stories."

However scholars choose to look at them, folktales and myths are literature derived from human imagination to explain the human condition. Literature today continues to express our concern about human strengths, weaknesses, and the individual's relationships to the world and to other people. Traditional literature forms the foundation of understandings of life as expressed in modern literature.

The Value of Folk Literature for Children

When Jacob and Wilhelm Grimm published the first volume of their "Household Stories" in 1812, they did not intend it for children. These early philologists were studying the language and grammar of such traditional tales. In recent years, as we have seen, anthropologists study folklore in order to understand the inherent values and beliefs of a culture. Psychologists look at folktales and myths and discover something of the motivation and inner feelings of humans; folklorists collect and categorize various stories, types, and motifs from around the world. These are all adult scholars of folk literature, which itself was first created by adults and usually told to an adult community. How, then, did folk literature become associated with children's literature, and what value does this kind of literature have for children?

Originally, folklore was the literature of the people; stories were told to young and old alike. Families or tribes or the king's court would gather to hear a famous storyteller in much the same way that an entire family today will watch their favorite television program. With the age of scientific enlightenment, these stories were relegated to the nursery, kept alive, in many instances, by resourceful nursemaids or grandmothers, much to the delight of children.

Children today still enjoy such tales because they are good stories. Born of the oral tradition, these stories are usually short and have fast-moving plots. They are frequently humorous and almost always end happily. Poetic justice prevails; the good and the just are eventually rewarded; the evil are punished. This appeals to the child's sense of justice and his moral judgment. Wishes come true, but usually not without the fulfillment of a task or trial. The littlest child, the youngest son, or the smallest animal succeeds; the oldest or the largest is frequently defeated. Youngsters who are the little people of their world thrive on such a turn of events.

Beyond the function of pure entertainment, folktales can kindle the child's imagination. Behind every great author, poet, architect, mathematician, or diplomat is a dream of what the person hopes to achieve. This dream or ideal has been created by the power of imagination. If we always give children stories of "what is," stories that only mirror the living of today, then we have not helped them to imagine what "might have been" or "what might be."

Bruno Bettelheim, in his remarkable book *The Uses of Enchantment*, maintains that fairy tales help children to cope with their dreams and inner turmoil. "Each fairy tale," he says, "is a magic mirror which reflects some aspects of our inner world and of the steps required by our evolution from immaturity to maturity."[10]

Kornei Chukovsky, the Russian poet, tells of a time when it was proposed that all folktales and fairy tales be eliminated from the education of the Russian child in favor of simple realistic stories. Then one of the major Russian educators began keeping a diary of her child's development. She found that her child, as if to compensate for the fairy tales which he had been denied, began to make up his own. He had never heard a folktale, but his world was peopled with talking tigers, birds, and bugs. Chukovsky concludes this story with this statement: "Fantasy is the most

[10]Bruno Bettelheim, *The Uses of Enchantment* (New York: Knopf, 1976), p. 309.

Anthony Browne's contemporary setting for the Grimms' story of *Hansel and Gretel* contrasts with Paul O. Zelinsky's more traditional one. How does a change in setting affect the meaning of the story?

valuable attribute of the human mind and should be diligently nurtured from earliest childhood."[11]

Traditional literature is a rightful part of a child's literary heritage and lays the groundwork for understanding all literature. Poetry and modern stories allude to traditional literature, particularly the Greek myths, Aesop's fables, and Bible stories. Northrop Frye maintains that "all theme and characters and stories that you encounter in literature belong to one big interlocking family."[12] As you meet recurring patterns or symbols in mythlike floods, savior heroes, cruel stepmothers,

the seasonal cycle of the year, the cycle of a human life, you begin to build a framework for literature. Poetry, prose, and drama become more emotionally significant as you respond to these recurring archetypes.

Our speech and vocabulary reflect many contributions from traditional literature. Think of the figures of speech that come from Aesop's fables: "sour grapes," "dog in the manger," "boy who cried wolf." Our language is replete with words and phrases from the myths—"narcissistic," "cereal," "labyrinth," "siren," and many more.

Every culture has produced a folklore. A study of the folktales of West Africa, Russia, Japan or North America provides insights into the beliefs of these peoples, their values, their jokes, their lifestyles, their histories. A cross-cultural study of folk literature helps children discover the universal qualities of humankind.

[11]Kornei Chukovsky, *From Two to Five,* translated and edited by Miriam Morton (Berkeley: University of California Press, 1963), p. 119.
[12]Northrop Frye, *The Educated Imagination* (Bloomington: Indiana University Press, 1964), p. 48.

FOLKTALES

Definition of Folktales

Folktales have been defined as "all forms of narrative, written or oral, which have come to be handed down through the years."[13] This definition would include epics, ballads, legends, and folk songs, as well as myths and fables. In using folk literature in the elementary school we have tended to confine the rather simple folktales—such as the popular "The Three Billy Goats Gruff," "Little Red Riding Hood," and "Rumpelstiltskin"—to the primary grades; we recommend the so-called fairy tales—such as "Snow White" and "Cinderella"—for slightly older children, since these tales are longer and contain romantic elements. Such a division appears arbitrary; it is based more on use than any real difference in the stories. To complicate matters even further, modern fanciful stories created by a known author are often also referred to as fairy tales. Hans Christian Andersen's stories are becoming part of the heritage that might be described as folktales, but *many originated in written rather than oral form.* Thus they are distinguished from the stories told by the common folk that were finally collected and recorded. Stories written in a folktale style, but which originated in an author's imagination, are often referred to as "literary folktales" (see Chapter 5, "Modern Folktale Style").

Questions often arise about which of the available print versions of a tale is the "correct" or authentic text. From a folklorist's point of view, a tale is recreated every time it is told and therefore *every* telling is correct in its own way. A great deal of variation is also acceptable in print versions, where literary style carries the same uniqueness as the teller's voice. Authors and illustrators may also add original twists, customize their stories for a chosen audience, or adapt a familiar tale to an unfamiliar setting, as oral storytellers do. There may be a problem, however, when a print version suggests by its title, or lack of an author's note, that it represents a tale derived directly from a previously printed source. Readers of a story

identified as recorded and published by the Brothers Grimm, for instance, have a right to find this tale then subsequently published without major additions, omissions, or distortions.

This chapter discusses folktales in children's literature that come from the oral tradition. It also includes a description of the epics, myths, and stories from the Bible, which are all a part of traditional literature. Modern fanciful stories written by known authors are discussed in Chapter 7.

Types of Folktales

CUMULATIVE TALES

Very young children are fascinated by such cumulative stories as "The Old Woman and Her Pig" (248) with its "Rat! rat! gnaw rope; rope won't hang butcher; butcher won't kill ox; ox won't drink water; water won't quench fire; fire won't burn stick; stick won't beat dog; dog won't bite pig; piggy won't get over the stile; and I shan't get home tonight." The story itself is not as important as the increasing repetition of the details building up to a quick climax. The story of *The Gingerbread Boy* (83) who ran away from the old woman defiantly crying "Catch me if you can" has been told in many different versions, including the Russian *The Bun* (29), and Ruth Sawyer's Appalachian *Journey Cake, Ho!* (263).

In another familiar cumulative tale, one day an acorn falls on *Henny Penny* (36, 231). Thinking the sky is falling down, she persuades Cocky-Locky, Ducky-Daddles, Goosey-Poosey, and Turkey-Lurkey to go along with her to tell the king. Children delight in the sound of the rhyming double names which are repeated over and over. Young children, especially, enjoy extending and personalizing these cumulative tales through dramatic play.

The Fat Cat (186) is a humorous Danish cumulative folktale that Jack Kent has illustrated. The fat cat eats the gruel he was watching for the little old lady; then he eats the pot and the little old lady herself! He continues his eating binge, growing larger and larger with each victim. Finally, the fat cat is stopped when he makes the mistake of trying to eat the woodcutter. All his victims are released, and the last picture shows the woodcut-

[13]Frye, *The Educated Imagination*, p. 48.

ter carefully applying a Band-Aid to the fat cat's tummy. Certainly the best known of all cumulative tales is the popular *The House That Jack Built* (289). You will find repetitive stories in practically all folklore.

POURQUOI TALES

Some folktales are "why" or *pourquoi* stories that explain certain animal traits or characteristics or customs of people. In "How the Animals Got Their Tails" (33), Ashley Bryan tells an African tale of a time when all animals were vegetarians. Then, Raluvhimba created a mistake, the flies who were flesh-eaters and blood-suckers. "I can't take back what I've done. After all, that's life," the god said. But he did give the rest of the animals tails with which to swish away the flies.

Many American Indian stories are "why" stories that explain animal features, the origin of certain natural features, or how humans and their customs came to be. William Toye has retold the Micmac Indian legend of how Glooskap saved the people from the giant Winter by persuading the lovely Summer to return north with him for half of the year. Elizabeth Cleaver has illustrated this book, *How Summer Came to Canada* (292), with brilliant collage pictures that make intriguing use of torn paper, pine needles, and hemlock. Paul Goble's retelling of a Sioux myth, *The Great Race of the Birds and the Animals* (99), explains the origins of the Milky Way and the reason why the magpie's tail feathers are iridescent. Susan Roth uses dramatic black-and-white woodcuts with yellow to highlight a Cherokee myth, *The Story of Light* (255), which explains how each animal was marked in its failure to capture light for earth until the tiny spider succeeded. It also explains how dark earth received the first sunlight.[14]

BEAST TALES

Probably the favorite folktales of young children are the beast tales in which animals act and talk like human beings. The best known of these frequently appear in newly illustrated versions. In *The Three Little Pigs*, Paul Galdone (92) portrays the wolf as a ferocious doggy creature; Lorinda

Bryan Cauley's wolf (173) is presented as a country gentleman among bumpkins; James Marshall's red-capped wolf looks like a thug in his red-striped polo shirt (212); and Tony Ross shows a modern-day wolf (254) in a gray flannel topcoat pursuing the pigs, who have moved to the country to escape an overcrowded city high-rise apartment! Other beast tales found in several versions include *The Three Billy Goats Gruff* (16, 91), *The Little Red Hen* (86, 318), and *Puss in Boots* (88, 240). In *The Three Bears and 15 Other Stories* (249), Anne Rockwell has included many of these favorite beast stories in a delightful collection for the very young child. Clear, glowing watercolors are used throughout to help the child follow the action of the stories.

Improbable details and humorous exaggeration in the pictures as well as asides, puns, and allusions in the text are typical of James Marshall's irreverent beast tales such as *Goldilocks and the Three Bears*.

[14]For modern *pourquoi* tales, see the section on Rudyard Kipling's *Just-So Stories* in Chapter 5.

CREATING POURQUOI STORIES WITH FIFTH GRADERS

A fifth-grade teacher assembled many African *pourquoi* stories and led her class in reading and discussing the patterns. Children noted that most explained animal characteristics or habits and natural phenomena. Children also discussed the illustrations and were particularly impressed with the clear colors and white-outlined shapes that Leo and Diane Dillon used for the Caldecott award-winning pictures in Verna Aardema's *Why Mosquitoes Buzz in People's Ears* (7). When the teacher asked children to produce their own "how" or "why" stories and illustrate them, here is what one child created:

Why Flies Eat Rotten Food

A long time ago, in a jungle Fly was very hot. So he flew to the river and rolled around in the mud. After that Fly was very hungry so he flew home. On the way he looked down and saw a big juicy steak lying on the ground.

Now fly was *very* hungry so he flew down and started eating it. But he was so dirty that when he landed he got mud on the steak and as he walked around eating it he got even more mud on it.

By the time Fly was done eating, the whole steak was covered with mud. Just then King Lion (the owner of the steak who had been taking a nap) walked into the clearing. "What have you done to my steak you stupid fly?" roared his majesty.

"Oh," said Fly, "I was just—." Then he looked at the steak. "Oh your majesty! I am very sorry. So very sorry," apologized Fly.

Then the King said, "As a punishment you can never eat fresh food again. You must always eat things like this steak."

Fly was so ashamed that he flew off with his head down but because he does not dare oppose King Lion he has eaten dirty and rotten food ever since.

A fifth grader, after seeing Leo and Diane Dillon's illustrations for Verna Aardema's *Why Mosquitoes Buzz in People's Ears,* used felt-tip markers and a white outline to imitate the Dillons' artwork for her pourquoi story of "Why Flies Eat Rotten Food."

Allison Fraser, fifth grade
Susan Steinberg, teacher
George Mason Elementary School
Alexandria, Virginia

Many African stories are wise beast–foolish beast tales of how one animal, such as a spider or rabbit, outwits lion, hyena, leopard, or other foes. In Verna Aardema's *Rabbit Makes a Monkey of Lion* (4), Rabbit and Turtle steal Lion's honey and continually trick him into letting them go. So Lion hides in Rabbit's house in hope of eating him for supper. But Rabbit notices the beast's footprints and calls out, "How-de-do, Little House." When the house doesn't reply, Rabbit pretends to be puzzled. "Little House, you always tell me *how-de-do*. Is something wrong today?" Of course, the confused Lion answers for the house, reveals his presence, and is tricked once again. Many beast tales that traveled to the United States with African slaves were collected by Joel Chandler Harris in the late 1800s. These have been retold in two series, one by Julius Lester that begins with *The Tales of Uncle Remus: The Adventures of Brer Rabbit* (197) and the other by Van Dyke Parks beginning with *Jump: The Adventures of Brer Rabbit* (151).

Talking animals appear in folktales of all cultures. Fish are often found in English, Scandinavian, German, and South Sea stories. Tales of bears, wolves, and the firebird are found in Russian folklore. Spiders, rabbits, tortoises, crocodiles, monkeys and lions are very much a part of African tales; rabbits, badgers, monkeys, and even bees are represented in Japanese stories. A study of just the animals in folklore would be a fascinating search.

WONDER TALES

Children call wonder tales of magic and the supernatural "fairy tales." Very few tales have even a fairy godmother in them, but the name persists. These are the stories that include giants, such as *Jack and the Beanstalk* (40), or fairies, as in *Tam Lin* (53). Wicked witches, Baba Yaga in Russian folklore, demons such as the *oni* of Japanese tales, or monsters and dragons abound in these stories. Traditionally, we have thought of the fairy tale as involving romance and adventure. "Cinderella," "Snow White and the Seven Dwarfs," or "Beauty and the Beast" all have elements of both. The long quest tales—such as the Russian *The Firebird* (184) or the Norwegian *East o' the Sun and West o' the Moon* (14)—are complex

wonder tales in which the hero, or heroine, triumphs against all odds to win the beautiful princess, or handsome prince, and makes a fortune. Children know that these tales will end with ". . . and they lived happily ever after." In fact, one of the appeals of the fairy tale is the secure knowledge that no matter what happens the virtues of love, kindness, and truth will prevail; hate, wickedness, and evil will be punished. Wonder tales have always represented the glorious fulfillment of human desires.

REALISTIC TALES

Surprisingly, there are a few realistic tales included in folklore. The story of *Dick Whittington and His Cat* (30) could have happened; in fact, there is evidence that a Richard Whittington did indeed live and was mayor of London. Like the American story of *Johnny Appleseed* (9), the tale began with a real person but has become so embroidered through various tellings that it takes its place among the folklore of its culture.

"Zlateh the Goat" (280), the title story in a collection of Jewish tales by Isaac Bashevis Singer, is a survival story. The son of a poor peasant family is sent off to the butcher to sell Zlateh, the family goat. On the way, he and the goat are caught in a fierce snowstorm. They take refuge in a haystack where they stay for three days. Zlateh eats the hay while the boy survives on Zlateh's milk and warmth. When the storm is over, they return home to a grateful family. No one ever again mentions selling Zlateh.

Two Japanese stories are very different in feeling but are realistic nonetheless. In *The Boy of the Three-Year Nap* (283), Diane Snyder tells how a poor mother tricks her lazy son into a marriage and employment. Margaret Hodges has retold *The Wave* (163) in which a poor man sacrifices his own rice fields in order to warn other villagers of an approaching tidal wave. Blair Lent worked in a technique rarely seen in children's books, using cardboard cutouts to print the illustrations for the story.

The box that follows, "A Cross-Cultural Study of Folktale Types," is the first of three boxes that group folktales from various countries in specific ways. These groups provide easy access to similar-tale titles so that teachers may more easily

RESOURCES FOR TEACHING

♦ A CROSS-CULTURAL STUDY OF FOLKTALE TYPES ♦

TYPE OF FOLKTALE	TALE	CULTURE
Cumulative tales	"The Old Woman and Her Pig" (248)	England
	The Fat Cat	Denmark
	Henny Penny (36)	England
	One Fine Day (164)	Armenia
	Bringing the Rain to Kapiti Plain (3)	Africa, Kenya
Pourquoi tales	*The Great Race of the Birds and the Animals* (99)	Native American
	"Jack and the Devil" (147)	African American
	The Cat's Purr (34)	West Indian
	Why the Sun and the Moon Live in the Sky (59)	Africa
	How Summer Came to Canada (292)	Native American
	"Tia Miseria's Pear Tree" (304)	Puerto Rico
	"How Animals Got Their Tails" (33)	Africa
	Feathers Like a Rainbow (78)	South America
	A Song of Stars (23)	China/Japan
Beast tales	*The Three Billy Goats Gruff* (16)	Norway
	The Bremen-Town Musicians (108)	Germany
	Rabbit Makes a Monkey of Lion (4)	Africa, Tanzania
	The Three Little Pigs (92)	England
	Foolish Rabbit's Big Mistake (213)	India
	"Brer Terrapin" (151)	African American
	Beat the Story Drum, Pum Pum (33)	Africa
	Rockabye Crocodile (13)	Philippines
Wonder tales	*Ali Baba and the Forty Thieves* (206)	Middle East
	Jack and the Beanstalk (40)	England
	Beauty and the Beast (239)	France
	Snow White (133)	Germany
	Momotaro, The Peach Boy (276)	Japan
	Tam Lin (53)	Scotland
	Vasilissa the Beautiful (303)	Russia
Realistic tales	*Dick Whittington and His Cat* (30)	England
	Brothers (79)	Jewish
	The Boy of the Three-Year Nap (283)	Japan
	"The Case of the Uncooked Eggs" (304)	Haiti
	My Mother Is the Most Beautiful Woman in the World (246)	Russia
	"Zlateh the Goat" (280)	Jewish
	The Empty Pot (63)	China

plan curricula. The other boxes group tales by motif and by variants.

Characteristics of Folktales

Since folktales have been told and retold from generation to generation within a particular culture, we may ask how they reflect the country of their origin and their oral tradition. An authentic tale from Africa will include references to the flora and fauna of Africa, to the food that was eaten by the tribespeople, their huts, their customs, their foibles, and their beliefs; and it will sound as if it is being *told*. While folktales have many elements in common, it should not be possible to confuse a folktale from Japan with a folktale from the fjords of Norway. What then are the characteristics common to all folktales?

PLOT STRUCTURES OF FOLKTALES

Among the folktales best known in children's literature, the longer stories are usually simple and direct. A series of episodes maintains a quick flow of action. If it is a wise beast–foolish beast story, the characters are quickly delineated; the action shows the inevitable conflict and resolution; and the ending is usually brief. If the tale is a romance, the hero sets forth on his journey, often helps the poor on his way, frequently receives magical power, overcomes obstacles, and returns to safety. The plot that involves a weak or innocent child going forth to meet the monsters of the world is another form of the "journey-novel." *Hansel and Gretel* (118) go out into a dark world and meet the witch, but goodness and purity triumph. Almost all folktale plots are success stories of one kind or another.

Repetition is a basic element in many folktale plots. Frequently, three is the magic number. There are three little pigs whose three houses face the puffing of the wolf. The wolf gives three challenges to the pig in the brick house—to get turnips and apples and to go to the fair. In the longer tales each of the three tasks becomes increasingly more difficult, and the intensity of the wonders becomes progressively more marvelous. For example, each of three prince brothers tries to determine who or what steals the golden apples that ripen each night in their garden. The youngest sees *The Firebird* (184) and manages to

bring back one of its brilliant feathers. So the three princes go their separate ways to find the glorious bird. Helped by a vixen, the youngest prince finally succeeds by performing tasks, winning a bride, and overcoming the treachery of his two older brothers. This repetition satisfies listeners or readers with its orderliness.

Repetition of responses, chants, or poems is frequently a part of the structure of a tale. "Mirror, mirror on the wall, who is fairest of them all?" And "Fee, fi, fo, fum" are repetitive verses familiar to all. Some versions of *Hansel and Gretel* (117) end with a storyteller's coda: "My tale is done, and there a mouse does run. Whoever catches it can make a big fur cap of it." These serve both the storyteller and the listener as memory aids and familiar markers of the unfolding plot.

Time and place are established quickly in the folktale. "Long ago, in the land of Egypt, where the Nile River widens to meet the blue sea, there lived a maiden called Rhodopis" begins *The Egyptian Cinderella* (44). Time is always past, and frequently described by such conventions as "Once upon a time" or "In olden times when wishing still helped." Time also passes quickly in the folktale. The woods and brambles encircle Sleeping Beauty's palace (132) in a quarter of an hour, and "when a hundred years were gone and passed," the prince appears at the moment the enchantment ends. The setting of the folktale is not specific, but in some faraway land, in a cottage in the woods, in a beautiful palace.

The introduction to the folktale usually presents the conflict, characters, and setting in a few sentences. In "Anansi and Nothing Go Hunting for Wives" (54) the problem is established in the first two sentences:

> ❧ It came to Anansi one time, as he sat in his little hut, that he needed a wife. For most men this would have been a simple affair, but Anansi's bad name had spread throughout the country and he knew that he wouldn't be likely to have much luck finding a wife in near-by villages.[15]

With little description, the storyteller goes to the heart of his story, capturing the interest of his audience.

[15]Harold Courlander and George Herzog, *The Cow-Tail Switch and Other West African Stories* (New York: Holt, Rinehart and Winston, 1947), p. 95.

"Now, I'm coming to gobble you up!" roared the troll.
"Well, come along! I've got two spears,
And I'll poke your eyeballs out at your ears.
I've got besides two great big stones,
And I'll crush you to bits, body and bones."

Traditional characteristics of the Norse tale of *The Three Billy Goats Gruff* include repetition of "trip, trap, trap" and the patterned responses of the troll to each of the three goats. In Marcia Brown's bold woodcut the powerful diagonal thrust of the biggest billy goat foreshadows its upcoming destruction of the evil troll.

The conclusion of the story follows the climax very quickly and includes few details. After the small sister finds her brothers who have been bewitched as *The Seven Ravens* (131), she leaves her tiny ring in one of the ravens' cups. He sees it and wishes:

🦋 "Would God that our own little sister were here, for then we should be free!"

When the maiden, who was standing behind the door listening, heard the wish, she came out, and then all the ravens regained human forms again. And they embraced and kissed one another and went joyfully home."[16]

[16]Grimm Brothers, *The Seven Ravens*, translated by Elizabeth D. Crawford, illustrated by Lisbeth Zwerger (New York: Morrow, 1981), unpaged.

Even this is a long ending compared with, "and so they were married and lived happily ever after."

The structure of the folktale, with its quick introduction, economy of incident, and logical and brief conclusion maintains interest through suspense and repetition. Because the storyteller has to keep the attention of the audience, each episode must contribute to the theme of the story. Written versions, then, should follow the oral tradition, adding little description and avoiding lengthy asides or admonitions.

CHARACTERIZATION IN FOLKTALES

Characters in folktales are shown in flat dimensions, symbolic of the completely good or entirely evil. Character development is seldom depicted. The beautiful girl is usually virtuous, humble, patient, and loving. Stepmothers are ugly, cross, and mean. The hero, usually fair-haired, or curly-haired, is strong, virile, brave, kind, and sympathetic. The poor are often kind, generous, and long suffering; the rich are imperious, hardhearted, and often conniving, if not actually dishonest. Physical characteristics may be described briefly, but readers form their own pictures as they read. In describing "The Daughter of the Dragon King" the Chinese grandmother says: "Now this young woman was poorly dressed, but her face was as fair as a plum blossom in spring, and her body was as slender as a willow branch."[17]

Qualities of character or special strengths or weaknesses of the characters are revealed quickly, because this factor will be the cause of conflict or lead to resolution of the plot. The lazy daughter and virtuous stepdaughter are contrasted in the Russian tale *The Month-Brothers* (208). "The daughter used to loll about the whole day long on a featherbed devouring sweetmeats, while the stepdaughter never got a chance to rest from morn to night."[18] The trickster character of Brer Rabbit in *Jump Again!* (152) is established in a few swift phrases: "Brer Rabbit could cut more capers than a hive has bumbly-bees. Under his hat, Brer Rabbit had a mighty quick thinking apparatus. . . ."[19]

Seeing folktale characters as symbols of good, evil, power, trickery, wisdom, and other traits, children begin to understand the basis of literature that distills the essences of human experience.

STYLE OF FOLKTALES

Folktales offer children many opportunities to hear rich qualitative language and a wide variety of language patterns. Story introductions may range from the familiar "once upon a time" to the

Persian "there was a time and there wasn't a time" or the African tale that starts: "We do not mean, we do not really mean that what we are going to say is true."

The introductions and language of the folktale should maintain the "flavor" of the country but still be understood by its present audience. Folktales should not be "written down" to children, but they may need to be simplified. Wanda Gág describes her method of simplification in adapting folktales for children:

> By simplification I mean:
>
> (a) freeing hybrid stories of confusing passages
> (b) using repetition for clarity where a mature style does not include it
> (c) employing actual dialogue to sustain or revive interest in places where the narrative is too condensed for children.
>
> However, I do not mean writing in words of one or two syllables. True, the careless use of large words is confusing to children; but long, even unfamiliar words are relished and easily absorbed by them, provided they have enough color and sound value.[20]

Some folktales include proverbs of the country. For example, a king speaks to his followers after hearing a story of a man whose second wife murdered his son: "Choose whom you want to marry, but if you choose a tree that has fruit, you must care for the fruit as much as for the tree."[21] In the Russian story of *Vasilissa the Beautiful* (303) a small doll counsels the sorrowful Vasilissa to shut her eyes and sleep for "The morning is wiser than the evening."

Although there is a minimum of description in the folktale, figurative language and imagery are employed by effective narrators. Isaac Singer (278) uses delightful prose to introduce the Jewish tale about the wager between the spirits of good luck and bad luck:

> In a faraway land, on a sunny spring day, the sky was as blue as the sea, and the sea was as blue as

[17]Frances Carpenter, *Tales of a Chinese Grandmother*, illustrated by Malthe Hasselriis (New York: Doubleday, 1949), p. 75.

[18]Samuel Marshak, *The Month-Brothers: A Slavic Tale*, translated by Thomas P. Whitney, illustrated by Diane Stanley (New York: Morrow, 1983), unpaged.

[19]Joel Chandler Harris, *Jump Again! More Adventures of Brer Rabbit*, retold by Van Dyke Parks, illustrated by Barry Moser (San Diego: Harcourt Brace Jovanovich, 1987), p. 2.

[20]Wanda Gág, *Tales from Grimm* (New York: Coward-McCann, 1936), p. ix.

[21]Diane Wolkstein, *The Magic Orange Tree and Other Haitian Folktales*, illustrated by Elsa Henriquez (New York: Knopf, 1978), p. 97.

the sky, and the earth was green and in love with them both.[22]

In the East African story *Bimwili & the Zimwi* (1), a little girl was playing by the ocean and "something that looked like a daytime moon came rolling in with a wave, and it tumbled at Bimwili's feet."[23] The daytime moon, a simile for a seashell, begins all of Bimwili's many nights of troubles.

Frequently, storytellers imitate the sounds of the story. In Katherine Paterson's poetic translation from the Japanese of the traditional tale *The Crane Wife* (306), Yohei goes out into the winter snow on an errand. "Suddenly, *basabasa*, he heard a rustling sound. It was a crane dragging its wing, as it swooped down and landed on the path."[24] Later in the story, the sound of a weaver at a loom is heard—*tonkara, tonkara*. In Verna Aardema's retelling of the West African tale of *Why Mosquitoes Buzz in People's Ears* (7), a python slithers into a rabbit's hole *wasawusu, wasawusu, wasawusu* and the terrified rabbit scurries away *krik, krik, krik*. These onomatopoeic words help listeners hear the story and are wonderful additions for those who tell and read stories to children.

When the tales are written as though the storyteller is speaking directly to the reader, the oral tradition is more clearly communicated. Joyce Arkhurst uses this style effectively in *The Adventures of Spider* (12):

> I have already told you, and you have already seen for yourselves, that Spider was very full of mischief. He was often naughty and always greedy. But sometimes, in his little heart, he wanted very much to be good. . . . He tried hard, but his appetite almost always got in the way. In fact, that is why Spider has a bald head to this day. Would you like to hear how it got that way?[25]

Surely children in the primary grades would be cheated linguistically if the only version they heard was Gerald McDermott's *Anansi the Spider* (203):

> One time Anansi went a long way from home. Far from home. He got lost. He fell into trouble. Back home was See Trouble. "Father is in danger!" he cried. He knew it quickly and he told those other sons.[26]

This kind of simplification of text deprives children not only of meaning but also of language of the folktale, a key feature of literature based on an oral tradition. Without the pictures, it would be difficult to comprehend this story.

Dialect enhances a story, but it is difficult for children to read. The teacher will need to practice reading or telling a story with dialect, but it is worth the effort if it is done well. Richard Chase recorded stories from the Appalachian mountain folk in *The Jack Tales* (43). He notes: "The dialect has been changed enough to avoid confusion to the reading eye; the idiom has been kept throughout." In this dialogue from "The Heifer Hide" the mountaineer vocabulary and dialect are clear:

> "Well, now," she says, "hit's just a little I was a-savin' for my kinfolks comin' tomorrow."
> "Me and Jack's your kinfolks. Bring it on out here for us."
> So Jack and him eat a lot of them good rations. Jack was awful hungry, and he knowed she hadn't brought out her best stuff yet, so he rammed his heifer hide again, says, "You blabber-mouthed thing! I done told you to hush. You keep on tellin' lies now and I'll put you out the door."[27]

Julius Lester, in his retellings of the Uncle Remus stories collected by Joel Chandler Harris, tried to do what Harris had done: namely, to write tales "so that the reader (listener) would feel as if he or she were being called into a relationship of warmth and intimacy with another human

[22]Isaac Bashevis Singer, *Mazel and Shlimazel, or The Milk of a Lioness,* illustrated by Margot Zemach (New York: Farrar, Straus, Giroux, 1967), p. 1.
[23]Verna Aardema, *Bimwili & the Zimwi,* illustrated by Susan Meddaugh (New York: Dial, 1985), unpaged.
[24]Sumiko Yagawa, *The Crane Wife,* translated by Katherine Paterson, illustrated by Suekichi Akaba (New York: Morrow, 1981), unpaged.
[25]Joyce Cooper Arkhurst, *The Adventures of Spider: West African Folk Tales,* illustrated by Jerry Pinkney (Boston: Little, Brown, 1964), p. 21.

[26]Gerald McDermott, *Anansi the Spider* (New York: Holt, Rinehart and Winston, 1972), unpaged.
[27]Richard Chase, *The Jack Tales,* illustrated by Berkeley Williams (Boston: Houghton Mifflin, 1943), p. xi.

body."[28] His contemporary storyteller communicates through asides, imagery, and allusions. For instance, in "Brer Rabbit Gets Even" (197) Brer Rabbit decides to visit with Miz Meadows and the girls:

🐾 "Don't come asking me who Miz Meadows and her girls were. I don't know, but then again, ain't no reason I got to know. Miz Meadows and the girls were in the tale when it was handed to me, and they gon' be in it when I hand it to you. And that's the way the rain falls on that one."[29]

The major criteria for style in the written folktale, then, are that it maintain the atmosphere of the country and culture from which it originated and that it sound like a tale *told* by a storyteller.

THEMES IN FOLKTALES

The basic purpose of the folktale is to tell an entertaining story, yet these stories do present important themes. Some tales may be merely humorous accounts of foolish people who are so ridiculous that the listeners see their own foolish ways exaggerated. Many of the stories once provided an outlet for feelings against the kings and nobles who oppressed the poor. Values of the culture are expressed in folklore. The virtues of humility, kindness, patience, sympathy, hard work, and courage are invariably rewarded. These rewards reflect the goals of people—long life, a good spouse, beautiful homes and fine clothing, plenty of food, freedom from fear of the ogre or giant. The power of love, mercy, and kindness is one of the major themes of folktales. The Latvian tale of *The Hedgehog Boy* (191) tells of an old couple who longed for a child and get instead a peasant boy who is covered with ugly hedgehoglike prickers. He is finally released from his spell by the love of a princess much to the pride of his loving parents. The thematic wisdom of *Beauty and the Beast* (233) is that we should not trust too much to appearances. The valuing of the inner

qualities of kindness and a loving heart above outward appearance is dramatically presented.

Many folktales feature the small and powerless achieving good ends by perseverance and patience. In the traditional Japanese tale of *Momotaro, The Peach Boy* (276), a peasant goes off to battle against wicked demons armed only with a banner, three *kibi dango* or dumplings baked by his mother, and the companionship of a dog and a monkey. But courage and quick wits help him persevere. In the African tale of *A Story, A Story* (142), Anansi the spider man wins stories for his people by outsmarting a leopard, the hornets, and a fairy, and presenting them all to the Sky God. Both Marina, the good child in *Baba Yaga* (187), and Sasha, the kind girl in *Bony-Legs* (49), have good luck when they are kind to objects and animals. Thus they are able to outwit the formidable old Russian witch, Baba Yaga. In the Grimm tale, *The Brave Little Tailor* (107) can outwit even huge ogres.

Feminists have expressed concern that folktale themes most often favor courageous, independent boy adventurers, while girls languish at home. Though it is true that it is easier to find tales that feature plucky boys, there are folktales that portray resourceful, courageous, clever, and independent girls. *Mollie Whuppie* (62), the youngest daughter of a woodcutter, rescues her two older sisters and herself from the murderous giant. She then bravely returns to the giant's castle to steal a sword, a purse, and a gold ring. Thus she wins for each sister and herself a king's son for a husband. In Jane Yolen's *Tam Lin* (312), outspoken, 16-year-old Jennet MacKenzie perseveres in saving a young man bewitched by the fairies even though they change his shape to many fearsome animals. *Princess Furball* (127) doesn't need a fairy godmother; she wins a prince because of her own cleverness. *Duffy and the Devil.* (314) make a pact, but she finally outwits him—and manages to get out of spinning and knitting for the rest of her days. Clever Oonagh helps her giant husband, *Fin M'Coul* (64), outsmart the giant Cucullin. Tales that feature spirited and courageous heroines have been gathered in several collections. *The Maid of the North* (241), *The Skull in the Snow* (201), and *Womenfolk and Fairy Tales* (220) are examples of the way collec-

[28]Julius Lester, "The Storyteller's Voice: Reflections on the Rewriting of Uncle Remus," *The New Advocate*, vol. 1, no. 3 (Summer 1988), p. 144.
[29]Julius Lester, *The Tales of Uncle Remus: The Adventures of Brer Rabbit*, illustrated by Jerry Pinkney (New York: Dial, 1987), p. 16

tions from the world over preserve and honor stories of strong, clever, and often brave women.

Parents, teachers, and some psychologists have expressed concern about themes of cruelty and horror in folktales. "Little Red Riding Hood," for example, has been rewritten so that the wolf eats neither the grandmother nor the heroine. Goals are not accomplished easily in folktales; they frequently require sacrifice. But usually harsh acts occur very quickly with no sense of pain and no details. In *The Seven Ravens* (131), no blood drips from the sister's hand when she cuts off a finger; not an "ouch" escapes her lips. *The Fat Cat* (186) is cut open so that the people he has eaten may escape. Tape closes the bloodless cut. Children accept these stories as they are—symbolic interpretations of life in an imaginary land of another time.

MOTIFS IN FOLKTALES

Folklorists analyze folktales according to motifs or patterns, numbering each tale and labeling its episodes.[30] *Motifs* have been defined as the smallest part of a tale that can exist independently. These motifs can be seen in the recurring parade of characters in folktales—the younger brother, the wicked stepmother, the abused child, the clever trickster—or in such supernatural beings as the fairy godmother, the evil witch, or the terrifying giant. The use of magical objects—a slipper, a doll, a ring, or tablecloth—is another pattern found in many folktales. Stories of enchantment, long sleeps, or marvelous transformations are typical motifs. Some of the motifs have been repeated so frequently that they have been identified as a type of folk story. Thus we have beast tales about talking animals and the wonder tales of supernatural beings.

Even the plots of the stories have recurring patterns—three tasks to be performed, three wishes that are granted, or three trials to be endured. A simple tale will have several motifs; a complex one will have many. Recognizing some of the most common motifs in folklore will help a

teacher to suggest points of comparison and contrast in a cross-cultural approach to folk literature.

Magical Powers

Magical powers are frequently given to persons or animals in folktales. A common pattern in folklore is the "helpful companions" who all have magical talents. *The Fool of the World and the Flying Ship* (245) sail away with eight companions who can eat huge quantities, hear long distances, or drink whole lakes. Later, these talents help them overcome trials the czar imposes on the fool. *The Month-Brothers* (208) have magical powers to control the coming of the seasons and each brother oversees his month. The gris-gris woman can make a girl fly as well as create for her a *Moss Gown* (165) in which she is able to attend the Carolina plantation owner's ball. Of course, *Rumpelstiltskin* (257) can spin straw into gold. The possessors of magical powers always aid each hero in obtaining his or her goal.

Transformations

The transformation of an animal to a person, or the reverse, is a part of many folktales. *Beauty and the Beast* (235) and *The Princess and the Frog* (126) are perhaps the most well known of tales in which a bewitched animal is transformed by love. A crane turns into a woman and back into a crane when her spouse is disloyal in the Japanese tale of *The Crane Wife* (306). Errol Le Cain's decorative illustrations for *Cinderella* (238) skillfully capture the exact moments of two transformations. The mouse is changed into a horse in eight overlapping figures; in another sequence of illustrations, Cinderella goes from rags to riches as images of floating clocks pursue her. Illustrations such as these may inspire children to render transformations creatively in their own stories.

Magic Objects

Magic objects are essential aspects of many tales that also reflect other themes or motifs. Both a ring and a lamp play an essential part in the story of *Aladdin* (188). *Vasilissa the Beautiful* (303) is able to outwit Baba Yaga's demands with the help of a magic little doll given to her by her mother. *Strega Nona* (66) owns a magic cooking pot that may be started by saying "Bubble, bubble, pasta

---

[30]Stith Thompson, *Motif Index of Folk-Literature* (Bloomington: Indiana University Press, 1955–1958), 6 vols.

pot" to make all the pasta anyone needs. But Big Anthony, a true noodlehead, starts the pot without observing Strega Nona's method of getting it to stop: blowing three kisses. *The Funny Little Woman* (225) has a magic rice paddle that she uses to good advantage both underground and above. In *The Badger and the Magic Fan* (177), a trickster badger steals a magic fan that has the power to make noses grow or shrink. He uses it on a beautiful girl's nose and she agrees to marry him if he will restore her beauty. But Badger's thievery is also his undoing when those from whom he stole the fan steal it back and make Badger's nose grow to the heavens. Other magic objects that figure in folktales are purses, harps, a hen that lays golden eggs, tables, sticks, and tinderboxes. A magical object often heightens a good character's courage and cleverness while in other stories the misuse of a magical object may cause disaster for a bad character.

Wishes

Many stories are told of wishes that are granted and then used foolishly or in anger or greed. *The Three Wishes* (320) is the tale of the woodsman who

A magic pot as well as an ignored warning are two of the motifs found in Tomie de Paola's popular Italian tale of *Strega Nona*.

was so hungry that he wished for a sausage; his wife was so angry at this wish that she wished the food would stick to his nose; then, of course, they have to use the third wish to get it off. The earth tones and blues of Margot Zemach's watercolor illustrations capture perfectly the rustic setting of this humorous story. *The Stonecutter* (205) wishes to have more power and the spirit of the mountain grants his wish. But in this Japanese tale, each time the stonecutter is transformed, he discovers something more powerful than he. Finally, left alone as a towering mountain, he feels a stonecutter chip away at his base and he trembles. As in *The Fisherman and His Wife* (112), greed destroys any gains a character may make.

Trickery

Both animals and people trick their friends and neighbors in folk literature. The wolf tricks Little Red Riding Hood into believing he is her grandmother; Hansel and Gretel trick the mean old witch into crawling into the oven.

Almost every culture has an animal trickster in its folklore. In European folktales it is usually a wolf or a fox; in Japan it is a badger or a hare; Indonesia has Kantjil, a tiny mouse deer; Africa has three well-known tricksters, Anansi the spider, Zomo the rabbit, and Ijapa the tortoise; and Coyote and the raven play this role in Native-American tales.

Two realistic tales feature humans tricking others. The familiar *Stone Soup* (32) presents three poor soldiers who dupe greedy peasants into contributing all of the ingredients to a pot of soup save one—a stone, which they generously contribute. *The Boy of the Three-Year Nap* (283) tricks a rich merchant, but the lazy boy is tricked into a lifetime occupation by his wise old mother.

In the African-American tale *Wiley and the Hairy Man* (19), Wiley twice tricks the Hairy Man, who lives in the Tombigbee Swamp land. But it is Wiley's mother who plays the third trick. When the Hairy Man comes to take Wiley away, his mother promises, from inside her cabin, to give him "the young 'un." However, she does not say *which* young one she means and she has substituted a piglet in Wiley's bed. The Hairy Man, realizing that he has been foiled, angrily snatches the piglet and disappears in a rage. According to tradition, since he has been tricked three times, he can never bother Wiley and his mother again.

Magical powers, transformations, use of magic objects, wishes, and trickery are just a few of the motifs that run through the folklore of all countries, as we have seen. Others may include the power of naming, as in *Rumpelstiltskin* (89); the ability to make yourself invisible as the man did in *The Twelve Dancing Princesses* (216); becoming stuck to a person or object, as in the African-American tale of "The Wonderful Tar-Baby Story" (152); or the enchanted or lengthy sleep as in "Urashima Taro and the Princess of the Sea" (296) or *Snow White* (133). One way to understand the common elements of all folklore is to make your own lists of motifs or have the children in your classroom do so.

The following box, "A Cross-Cultural Study of Folktale Motifs," mentions both well-known and lesser known tales as a beginning for those wishing to pursue a study of motifs. There are many other titles that could be added to these five motifs and, of course, there are many more motifs around which to group folklore.

VARIANTS OF FOLKTALES

The number of variants of a single folktale fascinates beginning students of folklore. A variant has basically the same story or plot as another, but it may have different characters and a different setting or it may use different motifs. For example, in an African-American story of *The Talking Eggs* (259), a poor girl goes to the old woman in the woods and in return for being help-

---

RESOURCES FOR TEACHING

♦ A CROSS-CULTURAL STUDY OF FOLKTALE MOTIFS ♦

SAMPLE MOTIFS	TALE	CULTURE
Magical powers	*The Fool of the World and the Flying Ship* (245)	Russia
	Rumpelstiltskin (89)	Germany
	The Month-Brothers (208)	Russia
	Raven's Light (273)	Native American
	The Seven Chinese Brothers (207)	China
	Moss Gown (165)	United States
	Yeh-Shen (200)	China
Transformations	*Beauty and the Beast* (234)	France
	The Crane Wife (306)	Japan
	The Story of Jumping Mouse (287)	Native American
	The Little Snowgirl (55)	Russia
	The Hedgehog Boy (191)	Latvia
	Cinderella (239)	France
	Tam Lin (312)	Scotland
	Snow White and Rose Red (134)	Germany
	The Princess and the Frog (126)	Germany
	The Selkie Girl (51)	Scotland
	The Orphan Boy (221)	Africa, Kenya
Magic objects	*The Talking Eggs* (259)	African American
	The Badger and the Magic Fan (177)	Japan
	Vasilissa the Beautiful (303)	Russia
	Aladdin (188)	Middle East

RESOURCES FOR TEACHING

◆ A CROSS-CULTURAL STUDY OF FOLKTALE MOTIFS (CONTINUED) ◆

SAMPLE MOTIFS	TALE	CULTURE
	The Twelve Dancing Princesses (216)	France
	The Magic Horse (266)	Middle East
Wishes	*The Stonecutter* (205)	Japan
	The Fisherman and His Wife (112)	Germany
	The Seven Ravens (131)	Germany
	Momotaro, the Peach Boy (276)	Japan
	The Three Wishes (320)	Germany
	The Fool and the Fish (8)	Russia
Trickery	*Borreguita and the Coyote* (2)	Mexico
	"Shrewd Todie and Lyzer, the Miser" (279)	Jewish
	Rabbit Makes a Monkey of Lion (4)	Africa, Tanzania
	The Quail Song (37)	Native American
	Stone Soup (288)	France
	"Anansi and the Old Hag" (271)	Jamaica
	The Boy of the Three-Year Nap (283)	Japan
	Wiley and the Hairy Man (19)	African American
	"Firefly and the Apes" (268)	Philippines
	Clever Tom and the Leprechaun (275)	Ireland
	The Merry Pranks of Till Eulenspiegel (321)	Germany
	Lon Po Po (313)	China

ful and uncritical, she is allowed to take plain eggs and warned to avoid the jeweled ones in the henhouse. The eggs, when tossed behind her, become riches. Her greedy stepsister then goes to the same woman and is critical and unhelpful. However, she is promised gifts and is warned in the same way, but chooses the fancy eggs instead. When they are tossed, out comes a veritable Pandora's box; the eggs are full of stinging insects. A choice of two chests is a motif of the Japanese tale, *The Tongue-Cut Sparrow* (172). The kind old man gains coral and riches from the smaller chest he chooses but his ill-tempered old wife is chased home by a snake and a toad when she opens her choice of the larger chest. In the Philippine tale of *Rockabye Crocodile* (13), a kind boar and a greedy one end up in a similar situation when one rocks a cranky baby crocodile while the other ignores it. The theme of rewards for a generous and willing person and punishment for a greedy and disobedient one seems to be universal.

A comparison of the variants of Cinderella illustrates differences in theme and motif. Scholars have found versions of this story in ancient Egypt, in China in the ninth century, and in Iceland in the tenth century. Cinderella receives her magic gifts in many different ways; in the French and most familiar version, a fairy godmother gives them to her (237); in Grimm's version (109) a dove appears on the tree that grew from the tears she had shed on her mother's grave; in the English *Tattercoats* (174) she receives her beautiful gowns from a herdboy; in the Chinese *Yeh-Shen* (200) magic fish bones bestow gifts on her. She attends three balls in some stories; for example, in the Italian version (155), Cenerentola throws coins as she leaves the ball the first night and pearls on the second escape and loses her slipper on the third night. Her treatment of the stepsisters varies from blinding them to inviting them to live at the palace. The Vietnamese version, "The Brocaded Slipper" (299), is made longer by the narrative of the stepsister finally meeting her own death after "killing" her Cinderella sister, Tam, three times. In "The Indian Cinderella" (156), the lovely young daughter of a chief is cruelly treated by her jealous elder sisters who frequently beat her and burn her face with hot coals. For this reason she is often called "Little Burnt Face" (in other versions of this tale).

Variants of the story of *Rumpelstiltskin* (130) include the hero's need to know the antagonist's name in order to have his services or to be safe from his magic powers. A character in these stories is able to discover the name and trick an imp, dwarf, or devil. Several variations on this theme may be found in the Cornish *Duffy and the Devil* (314), the English *Tom Tit Tot* (227), and the Scottish "Whippety Stourie" (302), all discussed under "British Folktales."

Another form of trickery is the "Helpful Companions" story in which a number of friends all have magical powers that assist the hero in completing his quest. *Jack and the Beanstalk* (40) comes in many versions, but Appalachian variants change not only the language of the telling but also the typical objects that Jack covets. These include a coverlet with small bells on it or a rifle. Humorous literary variants on this tale have been retold by Raymond Briggs in *Jim and the Beanstalk* (27) and by Tony Ross in *Jack and the Beanstalk* (252).

We have provided boxes that organize folktales by tale type and by common motif. The following box, "A Cross-Cultural Study of Folktale Variants," provides yet a third way of organizing tales for classroom presentation. These variants make excellent comparison material and elemen-

---

RESOURCES FOR TEACHING

◆ A CROSS-CULTURAL STUDY OF FOLKTALE VARIANTS ◆

VARIANTS OF A THEME	CULTURE
Cinderella (239)	France
Tattercoats (174)	England
Yeh-Shen (200)	China
"The Indian Cinderella" (156)	Native American
The Egyptian Cinderella (44)	Egypt
Moss Gown (165)	United States
Vasilissa the Beautiful (303)	Russia
Princess Furball (127)	Germany
"Mossycoat" (94)	England
Jack and the Beanstalk (40)	England
The History of Mother Twaddle and the Marvelous Achievements of Her Son Jack (85)	England
Jim and the Beanstalk (27)	Modern Literary
The Giant's Toe (48)	Modern Literary
"Jack and the Bean Tree" (43)	Appalachian American
Jack and the Beanstalk (252)	Modern Literary
Jack and the Bean Tree (143)	Appalachian American
The Magic Porridge Pot (87)	Germany
Strega Nona (66)	Italy
The Funny Little Woman (225)	Japan
The Magic Cooking Pot (291)	India

RESOURCES FOR TEACHING

♦ A CROSS-CULTURAL STUDY OF FOLKTALE VARIANTS (CONTINUED) ♦

VARIANTS OF A THEME	CULTURE
Generous person/greedy person	
Mufaro's Beautiful Daughters (286)	Africa, Zimbabwe
Baba Yaga (187)	Russia
The Talking Eggs (259)	African American
Rockabye Crocodile (13)	Philippines
"Toads and Diamonds" (189)	France
The Tongue-Cut Sparrow (172)	Japan
Mother Holly (125)	Germany
The Month-Brothers (208)	Russia
Helpful companions	
The Seven Chinese Brothers (207)	China
The Fool of the World and the Flying Ship (245)	Russia
Anansi the Spider (203)	West Africa
The Five Chinese Brothers (24)	China
Rum Pum Pum (73)	India
Rumpelstiltskin (130)	Germany
Duffy and the Devil (314)	England
"Whippety Stourie" (302)	Scotland
Tom Tit Tot (227)	England
The Table, the Donkey, and the Stick (136)	Germany
"The Lad Who Went to the North Wind" (14)	Norway
"Jack and the North West Wind" (43)	Appalachian American
"Clever Peter and the Two Bottles" (243)	Germany
Stone Soup (32)	France
The Soup Stone (297)	American Literary
Stone Soup (253)	Modern Literary
Nail Soup (315)	Sweden
Stone Soup (288)	France

tary children enjoy discovering the similarities and differences. Classroom-made charts, with the tale titles going down the left margin and topics listed across the top, allow children to compare such aspects as:

♦ opening and ending conventions
♦ origin of the tale
♦ clues to the country or region of origin
♦ talents of the characters

♦ tasks to be done
♦ verses, refrains, chants, and their outcomes
♦ illustrations
♦ special or unique vocabulary

Each group of variants will have other categories to compare as well. For example, categories might be "Instructions for Stopping a Pot from Cooking," "How Rumpelstiltskin's Name Is Discovered," or "Greedy Person's Reward."

Children should be encouraged to develop their own category titles whenever possible.

Knowledge of the different variants of a tale, common motifs, and common types of folktales enable a teacher to help children see similar elements in folktales across cultures. Knowledge of the folklore of a particular country or cultural group aids in identifying the uniqueness and individuality of that group. Both approaches to a study of folklore seem essential.

Folktales of the World

BRITISH FOLKTALES

The first folktales that most children in the United States hear are the English ones. This is because Joseph Jacobs, the folklorist who collected many of the English tales, deliberately adapted them for young children, writing them, he said, "as a good old nurse will speak when she tells Fairy Tales." His collection includes cumulative tales such as "The Old Woman and Her Pig" and "Henny Penny" and the much-loved talking-beast stories, "The Little Red Hen," "The Three Bears," and "The Three Little Pigs." Both Helen Oxenbury (231) and Anne Rockwell (248, 249) have retold and illustrated these in excellent collections. Paul Galdone has illustrated single editions of all of these nursery tales with large, colorful, and humorous pictures that appeal to the young child. Galdone's retelling of *The Three Bears* (90) reads aloud well. His clever pictures depict three sizes of bowls, chairs, and beds and use varying print size as each bear speaks; this practically invites 5- and 6-year-olds to read along. Small touches of humor, such as the baby reading a huge book while Papa has the tiniest, are found in many illustrations. James Marshall is even more broadly humorous in his *Goldilocks and the Three Bears* (209). His flippant telling seldom strays in content from the story's "bones," but Goldilocks cries "Patooie" as she tastes the too-hot porridge and his cartoonish illustrations show Baby Bear's room as a mess of football pennants, books, and toys. Marshall has also given *The Three Little Pigs* (212) a verbal and visual topspin.

In the original British tale of *Chicken Licken* (25) or *Henny Penny* (84), the fox eats the accumulation of animals rushing to tell the king that the sky is falling. However, Steven Kellogg gives Foxy Loxy his comeuppance in *Chicken Little* (180) by having a police helicopter pilot, a hippopotamus, fall onto the fox's poultry truck. The hapless fox is sentenced to jail and a diet of green bean gruel, and the foolish fowl are freed. Chicken Little is able to tell her tale to her grandchildren beside the giant oak which grew from the acorn that started it all. While purists may object, these humorous treatments of well-known beast tales keep the stories alive for slightly older elementary school audiences who are familiar with the original story from having heard it in preschool, on television, or at library story hours. (For more about folktale spinoffs, see "Fooling with Folktales," Chapter 13.)

The Three Sillies is a droll realistic story about people who borrow trouble before it comes. Comic illustrations by Paul Galdone (93) and Margot Zemach (319) and exaggerated ones by Kathryn Hewett (157) depict a young girl who goes down in the cellar to draw beer for her suitor and parents. Seeing an axe stuck in the cellar beam, she imagines what might happen if, after her marriage, she has a son and he goes down in the cellar and is struck by the axe. Her parents soon join her in weeping over this imagined tragedy.

An element of realism runs through some English folktales. The story of Dick Whittington and his cat has its basis in history. There was once a real Richard Whittington who was three times mayor of London, in 1396, 1406, and 1419. And what an exceptional mayor he must have been—enacting prison reforms, providing the first public lavatory and drinking fountain, and building a library and a wing on the hospital for unmarried mothers. It is no wonder that the common people made him the popular hero of one of their most cherished tales. The story of "Dick and His Cat" was found in some of the very earliest chapbooks of the day. Marcia Brown's picture storybook, *Dick Whittington and His Cat* (30), portrays this realistic tale with handsome linoleum block prints appropriately printed in gold and black.

The British version of Cinderella, called *Tattercoats* (174), is a more poignant romance than the better known French story, for in this tale the prince falls in love with Tattercoats even when she is dirty and wearing an old torn petticoat. To prove his love he invites her to come as she is with her gooseherd friend and his geese to the king's ball that evening. Only after the prince greets them and presents her to the king as the girl he has chosen for his bride does the gooseherd begin to play his magical pipe and Tattercoats's rags are changed to shining robes while the geese become dainty pages. The gooseherd is never seen again. Margot Tomes's illustrations depict this story of a former princess reduced to and rescued from poor circumstances in warm earthy tones of charcoals and browns with tints of rose and rust.

Giant killers are also characters in some English stories. Everyone knows the story of *Jack and the Beanstalk* (40). Less well known in the United States is *Mollie Whuppie*, retold by Walter de la Mare (62). Mollie is a girl who would delight the heart of any feminist, for she is clever enough to trick a giant four times and escape over the Bridge of One Hair. The original version (285) is more gruesome, in that Mollie tricks the giant into choking his own children instead of her sisters and beating his wife to death in Mollie's place. De la Mare's retelling softens the story so that readers don't know the outcome for the giant's family.

A strong giant with a clever wife is *Fin M'Coul: The Giant of Knockmany Hill* (64). When Cucullin, an even stronger giant, comes looking for Fin, clever Oonagh makes a plan with the fairies who are everywhere in evidence in Tomie de Paola's illustrations. Fin is disguised as his own baby and placed in a cradle. Then, Oonagh sets up tricks to ensure that Cucullin loses his power and Fin's future is assured. Patterns from early Irish metalwork decorate the bordered pictures. A similar version of this story may be found in "Oonagh and the Giants." (241).

A variation on the German "Rumpelstiltskin" is Harve Zemach's telling of the Cornish *Duffy and the Devil* (314). Margot Zemach depicts the devil as a "squinny-eyed creature" who dances and sings:

🐌 Tomorrow! Tomorrow! Tomorrow's the day!
I'll take her! I'll take her! I'll take her away!

Let her weep, let her cry, let her beg, let her pray—
She'll never guess my name is Tarraway![31]

However, Duffy's outwitting of the Devil makes all of her husband's hand-spun clothes disappear! Both the language and the pen-and-wash illustrations retain the Cornish flavor of this folklore comedy. In the Scottish "Whippety Stourie" (310) six wee ladies help a young wife outmaneuver her husband.

Four versions of the story told in the Scottish ballad, "Tamlane," show how storytellers and illustrators give new meanings to a story. In Jane Yolen's *Tam Lin* (312), Jennet MacKenzie has a mind of her own: "No man would want her, even for all her beauty and her father's name. For she always spoke what she thought. And *what* she thought was never quite proper for a fine young lady."[32] On her sixteenth birthday, she wishes to claim her inheritance, the ancient family home of Carterhaugh stolen by the fairies many years ago. But the house and land are ruined after years of neglect. Pledging to take back the house for humankind, she plucks a rose, the only thing of beauty left. Suddenly a young man appears. Claimed by the fairies over a hundred years ago, he is Tam Lin, and if she cannot save him by Hallow's Eve, he shall die. The way she must save him is to pull him from his horse when the fairy procession passes, and hold him no matter what shape he assumes. Vivid and bold illustrations by Charles Mikolaycak depict Tam Lin's transformation from a serpent still partially clad in tartan to a lion. Jennet perseveres, outwits the fairies, and wins herself a husband and a home. In Susan Cooper's retelling (53), Margaret meets Tam Lin in the forest in June and must save him by Midsummer's Eve. Warwick Hutton's ethereal watercolors give this version a more dreamlike appearance and his depiction of Tam Lin's transformation is dramatically rendered over three

[31]Harve Zemach, *Duffy and the Devil*, illustrated by Margot Zemach (New York: Farrar, Straus, 1973), unpaged.
[32]Jane Yolen, *Tam Lin*, illustrated by Charles Mikolaycak (San Diego: Harcourt Brace Jovanovich, 1990), unpaged.

pages. In a third variation, Susan Jeffers's *Wild Robin* (176), it is a young girl who saves her impetuous brother from the fairies. In a fourth, Betsy James in *The Red Cloak* (175), tells a similar story of two childhood friends in a poor fishing village who outwit the fairies with the help of a red cloak. Illustrations make explicit the many changes young Tam endures before he is saved. Children may compare the moods created by different illustrators, the character of the girl, the relationship of the two characters, the supernatural aids or advice given, and the outcomes. Yolen's version includes an informative note about the history of this ballad.

In *The Selkie Girl* (51), Cooper and Hutton present another legend of Scottish or Irish origin concerning a man who takes as his wife a selkie, a gray seal in the water, but a woman on land. He hides her sealskin and for many years the woman lives as his wife and mother to their five children. But when the youngest child finds his mother's sealskin, she confesses that she also has a family of five children in the sea, bids farewell to her landbound family, and disappears into the sea. Mordicai Gerstein's *The Seal Mother* (95) softens the ending by having the son accompany his mother under water. Each Midsummer's Eve thereafter, the human and the selkie branches of the family meet to cavort on the rocks. Jane Yolen's *Greyling* (310) is yet a third variation. Children familiar with "Tam Lin" or selkie stories can recognize the shape-changing or transformation motif, which is found in ancient mythology as well as modern fantasy. (See Chapter 7.) Cooper and Hutton have produced a third tale of transformation in their Welsh story of *The Silver Cow* (52). In this story the Scottish fairies, the Fey, turn cows into waterlilies when a farmer's greed gets the better of his judgment.

British folklore includes giants and wee folk but has developed relatively few of the complicated wonder tales that abound in French and Russian folklore. It is often more robust and humorous than some other European tale traditions. Its greatest contribution has been made to the youngest children in providing such nursery classics as "The Three Little Pigs," "Henny Penny," and "The Little Red Hen."

GERMAN FOLKTALES

Next in popularity to the English folktales are those of German origin. Jacob and Wilhelm Grimm spent over twelve years collecting the tales which they published in 1812 as the first volume of *Kinder und Hausmärchen* (121). They did not adapt their stories for children as Joseph Jacobs did for British folktales, but were very careful to preserve the form and content of the tales as they were told (without benefit of a tape recorder). These were then translated into English by Edgar Taylor from 1823 to 1826.

New and beautiful collections and single tales of the Grimms' stories continue to be published. Maurice Sendak visited Kassel, Germany, before illustrating his two volumes of *The Juniper Tree and Other Tales from Grimm* (122). In the museum there he was fortunate enough to find a version illustrated by none other than the Grimms' younger brother, Ludwig. The size of this little-known version with only six engravings served as the inspiration for Sendak's small volumes. Mindful of the fact that these tales were told to country folk, Sendak used adults as his subjects. His view of Rapunzel is from within her room looking out, rather than the cliché of Rapunzel hanging her hair out of the castle window. Sendak has pictured a pregnant Rapunzel, for the story states that she had her twin babies with her when she was at last united with her prince. This is an authentic and distinguished edition of Grimm that reflects the origin of the stories, yet makes us look at them with new wonder and delight.

German folklore is enlivened by elves, dwarfs, and devils, rather than the fairies of other cultures. *The Elves and the Shoemaker* (111) tells of a kindly but poor shoemaker who is aided in his work by elves until he and his wife return the favor by making the elves clothes. Then, off they scamper never to be seen again. Elegant marbleized endpapers with a hairy tail curling around the margins introduce Nonny Hogrogian's retelling of *The Devil with the Three Golden Hairs* (110). Similar to the Russian story of *The Three Wonderful Beggars* (267), it tells of a boy who wins the hand of the king's daughter by obtaining three hairs from the devil. In addition, he discovers the answers to three questions that enable him to return with four gold-laden donkeys and a way of outwitting the greedy king. Hogrogian has also illustrated the German tale of *The Glass Mountain* (115), framing each watercolor illustration with a complementary marbleized paper border.

Rumpelstiltskin (257) is another well-known tale that features a clever but demanding tiny man. He agrees to help the miller's daughter spin straw into gold to save her life, as her father has bragged too loudly to the king about her talents. Gennady Spirin's version features sharply delineated characters and settings in the manner of Brueghel's sixteenth-century paintings. Paul O. Zelinsky's elegant paintings set the tale in a medieval castle and the gold of the spun straw shines richly from the pages (130). Paul Galdone's version (129) presents a weepier daughter, a less elegant castle, and a more dwarf-like little man. In comparing three versions, children would discover these subtle differences in aspects of the illustrations, as well as the demise of the little man, the verse in which he reveals his name, and the name guesses the miller's daughter offers.

Many children know a version of "Snow White" only from the cartoon story created by Walt Disney studios. However, Nancy Ekholm Burkert's illustrations and Randall Jarrell's telling of *Snow-White and the Seven Dwarfs* (135) more faithfully recreate the original Grimm story. Burkert used her own 14-year-old daughter as the model for Snow White. Her drawings of dwarfs are based on weeks of medical library research studying characteristic proportions of dwarfs. And so Burkert's dwarfs are not grotesque elves, but real people who are loving and proud. The medieval cottage of the dwarfs is an authentic depiction: every architectural detail, the rich fabrics on floor or wall, the very plates and mugs on the table were copied from museum pieces. Burkert used images symbolically: the white dog, the basket of cherries, and the lilies on the table signify virginity; the meadow rue embroidered on the girl's apron was supposed to protect the wearer against witches; a Tarot card, the red mushrooms, spiders, and other articles in the witch's workroom signify evil. In Disney's version, a "Sleeping Beauty" kiss awakes the sleeping girl. But Randall Jarrell was true to the Grimm story in

which the apple lodged in Snow White's throat is shaken free when the prince carries her off to Italy. Perhaps such a beautiful edition of this story restores its dignity, beauty, and symbolic meaning. Another edition of *Snow White* (133) has been faithfully translated by Paul Heins and illustrated with robust, more romantic pictures by Trina Schart Hyman. In this version, the artist skillfully portrays the ravaging effects of the queen's jealous madness through the changing appearance of her face.

The wolf is usually the villain in the few beast tales in German folklore. Perhaps the best known wolf appears in the Grimm story "Little Red Cap." In the familiar story, the heroine ignores her mother's warnings and, as a result, she and her grandmother are eaten. Both escape through the intervention of a passing hunter who thinks that the wolf's loud snores couldn't be coming from a healthy grandmother. After her adventure, the little girl vows always to obey her mother's advice. Both Lisbeth Zwerger, in *Little Red Cap* (123) and Trina Schart Hyman, in *Little Red Riding Hood* (124), have portrayed this story with striking but differing illustrations. Hyman presents a younger, more innocent child distracted by the wolf. Small vignettes depicting household details, wildflowers, and insects are enclosed in changing border frames, giving the whole book a delightfully old-fashioned look. Children will look to find the cat in nearly every illustration that features Little Red Riding Hood. In *Self-Portrait: Trina Schart Hyman* (170), the author-illustrator recounts the importance of this story to her childhood. Beautiful, spare watercolors by Zwerger portray a contrastingly older Red Cap and the essential props against a soft and muted backdrop. Her use of gray and brown washes highlights the essentials while Hyman elaborately details forest and cottage backgrounds. Another version of this tale has been illustrated by James Marshall in his characteristically humorous way (211).

Some of the Grimm tales can be just that—grim, dark, and forbidding. Small children can be frightened by the story of *Hansel and Gretel* (120), the somber tale of a brother and sister abandoned in the woods by their parents and nearly eaten by a horrible witch. However, justice does prevail in this wonder tale: the witch dies in the same way as she had intended to kill the children; the stepmother also dies, and the children, laden with wealth, are reunited with their joyful father. Several very different illustrated versions present this tale to children. Paul Zelinsky's oil paintings somberly recreate the forest settings and interior of the poor woodcutter's house, and we can almost smell the witch's tasty house. Lisbeth Zwerger (117) portrays characters against a brown wash that gives the action a dreamlike, long-ago appearance. Susan Jeffers's exquisitely rendered forest scenes detail each leaf and bird, but her renditions of the children's experiences with the witch suffer from a sameness both of color and of size (119). Jeffers's witch is wrapped in a shawl identical to the stepmother's, hinting that the two may be the same person. Anthony Browne, in his startling contemporary version (116), makes the same connection by placing a mole on each woman's cheek. Browne's illustrations are full of reflected images, symbols of cages and flight, and the triangular shape that resembles a witch's hat. One writer has suggested that "Hansel and Gretel" is a story about the child's psychological and symbolic journey to independence. The cages and bars represent regression to an earlier infantile dependency; the many birds represent a child's growth and development into an independent being.[33] The story concludes with hope as blue sky is reflected in the doorway framing the reunion of father and children. On a shelf a green shoot emerges from a potted plant. While adults may feel that Browne's interpretation brings the story too close to children today, this violation of the folktale convention of distancing in "a long time ago" may be treated by older children simply as one more interesting variation.

Other Grimm stories featuring witches have been illustrated and retold. In the less well-known *Jorinda and Joringel* (81), a wicked witch transforms a lovely girl into a nightingale. Joringel, a shepherd, finds a magic flower. With it and his love to protect him, he goes to the castle in the dense forest and frees Jorinda and the 7,000 other girls who had all been transformed into birds.

Another witch, though never unkind to *Rapunzel* (128), nevertheless keeps her locked in a tower until a prince climbs her braids. When the witch discovers the prince, she throws him from the tower and he is blinded by the sharp thorns below. However, a year later, he and Rapunzel are reunited and her tears restore his sight. Trina Schart Hyman's dark and mysterious illustrations for this story have a Slavic appearance and owe a debt to Russian illustrator Ivan Biliban's use of small rectangular vignettes and borders.

A well-known morality tale is Randall Jarrell's translation of *The Fisherman and His Wife* (112) in which a foolish woman wishes her way from living in a smelly pigsty to being the pope. When her husband spares the life of an enchanted flounder the wife insists that the fish owes him a wish. The husband dutifully, and in the tradition of folktale refrains, asks for the wish:

> "Flounder, flounder in the sea,
> Come to me, O come to me!
> For my wife, good Ilsebill,
> Wills not what I'd have her will."[34]

However, the woman goes too far when she asks to control the sun and the moon so the two end up, predictably, in the pigsty, where they started. In Margot Zemach's watercolor illustrations, the dwellings of the peasant couple go through several transformations before their clothes catch up to their circumstances. In the more orderly depictions of Margot Tomes's illustrations (113), reds and pinks replace browns and blues as the woman's desires escalate. In contrast, Zemach crowds her scenes with jumbles of people while angry swirls of black watercolor wash depict the increasing agitation of the fish over the woman's unreasonable demands.

Another tale with a moral is *The Frog Prince* (114), which stresses the importance of keeping a promise, even if it is made by a princess to a frog. So the king makes his daughter honor her promise to welcome a frog that has retrieved her golden ball from a deep, dark pond. After the princess lets the frog sit by her side, eat from her

---

[33]Jane Doonan, "Talking Pictures: A New Look at 'Hansel and Gretel,'" *Signal*, no. 42 (September 1983), pp. 123–131.

[34]Grimm Brothers, *The Fisherman and His Wife*, translated by Randall Jarrell, illustrated by Margot Zemach (Farrar, Straus, Giroux, 1980), unpaged.

Charlotte Huck's *Princess Furball* is a clever girl who overcomes many obstacles to get what she wants in this Cinderella variant illustrated in glowing colors by Anita Lobel.

❦ ❦ ❦

Charlotte Huck's "Cinderella" variation on the Grimm story of "Many Furs" is called *Princess Furball* (127). A cruel king betroths his mother-less daughter to an ogre in exchange for fifty wag-onloads of silver. But, the princess hopes to foil his plan by first demanding that her father give her three dresses, one as golden as the sun, anoth-er as silvery as the moon, and the last as glittering as the stars, as well as a coat made of a thousand pieces of fur, one from every animal in the king-dom. When the king actually fulfills these demands, the princess runs away with her dresses and three tiny treasures that had belonged to her mother. Disguised in her fur coat, she is discov-ered and taken to another king's castle where she becomes a scullery maid known as Furball. When the King gives a ball, she appears in one of her dresses and the following day leaves a token in

plate, and sleep in her bed for three nights, the frog becomes a prince and the two are married. While some versions end with the princess dash-ing the frog against a wall, or beheading it, Jan Ormerod chose a gentler ending for her version. A similar tale, *The Princess and the Frog* with illustra-tions by Rachel Isadora (126), pictures a redhead-ed princess in turn-of-the-century attire.

Wicked enchantments and magical transforma-tions are typical of German folktales. Seven boys are changed into *The Seven Ravens* (131) by the curse of their father when they break a jug of water which was to be used to christen their new baby sister. When the sister is old enough to real-ize what has happened, she sets off for the glass mountain to find them. Coming at last to a locked door, she must cut off her finger in order to pass through. There she is able to release her brothers.

There are many differences between the German Cinderella and this early Chinese variant, *Yeh-Shen* by Ai-Ling Louie. Ed Young depicts Yeh-Shen in a fish shape that honors her magical mentor.

❦ ❦ ❦

the King's soup. At the third ball, the King slips a ring on Furball's finger and is later able to identify the scullery maid as his own true love, saying, "You are as clever as you are lovely." Practical, independent, and resourceful, Furball has capably managed to create a happy future. Anita Lobel uses opening portraits to personify Furball's dead mother while a portrait of the Ogre looks like the father-King. A series of imprisoning enclosures such as long hallways, deep forests, and windowless kitchens symbolically give way to more open scenes in lighter and brighter colors, with more windows, and finally to the fresh air of an outdoor wedding. In contrast to many other "Cinderella" characters, *Princess Furball* is a strong, responsible female who actively brings about her own happy end.

While there is little mercy for the wicked in these German tales, there is much joy for the righteous. The plots are exciting, fast-moving, and a little frightening. Evil stepmothers, wicked witches, and an occasional mean dwarf hold princes and princesses in magical enchantments that can be broken only by kindness and love. Such were the dreams and wishes of the common folk of Germany when the Grimm brothers recorded their tales.

Scandinavian Folktales

Most of the Scandinavian folktales are from the single Norwegian collection titled *East of the Sun and West of the Moon*. These stories were gathered in the early 1840s by Peter Christian Asbjørnsen and Jorgen Moe. The collection ranks in popularity with Grimm's fairy tales for much the same reason; they capture the vigorous language of the storyteller. Ten years after their publication in Norway, they were ably translated by an Englishman, George Dasent, and made available to the English-speaking world (14, 15).

Perhaps the best known of all of these stories is *The Three Billy Goats Gruff* (16) who "trip-trapped" across the troll's bridge to eat the green grass on the other side. It is the perfect example of folktale structure: the use of three billy goats, the increasing size of each one, and the anticipated downfall of the mean old troll. Fast action and an economy of words lead directly to the storyteller's conventional ending: "Snip, snap, snout/This tale's told out." Marcia Brown's matchless picture-book version is faithful to the Norwegian origin of this tale in both the setting of her lively illustrations and in the text. Paul Galdone's picture book (91), showing large close-up illustrations of the goats and the troll, will appeal particularly to the younger child.

Another story that delights young children is Nancy Polette's *The Little Old Woman and the Hungry Cat* (242). When his owner leaves him alone, the cat eats the sixteen cupcakes she left cooling, and proceeds down the road eating everyone and everything in his path. When he meets his owner, he gobbles her up as well. But her sewing scissors save the day when she is able to cut her way out, and she and the rest of the cat's victims escape. Now free, all have a party except for the hungry cat who has to stitch himself up. Either this story or Jack Kent's paperback version, *The Fat Cat* (186), can make a lively drama when the child playing the cat wears a blanket under which the eaten may disappear.

Two very funny Norwegian folktales deserve to be told together, for they complement each other. One, "Gudbrand on the Hillside" (58), tells of the contented wife who thinks everything her husband does is fine. One miserable day things go wrong for him—he sets out to buy a cow and trades it for one thing after another until he has nothing left. Still certain of his wife's infinite faith in his judgment, he bets his neighbor that she will not say a word against him. The good woman does not disappoint him and he wins his bet. Wanda Gág's *Gone Is Gone* (80) presents a bragging husband who tells his wife how hard he works while she just "putters and potters about the house." His wife suggests that they trade places; he can take care of the house and she'll do his work in the field. The next day is an utter disaster for the husband and he never again says that his work is harder than his wife's!

George Dasent's *East o' the Sun & West o' the Moon* (57) is a complex tale in which a poor man gives his youngest daughter to a white bear, who promises to make the family rich. The white bear comes to her every night and throws off his beast shape, but he leaves before dawn so she never sees him. When her mother tells her to light a candle and look into his face, she sees a handsome prince, but three drops of hot tallow awaken him. He then tells her of his wicked enchantment in which for one year he must be a bear by day. Now that she has seen him, he must return to the castle which lies east of the sun and west of the moon and marry the princess with a long nose. So the girl seeks the castle, finally arriving there on the back of the North Wind. Before the prince will marry, he sets one condition: he will only marry the one who can wash out the tallow spots on his shirt. Neither his long-nose troll bride-to-be nor an old troll hag can do it, but the girl who has posed as a beggar can wash it white as the snow. The wicked trolls burst and the prince and princess marry and leave the castle that lies east of the sun and west of the moon. Gillian Barlow's framed paintings in the style of folk art glow with warm colors. Children who know the Greek myth of "Cupid and Psyche" (20) will recognize similarities in the girl's nighttime curiosity and the trouble it begets. Kathleen and Michael Hague's retelling of *East of the Sun and West of the Moon* (141) follows the original structure of the story faithfully. However, Mercer Mayer's version (217) is a fabrication of parts of many folktales with a frog-prince who is carried away, a girl who journeys not to the four winds but to a giant salamander, a unicorn, and so forth.

The Norwegians tell of Cinderlad, rather than a Cinderella, in "The Maid on the Glass Mountain" (58). In it, a brave youngest son guards a hayfield and captures three horses on three successive nights. With these, he is able to ride up a glass hill, obtain three golden apples, and win the hand of a beautiful princess.

In many of the Norwegian tales the hero is aided in the accomplishment of seemingly impossible tasks by animals that he has been kind to. For example, in "The Giant Who Had No Heart in His Body" (15), a raven, a salmon, and a wolf all help to find the giant's heart. Then Boots squeezes it and forces the giant to restore to life his six brothers and their wives who had been turned to stone. Linda Allen has created a handsome single-tale edition of this story (10). In "Lord Per" (58), the Norwegian "Puss in Boots," the cat presents the king with the gifts of a reindeer, a stag, an elk, and a troll's castle. Then she asks him to cut off her head. When he reluctantly does, she becomes a lovely princess and he makes her his queen.

Scandinavian tales often seem to reflect the harsh elements of the northern climate. Animal helpmates assist heroes in overcoming giants or wicked trolls. Frequently, heroes are human beings who are held by an evil spell. The Scandinavian tales, characterized by many trolls, magic objects, and enchantments, often are also humorous, exciting, and fast-moving. The youngest son performs impossible tasks with ease and a kind of practical resourcefulness.

FRENCH FOLKTALES

French folktales were the earliest to be recorded, and they are also the most sophisticated and adult. This is probably because these tales were the rage among the court society of Louis XIV. In 1697 Charles Perrault, a distinguished member of the French Academy, published a little volume of fairy tales. The title page bore no name and there has been some debate as to whether they were the product of Charles Perrault or his son, Pierre. While the stories were probably very close to the ones told to Pierre by his governess, they have the consciously elegant style of the "literary tale" rather than the "told tale" of the Grimms.

The godmother in Cinderella is Perrault's invention, as are the pumpkin coach, the six horses of dappled mouse gray, and the glass slipper. In this French version Cinderella is kind and forgiving of her two stepsisters, inviting them to live at the palace with her. Marcia Brown was faithful to both the French setting and original text in her Caldecott award-winning book *Cinderella* (237). Ethereal illustrations in delicate blues and pinks portray the splendid palace scenes. Cinderella's stepsisters are haughty and homely, but hardly cruel. Another beautiful picture-book rendition of *Cinderella* has been created by Errol Le Cain (239). The rich, lavish illustrations are interesting to compare with Brown's delicate ones. Paul Galdone (82), Susan Jeffers (238), and James Marshall (178) have all illustrated colorful and humorous versions for younger children.

The sister story to "Cinderella" is the well-known "Sleeping Beauty." The opening suggests that this is not a story told for peasants but one to be enjoyed by a wealthy and traveled society:

🐦 Once upon a time there were a king and a queen who were very unhappy that they did not have any children, so unhappy that it can hardly be expressed. They went to all the watering places in the world, tried vows, pilgrimages, and acts of devotion but nothing would do. Finally, however, the queen did become pregnant and gave birth to a daughter.[35]

It is interesting to compare the wishes that the fairies gave to the newborn baby. In the German tale they endow Briar Rose with virtue, beauty, riches, and "everything in the world she could wish for"; in the French version they bestow her with beauty, an angelic disposition, the abilities to dance, sing, and play music. In both versions the jealous uninvited fairy predicts the child will prick her finger on a spindle and die. This wish is softened by the last fairy who changes it to the long sleep of a hundred years to be broken by the kiss of a prince.

Several beautiful picture-book editions of "Sleeping Beauty" have been published. English artist Errol Le Cain went to the Brothers Grimm for his retelling of the German *Thorn Rose or The Sleeping Beauty* (138). His rich, opulent pictures give the impression of early German paintings and royal tapestries. We wish his retelling of the tale might have been as rich as his illustrations. Trina Schart Hyman has painted robust romantic scenes for her interpretation of *The Sleeping Beauty* (132). Her many close-up pictures of the characters place the reader in the midst of the scenes rather than providing the distancing and mystical mood of the others.

On the cover of Fred Marcellino's *Puss in Boots* (240), a very French Puss looks out past the reader as if plotting his next moves. While he is the only inheritance of the youngest son of a poor miller, he proves his worth. The cat presents the King with gifts telling him that they are from his master, the imaginary Marquis of Carabas. When the King drives out one morning, Puss runs ahead and places his naked master in the pond shouting, "Help, the Marquis of Carabas is drowning." The King clothes the poor young man and is

impressed when they pass by peasants who proclaim (under dire threats from Puss) that they work for the imaginary Marquis. Puss races ahead and tricks an ogre into changing his shape from lion to mouse, eats the ogre, and proclaims the castle as his master's. At a lavish banquet, the "Marquis" marries the King's daughter and the exhausted Puss sleeps bootless on a rug in the foreground. Marcellino's illustrations and large type crowd the page as if the story would burst the confines of the book. Children familiar with this elegant version could compare it with Lorinda Cauley's colored pencil renditions of the sleek cat (41) or with Paul Galdone's swashbuckler (88).

The French telling of "The Twelve Dancing Princesses" is more ornate than the German version. Anne Carter's text (139) reads smoothly and elegantly, but Anne Dalton's illustrations do not do this tale justice. Errol Le Cain used the Grimm version of *The Twelve Dancing Princesses* (140) for this story of the poor soldier who discovers the underground kingdom where the twelve girls dance their shoes to pieces nightly. However, the depictions of tapestry borders, powdered wigs, and elegant dress of the masked ball give Le Cain's version a very French look. Marianna Mayer's cumbersome retelling of the story introduces new elements as well but Kinuko Y. Craft's luminous paintings (216) are well suited to the spirit of the original tale.

The best known French wonder tale, other than those by Perrault, is "Beauty and the Beast," adapted from a long story written in 1757 by Madame de Beaumont. This story of love based on one's essence rather than appearance has been variously illustrated. Mordicai Gerstein's *Beauty and the Beast* (234) features pastel-tinted line drawings that reveal its source as an animated film. In his story, a courageous Beauty rides to the Beast's castle by herself while in Warwick Hutton's robust version, a more timid Beauty is accompanied by her father. Hutton's vaguely Moorish palace contrasts with Mercer Mayer's ornately decorated interiors (236). Jan Brett's economic text and rich illustrations are framed in jeweled borders and the elegant tapestries in the background reveal the boar-beast's true identity (233).

Marcia Brown's *Stone Soup* (32) has long been staple primary-grade fare. As the French villagers

[35]Charles Perrault, "Sleeping Beauty" in *The Twelve Dancing Princesses and Other Fairy Tales,* edited by Alfred David and Mary Elizabeth David (New York: New American Library, 1964), p. 125.

In Fred Marcellino's illustration for Perrault's French tale of *Puss in Boots,* the clever cat establishes an immediate bond with the reader as he gazes thoughtfully from the wordless cover.

clad in wooden shoes and smocks hurry their contributions to the huge soup kettle, the three soldiers maintain a subtly earnest but amused look. In John Stewig's version (288), Grethel is a solo hungry traveler. When villagers turn down their mouths "like unlucky horseshoes" at her request for food, the girl goes to work with her magic stone and soon has created an evening, and a soup, to remember. Margot Tomes's soft flat tones give the story a homespun look. Iris Van Rynbach's version, called *The Soup Stone* (297), features a single soldier who works his magic on one New England family.

The folktales of France are not usually the tales of the poor but those of the rich. Most have all the trappings of the traditional fairy tale, including fairy godmothers, stepsisters, and handsome princes. Tales of romance and sophisticated intrigue, they must surely have been the "soap operas" of their day.

RUSSIAN FOLKTALES

Folktales from Russia feature universal patterns of tasks and trials, tricks, and transformations. Russian folktales are often longer, more complicated ones than those of other countries and frequently involve several sets of tasks. In *The Firebird* (184), three sons are charged to find who steals the golden apple from a certain tree. When Ivan the youngest discovers that the thief is a firebird, he shoots it with his bow and arrow, but only gains a feather for his trouble. Next, the father wants the firebird. This time, a shape-changing vixen helps the youngest find the castle where the firebird lives, but there the king demands Ivan perform three tasks. With the vixen's help, he completes the tasks only to be killed by his jealous brothers as he returns with a princess, a horse, and the firebird. Once again, the vixen helps by bargaining with a raven for the water of life, and Ivan lives again to regain what is rightfully his. Moira Kemp's glowing illuminations of the story lend a mystical aura to this version.

In Margaret Hodges's *The Little Humpbacked Horse* (162), a horse rather than a vixen advises his young and foolish master. Ivan must capture a firebird, win a princess, and pass through boiling water. While the hot water makes Ivan even more handsome, it kills the old tsar who is standing in the way of Ivan's success with the Tsarevna, and the two are free to marry.

Sally Scott's precise and richly textured paintings for *The Three Wonderful Beggars* (267) tell the story of Vassili, a seventh son of a villager whose destiny is foretold by three old beggars. Mark the Rich does everything he can to thwart the prophecy, but Vassili is able to trick Mark, win his daughter and riches as well by outwitting the Serpent King. As for Vassili, "he never turned a beggar from his door." As in many Russian folktales, the greedy rich and the heartless nobility are soon brought down by honest and hard-working commoners.

Russian folklore is replete with stories of poor but lucky men. In Harve Zemach's *Salt* (316), Ivan the fool takes the ship his father has given him and much to his father's surprise, returns as the richest of the three brothers who started out. With the help of an irresistible magic sack, an old soldier outwits *The Devils Who Learned to Be Good* in Michael McCurdy's tale (202) and another soldier saves a helpless tsar in Uri Shulevitz's *Soldier and Tsar in the Forest* (274). In Shulevitz's *The Fool of the World and the Flying Ship* (245), a youngest son goes forth, accompanied by eight companions, each of whom has a magic power that helps in outwitting the treacherous tsar. The fool wins the princess and riches for them both in this Caldecott award-winning story. A poor archer in Diane Wolkstein's *Oom Razoom or Go I Know Not Where, Bring Back I Know Not What* (305) keeps his beautiful wife from the clutches of the king while gaining riches and a magical servant.

The witch Baba Yaga is a complex character who figures in many Russian tales including *Oom Razoom*.[36] *Vasilissa the Beautiful* (303) is often called "the Russian Cinderella." In this tale, Vasilissa is sent by her stepmother to Baba Yaga to get a light for the cottage with the hope that the witch will eat her up. But Vasilissa carries with her a doll that her mother gave her before she died. When Baba Yaga gives Vasilissa impossible tasks to perform, the doll's magic and its advice to go to sleep for "the morning is wiser than the evening" save the unfortunate girl. The renown Russian illustrator Alexander Koshkin richly paints the story in a seventeenth-century setting. The arrival of Baga Yaga in her mortar and pestle is boldly lit by the glowing eyes of the picketed skulls surrounding her chicken-footed house.

In another story, *Vassilisa the Wise,* retold by Josepha Sherman (272), Vassilisa is now presented as the loving wife of the merchant Staver. When Staver's bragging about his wife's beauty and wisdom causes him to be imprisoned by the legendary Prince Vladimir, Vassilisa disguises herself as a Tartar prince. She outwits Vladimir and wins the release of her now contrite husband by performing three tasks. Daniel San Souci's use of rich browns, blues, and roses, bordered illustrations, and illuminated capitals reinforce the medieval setting of this tale.

Other stories about Baba Yaga present the fearsome witch in less frightening terms. Joanna Cole's *Bony-Legs* (49) tells how Sasha meets Baba Yaga under a different name but escapes being eaten by the witch because she is kind to a cat, a dog, and a squeaky gate. In yet another story of *Baba Yaga* (187), Eric Kimmel adds a "Generous person/Greedy person" motif in his story of Marina, a child with a horn growing out of her forehead, who is sent by her stepmother to Baba Yaga to get a needle. Her kindness to a frog earns her good advice in tricking the witch and good luck in having her horn removed. But when the stepsister Marusia rudely ignores the frog on her way to visit Baba Yaga so as to become "just like my stepsister," she is sent away with a horn on her forehead. Humorous illustrations in both stories remove some of the power of Baba Yaga's evil while providing an invitation to younger children to meet a well-known witch.

Old Koshchey, the demon, is another wicked character in Russian tales. In Elizabeth Isele's *The Frog Princess* (171), Baba Yaga helps rescue Vasilissa from him. *The Demon Who Would Not Die* (45) by Barbara Cohen also features this bad character. The same characters reappear in different guises in many Russian tales, and one story often braids into another.

Not all Russian folktales are dark and complex. The theme of cooperation is addressed in *The Turnip* (223). Dedoushka plants a turnip seed which grows so big that he needs to call his wife, Baboushka, to help by pulling him as he pulls. Eventually, their daughter Mashenka, a dog, a cat, and finally the mouse, are able to pull the turnip out. This humorous story would make a good primary drama. The theme of beauty being in the eye of the beholder is presented in another story. A child lost in the wheat fields sobs when she is separated from her mother and maintains that *My Mother Is the Most Beautiful Woman in the World* (246). After the townsfolk assemble all of the local beauties for Varya's inspection, a large toothless woman pushes through the crowd and mother and child are reunited.

[36]See the vivid description of one classroom's discovery of patterns when a teacher presented them with versions of "Baba Yaga Tales" in Joy F. Moss's *Focus on Literature: A Context for Literacy Learning* (Katonah, N.Y.: Richard C. Owen, 1990), pp. 49–62.

Jan Brett's *The Mitten* (26) is a Ukrainian tale in which animals small and large accumulate in Nicki's dropped mitten handknit by his grandmother, Baba. Jan Brett divides the pages with a birchbark window through which the increasingly stuffed mitten can be seen. A mitten-shaped panel on the left depicts Nicki's busy day; on the right, the next animal who will try to squeeze into the mitten is shown. Alvin Tresselt's version (294) features different animals and reads aloud as if it were a reminiscence. Both Yaroslava, the illustrator of this version, and Jan Brett have included traditional Ukrainian details, costumes, and patterns.

Carolyn Croll carefully researched Russian architecture, furnishings, toys, and clothing before illustrating a story set at Christmas, *The Little Snowgirl* (55). An old couple who wish for a child are delighted when the little girl the husband has made from snow comes to life. Caterina loves the snow girl but cannot bear to let her stay outside on Christmas Eve. In the morning, all the two find is a small puddle by the fireplace, but a soft laugh reveals that the little Snowgirl has been granted one wish by Baboushka, who gives good children what they want most on that special

Jan Brett uses birch bark to border the pictures for the Ukrainian tale of *The Mitten;* side panels foreshadow the next animal that will try to squeeze into the mitten.

❦ ❦ ❦

night. Reading aloud Charles Mikolaycak's story of *Baboushka* (219), who is destined to wander the world forever bestowing gifts on children, would forge a compelling link in the chain of Russian folklore.

In the Russian story of *The Month-Brothers* (208), a girl is given an impossible task by her stepmother: to go out in the winter snow and not return until she has gathered snowdrops. However, she luckily comes upon the twelve months of the year gathered about a fire in the forest. January and February agree to give the youngest month—brother March—one hour to create a forest floor dappled with snowdrops, and the girl is able to complete her task. However, the greedy stepmother next sends her own spoiled daughter into the snow to demand special summertime food to sell in the wintertime market. The rude girl accosts the men and is frozen in snow by old January. The greedy mother also perishes while searching for her daughter. The "Generous person/Greedy person" motif accompanies this personification and explanation of the changing seasons. In Diane Stanley's stunning watercolors, March is represented as a young boy, reflecting rural people's belief that the year of growing truly begins in March.

JEWISH FOLKTALES

Jewish tales have a poignancy, wit, and ironic humor that is not matched by any other folklore. Many of them have been preserved by the masterful writing of Isaac Bashevis Singer, who has retained the flavor of both the oral tradition and the Yiddish origin. In *Zlateh the Goat* (280) and *When Shlemiel Went to Warsaw* (279), Isaac Bashevis Singer's warm, humorous stories are based on tradition and his own childhood memories. The amiable fools of Chelm (that fabled village where only fools live), lazy shlemiels, and shrewd poor peasants who outwit rich misers are familiar characters in Singer's tales. In Chelm the wise elders are the most foolish of all, and their "solutions" to people's problems make for some hilarious stories. One night they plan to gather the pearls and diamonds of the sparkling snow so the jewels can be sold for money. Worried about how they can prevent the villagers from trampling the snow, they decide to send a messenger to each house to tell the people to stay inside. But the "wise elders" realize the messenger's feet will spoil the snow, so they have him carried on a table supported by four men so that he will not make any footprints as he goes from house to house!

The story of "Shrewd Todie and Lyzer the Miser" (278) is a delightful tale of chicanery in another book by Singer. Todie repeatedly borrows a silver tablespoon from Lyzer and always returns it along with the gift of a silver teaspoon, saying that the tablespoon had given birth to the teaspoon. When Todie then asks to borrow some silver candlesticks, Lyzer, eager to increase his wealth, presses eight of them on Todie, who immediately sells them. When Todie does not return them, saying that the "candlesticks died," Lyzer calls the rabbi for advice. The rabbi hears both sides and then tells Lyzer the miser that if he believes spoons can give birth, then he must accept the "fact" that candlesticks can die!

In *It Could Always Be Worse* (317), Margot Zemach tells the familiar tale of the poor farmer whose house is so crowded that he seeks the rabbi's advice. Following the rabbi's wise counsel, the farmer brings first one animal after another into the house until the noise and confusion become unbearable. The rabbi then advises their removal, and the house appears to be very large and peaceful. Zemach has created a humorous version of this tale with large robust pictures that seem to swarm with squalling children, rambunctious animals, and horrified adults.

Joanna Cole retells this story in a more simple style in *It's Too Noisy* (50). Kate Duke's cheerful cartoonish illustrations place this peasant family less clearly in the Jewish tradition than does Zemach.

The Hebrew legend, *Elijah the Slave* (277), has been retold by Isaac Singer and magnificently illustrated by Antonio Frasconi. In this story Elijah, a messenger from God, sells himself as a slave in order to help a poor faithful scribe. The pictures appear to be woodcut prints cut out and pasted on radiant backgrounds. The effect is breathtaking and reminiscent of medieval art. Florence B. Freedman tells another Hebrew legend in *Brothers* (79). In it, a father bequeaths his farm to be divided between two brothers, Joel, who marries and has three sons, and Dan, who remains single. When a bad year causes diminished crops, each brother tries to help the other by secretly taking wheat to the other's barn. When they discover each other at the border adjoining their fields one night, and as they wordlessly embrace, a voice comes from everywhere singing, "How good it is for brothers to live in friendship." Robert Andrew Parker's gentle watercolor illustrations with scratchy lines seem perfectly suited to this quiet story. In *The Diamond Tree* (265), Howard Schwartz and Barbara Rush have collected fifteen Jewish tales from around the world. Here readers may meet the giant Og, fools of Chusham, King Solomon, and even a Jewish Thumbelina, Katanya. Uri Shulevitz illustrated most of these tales with brilliant paintings.

FOLKTALES OF THE MIDDLE EAST AND INDIA

To determine the folktales of Middle Eastern countries and those of India would take several books, for this area is the cradle of civilization and the birthplace of many of our stories. Unfortunately, these tales are not as well known in the United States as they deserve to be. Rather than describe many unfamiliar stories available only in out-of-print collections, this section discusses only available tales or books that might serve as an introduction. Nonny Hogrogian's *One Fine Day* (164) is an Armenian cumulative story that begins when an old woman catches a fox licking up her pail of milk and cuts off his tail. She agrees to sew it back on only when he replaces the milk, which proves to be a difficult task. The simplicity of Hogrogian's drawings is perfect for the rustic humor and setting of this circular tale.

The collection of Scheherazade's tales told over *1001 Arabian Nights* has provided stories for generations since it was first published in 1712. Sir Richard Burton's translation of *The Arabian Nights* made them available to English speakers. Errol Le Cain selected one story from Burton's collection, *Aladdin* (188), and depicted it in pictures that resemble Persian miniature paintings. Details, ornate borders, and patterned surfaces lend an authenticity to the story. Carol Carrick's straightforward telling of *Aladdin and the Wonderful*

Lamp (39) relies on Donald Carrick's richly hued paintings for romance and drama. Marianna Mayer's *Aladdin and the Enchanted Lamp (214)* is a more inclusive story whose text captures some of the wonder of the story and is accompanied by Gerald McDermott's bold illustrations.

Another tale from this same source is *Ali Baba and the Forty Thieves* (206). Walter McVitty retells the story of Ali Baba's discovery of riches in the thieves' cave and of his clever servant Morgiana who saves his life. She kills the thieves by pouring hot oil in the olive jars where they are hiding and stabs the robber chief. Margaret Early's illustrations are decorated with ornate borders reflecting motifs from the story and each page of text begins with a decorated capital letter. Her use of gold and pictorial conventions from Persian art lend this story further authenticity and beauty.

Also from *The Arabian Nights* is Sally Scott's *The Magic Horse* (266), a romantic story of a loyal brother who, in saving his sister from marriage to an old Wizard, also wins himself a bride. The Wizard presents a flying horse to the King and asks for the princess's hand. When the Prince tries to intervene on his sister's behalf, he is carried away by the magic horse to a land where he meets a princess. Returning home with her, he is tricked by the Wizard into losing his princess, but he recovers her. After their marriage, the King has the magic horse, the source of all the trouble, broken up into a thousand pieces. Although the illustrations do not depict the triumphant marriage at the end of the story, their jewel-like colors illuminate the romantic tale and the arches, minarets, and towers frame the action with elegance.

Other rich sources of stories are the Hodja stories, known throughout the Mediterranean countries, Turkey, the Balkans, and Greece. Nasredden Hodja was thought to have lived several hundred years ago in Turkey, where he served as a religious teacher or judge when the occasion demanded. The wisdom of the Hodja is seen in the way he settles disputes. One day he watches a man cut wood while his companion rests nearby but groans helpfully each time the man swings his axe (300). When the woodcutter finally sells his wood at the bazaar, the companion demands half the pay. The Hodja listens to both sides, takes the coins, and drops them one by one on a stone. He awards the sound to the companion and the coins to the woodcutter.

Indian folklore tradition has its share of wise men, too. "The Sticks of Truth" in George Shannon's collection of *Stories to Solve* (269) tells of an Indian judge asked to determine who stole a gold ring. He gives each suspect a stick and says that only the stick of the thief will grow in the night. In the morning, he is able to accuse the one with the shortest stick of the thievery. Why? In this collection of short pieces, the reader is invited to guess before turning the page to discover the answer. In this case, the girl trims her stick in an effort to hide its growth thereby proving her guilt.

The *Jataka* (birth) stories found in India tell of the previous reincarnations of the Buddha and are known to have existed as early as the fifth century A.D. Many of these tales are moralistic or religious in nature. Later, beast tales were drawn from this collection to form the *Panchatantra*, which were used to instruct young princes in morality. When these stories are translated into English, their morals and teaching verses are usually eliminated. The resulting Indian tales sound more like folktales.

Rafe Martin retells an ancient ancestor of "Henny-Penny" or "Chicken Little" in the Jataka tale of *Foolish Rabbit's Big Mistake* (213). Rabbit hears an apple fall from a tree and wonders if the earth is breaking up. He panics and arouses a chain of animals who thoughtlessly run with him until a wise lion stops the stampede. He carries the silly rabbit back to the scene, proves it was only an apple that fell from the tree, and finally defends the rabbit from the anger of his friends by pointing out that they, too, ran without trying to find out the true cause of the alarm. Ed Young's large-scale paintings depict the action in dramatic close-ups and vibrant explosions of color.

In vigorous woodcuts, Marcia Brown illustrates the fable of *Once a Mouse* (31) which must have warned young princes about the folly of pride in one's origins. Seeing a mouse about to be eaten by a crow, a hermit rescues it. But a cat stalks the pet so the hermit changes the mouse into a bigger cat. Each change results in new dangers until finally the meek mouse is transformed into a huge tiger. But he "peacocked about the forest" until the hermit reminds him that he was once a mouse. When the tiger threatens the hermit, the hermit reduces it to its original shape of a mouse.

Pam Newton's retelling of the traditional Indian tale of *The Stonecutter* (228) shares a similar theme with the previous story as well as with the German "The Fisherman and His Wife." A circular tale, it demonstrates how you end up as you started when greed and dissatisfaction cannot be controlled. A poor stonecutter sees the house of a rich man when he comes to repair a wall and wishes that he, too, could be wealthy. The spirit of the mountain grants his wish and soon he is a rich merchant guiding a caravan to market. But he soon wants to be king. Even as king he is nearly overpowered by the sun's rays and so wishes to be the sun. A cloud obscures the sun, the wind blows away the cloud, and the stonecutter becomes each. But as the wind, he cannot blow down the mountain so he becomes the mountain. Then a stonecutter chips away at his surface and the first stonecutter realizes his mistake. Newton's use of gold and yellow tones plays off the gray mountain stone of this magical world. Gerald McDermott, in his spare telling of a Japanese version of *The Stonecutter* (205), used handpainted paper cut into collage for his stylized illustrations.

The lesson of *The Story of Wali Dad* (250), retold by Kristina Rodanas, is captured with gentle humor as a poor grasscutter decides to spend his hoard of coins on something beautiful. The bracelet he buys seems to be worthy of a princess, so he asks a merchant friend to present it to one who is most beautiful. The Princess of Khaistan accepts the gift and sends back a camel load of fine silks. But poor Wali Dad passes these on to the young Prince of Nekabad. As the size of the gifts escalate, Wali Dad is kept busy until he is horrified by the news that the Princess will visit her gracious admirer. But when Wali Dad arranges a meeting of the Prince and Princess, they fall in love. The generous and simple matchmaker is the happiest of all at the wedding for he recognizes on the bride's arm the small gold bracelet that started it all.

While these tales represent but a small portion of stories from the Middle Eastern countries and India, they are indicative of a rich source on which children's literature has yet to draw fully. Perhaps the next decades will provide a greater number of single-tale editions of stories such as these so that children might become more familiar with this important literary tradition.

FOLKTALES FROM CHINA AND JAPAN

While there are fewer folktales available from western and central Asia, there are increasing numbers of outstanding, well-illustrated single-tale editions of the folktales from Japan and China.

Ed Young, born in China and educated in the United States, has illustrated many folktales from China. His Caldecott award-winning *Lon Po Po* (313) comes from an ancient oral tradition and is thought to be over a thousand years old. In this story, three children are left alone by their mother who warns them to open the door to no one. But an old wolf claiming to be their grandmother, or Po Po, comes to the door. When the wolf answers the children's queries, they let him in and he promptly blows out the light. In the dark, the children into whose bed the wolf has crawled, say such things as, "Po Po, your hand has thorns on it" and the wolf replies, "Po Po has bought an awl to make shoes for you." Child readers will recognize similarities between this and "Red Riding Hood": the parental warning, the observations of the children, the woodland cottage setting, and the ultimate end of the wolf. However, this wolf perishes by falling from the gingko tree as a result of the three children's trickery and resourceful teamwork. Young's dedication, "To all the wolves of the world for lending their good name as a tangible symbol for our darkness" reminds us once again of the way in which we use stories to understand the world. Combining Chinese panel format with contemporary pastel and watercolors, Young creates a mysterious nighttime setting illuminated by candles, moonlight, and the shining eyes of the wolf.

Ai-Ling Louie's *Yeh-Shen* (200), also illustrated by Young, is one of the oldest written variants of "Cinderella," predating European versions by a thousand years. Left in the care of a stepmother and stepsister, Yeh-Shen is made to do the heaviest chores. Her only friend is a fish, which she feeds and talks with each day until the stepmother kills and eats it. However, its magic power lives on in the bones. Through it, Yeh-Shen is able to go to a festival dressed in a gown, a cloak made of kingfisher feathers, and gold slippers. There, the suspicious stepsister causes the girl to run away and she loses a slipper. Immediately, her fine clothes turn to rags. But the king, struck by her beauty, places the slipper in a roadside pavilion and hides in wait for the girl who will reclaim it. When Yeh-Shen creeps under cover of darkness to retrieve the slipper, they are reunited and later married. As in the German version of Cinderella, however, the stepsister and mother are punished, "crushed to death in a shower of flying stones." Young's depiction of costumes and footwear reflect his research into textiles, costuming, and festivals of the ancient Hmong people. In addition, each shimmering pastel and watercolor illustration reminds us in shape or shadow of the contours of the magic fish (see p. 332). A much longer but similar version of the tale is the title story in *The Brocaded Slipper and Other Vietnamese Tales* (299).

One of the most popular stories in the Chinese storytelling tradition is *The Seven Chinese Brothers* (207). In Margaret Mahy's retelling, each brother looks like the others but has one unique feature, such as unusual strength, amazing eyesight, acute hearing, bones that will not break, or unhappy tears that will flood an entire village. When Third Brother uses his enormous strength to repair singlehandedly a hole in the Great Wall, the emperor, worried about so powerful a man, imprisons him. So the "helpful companions," each of his six brothers, take his place as the emperor imposes new punishments. Finally, Seventh Brother is so distraught over the seeming inevitability of Sixth Brother's death that he begins to cry, and the emperor and his armies are washed away. The carefully researched details of Jean and Mou-Sien Tseng's watercolors reflect our contemporary concerns with authenticity in illustration as well as text. This version contrasts with Claire Huchet Bishop's simpler retelling and Kurt Weise's black-line stereotyped illustrations from an earlier era (1938) for *The Five Chinese Brothers* (24).

Caring for one's parents or others above oneself is also a theme of Chinese folktales. Rosalind Wang's *The Fourth Question* (301) is the one Yee-Lee must omit when he journeys to a wise man to

Three children consider whether it is truly their grandmother who is on the other side of the door in *Lon Po Po,* a Red-Riding Hood story from China, illustrated in watercolor and pastel panels by Ed Young.

🐾 🐾 🐾

ask, "Why, in spite of all my hard work, am I still so poor?" Carrying questions from a woman with a mute daughter, a man whose orchard will not bear fruit, and a third from a friendly dragon who cannot seem to rise to heaven, Yee-Lee discovers that according to the wise man's rules, one may ask only an odd number of questions. So Yee-Lee returns with three answers, which in turn give him riches, a bride, and the happiness of his old mother. In "The Wonderful Brocade" (160) as well as in Marilee Heyer's *The Weaving of a Dream* (158), a poor woman's embroidery comes to life due to her youngest son's efforts and sacrifices. Her two self-centered older sons are ashamed to see her because they have behaved so poorly and walk "away and away" dragging their walking sticks. In Carol Kendall's *The Wedding of the Rat Family* (185) a proud rat's desire, like the Japanese stonecutter and the German fisherman's wife, is to have power but in this case, through marriage. The rat is engaged to a member of the most powerful cat family with dire but predictable results for the proud rat clan. However, the poor, half-starved, and hard-working rat cousins who were not invited to the wedding triumph by inheriting the foolish rat clan's caves and wealth.

Pride is also the downfall of a village magistrate in Margaret Leaf's retelling of *Eyes of the Dragon* (192). Noticing that the new wall around the village is a bit plain, the magistrate commissions a famous painter to create a likeness of the Dragon King who controls lightning and thunder. Perhaps this likeness will bless the dry fields, too. The artist agrees with two conditions: they must accept his likeness and they must pay forth silver coins. The whole village watches as the painter completes the marvelous painting which surrounds the village so that its tail meets its head. But the magistrate will not pay until the artist completes the dragon: it lacks eyes. Reluctantly, and with a warning, the artist paints in the eyes, quickly retrieves his money, and departs. As he rides away, the dragon comes to life and departs for heaven while the wall surrounding the village crumbles away.

Arlene Mosel's humorous story of *Tikki Tikki Tembo* (226) is a Chinese pourquoi story. When the "first and honored" son with the grand long name of Tikki-Tikki-Tembo-no-sa-rembo-chari-bari-ruchi-pip-peri-pembo falls in the well, it takes so long for his brother Chang to tell someone that the elder son is nearly drowned! And that is why to this day all Chinese have short names. Young children love to repeat the rhythmical long name of the elder brother. Both the text and Blair Lent's stiff, stylized illustrations capture the tongue-in-cheek humor of the danger of too much respect!

Japanese folktales contain miniature people, monsters called *oni,* and like Chinese tales, themes of gentleness toward animals and other people, the value of hard work, and respect for the elderly. Mosel also retells a Japanese tale of *The Funny Little Woman* (225) who laughs at the wicked *Oni*-demons who capture her and take her underground to cook for their band. They give her a magic rice paddle that makes a potful of rice

from one grain. She steals the paddle and starts to escape, but the *Oni* suck all the water into their mouths, causing the woman's boat to become mired. Her infectious giggling, however, makes them laugh, and all the water flows back into the river. She floats back to her house and becomes the richest woman in Japan by making rice cakes with her magic paddle. Blair Lent won the Caldecott award for his imaginative pictures showing the wicked green demons underground and the detailed insets of the little woman's house during the passing seasons.

Said to be the most popular folktale in Japan, *Momotaro, The Peach Boy* (276) is held up to children as an example of kindness, courage, and strength. In Linda Shute's retelling, a tiny boy steps out of a huge split peach and into the lives of an elderly couple. When Momotaro grows up, he must go to fight the *Oni* who are robbing and attacking the people. Momotaro begins his journey armed with a sword, a war fan, a banner with his peach emblem on it, and his old mother's three dumplings. When he shares the dumplings with a dog, a monkey, and a pheasant, the companions help him storm the blue-bodied, horned *Oni*'s stronghold. Momotaro returns victorious, singing *"Enyara, enyara, enyara ya"* (a Japanese form of "Yo ho, heave ho") as they haul home all the gold and silver the *Oni* had stolen from the people. In an informative source note, Shute includes a glossary of Japanese words and explains the significance of symbols in her lively illustrations that draw on the style of Japanese narrative picture scrolls.

Another well-known Japanese story is *The Crane Wife* (306), a tale of the results of succumbing to poor advice and greed. Yohei, a poor peasant, removes an arrow from a wounded crane and dresses the injury. Later, a beautiful young woman appears at his door and asks to be his wife. To help pay for the extra mouth to feed, the woman offers to weave cloth but warns Yohei that he must never look at her as she works. The cloth brings a good price in the market and a greedy neighbor suggests that Yohei satisfy his curiosity and see what she is using for thread. Forgetting the warning, he looks in on her only to see a crane plucking feathers from her own breast in order to weave the beautiful cloth. No longer wishing to remain in human form, she flies away. Suekichi Akaba applied water-thinned ink to textured paper to create haunting and beautiful illustrations. A feather floats in the foreground of the screened weaver providing a visual clue to the weaver's identity. It would be interesting for children to compare Molly Bang's literary use of the tale in *Dawn* (18), which is set in nineteenth-century New England. The alert reader may spot clues to Dawn's true identity, such as pieces of eggshell under her bed when she gives birth to a daughter, and the quilt pattern she is piecing called "Wild Geese Flying."

In a humorous realistic folktale involving trickery, Diane Snyder relates *The Boy of the Three-Year Nap* (283). A poor widow, tired of supporting her son Taro who is "lazy as a rich man's cat," pesters him to go to work for a rich rice merchant. Declining to work, the boy disguises himself as the *ujigami*, the patron god of the town, and accosts the merchant by the roadside. He threatens to turn the merchant's daughter into a clay pot unless the merchant betroths her to "that fine lad who lives on your street," Taro himself. However, before the wedding may take place, Taro's mother says that the house must be repaired and enlarged for such a distinguished bride, so the merchant sends carpenters. Of course, says the widow, Taro must also have a job and so the merchant gives his future son-in-law a job but warns that there will be no napping. Tossing her head "like a cormorant that has caught a large fish," the widow consents to the marriage and Taro is pleasantly caught in his own tricks. He wasn't the only one who had plans. Allen Say's precise watercolor illustrations reflect the Japanese love of order as well as the artist's years of training as a cartoonist's apprentice in postwar Japan. The expressive faces of both the tricksters and the duped make readers laugh at the humorous situations.

Katherine Paterson's retelling of *The Tale of the Mandarin Ducks* (232) presents a greedy lord who captures a magnificently plumed drake so as to have a beautiful caged bird. When Shozo warns the lord that the wild bird will surely die in captivity, the lord shuns his advice because as a former mighty samurai, Shozo has lost an eye and is no longer handsome to look upon. The bird begins to pine for his mate, and Yasuko, a kitchen maid, secretly frees him. However, the lord blames Shozo, strips him of his rank, and puts him to work in the kitchen. There Yasuko and Shozo come to love each other, but the jealous and vindictive lord decides that they are both guilty of releasing the mandarin duck and sentences them to death by drowning. Just in time two messengers arrive from the emperor to say that anyone under a death sentence must be sent directly to him. In the nighttime march, the condemned couple are separated from the lord's guard, rescued by the messengers, and taken to a hut in the forest. In the morning, they wish to thank their saviors but find instead the mandarin duck and his mate who seem to bow before flying away. Shozo and Yasuko live on for many years in their forest hut in great happiness for they had learned that "trouble can always be borne when it is shared." Leo and Diane Dillon studied *ukiyo-e*, a Japanese art movement that depicted the everyday life of common people, before creating stunning watercolor and pastel illustrations for the story. Using woodcutlike illustrations painted in muted but warm tones, the Dillons suggest the natural beauty of a simple life with the company of a loving companion.

The many beautiful single-tale editions of folktales from Japan and China have made these old and magical tales more widely available to an English-speaking audience. Often illustrated in the pictorial styles of a particular period of Asian art, these stories may educate a child's artistic eye as well.

FOLKTALES FROM AFRICA

Children today are the fortunate recipients of a rich bounty of African folktales collected by folklorists such as Harold Courlander. Many of these tales have been retold in single editions by authors such as Verna Aardema or Ashley Bryan. More recent Caldecott awards have been given to African folktales than to tales from any other cultural tradition. The trickster tale of Anansi the spider told in *A Story, a Story* (142) by Gail Haley won a Caldecott award as did Aardema's pourquoi story of *Why Mosquitoes Buzz in People's Ears* (7) with illustrations by Leo and Diane Dillon. Caldecott honor books have included two other pourquoi stories, Elfinstone Dayrell's *Why the Sun and the Moon Live in the Sky* with Blair Lent's distinguished illustrations (59), and *The Village of Round and Square Houses* by Ann Grifalconi (106); a second story of the trickster *Anansi, the Spider* illustrated by Gerald McDermott (203); and John Steptoe's tale of a greedy and a generous sister, *Mufaro's Beautiful Daughters* (286).

Storytelling in Africa is a highly developed art, particularly in West Africa. These tales have a rhythm and cadence found in no other stories of the world. They ring of the oral tradition and are frequently written in the storyteller's voice, as in this tale of "How Spider Got a Thin Waist" (12):

> Many dry seasons ago, before the oldest man in our village can remember, before the rain and the dry and the rain and the dry that any of us can talk about to his children, Spider was a very big person. He did not look as he looks today, with his fat head and his fat body and his thin waist in between. Of course, he had two eyes and eight legs and he lived in a web. But none of him was thin. He was big and round, and his waistline was very fat indeed. Today, he is very different, as all of you know, and this is how it came to pass.[37]

Short sentences, frequent use of parallel constructions, repetition, and dialogue characterize the style of many of the African tales. All these elements are apparent in the story of "Ticky-Picky Boom-Boom" (271), an Anansi story that came to us by way of Jamaica. One can almost hear the storyteller increasing his tempo as he tells of the foolish tiger who is chased by the yams that he had tried to dig out of Anansi's garden:

> Tiger began to run. The yams ran, too. Tiger began to gallop. The yams galloped, too. Tiger jumped. The yams jumped. Tiger made for Brother Dog's house as fast as he could. . . . Down the road came the yams stamping on their two legs, three legs, four legs:
>
>> "Ticky-Picky Boom-Boom
>> "Ticky-Picky Boom-Boom, Boof!"[38]

[37]Joyce Cooper Arkhurst, *The Adventures of Spider, West African Folk Tales* (Boston, Mass.: Little, Brown, 1964), p. 5.
[38]Philip M. Sherlock, *Anansi the Spider Man, Jamaican Folk Tales*, illustrated by Marcia Brown (New York: Crowell, 1954), p. 79.

In Ashley Bryan's rhythmical tale from the Antilles, *The Dancing Granny* (35) can't resist the song of Spider Ananse, pictured as a vigorous man in the illustrations. Granny Anika dances far out of sight while the clever Ananse raids her vegetable plot. Three more times Brother Ananse tricks the old lady until she gets hold of him and makes him dance with her. The story itself sings with rhythmic prose and repeated refrains. Dark gray drawings capture the movements of the dancing Granny and Brother Ananse.

Many African tales are about personified animals, including those tricksters Anansi the spider, a rabbit, and a tortoise. Both Anansi and the rabbit are lazy creatures who are continually tricking the other animals into doing work for them. Storyteller Verna Aardema tells how *Rabbit Makes a Monkey of Lion* (4) when Rabbit and his friend Turtle steal Lion's honey. Lion finally catches the tricksters but both escape by telling Lion what he should not do with them. Of course, Lion tosses Rabbit into the brush and puts turtle in the mud. Aardema's stories, delightful to read aloud, are liberally laced with expressive words: Rabbit goes running, *yiridi, yiridi, yiridi* and a calabash gourd falls from a tree, *ngish!* Jerry Pinkney's watercolor illustrations capture the varying browns and greens of the hills and forests of this tale from the island of Zanzibar, now a part of Tanzania.

Verna Aardema has retold many other folktales from Africa. *Bimwili & the Zimwi* (1) is a wonder tale also from Zanzibar in which a little girl playing at the seashore finds a beautiful shell. When the shell transforms into a green-faced shrunken old manlike Zimwi, he greets her: "*Jambo*, Little Girl. How sweetly you sing!" He tricks the little girl and pops her into his drum so that he will have a singing drum, not one that just goes "*gum, gum, gum.*" As the two tour the island, each village gathers to hear the remarkable singing drum. However, when they come to Bimwili's own village, her voice is recognized by her own mother, and the family tricks the Zimwi into leaving them alone. Aardema's *Bringing the Rain to Kapiti Plain* (3) resembles the cumulative "House That Jack Built" as Ki-pat figures out how to bring much needed rain to his cows and crops on the Kenyan plain.

Leo and Diane Dillon won the Caldecott award for their beautiful illustrations in Aardema's West African tale of *Why Mosquitoes Buzz in People's Ears* (7). In this story the mosquito tells the iguana a tall tale that sets off a chain reaction which ends in disaster for a baby owl. Until the animals can find the culprit who is responsible for the owlet's death, Mother Owl refuses to hoot and wake the sun. King Lion holds a council and listens to everyone's excuse. Lively action words are used to tell this cumulative tale:

> So it was the mosquito
> who annoyed the iguana,
> who frightened the python,
> who scared the rabbit,
> who startled the cow,
> who alarmed the monkey,
> who killed the owlet—
> and now Mother Owl won't wake the sun
> so that day can come.[39]

The white outline of the stylized watercolors gives a cool but brilliant atmosphere to this West African story. The Dillons have also illustrated Aardema's humorous Masai tale, *Who's in Rabbit's House?* (6), as a play featuring masked actors.

Many other African stories may also be described as pourquoi stories. Ashley Bryan's wonderful retelling of "How the Animals Got Their Tails" (33) is a joy to read aloud. Gail Haley's *A Story, A Story* (142) tells how humans got their tales. Ann Grifalconi's *The Village of Round and Square Houses* (106) explains why, in a particular Cameroon village located at the base of a volcano, the women live in round huts while the men live in square ones. Little Osa of this story appears in other Grifalconi stories such as *Osa's Pride* (105).

A play on words is a favored form of humor in some African tales. Harold Courlander tells the story of the very wealthy man named Time (54). Change of fortune reduces him to a beggar and persons remark that "Behold, Time isn't what it used to be!"[40] The same collection has a story about the young hunters who try to capture "The One You Don't See Coming," which is their name for sleep. In another Anansi story, there is a character named Nothing. Anansi kills him and all the villagers "cry for nothing!" (54).

Frequently, an African tale will present a dilemma and then the storyteller will invite the audience to participate in suggesting the conclusion. The problem of which son should be given *The Cow-Tail Switch* as a reward for finding his lost father is asked in the title story of the book by Courlander (54). The boys undertake the search only after the youngest child learns to speak and asks for his father. Each of the sons has a special talent which he uses to help restore his father to life. It is then that the storyteller asks who should receive the father's cow-tail switch.

While searching for an African variant of "Cinderella," John Steptoe came upon the story of *Mufaro's Beautiful Daughters* (286) and turned it into a strikingly illustrated tale. Mufaro's daughters are very different. Manyara is bad-tempered, selfish, and scornful but predicts that one day she will be queen and her sister will be a servant. Nyasha cheerfully goes about her chores, protects a small garden snake she finds, and is delighted when the King might choose one of them to be his wife. Since the choice will be made at the royal palace in Zimbabwe, Manyara tries to sneak ahead of her sister by leaving in the night. Along the way she meets a hungry boy with whom she haughtily refuses to share her food, and she ignores the advice of an old woman. The next day, however, Nyasha shares her food with both people. When her sister arrives, Manyara comes running from the palace in hysterics because she has seen a five-headed snake on the throne. But Nyasha bravely approaches and is relieved to find the little garden snake who transforms itself, saying:

> "I am the king. I am also the hungry boy with whom you shared a yam in the forest and the old woman to whom you made a gift of sunflower seeds. . . .
> Because I have been all of these, I know you to be the Most Worthy and Most Beautiful Daughter in the Land. It would make me very happy if you would be my wife."[41]

[39]Verna Aardema, *Why Mosquitoes Buzz in People's Ears*, illustrated by Leo and Diane Dillon (New York: Dial, 1975), unpaged.
[40]Harold Courlander and George Herzog, *The Cow-Tail Switch and Other West African Stories* (New York: Holt, Rinehart and Winston, 1947), p. 77.
[41]John Steptoe, *Mufaro's Beautiful Daughters* (New York: Lothrop, Lee & Shepard, 1987), unpaged.

To accompany Nyasha, one of *Mufaro's Beautiful Daughters,* as she makes her way to the King, John Steptoe depicts bright-colored flowers and birds such as lovebirds and Carmine Bee-eaters that are found in the Zimbabwe region of Africa.

❦ ❦ ❦

After the wedding, Manyara is kept on as a servant in the Queen's household. Steptoe's careful research creates an accurate picture of the region. The Carmine Bee-eater bird that accompanies Nyasha, the intensely colored plants and animals living in the forest, architectural details from the actual ruined city of Zimbabwe, and a pair of Crowned Cranes that symbolize the royal couple all contribute authenticity to this Caldecott award winner.[42]

The Egyptian Cinderella by Shirley Climo (44) mixes fact and ancient legend in the story of a Greek slave girl, Rhodopis, who eventually mar-

---

[42]Darcy Bradley, "John Steptoe: Retrospective of an Imagemaker," *The New Advocate,* vol. 4, no. 1 (Winter 1991), p. 21.

ries the Pharoah. Rhodopis dances so beautifully that her master gives her a pair of dainty rose-red leather slippers. Jealous over her treatment, the other slave girls taunt her when they are allowed to go to Memphis to see the Pharoah and she must remain at home to wash linen, grind grain, and weed the garden. As she works, she places the slippers on the riverbank, but a great falcon carries one away to the Pharoah. Taking this as a sign, he searches up and down the Nile until he finds Rhodopis and makes her his queen. Recorded in the first century B.C., it is based on the story of a servant girl who actually came from Greece and married the Pharoah Amasis. The bird that steals the slipper was thought by story-tellers to be Horus, an Egyptian sky god and deity believed to appear on earth as a falcon.

Obviously, there is no dearth of folk literature from Africa, where oral tradition has been maintained. Children who hear these tales will become familiar with other cultures and the rhythmical chord of the ancient storytellers. They will learn of a land where baobab trees grow and people fear lions, leopards, droughts, and famines. More importantly, they will learn something about the wishes, dreams, hopes, humor, and despair of other peoples. They may begin to see literature as the universal story of humankind.

FOLKTALES OF NORTH AMERICA

When the early settlers, immigrants, and slaves came to North America, they brought their folktales with them from Europe, West Africa, and China. As they repeated their folktales, some of them took on an unmistakable North American flavor. Indigenous to the continent are those folktales told by Native Americans and those tall tales that developed from the pioneer spirit of the young American country.

In a discussion of folktales of North America it is impossible to describe any one body of folklore such as the Grimms discovered in Germany. However, the folklore of North America may be placed in four large categories:

1. Native-American, Eskimo and Hawaiian tales that were originally here.
2. Tales that came from other countries, primarily those from West Africa, and were

changed in the process to form the basis of African-American folktales.

3. Tales that came primarily from Europe and were modified into new variants.
4. Tall tales, legends, and other Americana that developed.

Virginia Haviland's collection of *North American Legends* (156) presents tales from each of these categories and gives a broad overview of folklore in the United States. Her excellent selection and accompanying annotations enable teachers to become acquainted quickly with common tales, motifs, and characters from each tradition.

The folktales told by Chinese immigrants in North America are well represented in three excellent collections. Laurence Yep's *The Rainbow People* (308) and *Tongues of Jade* (309) are tales Chinese immigrants told to remind themselves not only of home but to show how a wise man could survive in a strange new land. Collected by the WPA project in Oakland, California, in the 1930s and retold by Yep, these tales express the emotional realities of loneliness, anger, longing, and love that were a part of the Chinese-American immigrant experience. Yep's realistic fiction novels (see Chapters 9 and 10) reveal how deeply folklore and traditional tales were woven into the daily lives of Chinese Americans. Paul Yee's *Tales from Gold Mountain* (307) draws on the same wellspring of stories told by the Chinese who settled in Vancouver's Chinatown. Yee's original stories blend research and memory to evoke the world of the Chinese worker and frontier dweller.

Native-American Folktales

To try to characterize all the folklore of the various Native-American tribes as one cohesive whole is as unreasonable as it would be to lump all of the folklore of Europe together. Variations in Native-American dwellings, such as pueblos, longhouses, and teepees, or in symbolic artwork of totem poles, beading, story skins, and carvings are mirrored in the variations of Native-American folktales. The box, "Some Native-American Folktales by Region," is a useful grouping of tales for those wishing to study Native Americans specifically of a particular geographical area.

However, there are some common characteristics among the various tribes and between the folklore of Native Americans and that of northern Europeans.

Many Native-American tales might be categorized as mythology, for they include creation myths and sacred legends. *They Dance in the Sky* (385) is a collection of Native-American star myths that includes stories of the origin of the Pleiades, the Big Dipper, and other constellations. Some myths attempt to explain religious beliefs while telling people about tribal customs and how to act. Some of these tales were told as separate stories, but as with Greek or Roman mythology, they were heard by insiders who understood these tales within the context of a large interlocking set of stories.

Tales from the Native-American tradition, when originally told, were loosely plotted rather than highly structured as were European fairy tales. Thomas Leekley, who retold some of the stories of the Chippewa and Ottawa tribes in his book *The World of Manabozho* (193), says:

> Indian folklore is a great collection of anecdotes, jokes, and fables, and storytellers constantly combined and recombined these elements in different ways. We seldom find a plotted story of the kind we know. Instead, the interest is usually in a single episode; if this is linked to another, the relationship is that of two beads on one string, seldom that of two bricks in one building.[43]

The very act of storytelling was considered of ceremonial importance among various tribal groups. Storytelling took place at night and among certain tribes, such as the Iroquois, it was only permitted in the winter. Men, women, and children listened reverently to stories, which in some instances were "owned" by certain tellers and could not be told by any other person. The sacred number of four is found in all Indian tales, rather than the pattern of three common to other folktales. Four hairs may be pulled and offered to the four winds; or four quests must be made before a mission will be accomplished.

[43]Thomas B. Leekley, *The World of Manabozho: Tales of the Chippewa Indians*, illustrated by Yeffe Kimball (New York: Vanguard, 1965), pp. 7–8.

RESOURCES FOR TEACHING

◆ SOME NATIVE-AMERICAN FOLKTALES BY REGION ◆

PLAINS

Cohen, Caron Lee. *The Mud Pony*, illustrated by Shonto Begay. Scholastic, 1988. (Pawnee)
Goble, Paul. *Iktomi and the Berries: A Plains Indians Story*. Bradbury, 1989. (Lakota Sioux)
San Souci, Robert D. *The Legend of Scarface: A Blackfeet Indian Tale*, illustrated by Daniel San Souci. Doubleday, 1978.
Schoolcraft, Henry Rowe. *The Ring in the Prairie: A Shawnee Legend*, illustrated by Leo and Diane Dillon. Dial, 1970.
Steptoe, John. *The Story of Jumping Mouse: A Native American Legend*. Morrow, 1984.
Yolen, Jane. *Sky Dogs*, illustrated by Barry Moser. Harcourt, 1990. (Siksika)

WOODLAND

Esbensen, Barbara Juster. *Ladder to the Sky*, illustrated by Helen K. Davie. Little, Brown, 1989. (Ojibway)
_____. *The Star Maiden*, illustrated by Helen K. Davie. Little, Brown, 1988. (Ojibway)
Hamilton, Virginia. "Divine Woman the Creator" in *In The Beginning: Creation Stories from Around the World*, illustrated by Barry Moser. Harcourt, 1988. (Huron)
Haviland, Virginia. "How Glooskap Found Summer" in *North American Legends*, illustrated by Ann Strugnell. Collins, 1979. (Algonquin)
_____. "The Indian Cinderella" in *North American Legends*, illustrated by Ann Strugnell. Collins, 1979. (Eastern Canada)
Leekley, Thomas B. "The Giant Sturgeon" in *The World of Manabozho: Tales of the Chippewa Indians*, illustrated by Yeffe Kimball. Vanguard, 1985.
Martin, Rafe. *The Rough-Face Girl*, illustrated by David Shannon. Putnam, 1992. (Algonquin)
Norman, Howard. *How Glooscap Outwits the Ice Giants and Other Tales of the Maritime Indians*, illustrated by Michael McCurdy. Little, Brown, 1989.
Toye, William. *How Summer Came to Canada*, illustrated by Elizabeth Cleaver. Walck, 1969. (Micmac)

SOUTHWEST

Bierhorst, John. *Doctor Coyote: A Native American Aesop's Fables*, illustrated by Wendy Watson. Macmillan, 1987.
Baylor, Byrd, editor. *And It Is Still That Way*. Scribner's, 1976.
Carey, Valerie Scho. *The Quail Song: A Pueblo Indian Tale*, illustrated by Ivan Barnett. Putnam/Whitebird, 1990.
de Paola, Tomie. *The Legend of the Bluebonnet: An Old Tale of Texas*. Putnam's, 1983. (Comanche)
Durell, Ann, ed. "Coyote and the Bear" in *The Diane Goode Book of American Folk Tales & Songs*, illustrated by Diane Goode. Dutton, 1989. (Pueblo)
Hausman, Gerald. *Sitting on the Blue-Eyed Bear: Navajo Myths and Legends*. Lawrence Hill, 1975.
McDermott, Gerald. *Arrow to the Sun*. Viking, 1984. (Pueblo)
Rodanas, Kristina. *Dragonfly's Tale*. Clarion, 1991. (Zuni)

RESOURCES FOR TEACHING

◆ SOME NATIVE-AMERICAN FOLKTALES BY REGION (CONTINUED) ◆

NORTHWEST

Harris, Christie. *Once More upon a Totem*, illustrated by Douglas Tait. Atheneum, 1973.
Monroe, Jean Guard and Ray A. Williamson. "How Coyote Arranged the Night Stars" in *They Dance in the Sky: Native American Star Myths*, illustrated by Edgar Steward. Houghton Mifflin, 1987. (Wasco)
Shetterley, Susan Hand. *Raven's Light: A Myth from the People of the Northwest Coast*, illustrated by Robert Shetterly. Atheneum, 1991. (Haida)
Sleator, William. *The Angry Moon*, illustrated by Blair Lent. Little, Brown, 1970. (Tlingit)
Toye, William. *The Loon's Necklace*, illustrated by Elizabeth Cleaver. Oxford, 1977. (Tsimshian)

SOUTHEAST

Mayo, Gretchen Will. "Ice Man Puts Out the Big Fire" in *Earthmaker's Tales: North American Indian Stories from Earth Happenings*. Walker, 1989. (Cherokee)
Monroe, Jean Guard, and Ray A. Williamson. "What the Stars Are Like" in *They Dance in the Sky*, illustrated by Edgar Stewart. Houghton Mifflin, 1987. (Cherokee)
Roth, Susan. *The Story of Light*. Morrow, 1990. (Cherokee)
Troughton, Joanna. *How Rabbit Stole the Fire*. Bedrick/Blackie, 1986. (Creek)

ESKIMO

DeArmond, Dale. *The Boy Who Found the Light*. Sierra Club/Little, Brown, 1990.
_____. *The Seal Oil Lamp*. Sierra Club/Little, Brown, 1988.
Hamilton, Virginia. "Raven the Creator" in *In the Beginning: Creation Stories from Around the World*, illustrated by Barry Moser. Harcourt, 1990.
Haviland, Virginia. "Sedna the Sea Goddess" in *North American Legends*, illustrated by Ann Strugnell. Collins, 1979.
Houston, James. *The White Archer: An Eskimo Legend*. Harcourt, 1967.
McCarty, Toni. "The Skull in the Snow" in *The Skull in the Snow and Other Folktales*, illustrated by Katherine Coville. Delacorte, 1981.
Slote, Teri. *The Eye of the Needle*. Dutton, 1990.

Many of the Native-American tales are nature myths, pourquoi stories that explain how animals came to earth or why they have certain characteristics. Jane Yolen's retelling of *Sky Dogs* (311) captures perfectly the amazement and uncertainty with which a small tribe of Piegans might have greeted the first horses. Certain that the horses are a gift from the sky god called Old Man, a boy of the tribe explains:

❧ We fed the beasts dried meat like any dogs. We rubbed their noses with good backfat, which made them sneeze. We threw sticks before their faces so they could run and bring the sticks back. But they were startled by the throwing sticks, and one Sky Dog ran away. We did not see it again.[44]

Barry Moser's elegant watercolors are dominated by yellows and oranges that evoke the parched prairie grass and the heat of late summer. Paul Goble tells a similar story in which *The Gift of the Sacred Dog* (97) is the Great Spirit's attempt to help the Plains tribes hunt the buffalo more efficiently.

---

[44]Jane Yolen, *Sky Dogs*, illustrated by Barry Moser (San Diego: Harcourt Brace Jovanovich, 1990), unpaged.

In *The Loon's Necklace* (293), the bird receives his markings as a reward for his kindness in restoring the sight of a blind old man. Elizabeth Cleaver created stunning collage illustrations for this picture-book story of the origin of the "necklace." Several tales in the collection *The Talking Stone* (72), explain how the Winnebago people came to know "Thunderbird," who was formerly the giant Nasan; "Why Blackbird Has White Eyes," a Navajo tale; and the California Indian version of the origin of the Pleiades, "What Happened to Six Wives Who Ate Onions."

Perhaps one of the best known stories of explanation, which combines religious beliefs, how-and-why explanations, and references to Indian custom, is "Star Boy," which has many versions. Paul Goble retells this tale of *Star Boy* (104) with beautiful illustrations drawn from careful references to Blackfoot artistic traditions. In this story, Star Boy, expelled from the sky world with his mother and marked with a mysterious scar because of her disobedience, becomes known as Scarface. In order to marry, he must make a journey to the Sun, who removes the scar. When this happens, Star Boy is able to marry. To commemorate and honor the Sun's gesture, the Blackfeet have a sacred Sun Dance each summer. In Goble's version, Star Boy becomes another star and joins his father, Morning Star, and his mother, Evening Star. The original George B. Grinnell retelling on which Goble built his tale may be found in Virginia Haviland's *North American Legends* (156).

Without reference to scholarship, Robert San Souci has also retold this story in *The Legend of Scarface* (258). While the illustrations by Daniel San Souci are often striking, this edition has been criticized for its eclectic and embroidered retelling of this Blackfoot tale. Still another version of this story forms the skeleton of Jamake Highwater's novel, *Anpao* (159). In the tradition of "beads on a string" rather than "bricks in a building," Highwater lets Anpao meet many traditional Indian characters like Coyote, Grandmother Spider, Raven, and the Mouse People as he journeys to ask the sun for the removal of his scar. Parts of this novel are very humorous and would be fun to read aloud to middle schoolers familiar with the outline of the tale.

The tribes of the northeastern woodland nations also had their stories of visitors from the sky. Longfellow's lengthy poem, "The Song of Hiawatha," tells in part of Nokommis, daughter of the moon, who was cast from heaven by a jealous rival. Susan Jeffers begins her *Hiawatha* (199) with a pictorial reference to this tale and alludes to other sky people of the Algonquins and Ojibwa in her graceful illustrations for this short poetic excerpt.

In *Ladder to the Sky* (75), Barbara Esbensen tells another Ojibway story of how the Great Spirit, Gitchee Manitou, sent spirit messengers from the sky to earth on a vine that the Ojibway people were forbidden to touch. One day, a spirit messenger took a young man to the sky world and when his distraught grandmother tried to climb after him, the vine broke. Because, like Pandora, she had violated the warning, sickness and death were loosed on the world. But Gitchee Manitou pitied the people and sent a spirit messenger to show them how to use herbs, roots, and bark for medicine. Thus the Ojibway people learned to cure disease. Helen Davie uses traditional Ojibway textile patterns and motifs in her paintings for this story.

The woodland hero is Glooscap who, in some stories, is also known as Badger. Perhaps this is one of the "Glooskabe" stories Attean told to Matt as the two boys survived the long winter in Speare's *Sign of the Beaver* (see Chapter 10). William Toye's *How Summer Came to Canada* (292) tells how Glooscap journeyed south, when all of Canada was held in the giant Winter's cold power. When he returned with his bride the beautiful Summer, her stronger powers brought green back to Canada. Even Winter was melting away so Summer took pity on him and agreed that if he would return to the North, he could visit for six months of the year and she would leave his power alone. During the other six months she would rule and Canada would have spring and summer. Elizabeth Cleaver uses pine needles, twigs, and hand-colored torn paper in her collage illustrations for the story. Children would enjoy illustrating nature myths from other Native-American cultures using similar materials.

Almost all Native-American folklore traditions contain a trickster figure who mediates between the sky world and earth. The woodland tribes tell tales of Manabozho, a kind of half god, half superpower among the eastern tribes. But some of the stories of Manabozho picture him as less than a superhero. In "Sleepy Feet" (193), Manabozho is waiting for some rabbits to roast. He puts his feet in charge of watching them, while he goes to sleep! A canoeload of Indians comes by and quickly steals his dinner. Manabozho promptly punishes his feet by burning them because they have failed in their duty to guard his dinner! Both a rascal and a fool, cruel and admirable, Manabozho's favorite disguise is that of a hare. (His name, in fact, means "Great Hare.") He uses this shape to steal fire from the people in "The Theft of Fire" (72). The Great Plains trickster Coyote also snatches fire from the burning mountain in Margaret Hodges's *The Fire Bringer* (161), illustrated by Peter Parnall with clean line and an economy of color. To this day, says the legend, Coyote's fur is singed and yellow along his sides where the flames blew backward as he ran down the mountain carrying the burning brand.

Similar explanations of how fire or light came to the people are told in two southeastern tales, *How Rabbit Stole the Fire* (295) and the Cherokee tale, *The Story of Light* (255) in which a tiny spider carrying a small clay pot is able to carry a speck of light back to the other animals without getting burned. Each of these stories also explains physical characteristics or markings of certain animals.

Paul Goble has illustrated many tales from the Plains tribes, including several about the Plains trickster, Iktomi. Amusing stories that often have moral lessons within, they were meant to be told only after the sun had set. In *Iktomi and the Ducks* (103), Iktomi tricks some ducks into dancing with their eyes closed and then kills them. But as he cooks them in the fire, two trees rub together and their squeaking noise begins to bother the trickster. When he attempts to separate the rubbing trees, he is instead pinched between them and a hungry coyote steals his roast duck and substitutes hot coals. One trickster has been tricked by another. These stories were meant to elicit audience participation and Goble has incorporated this in an inviting way. Asides, such as "It looks like the end of Iktomi, doesn't it?" and Iktomi's often self-serving remarks, would make this very

Paul Goble uses three typefaces in the Plains Indian story of *Iktomi and the Ducks*—Iktomi's comments, the storyteller's story, and the storyteller's asides—to capture the essence of a live telling with plenty of audience participation.

🦃 🦃 🦃

funny as a shared reading. Alert readers will spot, too, the watchful coyote as he moves closer to his dinner. *Iktomi and the Boulder* (101), *Iktomi and the Buffalo Skull* (102), and *Iktomi and the Berries* (100) are three other tales of this Plains Indian trickster. Goble's illustrations for other titles such as *The Great Race of the Birds and the Animals* (99) and *Buffalo Woman* (96) are filled with patterns of flowers, trees, birds, and other animals indigenous to the prairie. Goble received the Caldecott medal for his stunning illustrations for *The Girl Who Loved Wild Horses*. All of Goble's work draws on Native-American artistic tradition as well.

In a tale adapted by Valerie Carey, the southwestern Pueblo Indians tell how Coyote had so much trouble learning *The Quail Song* (37) that the impatient Quail finally painted a rock to look like her. When the forgetful Coyote asked for singing lessons a third time and the stone refused to answer, Coyote ate what he thought was Quail but broke his teeth instead. Ivan Barnett's collage illustrations use the burnished colors and textures of oxidized metals, which give this tale the look of a story weathered by many tellings.

The trickster of the Pacific Northwest is Raven. While he is a wily, crafty being who loves to get the better of others, he is also a friend to humankind. *Raven's Light* (273) by Susan Shetterly tells how Raven created the earth from a stone and populated it with people and animals drawn from a sack around his neck. He then stole light for his world from the Kingdom of Day so that humans could see the world in its glory. Other Raven stories tell of how he brought salmon to the people (247) and in an Eskimo version, how he created the first man from a peavine (145).

Other Pacific Northwest stories have been collected by Christie Harris and illustrated by Douglas Tait. *Once More upon a Totem* (149) includes stories such as "The Prince Who Was Taken Away by the Salmon," which explains the mystery of the Pacific salmon's migration and return. Harris and Tait have also created several collections based on Mouse Woman, who appears either as a mouse or a tiny grandmother to set things aright. One of these is *Mouse Woman and the Muddleheads* (148).

Mouse Woman also figures prominently in Dale De Armond's story of *The Seal Oil Lamp* (61). Since Allegua was blind and Eskimo tribal law stated that no child may live if it cannot grow up to support itself, he was sadly left behind when the family moved to the summer fish camp. But the 7-year-old had fed a starving mouse that winter so the Mouse Woman and her family took care of Allegua:

> They told him wonderful stories about the mouse world and about the owls and foxes and eagles who try to catch them, and how the mouse people outwit their enemies. They told him about Raven and the magic that lives under the earth and in the sky country. And the mouse people sang their songs for him and did their dances on the back of his hand so he could feel how beautiful their dances were.[45]

[45]Dale De Armond, *The Seal Oil Lamp* (San Francisco: Sierra Club Books/Little, Brown, 1988), p. 20.

De Armond has also retold three Eskimo tales in *The Boy Who Found the Light* (60). His stylized wood engravings suggest dramatically the powerful beauty of Eskimo artwork.

Although survival themes are constant in Indian tales, they are particularly strong in Eskimo stories. James Houston, who spent many years among the Inuit, is especially sensitive to authentic depictions of Eskimo art and culture. His illustrations often look like renderings of Eskimo carvings. In *Tikta Liktak* (167) a legendary hunter is isolated when an ice pan breaks away. In a dream, he gains courage, kills a seal, and is able to find his way home. *The White Archer* (168) is a tale of a revengeful hunter who finally succumbs to the kindness and wisdom of an Eskimo couple.

The accompanying box, "A Study of Folktales by Culture" (pp. 354–5), provides a start for comparing characteristics, characters, collectors, and typical tales representative of specific areas.

European Variants in the United States

Richard Chase collected and published *The Jack Tales* (43) and *Grandfather Tales* (42), which are American variations of old stories brought to this country by English, Irish, and Scottish settlers in the seventeenth and eighteenth centuries. They are as much a part of Americana as the Brer Rabbit stories. In some respects Jack is an equivalent figure to Brer Rabbit. He is a trickster hero who overcomes his opponent through quick wit and cunning, rather than the strength that triumphs in the tall tales of the United States. All of these stories come from the mountain folk of the southern Appalachians. Cut off from the main stream of immigration and changing customs, these people preserved their stories and songs in the same way that they continue to weave the Tudor rose into their fabrics.

The Jack Tales represent a cycle of stories in which Jack is always the central figure. You'd expect to find him playing this role in "Jack in the Giant's Newground" and "Jack and the Bean Tree." However, he shows up again in "Jack and the Robbers," which is a variant of "The Bremen-Town Musicians". The delightful aspect of these tales is Jack's nonchalance about his exploits and the incongruous mixing of the mountaineer dialect with unicorns, kings, and swords. Yet another

RESOURCES FOR TEACHING

◆ A STUDY OF FOLKTALES BY CULTURE ◆

CULTURES AND COLLECTORS	TYPICAL TALES	CHARACTERS	CHARACTERISTICS
BRITISH FOLKTALES			
Joseph Jacobs (1854–1916)	*The Three Little Pigs* (92) *The Little Red Hen* (318) *Tam Lin* (312) *The Selkie Girl* (51) *Jack and the Beanstalk* (40) *Tattercoats* (174)	Talking beasts Lazy Jack Giants "Wee folk" Dick Whittington	Cumulative tales for youngest Beast tales Droll humor Transformations Giant killers
GERMAN FOLKTALES			
The Grimm Brothers Jacob (1785–1863) Wilhelm (1786–1859)	*Little Red Cap* (123) *Rumpelstiltskin* (257) *Hansel and Gretel* (120) *The Frog Prince* (114) *Snow-White and the Seven Dwarfs* (135) *The Elves and the Shoemaker* (111)	Tom Thumb Rumpelstiltskin Hansel and Gretel Red Riding Hood Witches, elves, dwarfs Bears, wolves Snow White, King Trushbeard	Somber stories Children as characters Harsh punishments Romances Transformations
SCANDINAVIAN FOLKTALES			
Peter Christian Asbjørnsen (1812–1885) Jorgen E. Moe (1813–1882) Translated into English by George Webbe Dasent (1817-1896)	*The Three Billy Goats Gruff* (16) "The Lad Who Went to the North Wind" (15) "Gudbrand on the Hillside" (59) *East o' the Sun and West o' the Moon* (57) *The Little Old Woman and the Hungry Cat* (242) *The Giant Who Had No Heart* (10)	Trolls, Tomte Many-headed giants Youngest sons or "Boots" North wind White bears Salmon Cats Reindeer, elk	Tongue-in-cheek humor Helpful animals Magic objects Magic enchantments Many trials and tasks Poor boy succeeds
FRENCH FOLKTALES			
Charles Perrault (1628–1703)	*Puss in Boots* (240) *Cinderella* (239) *The White Cat* (260) *Beauty and the Beast* (236) *The Sleeping Beauty* (132) *Stone Soup* (32)	Fairy godmothers Jealous stepsisters Royalty Talking cats Unselfish youngest daughter	Traditional fairy tale Romance Wicked enchantments Long sleep
RUSSIAN FOLKTALES			
Alexander Afanasyev (1855–1864)	*The Firebird* (184) *Baba Yaga* (187)	Vasilissa, beautiful and wise	Fool or youngest triumphs

RESOURCES FOR TEACHING

◆ A STUDY OF FOLKTALES BY CULTURE (CONTINUED) ◆

CULTURES AND COLLECTORS	TYPICAL TALES	CHARACTERS	CHARACTERISTICS
	Vasilissa the Beautiful (303)	Ivan, youngest brother	Peasants outwit tsars
	The Turnip (223)	Baba Yaga, the witch	Many tasks
	The Little Snowgirl (55)	Wolves, bears	Quest for firebird
	The Month-Brothers (208)	Firebird	Helpful animals
	The Fool and the Fish (8)	Koschay the Deathless	Dire punishments
JAPANESE FOLKTALES			
	The Boy of the Three-Year Nap (283)	Inch Boy	Transformation to birds
	The Crane Wife (306)	Momotaro	Childless couples have "different" children
	Momotaro, the Peach Boy (276)	Wicked Oni, ogres	
	"The Inch Boy" (224)	Trickster badger	
	The Funny Little Woman (225)	Urashima Taro	Respect for elderly
	Three Strong Women (284)	Poor farmers, fisherman	Self-sacrifice
	The Badger and the Magic Fan (177)		
AFRICAN FOLKTALES			
Harold Courlander and other present-day collectors	*Mufaro's Beautiful Daughters* (286)	Anansi, trickster spider	Pourquoi stories
	Rabbit Makes a Monkey of Lion (4)	Zomo, trickster rabbit	Talking beast tales
	A Story, a Story (142)	Various animals	Animal tricksters
	The Cow-Tail Switch (54)		Wry humor
	How Many Spots Does a Leopard Have? (194)		Onomatopoeia
	Traveling to Tondo (5)		Word play
NATIVE-AMERICAN FOLKTALES			
Henry Rowe Schoolcraft (1820s–1850s)	*Star Boy* (104)	Glooscap	Nature myths
	How Rabbit Stole the Fire (295)	Manabozho, the Hare	Tricksters
	Raven's Light (273)	Coyote	Transformation tales
	The Gift of the Sacred Dog (97)	Raven	
	Ladder to the Sky (75)	Iktomi	Pattern of four
	Iktomi and the Ducks (103)	Sky People	Pourquoi stories
	Mouse Woman and the Muddleheads (148)	Mouse Woman	Interaction with spirit world
	The Eye of the Needle (282)		
	The Dark Way (144)		

version is Gail Haley's *Jack and the Bean Tree* (143), cast as an Appalachian story told by Poppyseed, a character who is based on Haley's grandmother.

In *Moss Gown* (165) William H. Hooks retells an old story from North Carolina that melds elements of "Cinderella" with motifs from *King Lear*. Rejected by her father and banished from home by her two sisters, Candace meets a gris-gris woman in the cypress swamp who comforts her. The strange witch woman gives her a shimmering gown that will change back into Spanish moss when the morning star sets and a chant to call if she ever needs help. Candace finds work in the kitchen of a plantation where the Young Master is about to give a ball. Calling on the gris-gris woman for help, Candace wears her marvelous dress each night of the three-day frolic but is careful to leave before the morning star sets. At the ball she meets and falls in love with the Young Master, and when Candace is finally able to reveal herself, the Young Master has come to know her through conversation and, it is implied, to love her for more than her beauty. While Moss Gown has magic to help her, she is more similar in spirit to *Princess Furball* (127) and the traditional Cinderella than she is to the Disney and Perrault Cinderellas for it is her own intelligence and spirit that wins for Candace a husband, a home, and her father's love once again.

Others continue to Americanize European folktales. Hooks has also written an Appalachian version of *The Three Little Pigs and the Fox* (166) that depends on local detail, colloquial language, and mountain customs for flavor. In it, Hamlet rescues her two pig brothers from a "drooly-mouth fox" and comes home in time for Sunday dinner. Iris Van Rynbach illustrates and retells the French folktale of *The Soup Stone* (297) in a post-Revolutionary War New England setting. Barry Moser has taken the action of Hans Christian Andersen's tale of *The Tinderbox* (11) and set it in Appalachia after the Civil War. It is an ex-Confederate soldier who is sent to find the box by an East Tennessee mountain man instead of a witch. While purists may object, borrowing a tale from one tradition and retelling it in another is time honored, and these modern retellings will most likely be "found" in some other collection years from now.

African-American Folktales

When the slaves were brought to America from Africa, they continued to tell the tales they remembered, particularly the talking-beast tales. Some of these stories took on new layers of meaning about the relationship between the slaves and their masters. In the late 1800s, Joel Chandler Harris, a Georgia newspaperman, recorded these tales in a written approximation of the Gullah dialect in which the tales were told to him. In his book, *Uncle Remus: His Songs and His Sayings*, Harris invented Uncle Remus, an elderly plantation slave who told these talking-beast tales to a little white boy (see 150). Harris was later criticized for his portrayal of the Old South, but the "Brer Rabbit" stories live on in the retellings by other people.

Two excellent series have adapted these stories for today's children. In *Jump Again!* (152), Van Dyke Parks and Malcolm Jones present "The Wonderful Tar-Baby Story" in which Brer Fox sets up a sticky contraption and then, "Brer Fox, he lay low." When Brer Rabbit is finally stuck, Brer Fox saunters forth and laughs threateningly, showing "his teeth all white and shiny, like they were brand-new." Of course, Brer Rabbit pleads with the fox to do anything but throw him into a briar patch and the gullible fox is tricked once again into sparing the rabbit's life for he was "bred and born in a briar patch."[46] Two full-page watercolors depict portraits of Brer Fox in thought and the Tar Baby; two sketches depict "Brer Rabbit, All Stuck Up" and the briar patch itself. In contrast, Julius Lester's "Brer Rabbit and the Tar Baby" from his *The Tales of Uncle Remus* (150) is a more rambunctious version that sounds as if it is being told directly to the reader. Asides, contemporary allusions, creative figurative language, and interjections are characteristic of this storyteller. Lester describes Brer Rabbit as strutting "like he owned the world and was collecting rent from everybody in it."[47] But by the

[46]Joel Chandler Harris, *Jump Again! More Adventures of Brer Rabbit*, adapted by Van Dyke Parks, illustrated by Barry Moser (San Diego: Harcourt Brace Jovanovich, 1987), p. 9.
[47]Julius Lester, *The Tales of Uncle Remus*, illustrated by Jerry Pinkney (New York: Dial, 1987), p. 11.

The Rabbit Family's Riding Horse

Barry Moser's watercolor shows a supposedly sick, cigar-chomping Brer Rabbit astride "the Rabbit Family's Riding Horse" just before the trickster nudges the fox with his spurs. From *Jump! The Adventures of Brer Rabbit* by Joel Chandler Harris, adapted by Van Dyke Parks and Malcolm Jones.

time the poor rabbit is stuck, Brer Fox saunters out "as cool as the sweat on the side of a glass of ice tea."[48] Four full-color watercolors by Jerry Pinkney on one double-page spread depict incidents in the story. Julius Lester's foreword for his two collections dispel many of the myths surrounding the "Brer Rabbit" stories, discuss the nature of storytelling, and reflect on the role of the trickster figure in valuing a little disorder in today's society. Lester has also included several talking-beast tales in *The Knee-High Man and Other Tales* (195).

A funny tale collected by the Works Progress Administration (WPA) project in Alabama in the 1930s has been retold by Molly Bang in *Wiley and*

[48]Ibid, p. 14.

the Hairy Man (19). Wiley and his mother must figure out how to trick this "mighty mean man" three times. Then, by the laws of the Tombigbee Swamp where they live, the monster can never bother them again. While this tale is formatted as an easy-reading book, it makes a dramatic read-aloud choice for first and second grades.

The Talking Eggs by Robert D. San Souci (259) is a Creole folktale that seems to have its roots in European tales. A poor widow lives with her two daughters Rose and Blanche on a farm that looks like "the tail end of bad luck." Blanche has to do all the work, and is unfairly scolded one day. When she runs into the forest, she meets a strange old woman who offers to take her to her shack if she promises not to laugh at anything she sees. Blanche complies even though there are two-headed cows, strange chickens, and the old woman can remove her head! Before Blanche returns home, the old woman gives her the gift of special eggs, which will turn into riches when she throws them over her shoulder. But, she is warned, take only the ones that say "Take me." Blanche follows this advice even though the ones that she leaves are jewel-encrusted. When she arrives home with fancy clothes and a carriage, the mother plots to steal Blanche's things and send Rose for more. But Rose, who is rude and laughs at the old woman, steals the jeweled eggs, and is paid for her greediness by the release of whip snakes, wasps, and a cloud of bad things that chase her home. Blanche disappears to live a grand life in the city, and Rose and her mother never find the old lady's house again. Jerry Pinkney's rich and colorful illustrations magically evoke the forest and swamp settings of this Louisiana "generous person/greedy person" tale.

Virginia Hamilton has assembled a superior collection of stories representing the main body of African-American folktales in *The People Could Fly* (147). Twenty-four tales are divided into four sections. The animal tales contain such familiar stories as "Doc Rabbit, Bruh Fox, and the Tar Baby" and a lesson to the rich folks from their poor neighbors, "Bruh Alligator Meets Trouble." Motifs of transformation, trickery, and tall tales are found in the second section, which includes a version of "Wiley, His Mama, and the Hairy Man" that would compare well with Bang's version (19). A third contains tales of Jacks and one of John de Conquer. This section also contains tales of slaves who outwit slaveowners to win their freedom. Readers may recognize "The Peculiar Such Thing" as a variation of the British "Tailypo." Another pourquoi tale, "Jack and the Devil," explains the origins of foxfire or marsh light. The final section contains slave tales of freedom, including one handed down in the author's own family. The poignant title story, a moving one of fieldhands escaping from a cruel overseer, is typical of the stories often told on "Juneteenth," the day on which descendants of slaves in the South remember Emancipation. Hamilton has preserved the individual voices of the storytellers from whom the stories were collected. Some are in Gullah or plantation dialect

The plain eggs in Robert D. San Souci's *The Talking Eggs* cry out "Take me" while the jeweled eggs warn "Don't take me." Blanche obeys in Jerry Pinkney's watercolor and colored pencil illustrations for this story set in the rural southern United States.

and others include African words whose meanings are lost to us today. An excellent classroom resource, the collection contains author notes and an extensive bibliography. Bold black-and-white illustrations by Leo and Diane Dillon evoke the humor, beauty, and liveliness of these traditional stories.

According to Steve Sanfield's introduction to *The Adventures of High John the Conqueror* (261), the High John stories were popular among slaves, but for obvious reasons were never shared with white people. Although John was a slave, he spent his time doing as little slaving as possible, tricking the Old Master out of a roasting pig or a few hours of rest. Sanfield prefaces eight of the sixteen tales with notes explaining historical context or giving background. In one story of "Tops and Bottoms," a motif found in many tales, John asks Boss which half of the planting he wants. Thinking that High

John will plant cotton, Boss answers accordingly. But John has planted sweet potatoes. Each of the next three years, Boss is tricked by John. Finally, he chooses *both* tops and bottoms, which leaves High John the middle. But John, no fool, plants corn, and Boss is left with a heap of tassles and stalks while High John takes the corn. Virginia Hamilton extended the adventures of this sometimes mythical hero into a folktale-like novel, *The Magical Adventures of Pretty Pearl* (146).

Tall Tales

Ask any visitor to the United States what he has seen and he is apt to laugh and reply that whatever it was, it was the "biggest in the world"—the longest hot dog, the highest building, the largest store, the hottest spot. This is the land of superlatives, "the best." While many countries have tall tales in their folklore, only the United States has developed such a number of huge legendary heroes. Perhaps the vast frontier made settlers seem so puny that they felt compelled to invent stories about superheroes. Whatever the reasons, North American tall tales contain a glorious mixture of the humor, bravado, and pioneer spirit that was needed to tame a wilderness.

Paul Bunyan was a huge lumberjack who bossed a big gang of lumbermen in the North Woods of Michigan, Minnesota, and Wisconsin. Paul's light lunch one day was "three sides of barbecued beef, half a wagon load of potatoes, carrots and a few other odds and ends,"[49] Glen Rounds reports in *Ol' Paul, the Mighty Logger* (256). Rounds asserts, as do most chroniclers of Paul's doings, that he worked for Paul and was the biggest liar ever in camp. By switching from past to present tense, Rounds gives these eleven tales special immediacy. Esther Shephard's telling of *Paul Bunyan* (270) is somewhat windy and colloquial, but Rockwell Kent's powerful illustrations and unique capital letters intrigue children. Steven Kellogg synopsizes the life of *Paul Bunyan* (182) in his humorously illustrated picture-book version. Tidy endpapers depict Paul's New England seacoast beginnings and a U.S. map highlights Paul's feats. This action-packed version serves as an introduction to exploits like Paul's digging of the Great Lakes and the Grand Canyon and his famous popcorn blizzard. However, the extended text of the other versions fleshes out individual tall tales and makes them better choices for reading aloud.

Pecos Bill (183) was a Texan who, as a child, fell out of his parents' wagon as they moved West. Raised by coyotes, Bill could howl with the best of them. He even thought he was a coyote until a passing cowboy convinced him otherwise. Bill's exploits include squeezing the poison from a rattler to create the first lasso, and inventing cattle roping. He also bred cattle with shorter legs on the uphill side so that they could graze steep pinnacles without falling off. His taming of a wild horse eventually won him a bride, Slewfoot Sue. Kellogg's depiction of this exuberant tall-tale hero is full of humor, exaggeration, and boundless energy. Ariane Dewey's *Pecos Bill* (71) follows the same story line in easy-reader format with attractive but less active and less colorful pictures.

Of all the heroes, only *Johnny Appleseed* (198) was a gentle, tame one who lived to serve others. His real name was John Chapman and he grew up in the Connecticut Valley before setting out for Pennsylvania, Ohio, and Indiana. Reeve Lindbergh's poetry captures the quiet spirit of the man of whom it was said:

> He'd walked all through America
> And all his seeds he'd sown.
> He'd planted apples, sharp and sweet,
> And swiftly they had grown.[50]

Kathy Jakobsen's full-page folk-art paintings capture the changing face of the land as settlers moved west. Small illustrations bordered by checkered squares look like quilt squares and depict Chapman's life and the natural world to which he was so closely bound. Steven Kellogg's *Johnny Appleseed* (181), in contrast, focuses on the more rollicking incidents that grew around the tales which Chapman told to settlers and their own embellishments of these stories. Both authors include notes that help readers see how storytellers select events to shape into tales.

---

[49]Glen Rounds, *Ol' Paul, the Mighty Logger* (New York: Holiday House, 1949), p. 28.

[50]Reeve Lindbergh, *Johnny Appleseed*, illustrated by Kathy Jakobsen (Boston: Little, Brown, 1990), unpaged.

RESOURCES FOR TEACHING

♦ SOME AMERICAN TALL-TALE HEROES ♦

NAME	OCCUPATION/LOCALE	CHARACTERISTICS
JOHNNY APPLESEED (John Chapman) (1774–1845) *The Story of Johnny Appleseed* (9) *Johnny Appleseed* (181, 198) "Johnny Appleseed" (156, 230) "Rainbow Walker" (290)	Born in Massachusetts, wanderer in Pennsylvania, Indiana, and Ohio; planter of apple trees.	Selfless; friend to animals; dressed in rags with cook pot for hat.
PAUL BUNYAN *Ol' Paul, the Mighty Logger* (256) *Paul Bunyan* (270, 182) "Babe the Blue Ox" (156) "Sky Bright Axe" (290) "Paul Bunyan" (230)	Lumberjack; North American woods; created the Great Lakes, St. Lawrence Seaway, and Grand Canyon	Huge; strong even as a baby; Babe the Blue Ox was his pet; inventive problem solver.
JOE MAGARAC "Steelmaker" (290)	Steel worker; Pittsburgh, or "Hunkietown"	Made of steel; works and eats like a mule; born from an ore pit; could stir steel with bare hands.
PECOS BILL "Pecos Bill Becomes a Coyote" (156) *Pecos Bill* (183, 71) "Coyote Cowboy" (290) "Pecos Bill" (230)	Cowboy; first rancher; Texas panhandle and the Southwest.	Raised by coyotes; Widow-maker was his horse; Slewfoot Sue was his wife; invented lasso, six-shooter, cattle roping.
JOHN HENRY *John Henry* (179) *A Natural Man* (262) "Hammerman" (290) "John Henry" (230) "The Working of John Henry" (28)	Railroad man; West Virginia west to the Mississippi.	African-American wanderer, exceedingly strong even as a baby; Polly Ann was his wife; companion was Little Willie.
DAVY CROCKETT (1786–1836) *The Narrow Escapes of Davy Crockett* (70) "Davy Crockett" (230) "Frontier Fighter" (290) *Quit Pulling My Leg!* (244)	Frontiersman; Tennessee	Tall; good hunter and fighter; Betsy was his rifle; tamed a bear; wore coonskin cap.
ALFRED BULLTOP STORMALONG "Five Fathoms Tall" (290) "Stormalong Fights the Kraken" (156) "Stormalong" (230)	Sailor, whaler, ship's captain; Massachusetts and northern coasts.	Giant man, huge appetite; ship called the Tuscarora; made the White Cliffs of Dover with soap.

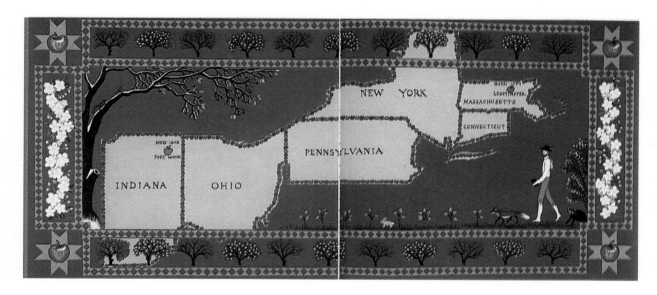

Kathy Jakobsen's folk-art paintings, with quilt-patterned borders, are in perfect harmony with Reeve Lindbergh's poetic story of the legendary hero, *Johnny Appleseed*.

Ariane Dewey has also brought less well-known American tall-tale figures to light in an easy-reader format illustrated simply but with humor. Her *Febold Feboldson* (68) tells of the Nebraska farmer who had a way with weather. *Gib Morgan* (69) was a real oilman whose tall tales chronicled the rise of the American oil business. *The Narrow Escapes of Davy Crockett* (70) and his wife, *Sally Ann Thunder Ann Whirlwind Crockett* (47) are tall tales surrounding this legendary couple.

Industry has its heroes, too. "Joe Magarac" (290) was a man of steel who came to Hunkietown. The word *magarac* means jackass, and Joe Magarac worked and ate like one. He finally melted himself down to become part of a new steel mill. John Henry was a powerful African American who swung his mighty hammer in a contest with a steam drill to build the transcontinental railroad. Steve Sanfield's illustrated short story, *A Natural Man* (262), tells of John Henry's life from childhood to his death after defeating the steam drill. Ezra Jack Keats created bold figures to depict this legendary hero in his picture book *John Henry* (179). In "The Working of John Henry" (28), William J. Brooke narrates a variation in which the steel-driving man triumphs by changing with the times and learning to use the newfangled machine.

Mary Pope Osborne has selected nine heroes whose stories she tells in *American Tall Tales* (230). In the tradition of nineteenth-century storytellers, she uses figurative language easily and has combined, edited, and added her own touches to these stories. Michael McCurdy's watercolor-washed bold wood engravings of Pecos Bill, John Henry, and Stormalong perfectly suit the exaggerated language of the tall tale.

The box, "Some American Tall-Tale Heroes," outlines some of the characteristics of seven of these legendary heroes. Others whom children might research and add to the list include Casey Jones, Old Stormalong, Tony Beaver, Mike Fink, and more.

FOLKTALES OF CENTRAL AND SOUTH AMERICA

Each year a little more of the rich story heritage of Central and South America becomes available. Many stories from this area appear in excellent collections of folktales, myths, or fables edited by John Bierhorst. *The Monkey's Haircut and Other Stories Told by the Maya* (22) includes stories collected in Guatemala and southeastern Mexico from Mayan Indians since 1900. Some are obvious variations of European tales and other are *ejemplos* (explanatory myths). Robert Andrew Parker's gray-washed drawings and Bierhorst's informative introduction both contribute appeal for middle-grade readers. (See "Fables" and "Myths" for other Bierhorst titles.)

Verna Aardema's tale from Mexico tells how *Borreguita and the Coyote* (2) meet in the field where the crafty "little lamb" outwits the coyote. Petra Mathers's stylish watercolor paintings feature bright saturated colors and primitive figures reminiscent of Henri Rousseau. Harriet Rohmer's *The Invisible Hunters* (251) is a Nicaraguan Miskito Indian folktale about an isolated tribe's first contact with the outside world when a magic vine bestows the gift of invisibility on three brother hunters. In *Brother Anansi and the Cattle Rancher* (67), a folktale from Nicaragua, James de Sauza tells a bilingual tale of the exploits of the trickster spider found throughout the Caribbean countries and West Africa. When Tiger wins the lottery, Anansi outwits him and becomes a partner in a cattle ranch.

Ellen Alexander's *Llama and the Great Flood* (343) is a Quechua story from Peru. Llama foresees the future ruin of the tribe when the sea overflows and warns the man. He and his wife gather three of every animal and flee to the top of the highest mountain in the Andes. After five days of flooding, the waters recede and the world may be inhabited again. Alexander's note links this story to other flood myths worldwide.

Two South American pourquoi stories tell different versions of how birds became brightly colored. "Humming-Bird and the Flower" appears in Charles Finger's *Tales from Silver Lands* (77), a collection of South American stories illustrated with woodcuts that won a Caldecott award in 1925. The story attributes the hummingbird's colors to clay, jewels, the color of the sunset, and the greens of the forests, which Panther helped the bird to gather after it helped restore Panther's eyesight. Flora's *Feathers Like a Rainbow* (78) explains how the Amazonian birds received their own bright colors by stealing poor Hummingbird's pot of colors, which she gleaned as she kissed the flowers. Colorful paintings depict the vegetation and birds of the Amazon River basin.

Colorful Amazonian birds decorate the endpapers of Beatriz Vidal's *The Legend of El Dorado* (298). The name *El Dorado* symbolized for the Spanish conquistadors everything related to the search for gold in the unexplored jungles of South America. But El Dorado, "the gilded man,"

comes from a story first recorded in Colombia. A tribal king once lived by an enchanted lake. When the serpent of the lake bewitched the king's wife and son into the water to join its kingdom, the tribe worried that the king would die of grief. But the serpent promised that the family would be reunited if the king ruled his kingdom wisely. The king ruled well, but to remind the serpent of its promise, each year he oiled his body and covered it with gold dust. Then his boat carried him upon the waters as he threw treasures to the serpent. Finally, the king was accepted into the serpent's world to join his family but to this day, the treasures of the gilded king, El Dorado, are locked in the depths of Lake Guatavita.

With the changing population of North America, we need more editions of traditional folktales, myths, and legends that reflect South and Central American cultural heritage. Small publishers have begun to feature folktales of the region and teachers will need to be persistent in finding these sources.

FABLES

Origin of Fables

Fables are usually associated with the name Aesop, a Greek slave who is supposed to have been born in Asia Minor about 600 B.C. Some scholars doubt his actual existence and believe that his works were the product of several storytellers. We know that some of the fables appeared in Greek literature two centuries before Aesop's birth, and in India and Egypt before that. The first written fables were in Greek, translated into Latin and again into English by William Caxton, and printed in 1484.

Another source for fables, as we have seen, was the *Jatakas*, animal stories that told of the previous births of the Buddha, and the *Panchatantra*, which was written for the purpose of instructing the young princes of India. These stories, longer than Aesop's fables, have moralistic verses interspersed throughout. When these are removed, the tales are closer to folktales, where they were discussed.

A third common source for fables is the work of La Fontaine, a French poet, who wrote his fables in verse form. However, he drew largely on the collections of Aesop's fables that were available in the seventeenth century.

Characteristics of Fables

Fables are brief, didactic tales in which animals, or occasionally the elements, speak as human beings. Examples of these might be the well-known race between "The Hare and the Tortoise" or the contest between "The Sun and the North Wind." Humans do appear in a few fables, such as "The Country Maid and the Milk Pail" or "The Boy Who Cried Wolf." The characters are impersonal, with no name other than "fox," "rabbit," or "cow." They do not have the lively personalities of Anansi the spider or Raven the trickster of folktale fame. The animals are merely representative of different aspects of human nature—the lion stands for kingliness, the fox for cunning, the sheep for innocence and simplicity, and so on. Fables seldom have more than three characters, and the plots are usually based on a single incident. Primarily, fables were meant to instruct. Therefore, all of them contain either an implicit or an explicit moral.

Because of their brevity fables appear to be simple. However, they convey an abstract idea in relatively few words, and for that very reason are highly complex stories. In selecting fables, then, it is wise to look at the quality of both language and illustrations. Compare the following two interpretations of the beginning of "The Town Mouse and the Country Mouse":

> A Town Mouse went to visit his cousin in the country. This Country Mouse lived simply, and he was not rich, but he brought out all that he had to feed and entertain his honored guest.[51]

Contrast the spare prose of Lisbeth Zwerger with the following version by Heidi Holder:

> An honest, plain, sensible Country Mouse invited her city friend for a visit. When the City Mouse arrived, the Country Mouse opened her heart and hearth in honor of her old friend. There was not a morsel that she did not bring forth out of her larder—peas and barley, cheese and parings and nuts—hoping by quantity to make up for what she feared was wanting in quality, eating nothing herself, lest her guest should not have enough.[52]

Holder's illustrations are framed with borders suggesting medieval embellishments; Zwerger chooses a simple picture of two mice conversing on a hillside. These reflect some of the unique and various treatments given to Aesop's stories for today's readers.

Various Editions of Fables

While younger children may appreciate some fables, they are not usually able to extract a moral spontaneously until about second or third grade. Eve Rice's *Once in a Wood* (331) is a collection of ten well-known fables in easy-reader format with rhyming morals. Fulvio Testa's *Aesop's Fables* (324) are concisely told with morals concealed in the conversation rather than appended. His use of crisp line and bright borders makes this version especially useful in reading aloud to larger groups.

Tom Paxton's lively verses in *Aesop's Fables* (323) and *Belling the Cat* (327) are a rhythmical delight. In "The Tortoise and the Hare," the first speaker says,

> Zip! Zap! Zoom! Look at me go!
> I am the hare, and I hope you know
> A streak of lightning could not catch me;
> I am as fast as fast can be.[53]

Animals and humans in medieval dress fool and are fooled by each other in Robert Rayvesky's illustrations, which have the look of richly tinted hand engravings. Eric Carle in *Twelve Tales from Aesop* (332) took some liberties in retelling so that in "The Grasshopper and the Ant" instead of being left out in the cold as a result of his lack of foresight, the grasshopper is invited into a second house as an honored musician.

In *The Exploding Frog and Other Fables from Aesop* (329) John McFarland retells more than thirty fables with a contemporary flair. Cheerfully humorous illustrations by James Marshall add much to these fables and since the morals are

---

[51]Lisbeth Zwerger, "Town Mouse and Country Mouse," from *Aesop's Fables* (Saxonville, Mass.: Picture Book Studio, 1989), unpaged.

[52]Aesop, *Aesop's Fables*, illustrated by Heidi Holder (New York: Viking, 1981), p. 5.
[53]Tom Paxton, *Aesop's Fables*, illustrated by Robert Rayevsky (New York: Morrow, 1988), unpaged.

Wendy Watson traveled to the American Southwest to sketch and paint on location for her pictures for *Doctor Coyote,* John Bierhorst's collection of stories that weave together Native-American coyote tales and the Old World fables of Aesop.

omitted, this collection may challenge children to add their own. A reissue of *The Caldecott Aesop* (328) shows how Randolph Caldecott applied the moral of a fable to a contemporary (for Caldecott) setting. Each fable has two pictures—one, a literal animal scene, and the second, a human one. "The Ass in the Lion's Skin" impresses the other animals until the disguise blows off. In Caldecott's satiric second interpretation, a pompous art critic is discovered to know nothing.

John Bierhorst, a distinguished collector and editor of Native-American literature, discovered Aesop's fables had been recorded by the Aztecs in the sixteenth century. *Doctor Coyote* (334) is a collection of these stories translated from the Aztec manuscript in which the main character of each fable became Coyote, a Native-American trickster. Bierhorst's cohesive collection of twenty fables weaves one story into the next and shows

Coyote getting a little wiser with each "lesson." With ample use of blues and roses Wendy Watson's full-color illustrations warmly depict the desert and mountain settings of New Mexico.

As in his many other books, Mitsumasa Anno in *Anno's Aesop* (333) challenges readers both visually and verbally. Little Freddy Fox finds a book of fables, which he asks his father to read to him. Readers see the original fable with a literal or enigmatic illustration on the top three-quarters of the page. At the bottom, Mr. Fox spins out his version of the story, which may be humorous, parallel, crazily imaginative, or part of a longer story he weaves from picture to picture. Older readers recognize Anno's trademark optical illusions, puzzles, allusions, and inclusions.

Other illustrators have chosen fewer tales for interpretation. Paul Galdone's *Three Aesop Fox Fables* (337) includes two stories in which the same fox is outsmarted and one in which he triumphs. Galdone has also illustrated a Jataka tale, *The Monkey and the Crocodile* (336) as did Marcia Brown in *Once a Mouse* (335). Ed Young illustrated *The Lion and the Mouse* (330) using black-and-white and startling close-ups to heighten the drama of "little and big." La Fontaine based many of his fables on Aesop, and Brian Wildsmith illustrated *The Miller, The Boy and the Donkey* (340), *The Hare and the Tortoise* (338), and *The Lion and the Rat* (339) in his familiar splashes of color.

Older children might enjoy comparing the treatment of several of these fables. In this way they would become familiar with the spare language, the conventional characters, and the explicit or implied morals of fables. They might appreciate modern writers of fables, such as Leo Lionni whose *Frederick* (341) is similar to Carle's version of "The Grasshopper and the Ant," or William Steig, whose *Amos & Boris* (342) mirrors "The Lion and the Mouse." After such comparisons, discussions, and readings, they would then be well prepared to write their own fables and variations.

MYTHS

The Nature of Myth

Mythology evolved as primitive peoples searched their imaginations and related events to forces, as they sought explanation of the earth, sky, and human behavior. These explanations moved slowly through the stages of a concept of one power or force in human form, who controlled the phenomena of nature; to a complex system in which the god or goddess represented such virtues as wisdom, purity, or love; to a worshipping of the gods in organized fashion. Gods took the forms of men and women, but they were immortal and possessed supernatural powers.

Myths deal with human relationships with the gods, with the relationships of the gods among themselves, with the way people accept or fulfill their destiny, and with the struggle of people within and without themselves between good and evil forces. The myths are good stories, too, for they contain action, suspense, and basic conflicts. Usually, each story is short and can be enjoyed by itself, without deep knowledge of the general mythology.

Types of Myths

CREATION MYTHS

Every culture has a story about how the world began, how people were made, how the sun and the moon got in the sky. These are called creation myths, or origin myths; they give an explanation for the beginnings of things. Deborah Nourse Lattimore based *Why There Is No Arguing in Heaven* (378) on myths found in the Mayan codices, books painted on bark or deerskin and preserved from invading Spaniards. In this creation story, Hunab Ku spits in a jar of rainwater and pours out the world. Two other gods, Lizard House and Moon Goddess, compete to create a being worthy of worshipping the gods. But it is the watchful Maize God who is finally successful in creating men and women and is allowed to take his place beside Hunab Ku. Lattimore's illustrations resemble the Mayan stonework and paintings found in Gautemala and parts of Mexico. Virginia Hamilton chose creation stories from around the world for her collection titled *In the Beginning* (369).

❦ These myths from around the world were created by people who sensed the wonder and glory of the universe. Lonely as they were, by themselves, early people looked inside themselves and expressed a

longing to discover, to explain who they were, why they were, and from what and where they came.[54]

Barry Moser's watercolor portraits and representations create mysterious and dramatic accompaniments to these tales. An Eskimo story tells how Raven the Creator made a pea pod from which sprang man. A Chinese story explains how Phan Ku burst from a cosmic egg to create the world. A California Indian legend, "Turtle Dives to the Bottom of the Sea," begins with a sea turtle that dives under water to bring up enough earth to make dry land. This is similar to a Papua New Guinea creation myth retold by Barbara Ker Wilson, *The Turtle and the Island* (402) which Frané Lessac has illustrated with her colorful folk-art paintings.

John Bierhorst's expertise in Aztec literature is the basis for *The Mythology of Mexico and Central America* (348). This book traces twenty basic myths and explains how they functioned among the ancient Aztec and Maya people and how they survive today. This volume, as well as its two companions, *The Mythology of South America* (350) and *The Mythology of North America* (349), which deal with North and South American mythology, would give teachers and older students the background needed to understand these creation stories. *The Hungry Woman: Myths and Legends of the Aztecs* (347) is for a younger audience than the previous series and includes reproductions of early Aztec paintings that functioned as a way of preserving stories.

Beginnings (361) is Penelope Farmer's collection of creation myths grouped under such categories as man, fire, food, or floods. Stories range from a Finnish one telling how earth was shaped from the broken pieces of a teal's egg to an Indonesian one that tells how a flood covered two arguing mountains and people and animals were saved when they climbed the third even higher mountain. Climbing a mountain in a flood is a motif also found in Ellen Alexander's *Llama and the Great Flood* (343) from Peru.

Children who compare myths may marvel at the human imagination and see the world in a

[54]Virginia Hamilton, *In the Beginning: Creation Stories from Around the World*, illustrated by Barry Moser (San Diego: Harcourt Brace Jovanovich, 1988), p. xi.

different way. Comparing myths often raises interesting questions for children about the similarities, connections, and migrations of early peoples as well.

NATURE MYTHS

The nature myths include stories that explain seasonal changes, animal characteristics, earth formations, constellations, and the movements of the sun and earth. Many Native-American nature myths are easier for young children to comprehend than are the creation myths. Some of these myths have been previously discussed in "Native-American Folktales."

The Greek story of "Demeter and Persephone" explains the change of seasons. Hades, god of the underworld, carried Persephone off to his land to be his bride, and Demeter, her mother, who made plants grow, mourned for her daughter. When she learned of Persephone's fate, she asked Zeus to intercede, and it was granted that the girl might return if she had eaten nothing in Hades. Since she had eaten four seeds of a pomegranate, she was compelled to return to Hades for four months each year during which time the earth suffered and winter came. Gerald McDermott in *Daughter of Earth* (382) contrasts the cool greens of earth above with the smoke reds of the underworld. By stroking the prepared canvas with a hard bristle brush, he has given the paintings a surface that resembles the ancient frescoes of Roman art.

HERO MYTHS

The hero myths, found in many cultures, do not attempt to explain anything at all. These myths have some of the same qualities as wonder stories in that the hero is given certain tasks or, in the case of Heracles, labors, to accomplish. Frequently the gods help (or hinder) a particular favorite (or disliked) mortal. Monsters such as gorgons, hydras, and chimaeras in the Greek stories are plentiful, but these provide the hero with his challenge. Characteristic of the hero role is that he accepts all dangerous assignments and accomplishes his quest or dies in one last glorious adventure.

Greek Mythology

The myths with which we are most familiar are those of the ancient Greeks collected by the poet

Hesiod sometime during the eighth century B.C. The Roman versions of these myths were adapted by the poet Ovid during the first century B.C. in his well-known work, *Metamorphoses*. This has caused some confusion in that the Roman names for the gods are better known than the Greek, even though the stories originated with the Greeks. However, the more recent versions of these myths are using Greek names. In working with children it is best to be consistent in your choice of names, or they will become confused. You might wish to reproduce the accompanying box, "Some Gods and Goddesses of Greek and Roman mythology," for their reference. Leonard Everett Fisher's *The Olympians* (359) provides an introduction to the pantheon. Each double-page spread features a painting as well as a paragraph about a particular god or goddess, and lists both Greek and Roman names, parentage, and the symbols representing that deity.

Greek mythology is composed of many stories of gods and goddesses, heroes, and monsters. The Greeks were the first to see their gods in their own image. As their culture became more sophisticated and complex, so, too, did their stories of the gods. These personified gods could do anything that humans could do, but on a much mightier scale. The gods, while immortal, freely entered into the lives of mortals, helping or hindering them, depending on their particular moods. Their strength was mighty and so was their wrath. Many of the myths are concerned with conflicts and the loves of the gods. Jealousy and the struggle for power among them often caused trouble for humans. Some of the stories concerning the loves and quarrels of the immortals, however, are inappropriate for children.

Greek mythology includes the creation story that Earth and Sky were the first gods. Their children were giant Cyclops and the Titans, one of whom was Cronus who drove his father away with a scythe (thus the picture of Father Time). Cronus swallowed each of his children so they would not usurp his place, but his wife gave him a stone instead of her last child, Zeus. Of course Zeus overthrew his father and made him disgorge his brothers and sisters, who were still alive. Zeus married the jealous Hera who caused all kinds of trouble. Prometheus was a Titan who defied the other gods in order to give fire to humankind.

Zeus punished his disobedience by chaining him to Mount Caucasus, where an eagle devoured his liver each day, but it was renewed each night. Zeus also sent "Pandora" (369) and a box of trouble to punish Prometheus and humankind. Warned not to open the box, Pandora was so curious that she could not help herself. All evils of the world were released but hope remained in the box and gave humankind the ability to endure.

Another story concerned Zeus's punishment of the greedy "King Midas" (380) whose curse was that everything he touched, including his little daughter, turned to gold. Children who have a good background in folktales will find that many of the same elements are present in the Greek myths. In the *d'Aulaires' Book of Greek Myths* (353) the story of "King Midas" is economically told in two pages with a bold stone lithograph illustration. The d'Aulaires' collection presents a well-woven selection of tales from the birth of Cronus's children to the stories of the mortal descendants of Zeus and the heroic adventures.

The gods could not tolerate human pride, which the Greeks called *hubris*. Arachne was transformed into a spider because of her pride when she foolishly challenged the goddess Athena to a weaving contest. Bellerophon slew the monster Chimaera, defeated the Amazons, and rode Pegasus. But when he boasted that he would fly to Olympus, the offended Zeus caused a gadfly to sting Pegasus, who bucked and tossed Bellerophon to his death.

Other stories of the disastrous results of *hubris* include the myths of "Daedalus" and "Phaethon." In Jane Yolen's *Wings* (404) Daedalus is presented as a proud Athenian inventor who is banished for inadvertently killing a nephew. Exiled to Crete, he designs and builds a labyrinth for King Minos but years later gives the Athenian Theseus the key to its maze. Thus Theseus is able to kill the Minotaur, free the Athenian youths, and escape with Minos's daughter. For these traitorous acts, his host Minos places Daedalus and his young son Icarus in a

RESOURCES FOR TEACHING
◆ SOME GODS AND GODDESSES OF GREEK AND ROMAN MYTHOLOGY ◆

GREEK	ROMAN	TITLE	RELATIONSHIP
Zeus	Jupiter or Jove	Supreme Ruler, Lord of the Sky	
Poseidon	Neptune	God of the Sea	Brother of Zeus
Hades or Pluto	Dis	God of the Underworld	Brother of Zeus
Hestia	Vesta	Goddess of the Home and Hearth	Sister of Zeus
Hera	Juno	Goddess of Women and Marriage	Wife and sister of Zeus
Ares	Mars	God of War	Son of Zeus and Hera
Athena	Minerva	Goddess of Wisdom	Daughter of Zeus
Apollo	Apollo	God of Light and Truth, the Sun God	Son of Zeus and Leto
Aphrodite	Venus	Goddess of Love and Beauty	Daughter of Zeus, wife of Hephaestus
Hermes	Mercury	Messenger of the Gods	Son of Zeus and Maia
Artemis	Diana	Goddess of the Moon and Hunt	Twin sister of Apollo
Hephaestus	Vulcan	God of Fire	Son of Hera
Eros	Cupid	God of Love	Son of Aphrodite (in some accounts)
Demeter	Ceres	Goddess of Grain	Daughter of Cronus and Rhea
Dionysus or Bacchus	Bacchus	God of Wine	Son of Zeus and Semele
Persephone	Proserpine	Maiden of Spring	Daughter of Demeter

That night, when her husband was asleep, she lit the lamp and saw him—not a monster, but the most beautiful of beings, a fair and graceful youth with golden wings, smiling even in his sleep. Psyche was moved by a deeper love than she had ever felt. She bent over her husband, and from the lamp, a drop of oil, burning hot, fell on his shoulder. Stung by the pain, he opened his eyes and looked at her

sternly. "Foolish Psyche," he said, "I knew how it would be. You could not trust me. You had to see for yourself. Now you will lose everything that I could give you, and I must lose you." Too late she knew who he was: Eros, the son of Aphrodite. There was a flash of golden wings and he was gone. The palace too was gone, and Psyche found herself alone again on the mountaintop.

In Donna Diamond's painting the theme is romantically illuminated by the light from Psyche's lamp just as a drop of hot oil awakens the sleeping Eros in *The Arrow and the Lamp* by Margaret Hodges.

high tower. Daedalus makes wings from bird feathers and fastens them to a frame with candle wax. Before the two soar away, he warns his son not to fly too low or water will soak his wings nor too high or the sun will melt the wax. Bordered in bleached tan lines, Dennis Nolan's watercolors capture the light of the Greek islands and the many blues of the sea; swirling pearly clouds and flowing lines are actually the gods watching the action as if viewing a play. In italics, Yolen's text provides a Greek chorus, or a commentary of the gods who give approval, observe, laugh, or listen gravely. While the gods express concern over the youth's flight and anguish over his death, they do not intervene. Daedalus is left to mourn.

Descended from the sun god Helios, "Phaethon" desires to drive the sun chariot to prove his parentage to his friends. When his father is finally tricked into agreeing, Phaethon

cannot control the sun chariot and nearly burns up the earth. Zeus saves humankind by killing Phaethon with a thunderbolt. Alice Low retells both of these stories and many others in *The Macmillan Book of Greek Gods and Heroes* (380). An excellent, invitingly illustrated collection of stories that features more dialogue than the d'Aulaire versions, Low's book also includes hero tales of Perseus, Heracles, Jason, Theseus, and Odysseus.

Margaret Hodges retells the story of Eros (or Cupid) and Psyche in *The Arrow and the Lamp* (372). Psyche is so beautiful that a jealous Aphrodite sends Eros to find an ugly and vile mate for her. Instead Eros falls in love with Psyche and becomes her unseen husband. Psyche's jealous sisters are so incredulous that Psyche has never seen her husband, they convince her to sneak a look while he is asleep. A drop of oil from Psyche's small lamp awakens Eros and he flies away. Psyche prays to Aphrodite for the return of her husband, but the goddess then sets impossible tasks for the girl to perform. When the last one finally kills Psyche, Eros carries her to Olympus and pleads successfully for her to become an immortal. Donna Diamond's delicate paintings, like the beauty of hand-tinted old photographs, give readers a glimpse of a time long gone. Edna Barth, in *Cupid and Psyche* (346), tells a shorter version of this myth. Children will be struck by the similarity of patterns in this tale with those in *East of the Sun and West of the Moon* (14, 15, 217).

Doris Gates has written a series of books featuring all of the stories related to one god or goddess. These provide a continuing theme and avoid the fragmentation of books that attempt to give a complete coverage of the myths. *Lord of the Sky: Zeus* (364) includes the lovely story of the poor couple, "Baucis and Philemon," who were willing to share all that they had with the stranger who stopped at their humble hut, never dreaming that he was Zeus. The longer stories of Theseus and Daedalus are well written, as are the other books in the series: *The Warrior Goddess: Athena* (366), *The Golden God: Apollo* (363), and *Two Queens of Heaven: The Story of Demeter and Aphrodite* (365). These would be fine stories to read aloud to 10- to 12-year-olds.

Older children who have been introduced to Greek mythology through the simpler stories will be ready for the longer hero tales of Perseus, the gorgon-slayer; Theseus, killer of the minotaur; Heracles and his many labors; Jason and his search for the golden fleece; and the wanderings of Odysseus. Fortunately, several of these stories are now published in single-tale editions. Leonard Everett Fisher's *Jason and the Golden Fleece* (358) is told in spare prose with dramatic paintings to underscore Jason's trials in overcoming Harpies, avoiding the crashing rocks of the Symplegades, and numerous other tasks. When Jason faces two snorting, firebreathing bulls with which he is supposed to plow a field, Fisher builds intensity:

❦ Their flaming nostrils heated the air as they trotted around the field, kicking up a thunderous cloud of

dust. They wheeled and charged, their flames reaching out and searing his skin.[55]

Jason wins the fleece with the help of Medea, sails home victoriously, and betrays his wife, finally to come to a lonely end. Fisher has also illustrated and retold *Theseus and the Minotaur* (360). Both stories features a simple map and sources.

Warwick Hutton's story of *Theseus and the Minotaur* (376) is more poetic and evocative of an Aegean setting than the previous version. Theseus tells his father, King Aegeus, that he will go with the fourteen youths sacrificed each year to King Minos's monster, the Minotaur. There, with the help of Ariadne who has fallen in love with him, he is able to find his way into the labyrinth and kill the evil creature. He finds his way out by following a cord held by Ariadne. Theseus's tragedy is that he must abandon Ariadne to the god Dionysus and in his misery he forgets to change the sail of his boat from black to white to indicate to his father that he is alive. The grief-stricken King Aegeus hurls himself into the sea from whence comes its name—the Aegean Sea. While Theseus later becomes King of Athens, he is never truly happy and finally steps down. Hutton's artwork reflects designs and motifs of Minoan architecture, clothing, and artifacts.

Bernard Evslin's *Hercules* (355) is told in modern language and allusion, which makes for an exciting and fast-paced narrative. By heightening the action and emphasizing characterization of the villainous Hera or the faithful and brave Iole, Evslin makes Hercules into a hero very much in keeping with those children already know from television and fantasy movies. Evslin's *Jason and the Argonauts* (356) is also part of this series.

Evslin also employs modern vernacular in *Heroes and Monsters of Greek Myth* (357). For example, Procrustes is showing Perseus his remarkable six-foot bed into which he fits everyone by the expedient of either cutting off their feet or stretching them. He explains:

❦ "And I am a very neat, orderly person. I like things to fit. Now, if the guest is too short for the bed, we

[55]Leonard Everett Fisher, *Jason and the Golden Fleece* (Holiday House, 1990), unpaged.

attach those chains to his ankles and stretch him. Simple."

"And if he's too long?" said Theseus.

"Oh, well then we just lop off his legs to the proper length."

"I see."

"But don't worry about that part of it. You look like a stretch job to me. Go ahead, lie down."[56]

Like Evslin, Robert Graves in *Greek Gods and Heroes* (367) utilizes the same rather flippant approach in his telling. This style makes the stories seem more contemporary, but at the same time, they lose part of their mystery and grandeur. *Tales of the Greek Heroes* (368) by Roger Lancelyn Green is a somewhat more difficult but well-written collection. Pamela Oldfield's *Tales from Ancient Greece* (386), like the Low and d'Aulaire collections, presents several well-known myths in formal prose and includes enough of the hero tales to pique children's curiosity. With the increased interest in giving children a literary foundation, perhaps we will in the future see more Greek myths elegantly presented in single-tale editions, as well as in lively collections.

Norse Mythology

A mythology derives its characteristics from the land and peoples of its origin. The land of the Norsemen was a cold, cruel land of frost, snow, and ice. Life was a continual struggle for survival against these elements. It seems only natural that Norse mythology was filled with gods who had to battle against huge frost giants also. These were heroic gods who, unlike the immortal Greek gods safe in their home on sunny Mount Olympus, knew that they and their home on Asgard would eventually be destroyed. And in a way their prophecy was fulfilled, for Christianity all but extinguished the talk of the old gods, except in Iceland. There, in the thirteenth century, Snorri Sturluson—a poet, scholar, and historian—collected many of the Norse myths and legends into a book called the *Prose Edda*. Much of his writing

was based on an earlier verse collection called the *Poetic Edda*. These two books are the primary sources for our knowledge of Norse mythology.

It is too bad that children do not know these myths as well as they know those of the Greeks. In some ways the Norse tales seem more suited to children than the highly sophisticated, gentle Greek tales. These stories appeal to the child's imagination, with their tales of giants and dwarfs, eight-legged horses and vicious wolves, magic hammers and rings. Primarily they are bold, powerful stories of the relationships among the gods and their battles against the evil frost giants. Odin is the serious protector of the men he created, willingly sacrificing one of his eyes to obtain wisdom that would allow him to see deep into the hearts of men. The largest and the strongest of the gods is Thor, owner of a magic hammer that will hit its mark and then return to his hands. And Balder, the tragic god of light, is the most loved by all the other gods.

Some of the stories are amusing. Seven- and 8-year-olds would enjoy the picture-book version of *The Hammer of Thunder* (389), retold by Ann Pyk. In this tale the enormous Thor is dressed as a bride and goes with Loki, who is his "bridesmaid," to trick the giant Thrym into returning Thor's magic hammer. Loki is a puzzling character who seems a likable mischief maker in the beginning of the tales but becomes increasingly evil. Finally, he is responsible for the death of Balder. He guides the hand of Hoder, Balder's blind brother, who shoots a fatal arrow made of mistletoe, the only object that could harm Balder. The gods impose a cruel punishment on Loki that reminds one of the punishment of Prometheus. This story is retold by Edna Barth in *Balder and the Mistletoe* (345).

While one of the best collection of these myths remains the classic Padraic Colum one, *The Children of Odin* (351), there are other notable collections. The d'Aulaires have provided a continuous narrative of these stories along with handsome lithographs, in their book *Norse Gods and Giants* (354). Their retellings maintain the flavor of the original *Edda*. For example, the description of the making of a special bond to chain the fierce Fenris wolf reminds us of the Witches' Chant in Macbeth:

---

[56]Bernard Evslin, Dorothy Evslin, and Ned Hoopes, *Heroes and Monsters of Greek Myth* (New York: Scholastic, 1970), p. 53.

🐿 [The gnomes] spell-caught the sound of cat paws, the breath of fish, the spittle of birds, the hairs of a woman's beard, the root of a mountain, and spun them around the sinews of a bear. That made a bond that looked as fine as a ribbon of silk, but since it was made of things not in this world, it was so strong nothing in the world could break it.[57]

If children have time to become acquainted with only one mythology, they should know the Greek stories (or their Roman adaptations). No other tales have so influenced the literature and art of the Western world. Norse mythology, too, has left its mark on Western culture, as in the names for Thursday (Thor's day) and Friday (Freya's day). Also, these tales have a special appeal for children. However, there are many other important mythologies that may be sampled as a part of the study of a culture or simply be enjoyed as literature.

EPIC AND LEGENDARY HEROES

The epic is a long narrative or cycle of stories clustering around the actions of a single hero. Epics grew out of myths or along with them, since the gods still intervene in earlier epics like the *Iliad* and the *Odyssey*. Gradually, the center of action shifted from the gods to a human hero, so that in such tales as Robin Hood the focus is completely on the daring adventures of the man himself.

The epic hero is a cultural or national hero embodying all the ideal characteristics of greatness in his time. Thus Odysseus and Penelope, his wife, represented the Greek ideals of intelligence, persistence, and resourcefulness. He survived by his wit rather than his great strength. Both King Arthur and Robin Hood appealed to the English love of justice and freedom: King Arthur and his knights represented the code of chivalry; Robin Hood was the champion of the common man—the prototype of the "good outlaw." The epics, then, express the highest moral values of a society. A knowledge of the epics gives children an understanding of a particular

[57]Ingri d'Aulaire and Edgar d'Aulaire, *Norse Gods and Giants* (Garden City, N.Y.: Doubleday, 1967), p. 52.

culture; but, more importantly, it provides them with models of greatness through the ages.

The *Iliad* and the *Odyssey*

According to tradition, a blind minstrel named Homer composed the epic poems the *Iliad* and the *Odyssey* about 850 B.C.; but scholars generally believe that parts of the stories were sung by many persons and that they were woven into one long narrative before they were written. The *Iliad* is an account of the Trojan War fought over Helen, the most beautiful woman in the world. When Paris, son of King Priam of Troy, kidnaps Helen from the Greek king Menelaus, the Greeks unleash a ten-year siege on Troy led by the Greek warriors Agamemnon and Achilles. The gods and goddesses have their favorites, and they, too, quarrel among themselves as they witness the battles, almost as one would watch a football game! The complex story is long and difficult to understand, although specific incidents such as the final defeat of the Trojans by the cunning device of the Trojan Horse do intrigue some children.

The *Odyssey* is the story of the hazardous ten-year journey of Odysseus (called Ulysses by the Romans) from Troy to his home in Ithaca, following the end of the war. Odysseus has one terrifying experience after another, which he manages to survive by his cunning. For example, he defeats the horrible one-eyed Cyclops by blinding him and then strapping his men to the undersides of sheep, which were allowed to leave the cave. No one has heard the song of the Sirens and lived, until Odysseus puts wax in his men's ears and has himself bound to the mast of his ship with strict orders to his men to ignore his pleas for release. His ship safely passes between the whirlpool of Charybdis and the monster Scylla, but later is shipwrecked and delayed for seven years. A loyal servant and his son aid the returned hero in assuming his rightful throne and saving his wife; Penelope has had a difficult time discouraging the many suitors who wish to become king. While children or teachers may be acquainted with episodes from the story, it is the total force of all his trials that presents the full dimensions of this hero.

Both of Barbara Picard's retellings, *The Odyssey of Homer Retold* (388) and *The Iliad of Homer* (387), are distinguished and emphasize the development of characters. Padraic Colum's version, *The Children's Homer* (352), keeps the essence of the traditional poem and Pogany's illustrations distinguish this book from others.

The *Ramayana*

The *Ramayana* is the great epic tale of India that tells how the noble Rama, his devoted brother, and his beautiful virtuous wife Sita manage to defeat the evil demon Ravana. Heir to the throne, Rama is banished from his home through the trickery of his stepmother. Prince Rama, his brother, and the devoted Sita spend fourteen years in wandering and adventure. One day Sita vanishes, kidnapped by Ravana. Rama searches for her unsuccessfully and then turns to a tribe of monkeys, for their help. Finally Sita is found, and with the help of an entire army of monkeys, Rama rescues her. In order to be cleansed from her association with the demon, Sita must stand a trial by fire. Her faithfulness proved, she is united with her beloved Rama. Peace and plenty prevail during the reign of Rama.

Composed in India by the sage Valmiki during the fourth century B.C., the *Ramayana* represented some 24,000 couplets that were memorized and repeated. It constitutes part of the gospel of Hindu scripture, for Rama and his wife are held as the ideal man and woman. Rama is believed to be an incarnation of the god Vishnu come to earth in human form.

Elizabeth Seeger created a prose version of *The Ramayana* (394) that reads smoothly as one long and exciting narrative. Joseph Gaer relates the story for children in *The Adventures of Rama* (362). Surely Western children should know something of this epic hero who is so important to a large part of the world.

Heroes of the Middle Ages

Some historians believe there was a King Arthur who became famous around the sixth century. Defeated by the invading Saxons, his people fled to Wales and Brittany and told stories of his brav-ery and goodness. Other stories became attached to these, and the exploits of Tristram, Gawaine, and Lancelot were added to the Arthurian cycle. The religious element of the quest for the Holy Grail, the cup used by Christ at the Last Supper, was also added. Whether or not the chalice actually existed, it remains as a symbol of purity and love. In the fifteenth century Sir Thomas Malory's *Morte d'Arthur* was one of the first books printed in England and became a major source of later versions. Margaret Hodges has recounted how Malory came to tell these stories in her nonfiction *Knight Prisoner: The Tale of Sir Thomas Malory and His King Arthur* (374).

In a short novel, Jane Yolen tells of the boyhood of Arthur, here called Artos, who becomes *The Dragon's Boy* (403). Artos has been raised by Sir Ector in a small castle along with the lord's son and other boys. One day while searching for a prized dog supposedly lost on the Fens, he discovers a cave in which a dragon dwells. Both fascinated and terrified, Artos agrees to seek wisdom from the dragon when he is not doing his work at the castle. Those who know the story will recognize clues that echo through the telling: the High King's son supposedly given to witches on the Tor and seen no more; the dragon's calling Artos "Pendragon"; Artos spending a jewel for a weapon, "a sword from a stone"; and the crusty old apothecary, Old Linn. Children who do not know the story will nonetheless find this a compelling introduction as they sympathize with the lonely boy who confronts his fears to discover the truth about the supposed dragon, his own parentage, and his future as the great King Arthur.

Numerous lavishly illustrated books about Arthur and Merlin introduce children to these stories. In Robert D. San Souci's *Young Merlin* (393), Merlin, whose parentage was thought to be half human and half fairy, is dragged before Vortigern, King of Britain, to be sacrificed as the priests have prophesied that only the blood of a half human can save Vortigern's defense tower. Merlin instead is able to see that underneath the tower's foundation, a red dragon fights the white one. When they are freed, the tower will stand. Merlin foretells the victory of Uther Pendragon over Vortigern as well, and is taken into the new king's household. Daniel Horne depicts the magician's childhood in paintings fittingly lit by eerie yellows and diffused by mists and smoke. Pamela Service shortens this tale for younger children in *Wizard of Wind and Rock* (395). Hudson Talbott's *King Arthur: The Sword in the Stone* (400) tells a single episode in Arthur's life and his vivid watercolors reflect the romance of the tale. Older children will appreciate Robin Lister's *The Legend of King Arthur* (379) for its fourteen stories told as Merlin reminisces. Alan Baker's full-color illustrations illuminate nearly every page. T. H. White's *The Sword in the Stone* (401) is an imaginative retelling of Arthur's boyhood and growth under Merlin's tutelage. Middle-school readers enjoy this novel for its humor.

Rosemary Sutcliff brings thirteen stories from the Arthurian cycle to life in *The Sword and the Circle* (398). Beginning with the events surrounding Arthur's accession to the throne, she weaves other stories into the text in separate chapters. "Tristan and Iseult," "Beaumains, the Kitchen Knight," "Sir Gawain and the Green Knight," and "Gawain and the Loathly Lady" are but a few of the tales included. Two other volumes, though concerning important parts of Arthurian legend, deal with less adventurous or romantic aspects of the story and may be of less interest to middle-grade readers. *The Light Beyond the Forest: The Quest for the Holy Grail* (396), details the wanderings of Lancelot, Galahad, Percival, and others in search of the grail but also in search of their own salvation. *The Road to Camlann* (397) tells of the sad end of Arthur and the Round Table fellowship. Sutcliff has also retold the romantic *Tristan and Iseult* in a full-length novel (399). The language has a lyrical quality reminiscent of the old storytellers:

> It was young summer when they came to the hidden valley; and three times the hawthorn trees were rusted with berries and the hazelnuts fell into the stream. And three times winter came and they huddled about the fire in the smoky bothie and threw on logs from the wood-store outside. . . .[58]

Sidney Lanier's *The Boy's King Arthur* (377), which first appeared in 1880, and Howard Pyle's *The Story of King Arthur and His Knights* (392), which was published as a four-volume work between 1902 and 1910, are classic works told in a stately mode.

Children who wish to learn more about the legendary King Arthur would appreciate *Quest for a King: Searching for the Real King Arthur* (344). Here, Catherine M. Andronik presents the various legends connected with King Arthur and carefully explores the historical facts behind them.[59]

Several stories set in King Arthur's time and retold with pictoral conventions of the Middle Ages are available in picture storybook format. In *Sir Gawain and the Loathly Lady* by Selina Hastings (371), King Arthur is caught without his sword Excalibur and must answer a riddle to save his life: What is it that women most desire? On the way home, a despairing Arthur meets a Loathly Lady (rendered in truly horrible detail by Juan Wijngaard) who offers him the riddle's answer if he will marry her to one of his knights. Arthur agrees but is heartbroken when valiant Sir Gawain offers himself. They are married, much to the chagrin of the court. However, once alone in the bedchambers, the Lady turns into a beautiful young woman who gives her new husband a choice. Will she be beautiful by day and ugly by night, or the opposite? When Gawain cannot bear to make the decision, he answers, "You must decide whichever you prefer." This breaks the spell and is also the key to the riddle. What every woman desires is to have her own way. This exquisitely illuminated story features bordered and decorated illustrations full of medieval detail and suffused with light. The story is a companion to *Sir Gawain and the Green Knight* (371).

Margaret Hodges retells the first part of "The Tale of Sir Gareth of Orkney" taken from Malory's *Le Morte D'Arthur* in *The Kitchen Knight* (373). In this story, Gareth, who is a nephew of King Arthur, wishes to earn his knighthood by deeds, not by birthright. So he becomes a kitchen lad in Arthur's castle and accepts a quest which no other knight will undertake, that of saving the beautiful Linette's sister, Linesse, from imprison-

[58]Rosemary Sutcliff, *Tristan and Iseult* (New York: Dutton, 1971). p. 90.

[59]See Barbara Elleman's annotated list of other books that relate to King Arthur, "The Days of Camelot," *Book Links*, vol. 1, no. 1 (September 1991), pp. 23–27.

The frame used by Trina Schart Hyman distances viewers while the arch of the dragon's body and the furl of its wings concentrates attention on the endangered knight in Margaret Hodges's retelling of *Saint George and the Dragon.*

❦   ❦   ❦

ment in the castle of the Knight of the Red Plain. While he vanquishes the Red Knight, it takes extra effort to win the gratitude of Linette and the acceptance of the highly selective Lady Linesse, whom he has rescued. Trina Schart Hyman researched weaponry before depicting accurately a leather rather than metal shield and an early horned helmet that was discovered recently in the Thames River.

Hyman also conducted painstaking research to set the illustrations accurately for Hodges's story of *Saint George and the Dragon* (375) in fourth-century England. She studied ancient lore of wildflowers and herbs in order to use them symbolically in the borders of each picture. For example, when Saint George engages the dragon in battle, agrimony, or fairy wand, which was a charm against serpents, appear in the borders; as he lies wounded in a streambed, the borders depict mandrake, which was thought to be a powerful anesthetic; in the last pages, white roses entwine as the king offers the hand of his daughter Una in marriage to George. White roses bloomed so profusely that the Romans gave England the name of Albion, from Rosa Alba, for the white rose. The fourth century was a time in which Christianity and ancient beliefs competed, so red-winged angels and pale fairies are both part of the borders. A pre-Norman sailing vessel appears in small pictures as a symbol of the hero's progress. Children are appropriately awed and thrilled by the truly terrible dragon, which Hyman drew after a long siege she had with a snapping turtle in her New Hampshire pond. While the story of St. George has little to do with King Arthur, it shares a similar time, theme, and conventions with other tales told in the Middle Ages.

All of these books contribute to a child's knowledge of the mystique that surrounds the story of King Arthur. Students seldom discover these tales on their own, but once introduced to them, they delight in taking their place at that round table of adventure.

Another legendary hero who captures the imagination of children is Robin Hood. Scholars have been unable to agree over whether there was indeed a medieval outlaw by the name of Robin Hood or whether he was really a mythical character derived from festival plays that took place in France at Whitsuntide. But by the fifteenth century May Day celebrations in England were called "Robin Hood's Festivals," and the story of Robin Hood had become a legend for all time.

Children love this brave hero who lived in Sherwood Forest, outwitted the Sheriff of Nottingham, and shared his stolen goods with the poor. Others in the band included the huge Little John, Friar Tuck, the minstrel Alan-a-Dale, and Robin's sweetheart Maid Marian. Howard Pyle's *Some Merry Adventures of Robin Hood* (390) is a shorter version of his classic, *The Merry Adventures of Robin Hood* (391). Ann McGovern retells this familiar legend in clear, direct language. A few words, such as "perchance" and "thou," retain the spirit of the medieval language without making *Robin Hood of Sherwood Forest* (383) too difficult to read. Virginia Lee Burton's illustrations for Malcolmson and Castagnetta's poetic edition of *The Song of Robin Hood* (381) are almost rhythmical in their use of swirling patterns.

Robin McKinley's *The Outlaws of Sherwood* (384) presents a Robin Hood for modern times. The unwilling outlaw leader is dressed in Lincoln green only because Marian is able to find several bolts of material cheaply because of an inferior dyeing job. Robin is not much of a good shot, but others in his band do the hunting while Robin broods over how to manage, shelter, and feed his ever-growing group. McKinley fleshes out the emotions of Little John, Robin Hood, Maid Marian, and others while exploring various dimensions of heroism. Some authors end the story with the death of Robin Hood in the hands of a treacherous prioress. McKinley creates an alternative ending that allows readers to carry the story on in their imaginations. While King Richard Lionheart imposes a fitting punishment on the outlaws, they keep their freedom in a most plausible way. Older readers who understand loyalty and appreciate the romance of a good tale will find this a rewarding and compelling story.

THE BIBLE AS LITERATURE

The Place of the Bible in Literary Study

The Bible has an important and rightful place in any comprehensive discussion of traditional literature because it is a written record of people's continuing search to understand themselves and their relationships with others and their creator. It makes little sense to tell children the story of Jack the Giant Killer but to deny them the stories about David and Goliath or Samson. They read of the wanderings of Odysseus, but not those of Moses. They learn that Gilgamesh built an ark and survived a flood, but do not know the story of Noah. Our fear should not be that children will know the Bible; rather it should be that they will *not* know it. Whatever our religious persuasion or nonpersuasion, children should not be denied their right to knowledge of the traditional literature of the Bible. Other literature cannot be fully understood unless children are familiar with the outstanding characters, incidents, poems, proverbs, and parables of this literature of the Western world of thought.

We must clarify the difference between the practice of religious customs and indoctrination of one viewpoint and the study of the Bible as a great work of literature. In 1963 the Supreme Court asserted that "religious exercises" violated the First Amendment, but the Court also encouraged study of the Bible as literature:

> In addition, it might well be said that one's education is not complete without a study of comparative religion or the history of religion and its relationship to the advancement of Civilization. It certainly may be said that the Bible is worthy of study for its literary and historic qualities.[60]

The literary scholar Northrop Frye believes it essential to teach the Bible, for it presents humans in all their history. "It's the *myth* of the Bible that should be the basis of literary training, its imaginative survey of the human situation which is so broad and comprehensive that everything else finds its place inside it."[61] Some critics will be disturbed by the use of the term *myth* unless they understand its larger literary context as the human search for and expression of truth and meaning.

Books for the Study of the Bible

COLLECTIONS OF BIBLE STORIES

When a school staff agrees that children should have an opportunity to hear or read some of the great stories from the Bible, it faces the task of selecting material. Walter de la Mare's introduction to *Stories from the Bible* (412) provides an excellent background for understanding the problems of translation. He compares versions of the story of Ruth in the *Geneva Bible* (1560), the *Douai Bible* (1609), and the *Authorized Version* (1611). The old form of spelling is used in his quotations from Wycliffe of 1382, John Purvey of 1386, and Miles Coverdale of 1536. He clearly explains the differences between literal, allegorical, moral, and analogical meanings given words and phrases. This book presents the Creation, the flood, and stories of Moses, Joseph, Samson, Samuel, Saul, and David. The text combines modern descriptive imagery with a biblical style of narration. For

[60]Quoted by Betty D. Mayo, "The Bible in the Classroom," *The Christian Science Monitor* (September 30, 1966), p. 9.
[61]Northrop Frye, *The Educated Imagination* (Bloomington: Indiana University Press, 1964), p. 111.

example: "As Joseph grew older, and in all that he was and did showed himself more and more unlike themselves, jealousy gnawed in their hearts like the fretting of a cankerworm."[62]

In *Moses' Ark* (408), a collection ranging from Genesis through Kings, Alice Bach and J. Cheryl Exum retain the spirit of the original stories as they expand the narration with subtle details. Conversation, based on archaeological and anthropological research, and borrowings from other parts of the Bible enrich our understanding. In the title story, the Pharoah muses that his Hebrew slaves may leave him so he shortsightedly imposes even harsher laws. Eventually, his order to kill all of the Hebrew boy children brings the Hebrew baby, Moses, to be raised in his palace. The following story, "The Exodus," shows the consequences of the Pharoah's actions. In a note, the authors point out that the use of "ark" instead of "basket" directs attention to a crucial parallel that Hebrew listeners would recognize. The Hebrew word for "ark" is used only twice in the Bible: once in Noah's story and here. Whereas Noah's ark saved humanity, Moses' ark saves the future leader of his people.[63] Stunning pastel and watercolor illustrations in varied shades of gray and black depict the stories of Sampson, Saul, Deborah, David, Solomon, Elijah, and others.

In *Does God Have a Big Toe?* (416), Marc Gellman, a rabbi, follows a long-held Jewish tradition of telling *midrashim*, stories about stories in the Bible. These involve readers with their humorous, contemporary tellings. For instance, Noah doesn't have the heart to tell his friends what God has told him so he hints: "You know, Jabal, this might be a very good time for you to take those swimming lessons you have been talking about for so long."[64] A more serious undertaking is *The Bible Story* (428) written by Philip

Turner and illustrated by Brian Wildsmith. Presented in chronological order, stories from both the Old Testament and the New Testament are told with dignity and illustrated with colorful flair.

SINGLE BIBLE STORIES

Many individual picture books based on individual stories from the Bible are especially useful to introduce children to this literature. Leonard Everett Fisher adapted *The Seven Days of Creation* (415) and used bold colorful paintings to excite the imagination of readers. Several illustrators such as Warwick Hutton, Charles Mikolaycak, Peter Spier, and Tomie de Paola have also contributed beautiful editions of single Bible stories. Hutton's *Adam and Eve* (417) is illustrated with quietly powerful watercolors depicting the Garden of Eden in all its splendor. A snake encircles the final illustration of two people walking away. Beautiful watercolors for his adapted King James version of *Noah and the Great Flood* (420) are like tableaux in contrast to the action and chaos presented in Peter Spier's paintings for *Noah's Ark* (427). Spier's version begins with a poem and proceeds in wordless but eloquent fashion to show us the consequences when animals share an ark for forty days and nights. Numerous small pictures as well as double-page spreads, humor as well as pathos, and a changing palette vary the rhythm of the story.

Moses in the Bulrushes (419) is more intimate in scale. Hutton uses close-up views of Moses being cared for by his mother and the Pharoah's daughter discovering him as she bathes in a gossamer bathing dress. This version ends with a short paragraph and an illustration of the resolute Moses followed by his people as they leave Egypt. Miriam Chaikin's *Exodus* (411) reveals what happened from the time Moses arrived in the Pharoah's palace until his final march across the desert. Charles Mikolaycak's dramatic illustrations bordered in weathered browns show Moses confronting the Pharoah as he conveys God's words to *"Let my people go,"* the plagues which were visited on the Egyptians, Moses receiving the Ten Commandments, and the Israelites' march toward the Promised Land. A contrast in artistic styles, these two books show how two different illustrators may depict the

[62]Walter de la Mare, *Stories from the Bible*, illustrated by Edward Ardizzone (New York: Knopf, 1961), p. 62.
[63]Alice Bach and J. Cheryl Exum, *Moses' Ark: Stories from the Bible*, illustrated by Leo and Diane Dillon (New York: Delacorte, 1989), p. 45.
[64]Marc Gellman, *Does God Have a Big Toe? Stories About Stories in the Bible*, illustrated by Oscar de Mejo (New York: Harper & Row, 1989), p. 31.

Charles Mikolaycak's use of warm earth tones and borders of desert brown give his paintings an ancient cast that perfectly suits the Egyptian setting for Miriam Chaikin's adaptation of the Bible story of *Exodus*.

🍎 🍎 🍎

same story in unique but equally compelling ways.

Both Warwick Hutton and Peter Spier have retold the story of Jonah. Hutton's paintings in *Jonah and the Great Fish* (418) present a rose-clad Jonah against an increasingly angry and darkening backdrop of sky and sea. When Jonah rests, his legs are crossed to resemble a fish tail as if to remind readers of his predicament. Spier's *The Book of Jonah* (426) is more literal, filled with details of life in this time, the contents of the fish's belly, and the crowded streets of Nineveh where Jonah reluctantly ends up. Maps, a historical note, and an annotated cross-section of a typical ship of Tarshish show the lengths to which Spier went in his research for this story.

Isaac Bashevis Singer vividly retold the Old Testament story of the destruction of Sodom in *The Wicked City* (425). The text is substantial, with a strong sense of story and an underlying layer of meaning for today's world. For example, when Abraham comes to visit Lot, neighbors talk:

🍎 "Why did Lot allow his crazy uncle to come here?" one of the bystanders asked. Others pelted Abraham and his two companions with the dung of asses.

"This is what happens when one admits strangers," said another. "Sooner or later they bring foreigners with them."[65]

The scratchboard pictures by Fisher provide fine details of texture and facial expression.

From the New Testament, Mikolaycak has depicted two stories both adapted by Elizabeth Winthrop. Illustrations for *A Child Is Born* (429) give a more active and protective role to Joseph. *He Is Risen* (430) portrays the central events of the Easter story in strong diagonals and a muted palette of rusts, browns, and reds. As in all of his stories from the Bible, Mikolaycak's authentic depiction of textile patterns, everyday details, armor, and headgear are based on research he conducts in such places as the Metropolitan Museum of Art in New York.

The Christmas story has been retold in words and pictures many times. Among the traditional tellings, Maud and Miska Petersham's *The Christ Child* (405) has long been a favorite. Isabelle Brent's *The Christmas Story* (407) resembles medieval manuscripts with its burnished gold, illuminated capitals, patterned backgrounds, and embellishments. Jan Pienkowski also uses gilt for the borders in his exquisite *Christmas: The King James Version* (406). Detailed black silhouettes against softly colored backgrounds give this telling the look of a pageant. Jacqueline Rogers's *The Christmas Pageant* (424), on the other hand, is a real one. While the text is from the traditional King James version, the pictures humorously and lovingly depict contemporary families gathering in a country meeting house to see the children's

[65]Isaac Bashevis Singer, *The Wicked City*, translated by the author and Elizabeth Shub, illustrated by Leonard Everett Fisher (New York: Farrar, Straus, 1972), unpaged.

annual play. John Bierhorst discovered an Aztec version of *Spirit Child* (419) and Barbara Cooney's beautiful paintings portray the story against a background of Central American mountains abloom with yucca and poinsettia.

Told from Mary's point of view, Cecil Bødker's *Mary of Nazareth* (410) is an insightful narrative of Mary's life from the time she receives bewildering news from an angel until her son begins to learn the carpenter's trade. This psychological portrait of a young woman is illustrated in richly detailed watercolors depicting everything from quiet evenings in outdoor courtyards to the busy work of a shipyard. The everyday life of people two thousand years ago is richly realized.

Many legends are associated with the Christmas story as well. *The Cobweb Curtain* by Jenny Koralek (421) tells how a friendly spider wove a web across a cave where Mary and Joseph hid from soldiers. Mikolaycak's *Babushka* (422) depicts the Russian story of the old woman too busy sweeping to follow the Three Wise Men and so destined to wander the world forever. Tomie de Paola's Italian version is *The Legend of Old Befana* (413). His *The Story of the Three Wise Kings* (414) begins with a historical note of how this story has developed over the centuries. It would make a good companion to either of the previous stories as would Ruth Robbins's *Baboushka and the Three Kings* (423). The stories concerning Befana would be ripe for reading on January 6, or Twelfth Night, the traditional "Feast of the Three Kings."

The Bible, myths and legends, fables, and folktales represent literature of people through the ages. Folk literature has deep roots in basic human feelings. Through this literature, children may form a link with the common bonds of humanity from the beginnings of recorded time. It is through this literature, as well, that children may form a foundation on which much of their future reading will stand.

SUGGESTED LEARNING EXPERIENCES

1. Choose one motif, such as transformations, wishes, or magical objects, and see how many different tales you can find, and how many different cultures or countries your collection represents.
2. Read folktales and myths from one country or one geographical or cultural region. Assume that these stories provide your only basis for understanding the country. Chart what you might derive from these tales using such categories as climate, food, animals, typical occupations, customs, geography, values, expressions, story conventions, and so forth.
3. Find as many different editions as you can of such well-known stories as "Cinderella," "Hansel and Gretel," "Sleeping Beauty," "Noah's Ark," or "Puss in Boots." Chart or compare both the language of the retellings and the illustrations.
4. Find as many variations as you can on a particular theme, such as "Helpful Companions," "Jack and the Beanstalk," or "Cinderella." Bring them to class and share them in small groups.
5. Select one folktale that you think you would like to learn to tell. Prepare it and tell it to four or five members of your class or to a group of children. What suggestions do they or you have for improving your presentation?
6. Beginning with a moral chosen from one of the fable collections, write a modern fable. Use present-day animals, people, or objects.
7. Collect advertisements and references that show our use of words from the myths: for example, Ajax cleanser, Mercury as a floral delivery symbol, or Atlas tires. Using a collection of myths, determine the story behind the reference and decide why the advertiser may wish consumers to connect this reference with their product.
8. On the basis of your knowledge of the characteristics of an epic, what do you think the hero of a North American epic might be like? Consider personal qualities, obstacles, achievements, and so forth.
9. Develop a simple inventory of names from folktales, myths, legends, and the Bible. Give it to your class or ask to give it to a group of children. How well known is traditional literature today?

RELATED READINGS

1. Bettelheim, Bruno, *The Uses of Enchantment*. New York: Knopf, 1976.

   A noted child psychologist maintains that fairy tales have a unique place in the development of children, satisfying many of their deepest emotional needs. He offers detailed analysis of several individual tales to show how they enable children to cope with their emotions and their world.

2. Caduto, Michael J., and Joseph Bruchac. *Keepers of the Earth: Native American Stories and Environmental Activities for Children*. Foreword by N. Scott Momaday, illustrated by John Kahionhes and Carol Wood. Golden, Col.: Fulcrum, 1989.

   Native-American folktales grouped under such headings as Creation, Fire, Earth, and Life/Death/Spirit are retold and illustrated with black line drawings. Stories are followed by discussion and many far-ranging activities for the elementary age child. Map of Native-American tribes and culture boundaries is a helpful teacher organizer as well.

3. Campbell, Joseph, and Bill Moyers. *The Power of Myth*. New York: Doubleday, 1988.

   Campbell, a preeminent teacher and scholar of mythology, converses with Moyers about myth in the modern world, the first storytellers, the power of myth in our lives, and mythical themes across cultures.

4. Dundes, Alan, ed. *Cinderella: A Casebook*. New York: Wildman Press, 1983.

   A collection of scholarly essays spanning the history of folklore research on the Cinderella theme. Of special interest to teachers and librarians are discussions of "Cinderella in Africa," a Jungian approach to "The Beautiful Wassilissa," and Jane Yolen's look at Cinderella in the mass market in "America's Cinderella."

5. Favat, André. *Child and Tale: The Origins of Interest*. NCTE Research Report No.19. Urbana, Ill.: The National Council of Teachers of English, 1977.

   Favat traces parallels between the components of traditional fairy tales and the concepts of reality as held by children 6 to 8 years of age, the period of peak interest in fairy tales.

6. Frye, Northrop. *The Great Code: The Bible in Literature*. San Diego: Harcourt Brace Jovanovich, 1982.

   The eminent literary critic develops a theory of literature based on patterns found in the Bible.

7. Hamilton, Edith. *Mythology*. New York: New American Library, 1953.

   An introduction for this literary standard summarizes the emergence of Greek ideas, followed by a readable presentation of Creation, Stories of Love and Adventure, and Heroes of the Trojan War. Genealogical tables are helpful inclusions.

8. Hearne, Betsy. *Beauty and the Beast: Visions and Revisions of an Old Tale*. Chicago: University of Chicago Press, 1989.

   An analysis of one of our culture's most persistent tales in chronological order from 1740 to Warwick Hutton's version in 1985. Hearne's comparions of versions told by women with those told by men is especially provocative.

9. Moss, Joy F. *Focus on Literature: A Context for Literacy Learning*. Katonah, N.Y.: Richard C. Owen, 1990.

   With classroom examples, Moss presents ten "focus units" developed around such themes as "Baba Yaga Tales," "Cat Tales," "Magic Object Tales," and "Bird Tales." Units involve traditional as well as all genres of literature, thoughtful discussions of children's learnings and curriculum development, and excellent bibliographies. A valuable teacher resource and a companion volume to *Focus Units in Literature* (Urbana, Ill.: National Council of Teachers of English, 1984).

10. Opie, Iona, and Peter Opie. *The Classic Fairy Tales*. New York: Oxford University Press, 1974.

    Twenty-four of the best known fairy tales are presented as they first appeared in print in English. Pictures are gleaned from two centuries of illustrators. An invaluable source of information on primary sources is the Opies' introductory essay for each tale.

11. Thompson, Stith. *The Folktale*. New York: Holt, Rinehart and Winston, 1951.

    Various theories of the origins of folktales and folktale themes are presented in a thorough manner in this book.

12. Yolen, Jane. *Touch Magic: Fantasy, Faerie and Folklore in the Literature of Childhood*. New York: Philomel, 1981.

    In short lively essays the author, herself a writer of fantasy and the literary tale, discusses the history of folklore and its role in the social, emotional, and intellectual growth of the child.

REFERENCES[66]

FOLKTALES

1. Aardema, Verna. *Bimwili & the Zimwi*, illustrated by Susan Meddaugh. Dial, 1985 (S—Africa, Zanzibar)
2. _____. *Borreguita and the Coyote*, illustrated by Petra Mathers. Knopf, 1991. (S—Mexico)
3. _____. *Bringing the Rain to Kapiti Plain*, illustrated by Beatriz Vidal. Dial, 1981. (S—Africa, Kenya)
4. _____. *Rabbit Makes a Monkey of Lion*, illustrated by Jerry Pinkney. Dial, 1989. (S—Africa, Tanzania)
5. _____. *Traveling to Tondo: A Tale of the Nkundo of Zaire*, illustrated by Will Hillenbrand. Knopf, 1991. (S)
6. _____. *Who's in Rabbit's House?*, illustrated by Leo and Diane Dillon. Dial, 1977. (S—West Africa)
7. _____. *Why Mosquitoes Buzz in People's Ears*, illustrated by Leo and Diane Dillon. Dial, 1975. (S—Africa, Kenya)
8. Afanasyev, Alexander Nikolayevich. *The Fool and the Fish*, retold by Lenny Hort, illustrated by Gennady Spirin. Dial, 1990. (S—Russia)
9. Aliki. *The Story of Johnny Appleseed*. Prentice-Hall, 1987. (S—United States)
10. Allen, Linda, reteller. *The Giant Who Had No Heart*. Philomel, 1988. (S—Norway)
11. Andersen, Hans Christian. *The Tinderbox*, illustrated by Barry Moser. Little, Brown, 1990. (S—United States Literary)
12. Arkhurst, Joyce Cooper. *The Adventures of Spider: West African Folk Tales*, illustrated by Jerry Pinkney. Little, Brown, 1964.
13. Aruego, Jose and Ariane Dewey. *Rockabye Crocodile*. Greenwillow, 1988. (S—Philippines)
14. Asbjørnsen, Peter Christian and Jorgen E. Moe. *East o'the Sun and West o'the Moon*, translated by George Webbe Dasent. Dover, 1970 (Norway)
15. _____. *East of the Sun and West of the Moon and Other Tales*, illustrated by Tom Vroman. Macmillan, 1963. (Norway)
16. _____. *The Three Billy Goats Gruff*, illustrated by Marcia Brown. Harcourt, 1957. (S—Norway)
17. Baker, Olaf. *Where the Buffaloes Begin*, illustrated by Stephen Gammell. Frederick Warne, 1981. (S—Native American)
18. Bang, Molly. *Dawn*. Morrow, 1983. (S—United States Literary)
19. _____. *Wiley and the Hairy Man*. Macmillan, 1976. (S—African American)
20. Barth, Edna. *Cupid and Psyche: A Love Story*, illustrated by Ati Forberg. Houghton Mifflin, 1976 (S—Greece)
21. Baylor, Byrd, ed. *And It Is Still That Way*. Scribner's, 1976. (Native American)
22. Bierhorst, John, ed. *The Monkey's Haircut and Other Stories Told by the Maya*, illustrated by Robert Andrew Parker. Morrow, 1986. (Central American)
23. Birdseye, Tom. *A Song of Stars: An Asian Legend*, illustrated by Ju-Hong Chen. Holiday, 1990. (S—China/Japan)
24. Bishop, Claire Huchet. *The Five Chinese Brothers*, illustrated by Kurt Wiese. Coward-McCann, 1938. (S)
25. Bishop, Gavin. *Chicken Licken*. Oxford, 1984. (S—England)
26. Brett, Jan. *The Mitten*. Putnam, 1989. (S—Ukrainian)
27. Briggs, Raymond. *Jim and the Beanstalk*. Coward, 1970. (Modern Literary)
28. Brooke, William J. *A Telling of the Tales: Five Stories*, illustrated by Richard Egielski. Harper, 1990. (Modern Literary)
29. Brown, Marcia. *The Bun: A Tale from Russia*. Harcourt, 1972. (S)
30. _____. *Dick Whittington and His Cat*. Scribner's, 1950. (S—England)
31. _____. *Once a Mouse*. Scribner's, 1961. (S—India)
32. _____. *Stone Soup*. Scribner's, 1947. (S—France)
33. Bryan, Ashley. *Beat the Story Drum, Pum-Pum*. Atheneum, 1980. (Africa)
34. _____. *The Cat's Purr*. Atheneum, 1985. (S—Antilles)
35. _____. *The Dancing Granny*. Atheneum, 1977. (S—Antilles)
36. Butler, Stephen. *Henny Penny*. Tambourine, 1991. (S—England)

[66]Except where it is obvious from the title, following each entry is the country of origin. (S) stands for a single-tale edition.

37. Carey, Valerie Scho. *The Quail Song: A Pueblo Indian Tale*, illustrated by Ivan Barnett. Putnam/Whitebird, 1990. (S—Native American)
38. Carpenter, Francis. *Tales of a Chinese Grandmother*, illustrated by Malthe Hasselriis. Doubleday, 1949.
39. Carrick, Carol. *Aladdin and the Wonderful Lamp*, illustrated by Donald Carrick. Scholastic, 1989. (S—Middle East)
40. Cauley, Lorinda Bryan. *Jack and the Beanstalk*. Putnam, 1983. (S—England)
41. _____. *Puss in Boots*. Harcourt, 1986. (S—France)
42. Chase, Richard. *Grandfather Tales*. Houghton Mifflin, 1948. (United States)
43. _____. *The Jack Tales*, illustrated by Berkeley Williams, Jr. Houghton Mifflin, 1943. (United States)
44. Climo, Shirley. *The Egyptian Cinderella*, illustrated by Ruth Heller. Crowell, 1989. (S—Egypt)
45. Cohen, Barbara. *The Demon Who Would Not Die*, illustrated by Anatoly Ivanov. Atheneum, 1982 (S—Russia)
46. Cohen, Caron Lee. *The Mud Pony*, illustrated by Shonto Begay. Scholastic, 1988. (S—Native American)
47. _____. *Sally Ann Thunder Ann Whirlwind Crockett*, illustrated by Ariane Dewey. Greenwillow, 1985. (S—United States)
48. Cole, Brock. *The Giant's Toe*. Farrar, Straus, 1988. (S—Modern Literary)
49. Cole, Joanna. *Bony-Legs*, illustrated by Dirk Zimmer. Four Winds, 1983. (S—Russia)
50. _____. *It's Too Noisy*, illustrated by Kate Duke. Crowell, 1989. (S—Jewish)
51. Cooper, Susan. *The Selkie Girl*, illustrated by Warwick Hutton. McElderry, 1986. (S—Scotland)
52. _____. *The Silver Cow: A Welsh Tale*, illustrated by Warwick Hutton. McElderry, 1983. (S)
53. _____. *Tam Lin*, illustrated by Warwick Hutton. McElderry, 1990. (S—Scotland)
54. Courlander, Harold and George Herzog. *The Cow-Tail Switch and Other West African Stories*, illustrated by Madye Lee Chastain. Holt, 1947.
55. Croll, Carol. *The Little Snowgirl*. Putnam, 1989. (S—Russia)
56. Crompton, Anne Eliot. *The Winter Wife*, illustrated by Robert Andrew Parker. Little, Brown, 1975. (S—Native American)
57. Dasent, George. *East o'the Sun & West o'the Moon*, illustrated by Gillian Barlow. Philomel, 1988. (S—Norway)
58. D'Aulaire, Ingri, and Edgar d'Aulaire, editors and illustrators. *East of the Sun and West of the Moon*. Viking, 1969. (Norway)
59. Dayrell, Elphinstone. *Why the Sun and the Moon Live in the Sky*, illustrated by Blair Lent. Houghton Mifflin, 1968. (S—Africa)
60. De Armond, Dale. *The Boy Who Found the Light*. Sierra Club/Little, Brown, 1990. (S—Eskimo)
61. _____. *The Seal Oil Lamp*. Sierra Club/Little Brown, 1988. (S—Eskimo)
62. de la Mare, Walter. *Mollie Whuppie*, illustrated by Errol Le Cain. Farrar, Straus, 1983. (S—England)
63. Demi. *The Empty Pot*. Holt, 1990. (S—China)
64. de Paola, Tomie. *Fin M'Coul: The Giant of Knockmany Hill*. Holiday, 1981. (S—Ireland)
65. _____. *The Legend of the Bluebonnet: An Old Tale of Texas*. Putnam, 1983. (S—Native American)
66. _____. *Strega Nona*. Prentice-Hall, 1975. (S—Italy)
67. de Sauza, James. *Brother Anansi and the Cattle Rancher*, illustrated by Stephen Von Mason. Children's Book Press, 1989. (S—Nicaragua)
68. Dewey, Ariane. *Febold Feboldson*. Greenwillow, 1984. (S—United States)
69. _____. *Gib Morgan, Oilman*. Greenwillow, 1987. (S—United States)
70. _____. *The Narrow Escapes of Davy Crockett*. Greenwillow, 1990. (S—United States)
71. _____. *Pecos Bill*. Greenwillow, 1983. (S—United States)
72. de Wit, Dorothy, ed. *The Talking Stone: An Anthology of Native American Tales and Legends*, illustrated by Donald Crews. Greenwillow, 1984.
73. Duff, Maggie. *Rum Pum Pum: A Folk Tale from India*, illustrated by Jose Aruego and Ariane Dewey. Macmillan, 1978. (S)
74. Durell, Ann, ed. *The Diane Goode Book of American Folk Tales & Songs*, illustrated by Diane Goode. Dutton, 1989.
75. Esbensen, Barbara Juster. *Ladder to the Sky*, illustrated by Helen K. Davie. Little, Brown, 1989. (S—Native American)
76. _____. *The Star Maiden*, illustrated by Helen K. Davie. Little, Brown, 1988. (S—Native American)

77. Finger, Charles. *Tales from Silver Lands*, illustrated by Paul Honore. Doubleday, 1924. (Central and South America)
78. Flora. *Feathers Like a Rainbow: An Amazon Indian Tale.* Harper, 1989. (S)
79. Freedman, Florence B. *Brothers: A Hebrew Legend*, illustrated by Robert Andrew Parker. Harper, 1985. (S)
80. Gág, Wanda. *Gone Is Gone.* Coward-McCann, 1935. (S—Norway)
81. _____. *Jorinda and Joringel*, illustrated by Margot Tomes. Coward-McCann, 1978. (S—Germany)
82. Galdone, Paul. *Cinderella.* McGraw-Hill, 1978. (S—France)
83. _____. *The Gingerbread Boy.* Clarion, 1975. (S—England)
84. _____. *Henny Penny.* Seabury, 1968. (S—England)
85. _____. *The History of Mother Twaddle and the Marvelous Achievements of Her Son Jack.* Seabury, 1974. (S—England)
86. _____. *The Little Red Hen.* Seabury, 1974. (S—England)
87. _____. *The Magic Porridge Pot.* Seabury, 1976. (S—France)
88. _____. *Puss in Boots.* Seabury, 1976. (S—France)
89. _____. *Rumpelstiltskin.* Houghton Mifflin, 1985. (S—Germany)
90. _____. *The Three Bears.* Clarion, 1985. (S—Germany)
91. _____. *The Three Billy Goats Gruff.* Seabury, 1973. (S—Norway)
92. _____. *The Three Little Pigs.* Seabury, 1970. (S—England)
93. _____. *The Three Sillies.* Houghton Mifflin, 1981. (S—England)
94. Garner, Alan. *Alan Garner's Book of British Fairy Tales*, illustrated by Derek Collard. Delacorte, 1984.
95. Gerstein, Mordicai. *The Seal Mother.* Dial, 1986. (S—Scotland)
96. Goble, Paul. *Buffalo Woman.* Bradbury, 1984. (S—Native American)
97. _____. *The Gift of the Sacred Dog.* Bradbury, 1980. (S—Native American)
98. _____. *The Girl Who Loved Wild Horses.* Bradbury, 1978. (S—Native American)
99. _____. *The Great Race of the Birds and the Animals.* Bradbury, 1985. (Native American)
100. _____. *Iktomi and the Berries: A Plains Indian Story.* Orchard, 1989. (S)
101. _____. *Iktomi and the Boulder: A Plains Indian Story.* Orchard, 1988. (S)
102. _____. *Iktomi and the Buffalo Skull: A Plains Indian Story.* Orchard, 1991. (S)
103. _____. *Iktomi and the Ducks: A Plains Indian Story.* Orchard, 1990. (S)
104. _____. *Star Boy.* Bradbury, 1983. (S—Native American)
105. Grifalconi, Ann. *Osa's Pride.* Little, Brown, 1990. (Picture Book—West Africa, Cameroon)
106. _____. *The Village of Round and Square Houses.* Little, Brown, 1986. (S—West Africa, Cameroon)
107. Grimm Brothers. *The Brave Little Tailor*, translated by Anthea Bell, illustrated by Eve Tharlet. Picture Book Studio, 1989. (S)
108. _____. *The Bremen-Town Musicians*, retold and illustrated by Ilse Plume. Doubleday, 1980. (S)
109. _____. *Cinderella*, illustrated by Nonny Hogrogian. Greenwillow, 1981. (S)
110. _____. *The Devil with the Three Golden Hairs*, illustrated by Nonny Hogrogian. Knopf, 1983. (S)
111. _____. *The Elves and the Shoemaker*, illustrated by Paul Galdone. Clarion, 1984. (S)
112. _____. *The Fisherman and His Wife*, translated by Randall Jarrell, illustrated by Margot Zemach. Farrar, Straus, 1980. (S)
113. _____. *The Fisherman and His Wife*, retold by John Warren Stewig, illustrated by Margot Tomes. Holiday, 1988. (S)
114. _____. *The Frog Prince*, retold by Jan Ormerod and David Lloyd, illustrated by Jan Ormerod. Lothrop, 1990. (S)
115. _____. *The Glass Mountain*, illustrated by Nonny Hogrogian. Knopf, 1985.(S)
116. _____. *Hansel and Gretel*, illustrated by Anthony Browne. Knopf, 1988. (1981) (S)
117. _____. *Hansel and Gretel*, translated by Elizabeth D. Crawford, illustrated by Lisbeth Zwerger. Morrow, 1979. (S)
118. _____. *Hansel and Gretel*, illustrated by Paul Galdone. McGraw-Hill, 1982. (S)
119. _____. *Hansel and Gretel*, illustrated by Susan Jeffers. Dial, 1980. (S)
120. _____. *Hansel and Gretel*, retold by Rika Lesser, illustrated by Paul O. Zelinsky. Dodd Mead, 1984. (S)
121. _____. *Household Stories of the Brothers Grimm*, translated by Lucy Crane, illustrated by Walter Crane. Dover, n.d. (1886).
122. _____. *The Juniper Tree and Other Tales from Grimm*, translated by Lore Segal and Maurice Sendak, illustrated by Maurice Sendak. Farrar, Straus, 1973.
123. _____. *Little Red Cap*, translated by Elizabeth D. Crawford, illustrated by Lisbeth Zwerger. Morrow, 1983. (S)

124. _____. *Little Red Riding Hood*, illustrated by Trina Schart Hyman. Holiday 1983. (S)
125. _____. *Mother Holly*, retold and illustrated by Bernadette Watts. North-South, 1988. (S)
126. _____. *The Princess and the Frog*, illustrated by Rachel Isadora. Greenwillow, 1989. (S)
127. _____. *Princess Furball*, retold by Charlotte Huck, illustrated by Anita Lobel. Greenwillow, 1989. (S)
128. _____. *Rapunzel*, retold by Barbara Rogasky, illustrated by Trina Schart Hyman. Holiday, 1982. (S)
129. _____. *Rumpelstiltskin*, illustrated by Paul Galdone. Clarion, 1985. (S)
130. _____. *Rumpelstiltskin*, retold and illustrated by Paul O. Zelinsky. Dutton, 1986. (S)
131. _____. *The Seven Ravens*, translated by Elizabeth D. Crawford, illustrated by Lisbeth Zwerger. Morrow, 1981. (S)
132. _____. *The Sleeping Beauty*, retold and illustrated by Trina Schart Hyman. Little, Brown, 1974. (S)
133. _____. *Snow White*, translated by Paul Heins, illustrated by Trina Schart Hyman. Little, Brown, 1974. (S)
134. _____. *Snow White and Rose Red*, illustrated by Barbara Cooney. Delacorte, 1991 (1965). (S)
135. _____. *Snow-White and the Seven Dwarfs*, translated by Randall Jarrell, illustrated by Nancy Ekholm Burkert. Farrar, Straus, 1972. (S)
136. _____. *The Table, the Donkey, and the Stick*, illustrated by Paul Galdone. McGraw-Hill, 1976. (S)
137. _____. *Tales from Grimm*, illustrated by Wanda Gág. Coward McCann, 1936.
138. _____. *Thorn Rose or the Sleeping Beauty*, illustrated by Errol Le Cain. Bradbury, 1975. (S)
139. _____. *The Twelve Dancing Princesses*, retold by Anne Carter, illustrated by Anne Dalton. Lippincott, 1989. (S)
140. _____. *The Twelve Dancing Princesses*, illustrated by Errol Le Cain. Bradbury, 1975. (S)
141. Hague, Kathleen, and Michael Hague. *East of the Sun and West of the Moon*, illustrated by Michael Hague. Harcourt, 1980. (S—Norway)
142. Haley, Gail E. *A Story, a Story*. Atheneum, 1970. (S—Africa)
143. _____. *Jack and the Bean Tree*. Crown, 1986. (S—United States)
144. Hamilton, Virginia. *The Dark Way: Stories from the Spirit World*, illustrated by Lambert Davis. Harcourt, 1990.
145. _____. *In the Beginning: Creation Stories from Around the World*, illustrated by Barry Moser. Harcourt, 1988.
146. _____. *The Magical Adventures of Pretty Pearl*. Harper, 1983. (African American)
147. _____. *The People Could Fly*, illustrated by Leo and Diane Dillon. Knopf, 1985. (African American)
148. Harris, Christie. *Mouse Woman and the Muddleheads*, illustrated by Douglas Tait. Atheneum, 1976. (Native American)
149. _____. *Once More upon a Totem*, illustrated by Douglas Tait. Atheneum, 1979. (Native American)
150. Harris, Joel Chandler. *The Complete Tales of Uncle Remus*, compiled by Richard Chase, illustrated by Arthur Frost and others. Houghton Mifflin, 1955. (African American)
151. _____. *Jump! The Adventures of Brer Rabbit*, adapted by Van Dyke Parks and Malcolm Jones, illustrated by Barry Moser. Harcourt, 1986. (African American)
152. _____. *Jump Again! More Adventures of Brer Rabbit*, adapted by Van Dyke Parks, illustrated by Barry Moser. Harcourt, 1987. (African American)
153. _____. *Jump on Over! The Adventures of Brer Rabbit and His Family*, adapted by Van Dyke Parks, illustrated by Barry Moser. Harcourt, 1989. (African American)
154. Hausman, Gerald. *Sitting on the Blue-Eyed Bear: Navajo Myths and Legends*. Lawrence Hill, 1975.
155. Haviland, Virginia. *Favorite Fairy Tales Told in Italy*, illustrated by Evaline Ness. Little, Brown, 1965.
156. _____. *North American Legends*, illustrated by Ann Strugnell. Collins, 1979.
157. Hewitt, Kathryn. *The Three Sillies*. Harcourt, 1986. (S—England)
158. Heyer, Marilee. *The Weaving of a Dream: A Chinese Folktale*. Penguin, 1986. (S)
159. Highwater, Jamake. *Anpao*, illustrated by Fritz Scholder. Lippincott, 1977. (Native American)
160. Hi Liyi. *The Spring of Butterflies and Other Folktales of China's Minority Peoples*, edited by Neil Philip, illustrated by Pan Aiqing and Li Zhao. Lothrop, 1986.
161. Hodges, Margaret. *The Fire-Bringer: A Paiute Indian Legend*, illustrated by Peter Parnall. Little, Brown, 1972. (S)
162. _____. *The Little Humpbacked Horse*, illustrated by Chris Conover. Farrar, Straus, 1980. (S—Russia)
163. _____. *The Wave*, illustrated by Blair Lent. Houghton Mifflin, 1964. (S—Japan)

164. Hogrogian, Nonny. *One Fine Day*. Macmillan, 1971. (S—Armenia)
165. Hooks, William. *Moss Gown*, illustrated by Donald Carrick. Clarion, 1987. (United States)
166. _____. *The Three Little Pigs and the Fox*, illustrated by S. D. Schindler. Macmillan, 1989. (S—United States)
167. Houston, James. *Tikta Liktak: An Eskimo Legend*. Harcourt, 1965. (S)
168. _____. *The White Archer: An Eskimo Legend*. Harcourt, 1967. (S)
169. Hutton, Warwick. *Beauty and the Beast*. Atheneum, 1985. (S—France)
170. Hyman, Trina Schart. *Self-Portrait: Trina Schart Hyman*. Harper, 1989. (1981) (Autobiography)
171. Isele, Elizabeth. *The Frog Princess*. Crowell, 1984. (S—Russia)
172. Ishii, Momoko. *The Tongue-Cut Sparrow*, translated by Katherine Paterson, illustrated by Suekichi Akaba. Dutton, 1982. (S—Japan)
173. Jacobs, Joseph. *The Story of the Three Little Pigs*, illustrated by Lorinda Bryan Cauley. Putnam, 1980. (S—England)
174. _____. *Tattercoats*, illustrated by Margot Tomes. Putnam, 1989. (S—England)
175. James, Betsy. *The Red Cloak*. Chronicle, 1989. (S—Scotland)
176. Jeffers, Susan. *Wild Robin*. Dutton, 1976. (S—Scotland)
177. Johnston, Tony. *The Badger and the Magic Fan: A Japanese Folktale*, illustrated by Tomie de Paola. Putnam, 1990. (S)
178. Karlin, Barbara. *Cinderella*, illustrated by James Marshall. Little, Brown, 1989. (S—France)
179. Keats, Ezra Jack. *John Henry: An Amerian Legend*. Pantheon, 1965. (S—African American)
180. Kellogg, Steven, *Chicken Little*. Morrow, 1985. (S—Modern Literary)
181. _____. *Johnny Appleseed*. Morrow, 1988. (S—United States)
182. _____. *Paul Bunyan*. Morrow, 1984. (S—United States)
183. _____. *Pecos Bill*. Morrow, 1986. (S—United States)
184. Kemp, Moira. *The Firebird*. Godine, 1984. (S—Russia)
185. Kendall, Carol. *The Wedding of the Rat Family*, illustrated by James Watt. Margaret K. McElderry, 1988. (S—China)
186. Kent, Jack. *The Fat Cat: A Danish Folktale*. Scholastic, 1972. (S)
187. Kimmel, Eric A. *Baba Yaga: A Russian Folktale*, illustrated by Megan Lloyd. Holiday, 1991. (S)
188. Lang, Andrew. *Aladdin*, illustrated by Errol Le Cain. Viking, 1981. (S—Middle East)
189. _____. *The Blue Fairy Book*, illustrated by Reisie Lonette. Random House, 1959.
190. _____. *The Twelve Dancing Princesses,* illustrated by Adrienne Adams. Holt, 1966. (S—France)
191. Langton, Jane. *The Hedgehog Boy: A Latvian Tale*, illustrated by Ilse Plume. Harper, 1985. (S)
192. Leaf, Margaret. *Eyes of the Dragon*, illustrated by Ed Young. Lothrop, 1987. (S—China)
193. Leekley, Thomas B. *The World of Manabozho: Tales of the Chippewa Indians*, illustrated by Yeffe Kimball. Vanguard, 1965.
194. Lester, Julius. *How Many Spots Does a Leopard Have? and Other Tales*, illustrated by David Shannon. Scholastic, 1989.
195. _____. *The Knee-High Man and Other Tales*, illustrated by Ralph Pinto. Dial, 1972. (African American)
196. _____. *More Tales of Uncle Remus: Further Adventures of Brer Rabbit, His Friends, Enemies, and Others*, illustrated by Jerry Pinkney. Dial, 1988. (African American)
197. _____. *The Tales of Uncle Remus: The Adventures Of Brer Rabbit*, illustrated by Jerry Pinkney. Dial, 1987. (African American)
198. Lindbergh, Reeve. *Johnny Appleseed*, illustrated by Kathy Jakobsen. Little, Brown, 1990. (S—United States)
199. Longfellow, Henry Wadsworth. *Hiawatha*, illustrated by Susan Jeffers. Dial, 1983. (Poetry)
200. Louie, Ai-Ling. *Yeh-Shen: A Cinderella Story from China*, illustrated by Ed Young. Philomel, 1982. (S)
201. McCarty, Toni. *The Skull in the Snow and Other Folktales*, illustrated by Katherine Coville. Delacorte, 1981.
202. McCurdy, Michael. *The Devils Who Learned to Be Good*. Little, Brown, 1987. (S—Russia)
203. McDermott, Gerald. *Anansi the Spider*. Holt, 1972. (S—Africa)
204. _____. *Arrow to the Sun*. Viking, 1974. (S—Native American)
205. _____. *The Stonecutter: A Japanese Folk Tale*. Penguin, 1975. (S)
206. McVitty, Walter. *Ali Baba and the Forty Thieves*, illustrated by Margaret Early. Abrams, 1989. (S—Middle East)
207. Mahy, Margaret. *The Seven Chinese Brothers*, illustrated by Jean and Mou-Sien Tseng. Scholastic, 1990. (S)
208. Marshak, Samuel. *The Month-Brothers: A Slavic Tale*, translated by Thomas P. Whitney, illustrated by Diane Stanley. Morrow, 1983. (S—Russia)

209. Marshall, James. *Goldilocks and the Three Bears*. Dial, 1988. (S—England)
210. _____. *Hansel and Gretel*. Dial, 1990. (S—Germany)
211. _____. *Red Riding Hood*. Dial, 1987. (S—Germany)
212. _____. *The Three Little Pigs*. Dial, 1989. (S—England)
213. Martin, Rafe. *Foolish Rabbit's Big Mistake*, illustrated by Ed Young. Putnam, 1985. (S—India)
214. Mayer, Marianna. *Aladdin and the Enchanted Lamp*, illustrated by Gerald MacDermott. Macmillan, 1985. (S—Middle East)
215. _____. *Beauty and the Beast*, illustrated by Mercer Mayer. Four Winds, 1978. (S—France)
216. _____. *The Twelve Dancing Princesses*, illustrated by Kinuko Y. Craft. Morrow, 1989. (S—France)
217. Mayer, Mercer. *East of the Sun and West of the Moon*. Four Winds, 1978. (S—Modern Literary)
218. Mayo, Gretchen Will. *North American Indian Stories from Earth Happenings*. Walker, 1989.
219. Mikolaycak, Charles. *Babushka: An Old Russian Folktale*. Holiday, 1984. (S)
220. Minard, Rosemary, ed. *Womenfolk and Fairy Tales*, illustrated by Suzanne Klelin. Houghton Mifflin, 1975.
221. Mollel, Tololwa M. *The Orphan Boy*, illustrated by Paul Morin. Clarion, 1991. (S—Africa)
222. Monroe, Jean Buard, and Ray A. Williamson. "What the Stars are Like" in *They Dance In the Sky*, illustrated by Edgar Stewart. Houghton Mifflin, 1987. (Cherokee)
223. Morgan, Pierr. *The Turnip: An Old Russian Folktale*. Philomel, 1990.
224. Morimoto, Junco. *The Inch Boy*. Viking, 1986. (S—Japan)
225. Mosel, Arlene. *The Funny Little Woman*, illustrated by Blair Lent. Dutton, 1972. (S—Japan)
226. _____. *Tikki Tikki Tembo*, illustrated by Blair Lent. Holt, 1968. (S—China)
227. Ness, Evaline. *Tom Tit Tot*. Scribner's, 1965. (S—England)
228. Newton, Pam. *The Stonecutter*. Putnam, 1990. (S—India)
229. Norman, Howard. *How Glooscap Outwits the Ice Giants and Other Tales of the Maritime Indians*, illustrated by Michael McCurdy. Little, Brown, 1989.
230. Osborne, Mary Pope. *American Tall Tales*, illustrated by Michael McCurdy. Knopf, 1991.
231. Oxenbury, Helen. *The Helen Oxenbury Nursery Story Book*. Knopf, 1985.
232. Paterson, Katherine. *The Tale of the Mandarin Ducks*, illustrated by Leo and Diane Dillon. Lodestar, 1990. (S—Japan)
233. de Beaumont, Mme. *Beauty and the Beast*, illustrated by Jan Brett. Houghton Mifflin, 1989. (S—France)
234. _____. *Beauty and the Beast*, retold and illustrated by Mordicai Gerstein. Dutton, 1989. (S—France)
235. _____. *Beauty and the Beast*, illustrated by Michael Hague. Holt, 1988. (S—France)
236. _____. *Beauty and the Beast*, retold and illustrated by Warwick Hutton. Atheneum, 1985. (S—France)
237. Perrault, Charles. *Cinderella*, illustrated by Marcia Brown. Scribner's, 1954. (S—France)
238. _____. *Cinderella*, retold by Amy Ehrlich. Illustrated by Susan Jeffers. Dial, 1985 (S—France)
239. _____. *Cinderella, or the Little Glass Slipper*, illustrated by Errol Le Cain. Bradbury, 1973. (S—France)
240. _____. *Puss in Boots*, translated by Malcolm Arthur, illustrated by Fred Marcellino. Farrar, Straus, 1990. (S—France)
241. Phelps, Ethel Johnston. *The Maid of the North: Feminist Folk Tales from Around the World*, illustrated by Lloyd Bloom. Holt, 1981.
242. Polette, Nancy. *The Little Old Woman and the Hungry Cat*, illustrated by Frank Modell. Greenwillow, 1989. (S—Norway)
243. Pyle, Howard. *Pepper and Salt, or Seasoning for Young Folks*. Harper, 1913.
244. Quackenbush, Robert. *Quit Pulling My Leg! A Story of Davy Crockett*. Simon & Schuster, 1987. (Biography)
245. Ransome, Arthur. *The Fool of the World and the Flying Ship*, illustrated by Uri Shulevitz. Farrar, Straus, 1968. (S—Russia)
246. Reyher, Becky. *My Mother Is the Most Beautiful Woman in the World*, illustrated by Ruth Gannett. Lothrop, 1945. (S—Russia)
247. Robinson, Gail. *Raven the Trickster*. Atheneum, 1982. (Native American)
248. Rockwell, Anne. *The Old Woman and Her Pig and 10 Other Stories*. Crowell, 1979.
249. _____. *The Three Bears & 15 Other Stories*. Crowell, 1975.
250. Rodanas, Kristina. *The Story of Wali Dad*. Lothrop, 1988. (S—India)
251. Rohmer, Harriet. *The Invisible Hunters*, illustrations by Joe Sam. Children's Book Press, 1987. (S—Nicaragua)

252. Ross, Tony. *Jack and the Beanstalk*. Delacorte, 1981. (S—England)
253. _____. *Stone Soup*. Dial, 1990. (S—Modern Literary)
254. _____. *The Three Pigs*. Pantheon, 1983. (S—England)
255. Roth, Susan. *The Story of Light*. Morrow, 1990. (S—Native American)
256. Rounds, Glen. *Ol' Paul, the Mighty Logger*. Holiday, 1949. (S—United States)
257. Sage, Alison, reteller. *Rumpelstiltskin*, illustrated by Gennady Spirin. Dial, 1991. (S—Germany)
258. San Souci, Robert D. *The Legend of Scarface: A Blackfeet Indian Tale*, illustrated by Daniel San Souci. Doubleday, 1978. (S)
259. _____. *The Talking Eggs*, illustrated by Jerry Pinkney. Dial, 1989. (S—African American)
260. _____. *The White Cat*, illustrated by Gennady Spirin. Orchard, 1990. (S—France)
261. Sanfield, Steve. *The Adventures of High John the Conqueror*, illustrated by John Ward. Orchard, 1989. (African American)
262. _____. *A Natural Man*, illustrated by Peter J. Thornton. Godine, 1986. (S—African American)
263. Sawyer, Ruth. *Journey Cake, Ho!*, illustrated by Robert McCloskey. Viking, 1953. (S—United States)
264. Schoolcraft, Henry Rowe. *The Ring in the Prairie: A Shawnee Legend*, illustrated by Leo and Diane Dillon. Dial, 1970. (S)
265. Schwartz, Howard, and Barbara Rush. *The Diamond Tree: Jewish Tales from Around the World*, illustrated by Uri Shulevitz. HarperCollins, 1991.
266. Scott, Sally. *The Magic Horse*. Greenwillow, 1985. (S—Middle East)
267. _____. *The Three Wonderful Beggars*. Greenwillow, 1987. (S—Russia)
268. Shannon, George. *More Stories to Solve: Fifteen Folktales from Around the World*, illustrated by Peter Sis. Greenwillow, 1990.
269. _____. *Stories to Solve: Folktales from Around the World*, illustrated by Peter Sis. Greenwillow, 1985.
270. Shephard, Esther. *Paul Bunyan*, illustrated by Rockwell Kent. Harcourt, 1924. (United States)
271. Sherlock, Philip M. *Anansi the Spider Man: Jamaican Folk Tales*, illustrated by Marcia Brown. Crowell, 1954.
272. Sherman, Josepha. *Vassilisa the Wise: A Tale of Medieval Russia*, illustrated by Daniel San Souci. Harcourt, 1988. (S)
273. Shetterly, Susan Hand. *Raven's Light: A Myth from the People of the Northwest Coast*, illustrated by Robert Shetterly. Atheneum, 1991. (S—Native American)
274. Shulevitz, Uri. *Soldier and Tsar in the Forest: A Russian Tale*, translated by Richard Lourie. Farrar, Straus, 1972. (S)
275. Shute, Linda. *Clever Tom and the Leprechaun*. Lothrop, 1988. (S—Ireland)
276. _____. *Momotaro, The Peach Boy*. Lothrop, 1986. (S—Japan)
277. Singer, Isaac Bashevis. *Elijah the Slave*, translated by the author and Elizabeth Shub, illustrated by Antonio Frasconi. Farrar, Straus, 1970. (S—Jewish)
278. _____. *Mazel and Shlimazel*, or *The Milk of a Lioness*, illustrated by Margot Zemach. Farrar, Straus, 1967. (S—Jewish)
279. _____. *When Shlemiel Went to Warsaw and Other Stories*, translated by the author and Elizabeth Shub, illustrated by Margot Zemach. Farrar, Straus, 1968. (Jewish)
280. _____. *Zlateh the Goat, and Other Stories*, translated by the author and Elizabeth Shub, illustrated by Maurice Sendak. Harper, 1966. (Jewish)
281. Sleator, William, *The Angry Moon*, illustrated by Blair Lent. Little, Brown, 1970. (Native American).
282. Slote, Teri. *The Eye of the Needle*. Dutton, 1990. (S—Native American)
283. Snyder, Diane. *The Boy of the Three-Year Nap*, illustrated by Allan Say, Houghton Mifflin, 1988. (S—Japan)
284. Stamm, Claus. *Three Strong Women: A Tall Tale from Japan*, illustrated by Jean and Mou-Sien Tseng. Viking, 1991 (1962). (S)
285. Steel, Flora Annie. *English Fairy Tales*, illustrated by Arthur Rackham. Macmillan, 1962 (1918).
286. Steptoe, John. *Mufaro's Beautiful Daughters: An African Tale*. Lothrop, 1987. (S—Africa, Zimbabwe)
287. _____. *The Story of Jumping Mouse: A Native American Legend*. Morrow, 1984. (S)
288. Stewig, John Warren. *Stone Soup*, illustrated by Margot Tomes. Holiday, 1991. (S—France)
289. Stobbs, William. *The House That Jack Built*. Oxford, 1983. (S—England)
290. Stoutenberg, Adrien. *American Tall Tales*, illustrated by Richard M. Powers. Penguin, 1976.
291. Towle, Faith. *The Magic Cooking Pot*. Houghton Mifflin, 1975. (S—India)
292. Toye, William. *How Summer Came to Canada*, illustrated by Elizabeth Cleaver. Walck, 1969. (S—Native American)
293. _____. *The Loon's Necklace*, illustrated by Elizabeth Cleaver. Oxford, 1977. (S—Native American)

294. Tresselt, Alvin. *The Mitten*, illustrated by Yaroslava. Lothrop, 1964. (S—Ukrainian)
295. Troughton, Joanna. *How Rabbit Stole the Fire*. Bedrick/Blackie, 1986. (S—Native American)
296. Uchida, Yoshiko. *The Dancing Kettle and Other Japanese Folk Tales*, illustrated by Richard C. Jones. Harcourt, 1949.
297. Van Rynbach, Iris. *The Soup Stone*. Greenwillow, 1988. (S—United States/Literary)
298. Vidal, Beatriz. *The Legend of El Dorado*, adapted by Nancy Van Laan. Knopf, 1991. (S—Colombia)
299. Vuong, Lynette Dyer. *The Brocaded Slipper and Other Vietnamese Tales*, illustrated by Vo-Dinh Mai. HarperCollins, 1991.
300. Walker, Barbara. *Watermelons, Walnuts* and the *Wisdom of Allah and other Tales of the Hoca*, illustrated by Harold Berson. Parents', 1967. (Middle East)
301. Wang, Rosalind C. *The Fourth Question: A Chinese Tale*, illustrated by Ju-Hong Chen. Holiday, 1991. (S)
302. Wilson, Barbara Ker. *Scottish Folk-Tales and Legends*, illustrated by Joan Kiddell-Monroe. Walck, 1954.
303. Winthrop, Elizabeth. *Vasilissa the Beautiful*, illustrated by Alexander Koshkin. HarperCollins, 1991. (S—Russia)
304. Wolkstein, Diane. *The Magic Orange Tree and Other Haitian Folktales*, illustrated by Elsa Henriquez. Knopf, 1978.
305. _____. *Oom Razoom or Go I Know Not Where, Bring Back I Know Not What*, illustrated by Dennis McDermott. Morrow, 1991. (S—Russia)
306. Yagawa, Sumiko. *The Crane Wife*, translated by Katherine Paterson, illustrated by Suekichi Akaba. Morrow, 1981. (S—Japan)
307. Yee, Paul. *Tales from Gold Mountain*, illustrated by Simon Ng. Macmillan, 1990. (Chinese American)
308. Yep, Laurence. *The Rainbow People*, illustrated by David Wiesner. Harper, 1989. (Chinese American)
309. _____. *Tongues of Jade*, illustrated by David Wiesner. Harper, 1991. (Chinese American)
310. Yolen, Jane. *Greyling*, illustrated by David Ray. Philomel, 1991 (1968). (S—Shetland Islands)
311. _____. *Sky Dogs*, illustrated by Barry Moser. Harcourt, 1990. (S—Native American)
312. _____. *Tam Lin*, illustrated by Charles Mikolaycak. Harcourt, 1990. (S—Scotland)
313. Young, Ed. *Lon Po Po: A Red Riding Hood Story from China*. Philomel, 1989. (S)
314. Zemach, Harve. *Duffy and the Devil*, illustrated by Margot Zemach. Farrar, Straus, 1973. (S—England)
315. _____. *Nail Soup*, adapted from the text of Nila Djurklo, illustrated by Margot Zemach. Farrar, Straus, 1964. (S—Sweden)
316. _____. *Salt: A Russian Tale*, illustrated by Margot Zemach. Follett, 1965. (S)
317. Zemach, Margot. *It Could Always Be Worse*. Farrar, Straus, 1977. (S—Jewish)
318. _____. *The Little Red Hen*. Farrar, Straus, 1983. (S—England)
319. _____. *The Three Sillies*. Holt, 1963. (S—England)
320. _____. *The Three Wishes: An Old Story*. Farrar, Straus, 1986. (S—England)
321. Zwerger, Lisbeth. *The Merry Pranks of Till Eulenspiegel*. Picture Book Studio, 1990. (Germany)

FABLES

322. Aesop. *Aesop's Fables*, illustrated by Heidi Holder. Viking, 1981.
323. _____. *Aesop's Fables*, retold by Tom Paxton, illustrated by Robert Rayevsky. Morrow, 1988.
324. _____. *Aesop's Fables*, illustrated by Fulvio Testa. Barron's, 1989.
325. _____. *Aesop's Fables*, illustrated by Lisbeth Zwerger. Picture Book Studio, 1989.
326. _____. *Androcles and the Lion: An Aesop Fable*, illustrated by Janet Stevens. Holiday, 1989.
327. _____. *Belling the Cat*, retold by Tom Paxton, illustrated by Robert Rayevsky. Morrow, 1990.
328. _____. *The Caldecott Aesop*, illustrated by Randolph Caldecott. Doubleday, 1978 (1883).
329. _____. *The Exploding Frog and Other Fables from Aesop*, retold by John McFarland, illustrated by James Marshall. Little, Brown, 1981.
330. _____. *The Lion and the Mouse*, illustrated by Ed Young. Doubleday, 1980.
331. _____. *Once in a Wood: Ten Tales from Aesop*, illustrated and adapted by Eve Rice. Greenwillow, 1979.
332. _____. *Twelve Tales from Aesop*, retold and illustrated by Eric Carle. Putnam, 1980.
333. Anno, Mitsumasa. *Anno's Aesop: A Book of Fables by Aesop and Mr. Fox*. Orchard, 1987.

334. Bierhorst, John. *Doctor Coyote: A Native American Aesop's Fables*, illustrated by Wendy Watson. Macmillan, 1987.
335. Brown, Marcia. *Once a Mouse*. Scribner's, 1961. (S)
336. Galdone, Paul. *The Monkey and the Crocodile*. Seabury, 1969. (S)
337. _____. *Three Aesop Fox Fables*. Seabury, 1971.
338. La Fontaine. *The Hare and the Tortoise*, illustrated by Brian Wildsmith. Oxford, 1982. (S)
339. _____. *The Lion and the Rat*, illustrated by Brian Wildsmith. Oxford, 1986.
340. _____. *The Miller, the Boy and the Donkey*, illustrated by Brian Wildsmith. Oxford, 1984.
341. Lionni, Leo. *Frederick*. Pantheon, 1967. (S—Modern)
342. Steig, William. *Amos & Boris*. Farrar, Straus, 1971. (S—Modern)

MYTHS AND EPICS

343. Alexander, Ellen. *Llama and the Great Flood: A Folktale from Peru*. Crowell, 1989. (S)
344. Andronik, Catherine M. *Quest for a King: Searching for the Real King Arthur*. Atheneum, 1989. (nonfiction)
345. Barth, Edna. *Balder and the Mistletoe*, illustrated by Richard Cuffari. Houghton Mifflin, 1979. (S)
346. _____. *Cupid and Psyche*, illustrated by Ati Forberg. Seabury, 1976. (S)
347. Bierhorst, John. *The Hungry Woman: Myths and Legends of the Aztecs*. Morrow, 1984.
348. _____. *The Mythology of Mexico and Central America*. Morrow, 1990.
349. _____. *The Mythology of North America*. Morrow, 1985.
350. _____. *The Mythology of South America*. Morrow, 1988.
351. Colum, Padraic. *The Children of Odin*, illustrated by Willy Pogany. Macmillan, 1920.
352. _____. *The Children's Homer: The Adventurers of Odysseus and the Tale of Troy*, illustrated by Willy Pogany. Macmillan, 1962.
353. D'Aulaire, Ingri, and Edgar Parin d'Aulaire. *D'Aulaires' Book of Greek Myths*. Doubleday, 1962.
354. _____. *Norse Gods and Giants*. Doubleday, 1967.
355. Evslin, Bernard. *Hercules*, illustrated by Joseph A. Smith. Morrow, 1984.
356. _____. *Jason and the Argonauts*, illustrated by Bert Dodson. Morrow, 1986.
357. Evslin, Bernard, Dorothy Evslin, and Ned Hoopes. *Heroes and Monsters of Greek Myth*, illustrated by William Hunter. Scholastic, 1970.
358. Fisher, Leonard Everett. *Jason and the Golden Fleece*. Holiday, 1990. (S)
359. _____. *The Olympians*. Holiday, 1984.
360. _____. *Theseus and the Minotaur*. Holiday, 1988. (S)
361. Farmer, Penelope. *Beginnings: Creation Myths of the World*, illustrated by Antonio Frasconi. McElderry, 1979.
362. Gaer, Joseph. *The Adventures of Rama*, illustrated by Randy Monk. Little, Brown, 1954.
363. Gates, Doris. *The Golden God: Apollo*, illustrated by Constantinos Coconis, Viking, 1973.
364. _____. *Lord of the Sky: Zeus*, illustrated by Robert Handville. Viking, 1972.
365. _____. *Two Queens of Heaven: The Story of Demeter and Aphrodite*, illustrated by Trina Schart Hyman. Viking, 1974.
366. _____. *The Warrior Goddess: Athena*, illustrated by Don Bolognese. Viking, 1972.
367. Graves, Robert. *Greek Gods and Heroes*. Doubleday, 1960.
368. Green, Roger Lancelyn. *Tales of the Greek Heroes*. Penguin, 1958.
369. Hamilton, Virginia. *In the Beginning: Creation Stories from Around the World*, illustrated by Barry Moser. Harcourt, 1988.
370. Hastings, Selina. *Sir Gawain and the Green Knight*, illustrated by Juan Wijngaard. Lothrop, 1981. (S)
371. _____. *Sir Gawain and the Loathly Lady*, illustrated by Juan Wijngaard. Lothrop, 1985. (S)
372. Hodges, Margaret. *The Arrow and the Lamp: The Story of Psyche*, illustrated by Donna Diamond. Little, Brown, 1989. (S)
373. _____. *The Kitchen Knight: A Tale of King Arthur*, illustrated by Trina Schart Hyman. Holiday, 1990. (S)
374. _____. *The Knight Prisoner: The Tale of Sir Thomas Malory and His King Arthur*. Farrar, Straus, 1976. (nonfiction)
375. _____. *Saint George and the Dragon*, illustrated by Trina Schart Hyman. Little, Brown, 1984. (S)
376. Hutton, Warwick. *Theseus and the Minotaur*. McElderry, 1989. (S)
377. Lanier, Sidney. *The Boy's King Arthur*, illustrated by N. C. Wyeth. Scribner's, 1989. (1917)

378. Lattimore, Deborah Nourse. *Why There Is No Arguing in Heaven: A Mayan Myth*. Harper, 1989. (S)
379. Lister, Robin. *The Legend of King Arthur*, illustrated by Alan Baker. Doubleday, 1990.
380. Low, Alice. *The Macmillan Book of Greek Gods and Heroes*, illustrated by Arvis Stewart. Macmillan, 1985.
381. Malcolmson, Anne, ed. *The Song of Robin Hood*, music arranged by Grace Castagnetta, illustrated by Virginia Lee Burton. Houghton Mifflin, 1947. (S)
382. McDermott, Gerald. *Daughter of Earth: A Roman Myth*. Delacorte, 1984. (S)
383. McGovern, Ann. *Robin Hood of Sherwood Forest*, illustrated by Tracy Sugarman. Scholastic, 1970.
384. McKinley, Robin. *The Outlaws of Sherwood*. Greenwillow, 1988.
385. Monroe, Jean Guard, and Ray A. Williamson. *They Dance in the Sky: Native American Star Myths*, illustrated by Edgar Stewart. Houghton Mifflin, 1987.
386. Oldfield, Pamela. *Tales from Ancient Greece*, illustrated by Nick Harris. Doubleday, 1988.
387. Picard, Barbara Leonie. *The Iliad of Homer*. Walck, 1960.
388. _____. *The Odyssey of Homer Retold*. Walck, 1952.
389. Pyk, Ann. *The Hammer of Thunder*, illustrated by Jan Pyk. Putnam, 1972.
390. Pyle, Howard. *The Merry Adventures of Robin Hood*. Scribner's, 1946 (1888).
391. _____. *Some Merry Adventures of Robin Hood*. Scribner's, 1954.
392. _____. *The Story of King Arthur and His Knights*. Scribner's, 1954.
393. San Souci, Robert D. *Young Merlin*, illustrated by Daniel Horne. Doubleday, 1990. (S)
394. Seeger, Elizabeth. *The Ramayana*, illustrated by Gordon Laite. Young Scott, 1969.
395. Service, Pamela F. *Wizard of Wind and Rock*, illustrated by Laura Marshall. Atheneum, 1990. (S)
396. Sutcliff, Rosemary. *The Light Beyond the Forest: The Quest for the Holy Grail*. Dutton, 1980.
397. _____. *The Road to Camlann*. Dutton, 1982.
398. _____. *The Sword and the Circle*. Dutton, 1981.
399. _____. *Tristan and Iseult*. Dutton, 1981.
400. Talbott, Hudson. *King Arthur: The Sword in the Stone*. Morrow, 1991. (S)
401. White, T. H. *The Sword in the Stone*. Putnam, 1939.
402. Wilson, Barbara Ker. *The Turtle and the Island: A Folktale From Papua New Guinea*, illustrated by Frané Lessac. Lippincott, 1990. (S)
403. Yolen, Jane. *The Dragon's Boy*. Harper, 1990.
404. _____. *Wings*, illustrated by Dennis Nolan. Harcourt Brace, 1991. (S)

BIBLE

405. Bible, New Testament. *The Christ Child*, illustrated by Maud and Miska Petersham. Doubleday, 1931. (S)
406. _____. *Christmas: The King James Version*, illustrated by Jan Pienkowski. Knopf, 1984. (S)
407. _____. *The Christmas Story*, illustrated by Isabelle Brent. Dial, 1989. (S)
408. Bach, Alice, and J. Cheryl Exum. *Moses' Ark: Stories from the Bible*, illustrated by Leo and Diane Dillon. Delacorte, 1989.
409. Bierhorst, John, translator. *Spirit Child: A Story of the Nativity*, illustrated by Barbara Cooney. Morrow, 1984. (S—Mexico)
410. Bødker, Cecil. *Mary of Nazareth*, translated by Eric Bibb, illustrated by Bengt Arne Runnerström. R & S Books/Farrar, Straus, 1989.
411. Chaikin, Miriam, adapter. *Exodus*, illustrated by Charles Mikolaycak. Holiday, 1987. (S)
412. de la Mare, Walter. *Stories from the Bible*, illustrated by Edward Ardizzone. Knopf, 1961.
413. de Paola, Tomie. *The Legend of Old Befana*. Harcourt, 1980. (S)
414. _____. *The Story of the Three Wise Kings*. Putnam, 1983. (S)
415. Fisher, Leonard Everett. *The Seven Days of Creation*. Holiday, 1981.
416. Gellman, Marc. *Does God Have a Big Toe? Stories About Stories in the Bible*, illustrated by Oscar de Mejo. Harper, 1989.
417. Hutton, Warwick. *Adam and Eve*. McElderry, 1987. (S)
418. _____. *Jonah and the Great Fish*. McElderry, 1983. (S)
419. _____. *Moses in the Bulrushes*. McElderry, 1986. (S)
420. _____. *Noah and the Great Flood*. Atheneum, 1977. (S)
421. Koralek, Jenny. *The Cobweb Curtain: A Christmas Story*, illustrated by Pauline Baynes. Holt, 1989. (S)
422. Mikolaycak, Charles. *Babushka: An Old Russian Folktale*. Holiday, 1984. (S)

423.   Robbins, Ruth. *Baboushka and the Three Kings*, illustrated by Nicolas Sidjakov. Parnassus, 1960. (S)
424.   Rogers, Jacqueline. *The Christmas Pageant*. Grosset, 1989. (S)
425.   Singer, Isaac Bashevis. *The Wicked City*, translated by the author and Elizabeth Shub, illustrated by Leonard Everett Fisher. Farrar, Straus, 1972.
426.   Spier, Peter. *The Book of Jonah*. Doubleday, 1985. (S)
427.   _____. *Noah's Ark*. Doubleday, 1977. (S)
428.   Turner, Philip. *The Bible Story*, illustrated by Brian Wildsmith. Oxford, 1987.
429.   Winthrop, Elizabeth. *A Child Is Born*, illustrated by Charles Mikolaycak. Holiday, 1983. (S)
430.   _____. *He Is Risen*, illustrated by Charles Mikolaycak. Holiday, 1985. (S)

Chapter Seven

Modern Fantasy

A wonderfully perceptive teacher maintained a diary in which she recorded significant events in her teaching day. These excerpts reveal her students' responses to a reading aloud of the well-known fantasy *Charlotte's Web* by E. B. White:

January 18

A wisp of a girl with dark dreaming eyes, Judy F. sits transfixed, listening to *Charlotte's Web*. When I read aloud, I'm aware of an irreplaceable group feeling. But beyond that, if children aren't read to, how will they see the purpose of such a difficult skill? . . .

February 6

Judy came in glowing.

"We've bought a baby pig. Mother took me to a nearby farm."

"How marvelous. What's his name?"

"Wilbur," she said, in a matter-of-fact voice—as if the name of the pig in *Charlotte's Web* was the only one possible. "He's quite cuddly for a pig. We bathe him every day."

February 20

When I'm alone with Judy, I ask about Wilbur.

"Oh, he's getting along just fine. We bought him a large pink ribbon and only take it off when he goes to bed."

"Where does he sleep?"

"In my bed," said Judy, as if I ought to know.

March 2

Everyone was silent at the end of *Charlotte's Web*. David wept when Charlotte died. Later he asked to borrow the book. It'll be interesting to see how he maneuvers such difficult reading. But there's the motivation they talk about.

April 3

Judy's mother hurried over to me at the P.T.A. meeting.

"What's all this about your pig?" she queried.

"My pig?" I answered incredulously. "You mean your pig; the one you and Judy bought at the farm."

"Come now," said Mrs. F. "This is ridiculous. Judy's been telling me for weeks about the class pig. The one you named for Wilbur in *Charlotte's Web*."

We looked at each other, puzzled, and suddenly the truth dawned upon us.

Wilbur, that immaculately clean pig in his dazzling pink ribbon, belonged to neither Mrs. F. nor me. He was born in dreams—a creature of Judy's wonderful imagination.[1]

A book of fantasy had seemed so real to these children that 7-year-old David had cried at its end, and Judy had continued the story in her imagination, convincing both her teacher and her mother that Wilbur did indeed exist.

FANTASY FOR TODAY'S CHILD

Some educators and parents question the value of fantasy for today's child. They argue that children want contemporary stories that are relevant and speak to the problems of daily living—"now" books about the real world, not fantasies about unreal worlds. They point to books by Lois Lowry, Gary Paulsen, Jerry Spinelli, Betsy Byars, and others (see Chapter 9) as examples of books that speak directly to today's child.

The tremendous increase in the publication of informational books also indicates that librarians buy what children seek: "useful" books that provide real facts, such as the most recent NFL statistics on football players or a report on underwater archeology. Of what use, the realists ask, is a 400-page story about talking rabbits (*Watership Down* by Richard Adams) or a series about a strange little man who can grant wishes (The Coven Tree series by Bill Brittain)?

Children themselves have denied the truth of some of these statements by choosing many books of fantasy as their favorites. Certainly *Charlotte's Web* is one of the most popular children's books to be published within the past fifty years. C. S. Lewis's Narnia series, Roald Dahl's *Charlie and the Chocolate Factory*, and Madeleine L'Engle's *A Wrinkle in Time* are all fantasies that rank among children's favorite books. And many of the classics, books that have endured through several generations—such as *Winnie-the-Pooh*, *The Wind in the Willows*, and *Alice's Adventures in Wonderland*—are also fantasies.

The great fantasies frequently reveal new insights into the world of reality. Both *Charlotte's Web* and *The Wind in the Willows* detail the responsibilities and loyalties required of true friendship. The fundamental truth underlying Ursula Le Guin's story *A Wizard of Earthsea* is that people are responsible for the evil they create and are only free of it when they face it directly. Such a theme might appear to be a thinly disguised Sunday School lesson in a book of realism; in fantasy it becomes an exciting quest for identity and self-knowledge. Fantasy consistently asks the universal questions concerning the struggle of good versus evil, the humanity of man, the meaning of life and death.

A modern realistic fiction novel may be out of date in five years, but well-written fantasy endures. Hans Christian Andersen's *The Nightingale* speaks directly to this century's adoration of mechanical gadgetry to the neglect of what is simple and real. Alan Arkin's *The Lemming Condition* portrays the ultimate hazard of following the crowd. Natalie Babbitt's *Tuck Everlasting* questions whether anything or anyone would wish to live forever. In considering the enduring qualities of fantasy, Lillian H. Smith wrote:

> It goes to the heart of the unseen, and puts that which is so mysteriously hidden from ordinary mortals into the clear light of their understanding, or at least of their partial understanding. It is more true, perhaps, of writers of fantasy than of any other writers except poets that they struggle with the inexpressible. . . . [T]hey are able to evoke ideas and clothe them in symbols, allegory, and dream.[2]

More importantly, however, fantasy helps the child to develop imagination. The ability to imag-

[1]Jean Katzenberg, "More Leaves from a Teacher's Diary: On Reading" in *Outlook*, Issue II (Spring 1974), pp. 28–29. Published by the Mountain View Center for Environmental Education, University of Colorado.

[2]Lillian H. Smith, *The Unreluctant Years: A Critical Approach to Children's Literature.* (Chicago: American Library Association, 1953). Viking Penguin, 1976, p. 150.

ine, to conceive of alternative ways of life, to entertain new ideas, to create strange new worlds, to dream dreams are all skills vital to the survival of humankind. Paul Fenimore Cooper wrote of the importance of imagination:

> He who lacks imagination lives but half a life. He has his experiences, he has his facts, he has his learning. But do any of these really live unless touched by the magic of the imagination? So long as the road is straight he can see down it and follow it. But imagination looks around the turns and gazes far off into the distance on either side. And it is imagination that walks hand in hand with vision.[3]

Susan Cooper suggests that the heterogeneous mix of cultures in the United States is such that children have no shared myths to inherit as they do in more homogeneous cultures. She believes that the role of fantasy, with its heroes, struggles, and allegories, becomes even more important because it satisfies the modern-day human hunger for myth.[4]

The Roots of Fantasy

The modern literature of fantasy is diverse. We have contemporary fairy tales; stories of magic, talking toys, and other wonders; quests for truth in lands that never were; and narratives that speculate on the future. While these types of stories may seem very different, they do have something in common: they are rooted in earlier sources—in folktales, legends, myths, and the oldest dreams of humankind.

All literature borrows from itself, but the fantastic genre is particularly dependent. Motifs, plots, characters, settings, and themes of new fantasy books often seem familiar. And well they should, for we have met them before, in other, older stories.

Jane Yolen, in an essay on the importance of traditional literature, says:

Stories lean on stories, art on art. This familiarity with the treasure-house of ancient story is necessary for any true appreciation of today's literature. A child who has never met Merlin—how can he or she really recognize the wizards in Earthsea? The child who has never heard of Arthur—how can he or she totally appreciate Susan Cooper's *The Grey King?*[5]

Many authors borrow directly from the characters and motifs of folklore. The African-American folk heroes John de Conquer and John Henry Roustabout in *The Magical Adventures of Pretty Pearl* enliven this unusual fantasy by Virginia Hamilton. Mollie Hunter's fantasy books are filled with the magic folk of her native Scotland. There are, among others, worrisome trows; the Selkies, who are seals capable of taking human form on land; and water sprites called kelpies, often seen as horses.

Such shape shifting often occurs in folk and fairy tales, and similar transformations are frequently arranged by authors of modern fantasy. In *The Cat Who Wished to Be a Man*, Lloyd Alexander's wizard transforms his cat Lionel into a young man whose catlike ways wear off only gradually. The wizard himself, of course, is a character drawn from the magician figures of old tales. In the same book, a good-hearted rogue named Tudbelly invites inhospitable townspeople to a feast, promising them a special stew, and then tricks them into furnishing the ingredients themselves. Readers who have had prior experience with folktales may recognize that Alexander's "delicious Pro Bono Publico" stew is made from the same basic recipe as *Stone Soup,* in the retelling by Marcia Brown.

In the case of Robin McKinley's *Beauty*, the debt to an earlier source is immediately clear. McKinley recasts the tale of "Beauty and the Beast" in the form of a novel by exploring character, motive, and the everyday details that do not fit within the frame of a conventional fairy tale. The result is a rich and satisfying book that manages to sustain a sense of anticipation even in those readers who know the outcome. Shirley

[3]Paul Fenimore Cooper, "On Catching a Child's Fantasy," in *Three Owls,* Third Book, Anne Carroll Moore, ed. (New York: Coward-McCann, 1931), pp. 56–57.

[4]Susan Cooper, "Fantasy in the Real World," *The Horn Book Magazine* (May/June, 1990), pp. 304–315.

[5]Jane Yolen, "How Basic Is Shazam?" in *Touch Magic: Fantasy, Faerie and Folklore in the Literature of Childhood* (New York: Philomel Books, 1981), p. 15.

Rousseau Murphy incorporates several variants of the Cinderella story in *Silver Woven in My Hair*, another fully developed fantasy for young readers built on the simpler structure of a familiar tale.

Some bodies of traditional lore have proven to be more popular than others as sources of new stories. Echoes of King Arthur—both the Arthur of the Medieval romances (as in Malory's *Le Morte d'Arthur*) and his historic precursor, Arthur the tribal chieftain of early Britain—are found in a great many modern fantasies. In *The Acorn Quest* by Jane Yolen, a short book with a light touch, the animal knights searching for the Golden Acorn that will save Woodland from hunger are sly parodies of Arthur's Knights of the Round Table and their pursuit of the Holy Grail. Among fantasies that treat the legends more seriously, William Mayne's *Earthfasts*, Pamela Service's *Winter of Magic's Return*, and Peter Dickinson's *Merlin Dreams* are three books much in Arthur's debt. Susan Cooper's five books that make up *The Dark Is Rising* sequence weave together elements of the Arthurian legends and broader themes from Celtic mythology, with its emphasis on ancient powers. Lloyd Alexander's Prydain Chronicles borrow extensively from the Welsh stories known as the *Mabinogion*.

Most of the authors who draw on the Celtic stories use those versions most familiar in England and Wales. But some of the same tales have Irish variants or analogues where Finn McCool is the hero of record. Mary Tannen has tapped this source in *The Wizard Children of Finn* and *The Lost Legend of Finn*, in which a modern sister and brother are time travelers to ancient Ireland, caught up in Finn's destiny, Druid magic, and finally Viking bloodshed.

Many fantasies are based on multiple sources. Perhaps it is this striking of several familiar notes at once that brings them such enduring popularity. *The Hobbit* by J. R. R. Tolkien places the archetypal hero of mythology against a smaller scale setting more common to folklore. C. S. Lewis's Narnia series puts centaurs and fauns from classical myths in company with modern children fighting medieval battles parallel to those recounted in Christian theology. Madeleine L'Engle draws on a similar array of referents. The volumes of her Time Trilogy (*A Wrinkle in Time, A*

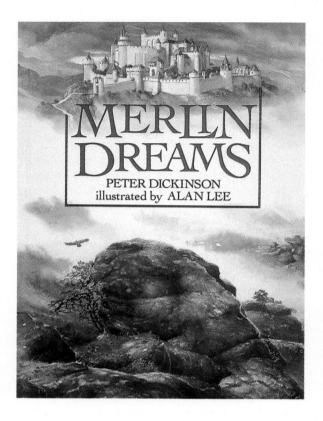

The times and characters of Merlin and King Arthur are the traditional lore on which many fantasies for both children and adults are built. Alan Lee's jacket illustration for Peter Dickinson's *Merlin Dreams* suggests the massive rock under which Merlin is supposed to lie waiting.

❦   ❦   ❦

Wind in the Door, A Swiftly Tilting Planet) explore intriguing possibilities of astrophysics and cellular biology, as befits science fiction, but the books also reflect her knowledge of theology, classical literature, myths, legends, and history. Pamela W. Service's *Winter of Magic's Return*, in which King Arthur and three children unite to save a ruined future earth, is a blend of legend, science fiction, and myth.

L'Engle's *Wrinkle in Time* as well as Robert C. O'Brien's *Mrs. Frisby and the Rats of NIMH* are termed science fiction as well as fantasy. Often fantasies that draw on various sources are difficult to classify. Dennis Hamley's *Hare's Choice* is a multilayered story of an elementary class's need to create a story for a hare they found dead by the roadside. The story the children create is science fiction, but the hare's own story, which alternates in italics, shows how the children's storytelling imbues the hare with mythic powers. Hare may choose a pastoral hare heaven where real rabbits go or the place where animals such as Peter Rabbit, Fiver and Hazel, Stuart Little, and Tom Kitten, who have been brought to life in stories, now dwell.

No matter how we classify these stories, however, the ultimate taproot of all fantasy is the human psyche. Like the ancient tale-tellers and the medieval bards, modern fantasy writers speak to our deepest needs, our darkest fears, and our highest hopes. Maurice Sendak, for instance, relies on such themes in his picture storybooks and in the singular small volume entitled *Higglety, Pigglety, Pop!* In this book a dog named Jennie sets out on an unspecified quest because "There must be more to life than having everything."[6] Her experiences are childlike and highly symbolic: the comforts of eating and the fear of being eaten, in turn, by a lion; the importance of one's own real name; the significance of dreams. Jennie's quest, as it turns out, may be read as the search for maturity and personal identity.

Ursula K. Le Guin conducts a similar psychic adventure for an older audience in *A Wizard of Earthsea*, where a young magician must learn the power of naming and recognize the Shadow that pursues him as part of himself. Adults may find, in these and similar stories, many of the collective images or shared symbols called archetypes by the great psychologist Carl Jung. Children will simply recognize that such a fantasy is "true." All our best fantasies, from the briefest modern fairy tale to the most complex novel of high adventure, share this quality of truth.

MODERN FAIRY TALES

The traditional folklore or fairy tale had no identifiable author but was passed by word of mouth

6Maurice Sendak, *Higglety, Pigglety, Pop!* (New York: Harper & Row, 1967), p. 5.

from one generation to the next. While the names of Grimm and Jacobs have become associated with some of these tales, they did not *write* the stories; they compiled and edited the folktales of Germany and England. The modern literary fairy tale utilizes the form of the old but has an identifiable author.

The Beginnings of the Modern Fairy Tale

Hans Christian Andersen is generally credited with being the first *author* of modern fairy tales, although even some of his stories, such as *The Wild Swans*, are definite adaptations of the old folktales. (Compare Andersen's *The Wild Swans* with the Grimm brothers' "The Six Swans," for example.) Many of Andersen's stories bear his unmistakable stamp of gentleness, melancholy, and faith in God. Often even his retellings of old tales are embellished with deeper meanings, making them very much his creations.

Some of Andersen's tales are really commentaries on what he saw as the false standards of society. In *The Princess and the Pea*, Andersen laughs at the snobbish desire of a prince to determine the true nature of his intended spouse by means of a dried pea. The farce of *The Emperor's New Clothes* is disclosed by a child who tells the truth—that the Emperor indeed has no clothes. Others of Andersen's tales are thought to be autobiographical commentaries. *The Ugly Duckling*, the jest of the poultry yard, became a beautiful swan just as the gawky Andersen suffered in his youth but was later honored by the Danish king and the world. *The Steadfast Tin Soldier* was rejected by his ballerina love just as Andersen was rejected by the woman he loved.

Andersen was not afraid to show children cruelty, morbidity, sorrow, and even death in his stories. In the long tale of *The Snow Queen*, a glass splinter enters Kai's (or Kay's) eye and stabs his heart. He becomes spiteful and angry with his friend Gerda, who is hurt by the change in his behavior. When he disappears with the Snow Queen, Gerda searches for and finds him and her tears melt the splinter and dissolve his icy demeanor. Susan Jeffers has illustrated three retellings of Andersen tales by Amy Erlich. In her illustrations for *The Snow Queen*, she features close-ups and swirling images of the dreams and snowstorms the two children encounter. With brilliantly colored and ornately patterned surfaces, Errol Le Cain's version emphasizes the strangeness of Gerda's journey to find Kai. Le Cain borrows from a Brueghel painting, "Hunters in the Snow," for an opening scene of children sledding. Children would be fascinated by seeing the way an artist may pay homage to another.

The Little Match Girl freezes to death on Christmas Eve while seeing a vision of her grandmother, the only person who truly loved her, in the flames of her unsold matches. The grandmother carries the girl to heaven. Rachel Isadora's version relies heavily on pinks and blues to depict this sentimental story; Blair Lent's version is more austere with its towering buildings and depiction of the helpless girl in a snowstorm.

Many of Andersen's stories have been beautifully illustrated in single editions. Nancy Ekholm Burkert's pictures for *The Nightingale* resemble paintings on old Chinese silk screens. Demi's outlined landscapes on golden green silk backgrounds appear in a more decorative version; Lisbeth Zwerger's simple composition and sure sepia line illustrate the story in another edition. Warwick Hutton's bright watercolors for *The Tinderbox* depict with humor the three large-eyed dogs that help a common soldier win riches and the princess while outwitting her father. Barry Moser reimagines the tale in a post–Civil War setting and illustrates it with watercolor portraits: the hero is an ex-Confederate soldier, the witch becomes an old east Tennessee man, and the princess is a politician's daughter. Illustrators such as these have done much to attract a new generation of readers to Andersen's stories.

The Complete Fairy Tales and Stories of Andersen have been faithfully translated by Erik Haugaard. Here we find the original telling of "The Little Mermaid" and "Thumbelina." Eighteen of these stories, selected for a single volume and illustrated by Michael Foreman, provide children with several of the most popular and well known of Andersen's stories. Many other illustrators, such as Michael Hague, Edward Ardizzone, and Maurice Sendak have illustrated their own favorite tales from the body of Andersen's work.

Two other early authors of the modern literary fairy tale are Oscar Wilde and George MacDonald. Wilde's *The Happy Prince*, strikingly illustrated by both Jean Claverie and by Ed Young, is the sentimental story of a bejeweled statue who little by little gives his valuable decorations to the poor. His emissary and friend is a swallow who faithfully postpones his winter migration to Egypt to do the prince's bidding, only to succumb to the cold at the statue's feet. When the town councilors melt down the now shabby statue for its lead, all burns except the heart, which is cast on the same ash heap as the body of the dead bird. Together, the two are received in Heaven as the most precious things in the city. Wilde's *The Selfish Giant* has even more religious symbolism.

Many of MacDonald's fairy tales are also religious in nature, including *The Golden Key*, which has been sensitively illustrated by Maurice Sendak. Sendak also illustrated MacDonald's *The Light Princess*, the story of a princess deprived of gravity by an aunt who was angry at not being invited to her christening. It is interesting to compare Sendak's tender yet humorous illustrations for this story with the detailed, amusing, and colorful pictures by William Pène du Bois. MacDonald is also remembered for *At the Back of the North Wind*, published in 1871 and one of the foundation stories of modern fantasy.

Fairy Tales Today

In many instances modern authors have written farcical versions of the old fairy-tale form. The story may be set in the days of kings and queens and beautiful princesses, the language will reflect the manners of the period, and the usual "Once upon a time" beginning and "They lived happily ever after" ending will be present—but the conflict usually has a modern twist. True to all fairy tales, virtue will be rewarded and evil overcome.

James Thurber's *Many Moons*, with new illustrations by Marc Simont, is the story of a petulant princess who desires the moon. The characterizations of the frustrated king, the perplexed wise men, and the understanding jester are well realized. Princess Lenore solves the problem of obtaining the moon in a completely satisfying and childlike manner. Thurber's *Thirteen Clocks* is a more sophisticated folktale for older readers. A cold duke who is afraid of "now" freezes time in Coffin Castle, where he keeps the beautiful Princess Saralinda. A prince in disguise accomplishes impossible tasks set by the duke and thus wins her hand. However, it is only with the bungling and amusing help of the Golux that the prince is able to obtain the one thousand jewels and start the thirteen clocks, so that time is Now and he may marry the princess. This imaginative spoof on folktales is one that middle graders thoroughly enjoy.

Jane Yolen writes lyrical tales that make use of modern psychological insights while following traditional patterns found in folk literature. Ed Young's illustrations in the style of Chinese cut paper artwork grace *The Emperor and the Kite,* in which the youngest daughter rescues her emperor father from imprisonment by means of a kite. In *The Girl Who Loved the Wind,* Yolen tells of the princess Danina who is protected by her father from all the unlovely things of the world by a high wall he has constructed around the palace. But when Danina hears the wind sing a true song of the world, she spreads her cape and off she flies with the wind. Ed Young studied Persian miniatures before designing the richly textured pictures for this beautiful book. A blind Chinese princess learns to "see" from the remarkable vision of a wise blind man in *The Seeing Stick.* Color is used selectively by Remy Charlip and Demetra Maraslis to help the reader see and feel the excitement of the princess.

In another story by Jane Yolen, the heroine *Dove Isabeau* is pure of heart, slender, and soft-spoken:

🕊 Her hair was the color of the tops of waves when the sun lights them from above, and her eyes were as dark blue as the sea. . . . And because she always dressed in gray or white, the color of a dove, she was known as Dove Isabeau.[7]

But when her mother dies, and her father remarries a witch, Dove Isabeau and her companion-

[7]Jane Yolen, *Dove Isabeau,* illustrated by Dennis Nolan (San Diego: Harcourt Brace Jovanovich, 1989), unpaged.

In Jane Yolen's story of *Dove Isabeau,* Dennis Nolan captures the moment when an unsuspecting Isabeau is cursed and enchanted by her jealous stepmother.

🕊 🕊 🕊

able white cat are barred from the witch's chambers. The evil and jealous woman transforms Isabeau into a terrible dragon whose destiny is to kill young men beneath her claws and to be cursed by all. While kisses may save Isabeau, the one who bestows them will himself turn to stone. This story of a spirited heroine and faithful love is a fine introduction to many longer fantasy novels.

Two other modern folktales present contrasting characterizations of dragons. Jay Williams suggests in *Everyone Knows What a Dragon Looks Like* that appearances can be deceiving. For no one except Han, the poor little gate sweeper, will believe the small fat man with a long white beard who says that he is a dragon come to defend the city. While the city fathers and the Mandarin won't bother with the old man's demands for polite treatment, food, and drink, Han supplies the three and the old man in dragon form rescues the city. Mercer Mayer's quasi-Oriental illustrations are full of detail and movement. Kenneth Grahame's *The Reluctant Dragon* is the droll tale of a peace-loving dragon who is forced to fight Saint George. The dragon's friend, called simply the Boy, arranges a meeting between Saint George and the dragon, and a mock fight is planned. Saint George is the hero of the day, the dragon is highly entertained at a banquet, and the Boy is pleased to have saved both the dragon and Saint George. Black line drawings by Ernest Shepard add to the subtle humor of this book.

A monster of another sort is finally charmed by the fiddle music of Sep, seventh son of a seventh son, in Joan Aiken's *The Moon's Revenge*. This story, illustrated in glowing and dramatic watercolors by Dennis Lee, tells of the consequences when Sep provokes the moon by asking a favor of it. He wishes to be the best fiddler in the land. While the moon grants his wish, the price is a baby sister born mute and a great scaly sea monster who comes to terrify the seaside village. Readers of traditional literature will recognize motifs and patterns common to folktales in this eerie tale.

A popular fairy tale of our time for adults and children is the haunting story of *The Little Prince* by Antoine de Saint-Exupéry. Written in the first person, the story tells of the author's encounter with the Little Prince on the Sahara Desert, where he has made a forced landing with his disabled plane. Bit by bit, the author learns the strange history of the Little Prince, who lives all alone on a tiny planet no larger than a house. He possesses three volcanoes, two active and one extinct, and one flower unlike any other flower in all the galaxy. However, when he sees a garden of roses, he doubts the uniqueness of his flower until a fox shows him that what we love is always unique to us. This gentle story means many things to different people, but its wisdom and beauty are for all.

MODERN FANTASY

Fantasy, like poetry, means more than it says. Underlying most of the great books of fantasy is a metaphorical comment on society today. Some children will find deeper meanings in a tale such as *The Little Prince*, others will simply read it as a good story, and still others will be put off reading it altogether because it isn't "real." Children vary in their capacity for imaginative thinking. The literal-minded child finds the suspension of reality a barrier to the enjoyment of fantasy; other children relish the opportunity to enter the world of enchantment. Children's reactions to books of modern fantasy are seldom predictable or mild; they appear to be either vehemently for or against them. Frequently, teachers may help children develop a taste for fantasy by reading aloud favorite books, such as Beverly Cleary's *Ralph S. Mouse*, Jean Merrill's *The Pushcart War*, or Sid Fleischman's *The Whipping Boy*.

Evaluating Modern Fantasy

Well-written fantasy, like other fiction, has a well-constructed plot, convincing characterization, a worthwhile theme, and an appropriate style. However, additional considerations are needed to guide the evaluation of fantasy. The primary concern is the way the author makes the fantasy believable. A variety of techniques may be used to create belief in the unbelievable. Many authors firmly ground a story in reality before gradually moving into fantasy. Not until Chapter 3 in *Charlotte's Web* does author E. B. White suggest that Fern can understand the farm animals as they talk. And even then, Fern never talks to the animals; she only listens to them. By the end of the story Fern is growing up and really is more interested in listening to Henry Fussy than to the animals. White's description of the sounds and smells of the barnyard allows readers to experience the setting as well.

Creating belief by careful attention to the detail of the setting is a technique also used by Mary Norton. Her graphic description of the Borrowers' home beneath the clock enables the reader to visualize this domestic background and to feel what it would be like to be as small as *The Borrowers*.

Having one of the characters mirror the disbelief of the reader is another device for creating convincing fantasy. In *Jeremy Visick*, David

Wiseman has portrayed his protagonist, Matthew, as a boy who thinks history is rubbish. Therefore, when even he is persuaded that the past lives again, the reader shares his terror as he descends to sure disaster within the depths of the Wheal Maid mine. In another well-written fantasy, *The Indian in the Cupboard* by Lynne Reid Banks, the boy Omri so respects the integrity of his toy cowboy and Indian come-to-life that the reader also begins to think of them as real. If they did not indeed exist, why should this thoroughly believable child take such pains with them?

The use of appropriate language adds a kind of documentation to fantasy. Underground for nearly two hundred years, the drummer uses such obsolete words as "arfish" for "afraid" in *Earthfasts*, by William Mayne, and his lack of understanding of such modern words as "breakfast" seems very authentic indeed.

In *The Fox Busters*, a clever story full of wordplay and puns, Dick King-Smith creates languages for a farm community in which chickens speak Hennish while the foxes speak Volpine. When one of the hens curses, using "fowl language," she tells a fox to "go fricassee yourself" and calls a human a "stupid scrambled boy." The hens, named after famous farm implement companies like Massey-Harris or Allis-Chalmers, add further authenticity to this delightful fantasy.

The proof of real objects gives an added dimension of truth in books. How can we explain the origin of Greta's kitten or her father's penknife if not from Blue Cove in Julia Sauer's story *Fog Magic*? In *Tom's Midnight Garden* by Philippa Pearce, it is the discovery of a pair of ice skates that confirms the reader's belief in Tom's adventures.

Another point to be considered when evaluating fantasy is the consistency of the story. Each fantasy should have a logical framework and an internal consistency in the world set forth by the author. Characters cannot become invisible whenever they face difficulty unless invisibility is a well-established part of their natures. The laws of fantasy may be strange indeed, but they must be obeyed.

Lloyd Alexander, master of the craft of writing fantasy, explains the importance of internal consistency within the well-written fantasy:

> Once committed to his imaginary kingdom, the writer is not a monarch but a subject. Characters must appear plausible in their own setting, and the writer must go along with the inner logic. Happenings should have logical implications. Details should be tested for consistency. Shall animals speak? If so, do *all* animals speak? If not, then which—and how? Above all, why? Is it essential to the story, or lamely cute? Are there enchantments? How powerful? If an enchanter can perform such-and-such, can he not also do so-and-so?[8]

[8]Lloyd Alexander, "The Flat-Heeled Muse," in *Children and Literature* by Virginia Haviland (Glenview, Ill.: Scott Foresman, 1973), p. 243.

GUIDELINES

Evaluating Modern Fantasy

The following specific questions might guide evaluation of modern fantasy:

- ♦ What are the fantasy elements of the story?
- ♦ How has the author made the story believable?
- ♦ Is the story logical and consistent within the framework established by the author?
- ♦ Is the plot original and ingenious?
- ♦ Is there a universal truth underlying the metaphor of the fantasy?
- ♦ How does it compare to other books of the same kind or by the same author?

Finally, while all plots should be original, the plots of fantasy must be ingenious and creative. A contrived or trite plot seems more obvious in a fanciful tale than in a realistic story.

Animal Fantasy

Children may first be introduced to fantasy through tales of talking animals, toys, and dolls. The young child frequently ascribes powers of thought and speech to pets or toys and may already be acquainted with some of the Beatrix Potter stories or the more sophisticated tales of William Steig.

A humorous introduction to animal fantasy is *Bunnicula* by Deborah and James Howe. When the Monroe family return from seeing "Dracula" with a small rabbit they found on a theater seat, the family cat Chester is immediately suspicious. Evidence mounts up: a note written in an obscure Transylvanian dialect is tied around the rabbit's neck; in the kitchen a white tomato and other vegetables appear drained of their juices; and the rabbit can go in and out of his locked cage. Is Bunnicula a vampire? Chester is convinced of it, and his efforts to protect the Monroes are laconically observed and recounted by Harold, the family dog. Older children can appreciate Harold's clever observations and his very doglike concern for food. There are several pun-filled sequels in this series including *The Celery Stalks at Midnight* and *Howliday Inn*.

Other introductions to animal fantasy are Beverly Cleary's *The Mouse and the Motorcycle*, *Runaway Ralph*, and *Ralph S. Mouse*. In the first story, Ralph makes friends with a boy who gives him a small toy motorcycle. *Runaway Ralph* continues Ralph's adventures with the motorcycle. In the third story, to escape his jealous mouse relatives, Ralph goes to school in the pocket of his friend Ryan, becomes a class project, and loses his precious motorcycle but gains a sports car. Cleary's excursions into the world of fantasy are as well accepted by children as are her realistic humorous stories of Henry Huggins and Ramona Quimby.

Michael Bond's Paddington series continues to please children who are just discovering the pleasures of being able to read longer books. Bond's first book, *A Bear Called Paddington*, introduces readers to the bear found in a London railway station and taken by the Brown family to their home. Paddington earnestly tries to help the Browns, but invariably ends up in difficulty. There are many other books in the series and the numerous commercial spinoffs from this popular series have made Paddington a household word.

Poet Lilian Moore gives younger readers a chance to think about the art of poetry in *I'll Meet You at the Cucumbers*. Adam Mouse loves the country and can hardly listen to the other mice when he is busy thinking his long thoughts about grass or stone walls or the view from the scarecrow pocket. Sometimes he shares these thoughts with his mouse pen-pal friend, Amanda, who lives in the city. When his friend Junius takes the reluctant Adam to the city to meet Amanda, Adam is nearly overwhelmed by all that the city has to offer. But his best discovery is the Library where Amanda sometimes goes to listen to the human Story Hour. She says, "Adam, you wouldn't believe how many wonderful stories have been written about us—mice heroes and mice heroines, mice adventurers, mice detectives, mice families. The children love us."[9] Amanda finally shows Adam that the thoughts he has written to her are really poems when she reads aloud poetry by Judith Thurman and Valerie Worth. When Adam returns to the country, he secures a promise from Amanda to come and visit him. In this gentle and humorous book, Moore skirts the "city mouse/country mouse" issue of which place is best in order to deal with larger themes. She helps readers think about the value of new experiences and new friendships, and the way poetry helps us see the world from a fresh perspective.

Adam and Amanda might have enjoyed the gentle and poignant tale of *The Mousewife* by Rumer Godden. It tells of the friendship between an industrious mouse and a caged turtledove. The dove remembers the outside world and speaks so wondrously about its magic—the dew, the night, the glory of flying—that the

[9]Lilian Moore, *I'll Meet You at the Cucumbers*, illustrated by Sharon Wooding (New York: Atheneum, 1988), p. 45.

A loyal Charlotte spins out her opinion of her friend Wilbur in Garth Williams's illustration for E. B. White's *Charlotte's Web*.

🐛   🐛   🐛

mouse must finally let her friend go by releasing the catch on his cage. Reminiscent of Hans Christian Andersen tales, this story has been realistically illustrated by Heidi Holder with soft pencil drawings emphasizing the limited sphere of the mousewife's world.

The same qualities of wonder and tenderness are found in the story of a small brown bat who becomes *The Bat-Poet* in Randall Jarrell's story. A perfect story and a commentary on the writing of poetry itself, it features a bat who cannot sleep during the day. He opens his eyes and sees squirrels and chipmunks, the sun and the mockingbird. Inspired by the mockingbird's songs, he makes up poems but the other bats aren't interested. The mockingbird deigns to listen, but comments only on the form, not the content of his poem. At last, the bat finds the perfect listener, the chipmunk, who is delighted with his poems and believes them. The fine pen-and-ink

drawings by Maurice Sendak are as faithful to the world of nature as the animals and the poetry in this story.

Unquestionably the most beloved animal fantasy of our time is E. B. White's delightful tale, *Charlotte's Web*. While much of our fantasy is of English origin, *Charlotte's Web* is as American as the Fourth of July and just as much a part of our children's heritage. Eight-year-old Fern can understand all of the animals in the barnyard—the geese who always speak in triplicate ("certainly-ertainly-ertainly"); the wise old sheep; and Templeton, the crafty rat—yet she cannot communicate with them. The true heroine of the story is Charlotte A. Cavatica—a beautiful, large gray spider who befriends Wilbur, a humble little pig. When the kindly old sheep inadvertently drops the news that as soon as Wilbur is nice and fat he will be butchered, Charlotte promises to save the hysterical pig. By miraculously spinning words into her web that describe the pig as "radiant," "terrific," and "humble," she makes Wilbur famous. The pig is saved, but Charlotte dies alone on the fairgrounds. Wilbur manages to bring Charlotte's egg sac back to the farm so that the continuity of life in the barnyard is maintained. Wilbur never forgets his friend Charlotte, though he loves her children and grandchildren dearly. Because of her, Wilbur may look forward to a secure and pleasant old age:

🐛 Life in the barn was very good—night and day, winter and summer, spring and fall, dull days and bright days. It was the best place to be, thought Wilbur, this warm delicious cellar, with the garrulous geese, the changing seasons, the heat of the sun, the passage of swallows, the nearness of rats, the sameness of sheep, the love of spiders, the smell of manure, and the glory of everything.[10]

This story has humor, pathos, wisdom, and beauty. Its major themes speak of the web of true friendship and the cycle of life and death. All ages find meaning in this most popular fantasy.

Children also enjoy two other animal fantasies by White, *Stuart Little* and *The Trumpet of the Swan*. While neither book has all the strengths of

[10]E. B. White, *Charlotte's Web*, illustrated by Garth Williams (New York: Harper & Row, 1952), p. 183.

Charlotte's Web, both appeal to children for their curious blend of fantasy and reality.

The English counterpart of Wilbur the pig is Daggie Dogfoot, the runt hero of Dick King-Smith's *Pigs Might Fly*. Saved by luck and his own determination from the Pigman's club, Daggie watches birds and aspires to fly. He discovers instead a talent for swimming that allows him to help rescue all the pigs from a flood. Like E. B. White's barn, the pigyard and pastures here are described in sharp, sensory detail, and the animals' conversation reflects the author's shrewd perceptions about human as well as animal nature. Another pig hero is King-Smith's *Babe: The Gallant Pig*, whose remarkable ability to speak politely to sheep gains him a stunning victory in a sheepdog trial meet. Babe's great-grandson *Ace: The Very Important Pig* even manages to communicate with his owner in this joyful and absurd continuation of a barnyard saga.

Robert Lawson has written a satisfying and tender story about all the little animals who live on *Rabbit Hill*. When they discover new folks are moving into the big house on the hill, they are worried: Will they be planting folks, who like small animals, or shiftless, mean people? Mother Rabbit is a worrier who tends to be pessimistic; Father Rabbit, stately and always eloquent, feels that there are many auspicious signs (he is a Southern gentleman and always speaks in this fashion); and young Georgie delightedly leaps down the hill chanting, "New folks coming, new folks coming!" Although on probation for several days after their arrival, the new folks win approval by putting up a large sign that says: "Please Drive Carefully on Account of Small Animals." *The Tough Winter* is a sequel to *Rabbit Hill*, describing the plight of all the animals when the "Folks" go away for the winter and leave a neglectful caretaker and a mean dog in charge.

The urban counterpart of *Charlotte's Web* and *Rabbit Hill* is *The Cricket in Times Square* by George Selden. A fast-talking Broadway mouse named Tucker and his pal, Harry the Cat, initiate a small country cricket called Chester into the vagaries of city living. Chester spends only one summer in New York City, having been transported in someone's picnic lunch basket. The climax of Chester's summer adventures comes when the cricket begins giving nightly concerts from the Bellinis' newsstand, saving his benefactors from bankruptcy. In several sequels the animal friends reunite for further adventures. In all these warm and witty books, illustrator Garth Williams creates human expressions for each animal to complement their very real personalities.

Garth Williams also illustrated Margery Sharp's series of tongue-in-cheek melodramas about the pure and beautiful white mouse *Miss Bianca*. The first story, *The Rescuers*, tells of the breathtaking adventure of three mice—Miss Bianca, Bernard, and Nils—as they rescue a Norwegian poet from the grim, windowless Black Castle. *Miss Bianca* is the exciting story of the rescue of a little girl, Patience, from the clutches of a hideous wicked duchess, who lives in the Diamond Palace. The duchess has twelve mechanical ladies-in-waiting who regularly bow to her every hour and say, "as your Grace pleases." The fiendish duchess wants at least one human being who will react to her cruelty, however, so Patience is kidnapped for this purpose. The beautiful and gracious Miss Bianca and the humble and resolute Bernard rescue Patience with the aid of the mouse members of the Ladies Guild. Williams's illustrations portray the hideousness of the duchess, as well as the gentle beauty of Miss Bianca. *The Turret* and *Miss Bianca in the Salt Mines* continue the adventures of these intrepid mice.

In chronicling the year-long survival of a mouse on an island, William Steig firmly establishes himself as a superb author as well as illustrator. *Abel's Island* details the survival of Abel, a very Victorian mouse, who is trapped on an island after being caught in a torrential rainstorm while attempting to retrieve his wife's scarf. Abel tries one ingenious escape plan after another, all without success. Left on his own, this rodent Crusoe finds a hollow log and learns to feed off the land. In addition to battling physical elements, he overcomes the psychological fears of loneliness and overwhelming despair. Finally, after almost a year of foraging for himself, Abel is able, and easily swims the distance to shore. Creating more than a mouse melodrama, Steig shows us what qualities help a mouse or person survive. Stripped of his possessions, Abel relies on his resourcefulness, but he is kept alive by his love for his wife Amanda, his art, his friendship with the forgetful frog, his hatred of the owl, and his joy of life. He is also sustained by two lucky finds, a pocket watch and a book:

🐝 . . . the steady, mechanical tempo of the watch gave him something he had been wanting in this wild place. It and the book helped him feel connected to the civilized world he'd come from. He had no use for the time the watch could tell, but he needed the ticking.[11]

Using the patterns familiar to folktale readers, Steig has also written *Dominic*, the story of an adventuring dog who meets good and evil on his road to happiness, and *The Real Thief*, a tale of a goose wrongly accused. Children delight in Steig's use of language and his allusions to traditional literature's settings, themes, and characters.[12]

What E. B. White did to popularize and humanize spiders, Robert C. O'Brien has accomplished for rats in *Mrs. Frisby and the Rats of NIMH*. Part of the story, which could be categorized as animal fantasy or as science fiction, concerns the widowed mouse Mrs. Frisby and her efforts to save her family and their cement-block house in the garden from the spring plowing. The other part gradually reveals the history of a remarkable band of rats who—along with Mrs. Frisby's late husband—were trained to read and write in a NIMH laboratory (National Institute for Mental Health—although it is never so identified in the story). When Mrs. Frisby meets the rats of NIMH, they are just completing a plan to move to a wilderness preserve where they can establish a self-sufficient community without having to steal from humans. The rats agree to help move the cement block, thus saving Mrs. Frisby's family, and she returns the favor by warning them about government exterminators who are coming with cyanide gas. All but two of the rats escape to their valley, but readers never learn if the unlucky ones include Justin, Mrs. Frisby's friend. Jane Conly,

O'Brien's daughter, has written two sequels. In *Racso and the Rats of NIMH*, Mrs. Frisby's son Timothy meets a cocky and streetwise rat from the city. The self-centered Racso, son of an original rat of NIMH who was thought to have been killed, locates the valley and cooperates with the rats to thwart the building of a dam that would flood their home. *R-T, Margaret, and the Rats Of NIMH* introduces the danger two lost children pose to a nervous rat colony. Short chapters, fast-moving plots advanced frequently by conversation, and memorable characters help make these longer books accessible and exciting to readers.

Another exodus is the focus of Alan Arkin's *The Lemming Condition*. When his friend Crow asks bothersome questions, young Bubber begins to doubt the wisdom of the other lemmings' intention to march over the cliffs to the sea. Can lemmings swim? Still the young lemming finds himself unable to resist the run toward mass suicide, finally feeling at "one with his people." Only at the last moment does Bubber recover his senses and manage to cling to safety in a rock crevice. He sets his course away from the few survivors, declaring that he is "not a lemming anymore." Shorter than *Mrs. Frsiby and the Rats Of NIMH*, this book may prove more difficult for inexperienced readers because of its heavy ironic tone and allegory. Children could discuss ways human beings may act like lemmings by acting irresponsibly about voting, pollution control, saving energy, or deforestation. Writing during the Cold War Era, Arkin made a personal statement about humankind's mad rush to possible extinction in an atomic war.

The well-loved *The Wind in the Willows* by Kenneth Grahame endures even though it is slow-paced, idyllic, and more sentimental than more modern animal fantasy. It is the story of four friends: kindly and gruff old Badger, practical and good-natured Ratty, gullible Mole, and boisterous, expansive, and easily misled Toad. While Toad gets into one scrape after another, the other three loyally rescue their errant friend and finally save his elegant mansion from a band of wicked weasels and stoats. The themes of friendship, the importance of a home place, and the love of nature pervade this pastoral fantasy. Not all children have the experience or patience

[11]William Steig, *Abel's Island* (New York: Farrar, Straus & Giroux 1976), p. 58.
[12]See "*The Real Thief: Reading Like a Writer*" in Joy Moss's *Focus Units on Literature: A Context for Literacy Learning* (Katonah, N.Y.: Richard C. Owen, 1990) for a discussion of this book's classroom use and its impact on older elementary school readers.

TEACHING FEATURE

KEEPING JOURNALS HELPS CHILDREN
UNDERSTAND FANTASY

In September, a sixth-grade language arts teacher asked her students to keep a journal and react to Robert C. O'Brien's *Mrs. Frisby and the Rats of NIMH*. She divided the book into about ten parts and children responded in their journals after reading each assignment. The diversity of children's responses showed how differently individual readers engage with a story.

One girl challenged the believability of this fantasy:

"I wonder where Mr. Ages gets the paper for the bags for medicine? . . . . I wonder how Mrs. Frisby can hold on to Jeremy's back. She's too small to wrap her 'arms' around it. I also wonder how mice can understand people talk." The teacher acknowledged her concerns and invited her to try to find some answers. She also reminded her that this was an animal fantasy which had its own rules.

Another girl sympathized with Mrs. Frisby's very modern predicament and mused about the humor of the story:

"Mrs. Frisby has a lot on her mind being a single parent with four children and one sick in bed with pneumonia. I would feel really pressured like that and Moving Day coming. . . . I like the crow Jeremy. He's funny and stupid. He picked up the string because it was *sparkly*. (That's cute.)" The teacher called attention to the way an author creates believability when she wrote back, "O'Brien has given the crow some human characteristics but has kept the animal habits faithful to the species."

Children asked questions: "I don't understand what the Boniface Estate is," said one. "I still have a question. What does *NIMH* stand for?" asked another. A third lamented, "All my questions aren't answered yet. I may seem like a bottomless pit of questions." The teacher reassured them that it is fine to have questions, clarified meanings, or referred a child to a classmate or back to a page in the book.

Some children worried about the morality of experimenting on animals: "I am very very very very very mad that they give those poor rats shocks plus giving the rats injections. I think it is very mean"; "It made me wonder if given injections, animals are in as much pain as they look." The teacher asked children to talk about the animal experimentation in this story and scientific experimentation in general.

In their final journal entries, some children were dissatisfied with the ending. "I think he should have put more pictures in and made the story a couple of chapters longer. He should have said something about like how Jeremy had a family." "Who died in the rat hole?" Others found the sequels and filled themselves in on what happened next.

Writing journals allowed the children to work out the meaning of the story for themselves. They also revealed themselves to the teacher in ways that would help her plan discussions, choose books, select writing topics, and diversify instruction for the rest of the school year.

Based on journals selected from the sixth-grade language arts class
taught by Susan Steinberg, George Mason Elementary School, Alexandria, Virginia.

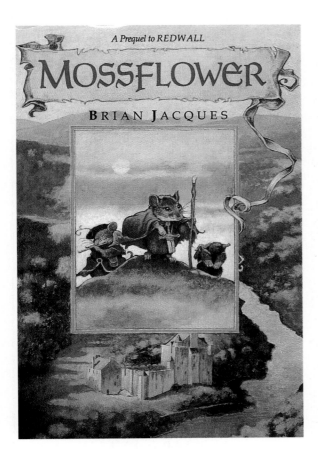

The brave Martin the Mouse leads his followers on a dangerous quest in Brian Jacques's *Mossflower*, a prequel to his *Redwall*.

Jacket illustration by Troy Howell.

with words to appreciate this book, but generations of parents have read it aloud a chapter at a time, which is, perhaps, the best way to introduce the book. One other way would be to share Adrienne Adams's beautifully illustrated picture book of just the first chapter titled *The River Bank* or one of two excerpts illustrated by Beverly Gooding, *The Open Road* and *Wayfarers All: From the Wind in the Willows*.

The villainous animals threatening Toad Hall in *The Wind in the Willows* are the same sorts who threaten Redwall Abbey in Brian Jacques's "Redwall" trilogy. But this series is swiftly told,

complexly plotted, and action-packed by comparison. In *Mossflower*, readers are introduced to Martin the Warrior, the mouse who leads a band of animals against the evil wildcat, Tsarmina. The wildcats have taken over Redwall Abbey and are decimating the population and demanding huge food tariffs. Frequent scene changes and a memorable but huge cast of characters make this lengthy story a challenge to readers. Although it is a sequel to *Mossflower*, *Redwall* seems an easier starting place. It tells of Matthias, a clumsy, young, and peace-loving mouse who galvanizes himself to defeat the evil rat, Cluny the Scourge. Aided by Cornflower the Fieldmouse, Constance the Badger, and Brother Methuselah, Matthias's efforts to fortify the Abbey alternate with chapters of the terrible Cluny subduing woodland creatures to his will. The sinister names of Cluny's band (Fangborn, Cheesethief, Ragear, Mangefur) alert young readers to the evil characters. In fact, one of the major appeals of the story is that one never doubts good will triumph. While one ancient adviser to Matthias dies, most other heroes are merely wounded in the endless skirmishes and battles. The mystery of a lost sword, curious clues on a stairway, secret passages, adventures on the Abbey roof and underground, plus the cliffhanger structure of alternating chapters, keep children on the edges of their seats. In a third story *Mattimeo*, son of Matthias, is kidnapped along with other animals and led to the underground rat kingdom of Malkarris. In the exciting fourth book of the series, *Mariel of Redwall*, a feisty mousemaid leads a successful fight to recover the bell her father made for the Abbey. This series resembles high fantasy (discussed later in this chapter) in that good and evil battle for possession of the Redwall Abbey world; quests are undertaken; the heroes are small, unprepared, and sometimes unwilling; and courage, truth, wisdom, and goodness are finally rewarded. While these books are long, they provide satisfaction to readers who enjoy adventurous quests, humor, and intrigue but are not yet ready for the deeper themes, ambiguous characters, or created worlds of high fantasy.

When *Watership Down* by Richard Adams was first published in England, one reviewer maintained that the "story is what one might expect had *The Wind in the Willows* been written after two world wars, various marks of nuclear bomb, the Korean and Vietnam obscenities and half a dozen other hells created by the inexhaustibly evil powers of man."[13] Published as adult fiction in the United States, this remarkable story of a rabbit band who cherish their freedom enough to fight for it is presented in a lengthy and complex book inaccessible to many children. Adams has created a complete rabbit civilization including a history, religion, mythology, and even a lapine language with a partial set of accompanying linguistic rules. The central character is Hazel, a young buck who leads a little band of bucks away from their old warren that is doomed by a new housing tract. He does so reluctantly but at the urging of his younger and weaker brother, Fiver, who has a form of extrasensory perception. The slow, steady growth of Hazel as a leader is told in this surprisingly unsentimental, even tough story. It is more realistic than most "realism" because the story is firmly rooted in a world we know: rabbits mate, make droppings, and talk and joke about both, very much as humans do. They get hurt, bleed, and suffer; they grow ugly with age and they die. During their storytelling sessions readers learn of El-ahrairah, the great chief rabbit and trickster. In a remarkable creation legend and a deeply moving story, a rabbit redeemer braves the palace of death to offer his own life for his people. And at the end of the book, when one of the does tells her little one a new story of El-ahrairah, we know that she is telling a garbled version of the story of the establishment of Watership Down and adding Hazel's accomplishments to those of the legendary rabbit—a comment on the entire process of mythmaking.

The World of Toys and Dolls

As authors have endowed animals with human characteristics, so, too, have they personified toys and dolls. Young children enjoy stories that bring inanimate objects such as a tugboat or a steamshovel to life. Seven-, 8-, and 9-year-olds still like to imagine that their favorite playthings have a life of their own. Hans Christian Andersen appealed to this in his stories of "The Steadfast Tin Soldier," "The Fir Tree," and many others.

Probably no one has made toys seem quite so much like people as has A. A. Milne in his well-loved Pooh stories. Each chapter contains a separate adventure about the favorite stuffed toys of Milne's son, Christopher Robin. The good companions include *Winnie-the-Pooh*, a bear of little brain; Eeyore, the doleful donkey; Piglet, the happy follower and devoted friend of Pooh; and Rabbit; Owl; Kanga; and little Roo. A bouncy new friend, Tigger, joins the group in Milne's second book, *The House at Pooh Corner*. They all live in the "100 Aker Wood" and spend most of their time getting into—and out of—exciting and amusing situations. Eight- and 9-year-olds thoroughly enjoy the humor of the Heffalump story, the self-pity of gloomy Eeyore on his birthday, and kindly but forgetful Pooh, who knocks at his own door and then wonders why no one answers. The humor in these stories is not hilarious but quiet, whimsical, and subtle. Such humor is usually lost on young children, but is greatly appreciated by third graders. However, younger children may enjoy the Pooh stories when they are read within a family circle. Parents' chuckles are contagious, and soon the whole family become Pooh admirers.

Rumer Godden makes the world of toys seem very much alive in several of her books—*The Dolls' House*, *Fu-Dog*, *Miss Happiness and Miss Flower*, and *Little Plum*. The idea expressed in all Godden's doll books is stated best by Toddie in *The Dolls' House*. She says: "It is an anxious, sometimes a dangerous thing to be a doll. Dolls cannot choose; they can only be chosen; they cannot 'do'; they can only be done by."[14]

A doll who tries to "do" rather than be "done by" is portrayed in *Caitlin's Holiday* by Helen V. Griffith. Caitlin gives in to an irresistible urge at a resale shop and trades her old doll for the most perfect doll she has ever seen. "She had big violet eyes, a smooth deep tan, and lots of fluffy,

---

[13]Aidan Chambers, "Letter from England: Great Leaping Lapins!" in *The Horn Book Magazine*, vol. 49, no. 3 (June 1973), p. 255.

[14]Rumer Godden, *The Dolls' House*, illustrated by Tasha Tudor (New York: Viking, 1962; first published in England in 1947), p. 13.

gold-silver hair. She was wearing a khaki shirt and shorts and high white boots. A little stereo hung from a strap over her shoulder."[15] Sure that this doll is worth the guilt she feels over practically stealing the doll, Caitlin is rewarded by being awakened by the doll's stereo playing in the night. But the doll is not only alive, she is also rude and self-centered, aggressively intent on keeping her tan and regaining her wardrobe, which Caitlin has left at the resale shop. Holiday, the doll, insists on spending Caitlin's allowance on fancy doll clothes, refusing to wear the old doll's less fashionable ones. Holiday also refuses to play with Caitlin and her friends and will not turn down her stereo at night. After trying to reason with the amoral doll, Caitlin angrily relegates her to the garage where she scares a would-be intruder and redeems herself. Caitlin's struggle to explain what a friend is and Holiday's promise to try to be one set the stage for sequels. Girls who have enjoyed playing with fashion-model dolls will enjoy the vicarious experience of owning a live doll. Susan Condie Lamb's pencil drawings of Caitlin and her friends lend further appeal to this story.

Miss Hickory by Carolyn Bailey is the story of a unique country doll whose body is an applewood twig and whose head is a hickory nut. Miss Hickory has all the common sense and forthright qualities that her name implies. She survives a severe New Hampshire winter in the company of her friends—Crow, Bull Frog, Ground Hog, and Squirrel. It is Squirrel who nearly ends it all when he eats Miss Hickory's head, but the headless twig becomes a graft on an old McIntosh apple tree.

In *The Indian in the Cupboard* by Lynne Reid Banks, a toy plastic Indian comes to life when Omri puts it inside a cupboard, locks it, and then unlocks it with a special key. Nine-year-old Omri feels pride and responsibility in caring for "his" Indian, Little Bear, and is quickly involved in providing for his needs. But trouble begins when Omri's friend Patrick places a cowboy in the cupboard. The British author gives stereotypical lan-

[15]Helen V. Griffith, *Caitlin's Holiday*, illustrated by Susan Condie Lamb (New York: Greenwillow, 1990), p. 12.

guage to Little Bear ("Little Bear fight like mountain lion. Take many scalps!") and the cowboy Boone ("I ain't sharin' m'vittles with no lousy scalp-snafflin' Injun and that's m'last word!"), but the characters transcend this in their growing concern for each other's welfare. Banks suggests once again to readers that we are responsible for what we have tamed or brought to life. In sequels, *The Return of the Indian* carries Omri back to Little Bear's world; *The Secret of the Indian* takes place in a contemporary setting where Omri and the tiny beings frighten "skinhead" robbers away.

As in the previous title, Elizabeth Winthrop's *The Castle in the Attic* also examines responsibility for one's own actions. Although an accomplished gymnast, 10-year-old William lacks confidence in himself. When he hears that Mrs. Phillips, his lifelong friend and live-in babysitter, is returning to her native England, he is crushed but determined to find a way to make her stay. After she brings him her parting gift, a huge model of a castle which has been in her family for generations, William discovers that one tiny lead knight comes to life at his touch. The knight reveals the presence of a wizard's amulet from another time and place, a charm that can be used to miniaturize objects or people. Almost at once William regrets his decision to reduce his babysitter to toy size and keep her in the castle. To undo this wrong, he must submit himself to the charm, travel back in time with the knight, and recover the amulet that will reverse the spell. Away from Mrs. Phillips for the first time, he discovers unexpected strengths and returns victorious. He is also prepared to wish his friend farewell and has become a more confident gymnast as well. The strong grounding in reality and the elaborately described castle give this fantasy special appeal for upper elementary students.

The inventive plot and memorable characters created by Richard Kennedy in *Amy's Eyes* help sustain reader interest in this lengthy but compelling story. Left at an orphanage by her sailor father, Amy is delighted when her sailor doll comes to life and becomes a ship's captain. In spite of wicked doings at the orphanage, and Amy's pining away until she becomes a doll, the captain is able to take her off on a voyage to hunt for treasure. The ship is "manned" by an odd lot: Skivvy who is made from long underwear, a crew of stuffed animals brought to life by a dose of Mother Goose and a needle-prick in the head, an evil cook who is not what she seems, and a lovesick frog. Together, they eventually outwit the pirate Goldnose and discover Amy's father, but not without a terrible price. The language is unusual, often poetic, and frequent humorous passages move the story to its serious conclusion. While fourth graders have enjoyed hearing the story read aloud, its length, complexity, and numerous philosophical and nautical digressions make it more suitable for older and more proficient readers of fantasy.

A strangely cruel yet tender tale by Russell Hoban, *The Mouse and His Child*, tells of two wind-up toys and their efforts to become "self-winding." New and shiny in the toy shop the day before Christmas, the naive little toys end up on the rubbish heap in the cruel clutches of Manny Rat. In their long and tedious journey to the outside world they search for a home, a family, and "their territory." A combination of many coincidences returns them to the dump, where they find "their doll house," establish their family, and defeat Manny Rat. In fact, Manny becomes "Uncle Manny" in his total conversion. The story is not a gentle one. It is filled with images of death and decay, violence and vengeance, tears and laughter. Like *Alice's Adventures in Wonderland*, the complex ideas, satire, and symbolism may appeal more to adults than to children. Yet it is a fantasy that is not easily forgotten.

Eccentric Characters and Preposterous Situations

Many humorous fantasies for children are based on eccentric characters or preposterous situations. Cars or people may fly, eggs may hatch into dinosaurs or dragons, and lizard bands may appear on television. Often these characters and situations occur in otherwise very normal settings—which allows readers to believe more readily.

Pippi Longstocking, a notoriously funny character created by Astrid Lindgren, has delighted children for more than forty years. Pippi is an orphan who lives alone with her monkey and her horse in a child's utopian world where she tells herself when to go to bed and when to get up! Pippi takes care of herself most efficiently and has a wonderful time doing it. Although she is only 9 years old, Pippi can hold her own with anyone, for she is so strong that she can pick up a horse or a man and throw him into the air. Children love this amazing character who always has the integrity to say what she thinks, even if she shocks adults. Actually, children admire Pippi's carefree existence. Seven-, 8-, and 9-year-olds enjoy her madcap adventures in the sequels to the original Pippi book, *Pippi Goes on Board*, *Pippi in the South Seas*, and *Pippi on the Run*.

When the east wind blew *Mary Poppins* by P. L. Travers into the Bankses' house in London to care for Michael and Jane, it blew her into the hearts of many thousands of readers. Wearing her shapeless hat and white gloves, carrying her parrot-handled umbrella and a large carpetbag, Mary Poppins is as British as tea, yet many children in the United States also love this nursemaid with strange magical powers. One favorite story is that of the laughing-gas party. Jane, Michael, and Mary Poppins visit Mary Poppins's uncle for tea, only to be overcome by fits of uncontrollable laughter. As a result, they all float right up to the ceiling. Mary Poppins raises the table in some way, and they have birthday tea suspended in midair! Nothing seems impossible for this prim autocrat of the nursery to perform. Mary Poppins goes serenely on her way through other funny adventures in *Mary Poppins Comes Back*, *Mary Poppins Opens the Door*, and *Mary Poppins in the Park*.

The story of *Mr. Popper's Penguins* by Richard and Florence Atwater has long been the favorite funny story of many primary-grade children. This is the tale of Mr. Popper, a mild little house painter whose major interest in life is the study of the Antarctic. An explorer presents Mr. Popper with a penguin, which he promptly names Captain Cook. In order to keep Captain Cook from becoming lonely, Mr. Popper obtains Greta from the zoo. After the arrival of ten baby penguins, Mr. Popper puts a freezing plant in the basement of his house and moves his furnace upstairs to the living room. The Atwaters' serious account of a highly implausible situation adds to the humor of this truly funny story.

In *James and the Giant Peach* by Roald Dahl, James, one of the saddest and loneliest boys in the world, lives with his wicked aunts in an old, ramshackle house on a high hill in the south of England. James meets a queer old man who thrusts a bag of green crystals into his hands and tells him that if he adds water to the crystals and then drinks the mixture, he'll never be miserable again. Intent upon getting to the kitchen without being seen by his aunts, James falls, and all of the magic crystals disappear into the ground right under the old peach tree. In the enormous peach that grows on the tree, James discovers six amazing creatures who have been waiting for him—a grasshopper the size of a large dog, a giant ladybug, an enormous spider, a centipede, an earthworm, and a silkworm. Early the next morning the centipede gnaws off the stem, the huge peach rolls down the hill, incidentally crushing the aunts, on its mad dash to the sea, and the marvelous adventure begins. This wonderful spoof on Victorian morality tales features well-drawn characters whose grumbling conversations are very believable. The illustrations by Nancy Burkert are beautifully detailed and reflect the pathos and joy of James's "fabulous flight." This book is popular with children of all ages. Its short chapters make it a good read-aloud selection for first and second graders, as well as for older children.

Another popular book is Dahl's *Matilda*, which tells the sad story of a little girl genius who is cursed with stupid and self-centered parents and victimized by her school's headmistress, Miss Trunchbull. The precocious Matilda uses her brainpower to overcome injustice, get rid of her awful parents, and move into a mansion with her dear teacher Miss Honey. While older children respond to revenge and Dahl's use of vulgarity and caricature to evoke humor, adults may wish for less cruelty and violence in this and other books by Dahl.

Still another fabulous flight is recorded in the story of *The Twenty-One Balloons* by William Pène du Bois. Professor Sherman leaves San Francisco on August 15, 1883, in a hot air balloon, telling reporters that he hopes to be the first man to fly across the Pacific Ocean. He is picked up three weeks later in the Atlantic Ocean clinging to the wreckage of a platform that has been flown through the air by twenty-one balloons. The story, told as the professor's speech to the Explorers' Club, recounts his forced landing on the island of Krakatoa where he discovers that he is to be a permanent visitor, since the twenty families who live over the most fabulous diamond mine in the world wish to remain unknown. They are extremely gracious to the professor and escort him on a tour of their amazing volcanic island, where houses are built on diamond foundations. The professor describes in graphic detail the inventions and customs of Krakatoans and their escape when the volcano erupts. As usual, the minute description of du Bois's text is matched only by the meticulous perfection of his pen-and-ink drawings.

It seems preposterous to try to raise a dinosaur in a small New Hampshire town. However, that is precisely what Nate Twitchell does when *The Enormous Egg* he is taking care of hatches into a baby triceratops. When government officials in Washington, D.C., are consulted about the problem, members of Congress attempt to have "Uncle Beazley" (the dinosaur) destroyed, since he is extinct and probably un-American! Oliver Butterworth's satire on politics in the United States is a delightful mixture of humor and truth.

Lizards rather than dinosaurs complicate an 11-year-old's life in Daniel Pinkwater's *Lizard Music*. With his older sister on an unauthorized camping trip and his parents away for two weeks, Victor has taken to watching late-night television. The only trouble is that he has begun to see large lizards peering over newscasters' shoulders, making music after the late late movie, or answering questions on a lizard quiz show. On a bus, Victor meets the cheerful but strange Chicken Man, so named for the chicken Claudia who roosts under his hat. The Chicken Man seems to know all about lizards. Back home, Victor muses:

> I like things neat. This situation wasn't neat at all, I decided that I was going to do something about it. Up till now, things had just been happening—not even happening *to* me—just happening in front of me. I wanted to know what was going on. I wanted to make some things happen.[16]

[16]Daniel M. Pinkwater, *Lizard Music* (New York: Dodd Mead, 1976), p. 47.

Victor's determination eventually gains him a tour of a floating island run by lizards. Pinkwater's story is fast-paced, full of zany names, hilarious observations on contemporary society, and bad puns. After one middle-school teacher jokingly awarded an enthusiastic seventh grader a "lizard lover's" card, he and other students formed a school club. Potential members had to pass a student-made test on the book, and many students went on to read other Pinkwater books. Other books by Pinkwater, including *The Magic Moscow*, and *Slaves of Spiegel*, rely on the same crazy blend of humor, eccentric characters, and preposterous situations. While these slim books are more accessible to younger readers than *Lizard Music*, they are read with enthusiasm by older readers as well.

Freaky Friday by Mary Rodgers hinges on one impossible situation: when Annabel wakes up one morning, she finds she has switched places with her mother. She looks like her mother, must meet her mother's obligations and appointments, but thinks and acts as Annabel. In Rodgers's *Summer Switch*, Ape Face suddenly finds himself in the body of his father. Instead of going to summer camp, he is about to leave for Beverly Hills and a new job. While *Freaky Friday* is told by Annabel, *Summer Switch* is hilariously related, in alternating typefaces, first by Ape Face in California and then by his father at Camp Soonawissakit. While in both sets of switches the characters gain a new understanding of each other, it is the humor that carries the stories along and makes either a good candidate for reading aloud in fifth- or sixth-grade classrooms.

A preposterous situation is presented in one of the few satires really enjoyed by children, Jean Merrill's *The Pushcart War*. The story is presented as a "documented report" of the famous Pushcart War of 1986. Believing that we cannot have peace in the world unless people understand how wars start, the "author-historian" proceeds to describe the beginning of the war between the giant trucks of New York City and the pushcarts that began when Mack, driver of the Mighty Mammoth, rode down the cart of Morris the Florist. Like the Minutemen of the American Revolution, the 509 pushcart peddlers unite in their fight against the three largest trucking firms in the city. At first their fragile carts are crushed like matchboxes,

but then the loyal band of defenders develops the old-fashioned peashooter into a highly effective weapon. The straight-faced account of the progress of the war and the eventual triumph of the pushcart peddlers provide a funny and pathetic commentary on life today. Children thoroughly enjoy this satire; in fact, one fifth-grade class returned for report cards on the last day of school and stayed an extra hour while their teacher finished reading the book. Few books can claim such devotion!

Extraordinary Worlds

When Alice followed the White Rabbit down his rabbit hole and entered a world that grew "curiouser and curiouser," she established a pattern for many modern books of fantasy. Starting in the world of reality they move quickly into a world where the everyday becomes extraordinary, yet still believable. The plausible impossibilities of Lewis Carroll's *Alice's Adventures in Wonderland* include potions and edibles that make poor Alice grow up and down like an elevator. At the famous "Mad Hatter's Tea Party" no one has the time to drink tea. The Mad Hatter, the Dormouse, and the Rabbit are just a few of the individuals Alice meets in her wanderings. Other characters include the Red Queen, who has to keep running in order to stay "in the same place"; the hurrying White Rabbit, who keeps murmuring that he'll be late—yet no one knows where he is going; Humpty Dumpty, whose words mean exactly what he chooses them to mean; and the terrifying Queen of Hearts, who indiscriminately shouts, "Off with her head." Always the proper Victorian young lady, Alice maintains her own personality despite her bizarre surroundings, and her acceptance of this nonsense makes it all seem believable. She is the one link with reality in this amazingly fantastic world.

Children are often surprised to find *Alice* and *Through the Looking Glass* the source of many words and expressions used in the popular culture. While many children do not have the maturity or sense of wordplay required to appreciate this fantasy, teachers or librarians might read aloud popular selections, such as the Jabberwocky or the Mad Hatter's Tea Party and encourage those who enjoy them to read the entire book.

The cyclone that blew Dorothy into the Land of Oz continues to blow swirling controversies around this series of books by L. Frank Baum and others. Some maintain that *The Wizard of Oz* is a skillfully written fantasy, a classic in its own right. Others condemn the first book because some of the forty-plus volumes that followed are poorly written. Dorothy, her dog Toto, the Scarecrow, the Tin Woodman, and the Cowardly Lion make the long, hazardous trip to the Emerald City to seek special gifts from the Wonderful Wizard. Eventually each of the characters achieves his or her particular wish, but the wizardry is what they do for themselves, rather than anything that the Wizard does for them. For the most part this fantasy depends on the strange situations and creatures that Dorothy and her companions meet. Adults never doubt that the four will overcome all odds and achieve their wishes. Even the Wizard holds no terror for practical, matter-of-fact Dorothy. This lack of wonder and awe—the basic ingredients of most fantasy—make *The Wizard of Oz* seem somewhat pedestrian when compared with other books of its kind.

For many years the Moomintroll family has delighted the children of Sweden. Strange but endearing creatures that look slightly like hippopotamuses, the Moomin live in a lonely valley with various peculiar friends. Each member of the Moomin family is an individual and remains faithful to his or her characterization throughout the series of books. *Tales from Moominvalley* by Tove Jansson is the first and, perhaps, best of this fantastic series.

Mary Norton tells a fascinating story about tiny people and their miniature world under the grandfather clock in *The Borrowers*. The Borrowers derive their names from their occupation, which is "borrowing" from human "beans," those "great slaves put there for them to use." "Borrowing" is a dangerous trade, for if one is seen by human beings, disastrous things may happen. Therefore, Pod and Homily Clock are understandably alarmed when they learn of their daughter Arrietty's desire to explore the world upstairs. Finally, Pod allows Arrietty to go on an

Illustrators Beth and Joe Krush have skillfully shown the comparative sizes of the tiny borrower and the boy when Arrietty meets a "human bean" in Mary Norton's *The Borrowers*.

expedition with him. While Pod is borrowing fibers from the hall doormat to make a new brush for Homily, Arrietty wanders outside, where she meets the boy. Arrietty's disbelief about the number of people in the world who are the boy's size, compared to those of her size, is most convincing:

> "Honestly—" began Arrietty helplessly and laughed again. "Do you really think—I mean, whatever sort of world would it be? Those great chairs . . . I've seen them. Fancy if you had to make chairs that size for everyone? And the stuff for their clothes . . . miles and miles of it . . . tents of it . . . and the sewing! And their great houses, reaching up so you can hardly see the ceilings . . . their great beds . . . the food they eat . . . great smoking mountains of it, huge bags of stew and soup and stuff."[17]

In the end, the Borrowers are "discovered" and flee for their lives. This surprise ending leads directly to the sequel called *The Borrowers Afield*. Strong characterizations, apt descriptions of setting, and detailed illustrations by Beth and Joe Krush make the small-scale world of the Borrowers come alive. Other titles continue the series.

The story of the Minnipins, mostly sober, sedate, and tradition-bound little folk in The Land Between the Mountains, is told in *The Gammage Cup* by Carol Kendall. When a "best village" contest is announced, the people of Slipper-on-the-Water decide that in order to win the coveted Gammage cup, all homes must be painted green and all Minnipins must wear green. Muggles speaks for the nonconforming few who insist on bright doors and orange sashes:

> ". . . it's no matter what color we paint our doors or what kind of clothes we wear, we're . . . well, we're those colors inside us. Instead of being green inside, you see, like other folk. So I don't think it would do any good if we just changed our outside color."[18]

The rebellious ones are exiled to the mountains, where by chance they discover a threat to the village from the Minnipins' ancient enemies, the Mushrooms. Muggles and her companions sound the alarm, save the village, and are welcomed back as heroes. This well-written fantasy offers tart commentary on false values in society and the theme of the individual versus the group. Ironically, the gentle Minnipins prove to be surprisingly fierce in their encounter with the Mushrooms.

One of the most popular fantasies for children is Roald Dahl's tongue-in-cheek morality tale, *Charlie and the Chocolate Factory*. Mr. Willie Wonka, owner of the mysterious locked chocolate factory, suddenly announces that the five children who find the gold seal on their chocolate bars will be allowed to visit his fabulous factory. And what an assortment of children win—Augustus Gloop, a greedy fat pig of a boy; Veruca Salt, a spoiled little rich girl whose parents always buy her what she wants; Violet Beauregarde, the world's champion gum chewer; Mike Teevee, a fresh child who spends every waking moment in front of the television set; and Charlie Bucket, a hero, who is honest, brave, trustworthy, obedient, poor, and starving. One by one the children disobey and meet with horrible accidents in the chocolate factory. Nothing, of course, happens to the virtuous Charlie, who by the story's conclusion has brought his poor family to live in the chocolate factory and is learning the business from his benefactor. The 1964 edition of this book was criticized for its stereotypical depiction of the Oompa-Loompas, black pygmies supposedly imported from Africa by Mr. Wonka and exploited as factory workers.[19] In the 1973 edition, Dahl revised the text so that the Oompa-Loompas were long-haired little people imported from Loompaland. The sequel to this book, *Charlie and the Great Glass Elevator*, lacks the humor and the imaginative sparkle of the first book.

Going through *The Phantom Tollbooth*, Milo discovers a strange and curious world indeed. Norton Juster creates "The Lands Beyond," which include the Foothills of Confusion, the Mountains of Ignorance, the Lands of Null, the

[17]Mary Norton, *The Borrowers*, illustrated by Beth and Joe Krush (New York: Harcourt Brace Jovanovich, 1953), p. 78.

[18]Carol Kendall, *The Gammage Cup*, illustrated by Erik Blegvad (New York: Harcourt Brace Jovanovich, 1959), pp. 91–92.

[19]Lois Kalb Bouchard, "A New Look at Old Favorites: 'Charlie and the Chocolate Factory'," *Interracial Books for Children*, vol. 3 (Winter/Spring 1971), pp. 3, 8.

Doldrums, and the Sea of Knowledge. Here Milo meets King Azoz the Unabridged, the unhappy ruler of Dictionopolis, the Mathemagician who serves them subtraction stew and increases their hunger, and the watchdog Tock, who keeps on ticking throughout all their adventures. The substance of this fantasy is in its play on words rather than its characters or situations. Its appreciation is dependent on the reader's knowledge of the definitions of various words, phrases, and allusions. For this reason children with mature vocabularies particularly enjoy its humor.

In Emily Rodda's *The Pigs Are Flying!*, readers are introduced to a world, "Inside," which parallels our own—with a few small differences. Rachel, sick in bed and bored, wishes something would happen and finds herself Inside with a terrible storm about to begin. During these storms, called Grunters, pigs actually do fly. Other strange things also happen during storms: a mailman bites dogs, fire fighters set their own firehouse ablaze, and children wander away. So people keep tethered pigs that float in the sky during storms and thus warn everyone to get inside or risk the consequences. Since Rachel arrives during a "force ten Grunter," an elderly couple takes her in to replace their lost daughter who wandered away in a previous storm. Although people here are kind to her, Rachel longs to return to her own life Outside and finally finds the key in the children's room of the library. Porcine word play and funny occurrences are enhanced by Noela Young's clever black line illustrations. A small mystery of a family friend's identity in real time neatly frames Rachel's suspenseful adventure in this extraordinary world where "pigrise" is a dangerous occasion.

Magical Powers

The children in books of fantasy often possess a magic object, know a magic saying, or have magical powers themselves. In *Half Magic* by Edward Eager, the nickel Jane finds turns out to be a magic charm, or at least half of a magic charm, for it provides half of all the children's wishes. Soon the children learn to double their wishes, so that half of them will come true. Eager's *Seven-Day Magic* tells of a magic book that the children borrow from the library. When they open the book, they find it is about themselves; everything they did that morning is in the book and the rest of the book is shut tight waiting for them to create it. Logic and humor are characteristic of the many books of fantasy that were Eager's legacy of modern magic to today's children.

Frequently, less demanding fantasy relies on magical powers, slight characterization, and fast-moving plots to interest less able readers. For instance, Ruth Chew's *Mostly Magic* features two children whose discovery of a magical ladder and pencil transports them to other places and allows them to transform objects. Scott Corbett's "trick" books, such as *The Lemonade Trick*, rely on Kirby Maxwell's use of a magic chemistry set belonging

In Lane Smith's drawing, Joe finds himself on the point of a dilemma when he is magically transported back in time in Jon Scieszka's *Knights of the Kitchen Table.*

to Mrs. Greymalkin, a neighborhood witch. Greedy John Midas suffers the consequences of his newly acquired magical power, *The Chocolate Touch,* in Patrick Skene Catling's new twist on an old story. While none of these stories challenge an accomplished reader, many children come to discover the pleasures of wide reading through books such as these.

The magical object in Jon Scieszka's two "Time Warp Trio" stories is *The Book.* In *Knights of the Kitchen Table,* Joe explains that he had just opened *The Book,* a birthday present from his magician uncle. Suddenly, he and his friends Fred and Sam are whisked back into King Arthur's time and the Black Knight is about to run them down. The boys' quick thinking saves them from this, a foul-smelling giant, and a fire-breathing dragon, before they find their way back to modern time. In *The Not-So-Jolly Roger,* the boys materialize on the island where Blackbeard is about to bury his treasure. In *The Good, the Bad, and the Goofy,* the boys are transported to the Old West. Ten short chapters, broad humor and gross characters, Lane Smith's quirky line illustrations, a fast-moving plot, and contemporary-sounding dialogue appeal especially to fourth- and fifth-grade boys.

Jane Langton has created several stories of mystery and magical powers surrounding the Halls, who live in a strange old turreted house in Concord, Massachusetts. In *The Diamond in the Window,* Uncle Freddy had been a world-renowned authority on Emerson and Thoreau until the mysterious disappearance of his younger brother and sister left him slightly deranged. In the tower room two beds are made up in a vain hope for the return of the two children. Edward and Eleanor move to the tower room and search in their dreams for the two missing members of the family.

Another story of the Hall family, *The Fledgling,* centers upon 8-year-old Georgie's desire and eventual ability to fly. She is befriended by the Goose Prince, who takes her on his back and teaches her to glide in the air by herself. Although Georgie outgrows her gift and the goose falls prey to a gun, he leaves her with a magical present, a ball that projects an image of the whole world, and the admonition, *"Take good care of it."* While

the villains Preak and Prawn are presented as satirizations of the world's attitudes, Georgie and her family are lovingly portrayed. Langton's descriptions give the story a warm and comfortable tone (the closet "smelled of warm rubbers and moth flakes and woolen cloth"); her evocation of flying may make earthbound readers' spirits soar. Another story, *The Summer Birds* by Penelope Farmer, presents child flyers taught by a strange boy who hopes to draw them to his island to restore his birdlike race. However, Farmer's story is darker and its conclusion less hopeful than in *The Fledgling.*

In a much lighter vein, Sid Fleischman sets his fantasy *The Midnight Horse* near another New England town of Cricklewood, New Hampshire: "Population 217. 216 Fine Folks & 1 Infernal Grouch." An orphan comes to claim his inheritance from the infernal grouch, a shady judge who is his great-uncle. Fleischman, in setting the scene, minces no words:

> It was raining bullfrogs. The coach lurched and swayed along the river road like a ship in rough seas. Inside clung three passengers like unlashed cargo.
>
> One was a blacksmith, another was a thief, and the third was an orphan boy named Touch.[20]

On the stormy ride, the honest blacksmith points out a real "haunt" who is riding the roof of the carriage for sport. It is "The Great Chaffalo," a magician who can among other tricks turn a heap of straw into a horse. (Chaffalo became a ghost in an unsuccessful attempt to catch a bullet in his teeth.) When Touch arrives in Cricklewood, his great-uncle Judge Wigglesforth tries to force him to sign for his inheritance, thirty-seven cents. No fool, Touch refuses to sign and escapes to a ramshackle inn run by a young woman who is about to sell it for a poor price to the conniving judge. In fast-paced, humorous short chapters, Touch discovers his real inheritance, saves the inn, and unmasks both the thief and the judge. Fleischman's ear for comic dialogue, his inspired similes, and his ability to strip a tale to its essen-

[20]Sid Fleischman, *The Midnight Horse,* illustrated by Peter Sis (New York: Greenwillow, 1990), p. 1.

Peter Sis's fine line drawing depicts the orphan Touch as he escapes on a bundle of straw magically turned into *The Midnight Horse,* in the book by Sid Fleischman.

❦ ❦ ❦

tials make this a lively story in the same vein as his *The Whipping Boy* (see p. 427).

Older readers with a tolerance for invented worlds and the ability to follow a large cast of characters will enjoy the work of Diana Wynne Jones. Stories featuring the magician Chrestomanci are a good place to begin. In *Charmed Life,* young Eric Chant (called Cat for short) and his haughty, conniving sister Gwendolyn are invited to live at a castle where time seems to exist on its own. While Cat is unaware of his own magic talents, his sister has been using minor witchcraft to borrow power from her brother to make her magic the most potent of all. Chrestomanci, the master of the castle, must help Cat realize his own powers while he preserves his own household of eccentric magicians against the evil that assails them from outside the castle walls. *The Lives of Christopher Chant,* a prequel, is about the boyhood of Chrestomanci, who is able to dream himself into strange worlds and bring back from these places what others cannot. Like Eric he is naive about adult motives, an unwitting accomplice to his uncle's wicked plans, and an unwilling heir to the previous Chrestomanci's power. These imaginatively plotted stories reveal the author's wry humor, her love of language, and her ability to balance aspects of time and space in impossible but believable ways.

Suspense and the Supernatural

Interest in the occult and the supernatural, always an adult preoccupation, also captures the imagination of children. They enjoy spooky, scary stories, just as they like being frightened by TV or theater horror stories. This may in part explain the popularity of such authors as John Bellairs, whose mysteries such as *The House with a Clock in Its Walls* are full of spooky old houses, scary characters, fast-moving plots, and plenty of dialogue. Increasingly, publishers issue finely crafted suspense fantasies that are often superior to the usual ghost story or mystery tale. These well-written tales of suspense and the supernatural deserve attention.

Paul Fleischman's *The Half-A-Moon Inn* has the tone of a folktale and a setting to match. Born mute, 12-year-old Aaron feels a new independence when his mother lets him stay home while she takes the cart to market. When it later becomes apparent that his mother is lost in a great snowstorm, Aaron sets off to find her. He accidentally stumbles into the Half-A-Moon Inn, where he is imprisoned by the evil Miss Grackle, who needs a boy to tend the bewitched fires none but honest folk may kindle. Aaron soon discovers that Miss Grackle reads her patrons' dreams and robs them of their riches but he is unable to run away because she has stolen his boots and his warm clothes. Aaron's escape, his reunion with his mother, and the folktale-like demise of the witch (she freezes to death beside her unlit fireplace) provide a satisfying conclusion. The narration is lighter than the content, and the well-wrought dialogue makes this a challenging and entertaining choice for reading aloud to 9- and 10-year-olds.

Mollie Hunter mingles long-ago legend with present-day mystery in *The Haunted Mountain*. In the lonely mountain passes of the Scottish Highlands the country folk still heed the ancient lore, which bids them to give a parcel of their land to the "Good People," so called to disguise their evil nature. But MacAllister, a strong and stubborn crofter, ignores a warning not to defy these shadowy creatures. He needs money to marry his Peigi-Ann, and so he dares to plow the Goodman's Croft. Later, the Good People capture him and chain him to the haunted mountain for seven years. His young son Fergus, cast in the same rugged mold as his father, breaks the evil spell by holding on to his father's hand through the many shape changes the Good People cause MacAllister to endure. This shape-changing motif, common in folktales, is boldly presented in several modern-day retellings such as Jane Yolen's *Tam Lin*. (See box, "Books That Introduce Aspects of Fantasy Novels" for other connections.)

The Mermaid Summer, also by Hunter, explores the ancient legend of a mermaid who was thought to live near "the Drongs" and could lure poor fishermen to their deaths on these rocks. Like MacAllister in *The Haunted Mountain*, Eric Anderson refuses to believe in the legend until he nearly loses his entire fishing crew to her singing. No one will sail with Eric after that and he is forced to leave his wife, son, and two grandchildren named Jon and Anna, and find a place on a large ship leaving for faraway ports. But Anna never gives up hope that her Granda will someday return to the village. Finally, years later he does, but only after Anna and Jon trick the vain and deadly mermaid into removing the curse from their grandfather. Filled with the cadenced language of the storyteller, this tale evokes the rich heritage of Scottish folklore.

Mollie Hunter has based another eerie tale, *A Stranger Came Ashore*, on the old legends of the Shetland Islands that tell of the Selkie Folk, seals who can take on human form. Only young Robbie Henderson and his grandfather are suspicious of the handsome stranger who appears in their midst

In the traditional tale of *Tam Lin*, retold by Jane Yolen, Charles Mikolaycak depicts the moment when Jennet MacKenzie maintains her grip on her shape-changing true love, a motif found in fantasy stories as well.

on the stormy night of a shipwreck. After Old Da dies, Robbie must put together the clues that reveal the real identity of Finn Learson and the sinister nature of his interest in the golden-haired Elspeth, Robbie's sister. Events build to a fearful climax on a night of ancient magic, when the dark powers of the sea are pitted against the common folk dressed as earth spirits and celebrating the last of the yule festival. Teachers who read aloud *A Stranger Came Ashore* find Jane Yolen's picture book *Greyling* or Susan Cooper's *The Selkie Girl*, a good introduction to Selkie lore. Children familiar with these stories are much more sensitive to Hunter's use of foreshadowing, folk beliefs, mood, and setting in this finely crafted novel.

Friendship binds a child from the present with a child from the past in two well-crafted ghost stories. In Pam Conrad's *Stonewords*, Zoe, who lives with her grandparents in an old farmhouse while her flighty mother "shows up when she shows up," makes friends with a strange transparent girl from the past named Zoe Louise whom only she can see. Over the years, the ghost girl appears, plays with Zoe, and enigmatically states that she is looking in Zoe's eyes for "the truth." On a rare visit, Zoe's mother points out the memory roses planted for a child who died on the property. When Zoe realizes that her ghost friend is that child, she must find out how her death occurs in order to prevent it from happening. A stack of old newspapers moldering away in the basement provides a clue and the real Zoe is able to go up the back stairs into the past and change history and the present as well.

In Mary Downing Hahn's *Wait Till Helen Comes*, another ghost child named Helen has perished in a fire and now waits by a pond to drag children to

RESOURCES FOR TEACHING

♦ BOOKS THAT INTRODUCE ASPECTS OF FANTASY NOVELS ♦

BOOK/AUTHOR	MOTIF, THEME, OR TOPIC	FANTASY NOVEL
Tam Lin, Yolen *Wild Robin*, Jeffers *The Red Cloak*, James *Tam Lin*, Cooper	Shape changing	*The Haunted Mountain*, Hunter
Stone Soup, Brown *The Soup Stone*, Van Rynbach *Stone Soup*, Stewig	"Stone Soup" motif	*The Cat Who Wished to Be a Man*, Alexander

The Tunnel, Browne
The Snow Queen, Andersen
*Elizabeth and the Water
    Troll*, Wangerin
Beauty and the Beast, de Beaumont
	Transformation by love	*The Lion, the Witch, and
		    the Wardrobe*, Lewis
		Amy's Eyes, Kennedy
		A Wrinkle in Time, L'Engle
		The Darkangel, Pierce

The Seal Mother, Gerstein *The Selkie Girl*, Cooper *Greyling*, Yolen	Selkie legend	*A Stranger Came Ashore*, Hunter *Seal Child*, Peck
Rumpelstiltskin, Grimm *Duffy and the Devil*, Zemach	Power of naming	*A Wizard of Earthsea*, Le Guin

Dove Isabeau, Yolen
St. George and the Dragon,
    Hodges
	Nature of western dragons	*The Hobbit*, Tolkien
		Dragon's Blood, Yolen
		Dealing with Dragons,
		    Wrede
		Tristan & Iseult, Sutcliff

Coll and His White Pig,
    Alexander
The Truthful Harp,
    Alexander
	Setting, characters	Prydain Chronicles, Alexander

their deaths as playing companions. When Molly and Michael's mother remarries, their new father's child joins the family, but Heather is a brat who forever whines about imagined injustices. Nobody believes Heather's stories of the ghostly Helen until Molly begins to develop some sympathy for her stepsister's point of view. In a chilling ending, Molly pieces together the mystery, saves Heather from a sure death, and forges a hopeful beginning of a loving family. Hahn's fast-paced story has won numerous state young readers awards showing how much children appreciate a good and scary ghost story.

Margaret Mahy's *The Haunting* blends a ghost story with deft observations of family interactions. Shy Barney Palmer is receiving unwanted messages from a ghostly relative but is afraid to tell anyone, especially his beloved new stepmother who is about to have a baby. At a family gathering, writing appears on a page of a book Barney is looking at and his oldest sister Tabitha pushes him for an explanation while his middle sister Troy seems oblivious to Barney's dilemma. Barney soon discovers that on his real mother's side of the family, there is in each generation a magician or psychic and his black sheep Uncle Cole is the one trying to contact Barney. Cole holds the magic power for his generation, is lonesome for other psychics, and is trying to possess Barney's mind. In an effort to remain normal, Barney struggles against his uncle's mounting frustration and anger. When the malevolent Uncle Cole finally arrives in Barney's house, different family members reveal individual strengths with surprising results. Mahy's trenchant observations of family communications, her deft and often humorous turns of phrases, and a riveting plot make this an excellent choice for reading aloud to older elementary school children.

For sheer nightmare quality, no one can compete with the books of Leon Garfield. He establishes an eerie ominous mood from the very first of *Mister Corbett's Ghost:*

❦ A windy night and the Old Year dying of an ague. Good riddance! A bad Old Year, with a mean spring, a poor summer, a bitter autumn—and now this cold, shivering ague. No one was sorry to see it go. Even

the clouds, all in black, seemed hurrying to its burying—somewhere past Hampstead.[21]

Benjamin wishes his harsh taskmaster, Mr. Corbett, dead when he is ordered to go off on a long delivery errand and is likely to miss the New Year's party. The recipient of the delivery, either the devil himself or a close relative, offers to arrange this for a simple fee, and Benjamin discovers Mr. Corbett's body in the road on the way home. The sad ghost eventually begins to plague the guilty boy, and Ben must bargain once more with the strange old man for the restoration of Mr. Corbett. Ever afterward, Ben thinks differently about his master. Children may recognize the similarities to Dickens's *A Christmas Carol:* in Dickens's story, the man develops compassion for the boy; here, the boy develops compassion for the man.

Another restless spirit is found in *The Ghost of Thomas Kempe* by Penelope Lively. Released from a bottle dislodged by workmen refinishing James Harrison's room, the ghost is determined to harass James into being his apprentice in matters of "Sorcerie, Astrologie, Geomancie, Alchemie, and Recoveries of Goodes Loste." This seventeenth-century poltergeist blows through rooms, causes some small accidents and a near tragedy, and leaves accusing notes in an effort to control James and make his own presence felt in this century. When at last with the help of old Bert Ellis, a handyman and amateur exorcist, the ghost is returned to his final resting place, James experiences a sense of the layers of time coexisting in his English village. Penelope Lively tells a good story with humor, and readers are left with the feeling of being, like James, in the middle of time that reaches away behind and before us.

The opening paragraph of *Sweet Whispers, Brother Rush* by Virginia Hamilton quickly draws the reader into a remarkable story:

❦ The first time Teresa saw Brother was the way she would think of him ever after. Tree fell head over heels for him. It was love at first sight in a wild

[21]Leon Garfield, *Mister Corbett's Ghost*, illustrated by Alan E. Cober (New York: Pantheon, 1968), p. 1.

beating of her heart that took her breath. But it was a dark Friday three weeks later when it rained, hard and wicked, before she knew Brother Rush was a ghost.[22]

Fourteen-year-old Tree takes care of her older brother Dab while her mother, Viola, works in another city as a practical nurse. Viola comes home sporadically to stock the pantry and to leave money for Tree and Dab. Loving "M'Vy," Tree

[22]Virginia Hamilton, *Sweet Whispers, Brother Rush* (New York: Philomel, 1982), p. 9.

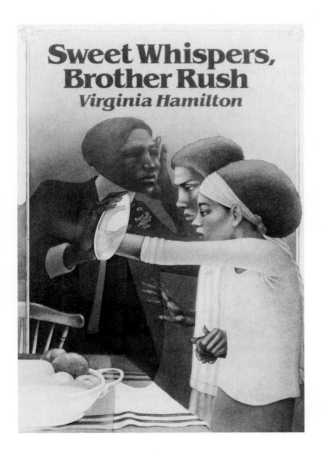

Teresa reaches for images in the mirror held by her uncle's ghost to try to grasp what she has seen but has yet to understand in Leo and Diane Dillon's painting for the jacket of Virginia Hamilton's story *Sweet Whispers, Brother Rush.*

painfully accepts these absences and devotes her time to schoolwork and caring for her brother. As Dab's occasional bouts of sickness suddenly become more frequent, Brother Rush appears to Tree. He has come to "take her out" through a small space he holds in his hand. Looking into this space, Tree becomes an observer of her family's recent past which, until now, she has not questioned. Through Brother Rush, Tree begins to understand why her mother has always avoided Dab, the hereditary nature of Dab's sickness, and something about her father. When Dab is moved to a hospital where he succumbs to the disease, Tree's experiences with Brother Rush enable her to understand what has happened. But it is M'Vy's love and the gentle strength of her companion Silversmith that pull Tree through her anger and despair toward an acceptance of her brother's death and the promise of new extended family relationships. Making use of cadences and inflections of African-American speakers, Hamilton moves surely from narration to dialogue and into Tree's thoughts. She has created complex characters whose steady or fumbling reachings for each other may linger with middle-school readers long past the end of this story.

Time-Shift Fantasy

Probably everyone at one time or another has wondered what it would be like to visit the past. We have looked at old houses and wished they could tell us of their previous occupants; we have held antique jewelry in our hands and wondered about its former owners. Our curiosity has usually been more than just an historical interest; we have wished to communicate, to enter into the lives of the past without somehow losing our own particular place in time.

Recognizing this, authors of books for children have written many fantasies that are based on characters who appear to shift easily from their particular moment in the present to a long-lost point in someone else's past. Usually these time leaps are linked to a tangible object or place that is common to both periods. In *Tom's Midnight Garden* by Philippa Pearce, the old grandfather clock that strikes thirteen hours serves as the fixed point of entry for the fantasy. And in *Playing Beatie Bow* by Ruth Park, Abby slips into the 1870s by virtue of the antique crochet work she wears on her dress; she cannot return to her own time without it.

Julia Sauer's *Fog Magic* is the tender, moving story of Greta Addington, a young girl of Nova Scotia. One day, while walking in the fog, Greta discovers a secret world, the village of Blue Cove. This fishing village is only present in the fog; on sunny days there are just empty cellar holes of houses from the past. Midst the fog magic, Greta meets a girl her own age whose mother senses that Greta is from "over the mountain" and quietly reminds her each time the fog is lifting that it is time to go home. Some occasional knowing looks and comments from Greta's father make her realize that he, too, has visited Blue Cove. Greta is particularly anxious that her twelfth birthday be a foggy day. That evening, when she is on the way home from a church picnic with her father, the fog comes in. She runs back to enter Blue Cove, where her friend's mother gives her a soft gray kitten and quietly wishes her a "Safe passage for all the years ahead." Greta senses that this will be the last time that she will be able to visit Blue Cove. She walks slowly down the hill to find her father waiting. As she shows him her kitten, he reaches into his pocket and pulls out an odd little knife that he had received on his twelfth birthday at Blue Cove. This is a hauntingly beautiful story, memorable for its mood and setting. Part of its appeal may come from the underlying view, common in mystical fantasy, that childhood confers special sensibilities that adults can no longer share.

No one is more skillful in fusing the past with the present than L. M. Boston in her stories of Green Knowe, that mysterious old English house in which the author lived. In *The Children of Green Knowe*, the first in this series, Boston tells the story of Tolly, who is sent to live with his great-grandmother. Over the large fireplace in the drawing room hangs a picture of three children who grew up at Green Knowe in the seventeenth century. When Tolly's great-grandmother tells him stories about the children, they seem so real that Tolly is convinced they often play hide and seek with him. His great-grandmother believes him, and soon the reader does too. Each story of Green Knowe blends a child of the present with characters and situations from previous centuries while creating for the reader a marvelous sense of place.

One of the finest time fantasies ever written is the mysterious and exciting *Tom's Midnight Garden* by Philippa Pearce. Forced to spend part of a summer with a rather boring aunt and uncle, Tom finds his visit quite dull until he hears the grandfather clock in the hall strike thirteen. Then he is able to slip into the garden and play with Hatty, a child of the past. Tom becomes so absorbed in his midnight visits when "there is time no longer," that he does not wish to return home. One fateful night Tom opens the back door and sees only the paving and the fences that stand there in daylight—Hatty and her garden have vanished. When Tom meets the real Hatty Bartholomew, a little old lady, he understands why the weather in the garden has always been perfect, why some nights it has been one season and the next night a different one, why Hatty was sometimes young and sometimes older; it all depended on what old Mrs. Bartholomew had been dreaming. Lonely and bored, Tom joined her in her dreams. This is a fascinating story that should please both boys and girls in the middle grades.

While the characters in most time fantasies slip in and out of the past, the problem in *Tuck Everlasting* is that the Tuck family is trapped forever in the present. Natalie Babbitt's elegant prose leads the reader to expect a quiet Victorian fantasy, but the book holds many surprises—including a kidnapping, a murder, and a jailbreak. The story opens with Winnie Foster, an overprotected 10-year-old, sitting in front of her family's prim touch-me-not cottage on a hot August day talking to a large plump toad. She informs the toad that she wants to do something interesting, something that will make a difference to the world. The very next morning Winnie "runs away" to the nearby woods owned by her parents and sees a young man of 17 (although he first says he is 104 years old) drinking from a spring. When Winnie asks for a drink, Jesse Tuck warns her not to take one. Just at that moment his mother, Mae Tuck, and brother Miles arrive. With all due apologies to Winnie, they bundle her onto their horse to go back to their home to have a talk with Mae's husband, Angus Tuck. On the way, Mae tells Winnie that drinking the spring water has given them everlasting life. Back at the shabby three-room cottage of the Tucks, they all gently try to persuade Winnie to guard their secret. In the morning Angus Tuck takes Winnie rowing on the lake and explains to her what it is like to live forever. He longs for a natural conclusion to his life. "I want to grow again, . . . and change. And if that means I got to move on at the end of it, then I want that, too."[23] Although the Tucks intend to let Winnie Foster make her own decision, they do not know that a man in a yellow suit, who has been searching for them for years, has overheard Mae Tuck reveal their secret to Winnie. Caught in the melodrama of the Tucks' lives, Winnie decides to protect and help them, a decision that does indeed change her life. The simplicity of the Tucks and their story belies the depth of the theme of *Tuck Everlasting*. With its prologue and epilogue, the story is reminiscent of a play, a kind of *Our Town* for children.

Many fantasies written in the United States seem more lighthearted than those of the British. For example, Edward Ormondroyd's *Time at the Top* is a refreshingly different time fantasy. It starts out with a windy, wretched day when everything goes wrong, until Susan meets and helps a funny little old "Mary Poppins-ish" woman who says she will "give her three." When Susan pushes the elevator button for the top floor where she and her father live, the elevator keeps right on going to the eighth floor—except there is no eighth floor. Susan gets off and finds herself in a different time and different place. How she makes friends with Victoria and her brother Robert and solves their financial difficulties and their widowed mother's marital problems makes for a fast-paced, amusing story. *All in Good Time* is a sequel to this time fantasy.

Mystery is also an important part of the complex fantasy by Eleanor Cameron titled *The Court of the Stone Children*. The story of modern-day Nina, who has a "Museum Feeling" and thinks she would like to be a curator, is intertwined with the story of Dominique, a young noblewoman of nineteenth-century France whose father was executed by Napoleon's regime and whose family possessions are now housed in a French museum in San Francisco. Domi enlists Nina's help in the task of clearing her father's name of the charge of murder. A suspenseful mystery, with telling clues foreshadowed in one of Nina's "real-life" dreams, leads to a painting that serves as evidence of the count's innocence. The Chagall painting "Time Is a River Without Banks," which hangs in the museum, is used throughout the story as a symbol of Nina's unusual interest in the abstract nature of time. This is a profound theme explored by a truly accomplished writer. However, young readers will more likely value the book for its exciting events and for the haunting presence of Domi in her museum domain than for its eloquent abstractions.

Like the "Green Knowe" stories, *A String in the Harp* gains strength from its setting and also from its connection to legend. Nancy Bond tells of an American family's adjustment to living in Wales when their newly widowed father accepts a university post. It is a particularly difficult time for 12-year-old Peter, who is stubborn, lonely, and hateful until he finds a strange object later identified as the harp key of Taliesin, the great sixth-century bard who lived in this part of Wales. While the key draws Peter back in time, his present-day life is adversely affected. Eventually, he is able to return the key to its proper place and assume a responsible place in the family. This strongly characterized but lengthy story mingles past and present time in a believable and involving way.

In *Earthfasts* William Mayne also draws on legendary characters to tell his story of three interwoven times. When two boys meet at a swelling in the earth, the ground begins to vibrate with the sound of drumming. Out of the earth emerges a stranger beating a drum and clutching a steady, cold white flame. It is Nellie Jack John, who according to local legend went underground two hundred years ago to seek the treasure of King Arthur. Nellie Jack John's disturbance of time causes many bizarre events: ancient stones called earthfasts work up in a farmer's field; a family's

[23]Natalie Babbitt, *Tuck Everlasting* (New York: Farrar, Straus & Giroux, 1975), p. 63.

poltergeist returns after a long absence; and one boy vanishes in what looks like a flash of lightning. Only by restoring the candle to its proper place because "King Arthur's time has not yet come" can the boys right the imbalance of time. This unforgettable book owes much of its impact to Mayne's use of language and his finely realized setting.

Another story that alludes to King Arthur, *Merlin Dreams* by Peter Dickinson, defies categorizing. Nine highly original short stories or dreams are each prefaced by Merlin's remembrance of some event in his long life. Whether the dreams are of time to come, time that was, or time that never will be is for the reader to decide. In one story, a damsel from the north and a knight use their powers to change into hunting dogs to outwit her greedy uncle whose other body is that of a wolf. In another, a different genus of human possessing a ten-toed, fan-shaped foot is protected from a roving band of scoundrels by mountain villagers, one of whom she eventually marries. But when the scoundrel band returns, tragedy results. In a humorous story, a basilisk turns on its evil master with predictable results. Between the short stories, Merlin's dreams allude to the many exploits of the famous magician as he helped King Arthur regain and hold the throne. Illustrator Alan Lee contrasts watercolor paintings for the stories and black line drawings for the dreams. His depiction of the woodland castles and poisoned wells, the threadbare knights, or the needful damsels highlights the subtleties and moods of this remarkable book for middle school readers.

Often time travelers learn to deal with a troubled present through experiences in an equally troubled past. In the Australian prize winner *Playing Beatie Bow*, Ruth Park presents Abigail, a contemporary 14-year-old who has been deeply hurt first by her father's defection from the family and then by her mother's quick agreement when he wants to come back. In this resentful mood, Abigail follows a strangely dressed child who has been watching a neighborhood street game called "Beatie Bow." The little girl, the original Beatie Bow, leads Abigail through increasingly unfamiliar streets to her home in The Rocks area of Sydney—in the year 1873. Injured in a fall and

divested of the dress with antique crochet work that has made her time passage possible, Abigail is trapped with Beatie's family. She comes to care for them all, especially charming cousin Judah, engaged to Beatie's older sister but attracted to Abby as well. Through her courage during a fire in the Bow family candy shop, Abigail earns her return to the twentieth century, where she finds that she is now more tolerant of her father's lapse of affection.

Self-understanding and better family relationships are also the outcomes for characters in two time-shift fantasies by Canadian authors. In *A Handful of Time* by Kit Pearson, a 12-year-old girl

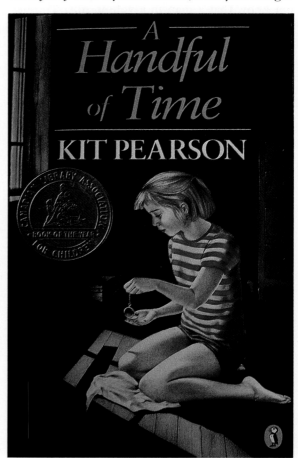

Patricia contemplates an antique pocket watch that will transport her into the past in Kit Pearson's time-shift fantasy, *A Handful of Time*.

Jacket illustration by Laura Fernandez.

is sent west to her cousins' camp on a lake near Edmonton while her parents' divorce becomes final. Patricia is definitely the "city cousin" who knows little about boating or horseback riding and is the constant butt of her cousins' jokes. When she discovers an old watch hidden under the floor of a guest house, she finds herself taken back in time to the same summer cabin where her mother was 12 and equally miserable. In her frequent trips to view the past, Patricia learns much about her short-tempered grandmother and her beautiful but reserved mother. By coming to understand her mother, Patricia moves toward understanding herself.

The Haunting of Frances Rain (published in Canada as *Who Is Frances Rain?*) by Margaret Buffie might well be a script for a Canadian *On Golden Pond* movie. When Lizzie, her egotistical brother, little sister, mother, and new stepfather drive from Winnipeg to a northern lake to see her grandmother, Lizzie thinks the holiday will be a disaster. Then while exploring deserted Rain Island, she finds a pair of old glasses that enable her to see a log cabin and its inhabitants, a young girl and her mother. Lizzie is haunted by them. Who are they? And who is the fat man who takes the girl away in a canoe while the mother is gone? Slowly she discovers that the young girl is her Gran, now old and confined to bed but remembering the same vivid scenes Lizzie is seeing. This mysterious story is as haunting and memorable as the cry of a loon on northern waters. Both stories feature girls who are in danger of using the past to escape their problems in the present. But when her entry into the past is blocked each girl faces the present with new resolve.

In some books where characters are shifted from modern times into specific periods of history, the concern with social and political issues of the past is very strong. Several notable examples serve the purposes of historical fiction as well as fantasy. In *A Chance Child* by Jill Paton Walsh, Creep, a present-day English boy abused and kept locked in a closet, gets out by chance, and follows a canal that takes him back to the Industrial Revolution. As a child laborer, he travels from one exhausting and dangerous job to another, eventually losing his grip on the present altogether. His half-brother, the only person with

any clue to his disappearance, searches historical documents from the early 1800s and is at last satisfied that Creep has escaped into the past and lived out his life there. The amount of technological information about work in the coal mines, the nailer's forge, the pottery, and the textile mill attests to the research necessary for recreating these settings. Walsh's juxtaposition of the abusive treatment of children in the nineteenth century and Creep's contemporary plight makes a strong statement about children and society.

David Wiseman's *Jeremy Visick* explores the conditions of child laborers in England's nineteenth-century copper mines when Matthew's school assignment leads him into a mine disaster of a previous century. In *A Traveler in Time* by Alison Uttley, readers are led by a child back into the intrigue surrounding a tragic plot to save Mary Queen of Scots. These novels demand much of readers because they blur the distinctions between time fantasy and historical fiction.

The time of slavery in America is explored in *A Girl Called Boy* by Belinda Hurmence. Blanche Overtha Yancey (Boy) is bored by her father's obvious pride in their African-American heritage and no longer impressed by the tiny African soapstone "freedom bird" passed down by his great-great-grandfather. But in response to her sarcastic command, the stone takes her "over the water" (a North Carolina stream near the picnic grounds where she has come for a family outing) and into the past when her father's ancestors were slaves. Boy's panic is entirely believable as she gradually realizes that she has lost touch with the present and, with her jeans and short-cropped hair, is being mistaken for a male runaway slave. The reader who discovers the injustices of slavery as Boy does is likely to develop strong feelings about the issues. Boy's flight toward freedom is exciting, and she becomes a memorable character. Her growing admiration and affection for the slaves who befriend and protect her are a counterpoint to her earlier attitudes and a testimony to the determination and sense of community among her people. The author's use of actual slave narratives and plantation records provides the same authenticity of background that would be expected in historical fiction. Using the device of time travel strengthens this story, however, for it allows the interjection of a contemporary perspective to balance the impact of that era's distorted values.

In Cora Taylor's *Yesterday's Doll* (called *The Doll* in Canada), a family heirloom becomes Meg's entry into the past and enables her to join her ancestors as they crossed the Canadian prairies in the 1880s with Red River Carts. Ten-year-old Meg is sent to her grandmother's old house outside of Saskatoon to recuperate from rheumatic fever while her parents are finalizing their divorce. Lonely, she plays with a 100-year-old doll that belonged to her great-grandmother. As she goes to sleep holding the doll, Meg becomes Morag and enters pioneer times. While life in the past is far more difficult than she ever realized, she even considers staying. Caught in a raging prairie fire, Morag/Meg saves her little sister but nearly loses her doll. Only when Meg looks through the family album with her grandmother does she learn the truth about "angel Morag." This well-written story vividly contrasts life in the pioneer past with that of the present. Like the girls in Buffie's *The Haunting of Frances Rain* and Pearson's *A Handful of Time*, Meg is also better able to face her own future with courage.

Janet Lunn, American born but now living in Canada, weaves together a haunting tale of a contemporary child, an old Canadian farmhouse, and the American Civil War in her book, *The Root Cellar*. When her grandmother dies, Rose is sent to live with her Aunt Nan's family in their country home on the northern shore of Lake Ontario. A shy child who has lived only with adults in New York City, 12-year-old Rose feels desperately lonely in the midst of Aunt Nan's and Uncle Bob's lively family. When she discovers an old root cellar door covered with vines and grass, she opens it and finds herself in a world more than a hundred years ago. She is more comfortable in this world and easily makes friends with Susan and Will. When Will runs off to fight in the Civil War and does not return, Rose and Susan set out on a hazardous journey that eventually takes them across the United States to an army hospital in Washington, D.C. Rose, who has traveled to Paris with her grandmother, is not prepared for the difficulties of this trip. She discovers, however, a strength and determination she did not know

she had that helps her when she returns to her own time. Some of the reverberations from this well-written fantasy echo the feelings created in other notable books. For instance, Rose's delight in the orchard and finding the root cellar door is reminiscent of Mary's experiences in Burnett's *The Secret Garden*. In another instance, Rose finally realizes that the old Mrs. Morrissay who helped her cook Christmas dinner for the family is really Susan, her friend in the past. A similar moment of understanding occurs in *Tom's Midnight Garden* by Pearce.

Imaginary Kingdoms

Many authors of fantasy create believability by setting their stories in an imaginary medieval society where kings rule a feudal society. Often lighter in tone than high fantasy, these stories may nonetheless feature some of its attributes such as a human character's search for identity, a quest, or the struggle against evil. Children are often drawn to this kind of fantasy as it seems so closely related in many ways to folktales and traditional literature.

Two of Natalie Babbitt's stories, *The Search for Delicious* and *Kneeknock Rise*, are set in an imaginary medieval kingdom. In the first story, young Gaylen is sent out as the King's messenger to poll the kingdom as to which food should stand for the word "delicious" in the dictionary that the prime minister is compiling. Before he finishes, Gaylen uncovers Hemlock's plot to overthrow the king. With the help of all the supposedly fictitious creatures that the minstrel sings about—such as woldwellers, the dwarfs, and Ardis the mermaid—Gaylen is able to foil Hemlock and save his king. In the epilogue the minstrel returns and the prime minister tells him Gaylen's strange story, thinking that it would make a very pretty song indeed. And so mythmaking continues. In *Kneeknock Rise*, Egan climbs the mountain and finds a perfectly rational explanation for the groaning noises of the mythical Megrimum. When he eagerly relates his findings to the villagers, they refuse to listen to him, and Egan discovers that people do not relinquish their myths easily; harmless monsters may be preferable to facts.

Patricia Wrede's *Dealing with Dragons* and *Searching for Dragons* are two books in a series that features the unconventional Princess Cimorene. In the first story, Cimorene runs off to be librarian and cook to the dragon Kazul rather than stay in the palace, sew, and wait for a suitor. Cimorene organizes the dragon's hoard, reads ancient books, and makes friends with neighboring princesses captured by dragons and awaiting rescue. Cimorene's gradual mastery of rudimentary magic and her friendship with the witch Morwen allow her to defeat an evil band of wizards who are trying to influence the choice of the new dragon ruler. In *Searching for Dragons* Cimorene and the young king of an enchanted forest join forces, borrow a faulty magic carpet from a giant, and set off to find Kazul, now king of the dragons, who has disappeared. Both stories make many sly references to folktale and fantasy conventions. While Cimorene and Menolly in Anne McCaffrey's high fantasy "Dragonsinger" series (discussed in the next section), are sisters under the skin, the tone of the two series differs. Children who enjoy Wrede's unconventional feminine adventurer would appreciate being guided to the works of McCaffrey, as well as those of Robin McKinley and Lloyd Alexander, whose heroines appeal to slightly older readers.

William Mayne's remarkable *Antar of the Eagles* takes place in a mountainous kingdom. Antar is plucked by eagles off the steeple of a church where he has perched while disobeying his father. The eagles carry him to their aerie where they peck and prod him to eat raw meat, to sew feathers on his now-ragged clothes, and to learn to fly. His eagle tutor is Garak who teaches him how to behave among eagles, how to find food, how to distinguish wing and eye signals, and how to survive in the cold and adverse conditions on the mountaintop. After gradually learning the eagles' language, Antar understands that only he can accomplish an important mission. The Great Eagle, their leader, is dying and the beautiful egg from which his successor would hatch has been stolen by men and stored in the king's treasury. Wishing only to go home, Antar undertakes this quest, surviving near burial in an erupting volcano, the weapons of the men, and near imprisonment by the king. As "egg-mother" to the new Great Eagle, Antar once again remains in the aerie until the eagles let him return to his own family. Told with a minimum of dialogue, this riveting story leads readers to consider not only the nature of a majestic bird but also the boundless possibilities of the human imagination.

In Zilpha Keatley Snyder's fast-paced adventure, *Song of the Gargoyle*, 13-year-old Tymmon eludes capture when his court-jester father is mysteriously kidnapped. The boy is befriended by a huge and ugly dog, which he, mistakenly or not, refers to as a stone gargoyle come to life. Since the dog Troff displays a talent for singing along with Tymmon's flute music, the two are able to make a living as itinerant musicians. As Tymmon searches for his father, he chafes at the discovery that his father threw away his noble heritage to become a fool. But in his travels Tymmon also sees the poverty and suffering that peasants endure because of the greed of the nobility, and he takes on the responsibility for two homeless children. When the tale of a mysterious old man sends Tymmon back to Austerneve to rescue or avenge his father, the boy and dog are thrown into the dungeon. Music again saves boy, dog, and father, who reunite with the two children in an exciting conclusion.

Sid Fleischman sets *The Whipping Boy*, his humorous variation on a prince-and-the-pauper theme, in a time of velvet britches, princely tutors, and robber brigands. Jemmy, the whipping boy for Prince Brat, has taken all the abuse for the prince that he can stand. Each time the bored prince makes mischief and is caught, Jemmy must receive the twenty whacks. But before Jemmy can leave, the Prince commands the former street urchin to sneak away from the dull palace with him to see what the world holds. When the boys are kidnapped by two notorious outlaws, Hold-Your-Nose-Billy and Cutwater, one of the boys' identities is given away: Prince Brat had thoughtfully stowed his crown in his picnic basket. But which one is the prince? Since Jemmy had learned to read and write as a tutor futilely labored to teach the prince, the cutthroats consider the whipping boy the one to be ransomed. When the two boys escape, they lead the ruffians on a chase through the woods and into the sewers of the town finally to be rescued by a dancing bear. The exaggerated characters in humorous situations are balanced by the prince's gradual transition to a decent person when he finds that none of his future subjects think much of him. Fleischman's appealing use of colorful figurative language, witty repartee, broadly drawn characters, and clever chapter titles make this a good shared-reading choice for fourth or fifth graders. Peter Sis's quirky drawings and small chapter openings are perfectly suited to this spoof.

In an essay about his father and his love of words and magic, Paul Fleischman said:

> When he gave up being a professional magician, he became instead a prestidigitator of words, palming plot elements, making villains vanish, producing solutions out of thin air. He knows how to keep an audience guessing, how to create suspense, how to keep readers reading.[24]

Joan Aiken sets her stories within imaginary kingdoms with a nod to history as well. *The Wolves of Willoughby Chase* has all of the ingredients of a nineteenth-century chiller, including wicked wolves without and an outrageously wicked governess within. It takes place in a period of history that never existed—the Stuarts in the person of good King James III are on the throne in the nineteenth century. *Black Hearts in Battersea* is the mad and exciting sequel, with shipwrecks, stowaways, more wolves, and a desperate climax to save the king by means of a balloon. *Nightbirds on Nantucket* is the tale of the quest for a pink whale. Feminists will applaud the return of the resourceful 11-year-old Dido as much as they will dislike the quaking 9-year-old Dutiful Penitence and her sinister Aunt Tribulation. Dido is also at the center of a still more inventive book, *The Stolen Lake*. Here Roman Britain history is superimposed on South American geography, with a 1,300-year-old Queen Guinevere awaiting Arthur just for good measure! While these books are not typical fantasies, their perpetual-motion plots represent suspenseful melodrama at its best.

Lloyd Alexander has a gift for portraying comic adventures in which serious themes lie under a surface of fast action and polished wit. *The Cat Who Wished to Be a Man* and *The Wizard in the Tree* are books of this sort. *The Marvelous Misadventures of Sebastian* is equally lighthearted, with all the trappings of madcap adventure. Sebastian finds an enchanted violin in which he hears the sound of what he might have become and in the end sets off to rediscover that lost self. Alexander's books share certain common elements: rich use of language, comic tone, usually a strong-willed female foil to the likeable, all-too-human hero, and the setting in an imaginary kingdom.

Older readers find satisfaction with Lloyd Alexander's two series, both of which take place in unmagical but imagined settings. *Westmark* is the story of Theo, a printer's apprentice, who pursues questions of honor, justice, and freedom of the press as he tries to avoid the villainous chief minister of the kingdom. Theo helps restore his street urchin friend Mickle to her rightful place as princess but he also questions the concept of a monarchy: Does anyone have a rightful place on a throne? *The Kestrel* and *The Beggar Queen* are sequels in which Theo and Mickle, now the "Beggar Queen," prove their worth in battle but learn the cost of personal victory. In a lighter vein, Vesper Holly is the intrepid young woman who, with her guardian Brinnie, embarks on *The Illyrian Adventure, The El Dorado Adventure, The Drackenburg Adventure, The Jedera Adventure* and *The Philadelphia Story*. The high-minded heroine and her guardian journey to imaginary places in Europe, Africa, and Central America where they discover treasure, recover important antiquities, foil villians, and narrowly escape all dangers. Told with Alexander's usual wit, these five stories invite middle-grade readers to create their own adventure "movies of the mind."

High Fantasy

Many readers who learn to enjoy popular stories of magic, ghosts, time travel, and the like, go on to become fans of a more serious and demanding type of story called high fantasy. These complex narratives, which often extend into sequels, are characterized by certain recurring themes and motifs. For instance, the stories frequently take

[24]Paul Fleischman, "Sid Fleischman," *The Horn Book Magazine*, vol. 63 (August 1987), p. 432.

place in created worlds or imaginary kingdoms. Characters may call on ancient and fundamental powers, for good or ill. The conflict between these opposing forces becomes the focus of many stories. Frequently, the protagonists of high fantasy have a quest to fulfill. Finally, although there may be touches of humor, the overall tone of high fantasy is serious, because its purpose is serious. High fantasy concerns itself with cosmic questions and ultimate values: goodness, truth, courage, wisdom.

In accepting the National Book Award for *The Farthest Shore*, Ursula K. Le Guin spoke about the intent of fantasy at this level:

> The fantasist, whether he uses the ancient archetypes of myth and legend or the younger ones of science and technology, may be talking as seriously as any sociologist—and a good deal more directly—about human life as it is lived, and as it might be lived, and as it ought to be lived. For after all, as great scientists have said and as all children know, it is above all by the imagination that we achieve perception, and compassion, and hope.[25]

High fantasy's best audience stretches over a wide age range, from preadolescents to adults. Some of its most enthusiastic readers are the same young people who are devoted to video games of imagined adventures. Many older readers simply call themselves science-fiction fans and make little distinction between the two types of books. In fact, much science fiction is also high fantasy; Madeleine L'Engle's *A Wrinkle in Time* is one familiar example. Some stories, like Anne McCaffrey's *Dragonsong*, appear to be science fiction by their extraterrestrial settings and the use of precepts of science (in this case, the bonding of a newborn animal and a mother figure). But *Dragonsong* seems more fantasy than science, since the newborns are traditional dragons and "fire lizards."

Not all critics will agree about the proper categorization of books like these. But it is the book itself, not its label, that matters to the reader.

However it may be identified, well-written high fantasy rewards its audience.

THE STRUGGLE BETWEEN GOOD AND EVIL

The age-old conflict between good and evil, light and darkness, life and death is a recurring theme in modern fantasy as well as in traditional literature. The setting for the struggle may be in the world as we know it, or in an invented land like Narnia, which some children know as well as their own backyards or city blocks. C. S. Lewis, a well-known English scholar and theologian, created seven fantasies about the country of Narnia. The best of the series is the first one published, *The Lion, the Witch, and the Wardrobe*, although it was the second in the sequence according to the history of Narnia. Beginning quite realistically in our time and world, four children find their way into the land of Narnia through the back of a huge wardrobe (or closet) in one of the large rooms of an old English house. The land, blanketed in snow and ice, is under the wicked Snow Queen's spell that controls the weather so it is "always winter and never Christmas." The children and the Narnians pit themselves against the evil witch and her motley assortment of ghouls, boggles, minotaurs, and hags. With the coming, sacrifice, and resurrection of the great Aslan the Lion, signs of spring are seen in the land. The children successfully aid the lion king in destroying the evil forces, and he crowns them Kings and Queens of Narnia. Narnia has its own history and time, and in *The Magician's Nephew* the reader is told of the beginnings of Narnia.[26] In the last of the books of Narnia, King Tirian calls on the Earth Children to come to his aid in this, *The Last Battle*. Narnia is destroyed; yet the real Narnia, the inner Narnia, is not. The children learn that no good thing is ever lost, and the real identity of Aslan is finally revealed to them. These stories are mysterious, intriguing, and beautifully written. If children do not always understand their religious allegory, they may appreciate them as

[25]Ursula K. Le Guin, "National Book Award Acceptance Speech," in *The Language of the Night: Essays on Fantasy and Science Fiction*, edited by Susan Wood (New York: Putnam, 1979), p. 58.

[26]See Brian Sibley's *The Land of Narnia*, with illustrations by Pauline Baynes (New York: HarperCollins, 1990) for help in sorting out the chronology of Narnia, notes on the creation of the series, and a simplified biography of C. S. Lewis.

wondrous adventures that somehow reveal more than they say.

Susan Cooper has written a series of five books about the cosmic struggle between light and dark. *Over Sea, Under Stone* introduces the three Drew children who, on holiday in Cornwall, find an ancient treasure map linked to King Arthur. The third book in the series, *Greenwitch*, continues this quest story. Both stories are less complex than the remarkable second book, *The Dark Is Rising*. On Midwinter Day that is his eleventh birthday, Will Stanton discovers that he is the last of the Old Ones, immortals dedicated throughout the ages to keeping the world from the forces of evil, the Dark. Will must find the six Signs of Life in order to complete his power and defeat, even temporarily, the rising of the Dark. Strange powers enable him to move in and out of time where he meets Merriman Lyon, the first of the Old Ones, who becomes his teacher and mentor. While rich in symbolism and allegory, the story is grounded in reality so that both Will's "real" life and his quest in suspended time are distinct, yet interwoven. In the fourth book of the series, *The Grey King*, Will once again must prepare for the coming battle between the Dark and the Light. Special help comes from Bran, a strange albino boy, and his dog Cafall. Set in Wales, the story works on many levels with the feud over a sheep-killing dog taking on more significance when Bran's mysterious background is revealed. *Silver on the Tree* draws characters from the previous four novels together for a final assault on the Dark. Much that was hidden in the other tales is made explicit here and knowledge of the major threads of the first four books is necessary to understand this exciting and fulfilling climax to the saga.

A more exotic setting for the encounter between good and evil is created by Meredith Ann Pierce for the series that begins with *The Darkangel*. In some far-off future time on the moon, a young woman is carried away to be the bride of a "vampyre," a fair young man with "wings of pure shadow." The abductor is pursued by the victim's servant girl, Aeriel, who is in turn captured. Her fate is to wait upon the spirit-forms of the darkangel's thirteen brides, whose souls are held in tiny vials on his neckchain. In her efforts to free them, Aeriel discovers that the darkangel

himself is enslaved, and that she is the only one who can save him from becoming completely and utterly evil. The act of faith required is reminiscent of tales such as "Beauty and the Beast," but far more dramatic. For experienced readers, one of the pleasures of this book might be in recognizing its links with other fantasies; for instance, the great lion Pendarlon, who carries Aeriel across the desert, is an echo of Aslan in Lewis's Narnia series. *The Darkangel* stands on its own imaginative merits, however, as a fantasy romance that celebrates the power of love over hate.

QUESTS AND ADVENTURES

High fantasy is almost always the story of a search—for treasure, justice, identity, understanding—and of a hero-figure who learns important lessons in the adventuring. One of the most famous seekers in all fantasy is J.R.R. Tolkien's Bilbo Baggins, *The Hobbit*. Generally hobbits are very respectable creatures who never have any adventures or do anything unexpected.

> They are (or were) small people, smaller than dwarves (and they have no beards) but very much larger than lilliputians. There is little or no magic about them, except the ordinary everyday sort which helps them to disappear quickly when large stupid folk like you and me come blundering along making a noise like elephants which they can hear a mile off. They are inclined to be fat in the stomach; they dress in bright colors (chiefly green and yellow); wear no shoes, because their feet grow natural leather soles and thick warm brown hair like the stuff on their heads (which is curly); have long clever brown fingers, good-natured faces, and laugh deep fruity laughs (especially after dinner, which they have twice a day when they can get it).[27]

Bilbo Baggins, however, has an adventure and finds himself doing and saying altogether unexpected things. He is tricked by the dwarfs and the elves into going on a quest for treasure when he would much rather stay at home where he could be sure of six solid meals a day rather than be off fighting dragons. On the way, he is lost in a tunnel and nearly consumed by a ghoulish crea-

---

[27] J.R.R. Tolkien, *The Hobbit* (Boston: Houghton Mifflin, 1938), p. 12.

ture called Gollum, who is "dark as darkness except for his two big round pale eyes." Gradually the hobbit's inner courage emerges, as he struggles on through terrifying woods, encounters with huge hairy spiders, and battles with goblins to a somewhat enigmatic victory over the dragon (a more heroic figure is allowed to slay it). *The Hobbit* gives children an introduction to Middle-earth and its creatures. Later they may pursue this interest in Tolkien's vastly expanded view of Middle-earth in *The Lord of the Rings*, a 1,300-page trilogy that again draws on the author's scholarly knowledge of the myth and folklore of northwestern Europe.

Welsh legends and mythology are the inspiration for the intriguing chronicles of the imaginary land of Prydain as told by Lloyd Alexander. In *The Book of Three* the reader is introduced to Taran, an assistant pigkeeper who dreams of becoming a hero. With a strange assortment of companions he pursues Hen Wen, the oracular pig, and struggles to save Prydain from the forces of evil. The chronicles are continued in the most exciting of all of the books, *The Black Cauldron*. Once again the faithful companions fight evil as they seek to find and destroy the great cauldron in which the dread Cauldron-Born are created, "mute and deathless warriors" made from the stolen bodies of those slain in battle. Taran is proud to be chosen to fight for Lord Gwydion, for now he will have more opportunity to win honor than when washing pigs or weeding a garden. His wise and sensitive companion, Adaon, tells him:

> "I have marched in many a battle host . . . but I have also planted seeds and reaped the harvest with my own hands. And I have learned there is greater honor in a field well plowed than in a field steeped in blood."[28]

Gradually, Taran learns what it means to become a man among men—the sacrifice of his gentle Adaon, the final courage of the proud Ellidyr, and the faithfulness of his companions. He experiences treachery, tragedy, and triumph; yet a thread of humor runs throughout to lighten the tension. Good does prevail, and Taran has

[28]Lloyd Alexander, *The Black Cauldron* (New York: Holt, Rinehart and Winston, 1965), p. 43.

matured and is ready for his next adventure. In the third book of the series, *The Castle of Llyr*, Taran escorts Princess Eilonwy to the Isle of Mona, where Queen Teleria is expected to teach the temperamental Eilonwy to behave in the manner of a proper princess—not an easy task. In the fourth book, *Taran Wanderer*, Taran searches for his parentage. More important than the identity of his parents, however, is Taran's self-discovery of who he is and what he dares to become. *The High King*, the masterful conclusion to this cycle of stories about the kingdom of Prydain, received the Newbery award. However, the recognition carried praise for all five of these chronicles. Each may be read independently, but together they represent an exciting adventure in some of the best-written fantasy of our time.

Lloyd Alexander writes another quest story in *The Remarkable Journey of Prince Jen*. Set in China during the Tang Dynasty, young Prince Jen, heir to the Dragon Throne, starts off to find T'ien-kuo, or Heavenly Kingdom, the utopia described by a wandering scholar. Jen sets off with six gifts for the ruler of T'ien-kuo, a retinue of soldiers, and a loyal servant. As his journey progresses, he loses everything but gains his manhood, love, and friendship. Filled with excitement and wisdom, this would be a superb story to read aloud to middle-grade students.

Often in high fantasy, an unsuspecting or reluctant hero born to be leader, princess, or king accepts true identity in a way that symbolizes each young person's own discovery of the powers and burdens of maturity. In Grace Chetwin's series, which begins with *Gom on Windy Mountain*, Gom Gobblechuck is such a hero. At 11, he can converse with animals but is content to follow in his woodchopper father's footsteps. However, his father tells him about his mother, Harga the Brown, who left her eleven children when Gom was born. Upon his father's death, Gom sets forth from his sequestered valley to find his wizard mother in *The Riddle and the Rune*. Armed with a magic rune, a gift from his mother, Gom wards off attacks of the evil skull-bird, nearly loses his rune to a shape changer, and naively trusts an oily cheat, Mat, who continues to cause trouble for the boy. Successive novels take Gom deeper beneath his own world and finally out of it into another time and space as he becomes more aware of the evil threatening his land of Ulm. Chetwin's stories feature a familiar earthiness, a celebration of a simple life, and the virtues of a steadfast heart. Readers will identify with Gom's unready demeanor, his hasty actions that cause later difficulties, and his gradual understanding of the dangers of wielding power unwisely. More unexpected is Chetwin's creation of a universe in which this small world exists. Like Sylvia Engdahl in *Enchantress from the Stars* and Ursula K. Le Guin in *A Wizard of Earthsea*, she explores the moral responsibility each person holds to maintain the balance of the universe.

Just as Grace Chetwin's woodcutter Gom and Lloyd Alexander's pigkeeper Taran discover that they have been chosen from the beginning for high purpose, so does Patricia McKillip's Morgon of Hed find an undreamed-of destiny in the trilogy that begins with *The Riddle-Master of Hed*. While Morgon knows he is a prince and a land-ruler, he does not know the significance of the three stars he bears on his forehead. As a student at the College of Riddle-Masters, he comes upon riddles that concern the stars, but he is reluctant to accept the powers which are his to claim. In the second book, *Heir of Sea and Fire*, Morgon disappears into Erlenstar Mountain on a search for the High One, and Raederle, the beautiful girl who is pledged to him, comes into full possession of her own magic. In *Harpist in the Wind*, the two are together once more, and the solution to the riddle of the Star-Bearer is known at last. These are difficult books, dense with allusions to the history and geography of their imaginary setting. Fantasy fans who are proficient readers are easily caught up in the compelling narrative, however. To avoid dissatisfaction with the abrupt endings of the first two books, it may be a good idea to begin this series with all three volumes at hand.

In Robin McKinley's *The Blue Sword*, a book with closer ties to the world as we know it, a young woman called Harry discovers that her heritage has destined her to be a "Lady Hero." A ward of her brother, Harry feels vaguely out of place in the military outpost where he has brought her to live. She feels strangely drawn by the mountains where Free Hillfolk still live in an uneasy truce with the conquering Homelanders, Harry's people. When Corlath the Hill-King comes to ask the Homelanders' cooperation in turning back the Northerners, who have demonic powers in battle, he is rebuffed. But his visionary gift of *kelar* drives him back to take Harry off across the desert to the hills, where she is treated as an honored captive, privileged to sit among his select troop of Riders. When she first tastes the Water of Sight, it is apparent that Harry has her own *kelar* and that she is destined to play a part in the Hillfolk's efforts against the hordes of the North. More and more at ease with her abductors, Harry trains for battle and earns the right to be a king's Rider and to bear the treasured Blue Sword, whose special power in her hand must finally stand between the Hillfolk and their enemies. The girl's poignant relationship with Corlath and his people is put in new perspective by her defiant courage and by her discovery of an ancestral link that proves she is in truth one of them. The story is rich with details of horsemanship, combat, and the romance of a nomadic life. It also speaks directly about women's roles and responsibilities, a message all the more intriguing for being set in a frame of military and desert life, where traditional roles for women are often rigid. *The Hero and the Crown* happens in time before *The Blue Sword* and features many of the same themes. It chronicles the coming of the king's only child Aerin into her powers while leaving the reader with the desire to know more of what Aerin's future will bring.

In *Dragonsong*, Anne McCaffrey writes of another young woman, Menolly, whose special power is tied to her remarkable talent for music. Her family denies her dream of becoming a Harper because tradition dictates that the making of music is a man's task. Menolly runs away, taking shelter from her planet's fiery scourge of "Threadfall" in a hollow cliff by the sea. Here she stumbles on a hatching clutch of coveted fire lizards, kin to the great dragons that patrol the skies. Being the first to feed and touch the new creatures, she "bonds" with nine of them, commanding their loyalty for life. Menolly's beautiful lizards help give her the confidence she needs to take up a new life when she is rescued by a dragonrider and brought to the attention of the Master Harper. *Dragonsinger* tells of Menolly's trials and successes as an apprentice at the Harper Hall, and *Dragondrums* takes up the story of her fellow student Piemur, who has his own role to play in protecting the kingdom of Pern. Except for the unusual proper names, these books are less complex and easier to read than many of the high fantasies previously discussed. *Dragonsong* in particular has great reader appeal; but it may be worth noting that in comparison to other fantasy protagonists, Menolly pays a small price for getting her heart's desire.

Dragon's Blood by Jane Yolen has some similarity to the McCaffrey books although it embodies a sterner view of the world. On a mythical planet dragons who fight for sport must be trained from hatchlings by one who has the gift for mind-bonding with them. Yolen tells the story of Jakkin, a bond servant who steals a newly hatched dragon and trains it in the hope of earning his bond price and his freedom. His surprising success is due in part to the help of a girl named Akki, who has distinct ideas about running her own life. Her brusque manner, her skills of healing, and her uncertain identity combine to make her an unusually interesting secondary character. In *Heart's Blood*, Jakkin's plans to enter his own dragon in the gaming pits are disrupted when he agrees to infiltrate a treacherous rebel group.

A superior tale against which other novels of high fantasy may be judged is *A Wizard of Earthsea* by Ursula K. Le Guin. Studying at the School for Wizards, Sparrowhawk is taunted by a jealous classmate to use his powers before he is ready. Pride and arrogance drive him to call up a dreadful malignant shadow that threatens his life and all of Earthsea. Thus begins a chase and the hunt between the young wizard and the shadow-beast across the mountains and the waters of this world. Sparrowhawk, or Ged, his true name known only by his must trusted friends, is a well-developed character who grows from an intelligent, impatient adolescent to a wise and grateful mage, or wizard. A major theme of the story is the responsibility that each choice carries with it. When Ged asks one of his teachers at the school how transformation of objects can be made permanent, he is answered:

> ❦ . . . you will learn it, when you are ready to learn it. But you must not change one thing, one pebble, one grain of sand, until you know what good and evil will follow the act. The world is in Equilibrium.

> A wizard's power of Changing and of Summoning can change the balance of the world. It is dangerous, that power. It is most perilous. It must follow knowledge, and serve need. To light a candle is to cast a shadow.[29]

The word *shadow* is one of the recurring motifs of the story: Ged's boat bears this name; the evil he releases into the world is called a shadow; and in the end, Ged recognizes this evil as a shadow of himself and his hasty deed. The power of knowing the true name of someone or something, a common motif in traditional literature, is of central importance to this story. So, too, is the value of self-knowledge:

> ❦ Ged's ultimate quest . . . had made him whole: a man who knowing his whole true self, cannot be used or possessed by any other power other than by himself, and whose life therefore is lived for life's sake and never in the service of ruin, or pain, or hatred, or the dark.[30]

The next story in this quartet of Earthsea is the sinister tale of a child priestess given at the age of 5 to a cult of darkness and evil. At 15, Tenar discovers Ged trapped in *The Tombs of Atuan*, a place where no man is allowed, and she must decide whether to save him. This more somber story provides important insights into trust and the price of freedom. *The Farthest Shore* in a sense completes the mighty deeds of Ged, as the wizard must use all of his wisdom to defeat evil forces threatening to overcome Earthsea. *Tehanu* returns to Tenar and her attempts to save a child, who has been abused both physically and sexually. Ged returns to these hills entirely spent of his powers and humiliated, but it is his human act, rather than his powers of wizardry, that saves Tenar and the child, who must herself come into her own powers. This final volume explores the many sources of a woman's strength—hearth, heart, and humanity—that she draws upon to arrive at mature and vital love. The metaphors in all four stories speak clearly and profoundly to today's world.

[29]Ursula K. Le Guin, *A Wizard of Earthsea*, illustrated by Ruth Robbins (Berkeley, Calif.: Parnassus, 1968), p. 57.
[30]Le Guin, *A Wizard of Earthsea*, p. 203.

Ruth Robbins's detailed map gives substance to the geography of Earthsea, the imaginary land created by Ursula Le Guin in *A Wizard of Earthsea*.

Patricia Wrightson, like Mollie Hunter, also mingles long-ago legends in stories with contemporary settings. Wrightson peoples her fantasies with legendary Australian creatures such as Narguns, Ninya, and water spirits. In *The Nargun and the Stars*, men disturb the ancient ones at Wongadilla, a sheep ranch in northern Australia. Simon Brett, a city boy, is awed by the size of the ranch where he has come to live following the death of his parents. He meets a Potkoorok, a froglike creature who lives in a swamp, and elusive tree spirits called Turongs. But on the night of a terrible storm, Simon is terrified by another, older presence, the ancient Nargun who has been disturbed by road-building machinery and is moving from its primeval silence to crush everything

in its path. Simon and his middle-aged cousin Charlie must bring all their cleverness and ingenuity to bear in trapping the Nargun in a cavern. Wrightson has also written a trilogy: *The Ice Is Coming, The Dark Bright Water*, and *Journey Behind the Wind*. In it, Wirrun who is called to save the land from restless ancient spirits, must confront gathering cold, the Eldest Nargun, and the monstrous Wulgaru, keeper of death.

In *Balyet*, also by Wrightson, a 14-year-old girl inadvertently discovers the power of ancient aboriginal sites to preserve spirits. Mrs. Willet, who is an elderly aboriginal woman and Jo's former babysitter, drives to the mountains to perform certain traditional rites only to discover that Jo has stowed away in the back seat of the car. Left on her own by her mother, Jo plans to surprise a classmate who is camping with his older brother. She obeys Granny Willet's warnings to stay off the mountainside only as long as the old lady can see her. But when Jo finds her friends and climbs the mountain, her playful calling awakens Balyet, the spirit of a young girl banished from her tribe a thousand years ago for irresponsibly causing the death of two brothers within a tribe. Jo sympathizes with the ostracized girl, who was flirting for fun, doing "what any girl might do." Angry at Granny Willet's treatment of her friends and longing for the friendship of the wistful spirit, Jo is almost led to her death when the ghost lures her to the highest crag. Wrightson's personification of the ancient mountains, depiction of aboriginal rites, and totally believable blending of contemporary vernacular with old ways are compelling examples of this storyteller's power. For non-Australian readers, the little known traditions underlying Wrightson's books and their emphasis on magical rather than human characters make unusual demands. However, a dramatic story and the force of Wrightson's language plus the idea of living in harmony with nature make this a compelling book for older readers.

SCIENCE FICTION

The line between fantasy and science fiction has always been difficult to draw, particularly in children's literature. Children are likely to use the label "science fiction" for any book that includes the paraphernalia of science, although critics make finer distinctions. It has been suggested that fantasy (even "science fantasy") presents a world that never was and never could be, whereas science fiction speculates on a world that, given what we now know of science, might just one day be possible. Sylvia Engdahl says that "science fiction differs from fantasy not in subject matter but in aim, and its unique aim is to suggest real hypotheses about mankind's future or about the nature of the universe."[31] Of course the difficulty comes in deciding what constitutes a "real

hypothesis." Are talking cats possible? Plants with a crystalline structure? Spaceships that think and are self-repairing? All these ideas have been put forth by science-fiction writers asking themselves "What if . . .?"

Science fiction is relevant for today's rapidly changing world. Writers must speculate about future technology and how new discoveries will affect our daily lives and thoughts. In order to do this, authors must construct a world in which scientific frontiers of genetic engineering, artificial intelligence, space exploration, or robotics have advanced beyond our present knowledge. As in modern fantasy, detailed descriptions of these "scientific principles" and the characters' acceptance of them make the story believable. H. M. Hoover speaks about the author's responsibility to be consistent with "facts":

> If the story takes place on an alien world, the reader must be able to believe humans can walk there. Everything, from gravity and atmosphere, geology and life forms, must fit and be a part of that world if it is to ring true. . . . If not, somewhere a bright child will say "baloney" or a less polite equivalent, and toss the book aside. Children may be gullible from lack of time to learn, but they're not stupid, and they remember details.[32]

In addition, authors who speak to today's reader about the future must consider the ethical or social implications inherent in the scientific issues they raise.

One of the values of science fiction is its ability to develop a child's imagination and intuition as well as exercising his or her speculative and improvisational abilities. While most literature offers a view of society as it is, science fiction assumes a vastly different society. Madeleine L'Engle suggests that children enter this world of speculation more easily than adults do: "Children have always been interested in these cosmic questions and riddles that adults often attempt to tame by placing into categories fit only for scientists or adults or theologians."[33]

[31]Sylvia Louise Engdahl, "The Changing Role of Science Fiction in Children's Literature," *The Horn Book Magazine*, vol. 47 (October 1971), p. 450.

[32]H. M. Hoover, "Where Do You Get Your Ideas?," *Top of the News*, vol. 39 (Fall 1982), p. 61.
[33]Madeleine L'Engle, "Childlike Wonder and the Truths of Science Fiction," *Children's Literature*, vol. 10 (Yale University Press, 1982), p. 102.

Much science fiction that considers cosmic questions falls within the realm of young adult novels. For instance, Peter Dickinson in *Eva* considers the consequences when the memory and the mind of a human girl is transferred from her ruined body to that of a healthy chimpanzee. H. M. Hoover's *Orvis* suggests what might happen if a robot developed human emotions. *The Duplicate* by William Sleator gives a teenage boy the power to be in two places at once with chilling results. Occasionally, however, older elementary school readers, drawn by a love of science, may read well above what adults consider their usual reading levels. Since newer science fiction tends to emphasize a concern with the complex emotional and physical consequences of technological breakthroughs to the future of humankind rather than the dangers posed by aliens or intergalactic warfare, perhaps science-fiction readers may be more compassionate and informed in choosing the future.

Through the Door

Many children come easily to science fiction by way of books that may not fit a purist's definition of the genre but which incorporate some of its trappings, such as robots, spaceships, futuristic settings, or scientific terminology. Eleanor Cameron's *The Wonderful Flight to the Mushroom Planet* begins a series of stories about Mr. Bass who lives on the planet Basidium. Alfred Slote has written a popular series that begins with *My Robot Buddy* in which Jack Jameson and his robot Danny One switch places to foil robot-nappers. Older readers are often entertained by Isaac Asimov's "Norby" series about an adolescent boy and his robot. While few of these books tackle weighty themes, they provide satisfaction to readers who can follow the characters through a series of adventures or who relish the ultimately happy conclusions in a science-fiction setting.

An exceptional book that presents a hopeful view of the future is Jill Paton Walsh's *The Green Book*. A family escapes Earth with others in a preprogrammed spacecraft before the "Disaster." Father tells Joe, Sarah, and Pattie that they can take very little with them but that this includes "one book per voyager." Pattie is ridiculed for

From the porthole of their departing spaceship, two sisters watch as the world diminishes and finally disappears in Lloyd Bloom's illustration from *The Green Book* by Jill Paton Walsh.

🐞   🐞   🐞

wasting her choice on a blank green-covered book. When they arrive at their destination planet, Pattie, as the youngest, has the privilege of naming their new home, a place of red foliage and shimmering silver plains. "We are at Shine, on the first day," says Pattie. Ironically, this shine is produced by the crystalline structure of the plant life on the planet. When the wheat seeds brought from Earth produce a crop of grains like "hexagonal yellow beads, shining like golden glass," it appears that the colony will face starvation. The children secretly grind the glasslike beads, mix and bake the dough, and eat the bread without harm. It is then that Pattie's blank book is needed to keep records, and the story-starved people discover that the green book is now full of the most satisfying story of all—their own. An excellent choice for reading aloud and discussing with third and fourth graders, this brief high-quality book raises thought-provoking speculations about life and survival on another planet. The writing is vivid and tight, evocative without being obscure, and an interesting twist in the narrative voice neatly brings together the opening and closing sentences. Illustrations by Lloyd Bloom match the solemn tone of the text and are memorable for their rounded shapes softened by the light on Shine.

Visitors to Earth

Television and motion pictures have eased our acceptance of the possibility of visitors from other parts of the universe. Whether the visitor arrives purposefully or inadvertently, young readers today are willing to suspend disbelief and are usually prepared to consider the dilemmas that visitor and human interactions present.

In *Star Ka'at* André Norton and Dorothy Madlee introduce readers to a superior breed of cats that visit earth in hopes of saving other cats before the world destroys itself. When orphans Jim and Elly Mae discover the Ka'at spaceship and go aboard, two Ka'ats they have befriended are able to communicate with them and so become their sponsors for the journey from Earth. In other books in the series, the children continue to aid Ka'ats Tiro and Mer in their efforts to protect Ka'at populations on other planets. Spunky African-American Elly Mae learns quickly and develops her powers of telepathy, but it is regrettable that the authors' representation of this child's speech relies more on errors in grammar than on use of an authentic dialect.

Tsynq Yr, an ace pilot from the Sylon Confederacy, crashes his cheap scout ship on Earth as he flees from a Zarnk attack. In *Stinker from Space*, Pamela Service tells the humorous story of how the dying spaceman tranfers to a new host body, that of a skunk. The skunk, now called Stinker, enlists the help of two children, Karen and her computer hacker friend Jonathan, in his plan to hijack a space shuttle to return to his galaxy. While adults in the story are slightly drawn and ineffectual, the suspicious alliance between the two new friends and the way their knowledge of outer space and computers help the visitor from space return to his galaxy are well realized.

Alexander Key presents another visitor to earth in *The Forgotten Door*, which explores the rights of

individuals and challenges readers' assumptions about the nature of human society. Little Jon wakens cold and bruised in a mossy cave and cannot remember who he is or where he came from. He is found by the kindly Bean family, who gradually discover some amazing facts about the quiet, sensitive boy. He cannot speak English, but he understands thought and gradually translates it into words. He can communicate with animals, even their cross dog. He eats only vegetables and knows nothing of money, guns, robbery, murder, war, or other evils. It soon becomes apparent to the Beans that he is not from this world. Rumors spread, however, and soon the federal government demands custody of Little Jon. Other political groups would like to use Jon's powers and the Beans are desperate for help. Finally, Jon is able to hear his parents calling him, and he communicates his concern for his friends, the Beans. As various forces close in on the tiny cabin, Jon and the Beans disappear through the Forgotten Door to the world Jon has described to them—a world so simple as to need no laws, leaders, or money, and one where intelligent people work together. The fast pace of the story and its substantial characters and challenging themes have made this a good discussion choice for small groups of fourth and fifth graders. For slightly older readers, *Star Lord* by Louise Lawrence considers a similar situation, further complicated by the supernatural powers present within a Welsh mountainside where the visitor's spacecraft lands.

Daniel Pinkwater's visitor to this planet is *Borgel*, who moves into Melvin Spellbound's family guest room as a sort of long-lost uncle. The special occasions when Melvin is invited into Uncle Borgel's room to drink Norwegian volemoss tea lead to an invitation to travel in time, space, and the other. But first Uncle Borgel must define a few terms:

❧ "The first thing you have to understand is that time is not like a string. . . . *[T]ime* is like a map of the state of New Jersey—not like the state of New Jersey or even the state of New Jersey seen from the air, or from a satellite—it is like a *map* of the state of New Jersey. Got that?"

"Sure."

"Okay, next is *space*. Space is sort of like a bagel,

but an elliptical one, with poppy seeds. You got that?"

"Sure."

"Good. Next is *the other*. This is the hardest to explain. The best I can do is that the other is like a mixed salad in which there is only one ingredient you like."[34]

Borgel takes on the education of Melvin. Before long, Melvin, the unlovable family dog Fafnir who can suddenly speak, and Borgel are off to outer space to visit a time traveler's root beer stand managed by a Bloboform. There they begin their search for the Great Popsicle, which is a coveted sort of energy bundle. Pinkwater's puns, jokes, asides, and the flip "science" he invents are bound to be traded back and forth by older readers who relish the social aspects of reading a truly funny book.

Terry Pratchett's "Bromeliad Trilogy" concerns a race of nomes, tiny four-inch beings who were stranded on earth when their scout ship crashed thousands of years ago. The dwindling band is guided by a black box, called The Thing, which is actually a powerful computer. In *Truckers*, part of the Borrower-like people live under the floorboards in a department store scheduled for demolition. A group of nomes who have been living outside in the fields and hedges move into "Arnold Bros. (Est. 1905)" and realize that the highly regimented nome society in the store has traditions, regulations, and superstitions, but no true knowledge of the outside world or of their impending doom. Under the leadership of young Masklin, the practical girl Grimma, and the irascible old harridan Granny Morkle, the group commandeers a truck and escapes into the wintry world. In *Diggers*, they arrive at a seemingly abandoned quarry only to run into human trouble. But they manage to combine efforts to start the Cat, a terrible yellow beast that can defeat the humans. In *Wings*, the nomes struggle to place The Thing on the space shuttle so that it can inform the mother ship of the nomes' whereabouts. Pratchett's wit is most evident in the first story, which challenges readers with, among other things, puns based on knowledge of department

stores. Pratchett's contrasting of the timid, unadventurous store nomes with the scrappy and inventive outdoor nomes is a satiric commentary on human foibles. In addition, his descriptions of how small beings might go about driving trucks and bulldozers, tricking humans, or contacting outer space are believable, humorous, and often moving accounts.

Views of the Future

Science fiction of the highest level presents the reader with complex hypotheses about the future of humankind. Many of H. M. Hoover's novels raise questions about the organization of society and the nature of the world following a massive ecological disaster. Writers such as John Christopher and Madeleine L'Engle imagine other life-forms and their interactions with our world. William Sleator in *The Green Futures of Tycho* asks how present time may be altered to affect the future; in L'Engle's *A Swiftly Tilting Planet*, the past is altered to change the present and future. Throughout these novels of speculation runs the question of which human qualities and responsibilities will become—or remain—essential in time to come.

A Wrinkle in Time suggests that love and individuality will continue to be important for the future. If there is a classic in the field of science fiction for children, it may be this Newbery award winner by Madeleine L'Engle. The exciting story concerns Charles Wallace, a 5-year-old brilliant beyond his age and time, and Meg, his 12-year-old sister, whose stubbornness later becomes an asset. With the help of Calvin O'Keefe, a 14-year-old on whose stability the two often rely, the children begin a frenzied search for their missing father, a scientist working for the government. They are aided in their search by three women who have supernatural powers—Mrs. Whatsit, Mrs. Who, and Mrs. Which. To rescue Mr. Murry, the children travel by means of a wrinkle in time, or a tesseract, to the evil planet of Camazotz. The people of Camazotz, having given up their identities to It, do everything in synchronization. When Charles Wallace attempts to resist It by reason, he, too, is captured. Though Meg is able to save her father, they must leave Charles Wallace

[34]Daniel Pinkwater, *Borgel* (New York: Macmillan, 1990), pp. 36–37.

behind. Exhausted and still under the evil influence of It, Meg is slowly nursed back to love and peace by another strange but loving creature, Aunt Beast. When Meg realizes that only she can save Charles Wallace, she returns to confront It with what she knows It does not have or understand—the power of love. This many-layered story may be read for the exciting plot alone or for the themes and the values it espouses.

A Wind in the Door, also by L'Engle, is a companion story involving many of the previous characters with new situations and other creatures. The story concerns the fight to save Charles Wallace from a baffling illness. Meg, Calvin, and Mr. Jenkins, the cold, remote principal of the school, are led to a planet in galactic space where size does not exist. Here they are made small enough to enter Charles Wallace's body and help fight the attacking forces of evil, the Echthroi. Only when Meg names them with her own name does she overcome the Echthroi and save Charles. The story emphasizes the importance of every minuscule part of the universe in carrying out its purpose in living. *A Wind in the Door* is more complex than *A Wrinkle in Time*, but L'Engle is capable of conveying her message to perceptive children of 9 or 10 and up.

A Swiftly Tilting Planet completes L'Engle's Time Trilogy. Charles Wallace has been saved, first from the dehumanization of It, and second from a rare blood disease. Now, in this story, the reader discovers why Charles Wallace has been twice rescued, for his ultimate mission involves saving the world from total destruction. He must journey back in historical time to change some seemingly small part of past relationships so that a potential world war in the present may be averted. The cast of characters has grown older, with Meg now married to Calvin and expecting a baby and Charles Wallace a teenager. This is by far the most demanding of the three volumes, as there are many characters in several time frames to attend to. The Time Trilogy is a unique and wonderful combination of science fiction, modern fantasy, traditional lore, and religious symbolism by which L'Engle stretches the minds and the spirits of her readers.

The White Mountains quartet by John Christopher describes a future world that has been reduced to a primitive society. However, people in this twenty-first-century world are controlled by machine creatures called Tripods. At 14 each human being must be "capped," a ceremony in which a steel plate is inserted into the skull to make the wearer a servant of the state. No one is allowed to discuss the capping ceremony, but Will finds out that his friend Jack has some real reservations about it. After Jack's capping he appears to be a different person—docile, too busy working to be a friend. Will talks to a seemingly crazy Vagrant and finds out that there is a colony of free people living in *The White Mountains* to the south. Will describes the terrifying journey that he and two other boys make to reach this refuge. In the second book, *The City of Gold and Lead*, Will wins an athletic contest in order to have "the privilege" of serving the master Tripods. Actually, he goes as a spy to learn the secrets of this alien culture. In the third book of the series, *The Pool of Fire*, the Tripods are defeated and humankind is free to set up its own government. The reader hopes that Will's plan for world unity will succeed, but realistically Will is forced by quarreling, dissident groups to give up his plans for world peace. Christopher explains in an ingenious prequel how the Tripods assumed power in *When the Tripods Came*.

Christopher's second science-fiction series (*The Prince in Waiting, Beyond the Burning Lands*, and *The Sword of the Spirits*) deals with England in the twenty-first century. People measure time since "The Disaster," a period of volcanic activity, earthquakes, and strong radiation from the sun, which destroyed all of humans' technical accomplishments. Amid the ruins a kind of medieval society has sprung up, with independent city-states not far advanced from barbarian tribes. Religion takes the form of Spiritism in this society, and the use of machines or the pursuit of science is strictly forbidden. These books are much more violent than the White Mountain trilogy, which is in keeping with their imagined setting. However, the violence may be justified because it raises the ethical questions of whether violence impersonalized by distance and machine is any different from hand-to-hand violence and whether it is possible to keep "rules" in war. All of John Christopher's books help children consider the problems of the future of humankind, but the themes never overburden the suspense or action of the stories.

H. M. Hoover is a prolific writer of science fiction for children and young adults. Many of her novels include complex political and social systems, challenging ideas, multiple species of thinking beings, and large casts of characters. *This Time of Darkness* presents a future in which most people live underground inside domed, multi-level cities, crowded and dirty but safe from the uncertainties of the outside atmosphere. Eleven-year-old Amy has been taught by her learning center that all layers of the city are alike, that there is nothing left or living outside the walls. However, unlike other citizens, Amy can read, and when she befriends Axel, who says he once lived outside, the two plan an escape. Their flight takes them on a terrifying but fascinating tour to the highest levels of the city where they are finally ejected as undesirables. Once outside, they must survive sunburn, starvation, an attack by mutants, and a brush fire before they, and the ever-present watcher following them, are reunited with Axel's people. Hoover imagines a very different view of future civilization after "the Great Destruction" in *Children of Morrow* and its sequel, *Treasures of Morrow*.

In *The Lake at the End of the World* by Caroline Macdonald, Diana and her parents think they are the last lonely survivors on earth. Nuclear accidents, toxic spills, and the pollution of the earth from overuse of herbicides and fertilizers have destroyed civilization in the twenty-first century. However, while gliding on wings her scientist father has made for her, Diana spots a boy and a dog near the mouth of a cave. The boy is one of about a hundred survivors living in an underground colony ruled by a power-hungry Utopian. Macdonald alternates chapters between Diana's and Hector's present-tense journal entries and thoughts as the two become friends. Hector's arrival causes friction between Diana and her parents, but Hector proves his mettle when he returns below ground for some much needed medicine to cure Diana's mother of a leg infection. When Hector discovers his colony is plotting to discharge their wastes into the unpolluted lake where Diana and her family live, he acts deci-

sively rather than in the passive way his leader had conditioned him. Older readers must use inferential skills and patience to fill in the actions of the past, but the strong characterizations, believable dialogue, and the carefully plotted, hopeful conclusion make this an excellent read-aloud choice for middle school children.

Teenager Ann Burden in *Z for Zachariah* by Robert C. O'Brien thinks she is the last living person on earth. As the radio stations go off the air one by one, it becomes apparent that no one is ever going to return to her valley. Ann begins to carve out a solitary life, accompanied only by the family dog, when she sees what appears to be smoke from a campfire on the horizon. Drawing closer, she sees it is indeed another person, who is wearing a radiation-proof safe-suit. After initially hiding from John Loomis, Ann becomes his caretaker when he falls ill from radiation sickness. But Loomis does not provide Ann with hoped-for companionship; instead, he becomes more and more possessive of Ann's work time and property while protecting his safe-suit. Eventually, Ann must hide in the hills to avoid Loomis and the possibility of being killed. At last, she decides on a plan to steal the safe-suit and leave the valley in hopes that she will find other survivors she has dreamed about. Her last encounter with Loomis leaves him in the valley and finds Ann headed toward the west where she once saw circling birds. Written in the form of a diary kept by Ann, this story is rich in the details of her survival and growing resolve. Ann traces her doubt and anger about the many choices she must make, but the reader does not doubt that Ann will find the others for whom she searches.

Enchantress from the Stars by Sylvia Louise Engdahl is an unusual story that almost exceeds the boundaries of science fiction. The mission of Elana and her party is to save the Andrecians from the Imperialists. Elana belongs to an anthropological service of the future which represents the most advanced humanity in the universe. By contrast, the Andrecians are at a medieval stage of development; people still believe in magic and will reward anyone who can kill the "terrible dragon." The dragon, however, is really an earth-mover with which the Imperialists intend to destroy forests and colonize. Eventually the fourth son of an Andrecian woodcutter and Elana defeat the invaders with the values of love, faith, and sacrifice that transcend all levels of development. The story helps readers see their own world in a different perspective, a function of all good literature. In a somewhat didactic sequel, *The Far Side of Evil,* Engdahl deals with the consequences of misuse of nuclear power. *This Star Shall Abide* and *Beyond the Tomorrow Mountains* are other contributions by this major writer of science fiction for young adults.

Fantasy for children needs no defense.

Whether a modern fairy tale like *Many Moons* or *The Little Prince,* modern fantasy like *Charlotte's Web* or *The Dark Is Rising,* or the science fiction of *A Wrinkle in Time* or *The Green Book,* these lasting books can speak for our time and the times to come. They stretch children's imaginations, present our own world in a new perspective, and ask readers to consider how present actions may affect earth's ecological, political, and social future. (See Chapter 12, "Stewards of the Earth," a curriculum web that partially deals with this topic.)

SUGGESTED LEARNING EXPERIENCES

1. Ask a group of middle graders, or your friends, to list their ten favorite children's books. How many of these could be categorized as modern fantasy?
2. Write a modern fairy tale, fable, or tall tale using the old forms, but with twentieth-century content reflecting today's changing values. For example, you might want to consider reversing the stereotyped sex roles of the prince and princess.
3. Working with children, or your peers, make an illustrated map to show an extraordinary world or imaginary kingdom that you have discovered in a book. Make a key to locate events of the story.
4. Compare the Chronicles of Narnia by C. S. Lewis with Lloyd Alexander's Prydain series; or compare two animal fantasies, such as *Charlotte's Web* with *Pigs Might Fly.* In what ways are they alike; how are they different?
5. Choose a book of high fantasy or time fantasy and identify motifs that seem derived from folklore, myth, or legend. Which of these motifs are common in other modern fantasies?
6. Make a display or a chart of the many symbols and their meaning found in *The Dark Is Rising* by Susan Cooper.
7. Think of some family heirloom that might act as a magical amulet that would take you back to the time when your mother or father was 12 years old. How does the heirloom "work"? Where would you be? What might you witness?
8. Ask yourself what might happen to the world of tomorrow if hunger were eliminated or if robots took over your school, or if hydrogen fusion were made a workable source of energy. Think through the impact of one such scientific advancement.

RELATED READINGS

1. Anderson, Douglas A. *The Annotated Hobbit,* illustrated by J. R. R. Tolkien. New York: Houghton Mifflin, 1988.
    Fascinating background information on Tolkien's sources for story, choices of names, scholarship, revisions, and illustrations, including many examples from foreign editions.

2. Cameron, Eleanor. *The Green and Burning Tree*. Boston: Little, Brown, 1969.

   The title essay in this fine book of literary criticism is a study of time fantasy. As the author of many fantasies herself, Cameron is in a unique position to evaluate the fantasies in this category.

3. Campbell, Joseph, *The Hero with a Thousand Faces*, 2nd ed. Princeton, N.J.: Princeton University Press, 1968.

   This standard scholarly work on the "monomyth," or the archetypal story of the hero, helps the serious student of high fantasy to see the protagonist of the quest in a universal perspective.

4. Egoff, Sheila. *Worlds Within: Children's Fantasy from the Middle Ages to Today*. Chicago: American Library Association, 1988.

   A study of the development of children's fantasy from its roots in ancient myth and legend to the intense and sometimes violent novels being written today.

5. Egoff, Sheila, G. T. Stubbs, and L. F. Ashley. *Only Connect: Readings on Children's Literature*, 2nd ed. New York: Oxford University Press, 1980.

   All the selections under "Fairy Tales, Fantasy, Animals" would be appropriate reading for this chapter. However, don't miss reading the article by C. S. Lewis, "On Three Ways of Writing for Children," or P. L. Travers's (creator of Mary Poppins) fine article, "Only Connect."

6. Haviland, Virginia. *Children and Literature: Views and Reviews*. Glenview, Ill.: Scott, Foresman, 1973.

   The former children's librarian of the Library of Congress has made an excellent selection of readings for this book. All of the entries for Chapter 6 would be appropriate, but two seem to have great significance for this chapter: Lloyd Alexander's "The Flat-Heeled Muse" and Sylvia Engdahl's "The Changing Role of Science Fiction in Children's Literature."

7. Hunter, Mollie. *Talent Is Not Enough*. New York: Harper & Row, 1975.

   A talented author discusses writing for children. In the essay titled "One World," Hunter maintains that true fantasy so integrates the real and the imagined worlds that it becomes believable. She also acknowledges fantasy's debt to ancient folklore, describing the basis for her own writing of *A Stranger Came Ashore*.

8. Le Guin, Ursula K. *The Language of the Night: Essays on Fantasy and Science Fiction*, Susan Wood, ed. New York: Putnam, 1979.

   Excellent essays by an outstanding writer of fantasy and science fiction discuss "Myth and Archetype in Science Fiction" and ask "Why are Americans Afraid of Dragons?," among other questions.

9. Mahy, Margaret. "A Dissolving Ghost: Possible Operations of Truth in Children's Books and the Lives of Children" in *The Arbuthnot Lectures 1980–1989*. Chicago: American Library Association, 1990.

   Mahy's intriguing essay describes the transformation of a real-life experience into a fantastic tale. See, also, Patricia Wrightson's essay, "Stones in Pools," in which she discusses the continuity of story from ancient times and the wonder found in fantasy.

10. May, Jill P. *Lloyd Alexander*. New York: Twayne, 1991.

    A twelve-page biographical essay is followed by a critical examination of each of Alexander's books. Among others, May discusses Alexander's innovative abilities and the diverse sources on which his books draw.

11. Meek, Margaret, Aidan Warlow, and Griselda Barton. *The Cool Web: The Pattern of Children's Readings*. New York: Atheneum, 1978.

    This fine collection of some fifty essays on children's literature was first published in England. James Britton's article on "The Role of Fantasy" and Arthur Applebee's "Where Does Cinderella Live?" have particular importance for this chapter.

12. Nadelman, Ruth Lynn. *Fantasy Literature for Children and Young Adults: An Annotated Bibliography*, 3rd ed. New York: Bowker, 1989.

    A helpful reference tool, especially for reader advisory and the discovery or sorting out of fantasy series.

REFERENCES[35]

Adams, Richard. *Watership Down*. Macmillan, 1974.

Aiken, Joan. *Black Hearts in Battersea*, illustrated by Robin Jacques. Doubleday, 1964.

_____. *The Moon's Revenge*, illustrated by Alan Lee. Knopf, 1987.

_____. *Nightbirds on Nantucket*, illustrated by Robin Jacques. Doubleday, 1966.

_____. *The Stolen Lake*. Delacorte, 1981.

_____. *The Wolves of Willoughby Chase*, illustrated by Pat Marriott. Doubleday, 1963.

Alexander, Lloyd. *The Beggar Queen*. Dutton, 1984.

_____. *The Black Cauldron*. Holt, 1965.

_____. *The Book of Three*. Holt, 1964.

_____. *The Castle of Llyr*. Holt, 1966.

_____. *The Cat Who Wished to Be a Man*. Dutton, 1973.

_____. *Coll and His White Pig*, illustrated by Evaline Ness. Holt, 1965.

_____. *The Drackenburg Adventure*. Dutton, 1988.

_____. *The El Dorado Adventure*. Dutton, 1987.

_____. *The Foundling and Other Tales of Prydain*. Dell, 1982.

_____. *The High King*. Holt, 1968.

_____. *The Illyrian Adventure*. Dutton, 1986.

_____. *The Jedera Adventure*. Dutton, 1989.

_____. *The Kestrel*. Dutton, 1982.

_____. *The Marvelous Misadventures of Sebastian*. Dutton, 1970.

_____. *The Philadelphia Adventure*. Dutton, 1990.

_____. *The Remarkable Journey of Prince Jen*. Dutton, 1991.

_____. *Taran Wanderer*. Holt, 1967.

_____. *The Truthful Harp*, illustrated by Evaline Ness. Holt, 1971.

_____. *Westmark*. Dutton, 1981.

_____. *The Wizard in the Tree*, illustrated by Laszlo Kubinyi. Dutton, 1975.

Andersen, Hans Christian. *The Emperor's New Clothes*, illustrated by Virginia Lee Burton. Houghton Mifflin, 1949.

_____. *The Fir Tree*, illustrated by Nancy Ekholm Burkert. Harper, 1970.

_____. *Hans Christian Andersen: The Complete Fairy Tales and Stories*, translated by Erik Haugaard. Doubleday, 1974.

_____. *The Little Match Girl*, illustrated by Rachel Isadora. Putnam's, 1987.

_____. *The Little Match Girl*, illustrated by Blair Lent. Houghton Mifflin, 1968.

_____. "The Little Mermaid" in *Hans Christian Andersen: The Complete Fairy Tales and Stories*, translated by Erik Christian Haugaard. Doubleday, 1974.

_____. *The Nightingale*, translated by Anthea Bell, illustrated by Lisbeth Zwerger. Picture Book Studio, 1985.

_____. *The Nightingale*, adapted by Anna Bier, illustrated by Demi. Harcourt, 1985.

_____. *The Nightingale*, translated by Eva Le Gallienne, illustrated by Nancy Ekholm Burkert. Harper, 1965.

_____. "The Princess and the Pea" in *Seven Tales*, translated by Eva Le Gallienne, illustrated by Maurice Sendak. Harper, 1990 (1959).

_____. *The Princess and the Pea*, illustrated by Paul Galdone. Seabury, 1978.

_____. *The Snow Queen*, illustrated by Marcia Brown. Scribner, 1972.

_____. *The Snow Queen*, retold by Amy Ehrlich, ilustrated by Susan Jeffers. Dial, 1982.

_____. *The Snow Queen*, adapted by Naomi Lewis, illustrated by Errol Le Cain. Viking, 1979.

_____. *The Snow Queen*, retold by Neil Philip, illustrated by Sally Holmes. Lothrop, 1989.

_____. *The Steadfast Tin Soldier*, illustrated by Paul Galdone. Clarion, 1979.

_____. *The Steadfast Tin Soldier*, illustrated by David Jorgensen. Knopf, 1986.

_____. *Thumbelina*, retold by Amy Ehrlich, illustrated by Susan Jeffers. Dial, 1979.

_____. *The Tinderbox*, illustrated by Barry Moser. Little, Brown, 1990.

_____. *The Tinderbox*, illustrated by Warwick Hutton. McElderry Books, 1988.

_____. *The Ugly Duckling*, illustrated by Troy Howell. Putnam, 1990.

[35]All books listed at the end of this chapter are recommended, subject to the qualifications noted in the text. See Appendix for publishers' complete addresses.

_____. *The Ugly Duckling*, retold by Marianna Mayer, illustrated by Thomas Locker. Macmillan, 1987.

_____. *The Wild Swans*, retold by Amy Ehrlich, illustrated by Susan Jeffers. Dial, 1981.

Arkin, Alan. *The Lemming Condition*. Harper, 1976.

Asimov, Janet, and Isaac Asimov. *Norby, the Mixed-Up Robot*. Walker, 1983.

_____. *Norby Finds a Villain*. Walker, 1987.

_____. *Norby and Yobo's Great Adventure*. Walker, 1989.

Atwater, Richard, and Florence Atwater. *Mr. Popper's Penguins*, illustrated by Robert Lawson. Little, Brown, 1938.

Babbitt, Natalie. *Kneeknock Rise*. Farrar, Straus, 1970.

_____. *The Search for Delicious*. Farrar, Straus, 1969.

_____. *Tuck Everlasting*. Farrar, Straus, 1975.

Bailey, Carolyn Sherwin. *Miss Hickory*, illustrated by Ruth Gannett. Viking, 1962 (1946).

Banks, Lynne Reid. *The Indian in the Cupboard*, illustrated by Brock Cole. Doubleday, 1981.

_____. *The Return of the Indian*, illustrated by William Geldard. Doubleday, 1986.

_____. *The Secret of the Indian*, illustrated by Ted Lewin. Doubleday, 1989.

Baum, L. Frank. *The Wizard of Oz*. World, 1972 (1900).

Bellairs, John. *The House with a Clock in Its Walls*. Dial, 1973.

Bond, Michael. *A Bear Called Paddington*, illustrated by Peggy Fortnum. Houghton Mifflin, 1960.

_____. *More about Paddington*, illustrated by Peggy Fortnum. Houghton Mifflin, 1962.

_____. *Paddington at Large*, illustrated by Peggy Fortnum. Houghton Mifflin, 1963.

_____. *Paddington Helps Out*, illustrated by Peggy Fortnum. Houghton Mifflin, 1961.

_____. *Paddington Marches On*, illustrated by Peggy Fortnum. Houghton Mifflin, 1965.

_____. *Paddington Takes the Air*, illustrated by Peggy Fortnum. Houghton Mifflin, 1971.

Bond, Nancy. *A String in the Harp*. Atheneum, 1976.

Boston, L. M. *The Children of Green Knowe*, illustrated by Peter Boston. Harcourt, 1955.

_____. *An Enemy at Green Knowe*, illustrated by Peter Boston. Harcourt, 1964.

_____. *The River at Green Knowe*, illustrated by Peter Boston. Harcourt, 1959.

_____. *The Treasure of Green Knowe*, illustrated by Peter Boston. Harcourt, 1958.

Brittain, Bill. *The Devil's Donkey: A Tale of Coven Tree*, illustrated by Andrew Glass. Harper, 1981.

_____. *Dr. Dredd's Wagon of Wonders: A Tale of Coven Tree*, illustrated by Andrew Glass. Harper, 1987.

_____. *Professor Popkin's Prodigious Polish: A Tale of Coven Tree*, illustrated by Andrew Glass. Harper, 1990.

_____. *The Wish Giver: A Tale of Coven Tree*, illustrated by Andrew Glass. Harper, 1983.

Brown, Marcia. *Stone Soup*. Scribner's, 1947. (Traditional)

Browne, Anthony. *The Tunnel*. Knopf, 1990. (Picture Book)

Buffie, Margaret. *The Haunting of Frances Rain*. Scholastic, 1989. (Published in Canada as *Who Is Frances Rain?* Kids Can Press, 1987).

Butterworth, Oliver. *The Enormous Egg*, illustrated by Louis Darling. Little, Brown, 1956.

Cameron, Eleanor. *The Court of the Stone Children*. Dutton, 1973.

_____. *The Wonderful Flight to the Mushroom Planet*, illustrated by Robert Henneberger. Little, Brown, 1954.

Carroll, Lewis, pseud. (Charles L. Dodgson). *Alice's Adventures in Wonderland and Through the Looking Glass*, illustrated by John Tenniel. Macmillan, 1963 (1865, 1872).

Catling, Patrick Skene. *The Chocolate Touch*, illustrated by Margot Apple. Morrow, 1979 (1952).

Chew, Ruth. *Mostly Magic*. Holiday, 1982.

Chetwin, Grace. *The Crystal Stair*. Bradbury, 1988.

_____. *Gom on Windy Mountain*. Lothrop, 1986.

_____. *The Riddle and the Rune*. Bradbury, 1987.

_____. *The Starstone*. Bradbury, 1989.

Christopher, John. *Beyond the Burning Lands*. Macmillan, 1971.

_____. *The City of Gold and Lead*. Macmillan, 1967.

_____. *The Guardians*. Macmillan, 1970.

_____. *The Pool of Fire*. Macmillan, 1968.

_____. *The Prince in Waiting*. Macmillan, 1970.

_____. *The Sword of the Spirits*. Macmillan, 1972.

_____. *When the Tripods Came*. Dutton, 1988.

_____. *The White Mountains*. Macmillan, 1967.

Cleary, Beverly. *The Mouse and the Motorcycle*, illustrated by Louis Darling. Morrow, 1965.

_____. *Ralph S. Mouse*, illustrated by Paul O. Zelinsky. Morrow, 1982.

_____. *Runaway Ralph*, illustrated by Louis Darling. Morrow, 1970.

Conly, Jane. *Racso and the Rats of NIMH*, illustrated by Leonard Lubin. Harper, 1986.

_____. *R-T, Margaret, and the Rats of NIMH*, illustrated by Leonard Lubin. Harper, 1990.

Conrad, Pam. *Stonewords*. Harper, 1990.

Cooper, Susan. *The Dark Is Rising*, illustrated by Alan E. Cober. Atheneum, 1973.

_____. *Greenwitch*. Atheneum, 1974.

_____. *The Grey King*. Atheneum, 1975.

_____. *Over Sea, Under Stone*, illustrated by Marjorie Gill. Harcourt, 1966.

_____. *The Selkie Girl*, illustrated by Warwick Hutton. Macmillan, 1986. (Traditional)

_____. *Silver on the Tree*. Atheneum, 1977.

_____. *Tam Lin*, illustrated by Warwick Hutton. Macmillan, 1990. (Traditional)

Corbett, Scott. *The Lemonade Trick*, illustrated by Paul Galdone. Little, Brown, 1972 (1960).

Dahl, Roald. *Charlie and the Chocolate Factory*, illustrated by Joseph Schindelman. Knopf, 1972.

_____. *Charlie and the Great Glass Elevator*, illustrated by Joseph Schindelman. Knopf, 1972.

_____. *James and the Giant Peach*, illustrated by Nancy Ekholm Burkert. Knopf, 1961.

_____. *Matilda*, illustrated by Quentin Blake. Viking Kestrel, 1988.

de Beaumont, Mme. *Beauty and the Beast*, illustrated by Jan Brett. Houghton Mifflin, 1989. (Traditional)

Dickinson, Peter. *Eva*. Delacorte, 1989.

_____. *Merlin Dreams*, illustrated by Alan Lee. Delacorte, 1988.

du Bois, William Pène. *The Twenty-One Balloons*. Viking, 1947.

Eager, Edward. *Half Magic*, illustrated by N. M. Bodecker. Harcourt, 1954.

_____. *Seven-Day Magic*, illustrated by N. M. Bodecker. Harcourt, 1962.

Engdahl, Sylvia Louise. *Beyond the Tomorrow Mountains*, illustrated by Richard Cuffari. Atheneum, 1973.

_____. *Enchantress from the Stars*, illustrated by Rodney Shackell. Atheneum, 1970.

_____. *The Far Side of Evil*, illustrated by Richard Cuffari. Atheneum, 1971.

_____. *This Star Shall Abide*, illustrated by Richard Cuffari. Atheneum, 1972.

Farmer, Penelope. *The Summer Birds*, illustrated by James Spanfeller. Harcourt, 1962.

Fleischman, Paul. *The Half-A-Moon Inn*, illustrated by Kathy Jacobi. Harper, 1980.

Fleischman, Sid. *The Midnight Horse*, illustrated by Peter Sis. Greenwillow, 1990.

_____. *The Whipping Boy*, illustrated by Peter Sis. Greenwillow, 1986.

Garfield, Leon. *Mister Corbett's Ghost*, illustrated by Alan E. Cober. Pantheon, 1968.

Gerstein, Mordicai. *The Seal Mother*. Dial, 1986. (Traditional)

Godden, Rumer. *The Dolls' House*, illustrated by Tasha Tudor. Viking, 1962 (1947).

_____. *Fu-Dog*, illustrated by Valerie Littlewood. Viking, 1990.

_____. *Little Plum*. Viking, 1987.

_____. *Miss Happiness and Miss Flower*. Viking, 1987.

_____. *The Mousewife*, illustrated by Heidi Holder. Viking, 1982 (1951).

Grahame, Kenneth. *The Open Road*, illustrated by Beverly Gooding. Scribner's, 1980.

_____. *The Reluctant Dragon*, illustrated by Ernest H. Shepard. Holiday, 1938.

_____. *The River Bank: From The Wind in the Willows*, illustrated by Adrienne Adams. Scribner's, 1977.

_____. *Wayfarers All: From The Wind in the Willows*, illustrated by Beverly Gooding. Scribner's, 1981.

_____. *The Wind in the Willows*, illustrated by E. H. Shepard. Scribner's, 1940 (1908).

Griffith, Helen V. *Caitlin's Holiday*, illustrated by Susan Condie Lamb. Greenwillow, 1990.

Grimm Brothers. *Rumpelstiltskin*, illustrated by Paul O. Zelinsky. Dutton, 1986. (Traditional)

Hahn, Mary Downing. *Wait Till Helen Comes: A Ghost Story*. Houghton Mifflin, 1986.

Hamilton, Virginia. *The Magical Adventures of Pretty Pearl*. Harper, 1983.

_____. *Sweet Whispers, Brother Rush*. Philomel, 1982.

Hamley, Dennis. *Hare's Choice*, illustrated by Meg Rutherford. Delacorte, 1990.

Hoban, Russell. *The Mouse and His Child*, illustrated by Lillian Hoban. Harper, 1967.

Hodges, Margaret. *St. George and the Dragon*, illustrated by Trina Schart Hyman. Little, Brown, 1984. (Traditional)

Hoover, H. M. *The Children of Morrow*. Four Winds, 1973.

_____. *Orvis*. Penguin, 1987.

_____. *This Time of Darkness*. Viking, 1980.

_____. *Treasures of Morrow*. Four Winds, 1976.

Howe, Deborah, and James Howe. *Bunnicula*, illustrated by Leslie Morrill. Atheneum, 1983.

Howe, James. *The Celery Stalks at Midnight*, illustrated by Leslie Morrill. Atheneum, 1983.

_____. *Howliday Inn*, illustrated by Lynn Munsinger. Atheneum, 1982.

Hunter, Mollie. *The Haunted Mountain*, illustrated by Laszlo Kubinyi. Harper, 1972.

_____. *The Mermaid Summer*. Harper, 1988.

_____. *A Stranger Came Ashore*. Harper, 1975.

Hurmence, Belinda. *A Girl Called Boy*. Clarion, 1982.

Jacques, Brian. *Mariel of Redwall*, illustrated by Gary Chalk. Philomel, 1992.

_____. *Mattimeo*, illustrated by Gary Chalk. Philomel, 1990.

_____. *Mossflower*, illustrated by Gary Chalk. Philomel, 1988.

_____. *Redwall*, illustrated by Gary Chalk. Philomel, 1987.

James, Betsy. *The Red Cloak*. Chronicle Books, 1989. (Traditional)

Jansson, Tove. *Tales from Moominvalley*, translated by Thomas Warburton. Walck, 1964.

Jarrell, Randall. *The Bat-Poet*, illustrated by Maurice Sendak. Macmillan, 1964.

Jeffers, Susan. *Wild Robin*. Dutton. 1976. (Traditional)

Jones, Diana Wynne. *Charmed Life*. Greenwillow, 1989.

_____. *The Lives of Christopher Chant*. Greenwillow, 1988.

Juster, Norton. *The Phantom Tollbooth*, illustrated by Jules Feiffer. Random, 1961.

Kendall, Carol. *The Gammage Cup*, illustrated by Erik Blegvad. Harcourt, 1959.

Kennedy, Richard. *Amy's Eyes*, illustrated by Richard Egielski. Harper, 1985.

Key, Alexander. *The Forgotten Door*. Westminster, 1965.

King-Smith, Dick. *Ace: The Very Important Pig*, illustrated by Lynette Hemmant. Crown, 1990.

_____. *Babe the Gallant Pig*, illustrated by Mary Rayner. Crown, 1985.

_____. *The Fox Busters*, illustrated by Jon Miller. Delacorte, 1988.

_____. *Pigs Might Fly*, illustrated by Mary Rayner. Viking, 1982.

Langton, Jane. *The Diamond in the Window*, illustrated by Erik Blegvad. Harper, 1962.

_____. *The Fledgling*. Harper, 1980.

Lawrence, Louise. *Star Lord*. Harper, 1978.

Lawson, Robert. *Rabbit Hill*. Viking, 1944.

_____. *The Tough Winter*. Viking, 1954.

Le Guin, Ursula K. *The Farthest Shore*, illustrated by Gail Garraty. Atheneum, 1972.

_____. *Tehanu: The Last Book of Earthsea*. Atheneum, 1990.

_____. *The Tombs of Atuan*, illustrated by Gail Garraty. Atheneum, 1971.

_____. *A Wizard of Earthsea*, illustrated by Ruth Robbins. Parnassus, 1968.

L'Engle, Madeleine. *A Swiftly Tilting Planet*, Farrar, Straus, 1978.

_____. *A Wind in the Door*. Farrar, Straus, 1973.

_____. *A Wrinkle in Time*. Farrar, Straus, 1962.

Lewis, C. S. *The Horse and His Boy*, illustrated by Pauline Baynes. Macmillan, 1962.

_____. *The Last Battle*, illustrated by Pauline Baynes. Macmillan, 1964.

_____. *The Lion, the Witch, and the Wardrobe*, illustrated by Pauline Baynes. Macmillan, 1961.

_____. *The Magician's Nephew*, illustrated by Pauline Baynes. Macmillan, 1964.

_____. *Prince Caspian, the Return to Narnia*, illustrated by Pauline Baynes. Macmillan, 1964.

_____. *The Silver Chair*, illustrated by Pauline Baynes. Macmillan, 1962.

_____. *The Voyage of the "Dawn Treader,"* illustrated by Pauline Baynes. Macmillan, 1962.

Lindgren, Astrid. *Pippi Goes on Board*, translated by Florence Lamborn, illustrated by Louis S. Glanzman. Viking, 1957.

_____. *Pippi in the South Seas*, translated by Florence Lamborn, illustrated by Louis S. Glanzman. Viking, 1959.

_____. *Pippi Longstocking*, illustrated by Louis S. Glanzman. Viking, 1950.

_____. *Pippi on the Run*. Viking, 1976.

Lively, Penelope. *The Ghost of Thomas Kempe*, illustrated by Anthony Maitland. Dutton, 1973.

Lunn, Janet. *The Root Cellar*. Scribner's, 1983.

McCaffrey, Anne. *Dragondrums*, illustrated by Fred Marcellino. Atheneum, 1979.

_____. *Dragonsinger*. Antheneum, 1977.

_____. *Dragonsong*, illustrated by Laura Lydecker. Atheneum, 1976.

Macdonald, Caroline. *The Lake at the End of the World*. Dial, 1988.

MacDonald, George. *At the Back of the North Wind*. Garland, 1976 (1871).

_____. *The Golden Key*, illustrated by Maurice Sendak. Farrar, Straus, 1967 (1867).

_____. *The Light Princess*, illustrated by William Pène du Bois. Crowell, 1962.

_____. *The Light Princess*, illustrated by Maurice Sendak. Farrar, Straus, 1969.

McKillip, Patricia. *Harpist in the Wind*. Atheneum, 1979.
_____. *Heir of Sea and Fire*. Atheneum, 1977.
_____. *The Riddle-Master of Hed*. Atheneum, 1976.
McKinley, Robin. *Beauty: A Retelling of the Story of Beauty and the Beast*. Harper, 1978.
_____. *The Blue Sword*. Greenwillow, 1982.
_____. *The Hero and the Crown*. Greenwillow, 1985.
Mahy, Margaret. *The Haunting*. Macmillan, 1982.
Mayne, William. *Antar and the Eagles*. Delacorte, 1989.
_____. *Earthfasts*. Dutton, 1967.
Merrill, Jean. *The Pushcart War*, illustrated by Ronni Solbert. W. R. Scott, 1964.
Milne, A. A. *The House at Pooh Corner*, illustrated by Ernest H. Shepard. Dutton, 1928.
_____. *Winnie-The-Pooh*, illustrated by Ernest H. Shepard. Dutton, 1926.
Moore, Lilian. *I'll Meet You at the Cucumbers*, illustrated by Sharon Wooding. Atheneum, 1988.
Murphy, Shirley Rousseau. *Silver Woven in My Hair*, illustrated by Alan Tiegreen. Atheneum, 1977.
Norton, André and Dorothy Madlee. *Star Ka'at*. Walker, 1976.
Norton, Mary. *The Borrowers*, illustrated by Beth and Joe Krush. Harcourt, 1953.
_____. *The Borrowers Afield*, illustrated by Beth and Joe Krush. Harcourt, 1955.
_____. *The Borrowers Afloat*, illustrated by Beth and Joe Krush. Harcourt, 1959.
_____. *The Borrowers Aloft*, illustrated by Beth and Joe Krush. Harcourt, 1961.
_____. *The Borrowers Avenged*, illustrated by Beth and Joe Krush. Harcourt, 1982.
O'Brien, Robert C. *Mrs. Frisby and the Rats of NIMH*, illustrated by Zena Bernstein. Atheneum, 1971.
_____. *Z for Zachariah*. Atheneum, 1975.
Ormondroyd, Edward. *All in Good Time*, illustrated by Ruth Robbins. Parnassus, 1975.
_____. *Time at the Top*, illustrated by Peggy Bach. Parnassus, 1963.
Park, Ruth. *Playing Beatie Bow*. Atheneum, 1982.
Pearce, Phillipa. *Tom's Midnight Garden*, illustrated by Susan Einzig. Lippincott, 1959.
Pearson, Kit. *A Handful of Time*. Viking Penguin, 1988.
Peck, Sylvia. *Seal Child*, illustrated by Robert Andrew Parker. Morrow, 1989.
Pierce, Meredith. *The Darkangel*. Little Brown, 1982.
_____. *A Gathering of Gargoyles*. Little, Brown, 1984.
_____. *The Pearl of the Soul of the World*. Little, Brown, 1989.
Pinkwater, Daniel. *Borgel*. Macmillan, 1990.
_____. *Lizard Music*. Dodd, Mead, 1976.
_____. *The Magic Moscow*. Dodd, Mead, 1976.
Pratchett, Terry. *Diggers*. Delacorte, 1991.
_____. *Truckers*. Delacorte, 1990.
_____. *Wings*. Delacorte, 1991.
Rodda, Emily. *The Pigs Are Flying!*, illustrated by Noela Young. Morrow, 1988.
Rodgers, Mary. *Freaky Friday*. Harper, 1972.
_____. *Summer Switch*. Harper, 1982.
Saint-Exupéry, Antoine de. *The Little Prince*, translated by Katherine Woods. Harcourt, 1943.
Sauer, Julia. *Fog Magic*, illustrated by Lynd Ward. Viking, 1943.
Scieszka, Jon. *The Good, the Bad, and the Goofy*, illustrated by Lane Smith. Viking, 1992.
_____. *Knights of the Kitchen Table*, illustrated by Lane Smith. Viking, 1991.
_____. *The Not-So-Jolly Roger*, illustrated by Lane Smith. Viking, 1991.
Selden, George. *Chester Cricket's Pigeon Ride*, illustrated by Garth Williams. Farrar, Straus, 1981.
_____. *The Cricket in Times Square*, illustrated by Garth Williams. Farrar, Straus, 1960.
_____. *Harry Cat's Pet Puppy*, illustrated by Garth Williams. Farrar, Straus, 1974.
_____. *Tucker's Countryside*, illustrated by Garth Williams. Farrar, Straus, 1969.
Sendak, Maurice. *Higglety, Pigglety, Pop!* Harper, 1967.
Service, Pamela. *Stinker from Space*. Scribner's, 1988.
_____. *Winter of Magic's Return*. Atheneum, 1985.
_____. *Tomorrow's Magic*. Atheneum, 1987.
Sharp, Margery. *Miss Bianca*, illustrated by Garth Williams. Little, Brown, 1962.
_____. *Miss Bianca in the Salt Mines*, illustrated by Garth Williams. Little, Brown, 1967.
_____. *The Rescuers*, illustrated by Garth Williams. Little, Brown, 1959.
_____. *The Turret*, illustrated by Garth Williams. Little, Brown, 1963.
Sibley, Brian. *The Land of Narnia*, illustrated by Pauline Baynes. HarperCollins, 1990.

Sleator, William. *The Duplicate*. Dutton, 1988.

_____. *The Green Futures of Tycho*. Dutton, 1981.

Slote, Alfred. *C.O.L.A.R.*, illustrated by Anthony Kramer. Harper, 1981.

_____. *My Robot Buddy*. Lippincott, 1975.

Snyder, Zilpha Keatley. *Song of the Gargoyle*. Delacorte, 1991.

Steig, William. *Abel's Island*. Farrar, Straus, 1976.

_____. *Dominic*. Farrar, Straus, 1972.

_____. *The Real Thief*. Farrar, Straus, 1973.

Stewig, John. *Stone Soup*, illustrated by Margot Tomes. Holiday, 1991. (Traditional)

Sutcliff, Rosemary. *Tristan & Iseult*. Farrar, Straus, 1991 (1971).

Tannen, Mary. *The Lost Legend of Finn*. Knopf, 1982.

_____. *The Wizard Children of Finn*. Knopf. 1981.

Taylor, Cora. *Yesterday's Doll*. Scholastic, 1990. (Published in Canada as *The Doll*, Western Producer Prairie Books, 1987).

Thurber, James. *Many Moons*, illustrated by Marc Simont. Harcourt, 1990.

_____. *The 13 Clocks*, illustrated by Marc Simont. Simon & Schuster, 1950.

Tolkien, J. R. R. *The Hobbit*. Houghton Mifflin, 1938.

_____. "The Lord of the Rings" trilogy: *The Fellowship of the Ring, The Two Towers, The Return of the King*. Houghton Mifflin, 1965.

Travers, P. L. *Mary Poppins*, illustrated by Mary Shepard. Harcourt, 1934.

_____. *Mary Poppins Comes Back*, illustrated by Mary Shepard. Harcourt, 1935.

_____. *Mary Poppins in the Park*, illustrated by Mary Shepard. Harcourt, 1952.

_____. *Mary Poppins Opens the Door*, illustrated by Mary Shepard and Agnes Sims. Harcourt, 1943.

Uttley, Alison. *A Traveler in Time*, illustrated by Christine Price. Viking, 1964 (1939).

Van Rynbach, Iris. *The Soup Stone*. Greenwillow, 1988. (Traditional)

Walsh, Jill Paton. *A Chance Child*. Farrar, Straus, 1978.

_____. *The Green Book*, illustrated by Lloyd Bloom. Farrar, Straus, 1982.

Wangerin, Walter, Jr. *Elizabeth and the Water Troll*, illustrated by Deborah Healy. HarperCollins, 1991.

White, E. B. *Charlotte's Web*, illustrated by Garth Williams. Harper, 1952.

_____. *Stuart Little*, illustrated by Garth Williams, Harper, 1945.

_____. *The Trumpet of the Swan*, illustrated by Edward Frascino. Harper, 1970.

Wilde, Oscar. *The Happy Prince*, illustrated by Jean Claverie. Oxford, 1981.

_____. *The Happy Prince*, illustrated by Ed Young. Simon & Schuster, 1989.

_____. *The Selfish Giant*, illustrated by Lisbeth Zwerger. Picture Book Studios, 1984.

Williams, Jay. *Everyone Knows What a Dragon Looks Like*, illustrated by Mercer Mayer. Four Winds, 1976.

Winthrop, Elizabeth. *The Castle in the Attic*. Holiday, 1985.

Wiseman, David. *Jeremy Visick*. Houghton Mifflin, 1981.

Wrede, Patricia C. *Dealing with Dragons*. Harcourt, 1990.

_____. *Searching for Dragons*. Harcourt, 1991.

Wrightson, Patricia. *Balyet*. Macmillan, 1989.

_____. *The Dark Bright Water*. Atheneum, 1979.

_____. *The Ice Is Coming*. Atheneum, 1977.

_____. *Journey Behind the Wind*. Atheneum, 1981.

_____. *The Nargun and the Stars*. Atheneum, 1979.

Yolen, Jane. *The Acorn Quest*, illustrated by Susanna Natti. Crowell, 1981.

_____. *Dove Isabeau*, illustrated by Dennis Nolan. Harcourt Brace Jovanovich, 1989.

_____. *Dragon's Blood*. Delacorte, 1982.

_____. *The Emperor and the Kite*, illustrated by Ed Young. World, 1967.

_____. *The Girl Who Loved the Wind*, illustrated by Ed Young. Crowell, 1972.

_____. *Greyling*, illustrated by David Ray. Philomel, 1991. (Traditional)

_____. *Heart's Blood*. Delacorte, 1984.

_____. *The Seeing Stick*, illustrated by Remy Charlip and Demetra Maraslis. Crowell, 1977.

_____. *Tam Lin*, illustrated by Charles Mikolaycak. Harcourt Brace Jovanovich, 1990. (Traditional)

Zemach, Harve. *Duffy and the Devil*, illustrated by Margot Zemach. Farrar, Straus, 1986. (Traditional)

Chapter Eight
Poetry

A fifth-grade teacher finished reading aloud Katherine Paterson's *Bridge to Terabithia* to her class. This is the well-loved story of friendship between a highly imaginative girl, Leslie, and Jess—middle child in a rural family of five. It was Leslie's idea to create Terabithia, their secret kingdom in the woods that could be approached only by swinging across a stream on a rope. And it was this frayed rope that brought about the tragedy in the story. Following the completion of the story, the group was silent for a moment thinking about Leslie's death and the legacy she had left Jess. Wisely, the teacher respected their silence, recognizing that this book had moved them deeply. They did not discuss it immediately but quietly began to do other work. That evening one of the girls in the class wrote this poem:

> As the stubborn stream swirls and pulls out a song,

The hillside stands in the cold dark sky.
Over the hillside stands a lonely palace.
Before it shook with joy
But now its queen is dead
So the sour sweet wind blows the tassels of the weak rope,
And the tree mourns and scolds the rope,
Saying "Couldn't you have held on a little longer?"

Cheri Taylor
Highland Park School
Grove City, Ohio
Linda Charles, teacher

Poetry was as much a part of this classroom as prose was. The teacher shared some poetry every day, as well as reading stories. Frequently she read a poem that reflected the same content or feeling as the novel she was reading. So it was natural for Cheri to write a poem in response to her feelings about *Bridge to Terabithia*.

Poetry is the language of emotions. It can encapsulate a deep response in a few words. For Cheri, poetry was the only way to capture her feelings about a book that had moved her as no other one had ever done before.

THE MEANING OF POETRY

What Is Poetry?

There is an elusiveness about poetry that defies precise definition. It is not so much what it is that is important as how it makes us feel. Eleanor Farjeon tells us that "Poetry" (58) is "not a rose, but the scent of the rose . . . Not the sea, but the sound of the sea." Fine poetry is this distillation of experience that captures the essence of an object, feeling, or thought. Such intensification requires a more highly structured patterning of words than prose does. Each word must be chosen with care, for both its sound and meaning, since poetry is language in its most connotative and concentrated form. Laurence Perrine defines poetry as "a kind of language that says more and says it more intensely than ordinary language."[1]

Poetry may both broaden and intensify experience, or it may present a range of experiences beyond the realm of personal possibility for the individual listener. It may also illuminate, clarify, and deepen an everyday occurrence in a way the reader never considered, making the reader see more and feel more than ever before. For poetry does more than mirror life; it reveals life in new dimensions. Robert Frost stated that a poem goes from delight to wisdom. Poetry does delight children, but it also helps them develop new insights, new ways of sensing their world.

Poetry communicates experience by appealing to both the thoughts and feelings of its reader. It has the power to evoke in its hearers rich sensory images and deep emotional responses. Poetry demands total response from the individual—all the intellect, senses, emotion, and imagination. It does not tell *about* an experience as much as it invites its hearers to *participate in* the experience. Poetry can only happen when the poem and the reader connect. Eve Merriam writes about the process in this way:

🐛 "I," says the poem matter-of-factly,
   "I am a cloud,

I am a tree.

I am a city,
I am the sea,

I am a golden
Mystery."

But, adds the poem silently,
I cannot speak until you come.
Reader, come, come with me.

Eve Merriam (162) [2]

Much of what poetry says is conveyed by suggestion, by indirection, by what is not said. As Carl Sandburg put it, "What can be explained is not poetry. . . . The poems that are obvious are like the puzzles that are already solved. They deny us the joy of seeking and creating."[3] A certain amount of ambiguity is characteristic of poetry, for more is hidden in it than in prose. The poet does not tell readers "all," but invites them to go beyond the literal level of the poem and discover its deeper meanings for themselves.

Robert Frost playfully suggested that poetry is what gets lost in translation—and translation of poetry into prose is as difficult as translation of poetry into another language. To paraphrase a poem is to destroy it. Would it be possible to reduce Frost's "Mending Wall" to prose? The scene, the situation, the contrast of the two men's thoughts about the wall they are repairing may be described, but the experience of the poem cannot be conveyed except by its own words.

Poetry for Children

Poetry for children differs little from poetry for adults, except that it comments on life in dimensions that are meaningful for children. Its language should be poetic and its content should

---

[1]Laurence Perrine, *Sound and Sense: An Introduction to Poetry*, 5th ed. (New York: Harcourt Brace Jovanovich, 1981), p. 3.

[2]If the source of a poem is not obvious, the number following a poem in this chapter refers to the number in the References at the end of the chapter where the poem may be found. Many of the poems appear in several anthologies, however.

[3]Carl Sandburg, "Short Talk on Poetry," in *Early Moon* (New York: Harcourt Brace Jovanovich, 1930), p. 27.

appeal directly to children. Bobbi Katz describes the feel of "Cat Kisses" in a way that appeals to children's sensory experiences and helps them think about a cat in a new imaginative way.

CAT KISSES

Sandpaper kisses
on a cheek or a chin—
that is the way
for a day to begin!

Sandpaper kisses—
a cuddle, a purr
I have an alarm clock
that's covered with fur.

Bobbi Katz (46)

The comparison of the rough feel of a cat's tongue to sandpaper kisses and a cat's function as an alarm clock are both metaphors that will delight a child. These metaphors are childlike, but not "childish."

Modern children need fresh comparisons that are relevant to their background of experiences. The child's hero of today works in space and not under the spreading chestnut tree. Many children who would have little understanding of "The Village Blacksmith" (54) would comprehend the comparison that Eve Merriam makes in her poem:

SATELLITE, SATELLITE

Satellite, satellite
The earth goes around the sun.

Satellite, satellite,
The moon goes around the earth.

Satellite, satellite,
I have a little satellite:

My little brother orbits me
And pesters day and night.

Eve Merriam (163)

Children might be encouraged through discussion to think of other satellite situations in their lives—a little dog that faithfully follows its master, a bee buzzing around a clover blossom, even Mary's little lamb.

The emotional appeal of children's poetry should reflect the real emotions of childhood. Poetry that is cute, coy, nostalgic, or sarcastic may be *about* children, but it is not *for* them. Whittier's "The Barefoot Boy" (54) looks back on childhood in a nostalgic fashion characteristic of adults, not children. "The Children's Hour" (54) by Longfellow is an old man's reminiscences of his delight in his children. Some poems patronize childhood as a period in life when children are "cute" or "naughty." Joan W. Anglund's poetry is as cute and sentimental as her pictures of "sweet little boys and girls." Even the best of children's poets occasionally have been guilty of this kind of portrayal of childhood. For example, "Vespers" (167) by A. A. Milne appeals more to adults who are amused and pleased by the sweet description of a child's desultory thoughts during prayer; children find little humor in this poem that makes them the object of laughter.

Many poems are didactic and preachy. Unfortunately, some teachers will accept moralizing in poetry that they would never accept in prose. Sentimentality is another adult emotion, seldom felt by children. The poem "Which Loved Best," frequently quoted before Mother's Day, drips with sentiment and morality. Poems that are *about* childhood or aim to instruct are usually disliked by children.

Yet children do feel deep emotions; they can be hurt, fearful, bewildered, sad, happy, expectant, satisfied. Almost all surveys show that adults believe children have a harder time growing up today than their parents did. According to Kati Haycock,[4] *every day* in America:

1,849 children are abused.
2,407 children are born out of wedlock.
2,987 children see their parents divorced.

More and more modern poetry for children reflects the despair of struggling to grow up in America today. Some poets have been successful in capturing the real feelings of troubled children. For example, Elizabeth Smith, an African-

[4]Kati Haycock, "Producing a Nation of Achievers," *Journal of Youth Services in Libraries*, Vol. 4 (Spring 1991), p. 237.

American poet, describes the mixed feelings of pride and loneliness felt by a latchkey child:

🐞 MY KEY

I don't go to daycare
Or a sitter any more.
Now that I am grown-up
I've a key to my front door.

I check my pocket through the day,
Making sure I have my key.
I call my mom when I get home
To tell her all is right with me.

I get a little scared sometimes
When there's no one else at home.
The TV keeps me company—
I'm not all that alone.

I like the grown-up feeling
Of having my own key.
But every now and then I wish
My mom was home with me.

Elizabeth Smith (90)

Many of the poems in Myra Cohn Livingston's book *There Was a Place and Other Poems* are written from the perspective of children from broken homes and one-parent families. The constant tug-of-war feeling of a child caught in the middle of a divorce is reflected in one of her poems from this book:

🐞 IN THE MIDDLE

Mom
says
she wants me
more than Dad.
How do I ever choose?
Dad
says
he wants me
more than Mom.
Somebody has to lose.

Myra Cohn Livingston (145)

Not only has she described the feelings of a child caught in the middle of a divorce, she has even spaced her words to convey the tension in this household—the constant seesawing back and

forth. Poets have many ways to reinforce the meaning of a poem.

The Elements of Poetry

A child responds to the total impact of a poem and should not be required to analyze it. However, teachers need to understand the language of poetry if they are to select the best to share with children. How, for example, can you differentiate between real poetry and mere verse? *Mother Goose,* jump-rope rhymes, tongue twisters, and the lyrics of some songs are not poetry; but they *can* serve as a springboard for diving into real poetry. Elizabeth Coatsworth, who has written much fine poetry and verse for children, refers to rhyme as "poetry in petticoats."[5] Such rhymes may have the sound of poetry, but they do not contain the quality of imagination or the depth of emotion that characterizes real poetry.

It is a difficult task to identify elements of poetry for today's children, for modern poets are breaking traditional molds in both content and form. These poems speak directly to the reader about all subjects. Frequently the words are spattered across pages in a random fashion or they become poem-pictures, as in concrete poetry. As children become more sophisticated by their exposure to films and television, the dividing line between what is poetry for adults and what is poetry for children becomes fainter and fainter. It is, however, possible to identify those poems that contain the elements of fine poetry, yet still speak to children.

RHYTHM

The young child is naturally rhythmical. She beats on the tray of her high chair, kicks her foot against the table, and chants her vocabulary of one or two words in a singsong fashion. She delights in the sound of "Pat-a-cake, pat-a-cake, baker's man," or "Ride a cock-horse to Banbury Cross" before she understands the meaning of the words. She is responding to the monotonous rocking-horse rhythm of Mother Goose. This response to a measured beat is as old as humans

[5]Elizabeth Coatsworth, *The Sparrow Bush,* illustrated by Stefan Martin (New York: Norton, 1966), p. 8.

themselves. Primitive people had chants, hunting and working songs, dances, and crude musical instruments. Rhythm is a part of the daily beat of our lives—the steady pulse rate, regular breathing, and pattern of growth. The inevitability of night and day, the revolving seasons, birth and death provide a pattern for everyone's life. The very ebb and flow of the ocean, the sound of the rain on the window, and the pattern of rows of corn in a field reflect the rhythm of the world around us.

Poetry satisfies the child's natural response to rhythm. A poem has a kind of music of its own and the child responds to it. The very young child enjoys the rocking rhythm of Mother Goose and expects it in all other poems. Mary Ann Hoberman explores other rhythms in the child's life as she links weather and seasonal patterns to the rhythm of a child's swinging:

🍂 *Hello and good-by*
Hello and good-by

When I'm in a swing
Swinging low and then high,
Good-by to the ground
Hello to the sky.

Hello to the rain
Good-by to the sun,
Then hello again sun
When the rain is all done.

In blows the winter,
Away the birds fly.
Good-by and hello
Hello and good-by.

Mary Ann Hoberman (75)

This poem could be compared to Robert Louis Stevenson's well-known poem "The Swing" (46), which suggests a different meter for the physical sensation of swinging. Read both these poems to children and let them pantomime swinging as they listen. They may want to discuss which poem is the easier one to respond to, ways they are alike and ways they are different.

The galloping rhythm of Stevenson's "Windy Nights" (46) compares the sound of the wild wind

to a mysterious horseman riding by. Stevenson has also captured the fast pace of a train with the clipped rhythm of his poem "From a Railway Carriage" (219), while the slow steady beat of "Lullaby" by Hillyer (50) imitates the strong strokes of the paddle moving a canoe slowly toward the shore. The rhythm of a poem, then, should be appropriate to its subject matter, reinforcing and creating its meaning.

In some poems both the rhythm and pattern of the lines are suggestive of the movement or mood of the poem. The arrangement of these poems forces the reader to emphasize a particular rhythm. For example, the words of Eleanor Farjeon's "Mrs. Peck-Pigeon" (47) and the repetition of the hard sounds of "b" and "p" help to create the bobbing rhythm of the pigeon herself. The somewhat pensive mood of A. A. Milne's "Halfway Down" (167) is heightened by the arrangement of the words and lines. The reader has to interpret the slow descent of a little boy going down the stairs until he stops at his favorite step, halfway down.

A change of rhythm is indicative of a new element in the poem: a contrast in mood, a warning, or a different speaker, for example. Lilian Moore's poem "Wind Song" gathers momentum with the sound of all the things the wind blows and then becomes suddenly quiet when the wind dies down.

🍂 WIND SONG
When the wind blows
the quiet things speak.
Some whisper, some clang,
Some creak.

Grasses swish.
Treetops sigh.
Flags slap
and snap at the sky.
Wires on poles
whistle and hum.
Ashcans roll.
Windows drum.

When the wind goes—
suddenly
then,

the quiet things
are quiet again.

Lilian Moore (46)

RHYME AND SOUND

In addition to the rhythm of a poem children respond to its rhyme. For rhyme helps to create the musical qualities of a poem, and children enjoy the "singingness of words." The Russian poet Kornei Chukovsky[6] maintains that in the beginning of childhood we are all "versifiers," and that it is only later in life that we begin to speak in prose. He is referring to the young child's tendency to double all syllables so that "mother" is first "mama" and water "wa-wa." This, plus the regular patterning of such words as daddy, mommy, granny, and so on, makes for a natural production of rhyme. The young child's enjoyment of Mother Goose is due almost entirely to the rhyme and rhythm of these verses. "Rope Rhyme" by Eloise Greenfield captures the rhythm of the turning rope and the slapping sound of the rope itself.

🐚 ROPE RHYME

Get set, ready now, jump right in
Bounce and kick and giggle and spin
Listen to the rope when it hits the ground
Listen to that clappedy-slappedy sound
Jump right up when it tells you to
Come back down, whatever you do
Count to a hundred, count by ten
Start to count all over again
That's what jumping is all about
Get set, ready now,
    jump
      right
        out!

Eloise Greenfield (69)

Joanna Cole collected many jump-rope rhymes for her book *Anna Banana: 101 Jump-Rope Rhymes*. Street rhymes, hand clapping and ball bouncing rhymes, and counting out rhymes are all found in *Miss Mary Mack* by Joanna Cole and Stephanie

[6]Kornei Chukovsky, *From Two to Five*, translated and edited by Miriam Morton (Berkeley: University of California Press, 1963), p. 64.

The Dillons' illustrations for the poems in *Honey I Love* by Eloise Greenfield are as joyous and thoughtful as the poems themselves.

Calmenson. If children have not heard any poetry or do not know any Mother Goose rhymes, teachers may want to introduce poetry with street rhymes, jump-rope rhymes, or raps. But children need to be freed from the notion that all poetry must rhyme. They should be introduced to some poetry that doesn't rhyme, such as free verse or haiku, so that they begin to listen to the meaning of a poem as well as the sound of it.

Rhyme is only one aspect of sound; alliteration, or the repetition of initial consonant sounds, is another; assonance, or the repetition of particular vowel sounds, is still another. Jack Prelutsky frequently uses alliteration to create the humor in his verse. Read "The Lurpp Is on the Loose" (200) for example, and listen to the repetition of the "l" sounds. Younger children delight in the sounds of Susie's galoshes in Rhoda Bacmeister's well-known poem:

❦ GALOSHES

Susie's galoshes
Make splishes and sploshes
And slooshes and sloshes
As Susie steps slowly
Along in the slush.

They stamp and they tramp
On the ice and concrete,
They get stuck in the muck and the mud;
But Susie likes much best to hear

The slippery slush
As it slooshes and sloshes,

Marcia Brown portrays a vigorous young girl stamping along in her "Galoshes." Nine Caldecott award winners illustrated this stunning collection of poetry selected by Beatrice Schenk de Regniers and others and titled *Sing a Song of Popcorn.*

❦ ❦ ❦

And splishes and sploshes,
All around her galoshes!

Rhoda Bacmeister (46)

The quiet "s" sound and the repetition of the double "o" in "moon" and "shoon" suggest the mysterious beauty of the moon in Walter de la Mare's poem, "Silver" (54). *Onomatopoeia* is a term that refers to the use of words that make a sound like the action represented by the word, such as "crack," "hiss," and "sputter." Occasionally, a poet will create an entire poem that resembles a particular sound. David McCord has successfully imitated the sound of hitting a picket fence with a stick in his popular chant:

❦ The pickety fence
The pickety fence
Give it a lick it's
The pickety fence
Give it a lick it's
A clickety fence
Give it a lick it's
A lickety fence
Give it a lick
Give it a lick
Give it a lick
With a rickety stick
Pickety
Pickety
Pickety
Pick

David McCord (156)

Repetition is another way the poet creates particular sound effects in a poem. Certainly, David McCord employed repetition along with onomatopoeia to create his poem "The Pickety Fence" (156). Felice Holman appropriately uses repetition to describe the way we all feel when we can't get a particular tune out of our heads in her poem "The Song in My Head" (76). Robert Frost frequently used repetition of particular lines or phrases to emphasize meaning in his poems. The repetition of the last line "miles to go before I sleep" in his famous "Stopping by Woods on a Snowy Evening" (47) adds to the mysterious element in that poem.

Children are intrigued with the sound of language and enjoy unusual and ridiculous combinations of words. The gay nonsense of Laura Richards's "Eletelephony" (47) is as much in the sound of the ridiculous words as in the plight of the poor elephant who tried to use the "telephant." Children love to trip off the name of "James James Morrison Morrison Weatherby George Dupree," who complained about his mother's "Disobedience" (167). They delight in the sound of David McCord's introduction to ladybugs in "I Want You to Meet . . ." (156). Poets use rhyme, rhythm, and the various devices of alliteration, assonance, repetition, and coined words to create the melody and sound of poetry loved by children.

IMAGERY

Poetry draws on many kinds of language magic. To speak of the imagery of a poem refers to direct sensory images of sight, sound, touch, smell, or taste. This aspect of poetry has particular appeal for children, as it reflects one of the major ways they explore their world. The very young child grasps an object and immediately puts it in her mouth. Children love to squeeze warm, soft puppies or they squeal with delight as a baby pet mouse scampers up their arms. Taste and smell are also highly developed in the young child.

The sadness of our modern society is that children are increasingly deprived of natural sensory experiences. One of the first admonitions they hear is "Don't touch." In the endless pavements of our cities, how many children have an opportunity to roll in crunchy piles of leaves? Air-pollution laws assure that they will never enjoy the acrid autumn smell of burning bonfires (rightly so, but still a loss). Many also miss the warm yeasty odor of homemade bread or the sweet joy of licking the bowl of brownie batter. Some of our newest schools are windowless, so children are even deprived of seeing the brilliant blue sky on a crisp cold day or the growing darkness of a storm or the changing silhouette of an oak tree on the horizon.

Poetry can never be a substitute for actual sensory experience. A child can't develop a concept of texture by hearing a poem or seeing pictures of the rough bark of a tree; he must first touch the bark and compare the feel of a deeply furrowed oak with the smooth surfaced trunk of a beech tree. Then the poet can call up these experiences, extend them or make the child see them in a new way.

Since most children are visual-minded they respond readily to the picture-making quality of poetry. Marie Louise Allen has looked with the eyes of a child at a familiar world made strange by snow. Her poem "First Snow" may well be the first snow of the season or the child's first experience with snow:

🐦 FIRST SNOW
Snow makes whiteness where it falls,
The bushes look like popcorn balls.
And places where I always play,
Look like somewhere else today.

Marie Louise Allen (89)

Robert Frost has made us see a "Patch of Old Snow" (50) in the city as if it were an old blown-away newspaper bespeckled with grimy print. How many different ways can snow be described?

Tennyson's description of "The Eagle" is rich in the use of visual imagery. In the first verse the reader can see the eagle perched on the crest of a steep mountain, poised ready for his swift descent whenever he sights his quarry. But in the second verse the poet "enters into" the eagle's world and describes it from the bird's point of view. Looking down from his lofty height, the might of the waves is reduced to wrinkles and the sea seems to crawl:

🐦 THE EAGLE
He clasps the crag with crooked hands;
Close to the sun in lonely lands,
Ringed with the azure world, he stands.

The wrinkled sea beneath him crawls;
He watches from his mountain walls,
And like a thunderbolt he falls.

Alfred, Lord Tennyson (110)

The lonely, peaceful scene is shattered by the natural metaphor of the final line, "And like a thunderbolt he falls." In your mind's eye you can see, almost feel, the wind on your wings as you plunge down the face of the cliff.

Jane Yolen uses all kinds of auditory and visual images to portray a woodpecker drilling on a tree

Jane Yolen's poem invites you to hear the woodpecker's jackhammer drumming; Ted Lewin's detailed watercolors let you almost feel the texture of this red-bellied woodpecker's world.

From *Bird Watch* by Jane Yolen.

in her book, *Bird Watch*. The realistic picture painted by Ted Lewin lets us feel with our eyes the rough bark of the old tree on which the bird is tapping.

    WOODPECKER
    His swift
    ratatatatat
    is
    as casual as a jackhammer
    on a city street,
    as thorough as an oil drill
    on an Oklahoma wellsite,
    as fine as a needle

    in a record groove,
    as cleansing as a dentist's probe
    in a mouthful of cavities,
    as final as a park attendant's stick
    on a lawn of litter.
    Ratatatatatat.
    He finishes his work
    on the maple tree,
    then wings off again
    to the pine,
    leaving his punctuation
    along the woody line.

                    Jane Yolen (234)

Most poetry depends on visual and auditory imagery to evoke a mood or response, but imagery of touch, taste, and smell is also used. Children have always enjoyed the poem that begins, "Mud is very nice to feel/all squishy—squash between the toes! . . ." (38). Or you could compare what feet know with what hands discover through sensory experiences. Dorothy Aldis does this for very young children in her poem "Feet" (8).

Psychologists tell us that some of children's earliest memories are sensory, recalling particularly the way things smell and taste. Most children have a delicate sense of taste that responds to the texture and smell of a particular food. In "Hard and Soft" (4) Arnold Adoff contrasts the crunch of eating a carrot with the quiet sound of swallowing raisins. In "A Matter of Taste" (163) Eve Merriam relates the way food tastes to the way it feels and sounds when being chewed. Rose Rauter captures both the feel of a fresh picked peach and its delicious taste in her poem:

    PEACH
    Touch it to your cheek and it's soft
    as a velvet newborn mouse
    who has to strive
    to be alive.
    Bite in. Runny
    honey
    blooms on your tongue—
    as if you've bitten open
    a whole hive.

                    Rose Rauter (100)

Certain smells can recapture a whole experience that may have happened years before. In "That Was the Summer" (38) Marci Ridlon recalls summer smells of grass and hot wet pavement. Joanna Cole contrasts the smells of the road with the smells of the beach in her poem, "Driving to the Beach" (78).

FIGURATIVE LANGUAGE: COMPARISON AND CONTRAST

Since the language of poetry is so compressed, every word must be made to convey the message of the poem. Poets do this by comparing two objects or ideas with each other in such a way that the connotation of one word gives added meaning to another.

In "Peach" (100) Rose Rauter compared the soft fuzzy feel of a peach to a velvet newborn mouse; its sweet taste made her think of a whole hive of honey. X. J. Kennedy portrays the observations of a passenger who is riding backward on a speeding train:

FLYING UPTOWN BACKWARDS
Squeezing round a bend, train shrieks
Like chalk on gritty blackboards.

People talk or read or stare.
Street names pass like flashcards.

Hope this train keeps going on
Flying uptown backwards.

X. J. Kennedy (97)

When writers compare one thing with another, using such connecting words as *like* or *as*, they are using a *simile*. Using two similes that call up common school experiences, Kennedy compares the shrieking sound of the train with the piercing shriek of chalk on a blackboard and the quickly passing street names with the use of old-fashioned flashcards. In a *metaphor* the poet speaks of an object or idea as if it *were* another object. In recent years we have paid little attention to the difference between these two techniques, referring to both as examples of metaphorical or figurative language.

It is not important that children know the difference between a simile and a metaphor. It is important that they know what is being compared and that the comparison is fresh and new and helps them view the idea or object in a different and unusual way. Two well-known poems which contain metaphors that help children see their world afresh are "The Moon's the North Wind's Cooky" (38) and the first line of "On a Snowy Day" (8), which describes fenceposts as wearing marshmallow hats. Perhaps the reason these poems have endured is that they also reveal a true understanding of a child's point of view.

Some figurative language is so commonplace that it has lost its ability to evoke new images. Language and verse are filled with such clichés as "it rained cats and dogs," "a blanket of snow," "quiet as a mouse," or "thin as a rail." Eve Merriam describes a "Cliché" (162) as what lazy people use in their writing. Her poem "Metaphor Man" (164) also pokes fun at such expressions as "drives a hard bargain," "stands four square," or "flies in a rage."

Valerie Worth received the NCTE Award for Excellence in Poetry for Children with four "Small Poems" books. These have been combined in a fifth one titled *All the Small Poems*. Her simple free verse contains vivid metaphors that describe such ordinary objects as a safety pin, chairs, or earthworms. Her poem about a library describes the smell and quiet sounds of this room. It also suggests that books may provide life and song.

LIBRARY
No need even
To take out
A book: only
Go inside
And savor
The heady
Dry breath of
Ink and paper,
Or stand and
Listen to the
Silent twitter
Of a billion
Tiny busy
Black words.

Valerie Worth (229)

Some poets sustain a metaphor throughout the poem. Most children are intrigued with the subject of dinosaurs and readily respond to Charles Malam's poem that compares a steam shovel with those enormous beasts.

❦ STEAM SHOVEL

The dinosaurs are not all dead.
I saw one raise its iron head
To watch me walking down the road
Beyond our house today.
Its jaws were dripping with a load
Of earth and grass that it had cropped.
It must have heard me where I stopped,
Snorted white steam my way,
And stretched its long neck out to see,
And chewed, and grinned quite amiably.

Charles Malam (50)

Personification is a way of speaking about inanimate objects as though they were living creatures. Human beings have always personified inanimate objects. Young children personify their toys and pets; adolescents and adults name their computers, their cars and boats. Poetry simply

The proud *Sierra* provides a home for this brilliant stellar jay. Wendell Minor's vivid acrylic paintings portray other birds and animals sheltered by this majestic mountain range.

From *Sierra* by Diane Siebert.

extends this process to a wider range of objects. In "Flashlight" (173) Judith Thurman compares a flashlight to a hound straining on his leash. James Stephens's well-known poem personifies "The Wind" (52) as a person who will "kill, kill." Diane Siebert personifies the desert in her book, *Mojave*, and the Sierra Nevada Mountains in *Sierra*. In *Sierra* a majestic mountain shelters the many birds, animals, and trees that Wendell Minor portrays in brilliant acrylic paintings. The last poem suggests a new force in the life of the mountain and "its name is MAN."

❦ From *SIERRA*

I am the mountain,
Tall and grand,
And like a sentinel I stand.
Yet I, in nature's wonders draped,
Now see this mantle being shaped
By something new—a force so real
That every part of me can feel
Its actions changing nature's plan.
Its numbers grow. Its name is MAN.
And what my course of life will be
Depends on how man cares for me.

I am the mountain,
Tall and grand.
And like a sentinel I stand.

Diane Siebert (210)

Another way of strengthening an image is through contrast. Elizabeth Coatsworth employs this device in much of her poetry. Her best known "Poem of Praise" (50) contrasts the beauty of swift things with those that are slow and steady. Marci Ridlon presents two points of view concerning life in the city in her poem "City City" (196). By contrasting a view of a bridge by day and night, Lilian Moore gives us two images, one of strength and one of lacy lightness in her poem "The Bridge" (174). In the poem "Fueled," the poet compares the launching of a man-made rocket with the miraculous growth of a seedling pushing its way through the earth. The first feat receives much acclaim; the second goes virtually unnoticed. There seems to be no doubt in the poet's mind which is the greater event, for she has even shaped her poem to resemble half of a tree:

❦ FUELED
Fueled
by a million
man-made
wings of fire—
the rocket tore a tunnel
through the sky—
and everybody cheered.
Fueled
only by a thought from God—
the seedling
urged its way
through the thickness of black—
and as it pierced
the heavy ceiling of the soil—
and launched itself
up into outer space—
no
one
even clapped.

Marcie Hans (50)

Even though all children know about rockets and seeds, they may not be able to see the connection between the two images that the poet has created. Among one group of educationally and economically advantaged 8-year-olds, not one child saw both of these ideas; yet 11-year-olds in the same school easily recognized them. This suggests the importance of knowing the developmental level of a group before selecting poetry for them.

THE SHAPE OF A POEM

The first thing children notice about reading a poem is that it looks different from prose. And usually it does. Most poems begin with capital letters for each line and have one or more stanzas.

Increasingly, however, poets are using the shape of their poems to reinforce the image of the idea. David McCord describes the plight of "The Grasshopper" (157) that fell down a deep well. As luck would have it, he discovers a rope and up he climbs one word at a time! The reader must read up the page to follow the grasshopper's ascent. Eve Merriam's "Windshield Wiper" (100) not only sounds like the even rhythm of a car's wiper but has the look of two wipers. Lillian Morrison's poem about a sidewalk racer describes the thrill

of the rider at the same time it takes the shape of a skateboard and strengthens her image.

❦ THE SIDEWALK RACER
or
On the Skateboard

Skimming
an asphalt sea
I swerve, I curve, I
sway; I speed to whirring
sound an inch above the
ground; I'm the sailor
and the sail, I'm the
driver and the wheel
I'm the one and only
single engine
human auto
mobile

Lillian Morrison (100)

Children enjoy mounting their own poems on a piece of paper shaped in the image of their poem, such as a verse about a jack-o'-lantern on a pumpkin shape or a poem about a plane mounted on the silhouette of a plane. Later the words themselves may form the shape of the content, as in concrete poetry.

THE EMOTIONAL FORCE OF POETRY

We have seen how sound, language, and the shape of a poem may all work together to create the total impact of the poem. Considered individually, the rhyme scheme, imagery, figurative language, or the appearance of the poem are of little importance unless all of these interrelate to create an emotional response in the reader. The craft of the poem is not the poem.

In the poem "Listening to grownups quarreling," a modern poet writes of the way two children feel when caught in the vortex of their parents' quarrel:

❦ LISTENING TO GROWNUPS
QUARRELING,
standing in the hall against the
wall with my little brother, blown
like leaves against the wall by their
voices, my head like a pingpong ball
between the paddles of their anger:

I knew what it meant
to tremble like a leaf.

Cold with their wrath, I heard
the claws of the rain
pounce. Floods
poured through the city,
skies clapped over me,
and I was shaken, shaken
like a mouse
between their jaws.

Ruth Whitman (100)

A teacher could destroy the total impact of this poem for children by having them count the number of metaphors in it, looking at their increasing force and power. Children should have a chance to hear it, comment on it if they wish, or compare it with Myra Cohn Livingston's poem "In the Middle" (see p. 454). With more than half the marriages in this country ending in divorce, children frequently are caught in the middle, "shaken, shaken" by the experience. All elements of these poems work together to create the feeling of being overpowered by a quarrel between those you love most.

Good poetry has the power to make the reader moan in despair, catch the breath in fear, gasp in awe, smile with delight, or sit back in wonder. For poetry heightens emotions and increases one's sensitivity to an idea or mood.

Teachers need to be able to identify the characteristics of good poetry in order to make wise selections to share with children. They need to know the various kinds of poetry and the range of content of poetry for children. Then they can provide children with poetry that will gradually develop an increasing sense of form and appreciation. The following questions for evaluating poetry may be helpful. All these questions would not be appropriate to use for every poem. However, they can serve as a beginning way to look at poetry for children (see p. 464).

Forms of Poetry for Children

Children are more interested in the "idea" of a poem than in knowing about the various forms of poetry. However, teachers will want to expose children to various forms of poetry and note their reactions. Do these children like only narrative poems? Do they think all poetry must rhyme, or will they listen to some free verse? Are they ready for the seemingly simple, yet highly complex form of haiku? Understanding of and appreciation for a wide variety of poetry grow gradually as children are exposed to different forms and types.

BALLADS

Ballads are narrative poems that have been adapted for singing or that give the effect of a song. Originally, they were not made or sung for children but were the literature of all the people. Characteristics of the ballad form are the frequent use of dialogue in telling the story, repetition, marked rhythm and rhyme, and refrains that go back to the days when ballads were sung. Popular ballads have no known authors, as they were handed down from one generation to the next; the literary ballad, however, does have a known author. Ballads usually deal with heroic deeds and include stories of murder, unrequited love, feuds, and tragedies.

Children in the middle grades enjoy the amusing story of the stubborn man and his equally stubborn wife in "Get Up and Bar the Door" (19). As in many ballads, the ending is abrupt, and the reader never does find out what happened to the two sinister guests, other than that the good husband finally locked them all in the house together! In the story of the "Wraggle Taggle Gypsies" (52), the newlywed wealthy lady leaves her lord to run off with gypsies. Whereas in the ballad of "The Outlandish Knight" (52) the pretty maid turns the table on the knight who would drown her as he has six other maidens and drowns him instead. (For a discussion of the Scottish ballad "Tam Lin" see Chapters 6 and 7).

American ballads were frequently popular songs such as "On Top of Old Smoky" (100) and "The Foggy Foggy Dew" (52). Few literary ballads are being written today. One titled the "Ballad of Birmingham" (52) by Dudley Randall is a civil rights ballad about the tragic death of a child in the bombing of a church in Birmingham, Alabama, in 1963. When a young girl begs to go to the freedom march in the streets of Birmingham,

GUIDELINES

Evaluating Poetry for Children

♦ How does the rhythm of the poem reinforce and create the meaning of the poem?

♦ If the poem rhymes, does it sound natural or contrived?

♦ How does the sound of the poem add to the meaning? Is alliteration used? Onomatopoeia? Repetition?

♦ Does the poem create sensory images of sight, touch, smell, or taste? Are these related to children's delight in their particular senses?

♦ What is the quality of the imagination in the poem? Does it make the child see something in a fresh new way, or does it rely on old tired clichés?

♦ Is the figurative language appropriate to children's lives? Are the similes and metaphors those that a child would appreciate and understand?

♦ What is the tone of the poem? Does it patronize childhood by looking down on it? Is it didactic and preachy? Does it see childhood in a sentimental or nostalgic way?

♦ Is the poem appropriate for children? Will it appeal to them, and will they like it?

♦ How has the poet created the emotional intensity of the poem? Does every word work to heighten the feelings conveyed?

♦ Does the shape of the poem, the placement of the words, contribute to the meaning of the poem?

♦ What is the purpose of the poem? To amuse, describe in a fresh way, comment on humanity, draw parallels in our lives? How well has the poet achieved this purpose?

her mother tells her it is too dangerous. Instead the mother sends the girl off to the children's choir where she thinks she will be safe. That day the church is bombed and the daughter is killed. Ballads frequently have this ironic twist to their stories.

NARRATIVE POEMS

The narrative poem relates a particular event or episode or tells a long tale. It may be a lyric, a sonnet, or written in free verse; its one requirement is that it *must* tell a story. Many of children's favorite poems are these so-called story poems. One of the best known narrative poems is Robert Browning's *The Pied Piper of Hamelin*. First illustrated by Kate Greenaway in 1888, it continues to

be published with such new illustrators as Terry Small.

The most popular narrative poem in this country is Clement Moore's *The Night Before Christmas*. Every artist from Grandma Moses to Tasha Tudor to Tomie de Paola and Wendy Watson has illustrated this Christmas story. Presently there are nearly forty editions of *The Night Before Christmas*.

One of the favorite narrative poems of young children is the simple story of the parents who lovingly pretend to look for their child in the poem "Hiding" (8) by Dorothy Aldis. A. A. Milne's narrative poems are favorites of many young children. They love his story of a lost mouse in "Missing" (167) and the disappearing beetle in "Forgiven" (167). Six-, 7-, and 8-year-olds delight in Milne's "The King's Breakfast" (167) and "King John's Christmas" (167), those petulant kings, one of whom wants a "bit of butter" for his bread and the other one, a big red India-rubber ball. Other favorite story poems for this age group are Karla Kuskin's ridiculous tale of "Hughbert and the Glue" (103) and the loving story of the stuffed "Bear with Golden Hair" (103). The long narrative tale of "Custard the Dragon" by Ogden Nash has been humorously illustrated by Quentin Blake in the book *Custard & Company*. John Ciardi's story of the disastrous day "Mummy Slept Late and Daddy Fixed Breakfast" (110) continues to be a favorite among children, even though it perpetuates the stereotype of the mother as the only one capable of making waffles and the father as somewhat of a dolt in the kitchen.

Without a doubt the all-time favorite narrative poems of children today are the outrageously funny ones in Shel Silverstein's *Where the Sidewalk Ends* and *The Light in the Attic*. Some of their favorite story verses include "Sick" (212), in which Peggy Ann McKay claims to have every known symptom of dreadful diseases until she realizes it is Saturday; the sad tale of "Sarah Cynthia Sylvia Stout Who Would Not Take the Garbage Out" (210), and the man who is slowly being swallowed alive by a "Boa Constrictor" (212).

Children also enjoy the story verse of Jack Prelutsky, particularly the collection of poems about the bully Harvey and the children's ultimate revenge on him in *Rolling Harvey Down the Hill*. Middle graders delight in Prelutsky's macabre tales in *Nightmares*, enriched by Arnold Lobel's grisly black-and-white illustrations.

Not all narrative poems for children are humorous. Older children, for example, respond to the pathos of "Nancy Hanks" (38) and Eve Merriam's poem "To Meet Mr. Lincoln" (47). They are stirred by the galloping hoofbeats in Longfellow's *Paul Revere's Ride*, recently illustrated with vibrant moonlit pictures by Ted Rand. A favorite romantic tale is the dramatic *The Highwayman* by Alfred Noyes, which has been illustrated in three stunning picture-book editions, one by Charles Mikolaycak (180), one by Charles Keeping (179), and one by Neil Waldman (181). Waldman uses dramatic silhouettes against soft-colored pastels.

Each of Mikolaycak's black-and-white illustrations are contrasted with a bit of brilliant red echoing the dark red love knot plaited in the landlord's daughter's hair. After the death of the highwayman and his black-eyed Bess, Keeping reverses his striking pictures from black on white to a ghostly white on black. This is a dramatic edition that pictures the tragedy and darkness of this tale of love, suicide, and haunting.

One of the best ways to capture children's interest in poetry is to present a variety of narrative poems. Teachers will want to build a file of story poems appropriate to the interests of children in their classes and use them to introduce poetry to children.

LYRICAL POETRY

Most of the poetry written for children is lyrical. The term is derived from the word "lyric," and means poetry that sings its way into the minds and memories of its listeners. It is usually personal or descriptive poetry, with no prescribed length or structure other than its melody.

Much of William Blake's poetry is lyrical, beginning with the opening lines of his introductory poem to *Songs of Innocence:* "Piping down the valleys wild/Piping songs of pleasant glee" (110). Stevenson's poems have a singing quality that makes them unforgettable. Everyone knows his poems "The Swing" and "The Wind" (219). Equally popular is his mysterious "Windy Nights" (47), which compares the sound of the wind to a galloping horseman:

❦ WINDY NIGHTS

Whenever the moon and stars are set,
   Whenever the wind is high,
All night long in the dark and wet,
   A man goes riding by.
Late in the night when the fires are out,
Why does he gallop and gallop about?

Whenever the trees are crying aloud,
   And ships are tossed at sea,
By, on the highway, low and loud,
   By at the gallop goes he.
By at the gallop he goes, and then
By he comes back at the gallop again.

Robert Louis Stevenson (47)

After the death of *The Highwayman*, Charles Keeping uses negative ghostlike images in his powerful pictures.

From *The Highwayman* by Alfred Noyes.

🐛   🐛   🐛

Eleanor Farjeon's lovely "The Night Will Never Stay" (52) is another thoughtful lyrical poem. Masefield's well-known poem "Sea Fever" (54) would be a good one to read *after* sharing *The True Confessions of Charlotte Doyle* by Avi. Children always respond to the sound of the internal rhyme of "The Lone Dog" by Irene Rutherford McLeod that begins with "I'm a lean dog, a keen dog, a wild dog and lone" (54). Lyrical poetry is characterized by this lilting use of words that gives children an exhilarating sense of melody.

LIMERICKS

A nonsense form of verse that is particularly enjoyed by children is the limerick. This is a five-line verse with the first and second lines rhyming, the third and fourth agreeing, and the fifth line usually ending in a surprise or humorous statement. Freak spelling, oddities, and humorous twists characterize this form of poetry. David McCord in his book *One at a Time* suggests that "a limerick, to be lively and successful, *must* have

perfect riming and *flawless* rhythm." He gives several suggestions on how to write a limerick using the limerick form itself. He also describes the shape of a limerick in this poem:

🐛 A limerick shapes to the eye
   Like a small very squat butterfly,
       With its wings opened wide,
       Lots of nectar inside,
   And a terrible urge to fly high.

David McCord (157)

Other modern poets who continue to produce limericks include William Jay Smith and Myra Cohn Livingston. Arnold Lobel wrote a most humorous book of limericks, which instead of being about very old persons from places in England were verses about different pigs from various cities in the United States. For example:

🐛 There was a young pig from Schenectady
   Who cried, "What is wrong with my neck today?
       At ten minutes to two

It just sprouted and grew.
Now I'm taller than all of Schenectady!"

Arnold Lobel (151)

His illustrations of humanized pigs are as funny as the limericks.

Children in the middle grades enjoy writing limericks, whether based on nursery rhymes, pigs, or their own names. It is certainly a far easier form for them to write than the highly abstract form of the haiku.

FREE VERSE

Free verse does not have to rhyme but depends on rhythm or cadence for its poetic form. It may use some rhyme, alliteration, and pattern. It frequently looks different on a printed page, but it sounds very much like other poetry when read aloud. Children who have the opportunity to hear this form of poetry will be freed from thinking that all poetry must rhyme. Many of Valerie Worth's deceptively simple *Small Poems* are written in free verse. For example, her fine metaphorical description of "chairs" makes them come alive.

Chairs
Seem
To
Sit
Down
On
Themselves, almost as if
They were people,
Some fat, some thin
Settled comfortably
On their own seats,
Some even stretch out their arms
To
Rest.

Valerie Worth (233)

Sylvia Cassedy's book, *Roomrimes*, characterizes various rooms such as an attic, a closet, or the very proper "Parlor" (30). Children would enjoy writing their own room descriptions in free verse after hearing these. While much of Eve Merriam's poetry rhymes, she has also written free verse. Her well-known poem "How to Eat a Poem" (162) is written in free verse. Langston Hughes's

melodic "April Rain Song" (38) is another example of the effective use of free verse. Probably one of the best known poems of our day is "Fog" (84) by Carl Sandburg. This metaphorical description of the fog characterized as a cat is written in free verse.

HAIKU

Haiku is an ancient Japanese verse form that can be traced back to the thirteenth century. There are only seventeen syllables in the haiku; the first and third lines contain five syllables, the second line seven. Almost every haiku may be divided into two parts; first, a simple picture-making description that usually includes some reference, direct or indirect, to the season; and second, a statement of mood or feeling. A relationship between these two parts is implied, either a similarity or a telling difference.

The greatest of haiku writers, and the one who crystallized the form, was Basho. In his lifetime Basho produced more than 800 haiku. He considered the following poem to be one of his best:

An old silent pond . . .
A frog jumps into the pond,
splash! Silence again.

Basho (119)

The silence reverberates against the sudden noise of the splash, intensified by the interruption. Richard Lewis collected the haiku for *In a Spring Garden*, a book that Ezra Jack Keats illustrated with stunning pictures featuring silhouettes projected against a background of marbleized paper. Older students in middle school would enjoy attempting this form of poetry and using the same media employed by Keats. However, the meaning of haiku is not expected to be immediately apparent. The reader is invited to add his or her own associations and meanings to the words, thus completing the poem in the mind. Each time the poem is read, new understandings will develop.

Haiku is deceiving in that the form appears simple, yet it requires much from its reader. Unless children have reached the Piagetian level of formal operations in their thinking, haiku may be too abstract a form of poetry for them to fully understand. The common practice of asking

Just simply alive,
Both of us, I
And the poppy.
—*Issa*

Ezra Jack Keats captures the joy of this haiku with a simple silhouette of a boy and his poppy shown against a sunny orange background made of marbleized paper.

From *In a Spring Garden* edited by Richard Lewis.

young children to write haiku suggests that teachers do not understand its complexity. In this case, short is not simple!

CONCRETE POETRY

Many poets today are writing picture poems that make you see what they are saying. The message of the poem is presented not only in the words (sometimes just letters or punctuation marks) but in the arrangement of the words. Meaning is reinforced, or even carried, by the shape of the poem. We have seen how Lillian Morrison formed her poem about "The Sidewalk Racer" into the shape of a skateboard (p. 462) and how "Fueled" by Marcie Hans was written to resemble half of a tree (p. 462).

Eve Merriam uses concrete poetry to create the image of a windshield wiper while her words imitate its sound:

WINDSHIELD WIPER

fog smog	fog smog
tissue paper	tissue paper
clear the blear	clear the smear

fog more	fog more
splat splat	downpour
rubber scraper	rubber scraper
overshoes	macintosh
bumbershoot	muddle on
slosh through	slosh through

drying up	drying up
sky lighter	sky lighter
nearly clear	nearly clear
clearing clearing veer
clear here clear

Eve Merriam (100)

Robert Froman's pictures and words provide an innovative way of *Seeing Things* in a book by that title. His "A Seeing Poem" is drawn in the shape of a light bulb. He suggests that concrete poetry helps children turn on a light in their minds.

Once children have been exposed to concrete poetry, they invariably want to try creating some of their own. However, some children become so involved in the picture-making process, they forget that the meaning of the poem is carried by both words and arrangement. If emphasis is placed on the meaning first, then the shaping of the words will grow naturally from the idea of the poem.

SELECTING POETRY FOR CHILDREN

Children's Poetry Preferences

Children's interest in poetry has been the subject of many research studies starting in the early 1920s. The interesting fact about all these studies is the similarity of their findings and the stability of children's poetry preferences over the years.

Before conducting her own research on children's response to poetry, Ann Terry[7] summarized the findings of these earlier studies:

1. Children are the best judges of their preferences.
2. Reading texts and courses of study often do not include the children's favorite poems.
3. Children's poetry choices are influenced by (1) the poetry form, (2) certain poetic elements, and (3) the content, with humor and familiar experience being particularly popular.
4. A poem enjoyed at one grade level may be enjoyed across several grade levels.
5. Children do not enjoy poems they do not understand.
6. Thoughtful, meditative poems are disliked by children.
7. Some poems appeal to one sex more than another; girls enjoy poetry more than boys.
8. New poems are preferred over older, more traditional ones.
9. Literary merit is not necessarily an indication that a poem will be liked.

In her national survey of children's poetry preferences in fourth, fifth, and sixth grade, Terry[8] found much consistency with the results of these earlier studies. Narrative poems, such as John Ciardi's "Mummy Slept Late and Daddy Fixed Breakfast" (34), and limericks, including both modern and traditional, were the favorite forms of poetry for children. Haiku was consistently disliked by all grade levels. Elements of rhyme, rhythm, and sound increased children's enjoyment of the poems, as evidenced by their preference for David McCord's "The Pickety Fence" (157) and "Lone Dog" (54). Poems that contained much figurative language or imagery were disliked. Children's favorite poems at all three grade levels contained humor or were about familiar experiences or animals. All children preferred contemporary poems containing modern content

and today's language more than the older, more traditional poems.

Carol Fisher and Margaret Natarella[9] surveyed the poetry preferences of first, second, and third graders, using the same schools and techniques as the Terry study. Again, they found children in these grades also preferring narrative poetry and limericks, followed by rhymed verse, free verse and lyric poetry, with haiku ranking last. Both studies found children liked poems that were funny and poems about animals and familiar experiences. The younger children enjoyed poems about strange and fantastic events, such as "The Lurpp Is on the Loose" (200) by Prelutsky and Nash's "Adventures of Isabel" (47); the older children opted for more realistic content. Younger children appeared to like more traditional poems than the older children did. However, they insisted that poetry must rhyme, and all of the traditional poems did. Thus they could have been selecting on the basis of rhyme rather than content. Again a consistent finding of this study was that adults cannot accurately predict which poems children will like.

How then can we most effectively select poetry for children? Certainly a teacher will want to consider children's needs and interests, their previous experience with poetry, and the types of poetry that appeal to them. A sound principle to follow is to begin where the children are. Using some of the findings from the research we mentioned, teachers can share poems that have elements of rhyme, rhythm, and sound, such as "Galoshes" (47) or "The Pickety Fence" (47). Teachers can read many narrative verses and limericks and look for humorous poems and poems about familiar experiences and animals. Finally, they should share only those poems that they really like themselves; enthusiasm for poetry is contagious. Teachers will not want to limit their sharing only to poems that they know children will like. For taste needs to be developed, too; children should go beyond their delight in

[7]Ann Terry, *Children's Poetry Preferences: A National Survey of the Upper Elementary Grades* (Urbana, Ill.: National Council of Teachers of English, 1974, 1984), p. 10.
[8]Ann Terry, *Children's Poetry Preferences.*

[9]Carol J. Fisher and Margaret A. Natarella, "Young Children's Preferences in Poetry: A National Survey of First, Second and Third Graders," *Research in the Teaching of English*, vol. 16 (December 1982), pp. 339–353.

humorous and narrative poetry to develop an appreciation for variety in both form and content. We want children to respond to more poetry and to find more to respond to in poetry.

It may well be that the consistency in children's poetry preferences over the years simply reflects the poverty of their experience with poetry. We tend to like the familiar. If teachers only read traditional narrative poems to children, then these children will like narrative poems. Or having had little or no exposure to fine imaginative poetry, children may not have gone beyond their natural intuitive liking for jump-rope rhymes or humorous limericks. In brief, the results of the studies of children's interests in poetry may be more of an indictment of the quality of their literature program than of the quality of their preferences. We need to ascertain children's poetry preferences *after* they have experienced a rich, continuous exposure to poetry throughout the elementary school. It is hoped that as children have increased experience with a wide range of quality poetry by various poets, they will grow in appreciation and understanding of the finer poems.

Poets and Their Books

Recent years have seen an increase in the number of writers of verse for children and the number of poetry books published for the juvenile market. Poetry itself has changed, becoming less formal, more spontaneous and imitative of the child's own language patterns. The range of subject matter has expanded with the tremendous variation in children's interests. It is difficult to categorize the work of a poet on the basis of the content of his or her poems, for many poets interpret various areas of children's experience. However, an understanding of the general subject matter of the works of each poet will help the teacher select poems and make recommendations to children.

HUMOROUS VERSE

In every preference study that has been done, children prefer narrative rhyme and humorous verse. Today the popularity of the verse of Shel Silverstein and Jack Prelutsky attests to this. The use of imaginative symbols and vivid imagery and metaphor mark the difference between real poetry and verse. The versifiers provide instant gratification but leave the reader with little to ponder about. However, since children begin here in their enjoyment of poetry, it seems appropriate to start this section with writers of humorous verse.

Almost all poets have written some humorous verse, but only a few have become noted primarily for this form. In the nineteenth century the names of Edward Lear and Lewis Carroll became almost synonymous with humorous nonsense poems. Lear's limericks, alphabet rhymes, and narrative poems have been compiled into one book, *The Complete Nonsense Book*. Each absurd verse is illustrated by the poet's grotesque drawings, which add greatly to Lear's humor.

Several of our modern poets are following in the tradition of Lear. William Jay Smith included limericks, rhyming ABCs, and imaginary dialogue in much of his nonsense verse. The best of his poetry has been reissued in a new *Laughing Time* illustrated with amusing pictures by Fernando Krahn. His poems "Elephant," "Rhinoceros," and the "Coati-Mundi" are much fun and would add to a unit on zoo animals. One of the best of Smith's poems is the well-known "Toaster" that compares that kitchen utensil to a dragon. J. Patrick Lewis writes wonderfully funny verse in his book *A Hippopotamusn't*. Victoria Chess illustrates all these poems of beasts and birds with most amusing pictures of fat dumpy-looking creatures. The puns in the poem "Tom Tigercat" are reminiscent of the work of Ogden Nash and John Ciardi.

Much of the sophisticated light verse and limericks of Ogden Nash is out of print. Quentin Blake illustrated a new edition of his poems under the title of *Custard & Company*. It includes the long narrative verse about the cowardly dragon and some eighty-four other poems. "The Adventures of Isabel" (47) who eats a bear continues to be one of children's favorite story-poems. Maurice Sendak illustrates this poem in the fine collection titled *Sing a Song of Popcorn* (47). James Marshall's picture book rendition of Nash's legendary Isabel (177) is outrageously funny. Isabel may wear hair bows and nail polish but she is as tough as the bear she encounters.

John Ciardi's light verse for children is enjoyed by boys and girls with enough sophistication to

TOM TIGERCAT

Tom Tigercat is noted
for his manners and his wit.
He wouldn't think of lion,
no, he doesn't cheetah bit.
Tom never has pretended
to be something that he's not.
I guess that's why we like him
and why he likes ocelot.

The witty humor of "Tom Tigercat" is as funny as the fat dumpy-looking dogs and cat that Victoria Chess created to illustrate this poem.

From *A Hippopotamusn't* by J. Patrick Lewis.

appreciate his tongue-in-cheek humor. One particular favorite is "The Cat Heard the Cat Bird" (31) which tells the story of "Thin-grin Cat" who became a fat cat when the catbird disappeared! His "Mummy Slept Late and Daddy Fixed Breakfast" (110) was the most popular poem of the children in the fourth, fifth, and sixth grades in the Terry study (See p. 469). A former poetry editor for *The Saturday Review*, Ciardi could write serious verse as well as light verse. His "How to Tell the Top of the Hill" (33) and "The River Is a Piece of the Sky" (37) are both proof of this. Over the years, he wrote over a dozen books of poetry for children and his last, *Mummy Took Cooking Lessons and Other Poems*, was published posthumously. Ciardi was an early winner of the NCTE Poetry Award.

X. J. Kennedy has a wonderfully weird sense of humor. Most of his poetry is pure nonsense and delights children. His poem "Wildlife Refuge" (99), in which he describes "a reindeer in rain gear," is just one example of his talent for word play. "A Stupendous Pincushion" (99) is a pin-cushion not only for pins but for rolling pins and bowling pins besides. In "Backyard Volcano" (99), Uncle Jack delights in swimming in this phenomenon and Mother props her feet up to keep them warm. His books include *Brats, Fresh Brats, The Forgetful Wishing Well,* and *Ghastlies, Goops and Pincushions.*

Much of what children consider funny is frequently sadistic and ghoulish. Jack Prelutsky's macabre poems in *Nightmares* and Lobel's black-and-white illustrations are splendidly terrifying. One seventh-grade teacher of children in the inner city maintained that this book got her through her first year of teaching! Prelutsky is also a master at creating such zany imaginary creatures as "The Wozzit" who is hiding in the closet and "The Grobbles" who quietly wait to gobble someone up. These both appear along with *The Snopp on the Sidewalk* in a book by that name. He creates softer more lovable creatures in *The Baby Uggs Are Hatching,* including "The Sneezy-snoozer," "The Dreary Dreeze," and "The Sneepies." All ages enjoy Prelutsky's large collection of more than a hundred poems titled *The New Kid on the Block,* which includes humorous realistic poems such as "I'm Disgusted with My Brother" or "My Sister Is a Sissy," plus many funny characters and more zany creatures. *Something Big Has Been Here* is another large collection of amusing poems such as "Wilhelmina Wafflewitz" who can't make up her mind, slow slow "Slomona," and "The Addle-pated Paddlepuss." Children love to listen to "The Wumpaloons, Which Never Were" and then draw what they think they looked like according to the description in the poem. They also enjoy creating their idea of the animal that left the huge footprints in the title poem of this collection.

Prelutsky has written some lighthearted realistic verse for younger children about special holidays and seasons. These include some useful poems in *It's Halloween* and *It's Thanksgiving* and some very amusing ones in *Rainy Rainy Saturday,* and *It's Snowing! It's Snowing.* His two books, *Ride a Purple Pelican* and *Beneath a Blue Umbrella,* are filled with Mother Goose-type verses that appeal to preschoolers. Garth Williams has made large, handsome, colored illustrations for each of these

James Stevenson's cover illustration for the title poem *Something Big Has Been Here* by Jack Prelutsky captures children's horrified expressions as they look at the enormous footprints.

joyous poems which play with place names such as "Grandma Bear from Delaware" (198) and "Cincinnati Patty" (198).

Shel Silverstein's *Where the Sidewalk Ends* was on the *New York Times* bestseller list for three years. It is the one poetry book that all teachers, children, and parents seem to know. Librarians complain that they can't keep the book on the shelf, no matter how many copies they have. Here you meet a boy who turns into a TV set, a king who eats only a "Peanut-Butter Sandwich," and those three characters "Ickle Me, Pickle Me, Tickle Me Too." Much of the humor of these poems is based on the sounds of words, the preposterous characters, and amusing situations. While some verses are slightly unsavory, others surprise you with their sensitivity, such as

"Invitation," "Listen to the Mustn'ts," and the title poem, "Where the Sidewalk Ends." *The Light in the Attic* is more of the same and equally popular.

Poetry is neglected in our schools today, but there is no dearth of humorous verse. Children take to it as they do to a Big Mac, fries, and a shake. And like a McDonald's meal, it is enjoyable but not memorable—certainly not nutritious enough for a steady diet.

INTERPRETERS OF THE WORLD OF CHILDHOOD

Robert Louis Stevenson was the first poet to write of childhood from the child's point of view. *A Child's Garden of Verses*, published in 1885, continues in popularity today. Stevenson was himself a frail child and spent much of his early life in bed or confined indoors. His poetry reflects a solitary childhood, but a happy one. In "Land of Counterpane" and "Block City," he portrays a resourceful, inventive child who can create his own amusement. He found playmates in his shadow, in his dreams, and in his storybooks. The rhythm of Stevenson's "The Swing," "Where Go the Boats," and "Windy Nights" appeals to children today as much as to the children of a century ago. Currently, some ten illustrated editions of *A Child's Garden of Verses* are in print. They range in interpretation from Tasha Tudor's (218) quaint pastel pictures that portray Stevenson as a young child to Brian Wildsmith's (219) edition that is a brilliant kaleidoscope of color. Ted Rand has created a stunning picture-book edition of *My Shadow*, expanding the meaning of this poem to incorporate children from all over the world.

And he sometimes gets so little that there's none of him at all.

Everyone has a shadow. Ted Rand uses this universal image to portray children from all over the world in his illustrations for Robert Louis Stevenson's poem *My Shadow*. In this picture an African mother and child observe their noonday shadows.

474 Knowing Children's Literature

Whether skating in the Netherlands, leapfrogging in Russia, kicking a ball in China, or swinging beneath a tree in America, children are playing everywhere and their shadows are not far behind. This is a fresh vital look at a familiar poem. Ashley Wolff's illustrations extend *Block City* from a boy building with blocks at home to creating an elaborate landscape that seems to come alive. Such new picture books make fine introductions to Stevenson's poems.

Perhaps the best loved of British children's poets is A. A. Milne. Some of his poems show perceptive insight into the child's mind, such as "Halfway Down" and "Solitude." "Happiness" captures a child's joy in such delights as new waterproof boots, a raincoat, and hat. Told in the first person, "Hoppity" reveals a young child's enjoyment of the state of perpetual motion! The majority of Milne's poems are delightfully funny. The poetry from both of Milne's poetry books has now been collected into one volume titled *The World of Christopher Robin*. Illustrations by Ernest Shepard seem to belong with Milne's poetry as much as Pooh belongs with Christopher Robin; it is hard to imagine one without the other.

Another well-loved British poet for children is Eleanor Farjeon. Her knowledge and understanding of children's thoughts and behavior are reflected in her book, *Eleanor Farjeon's Poems for Children*. The simple poem "New Clothes and Old" tells of a child's preference for old things. "Over the Garden Wall" is a hauntingly beautiful poem that makes the reader feel as lonely as the child who is left out of the ball game on the other side of the wall. This poet also wrote the lovely nature poem "The Night Will Never Stay" and the graphic description of "Mrs. Peck-Pigeon."

Before her death in 1965 Eleanor Farjeon had received notable recognition for her poetry and prose. She was the first recipient of the international Hans Christian Andersen Medal and she received the Regina Medal for her lifework. A prestigious British award "for distinguished services to children's books" that bears the name of this well-known poet and writer is given annually. No other poet who has written exclusively for children has received such recognition.

Dorothy Aldis was one of the first American poets to celebrate children's feelings and every-day experiences with simple childlike verses. With rhyme and singsong meter, she captures the child's delight in the ordinary routines of home life, as in "After My Bath," "Going to Sleep" and even brushing teeth:

❦ SEE I CAN DO IT
    See, I can do it all myself
    With my own little brush!
    The tooth paste foams inside my mouth.
    The faucet waters rush

    In and out and underneath
    And round and round and round:
    First I do my upstairs teeth
    And then I do my down—

    The part I like the best of it
    Is at the end, though, when, I spit.

                    Dorothy Aldis (8)

Aldis is particularly sensitive to the emotions of childhood in "Bad," "Alone," and "No One Heard Him Call." Family relationships are lovingly portrayed in "Little," "My Brother," and "Hiding." Poems from the first four books by Dorothy Aldis were collected in a single volume entitled *All Together*, which can still be found in most library collections.

Mary Ann Hoberman writes lively rhythmical verse for young children. The poems in the collection *Yellow Butter Purple Jelly Red Jam Black Bread* range from such delightful nonsense as "The Llama Who Had No Pajama" to the swinging rhythm of "Hello and Goodbye" (see p. 455). The poem "Brother" (47), who is a bit of a bother to everyone, is a favorite with children and could well be shared as an introduction to books on sibling rivalry. Mary Ann Hoberman wrote the poems for *A Fine Fat Pig* after Malcah Zeldis created brilliant folk-art paintings of various animals. Each poem captures the uniqueness of the animals described from the giraffe to the walrus. This poetry book could be shared with a class of children, for the pictures are large and clear and both poems and illustrations maintain a child's point of view as seen in this poem about elephants:

❦ HOW ELEGANT THE ELEPHANT

How elegant the elephant
How mighty yet how mild
How elegant its mighty mate
How elegant its child
How toothsome are its ivory tusks
How luminous its eyes
How supple are its floppy ears
How jumbo is its size
How flexible its pudgy knees
How delicate its tail
But best of all
How nice its nose
Which works just like
A garden hose

Mary Ann Hoberman (73)

Primary children also enjoy the long sustained poems in Hoberman's picture book *A House Is a House for Me*. In this book she plays with the concept of houses, including regular houses and animals' houses, and then looks at other possibilities, such as a glove becoming a house for a hand and a pocket as a house for pennies. Once children hear

Mary Ann Hoberman wrote her delightful poem "How Elegant the Elephant" after viewing the brilliant folk-art paintings of Malcah Zeldis. Both artist and poet have presented a child's point of view in this fine collection of animal poems titled *A Fine Fat Pig*.

❦ ❦ ❦

these poems, they like to make up their own "house" poems. All of Hoberman's poetry can be distinguished by its fast-paced rhymes and marked rhythms.

Karla Kuskin also sees with the eyes of a child as she creates her well-known poems. Her book titled *Dogs & Dragons, Trees & Dreams* includes many of her best known narrative poems such as "I Woke Up This Morning," which tells of a child who feels she/he hasn't done anything right since "quarter past seven," or "Lewis Has a Trumpet," or "The Bear with the Golden Hair." She can write mysterious poems such as the haunting "Where Would You Be?" or play with the sounds of words as in "The Full of the Moon". Her book *Any Me I Want to Be* is written from the point of view of the subject. Instead of writing how a cat or the moon or a pair of shoes appear to her, the poet tries to get inside the object and be its voice. Children then enjoy guessing what the verse is about. In *Near the Window Tree* the poet attaches a note to each of her poems explaining what prompted her to write it. This was in response to the number of letters she receives from children asking her where she gets her ideas. Many of her poems contain both humor and wisdom as in this quizzical one:

❦ THE QUESTION

People always say to me
"What do you think you'd like to be
When you grow up?"
And I say "Why,
I think I'd like to be the sky
Or be a plane or train or mouse
Or maybe a haunted house
Or something furry, rough and wild. . .
Or maybe I will stay a child."

Karla Kuskin (103)

Something Sleeping in the Hall is a collection of easy-to-read poems about all kinds of pets. Six- and 7-year-olds would like to write about the pets, big or small, that might be "sleeping in their halls" after reading this delightful book. Karla Kuskin illustrates all her own poetry books with tiny precise pen-and-ink drawings. She designed the artwork for the NCTE Poetry Award and then was the third recipient of that coveted prize.

MULTICULTURAL POETRY

Long before black experiences became recognized in literature, Pulitzer Prize winner Gwendolyn Brooks wrote poignant poetry about African-American children living in the inner city. *Bronzeville Boys and Girls* contains some thirty-four poems, each bearing the name, thoughts, and feelings of an individual child. There is "John, Who Is Poor"; "Michael," who is afraid of the storm; and "Otto," who did not get the Christmas presents he had hoped for. But there is some joy—the happiness that "Eunice" feels when her whole family is in the dining room; "Beulah's" quiet thoughts at church; and "Luther and Breck," who have a make-believe dragon fight. Unfortunately, this poet has written only one volume of poetry for children.

A more joyous book is *Honey, I Love* by Eloise Greenfield, who has a great capacity for speaking in the voice of a young African-American child. This little book of sixteen poems includes a chant, a jump-rope rhyme (see p. 456), and thoughtful observations on such experiences as dressing up ("I Look Pretty") or thinking about a neighbor who left her a nickel as a "Keepsake" before she died. The Dillons' illustrations are as sensitive as these poems that celebrate the rich content of a child's world.

Greenfield portrays a slightly older child in the eighteen first-person poems that make up the collection of *Nathaniel Talking*. Nathaniel gives us his "philosophy" of life in these poems. Some are bittersweet memories; others look to the future. In the poems about his family, each generation is represented by a musical form associated with that time period, from "Nathaniel's Rap" to "My Daddy," which is written to the rhythm of a twelve-bar blues, to "Grandma's Bones," which imitates the sound of an African folk instrument. Sharp, clear pencil drawings by Jan Spivey Gilchrist help to make this a distinguished book of poetry. Gilchrist also illustrated the eighteen poems that Greenfield included in her *Night on Neighborhood Street*. These poems are about family, friends, and neighbors. Two of them focus on the father who is out of work and a drug seller with his "packages of death." Greenfield has written poems to go with Mr. Amos Ferguson's Bahamian folk-art paintings in *Under the Sunday Tree*.

Nikki Giovanni is well known for her adult poetry, but she has also written for children. *Spin a Soft Black Song* has been reissued with new illustrations. "Poem for Rodney" expresses both a child's point of view and an adult's. Rodney is tired of everyone asking him what he is going to do when he grows up; his reply is simply that he'd like to grow up. Rodney's answer is typical of childhood; but projected against adults' knowledge of life and death in our cities, it carries a more pathetic plea.

Arnold Adoff writes strong poems about the inner thoughts and feelings of a girl born of a mixed marriage. In *All the Colors of the Race*, he spatters his words across the page to slow down the reader and emphasize the meaning of each word. His poem "The way I see any hope for later" (1) is one that everyone should read and heed. His story-poem, *Black Is Brown Is Tan*, describes a family of different races growing up happy in a house full of love:

> Black is brown is tan
> is girl   is boy
> is nose   is face
> is all the colors
> of the race
> is dark   is light
> singing songs
> in singing night
> kiss big woman   hug big man
> black   is brown   is tan
>
> Arnold Adoff (2)

These poems not only reflect Arnold Adoff's love for his own family but celebrate diversity and individuality. While many of his poems are about caring and friendship between races, others are about seasons and eating. *In for Winter, Out for Spring* is a journal of poems of the changing seasons, capturing the joy of the first snowflake to the coming of the monarch butterflies in May, to fireflies in August and pumpkins in late October. Adoff creates vivid images in these poems of people and seasons. *Eats* celebrates food and is filled with poems that delight youngsters. One of them even gives a recipe for "Peanut Butter Batter Bread." In *Chocolate Dreams* the poet sees humor

Emily McCully's small watercolor illustrations portray the fun and joy of this multiracial family growing up in a house full of love.

From *Black Is Brown Is Tan* by Arnold Adoff.

❦   ❦   ❦

in his own passion for this sweet. Arnold Adoff is also a recipient of the prestigious NCTE Poetry Award.

Beginning in the 1920s, Langston Hughes was the first African American to write poems of black protest and pride. It was his voice that first asked "What Happens to a Dream Deferred?" While most of his poetry is for adults, some fine poems are found in anthologies for youngsters. Unfortunately, *Don't You Look Back*, the one collection of Hughes's poems for young people, is out of print. Some of Ann Grifalconi's finest woodcuts illustrate this outstanding collection put together by Lee Bennett Hopkins. Perhaps *Don't You Look Back* will be reissued; if not, it is still available in most libraries. The well-known poems "Dreams" (50) and "April Rain Song" (38) can be found in several anthologies.

The poems by Cynthia Rylant in her book *Waiting to Waltz* capture the essence of growing up in a small town in Appalachia. Her vivid images chronicle the minor crises that make up a childhood: the day a girl's mother runs over "Little Short Legs," the black dog down the road; the time the girl loses the spelling bee; and her dismay at being reprimanded for swearing. The most poignant poem of all, "Forgotten," describes her mixed feelings when she hears that her long-absent father has died. Stephen Gammell's soft pencil drawings are as sensitive as these poems, each picturing a fleeting moment of childhood—that suddenly is gone.

Gerald Milnes collected mountain rhymes for his book titled *Granny Will Your Dog Bite?* Reminiscent of some Mother Goose rhymes, the collection sings to the sound of an imaginary fiddle. Milnes himself plays the banjo and guitar for the cassette of this book and a 9-year-old girl accompanies him with her clear mountain voice. Kimberly Bulcken Root's soft earth-toned watercolors have a rustic appeal that seems just right for this collection of poems from the mountains.

Jo Carson's *Stories I Ain't Told Nobody Yet* contains forty-nine first-person prose poems. Most of these poems are for teenagers but some speak to a universal audience. The poems are numbered rather than titled. One (number 20) on "progress" in the mountains would be excellent for a unit on the environment. The voices in this book sound authentic and vary in tone from humorous and kindly to bitter.

While Charlotte Pomerantz is not Hispanic, she and her husband and two children spend winters in Puerto Rico. This experience encouraged her to write poetry in two languages, English and Spanish. She does this so skillfully in her poems for *The Tamarindo Puppy* that the child easily learns words in both languages while reading and hearing these poems. Illustrations by Byron Barton also help indicate meaning. Another book by Pomerantz is *If I Had a Paka: Poems in Eleven Languages*. In this collection, Pomerantz builds the child's cross-cultural vocabulary by repeating a key word in a different language, such as Swahili. With the help of English language clues and the clear pictures by Nancy Tafuri, young children can easily guess the meaning of the words and poems.

POETS OF NATURE

Children, like poets, are very attuned to the world around them. They are fascinated by the constant changes in nature and enjoy poems that communicate their delight in the first snow, for example, or their sense of wonder when they touch a pussy willow or hear a foghorn or see a deer.

Aileen Fisher is adept at observing both nature and children. She views the natural world through the eyes of the child, preserving a remarkable sense of wonder. Her poems are filled with sensory imagery, as in this verse:

> ❦ PUSSY WILLOWS
> Close your eyes
> and do not peek
> and I'll rub Spring,
> across your cheek—
> smooth as satin,
> soft and sleek—
> close your eyes
> and do not peek.
>
> Aileen Fisher (56)

Fisher's comparisons are simple and fresh, very much within the experience of a child. A collection of some of Aileen Fisher's favorite poems appears in her book *Always Wondering*. Included are such popular nature poems as "Bird Talk," "Pussy Willow," and "I Like Fall," as well as poems about children's interests such as "First Day of School" and "When It's Thanksgiving." *Listen Rabbit* is a long narrative poem about a boy who finds a nest of baby rabbits and anticipates watching them grow up. Sensitive realistic pictures by Symeon Shimin add to the enjoyment of this book. *Rabbits Rabbits* provides more poems about these woodland animals. Aileen Fisher was the second recipient of the Award for Excellence in Poetry for Children given by the National Council of Teachers of English.

Lilian Moore describes the changing moods and seasons of both the city and the country in her short-lined free verse. Her poems frequently appeal to the senses as she talks about the moaning of foghorns or the "tree-talk" or "wind-swish" of the night. One that children enjoy is "Encounter" (174), which tells of a "heart-stopping" meeting with a deer. In "Wind Song" (see pp. 455–6) she describes the flapping and snapping noise the wind makes as it blows flags and ashcans. In "Snowy Morning" (174) she speaks of waking to a hushed morning of snow in the city. Her poem "Until I Saw the Sea" (47) provides a fresh new image of the "wrinkled sea." A former teacher, reading specialist, and editor who lived in the city, Lilian Moore now lives on a farm in the country. Her poetry reflects her knowledge of what children enjoy and her close observations of her surroundings. Many of her poems from her earlier books have been included in a book titled *Something New Begins*. Lilian Moore is also a recipient of the NCTE Poetry Award.

J. Patrick Lewis includes seventeen poems in *Earth Verses and Water Rhymes*. He begins with poems about the fall and progresses through the seasons. These poems provide fresh new images; for example, he describes trees as "Earth umbrellas." Robert Sabuda's handcut linoleum block prints in soft muted colors seem just right for the contemplative tone of these poems.

Byrd Baylor writes long story-length poems that reflect her appreciation for nature and the beauty of the southwestern landscape. In *The Other Way to Listen*, an older man tells a young girl how you can hear wildflower seeds burst open or a rock murmuring or hills singing—of course it takes practice! *Your Own Best Secret Place*, *Everybody Needs a Rock*, and *I'm in Charge of Celebrations* are fine poetry workshop starters as children describe their secret places or plan special celebrations. Peter Parnall incorporates the text as part of his bold illustrations.

Two unusually fine picture books of nature poems are Marilyn Singer's *Turtle in July* and *The Hornbeam Tree and Other Poems* by Charles Norman. In *Turtle in July*, Singer writes from the animal, fish, or insect's point of view. She includes a different animal for each month of the year, describing, for example, a deer who runs over the hard-packed January snow or the beavers in November who add mud and more mud, sticks and more sticks to their winter homes. The turtle is the only one who knows how to stay cool in July.

> ❦ TURTLE IN JULY
> Heavy
> Heavy hot

Heavy hot hangs
Thick sticky
Icky
But I lie
Nose high
Cool pool
No fool
A turtle in July.

Marilyn Singer (213)

Jerry Pinkney's clear watercolors portray each creature in its natural habitat. In the nineteen poems written for *The Hornbeam Tree*, Charles Norman describes the characteristics of creatures as small as a snail and as large as a polar bear, as common as a squirrel and as exotic as the duck-billed platypus. Ted Rand's vibrant watercolor illustrations for this book capture the dive of a kingfish or the drumming of a woodpecker. Jane Yolen's poems for *Bird Watch* are filled with wonderful images such as a cardinal as a "brilliant blob" on the page of winter. See page 459 for her poem "Woodpecker."

While Carl Sandburg is noted for his sage commentary on people, he did make two collections of poetry with young people in mind, *Early Moon*

A turtle in July

Jerry Pinkney's painting of a turtle partially submerged in the water shows the wise turtle "nose high/cool pool/no fool." The poems for *Turtle in July* were written by Marilyn Singer.

and *Wind Song*. Only *Early Moon* is still available, in paperback. Lee Bennett Hopkins has made a handsome new edition of selected poems of Carl Sandburg titled *Rainbows Are Made*, illustrated with six of Fritz Eichenberg's wood engravings—themselves as powerful as some of Sandburg's poetry. This collection includes selections from *The People, Yes* and poems about nature, people, the seasons, the sea, and the stars. Old favorites such as "Arithmetic," "Phizzog," and "Buffalo Dusk" are here. But children may become newly acquainted with "Doors," "Pencils," and "The Young Sea" as well. This handsome book will introduce them to the thoughtful, quizzical nature of Carl Sandburg's poetry.

Many poems of Robert Frost are both simple enough for a child to understand and complex enough for graduate study. Before his death, Frost selected some of his poems to be read to, or by, young people. Interestingly, the title of this collection, *You Come Too*, was taken from a line of "The Pasture," the first poem in this book and the introductory poem of the very first book of Frost's ever to be published. Upon initial reading this poem seems no more than a literal invitation to join someone as he cleans the pasture spring. However, the poem takes on more meaning when viewed in the context of its placement; the trip to the pasture to clean the spring may well be an invitation to the enjoyment of poetry itself—"you come too!" Robert Frost seems to have had a preoccupation with clearing muddied waters, and it is significant that his last book for adults was titled *In the Clearing*. By reading *You Come Too*, children can enjoy "The Runaway," "Dust of Snow," "The Last Word of a Bluebird," and "The Pasture," poems on their level of understanding. Older children will begin to comprehend the deeper meanings in "Mending Wall," "The Road Not Taken," and "The Death of the Hired Man."

VERSATILE POETS

It is almost impossible to characterize the wide variety of poems produced by certain poets. David McCord's poetry, for example, ranges in subject matter from poems about everyday experiences to nature poems to verses about verse. He plays with sound in "The Pickety Fence" and

"Song of the Train"; with form, including couplets, quatrains, limericks, and triolets, in "Write Me a Verse"; and with words and their meanings in many of his poems, for example "Glowworm," "Ptarmigan," and "Goose, Moose and Spruce." He can write with a lively wit or quietly enter the serious inner world of the child. For example, in "This Is My Rock" he reflects the feelings of all children who have a special place they love.

🌿 THIS IS MY ROCK

This is my rock,
And here I run
To steal the secret of the sun;

This is my rock,
And here come I
Before the night has swept the sky;

This is my rock,
This is the place
I meet the evening face to face.

David McCord (157)

Every Time I Climb a Tree was among the first poetry books to be illustrated by a well-known picture-book illustrator, Caldecott award-winning Marc Simont. All of David McCord's poetry was collected in a single volume titled *One at a Time*. It is appropriate that this book was published in the same year that David McCord received the first award for Excellence in Poetry for Children given by the National Council of Teachers of English.

Eve Merriam's poetry has a lilt and a bounce that will capture the most disinterested child's attention, beginning with her narrative poems about the "Alligator on the Escalator" (163) and "Teevee" (163), the story of the married couple who watched so much TV they became strangers to each other. Her books for primary children, *You Be Good & I'll Be Night*, *A Poem for a Pickle*, and *Blackberry Ink*, contain bouncy jump-rope rhymes such as "Jump, Jump" or the rhythmical "Swing Me Swing Me" and the loving "You're My Turtle." *Fresh Paint* contains lovely fresh images of new snow, "The First Day of Spring," and "Sunset." Older students, once they have read

her "A Throw of Threes" might like to try writing three things that they think go together. *Chortles* is full of wordplay including "Gazinta," "Whodunnit," and "A Token of Unspoken." Here too, students can find "Windshield Wiper" (see p. 468). *Halloween ABC* provides chilling poems for older students to enjoy on that holiday. Lane Smith's spooky illustrations are perfect for some of these shivery poems. Many of Eve Merriam's most popular poems including "Satellite, Satellite" (see p. 453), "To Meet Mr. Lincoln," "A Commercial for Spring," and a "Yell for Yellow" all appear in the paperback edition of *Jamboree*. It seems obvious that such a versatile poet received the NCTE Poetry Award.

Another NCTE Poetry Award winner is Myra Cohn Livingston, a prolific and versatile writer of poetry for all ages of children. She handles a variety of styles and forms masterfully, including rhymes, free verse, limerick, triolet, haiku, concrete poems, and others. Her first books of poetry appealed more to the younger child and included such well-known poems as "Whispers," "The Night," and "Bump on My Knee." Many of these poems for younger children have been gathered together in a small-sized book, *A Song I Sang for You*, illustrated with Margot Tomes's appropriately naive black-and-white illustrations. In *Worlds I Know*, Livingston echoes the emotions of slightly older children. Here she talks about the aunts and uncles that people a child's world and "The Grandfather I Never Knew." "Secret Door" and "Secret Passageway" would intrigue children.

🌿 SECRET DOOR

The upstairs room
has a secret door.
Dad says someone
used it for
some papers many years ago,
and if I want to, I can go
and bring a treasured thing
to hide
and lock it up
all dark inside
and it can be
a place for me
to open

with

its

tiny

key.

Myra Cohn Livingston (150)

Myra Cohn Livingston gets inside of older children's thoughts in such poems as "Lonesome," "I'm Sorry," and "Poor" in *The Way Things Are and Other Poems*. Her poems in *There Was a Place* are remarkable for reflecting how children from broken homes and one-parent families feel (see "In The Middle," p. 454).

Increasingly, Livingston is combining her poetry with the artwork of Leonard Everett Fisher to produce such striking books as *Circle of Seasons, Sky Songs, Earth Songs, Sea Songs, Space Songs*, and *Up in the Air*. In some of these books, the abstract artwork almost overpowers her fine poetry; in *Celebrations* both the art and the poems present a moving panorama of sixteen holidays, including Martin Luther King Day, Columbus Day, Presidents' Day, and all birthdays. Not only is Myra Cohn Livingston a versatile poet, but she is also a well-known anthologist and teacher of creative writing to children.

Anthologies of Poems for Children

Today poetry anthologies do not stay in print as long as they used to because time limits are usually placed on permissions to use certain poems. This has meant the publication of fewer large anthologies and the proliferation of many specialized collections containing fewer than twenty poems. For this reason only a selected number of anthologies are reviewed here; others will be found in the box beginning on page 483.

COMPREHENSIVE POETRY COLLECTIONS

Every family will want to own at least one excellent anthology of poetry for children. Teachers will want to have several, including some for their personal use and some for the children. In selecting a general anthology of poetry, the following criteria need to be considered.

Sing a Song of Popcorn, edited by Beatrice Schenk deRegniers and others, is a stunning collection of poetry for all children. The poems were first selected for a popular paperback called *Poems Children Will Sit Still For* (now out of print, this Scholastic title sold over a quarter of a million copies). The selection of poetry for *Sing a Song of*

GUIDELINES

Evaluating Poetry Anthologies

- ◆ What is the age-level appeal of this book?
- ◆ How many poems are included?
- ◆ What type of poems are included?
- ◆ How many poets are represented?
- ◆ What is the quality of the poetry?
- ◆ Are there recent contemporary poems as well as old favorites?
- ◆ What is the subject matter of the poems?
- ◆ How are the poems arranged and organized?
- ◆ How adequate are the indexes in helping the reader find a poem?
- ◆ How helpful are the introduction and commentaries?
- ◆ Has the compiler achieved the stated or implied purpose in making the collection?
- ◆ Are the illustrations and format appropriate for the poems and age appeal of the collection?

Popcorn has been updated and is now illustrated in full color by nine Caldecott Medal-winning artists. Marcia Brown evokes scenes of all kinds of weather and gives visual impressions of haiku. Maurice Sendak interprets story poems; Richard Egielski's weird pictures add to the fun of non-sense verse. The Dillons' soft batik-like illustrations sensitively convey feelings and thoughts. The volume contains over 128 poems that had to meet the criteria of captivating children's interest. The represented poets range from Mary Ann Hoberman to Emily Dickinson. It includes such well-known poems as "Galoshes" (see p. 457), "Eletelephony," "Brother," and "Stopping by Woods on a Snowy Evening." If a teacher or a parent could only have one collection, this would be the one to buy.

Tomie de Paola's Book of Poems is also a handsome anthology. He uses Emily Dickinson's poem "There is no frigate like a book" to symbolically unite the cover, title page, introduction, and final page. His eighty-six poems are well chosen including classics such as Stevenson's "Land of Counterpane" and "Windy Nights" and such contemporary poems as Myra Cohn Livingston's "Secret Door," Valerie Worth's "Hose," and Eve Merriam's funny "Alligator on the Escalator." A unique addition is some poems in Spanish.

Jack Prelutsky has produced two very popular anthologies. *Read-Aloud Rhymes for the Very Young* contains over two hundred of the most popular poems for very young children including a few Mother Goose and jump-rope rhymes, Karla Kuskin's "The Gold Tinted Dragon," Dennis Lee's "Dreadful Doings of Jelly Belly," and Milne's "Halfway Down." Lively illustrations by Marc Brown emphasize the fun and nonsense of some of these verses.

Many parents and teachers will be attracted to the large *Random House Book of Poetry*, with its 572 poems selected by Jack Prelutsky and profusely illustrated with Arnold Lobel's lively pictures. If children have only known Shel Silverstein's and Prelutsky's humorous verse, this is a good place to begin. Though much of the book is dominated by humorous verse (some thirty-eight poems by Prelutsky himself), fine poems by Robert Frost, Eve Merriam, Eleanor Farjeon, Emily Dickinson, Myra Cohn

Tomie de Paola captures the amazed expressions of the shoppers who encounter an alligator thoroughly enjoying his ride on the escalator. "Alligator on the Escalator" by Eve Merriam is one of children's favorites in *Tomie de Paola's Book of Poems.*

Livingston, Dylan Thomas, and others are interspersed with them—a little like putting a bunch of beautiful cold grapes on a plate of fudge: you hope they will be tasted even if they don't go together. Arnold Lobel's humorous full-color illustrations also draw children to this anthology.

David Booth's *Til All the Stars Have Fallen* is an exciting collection of over seventy Canadian poems for children ages 8 and up. These include poems by such well-known poets as Dennis Lee and Jean Little and some wonderful new voices such as Duke Redbird, A. M. Klein, Lois Simmie, and George Swede. Kady Denton has echoed the poetic imagery of many of these poems in her expressive watercolors and collage illustrations.

RESOURCES FOR TEACHING

◆ COMPREHENSIVE POETRY ANTHOLOGIES ◆

COMPILER	TITLE	AGE LEVEL	DESCRIPTION
Tomie de Paola	*Tomie de Paola's Book of Poems*	6–10	See text.
Lee Bennett Hopkins	*Side by Side*	6–10	Some fifty-seven poems ranging from traditional to such modern poets as McCord, Kuskin, Lilian Moore, plus Robert Frost and Lewis Carroll.
Beatrice Schenk de Regniers et al.	*Sing a Song of Popcorn*	6–12	See text.
Jack Prelutsky	*Read Aloud Rhymes for the Very Young*	5–10	See text.
Jack Prelutsky	*The Random House Book of Poetry*	7–12	See text.
Sara and Stephen Corrin	*Once upon a Rhyme*	6–10	Illustrated by Jill Bennett, this collection of about a hundred poems contains many narrative verses.
Joanna Cole	*A New Treasury of Children's Poetry*	8–12	A comprehensive collection of more than two hundred poems. Poems are arranged from nonsense poems to more complex. A good family collection.
Nancy Larrick	*Piping down the Valleys Wild*	8–12	A distinctive collection of some 250 poems ranging from traditional to such modern poets as Kuskin, Milne, Merriam, Livingston, plus favorites by Frost and Sandburg.
Nancy Larrick	*To the Moon and Back*	9–up	A fresh new collection of sixty-six poems including such well-known poets as X. J. Kennedy, Lucille Clifton, Lillian Morrison, and some fine Native-American and Eskimo poems.

RESOURCES FOR TEACHING

◆ COMPREHENSIVE POETRY ANTHOLOGIES (CONTINUED) ◆

COMPILER	TITLE	AGE LEVEL	DESCRIPTION
Mary Alice Downie, Barbara Robertson	*The New Wind Has Wings* *The Wind Has Wings*	8–12	Two fine Canadian collections illustrated with unusual collage pictures by the well-known illustrator Elizabeth Cleaver. Includes such exciting poems as "There's a Fire in the Forest" and "Rattlesnake."
David Booth	*Til All the Stars Have Fallen*	8–12	See text.
X. J. Kennedy, Dorothy M. Kennedy	*Knock at a Star*	9–12	See text.
Paul Janeczko	*This Delicious Day*	12–up	Contains sixty-five poems with fresh new images. The title refers to various "meals" for the eye and mind that each day provides.
Steve Dunning, Edward Lueders and Hugh Smith	*Reflections on a Gift of Watermelon Pickle and Other Modern Verses*	12–up	See text.
Helen Ferris	*Favorite Poems Old and New*	8–12	First published in 1957 when there was no time limit on poetry permissions, this collection has over seven hundred poems! Now in paperback, it is still an excellent source for teachers.
Edward Blishen	*The Oxford Book of Poetry for Children*	8–12	Recently reissued, this collection of such traditional poets as Lear, Carroll, de la Mare, Stevenson, even Shakespeare and Shelley, has been beautifully illustrated in a kaleidoscope of color by Brian Wildsmith.
Scott Elledge	*Wider Than the Sky*	10–up	Over two hundred poems mostly written by traditional

Knock at a Star is subtitled "A Child's Introduction to Poetry." Selected by the well-known adult poet and anthologist X. J. Kennedy and his wife Dorothy, this is a memorable collection of poetry for children 8 years old and up. The poets represented range widely from such adult poets as James Stephens, Emily Dickinson, Robert Frost, and William Stafford to children's poets Aileen Fisher, David McCord, and Lillian Morrison. Many familiar poems are here, but most of them are new and fresh to children's collections. The three section headings in this book also are addressed to children; they provide an understanding of how poetry does what it does: (1) What Do Poems Do? (make you laugh, tell stories, send messages, share feelings, start you wondering); (2) What's Inside a Poem? (images, word music, beats that repeat, likenesses); (3) Special Kinds of Poems. Teachers, librarians, and parents as well as children can learn from this wise book, which teaches at the same time that it develops enthusiasm for poetry.

Another unique anthology that provides insight into how some thirty-nine poets work and feel about their poems is Paul Janeczko's *The Place My Words Are Looking For.* Here Jack Prelutsky, X. J. Kennedy, Myra Cohn Livingston, and others talk about how they create their poetry by providing personal comments and examples of their poems. Pictures of the poets accompany each section so children can see what their favorite poet looks like. Lillian Morrison comments on how she wrote "The Sidewalk Racer" (see page 462), for example. She says:

> Writing poems can be a way of pinning down a dream (almost); capturing a moment, a memory, a happening; and, at the same time, it's a way of sorting out your thoughts and feelings. Sometimes words tell you what you didn't know you knew.[10]

One of the most exciting current anthologies is *Reflections on a Gift of Watermelon Pickle and Other Modern Verses* by Dunning, Lueders, and Smith. Illustrated with superb black-and-white photographs surrounded by much space, this anthology appeals to the eye as well as the ear of older students in middle school. They will take delight in "Sonic Boom" by John Updike, "Ancient History" by Arthur Guiterman, "Dreams" by Langston Hughes, and "How to Eat a Poem" by Eve Merriam. They will appreciate the honesty and realistic viewpoint of "Husbands and Wives," in which Miriam Hershenson tells of couples who ride the train from station to station without ever speaking to each other. The sharply cynical "Forecast" by Dan Jaffe suggests that when the end of the world comes, humankind will probably hear about it on the weather report on television. But the poems of despair are balanced in this fine anthology with poems of hope and beauty.

[10]Lillian Morrison in *The Place My Words Are Looking For* by Paul B. Janeczko (New York: Bradbury Press, 1990), p. 11.

SPECIALIZED COLLECTIONS

As poetry permissions become more expensive and more difficult to obtain for long lengths of time, anthologists have turned to making small specialized collections. Most of these are organized for a particular age level or around certain subjects, such as dogs or seasons. Some are related to the ethnic origin of the poems, such as poetry of Native Americans or poems that celebrate the experiences of African Americans. An increasing number of specialized collections contain stunning illustrations. Some of the best of these are noted in the text; others are included in the list of specialized anthologies.

Laura Whipple is the anthologist for *Eric Carle's Animals Animals* although her name appears only on the flap of the jacket! Carle's large painted collage pictures will unquestionably attract children to this collection of nearly seventy-five poems. But the poems themselves have been well chosen and range in subject from animals to insects to birds and fish. Along with the art, children will enjoy Prelutsky's poem "Long Gone" about dinosaurs, Bobbi Katz's poem about a kangaroo, and X. J. Kennedy's "Electric Eel." Whipple and Carle have also teamed together to produce a very handsome collection of poems about mythological and fantasy creatures in *Eric Carle's Dragons Dragons & Other Creatures That Never Were*. These books represent the current trend for more visually oriented poetry books.

Nancy Larrick's books *Cats Are Cats* and *Mice Are Nice* are superbly illustrated with Ed Young's charcoal and pastel pictures. Each book contains some twenty-five well-chosen poems. The illustrations for *Cats Are Cats* were quickly drawn on brown wrapping paper, but they make a stunning book. Lee Bennett Hopkins is a prolific anthologist, collecting poems on subjects as varied as in his book *Dinosaurs* and *Good Books, Good Times!* a superb collection of poems about enjoying reading. Myra Cohn Livingston not only writes fine poetry for children but she creates excellent anthologies for them, such as her five collections of poems about various members of families.

In My Mother's House by Ann Nolan Clark was a breakthrough book when it was first published in 1941. Now reissued, it contains poems describing the close-knit farming community of the Pueblo Indians. Based on stories told by the Pueblo children, it was the first book to represent a Native-American point of view. Velino Herrera did the beautifully clear pictures for this fine book of poems.

Stephen Gammell illustrates *Dancing Teepees* edited by Virginia Driving Hawk Sneve with sensitive full-color watercolors. This is a handsome book of some twenty poems chosen from various tribes. Unfortunately, Aline Amon's book *The Earth Is Sore*, which contained poetry and early speeches of Native Americans, is out of print. This book was beautifully illustrated with black-and-white prints of natural objects such as leaves, pine needles, and spider webs. Such an outstanding book deserves to be reissued. John Bierhorst also emphasizes humanity's close relationship to nature in his anthology *In the Trail of the Wind: American Indian Poems and Ritual Orations*. This

Drawing on brown wrapping paper, Ed Young portrays an elusive cat who will only reveal half of himself for the cover of *Cats Are Cats,* a collection of cat poems selected by Nancy Larrick.

🐾 🐾 🐾

RESOURCES FOR TEACHING

◆ SPECIALIZED COLLECTIONS OF POETRY ◆

COMPILER/POET	TITLE	AGE LEVEL	DESCRIPTION
	CHILDREN'S EVERYDAY EXPERIENCES		
Myra Cohn Livingston	*Dilli Dilli Piccalilli*	6–10	Contains fifty-five poems for young children ranging from Edward Lear to Karla Kuskin, Eve Merriam, and Clyde Watson. An appealing selection.
Nancy Larrick	*The Merry-Go-Round Poetry Book*	6–10	Black-and-white sketches by Karen Gundersheimer add to the appeal of these nearly sixty lively poems for youngsters.
Lee Bennett Hopkins	*Morning, Noon and Nighttime, Too*	6–8	Hopkins has selected over forty excellent poems that take us through a child's day.
Lee Bennett Hopkins	*By Myself*	6–8	Contains sixteen poems that describe children's thoughts and feelings.
Lee Bennett Hopkins	*Best Friends*	6–8	Includes the fun of sledding, fishing, and slumber parties with best friends.
Lee Bennett Hopkins	*Surprises*	6–8	With unerring taste for good poetry and what children enjoy, Hopkins has selected nearly forty poems that children can read independently.
Lee Bennett Hopkins	*More Surprises*	6–8	More poems for children to read and enjoy by themselves.
Lee Bennett Hopkins	*Through Our Eyes: Poems and Pictures About Growing Up*	8–12	A collection of poems depicting children of various backgrounds—their thoughts, hopes, lifestyles. Full-color photographs help make these voices come alive.

RESOURCES FOR TEACHING

♦ SPECIALIZED COLLECTIONS OF POETRY (CONTINUED) ♦

COMPILER/POET	TITLE	AGE LEVEL	DESCRIPTION
Myra Cohn Livingston	*I Like You, If You Like Me*	10–up	Contains nearly a hundred poems that celebrate friends and comradeship. Some poems are funny; others sad or lonesome.

NIGHT POEMS

Helen Plotz	*A Week of Lullabies*	3–6	Fourteen goodnight poems, containing childlike illustrations by Marisabina Russo. The colored borders of each picture create a cozy feeling.
Lee Bennett Hopkins	*Still as a Star: A Book of Nighttime Poems*	5–8	Contains many well-known and some fresh goodnight poems.
Nancy Larrick	*When the Dark Comes Dancing*	5–8	Subtitled "a bedtime poetry book," contains some forty-five poems by such well-known poets as Aileen Fisher and Karla Kuskin, plus songs and familiar nursery rhymes.
Nancy Larrick	*Bring Me All Your Dreams*	10–up	Includes a wide range of exciting poems by many contemporary poets. Dreams include daydreams, wishes, night dreams.

FAMILIES

Myra Cohn Livingston	*Poems for Fathers*	5–8	Well-chosen poems that avoid typical stereotypes of father roles.
Myra Cohn Livingston	*Poems for Mothers*	5–8	Provides a good balance between humor and affection; also avoids stereotyping mothers.
Myra Cohn Livingston	*Poems for Brothers, Poems for Sisters*	5–8	Some nineteen poems about siblings; some are humorous poems, others serious.

RESOURCES FOR TEACHING

◆ SPECIALIZED COLLECTIONS OF POETRY (CONTINUED) ◆

COMPILER/POET	TITLE	AGE LEVEL	DESCRIPTION
Myra Cohn Livingston	*Poems for Grandmothers*	5–8	Eighteen poems about grandmothers, great-grandmothers, and a stepgrandmother. Shows various races, ages, and economic backgrounds.

POETRY OF NATURE AND SEASONS

Lee Bennett Hopkins	*The Sky Is Full of Song*	6–8	A jewel of a book: poems about the seasons described from a young child's point of view. Illustrated with small colored linocuts by Dirk Zimmer.
Lee Bennett Hopkins	*The Sea Is Calling Me*	7–10	Contains over twenty poems about the ocean, seashore, lighthouses, seashells, and sand castles.
David Booth	*Voices on the Wind: Poems for All Seasons*	6–9	Over twenty poems with a wide range of poets from William Blake to John Ciardi. Lovely full-page acrylic paintings by Michele Lemieux.
Josette Frank	*Snow Toward Evening*	7–10	Thirteen poems, one for each month and the introductory one. Thomas Locker has painted a full-sized oil landscape for each poem.
Myra Cohn Livingston	*If the Owl Calls Again*	9–up	Over seventy owl poems from Shakespeare to Eve Merriam to David McCord. Nursery rhymes and poems from the Navajo and Chippewa are included.

ANIMAL POEMS

Laura Whipple	*Eric Carle's Animals Animals*	5–9	See text.
Nancy Larrick	*Cats Are Cats*	5–9	See text.

RESOURCES FOR TEACHING

♦ SPECIALIZED COLLECTIONS OF POETRY (CONTINUED) ♦

COMPILER/POET	TITLE	AGE LEVEL	DESCRIPTION
Nancy Larrick	*Mice Are Nice*	5–9	See text.
Myra Cohn Livingston	*Cat Poems*	5–9	Over twenty poems about cats. Stylish black-and-white illustrations by Trina Schart Hyman.
Myra Cohn Livingston	*Dog Poems*	5–9	Some twenty poems illustrated by Leslie Morrow. Contemporary and traditional poems included.
Bobbye S. Goldstein	*Bear in Mind*	5–8	Nearly thirty poems about bears—live ones and teddy bears. Wonderful full-color pictures by William Pène DuBois.
Lee Bennett Hopkins	*Dinosaurs*	8–up	Some eighteen poems including one on "The Last Dinosaur" and "How the End Might Have Been" good for discussion and dinosaur units.
Laura Whipple	*Eric Carle's Dragons Dragons & Other Creatures That Never Were*	8–up	See text.

HUMOROUS POETRY

COMPILER/POET	TITLE	AGE LEVEL	DESCRIPTION
Emma Chichester Clark	*I Never Saw a Purple Cow*	4–9	A superb collection of 117 nonsense rhymes including verses by Carroll, Lear, and Hilaire Belloc. Action-packed watercolors add to the appeal.
Jack Prelutsky	*For Laughing Out Loud: Poems to Tickle Your Funnybone*	5–10	Prelutsky has included over 130 of the funniest poems in this book. Lively colored illustrations by Marjorie Priceman add to the humor.

RESOURCES FOR TEACHING

◆ SPECIALIZED COLLECTIONS OF POETRY (CONTINUED) ◆

COMPILER/POET	TITLE	AGE LEVEL	DESCRIPTION
Jack Prelutsky	*Poems of A. Nonny Mouse*	5–10	Prelutsky collected some seventy of the silliest poems attributed by publishers to "anonymous." Absurdly brilliant illustrations of Henrik Drescher seem most appropriate.
William Cole	*Oh, What Nonsense!* *Oh, How Silly!* *Oh, That's Ridiculous!*	7–12	These collections contain some of Shel Silverstein's verses and other favorites of children.
William Cole	*Poem Stew*	6–12	A hilarious feast of poems about food. Children love this collection.
John E. Brewton, Lorraine A. Blackburn	*They've Discovered a Head in the Box for the Bread*	6–12	Humorous limericks that delight all children.
Sara Brewton	*My Tang's Tungled & Other Ridiculous Situations*	9–12	Humorous play on words for older children.
Sara and John E. Brewton	*Of Quarks, Quasars and Quirks: Quizzical Poems for the Supersonic Age*	10–up	Lighthearted poems that are both humorous and scientific.

HOLIDAY COLLECTIONS

Lee Bennett Hopkins	*Hey-How for Halloween*	6–9	Some twenty poems that celebrate one of children's favorite holidays.
Myra Cohn Livingston	*Christmas Poems* *Easter Poems* *Halloween Poems* *Thanksgiving Poems* *Valentine Poems* *Poems for Jewish Holidays* *New Year's Poems*	6–9	Each of these illustrated books contains a fine collection of approximately twenty poems. Some are well-known favorites; others are new, having been commissioned for these books.

RESOURCES FOR TEACHING

♦ SPECIALIZED COLLECTIONS OF POETRY (CONTINUED) ♦

COMPILER/POET	TITLE	AGE LEVEL	DESCRIPTION
Myra Cohn Livingston	*Why Am I Grown So Cold? Poems of the Unknowable*	10–up	Contains some 150 ghostly poems. Some are appropriate for Halloween but many can be read throughout the year. Children would enjoy comparing the four poems about haunted houses.
Sara and John E. Brewton	*Shrieks at Midnight: Macabre Poems, Eerie and Humorous*	8–12	An excellent collection that includes many eerie poems, plus ironic takeoffs on nursery rhymes and other humorous poems.

MULTIETHNIC POETRY COLLECTIONS

COMPILER/POET	TITLE	AGE LEVEL	DESCRIPTION
Arnold Adoff	*My Black Me*	8–up	A collection of contemporary poems that mixes black pride with power and protest. Brief biographical notes on each of the poets add interest.
Arnold Adoff	*I Am the Darker Brother: An Anthology of Modern Poems by Black Americans*	10–up	Contains some of the best known poetry of Langston Hughes, Gwendolyn Brooks, and Countee Cullen, as well as some modern poets.
Ann Nolan Clark, Velino Herrera	*In My Mother's House*	6–10	See text.
Virginia Driving Hawk Sneve	*Dancing Teepees*	8–12	See text.
Aline Amon	*The Earth Is Sore*	8–up	See text.
John Bierhorst	*In the Trail of the Wind*	12–up	See text.

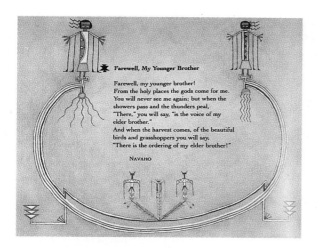

Stephen Gammell illustrates the Navaho poem "Farewell My Younger Brother" with a design that suggests a sand painting. Virginia Driving Hawk Sneve selected these Native-American poems for her book *Dancing Teepees*.

authentic collection includes poems of the Aztec, Maya, and Eskimo as well as North American Indians. It is more appropriate for older students.

We can be grateful for the reissue of . . . *I Never Saw Another Butterfly* (93). This book contains poems and pictures created by children in the Terezin concentration camp between 1942 and 1944. These drawings and poems are all that are left of the 15,000 children who passed through this camp on their way to Auschwitz. They are an eloquent statement of their courage and optimism in the midst of despair.

PICTURE-BOOK EDITIONS OF SINGLE POEMS

It was inevitable that poetry should also follow the trend to single-poem editions already established by the many beautifully illustrated editions of single fairy tales and folk songs.

The first book of poetry to be presented with the Newbery award was *A Visit to William Blake's Inn* by Nancy Willard. In the same year illustrators for this book, Alice and Martin Provensen, received a Caldecott Honor award. Inspired by Blake's work, Nancy Willard created a book of magical poems about life at an imaginary inn run by William Blake himself. In this inn a rabbit shows you to your room and makes the beds. Two mighty dragons are the bakers, and a bear, a tiger, and the King of Cats appear to be inhabitants. Each poem creates a story of all the activities going on in this remarkable place. Children ages 8 and up will be intrigued by the detailed pictures of the inn and its guests. They may particularly enjoy the poems "A Rabbit Reveals My Room" and "The King of Cats Sends a Postcard to His Wife."

Susan Jeffers has illustrated two well-known poems in picture-book format. Her pictures for Frost's *Stopping by Woods on a Snowy Evening* evoke the quiet stillness of the forest in contrast to the staid New England village. No one can depict the deep woods as well as Jeffers. She uses this vision again as she illustrates Longfellow's *Hiawatha*. Here she pictures the romantic Indian in keeping with Longfellow's poem and time. Lovely pictures of Nokomis and a growing Hiawatha hold children's interest. The artist is not always consistent in portraying the age of the Iroquois lad, however;

RESOURCES FOR TEACHING				
◆ PICTURE-BOOK EDITIONS OF SINGLE POEMS ◆				
POEM, POET	ILLUSTRATOR		AGE LEVEL	DESCRIPTION
Block City Robert Louis Stevenson	Ashley Wolff		5–8	See text.
My Shadow Robert Louis Stevenson	Ted Rand		5–8	See text.

RESOURCES FOR TEACHING

◆ PICTURE-BOOK EDITIONS OF SINGLE POEMS (CONTINUED) ◆

POEM, POET	ILLUSTRATOR	AGE LEVEL	DESCRIPTION
General Store Rachel Field	Nancy Winslow Parker	5–8	A little girl dreams of having a general store like the old-fashioned ones of the 1920s. Clear, childlike pictures.
The Owl and the Pussy Cat Edward Lear	Jan Brett	5–8	A dapper owl and a demure cat set off in their boat "Promise" to find a paradise in the Caribbean. Lush colors and intricate detail in the pictures extend this poem.
The Quangle Wangle's Hat Edward Lear	Janet Stevens	5–8	A cast of amazing characters decide to nest on the mysterious Quangle Wangle's beribboned hat.
The Adventures of Isabel Ogden Nash	James Marshall	5–8	See text.
The Scroobious Pip Edward Lear, Ogden Nash	Nancy Ekholm Burkert	7–up	Delicate line drawings and jewel-like watercolors and pastels illustrate this long nonsense poem.
Hist Whist e.e. cummings	Deborah K. Ray	7–up	Ray's illustrations create a spooky Halloween story from this poem.
A Visit to William Blake's Inn Nancy Willard	Alice and Martin Provensen	8–up	See text.
Mr. Mistoffelees with Mungojerrie and Rumpelteazer T. S. Eliot	Errol LeCain	8–up	LeCain has given us precise detailed pictures of this "conjuring cat," plus pictures of a notorious couple of cats with bad reputations. Pictures are as clever as the poems.

RESOURCES FOR TEACHING

♦ PICTURE-BOOK EDITIONS OF SINGLE POEMS (CONTINUED) ♦

POEM, POET	ILLUSTRATOR	AGE LEVEL	DESCRIPTION
Casey at the Bat Ernest Thayer	Wallace Tripp	8–up	These humorous illustrations portray the Mudville team as animals who are in deep despair when Casey strikes out.
Casey at the Bat Ernest Thayer	Barry Moser	8–up	A centennial edition with an afterword by Donald Hall discussing the poem's history. Moser's watercolors look almost like real photos of baseball players.
Paul Revere's Ride Henry Wadsworth Longfellow	Nancy Winslow Parker	6–up	Provides a foreword on the setting and an illustrated map of both Revere's and Prescott's rides. Pictures are flat-colored wash painted in much the same way as a child would depict the action.
Paul Revere's Ride Henry Wadsworth Longfellow	Ted Rand	6–up	Rand's moonlit vision of this famous ride adds to its drama. He provides fresh new perspectives such as the inside view of the steep belfry chambers where the lanterns are placed. A handsome book.
Hiawatha Henry Wadsworth Longfellow	Susan Jeffers	7–up	See text.
Hiawatha's Childhood Henry Wadsworth Longfellow	Errol LeCain	7–up	Indian designs and borders are handsome, but Hiawatha appears as a stereotyped Indian figure.
The Legend of William Tell Terry Small (author/illustrator)		7–up	The well-known story of William Tell, who must shoot an apple off his son's head, is told in metered beat. Authentic full-color pictures capture the action of this adventure story.

RESOURCES FOR TEACHING

◆ PICTURE-BOOK EDITIONS OF SINGLE POEMS (CONTINUED) ◆

POEM, POET	ILLUSTRATOR	AGE LEVEL	DESCRIPTION
Johnny Appleseed Reeve Lindbergh	Kathy Jakobsen	7–up	The traditional story of Johnny Appleseed is told in verse form. Lively folk-art paintings illustrate his travels.
The Cremation of Sam McGee *The Shooting of Dan McGrew* Robert W. Service	Ted Harrison Ted Harrison	8–up	Glorious illustrations in brilliant colors bring to life these classic poems of the gold rush days.
The Highwayman Alfred Noyes	Charles Keeping	10–up	See text.
The Highwayman Alfred Noyes	Charles Mikolaycak	10–up	See text.
The Highwayman Alfred Noyes	Neil Waldman	10–up	See text.
Birches Robert Frost	Ed Young	10–up	Ed Young never pictures the swinger of birches but leaves that to the reader's imagination. He does portray lovely birches seen from various perspectives. The complete poem is given at the end.
Stopping by Woods on a Snowy Evening Robert Frost	Susan Jeffers	10–up	See text.

he·seems older, then younger, before he reaches manhood and leaves the tribe.

In some instances these stunning picture books may create a new interest in a poem like *Hiawatha* or *Paul Revere's Ride*. It is generally a good idea to read the poem through once before sharing the pictures, since turning the pages to look at the illustrations interrupts the flow of the poem. Many of these picture/poetry books provide the text of the complete poem at the end of the book. Since poetry is the most concentrated and connotative of language, it needs to be shared several times anyway.

SHARING POETRY WITH CHILDREN

Developing Enjoyment of Poetry

THE MISUSE OF POETRY IN THE CLASSROOM

Very young children respond spontaneously to the sensory-motor action of "Ride a Cock Horse" or "Peas porridge hot/Peas porridge cold." They enjoy the damp adventures of poor old Dr. Foster, and they delight in the misfortune of

"The Three Blind Mice." Children in the primary grades love to pantomime "Hiding" (8) by Dorothy Aldis or join in the chant of "Cheers" (163) by Eve Merriam. The young child naturally delights in the sound, the rhythm, the language of poetry.

However, at some time toward the end of the primary grades, children begin to lose interest in poetry. The poet William Jay Smith comments: "How natural and harmonious it all is at the beginning; and yet what happens along the way later to make poetry to many children the dullest and least enjoyable of literary expressions?"[11] Norvell, in his classic study of children's reading interests, indicated that boys and girls begin to show a dislike for both juvenile and adult poems between grades three and five.[12] Terry[13] also reported a decreasing interest in poetry as children progressed through the middle grades, with fourth graders evidencing more interest in poetry than sixth graders. These findings suggest that rather than develop enjoyment of poetry, many teachers may actually destroy children's natural liking for this form of literature.

There are several ways in which teachers have alienated children from poetry. Poor selection of poetry is one of the most common mistakes made by both teachers and textbook publishers. The Tom study[14] found that teachers in the middle grades read many more traditional poems than contemporary ones that would be more suited to the modern child's maturity, experiences, and interests. Sentimental poems or poems that are about childhood rather than for children will turn today's young people from poetry very quickly. Poems that are too difficult, too abstract for children to understand, will also be rejected.

Several studies have indicated teachers' neglect of poetry. Terry[15] found, for example, that over 75 percent of the teachers in the middle grades admitted reading poetry to their children only once a month or less. Children can hardly be expected to develop a love of poetry when they hear it less than nine times a year! It is also possible to hear too much poetry, particularly at one time. Teachers who read poetry for one hour or have every child read one poem on a Friday afternoon are contributing to children's dislike of poetry as much as those who simply neglect it. This also happens when we relegate poetry to a "Poetry Week" in the spring. Poetry needs to be shared naturally every day by a teacher who loves it.

Another way to create distaste for poetry is by requiring memorization of certain poems, usually selected by the teacher. When everyone has to learn the same poem, it is especially dull. Many children do enjoy memorizing favorite poems, provided it is done voluntarily and that they may select the poem. But choosing to commit a certain poem to memory is quite different from being required to do so.

Too detailed analysis of every poem is also detrimental to children's enjoyment of poetry. An appropriate question or comment to increase meaning is fine; but critical analysis of every word in a poem, every figure of speech, and every iambic verse is lethal to appreciation. Jean Little captures one student's reaction to too much analysis in her poem:

AFTER ENGLISH CLASS
I used to like "Stopping by Woods on a Snowy Evening."
I liked the coming darkness,
The jingle of harness bells, breaking—and adding to—the stillness,
The gentle drift of snow....

But today, the teacher told us what everything stood for.
The woods, the horse, the miles to go, the sleep—
They all have "hidden meanings."

[11]Virginia Haviland and William Jay Smith, *Children and Poetry* (Washington, D.C.: Library of Congress, 1969), p. iv.
[12]George W. Norvell, *What Boys and Girls Like to Read* (New York: Silver Burdett, 1958), p. 26.
[13]Ann Terry, *Children's Poetry Preferences: A National Survey of the Upper Elementary Grades* (Urbana, Ill.: National Council of Teachers of English, 1974, 1984), p. 29.
[14]Chow Loy Tom, "Paul Revere Rides Ahead: Poems Teachers Read to Pupils in the Middle Grades," *The Library Quarterly*, vol. 43 (January 1973), pp. 27–38.
[15]Terry, *Children's Poetry Preferences*, p. 53.

It's grown so complicated now that,
Next time I drive by,
I don't think I'll bother to stop.

Jean Little (121)

CREATING A CLIMATE FOR ENJOYMENT

There have always been teachers who love poetry and who share their enthusiasm for poetry with students. There are teachers who make poetry a natural part of the daily program of living and learning. They realize that poetry should not be presented under the pressure of a tight time schedule, but should be enjoyed every day.

Children should be able to relax and relish the humor and beauty that the sharing of poetry affords.

Such teachers will provide an abundance of many poetry books and not rely on a single anthology that may overpower children with its sheer quantity of poems. Students will be encouraged to buy their own copies of some of the fine paperback collections such as Eve Merriam's *Jamboree,* or Nancy Larrick's *Piping Down the Valleys Wild,* or *Reflections on a Gift of Watermelon Pickle* by Dunning and others. Beautiful poetry books such as Diane Siebert's *Sierra* and

---

RESOURCES FOR TEACHING

♦ DEVELOPING ENJOYMENT OF POETRY ♦

AWAY FROM *DISLIKE* OF POETRY	TOWARD *DELIGHT* IN POETRY
Away from selecting only traditional poems	Toward selecting modern contemporary poems
Away from adult selection of "appropriate poems"	Toward beginning with students' interests—nonsense verse, narrative verse, jump-rope rhymes, song lyrics
Away from teacher neglect and fear of poetry	Toward teachers and children discovering and enjoying poetry together
Away from reading poetry only once a month or less	Toward daily sharing of poetry
Away from study about a poem	Toward experiencing the poem
Away from dissection and analysis	Toward questions that contribute to the meaning and enjoyment of the poem
Away from teacher presentation of poetry from a single anthology	Toward use of many poetry books, records, and cassette tapes of poets reading their own works; student-recorded tapes with appropriate backgrounds of music or sound; slides, filmstrips, and pictures
Away from poetry presented in isolation	Toward poetry related to children's experiences, classroom activities, favorite books, art, music and drama
Away from required memorization of assigned poems	Toward voluntary memorization of self-selected poems
Away from required writing of poetry	Toward student's self-selection of the form of poetry as the most appropriate one for his or her thoughts
Away from assigned writing of a poem	Toward keeping a poetry journal
Away from an assigned topic for writing a poem	Toward students selecting what they want to write about
Away from teacher evaluation of every poem	Toward other students' critiques, self-evaluations, along with teacher conferences.

Heartlands or *Of Quarks, Quasars and Other Quirks* by Brewton could be featured in the science and math centers. In a primary classroom David McCord's wonderment about "The Shell" (157) could be displayed with a group of shells or his poem about a "Cocoon" (156) might be taped to the screen cage where a cocoon awaits spring hatching. Evidence of enjoyment of poetry should not be limited to one time or place.

The book center should contain many poetry books. One fifth- and sixth-grade class that really makes poetry central to their curriculum has more than two hundred poetry books in the classroom. They also have a listening area where children can hear poets reading from their own works on tapes or recordings. A bulletin board displays a list of children's current favorite poems, along with paintings and copies of their own poetry work. Many teachers and children have enjoyed setting up displays of real objects and pictures of a predominant color to highlight their favorite poem from *Hailstones and Halibut Bones* by Mary O'Neill.

The writing center should have all kinds of shapes, sizes, and colors of paper available including long skinny adding machine rolls, wide storybook paper, pastel-colored papers for pages, blank books in different shapes, and large or small index cards. Then let children choose what fits their poems the best. Art materials and bookbinding supplies should be nearby for when children are ready to illustrate their poems and publish their poetry books or personal anthologies.

A brief visit to a classroom, library, or school will reveal whether poetry is "alive and well" in that place, or sadly neglected and dying. A faculty might evaluate their own school by determining where they would place themselves on the continuum presented in the box "Developing Enjoyment of Poetry" (p. 498). Teachers might also evaluate their own practices against those described as producing dislike or delight.

FINDING TIME FOR POETRY

Teachers who would develop children's delight in poetry will find time to share it with them during some time each day. They know that any time is a good time to read a poem to children, but they will especially want to capitalize on such exciting experiences as the first day of snow, a birthday party, or the arrival of a classmate's new baby brother. Perhaps there has been a fight in the playground and someone is still grumbling and complaining—that might be a good time to share poetry about feelings. The teacher could read Eve Merriam's "Mean Song" (163) or Karla Kuskin's "I Woke Up This Morning" (103) and then everyone could laugh the bad feelings away. Poetry can also be thought of as a delicious snack to nibble on during transition times between going out to recess or the last few minutes of the day. Anytime is a good time for a poetry snack!

Such teachers frequently read poetry cycles, three or four poems with the same theme. One teacher capitalized on children's interest in "special places." She shared Byrd Baylor's poetic story *Your Own Best Secret Place* and Charlotte Huck's specialized collection of poems about *Secret Places* with a group of third graders. Later children wrote about their own secret places in both prose and poetry. Children also enjoy selecting a particular subject and creating their own poetry cycles from anthologies in the library or classroom.

One way to be sure to share poetry every day is to relate children's favorite prose stories to poetry. One teacher who keeps a card file of poems always slips one or two cards into the book that is to be read aloud that day. For example, after sharing *Whistle for Willie* by Ezra Jack Keats, "Whistling" (197) by Jack Prelutsky and "Where Is It?" (8) by Dorothy Aldis could be read. Teachers in the middle grades could read Byrd Baylor's *Hawk, I'm Your Brother* or Jean George's *On the Far Side of the Mountain*. Then they could share "Birdfoot's Grampa" (173) with the class and talk about the way freeing a hawk or a peregrine falcon was similar to Grampa caring for toads. Librarians and teachers will want to make their own poetry/prose connections. We hope the following list will get you started.

Other subjects or activities in the curriculum may be enriched with poetry. A "science discovery walk" could be preceded by reading Florence McNeil's "Squirrels in My Notebook" (20) in which a child records his observations of a squirrel including the fact that he couldn't repeat what the squirrel said to him! Older children would enjoy Moffitt's well-known poem "To Look at

RESOURCES FOR TEACHING

◆ POETRY/PROSE CONNECTIONS* ◆

SUBJECT/THEME	AGE LEVEL	POEMS	BOOKS
		PRIMARY	
Be Yourself	6–8	"Changing" (75), Mary Ann Hoberman "Everybody Says" (8), Dorothy Aldis "The Question" (103), Karla Kuskin "Who Am I?" (111), Felice Holman "When I Am Me" (78), Felice Holman	*Alexander and the Wind-Up Mouse*, Leo Lionni *Dandelion*, Don Freeman *Elmer*, David McKee *Leo, the Late Bloomer*, Robert Kraus
Bears	5–7	"Algy Met a Bear" (36), Anon. "The Bear with Golden Hair" (103), Karla Kuskin "Oh, Teddy Bear" (192), Jack Prelutsky "Grandpa Bear's Lullaby" (47), Jane Yolen "Koala" (103), Karla Kuskin *Bear in Mind*, Bobbye Goldstein *The Three Bears Rhyme Book*, Jane Yolen	*The Bear's Toothache*, David McPhail *Corduroy*, Don Freeman *Ira Sleeps Over*, Bernard Waber *Where's My Teddy?*, Jez Alborough *Koala Lou*, Mem Fox *Goldilocks and the Three Bears*, Jan Brett *Jamberry*, Bruce Degen
Bedtime/Dreams	5–7	"Bedtime" (53), Eleanor Farjeon "Conversation" (157), David McCord "The Middle of the Night" (103), Karla Kuskin "Bedtime Stories" (38), Lilian Moore "The Llama Who Had No Pajama" (75), Mary Ann Hoberman *When the Dark Comes Dancing*, Nancy Larrick	*Clyde Monster*, Robert Crowe *Bedtime for Frances*, Russell Hoban *The Quilt*, Ann Jonas *The Napping House*, Audrey Wood *There's a Nightmare in My Closet*, Mercer Mayer *What's Under My Bed?*, James Stevenson *Why Do Grown-Ups Have All the Fun?*, Marisabina Russo *Is Your Mama a Llama?*, Deborah Guarino

*References for prose will be found after the chapter references on poetry.

RESOURCES FOR TEACHING

◆ POETRY/PROSE CONNECTIONS (CONTINUED) ◆

SUBJECT/THEME	AGE LEVEL	POEMS	BOOKS
Color	5–7	"Yellow" (157), David McCord "A Yell for Yellow" (163), Eve Merriam "Lullaby" (163), Eve Merriam "Winter Cardinal" (174), Lilian Moore *Hailstones and Halibut Bones* (182), Mary O'Neill *My Head is Red*, (133) Myra Cohn Livingston	*Color Dance*, Ann Jonas Cohn Livingston *Color Farm*, Lois Ehlert *Color Zoo*, Lois Ehlert *Little Blue and Little Yellow*, Leo Lionni *The Mixed-Up Chameleon*, Eric Carle *Freight Train*, Donald Crews
Death/Loss	7–8	"For a Bird" (142), Myra Cohn Livingston "Skipper" (26), Gwendolyn Brooks "When My Dog Died" (38), Freya Littledale "Poem" (46), Langston Hughes	*The Accident*, Carol and Donald Carrick *Mustard*, Charlotte Graeber *The Tenth Good Thing About Barney*, Judith Viorst *Blow Me a Kiss, Miss Lilly*, Nancy W. Carlstrom *Granpa*, John Burningham *The Very Best of Friends*, Margaret Wild
Family	5–7	"Little" (46), Dorothy Aldis "My Brother" (196), Marci Ridlon "Father" (38), Myra Cohn Livingston "All Kinds of Grands" (47), Lucille Clifton "I Never Hear" (83), Dorothy Aldis "Happy" (83), Stacy Jo Crossen and Natalie Anne Crovell	*Aunt Nina, Good Night*, Franz Brandenberg *A Chair for My Mother*, Vera Williams *Dogger*, Shirley Hughes *Mr. Rabbit and the Lovely Present*, Charlotte Zolotow *The Whales' Song*, Dyan Sheldon *The Stories Julian Tells*, Ann Cameron
Feelings	6–8	"When I Woke Up This Morning" (103), Karla Kuskin "When I Was Lost" (196), Dorothy Aldis "Wrong Start" (196), Marchette Chute "A Small Discovery" (46), James Emannuel	*Alexander and the Terrible, Horrible, No Good, Very Bad Day*, Judith Viorst *Dinah's Mad, Bad Wishes*, Barbara M. Joosse *The Hating Book*, Charlotte Zolotow

RESOURCES FOR TEACHING

♦ POETRY/PROSE CONNECTIONS (CONTINUED) ♦

SUBJECT/THEME	AGE LEVEL	POEMS	BOOKS
		"I'm in a Rotten Mood" (192), Jack Prelutsky	*Lost in the Museum*, Miriam Cohen *Will I Have a Friend?*, Miriam Cohen *Osa's Pride*, Ann Grifalconi
Folktales	7–8	"Look Cinderella" (142), Myra Cohn Livingston "Fairy Tales: 4 poems" (224), Judith Viorst "The Gingerbread Man" (47), Rowena Bennett "Trimmed-down Tales" (99), X. J. Kennedy "The Troll Bridge" (174), Lilian Moore "In Search of Cinderella" (211), Shel Silverstein "Spaghetti" (212), Shel Silverstein "The Builders" (50), Sara Henderson Hay	*Cinderella*, Charles Perrault, illustrated by Susan Jeffers *The Gingerbread Boy*, Paul Galdone *Frog Prince*, Edith H. Tarcov *The Frog Prince Continued*, Jon Scieszka *The Three Little Pigs*, James Marshall *The True Story of the 3 Little Pigs by A. Wolf*, Jon Scieszka *Strega Nona*, Tomie de Paola
Secret Places	7–8	"Hideout" (46), Aileen Fisher "Secret Place" (8), Dorothy Aldis "Tree House" (212), Shel Silverstein *Secret Places* (91), Charlotte Huck	*Your Own Best Secret Place*, Byrd Baylor *The Little Island*, Golden MacDonald *Come Away from the Water, Shirley*, John Burningham *Dawn*, Uri Shulevitz *When I Was Young in the Mountains*, Cynthia Rylant
Sibling Rivalry	5–7	"Brother" (46), Mary Ann Hoberman "I'm Disgusted with My Brother" (192), Jack Prelutsky "For Sale" (212), Shel Silverstein "Satellite, Satellite" (163), Eve Merriam "Moochie" (69), Eloise Greenfield	*A Baby Sister for Frances*, Russell Hoban *Julius, the Baby of the World*, Kevin Henkes *She Come Bringing Me That Little Baby Girl*, Eloise Greenfield *Peter's Chair*, Ezra Jack Keats *Titch*, Pat Hutchins *Noisy Nora*, Rosemary Wells

RESOURCES FOR TEACHING

♦ POETRY/PROSE CONNECTIONS (CONTINUED) ♦

SUBJECT/THEME	AGE LEVEL	POEMS	BOOKS
Vacations	7–8	"Driving to the Beach" (78), Joanna Cole "Until I Saw the Sea" (47), Lilian Moore "Pretending to Sleep" (78), Judith Thurman "Encounter" (174), Lilian Moore "Picnic" (8), Dorothy Aldis "July" (20), Fran Newman "Leavetaking" (87), Eve Merriam	*Dawn*, Uri Shulevitz *Time of Wonder*, Robert McCloskey *Up North at the Cabin*, Marsha W. Chall *Sleep Out*, Carol and Donald Carrick *Stringbean's Trip to the Shining Sea*, Vera B. Williams *The Lost Lake*, Allen Say

MIDDLE GRADES

SUBJECT/THEME	AGE LEVEL	POEMS	BOOKS
Change	10–12	"The Errand" (16), Harry Behn "Running Away" (104), Karla Kuskin "Growing Up" (38), Harry Behn "Long-Ago Days" (145), Myra Cohn Livingston "Olive Street" (145), Myra Cohn Livingston	*The Stone-Faced Boy*, Paula Fox *From the Mixed-Up Files of Mrs. Basil E. Frankweiler*, E. L. Konigsburg *Tuck Everlasting*, Natalie Babbitt *Staying Nine*, Pam Conrad *Maniac Magee*, Jerry Spinelli *Anastasia Krupnik*, Lois Lowry *Two Under Par*, Kevin Henkes
Courage and Pride	10–12	"Mother to Son" (38), Langston Hughes "Troubled Mother" (92), Langston Hughes "I Too Sing America" (92), Langston Hughes "Which Washington?" (38), Eve Merriam "Otto" (26), Gwendolyn Brooks . . . *I Never Saw Another Butterfly* (93)	*Sounder*, William Armstrong *Roll of Thunder, Hear My Cry*, Mildred Taylor *The Most Beautiful Place in the World*, Ann Cameron *The Wednesday Surprise*, Eve Bunting *Number the Stars*, Lois Lowry *Lyddie*, Katherine Paterson *The Land I Lost: Adventures of a Boy in Vietnam*, Quang Nhuong Huynh
Decisions	11–12	"The Way Things Are" (148), Myra Cohn Livingston "The Road Not Taken" (65), Robert Frost "An Easy Decision" (111), Kenneth Patchen	*The Cry of the Crow*, Jean George *Sarah, Plain and Tall*, Patricia MacLachlan *Jacob Have I Loved*, Katherine Paterson

RESOURCES FOR TEACHING

◆ POETRY/PROSE CONNECTIONS (CONTINUED) ◆

SUBJECT/THEME	AGE LEVEL	POEMS	BOOKS
		"In the Middle" (145), Myra Cohn Livingston	*Homecoming*, Cynthia Voigt *Tuck Everlasting*, Natalie Babbitt
Dinosaurs	10–12	"Fossils" (174), Lilian Moore "The Steam Shovel" (46), Rowena Bennett "Steam Shovel" (50), Charles Malam *Dinosaurs* (79), Lee Bennett Hopkins *Tyrannosaurus Was a Beast* (202), Jack Prelutsky	*My Daniel*, Pam Conrad *The News About Dinosaurs*, Patricia Lauber *Living with Dinosaurs*, Patricia Lauber *Dinosaur Dig*, Kathryn Lasky
The Environment	12–13	"To Look at Anything" (50), Robert Francis "Birdfoot's Grampa" (173), Joseph Bruchac "The Earth Is Sore" (9), Aline Amon "Hurt No Living Thing" (196), Christina Rossetti "Ecology" (174), Lilian Moore "Recycled" (174), Lilian Moore "Quest" (160), Eve Merriam "Progress" (29), Jo Carson *Sierra* (210), Diane Siebert	*Window*, Jennie Baker *On the Far Side of the Mountain*, Jean George *Who Really Killed Cock Robin?*, Jean George *One Day in the Tropical Rain Forest*, Jean George *Hawk, I'm Your Brother*, Byrd Baylor *The Way to Start a Day*, Byrd Baylor *The Year of the Panda*, Miriam Schlein *The Great Kapok Tree*, Lynne Cherry
Friendship	10–12	"I Loved My Friend" (46), Langston Hughes *Hey World, Here I Am!* (121), Jean Little "Friendship" (212), Shel Silverstein *I Like You, If You Like Me, Poems on Friendship* (132), Myra Cohn Livingston	*Bridge to Terabithia*, Katherine Paterson *The Sign of the Beaver*, Elizabeth Speare *Look Through My Window*, Jean Little *Kate*, Jean Little *Other Bells for Us to Ring*, Robert Cormier

♦ POETRY/PROSE CONNECTIONS (CONTINUED) ♦

SUBJECT/THEME	AGE LEVEL	POEMS	BOOKS
Holocaust/War	11–12	"... I Never Saw Another Butterfly" (93) "Fear" (93) "Earth" (50), John Hall Wheelock "War" (50), Dan Roth	*Anne Frank: Diary of a Young Girl* *Hiroshima No Pika*, Toshi Maruki *Rose Blanche*, Christophe Gallaz and Roberto Innocenti *Number the Stars*, Lois Lowry *The Wall*, Eve Bunting
The Future	11–12	"Where Will We Run To?" (97), X. J. Kennedy "Neuteronomy" (228), Eve Merriam "I'm Sorry Says the Machine" (159), Eve Merriam "A New Song for Old Smokey" (165), Eve Merriam "Southbound on the Freeway" (50), May Swenson "The Forecast" (50), Dan Jaffe	*The Green Book*, Jill Paton Walsh *Z for Zachariah*, Robert C. O'Brien *When The Tripods Came*, John Christopher *Eva*, Peter Dickinson *The Green Futures of Tycho*, William Sleator *Winter of Magic's Return*, Pamela Service *The Lake at the End of the World*, Caroline MacDonald

Anything" (50). A math lesson might be introduced with Carl Sandburg's "Arithmetic" (84). Many poems may enhance the social studies including Rosemary and Stephen Vincent Benét's *Book of Americans*, which includes their well-known poetry about "Nancy Hanks," "Abraham Lincoln," and "Western Wagons." The first poem is about "Christopher Columbus," but the second one is about the people who were here first, "The Indians." In *Celebrations*, Myra Cohn Livingston has a poem on "Martin Luther King Day" and "Columbus." Eve Merriam's paperback *Jamboree* includes "Which Washington?" and "To Meet Mr. Lincoln."

Imaginary Gardens by Charles Sullivan pairs poetry and art together in a unique way. Famous American paintings and poems were selected by Sullivan. Some of his pairs seem obvious such as a Grandma Moses painting with Lydia Childs's

well-known Thanksgiving Day poem "Over The River and Through the Woods," but the coupling of "Afternoon on a Hill" by Edna St. Vincent Millay and "Spring" by Marjorie Frost Fraser with Andrew Wyeth's painting of "Christina's World" was pure genius. The repeated phrase "to tangled grass I cling" is so right for Christina who must pull her crippled body back to that bleak house on the hill. This is a beautiful book that middle graders would enjoy looking at and reading over and over again. Older children will also be delighted with two excellent poetry books on sports, *Sprints and Distances* by Lillian Morrison and *American Sports Poems* selected by R. R. Knudson and May Swenson. They also enjoy the superb tension captured by Hoey's basketball poem, "Foul Shot" (50). Every taut move of the player is felt as he prepares to make the free throw that can win the game. "Base Stealer" (50)

STUDYING POETRY AND NATURE

Linda Woolard combines poetry and nature study with her fifth-grade class on their visits to the school's William E. Miller Land Lab in Newark, Ohio. The students explore the trails of the land lab located on a wooded hillside by the school. Each student has selected a favorite spot and returns there each season. They usually spend the first ten minutes in silence to better use all their senses. They observe the woods carefully, sketching and recording their observations. They may list their sightings using books to identify wildflowers, rocks, animals, or other special finds. Linda encourages them to record their thoughts and feelings also.

Before they visit the wooded area, Linda reads books and poems to them such as Jean George's *My Side of the Mountain*, Jim Arnosky's books on sketching nature in different seasons and his *Secrets of a Wildlife Watcher*, John Moffitt's poem "To Look at Anything" (50), Marcie Hans's "Fueled" (50), Lew Sarrett's "Four Little Foxes" (110), and many more.

The children bring back their notebooks, nature specimens, such as interesting fossils, leaf rubbings, and sketches, lists of bird sightings and wildflowers, and so on. These are placed on a special bulletin board. Poems are reread, reference books consulted, and pictures mounted. Many of the careful observations now become part of poems. Two that came from these trips follow:

THE WOODS ARE SO STILL

Still
Still
The woods are very
Still;
Water dripping, dripping
Off the trees.
Nothing moves
It all stays very
Still.

Katie Hopkins

EAGLE

Soaring high
   Soaring low
From mountain to hill
   And back
Wind whispering under his
magnificent wings
   gently falling
climbing
   falling
     climbing
     then he lands.

Brian Dove

Linda writes poetry at the same time her students do, and she is brave enough to ask them to make suggestions on how she can improve! Obviously, this is another classroom where a love of poetry is nurtured by much sharing of poetry, relating it to children's experiences, and modeling the joy of writing it by the teacher herself.

Miller Elementary School
Newark, Ohio
Linda Woolard, teacher

by Robert Francis is another poem that combines sports with poetry. All areas of the curriculum can be enhanced with poetry; teachers should realize that there are poems on *every* subject from dinosaurs to quasars and black holes.

Finding the right poem for the right moment requires preparation and planning. Many teachers make their own collection of poems either on cards or in a notebook. These can be categorized in ways that teachers find the most appropriate for their own styles of teaching. Finding several poems on the same subject or developing cycles of poems gives students an opportunity to compare and contrast different points of view.

Students also can be encouraged to find poems that they think complement particular books. One fifth grader chose Felice Holman's poem "Who Am I?" (111) to go with the Prydain series by Lloyd Alexander because he felt the person in the poem was searching for her identity in the same way Taran was searching for who he was and how he fit in the world. Students have to read many poems in order to find one that connects with a book. It is a useful assignment, however, for it requires them to think of the main theme of both the poem and the story.

Children also need time to share and read poetry, write in their poetry journals, a kind of "poetry workshop" time. One middle-grade group reserves 15 to 20 minutes a day when everyone reads poetry. Frequently children work in pairs, for once they have found a poem they particularly like it is only natural that they want to share it. Children also enjoy making their own personal anthologies of favorite poems.

READING POETRY TO CHILDREN

Children need to be immersed in poetry from the very first day of school. Some lucky ones will have come from poetry-loving families and will have heard Mother Goose rhymes or some poems before they enter school, but increasingly teachers tell us that this group is very small. One kindergarten teacher reported only two children of her class of thirty-two knew any nursery rhymes. Teachers need to find out what children do know, however. Try reading some of the street rhymes in Joanna Cole and Stephanie Calmenson's *Miss Mary Mack* (39) and see which

ones they recognize. Or read some nonsense rhymes such as "Algy Met a Bear" (197) or "Way Down South Where the Bananas Grow" (197) or Ogden Nash's *The Adventures of Isabel* (177). Recite some popular Mother Goose rhymes such as "Jack and Jill," "Peter Peter Pumpkin Eater," or "Mary Had a Little Lamb." Sing songs that tell a story such as "The Little Turtle" (197) or chant "The Mitten Song" (197) when it is time to get dressed and go out in the snow. Let children move to the poem "Holding Hands" (197), which describes the heavy way that elephants walk.

Few children can resist the infectious rhythm and beat of Eloise Greenfield's "Rope Rhyme" (see p. 456) or her poem:

❧ THINGS
  Went to the corner
  Walked in the store
  Bought me some candy
  Ain't got it no more
  Ain't got it no more
  Went to the beach
  Played on the shore
  Built me a sandhouse
  Ain't got it no more
  Ain't got it no more
  Went to the kitchen
  Lay down on the floor
  Made me a poem
  Still got it
  Still got it

          Eloise Greenfield (69)

The trick is to read a variety of poems to children and find out what they do like. Read or recite the verses several times and encourage them to join in on the refrains. Let them clap or move to the rhythm of the poem if that seems appropriate.

Poetry should be read in a natural voice with a tone that fits the meaning of the poem. "Things" (69) is a joyous poem so you will want to have fun with its beat and refrains. The last stanza needs to be read a little slower, showing real triumph in your voice as you read the last two lines.

Generally, the appropriate pace for reading poetry is slower than for reading prose. It is usually recommended that a poem be read aloud a second time, perhaps to refresh children's memories, to clarify a point, or to savor a particular image. Most poetry, especially good poetry, is so concentrated and compact that few people can grasp its meaning in one exposure. Following the reading of a poem, discussion should be allowed to flow. In certain instances discussion is unnecessary or superfluous. Spontaneous chuckles may follow the reading of Kaye Starbird's "Eat-it-all Elaine" (196), while a thoughtful silence may be the response to Robert P. Tristram Coffin's "Forgive My Guilt" (50). It is not necessary to discuss or do something with each poem read other than enjoy it. The most important thing you as a teacher or librarian can do when you are reading poetry is to share your enthusiasm for the poem.

If you feel uncomfortable reading poetry, try taping it and see how you sound. There are also many tapes of poets reading their own poems aloud to help you find out how the authors themselves thought it should be read. The more you read poetry, the more comfortable you will become. Recordings may supplement the teacher's presentation, but they should never substitute for it. There is no substitute for a teacher reading and enthusiastically sharing poetry with a class.

Involving Children in Poetry

Assuming that the goal of teachers and librarians is not only to introduce poetry to children but to develop a love of poetry in them, how should they do it? The first principle, as we have seen, is to immerse children in poetry from kindergarten onward. Read it to them every day. Read several poems with the same theme and contrast them. Combine poetry and prose. Make poetry a part of every content area. Provide many poetry books in the classroom, along with time to read them and share them. Teachers need to convey enthusiasm for poetry by reading it well and often. Only then will poetry become alive and grow in our schools.

However, teachers want to know more; they want to know what to do with poetry that is positive. They want to know how to involve children in poetry.

DISCUSSING POETRY

After teachers or librarians have shared a poem with children, they frequently will discuss it.

They may want to link it to other poems children have read, comparing and contrasting how the poet dealt with the concept. Suppose a second-grade teacher reads the picture book *The Accident* by the Carricks to children. She or he may want to follow that book with Littledale's poem "When My Dog Died" (38) or Livingston's "For a Bird" (47). Children could then compare how the person in the poems felt about the dog, and the little bird. Were they as hurt by their loss as Christopher was when Bodger was struck by a truck? How much detail can an author and artist give? How much can a poet? With many such discussions children will eventually see how poetry has to capture the essence of a feeling in very few words and how important each of the words must be. Starting then with the content (children will want to tell of their experiences of losing pets—and they should have a chance to link these real-life experiences with literature), the teacher may gradually move into a discussion of the difference between prose and poetry. Discussion should center on meaning and feelings first. Only after much exposure to poetry does a teacher move into the various ways a poet may create meaning.

Children may help each other to find meaning in a poem by meeting in small discussion groups, or the teacher may lead a whole class discussion. In the following class discussion, the teacher had read aloud a short poem by Nikki Giovanni, titled "The Drum."

> Daddy says the world
> Is a drum
> Tight and hard
> And I told him
> I'm gonna beat out my own rhythm.
>
> Nikki Giovanni (67)

This fifth- and sixth-grade group of children had heard and discussed many poems, so they were eager to talk about the meaning of this one with their teacher, Sheryl. Aaron offered the following opinion in answer to his teacher's question of "What do you think about this poem?"

> "Well, when Mike said about when the father was telling what the world was going to be like—he said the world is a tight drum. He said it is, not it will be," Aaron answered, seemingly intent on

examining each word carefully so he understood the poet's message.

"Yes," agreed Sheryl. "Why did the father say the world is a drum, tight and hard. Why did he say it *is* instead of it *will be?*"

"Because it is right now," answered many voices.

"Because he is the one that has to pay all the taxes and make a living," said Stacie.

"Why does the father know that and the girl doesn't," Sheryl asked again, intent on helping them delve as far into the poem as they could.

Many voices again responded: "Because he's out in the world." "He knows about life." "He's lived longer." And similar comments were offered. . . .

Carrie had an interesting observation. "This reminds me of that poem by . . . I forget . . . the one you read yesterday to us about the crystal stairs." She was referring to Langston Hughes's moving poem, "Mother to Son," in which a black mother gives advice to her child about not giving up in the face of adversity. "The part . . . when he said the part about the drum, is tight," she continued, "that's the part that reminded me of the [Hughes] poem because it talks about nails and spots without any boards and no carpet. That sounded the same."

"That is an interesting connection because Langston Hughes and Nikki Giovanni could well have had similar experiences growing up," answered Sheryl. "Do people who heard 'Mother to Son' see any relationship between these poems?"

Jennifer had an idea. "They're both talking about how life is or was. Like the mother was talking about how hard hers was and the dad—he is talking about how hard his life was."

"It also seems like they're alive and it could happen," added Aaron.

"Like my dad," said Deon. "My mom and dad . . . he always says things like you can't get your own way—just like that poem."

"All right," responded Sheryl.

"I think that in both poems—that this one and the one we're comparing it to—that they're warning their children of what life will be and they should be ready for it," said Jennifer.

"And in 'The Drum,' how is the child responding to that?" Sheryl asked the group.

"She's gonna beat her own rhythm," answered Stacie and Deon together.

"Is it okay to do that?" Sheryl wanted to know. Many children shook their heads no. "If you didn't, what would you be like?"

"Boring," said Stacie, wrinkling up her nose in distaste.

"You would be the same as everybody else," added Mike.

"Or at least the same as what?" asked Sheryl. "Do you think the father was telling her she *had* to live her life a certain way?"

Her question was greeted by a strong chorus of "No."

"She chose to live that way," added Angela.

"But he is trying to warn her what life is going to be like. Nevertheless she is going to try—just like the mother in Langston Hughes's poem, she is going to climb her stairs," said Sheryl.[16]

Not only did the children understand the meaning of this poem, they connected it with their own lives and with another poem. Notice the teacher did not tell them the meaning of the poem but let them discover the meaning for themselves. In the total discussion, she reread the poem twice. By comparing this poem with the Langston Hughes poem "Mother to Son" (92), the children extended their understanding of both poems. They also considered the idea of creating their own individual lives—beating their own rhythms.

WRITING POETRY

Using Models from Literature

Children need to hear much poetry and discuss it before attempting to write it themselves. Their early efforts are usually based on the false notion that all poetry must rhyme. Acting on this assumption, beginning efforts may be rhyme-

[16]Amy A. McClure, Peggy Harrison, and Sheryl Reed, *Sunrises and Songs, Reading and Writing Poetry in an Elementary Classroom* (Portsmouth, N.H.: Heinemann Educational Books, 1990), pp. 61–62.

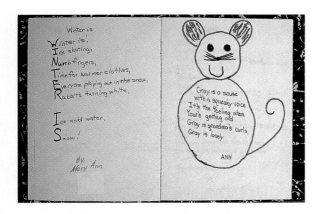

A class poetry book includes third graders' poems that are expressed in both visual and written form.

Greensview School, Upper Arlington Public Schools, Upper Arlington, Ohio. Susan Lee, teacher.

driven and devoid of meaning. One third-grade teacher, in an effort to avoid this rhyming trap, read her children Aileen Fisher's poem "All in a Word" (56), which is a Thanksgiving acrostic based on the word *Thanks*. She also shared William Smith's poem on an "Elephant" (215) which is placed in the shape of that animal. One child created her acrostic "Winter Is" and another one did a shaped poem about a mouse. These were then included in a bound book of class poems for all to read. The mouse poem shows the influence of hearing Mary O'Neill's well-loved poems about color in *Hailstones and Halibut Bones*. The first time children try to write their own take-offs on these poems they are apt to make a kind of grocery list of all the objects that are a particular color. By returning to the book they can begin to appreciate the craft of the poems, realizing that all lines do not begin in the same way. They see that the poems contain objects which are that color but also describe the way the color made the poet feel, smell, and taste. One sixth grader made several revisions of her poem before she was satisfied with it.

> MY RED MOOD
> Red is the heat from a hot blazing fire,
> A soft furry sweater awaiting a buyer.
> Red is the sweet smell of roses in the spring,
> Red are my cheeks that the winter winds sting.

> Red is a feeling that rings deep inside
> When I get angry and want to hide.
> Red is a sunset waving good-bye.
> Red is the sunrise shouting "Surprise!"

> Treeva
> **Ridgemont Elementary School**
> **Mt. Victory, Ohio**
> **Peg Reed, Peggy Harrison, teachers**

Looking at the way other poets have described color may extend children's thinking. Examples are Rossetti's well-known poem "What Is Pink?" (196), Lilian Moore's "Red" (174), David McCord's "Yellow" (157), and Eve Merriam's "A Yell for Yellow" (163).

One group of 5- and 6-year-olds responded to Mary Ann Hoberman's long picture-book poem *A House Is a House for Me* by creating pictures and ideas of other possible houses (see picture below).

We have seen how another kindergarten/first-grade group adapted Bill Martin, Jr.'s *Brown Bear Brown Bear* pattern to fit their study of bugs (see

After their teacher read aloud from Mary Ann Hoberman's *A House Is a House for Me*, 5- and 6-year-olds dictated and illustrated their ideas of other things that could be houses.

Martin Luther King, Jr., Lab School, Evanston, Illinois. Esther Weiss, teacher.

p. 227). In New Zealand, a group of primary children visited a park and also used the patterned sentence "Brown Bear, Brown Bear, What Do You See?" as a model for their group poem on "Trees." The poem was then made into a big book and illustrated with the children's glorious tissue paper collages.

TREES
We walked to the park
And what did we see?
　Big trees, small trees,
　Fat trees, tall trees
　And trees with coloured leaves.

We looked at the trees
And what did we find?
　Trees with branches,
　Trees with trunks,
　Rough bark, smooth bark
　And tiny little twigs.

Sun shining on the trees
What does it show?
　Shiny leaves, tiny buds
　Big branches, wide trunks

We looked at the trees and what did we find?

Trees with branches, Trees with trunks

While kindergarten children used *Brown Bear, Brown Bear, What Do You See?* as their model for a book on trees, they looked closely at the bark, the texture, and the shape of trees. This is reflected in their glorious tissue paper collage illustrations for their "Big Book of Trees."

Mt. Eden Normal School, Auckland, New Zealand.
Jo Massam-Windsor, teacher.

And giant shadows that
Grow and grow and grow . . . .

K–2 Children
Mt. Eden Normal School
Auckland, New Zealand
Jo Massam-Windsor, teacher

Many children have been inspired to be the voice of an animal and write its prayer after hearing Rumer Godden's translation of de Gasztold's *Prayers from the Ark* (66). One 10-year-old composed this poem about a worm:

God, I am but a wiggling worm.
Who sees beauty in me?
I am brown and squishy,
　and they feed me to the fish.
Is it because of *that;* they say I have no beauty?
They laugh and scream and run away.
I ask nothing of you
　but that you consider my humble plea.
Dress me in riches!
Feed me apples!
So that people will not say "worm holes" in disgust
　or fear that I might still be there.
I am just a worm,
　your creation to plow the earth
　　So why do I bother?

Lisa Schiltz, age 10
Martin Luther King, Jr., Lab School
Evanston, Ill.
Barbara Friedberg, teacher

Another student wrote a poem based on Jean George's *The Cry of the Crow* and Robert P. Tristram Coffin's poem "Forgive My Guilt" (50). While the work was his own, he carefully acknowledged the sources of his ideas.

THE CRY OF THE CROW
I sat in a tree
Waiting for a bird.
That day I sighted
Three large crows.

I sighted them with my gun,
I squeezed the trigger,
One wing pulled
From a bird's body.
I still hear
The cry of that crow.
As it haunts me forever.

Thoughts about this poem came from *Cry Of the Crow* and "Forgive My Guilt" by Jean Craighead George and Robert P. Tristram Coffin.

Matt Jennings
Ridgemont Elementary School
Mt. Victory, Ohio
Peg Reed, Peggy Harrison, teachers

Different forms of poetry may offer poetic structures to children and serve as models for creative poetry writing. We have seen how shaped poetry may get children started. Concrete poetry is another gateway. Using Robert Froman's *Seeing Things* or the poem titled "Flamingo" by J. Patrick Lewis (118), children could try creating their own concrete poems. Again the emphasis should be placed on the meaning of the poem first, then its shape.

Haiku frequently release children from the problem of rhyme and focus on the idea of the poem. However, this form of poetry has been overused with students too immature to understand the beauty of its concise thought and high level of abstraction. Frequently, the writer must imply a relationship between two disparate ideas, events, or scenes. These events must have some relationship to nature and take place at the present moment. To make matters even more complex, all these rules must be followed within a pattern of seventeen syllables, although an occasional deviation is allowed in English haiku. Obviously, haiku are not simple to write. Only when children are ready for the formal discipline imposed by haiku should they try it. Some middle graders are challenged by it; others are only confused. Certainly, primary-grade children who are still at the cognitive level of concrete operations should not be asked to try anything so abstract and foreign to their way of thinking. The examples here illustrate two 12-year-olds' success in writing haiku:

The cabin is small
in the vast whiteness. Only
the smoke reveals it.

Carol Bartlett

The leaves on a tree
Rustle, impatient, restless,
Waiting to fall off.

Patti Krog
Boulder Public Schools, Colorado
Allaire Stuart, teacher

Poetry Workshop

Using models may be a way to get children started in writing poetry. It provides the opportunity to "write like a poet" and the given structures usually produce an acceptable poem. In no way does this approach help a child *think* like a poet. That may happen only after much sustained writing and revisions.

In a small rural school in Ohio, two teachers, Peg Reed and Peggy Harrison, began a year-long poetry program with their combined group of fifth and sixth graders. Amy McClure[17] spent a year studying this poetry program and then writing an ethnographic research report on it. Still later this study was rewritten for a fine book[18] for teachers on how to include poetry in the classroom.

They begin their poetry workshop with reading poetry aloud several times a day. The classroom collection of over two hundred poetry books is extensive. Children read poetry for some 10 to 15 minutes a day and keep poetry journals in which they write every day. They do not have to produce a poem a day—they can list possibilities, revise a poem they have been working on, or invite one of their friends to critique a poem. Frequently, they illustrate one of their best poems, or they make anthologies of their own poetry, or create personal anthologies of their favorite poems from various books. This requires that the child read a wide variety of poetry and then decide on the organizing feature. Is it to be a book of animal poems or, as one child titled his, "deep feeling poems"?

One student wrote over four hundred poems in the two years he was in this class. He created an anthology with all the poems he had written about *Bats and Owls*, an interest that developed from his teacher's reading of Randall Jarrell's story of *The Bat-Poet*. He then asked one of his friends in the class who was known for his artistic ability to illustrate it with detailed black-and-white pencil drawings. These pictures were mounted on black, tan, and gray pages cut with scalloped edges to imitate the shape of an owl's

[17]Amy A. McClure, "Children's Responses to Poetry in a Supportive Literary Context" (unpublished Ph.D. dissertation, Ohio State University, Columbus, 1984).
[18]McClure, Harrison, and Reed, *Sunrises and Songs*.

 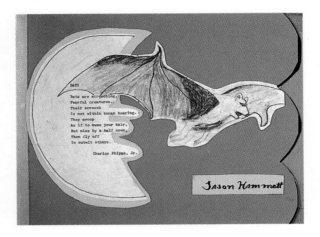

Two sixth graders worked together to create this book of poems titled *Bats and Owls*. Charles Phipps, Jr., created the poetry while his friend Jason Hammet drew the illustrations. Notice how the pages are scalloped like the wings of owls.

Ridgemont Elementary School, Mt. Victory, Ohio. Sheryl Reed and Peggy Harrison, teachers.

wing. Their finished book reflected the subject as well as the carefully crafted poems. One of the poems from their book follows:

A BAT
A bat
Feeds lavishly
On moths
And beetles
Flies loops
And twirls
Catches bugs
From behind
When the sun
Rises faintly
The bat
Retires to rest

Charles Phipps, Jr.
**Ridgemont Elementary School
Mt. Victory, Ohio
Peg Reed, Peggy Harrison, teachers**

Children write their best poetry when they write about what they know. The fifth-grade teacher who combined poetry with children's nature study at the school land laboratory (see p. 506) always encourages her students to make careful observations, even sketching what they are going to write about first. Corey lived in the country and so he sketched and wrote about the way he saw cornstalks.

GOOD-BYE CORNSTALKS
Wind
        whistling on the cornstalks
    in the field
                    Swishing
        back and forth
                Blowing the ears
    up and down
                And when they do
    go up and down
                    I think
They're waving to me
                Good-bye
Corey
                Good-bye
Cornstalks

Corey Duston
**Miller School
Newark, Ohio
Linda Woolard, teacher**

In New York City, Georgia Heard, a published poet herself, also encourages children to write what they know and what they feel when she conducts poetry workshops with all age groups. In conferring with children, she frequently asks them to close their eyes and visualize their topic. Jason had written a first draft of a poem about cats:

Cats are cats
Cats are great
Cats can't be beat

Jason

After reading his poem, Georgia Heard[19] writes:

The old me wants to evaluate Jason's poem. The researcher, the curious me, notices what Jason knows about poetry. There's some rhythm in his poem, repetition, and a little rhyme; it sounds like a chant or a cheer. He definitely knows the difference between a poem and a story. I tell him what I notice about his poem, but I also want to know why he chose cats as his subject.

When she discovered that Jason owned a cat, she asked him to close his eyes again and revisualize his cat. Slowly, he told her what he saw. She repeated his words back to him and he wrote his poem again:

MY CAT
My cat is black and white
I pretend he is my son
I love him.
His feet smell like popcorn.[20]

Jason

At another time, this child may want to play with the order of his lines. However, because he is just beginning to write poems, Georgia Heard wisely let his second draft stand. He has specifically described *his* cat and how he feels about him in this poem, a far cry from his first generic poem about all cats.

Children's poems do not have to be perfect. One of the reasons for having them write poetry is to increase their enjoyment of poetry; it is not necessarily to produce poets. In critiquing children's poems, it is important to evaluate improve-

ment. In Georgia Heard's evaluation conferences, she asks students to bring all of their poems to her, and then they spread them out on the floor. Some of the questions she offers as guidelines are:[21]

What things do you usually write about?
What kind of poems do you tend to write? Rhyming poems, long, short, narrative, lyric?
What kind of lines do you usually work with? Long or short?
What are you really good at? Titles, images, interesting words, repetition, rhyme?
What are you not so good at? How would you like to improve?
Do you revise? How do you do it? Do you change or add a word or overhaul the whole poem?
What is the hardest part of writing a poem for you? Where do you get stuck?
Are there any new things you'd like to learn?

This process enables the child, not the teacher, to be the evaluator. It is a learning process for both of them, however. Children who hear poetry every day, who read poetry every day, and who write it every day develop a deep love for poetry. Writing honest poems that reflect their own thoughts and feelings helps children develop a real appreciation for poetry.

CHORAL READING

The reading and sharing of poetry through choral speaking is another way to foster interest in poetry. Choral speaking or reading is the interpretation of poetry by several voices speaking as one. At first, young children *speak* it as they join in the refrains. Middle-grade children may prefer to *read* their poems. They are not always read in unison; in fact, this is one of the most difficult ways to present a poem.

Four types of choral speaking are particularly suited for use in the elementary school. In the first, the "refrain" type, one person (teacher or child) reads the narrative and the rest of the class

---

[19]Georgia Heard, *For the Good of the Earth and Sun: Teaching Poetry.* (Portsmouth, New Hampshire: Heinemann Educational Books, 1989.) pp. 40–41.
[20]Georgia Heard, p. 41.

[21]Georgia Heard, p. 53.

joins in the refrain, or "echo" as Nancy Larrick[22] calls it. In her book *Let's Do a Poem,* she suggests using the well-known folk poem that begins "In a dark, dark wood there was a dark dark house," and letting children join in on the "dark darks." She also recommends David McCord's "Windshield Wipers' Song" (100) and Vachel Lindsay's poem "The Mysterious Cat" (107) as good echo poems to try. Both of these poems are included in her book.

Another way, called antiphonal, is to divide the class into two groups. For example, in reading Rose Fyleman's "Witch, Witch" (228) one group can ask the witch the questions and the other group can give her answers. An effective approach with young children is the "line-a-child" arrangement, where different children say, or read, individual lines, with the class joining in unison at the beginning or end of the poem. "One, Two, Buckle My Shoe" is a good rhyme to introduce this type of choral reading. The dialogue of David McCord's "At the Garden Gate" (157) lends itself to this approach for children in the middle grades. A more difficult and formal version of this method is part speaking. Groups are divided according to the sound of their voices into high, middle, and low parts. The poem is then interpreted much as a song might be sung in parts. This is usually done with mature groups and is the method utilized by verse-speaking choirs. Another difficult method is to have children say the whole poem in unison, giving just one interpretation.

Many variations to these approaches will be used by creative teachers and children. A certain sound that complements both rhythm and the meaning of the poem may be an accompaniment; for example, "clickety clack" from the sound of "The Song of the Train" (157) by David McCord. One group may repeat this phrase as another group says the words of the poem. Another poem that provides an interesting sound is "What the Gray Cat Sings" (228) by Arthur Guiterman. Alternate groups or solo voices could say the verses with the entire class joining in the cat's weaving song. This would be a wonderful poem to share after reading Ashley Bryan's West Indian folktale, *The Cat's Purr.*

[22]Nancy Larrick, *Let's Do a Poem* (New York: Delacorte Press, 1991), pp. 45–47.

It is great fun to read Livingston's "Street Song" (148) while eating potato chips. The bag can pass from one group to another with each verse, or one person can start it and pick up a friend to walk along to the rhythm. Children love to think of sounds to go with this poem from "crunch crunch" to "smack smack." Be sure to bring a bag of potato chips to class the day you read this poem!

STREET SONG
O, I have been walking
with a bag of potato chips,
me and potato chips
munching along,

walking alone
eating potato chips,
big old potato chips,
crunching along,

walking along
munching potato chips,
me and potato chips
lunching along.

Myra Cohn Livingston (148)

Children also enjoy planning how to read Jack Prelutsky's "The Grobbles" (200). One person can be the innocent soul walking through the woods while individual children can each give a line describing the grobbles. Then the poem can grow with scary intensity as the person walks closer to the grobbles:

THE GROBBLES

The grobbles are gruesome	(Child 1)
The grobbles are green	(Child 2)
The grobbles are nasty	(Child 3)
The grobbles are mean	(All)
The grobbles hide deep	(Child 4)
in a hollowy tree	
just waiting to gobble	(All)
whomever they see	

I walk through the woods	(Solo)
for I'm quite unaware	
that the grobbles are waiting	
to gobble me there	

they suddenly spring   (Children 1–4)
from their hollowy tree
Oh goodness! the grobbles   (Solo)
are gobbling m . . .

Jack Prelutsky (200)

This interpretation of how to read "The Grobbles" is only one of many that could be developed. After you have worked with children in choral reading, they will suggest variations of different ways to interpret poems. Try these out and see which ones are the most pleasing to the ear and the most appropriate for the meaning of the poem. More serious poetry can also be read effectively. Lew Sarett's "Four Little Foxes" (228), Elizabeth Coatsworth's "Sea Gull" (228), or Eve Merriam's "Neuteronomy" (228) all lend themselves beautifully to choral speaking. More suggestions are given in Isabel Wilner's useful book *The Poetry Troupe*.

Older children particularly enjoy practicing reading Paul Fleischman's poems for two voices found in his Newbery Medal book, *Joyful Noise* and *I Am Phoenix*. All of the poems in *Joyful Noise* are about insects. In *I Am Phoenix*, all of the poems are about birds. One from the first book that older children particularly enjoy reading together in pairs is "Water Striders."

❦ WATER STRIDERS

Whenever we're asked	Whenever we're asked
if we walk upon water	if we walk upon water
we answer	we answer
	Of course.
To be sure.	
	It's quite true.
Whenever we're asked	Whenever we're asked
if we walk on it often	if we walk on it often
we answer	we answer
Quite often.	
	Each day.
All day through.	
Should we be questioned	Should we be questioned
on whether it's easy	on whether it's easy
we answer	we answer
	Quite easy.
A snap.	
	It's a cinch.
Should we be told	Should we be told
that it's surely a miracle	that it's surely a miracle
we reply	we reply
Balderdash!	
	Rubbish!
Nonsense!	
Whenever we're asked	Whenever we're asked
for instructions	for instructions
we always say	we always say
	Come to the pond's edge
and do as we do.	
	Put down one foot
and then put down another,	
	resting upon the thin film
	on the surface.
Believe me, there's no call	
at all to be nervous	
	as long as you're reasonably
	mindful that you—
But by that time our student	But by that time our student
no matter how prudent	
has usually	has usually
	don't ask me why
sunk from view.	sunk from view.

Paul Fleischman (60)

The values of reading poetry together are many. Children derive enjoyment from learning to respond as a group to the rhythm and melody of the poem. They learn much about the interpretation of poetry as they help plan various ways to read the poem. Shy children forget their fears when participating with the group, and all children learn to develop cooperation as they work together with a leader to present a poem. It is necessary to remember that the process of choral reading is much more important than the final product. Teachers must work for the enjoyment of poetry, not perfection of performance. Too frequently choral reading becomes a "stunt" or a quick way to entertain a P.T.A. group. If teachers and children are pressured for a "production," interpretation of poetry will be exploited for unnatural ends.

Boys and girls should have many opportunities to share poetry in interesting and meaningful situations, if they are to develop appreciation for the deep satisfactions that poetry brings. Appreciation for poetry develops slowly. It is the result of long and loving experience with poetry over a period of years. Children who are fortunate enough to have developed a love of poetry will always be the richer for it.

SUGGESTED LEARNING EXPERIENCES

1. Begin a poetry collection for future use with children. Make your own filing system. What categories will you include? Indicate possible uses for some poems, possible connections with prose, ways to interpret poems.
2. Make a study of one poet. How would you characterize his or her work in style and usual content? What can you find out about his or her background? How are these experiences reflected in the poetry?
3. Make a cycle of poems about one particular subject—for example, friends, secret places, the city, loneliness. Share these with the class.
4. Bring your favorite children's poem to present to the class or to tape-record. Invite class members to comment on both your selection and presentation.
5. Select three different kinds of poems and read them to a group of children. Record their responses. What poems had the greatest appeal? Why?
6. Select one or two poems that contain figurative language. Share them with children at different developmental stages. When do children appear to understand the metaphors being used? One way to link into their understanding is to ask them to draw a picture of the images they see.
7. Find a poem to go with a passage in a book or with your favorite picture book.
8. Compare two general anthologies of poetry, using criteria suggested in the text.
9. Select several poems you think would lend themselves to choral reading. Work with a group of children or classmates in planning ways to present one of these poems. If possible, tape-record these interpretations.
10. Make a survey of the teachers in an elementary school to see how often they read poetry to their students, what their favorite poems are, what their favorite sources for poetry are. Make a visual presentation of your results.
11. Listen to some recordings of poetry read by authors and by interpreters. Contrast the presentations and appropriateness of the records for classroom use. Share these with children. Which ones do they prefer?
12. Try writing some poetry yourself. You may want to use some experimental verse forms, such as concrete poetry or found poetry.

RELATED READINGS

1. Chukovsky, Kornei. *From Two to Five,* translated and edited by Miriam Morton. Berkeley: University of California Press, 1963.

   This is a classic review of the young child's delight in poetry. Written by a well-known Russian poet, it emphasizes that poetry is the natural language of little children.
2. Fisher, Carol J., and Margaret A. Natarella. "Young Children's Preferences in Poetry: A National Survey of First, Second and Third Graders," *Research in the Teaching of English,* vol. 16, no. 4 (December 1982), pp. 339–354.

   Using Terry's research as a model, this study researched the poetry preferences of primary children. Findings were almost identical to the Terry study done eight years earlier.

3. Heard, Georgia. *For the Good of the Earth and Sun: Teaching Poetry*. Portsmouth, N.H.: Heinemann Educational Books, 1989.
    A published poet describes her methods of teaching elementary children in New York City schools to enjoy poetry, to read poetry, and to write poetry. She describes the many poetry workshops she does with children from kindergarten through sixth grade. Filled with practical suggestions, this book offers the reader help and inspiration for ways to teach poetry to children.

4. Hopkins, Lee Bennett. *Pass the Poetry, Please*, rev. ed. New York: Harper & Row, 1987.
    This revised edition of a well-known book presents a wealth of ideas for making poetry come alive in the classroom. It contains suggestions for sparking children's interest in writing poetry. It also includes interviews with more than twenty contemporary poets. Teachers will want to read this book.

5. Larrick, Nancy. *Let's Do a Poem*. New York: Delacorte Press, 1991.
    Nancy Larrick's enthusiasm for poetry is obvious in this wonderfully useful book that suggests children should be introduced to poetry through listening, singing, chanting, impromptu choral reading, body movement, dance, and drama.

6. Livingston, Myra Cohn. *Climb into the Bell Tower: Essays on Poetry*. New York: Harper & Row, 1990.
    A noted poet and anthologist, Myra Cohn Livingston offers a collection of her own essays, articles, and speeches on poetry for children published between 1967 and 1987. This book brings together her insights into teaching and writing poetry for children, her sharp criticism, and praise for those who create poetry. A stimulating collection from someone courageous enough to take a stand for quality in children's literature.

7. Livingston, Myra Cohn. *The Child as Poet: Myth or Reality?* Boston: Horn Book, 1984.

8. _____. *Poem-Making: Ways to Begin Writing Poetry*. New York: A Charlotte Zolotow Book, HarperCollins, 1991.
    In the first text, Livingston disputes the widely believed statement that the child is a natural poet. She reacts strongly to some techniques used in teaching children to write poetry. In the second book, she provides positive help for middle-grade students or teachers who want to learn more about the form and elements of poem making. She clearly presents the process of writing poetry and gives many poems as examples. Teachers will find this a very useful book.

9. McClure, Amy A., Peggy Harrison, and Sheryl Reed. *Sunrises and Songs: Reading and Writing Poetry in an Elementary Classroom*. Portsmouth, N.H.: Heinemann Educational Books, 1990.
    This book has been rewritten for teachers from McClure's dissertation. Dropping the research voice, for an almost poetic description of one year in a classroom where poetry was the heart of the curriculum, this is a text middle-grade teachers should not miss.

10. Terry, Ann. *Children's Poetry Preferences: A National Survey of Upper Elementary Grades*. Urbana, Ill.: National Council of Teachers of English, 1974, reissued 1984.
    These findings from a national survey of children's poetry preferences emphasize the importance of selecting appropriate poems if we wish to increase children's enjoyment of poetry. In the last chapter, the author makes recommendations for ways classroom teachers can create a poetry program.

POETRY REFERENCES

1. Adoff, Arnold. *All the Colors of the Race*, illustrated by John Steptoe. Lothrop, 1982.
2. _____. *Black Is Brown Is Tan*, illustrated by Emily McCully. Harper, 1973.
3. _____. *Chocolate Dreams*, illustrated by Turi MacCombie. Lothrop, 1988.
4. _____. *Eats: Poems*, illustrated by Susan Russo. Lothrop, 1979.

5. _____, ed. *I Am the Darker Brother: An Anthology of Modern Poems by Black Americans*. Macmillan, 1970.
6. _____. *In for Winter, Out for Spring*, illustrated by Jerry Pinkney. Harcourt, 1991.
7. _____, ed. *My Black Me*. Dutton, 1974.
8. Aldis, Dorothy. *All Together*, illustrated by Marjorie Flack, Margaret Frieman, and Helen D. Jameson. Putnam, 1925, 1952. (o.p.)
9. Amon, Aline, adapter and illustrator. *The Earth Is Sore: Native Americans on Nature*. Atheneum, 1981. (o.p.)
10. Baylor, Byrd. *Everybody Needs a Rock*, illustrated by Peter Parnall. Scribner's, 1974.
11. _____. *Hawk, I'm Your Brother*, illustrated by Peter Parnall. Scribner's, 1976.
12. _____. *I'm in Charge of Celebrations*, illustrated by Peter Parnall. Scribner's, 1986.
13. _____. *The Other Way to Listen*, illustrated by Peter Parnall. Scribner's, 1978.
14. _____. *The Way to Start a Day*, illustrated by Peter Parnall. Scribner's, 1978.
15. _____. *Your Own Best Secret Place*, illustrated by Peter Parnall. Scribner's, 1979.
16. Behn, Harry. *Crickets & Bullfrogs & Whispers of Thunder: Poems & Pictures by Harry Behn*, edited by Lee Bennett Hopkins, illustrated by Harry Behn. Harcourt, 1984.
17. Benét, Stephen Vincent, and Rosemary Benét. *A Book of Americans*, illustrated by Charles Child. Henry Holt, paper, 1984.
18. Bierhorst, John, ed. *In the Trail of the Wind: American Indian Poems and Ritual Orations*. Farrar, Straus, 1971.
19. Blishen, Edward, compiler. *Oxford Book of Poetry for Children*, illustrated by Brian Wildsmith. Watts, 1963, reissued by Bedrick Books, 1984.
20. Booth, David, ed. *Til All the Stars Have Fallen: Canadian Poems for Children*, illustrated by Kady MacDonald Denton. Kids Can Press, 1989.
21. _____. *Voices on the Wind, Poems for All Seasons*, illustrated by Michele Lemieux. Morrow, 1990.
22. Brewton, John E., and Lorraine A. Blackburn, eds. *They've Discovered a Head in the Box for the Bread and Other Laughable Limericks*, illustrated by Fernando Krahn. Crowell, 1978.
23. Brewton, Sara, et al., eds. *Of Quarks, Quasars and Other Quirks: Quizzical Poems for the Supersonic Age*, illustrated by Quentin Blake. Harper, 1977.
24. _____, ed. *My Tang's Tungled and Other Ridiculous Situations*, illustrated by Graham Booth. Crowell, 1989.
25. Brewton, Sara, and John E. Brewton, compilers. *Shrieks at Midnight: Macabre Poems, Eerie and Humorous*, illustrated by Ellen Raskin. Crowell, 1969.
26. Brooks, Gwendolyn. *Bronzeville Boys and Girls*, illustrated by Ronni Solbert. Harper, 1965.
27. Browning, Robert. *The Pied Piper of Hamelin*, illustrated by Kate Greenaway. Warne, 1889.
28. _____. *The Pied Piper of Hamelin*, illustrated by Terry Small. Harcourt, 1988.
29. Carson, Jo. *Stories I Ain't Told Nobody Yet*. Orchard, 1989.
30. Cassedy, Sylvia. *Roomrimes*, illustrated by Michele Chessare. Crowell, 1987.
31. Ciardi, John. *I Met a Man*, illustrated by Robert Osborn. Houghton Mifflin, 1961.
32. _____. *Mummy Took Cooking Lessons and Other Poems*, illustrated by Merle Nacht. Houghton Mifflin, 1990.
33. _____. *The Reason for the Pelican*, illustrated by Mark Cocoran. Contemporary Books, 1989 (1959).
34. _____. *You Read to Me, I'll Read to You*, illustrated by Edward Gorey. Lippincott, 1962.
35. Clark, Ann Nolan. *In My Mother's House*, illustrated by Velino Herrera. Viking, 1991 (1941).
36. Clark, Emma Chichester, ed., illustrator. *I Never Saw a Purple Cow and Other Nonsense Rhymes*. Little, Brown, 1991.
37. Cole, Joanna. *Anna Banana: 101 Jump-Rope Rhymes*, illustrated by Alan Tiegreen. Morrow, 1989.
38. _____. *A New Treasury of Children's Poetry*, illustrated by Judith G. Brown. Doubleday, 1984.
39. Cole, Joanna, and Stephanie Calmenson. *Miss Mary Mack and Other Children's Street Rhymes*, illustrated by Alan Tiegreen. Morrow, 1990.
40. Cole, William, compiler. *Oh, How Silly!*, illustrated by Tomi Ungerer. Viking, 1970.
41. _____, compiler. *Oh, That's Ridiculous!*, illustrated by Tomi Ungerer. Viking, 1972.
42. _____, compiler. *Oh, What Nonsense!*, illustrated by Tomi Ungerer. Viking, 1966.
43. _____, ed. *Poem Stew*, illustrated by Karen Ann Weinhaus. Lippincott, 1981.
44. Corrin, Sara, and Stephen Corrin. *Once upon a Rhyme: 101 Poems for Young Children*, illustrated by Jill Bennett. Faber & Faber, 1982.
45. cummings, e. e. *Hist Whist*, illustrated by Deborah Kogan Ray. Crown, 1989.
46. de Paola, Tomie, ed. *Tomie de Paola's Book of Poems*. Putnam's, 1988.

47. deRegniers, Beatrice Schenk, et al., eds. *Sing a Song of Popcorn*, illustrated by nine Caldecott Medal artists. Scholastic, 1988.

48. Downie, Mary Alice, and Barbara Robertson, compilers. *The New Wind Has Wings*, illustrated by Elizabeth Cleaver. Oxford, 1987.

49. _____. *The Wind Has Wings*, illustrated by Elizabeth Cleaver. Oxford, 1978.

50. Dunning, Stephen, Edward Lueders, and Hugh Smith. *Reflections on a Gift of Watermelon Pickle and Other Modern Verses*. Lothrop, 1966.

51. Eliot, T. S. *Mr. Mistoffelees with Mungojerrie and Rumpelteazer*, illustrated by Errol LeCain. Harcourt, 1991.

52. Elledge, Scott, ed. *Wider Than the Sky: Poems to Grow Up With*. Harper, 1990.

53. Farjeon, Eleanor. *Eleanor Farjeon's Poems for Children*. Lippincott, 1985 (1951).

54. Ferris, Helen, compiler. *Favorite Poems Old and New*, illustrated by Leonard Weisgard. Doubleday, 1957.

55. Field, Rachel. *General Store*, illustrated by Nancy Winslow Parker. Greenwillow, 1988.

56. Fisher, Aileen. *Always Wondering*, illustrated by Joan Sandin. Harper, 1992.

57. _____. *Listen, Rabbit*, illustrated by Symeon Shimin. Crowell, 1964.

58. _____. *Rabbits Rabbits*, illustrated by Gail Niemann. Harper, 1983.

59. Fleischman, Paul. *I Am Phoenix: Poems for Two Voices*, illustrated by Ken Nutt. Harper, 1985.

60. _____. *Joyful Noise: Poems for Two Voices*, illustrated by Eric Beddows. Harper, 1988.

61. Frank, Josette, ed. *Snow Toward Evening*, illustrated by Thomas Locker. Dial, 1990.

62. Froman, Robert. *Seeing Things*. Crowell, 1974.

63. Frost, Robert. *Birches*, illustrated by Ed Young. Henry Holt, 1988.

64. _____. *Stopping by Woods on a Snowy Evening*, illustrated by Susan Jeffers. Dutton, 1978.

65. _____. *You Come Too*, illustrated by Thomas W. Nason. Holt, 1959.

66. Gasztold, Carmen Bernos de. *Prayers from the Ark*, translated by Rumer Godden, illustrated by Jean Primrose. Viking, 1962.

67. Giovanni, Nikki. *Spin a Soft Black Song: Poems for Children*, illustrated by George Martins. Hill and Wang, 1985 (1971).

68. Goldstein, Bobbye S., ed. *Bear in Mind*, illustrated by William Pène DuBois. Viking, 1989.

69. Greenfield, Eloise. *Honey, I Love: And Other Poems*, illustrated by Leo and Diane Dillon. Harper, 1978.

70. _____. *Nathaniel Talking*, illustrated by Jan Spivey Gilchrist. Black Butterfly Children's Books, 1988.

71. _____. *Night on Neighborhood Street*, illustrated by Jan Spivey Gilchrist. Dial, 1991.

72. _____. *Under the Sunday Tree*, illustrated by Mr. Amos Ferguson. Harper, 1988.

73. Hoberman, Mary Ann. *A Fine Fat Pig*, illustrated by Malach Zeldis. HarperCollins, 1991.

74. _____. *A House Is a House for Me*, illustrated by Betty Fraser. Penguin, 1982.

75. _____. *Yellow Butter Purple Jelly Red Jam Black Bread*, illustrated by Chaya Burstein. Viking, 1981.

76. Holman, Felice. *The Song in My Head*, illustrated by Jim Spanfeller. Scribner's, 1985.

77. Hopkins, Lee Bennett, ed. *Best Friends*, illustrated by James Watts. Harper, 1986.

78. _____, ed. *By Myself*, illustrated by Glo Goalson. Harper, 1980.

79. _____, ed. *Dinosaurs*, illustrated by Murray Tinkelman. Harcourt, 1987.

80. _____, ed. *Good Books, Good Times!*, illustrated by Harvey Stevenson. Harper, 1990.

81. _____, ed. *Hey-How for Halloween!*, illustrated by Janet McCaffrey. Harcourt, 1974.

82. _____, ed. *More Surprises*, illustrated by Megan Lloyd. 1987.

83. _____, ed. *Morning, Noon and Nighttime, Too*, illustrated by Nancy Hannans. Harcourt, 1980.

84. _____, ed. *Rainbows Are Made: Poems by Carl Sandburg*, illustrated by Fritz Eichenberg. Harcourt, 1984.

85. _____, ed. *The Sea Is Calling Me*, illustrated by Walter Gaffney-Kessell. Harcourt, 1986.

86. _____, ed. *Side by Side: Poems to Read Together*, illustrated by Hilary Knight. Simon & Schuster, 1988.

87. _____, ed. *The Sky Is Full of Song*, illustrated by Dirk Zimmer. Harper, 1983.

88. _____, ed. *Still as a Star: A Book of Nighttime Poems*, illustrated by Karen Milone. Little, Brown, 1989.

89. _____, ed. *Surprises*, illustrated by Megan Lloyd. Harper, 1984.

90. _____, ed. *Through Our Eyes: Poems and Pictures About Growing Up*, photography by Jeffrey Dunn. Little, Brown, 1992.

91. Huck, Charlotte, ed. *Secret Places*, illustrated by Lindsay Barrett George. Greenwillow, 1993.

92. Hughes, Langston. *Don't You Turn Back*, edited by Lee Bennett Hopkins, illustrated by Ann Grifalconi. Knopf, 1969.

93. . . . *I Never Saw Another Butterfly: Children's Drawings and Poems from Terezin Concentration Camp, 1942–1944*. Schocken, 1978.

94. Janeczko, Paul B., ed. *The Place My Words Are Looking For*. Bradbury, 1990.

95. _____, ed. *This Delicious Day*. Orchard, 1987.

96. Kennedy, X. J. *Brats*, illustrated by James Watts. Atheneum, 1986.

97. _____. *The Forgetful Wishing Well: Poems for Young People*, illustrated by Monica Incisa. Atheneum, 1985.

98. _____. *Fresh Brats*, illustrated by James Watts. Atheneum, 1990.

99. _____. *Ghastlies, Goops & Pincushions*, illustrated by Ron Barrett. Atheneum, 1989.

100. Kennedy, X. J. and Dorothy M. Kennedy, compilers. *Knock at a Star: A Child's Introduction to Poetry*, illustrated by Karen Ann Weinhaus. Little, Brown, 1982.

101. Knudson, R. R., and May Swenson. *American Sports Poems*. Orchard, 1988.

102. Kuskin, Karla. *Any Me I Want to Be*. Harper, 1972.

103. _____. *Dogs & Dragons, Trees & Dreams: A Collection of Poems*. Harper, 1980.

104. _____. *Near the Window Tree*. Harper, 1975.

105. _____. *Something Sleeping in the Hall*. Harper, 1985.

106. Larrick, Nancy, ed. *Bring Me All of Your Dreams*, photographs by Larry Mulvehill. M. Evans, 1980.

107. _____, ed. *Cats Are Cats*, illustrated by Ed Young. Philomel, 1988.

108. _____, ed. *The Merry-Go-Round Poetry Book*, illustrated by Karen Gundersheimer. Delacorte, 1989.

109. _____, ed. *Mice Are Nice*, illustrated by Ed Young. Philomel, 1990.

110. _____, ed. *Piping Down the Valleys Wild*, illustrated by Ellen Raskin. Delacorte, 1985 (1968).

111. _____, ed. *To the Moon and Back*, illustrated by Catherine O'Neill. Delacorte, 1991.

112. _____, compiler. *When the Dark Comes Dancing*, illustrated by John Wallner. Philomel, 1983.

113. Lear, Edward. *The Complete Nonsense Book*. Dodd, Mead, 1946.

114. _____. *The Owl and the Pussycat*, illustrated by Jan Brett. Putnam's, 1991.

115. _____. *The Quangle Wangle's Hat*, illustrated by Janet Stevens. Harcourt, 1988.

116. Lear, Edward, and Ogden Nash. *The Scroobious Pip*, illustrated by Nancy Ekholm Burkert. Harper, 1968.

117. Lewis, J. Patrick. *Earth Verses and Water Rhymes*, illustrated by Robert Sabuda. Atheneum, 1991.

118. _____. *A Hippopotamusn't*, illustrated by Victoria Chess. Dial, 1990.

119. Lewis, Richard, ed. *In a Spring Garden*, illustrated by Ezra Jack Keats. Dial, 1989 (1964).

120. Lindbergh, Reeve. *Johnny Appleseed*, illustrated by Kathy Jakobsen. Little, Brown, 1990.

121. Little, Jean. *Hey World, Here I Am!*, illustrated by Sue Truesdell. Harper, 1986.

122. Livingston, Myra Cohn, ed. *Cat Poems*, illustrated by Trina Schart Hyman. Holiday, 1987.

123. _____. *Celebrations*, illustrated by Leonard Everett Fisher. Holiday, 1985.

124. _____, ed. *Christmas Poems*, illustrated by Trina Schart Hyman. Holiday, 1985.

125. _____. *A Circle of Seasons*, illustrated by Leonard Everett Fisher. Holiday, 1982.

126. _____, ed. *Dilly Dilly Piccalilli, Poems for the Very Young*, illustrated by Eileen Christelow. McElderry, 1989.

127. _____, ed. *Dog Poems*, illustrated by Leslie Morrill. Holiday, 1990.

128. _____. *Earth Songs*, illustrated by Leonard E. Fisher. Holiday, 1986.

129. _____, ed. *Easter Poems*, illustrated by John Wallner. Holiday, 1985.

130. _____, ed. *Halloween Poems*, illustrated by Stephen Gammell. Holiday, 1989.

131. _____, ed. *If The Owl Calls Again, A Collection of Owl Poems*, illustrated by Antonio Frasconi. McElderry, 1990.

132. _____, ed. *I Like You, If You Like Me, Poems of Friendship*. McElderry, 1987.

133. _____. *My Head Is Red and Other Riddle Poems*, illustrated by Tere Lo Prete. Holiday, 1990.

134. _____, ed. *New Year's Poems*, illustrated by Margot Tomes. Holiday, 1987.

135. _____, ed. *Poems for Brothers, Poems for Sisters*, illustrated by Jean Zallinger. Holiday, 1991.

136. _____, ed. *Poems for Fathers*, illustrated by Robert Cassilla. Holiday, 1989.

137. _____, ed. *Poems for Grandmothers*, illustrated by Patricia Cullen-Clark. Holiday, 1990.

138. _____, ed. *Poems for Jewish Holidays*, illustrated by Lloyd Bloom. Holiday, 1986.

139. _____, ed. *Poems for Mothers*, illustrated by Deborah K. Ray. Holiday, 1988.

140. _____. *Sea Songs*, illustrated by Leonard E. Fisher. McElderry, 1986.

141. _____. *Sky Songs*, illustrated by Leonard E. Fisher. McElderry, 1984.

142. _____. *A Song I Sang to You: A Selection of Poems*, illustrated by Margot Tomes. Harcourt, 1984.
143. _____. *Space Songs*, illustrated by Leonard E. Fisher. McElderry, 1988.
144. _____, ed. *Thanksgiving Poems*, illustrated by Stephen Gammell. Holiday, 1985.
145. _____. *There Was a Place and Other Poems*. McElderry, 1988.
146. _____. *Up in the Air*, illustrated by Leonard E. Fisher. McElderry, 1989.
147. _____, ed. *Valentine Poems*. Holiday, 1987.
148. _____. *The Way Things Are and Other Poems*, illustrated by Jenni Oliver. Atheneum, 1974.
149. _____, ed. *Why Am I Grown So Cold? Poems of the Unknowable*. Atheneum, 1984.
150. _____. *Worlds I Know*, illustrated by Tim Arnold. McElderry, 1985.
151. Lobel, Arnold. *The Book of Pigericks*. Harper, 1983.
152. Longfellow, Henry Wadsworth. *Hiawatha*, illustrated by Susan Jeffers. Dial, 1983.
153. _____. *Hiawatha's Childhood*, illustrated by Errol Le Cain. Farrar, Straus, 1984.
154. _____. *Paul Revere's Ride*, illustrated by Nancy Winslow Parker. Greenwillow, 1985.
155. _____. *Paul Revere's Ride*, illustrated by Ted Rand. Dutton, 1990.
156. McCord, David. *Every Time I Climb a Tree*, illustrated by Marc Simont. Little, Brown, 1967.
157. _____. *One at a Time*, illustrated by Henry B. Kane. Little, Brown, 1977.
158. Merriam, Eve. *Blackberry Ink*, illustrated by Hans Wilhelm. Morrow, 1985.
159. _____. *Chortles*, illustrated by Sheila Hamanaka. Morrow, 1981.
160. _____. *Fresh Paint*, illustrated by David Frampton. Macmillan, 1986.
161. _____. *Halloween A B C*, illustrated by Lane Smith. Macmillan, 1987.
162. _____. *It Doesn't Always Have to Rhyme*, illustrated by Malcom Spooner. Atheneum, 1964.
163. _____. *Jamboree: Rhymes for All Times*, illustrated by Walter Gaffney-Kassell. Dell, 1984.
164. _____. *Out Loud*, illustrated by Harriet Sherman. Atheneum, 1973.
165. _____. *A Poem for a Pickle*, illustrated by Sheila Hamanaka. Macmillan, 1989.
166. _____. *You Be Good & I'll Be Night*, illustrated by Karen Lee Schmidt. Morrow, 1988.
167. Milne, A. A. *The World of Christopher Robin*, illustrated by E. H. Shepard. Dutton, 1958.
168. Milnes, Gerald. *Granny Will Your Dog Bite? And Other Mountain Rhymes*, illustrated by Kimberly Root. Knopf, 1990.
169. Moore, Clement C. *The Night Before Christmas*, illustrated by Tomie de Paola. Holiday, 1980.
170. _____, illustrated by Grandma Moses. Random, 1962.
171. _____, illustrated by Tasha Tudor. Macmillan, 1975.
172. _____, illustrated by Wendy Watson. Clarion, 1990.
173. Moore, Lilian. *Go with the Poem*. McGraw-Hill, 1979. (o.p.)
174. _____. *Something New Begins*, illustrated by Mary J. Dunton. Atheneum, 1982.
175. Morrison, Lillian, ed. *Sprints and Distances: Sports in Poetry and Poetry in Sport*, illustrated by Clara Ross and John Ross. Crowell, 1965.
176. Nash, Ogden. *Custard & Company*, selected and illustrated by Quentin Blake. Little, Brown, 1980.
177. _____. *The Adventures of Isabel*, illustrated by James Marshall. Little, Brown, 1991.
178. Norman, Charles. *The Hornbeam Tree and Other Poems*, illustrated by Ted Rand. Henry Holt, 1988.
179. Noyes, Alfred. *The Highwayman*, illustrated by Charles Keeping. Oxford, 1981.
180. _____. *The Highwayman*, illustrated by Charles Mikolaycak. Lothrop, 1983.
181. _____. *The Highwayman*, illustrated by Neil Waldman. Harcourt, 1990.
182. O'Neill, Mary. *Hailstones and Halibut Bones: Adventures in Color*, illustrated by John Wallner. Philomel, 1989 (1961).
183. Plotz, Helen, ed. *A Week of Lullabies*, illustrated by Marisabina Russo. Greenwillow, 1988.
184. Pomerantz, Charlotte. *If I Had a Paka: Poems in Eleven Languages*, illustrated by Nancy Tafuri. Greenwillow, 1982.
185. _____. *The Tamarindo Puppy and Other Poems*, illustrated by Byron Barton. Greenwillow, 1980.
186. Prelutsky, Jack. *The Baby Uggs Are Hatching*, illustrated by James Stevenson. Greenwillow, 1982.
187. _____. *Beneath a Blue Umbrella*, illustrated by Garth Williams. Greenwillow, 1990.
188. _____, ed. *For Laughing Out Loud: Poems to Tickle Your Funnybone*, illustrated by Marjorie Priceman. Knopf, 1991.
189. _____. *It's Halloween*, illustrated by Marylin Hafner. Greenwillow, 1977.
190. _____. *It's Snowing! It's Snowing!*, illustrated by Jeanne Titherington. Greenwillow, 1984.
191. _____. *It's Thanksgiving*, illustrated by Marylin Hafner. Greenwillow, 1982.
192. _____. *The New Kid on the Block*, illustrated by James Stevenson. Greenwillow, 1984.
193. _____. *Nightmares: Poems to Trouble Your Sleep*, illustrated by Arnold Lobel. Greenwillow, 1976.
194. _____, ed. *Poems by A. Nonny Mouse*, illustrated by Henrik Drescher. Knopf, 1989.
195. _____. *Rainy Rainy Saturday*, illustrated by Marylin Hafner. Greenwillow, 1980.

196. _____, ed. *The Random House Book of Poetry for Children*, illustrated by Arnold Lobel. Random House, 1983.
197. _____, ed. *Read-Aloud Rhymes for the Very Young*, illustrated by Marc Brown. Knopf, 1986.
198. _____. *Ride a Purple Pelican*, illustrated by Garth Williams. Greenwillow, 1986.
199. _____. *Rolling Harvey down the Hill*, illustrated by Victoria Chess. Greenwillow, 1980.
200. _____. *The Snopp on the Sidewalk and Other Poems*, illustrated by Byron Barton. Greenwillow, 1977.
201. _____. *Something BIG Has Been Here*, illustrated by James Stevenson. Greenwillow, 1990.
202. _____. *Tyrannosaurus Was a Beast*, illustrated by Arnold Lobel. Greenwillow, 1988.
203. Rylant, Cynthia. *Waiting to Waltz: A Childhood*, illustrated by Stephen Gammell. Bradbury, 1984.
204. Sandburg, Carl. *Early Moon*, illustrated by James Daugherty. Harcourt, 1930.
205. _____. *The People, Yes*. Harcourt, 1936.
206. Service, Robert W. *The Cremation of Sam McGee*, illustrated by Ted Harrison. Greenwillow, 1987.
207. _____. *The Shooting of Dan McGrew*, illustrated by Ted Harrison. Godine, 1988.
208. Siebert, Diane. *Heartland*, illustrated by Wendell Minor. Crowell, 1989.
209. _____. *Mojave*, illustrated by Wendell Minor. Crowell, 1988.
210. _____. *Sierra*, illustrated by Wendell Minor. HarperCollins, 1991.
211. Silverstein, Shel. *A Light in the Attic*. Harper, 1981.
212. _____. *Where the Sidewalk Ends: Poems and Drawings*. Harper, 1974.
213. Singer, Marilyn. *Turtle in July*, illustrated by Jerry Pinkney. Macmillan, 1989.
214. Small, Terry. *The Legend of William Tell*. Bantam, 1991.
215. Smith, William Jay. *Laughing Time*, illustrated by Fernando Krahn. Delacorte, 1990 (1980).
216. Sneve, Virginia Driving Hawk. *Dancing Teepees*, illustrated by Stephen Gammell. Holiday, 1989.
217. Stevenson, Robert Louis. *Block City*, illustrated by Ashley Wolff. Dutton, 1988.
218. _____. *A Child's Garden of Verses*, illustrated by Tasha Tudor. Oxford, 1947 (1885).
219. _____. *A Child's Garden of Verses*, illustrated by Brian Wildsmith. Oxford, 1966 (1885).
220. _____. *My Shadow*, illustrated by Ted Rand. Putnam, 1990.
221. Sullivan, Charles, ed. *Imaginary Gardens: American Poetry and Art for Young People*. Abrams, 1989.
222. Thayer, Ernest. *Casey at the Bat: A Ballad of the Republic, Sung in the Year 1888*, illustrated by Wallace Tripp. Putnam's, 1980.
223. _____. *Casey at the Bat: A Centennial Edition*, illustrated by Barry Moser. Godine, 1988.
224. Viorst, Judith. *If I Were in Charge of the World and Other Worries*, illustrated by Lynne Cherry. Atheneum, 1982.
225. Whipple, Laura, ed. *Eric Carle's Animals Animals*. Philomel, 1989.
226. _____. *Eric Carle's Dragons Dragons & Other Creatures That Never Were*. Philomel, 1991.
227. Willard, Nancy A. *A Visit to William Blake's Inn*, illustrated by Alice and Martin Provensen. Harcourt, 1981.
228. Wilner, Isabel, compiler. *The Poetry Troupe: An Anthology of Poems to Read Aloud*. Scribner's, 1977.
229. Worth, Valerie. *All the Small Poems*, illustrated by Natalie Babbitt. Farrar, Straus, 1987.
230. _____. *More Small Poems*, illustrated by Natalie Babbitt. Farrar, Straus, 1976.
231. _____. *Small Poems*, illustrated by Natalie Babbitt. Farrar, Straus, 1972.
232. _____. *Small Poems Again*, illustrated by Natalie Babbitt. Farrar, Straus, 1985.
233. _____. *Still More Small Poems*, illustrated by Natalie Babbitt. Farrar, Straus, 1978.
234. Yolen, Jane. *Bird Watch*, illustrated by Ted Lewin. Philomel, 1990.
235. _____. *The Three Bears Rhyme Book*, illustrated by Jane Dyer. Harcourt, 1987.

PROSE REFERENCES

Alborough, Jez. *Where's My Teddy?* Candlewick, 1992.
Alexander, Lloyd. *The Prydain Chronicles*. Holt, 1964–1968.
Avi. *The True Confessions of Charlotte Doyle*. Orchard, 1990.
Armstrong, William H. *Sounder*, illustrated by James Barkley. Harper, 1969.
Arnosky, James. *Secrets of a Wildlife Watcher*. Lothrop, 1983.
_____. *Sketching Outdoors in Autumn*. Lothrop, 1988.
_____. *Sketching Outdoors in Spring*. Lothrop, 1987.
_____. *Sketching Outdoors in Summer*. Lothrop, 1988.
_____. *Sketching Outdoors in Winter*. Lothrop, 1988.
Babbitt, Natalie. *Tuck Everlasting*. Farrar, Straus, 1975.
Baker, Jennie. *Window*. Greenwillow, 1991.

Baylor, Byrd. *Hawk, I Am Your Brother*, illustrated by Peter Parnall. Scribner's, 1976.

_____. *The Way to Start a Day*, illustrated by Peter Parnall. Scribner's, 1978.

Baylor, Byrd. *Your Own Best Secret Place*, illustrated by Peter Parnall. Scribner's, 1979.

Brandenberg, Franz. *Aunt Nina, Goodnight*, illustrated by Aliki. Greenwillow, 1989.

Brett, Jan. *Goldilocks and the Three Bears*. Dodd, Mead, 1987.

Bryan, Ashley. *The Cat's Purr*. Atheneum, 1985.

Bunting, Eve. *The Wall*, illustrated by Ronald Himler. Clarion, 1990.

_____. *The Wednesday Surprise*, illustrated by Donald Carrick. Clarion, 1989.

Byars, Betsy. *The House of Wings*, illustrated by Daniel Schwartz. Viking, 1972.

Burningham, John. *Come Away from the Water, Shirley*. Harper, 1977.

_____. *Granpa*. Crown, 1985.

Cameron, Ann. *The Most Beautiful Place in the World*, illustrated by Thomas B. Allen. Knopf, 1988.

_____. *The Stories Julian Tells*, illustrated by Ann Strugnell. Knopf, 1981.

Carle, Eric. *The Mixed-Up Chameleon*. Crowell, 1984.

Carlstrom, Nancy W. *Blow Me a Kiss, Miss Lilly*, illustrated by Amy Schwartz. Harper, 1990.

Carrick, Carol, and Donald Carrick. *The Accident*. Seabury, 1976.

_____. *Sleep Out*. Seabury, 1973.

Chall, Marsha Wilson. *Up North at the Cabin*, illustrated by Steve Johnson. Lothrop, 1992.

Cherry, Lynne. *The Great Kapok Tree*. Harcourt, 1990.

Christopher, John. *When The Tripods Came*. Dutton, 1988.

Cohen, Miriam. *Lost in the Museum*, illustrated by Lillian Hoban. Greenwillow, 1979.

_____. *Will I Have a Friend?*, illustrated by Lillian Hoban. Macmillan, 1967.

Conrad, Pam. *My Daniel*. Harper, 1989.

_____. *Staying Nine*, illustrated by Mike Wimmer. Harper, 1988.

Cormier, Robert. *Other Bells for Us to Ring*, illustrated by Deborah Kogan Ray. Delacorte, 1990.

Crews, Donald. *Freight Train*. Greenwillow, 1978.

Crowe, Robert. *Clyde Monster*, illustrated by Kay Chorao. Dutton, 1976.

Degen, Bruce. *Jamberry*. Harper, 1983.

de Paola, Tomie. *Strega Nona*. Prentice-Hall, 1975.

Dickinson, Peter. *Eva*. Delacorte, 1989.

Ehlert, Lois. *Color Farm*. Lippincott, 1990.

_____. *Color Zoo*. Lippincott, 1989.

Fox, Mem. *Koala Lou*, illustrated by Pamela Lofts, Harcourt, 1989.

Fox, Paula. *The Stone-Faced Boy*, illustrated by Donald A. Mackay. Bradbury, 1968.

Frank, Anne. *Anne Frank: Diary of a Young Girl*. Doubleday, 1952.

Freeman, Don. *Corduroy*. Viking, 1968.

_____. *Dandelion*. Viking, 1964.

Galdone, Paul. *The Gingerbread Boy*. Clarion, 1979.

Gallaz, Christophe, and Roberto Innocenti. *Rose Blanche*, illustrated by Roberto Innocenti. Creative Education, 1985.

George, Jean Craighead. *The Cry of the Crow*. Harper, 1980.

_____. *On the Far Side of the Mountain*. Dutton, 1990.

_____. *One Day in the Tropical Rain Forest*, illustrated by Gary Allen. Crowell, 1990.

_____. *Who Really Killed Cock Robin?* Harper, 1991 (1971).

Graeber, Charlotte. *Mustard*, illustrated by Donna Diamond. Macmillan, 1982.

Greenfield, Eloise. *She Come Bringing Me That Little Baby Girl*, illustrated by John Steptoe. Lippincott, 1974.

Grifalconi, Ann. *Osa's Pride*. Little, Brown, 1990.

Guarino, Deborah. *Is Your Mama a Llama?*, illustrated by Steven Kellogg. Scholastic, 1989.

Henkes, Kevin. *Julius, the Baby of the World*. Greenwillow, 1990.

_____. *Two Under Par*. Greenwillow, 1987.

Hoban, Russell. *A Baby Sister for Frances*, illustrated by Lillian Hoban. Harper, 1970.

_____. *Bedtime for Frances*, illustrated by Garth Williams. Harper, 1960.

Hughes, Shirley. *Dogger*. Lothrop, 1988.

Hutchins, Pat. *Titch*. Macmillan, 1971.

Huynh, Quang Nhuong. *The Land I Lost: Adventures of a Boy in Vietnam*, illustrated by Vo-Dinh Mai. Harper, 1982.

Jarrell, Randall. *The Bat-Poet*, illustrated by Maurice Sendak. Macmillan, 1964.

Jonas, Ann. *Color Dance*. Greenwillow, 1989.

_____. *The Quilt*. Greenwillow, 1984.

Joosse, Barbara M. *Dinah's Mad, Bad Wishes*, illustrated by Emily Arnold McCully. Harper, 1989.

Keats, Ezra Jack. *Peter's Chair*. Harper, 1967.

Konigsburg, Elaine. *From the Mixed-Up Files of Mrs. Basil E. Frankweiler*. Atheneum, 1967.

Kraus, Robert. *Leo the Late Bloomer*, illustrated by Jose Aruego. Harper, 1987 (1971).

Lasky, Kathryn. *Dinosaur Dig*, photography by Christopher G. Knight. Morrow, 1990.

Lauber, Patricia. *Living with Dinosaurs*, illustrated by Douglas Henderson. Bradbury, 1991.

_____. *The News About Dinosaurs*. Bradbury, 1989.

Le Guin, Ursula K. *A Wizard of Earthsea*, illustrated by Ruth Robbins. Parnassus, 1968.

Lionni, Leo. *Alexander and the Wind-Up Mouse*. Pantheon, 1969.

_____. *Little Blue and Little Yellow*. Astor-Honor, 1959.

Little, Jean. *Kate*. Harper, 1971.

_____. *Look Through My Window*, illustrated by Joan Sandin. Harper, 1970.

Lowry, Lois. *Anastasia Krupnik*. Houghton, 1979.

_____. *Number the Stars*. Houghton, 1989.

McCloskey, Robert. *One Morning in Maine*. Viking, 1952.

_____. *Time of Wonder*. Viking, 1957.

MacDonald, Caroline. *The Lake at the End of the World*. Dial, 1989.

MacDonald, Golden, pseud. (Margaret Wise Brown). *The Little Island*, illustrated by Leonard Weisgard. Doubleday, 1946.

McKee, David. *Elmer*. Lothrop, 1989 (1968).

MacLachlan, Patricia. *Sarah, Plain and Tall*. Harper, 1985.

McPhail, David. *The Bear's Toothache*. Little, Brown, 1972.

Marshall, James. *The Three Little Pigs*. Dial, 1989.

Maruki, Toshi. *Hiroshima No Pika*. Lothrop, 1980.

Mayer, Mercer. *There's a Nightmare in My Closet*. Dial, 1968.

O'Brien, Robert. *Z for Zachariah*. Atheneum, 1975.

Paterson, Katherine. *Bridge to Terabithia*, illustrated by Donna Diamond. Crowell, 1977.

_____. *Jacob Have I Loved*. Crowell, 1980.

_____. *Lyddie*. Dutton, 1991.

Perrault, Charles, retold by Amy Ehrlich. *Cinderella*, illustrated by Susan Jeffers. Dial, 1985.

Russo, Marisabina. *Why Do Grown-Ups Have All the Fun?* Greenwillow, 1987.

Rylant, Cynthia. *When I Was Young in the Mountains*, illustrated by Diane Goode. Dutton, 1982.

Say, Allen. *The Lost Lake*. Houghton Mifflin, 1989.

Schlein, Miriam. *The Year of the Panda*, illustrated by Kam Mak. Crowell, 1990.

Scieszka, Jon. *The Frog Prince Continued*, illustrated by Steve Johnson. Viking, 1991.

_____. *The True Story of the 3 Little Pigs! By A. Wolf*, illustrated by Lane Smith. Viking, 1989.

Service, Pamela. *Winter of Magic's Return*. Atheneum, 1985.

Sheldon, Dyan. *The Whales' Song*, illustrated by Gary Blythe. Dial, 1991.

Shulevitz, Uri. *Dawn*. Farrar, Straus, 1974.

Sleator, William. *The Green Futures of Tycho*. Dutton, 1981.

Speare, Elizabeth. *The Sign of the Beaver*. Houghton Mifflin, 1983.

Spinelli, Jerry. *Maniac Magee*. Little, Brown, 1990.

Stevenson, James. *What's Under My Bed?* Greenwillow, 1983.

Tarcov, Edith H. *The Frog Prince*, illustrated by James Marshall. Scholastic, 1987.

Taylor, Mildred. *Roll of Thunder, Hear My Cry*. Dial, 1976.

Viorst, Judith. *Alexander and the Terrible, Horrible, No Good, Very Bad Day*, illustrated by Ray Cruz. Atheneum, 1972.

_____. *The Tenth Good Thing About Barney*, illustrated by Erik Blegvad. Atheneum, 1971.

Voigt, Cynthia. *Homecoming*. Atheneum, 1983.

Waber, Bernard. *Ira Sleeps Over*. Houghton Mifflin, 1972.

Walsh, Jill Paton. *The Green Book*, illustrated by Lloyd Bloom. Farrar, Straus, 1982.

Wells, Rosemary. *Noisy Nora*. Dial, 1973.

Wild, Margaret. *The Very Best of Friends*, illustrated by Julie Vivas. Harcourt, 1990.

Williams, Vera B. *A Chair for My Mother*. Greenwillow, 1982.

Williams, Vera B., and Jennifer Williams. *Stringbean's Trip to the Shining Sea*. Greenwillow, 1988.

Wood, Audrey. *The Napping House*, illustrated by Don Wood. Harcourt, 1984.

Zolotow, Charlotte. *The Hating Book*, illustrated by Ben Shecter. Harper, 1969.

_____. *Mr. Rabbit and the Lovely Present*, illustrated by Maurice Sendak. Harper, 1962.

Chapter Nine

Contemporary Realistic Fiction

REALISM IN CONTEMPORARY
CHILDREN'S LITERATURE

VALUES OF CONTEMPORARY FICTION
ISSUES RELATING TO REALISTIC FICTION

WHAT IS REAL?
HOW REAL MAY A CHILDREN'S BOOK BE?
BIAS AND STEREOTYPING
THE BACKGROUND OF THE AUTHOR
CATEGORIZING LITERATURE

BECOMING ONE'S OWN PERSON

LIVING IN A FAMILY

FAMILY RELATIONSHIPS
EXTENDED FAMILIES
FAMILIES IN TRANSITION

LIVING WITH OTHERS

FINDING PEER ACCEPTANCE
MAKING FRIENDS

GROWING TOWARD MATURITY

DEVELOPING SEXUALITY
FINDING ONE'S SELF
SURVIVAL STORIES

COPING WITH PROBLEMS OF THE
HUMAN CONDITION

PHYSICAL DISABILITIES
DEVELOPMENTAL DISABILITIES

MENTAL ILLNESS
AGING AND DEATH

AGING
DEATH AND DYING

LIVING IN A DIVERSE WORLD

APPRECIATING RACIAL AND ETHNIC DIVERSITY

AFRICAN-AMERICAN EXPERIENCES IN BOOKS FOR
    CHILDREN

GUIDELINES: EVALUATING MULTICULTURAL
LITERATURE
BOOKS ABOUT OTHER MINORITIES
TOWARD UNDERSTANDING VARIOUS WORLD
    CULTURES

TEACHING FEATURE: TEACHERS DISCUSS
LITERATURE BY AND ABOUT MINORITIES

POPULAR TYPES OF REALISTIC FICTION

HUMOROUS STORIES
ANIMAL STORIES
SPORTS STORIES
SCHOOL STORIES
MYSTERIES

SUGGESTED LEARNING EXPERIENCES

RELATED READINGS

REFERENCES

GILLY IN ME

I think I am a lot like Gilly in some ways. One way is everything somebody says I can't do, I have to show them that I can do it or something like it. I think Gilly and I feel the same way about foster parents. If I had foster parents, I probably would feel that my mother would come and get me; but I wouldn't run away or steal money.

In school I don't act like she does, going to the principal or slipping notes in teacher's books. It seems she doesn't like to be with her friends. I like to be around with my friends. I don't like to be by myself. I think Gilly gets mad easy. I get mad easy like getting called names. I always have to call them a name back.

Amy Kauffman, seventh grade
Delaware Public Schools, Ohio
Christy Slavik, teacher

A small group of seventh graders read Katherine Paterson's *The Great Gilly Hopkins* in their in-depth reading group. One of their options when they finished the book was to write about ways they were like Gilly or ways in which they were different from Gilly. Obviously, Amy had identified with the character of Gilly Hopkins. By contrasting her perception of herself with Gilly, she learned more about Gilly and developed insight into her own personality.

A well-written contemporary story should do more than just mirror modern life. It should take children inside a character and help them understand the causes of behavior, while at the same time it should take them outside themselves to reflect on their own behavior. *The Great Gilly Hopkins* had opened a window of understanding for Amy and let her view herself and the world with slightly changed perception.

REALISM IN CONTEMPORARY CHILDREN'S LITERATURE

Realistic fiction may be defined as imaginative writing that accurately reflects life as it was lived in the past or could be lived today. Everything in such a story can conceivably happen to real people living in our natural physical world, in contrast to fantasy, where impossible happenings are made to appear quite plausible even though they are not possible. Historical fiction (see Chapter 10) portrays life as it may have been lived in the past; contemporary realism focuses on the problems of living today. Though other genres in children's literature, such as fantasy, enjoy popularity, realistic fiction consistently leads in studies of children's preferences. The books discussed in this chapter may be categorized as contemporary realistic fiction for children. Many of these are stories about growing up today and finding a place in the family, among peers, and in modern society. In addition, aspects of coping with the problems of the human condition may be found in contemporary literature for children. Books that are humorous or reflect special interests—such as animal or sports stories and mysteries—are also classified as realistic literature and so are included in this chapter.

The content of contemporary realism for children has changed dramatically in the past thirty years. A discussion of some of these changes was included in Chapter 1; Chapter 3 identified recent trends in publishing books for children. These changes have provoked controversy among writers, critics, librarians, teachers, and parents. For this reason we give attention to some of the values of contemporary realism for children and some of these issues.

Values of Contemporary Fiction

Realistic fiction serves children in the process of understanding and coming to terms with themselves as they acquire "human-ness." Books that honestly portray the realities of life help children toward a fuller understanding of human problems and human relationships and, thus, toward a fuller understanding of themselves and their own potential. In describing her purpose in writing for children, Nina Bawden states:

> If a children's writer presents his characters honestly and is truthful about their thoughts and their feelings, he is giving his readers "a means to gain a hold on fate" by showing them that they can trust their thoughts and their feelings, that they can have faith in themselves. He can also show them a bit of the world, the beginning of the path they have to tread; but the most important thing he has to offer is a little hope, and courage for the journey.[1]

This is not a function unique to contemporary realism. Other types of books can show children a slice of the world. Some fantasy may be nearer to truth than realism; biography and autobiography frequently provide readers with models of human beings who offer "hope and courage for the journey." The ability to maintain one's humanity and courage in the midst of deprivation becomes clear

in *Number the Stars*, Lois Lowry's story about Danish efforts to save Jewish citizens in World War II. Personal bravery and responsible behavior under dire circumstances is also one of the themes of the high fantasy *A Wizard of Earthsea* by Ursula Le Guin. However, most children appear to identify more readily with characters in books of contemporary realism than with those of historical fiction or fantasy.

Realistic fiction helps children enlarge their frames of reference while seeing the world from another perspective. The horror of racial inequality in South Africa is strongly realized in Beverley Naidoo's *Journey to Jo'burg*. The incidents portrayed in Peter Härtling's humorous as well as moving story of a German family's year with *Old John* depict the rewards and problems in living with an aging person. Stories such as these help young people develop compassion for and an understanding of human actions.

Realistic fiction also reassures young people that they are not the first in the world to have faced problems. They read of other children whose parents have divorced in Judy Blume's *It's Not the End of the World* or of someone concerned about relationships with the opposite sex in Betsy Byars's *The Burning Questions of Bingo Brown*. They gain some solace from the recognition of the problems a ghetto environment poses for Jamal in Walter Dean Myers's *Scorpions*. This knowledge that they are not alone brings a kind of comfort to the child reader. James Baldwin recognized the power of books to alleviate pain when he said:

> You think your pain and your heartbreak are unprecedented in the history of the world, but then you read. It was books that taught me that the things that tormented me the most were the very things that connected me with all the people who were alive, or who had ever been alive.[2]

Realistic fiction can also illuminate experiences that children have not had. A child with loving parents whose only chore consists of making a bed may have a deeper need to read Marilyn

[1]Nina Bawden, "Emotional Realism in Books for Young People," *The Horn Book Magazine* (February 1980), p. 33.

[2]James Baldwin, "Talk to Teachers," *Saturday Review* (December 21, 1963), pp. 42–44, 60.

Sachs's *The Bears' House* than a child of poverty whose life may more nearly reflect the story. A child who takes school for granted may gain much from Ann Cameron's poignant *The Most Beautiful Place in the World* that describes a Guatemalan who desperately wants an education. Realistic fiction may become one way of experiencing a world we do not know.

Some books also serve as a kind of preparation for living. Far better to have read Katherine Paterson's *Bridge to Terabithia* or Cynthia Voigt's *Dicey's Song* than to experience firsthand at age 10 or 12 the death of your best friend or your mother. For many years, death was a taboo subject in children's literature. Yet, as children face the honest realities of life in books, they are developing a kind of courage for facing problems in their own lives. Madeleine L'Engle, whose *Meet the Austins* was among the first works of modern children's

As the first in his Guatemalan family to attend school, Juan receives hugs from his proud grandmother when he brings home a letter from his teacher praising his abilities.

Drawing by Thomas B. Allen from *The Most Beautiful Place in the World* by Ann Cameron.

literature to treat the subject of death, maintained that "to pretend there is no darkness is another way of extinguishing light."[3]

Realistic fiction for children does provide many possible models, both good and bad, for coping with problems of the human condition. As children experience these stories, they may begin to filter out some meaning for their own lives. This allows children to organize and shape their own thinking about life as they follow, through story, the lives of others.

Issues Relating to Realistic Fiction

More controversy surrounds the writing of contemporary realistic fiction for children than perhaps any other kind of literature. Everyone is a critic of realism, for everyone feels he or she is an expert on what is real in today's world. But realities clash, and the issue of "what is real for one may not be real for another" is a true and lively concern. Some of the questions that seem uniquely related to contemporary realism in writing for children need to be examined.

WHAT IS REAL?

The question of what is "real" or "true to life" is a significant one. C. S. Lewis, the British author of the well-known Narnia stories (see Chapter 7, "Modern Fantasy"), described three types of realistic content:

> But when we say, "The sort of thing that happens," do we mean the sort of thing that usually or often happens, the sort of thing that is typical of the human lot? Or do we mean "The sort of thing that might conceivably happen or that, by a thousandth chance, may have happened once?"[4]

Middle graders reading the Narnia series know they are fantasy and couldn't happen. However, middle graders may read such stories as Vera and Bill Cleaver's *Where the Lilies Bloom* or Gary Paulsen's *Hatchet* and believe that children can survive any hardship or crisis if they only possess

---

[3]Madeleine L'Engle, in a speech before the Florida Library Association, Miami, May 1965.
[4]C. S. Lewis, *An Experiment in Criticism* (Cambridge, England: Cambridge University Press, 1961), p. 57.

determination. These well-written books cast believable characters in realistic settings facing real problems. But an adult reader might question whether this is the sort of thing that "by a thousandth chance, may have happened once."

How Real May a Children's Book Be?

Controversy also centers on how much graphic detail may be included in a book for children. How much violence is too much? How explicit may an author be in describing bodily functions or sexual relations? These are questions that no one would have asked twenty-five years ago. But there are new freedoms today. Childhood is not the innocent time we like to think it is (and it probably never was). Although youth may not need protection, it does still need the perspective that literature can give. A well-written book makes the reader aware of the human suffering resulting from inhumane acts by others, whereas television and films are more apt to concentrate on the acts themselves.

The TV newscasts of the local Saturday night killings or the body count in the latest "peace-keeping" effort seldom show the pain and anguish that each death causes. The rebuilding of human lives is too slow and tedious to portray in a half-hour newscast. Even video games are based on violence. The winner of the game is the one who can eliminate or destroy the "enemy." Reasons or motivations are never given, and the aftereffects are not a part of the game.

By way of contrast to the media world, a well-written story provides perspective on the pain and suffering of humankind. In a literary story the author has time to develop the characters into fully rounded human beings. The reader knows the motives and pressures of each individual and can understand and empathize with the characters. If the tone of the author is one of compassion for the characters, if others in the story show concern or horror for a brutal act, the reader gains perspective.

A story that makes violence understandable without condoning it is Suzanne Fisher Staples's story of *Shabanu, Daughter of the Wind*. In the Pakistani desert culture in which 12-year-old Shabanu lives, obedience to rules has enabled many tribes to live in peace in an environment that offers little material comfort. When Shabanu runs away to avoid an arranged marriage to a middle-aged man, she discovers her favorite camel has broken its leg. In choosing to remain with the camel, Shabanu tacitly agrees to the rules of her clan. Her father catches up with her and beats her severely. But she is soaked with his tears as he does what he must, and the reader realizes both are trapped in roles their society has defined for them. Another story in which a violent act seems understandable is related in Vera and Bill Cleaver's *Grover*. Grover's mother committed suicide rather than face a slow death from cancer. But a neighbor woman taunts the boy for his mother's "cowardice" and treats him unfairly in other ways. When Grover, with his friends watching, cuts the head off her tom turkey in retaliation, he and his friends can't speak to each other, so horrified are they by the act. But the reader sees the killing as cathartic for Grover. Both strong stories suggest we all have to wrestle with grim reality in our lives in the best ways that we know.

James Giblin, a former children's book editor, suggests that a book can be realistic without being overly graphic.

> For instance, if the young detective in a mystery story was attacked by a gang of bullies, I wouldn't encourage an author to have them burn his arms with a cigarette to get him to talk (although that might conceivably happen in an adult mystery). However, I would accept a scene in which the gang *threatened* to do so: that would convey the reality and danger of the situation without indulging in all the gory details.[5]

Giblin maintains that very few subjects are inappropriate in themselves; it is all in how the author treats them. The facts of a situation, ugly as they may be, can be presented with feeling and depth of emotion, which carry the reader beyond the particular subject.

The same criteria are appropriate for evaluating explicitness in sex and bodily functions in books for children. Betty Miles raises this issue in *Maudie and Me and the Dirty Book*. When seventh

[5]James Cross Giblin, *Writing Books for Young People* (Boston: The Writer, Inc., 1990), p. 73.

grader Kate Harris teams up with a classmate to read aloud to first graders, one of her choices—a story about a puppy being born—triggers a discussion among the 6-year-olds about human birth and conception. While Kate handles the discussion with poise, a parent complaint eventually brings about a town meeting concerning what is appropriate in the elementary classroom curriculum. Miles treats the topics of conception, birth, and censorship in an open and forthright way.

BIAS AND STEREOTYPING

Since children's books have always reflected the general social and human values of a society, it is not surprising they are also scrutinized for implied attitudes or biases of that society. Contemporary realistic fiction is examined for racism and accuracy in depicting cultural aspects, sexism, ageism, and treatment of people with physical or mental impairments. The general raised consciousness of the children's book world has increased the number of books that present diverse populations positively and fairly.

The political and social activism of the 1960s contributed to an awareness of racism in children's books. (See "Appreciating Racial and Ethnic Diversity" later in this chapter.) In the 1980s and 1990s, children may find fully realized African-American characters in books such as Virginia Hamilton's *Cousins,* Bruce Brooks's *Everywhere,* Katherine Paterson's *Come Sing, Jimmy Jo,* Walter Dean Myers's *The Mouse Rap,* and Jerry Spinelli's *Maniac Magee* who exist in their own right and not so that a white main character may "find" herself or himself. Still, adults need to be alert to reissues of books from an earlier era such as the 1945 Newbery honor book, *The Silver Pencil,*[6] with many racist descriptions of people in Trinidad. Books such as this help us recognize the gains of recent decades.

Because feminists in the 1970s made us more aware of the subtle ways in which literature perpetuated stereotypes, contemporary realistic fiction now does a much better job of portraying women in a variety of roles. Capable working mothers; caring female role models outside of a child's family; characters who fight sexism; intelligent, independent, and strong girls and women; and romance as a consequence of strong friendship are all found in realistic fiction of the present decade.

Decrying a work of historical realistic fiction as sexist has its own problems. Elizabeth George Speare's *The Witch of Blackbird Pond* has been crticized for depicting the heroine as someone whose greatest problem is whom she should marry. But in 1688, Kit had little other choice. Again, there is no point in denouncing fairy tales for their sexist portrayal of evil stepmothers, nagging wives, or beautiful young girls waiting for the arrival of princes. Such stories reflect the longings and beliefs of a society long past. To change the folktales would be to destroy our traditional heritage. A book should not then be criticized for being historically authentic or true to its traditional genre. However, we have every right to be critical when such stereotyped thinking is perpetuated in contemporary literature.

Boys have also been subtly victimized by the stereotypes of the past. They have been consistently reminded that men and boys don't cry, for example. But more modern realistic fiction shows that everyone may cry as they grieve, as do a boy and his father following the drowning of a friend in *On My Honor* by Marian Dane Bauer or following the death of a beloved old cat in *Mustard* by Charlotte Graeber. Boys have also been frequently stereotyped in animal stories as having to kill an animal they have loved as an initiation rite. In Marjorie Kinnan Rawlings's *The Yearling,* for instance, Jody is ordered to shoot his pet deer because it is destroying the family crops: "He did not believe he should ever again love anything, man or woman or his own child, as he loved the Yearling. He would be lonely all his life. But a man took it for his share and went on."[7] In Fred Gipson's *Old Yeller,* after the boy shoots his possibly rabid dog, his father tells him to try to forget and go on being a man. Stories such as these cause us to question the way some of our best literature conditions boys to be hard and strong.

---

[6]Alice Dalgliesh, *The Silver Pencil* (New York: Puffin, 1991). (1944)

[7]Marjorie Kinnan Rawlings, *The Yearling,* illustrated by Edward Shenton (New York: Scribner's 1938), p. 400.

People with mental or physical impairments have in the past been depicted as "handicapped" or "disabled." A more enlightened view suggests that the person in front of the impairment is more important than the impairment; one may *have* a disability without necessarily being disabled. Older people (and other adults) in children's literature have often been dismissed to an irrelevant position in a young person's life, as ineffectual in contrast to the vibrancy of young spirits, or as unable to do certain things because of their age. (See "Coping with Problems of the Human Condition" later in this chapter.) High-quality contemporary realistic fiction stories depict adults and the elderly in many ways—as mentors to a young person and as having their own romances, problems, and triumphs.

Children's books have made great gains in the depiction of our changing society. However, today's books need to continue to reflect the wide ranges of occupations, education, speech patterns, lifestyles, and futures that are possible for all, regardless of race, gender, age, or belief.

THE BACKGROUND OF THE AUTHOR

Another controversy swirls around the racial background of the author. Must an author be black to write about Africans, or Native American to write about Native Americans? As Virginia Hamilton states:

> It happens that I know Black people better than any other people because I am one of them and I grew up knowing what it is we are about . . . The writer uses the most comfortable milieu in which to tell a story, which is why my characters are Black. Often being Black is significant to the story; other times, it is not. The writer will always attempt to tell stories no one else can tell.[8]

It has been generally accepted that an author should write about what he or she knows. But Ann Cameron, the white author of *The Stories Julian Tells* and other books about an African-American family, maintains a different point of view:

> It seems to me that the people who advise "write about what you know" drastically underestimate the human capacity for imagining what lies beyond our immediate knowledge and for understanding what is new to us. Equally, they overestimate the extent to which we know ourselves. A culture, like a person, has blind spots. . . . Often the writer who is an outsider—an African writing about the United States, an American writing about China—sees in a way that enriches him as an observer, the culture he observes, and the culture he comes from.[9]

The hallmark of fine writing is the quality of imagining it calls forth from us. Imagination is not the exclusive trait of any race or gender but is a universal quality of all fine writers. No authors or artists want to be limited to writing about or portraying only an African-American or a Hispanic-American experience nor should they be. We need to focus on two aspects of every book: (1) What is its literary merit? and (2) Will children enjoy it?

CATEGORIZING LITERATURE

Reviewers, educators, and curriculum makers often categorize books according to their content. Categorizing serves textbook authors by allowing them to talk about several books as a group. It serves educators who hope to group books around a particular theme for classroom study. While one person might place Paterson's *Bridge to Terabithia* in a group of books about "making friends," it could just as easily be placed in another group: "growing up," "learning to accept death," or "well-written books." It is a disservice both to book and to reader if we apply a label and imply that this is all that the book is about. Readers with their own purposes and backgrounds will see many different aspects and strengths in a piece of literature. It is helpful to remember that our experiences with art occur at many different, unique, and personal levels. While teachers may wish to lead children to talk about a particular aspect of a book, they will not want to suggest that this is the only aspect worth pursuing.

A second issue in the categorizing of literature relates to its appropriateness for a specific age level. Realistic fiction is often categorized as for upper elementary or middle grade and junior high or young adult (YA) readers. Yet, anyone

[8]Virginia Hamilton, "Writing the Source: In Other Words," *The Horn Book Magazine*, vol. 54 (December 1978), p. 618.

[9]Ann Cameron, "Write What You Care About," *School Library Journal*, vol. 35, no. 10 (June 1989), p. 50.

who has spent time with 9- to 14-year-old readers has surely noticed the wide ranges of reading interests, abilities, and perceptions present. Betsy Byars's *The Pinballs* and Judy Blume's *Are You There, God? It's Me, Margaret* have challenged and entertained readers from fourth grade through high school. To suggest that these titles are "for 10- to 12-year-old readers" would ignore the ages of half of the readership of these popular authors.

In this chapter, books are arranged according to categories based on theme and content merely for the convenience of discussion. They could have been arranged in many other ways. The ages of main characters are noted, where appropriate, as a clue to potential readership. In some instances we have also noted, with references to actual classroom teachers' experiences, at which grade levels certain titles seem to have greatest impact.

BECOMING ONE'S OWN PERSON

The story of every man and every woman is the story of growing up, of becoming a person, of struggling to become one's own person. The kind of person you become has its roots in the experiences of childhood—how much you were loved, how little you were loved; the people who were significant to you, the ones who were not; the places you've been, and those you did not go to; the things you wanted, and the things you did not get. Yet a person is always more than the totality of these experiences; the way a person organizes, understands, and relates to those experiences makes for individuality.

Childhood is not a waiting room for adulthood but the place where adulthood is shaped by one's family, peers, society, and, most importantly, the person one is becoming. The passage from childhood to adulthood is a significant journey for each person. It is no wonder that children's literature is filled with stories about growing up in our society today.

Living in a Family

Within the family the human personality is nurtured; here the growing child learns of love and hate, fear and courage, joy and sorrow. The first "family-life" stories tended to portray life without moments of anger and hurt, emphasizing only the happy or adventurous moments. Today the balance scale has tilted in the other direction, and it is often more difficult to find a family story with well-adjusted children and happily married parents than it is to find a story about family problems.

In earlier stories like Eleanor Estes's pretelevision era books *The Moffats, The Middle Moffat,* and *Rufus M.,* parents tend to recede into the background and the emphasis is on the children's fun and problems. Elizabeth Enright's *The Saturdays* protrays the close-knit Melendy children in New York in the early 1940s. Sidney Taylor's *All-of-a-Kind Family* series recreates family life in a Lower East Side Jewish home in the 1930s. Titled "all-of-a-kind" because all are girls until a baby boy comes along, the children understand that this also means that they are Jewish and "we're all close and loving and loyal—and our family will always be that." Descriptions of Jewish feasts and holy days contribute much to readers' understanding of one family's religious faith. Children still enjoy these series, set as they are in the "olden days," and adults often point to them as evidence of the pleasures of a less fast-paced life.

However, many young readers prefer stories about today's children, those they might meet in the neighborhood, the shopping center, a playground, or the classroom. More recent books include adults with both strengths and weaknesses and show children interacting with them. Formula stories depict parents and adults as completely inept and unable to cope with or understand their children. If children are to see life wholly and gain some perspective from their reading, educators must help children balance their reading choices.

FAMILY RELATIONSHIPS

Episodic stories centered comfortably in a warm family setting are often the first chapter-book stories younger children read independently. Young readers who more readily follow episodic rather than complicated plots find Johanna Hurwitz's stories about *Russell and Elisa* satisfying reading. Chapters alternate between 4-year-old Elisa and her older brother Russell who is 7. When Elisa receives a rag doll as a present, she names it "Airmail" after she opens it at the post office. Russell offers to give it a haircut but settles

Ann Strugnell depicts Julian's father as he dramatically whips up a pudding that tastes "like a raft of lemons, like a night on the sea" in Ann Cameron's *The Stories Julian Tells*.

🐇 🐇 🐇

instead on trimming the hair of Elisa's best friend, Annie, which gets him into trouble. Hurwitz portrays character through authentic dialogue and description of the small tensions that make up many children's lives. Sibling rivalry, an older child's scorn for the younger one and the younger one's revenge, and exasperated but patient parents who set limits and warn of consequences are familiar to most readers. Hurwitz also creates stories about *Busybody Nora* and her brother *Superduper Teddy* who share the same apartment building with Russell. These stories are just right for readers who want to read or hear read aloud "longer books."

Ann Cameron's "Julian" tales begin with *The Stories Julian Tells* but may be read in any order as they chronicle the daily doings of Julian, his gullible younger brother, and their best friend Gloria. The humorous stories reflect children's universal concerns, such as losing teeth, telling fibs, imaginations working overtime when viewing post office "most-wanted" posters, compassion for dogs locked in hot cars in the summertime, and mastering a two-wheeler. Both of Julian's African-American parents keep track of his activities, but Julian's automobile repairman father is portrayed with special warmth in Cameron's stories and in the illustrations by various artists.

Following in a similar tradition, Christine McDonnell presents six chapters in the lives of first grader Ivy and her school friend the obstreperous Leo in *Don't Be Mad, Ivy*. Ivy's dilemmas, such as her reluctance to part with a toy bulldozer that is a birthday present to another child, or her "borrowing" of a friend's stuffed bear, are very true to 6- and 7-year olds. Leo's story is told in *Toad Food and Measle Soup;* the title represents his misinterpretation of his mother's vegetarian venturing into cooking with tofu and miso soup. In *Lucky Charms and Birthday Wishes*, Emily starts a new school year, discovers an intriguing dollhouse, and for her birthday receives a handmade rag doll that becomes an important link with her grandmother. *Just for the Summer* develops further the friendship of Emily, Ivy, and Lydia, whose father is in the hospital. Cameron, Hurwitz, and McDonnell write sensitive, perceptive, and often humorous stories about the lives of 6- to 9-year-olds.

Beverly Cleary's perennially popular and humorous stories about Ramona are enjoyed both by 7- to 9-year-olds who identify with Ramona's problems, and by 10- and 11-year-olds who remember "how I used to be." Cleary's stories concern "the problems which are small to adults but which loom so large in the lives of children, the sort of problems children can solve themselves."[10] In *Ramona the Pest*, Ramona can hardly wait for kindergarten to begin so that she can share her doll with the green hair, named "Chevrolet" after her aunt's car. The green hair is a result of the doll's encounter with soap and Dutch Cleanser. In *Ramona and Her Mother*, Ramona worries that her mother doesn't love her

[10]Beverly Cleary, "The Laughter of Children," *The Horn Book Magazine*, vol. 58 (October 1982), p. 557.

as much as she loves Beezus, her older sister. *Ramona and Her Father* are more frequently together now that she returns from school to find him waiting for telephone calls about jobs he has applied for. She is embarrassed about the makeshift sheep costume her overworked mother creates for her role in the Christmas pageant. However, the advice of "The Three Wise Persons" helps her change her mind. In *Ramona Forever*, Ramona's favorite aunt marries, the family's pet cat dies, and Mrs. Quimby expects a new baby. After the family thinks of all kinds of appropriate male names, Roberta arrives. Still a third grader, but a more mature *older* sister now, Ramona continues to be her irrepressible dra-

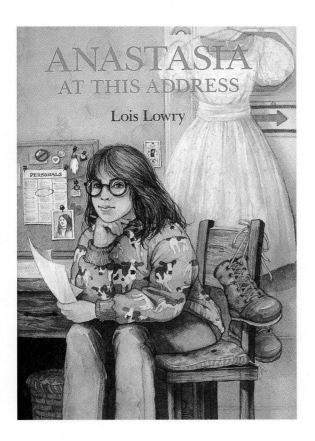

Anastasia contemplates answering an ad in the personals column of her father's magazine in Diane de Groat's jacket for Lois Lowry's *Anastasia at This Address.*

matic self. Ramona and her family are people worth knowing.

Lois Lowry's *Anastasia Krupnik* is the only girl in fourth grade whose name will not fit on the front of a sweatshirt. During Poetry Week at school, her teacher prefers the rhymed doggerel of her classmates to Anastasia's free verse. And to top off the list of "Things I Love/Things I Hate" that Anastasia keeps, one of the things she is sure she is going to hate is the arrival of a new baby brother. In an effort to appease her, Anastasia's parents let her choose the baby's name and she considers the worst one possible. But the death of her grandmother gives Anastasia some thoughts about the importance of family and of memories—and the new baby becomes Sam after her grandfather, who Anastasia knows only through the reminiscences of her grandmother. Anastasia's ever-changing lists appear at the end of each chapter and are humorous exclamation points to the preceding events. Each succeeding novel in the Anastasia series chronicles some new quandary—a move to the suburbs of Boston, a stint as a maid, a growing need to talk to someone who understands, and managing the household while her mother is away. In Lowry's stories, the Krupnik parents treat Anastasia and her brother with openness, humor, and respect; they are both literate and concerned parents whose careers as artist and English teacher do not interfere with their interactions with Anastasia. Lowry has a gift for natural-sounding dialogue and situational humor, anchored by keen observations of human nature and family relationships. She has also told baby brother Sam's story in the hilarious *All About Sam* and *Attaboy, Sam.*

In Claudia Mills's story, *Dynamite Dinah* is the performing artist of fifth grade. That is, she does anything for attention from waltzing with a wet mop in the school hall to going out the window to dance on the roof when the substitute teacher isn't watching. But Dinah's crowning moment, the memorization of Edna St. Vincent Millay's "Renascence," is eclipsed by the arrival of her new baby brother. As her distracted parents struggle to organize a now chaotic household, Dinah faces feelings of jealousy and loneliness, disappointment over not being chosen as the lead in a class play, and her best friend's exasperated accusation that "you only have one topic: yourself." When Dinah takes her brother for a walk, her angry inner monologue causes her to trip and let his stroller loose in the street. A near catastrophe shocks Dinah into contrition and the long climb back from her depression and self-centeredness to a new appreciation of her friends, her family, and finally herself in this warm and satisfying story.

A very different family life is portrayed by Paula Fox in *The Stone-Faced Boy*. Gus, a middle child, has learned to keep an expressionless face when his brothers and sisters tease him, thus earning himself the nickname "stone-face." During a snowstorm, his visiting great-aunt gives him a geode. That night Gus is talked into rescuing a stray dog that his sister has found in a fox trap. Although Gus is terrified, he does rescue the dog and the experience changes him so that when his brother goads him to break open the geode, he refuses:

> ❧ He knew how the stone would look inside, but he didn't choose to break it open yet. When he felt like it, he would take the hammer and tap the geode in such a way that is would break perfectly. . . .[11]

For behind Gus's stone face lies a personality as intact and as perfect as the crystals of the geode.

No book has revealed the complexities of sibling rivalry with as much depth as Katherine Paterson's challenging Newbery award-winning story, *Jacob Have I Loved*. Louise is convinced that she lives in her twin sister's shadow. Caroline, her beautiful, blond, delicate sister, is the talented one who leaves their island home of Rass each week to take piano lessons. Louise, or "Wheeze," the hated name Caroline has given her, believes her sister has stolen everything from her: her parents' affection, her friends Call and the Captain, and her chance for an education. Her half-crazed Bible-quoting grandmother recognizes her burning resentment of Caroline and taunts her with the quote "Jacob have I loved but Esau have I hated." Louise is horrified when she looks

up the passage to find that the speaker is God. So now, like the biblical Esau, even God must see her as the despised elder twin.

Paterson has skillfully woven the Bible story of Esau, first born, who was tricked into giving up his birthright to Jacob, the younger of the twin brothers, into this modern novel of sibling rivalry. Only maturity and a family of her own can help Louise to put her hatred and resentment of her sister to rest. The novel ends on a theme of reconciliation as Louise, now a midwife in a mountain community, fights to save the life of the weaker second-born baby of a pair of twins. In her Newbery acceptance speech for *Jacob Have I Loved*, the author, herself the middle child of five, said: " . . . among children who grow up together in a family there run depths of feeling that will permeate their souls for good and ill as long as they live."[12]

EXTENDED FAMILIES

The extended family of grandparents, uncles, aunts, or cousins often plays a significant role in a child's developing perception of the world. Children's literature presents other adults, and sometimes even children, acting in the place of absent or incapacitated parents.

In Eleanor Clymer's book the responsibility for *My Brother Stevie* is given to 12-year-old Annie Jenner. In fact, the last thing her mother told Annie before she left was to "Take care of your brother." Stevie is 8 years old and "full of the devil." Grandmother, who has reluctantly taken the children to live with her in a big city project apartment, can't cope with Stevie, either. He breaks into candy machines and throws rocks at trains, and Annie is frightened. Then Stevie gets a new teacher, Miss Stover, and Annie has someone who can help her with him. Stevie does behave better in school until suddenly Miss Stover moves away, and Stevie reverts to his old ways. Annie devises a desperate scheme resulting in a train ride to Miss Stover's house in the country. Stevie changes, but so, too, does his grandmother, as Annie's notes show:

---

[11]Paula Fox, *The Stone-Faced Boy*, illustrated by Donald A. Mackay (Englewood Cliffs, N.J.: Bradbury, 1968), p. 106.

[12]Katherine Paterson, "Newbery Medal Acceptance" in *Gates of Excellence* (New York: Elsevier/Nelson Books, 1981), p. 118.

🐦 So now everything is pretty much the same as before, but not quite the same, because as I said, we did this thing [the train ride] and it made us all a little different.[13]

This is an honest, realistic story that shows the influence of each character on the others.

Ann Cameron tells of 7-year-old Juan who lives in *The Most Beautiful Place in the World* in Guatemala where strollers talking in the street may interrupt traffic. "Stories are important, and cars aren't," he says. His young mother has remarried and since her new husband can't support Juan, he moves in with his grandmother. Grandmother owns her own four-room cement-block house and makes her living by selling *arroz con leche* in the market every day. Three uncles, some cousins, and other family members live with her when they are sick, out of work, or not getting along in their own families. Grandmother puts Juan to work helping her in the marketplace and when Juan is about 5, he becomes a shoeshine boy. As he waits for customers, he practices reading on scraps of newspaper, produce signs, and other print that comes his way. When Juan asks to go to school, his grandmother tries to enroll him, but they are nearly turned away until the next year. Juan shows that he has learned to read and is quickly placed in second grade. When his grandmother explains why she never went to school, Juan realizes how important an education could have been to her. He may live in the most beautiful place in the world, as the travel poster says, but he knows that truly the best place is where someone like his grandmother loves him. Thomas B. Allen's black line drawings capture the warmth of Juan's life, yet the artist also reveals the cold realities of the boy's poverty and abandonment.

Patricia MacLachlan's *Arthur for the Very First Time* chronicles the summer of a 10-year-old boy. From the moment his parents drop Arthur at the farm of his idiosyncratic Uncle Wrisby and Aunt Elda ("shaped like an uncertain circle, made up of large shifting spaces like an easy-to-color coloring book"), he begins to change. His aunt and uncle speak French to a pet chicken, sing to a pig,

and allow Arthur to check off the foods he doesn't like to eat. Always an observer, Arthur keeps copious notes in his journal: "I write about people, things I see, everything I think about," he tells his uncle. Uncle Wrisby is not impressed. Neither is his new friend Moira. Refusing to call Arthur anything but "Mouse," she accuses him of spending so much time writing in his journal that he doesn't really see what is going on around him. Arthur engineers and builds a pigpen and is justifiably proud. When he saves a piglet from dying and protects its mother from the rain with Moira's help, she later excitedly tells everyone "Arthur did it . . . Arthur really *did* it." She has called him "Arthur" for the very first time. MacLachlan's story is full of warmth, humor, and quirky characters, both human and animal. While the book has much to say about the values of *doing* as opposed to *observing*, it also suggests that what is important or real is often at first difficult to see. Her writing respects readers' intelligence.

In Betsy Byars's *The House of Wings*, Sammy's parents leave him behind with his aged grandfather, a recluse in an old run-down house, while they go ahead to find a place to stay in Detroit. When Sammy refuses to believe his parents have left and tries to follow them, the old man runs after the furious boy. But in the midst of the chase he calls him to come and look at a wounded crane. Together the two of them catch the crane and care for it. Suddenly the boy desperately wants his grandfather to know him the way he knows birds:

🐦 He wanted his grandfather to be able to pick him out of a thousand birds the way he could pick out the blackbird, the owls, the wild ducks. . . . He said, "My name's Sammy."[14]

His grandfather looks at Sammy and then, instead of calling him "Boy," calls him "Sammy," and the relationship is sealed. This is one of Betsy Byars's best books. Her two characters are well drawn: the eccentric old man, more interested in birds than in his grandson; the boy Sammy, furious at being left, uncertain of himself, and desperately wanting to love and be loved.

[13]Eleanor Clymer, *My Brother Stevie* (New York: Holt, Rinehart and Winston, 1967), p. 75.

[14]Betsy Byars, *The House of Wings*, illustrated by Daniel Schwartz (New York: Viking, 1972), p. 141.

A memorable girl is Eleanor Cameron's main character in *That Julia Redfern*. Julia throws herself into her activities, whether borrowing her older brother's bicycle or "skinning the rabbit" on the playground climber. "You live too hard, Julia," says her mother, and her grandmother clearly disapproves of Julia. One day, after Julia falls and knocks herself out, she dreams a curious dream about her father, who is away in World War I. In it, he tells her to "remember to tell Mama to go through my papers." Julia's dream results in the posthumous publication of her father's short story. Julia's imaginative gifts flower in *Julia and the Hand of God*, when she is given an elegant leather-bound journal as a twelfth birthday present by her favorite uncle. There she chronicles a falling-out with her friend Maisie for so simple an act as cremating a mouse in Maisie's mother's saucepan and her escape from a forest fire in the Berkeley hills. *A Room Made of Windows* is the way Julia describes her new room when her family moves into a new house where she begins to develop her perception as well as her writing skills. *The Private Worlds of Julia Redfern* follows Julia to high school and chronicles her increasing awareness of the vagaries of the adult world. Cameron's superb writing allows the reader to share not only Julia's world but also her unique perception of it. Potential readers of the series should be alerted to the fact that *Julia's Magic* and *That Julia Redfern*, written more recently than the other titles mentioned, take readers back to Julia's early childhood.

Both Rachel's mother and grandmother have warned Rachel not to question her great-grandmother Nana Sashie about the past. But in Kathryn Lasky's *The Night Journey*, old Nana Sashie wants to talk about her family's escape from Russia and suddenly Rachel is drawn into an exciting tale of family history. At age 9, Sashie and her family fled from Russian czarist persecution of the Jews in 1900. Lasky wisely frames Nana Sashie's story in a contemporary family setting complete with Rachel's trials over a school drama production. Chapters alternate; one is set in the present, and the next is part of Nana Sashie's continuing story about the family's flight from Russia disguised as Purim players, intinerant actors who recreate the ancient story of Queen

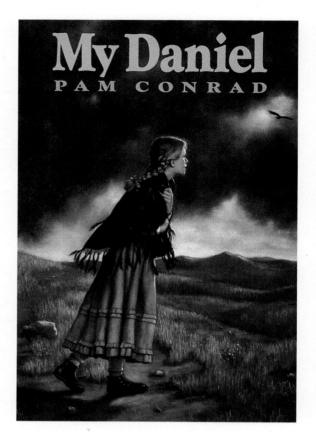

In a flashback from the present, 12-year-old Julia races an impending Nebraska storm to find her brother who is guarding newly discovered dinosaur bones in *My Daniel* by Pam Conrad.

Jacket by Darryl S. Zudeck.

Esther's saving of her people. Readers who might not readily be interested in historical fiction are gently moved in that direction, as is Rachel. Trina Schart Hyman's bold black-and-white drawings help children visualize places, characters, and possessions like the family samovar, which plays an important role in both past and present time. This is an excellent story to read aloud to fifth or sixth graders in conjunction with a study of family history.

Another story of family history neatly framed in the present is Pam Conrad's *My Daniel*. More complex in the telling than the previous novel, it concerns the pilgrimage of the 80-year-old Julia

Creath Summerwaite to a natural history museum back east where the bones of a dinosaur her brother once discovered now lie. In the course of a day, Julia takes her grandchildren, Ellie and Stevie, to the museum and tells them bits about her brother Daniel, silently recalls other moments, and gradually reveals to the children how he died. Daniel had discovered fossilized bones at a time when museums were battling for their possession and wrote to a field paleontologist, Mr. Crow, so that he might claim a reward and pay off the mortgage on the family's Nebraska farm. But prairie lightning killed Daniel and a dinosaur "claim jumper" tried to steal the bones before they could come safely into the hands of Crow. For the young Julia, parting with the bones meant parting with something precious:

> ❦ I was suddenly alone in the creek for the last time with the bones. All alone, and I was sad. I guess in my deepest heart I didn't want them taking the dinosaur. . . . I stood there and remembered tumbling down the bank with Daniel and seeing these old bones for the first time. A sob squeezed my ribs, and I wrapped my arms around myself for comfort.[15]

In the novel's enigmatic climax, Julia once more greets Daniel after passing on to the two children her own family secrets. This powerful story about Julia's life on the prairie and her love for her brother also captures the time when the discovery of dinosaur bones was beginning to suggest to humankind the evolution of life on the planet. Some readers will classify this novel, like time-slip fantasies, as historical fiction.

Thirteen-year-old Jane Tucker, *The Outside Child* in Nina Bawden's novel, has lived differently from other people. Instead of a proper family, she has lived with her two loving but eccentric aunts for as long as she can remember. But when she discovers a photograph of two other children while visiting her father's ship, she learns of Annabel and George, the children of her father's second marriage. With her best friend, an asthmatic outsider named Plato Jones, Jane

locates the family on the other side of London, spies on them, and finally meets them without telling her aunts. Jane's plan has near tragic results when her stepmother recognizes the melody a gift music box plays and realizes that this now grown child is the one she refused to raise ten years ago. Even though Jane repairs her relationship with her aunts and her father's wife apologizes for her outbursts, at the end of the novel, Jane sees the adult world and her own family a little less idealistically. Like Katherine Paterson, Nina Bawden suggests that what people most often wish for is not necessarily what is best for them.

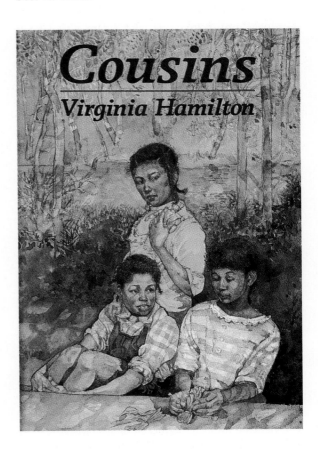

Cammy's relationships with members of her extended family help her work through her grief and guilt following the death of a cousin in Virginia Hamilton's *Cousins*.

Jacket illustration by Jerry Pinkney.

[15]Pam Conrad, *My Daniel* (New York: Harper & Row, 1989), p. 124.

Among Virginia Hamilton's many books are those that draw on her family experiences as part of the fifth generation of free African Americans to have lived in southern Ohio. *Cousins* is, on one level, the story of 10-year-old Cammy who is consumed with jealousy for her beautiful and probably bulimic cousin, Patty Ann. During a summer camp outing, Patty Ann disappears in a sinkhole of a fast-moving river after saving another cousin from drowning, and Cammy is convinced the death is her fault for having hated this perfect cousin so much. But on another level *Cousins* is a story about how interconnected tensions, complex relationships, and surprising discoveries can nurture and sustain each member of an extended family. Cammy loves her old Gram Tut who is now in a nursing home. Despite her divorced mother's warnings to stay away from the nursing home, she visits frequently on her own. When Cammy cannot overcome her guilt and grief, it is the presence of her estranged father and the promise that she may know him better in the future as well as her grandmother's temporary homecoming that help Cammy begin to cope with Patty Ann's death. "You got to stop this. . . . We, left behind . . . have to go ahead on," Gram Tut whispers to Cammy. Children who are just beginning to discover the rich and often confusing network of family relationships will appreciate the support Cammy's family gives to her. *Zeely*, another story set in Ohio, concerns 11-year-old Geeder Perry's need to make a Watusi queen out of Zeely Taber, a herder of pigs. It is Zeely who convinces Geeder that real beauty comes from accepting yourself and others for what they are.

Cynthia Voigt's saga about the Tillerman family spans at least six novels as it fills in the events of several families' lives in a small Chesapeake Bay town. *Homecoming* introduces 13-year-old Dicey Tillerman who, along with her two younger brothers and a younger sister, was abandoned in the parking lot of a Connecticut shopping mall by her mentally ill mother. Dicey decides the children must walk south along the Connecticut shoreline to Bridgeport to live with an aunt. But the aunt has died and her daughter, Cousin Eunice, wants to divide the family into foster homes. From Eunice, Dicey discovers that they have a grandmother living in Maryland.

Determined to keep her family together, Dicey manages against all odds to reach her grandmother's home on the Chesapeake Bay, only to find an eccentric, independent, and angry old lady. The children try to keep up the huge run-down house and garden and quickly grow to love the place. But they are less sure of their grandmother. Ten-year-old James asks Dicey:

> "Do you like her?" Dicey considered this. "You know? I could. I mean, she's so odd and prickly. She fights us, or anyway I feel like I'm fighting her and she's fighting back, as if we both know what's going on but neither of us is saying anything. It's fun . . . but she's a good enemy—you know? . . . So she might make a good friend."[16]

This believable survival story ends with a tentative understanding formed between Gram and the children. In the sequel, *Dicey's Song*, each child has the time to grow. Nine-year-old Maybeth tackles her reading problem and proves to have a beautiful singing voice, James struggles with balancing his bookish tendencies with his need for friendship, and 6-year-old Sammy's belligerence is gradually subdued by Gram's strong will and courage. However, the novel belongs to Dicey. She must learn to let her family change, accept her own move toward maturity, and acknowledge her feelings for others. It is the growing warmth the Tillermans take on as they learn to be a family that lets the children, and the reader, accept their mother's death at the story's end.

Other stories in the Tillerman saga include *A Solitary Blue*, the story of Jeff Green, a minor character in *Dicey's Song*. Again the story is about the gradual development of a loving relationship, this one between Jeff and his uncommunicative father. Two young adult novels continue the story. *The Runner* tells of Dicey's mother's brother whose defiance is echoed in the character of Sammy, Dicey's brother. *Seventeen Against the Dealer* returns to Dicey, now 21, and her dream of owning her own boatyard, which nearly crowds out what is truly important. In all of her novels about the Tillerman family, Voigt explores love

---

[16]Cynthia Voigt, *Homecoming* (New York: Atheneum, 1981), p. 289.

in its many forms—love that can't be expressed, learning to love, manipulative love, and family love.

FAMILIES IN TRANSITION

The 1990 U.S. census report found that one-fourth of American children live in single-parent families. In addition, although a majority of suburban children live with married parents, as many as two-thirds of city children do not. Nearly one out of every two marriages now ends in divorce. It is only natural, then, that books acknowledge children's attempts to deal with the disruption and confusion or pain and anger that often result.

Beverly Cleary won the Newbery award for *Dear Mr. Henshaw*, the story of Leigh Botts, a child of divorce. The plot is skillfully revealed through a series of letters to an author, Mr. Henshaw. Required to write a letter to his favorite author, sixth-grade Leigh writes Mr. Henshaw and asks for an immediate answer to ten questions. Mr. Henshaw responds with ten questions of his own. In the process of answering these questions (his mother says he has to) Leigh reveals how much he misses his truck-driver father and Bandit, his dog; his concern over who is stealing food from his lunch box; and his many attempts to write a prize story for the yearbook. While not as humorous as some of Beverly Cleary's other books, this one is more thoughtful and certainly presents an honest picture of a child living in a single-parent home. Leigh learns that there are some things he can't control (like his parents getting back together again), but he does figure out a way to scare away the lunch box thief and receives not first place but honorable mention for his story titled "A Day on Dad's Rig." Cleary's ear for portraying the way children think and speak is remarkably true.

Cleary's *Strider*, a buoyant sequel, begins four years later. Leigh is a high school student, a track runner, and still writes in his diary. When he and his best friend Barry discover an abandoned dog on the beach, they name it Strider and agree to have "joint ownership." The dog rests his foot on Leigh's and follows him wherever he goes. Leigh's hurt over his father's abandonment is also lessened by his new friend, a redheaded girl hurdler, and his success in school. But Leigh's spe-

cial bond with the new dog causes him to have a falling-out with Barry before the two reach a new agreement. Middle schoolers will enjoy this sequel but Paul O. Zelinsky's many black line illustrations seem designed to appeal to even younger readers.

Judy Blume's character Karen Newman thinks it is the end of the world when her father decides to go to Las Vegas to get a divorce. Suddenly she decides that if she could only get her parents together, they would change their minds. Her plan of showing them her Viking diorama isn't very successful, but when her brother Jeff runs away, they have to get together. Karen then learns that some very nice people are just impossible when they are together. She finds out that as much as she thought divorce was the awful end, *It's Not the End of the World*. This is one of Blume's best books. The characters are well realized, and she has realistically described the tension of the situation. In typical Blume fashion, real humor relieves the seriousness of the problem. *I, Trissy* by Norma Fox Mazer is also a girl's first-person account of the problems of being caught somewhere between divorced parents. Simultaneously funny and heartbreaking, this is another popular "divorce story" for middle graders.

Phyllis Reynolds Naylor's entertaining series about Alice, beginning with *The Agony of Alice*, is not about life after divorce but is instead about making one's own way toward adulthood without a mother's guidance. Alice, an 11-year-old whose mother died when she was 4, is searching for a female role model. Her father and 19-year-old brother are no help when it comes to buying jeans or bras, and she longs for a mother to help explain what being a teenager is all about. Like Anastasia Krupnik, Alice keeps lists of her successes and failures as she casts around for someone on whom to model her life. She hopes to be placed in a young and beautiful teacher's sixth-grade class but instead ends up with Mrs. Plotkin, shaped like "a human pear." But much to Alice's surprise, it is the human pear who becomes the hoped-for role model. In *Alice in Rapture, Sort Of*, Alice must work out for herself how she feels about her first romance with Peter, an old, good friend, because her understanding and loving father simply cannot answer questions about kissing and dating. *Reluctantly Alice* and *All but Alice* follow the sociable and forthright Alice into seventh grade. Realistic dialogue, humor, and the message that most people have to work out for themselves the answers to important questions give these stories high reader appeal.

Betsy Byars frequently writes about children who live in single-parent families and are often left on their own. While adult intervention eventually helps allay a crisis, Byars's main characters generally work things out for themselves while realizing a "little moment of growth." Eleven-year-old *Cracker Jackson* suspects his much loved former babysitter Alma is being abused by her husband. With his best friend Goat's help, he tries to drive his mother's car and take Alma to a shelter. In a classic response of battered women, Alma backs out and returns home. Cracker seeks help from his flight attendant mother, but it is nearly too late to save Alma's life. *The Night Swimmers* are three children who sneak into neighbors' pools under cover of darkness. They are raising themselves while their father tries to pursue a career as a country-western singer. Retta cares for her two younger brothers but is having trouble letting them become more self-reliant. It is only when the youngest nearly drowns that she realizes things can't go on as they have been. *The Animal, The Vegetable & John D Jones* explores the tentative blending of two families, one with a pair of sisters, and the other with the insufferable John D who, up to now, has the "constant companionship of the most intelligent, witty, and creative person in the world—himself." A keen ear for dialogue, deft flashbacks that reveal character, humor, and an accurate eye for the memorable incidents of childhood typify the novels by Betsy Byars.

The Pinballs, also by Byars, deals with three children who have been placed in a foster home. Carlie is a tough, likable 12-year-old girl who has been repeatedly beaten up by her third stepfather. She endures her world by watching television and making caustic comments. Harvey comes to the Masons' in a wheelchair because his alcoholic father accidentally ran him over and broke both his legs. The third child in this mismatched group is Thomas J., an 8-year-old boy going on 80. Elderly twin spinsters had tried to

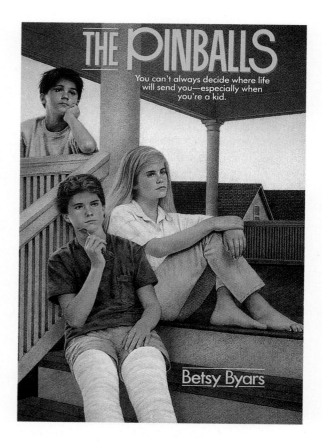

Betsy Byars uses the concept of pinballs as a metaphor for three foster children shot into the maze of society in *The Pinballs*.

Jacket by Richard Williams.

raise him without notifying the authorities, so Thomas J. had never gone to school. Carlie maintains that they are all "'. . . just like pinballs. Somebody put a dime and punched a button and out we come, ready or not, and settled in the same groove.'"[17] By the end of the story, Carlie has learned that life is determined not only by blind chance but also by initiative, for it is her creative planning that finally breaks through Harvey's depression and gives him some reason to live. By including Thomas J. in her plans, Carlie makes him feel important, too. Carlie's change, from a defensive, self-centered person to

[17]Betsy Byars, *The Pinballs* (New York: Harper & Row, 1977), p. 29.

a compassionate human being, is gradual and believable, and she never loses her comical perspective on life. Middle-grade students enjoy hearing this story read aloud and meeting this fine cast of characters.

In Katherine Paterson's story, *The Great Gilly Hopkins*, Gilly is not nearly the likable character that Carlie is. When Gilly arrives at her next foster home, she can't bear the huge, semiliterate Maime Trotter and her "retard" 7-year-old ward. So she sends a letter to her beautiful mother in California greatly exaggerating her situation. When she steals over a hundred dollars of Trotter's foster-care money and tries to buy a ticket to California, she is stopped by the police. Finally she understands the real love and trust that Trotter has for her as she refuses to let the social worker move Gilly to yet another home. It is too late, however, as Gilly receives an answer to her letter in the form of a visit from her grandmother who she never knew existed. Desperately sad about leaving Trotter, Gilly learns then that one has to accept responsibility for one's own actions. One of the consistent themes in Paterson's writings is that main characters always get their wishes—but not in the way they expected.[18] At the end of the story Gilly's wish for a real home comes true, but it is a home with her grandmother, not with Courtney, the beautiful idealized mother she has created in her dreams. However, life with Maime Trotter, in which she had learned to accept and give love for the first time, made her ready for her real family. The reader knows that Gilly is capable of healing the hurt in Nonnie's life and that her own will be healed in the process. These larger-than-life characters are superbly drawn and most believable. Children delight in the swearing, self-sufficient young Gilly, but they admire the more mature Gilly who has to learn her lessons the hard way.

Living with Others

Three- and 4-year-olds show momentary concern for their sandbox companions, but it is usually

[18]Christy Richards Slavik, "The Novels of Katherine Paterson: Implications for the Middle School." Unpublished Ph.D. dissertation, Ohio State University, 1983.

only when children go to school that the peer group becomes important. By the time children approach the middle of elementary school, what other children think is often more significant than what parents, teachers, or other adults think. By the time children reach middle or junior high school, the peer group and making friends are all important.

FINDING PEER ACCEPTANCE

A classic example of children's cruelty to others who are "different" is the well-known, somewhat didactic story of *The Hundred Dresses* by Eleanor Estes. Wanda, a poor Polish girl, attempts unsuccessfully to win a place in the group by telling of the hundred dresses she owns. It is only after she moves away, and the hundred dresses—all drawings—are displayed, that her peers understand that their cowardice in not befriending Wanda and their meanness have deprived them of both a friend and their own self-respect.

Louise Fitzhugh's *Harriet the Spy* has also achieved the status of a modern classic. It is the story of a precocious child who finds it difficult to relate to both her parents and her peers. Harriet tells her own story, interspersed with her notes about people she observes at school and after school. Her babysitter, Ole Golly, has been Harriet's consistent source of security, and when she leaves, Harriet's loneliness is compounded when her classmates find her journal. The underlying theme of this 30-year-old story is still relevant today. It contains serious statements about how children respond to teachers, to cliques, and to each other.

In two books by Mary Stolz, the same characters and events are examined from different points of view. In the first story, *A Dog on Barkham Street*, Edward is frightened of Martin, the bully next door, who threatens him each day. When his uncle comes with his collie dog to visit the family, he helps Edward learn how to handle a bully. When he leaves, he gives Edward what he has always wanted, his own dog. In the other book, *The Bully of Barkham Street*, the reader learns that Martin Hastings had once had a dog but that his parents had given it away when Martin had failed to care for it. Then the reader knows why Martin is so resentful of Edward and his collie dog. Martin, now 13 years old and an ex-bully, struggles to lose his old reputation in *The Explorer of Barkham Street*. His teacher has introduced him to the joys of reading (and day-dreaming) about explorers. While old problems continue to plague Martin, he begins to understand that he can be an explorer, and the discovery will be his own real self. Although there are touching scenes and a satisfying end, there is little action or suspense. Instead, this book may be enjoyed for its characters, vivid imagery, and lively dialogue. A rich discussion could center on Martin's fears and dreams, how these changed, and why.

MAKING FRIENDS

The theme of building friendships is often a part of realistic fiction. Stories about life in families often include one child's relationship with someone outside the home. Popular fiction traces the ups and downs of friendships in the classroom. Other stories, such as Nina Bawden's *The Outside Child*, Lois Lowry's *Rabble Starkey*, Ann Cameron's *Julian's Glorious Summer*, or Beverly Cleary's depiction of Ramona, Howie, and "Yard Ape," have multiple themes besides the tentative ways boys and girls form important friendships.

Johanna Hurwitz warmly portrays the friendship that develops between Aldo Sossi and DeDe in *Aldo Applesauce*. These two fifth-grade friends tolerate each other's differences: DeDe has trouble accepting her parents' divorce and Aldo has decided to be a vegetarian. Other books in the series include *Aldo Peanut Butter*, a humorous account of the year Aldo wishes for a dog for his eleventh birthday and receives not one but five of them.

Two other fifth-grade friendships are presented in Betsy Byars's *The Cybil War;* the first is a long-standing one between Simon Newton and Cybil Ackerman, and the other is a rocky one between Simon and his boastful, lying friend, Tony Angotti. While both boys vie for Cybil's attention, Tony tricks her into going out on a first date with him. However, his scheme backfires for Cybil recognizes Tony's true nature. Simon's triumphant bicycle ride with Cybil provides a satisfying conclusion to this lighthearted tale of friendship.

Wallis Greene has moved too many times and hates the prospect of trying to make friends in her new suburban neighborhood where all the streets are named for flowers and the houses all look alike. In Ellen Conford's novel, Wallis would do *Anything for a Friend*. She finally does make friends, including an unwanted one, only to discover the family is to move again. Wallis is angry and disappointed until she begins to realize that if she has made friends here, she can do it once more. Frequently, authors such as Conford, Judy Blume, and Paula Danziger have included the development of peer relationships and friendships as one of the themes in their popular novels about and for 10- to 14-year-olds.

Almost all children long for a "special friend," someone to pal around with, to call on the phone, or to "sleep over" with. *A Girl Called Al* by Constance Greene turns out to be this kind of friend for the unnamed narrator of her story. The two girls become fast friends; their second best friend is Mr. Richards, the assistant superintendent of their building. He lets them strap rags to their shoes and skate on his kitchen floor to polish it. And when the school won't let Al take shop, he helps both girls build a bookshelf. The girls find him after he has a heart attack and get Al's mother to call the doctor. They visit him once in the hospital before he dies in his sleep one night. Their friendship with each other and Mr. Richards is a part of their growing-up process. The first-person telling of this story adds to its contemporary sound and enables Greene to portray complex feelings and relationships with ease and humor.

Emily Blair is an only child until the summer when she and her mother and father move into an eighteen-room house and her four cousins come to stay with them. Not only does Emily have an instant family but she discovers Kate, a very special person who writes poetry as Emily does. In *Look Through My Window*, Jean Little has created the life that an only child might hope for. This is an affectionate story with real characters who come alive. Passages that are serendipitous for book lovers are Emily and Kate's rapt discussions about the books they love. In *Kate*, a sequel, the difficulties of friendship is one theme; Kate's search for her identity through her father's Jewish background becomes another. Kate also reveals her thoughts in poetry and prose in *Hey World, Here I Am!*

Characters in Zilpha Keatley Snyder's books are often intelligent children from differing backgrounds who develop strong friendships. In *The Egypt Game*, six young children in a Berkeley, California, neighborhood set up an imaginary game in an abandoned storage yard based on their research into the ceremonies and culture of ancient Egypt. When one of the game players is attacked and another neighborhood child is murdered, the children's outdoor play is curtailed until near Halloween. In this mystery, Snyder leads readers to believe that a junk dealer/professor who owns the storage yard is the murderer. But he is instrumental in apprehending the criminal, which forces the children to reconsider their appraisal of him. The children continue their friendship, this time with a game based on "Gypsies."

Snyder's *Libby on Wednesday* is about an 11-year-old who, because of her home schooling in the hands of well-educated adults, is placed in the eighth grade. Her actress mother, away in New York, thinks Libby needs to be "socialized." But Libby hates school because she is ridiculed for her height and intelligence. When she wins a writing competition and is placed in a five-person writers' group, she later retreats to her Victorian treehouse, a place that seems to confer "a mysterious promise of good news—of magic to be revealed or wishes granted, or sometimes simply of peace restored."[19] There she writes in her journal about the others in her group: Alex, a brilliant parodist with cerebral palsy; Wendy, whose clichéd writing reflects her concern for clothes and boyfriends; Tierney, angry because she did not inherit her family's good looks; and G.G., whose searing sarcasm and angry comments cover his fear of an alcoholic father. As Libby finds the courage to share herself, beginning with a tour of the rundown family mansion and the treehouse her eccentric author/grandfather built, her views of those in her writing group begin to change. Like Madeleine L'Engle, Snyder creates exceptional and gifted child characters whose intelligent thoughts and actions often lead older readers to reflect more widely on their own lives.

[19]Zilpha Keatley Snyder, *Libby on Wednesday* (New York: Delacorte Press, 1990), p. 27.

Life in an Australian school setting forms the backdrop for an absorbing and humorous novel about family relationships and making friends, *Hating Alison Ashley* by Robin Klein. Erica Yurken, known as "Yuk" to her friends and "Erk" to her family, feels totally superior to every single person in her whole elementary school, which is located in a poor blue-collar suburb. However, when the school district is redrawn, the wealthy and elegant Alison Ashley joins the sixth-grade class. The opposite of Erica, Alison is not allowed to eat junk food, dresses impeccably, has perfect school supplies, and worst of all, maintains an even temper and exquisite politeness in spite of Erica's jealousy and the class's general rudeness. Erica's first-person narration is filled with scathing observations, snappy dialogue, candor, and humor. The two girls form a tentative friendship based on Erica's inventions about her own motley family and her fascination with how Alison lives. The friendship ends abruptly when Erica thoughtlessly awakens Alison's mother and hears Alison apologize by saying Erica is "nobody, really. Just a kid from school." However, during a week-long school campout, Erica writes two plays, planning to star in and direct both. When Erica can't act because of stage fright, Alison overcomes her own disappointment at her mother's refusal to attend the play, and takes over. Both girls understand each other and their own imperfect families a little better and make a new start at friendship.

Imaginary play is the basis for a friendship that develops between 10-year-old Jess Aarons, an artistic boy who is a misfit in his family, and Leslie Burke, a newcomer who is a misfit at school. Her parents, both writers, have moved to rural Virginia in pursuit of a simpler lifestyle. In Katherine Paterson's Newbery award book, *Bridge to Terabithia*, these two lonely children invent a kingdom based on Leslie's image of Narnia and other fantasy worlds in literature. Their "Terabithia" is a real place, however, a private hideout in the woods reached by swinging on a rope across a dry creek bed. On a day when spring rains turn the creek into a torrent, Leslie goes alone to their meeting place, falls off the rope swing, and drowns. As Jess works through his complex feelings of grief, he comes to see a

In helping his little sister cross the swollen stream, Jess exercises the new self-confidence that is part of his friend's legacy.

Illustration by Donna Diamond from *Bridge to Terabithia* by Katherine Paterson.

more supportive side of his usually unsympathetic family and realizes that Leslie's gifts to him—a wider perspective and confidence in his own imaginative powers—are gifts that last, and can be shared.

> Now it occurred to him that perhaps Terabithia was like a castle where you came to be knighted. After you stayed for a while and grew strong you had to move on. . . . Now it was time for him to move out. She wasn't there, so he must go for both of them. It was up to him to pay back to the world in beauty and caring what Leslie loaned him in vision and strength.[20]

[20]Katherine Paterson, *Bridge to Terabithia*, illustrated by Donna Diamond (New York: Crowell, 1977), p. 126.

With lumber given him by Leslie's father, Jess builds a bridge to Terabithia, a safe entry for his younger sister May Belle as he leads her into the shining kingdom with the unspoken hope that her world, like his own, will grow. By asking fourth and fifth graders if there are any other "bridges" in this story, teachers have allowed children to discuss the many emotional or metaphorical bridges portrayed in Paterson's beautifully written story.

Cynthia Rylant's *A Fine White Dust* explores, among other themes, a child's development of religious feelings as a part of maturing. Seventh grader Peter Cassidy wishes his parents were more interested in religion. When one morning at breakfast he tells his father, "I think people in town are wondering why you and Mother never go to church," he gets an unsatisfying, and tolerant, answer. Better answers seem to come to him at a revival led by a charismatic Preacher Man who speaks straight to Pete's heart. Pete overflows with emotions he can't express even to his best friend Rufus. After attending the week of evening meetings, he is asked by the Preacher Man to leave with him and become an itinerant preacher, too. Pete packs, rebuffs Rufus, leaves an explanatory note for his parents, and waits at the designated spot. But it is after midnight before Pete realizes the Preacher Man has already left—without him. Rufus, hiding in some bushes, accompanies his friend home. Pete mourns his loss even more deeply when he discovers that the drugstore waitress has run off with the revivalist. Pete maintains his faith, believing that there is some lesson in this experience and while he may not need church, he does need God. His new appreciation of his parents despite their differences makes him better able to accept his own religious uncertainties. In spare prose, this story explores a child's acceptance of differences between himself and his friend, between himself and his family.

Robert Cormier also writes about spirituality and religion in a many-layered story, *Other Bells for Us to Ring*. Eleven-year-old Darcy has never had a best friend before she meets the indomitable Kathleen Mary O'Hara. Darcy's family are Unitarian, but since her father is away serving in World War II, her mother seldom attends church. Intrigued with Kathleen Mary's tales of Catholicism, Darcy goes with her one day to look inside the church. There, Kathleen Mary sprinkles her with holy water and pronounces her a Catholic, "forever and ever, world without end. Amen." Darcy worries about what this means. When she goes to her friend's house to ask, Darcy finds Kathleen Mary hiding from her drunken father. Her two brothers are bruised and subdued. The next time Darcy tries to visit, the family has moved away and Darcy must resolve her many questions by herself. In despair at losing first her best friend and then her father, who is missing in action, Darcy visits an old nun who is supposed to perform miracles. She prays with Darcy for her father's safe return. When Darcy learns from her mother that her father has been injured and will be returning to them, she believes a miracle has happened. On Christmas Eve, hurrying home to a joyful celebration with her parents, Darcy hears the bells of St. Jude ringing, the bells that were to remain silent until the end of the war. No one else hears the bells, however, and Darcy later realizes that her heart had acknowledged the death of her friend, Kathleen Mary, who had at that moment been hit by a car as she fled from her drunken father. Superbly crafted, this novel explores the true nature of prayer and religious belief, friendship and loss, that take place as one child makes the transition to adolescence.

Growing Toward Maturity

In building a concept of self, each person begins to answer such questions as "What kind of person am I?" "How am I changing?" "What do others think of me?" "What are my roles in society?" Based on the experiences they encounter, children begin to see themselves as worthy and successful people who can give and receive love and respect.

As children move toward adulthood, they may experience brief moments of awareness of this growth process. A conversation, an event, or a literary experience may give a child the sudden realization that he or she has taken a step toward maturity. The step may be toward understanding complex human emotions, acknowledgment of sexuality, or acceptance of responsibility for one's

actions. This process of becoming is never easy or painless. In modern realistic fiction, there are models of ordinary boys and girls who find the courage to grow and change, or to stand up for their beliefs.

DEVELOPING SEXUALITY

The first story to discuss menstruation, *The Long Secret* by Louise Fitzhugh, was published in 1965. In it, a girl explains menstruation to her friend in a matter-of-fact manner to correct misinformation the friend's grandmother had given her. None of the girls are pleased with the prospect, but they take some satisfaction that when they have their periods, they'll be able to skip gym. By way of contrast, Margaret, in the story *Are You There, God? It's Me, Margaret*, by Judy Blume, prays for her period because she doesn't want to be the last of her secret club to start menstruating. She regularly does exercises that she hopes will increase her size 28 bust and she practices wearing a sanitary napkin. Mixed with her desire for physical maturation is a search for a meaningful relation with God. Adults find this book very funny and reminiscent of their own preadolescence, but it is extremely serious for 10- and 11-year-old girls who share Margaret's concern for their own physical maturation.

Judy Blume has also written a book about the physical and emotional maturing of a boy, *Then Again, Maybe I Won't*. One strand of the story concerns the sexual awakening of Tony, a 13-year-old boy who is embarrassed and concerned about erection and nocturnal emissions. The other concerns the conflicts that Tony feels about his family's sudden adoption of a new lifestyle when they move from a cramped two-family house in Jersey City to an acre of land on Long Island. The title conveys the same ambiguity as the direction of Tony's life. There is no doubt that Tony has achieved physical maturation, but will he be able to sustain his personal values in the difficult task of growing toward psychological and emotional maturity?

In Brock Cole's remarkable novel *The Goats*, a boy and a girl are stripped of their clothes and left on an island in the night as a summer camp prank. Angry and humiliated, the two outcasts, or "goats," decide not to return to camp and instead to escape from the island. They float ashore holding on to a floating log, break into a cabin and find some clothes, crackers, and ginger ale. Then, penniless, they begin an aimless journey, finding food, coping with various new problems (including the arrival of the girl's period), and making do until the Saturday when the girl's mother plans to visit camp. As a gradual friendship develops, the two become awkwardly aware of each other and more self-aware. When they cleverly figure out a way to stay in a motel at someone else's expense, a suspicious cleaning woman accuses them of "spending the afternoon in the same bed." Ironically, it is the adult suspicion of sexual activity rather than the thievery of clothes, food, or a motel room that catches the two fugitives. The girl and boy, nameless to each other until the final chapter, are reunited with the girl's mother and other adults who will straighten things out. But Laura and Howie are different now: more self-reliant, able to form real friendships based on their own inner sense, and unlikely ever again to be gullible victims of peer cruelty or thoughtlessness. Emotionally gripping and thought provoking, this story leads individual young adult readers to consider what it means to be alienated from one's peers and what it means to have a trusted friend.

In C. S. Adler's *The Once in a While Hero*, Pat, a seventh grader, is confused about his own sexuality. His two best friends are Susan and Lucy; his longer hair makes him look more like a girl; and his gentle manner makes him the target of the class bully, McGrew, who calls him "Pattycakes." When Pat volunteers to show a new boy around, and the boy asks him outright, "You gay or something?", Pat is even more confused. When Pat finally decides to fight McGrew and earns the respect of his classmates, readers are left to wonder if fighting is what makes a boy more manly. Still, Pat's gentle father helps Pat to decide what is important for his self-respect and to value his own nature.

A more direct treatment of a boy's concern with his own sexuality is found in John Donovan's sensitively told story, *I'll Get There, It Better Be Worth the Trip*. Davy Ross and his 13-year-old friend Altschuler are playing with Davy's dog and, impelled by an "unusual" feeling, the two exchange a kiss. After that, they pretend to box, "like tough guys." A later incident causes Davy's divorced mother to call his father to come and have a talk with Davy. When Davy and Altschuler eventually cool their friendship, and Davy's dog dies, Davy seems to have lost more than he has gained—a move toward a future which, as the book's title says, better be worth the trip.

Perhaps because of ground-breaking books such as these, authors are now able to incorporate aspects of a child's acknowledgment of sexuality into stories with other themes as well.

FINDING ONE'S SELF

Most of the stories of physical maturing also suggest a kind of emotional growth or coming to terms with one's self. The process of becoming a mature person is a lifelong task that begins in the latter stages of childhood and continues for as long as a person lives. Many stories of children's literature chronicle the steps along the way to maturity.

In Pam Conrad's short novel *Staying Nine*, Heather wishes in the week before her tenth birthday that she "could stay just the same for millions of years." She doesn't like change and she especially doesn't want to lose the ability to edge up to the ceiling by way of the kitchen doorway. So Heather decides not to have a birthday party, to wear the same clothes for her school picture that she wore last year, and to stay the passing of time by ignoring it. Her mother wisely agrees to an unbirthday party, but it is Rose Rita, her uncle's young girlfriend, who sympathetically and humorously conveys to Heather that growing up just might be fun and that her wall-climbing skills won't atrophy with age. Conrad's depiction of a week in the life of a child who has trouble accepting changes is both humorous and poignant.

Characters in novels by Betsy Byars often have small moments of growing up, too. In *The 18th Emergency*, Benjie (better known as Mouse) has to face up to a beating by the school bully, Marv Hammerman, when he writes Marv's name under a picture of a Neanderthal man on a school evolution chart. As he avoids Marv, Mouse amuses himself by thinking of humorous things such as writing along a wall crack "to open building tear along dotted line." But in the end, it is a point of honor—Mouse faces Marv and no longer needs to think up escapes from imaginary or real "emergencies." In *After the Goat Man*, a miserable overweight Harold and his new friend Figgy decide to do something about Figgy's grandfather who has barricaded himself in his old cabin and refuses to leave so that a new highway can be built. When Figgy breaks his leg in the woods, Harold must take care of his friend as well as face alone the grandfather, also called "the Goat Man." During his confrontation with the Goat Man, Harold suddenly realizes what place means to the old man. This moment of empathy is a step toward maturity for Harold.

Lois Lowry's memorable character, 12-year-old *Rabble Starkey*, tells her own story of accepting growth and change, "about all kinds of loving, and about saying goodbye. And about moving on to where more things are in store."[21] Rabble (short for Parable Ann) lives with her mother Sweet Hosanna above the Bigelow family's garage where they take care of two children whose mother is hospitalized for depression. Veronica Bigelow and Rabble are like sisters; they share their love for Veronica's little 4-year-old brother Gunther; they work on a school project about family trees together; and they observe their neighbors and try to do right by them. Mr. Bigelow even buys both girls new dresses, treating Rabble as if he were the father she has never known. She feels she finally has a family. Her mother, Sweet-Ho, an abandoned wife at 14, is also trying to grow as she acknowledges she doesn't want to be a housekeeper or a waitress forever. In her acceptance of the 1987 Boston Globe-Horn Book Award for fiction, Lois Lowry maintains:

> In writing *Rabble Starkey*, I had a picture in my head. It was a complicated one, because it included not only Rabble and her mother, Sweet Hosanna, but it included the entire landscape of their lives, as well: the little town in West Virginia which molded them into what they would become and the rural hills beyond, where their heritage lay.[22]

[21]Lois Lowry, *Rabble Starkey* (Boston: Houghton Mifflin, 1987), p. 191.
[22]Lois Lowry, "Rabble Starkey," *The Horn Book Magazine*, vol. 64 (January/February 1988), p. 29.

Rabble is a sympathetic character, a clear-eyed and unsentimental observer, a lover of words, and a person who initially has trouble accepting her mother's decision to start college when Mrs. Bigelow returns to the family. But the strength of the story is its quiet assurance that while it is all right to be wary of change, love and a plan make growth not only bearable but rewarding.

Another aspect of growing up, accepting people as they are, including small pretenses and idiosyncrasies, is one of the themes of E. L. Konigsburg's *Journey to an 800 Number*. Hiding behind his prep school blazer, Maximilian Stubbs is spending the summer months with his father Woody, while his mother remarries. Max is a self-proclaimed expert on "normal" and "first class," both of which he is sure his father is not. Woody, a camel keeper, moves through the Southwest giving rides at shopping centers or making appearances at dude ranches, state fairs, and conventions. Max's disdain for his father and his father's life is revealed in his quick quips and disparaging remarks. Throughout the summer, Max meets others who care deeply about Woody and who seem able where Max is not. Only when Max discovers the facts about his real parentage is he able to show the love he has come to feel for Woody and to accept the love Woody has been showing him all along. Konigsburg's first-person narrative is sharp, humorous, and insightful. The gradual revelation to Max of the strange and wonderful possibilities in a world outside prep school suggests to him new definitions of "normal" and "first class."

A lighter look at the problems of growing up is presented in the Bingo Brown stories by Betsy Byars. In *The Burning Questions of Bingo Brown*, Bingo agonizes over which of three girls he should pay attention to in his sixth-grade class. He also thinks about how much mousse his hair needs ("You always overdo everything," says his mother) and how he can get one of these girls, Melissa, to hold hands but, more importantly, how he should then let go. As is usual in novels by Byars, a deeper issue—this time of attempted suicide—is raised when Bingo's teacher appears to have crashed his motorcycle on purpose after an argument with a woman he wished to date. In *Bingo Brown and the Language of Love*, Bingo's parents confront him with huge phone bills he has run up talking long distance to his girlfriend Melissa who has moved to Oklahoma. Not only that, but Bingo and his parents have to sort out their feelings over the news that his mother is going to have another baby. *Bingo Brown, Gypsy Lover* continues to develop this theme while Bingo decides what is an appropriate Christmas gift for Melissa who has sent him a "handmade notebook cover and carrier." Bingo is a contemporary, lovable, normal 12-year-old whose anxiety over being thrust into maturity is more than offset by his sense of humor and honor. While adults may laugh out loud as they remember their own childhoods or recognize themselves in the adults Byars creates, older children will recognize Bingo immediately as one of their own classmates.

Another sixth grader who is facing problems in growing up is Sara in Jan Slepian's *The Broccoli Tapes*. While her father completes a term as a visiting professor in Hawaii and her mother is distraught over the medical condition of her own mother, Sara and her older brother Sam are left on their own. Sara has agreed to send tape-recorded messages back to her class in Boston while she is in Hawaii. At first, the messages are about an injured wild cat she and her brother free from its trap in the rocks. Gradually, the tapes begin to include information about the strange Eddie Nutt and the wary way in which he approaches Sara and Sam when they build a rock pool on the beach. Later messages record Sara's feelings about her grandmother's impending death, her brother's inability to face this, and her growing attachment to the cat that the two name Broccoli because of its fondness for the vegetable scraps they bring to it. In private tapes that Sara erases, she records her feelings for Eddie and the moments of understanding which lead to her first kiss. In the five months in which the story takes place, Sara begins to realize that love has both risks and rewards, that nothing is gained from protecting yourself from caring, and that friends are where you find them. Slepian uses the word *click* to remind readers that Sara is now recording for her teacher and friends. This serves to place readers squarely in Sara's group of Boston friends as they listen to her tell her story.

Gilly Ground is also a loner, torn between his desire for freedom and his longing for peace and security. In Julia Cunningham's *Dorp Dead* Kobalt's house seems a haven of peace compared to the orphanage where Gilly first lived. But gradually Gilly realizes that while Kobalt provides clothing, good food, and shelter, he is cruel and evil. Gilly has begun to acquire the same dull and unresponsive look he had first noticed in Kobalt's beaten dog. When Gilly finally gathers the courage to escape, a mysterious hunter provides the human contact Gilly needs to choose freedom. As a last act of defiance, he scrawls on Kobalt's door the message "Dorp dead." This intense and allegorical novel deals with the problem all youth face in accepting some amount of insecurity while searching for love and freedom.

Another psychologically complex novel, *One-Eyed Cat* by Paula Fox, begins when 11-year-old Ned Wallis receives from his favorite uncle an unexpected birthday present—an air rifle. But Ned's minister father banishes the gun to the attic until Ned is older. Longing to shoot just once, Ned steals into the attic at night, points the gun out the window, and fires toward something moving near a shed. He is immediately guilt-stricken. Was it an animal? As he broods on his disobedience, he begins to lie and each lie "makes the secret bigger." He can't confide in his mother, who is wheelchair-bound by arthritis, or in the temperamental housekeeper Mrs. Scallop, or in his preoccupied father. As he carries his uncomfortable secret, Ned seems most at ease at the house of an elderly neighbor, Mr. Scully, for whom he does household chores and odd jobs after school. There he and the old man see a sickly one-eyed cat that they feed and observe during the winter. When Mr. Scully suddenly suffers a stroke and is taken to the hospital, Ned is afraid he has lost both his friend and the cat. Finally, on a visit to the home where Mr. Scully, unable to speak, resides, Ned gathers enough courage to tell his guilty secret to his friend. This release brings a change in Ned and enables him to repair the pains of separation. Although Mr. Scully dies, the cat returns in the spring with its own family, and his mother is able to ease her pain somewhat with a new treatment. Ned's rich interior monologues contrast with his inability to talk; this motif of being unable to speak about some of life's most important moments recurs throughout the story. Paula Fox's carefully chosen images, such as "people aging the way trees do, getting gnarled and dried out" or "the gun was a splinter in his mind" lend real depth to this perceptive and well-written story. Although it is set in 1935, children are not likely to see the book as historical fiction but rather as a story of one person's moral dilemmas that spiral round him as a result of his disobedience and lying.

The Village by the Sea, also by Fox, takes place in the two weeks that Emma spends with her Aunt Bea and Uncle Crispin while her father undergoes heart bypass surgery. Uncle Crispin understands 11-year-old Emma's apprehension and anxiety but bitter and self-centered Aunt Bea seems able to talk only in thinly veiled innuendos and accusations. Emma observes, "There was something lopsided about her as though she'd lost her balance a long time ago and couldn't get it back."[23] One day on the beach, Emma meets another girl, Bertie, and together they build a beautiful town filled with houses made of shells, stones, and glass polished by the sea. As they talk, Emma is able to piece together more about her formerly alcoholic aunt and the family history. When the town is finished, Emma proudly shows Uncle Crispin. But Aunt Bea, resentful over Emma's disinterest in a trunk of old things and her good cheer now that her father is recovering, refuses to go down to the beach. The night before Emma is to rejoin her parents in New York, she decides to make one last visit to the village by moonlight only to discover it kicked to pieces by someone who Emma realizes can only be Aunt Bea. Now furious and full of hate, Emma sobs to Uncle Crispin, who tries to help her understand how her aunt is consumed by memories and envy of anyone who seems to be able to live a joyful life. It is only when Emma sees an entry Aunt Bea has scratched in Emma's own diary that she can let go of her hate and understand this "sad bad old woman."

While readers know that Emma has made it through a difficult time, they are not so sure that 12-year-old Joel will be able to do the same in the powerful story *On My Honor* by Marion Dane Bauer. Goaded by his friend Tony, Joel asks his father if the two boys can ride to the bluffs outside of town and is surprised when his father gives permission. Joel promises on his honor to be careful, but when the two boys come to a bridge across a swiftly moving river, they agree to stop for a swim. When the two reach the fast current, Tony, who can't swim, is swept away and drowned. Joel, horrified, doesn't know what to do. When he reaches his home, he can't tell anyone what has happened and withdraws to his bed. Finally, the arrival of the police at Tony's house and the anguish of the adults not knowing forces Joel to tell his story. He angrily blames his father and himself. In a moving scene by Joel's bedside, his father says: "We all made choices today, Joel. You, me, Tony. Tony's the only one who doesn't have to live with his choice."[24] His father's admission of partial responsibility frees Joel to cry and begin to grieve. While for some children the book ends abruptly, it is not a story of dealing with the death of a friend. Instead, it is a story about facing the tragic consequences of your own actions with the help of a loving family. After reading this story, fifth graders are anxious to discuss honor, conscience, and parental obligations versus self-responsibility. They are also eager to predict a hopeful future for Joel.

Two differing novels by Katherine Paterson nonetheless are concerned with similar themes of growing up. In *Come Sing, Jimmy Jo*, James struggles to reconcile his singing talent and his growing love of performance in his Appalachian family's country-western band with his need for the quiet security of his grandmother and her country life. His friendship with an African-American classmate, Eleazer Jones, who is uncowed by adults, helps him acknowledge his real father as he confronts his feelings about his stepfather. James finds support for his growth both from inside and outside his family. A boy in Paterson's *Park's Quest* journeys from his home near Washington, D.C., to his dead father's home in rural Virginia. Like James, Park is trying to discover who he is, and his family both supports and interferes with his desire to know more. Park's

[23]Paula Fox, *The Village by the Sea* (New York: Orchard Books, 1988), p. 63.

[24]Marion Dane Bauer, *On My Honor* (Boston: Houghton Mifflin, 1986), p. 88.

father died in Vietnam and his mother wants nothing to do with Park's grandfather who has suffered a stroke and cannot speak. When he visits his ancestral home, he finally has a glowing moment of understanding and communication with the old man. He also forms a prickly friendship with a girl on the farm called Thanh, her Vietnamese mother and the mother's husband, but the reader realizes who this girl is long before Park does. Like the characters in *Bridge to Terabithia*, Park loves books, especially the story of King Arthur. Paterson's many allusions reinforce points in the story where Park demonstrates heroism as he seeks to know about his parents and their past, himself, and his future.

Manolo is a Spanish boy who has to decide whether to follow his own conscience or to conform to community expectations. *Shadow of a Bull* by Maia Wojciechowska describes the darkening shadow of Manolo's fear of failure to be like his father, a famous bullfighter. On the night before facing his first bull at age 12, he is told by his mother about how tired his father is after bullfights. But what he did was for himself. Manolo also hears a famous bullfight critic say that it is important to be what you want to be and if you don't know, to wait until you do. "Don't let anyone make that decision for you." Manolo proves himself by fighting the bull long enough to show his skill and bravery; then he makes his choice. He turns the fight over to his friend Juan while he goes and sits with a doctor friend. His future will be healing, not killing. For Manolo it took far greater courage to say no, to be what *he* wanted to be, than to follow in his father's footsteps.

His real name is Jeffrey Lionel Magee but the kids of Two Mills call the homeless boy who became a legend *Maniac Magee*. Jerry Spinelli's Newbery award-winning book is more a tale of a modern-day superman than it is realistic fiction. There is nothing Maniac can't do: he beats a kid called Mars Bar in a race running backward; he hits home runs, scores touchdowns, unties the famous Cobbles Knot, and goes into mean old Finsterwald's backyard; he teaches old Mr. Grayson to read and gets the famous McNab twins to go to school. Most importantly, he brings together the town, which is racially divided. Yet Maniac continues running. He finds many shelters for himself, but no home. He lives for a while with the Beals, a kind African-American family, and later with the McNabs, who are racist whites. He is happiest with Mr. Grayson, a locker room attendant at the YMCA who lives with him under a band shell. But when Grayson dies, Maniac is running again. Only when Amanda Beal goes to the zoo where Maniac is now spending his nights in the buffalo enclosure and forces Maniac to listen does he finally know that someone is calling him home. Maniac is bigger than life, a legend in his own world. In his Boston Globe-Horn Book Award acceptance speech, Jerry Spinelli mused, "I thought about the world that children inhabit . . . a world that, in many ways, I find indistinguishable from myth and legend."[25] Spinelli says he tried to capture the rhythms and life of the neighborhood gang from his own childhood. Short chapters, punchy dialogue, and nonstop action make this a book that readers will not want to put down.

In *Scorpions* by Walter Dean Myers, 12-year-old Jamal reluctantly takes his brother's place as leader of a Harlem gang, the Scorpions, after his brother is sent to prison. His best friend Tito constantly counsels him not to get involved with the gang while his long-suffering mother and his uppity sister Sassy fear that he might follow in his brother's footsteps. When Jamal is given the gang's gun, he finds courage he didn't know he had and briefly displays it to get away from a school bully. On his way to a meeting with dissatisfied older boys in the gang, Tito and Jamal reflect on their lives:

❦ "I don't like this park, man," Tito spoke under his breath to Jamal.

"How come?"

"You got guys laying on the ground, you got guys laying on the grass, you even got some women laying around in here."

"They either winos or crackheads," Jamal said.

"They look like they thrown-away people," Tito said. "That makes me scared, because I don't want to be no thrown-away guy."

[25]Jerry Spinelli, "*Maniac Magee:* Homer on George Street," *The Horn Book Magazine* (January/February 1991), p. 40.

"That's why we got to be like this"—Jamal held up two fingers close together—"So we don't let nobody throw us away."[26]

But in a nighttime encounter with two older boys in the gang, Jamal is beaten and Tito, who is holding the gun, shoots the assailants. Both boys are stunned by the incident but Tito worries and finally goes to the police. Because he is a minor, he may return to Puerto Rico to avoid prosecution. The novel leaves readers to wonder if Jamal, who has lost his best friend and his innocence, is strong enough to follow his own conscience and resist becoming a "thrown-away guy" himself.

SURVIVAL STORIES

Survival stories have powerful appeal to children in middle grades. Numerous stories in all genres portray an individual child or a small group of children, without adults, in situations that call for ingenuity, quick thinking, mastery of tools and skills, and strength of character. Survivors return to civilization or their former lives knowing that they have changed as a result of their experiences. In primitive societies, surviving a hazardous experience often marked the transition from childhood to adulthood. Today, we have forms of this in "survival training" conducted in schools, camps, or juvenile homes. Children in middle grades avidly read survival stories and wonder, "Could I do it? How? What would I do in this same situation?"

Armstrong Sperry's quintessential survival story *Call It Courage* begins and ends in the manner of a story told in the oral tradition:

It happened many years ago, before the traders and the missionaries first came into the South Seas, while the Polynesians were still great in numbers and fierce of heart. But even today the people of Hikueru sing this story in their chants and tell it over the evening fires. It is the story of Mafatu, the Boy Who Was Afraid.[27]

Taunted for his fears, Mafatu sets out to conquer his dread of the water by sailing to some other island, accompanied only by his pet albatross and his dog. On a distant island his character gradually develops as he proves his courage to himself: he defies a tabu; steals a much-needed spear from an idol; fights dangerous animals; and escapes from cannibals. These heroic deeds, which represent the many faces of courage, build his self-esteem. As in so many survival stories, having proven to himself that he could carve out an existence, Mafatu is ready to return to his former life as a changed person who knows his own worth. The first paragraph of the book is repeated at the end—only the last sentence is left off.

Jean George's well-loved *My Side of the Mountain* is about a city boy who chooses to spend a solitary winter in the Catskills on family land. Armed with knowledge from reading, he makes a home in a hollow tree, tames a falcon, sews buckskin clothing, and lays up stores for the winter. In his journal, he records his observations as he goes about the business of living. When a reporter discovers him in the spring, Sam realizes he is ready to be found. Thirty years after the publication of this story, George wrote a bittersweet but worthy sequel, *On the Far Side of the Mountain*, which picks up the plot immediately following the first story. Sam allows his younger sister Alice to become his neighbor while he continues to enrich his environment and his life in the wild. But a criminal posing as a conservation officer steals Sam's falcon and his sister vanishes. In both books George expresses concern about our relationship to the natural world and our responsibility to preserve it.

Another exciting story of survival also by George, is the Newbery award-winning novel *Julie of the Wolves*. Miyax, the Eskimo heroine of this beautiful story, finds herself alone on the Alaskan tundra. She realizes that her salvation or her destruction depends on a nearby pack of wolves. Julie (Miyax is her Eskimo name) watches the wolves carefully and gradually learns to communicate with them by glance, movement, and caress until Amaroq, their leader, acknowledges her as a friend. Because of the wolves Julie survives and finds her way back to civilization. But it is civilization that kills Amaroq, as white hunters wantonly shoot him down from a plane for the "sport" of killing. Much of the story is

[26]Walter Dean Myers, *Scorpions* (New York: Harper & Row, 1988), p. 161.
[27]Armstrong Sperry, *Call It Courage* (New York: Macmillan, 1940), p. 7.

Miyax mourns the wanton killing of Amaroq, leader of the wolves.
Illustration by John Schoenherr from *Julie of the Wolves* by Jean Craighead George.

🐾 🐾 🐾

based on research on wolves conducted at the Arctic Research Laboratory.[28]

Vera and Bill Cleavers' *Where the Lilies Bloom* is a well-known survival story set in Appalachia. The torturous death of Roy Luther from "worms in the chest" puts the full responsibility for the survival of the family on Mary Call, his 14-year-old daughter. She and Romey, her younger brother, carry Luther up the mountain in a wagon and bury him so the "county people" will not find out that they are orphaned and separate them. Then Mary Call strives to keep her "cloudy-headed" older sister, Devola, and her two younger siblings alive through the winter. Mary Call's fierce pride gives her fortitude to overcome a severe winter, a caved-in roof, and the constant pretense that Roy Luther still lives. At 14, Mary Call's strength and responsibility have made her mature beyond her years, but she pulls the family through the crisis:

🐾 My name is Mary Call Luther, I thought, and someday I'm going to be a big shot. I've got the guts to be one. I'm not going to let this beat me. If it does, everything else will for the rest of my life.[29]

Mary Call and her family do survive, through wildcrafting on the mountains, scheming, and pure grit. The authors have captured the beauty of the Smokies and of this memorable family who live in what an old hymn calls the land "Where the Lilies Bloom So Fair." Mary Call's story is continued in *Trial Valley*, a more contrived and less believable sequel.

This story's tone stands in sharp contrast to that in E. L. Konigsburg's *From the Mixed-Up Files of Mrs. Basil E. Frankweiler*. In it, two children decide to run away from home and live in comfort in the Metropolitan Museum of Art. Claudia's reasons for running away are based on what she considers injustice—she has to set the table and empty the dishwasher on the same

[28]See "Newbery Award Acceptance" speech by Jean Craighead George in *The Horn Book Magazine*, vol. 49 (August 1973), pp. 337–347.

[29]Vera Cleaver and Bill Cleaver, *Where the Lilies Bloom* (New York: Lippincott, 1969), p. 144.

night while her brothers do nothing. But Claudia is also bored with the sameness of her straight-A life; she wants to do something that is different and exciting. She chooses her brother Jamie to go along with her because he has money—$24.43. Claudia is a good organizer, and the two of them take up residence in the museum. They take baths in the museum's fountain, eat meals at the automat and the museum's cafeteria, and join tour groups for their education. Their adventure grows more exciting when Claudia becomes involved in the mystery surrounding the statue of a little angel. The children's research finally takes them to the home of Mrs. Basil E. Frankweiler, who arranges for Claudia to return home the way she had hoped she would—different in some aspect. Now she is different because she knows the secret of the angel. In return for this knowledge the two children tell Mrs. Frankweiler the details of their survival, she carefully records it, and then writes their story. This story-within-a-story is a sophisticated and funny account of two very modern and resourceful survivors.

Felice Holman has written a grim story of survival in New York City, *Slake's Limbo*. Slake is a 13-year-old nearsighted orphan who lives with his aunt and thinks of himself as a worthless lump. Slake has no friends; his vision makes him a poor risk for any gang, and a severe reaction to smoke and drugs makes him useless in other ways. Hunted and hounded for sport, Slake takes refuge in the subway, staying for 121 days. He earns a little money reselling papers he picks up on the trains and makes his home in a hidden cave in the subway wall. One day when the subway repair crew comes through, Slake realizes that his "home" will be destroyed. He becomes ill and is taken to the hospital, where he is given nourishment and proper eyeglasses. Later he slips out of the hospital. His first reaction is to return to the subway but when he hears a bird sing, he looks up and decides he could perhaps exist on the roofs of some of the buildings: "He turned and started up the stairs and out of the subway. Slake did not know exactly where he was going but the general direction was up."[30]

[30]Felice Holman, *Slake's Limbo* (New York: Aladdin, 1986), p. 117.

Canadian author James Houston has based his survival story, *Frozen Fire*, on the actual survival story of a boy in the Canadian Arctic. Two boys, Matthew Morgan and his Inuit friend Kayak, set forth on a snowmobile to search for Matthew's prospector father, whose plane has been downed by a snowstorm. Careless securing of the cap of a gas can leaves them stranded seventy miles from Frobisher Bay. Kayak is able to use the skills taught him by his grandfather and helps both boys eventually to walk out on the ice, where they are seen and rescued. They discover that Matthew's father has also been saved. Houston's crisp telling and cliff-hanger chapter endings make this a fast-paced story. Having spent twelve years among the Inuit people, he is able to weave aspects of a changing Eskimo culture and folk wisdom into the text. *Black Diamonds: A Search for Arctic Treasure* continues the adventure of the two boys as they help Matthew's father in searching for gold.

A more hopeful story is told in Paula Fox's *Monkey Island*. Eleven-year-old Clay Garrity is homeless and sleeping in the streets. Abandoned by his despondent and pregnant mother and not wishing to let his neighbor in the New York welfare hotel report him to the social worker, Clay runs away. On the street, he manages to survive because two men share their place in a park, a box where they sleep. Calvin, a retired high school math teacher who frequently succumbs to alcohol, and Buddy, a young African-American

James Houston's illustrations reflect the style of the Inuit people among whom he has spent many years.

From *Frozen Fire* by James Houston.

man, become his family, sharing their food and their life stories. Clay learns to wear all his clothes at once, where to find food, and how not to attract attention during the day. One terrifying November night, a street gang destroys the makeshift shelters of the homeless people living in the park, Calvin disappears, and Clay catches pneumonia. Realizing his friend needs help, Buddy makes the choice of taking him to a hospital even though it means Clay will lose his freedom. But in a hopeful conclusion, Clay, his mother, and his new baby sister are reunited. Paula Fox's story prompts readers to consider the causes of homelessness and to consider what may happen. Clay's dangerous journey is made at least partially bearable by the dog-eared copy of *Robinson Crusoe* he carries from the welfare hotel. Later, it is a copy of *David Copperfield* whose story of a life outside his lost family lends Clay some courage. Paula Fox creates memorable characters in an unsentimental but hopeful survival story in which the social services of a large city, as well as caring individuals who take action, are able to do well for at least one boy and one family.

Gary Paulsen's survival story *Hatchet* begins with a crash of a bush plane carrying a boy to meet his father. When the pilot suffers a heart attack, Brian Robeson manages to land the plane in a lake in the Canadian wilderness and swim to shore. Alone, 13-year-old Brian lets self-pity and anxiety over his parents' impending divorce distract him from the immediate needs of survival and is soon sick and frightened. But gradually he begins to act intelligently, building a shelter, finding ripe berries, fending off a bear, and discovering respect for a cow moose that nearly kills him. A hatchet his mother had given him as a parting gift becomes essential to his survival. When a huge storm disturbs the plane enough to raise its tail in the water, Brian ventures out to seek the survival kit all pilots carry with them. But his carelessness when he loses his hatchet in the water and his horror of what he might find when he dives to the cockpit nearly prevent his success in retrieving the kit. Ironically, Brian is cooking a delicious meal of trail food in a real pot and has survived for over two months when he is finally spotted from the air by a mapping plane. Paulsen ties up the whole story, perhaps a little too neatly,

in an epilogue, but readers know that Brian is a changed person for having met this challenge. Two years later in *The River*, Brian is once again pitted against the elements when he agrees to make a film to teach survival techniques to the military. But the man recording Brian's experiences is struck by lightning and will die unless Brian can build a raft and navigate himself and Derek downriver to a trading post. Other survival stories by Paulsen include *Dogsong*, which is partially based on the author's own experiences of training sled dogs for the Iditarod Trail race. *The Voyage of the Frog* reveals the courage of a boy who ventures out on the ocean to scatter his dead uncle's ashes and is caught unprepared in a sudden storm.

There are intriguing patterns in stories of survival. Many deal with questions and themes basic to humankind. Some survival stories suggest that surviving with another person provides comforting benefits as well as difficulties. Questions readers might ask while comparing survival stories of all genres include: What qualities make one able to survive? How does surviving an ordeal change a person's outlook? After basic wants are satisfied, what other needs do survivors seem to have? Which is more difficult, physical survival or emotional survival? What role does art or beauty play in the survivor's ability to endure?

COPING WITH PROBLEMS OF THE HUMAN CONDITION

People in all times and places must cope with problems of the human condition—birth, pain, and loneliness; poverty, illness, and death. Children do not escape these problems, but literature can give them windows for looking at different aspects of life, show them how some characters have faced personal crises, and help them ask and answer questions about the meaning of life.

In discussing the portrayal of emotionally significant themes in children's literature, Mollie Hunter points out:

A broken home, the death of a loved person, a divorce between parents—all these are highly charged emotional situations once considered unsuitable for children's reading, but which are nevertheless still part of some children's experience; and the writer's success in casting them in literary terms rests on the ability to create an emotional frame of reference to which children in general can relate.[31]

David Elkind, a psychologist, warns that we may nonetheless be overburdening our children with the ills of society before they have an opportunity to find themselves. He says:

> This is the major stress of the literature of young children aimed at making them aware of the problems in the world about them before they have a chance to master the problems of childhood.[32]

Certainly teachers and librarians should balance the reading of "problem books" with those that emphasize joy in living.

Physical Disabilities

Good stories about people with physical disabilities serve two purposes. They provide positive images with which disabled youngsters may identify, and they may help physically unimpaired children to develop a more intelligent understanding of some of the problems that disabled persons face. In stories, disabilities should neither be exaggerated nor ignored, neither dramatized nor minimized, neither romanticized nor belittled.[33] It is particularly important that stories of disabilities be well written, not sentimental or maudlin. They should not evoke pity for what children with disabilities cannot do, but respect for what they *can* do. As in all well-written stories, characters should be multidimensional persons with real feelings and frustrations. The author should be honest in portraying the condition and

future possibilities for the character. Illustrations should also portray disabilities in an honest and straightforward manner.

Literary treatment of disabilities may rely on time-honored themes: a disabled person has special powers, grace, or a predetermined destiny; a disabled person serves as a catalyst in the maturation of others; a disability is a metaphor for society's ills, such as a blind person who can "see" what others do not choose to acknowledge or are too insensitive to see. Occasionally, disabilities are somewhat misleadingly portrayed as being able to be overcome with determination, faith, and grit.[34] In the hands of a fine writer, themes such as these avoid becoming clichés and may present the reader with fresh insight into coping with the human condition.

Older stories have depicted children with cerebral palsy and families who deal courageously with this illness. In Marie Killilea's *Karen*, an older sister struggles to understand her younger sister's difficulty in walking and doing other things for herself. But her parents help her understand that Karen must learn to do things for herself in order to become more independent. The same theme of "what kind of help and how much" is also evident in Jean Little's *Mine for Keeps*. When Sally, who has cerebral palsy, returns from a special school to live at home, she attends regular school and faces several problems. But a dog that may be hers "for keeps" helps her gain physical skill and the emotional courage to help another child who has been ill.

In *The Alfred Summer*, Jan Slepian presents a 14-year-old boy with cerebral palsy who also chafes resentfully at the strings that he feels bind him to his overprotective mother and ignoring father. Lester describes himself self-mockingly as a walking "perpetual motion machine." When he falls, and someone asks him "Are you okay?" Lester thinks:

> Now here's the thing: I want to say, sure I'm okay, or, that's all right, I'm fine. Something like that. Well, if he has an hour or two to spare I'll get it out. I might in that time be able to tell him what's on

[31]Mollie Hunter, *Talent Is Not Enough* (New York: Harper & Row, 1990), p. 20.
[32]David Elkind, *The Hurried Child: Growing Up Too Fast Too Soon.* (Reading, Mass.: Addison-Wesley, 1981), p. 84.
[33]Barbara H. Baskin and Karen H. Harris, *More Notes from a Different Drummer: A Guide to Juvenile Fiction Portraying the Disabled* (New York: R. R. Bowker, 1984).

[34]Baskin and Harris, *More Notes from a Different Drummer*, Chapter 2.

my mind. In other words . . . in other words I have no words. Or none that I can get out without looking as if I'm strangling. . . .[35]

Lester one day makes a friend of Alfred, a retarded boy he sees collecting tinfoil from the gutters. Alfred's total acceptance of him frees Lester, and the two discover a third friend in Myron. As the three friends make a boat, each accomplishes something he thought he could not do and gains some self-respect. When the boat is finally launched, it sinks, but Myron and Lester realize that what they have built over the summer is much more important than a leaky old boat. By using Lester as a narrator in several chapters, Slepian injects humor and insight into this well-characterized, compassionate story. The sequel, *Lester's Turn*, is told entirely from Lester's point of view as he grows in independence.

Ivan Southall has vividly portrayed some of the desires and frustrations of a boy with a mild spastic condition in *Let the Balloon Go*. John Sumner attends a regular school in Australia and, except for occasional and unpredictable spasms and stuttering, he is like any other 12-year-old boy. And yet he has no friends. The children avoid him and his overanxious mother keeps telling him what he can't do. John longs to be free, to do what he wants. And one day, when he is home alone for the very first time, he does; he climbs a very tall tree all by himself. He once heard a man say that a balloon isn't a balloon until someone cuts the string. John has cut the string that bound him to his house and mother; at last he is truly free to grow in his own way.

In *Keeping It Secret*, Penny Pollock suggests some of the problems wearing a hearing aid poses for 11-year-old Wisconsin. Though everyone in her old school knows about and accepts the fact that she wears the aid, Wisconsin is apprehensive about facing a new school and new classmates. It is her determination to play baseball, in spite of her overprotective father's wishes, that helps her overcome her self-consciousness and acknowledge that her classmates knew about her hearing loss all along. Pollock treats hearing impairment in a straightforward manner, detailing Wisconsin's sensitivity to clapping and loud noises, her problems in hearing soft sounds, and her fear that her hearing aid will fall out when she participates in sports or that a battery will suddenly fail and there will be no place to change it discreetly. While Donna Diamond's pictures depict the characters in realistic detail, there is unfortunately no illustration of Wisconsin wearing the hearing devices that are such an important part of her story.

Veronica Robinson's *David in Silence* tells of a boy who learns to live with his profound deafness. Set in England, the story has plenty of action as the children make overtures to a new boy who can only make grunting noises. David is delighted when a classmate named Michael learns sign language so he can communicate through his wall of silence. The world of deafness, with its absolute absence of sound, is made quite clear to the reader. While the other boys eventually come to accept David and to have a new awareness of the joy of hearing, David will always remain in his silent world. (See also Riskind's *Apple Is My Sign*, Chapter 10, which portrays a boy learning to live among the hearing in one of the first schools for children with hearing impairment.)

In Colin Thiele's *Jodie's Journey*, Jodie thinks at first that the pain in her joints is a result of improper horseback riding techniques. She continues to train her horse and herself for other races but when the pain becomes too intense, she and her parents visit numerous doctors before she is told that she has rheumatoid arthritis and will never ride again. While Jodie can allow a friend to ride her beloved horse Monarch, she can't bear to part with the horse who is a companion as well as a prizewinner. Home with her disease temporarily in remission, Jodie learns to use a wheelchair and get around on her own. When her parents leave her alone for a day, a raging Australian range fire consumes hundreds of acres including the farm Jodie lives on but her courageous action saves both her and her horse. Fast-paced incidents and an unsentimental description of Jodie's illness propel this story to its life-affirming conclusion. Thiele, who has suffered for most of his life with rheumatoid arthritis, describes accurately the treatment and prognosis for this disease.

[35]Jan Slepian, *The Alfred Summer* (New York: Macmillan, 1980), p. 3.

During the summer of their mother's chemotherapy treatment following her mastectomy, 11-year-old twins Sally and Emily have grown apart. In *The Long Way Home* by Barbara Cohen, Sally is angry at her family and disappointed at not being in the same "tribe" as her sister at summer day camp. She is unpleasant to everyone until she makes friends with Claire, the overweight driver of the camp bus. Tensions at camp come to a head when Sally's group can't decide who should be leader and what they should do for the final camp show. This gradual resolution and Claire's friendship allow Sally to begin to talk with her close-knit Jewish family about her fears concerning breast cancer: Will her mother die? Will she contract the disease? A family doctor provides straight information which the twins and their older sister takes as a good sign that things have a chance of turning out well. Cohen builds a believable story in which friendship, independence, and growth are neatly balanced with dealing with family illness.

Developmental Disabilities

The opening line of *Take Wing* by Jean Little reads: "James had wet the bed again." As usual, 7-year-old James calls on his sister Laurel to help him, rather than on his mother because Laurel has a special way and a special love for this younger brother who is "different." Laurel has always tried to hide her fear that he isn't quite normal. Her mother won't talk about him and her father is too busy to notice how slow and unsure his son is. When Laurel's mother breaks her hip, her Aunt Jessica comes to stay at their house. Aunt Jessica recognizes that Laurel is carrying too much responsibility in having to care for James and finally an appointment is made for him to have an examination at the medical clinic. Their findings confirm Laurel's fears that her brother is retarded, but he is also educable. This is as much Laurel's story as James's. By refusing to face the facts of James's disability, the family had overburdened his older sister. The title, *Take Wing*, symbolizes Laurel's freedom to begin to have a childhood of her own, to make friends, and to grow.

"Slower Than the Rest" is how Leo's father describes him. In the first story from Cynthia

Rylant's collection, *Every Living Thing*, Leo discovers a turtle and makes it a pet. In his special education class, one he hates since he has been separated from the rest of the fourth grade, he writes a passionate school report on forest fires and the dangers they pose, especially to animals like his turtle: "It isn't fair for the slow ones." When Leo's essay wins a prize at an all-school assembly, he feels proud, happy, and for the first time in a long time, "Leo feels *fast*." In a dozen pithy short stories, Rylant explores the moments when people's lives change and they see something in a different way. These direct and powerful stories read aloud well and evoke discussion among third to sixth graders.

Betsy Byars won the Newbery award for her story about an adolescent girl and her retarded brother in *Summer of the Swans*. Sara feels very much like the ugly duckling in her difficult fourteenth summer. She weeps over her big feet, her skinny legs, and her nose, even over her gross orange sneakers. But when her retarded brother is lost in the woods, her tears vanish in the terror she feels for Charlie. In her anguish Sara turns to Joe Melby—whom she had despised the day before—and together they find Charlie. It is the longest day of the summer and Sara knows that she will never be the same again. Like the awkward flight of the swans with their "great beating of wings and ruffling of feathers," Sara is going to land with a long perfect glide. Sara's love and concern for her brother's safety help her break through her moody adolescent shell.

In Jan Slepian's *Risk 'n Roses*, a novel set in the Bronx just after World War II, it seems to 11-year-old Skip that her parents have been having the same argument forever. How responsible is Skip supposed to be for her older and mentally retarded sister, Angela? The family has moved to a new neighborhood so that Angela can be closer to a special school, and Skip is desperate for a friend. Then she meets the compelling Jean Persico who "didn't care about feelings or laws or being good so far as Skip could tell. She wasn't like the rest. She was untamed. Wonderful."[36] Jean forms a club, the Dares, in which she cruelly

---

[36]Jan Slepian, *Risk 'n Roses* (New York: Philomel, 1990), p. 107.

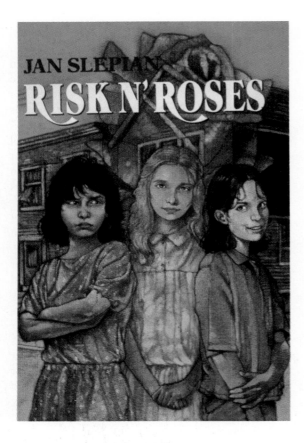

Skip must choose between the influence of her wild friend Jean and loyalty to her beautiful but mentally handicapped older sister in Jan Slepian's *Risk n' Roses.*

Jacket illustration by Stephen Marchesi.

preys on each member's weakness, getting each girl to do things such as shoplifting or disrupting an ice cream store by dropping a cockroach. Angela makes friends with a reclusive neighbor, Mr. Kaminsky, whose precious roses have all been named for family and friends he believes have been exterminated by Hitler. But Jean has targeted him for malice and her final act of cruelty, enticing Angela to cut down his prize roses, is her way of paying Angela back for inadvertently reporting on one of Jean's cruel jokes. Jean's manipulation of her sister shocks Skip into realizing that her desire for a friend has blinded and trapped her. But her realization and her actions

show the reader she has changed. This is as much a story of peer pressure and the desire for friendship as it is a story of accepting a sibling for herself and not for what one wishes she were. Like Betty Wright's *The Dollhouse Murders* (see Chapter 7) and Bauer's *On My Honor, Risk n' Roses* is also about taking responsibility for one's own actions.

It is summertime when 10-year-old Jill is *Between Friends,* following a family move. Although anxious to make friends, Jill nonetheless initially avoids Dede's first overtures because Dede has Down syndrome. But because there is no one else in the neighborhood her own age, Jill reluctantly becomes Dede's friend. Relying heavily on dialogue, Sheila Garrigue explores what retardation means to Jill, to Dede, and to her mother. Many of the adults as well as Jill's school friends display unbelievably cruel attitudes about Down syndrome, but Jill makes a courageous decision to accept Dede's invitation to attend her school's Christmas party. There, she sees firsthand all that these "special" children have accomplished, shares Dede's pride in the flowers she is raising, and discovers that her previous fears about this visit were based on her own misconceptions. Since Jill chooses to attend Dede's party rather than go to see a ballet with some of her snobby, cliquish classmates, she makes an important statement about what is important "between friends." In another book Marlene Shyer examines the complex feelings of a boy, Neil, as his mentally retarded 13-year-old sister returns home in *Welcome Home, Jellybean.* Upper elementary readers can identify with the concerns, feelings, and doubts of both Jill and Neil as they build these special relationships.

The ambivalent feelings of a rebellious 15-year-old toward her retarded 11-year-old brother are examined with compassion in Colby Rodowsky's novel, *What About Me?* It seems to Dorrie that her own life is swallowed up in the family's constant concern for Fred. Her frustration and anger boil to the surface as expressions of hatred for her brother; yet when she is left alone with him and his heart condition becomes critical, she finds herself caring for him, loving him, just as her parents have always done. In the story's poignant resolution Fred dies and, like Dorrie, the reader is left to consider what it means to grow up in a family that includes a retarded child.

In *All Together Now* Sue Ellen Bridgers portrays an important summer in 12-year-old Casey Flanagan's life. Casey, whose mother works at two jobs while her father is away fighting in the Korean War, has come to spend the summer with her grandparents in a small southern town. There she meets Dwayne Pickens, a retarded man who is her father's age. Dwayne has the mind of a 12-year-old and a passion for baseball. Their friendship grows when Dwayne, who dislikes girls but mistakes Casey for a boy, includes her in his endless baseball sessions, often with Casey's feisty Uncle Taylor playing, too. Casey contracts what may be polio and her anxious family sits with her through several terrible August days. Having forgiven Casey for being a girl, Dwayne faithfully visits during the long convalescence that follows and keeps her spirits up. By the summer's end, Casey has grown in awareness of herself and the nature of friendship. "Having responsibility made people responsible. Having someone to love gave you a chance to be loved yourself."[37] Humorous and sometimes poignant subplots involving Casey's observations and interactions with adults make this a complex and richly characterized novel. In this well-crafted story for middle school readers, Bridgers reveals the characters' thoughts and feelings with a shifting viewpoint, allowing readers to consider the potential of human relationships.

Mental Illness

Few stories about mental illness have been written for the elementary school child. In the title of the book, *(George)*, E. L. Konigsburg has let the name with parentheses stand for Ben's alter ego, a real and constant companion. Ben manages to keep his schizophrenic symptoms to himself until he enters sixth grade. Then, because of the fear that he might be sent away to live with his father and stepmother and the pressure of knowing that his lab partners are stealing equipment from chemistry class to make LSD, George begins to speak out loud. Part of this story is very witty, as

is typical of Konigsburg's stories, but part is very serious. George and Ben finally become one again and the book ends on a cheerful note of recovery.

Thirteen-year-old Carrie Stokes, in Zibby Oneal's *The Language of Goldfish*, does not like what is happening to her. She wishes her family could return to the days when they lived in a cramped Chicago apartment rather than in an affluent suburb. If only things didn't change, she would still be close to her sister Moira, and they would share all that they had as children. Instead, Carrie is under pressure by her mother and sister to wear more appropriate and stylish clothes, to go to school dances, and, somehow, be someone Carrie feels she is not. When she attempts suicide by overdosing on pills, her mother still avoids dealing with the real Carrie. Gradually, as Carrie mends, she is better able to understand her mother's denial. She is helped in this by a therapist, a trusted art teacher, and a new friend, the neighbor boy. Finally, she learns to accept changes in others and herself while those closest to her display various ways in which they, too, cope with mental illness.

While there are few books about mentally ill children, there are several that present a child or children dealing with a mentally ill adult. Voigt's *Homecoming* and *Dicey's Song,* for instance, portray the aftereffects of a depressed mother's abandonment of her children. Paula Fox's *The Village by the Sea* concerns a girl's two-week stay with a mentally ill aunt. Bruce Brooks, in *The Moves Make the Man,* shows through the eyes of a compassionate and articulate boy narrator how the mental breakdown of his friend's mother nearly brings about the breakdown of the friend as well. Jocelyn Riley's *Only My Mouth Is Smiling* follows 13-year-old Merle Carlson as she moves with her psychotic mother and two siblings first to camp in Wisconsin and then into a small rented house in town. Merle enjoys making friends until her mother's increasingly erratic behavior becomes more difficult to conceal. Eventually, Merle realizes she and her family cannot cope alone and a social worker intervenes. While the story ends with hope, the family will have to learn to live with their mother's illness. Merle's story is continued in *Crazy Quilt*. Sue Ellen Bridgers's *Notes*

[37]Sue Ellen Bridgers, *All Together Now* (New York: Knopf, 1979), p. 229.

for Another Life portrays the effects of a father's incurable mental illness and a mother's inability to cope with 13-year-old Wren and her older brother. While memorable grandparents help, it is up to Wren to make important decisions about her future in this young adult novel.

Aging and Death

In the early part of this century the aging and death of loved ones were accepted as a natural part of a child's firsthand knowledge. However, in most instances the modern child is removed from any such knowledge of senility and death. Few grandparents live with their families anymore and many relocate to apartments or retirement communities. When older relatives become ill they are shunted off to hospitals and nursing homes. Few people die at home today, and many children have never attended a funeral. Seldom is death discussed with children. Contemporary authors realize that there is enough genuine mystery about death, without hiding it under this false cloak of secrecy.

Today, realistic fiction for children reflects society's concern for honesty about aging and dying. We have moved from a time when the subject of death was one of the taboos of children's literature to a time when it is being discussed openly and frankly.

AGING

Many recent picture books have portrayed young people learning to accept older people as they are or to recall them fondly as they were (see Chapter 5). Realistic fiction portrays older people in all their rich variety, as treasured grandparents, as activists or as passive observers, as senile or vitally involved in events around them, and as still valuable contributors to a society they have helped to build.

The Hundred Penny Box written by Sharon Bell Mathis and illustrated by Leo and Diane Dillon tells of the love between Great-great-Aunt Dew, an aged African-American woman, and Michael, a young boy. Aunt Dew is 100 years old and she keeps a box full of pennies, one for each year of her life. Michael loves to count them out while Aunt Dew tells him the story behind each one,

relating it to life and historical events. Michael's mother wants to give the old box away but Michael plans a special hiding place for it. This story is remarkable for presenting three different viewpoints on the aged: Aunt Dew who is content to sing her long song and recall the past with her pennies, Michael's mother who has to take care of her, and Michael who loves her but in his childlike way also wants to be entertained by her storytelling. The Dillons have captured these sharply contrasting feelings in their fine brown-and-white pictures.

Two short novels with settings in earlier decades show the sustaining love a grandparent and child share. In Nancy Ruth Paterson's *The Christmas Cup,* nine episodes from a thoughtful third grader's life in the 1950s in Missouri are chronicled. In one story, Megan spends her hard-earned money at an auction to buy an old milkshake cup and is ridiculed by her friends. But her grandmother has a suggestion. They should use the cup to save small change, keep a record of all the people who have done nice things for them, and choose one to receive a secret special present at Christmas. Each episode suggests to the reader another person Megan and her grandmother might choose. While Megan may be from another era, her sense of honor and strong feelings about those who do right by her will surely resonate with contemporary readers.

Told from the point of view of its 10-year-old narrator who is unnamed in the story, Bruce Brooks's novel *Everywhere* depicts the love of the sensitive boy narrator for his grandfather who may be dying from a heart attack. In order to save his life, the boy and Dooley, nephew of his grandfather's African-American nurse, decide to try a "soul switch," which Dooley has read about in a comic book about Native Americans. Dooley finds a turtle that they plan to kill to "give the souls a chance to fly by each other in the sky." As the boy climbs the porch to see when his grandfather's soul is leaving, he witnesses another heart attack. Shocked, he cries out, which somehow calls his grandfather back from what seems to be the verge of dying. Whether Dooley actually kills the turtle isn't discovered until the final chapters when the boy and his grandfather are out in the garage working on a summer project before

Dooley returns to his family and school. Brooks has written a beautiful short novel filled with nuances, ambiguities, and depth. It will challenge sixth and seventh graders to wonder about the power of love and the gifts that friends may share with each other.

In *A Figure of Speech* by Norma Fox Mazer the problems of an older person in the home are presented more realistically. The theme that an older person is a person—not a senior citizen, a cliché, or figure of speech—is made very clear. This is a touching and poignant story of Jenny's love for her grandfather, who is tolerated by his family and then pushed aside when the older son and his wife come to live. The book ends tragically with the death of the old man. It is certainly a fine story to promote discussion of the way in which society treats older persons.

Peter Härtling's *Old John* is an independent, cantankerous, lovable and opinionated 75-year-old when he comes to live with Laura and Jacob's family. One of his prized possessions is a poster of Albert Einstein sticking out his tongue, a comment on Old John's belief that people should give themselves the freedom to put people on a little bit. Jacob comes to admire his independence and gradually learns about his Czech grandfather's involvement in anti-Nazi efforts during World War II. While each person in the family must cope with exasperation over the old man's habits, each loves him and learns from him. Old John finds raucous companions in the small German village where he now lives, paints and decorates his bedroom to his own tastes, picks up his former profession as a dyer, and even falls in love. However, he suffers a stroke and as the next year passes, becomes progressively more disoriented and crotchety. But the family rallies to care for him and he dies peacefully at home. In contrast to Mazer's story, this family copes as honorably as it can. Härtling lets incidents speak for themselves, leaving the reader to observe how life with an older person may be for one family. While Old John will "never be there again" on his favorite corner of the couch, the reader knows that he will be there in the minds of Jacob and Laura who are richer people for having known their grandfather so well.

There are also books that portray older people as active, lively, and interesting. Often children discover, much to their surprise, that old people can be interesting. In Lois Lowry's *Anastasia Again*, Anastasia devises a scheme for involving her grouchy neighbor with a group of lively older people at a local Senior Citizen center. In Eth Clifford's *The Rocking Chair Rebellion*, 14-year-old Opie (short for Penelope) volunteers at the Maple Ridge Home for the Aged when a former neighbor takes up residence there. She eventually is instrumental in helping several of the residents to leave and set up their own group home in her neighborhood. Although events are somewhat improbable, both Lowry and Clifford present older people as diverse, intelligent, active, and interesting as potential friends.

Another book which suggests that different generations have much to offer each other is Walter Dean Myers's *Won't Know Till I Get There*. Fourteen-year-old Steve Perry's family, who are African-American, decides to take in a foster child, but the one they are assigned is a street-tough 13-year-old named Earl Goins. When Earl and Steve trespass through a railroad yard with some of Steve's friends, Steve decides to show off and spray-paint a car with the name of his imaginary gang. They are caught by the transit police and eventually sent before a judge who sentences them to "volunteer" at an inner-city home for older people. There they become involved in the "seniors'" efforts to run the home themselves rather than move to larger facilities. Narrated by Steve, the story takes on a humorous upbeat style. The gradual revelation to Steve that "the more I get to know them the more I see them as individual people" is very believable. Realistically, the seniors do not get to keep their city-owned home and disband in the end, but Steve does gain a foster brother who needs him.

DEATH AND DYING

A child's first experience with death is frequently the loss of a pet. While picture books for younger children portray this experience with younger protagonists, several longer books have depicted slightly older children dealing with the death of a pet. In *The Growing Time* by Sandol Stoddard Warburg, Jamie's old collie dog King dies and Jamie is desolate. Eventually, the family buys Jamie a puppy, but he doesn't even want to look at it. In the middle of the night, however, the new pup cries and needs someone to love it. Jamie comes downstairs to comfort and claim him.

Charlotte Graeber's *Mustard* tells the story of a beloved old cat's eventual death from a series of strokes. Eight-year-old Alex stubbornly refuses to believe that his cat is dying. His father says, "I wish I could tell you Mustard will be okay, but we can only hope." After the sympathetic veterinarian puts Mustard to sleep, Alex tearfully helps his father bury the cat in the backyard. When he and his father go to the animal shelter to donate some of Mustard's things, they both agree that it is hard to consider another new cat. Alex thinks that maybe next Easter they will come back to the shelter, "But now he only had room for remembering Mustard." Emotions are portrayed honestly: both adults shed tears over their 14-year-old cat's death and Alex isn't ready yet to accept another pet. Donna Diamond's soft charcoal drawings portray family members and Mustard with warmth and truth.

Other children's first experience with death is the loss of a grandparent. Two warmly illustrated short stories show a child coping with the death of one grandparent while continuing a rewarding relationship with the remaining one. In Mavis Jukes's *Blackberries in the Dark*, Austin spends the summer on the farm with Grandma and everywhere around him are reminders of his grandfather: the tire swing he built, his fishing reel hanging in the barn, and his treasured old fishing knife now strangely out of place in the dining room cupboard. Grandpa had promised to teach him how to fish this summer and with him gone, there's no one to teach him or to help him pick blackberries at night. After Grandma and Austin recall the past summer, however, Austin starts out to pick blackberries on his own only to have his grandmother follow, complete with her husband's fishing gear, so the two of them can teach each other to fish. Readers can almost feel the two resolve to move on from grief to new challenges and the decision is neatly punctuated by Grandma's gift of Grandpa's fishing knife to Austin. Thomas B. Allen's black-and-white soft pencil illustrations capture poignancy, accept the pleasant loneliness of the farm, and depict the humor of Austin's story.

Overpowered by the scent of her deceased grandmother's cologne, Suzie privately grieves for her loss in Marcia Sewall's sensitive pastel-and-line drawing.

From *Saying Good-Bye to Grandma* by Jane Resh Thomas.

Marcia Sewall's full-color pastel and fine line illustrations reaffirm in a contrasting way that life goes on in the midst of one extended family's funeral gathering in *Saying Good-Bye to Grandma* by Jane Resh Thomas. Seven-year-old Suzie and her parents return to the small town where Mother grew up. While the many cousins play, the adults reminisce and occasionally weep as they fix meals and make arrangements. The narrator Suzie shares her concerns about not knowing what is going to happen at the funeral, her fears that she may not recognize Grandma in her casket, and her small guilt over "not being sad enough" because she played with her cousins.

Parents reassure her and Mom even says that funerals are for saying good-bye but also saying hello to family and friends. As in Jukes's story, sharing time by fishing with the remaining grandparent gives each child a time for reflection and reaffirmation.

A Taste of Blackberries by Doris Smith is a believable story of the sudden death of a young boy. Jamie and his friends are catching Japanese beetles for Mrs. Houser when Jamie shoves a slim willow limb down a bee hole. The bees swarm out and Jamie is stung. Allergic to bee stings, Jamie screams and gasps and falls to the ground. His best friend thinks Jamie is just showing off until the ambulance arrives. Jamie is dead by the time he arrives at the hospital. His friend goes to the funeral, and the author graphically describes his reaction to seeing Jamie:

❦ There was Jamie. He was out straight with one hand crossed over his chest. He didn't look like he was asleep to me. Jamie slept all bunched up. Jamie looked dead.[38]

After the funeral Jamie's friend picks blackberries because the two of them had planned to do so together. He shares the berries with Jamie's mother, who is very loving toward him. Because the story is told in the first person, the reader views death through a child's eyes. Simple, yet direct, this story seems very real. Titles such as Paterson's *Bridge to Terabithia* and Bauer's *On My Honor* are each about a child who suffers after the death of a friend (see earlier discussion in this chapter).

In *A Family Project* by Sarah Ellis, 11-year-old Jessica is increasingly annoyed with her 14-year-old brother Simon who has taken to wearing his Walkman to dinner. Mum, a distracted engineer, seems to parent in intense spurts governed by the latest magazine article she has read. Her oldest brother has moved into his own apartment and is making cloth bags for a living. When Jessica's parents announce that Mum is pregnant, Jessica is delighted and embarks on a class project of researching babies with her best friend Margaret.

Baby Lucie's arrival creates the expected chaos but also provides Jessica with special moments of love and appreciation including her overhearing Simon read *Motor Trends* aloud to the wailing Lucie. One night when Jessica is at a friend's slumber party, Lucie dies suddenly of sudden infant death syndrome. Following the funeral and a large gathering of friends and relatives, each member of the family grieves. Mum withdraws, Dad is frenetically busy, Simon is curt, and Jessica feels as if her life will never be joyous or whole again. Margaret acknowledges her friend's grief, saying that while time will help her feel less sad, she will always have a small sad spot in her memory for this baby sister. Weeks pass, and it is finally Simon and Jessica who help each other accept the death of their sister. Following Jessica's nighttime burst of tears, the two take a wild bicycle ride through the empty streets at three in the morning and stop for cocoa in an all-night restaurant. The companionship they feel for each other, and the peace and freedom they feel in the empty streets, returns them to the world. Ellis creates a totally believable contemporary family whose grief over the sudden death of a baby will be healed by their love for each other.

In two other stories, *Beat the Turtle Drum* by Constance Green and *A Summer to Die* by Lois Lowry, a sister also dies. Green's story, told by 13-year-old Kate, depicts the summer that Joss had saved her money, rented a horse, and finally in an accidental fall from a tree, was killed. Readers who have come to know the two sisters feel, along with Kate and her parents, the tragedy of Joss's death. Lowry's story presents two sisters who quarrel constantly until the older one contracts leukemia. While the author juxtaposes the celebration of birth with the sadness of a death, and Meg moves through the stages of dealing with her sister's death, the first story seems more compelling.

Robbie Farley felt that breaking his arm on the first day of summer vacation was the most terrible thing that could happen to him. But he finds out that *There Are Two Kinds of Terrible* when his mother goes to the hospital for tests and dies of cancer. Peggy Mann details Robbie's grief, anger, and bewilderment at his mother's sudden death. What makes it even harder to bear is that Robbie

[38]Doris Buchanan Smith, *A Taste of Blackberries*, illustrated by Charles Robinson (New York: Crowell, 1973), p. 34.

feels he doesn't really know the cool stranger who is his father. The adjustment to his loneliness and his father is slow and painful for them both. This is an honest and an intensely moving story of one boy's loss of his mother. *Grover*, by the Cleavers, reports the anger and frustration a young boy feels following his mother's suicide. Grover, too, has a difficult time relating to his father.

Crescent Dragonwagon's *Winter Holding Spring* is a simple poetic story with complex ideas about death, time, hope, and love. It begins as 11-year-old Sarah and her father can tomatoes just as her mother used to before she died. Both adult and child find it difficult to talk about their feelings, but they observe, as a yellow leaf falls, that the season of summer holds fall. The two go about the daily chores of living as fall turns into winter and winter holds tiny green promises of spring. Sarah uses the idea of a future embedded in the present to give herself hope and courage. This eventually allows Sarah to talk with her father about the small reminders of her mother: a twirly skirt she wore, the way she loved basil, and how much Sarah still misses her. As father and daughter talk, Sarah realizes that times past are also embedded in the present. Her mother's love will always remain with her. The elegant telling, the symbolism, and the philosophical discussion of death in the midst of life are grounded realistically for child readers in the ordinary events of Sarah's everyday life. Details are warmly depicted in Ron Himler's black pencil drawings of Sarah and her father in their New England town. This book enfolds the reader with comfort, courage, and warmth.

Another story that tells of a boy's emotional reconciliation following the death of a parent from cancer is told in Jean Little's *Mama's Going to Buy You a Mockingbird*. Eleven-year-old Jeremy and his little sister have spent an uneasy summer at their cottage with an aunt while their father has an operation in a nearby Canadian city. When his father returns, weak and pale, Jeremy refuses to accept his father's impending death. One evening his father and he share a sighting of two owls and his father commemorates the event with the gift of a small carved owl to Jeremy. Later in the fall when his father dies, Jeremy is unable to look at the owl and hides it on his bookshelf. He thinks,

Forgetting *was* the easiest way. When he forgot Dad was dead, when he forgot Dad altogether and concentrated on other things, then life was easier. When something made him think of his father—birds flying south, a song the two of them had liked coming over the radio, the sight of Dad's name written in the front of a book—he felt so mixed-up, lonely and scared that he wished with all his heart that he had not been made to remember.[39]

His new but tentative friendship with a lanky classmate Tess and a move to a new apartment where he adopts a grandfather help cheer him. It is only when he begins to think of the feelings of others that he can finally hold the small owl and realize the "more difficult" joy that remembering brings. Jean Little crafts an extraordinary story out of richly observed detail, humor, and the emotions of this loving family's reconciliation with their loss. The many references to other novels and poems with which Jeremy and his sister are familiar are a plus for readers. Another fine story, *Home from Far*, also by Jean Little, portrays a girl's resentment and anger following the death of her twin brother.

Previously discussed books deal with a child who recovers from the death of a friend, sibling, parent, or grandparent. *Hang Tough, Paul Mather* tells a memorable story of a boy who is anticipating his own death. Alfred Slote writes of Paul, a Little Leaguer who develops leukemia. The family moves from California to Michigan to be close to the university hospital where Paul will have special treatments. He is not supposed to play baseball, but the neighborhood team needs a pitcher for their big game. Paul slips out without his parents' knowledge, forges the permission slip, and pitches a great game. However, he injures himself and endures a long stay in the hospital. There, a young doctor becomes his friend. Their discussion of death is one of the most honest in children's literature. Paul leaves the hospital in his wheelchair, at least long enough to watch and help win another game. While Paul sounds hopeful at the end of the story, he is back in the hospital and his condition has worsened.

[39] Jean Little, *Mama's Going to Buy You a Mockingbird* (New York: Viking Kestrel, 1984), p. 151.

Two books for older readers discuss the impact of an awareness of death on life's possibilities. Mollie Hunter's compelling autobiographical novel *A Sound of Chariots* is the story of a young Scottish girl coming to terms with her father's death. Living with her nightmares about her father, Bridie finally faces the real meaning of death when her brother's pet rabbit dies. She makes her brother touch the cold stiff rabbit so he will finally know what dead means. Suddenly she is aware of her physical surroundings as if she could feel "the shape of the smallest stones on her feet . . . through all her senses she was filtering into their component parts the whole vast complex of smells and sounds, shapes, colors and textures through which she moved."[40] At last Bridie knows she is alive and despite her fear of death, she recognizes the present for the miracle it is.

Another powerful story which asserts that coming to terms with death can be an affirmation of life and hope is Madeleine L'Engle's *A Ring of Endless Light*. Vicky Austin, whom readers met in *Meet the Austins*, begins her sixteenth summer at graveside services for a family friend who has suffered a heart attack after rescuing a spoiled teenager from an attempted suicide. While Vicky is already grieving for the impending death of her family's beloved grandfather, she tries to understand what mortality and immortality mean. She also deals with the attentions of three different young men. Zachary, the boy who attempted suicide, is rich, impulsive, and exciting; Leo, whose father had tried to save Zachary, is plain and awkward but also reliable and candid; and Adam, a marine biologist studying the communication of dolphins, is warm, kind, and intensely eager to involve Vicky in his research after he sees her natural ability to communicate with dolphins. When the death of a child numbs Vicky, it is her experience with the dolphins that brings her back to an emotional present. Throughout the story shines the "ring of endless light" which her grandfather has been leading her to see. He tells Vicky, in the depths of her grief and denial:

"You have to give the darkness permission. It cannot take over otherwise . . . Vicky, do not add to the darkness. . . . This is my charge to you. You are to be a light-bearer. You are to choose the light."[41]

LIVING IN A DIVERSE WORLD

In a true pluralistic society it is essential that we learn to respect and appreciate the diversity of all cultures. Books can never substitute for firsthand contact with other people, but they can deepen our understanding of different cultures. Rather than falsely pretend that differences do not exist, children need to discover what is unique to each group of persons and universal to the experience of being human.

Appreciating Racial and Ethnic Diversity

The civil rights movement of the 1950s led to the publication of many books about integration (see Chapter 3). These books tended to emphasize similarity of groups rather than unique racial, cultural, or ethnic identities. Increasing activism in the 1960s further influenced the publication of books that featured Native Americans, Hispanic Americans, and African Americans. However, many of these titles went out of print rapidly when federal funds for schools and libraries diminished. Presently, we need more high-quality literature that reflects many ethnicities and the changing population of our schools. All readers should be able to find their own cultural heritage reflected in the literature they read. It is still necessary, however, to evaluate literature about minority people according to not only its general literary value but also the image of the minority group presented by the text and illustrations.

AFRICAN-AMERICAN EXPERIENCES IN BOOKS FOR CHILDREN

In the last decades many fine books have been published that reflect the social and cultural traditions associated with growing up as an African-American child in America. This "culturally con-

[40] Mollie Hunter, *A Sound of Chariots* (New York: Harper & Row, 1972), p. 135.

[41] Madeleine L'Engle, *A Ring of Endless Light* (New York: Farrar, Straus & Giroux, 1980), p. 318.

GUIDELINES

Evaluating Multicultural Literature

While the emphasis should be placed on selection of high-quality literature, the following guidelines[42] may be useful in evaluating literature that depicts minorities or other cultures:

1. *Diversity and range of representation.* In the portrayal of any minority group, a collection of books should show a wide range of representation of that particular race or ethnic group. While some African Americans live in city ghetto or rural settings, others live in middle-class suburbs and small towns. Although some Hispanic Americans make a living in migrant camps, most hold jobs that have nothing to do with seasonal crops. Only when a collection of books about a particular group offers a wide spectrum of occupations, educational backgrounds, living conditions, and lifestyles will we honestly be moving away from stereotyping in books and offering positive images about minorities.

2. *Avoidance of stereotyping.* Literature must depict the varieties of a particular culture or ethnic group. Illustrations should portray the distinctive yet varied characteristics of a group or race so that readers know they are looking at a people of, for example, Sioux, Jamaican, or Vietnamese descent. The portrayal of stereotypical articles should be avoided, such as the sombrero and poncho, a feathered headdress and moccasins, or the "pickaninny with a watermelon" so often pictured in children's books from earlier decades. Literature should avoid implying that specific occupations such as computer expert, recreational pastimes such as soccer, family organizational structure, or values are descriptive of any particular race or ethnic group. (For further discussion of stereotypes see Chapter 5, "Picture Books," and Chapter 11, "Informational Books.")

3. *Language considerations.* Derogatory terms for particular racial groups should not be used in stories about minorities unless these are essential to a conflict or used in historical context. Even then, it should be made clear that these unacceptable terms cast aspersion on the speaker, not the one spoken about or to. Another consideration is the use of dialect or "broken English." Some recent books about African Americans make a conscious effort to reproduce the cadence and syntax of certain language patterns without resorting to phonetically written spellings or stereotypic dialect. Books that incorporate the

---

[42] More detailed guidelines may be found in Augusta Baker, *The Black Experience in Children's Books*, New York Public Library, 1984; and Rudine Sims, *Shadow and Substance: Afro-American Experience in Contemporary Children's Fiction* (Urbana, Ill.: National Council of Teachers of English, 1982).

GUIDELINES

language of a minority group, such as Hispanic Americans, do not need to translate a word if context defines it. Children need to understand that all languages adequately serve their speakers and that no one language is better than another.

4. *The perspective of the book.* In evaluating a book about a minority group, we need to ask if it truly represents that minority's experience. This is a difficult guideline to define because we don't want to suggest there is only one sort of African-American experience, for example. Who solves the problems in stories? Do minority characters take the initiative in problem solving or are solutions provided by paternalistic whites? Are racial pride and positive self-image apparent in the story? How authentic are the details of the story to the experience of the represented minority?

No one is free from his or her own particular bias or background. Teachers or librarians in specific school settings may want to add other criteria to this list as they select books for children. It is essential to provide books about minorities for *all* children and to choose variety not merely reflecting the minority populations that specific schools serve. Books can help develop children's appreciation for our ever-changing pluralistic society.

scious fiction," says Rudine Sims, has certain recurring features which offer all children, but especially African-American children, a unique perspective in fiction. In culturally conscious fiction there often appear references to distinctive language patterns and vocabulary; relationships between a young person and a much older one; extended or three-generational families; descriptions of skin shades and positive comparisons made, such as "dark as a pole of Ceylon ebony"; and acknowledgment of African-American historical, religious and cultural traditions.[43]

Today, there is an increasing number of picture books and folktales by authors and illustrators such as Lucille Clifton, the late John Steptoe, Eloise Greenfield, Pat Cummings, Jerry Pinkney, and others, that portray an African-American

experience for younger readers (see Chapters 5 and 6). There are also an increasing but still small number of chapter books for younger readers. For instance, Ann Cameron's "Julian" series, such as *Julian, Dream Doctor*, portray a small-town family consisting of a soft-spoken mother, a stern but fun-loving father, and two brothers. In *Julian, Dream Doctor*, Julian's problem of what to give his father for his thirty-fifth birthday seems to be solved when he hears his father in his sleep seem to wish for "two big snakes." But Julian's problems just begin when he gives his terrified father a live snake. Another chapter book children of 7 or 8 can read easily is Lucille Clifton's *The Lucky Stone*. In four short chapters, Clifton traces the path of a black stone with a letter scratched on it as it is passed from generation to generation of African Americans, slave times to now.

Mildred Pitts Walter's *Justin and the Best Biscuits in the World* draws on information about African-American cowboys on the American frontier in the late 1800s while telling a contemporary story.

[43] Rudine Sims, *Shadow and Substance: Afro-American Experience in Contemporary Children's Fiction* (Urbana, Ill.: National Council of Teachers of English, 1982), pp. 49–77.

Tired of his family of sisters and his mother, 10-year-old Justin is relieved when his grandfather invites him to stay at his Missouri ranch. From Grandpa, Justin learns family history, how to clean fish, keep his room in order, and cook. When he goes home, Justin has developed self-confidence and his family is more appreciative of his talents. Walter's digressions about African Americans in the old west under the guise of books read by Justin may send some children to the library for further research. Another book by Walter, *Have A Happy . . .*, traces an 11-year-old boy's feelings as he tries to earn money to help out his family during the Christmas season. His participation in the events of Kwanzaa is presented so that even readers unfamiliar with this modern African-American holiday can visualize the celebration and understand its significance.

Using the device of a secret diary about her "special days," Eloise Greenfield has presented an intimate picture of Doretha, called *Sister* by her family. The diary begins when Doretha is 10 and details the sudden death of her father while they are all attending a picnic. At 11 Doretha learns the family's story of her freedom-fighting ex-slave ancestor. When she is 12 she records her tears and her mother's disappointment when her mother's friend jilts her. Throughout the book Doretha worries about her alienated sister, but gradually, Doretha emerges from the pages of her book and from her role of sister, to become a very real person in her own right.

A four-time winner of the Coretta Scott King Award, Walter Dean Myers sets many of his stories in Harlem, but he portrays a less grim, and even humorous, city existence in some of his stories. *The Mouse Rap*, which alternates between first and third person, is written in the vernacular and slang of jive-talking, rapping 14-year-old Mouse Douglas, boy "hoop" player. Mouse's parents are separated but his father wants to rejoin the family, and he and his best friend Styx like the same girl. Mouse is not clear about what he wants:

  Sometimes things you want in life come with little price tags on them that read "risk" and "not sure" and "confusion." The Mouse didn't want to give up anything. He didn't want to give up Mom to get Dad back, or Beverly so he'd be cool with Styx

again. The thought made The Mouse feel a little like Queasy Glider, so he Reeboked his psyche in the direction of the tube, where it was always safe from thoughts, good, bad, or otherwise.[44]

In addition, Mouse and his friends know an old man who used to be part of Tiger Moran's gang. The old fellow says there is money from a 1930s bank robbery hidden in an abandoned Harlem building. In an exciting and humorous conclusion, Mouse cleverly uses a television news reporter who is in the neighborhood covering a dance contest he and his friends have entered to gain a chance to explore the abandoned building. Myers also relies on the keen observations of an intelligent boy narrator in his *Fast Sam, Cool Clyde, and Stuff*, a story of the interdependence of a group of basketball-playing boys who inadvertently become involved with drugs while trying to help a former addict. The author's lighter books also show boys coping successfully with urban life. Myers has said, "I see most of my books as opportunities to say something in a nonpreachy way."[45]

In 1975, Virginia Hamilton was the first African American to win the Newbery award with *M.C. Higgins, The Great*. Like *Cousins*, it is set in southern Ohio where 13-year-old Cornelius Higgins and his family live on old family property just beneath a slag heap created by strip miners. M.C. dreams of moving his family away from the slow-moving heap that threatens to engulf their home. His place of refuge from which he surveys the world is a 40-foot steel pole. From there M.C. sees a "dude" who he imagines will make his mother a singing star and enable them to move. Another outsider, Lurhetta, who is hiking through this Appalachian section, awakens M.C.'s initiative and makes him see that he is never going to solve his problems by dreaming about them or swaying over them. M.C. is finally moved to a small but symbolic action. (Mildred Taylor in 1977 was the second African-American author to win the Newbery award. Her books are discussed in Chapter 10.)

[44] Walter Dean Myers, *The Mouse Rap* (New York: Harper & Row, 1990), p. 159.
[45] Stephanie Zvirin, "The Booklist Interview: Walter Dean Myers," *Booklist*, February 15, 1990, p. 1152.

Hamilton has also written *The Planet of Junior Brown*, which is really a story about three complementary "planets." The first planet is a huge mass added to a model solar system that Mr. Poole, the custodian, and Buddy have set up in the school basement. Like the 300-pound Buddy, the planet is larger than anything else in its area. The second is a set of sanctuaries for homeless boys throughout the forgotten places of New York City, held together by boys such as Junior Brown who act as leaders of homeless and familyless children. The final planet is the one that readers see as possible if people like Junior Brown could lead us there. This planet could be a place where everyone belongs, where people respect each other, and where all value themselves as well. Hamilton's books celebrate the uniqueness of an African-American experience in elegant and approachable prose. Her books speak to all readers, encouraging young people to take risks on behalf of others, to love all members of their immediate or extended or adopted families, and to do one's best to act responsibly and honorably, for all of these actions will improve a small part of humankind.

BOOKS ABOUT OTHER MINORITIES

There are far better quality and greater range in recent novels about African Americans than there are for other minorities. Informational books, folktales, biographies, and picture books do a much better job of reflecting the multicultural society in which we now live. In older books about Hispanic Americans, for instance, forced stories and thin characterizations tended to perpetuate stereotypes rather than dispel them. Other titles such as *Felita* by Nicolasa Mohr suggest that "stick to your own kind" is the only way 9-year-old Felita and her family can cope with prejudice from their new neighbors. They return to the ghetto rather than stay in an apartment building where they have no friends. In *Going Home*, Felita, now a sixth grader, spends a summer in Puerto Rico and recognizes the universality of prejudice when her friendliness and artistic talents cause jealousy from her Puerto Rican peers.

In striking contrast, Gary Soto's *Baseball in April and Other Stories* is an inspired collection of short stories that depicts a variety of Hispanic children

in daily life. Fausto longs for a guitar but his scheme to raise the money to buy one makes him feel so guilty that he finally gives the money to a church. When he becomes the owner of his grandfather's *guitarron*, his honorable behavior is amply rewarded. In other stories one girl becomes marbles champ while another learns that it may be more painful to stay home when your family goes on vacation than it is to endure their company. Soto's gentle portrayal of these central Californian children, through description and dialogue, reflects a sympathy for the universal experiences of growing up. A glossary helps those readers who cannot use context to translate the Spanish words and phrases that flow naturally through the story. His novel, *Taking Sides*, explores Lincoln Mendoza's divided loyalties when he moves from a barrio school to a suburban junior high school and competes in basketball against his former teammates.

An older story of a boy of Spanish descent is Joseph Krumgold's *. . . And Now Miguel*. Miguel is the middle brother of a Hispanic family living on a New Mexico sheep ranch. Pedro, the younger brother, seems satisfied with what he has, but Miguel thinks his 19-year-old brother Gabriel not only can do everything but also has everything. Miguel expresses the problem of all who feel "in between":

> Both of them, they are happy. But to be in between, not so little any more and not yet nineteen years, to be me, Miguel, and to have a great wish—that is hard.[46]

Miguel has one all-consuming desire, and that is to be able to go with the men when they take the sheep to the Sangre de Cristo Mountains. His prayers are answered, but not as Miguel wished. Because Hispanics are one of the fastest growing groups of immigrants to the United States, we still urgently need more contemporary realistic fiction that reflects Hispanic culture.

Asian Americans are among the most rapidly growing minority groups in North America. The few excellent stories set in this country that include children from countries in Asia are

[46] Joseph Krumgold, *. . . And Now Miguel*, illustrated by Jean Charlot (New York: Crowell, 1953), p. 9.

historical fiction titles such as Yoshiko Uchida's books which build on her experiences in the 1930s and in relocation camps for Japanese Americans in World War II. Jean Fritz's *Homesick: My Own Story* and Bette Bao Lord's *In the Year of the Boar and Jackie Robinson* are also in the past (see Chapter 10).

A notable exception is Laurence Yep's *Child of the Owl.* It is the fine story of a Chinese-American girl who finds herself and her roots when she goes to live with Paw Paw, her grandmother, in San Francisco's Chinatown. When Barney, Casey's gambling father, winds up in the hospital after being beaten and robbed of his one big win, he first sends Casey to live with her Uncle Phil and his family in suburbia. Casey doesn't get along with Uncle Phil's family and they are horrified by her, so she is sent to Chinatown. At first Casey doesn't like the narrow streets and alleys or the Chinese schools. But Paw Paw tells her about Jeanie, the mother Casey never knew, about her true Chinese name, and the story of the family's owl charm. Gradually she comes to appreciate it all and to realize that this place that was home to Paw Paw, Jeanie, and Barney is her home, too. *Child of the Owl* is as contemporary as the rock music that Paw Paw enjoys and as traditional as the owl charm, but Casey and Paw Paw are true originals.

Jamie Gilson's novel, *Hello, My Name Is Scrambled Eggs* takes its name from the stick-on labels Harvey Trumble uses to teach Vietnamese refugee Tuan Nguyen to speak English. He labels the ceiling, the dinner table items, and clothes in an effort to make learning fun while Tuan, his father, and grandmother are staying with Harvey until their own home is ready. Also sponsored by Harvey's church are Tuan's mother and baby sister who will follow later. Harvey further Americanizes Tuan by teaching him how to play computer games, and in an ill-advised caper, how to toilet-paper his Illinois town's monument to pork. Motivated by altruism but also by the power he feels over Tuan's welfare, he even gives Tuan an American name, Tom Win. But 12-year-old Tuan, eager to please, is nonetheless his own person, too. He teaches Harvey's rival Quint how to play marbles and is so adept at math that he eclipses even the "gift-ed" Quint in their seventh-grade class. And he decides that although he will be American, he will also keep his Vietnamese name. While Tuan wishes to be more American, he feels the tension between himself and his father who is unaccustomed to relying on his son to translate, and his grandmother who clings to her old ways. Gilson allows Tuan to reveal parts of his harrowing boat escape from Vietnam and a classmate's current events report fills in other details. Like Barbara Cohen's historical story *Molly's Pilgrim* (see Chapter 10), this novel culminates symbolically in a Thanksgiving celebration. Both would be excellent catalysts for discussing the many reasons, including political repression, that have caused people to emigrate to the United States.

Novels about Native-American minorities are also scarce. The following three novels, in geographically diverse settings, all depict teenagers involved in survival who must draw on their Native-American heritage in various ways.

In Kirkpatrick Hill's well-crafted survival story, *Toughboy and Sister* are suddenly on their own at the family summer fish camp in Canada's Yukon Territory after their widowed father, an alcoholic, literally drinks himself to death. The 11-year-old Toughboy, an Athabascan Indian, thinks what his future might have held had his father lived:

> Now he was old enough to go moose hunting, old enough to go trapping at the long trap line, old enough to go to the fish wheel by himself and learn everything he'd been waiting to learn. It was as if Daddy had cheated him, telling him to wait. . . . Then Daddy was gone.[47]

He and his sister expect to be rescued in a few days because their father's boat with his corpse in it will float downriver by their village. But when no one comes, the two must work together to cook, fish, make bread, deal with a pesky bear, and keep their clothes and the cabin clean. The survival of these two resourceful children doesn't compare to many other stories in this genre that feature greater dangers and deprivations. However, it does provide fourth- and fifth-grade readers with a sympathetic glimpse into the life of two self-reliant and strong Native-American children.

[47] Kirkpatrick Hill, *Toughboy and Sister* (New York: Margaret K. McElderry/Macmillan, 1990), p. 45.

In Jean Craighead George's *The Talking Earth*, Billy Wind, a Seminole Indian girl who has been to school at the Kennedy Space Center, scoffs at the legends of her ancestors. As Billy's punishment she is sent to stay in the Everglades for one night and two days to see if she then will believe in talking animals and little people who live under the ground. She is caught in a swamp fire and survives by hiding in one of the caves used by her ancestors. With the companionship of a pet otter, a baby panther, and a turtle, Billy Wind also lives through a hurricane and a tidal wave. After twelve weeks in the wilderness, she arrives home convinced that the animals do indeed know the earth as she and others do not. As in *Julie of the Wolves* (discussed previously in this chapter), George states a powerful ecological message.

Bearstone by Will Hobbs tells the story of 14-year-old Cloyd Atcitty, a Ute Indian who has lived resentfully in a group home in Durango, Colorado, for much of his life. Unable to live on the reservation with his remaining family, his grandmother and sister, Cloyd is placed for the summer on a ranch where he will work for an old widower named Walter. Angry, Cloyd runs off after he is driven to the remote ranch in the Colorado/Utah mountain country. Taking refuge in a small cave, he discovers a small carved stone bear, an animal important to Ute tribal beliefs. Adopting this bear as his totem, Cloyd decides to give Walter and ranch life a try. Later in the story, however, his violent encounters with bear hunters cause Cloyd to undo much of the good he has accomplished for himself and Walter. But a late summer pack trip into Walter's gold mine allows Cloyd to use some of his boyhood skills, to act intelligently to save a life, and to discover that, in the words of his grandmother, he might "live in a good way." While Cloyd and Walter develop respect for each other, Cloyd finds respect for himself. More important, in this excellent coming-of-age story, Cloyd's knowledge of his people's ways finally gives him the power to control his own life.

TOWARD UNDERSTANDING VARIOUS WORLD CULTURES

Despite the increasing number of fine books of nonfiction, and folklore and picture books from and about other countries, there are fewer novels that attempt to portray the lives of modern children and their families living in other places. Yet, as children study Australia or the countries of South America, Europe, or Africa, it is critical that they also be made aware of the stories that reveal the feelings of people in those countries. To emphasize this, the American Library Association annually gives the Batchelder Award to the publisher of the most outstanding book of that year which was first published in another country. These books, usually translated, are excellent firsthand accounts of life in other countries (see Appendix A). However, children may need to be reminded that no single book can convey a complete picture of a country and its people. In order to make this point clear, students might consider what book, if any, they would like to have sent to other countries as representative of life in the United States.

One of the few novels that reflects urban life for some in a Central American country is Ann Cameron's *The Most Beautiful Place in the World* (see p. 537). Third- or fourth-grade children who read this story learn something of the geography of Guatemala, the distant volcanoes and the cornfields, the customary stroll through the streets in the evening, and what a marketplace is like. However, they learn nothing about the political realities or the pervasive military influence in this country.

In contrast, one child's discovery of political realities is the focus of two books about South Africa. In Beverley Naidoo's *Journey to Jo'burg*, 13-year-old Naledi has lived a sheltered life in her village. While her mother works as a maid in Johannesburg over ninety miles away, their grandmother takes care of Naledi, her brother Tiro, and their little sister, Dineo. When Dineo sickens and it appears she may die, Naledi and Tiro decide to go to the city and bring their mother home. On the way, Naledi discovers what apartheid means to persons of color when she is rebuffed by the driver of a "whites" bus and witnesses a pass check. She contrasts her own family's values and lifestyle with those of the family where her mother works, and hears about political rallies in which people disappear. While the story concentrates on the children's efforts to return home and save Dineo from starvation and dehy-

Naledi convinces her brother that they must walk to Johannesburg to bring their mother home or their baby sister will die.

Illustration by Eric Velasquez for *Journey to Jo'burg* by Beverley Naidoo.

dration, Naledi, like the reader, is full of questions. Why is South Africa divided? What happens to those who want to see the system changed? Why is there such a contrast between the lives of whites and those of other races? While Naledi can't work this out by herself, she vows that she will begin to listen to the older children at school and will try to learn. In a sequel for older readers, *Chain of Fire*, Naledi learns that her village is to be relocated to a "homeland." A peaceful student demonstration is violently terminated by police, some of Naledi's neighbors betray their own peo-

ple, and homes are bulldozed. The move will eventually transpire, but not before Naledi and others unify to fight injustice.

Sheila Gordon's *The Middle of Somewhere* depicts the effects on two families of relocating their village. Nine-year-old Rebecca is frightened when the government threatens to bulldoze her house. Her friend Noni's family agrees to relocate, but Rebecca and her family stay. When Rebecca's father is arrested in a demonstration, the family must struggle to survive without him. Outside observers at his trial help gain his release at the time when Nelson Mandela is also released. Throughout this family crisis, Rebecca's constant friend is a beat-up white doll that she has treasured since childhood. But when she is given a new black doll, which she names Noni after her departed friend, she keeps both, a symbol of her hope that those of different races might be friends. This story of a family helping itself through difficult times is written for a younger reader than Gordon's earlier *Waiting for the Rain*, which also captures a feel for the geography, the people, and the language of South Africa.

In *The Year of the Panda* by Miriam Schlein, Lu Yi rescues a starving baby panda against his father's wishes, carries it around in a sling made of a pair of pants, and names it Su Lin. His Chinese village neighbors continue to chase away pandas from their beehives and out of their fields, but the starving pandas still move down from the high ground, where their food source, bamboo, has died out as it does every seventy years. They are seeking another kind of bamboo, but the villagers have cleared much of that to plant crops. If the villagers will relocate, a government official explains, their land will be made into a refuge for wild pandas. While his family refuses to move, Lu Yi agrees to accompany his pet by helicopter to a panda rescue center. There he witnesses what American and Chinese scientists are doing to save the giant pandas. His sadness at leaving Su Lin behind is tempered by the center's invitation for him to be a student aide the following year. Schlein's notes at the end of the story satisfy third and fourth graders' need to know "what happened next" while her research suggests the ways in which countries work together to save endangered species.

In Emily Cheney Neville's story 14-year-old Henrietta Rich spends *The China Year* in Beijing while her father is a "foreign expert" at the university. Through Henri's eyes, readers see modern Chinese city living just before the Chinese army drove into Tienanmen Square. When Henri befriends Li Minyuan, a boy her own age who spent a year in the United States, she is relieved to have someone with whom to talk, to bicycle to parks and stores, and to translate the language and culture for her. Misunderstandings result when Minyuan's nosy neighbor misinterprets the American family's visit to the Li family apartment as a black market contact and Henri nearly loses her friend. But Minyuan and Henri reach an understanding before the Riches must leave China suddenly because of Henri's mother's illness. The story unfolds in a variety of ways: Henri writes to friends back home, completes assignments for her correspondence courses, tells a 6-year-old American friend stories, and talks with Minyuan and others about the differences between Chinese and Americans. Cheney's slow-moving story both mirrors Henri's pace as she struggles to understand Chinese culture and subtly allows readers to absorb and visualize details of life in China in the early 1990s.

The Land I Lost: Adventures of a Boy in Vietnam by Quang Nhuong Huynh is a series of portraits remembered from the author's home village in the central highlands of Vietnam. Although it is "endless years of fighting" that make his homeland lost, his reminiscences barely mention war. Instead, his stories focus on people: farmers, hunters, bandits, his karate-expert grandmother, his older cousin who could capture pythons and train birds to sing popular tunes. Animals figure significantly in every episode—as pets, workers, or as formidable enemies. Tank, the family water buffalo, has knives strapped to his horns to help him defend the village herd from marauding tigers. Barriers are erected in the river to keep crocodiles from snatching luckless bathers. Vo-Dinh's illustrations capture the menace and fascination of many of these encounters. Each episode is sparely told, often humorous, and infused with the elusive meanings of folklore. *The Land I Lost* personalizes the Vietnamese people and may help children become acquainted with what has so often been represented as an alien land.

A Vietnamese girl comes to terms with the trauma of escaping from her country without knowing what has happened to the rest of her family in Diana Kidd's brief *Onion Tears*. In first-person narrative, Nam reveals her life with Auntie, and another refugee called Chu Minh who cooks in Auntie's restaurant, her cruel and thoughtless schoolmates in Miss Lily's class, and her constant longing to see her parents. As time passes, Nam is able to shed real tears over the sickness of her teacher instead of the onion tears she sheds as she helps in Auntie's kitchen. Instead of a lonely survivor, she is now a part of a school and neighborhood community. Based on interview accounts of girls who journeyed from Southeast Asia to Australia, this story has many gaps that readers must fill by inference. Children may be misled by Lucy Montgomery's line drawings, which misrepresent the characters' ages. This book would be a good small group choice for its excellent discussion possibilities about Nam and the qualities she possess that make her, too, a survivor.

Ivan Southall's *Josh* is also a story of survival, both psychological and physical, of a 14-year-old Australian boy who goes to visit the country town that was settled by his great-grandfather. Josh, a dreamer and a poet, seems to do everything wrong. During his three-day visit the young people of Ryan Creek treat him first with veiled hostility and later with open violence. While his aunt says that Josh has been a catharsis for the small town, his struggle to survive in this world he does not understand is more than he can bear. He cuts short his stay and starts to walk back to Melbourne. Other authors who set their novels in contemporary Australia include Patricia Wrightson, Ruth Park, Emily Rodda (see Chapter 7), and Robin Klein.

Two books that have won the Batchelder Award come from Scandinavia. Nina Ring Aamundsen's *Two Short and One Long* gets its title from the burping talent that 12-year-old Jonas and his friend Einar share with each other. The two have been friends ever since Einar came to Oslo to live with his grandparents following the death of his parents. Einar won't talk about his past and always leaves some token article of clothing in Jonas's house as a guarantee that he will be allowed to return. When Jonas befriends an Afghan boy, Hewad, Einar withdraws and Jonas is confused about how well he thought he knew his friend. The three boys eventually become friends after a racist incident provokes Jonas and his father into taking action. The first-person narrative, the plot advanced through dialogue and fast action, the theme of overcoming racism, and the realistic portrayal of a maturing friendship appeal to middle-school-aged readers. *If You Didn't Have Me* by Ulf Nilsson appeals to younger readers and takes place on a Swedish farm where two brothers are staying with their grandparents while their parents build a new house. The older brother details all the things that might go wrong on the farm "if you didn't have me."

Jan Mark was awarded a Carnegie Medal for *Thunder and Lightnings,* a story of friendship between two British boys. Andrew, a city boy who has recently moved to the country, doesn't quite know what to make of his classmate, the unconventional Victor. Victor wears several layers of clothes, has a cluttered bedroom full of model airplanes, and a generally loving but disorderly family life in contrast to Andrew's well-ordered and sterile one. As Victor introduces Andrew to the many aircraft that come and go from a nearby field, Andrew begins to understand Victor and value his friendship. The novel is concerned with the fine-tuning of observation—seeing what is actually there, whether drawing fish or airplanes—or sensing what may not be readily apparent: our need to care and be cared about. In *Handles,* Mark presents 11-year-old Erica who loves motorcycles. When she stays with her relatives in the country, she sneaks away to hang out at Mercury Motorcycles, a dingy repair shop where the owner gives imaginative nicknames, or handles, to the people who visit his muddy yards. Erica longs to be part of this kingdom, with a handle of her own, which is finally awarded. Jan Mark's subtle wordplay, her observations of everyday detail, and her ability to see the quirks of the adult world through the eyes of a child narrator make these stories rewarding to read.

The Cholistan desert area of modern Pakistan is the setting for the coming of age of *Shabanu: Daughter of the Wind* in Suzanne Fisher Staples's riveting portrait of a young girl in a family of nomadic camel herders. Shabanu, nearly 12, knows that she must accept an arranged marriage in the next year following the wedding of her older sister Phulan. However, as the time of Phulan's marriage draws near, the two girls are accosted by a rich landowner's hunting guests, who threatened to abduct and rape the pair. In seeking revenge, Phulan's intended husband is killed. Phulan is quickly married to her sister's betrothed, and Shabanu is promised against her will to an older man as his fourth wife. Shabanu struggles to reconcile her own independent spirit with her loyalty to her family. An aunt offers support, saying, "Keep your wits about you. Trust yourself. Keep your inner reserves hidden." Shabanu chooses to run away but when a much loved camel she has raised breaks his leg in the desert, she decides to stay with him and accept the beating she knows will follow when her father finds her. She will accept her marriage, too, but she vows to herself that no one can ever unlock the secrets of her heart. Telling her compelling story in present tense, Shabanu faces giving up her life as a camel herder, discovers and accepts her sexuality, and finds a place in the adult world. Vivid details of camel behavior, camel-trading fairs, feasts and celebrations, the differing roles of men and women, and the ever-changing desert are brilliantly evoked for older readers. It is difficult for Western readers to imagine that this story takes place today. Reading *Shabanu* would certainly lead readers to discussion of women's roles in other countries as well as their own.

Many young adult novels also deal with contemporary life in other lands. *The Honorable Prison* by Lyll Becerra de Jenkins depicts the internment of Marta's family in an Andean Mountain village when her father's political opinions fall out of favor. In *The Forty-Third War* by Louise Moeri, 12-year-old Uno is conscripted into the army and forced, like the reader, to learn of the harsh realities of a Central American military state. *The Return* by Sonia Levitin is a survival story of Ethiopian Jews trying to escape to Jerusalem. Minfong Ho's *Rice Without Rain* presents the class struggles for land reform in Thailand in the 1970s as seen by 17-year-old Jinda. While some middle schoolers may be ready for the complex political and emotional scopes of young adult novels such

TEACHERS DISCUSS LITERATURE BY AND ABOUT MINORITIES

Three curriculum specialists in Fairfax County Public Schools in northern Virginia were concerned that teachers were not incorporating books by and about minorities into their classroom reading programs. With a significant and growing population of minorities, the school system needed to modify its choices of assigned reading. The specialists noted that while they provided annually updated book lists and library media specialists added multicultural titles to school collections, these titles did not then become a part of classroom study. They concluded that teachers would not work recent books into their curriculum unless they had read and discussed the books. Providing book lists was not enough to change teacher behaviors.

A modest sum of grant money was available for programs that would "improve minority achievement." So they invited teachers in grades four through twelve to hold book discussion groups. Groups of at least three teachers agreed to discuss one book per month for a three-, four-, or five-month period. In-service credits could be earned for time spent in discussion. They supplied a list of paperback books (purchased with grant and other money) that could be checked out from a central office location and were available in multiple copies. Titles included Gary Soto's *Baseball in April*, *El Chino* by Allen Say, *The Talking Earth* by Jean Craighead George, Virginia Hamilton's *Cousins*, Diana Kidd's *Onion Tears*, and Mildred Taylor's *The Friendship*.

They were overwhelmed by the response. Over 300 administrators and teachers in all subject areas formed groups in 35 of the 37 schools in their area. The three facilitators drew up charts of which schools needed which books and shipped them via interoffice mail. The facilitators' advice to discussion leaders was to talk about the book. "Talk about whatever you want. Did you like it? Was it good? And save the inevitable question of how you would use it in the classroom for the very last." The groups began to meet.

As a result of these discussions, teachers discovered many books new to them, and also read beyond the book list to find additional titles to add to it. Their book evaluation skills increased. They became risk takers as they ventured opinions and discovered how the responses of others meshed, illuminated, or conflicted with their own responses. In fact, in evaluating the program, teachers indicated that what was most important to them was the experience of discussing books with their peers. Many of the books are now in children's hands. A grant provided some extra funding so that participating schools could purchase minority literature. The discussion groups are still meeting and continuing to add new books to their classroom reading plans.

This could happen anywhere, couldn't it? What it takes is some planning, some seed money to purchase multiple paperbacks of selected titles, and the belief that teachers are willing to change if given support.

This program was designed and carried out by Joan Lewis, Shirley Bealor, and Patricia M. Williams, Curriculum Specialists in Area II of the Fairfax County Public Schools.

as these, teachers should read first those titles that they plan to introduce into the classroom.

All children deserve a chance to read about the lives of children living in other lands. As our globe shrinks, books such as these contribute to a deeper, richer, more sympathetic and enduring communication between people.

POPULAR TYPES OF REALISTIC FICTION

Certain categories of realistic fiction are so popular that children ask for them by name. They want a good animal story, usually about a dog or horse; a sports book; a "funny" book; or a good mystery. Each decade seems to have a popular series, as well, which lingers on the bookshelves. From Gertrude Chandler Warner's "Boxcar Children" to Ann Martin's "Baby-sitters Club," from "Nancy Drew" and the "Hardy Boys" to Patricia Reilly Giff's "Kids of Polk Street School," children read one volume and demand the next. Many of these books are not high-quality literature, and we would hope children would not read these titles to the exclusion of other books.[48] Yet many of these stories do serve the useful function of getting children hooked on books so that they will move on to better literature. Children also develop fluency and speed as they quickly read through popular books or a series. Teachers and librarians need to identify and evaluate these popular books. Knowing and honoring the books children like increases an adult adviser's credibility, while also allowing him or her to recommend other titles that can broaden children's reading choices.

Humorous Stories

Children like to laugh. The humorous verses of contemporary poets such as Shel Silverstein or Jack Prelutsky represent children's favorite

---

[48] For a discussion of some of the values to the reader of reading series books, see Margaret Mackey's "Filling the Gaps: *The Baby-sitters Club,* the Series Book, and the Learning Reader," *Language Arts,* vol. 67, no. 5 (September 1990), pp. 484–489.

poetry (see Chapter 8). Collections of jokes and riddles circulate at all levels of the elementary school. Humorous realistic fiction often presents characters involved in amusing or exaggerated predicaments that are then solved in clever or unique ways. Often these stories are episodic in plot structure; each chapter might stand alone as a complete story.

The "Amelia Bedelia" stories are an easy-to-read series that feature the literal-minded maid of the Rogers family. Amelia follows Mrs. Rogers's instructions to the letter. She can't understand why Mrs. Rogers wants her to dress the chicken or draw the drapes, but she cheerfully goes about making a pair of pants for the chicken and drawing a picture of the drapes. Her wonderful lemon meringue pie saves the day—and her job. Peggy Parish wrote several Amelia Bedelia books, illustrated by various artists, in which the maid continues to misinterpret English expressions. These modern noodlehead stories include *Teach Us, Amelia Bedelia; Thank You, Amelia Bedelia;* and *Amelia Bedelia Helps Out* and are very funny to those who are just themselves learning to understand that simple words in special combinations have special meanings.

Young readers who ask for "longer books" have found repeated satisfaction with Carolyn Haywood's enduring and humorous series about "Little Eddie" or "Betsy." Eddie is portrayed as a typical American boy whose passion for collecting usually turns a profit for him. Betsy involves her friends and family in neighborhood and school activities. While the dialogue seems dated and the incidents often pedestrian, these stories provide a safe, predictable experience for fledgling readers.

Beverly Cleary's stories about Ramona have probably made more real readers than any basal reading series has. She has written another genuinely funny series of books about a very normal boy named *Henry Huggins.* In the first book Henry's problems center on a stray dog named Ribsy and Henry's efforts to keep him. In *Henry and Beezus,* Henry's major interest is in obtaining a new bicycle. At the opening of the Colossal Market he is delighted when he wins one of the door prizes but then horrified to find out it is $50 worth of Beauty Shoppe services. Cleary's intimate knowledge of boys and girls is evident as she describes their problems, adventures, and hilarious activities.

The opening chapter of Barbara Park's *Skinnybones* is also hilarious. The self-acclaimed funniest person in the sixth grade is telling his story about trying to enter a catfood commercial contest. In addition, Alex (also known as Skinnybones) has been a size "small" in Little League for six years, never is able to catch the ball or make a hit, and is the butt of the class bully's jokes. While the bully wins the baseball trophy, Alex wins, too, in this story of a wise-cracker with a knack for getting into trouble.

Peter Hatcher's endless problems with his brother begin in Judy Blume's *Tales of a Fourth Grade Nothing*. In this story, Fudge, whose real name is Farley Drexel Hatcher, aged 2, eats Peter's pet turtle but the long-suffering Peter earns a pet dog. In *Superfudge*, Peter narrates further complications in his life—new baby sister Tootsie, new school, and new friends—when his family moves to New Jersey. Fudge begins kindergarten much to Peter's embarrassment and dismay. *Fudge-a-Mania* chronicles a near disastrous summer vacation when the Hatchers and Sheila Tubman and her family share a Maine vacation home. Blume fans will recognize Sheila from *Otherwise Known as Sheila the Great*. Dialogue and plot unfold like television situation comedies in these entertaining stories appealing to children in second through fifth grades.

How to Eat Fried Worms by Thomas Rockwell begins with a dare and a $50 bet. To win it, Billy plans to eat fifteen worms in fifteen days. They are fried, boiled, and smothered with catsup, horseradish, and other toppings. Each ingestion becomes more bizarre the closer Billy comes to winning his bet. The brief chapters, extensive and amusing dialogue, and the plot make this a favorite story of less able middle-grade readers.

One of the funniest books to be published for children is Barbara Robinson's *The Best Christmas Pageant Ever*. The six Herdman children are the terror of the public school, so it is not surprising that they extend their reign of terror to Sunday School and take over the Christmas pageant. The poor unsuspecting substitute teacher cannot understand why only the Herdmans volunteer for parts in the pageant, unaware that they have threatened to stuff pussy willows down the ears of any children who raise their hands. Since the Herdmans have never heard the Christmas story before, their interpretation is contemporary, humorous, and surprisingly close to the true meaning of Christmas.

In the "Bagthorpe Saga," British author Helen Cresswell presents a family in which anything might happen—and usually does. Poor *Ordinary Jack* thinks he has no distinguishing qualities ("strings in his bow") to compete with the other members of this brilliantly talented British family. *Absolute Zero* features Jack's much maligned dog, who rises to fame as a result of the family's competition to win prizes by entering contests. Cresswell's humor derives from her ability to involve her zany characters in preposterous situations while writing with understatement and restraint. When Jack and Uncle Parker attempt to train the lethargic Zero to sit up, Jack must model the act:

> "Now," whispered Jack to Uncle Parker, "you say, 'Up!' and I'll sit up and beg. If I do it and he doesn't, you say 'Good boy!' and pat my head, and give me the biscuit."
>
> Uncle Parker nodded. He delved in the bag and came up with a chocolate digestive which he broke in half.
>
> "Right."
>
> He held the biscuit aloft halfway between Jack and Zero.
>
> "Up. Sit up. Beg. Good boy—boys, rather."[49]

Other books in the series pit the Bagthorpes against obnoxious relatives, send the family into frantic self-sufficiency preparations, and chronicle their ill-fated holiday in a haunted house in Wales.

There are certainly many other books in which humor plays a part. The fantasies of Roald Dahl and Daniel Pinkwater, for instance, often portray absurd situations that children find funny. The animal antics in stories by Farley Mowat or Nina Bawden cause readers to laugh out loud. The snappy retorts of Carlie in Betsy Byars's *The Pinballs* or her accurate and humorous observations of everyday school situations in *The Burning Questions of Bingo Brown* give readers a smile of

[49] Helen Cresswell, *Absolute Zero* (New York: Macmillan, 1978), p. 24.

recognition. The "Magic School Bus" series by Joanna Cole and Bruce Degen are examples of nonfiction packaged in child-appealing humorous asides and funny conversation balloons. Humorous books need no justification other than that they provide pure enjoyment. They are a healthy contrast to a reading diet that may be overburdened with contemporary social problems. Funny stories also beg to be shared with other readers in the classroom and are powerful reading catalysts. Children who laugh with books are building a love of reading in which enjoyment is the foundation.

Animal Stories

Stories about animals provide children with the vicarious experience of giving love to and receiving devotion and loyalty from an animal. Frequently, these animal tales are really stories of the maturing of their major characters. For example, the well-loved story of *The Yearling* by Marjorie Kinnan Rawlings is as much the story of Jody's growth and realization of the consequences of giving love as it is the story of a boy's discovery and raising of a pet deer. Sterling North's *Rascal: A Memoir of a Better Era* presents a boy who shares happy outings with his father, worries about his older brother serving in World War I, builds a canoe in the living room, and raises a crow and a raccoon as pets. But Sterling gradually and painfully realizes that his beloved companion raccoon, Rascal, will survive only in the wild.

Using the setting of Wales where her family moved to avoid the World War II bombings of London, Nina Bawden tells a humorous autobiographical tale about *Henry*, their pet squirrel. Shot out of a tree as a baby and adopted immediately, Henry sleeps in the sleeve of a jacket, makes nests or dreys from dirty laundry, swears "vut, vut, vut," eats nuts, apple "pips," or things he finds in the children's pockets, and generally intoxicates the family with his antics. At one point, Nina's two younger brothers discuss letting Henry go:

🐿 "Perhaps he'd rather be wild," James said. "He'd have other squirrels to play with."

"He's got us," Charlie said indignantly. "He's got four extra good trees. Not just nut trees but trees that grow biscuits and sweets and all sorts of nice things. I bet he's glad he hasn't got to find his own food."

"He can't be glad," James said. "I mean, he can't be glad because he's never had to look after himself, so he doesn't know if he'd like it better or not. He only knows what it's like to be a pet. He might rather be a real squirrel."[50]

Like Bawden's *The Peppermint Pig*, this novel is more than an animal story as the perceptive 12-year-old narrator reflects on rural life, the wartime absence of her father, the death of an elderly neighbor, and her own inadvertent release of Henry, which readers are alerted to on the first page of the story.

Like Nina Bawden, Jean Craighead George draws on her own experiences with animals to provide fascinating information and many humorous anecdotes about crows as part of her novel, *The Cry of the Crow*. Mandy is used to roaming the piney woods surrounding her family's Florida strawberry farm and rescues a fledgling crow shot from its nest. Naming it Nina Terrance, she secretly raises it over the summer, learns to recognize crow calls, and teaches it to make some human speech sounds. Torn between letting the maturing crow go with the flock and keeping it as a pet, she opts to keep the crow. But crows have been known to seek revenge and when Mandy, and finally Nina Terrance, discover that it was Mandy's brother who shot the crow's nest, she must face the consequences of having kept a wild animal as a pet when the crow attacks her brother. Jean George's careful research is skillfully woven into this story of the difficult choices people must make as they grow to maturity.

The companionship between a South Australian boy and his pet pelican, Mr. Percival, is poetically told in Colin Thiele's *Storm Boy*. With a friend, Storm Boy soon trains the pelican to drop a fishing line out beyond the breakers so that he and his father can fish even on stormy days. It is this skill that enables Mr. Percival to save a wrecked tugboat crew by dropping a line over the boat's bow. When Mr. Percival is killed by a

---

[50] Nina Bawden, *Henry*, illustrated by Joyce Powzyk (New York: William Morrow, 1988), p. 65.

hunter, Storm Boy decides to accept the captain's offer to send him to boarding school in Adelaide. But Storm Boy and his friend back home do not forget: "And everything lives on in their hearts— the wind-talk and wave-talk, and the scribblings on the sand; the coorong, the salt smell of the beach . . . and the long days of their happiness together."[51]

Horse and dog series comprise a great number of animal stories and are favorites of intermediate children. Walter Farley's popular series begins with *The Black Stallion* who, along with Alec Ramsey, are the only survivors of a shipwreck. Later, the boy secretly trains the horse to run in the Derby. Other titles in the series, such as *Son of Black Stallion*, emphasize the horse's training and racing over the development of the people characters. The best known of Marguerite Henry's well-researched horse stories is *Misty of Chincoteague*. The wild horse descendants of ship-wrecked Spanish horses are rounded up on Assateague Island and herded ashore and sold each year. When Paul and Maureen buy a wild horse and her colt, they train both, only to have the mother run away. *Stormy, Misty's Foal*, continues the story. *King of the Wind* won a Newbery award for Henry's portrayal of the devotion of a deaf-mute Arabian boy to a horse.

Dogs respond to human affection and return it warmly. This bond of love is one of the themes in Taylor's *The Trouble with Tuck*. Like Marguerite Henry, Theodore Taylor based his novel on a true story. Helen lacked self-confidence until she became involved in raising Tuck, a beautiful golden Labrador given to her by her parents. Tuck once saved Helen from drowning and is devoted to her. By the time Helen reaches 13, Tuck has grown totally blind. Rejecting the advice of the veterinarian to give Tuck to the university for research or have him put to sleep, Helen finds an alternative—she obtains a seeing-eye dog for Tuck. Jealous and confused, Tuck refuses to accept this stranger until Helen's patient and innovative training methods teach Tuck to follow the guide dog. As the two dogs parade before Helen and her proud family, the

reader rejoices in both canine and human triumphs. The focus shifts from Tuck to a Korean boy the family adopts in a sequel, *Tuck Triumphant*.

In Jane Resh Thomas's *The Comeback Dog*, Daniel must decide if he is once again going to risk his love on a dog who has already rejected him. While 9-year-old Daniel is still grieving for the loss of his old dog, Captain, he discovers a starved and nearly drowned English setter in the culvert near his family's Michigan farm. He brings the dog home, calls it Lady, and nurses her back to health, assuming that she will return his love in the same way Captain did. But Lady, who has been mistreated, cringes from Daniel's touch and refuses to wag her tail for him. One day, in anger at her lack of affection, Daniel yanks Lady's chain.

> "What's the matter with you," he said. "I'm the one who fed you when you were half dead."
> "You can't squeeze blood out of a turnip, Daniel," said his mother quietly at the kitchen door.
> "What's that supposed to mean?"
> "You can't get love by force, if she's not willing."[52]

Daniel angrily unleashes the choke chain that holds Lady and she bounds away over the fields. She is gone, only to return a week later bristling with porcupine quills. Sympathetic parents who show their love finally help Daniel to show his. In *Fox in a Trap*, a sequel which begins the day after the previous book ends, Daniel begs his uncle to teach him to trap. His father warns, "Trapping isn't pretty. I don't think you're going to like it." While Daniel struggles with his need to be different from his father and his mixed feelings over his uncle's nomadic career, he also gains the courage to admit to himself and to his family his detestation of trapping. Troy Howell's frequent illustrations, the believable dialogue, and short chapters make these two books easily approachable by independent 8- or 9-year-old readers.

Meindert DeJong's moving story *Hurry Home, Candy* tells of another dog's search for love and

[51] Colin Thiele, *Storm Boy*, illustrated by John Schoenherr (New York: Harper & Row, 1978), p. 62.

[52] Jane Resh Thomas, *The Comeback Dog*, illustrated by Troy Howell (Boston: Houghton Mifflin, 1981), pp. 45–47.

security. Candy had first been owned by two children and punished with a broom by their impatient mother. Finally, he would sleep: "A troubled broom-haunted sleep in which his paws twitched nervously because in his sleep he was fleeing from the fretful broom."[53] In a storm Candy is separated from the family, and fear of a broom across the ditch prevents him from crossing to them. Alone, hungry, lost, and sorrowful, he at last finds shelter with a man, a retired captain turned artist. One night, the artist interrupts some thieves, and the news story brings the original owners. But the children want only the reward, not the small dog. Candy hides again, but is drawn to the house by hunger. Once more, a broom stands between the dog and love and security. The captain discovers the source of the dog's fear; at the same time he gains understanding of his own. The big man tosses the broom aside, and the dog edges his way to food, to love, and home.

In Phyllis Reynolds Naylor's Newbery award-winning *Shiloh*, Marty Preston befriends a cringing stray beagle that surrounds the boy with joy. The dog, however, belongs to a neighbor known for abusing his animals; Marty, reluctantly but obedient to his father, returns the puppy. When the half-starved dog later slinks back to the field by the Preston home, Marty decides to hide the dog in the woods of his West Virginia mountain hollow. He deceives his family until a crisis forces him to fight for his principles and confront the owner of the dog he has named Shiloh. Well-drawn characters, a strongly realized setting, and a quick-paced plot are woven into this first-person narrative. Like Bauer's *On My Honor*, this story asks upper elementary students to think about what constitutes honorable and responsible behavior when rebelling against parents and their beliefs.

Heroic dogs who overcome obstacles are the subject of popular animal stories for children. Sheila Burnford's book of three runaway pets is an odyssey of courage and endurance, as a young Labrador retriever, an old bull terrier, and a Siamese cat make *The Incredible Journey*. Left with a friend of their owner, the animals try to reach their home more than 250 miles away. Hunger,

storms, dangerous river crossings, and fights are the nearly insurmountable problems of these three animals. Their survival and care for each other make a remarkable story.

A sled dog named Searchlight and his owner, little Willy, are the heroes of John Reynolds Gardiner's well-loved story, *Stone Fox*. Little Willy needs five hundred dollars to pay off the back taxes on his grandfather's farm or it will be taken from them. So the two enter a dogsled race but among the contestants is the legendary Indian Stone Fox with his five Samoyed sled dogs. Willy nearly wins the race but Searchlight's heart gives out in a final burst of speed just before the finish line. In the moving conclusion, Stone Fox and his team halt just short of the finish while Willy carries his dog across the line to win the race and save his farm. This short story, an excellent read-

Little Willie and Searchlight harvest the potatoes for his sick grandfather to help to make his payment on their Wyoming farm.

Drawing by Marcia Sewall for *Stone Fox* by John Reynolds Gardiner.

---

[53] Meindert DeJong, *Hurry Home, Candy*, illustrated by Maurice Sendak (New York: Harper, 1953), p. 39.

aloud choice, causes fourth- and fifth-grade readers to ask for tissues and more animal stories.

Where the Red Fern Grows by Wilson Rawls is a heartwarming sentimental tale of the love between two hound dogs and their master. Young Billy trains his two dogs, Old Dan and Little Ann, to be the finest hunting team in the Cherokee country of the Ozarks in northeastern Oklahoma. Twenty-five sets of hounds are entered in the big coon hunt. After five nights of hunting, catching the coons, skinning them, and turning in the hides, Billy's hounds win three hundred dollars and the first-place cup. During the hunt Old Dan and Little Ann nearly freeze to death after getting lost during an unexpected blizzard. When the family decides to move, Billy plans to remain behind with his beloved grandfather and the two dogs. But when both dogs die, one defending Billy against a mountain lion attack and one pining away, he regretfully joins his family's departure. Billy's decision is reaffirmed when a legendary red fern springs up at the dogs' gravesite. This story is memorable to 10-, 11-, and 12-year-olds because of its warmth and the strong portrayal of devotion between humans and animals.

Occasionally, books intended for an adult audience become part of the reading of older children. Jack London's *The Call of the Wild* was written for adults but is read by some gifted middle-grade students. The men in the story are ruthless and the dog Buck returns to the wildness of nature just as the men revert to force and cruelty to survive. Jim Kjelgaard communicates a love of wilderness through exciting dog stories like *Big Red*, a tale of an Irish setter groomed for championship showing who, along with his 17-year-old trainer, faces the bear Old Majesty. Farley Mowat's *The Dog Who Wouldn't Be* tells of his boyhood on the Saskatchewan prairie in the company of his "Prince Albert retriever" named Mutt and a score of other animal pets. In his shorter novel, *Owls in the Family*, Mowat recounts in hilarious detail his adventures in acquiring and training two pet great horned owls, the intrepid Wol and his timid companion, Weeps.

Sports Stories

Sports fiction for children reflects their energetic participation and interest in a variety of individual and team sports. Recent fiction includes team sports such as baseball, football, soccer, and basketball. It also includes books about such popular individual sports as tennis, running, gymnastics, dirt-bike racing, skateboarding, and swimming. Fiction, biography, and informational books about sports extend and enrich the personal experiences of the child who participates in or observes sports.

It is difficult to find well-written sports stories. Most of the characters are flat, one-dimensional figures. The dialogue tends to be stilted, and the plots predictable. Nevertheless, children continue to select these stories because they are so personally involved and interested in the activities. Series such as Dean Hughes's "Angel Park All-Stars" and "The Rookies" series by various authors cater to sports fans.

While there are now many more stories that feature girls in sports, the female athlete has made little impact on formula sports fiction. The same clichés—making the team through hard work or overcoming fear and triumphing over pain—are prevalent in both stories for boys and stories for girls. One important change, however, is that girls on boys' sports teams are no longer greeted with disbelief and protest.

Matt Christopher's many sports stories include titles for young readers as well as for those in middle school. Christopher's books depend on accounts of games or sports for their interest, but problem themes are usually developed as well. For example, in *Dirt Bike Racer*, a boy find a dirt bike in the bottom of a lake and restores it to working order. But the job he takes to earn money for bike parts is with an old man whose jealous nephew begins to make trouble. Christopher skirts the edges of fantasy in *Skateboard Tough* when Brett unearths a skateboard which seems to convey special powers to its owner. Brett's abilities multiply but so do his problems. Christopher always describes something of the thrill of the play and action of a sport—whether hockey, swimming, running, or baseball.

A more serious story that portrays characters of real depth and understanding is *Thank You, Jackie Robinson* by Barbara Cohen. While the story takes place in 1947–1948, it is written in the first person and told as a reminiscence to a contemporary child. Sam Green is the only son of a Jewish widow who runs an inn in New Jersey. He doesn't care much about sandlot ball, but he can recite the batting order and play-by-play for every Dodgers game since the time he became a fan. Sam's best friend is the inn's African-American cook, Davy, who takes Sam to his first Dodgers game. The two see other games together, and the hero of all the games for both of them is Jackie Robinson. In midseason Davy has a heart attack. Sam gathers his courage, buys a baseball, and goes alone to a Dodgers game, where he asks Jackie Robinson to autograph a ball for Davy. Then Davy's son-in-law, Elliott, helps Sam sneak into the hospital in a laundry cart so he can personally present the ball to Davy:

> ❦ There was no magic in the ball. He loved it, but there was no magic in it. It was not going to cure him, the way deep down in my heart I had somehow thought it would. I knew that, my whole self knew that now.[54]

This book succeeds at many levels: as a warm and understanding consideration of friendship across ages and races; as a realistic presentation of death; and as a retrospective look at Jackie Robinson and the Brooklyn Dodgers during the height of their baseball fame. Peter Golenbock's nonfiction story of *Teammates* would help children further understand Robinson's courageous entry into major league baseball.

Another book that succeeds on many levels is Alfred Slote's *The Trading Game*. Andy Harris, who loves to play baseball and collect baseball cards, receives the cards his deceased father had bequeathed to him. Among them is a precious 1953 Mickey Mantle worth over two thousand dollars. But the card Andy truly wants is Ace 459, the card of his idolized grandpa, a former major league player. Greedy Tubby Watson owns the card and won't part with it unless Andy will trade the Mickey Mantle card. When Grampa comes to visit, it is clear to Andy that the cards his father collected are of no importance to the old man and that Grampa has not reconciled himself to his son's death. When Andy's pal Alice grabs the card

from Tubby, flips a quarter in his direction, and says she has bought the card to give to Andy, things become complicated. Slote sorts out the ethics of this and includes a compelling scene where Grampa coaches Andy's failing ball team, showing each player how to be a little better. Andy discovers that Grampa's competitive spirit is something his own father did not possess and begins to understand something of father/son relationships. Andy realizes that friendships and the memories which the cards represent are more important than winning and the money the cards are worth. *Hang Tough, Paul Mather* was discussed among the books dealing with death. Slote's *My Father, the Coach* involves the challenge to a team when the president of the sponsoring bank insults their coach, a parking lot attendant. Slote's books, often told in first person, capture the emotions, actions, and conversation of typical fifth- and sixth-grade boys.

Upper elementary school students have laughed at the antics of Orp, or Orville Rudemeyer Pygenski, Jr. In one story in the series by Suzy Kline, *Orp Goes to the Hoop*, the seventh grader is trying to make the basketball team of his Connecticut middle school. With a mother who was a free-throw champion and a father with a terrific lay-up, Orp has great advice. While Orp's story is one of near continuous successes both on the court and in the social arena, readers will appreciate vicariously Orp's long pass to a teammate for the winning basket. R. R. Knudson's sports stories feature high schooler Zan Hagan as her interests progress from football, to basketball, to distance running in three titles: *Zanballer, Zanbanger,* and *Zanboomer.* Knudson's *Rinehart Lifts* recounts the time Zan helped skinny Rinehart with a grade school weight-lifting contest. Knudson sometimes relies on journal entries, first-person narrative, and thoughtlike fragments in her stories. Likable characters with loyal friendships that transcend age and gender bounds are typical of her novels.

Other stories depict the blurring of the lines between traditionally all-male or all-female teams. Mel Cebulash's fictional speculation about the first woman to break into major league baseball is chronicled in several stories. *Ruth Marini, Dodger Ace* and *Ruth Marini of the Dodgers* both

---

[54] Barbara Cohen, *Thank You, Jackie Robinson,* illustrated by Richard Cuffari (New York: Lothrop, 1974). p. 11.

relate Ruth's difficulties in being accepted for what she can do for the team, not for who she is or what she represents. In Thomas Dygard's *Winning Kicker*, Kathy Denver joins a football team as a place kicker but a broken ankle sidelines her. However, she has won the respect of coach and team. Dygard's *Rebound Caper* reverses the situation when a boy tries to join a girls' basketball team after being benched by the coach of the high school boys' team.

Middle schoolers ready to move into more complex novels that use sports to explore other subjects might be guided to Ilene Cooper's *Choosing Sides*, Bruce Brooks's *The Moves Make the Man*, Robert Lipsyte's *The Contender*, or Chris Crutcher's *Stotan!* Sports fiction at its best provides readers with the vicarious satisfactions of playing the sport as well as struggling with the problems and issues that arise in practice, in play, and at home.

School Stories

Stories that take place in school offer children the solace of the familiar. Settings furnished with desks and lockers; characters such as the friendly custodian or principal, the class bully, the understanding or hatchet-faced teacher; and situations such as a cheating student, the looming deadline for a project or paper, misunderstandings between friends, or seasonal celebrations are all recognizable to everyone. While books such as these do not always encourage readers to stretch their abilities, they do provide a kind of support for horizontal growth as children learn to read faster with more satisfaction. Unfortunately (or fortunately for readers), many of these stories are part of a numbered series and children want to read them in order. This challenges teachers and parents to help children find other books while they are "waiting for number 7 of the series."

Patricia Reilly Giff has written numerous stories about the second-grade "Kids of Polk Street School." The first series takes place over the months of the school year and the teacher, Ms. Rooney, usually has a good holiday celebration or project to mark the month. The series begins with *The Beast in Ms. Rooney's Room*, about a boy who is "held back" in second grade, and subse-

quent stories often refer back to previous ones. Often the first chapter book a child risks reading, these nonepisodic stories build to modest themes such as being a friend, doing your best, behaving honestly, being patient with learning difficulties, and so forth. Giff's other series include the "Polka Dot Private Eye" stories and the "New Kids of Polk Street School."

Third graders will recognize in Janice Lee Smith's stories the problems 7- or 8-year-old Adam Joshua encounters in *It's Not Easy Being George*. Adam Joshua brings his dog George to the school pet show, but George can't do tricks and gets his nose bitten by a sassy parrot. But when Adam Joshua tells the judges that George listens to all his problems and laughs at his jokes, George

Chagrined and embarrassed, Ramona waits while the raw egg she accidentally cracked on her head is removed from her hair in a humorous scene from Beverly Cleary's *Ramona Quimby, Age 8*.

Illustration by Alan Tiegreen.

wins a ribbon as "A Best Friend." Long funny chapters tell about the class sleepover in the library, which is interrupted by rubber insects, a pillow fight, a "gypsy storyteller," and finally the howls of George the dog. The series begins with *The Monster in the Third Dresser Drawer*, but the books may be read in any order.

Susan Shreve's school story about *The Flunking of Joshua T. Bates* is, like Giff's *The Beast in Ms. Rooney's Room*, also about being held back. Joshua hasn't mastered reading but through the thoughtful tutoring and friendship of his new teacher, he is able to pass a test at Thanksgiving and join his old class. Adults will wince as Joshua vents his frustration by threatening to move to East Africa or become a custodian in Japan, and they may find unrealistic the implication that children may be promoted after two months of tutoring. But children applaud the way the bully in Joshua's former class is subdued and the satisfying happy ending.

Beverly Cleary, Jamie Gilson, and Johanna Hurwitz make use of the humor of school situations for third and fourth graders. In Cleary's *Ramona Quimby, Age 8*, Ramona arrives in third grade where she enjoys her teacher's Dear time (Drop Everything And Read). She also stages a hilarious parody of a catfood commercial for her book report, makes a friend of "Yard Ape," and realizes that her teacher likes her. Hurwitz introduces Lucas Cott, *Class Clown*, and the most obstreperous boy his third-grade teacher has ever seen. Lucas settles down finally when he stands in for a sick classmate to become the ringmaster of the class circus. Cricket Kaufman thinks she will be the *Teacher's Pet* as well as the smartest and the best liked girl in fourth grade. But her teacher treats everyone equally, and a new girl, Zoe, challenges Cricket's academic prowess before the two become friends. The group moves to fifth grade where Julio Sanchez decides he might run for *Class President* instead of managing the campaign of his friend Lucas. While *School's Out* takes place at Lucas's home, the earlier books are really humorous stories of learning how to get along in school.

Jamie Gilson's humorous stories of Hobie Hanson, fourth-grade graduate, begin with *Hobie Hanson, You're Weird*. All of his classmates are having wonderful summers at camp, like his best friend Nick, or on vacation while Hobie is under

edict from his father to "do what Tom Sawyer did," just fool around. Hobie discovers that his pet peeve, Molly Bosco, may just make a decent friend even if she is a girl when the two of them win a pie-eating contest. *Hobie Hanson, Greatest Hero of the Mall*, a sequel, is set in school but this time Hobie's school is a mall while his flood-damaged school is being repaired. Gilson's *4B Goes Wild* and *Thirteen Ways to Sink a Sub* are also popular stories. Gilson's stories are fast-moving, full of pranks and funny dialogue, with reasonable adults who remain very much in the background.

Rebecca Jones has written a humorous series about Jeremy Bluett. Called *Germy Blew It* by his sixth-grade friends, Jeremy is always trying to raise money in various ventures that run awry. In *Germy Blew The Bugle*, he launches a school newspaper despite unwilling reporters, a principal who refuses to let him sell advertising, and deadline trouble. His father enthusiastically tries to become involved, as does an overeager classmate Margaret, but it is her computer ability that finally saves him. Jones inserts hilarious paragraphs about Jeremy imagining what the president would say about that amazing Bluett boy. Her observations of life in sixth grade ring true.

Other authors also set their stories for older readers within the cozy confines of a school. Gordon Korman's private school, MacDonald Hall, has been the setting for many of his slapstick stories. The characters of the popular paperback series "Sweet Valley High" and "Sweet Valley Twins" (created by Francine Pascal but written by a stable of authors) use school as a backdrop for their interactions. A giant step up from these series is Ilene Cooper's "The Kids from Kennedy Middle School" series in which themes and situations of more depth are treated both humorously and seriously. In *Choosing Sides*, for instance, sixth grader Jonathan Rossi is trying to be the basketball player his father wants him to be and his older brother already is. But Jonathan's heart isn't in it. His friend, Ham Berger, purposely gets cut from the team, but Jon continues to put up with pressure and lessons from his father. When his teacher, Mrs. Volini, asks the class to write about "moral dilemmas," Jon suddenly sees that his is not how to skip basketball practice but how to reconcile his own feelings with his father's unreasonable demands. *Queen of the Sixth Grade* introduces readers to Jon's friend Robin who suddenly becomes a class outcast when she rebels against the cruel Veronica's jokes. Each of Cooper's stories deals with a major theme against the backdrop of everyday school concerns such as what to do at a first sixth-grade coed dance, peer groups and making friends of both sexes, dealing with bad and good teachers, or handling difficult school assignments.

Mysteries

Most children enjoy mystery stories during some period in their lives. James Howe, author of the popular Sebastian Barth mysteries, has said that in adult mysteries "who done it?" is the question to be answered, but in children's mysteries, the question is more likely to be "What's going on here?"[55] Children enjoy figuring out the "rules of the game" in a mystery, and they are proud to be masterful solvers of the problem. They enjoy the order of a mystery's universe where loose ends are tied up, everything is explained, and evil is punished. They like escapist reading just as much as adult mystery fans do.

Even first- and second-grade readers demand mysteries. Whole series such as the "Something Queer" books by Elizabeth Levy, the "Miss Mallard" and "Sherlock Chick" animal detective stories by Robert Quackenbush, Crosby Bonsall stories, or Patricia Reilly Giff's "Polka Dot Private Eye" books satisfy a child's need to keep reading.

Slightly older children usually become enmeshed in the "Nancy Drew" or "Hardy Boys" series. These formula books have predictable plots, one-dimensional characters, stilted dialogue, and cliché-ridden prose. Although most librarians and teachers do not order these books, they continue to sell well. Rather than discount mystery stories in general because of popular series, teachers and librarians should look for better written mysteries and other books that contain the elements of mystery, such as "suspense and supernatural" fantasy (see Chapter 7) in order to expand children's interests.

Two popular mystery series give the reader a chance to match wits with clever boys. Both boys and girls enjoy the Encyclopedia Brown stories by Donald Sobol. In *Encyclopedia Brown Takes a Case*, Mr. Brown, chief of police of Idaville, brings home all the cases his men cannot solve. At dinner he describes them to his son, Encyclopedia Brown, who usually solves them before it is time for dessert. Each Encyclopedia Brown book presents ten cases whose solutions are included in the back of the book. Seymour Simon, author of many nonfiction titles, also features short mysteries in his Einstein Anderson series. In *Einstein Anderson Lights Up the Sky*, the brainy Einstein applies his knowledge of science to show that mysterious UFOs are really spotlight reflections off low nighttime clouds and "solves" another nine problems. While each series features both consistent format and a continuing cast of characters, Einstein's incidental jokes, puns, and riddles in each chapter and the scientific observations give this series extra appeal and depth.

Attics in two mystery stories hold clues to the past and keys to the future for two horse-loving girls. In Rumer Godden's *The Rocking Horse Secret*, 8-year-old Tibby is bored living in a wing of the Pomeroy mansion with her housekeeper mother until she discovers a rocking horse in an attic playroom. One day while playing in the forbidden room, she is dismayed to see the horse's tail fall off, revealing a piece of paper that looks like an important letter. She repairs the damage and hopes no one will notice. Later, when old Miss Pomeroy dies, terrible changes occur in the household brought about by her shrewish nieces who stand to inherit the mansion unless a will is found. In an exciting conclusion, it falls to Tibby to produce the will and keep the house from being destroyed. *The Horse in the Attic* by Eleanor Clymer is an old painting which, when restored, proves to be an important work of a long dead local artist. Twelve-year-old Caroline tracks down the painting's "bloodlines" and when she agrees that the family should sell it, the proceeds suggest her father might be able to make a career of painting and Caroline might continue to develop her skills in horseback riding. Both Clymer and Godden create memorable characters and provide satisfying endings sure to delight middle elementary mystery and horse lovers.

The attic of Marcus Mullen's house holds the answer to a mystery in Eve Bunting's *Is Anybody*

[55]James Howe, "Writing Mysteries for Children," *The Horn Book Magazine* (March/April, 1990), pp. 178–183.

There?. Thirteen-year-old Marcus is resentful of his widowed mother's affection for Nick, the man renting the apartment attached to their home. He is convinced it is Nick who has sneaked into the house to make peanut butter sandwiches, steal small articles, and leave grassy footprints on their kitchen floor. But Nick also seems mystified. Marcus nonetheless decides to visit Nick's apartment to see if he can find incriminating evidence. He discovers that Nick has a son from a previous marriage who he obviously hasn't seen for at least six years. Bunting's well-paced story also includes subplots of a first romance between Marcus and Angelica and Marcus's creation of a wonderful Christmas present for his mother—a bicycle made entirely of parts salvaged from a bicycle shop. Marcus finally solves the mystery of the intruder when he discovers Nick's son has been hiding in their attic. He also resolves his feelings for Nick when he declares to his son that Nick would make a pretty nice dad.

The House of Dies Drear by Virginia Hamilton is a compelling story of the weird and terrifying happenings that threaten and mystify an African-American professor and his family when they rent a house that was a former underground railway station. The brooding old house holds many secrets for Thomas Small and his family, who are threatened by dangers from outside as well as inside the house. The treasure of fleeing slaves that was discovered by Thomas in the previous title becomes one of the problems in a sequel, *The Mystery of Drear House*. Now the Small family must help determine the fate of the abolitionist's house, and the disposal of the goods. Hamilton's finely crafted plot, elegant prose, and well-developed characters provide gripping reading.

Philippa Pearce's *The Way to Sattin Shore* is the satisfying story of a girl's longing to understand the mystery surrounding the disappearance of her father the day she was born. Her mother and her grandmother both tell her that he is dead. Kate believes them until she discovers that the tombstone in the cemetery is her uncle's, not her father's, as she had thought. The clues to the mystery ebb and flow like the tide in which she learns her uncle drowned. The tension between her mother and disagreeable grandmother rises, and her older brother reveals that they had once lived somewhere else—at Sattin Shore. Kate rides her bicycle alone to the shore and discovers a grandmother she didn't know she had. Through her own determination and initiative she does find her father and brings about a reunion with her mother. While the plot provides suspense, it is the author's skill in creating believable relationships among the characters and a haunting sense of place that you admire. The eerie loneliness of the shore is as threatening as Kate's dark, unhappy home. It is up to Kate to discover what happened on that beach the day she was born and solve the mystery that has engulfed them all.

In the "Sebastian Barth" mysteries, which begin with *What Eric Knew*, James Howe develops situations and characters to a depth seldom found in mystery series. These stories appeal to an audience slightly older than his "Bunnicula" fantasy series. *Dew Drop Dead* concerns Sebastian and his friends Corrie and David who discover the body of a homeless man in the woods. The adults in this story are not relegated to the background as is typical in most children's mysteries. Sebastian is concerned about his father who may lose his job at the radio station; Corrie's father is a minister working with the homeless; and David's single-parent father, a mystery writer who has some trenchant observations on his art, becomes interested in a female detective who is working on the case. While the children help solve the mystery, they are also engaged in contemporary concerns such as parental unemployment and the plight of the homeless. It is not necessary to read the stories "in order," but readers who do will appreciate watching the characters develop and seeing situations change as the series unfolds.

Ellen Raskin cut apart the words to "America the Beautiful" and dispersed them among sixteen characters to begin her "puzzle-mystery," *The Westing Game*.[56] Heirs to the estate of millionaire Samuel W. Westing are invited to the reading of his will: a directive to discover the identity of his murderer and a series of clues cleverly hidden within the will. Characters, all with their own physical, moral, or emotional imperfections, play in pairs. They include a judge, a Chinese restauranteur, a dressmaker, a track star, a 15-year-old

---

[56]See Ellen Raskin, "Newbery Medal Acceptance," *The Horn Book Magazine*, vol. 55 (August 1979), pp. 385–391.

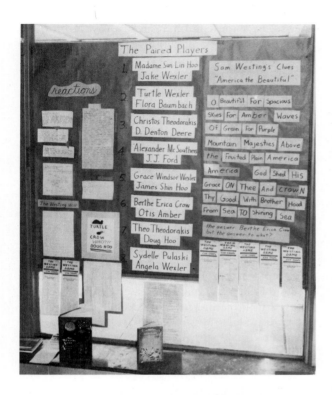

Fourth graders keep track of Ellen Raskin's intricate mystery, *The Westing Game*, by listing character pairs, assembling cut-up clues, and making predictions.

Barrington Road Elementary School, Upper Arlington Public Schools, Ohio. Pat Enciso, teacher.

palsied boy, a reluctant bride-to-be, and a 13-year-old terror, Turtle Wexler. It is Turtle who begins to link clues and discover patterns as she and readers piece together Westing's amazing game. In a tightly constructed story divided into many short sections, Raskin piles detail upon detail; rereading shows that what appears to be insignificant always proves otherwise. Warmly realized characters interrelate and grow in this Newbery award winner, but it is Turtle who, unbeknownst to any of the other players, quietly solves the puzzle and bikes up to the Westing house to receive her prize in the satisfying ending.

Popular mystery writer Vivien Alcock skirts the fantastic in novels such as *The Mysterious Mr. Ross* in which 12-year-old Felicity suspects the man she has saved from drowning, Albert Ross, may well be the human incarnation of an injured alba-

tross. Readers are kept in suspense, however, as Alcock's young gullible girl on the edge of adolescence moves through sympathy, doubt, anger, and remorse before defending Mr. Ross from nosy seacoast villagers. While Felicity and her curious friend Bony never satisfy their questions concerning Mr. Ross, and he departs, the two form a deeper appreciation of each other. Alcock's numerous other titles such as *The Monster Garden* and *The Stonewalkers* venture into supernatural and science-fiction territory and appeal to middle schoolers for their mixture of mystery, fantasy, and adolescent awareness of the adult world.

Like many of her books, two mysteries by Nina Bawden concern the interactions among "outside children," those who either are or feel themselves to be different. In *The Witch's Daughter*, Perdita is a lonely orphan shunned by village children because of her odd clothes, shy manner, and sensitivity to nature. The unschooled Perdita is especially kind to a blind girl, Janey, who comes with her family to this Scottish island for a holiday. When Tim, Janey's brother, notices a mysterious man who has rented a cottage to fish for lobster, which he doesn't even like, the boy puts together the pieces of a puzzle involving stolen jewels. *Squib* is the nickname two children give to a shy little boy with odd eyes and a bit of bruise on his leg. But Kate and Robin are drawn into a terrifying situation because of their curiosity about the child. All of Bawden's books have well-drawn characters with believable and exciting plots.

Joan Lowery Nixon's riveting story, *The Other Side of Dark*, won the Edgar Allan Poe Mystery Writer's Award for its distinct portrayal of a girl who, after witnessing the murder of her mother and being shot herself, loses her memory for four years. At 17, Stacy McAdams regains some memory and is adjusting to being an adolescent. When publicity suggests that she may remember the face of the killer, Stacy is placed once again in danger as she attempts to identify the killer before he kills her. The plot is complicated when new friends may not be what they seem. Stacy's first-person narrative reveals her desire for revenge, her confusion over who she is, and her growth toward adulthood in this thriller. Another of Nixon's thrillers, *A Candidate for Murder*, concerns Cary and the crank calls she begins to receive when her father runs for governor of Texas. Cary has unknowingly witnessed something that places her in the midst of political intrigue and danger. Older readers enjoy the compelling mysteries of Joan Lowery Nixon for their skilled combination of human emotions, suspense, romance, and terror with a fast-moving plot and cliff-hanging chapters.

Like Nixon, Lois Duncan writes about high school students who inadvertently stumble into mysteries. In *The Twisted Window*, for instance, she tells the story of high school junior Tracy Lloyd who believes Brad Johnson when he says his stepfather has stolen his little sister from his mother's house. Three days later she is involved in a kidnapping, a case of mistaken identity, and a dangerous game with a disturbed boy. Middle school girl readers pass Duncan's young adult mysteries from hand to hand.

Popular fiction should be evaluated with the same criteria used to consider all fiction, with the recognition that the major appeals are fast action, contemporary characters in familiar settings, straightforward plot development, humor, sus-pense, or some combination of these. Children develop the skills of rapid reading, vocabulary building, prediction, and the noticing of relevant details when they read popular fiction. They develop a love of reading with popular novels, and skillful teachers can extend and diversify readers' choices with all that realistic fiction has to offer.

Contemporary realistic fiction is diverse. It has moved away from the problem novels of the 1960s and 1970s to serious fiction balanced with characters less prone to despair. Contemporary novels encompass diverse themes and writing styles. While paperback series and popular novels continue to attract readers, these selections are counterbalanced by many well-written and com-pelling stories. The cultural diversity of the United States and many world cultures are repre-sented in literature for children and the number of titles available grows slowly. Contemporary realistic fiction, the most popular genre among child readers, continues to thrive in this decade.

SUGGESTED LEARNING EXPERIENCES

1. Find books about a specific minority group. Look for poetry, biography, fiction, picture storybooks, and nonfiction that would extend these books in a classroom. What kind of books were easiest and which most difficult to find?
2. Select a current subject in realistic fiction such as single-parent families, foster children, immigration, or disability and create an annotated bibliography. Find some nonfiction that can be grouped with the fiction.
3. Compare the treatment of a topic such as death of a pet, a child, or grandparent in a picture book, a novel, poetry, and in informational books.
4. Select several books from various decades that portray a particular minority group. Do you find stereotypical treatment? What themes prevail?
5. Compare several humorous stories. What kinds of things are funny, such as slapstick, exaggeration, puns or wordplay, situations, or satire? How would you rank these titles from lesser to greater sophistication?
6. Discuss with peers or a small group of children a novel such as Lowry's *Rabble Starkey*, MacLachlan's *Arthur for the Very First Time*, Howe's *Dew Drop Dead*, Paterson's *Park's Quest* or Bawden's *The Outside Child*. How is the main character influenced by other characters in the book? When the child character becomes an adult, which of these other characters might he or she want to thank? Why?
7. Compare the relationships of parents and children in several titles from the section "Living in a Family."
8. Compare several survival stories chosen from this chapter as well as from other genres. After basic wants are satisfied, what else does the surviving person seem to need? What qualities does each person possess or develop in order to survive? How does (or may) surviving change a person?

RELATED READINGS

1. Baskin, Barbara H., and Karen H. Harris. *More Notes from a Different Drummer: A Guide to Juvenile Fiction Portraying the Disabled.* New York: Bowker, 1984.

   Annotations and analysis of more than three hundred books published between 1976 and 1981, plus two introductory chapters that provide context, background, and excellent evaluative criteria. This supplements *Notes from a Different Drummer* (New York: Bowker, 1977), which covered titles published from 1940 to 1975.

2. Bernstein, Joanne E., and Masha K. Rudman. *Books to Help Children Cope with Separation and Loss,* 3rd ed. New York: Bowker, 1988.

   This book selection guide summarizes six hundred recent fiction and nonfiction titles grouped by topics such as divorce, mental illness, moving, tragic loss, disabilities, and others.

3. Bishop, Rudine Sims. *Presenting Walter Dean Myers.* New York: Twayne, 1990.

   A discussion and criticism of Myers's books about young urban African Americans including an analysis of humor, theme, characterization, and other patterns found in Myers's work. Other titles in this critical series discuss works by authors such as Sue Ellen Bridgers, Robert Cormier, Richard Peck, and Judy Blume.

4. *The Black Experience in Children's Literature.* New York: New York Public Library, 1989.

   This annotated list is the fourth revision of the 1971 list first edited by Augusta Baker. Some four hundred books are arranged by genre under the geographical headings of the United States, South and Central America, the Carribean, Africa, and England.

5. Dreyer, Sharon Spredeman. *The Bookfinder: A Guide to Children's Literature About the Needs and Problems of Youth Aged 2–15,* Volumes I, II, III, and IV. Circle Pines, Minn.: American Guidance Service, 1981, 1985, 1989.

   Titles are indexed and annotated under headings that suggest a range of problems in growing up: responsibility, parental absence, disabilities, friendship, and so on. Introductory essays discuss ways parents and teachers might plan thematic studies to develop children's understandings.

6. Hunter, Mollie. *The Pied Piper Syndrome.* New York: HarperCollins, 1992.

   In this collection of speeches and essays, Scotland's best known children's author shows how one person sees her craft. Since Hunter's first language was not English, her essay on "Writing from a Minority Literature" rings true. In an earlier collection, *Talent Is Not Enough* (New York: Harper, 1976, 1990), the author reflects on the challenges and demands of writing for children.

7. Lass-Woodfin, Mary Jo, ed. *Books on American Indians and Eskimos: A Selection Guide for Children and Young Adults.* Chicago: American Library Association, 1978.

   An annotated bibliography of some 750 titles that identifies the understandings and information available from each story. Ratings for quality and reading level are included.

8. Paterson, Katherine. *The Spying Heart: More Thoughts on Reading and Writing Books for Children.* New York: E.P. Dutton, 1989.

   A collection of eight essays and speeches and seven book reviews that develop the author's views on three themes: story, imagination, and hope. See also an earlier companion volume, *Gates of Excellence: On Reading and Writing Books for Children.* (New York: Elsevier/Nelson Books, 1981.)

9. Rees, David. *Painted Desert, Green Shade: Essays on Contemporary Writers of Fiction for Children and Young Adults.* Boston: Horn Book, 1984.

   Rees critiques the work of thirteen American and British writers, focusing new light on such authors as Betsy Byars, Katherine Paterson, Jan Mark, Robert Westall, Virginia Hamilton, and John Rowe Townsend. See also the companion volume, *Marble in the Water: Essays on Contemporary Writers of Fiction for Children and Young Adults.* (Boston: Horn Book, 1980.)

10. Sims, Rudine. *Shadow and Substance: Afro-American Experience in Contemporary Children's Fiction.* Urbana, Ill.: National Council of Teachers of English, 1982.

    The author surveys 150 books published between 1965 and 1979 that portray contemporary African-American experience. She categorizes images portrayed in three sections: fiction with a social conscience, "melting pot" fiction that essentially assumes a cultural homogeneity, and "culturally conscious fiction." Five African-American authors are discussed against a backdrop of other contemporary authors.

REFERENCES[57]

Aamundsen, Nina Ring. *Two Short and One Long*. Houghton Mifflin, 1990.
Adler, C. S. *The Once in a While Hero*. Coward, 1982.
Alcock, Vivien. *The Monster Garden*. Delacorte, 1988. (Fantasy)
_____. *The Mysterious Mr. Ross*. Delacorte, 1987.
_____. *The Stonewalkers*. Delacorte, 1983. (Fantasy)
Bauer, Marian Dane. *On My Honor*. Houghton Mifflin, 1986.
Bawden, Nina. *Henry*, illustrated by Joyce Powzyk. Lothrop, 1988.
_____. *The Outside Child*. Lothrop, 1989.
_____. *The Peppermint Pig*. Lippincott, 1975. (Historical Fiction)
_____. *Squib*. Lippincott, 1971.
_____. *The Witch's Daughter*. Lippincott, 1966.
Blume, Judy. *Are You There, God? It's Me, Margaret*. Bradbury, 1970.
_____. *Fudge-a-Mania*. Dutton, 1990.
_____. *It's Not the End of the World*. Bradbury, 1972.
_____. *Otherwise Known as Sheila the Great*. Dutton, 1972.
_____. *Superfudge*. Dutton, 1980.
_____. *Tales of a Fourth Grade Nothing*, illustrated by Roy Doty. Dutton, 1972.
_____. *Then Again, Maybe I Won't*. Bradbury, 1971.
Bridgers, Sue Ellen. *All Together Now*. Knopf, 1979.
_____. *Notes for Another Life*. Knopf, 1981.
Brooks, Bruce. *Everywhere*. Harper, 1990.
_____. *The Moves Make the Man*. Harper, 1984.
Bunting, Eve. *Is Anybody There?* Lippincott, 1988.
Burnford, Sheila. *The Incredible Journey*, illustrated by Carl Burger. Little, Brown, 1961.
Byars, Betsy. *After the Goat Man*, illustrated by Ronald Himler. Viking, 1974.
_____. *The Animal, the Vegetable, & John D Jones*, illustrated by Ruth Sanderson. Delacorte, 1982.
_____. *Bingo Brown and the Language of Love*. Viking, 1989.
_____. *Bingo Brown, Gypsy Lover*. Viking, 1990.
_____. *The Burning Questions of Bingo Brown*. Viking, 1988.
_____. *Cracker Jackson*, Viking, 1985.
_____. *The Cybil War*, illustrated by Gail Owens. Viking, 1981.
_____. *The 18th Emergency*, illustrated by Robert Grossman. Viking, 1973.
_____. *The House of Wings*, illustrated by Daniel Schwartz. Viking, 1972.
_____. *The Night Swimmers*. Delacorte, 1980.
_____. *The Pinballs*. Harper, 1977.
_____. *The Summer of the Swans*, illustrated by Ted CoConis. Viking, 1970.
Cameron, Ann. *Julian, Dream Doctor*, illustrated by Ann Strugnell. Random House, 1990.
_____. *Julian's Glorious Summer*, illustrated by Dora Leder. Random House, 1987.
_____. *Julian, Secret Agent*, illustrated by Diane Allison. Random House, 1988.
_____. *More Stories Julian Tells*, illustrated by Ann Strugnell. Knopf, 1986.
_____. *The Most Beautiful Place in the World*, illustrated by Thomas B. Allen. Knopf, 1988.
_____. *The Stories Julian Tells*, illustrated by Ann Strugnell. Knopf, 1981.
Cameron, Eleanor. *Julia and the Hand of God*, illustrated by Gail Owens. Dutton, 1977.
_____. *Julia's Magic*, illustrated by Gail Owens. Dutton, 1984.
_____. *A Room Made of Windows*. Little, Brown, 1971.
_____. *That Julia Redfern*, illustrated by Gail Owens. Dutton, 1982.
_____. *The Private Worlds of Julia Redfern*. Dutton, 1988.
Cebulash, Mel. *Ruth Marini, Dodger Ace*. Lerner, 1983.
_____. *Ruth Marini of the Dodgers*. Lerner, 1983.
Christopher, Matt. *Dirt Bike Racer*, illustrated by Barry Bomzer. Little, Brown, 1979.
_____. *Skateboard Tough*. Little, Brown, 1991.
Cleary, Beverly. *Dear Mr. Henshaw*, illustrated by Paul O. Zelinsky. Morrow, 1983.

[57]All books listed at the end of this chapter are recommended subject to the qualifications noted in the text. See Appendix for publishers' complete addresses. References to books of other genres are noted in parentheses.

_____. *Henry and Beezus*, illustrated by Louis Darling. Morrow, 1952.

_____. *Henry Huggins*, illustrated by Louis Darling. Morrow, 1950.

_____. *Ramona Forever*, illustrated by Alan Tiegreen. Morrow, 1984.

_____. *Ramona and Her Father*, illustrated by Alan Tiegreen. Morrow, 1977.

_____. *Ramona and Her Mother*, illustrated by Alan Tiegreen. Morrow, 1979.

_____. *Ramona Quimby, Age 8*, illustrated by Alan Tiegreen. Morrow, 1981.

_____. *Ramona the Brave*, illustrated by Alan Tiegreen. Morrow, 1975.

_____. *Ramona the Pest*, illustrated by Louis Darling. Morrow, 1968.

_____. *Strider*, illustrated by Paul O. Zelinsky. Morrow, 1991.

Cleaver, Vera, and Bill Cleaver. *Grover*, illustrated by Frederic Marvin. Lippincott, 1970.

_____. *Trial Valley*. Lippincott, 1977.

_____. *Where the Lilies Bloom*, illustrated by James Spanfeller. Lippincott, 1969.

Clifford, Eth. *The Rocking Chair Rebellion*. Houghton Mifflin, 1978.

Clifton, Lucille. *The Lucky Stone*, illustrated by Dale Payson. Delacorte, 1979.

Clymer, Eleanor. *The Horse in the Attic*, illustrated by Ted Lewin. Bradbury, 1983.

_____. *My Brother Stevie*. Holt, 1967.

Cohen, Barbara. *The Long Way Home*, illustrated by Diane de Groat. Lothrop, 1990.

_____. *Molly's Pilgrim*, illustrated by Michael J. Deraney. Lothrop, 1983. (Historical Fiction)

_____. *Thank You, Jackie Robinson*, illustrated by Richard Cuffari. Lothrop, 1974.

Cole, Brock. *The Goats*. Farrar, 1987.

Conford, Ellen. *Anything for a Friend*. Little, Brown, 1979.

Conrad, Pam. *My Daniel*. Harper, 1989.

_____. *Staying Nine*, illustrated by Mike Wimmer. Harper, 1988.

Cooper, Ilene. *Choosing Sides*. Morrow, 1990.

_____. *Queen of the Sixth Grade*. Morrow, 1988.

_____. *The Winning of Miss Lynn Ryan*. Morrow, 1987.

Cormier, Robert. *Other Bells for Us to Ring*, illustrated by Deborah Kogan Ray. Delacorte, 1990.

Cresswell, Helen. *Absolute Zero*. Macmillan, 1978.

_____. *Bagthorpes Abroad*. Macmillan, 1984.

_____. *Bagthorpes Haunted*. Macmillan, 1985.

_____. *Bagthorpes Liberated*. Macmillan, 1989.

_____. *Bagthorpes Unlimited*. Macmillan, 1978.

_____. *Bagthorpes v. the World*. Macmillan, 1979.

_____. *Ordinary Jack*. Macmillan, 1977.

Crutcher, Chris. *Stotan!* Greenwillow, 1986.

Cunningham, Julia. *Dorp Dead*, illustrated by James Spanfeller. Pantheon, 1965.

de Jenkins, Lyll Becerra. *The Honorable Prison*. Dutton, 1988.

DeJong, Meindert. *Hurry Home, Candy*, illustrated by Maurice Sendak. Harper, 1953.

Donovan, John. *I'll Get There, It Better Be Worth the Trip*. Harper, 1969.

Dragonwagon, Crescent. *Winter Holding Spring*, illustrated by Ronald Himler. Macmillan, 1990.

Duncan, Lois. *The Twisted Window*. Delacorte, 1987.

Dygard, Thomas J. *Rebound Caper*. Morrow, 1983.

_____. *Winning Kicker*. Morrow, 1978.

Ellis, Sarah. *A Family Project*. Macmillan, 1988.

Enright, Elizabeth. *The Saturdays*. Holt, 1941.

Estes, Eleanor. *The Hundred Dresses*, illustrated by Louis Slobodkin. Harcourt, 1944.

_____. *The Middle Moffat*, illustrated by Louis Slobodkin. Harcourt, 1942.

_____. *The Moffats*, illustrated by Louis Slobodkin. Harcourt, 1941.

_____. *Rufus M.*, illustrated by Louis Slobodkin. Harcourt, 1943.

Farley, Walter. *The Black Stallion*, illustrated by Keith Ward. Random, 1944.

_____. *The Black Stallion's Filly*, illustrated by Milton Menasco. Random, 1952.

_____. *The Blood Bay Colt*, illustrated by Milton Menasco. Random, 1950.

_____. *Son of the Black Stallion*, illustrated by Milton Menasco. Random, 1947.

Fitzhugh, Louise. *Harriet the Spy*. Harper, 1964.

_____. *The Long Secret*. Harper, 1965.

Fox, Paula. *Monkey Island*. Orchard, 1991.

_____. *One-Eyed Cat*. Bradbury, 1984.

_____. *The Stone-faced Boy*, illustrated by Donald A. Mackay. Bradbury, 1968.

_____. *The Village by the Sea*. Orchard, 1988.

Fritz, Jean. *Homesick: My Own Story*, illustrated by Margot Tomes. Putnam, 1982. (Historical Fiction)
Gardiner, John Reynolds. *Stone Fox*, illustrated by Marcia Sewall. Crowell, 1980.
Garrigue, Sheila. *Between Friends*. Bradbury, 1978.
George, Jean Craighead. *The Cry of the Crow*. Harper, 1980.
_____. *Julie of the Wolves*, illustrated by John Schoenherr. Harper, 1972.
_____. *My Side of the Mountain*. Dutton, 1959.
_____. *On the Far Side of the Mountain*. Dutton, 1990.
_____. *The Talking Earth*. Harper, 1983.
Giff, Patricia Reilly. *The Beast in Ms. Rooney's Room*, #1. Dell, 1985.
Gilson, Jamie. *4B Goes Wild*, illustrated by Linda S. Edwards. Lothrop, 1983.
_____. *Hello, My Name Is Scrambled Eggs*, illustrated by John Wallner. Lothrop, 1985.
_____. *Hobie Hanson, Greatest Hero of the Mall*, illustrated by Anita Riggio. Lothrop, 1989.
_____. *Hobie Hanson, You're Weird*, illustrated by Elise Primavera. Lothrop, 1987.
_____. *Thirteen Ways to Sink a Sub*, illustrated by Linda S. Edwards. Lothrop, 1982.
Gipson, Fred. *Old Yeller*, illustrated by Carl Burger. Harper, 1956.
Godden, Rumer. *The Rocking Horse Secret*, illustrated by Juliet S. Smith. Viking, 1978.
Golenbock, Peter. *Teammates*, illustrated by Paul Bacon. Harcourt, 1990. (Biography)
Gordon, Sheila. *The Middle of Somewhere: A Story of South Africa*. Orchard, 1990.
_____. *Waiting for the Rain*. Orchard, 1987.
Graeber, Charlotte. *Mustard*, illustrated by Donna Diamond. Macmillan, 1982.
Greene, Constance C. *Beat the Turtle Drum*, illustrated by Donna Diamond. Viking, 1976.
_____. *A Girl Called Al*, illustrated by Byron Barton. Viking, 1969.
Greenfield, Eloise. *Sister*. Crowell, 1974.
Hamilton, Virginia. *Cousins*. Philomel, 1990.
_____. *The House of Dies Drear*, illustrated by Eros Keith. Macmillan, 1968.
_____. *M.C. Higgins, the Great*. Macmillan, 1974.
_____. *The Mystery of Drear House*. Greenwillow, 1987.
_____. *The Planet of Junior Brown*. Macmillan, 1971.
_____. *Zeely*, illustrated by Symeon Shimin. Macmillan, 1967.
Härtling, Peter. *Old John*, translated by Elizabeth D. Crawford. Lothrop, 1990.
Haywood, Carolyn. *"B" Is for Betsy*. Harcourt, 1968 (1939).
_____. *Betsy's Busy Summer*. Harcourt, 1956.
_____. *Eddie and His Big Deals*. Morrow, 1955.
_____. *Little Eddie*. Morrow, 1947.
_____. *Snowbound with Betsy*. Morrow, 1962.
Henry, Marguerite. *King of the Wind*, illustrated by Wesley Dennis. Macmillan, 1948.
_____. *Misty of Chincoteague*, illustrated by Wesley Dennis. Macmillan, 1947.
_____. *Mustang, Wild Spirit of the West*, illustrated by Robert Lougheed. Macmillan, 1971.
_____. *Stormy, Misty's Foal*, illustrated by Wesley Dennis. Macmillan, 1963.
Hill, Kirkpatrick. *Toughboy and Sister*. McElderry, 1990.
Ho, Minfong. *Rice without Rain*. Lothrop, 1988.
Hobbs, Will. *Bearstone*. Atheneum, 1989.
Holman, Felice. *Slake's Limbo*. Scribner, 1974.
Houston, James. *Black Diamonds: A Search for Arctic Treasure*. Atheneum, 1982.
_____. *Frozen Fire*. Atheneum, 1977.
Howe, James. *Dew Drop Dead: A Sebastian Barth Mystery*. Atheneum, 1990.
_____. *Eat Your Poison, Dear: A Sebastian Barth Mystery*. Atheneum, 1986.
_____. *Stage Fright*. Atheneum, 1986.
_____. *What Eric Knew: A Sebastian Barth Mystery*. Atheneum, 1985.
Hughes, Dean. *Making the Team: Angel Park All-Stars*, #1. Random House, 1990.
Hunter, Mollie. *A Sound of Chariots*. Harper, 1972.
Hurwitz, Johanna. *Aldo Applesauce*, illustrated by John Wallner. Morrow, 1979.
_____. *Aldo Ice Cream*, illustrated by Sheila Hamanaka. Morrow, 1987.
_____. *Aldo Peanut Butter*, illustrated by Diane de Groat. Morrow, 1990.
_____. *Busybody Nora*, illustrated by Susan Jeschke. Morrow, 1976.
_____. *Class Clown*, illustrated by Sheila Hamanaka. Morrow, 1987.
_____. *Class President*, illustrated by Sheila Hamanaka. Morrow, 1990.
_____. *Much Ado About Aldo*, illustrated by John Wallner. Morrow, 1978.
_____. *Russell and Elisa*, illustrated by Lillian Hoban. Morrow, 1989.
_____. *School's Out*, illustrated by Sheila Hamanaka. Morrow, 1991.

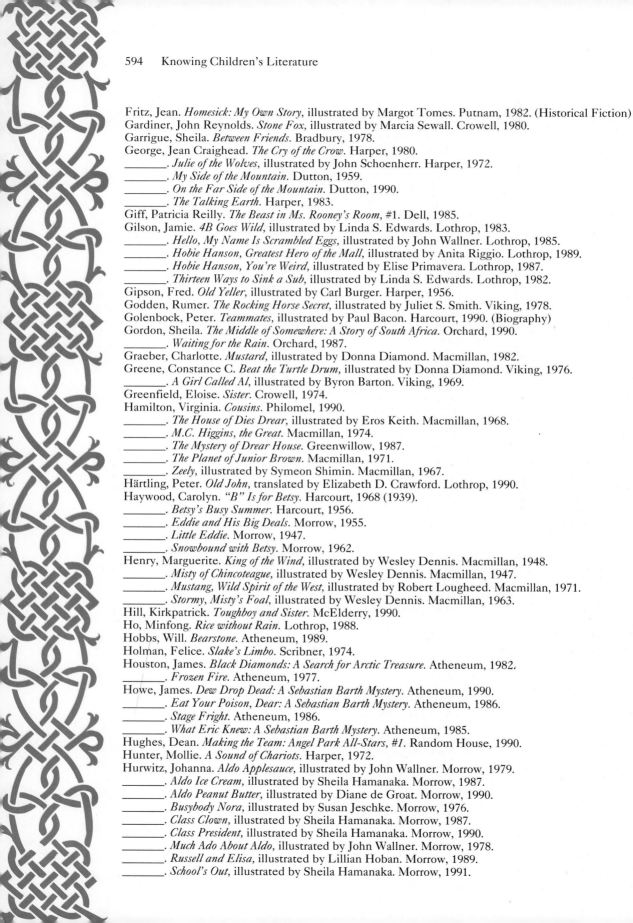

_____. *Superduper Teddy*, illustrated by Susan Jeschke. Morrow, 1980.

_____. *Teacher's Pet*, illustrated by Sheila Hamanaka. Morrow, 1988.

Huynh, Quang Nhuong. *The Land I Lost: Adventures of a Boy in Vietnam*, illustrated by Vo-Dinh Mai. Harper, 1982.

Jones, Rebecca. *Germy Blew It*. Dutton, 1987.

_____. *Germy Blew It Again*. Holt, 1988.

_____. *Germy Blew* The Bugle. Arcade, 1990.

Jukes, Mavis. *Blackberries in the Dark*, illustrated by Thomas B. Allen. Knopf, 1985.

Kidd, Diana. *Onion Tears*, illustrated by Lucy Montgomery. Orchard, 1991.

Killilea, Marie. *Karen*, illustrated by Bob Riger. Dodd, Mead, 1954.

Kjelgaard, Jim. *Big Red*, illustrated by Bob Kuhn. Holiday, 1956.

Klein, Robin. *Hating Alison Ashley*. Viking Kestrel, 1987.

Kline, Suzy. *Orp*. Putnam's, 1989.

_____. *Orp and the Chop Suey Burgers*. Putnam's, 1990.

_____. *Orp Goes to the Hoop*. Putnam's, 1991.

Knudson, R. R. *Rinehart Lifts*. Farrar, Straus, 1980.

_____. *Zanballer*. Harper, 1972.

_____. *Zanbanger*. Harper, 1977.

_____. *Zanboomer*. Harper, 1978.

Konigsburg, E. L. *From the Mixed-Up Files of Mrs. Basil E. Frankweiler*. Atheneum, 1967.

_____. *(George)*. Atheneum, 1970.

_____. *Journey to an 800 Number*. Atheneum, 1982.

Korman, Gordon. *This Can't Be Happening at Macdonald Hall*. Scholastic, 1978.

Krumgold, Joseph. *. . . And Now Miguel*, illustrated by Jean Charlot. Crowell, 1953.

Lasky, Kathryn. *The Night Journey*, illustrated by Trina Schart Hyman. Warne, 1981.

Le Guin, Ursula K. *A Wizard of Earthsea*, illustrated by Ruth Robbins. Houghton Mifflin, 1968. (Fantasy)

L'Engle, Madeleine. *Meet the Austins*. Dell, 1981. (1960)

_____. *A Ring of Endless Light*. Farrar, Straus, 1980.

_____. *A Wrinkle in Time*. Farrar, Straus, 1962. (Fantasy)

Levitin, Sonia. *The Return*. Atheneum, 1987.

Levy, Elizabeth. *Something Queer at the Lemonade Stand*, illustrated by Mordicai Gerstein. Delacorte, 1982.

Lipsyte, Robert. *The Contender*. Harper, 1967.

Little, Jean. *Hey World, Here I Am!*, illustrated by Sue Truesdell. Harper, 1989. (Poetry and prose)

_____. *Home from Far*, illustrated by Jerry Lazare. Little, Brown, 1965.

_____. *Kate*. Harper, 1971.

_____. *Look Through My Window*, illustrated by Joan Sandin. Harper, 1970.

_____. *Mama's Going to Buy You a Mockingbird*. Viking, 1984.

_____. *Mine for Keeps*, illustrated by Lewis Parker. Little, Brown, 1962.

_____. *Take Wing*. Little, Brown, 1968.

London, Jack. *The Call of the Wild*, illustrated by Charles Pickard. Dutton, 1968 (1903).

Lord, Bette Bao. *In the Year of the Boar and Jackie Robinson*, illustrated by Marc Simont. Harper, 1984. (Historical Fiction)

Lowry, Lois. *All About Sam*. Houghton Mifflin, 1988.

_____. *Anastasia Again!*, illustrated by Diane de Groat. Houghton Mifflin, 1981.

_____. *Anastasia, Ask Your Analyst*. Houghton Mifflin, 1984.

_____. *Anastasia at This Address*. Houghton Mifflin, 1991.

_____. *Anastasia at Your Service*, illustrated by Diane de Groat. Houghton Mifflin, 1982.

_____. *Anastasia Has the Answers*. Houghton Mifflin, 1986.

_____. *Anastasia Krupnik*. Houghton Mifflin, 1979.

_____. *Anastasia on Her Own*. Houghton Mifflin, 1985.

_____. *Attaboy, Sam*, illustrated by Diane de Groat. Houghton Mifflin, 1992.

_____. *Number the Stars*. Houghton Mifflin, 1989. (Historical Fiction)

_____. *Rabble Starkey*. Houghton Mifflin, 1987.

_____. *A Summer to Die*, illustrated by Jenni Oliver. Houghton Mifflin, 1977.

McDonnell, Christine. *Don't Be Mad, Ivy*, illustrated by Diane de Groat. Dial, 1981.

_____. *Just for the Summer*, illustrated by Diane de Groat. Viking, 1987.

_____. *Lucky Charms and Birthday Wishes*, illustrated by Diane de Groat. Viking, 1984.

_____. *Toad Food and Measle Soup*, illustrated by Diane de Groat. Dial, 1982.

MacLachlan, Patricia. *Arthur for the Very First Time*, illustrated by Lloyd Bloom. Harper, 1980.

Mann, Peggy. *There Are Two Kinds of Terrible*. Doubleday, 1977.

Mark, Jan. *Handles*. Atheneum, 1985.

_____. *Thunder and Lightnings*, illustrated by Jim Russell. Harper, 1979.

Martin, Ann. *Kristy's Great Idea: The Baby-Sitters Club*, #1. Scholastic, 1986.

Mathis, Sharon Bell. *The Hundred Penny Box*, illustrated by Leo and Diane Dillon. Viking, 1975.

Mazer, Norma Fox. *A Figure of Speech*. Delacorte, 1973.

_____. *I, Trissy*. Delacorte, 1971.

Miles, Betty. *Maudie and Me and the Dirty Book*. Knopf, 1980.

Mills, Claudia. *Dynamite Dinah*. Macmillan, 1990.

Moeri, Louise. *The Forty-Third War*. Houghton Mifflin, 1989.

Mohr, Nicolasa. *Felita*, illustrated by Ray Cruz. Dial, 1979.

_____. *Going Home*. Dial, 1986.

Mowat, Farley. *The Dog Who Wouldn't Be*. Little, Brown, 1957.

_____. *Owls in the Family*. Little, Brown, 1961.

Myers, Walter Dean. *Fast Sam, Cool Clyde, and Stuff*. Viking, 1975.

_____. *The Mouse Rap*. Harper, 1990.

_____. *Scorpions*. Harper, 1988.

_____. *Won't Know Till I Get There*. Viking, 1982.

Naidoo, Beverley. *Journey to Jo'burg*, illustrated by Eric Velasquez. Lippincott, 1986.

_____. *Chain of Fire*, illustrated by Eric Velasquez. Lippincott, 1990.

Naylor, Phyllis Reynolds. *The Agony of Alice*. Atheneum, 1985.

_____. *Alice in Rapture, Sort Of*. Atheneum, 1989.

_____. *All but Alice*. Atheneum, 1992.

_____. *Reluctantly Alice*. Atheneum, 1991.

_____. *Shiloh*. Atheneum, 1991.

Neville, Emily Cheney. *The China Year*. HarperCollins, 1991.

Nilsson, Ulf. *If You Didn't Have Me*, translated by Lone Thygesen Blecher and George Blecher, illustrated by Eva Eriksson. McElderry, 1987.

Nixon, Joan Lowery. *A Candidate for Murder*. Delacorte, 1991.

_____. *The Other Side of Dark*. Delacorte, 1986.

North, Sterling. *Rascal: A Memoir of a Better Era*, illustrated by John Schoenherr. Dutton, 1963.

Oneal, Zibby. *The Language of Goldfish*. Viking, 1980.

Parish, Peggy. *Amelia Bedelia*, illustrated by Fritz Siebel. Harper, 1963.

_____. *Amelia Bedelia Helps Out*, illustrated by Lynn Sweat. Greenwillow, 1979.

_____. *Teach Us, Amelia Bedelia*, illustrated by Lynn Sweat. Greenwillow, 1977.

_____. *Thank You, Amelia Bedelia*, illustrated by Fritz Siebel. Harper, 1964.

Park, Barbara. *Skinnybones*. Knopf, 1982.

Paterson, Katherine. *Bridge to Terabithia*, illustrated by Donna Diamond. Crowell, 1977.

_____. *Come Sing, Jimmy Jo*. Dutton, 1985.

_____. *The Great Gilly Hopkins*. Crowell, 1978.

_____. *Jacob Have I Loved*. Harper, 1980.

_____. *Park's Quest*. Dutton, 1988.

Patterson, Nancy Ruth. *The Christmas Cup*, illustrated by Leslie Bowman. Orchard, 1989.

Paulsen, Gary. *Dogsong*. Bradbury, 1985.

_____. *Hatchet*. Bradbury, 1987.

_____. *The River*. Delacorte, 1991.

_____. *The Voyage of the Frog*. Bradbury, 1989.

Pearce, Philippa. *The Way to Sattin Shore*, illustrated by Charlotte Voake. Greenwillow, 1983.

Peck, Robert Newton. *Soup*, illustrated by Charles Gehm. Knopf, 1974.

_____. *Trig*, illustrated by Pamela Johnson. Little, Brown, 1977.

Pollock, Penny. *Keeping It Secret*, illustrated by Donna Diamond. Putnam, 1982.

Raskin, Ellen. *The Westing Game*. Dutton, 1978.

Rawlings, Marjorie Kinnan. *The Yearling*, illustrated by Edward Shenton. Scribner, 1938.

Rawls, Wilson. *Where the Red Fern Grows*. Doubleday, 1961.

Riley, Jocelyn. *Crazy Quilt*. Morrow, 1983.

_____. *Only My Mouth Is Smiling*. Morrow, 1982.

Riskind, Mary. *Apple Is My Sign*. Houghton Mifflin, 1981. (Historical Fiction)

Robinson Barbara. *The Best Christmas Pageant Ever*, illustrated by Judith Gwyn Brown. Harper, 1972.

Rockwell, Thomas. *How to Eat Fried Worms*. Watts, 1973.

Rodowsky, Colby F. *What About Me?* Watts, 1976.

Rylant, Cynthia. *Every Living Thing*, illustrated by S. D. Schindler. Bradbury, 1985.
_____. *A Fine White Dust*. Bradbury, 1986.
Sachs, Marilyn. *The Bears' House*, illustrated by Louis Glanzman. Doubleday, 1971.
Say, Allen. *El Chino*. Houghton Mifflin, 1990. (Biography)
Schlein, Miriam. *The Year of the Panda*, illustrated by Kam Mak. Crowell, 1990.
Shreve, Susan. *The Flunking of Joshua T. Bates*, illustrated by Diane de Groat. Knopf, 1984.
Shyer, Marlene. *Welcome Home, Jellybean*. Scribner, 1978.
Simon, Seymour. *Einstein Anderson Lights Up the Sky*, illustrated by Fred Winkowski. Viking, 1982.
Slepian, Jan. *The Alfred Summer*. Macmillan, 1980.
_____. *The Broccoli Tapes*. Putnam, 1989.
_____. *Lester's Turn*. Macmillan, 1981.
_____. *Risk n' Roses*. Philomel, 1990.
Slote, Alfred. *Hang Tough, Paul Mather*. Lippincott, 1973.
_____. *My Father, the Coach*. Lippincott, 1972.
_____. *The Trading Game*. Lippincott, 1990.
Smith, Doris Buchanan. *A Taste of Blackberries*, illustrated by Charles Robinson. Crowell, 1973.
Smith, Janice Lee. *It's Not Easy Being George*, illustrated by Dick Gackenbach. Harper, 1990.
_____. *The Monster in the Third Dresser Drawer*, illustrated by Dick Gackenbach. Harper, 1981.
_____. *The Show-And-Tell War and Other Stories About Adam Joshua*, illustrated by Dick Gackenbach. Harper, 1988.
_____. *The Turkey's Side of It*, illustrated by Dick Gackenbach. Harper, 1990.
Snyder, Zilpha K. *The Egypt Game*, illustrated by Alton Raible. Atheneum, 1967.
_____. *Libby on Wednesday*. Delacorte, 1990.
Sobol, Donald. *Encyclopedia Brown Takes a Case*, illustrated by Leonard Shortall. Nelson, 1973.
Soto, Gary. *Baseball in April and Other Stories*. Harcourt, 1990.
_____. *Taking Sides*. Harcourt, 1991.
Southall, Ivan. *Josh*. Macmillan, 1972.
_____. *Let the Balloon Go*, illustrated by Jon Weiman. Bradbury, 1968.
Speare, Elizabeth George. *The Witch of Blackbird Pond*. Houghton Mifflin, 1958. (Historical Fiction)
Sperry, Armstrong. *Call It Courage*. Macmillan, 1968.
Spinelli, Jerry. *Maniac Magee*. Little, Brown, 1990.
Staples, Suzanne Fisher. *Shabanu: Daughter of the Wind*. Knopf, 1989.
Stolz, Mary. *The Bully of Barkham Street*, illustrated by Leonard Shortall. Harper, 1963.
_____. *A Dog on Barkham Street*, illustrated by Leonard Shortall. Harper, 1960.
_____. *The Explorer of Barkham Street*, illustrated by Emily A. McCully. Harper, 1985.
Taylor, Mildred. *The Friendship*, illustrated by Max Ginsburg. Dial, 1987. (Historical Fiction)
Taylor, Sidney. *All-of-a-Kind Family*, illustrated by Helen John. Follett, 1951.
_____. *All-of-a-Kind Family Uptown*, illustrated by Mary Stevens. Follett, 1958.
_____. *More All-of-a-Kind Family*, illustrated by Mary Stevens. Follett, 1954.
Taylor, Theodore. *Tuck Triumphant*. Doubleday, 1991.
_____. *The Trouble with Tuck*. Doubleday, 1981.
Thiele, Colin. *Jodie's Journey*. Harper, 1988.
_____. *Storm Boy*, illustrated by John Schoenherr. Harper, 1978.
Thomas, Jane Resh. *The Comeback Dog*, illustrated by Troy Howell. Houghton Mifflin, 1981.
_____. *Fox in a Trap*, illustrated by Troy Howell. Clarion, 1987.
_____. *Saying Good-Bye to Grandma*, illustrated by Marcia Sewall. Clarion, 1988.
Voigt, Cynthia. *Dicey's Song*. Atheneum, 1983.
_____. *Homecoming*. Atheneum, 1981.
_____. *The Runner*. Atheneum, 1985.
_____. *Seventeen Against the Dealer*. Atheneum, 1985.
_____. *A Solitary Blue*. Atheneum, 1984.
Walter, Mildred Pitts. *Have a Happy . . . .* Lothrop, 1989.
_____. *Justin and the Best Biscuits in the World*, illustrated by Catherine Stock. Knopf, 1986.
Warburg, Sandol Stoddard. *The Growing Time*, illustrated by Leonard Weisgard. Harper, 1969.
Warner, Gertrude Chandler. *The Boxcar Children*, #1. Whitman, 1942.
Wojciechowska, Maia. *Shadow of a Bull*, illustrated by Alvin Smith. Atheneum, 1964.
Wright, Betty Ren. *The Dollhouse Murders*. Holiday, 1983. (Fantasy)
Yep, Laurence. *Child of the Owl*. Harper, 1977.

Chapter Ten

Historical Fiction and Biography

The author of an historical novel visited a public library's after-school program to meet with a group of children. In her talk she described the research she had done to establish an authentic Civil War background for her book. To make the efforts seem more concrete, she had brought along many examples of source material: maps, reproductions of nineteenth-century photographs, books and pamphlets, and a three-ring binder bulging with notes. One 10-year-old girl regarded this display with a troubled expression, and when time came for questions quickly raised her hand.

"You found out a lot of things that you didn't put in the book, didn't you?" she asked. The author agreed, and the girl smiled. "Good!" she said. "If you had put all *that* stuff in, there wouldn't have been any room for the imagining!"

This child intuitively knew that historical fiction must draw on two sources, fact and imagination—the author's information about the past and his or her power to speculate about how it was to live in that time.

Biography for children also draws on both sources. Although biography is by definition a nonfiction genre, its success depends as much on its imaginative presentation of facts as on their accuracy. Both biography and historical fiction have narrative appeal. By personalizing the past and making it live in the mind of the reader, such books can help children understand both the public events that we usually label "history" and the private struggles that have characterized the human condition across the centuries.

HISTORICAL FICTION

Historical Fiction for Today's Child

Historical fiction is not as popular with readers today as it was a generation ago. Children generally select realistic fiction, the so-called "I" stories with modern-day characters and settings. Even so, children have more historical fiction available now than in the 1980s.

Publishers have capitalized on children's interest in series books by developing collectible sets of historical fiction titles. The "American Girl" books offer four different series, each chronicling the adventures of a girl in a particular time. These books, along with the expensive dolls and period costumes that go with them, have been phenomenally successful.

Other publishers, influenced by public debate about children's need to know their heritage, have also targeted the 7 to 11 age range. Viking's "Once upon America" books, written by many different authors, vary widely in quality. However, they offer an unusually wide range of settings, such as the flu epidemic of 1918 (*Hero Over Here* by Kathleen Kudlinski) and the 1889 Johnstown, Pennsylvania, flood (*The Day It Rained Forever* by Virginia Gross).

Another noticeable trend in historical fiction is the number of picture storybooks that portray the life of a particular period. For example, Barbara Cooney depicts the story of her mother's growing up in affluence in first Brooklyn and then Long Island in *Hattie and the Wild Waves*. Servants, dressmakers, a summer home on the ocean, a large sailing vessel, and the new enormous house on Long Island with its park full of deer were all a natural part of her childhood in the early 1900s. In *Island Boy*, Cooney shows the continuity of life as various generations of children grow to love their small island home in New England. Michelle Dionetti tells the story of her Italian-American grandfather, who grew up in a coal-mining town, went to New York to make his fortune, helped build the Brooklyn Bridge, and lived to tell joyous, exaggerated tales to his extended family. This book, *Coal Mine Peaches*, has illustrations by Anita Riggio that show many details of social history.

The increased use of books across the curriculum has created a demand for more historical fiction and biography in the social studies curriculum. Many books that were written in the 1950s such as Eloise McGraw's *Moccasin Trail* and William Steele's *Winter Danger*, *The Buffalo Knife*, and *Flaming Arrows* have been reissued in paperback in the 1990s. These are still exciting well-written stories of frontier living and will capture children's interest. *On to Oregon!* by Honoré Morrow is an almost unbelievable tale of the courage of the six Sager children who, after the death of their parents, walked over a thousand miles by themselves through the wilderness until they reached the Whitman missionary station. First published in 1926, then again in 1946 and 1954, and now in paperback in the 1990s, this novel proves the lasting quality of a true survival story.

While many books of American historical fiction are being reissued, many fine books such as Rosemary Sutcliff's books about early Britain have been allowed to go out of print. Except for an increase in the number of titles about the Holocaust, we have fewer books of historical fiction of other lands. This is a loss indeed for a world that is becoming increasingly interdependent. We need to know our history *and* the history of other countries.

VALUES OF HISTORICAL FICTION

Historical novels for children help a child to experience the past—to enter into the conflicts, the suffering, the joys, and the despair of those who lived before us. There is no way that children can feel the jolt of a covered wagon, the tediousness of the daily trek in the broiling sun, or the constant threat of danger, unless they take an imaginative journey in such books as *Trouble for Lucy* by Carla Stevens or *Beyond the Divide* by Kathryn Lasky. Well-written historical fiction

Illustrations help describe historical settings of an affluent era for the picture-book audience.

Illustration by Barbara Cooney from *Hattie and the Wild Waves*.

offers young people the vicarious experience of participating in the life of the past.

Historical fiction encourages children to think as well as to feel. Every book set in the past invites a comparison with the present. In addition, opportunities for critical thinking and judgment are built into the many novels that provide conflicting views on an issue and force characters to make hard choices. Readers of *My Brother Sam Is Dead* by the Colliers can weigh Sam's Patriot fervor against his father's Tory practicality as young Tim tries to decide which one is right. Readers will question Will Page's dislike of his uncle because he refused to fight the Yankees in Carolyn Reeder's story, *Shades of Gray*. And yet there have been conscientious objectors in every war that this nation has participated in. Mary Downing Hahn deals with the same issue in *Stepping on the Cracks*, a story set during World War II.

An historical perspective also helps children to see and judge the mistakes of the past more clearly. They can read such books as Paula Fox's *The Slave Dancer*, *Hide and Seek* by Ida Vos, or *Journey to Topaz* by Yoshiko Uchida and realize the cruelty that people are capable of inflicting on their own kind, whether by slavery, persecution, or the assignment of American Japanese to "relocation centers." Such books will quicken children's sensibilities and bring them to a fuller understanding of human problems and human relationships. We hope they will learn not to repeat the injustices of the past. Many years ago George Santayana cautioned: "Those who cannot remember the past are condemned to repeat it."

Stories of the past help children see that times change; nations do rise and fall; but the universal needs of humankind have remained relatively unchanged. All people need and want respect, belonging, love, freedom, security, regardless of whether they lived during the period of the Vikings or the pioneers or are alive today. It matters not how many different "Little Houses" the Ingalls family lived in as long as Pa's fiddle sang a song of love and security in each one. Children today living in tenements, trailers, or suburban homes seek the same feeling of warmth and family solidarity that Laura Ingalls Wilder portrayed so effectively in her Little House series.

Historical fiction also enables children to see the interdependence of humankind. We are all interconnected and interrelated. We need others as much as Matt needed Attean and Saknis in Elizabeth George Speare's *The Sign of the Beaver* or Ellen Rosen needed Annemarie Johansen's family in order to escape the Nazis in Lois Lowry's award-winning book *Number the Stars*. Such books also dramatize the courage and integrity of the thousands of "common folk" who willingly take a stand for what they believe. History does not record their names, but their stories are frequently the source of inspiration for books of historical fiction.

Children's perceptions of chronology are inexact and develop slowly. Even so, stories about the past can develop a feeling for the continuity of life and help children to see themselves and their present place in time as a part of a larger picture. Bonnie Pryor's *The House on Maple Street* provides this sense for younger elementary students. Lost objects from early times are unearthed in a contemporary child's yard. Paintings by Beth Peck link past and present, showing changes which came to that specific setting over the intervening centuries.

The concept of continuity is stated eloquently in Paul Fleischman's moving story of *The Borning Room*. Every crisis of Georgina Lott's life had taken place in this one room in the family's Ohio home called the "borning room." She had been born there in 1851, her mother had given birth there with the help of a runaway slave, her beloved grandfather had died there as had her mother in a subsequent childbirth, her two brothers had nearly died of diphtheria, and she herself had given birth to her first child there. After her daughter, named for her mother, is born, she was placed in the cedar cradle her grandfather had made, wrapped in a blanket woven by her grandmother, and placed alongside her was the cornhusk doll made by the runaway slave. This one room held the memory of the eternal cycle of birth, courtship, sickness, and death. The reading of historical fiction is one way to help children develop this sense of history and to begin to understand their place in the sweep of human destiny.

TYPES OF HISTORICAL FICTION

The term *historical fiction* can be used to designate all realistic stories that are set in the past.

Even though children tend to see these in one undifferentiated category (since all the action happened "in the olden days" before they were born), students of literature will want to keep in mind that various distinctions can be made on the basis of the author's purpose and the nature of the research and writing tasks required.

In the most obvious type of historical fiction, an author weaves a fictional story around actual events and people of the past. *Johnny Tremain* by Esther Forbes, the story of a fictional apprentice to Paul Revere, is a novel of this sort. The author had previously written a definitive adult biography of Revere and had collected painstakingly accurate details about life in Boston just before the Revolutionary War: the duties of apprentices, the activities of the Committee for Public Safety, and much, much more. Johnny Tremain's personal story, his development from an embittered boy to a courageous and idealistic young man, is inextricably connected with the political history and way of life of his place and time.

In other stories of the past, fictional lives are lived with little or no reference to recorded historical events or real persons. However, the facts of social history dictate the background for how the characters live and make their living; what they wear, eat, study, or play; and what conflicts they must resolve. Patricia MacLachlan's *Sarah, Plain and Tall* is a book of this type. The demands of life on the great mid-American prairie before the advent of mechanized farming and the practice of advertising for mail-order brides provide the frame for this moving story of a family that needs a mother. Authors who write within this generalized frame of social history have more freedom to imagine their story, since they are not bound to the chronology of specific historical events.

If we look at the author's task in another way, we can see that some deliberately reconstruct, through research, the life and times of a period long past. Others recreate, largely from memory, their own personal experiences of a time that is "history" to their child audience. The Little House books, for example, are all based on actual childhood experiences in the life of their author, Laura Ingalls Wilder, or those of her husband. Such books require searching the memory for details and then the sorting and imaginative

retelling of significant events, but extensive research is seldom done.

In other instances, a purely contemporary story about a significant event may endure until it acquires historical significance. *Snow Treasure* by Marie McSwigan is the exciting story of Norwegian children who strapped gold bullion under their sleds and slid down the hill to the port past the watchful Nazi commandant. Written as realism in 1942, this book is read by children today as historical fiction.

Some essentially historical stories defy commonly accepted classifications. A few authors tell stories of the past within the guise of another genre to draw the hesitant reader in more quickly. Jane Yolen's devastating story of the Holocaust, *The Devil's Arithmetic*, begins in the present when Hannah, bored with all the remembering of the Passover Seder, opens the door to welcome symbolically the prophet Elijah, and finds herself in the unfamiliar world of a Polish village in the 1940s. When the Nazi soldiers come to a wedding and take all of the villagers away, only Hannah knows where they are going. This is one of the few children's stories of the Holocaust that details the horrors within a concentration camp. Hannah's knowledge of the future brings a special poignancy to the hopes and actions of the people. Other fantasy devices are used to transport the main character (and the reader) from the present day to a carefully researched past in such books as Janet Lunn's *The Root Cellar* and *The Doll* by Cora Taylor (see Chapter 7). In all instances the characters return to the present as wiser, more understanding persons.

E. L. Konigsburg's unique story of Eleanor of Aquitaine, *A Proud Taste for Scarlet and Miniver*, combines fantasy, historical fiction, and biography. Categorizing books like these is far less important than bringing them to the attention of children, for they all tell good stories and make their subjects memorable.

No type of historical story is intrinsically better than another. However, the type of story might influence a teacher's selection process when choosing books for specific classroom purposes. And, in applying the criteria for evaluating historical fiction which are described in the following section, standards of authenticity must be applied most rigorously to stories that give a prominent place to real people and real events.

CRITERIA FOR HISTORICAL FICTION

Books of historical fiction must first of all tell a story that is interesting in its own right. The second, and unique, requirement is balancing fact with fiction. Margery Fisher maintains that fact must always be subordinated to the story:

> For the more fact he [the author] has to deal with, the more imagination he will need to carry it off. It is not enough to be a scholar, essential though this is. Without imagination and enthusiasm, the most learned and well-documented story will leave the young reader cold, where it should set him on fire.[1]

Historical fiction does have to be accurate and authentic. However, the research should be thoroughly digested, making details appear as an essential part of the story, not tacked on for effect. Mollie Hunter, a well-known Scottish writer of fine historical fiction for children, maintains that an author should be so steeped in the historical period of the book that "you could walk undetected in the past. You'd wake up in the morning and know the kind of bed you'd be sleeping in, . . . even to the change you'd have in your pocket!"[2] The purpose of research, she said, is:

> . . . to be able to think and feel in terms of a period so that the people within it are real and three-dimensional, close enough to hear the sound of their voices, to feel their body-warmth, to see the expression in their eyes.[3]

Although fictional characters and invented turns of plot are accepted in historical novels, nothing should be included that contradicts the actual record of history. If President Lincoln was busy reviewing Union troops in Virginia on a given day in 1863, an author cannot "borrow" him for a scene played in New York City, no matter how great the potential dramatic impact. It breaks the unwritten contract between author and child reader to offer misinformation in any form.

Stories must accurately reflect the spirit and values of the times, as well as the events. Historical fiction can't be made to conform to today's more enlightened point of view concerning women or minorities or knowledge of medicine. You can't save George Washington with a shot of penicillin any more than you can have the African-American mother in William Armstrong's *Sounder* become a militant in the 1890s. Characters have to act in accordance with the values and beliefs of the time. The father of Carol Ryrie Brink's *Caddie Woodlawn* allowed her to be a tomboy while she was growing up in the Wisconsin backwoods, but she had to become a "proper lady" during the Victorian era; there was no other choice. Avi's *The True Confessions of Charlotte Doyle* is a dramatic sea adventure story in the manner of Robert Louis Stevenson's *Kidnapped*. In 1832 13-year-old Charlotte Doyle boards the *Seahawk* to sail from Liverpool, England, to Providence, Rhode Island. Fresh from her proper boarding school experience in England, Charlotte is dismayed to find she is the only passenger and the only female on the ship. Within hours of her arrival aboard, the ship's cook gives her a dagger for her own protection. And that is just the beginning of this exciting sea yarn. Charlotte is a strong female character, yet some of her adventures stretch credibility as tightly as the full-blown sails that she climbs. Despite the many awards this book has received, we cannot help wondering if it wasn't written with today's values in mind rather than the New England of the early 1830s.

The historian Christopher Collier, who has collaborated with his brother James Lincoln Collier on several novels set during the era of the American Revolution, maintains that authors should pay careful attention to historiography, ". . . that is, the way that professional historians have approached and interpreted the central episode of the story."[4] Collier believes that authors should weigh opposing views on the causes or meaning of a conflict and decide which

[1] Margery Fisher, *Intent upon Reading: A Critical Appraisal of Modern Fiction for Children* (New York: Watts, 1962), p. 225.
[2] In a lecture given in Columbus, Ohio, November 1968.
[3] Mollie Hunter, "Shoulder the Sky" in *Talent Is Not Enough* (New York: Harper & Row, 1976), pp. 43–44.
[4] Christopher Collier, "Criteria for Historical Fiction," *School Library Journal*, vol. 28 (August 1982), p. 32.

should be predominant in the story, but also find a way to include the other significant interpretations. One way is to have different characters espouse different points of view. However, fiction that draws the reader into the thoughts and feelings of a central character cannot be truly impartial. In the middle of a massacre scene, a bleeding settler who cries ". . . but the Indians are only fighting for what is theirs!" will sacrifice the story's credibility. Many fine books, like Carolyn Reeder's *Shades of Gray* and Avi's *The Fighting Ground*, do let the reader feel more than one side of an issue. But for a more inclusive viewpoint, teachers and librarians will want to provide a variety of books, each with its own approach to the topic.

The authenticity of language in historical fiction should be given careful attention. We have no record of how people in other times actually talked, but the spoken word in a book with an historical background should give the flavor of the period. However, too many "prithees" and "thous" will seem artificial and may discourage children's further reading. Some archaic words can be used if they are explained in the content. For example, the book *The Cabin Faced West* notes that George Washington "bated" at the Hamiltons. The author, Jean Fritz, makes it very clear by the action in the story that "bated" meant "stopped by for dinner."

Some words commonly used in earlier times are offensive by today's standards. Authors must consider whether or not it would be misleading to omit such terms entirely and how necessary such language is for establishing character. In Sheila Garrigue's *The Eternal Spring of Mr. Ito*, residents of Vancouver in the panic of late 1941 contemptuously refer to their Japanese neighbors as "Japs." It would have defeated the purpose of the story to portray the residents as more understanding and compassionate than they actually were.

Well-written historical fiction also makes use of figurative language that is appropriate for the times and characters in the story. For example, in Katherine Paterson's powerful story of *Lyddie*, a farm girl who goes to work in the fabric mills of Lowell, Massachusetts, in the 1840s, every allusion and metaphor are those of an uneducated rural girl. When Lyddie first sees the city she thinks:

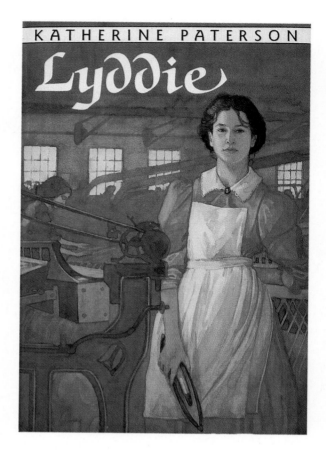

The cover of Katherine Paterson's *Lyddie* helps readers visualize the inside of a nineteenth-century textile mill. At the same time it introduces a main character whose fortitude is written in her face.

Art by Deborah Chabrain.

There were as many buildings crowded before her as sheep in a shearing shed. But they were not soft and murmuring as sheep. They were huge and foreboding. . . .[5]

When she receives fifty dollars in return for her gift to a runaway slave, she thinks her "bank account had bulged like a cow about to freshen."[6] In the very beginning of the story a bear gets into their farm cabin and Lyddie stares him down

[5]Katherine Paterson, *Lyddie* (New York: Dutton, 1991), p. 51.
[6]Paterson, *Lyddie*, p. 115.

while the children climb the ladder to the loft. Finally she herself backs up to the ladder, climbs it, and pulls it up behind her. Throughout the book Lyddie alludes to "staring down the bears." She thinks of the huge machines as "roaring clattering beasts . . . great clumsy bears."[7] And when she throws a water bucket at the overseer to get him to let go of a young girl, she laughs as she imagines she hears the sound of an angry bear crashing the oatmeal bucket in the cabin. Everything about this book works together to capture Lyddie's view of the world. At the same time the long thirteen hours of factory work, life in the dormitories, the frequency of TB, and the treatment of women all reflect the spirit and the values of the times. More important than the authenticity of the writing is the fast-paced story and the grit, determination, and personal growth of Lyddie herself.

A book of historical fiction should do even more than relate a good story of the past authentically and imaginatively. It should illuminate the problems of today by examining those of other times.

| [7]Paterson, *Lyddie*, p. 97.

The themes of many historical books are such basic ones as the meaning of freedom, loyalty and treachery, love and hate, acceptance of new ways, closed minds versus questing ones, and, always, the age-old struggle between good and evil. Many tales of the past echo recent experience. Books such as *Lyddie* by Katherine Paterson or *The Borning Room* by Paul Fleischman or *Prairie Songs* by Pam Conrad could well be used in a discussion of the history of women's roles. All these books are capable of shedding light and understanding on the problems of today.

To summarize, historical fiction must first meet the requirements of good writing, but it demands special criteria beyond that. In evaluating historical fiction the reader will want to consider whether the story meets these specialized needs.

Historical fiction can dramatize and humanize the sterile facts of history. It can give children a sense of participation in the past and an appreciation for their historical heritage. It should enable the child to see that today's way of life is a result of what people did in the past and that the present will influence the way people live in the future.

GUIDELINES

Evaluating Historical Fiction

- ♦ Does the book tell a good story?
- ♦ Is fact blended with fiction in such a way that the background is subordinate to the story?
- ♦ Is the story as accurate and authentic as possible?
- ♦ Does the author avoid any contradiction or distortion of the known events of history?
- ♦ Are background details authentic or in keeping with accurate information about the period?
- ♦ Does the story accurately reflect the values and spirit of the times?
- ♦ Are different points of view on the issues of the time presented or acknowledged?
- ♦ Is the dialogue constructed so as to convey a feeling of the period without seeming artificial? Does it reflect character as well as setting?
- ♦ Is the language of the narrative appropriate to the times, drawing figures of speech from the setting?
- ♦ Does the theme provide insight and understanding for today's problems as well as those of the past?

In the following sections, books are discussed chronologically, according to the periods and settings they represent. Another way to approach historical fiction is to look at common topics or themes as they are presented in different settings across the centuries. For examples of titles grouped in this way, see the box on page 624.

Stories of Prehistoric Times

Anthropologists and geologists are slowly uncovering scientific data that make it possible to imagine how life in prehistoric times might have been. Authors and their readers have been fascinated with trying to reconstruct the mind and feelings of primitive people. How did they discover that there were others living in the world? Were all the tribes at the same level of development, or did different groups mature ahead of others? What happened when two groups met? These and other questions have provided the stimulus for some remarkably fine stories.

In *Time of the Bison*, Ann Turner creates a story of the cave painters. Who were they? What did their pictures mean to them? Scar Boy hates his name and longs for the time when he will find his real name, his inner name. One night he dreams of a horse, a great stallion. The next day at the river he makes a remarkable red clay statue of the horse of his dreams. His father is astonished and decides he must take Scar Boy on a journey to see The Painter of the Caves, a wise man who belongs to his mother's tribe. When Scar Boy is allowed to visit the cave he discovers the true meaning of his gift and what his real name will someday be.

Another story of a boy who stands out because of his talent for drawing is told by Rosemary Sutcliff in *Sun Horse, Moon Horse*. Lubrin is the son of an early chieftain of the Horse People on the chalk downs of England. When invaders imprison his people and the leader demands that Lubrin draw a huge horse on the hillside, the boy bargains freedom for his tribe. He agrees to cut a likeness of a horse into the white chalk half a hill high if his people are allowed to go north with enough stallions and brood mares to establish a new herd. But the image is to be a horse-god, incomplete without the quickening force of

human blood. Lubrin gives his life as well as his art for his people in this powerful story of sacrifice and the demands of creativity. The author's fascination with the beautiful ancient White Horse of Uffington led her to write this tale speculating about its origin.

T. A. Dyer's *A Way of His Own* deals with early people of North America, a small band of hunters and gatherers on an inland prairie. According to their way, they abandon young Shutok because he cannot keep up and because they believe his crippled back houses an evil spirit responsible for all their misfortunes. But Shutok, a well-devel-

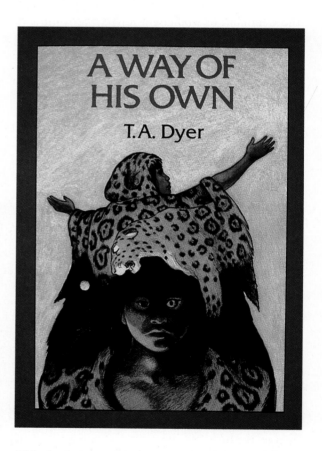

This dual view of a character with a jaguar-skin robe and eyes that hint of a transformation provides a glimpse of the drama in this prehistoric story.

From the paperback edition of *A Way of His Own* by T. A. Dyer.

🍎 🍎 🍎

oped character with great determination, does not die as expected. He is joined by the escaped slave girl Uita, and together the two outcasts kill the fearsome jaguar that invades their cave, struggle against bitter cold and hunger, and live to reclaim a position of worth with Shutok's people. The story is fast-paced, with lively dialogue.

Seth of the Lion People by Bonnie Pryor also tells the story of a boy crippled from birth. At first it was thought that Seth would follow in his father's footsteps and become the clan's storyteller, the one who kept their history alive. But the new leader's son is cruel and only measures a man's worth by his hunting and fighting skills. Seth, his best friend Esu, and the loyal Dog he has tamed set off across the mountains to see if it is really true that people there tend crops, domesticate animals, and live in warm huts. After a long and treacherous journey they discover all they had heard is true. They return to their tribe just in time to save them from an erupting volcano. Because of all he learned from the other tribe, Seth is chosen leader over the cruel Nar.

In *The Stronghold*, Mollie Hunter has created a character whose courage and imagination override a handicap. Coll's achievement is his plan for protection against the raiding Romans—the "brochs," or strongholds of stone that remain to intrigue present-day visitors to the North of Scotland. This is a story of conflict between tribal life and the religious domination of the Druids. It is also a story of devotion as Coll makes a daring attempt to save the girl he loves from Druid sacrifice. The power of the setting and of the language helped to make this challenging novel a Carnegie award winner.

J. H. Brennan's story of *Shiva* relates the warlike meeting of two groups of prehistoric peoples: the Neanderthals, called ogres by Cro-Magnon people, who in turn were called "The Weakling Strangers" by the ogres. One group kept to the forests and caves; the other was nomadic and hunted. No ogre had been seen for many years, and it was assumed they had all died until Shiva, an orphan girl, wanders too far from camp and is attacked by wolves. To her amazement, she is saved by a young ogre boy who jumps on the wolf and kills him. Her cries attract her own tribe who promptly capture the young ogre. Shiva frees him. This is a complex story of the distrust felt by one group for another group who look different from others. Only Shiva can see the humanity of both tribes.

The Faraway Lurs by Harry Behn is a hauntingly beautiful story of the love between a young Stone Age girl, Heather, and Wolfe Stone, son of the chieftain of the Sun People, a warlike group who would destroy the mighty tree that her peaceful Forest People worship. The two fall in love, but there is no solution for them other than death in this Romeo and Juliet story of the Bronze Age. The author was inspired to tell Heather's tale after a journey to Denmark to visit the birthplace of his mother. An important archeological find had been made on a nearby farm when they discovered the "wet grave" of an 18-year-old girl perfectly preserved for some three thousand years. Behn listened to the details of her burial and then wrote his own interpretation of what might have happened. In his foreword Behn points out the relative brevity of human history and the slow progress in human relations since Heather's time.

Stories of the Old World

Children in the United States are more interested in stories of the American frontier, the Civil War, or World War II than they are in the fiction of ancient or medieval days. However, there is some fine historical fiction of the Old World.

ANCIENT TIMES

The ancient world of Egypt with all of its political intrigue provides a rich background for Eloise McGraw's story of a slave girl, *Mara, Daughter of the Nile*. Mara, the mistreated slave of a wealthy jewel trader, is bought by a mysterious man who offers her luxury in return for her services as a spy for the queen. On a Nile riverboat Mara meets Lord Sheftu, who employs her as a spy for the king. In this exciting and sinister story of espionage and counterespionage, the transformation of Mara from a selfish, deceitful slave to a loyal and courageous young woman is made slowly and believably. Eloise McGraw has written another exciting complex story of this period of ancient history titled *The Golden Goblet*. It has recently been reissued in paperback.

Daniel Bar Jamin has but one all-consuming purpose in his life, to avenge the cruel death of his father and mother by driving the Romans out of his land of Israel. First with an outlaw band, and then with a group of boy guerrillas, Daniel nurses his hatred and waits for the hour to strike. He takes comfort in the verse from II Samuel 22:35—"He trains my hands for war, so that my arms can bend a bow of bronze." Seen as a symbol for what no man can do, *The Bronze Bow* is the title for Daniel's tormented journey from blind hatred to his acceptance and understanding of love. Only after he has nearly sacrificed his friends and driven his sister, Leah, deeper into mental darkness, does he seek the help of Simon's friend, Jesus. After he pours out his troubles and hatred, Jesus tells him:

🐦 It is hate that is the enemy, not men. Hate does not die with killing. It only springs up a hundred-fold. The only thing stronger than hate is love.[8]

The healing strength of Jesus cures Leah and, at that moment, Daniel can forgive the Romans. He understands at last that only love can bend the bow of bronze. Each character stands out in this startling story of the conflict of good and evil.

A bear, a boy, and a holy man are strange traveling companions in Peter Dickinson's novel, *The Dancing Bear*, set in sixth-century Byzantium. Silvester, a young Greek slave, is very happy at his master's large house, where he plays with Lady Adriane, the master's daughter, learns Latin and medicine, and has the sole responsibility of training Bubba, the bear, to dance. Silvester's world is destroyed on the night of Lady Adriane's betrothal feast, when a group of Huns enter the house, slaughter most of the guests, and eventually carry the girl away. Silvester takes Bubba to go in search of her. On his quest to find and free the Lady Adriane, Silvester is freed from his literal and psychological bondage to slavery. Gradually, as he learns to act and think like a free man, he loses "the look of a slave." This is a heady tale, rich in humor, high adventure, imagination, and historical detail.

TALES OF EARLY BRITAIN

No one has surpassed Rosemary Sutcliff in her ability to recreate the life and times of early Britain. More remarkable, she writes of the native peoples of Britain and of the Roman occupation forces with equal skill and sympathy.

The Eagle of the Ninth, The Silver Branch, and *The Lantern Bearers* form a trilogy that describes the period when Britain was ruled by Romans. In the third book the last of the Roman auxiliaries set sail in their galleys and abandon Britain to internal strife and the menace of invasion by Saxons. At the final moment, one Roman officer decides that his loyalties lie with Britain rather than the legions. Aquila returns to his family villa only to have all that he loves destroyed by the Saxons. His father is killed, his sister captured, and he is enslaved by a band of invaders. Three years later

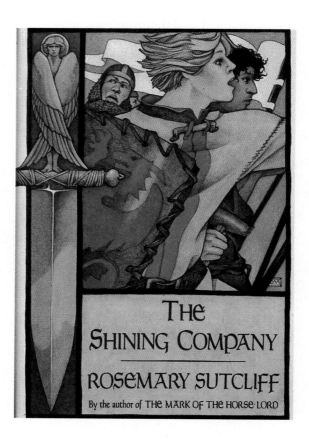

The dagger, shield, and flying banner are clues to a story of high adventure and heroism on this enticing cover.

Jacket art by Charles Mikolaycak for *The Shining Company* by Rosemary Sutcliff.

[8] Elizabeth George Speare, *The Bronze Bow* (Boston: Houghton Mifflin, 1961), p. 224.

he escapes his thralldom, but it is many years before he can rid himself of the black bitterness of his sister's marriage to a Saxon. As Aquila looks to the future, an old friend reflects his thoughts and the theme of this fine book:

> I sometimes think that we stand at sunset. . . . It may be that the night will close over us in the end, but I believe that morning will come again. Morning always grows again out of the darkness, though maybe not for the people who saw the sun go down. We are the Lantern Bearers, my friend; for us to keep something burning, to carry what light we can forward into the darkness and the wind.[9]

In her novel *The Shining Company*, Rosemary Sutcliff tells of the king's betrayal of his war host of three hundred younger sons sent to fight the invading Saxons. Among them is his own son, Gorthyn, and his shieldbearer, Prosper. Set in A.D. 600, the story is based on *The Gododdin*, the earliest surviving North British poem. It is a story of adventure and heroism, loyalty and betrayal.

MEDIEVAL TIMES AND TALES

In the Dark Ages, the chivalrous deeds of the knights were a window to the light. Young children of 7 and 8 are intrigued with stories of the days of knighthood. Some of them will be able to read Clyde Bulla's *The Sword in the Tree*, which is the story of a boy who saved his father and Weldon Castle by bravely going to King Arthur. Through treachery, Shan's uncle makes his own brother a captive and takes control of the castle. Remembering where he hid his father's sword in a tree, Shan establishes his identity as the rightful owner of Weldon Castle. This is an easy-reading book with excitement on every page. It has more than just a lively plot, however, for it presents an interesting picture of the justice of the time.

The entertainers of medieval times were minstrels, whose special way of life provides a natural frame for journey or chase stories. Thirteenth-century England is the setting for the Newbery award winner *Adam of the Road* by Elizabeth Janet Gray. It is the story of Adam, his minstrel father

Roger, and Adam's devoted dog Nick. Nick is stolen on their way to the great Fair of St. Giles. In the frantic chase that follows, Adam is separated from his father. It takes a whole long winter to find both Nick and Roger again. Adam has many adventures and some disasters, but he learns that the road is home to the minstrel and that people, generally, are kind.

Marguerite de Angeli has written many books, but her finest is *The Door in the Wall*, a Newbery award winner. Setting the book in fourteenth-century England, de Angeli painted in words and pictures the dramatic story of Robin, crippled son of Sir John de Bureford. Robin is to become a page to Sir Peter de Lindsay. He becomes ill with a strange malady, however, and is taken to the monastery by Brother Luke. There, Robin learns many things: to whittle, to swim, to read, to write, and above all to have patience—all "doors in the wall," according to Brother Luke. For:

> Whether thou'lt walk soon I know not. This I know. We must teach thy hands to be skilled in many ways, and we must teach thy mind to go about whether thy legs will carry thee or no. For reading is another door in the wall, dost understand, my son?[10]

Robin does learn to walk, but only with the aid of the crutches that he makes with his own hands. When he is well enough to travel, Brother Luke takes him to Sir Peter's castle. Robin is fearful of the reception a page on crutches might receive, but Sir Peter assures him that there are many ways to serve. It is during a siege of the castle that Robin finds a way to aid the king. Finally, Robin, or Sir Robin as he becomes for his exploits, is reunited with his father and mother. Robin's rebellion, final acceptance, and then challenge to live a rich life *with* his handicap should provide inspiration for children today.

THE EMERGENCE OF MODERN EUROPE

Poland is the setting for Eric Kelly's Newbery award winner *The Trumpeter of Krakow*. This is a complex tale of the quest for the shimmering Great Tarnov Crystal, coveted by a Tartar chief-

---

[9]Rosemary Sutcliff, *The Lantern Bearers*, illustrated by Charles Keeping (New York: Henry Z. Walck, 1959), pp. 250–251.

[10]Marguerite de Angeli, *The Door in the Wall* (New York: Doubleday, 1949), p. 28.

tain for supposed magical powers and zealously guarded by the ancestral oath of a Ukrainian family. Joseph and Elzbietka save the crystal through their knowledge of history. Ever since the Tartars had sacked the city of Krakow in 1241, the Trumpeter had ended the hourly hymn on a broken note to commemorate the steadfast soldier of that time who was killed in the midst of his playing. The year is now 1461 and a small band of Tartars who are again seeking the Tarnov Crystal have captured Joseph's father. When it is the time of the second hour, Joseph is allowed to play the hymn so no one will suspect anything is wrong. He signals for help by playing the hymn through to its completion, something that had not been done for two hundred years. The background of fifteenth-century Eastern Europe is vividly portrayed.

The political and personal intrigues surrounding the imprisonment of Mary, Queen of Scots are the focus of Mollie Hunter's *You Never Knew Her as I Did!* The narration is in the voice of young Will Douglas, page to the queen's custodian at the island castle of Lochleven. The action centers on attempts by Mary's supporters to rescue her and ends with a moment of triumph as she rides free before the battle that is to decide her fate. But the book is actually Will's memoir; and his postscript, which mentions her long captivity in England, is full of grief at the news of her death in 1587. Hunter's interpretation of the tragic queen leaves the reader with an appreciation for her matchless courage, unusual beauty, and ability to command the devotion of her followers.

In *Bartholomew Fair*, Mary Stolz weaves the story of six persons of varying stations of life from the aging Queen Elizabeth down to Will Shaw, a starveling apprenticed to a stonemaker, who are attending the last day of Bartholomew Fair. As the day progresses we see into the lives of these six fair-goers, all of whom but one return home that night. Mary Stolz has created a vivid six-teenth-century tapestry and brought it brilliantly to life.

In *Flame-Colored Taffeta*, Rosemary Sutcliff writes an exciting eighteenth-century story of smugglers on the Sussex Coast and an emissary of Bonnie Prince Charlie. Two young children find a wounded man and, with the help of the Wise Woman who is a healer, they hide and care for

him. Students will love this adventure story in which the young girl, Damaris, and Peter play the major role in hiding Tom and arranging for his escape. In her quiet conversations with him, Damaris reveals her desire to someday have a flame-colored taffeta petticoat. Four years after his escape, Tom sends her one as a wedding present for her marriage to Peter.

Leon Garfield writes with similar excitement about life in England during the eighteenth century. While he captures the flavor of the times and vividly describes the grim social conditions of the poor, he does not include any known historical events. Rather, his books have a Dickensian flavor compounded of violence, suspense, and intrigue. *Smith* is the story of a 12-year-old pickpocket in the grimy, shadow-filled underworld of eighteenth-century London. *Jack Holborn* is a story of a young orphan seeking his identity. He stows away on a ship attacked by pirates, endures bloody battles and a terrible shipwreck, marches through the sodden jungles of Africa, and witnesses the horrors of a slave market and a murder trial at Old Bailey in London. There is no doubt that these are exaggerated, swashbuckling tales, yet Garfield is a masterful storyteller. The larger-than-life drama is reminiscent of the Gothic novels of Joan Aiken. In contrast to Aiken's books, however, Garfield provides a real eighteenth-century setting. Certainly readers would get a feel for the times: its cruelty to children, the poor, and prisoners; its lawlessness; and its daily life.

One of the few stories of early Russia for English-speaking children is E. M. Almedingen's *The Crimson Oak*. A peasant boy named Peter has a chance encounter with the exiled Princess Elizabeth, saving her from the charge of a bear, but must wait for her return to power before speaking of his deed. The political climate of Russia in 1740 is repressive. Peter is caught up in a nightmare of injustice when his great desire to learn to read brings him to the attention and the suspicion of the Secret Chancery. Arrested, beaten, and imprisoned in a dungeon without trial, the boy does learn his letters from a fellow prisoner. Peter's eventual rescue is dramatic, and his second meeting with Elizabeth, now the empress, brings her promise that he will go to school. Grim moments in this book are balanced by the dream-come-true ending and the presence of compassionate characters who care about Peter and his cause.

Stories of the New World

COLONIAL AMERICA

The varied settings and conflicts of colonial America have inspired an unusually large number of books about this period. *A Lion to Guard Us* by Clyde Bulla tells of three motherless London children who sail to Jamestown in hope of finding their father, who has gone ahead to the new colony. When the ship is wrecked in a storm near Bermuda, the children manage to save their own treasure from home, a lion's head door knocker. The voyagers survive on the bounty of the island while other ships are built to take them to Virginia. There the children do find their father, weak and ill, one of the few who survived the Starving Time of 1609–1610. Young Jemmy hangs the lion's head on a peg above the door latch, a symbol of home. The carefully limited historical detail and simple writing style make this book accessible to readers as young as 8 or 9.

Many informational books tell us what the Pilgrims did, but there are few records that tell how they felt about what they did. *The Thanksgiving Story* by Alice Dalgliesh details the life of one family on the *Mayflower*, including their hardships on the voyage and during their first winter. It tells, too, of joy in the arrival of their new baby, of spring in their new home, of planting, harvest, and giving thanks. The large stylized pictures by Helen Sewell capture the spirit of American primitive paintings. *The Pilgrims of Plimoth*, written and illustrated with full-color illustrations by Marcia Sewall, provides a descriptive text that discusses the travels of the Pilgrims and their way of life at the settlement. Using George Ancona's black-and-white photographs of the reconstructed settlement at Plimouth Plantation, Joan Anderson presents her concept of *The First Thanksgiving Feast*. The text includes dialogue based on historical accounts from the era. All these informational picture books are appropriate for children from grade two and up. They may serve to celebrate Thanksgiving or as an introduction to a serious study of the Pilgrims.

One of the liveliest stories about the Pilgrims is *Constance: A Story of Early Plymouth* by Patricia Clapp. Written in the form of a diary, the story of Constance Hopkins, daughter of Stephen Hopkins, begins in November of 1620 on the deck of the *Mayflower* and ends seven years later with her marriage in Plymouth to Nicholas Snow. Constance describes the grim first winter at Plymouth with its fear of the Indians, the deaths of many of the colonists, and the difficulties with the English backers of the settlement. The device of a diary allows the author to use first-person narrative, which creates an immediate identification of the reader with Constance. An excellent romance, it is all the more fascinating for being the story of real people.

The Puritans soon forgot their struggle for religious freedom as they persecuted others who did not follow their beliefs or ways. Older students will thoroughly enjoy the superb story of *The Witch of Blackbird Pond* written by Elizabeth Speare. Flamboyant, high-spirited Kit Tyler is a misfit in the Puritan household of her aunt and stern-faced uncle. Kit is as different from her colorless cousins as the bleak barren shore of Wethersfield, Connecticut, differs from the shimmering turquoise bay of Barbados that had been her home for sixteen years. The only place in which Kit feels any peace or freedom is in the meadows near Blackbird Pond. Here she meets the lonely bent figure of Quaker Hannah, regarded as a witch by the colonists. Here, too, Kit meets Nathaniel Eaton, the sea captain's son, with his mocking smile and clear blue eyes. Little Prudence, a village child, also comes to the sanctuary in the meadows. One by one, outraged townspeople put the wrong things together and the result is a terrifying witch hunt and trial. The story is fast-paced and the characters are drawn in sharp relief against a bleak New England background.

Although the subject is the same, the tone of *Tituba of Salem Village* by Ann Petry is as forbidding as the rotten eggs found on the steps of the parsonage the day that the Reverend Samuel Parris, his family and slaves, John and Tituba, arrive in Salem Village in 1692. Tituba, too, has come from sunny Barbados and then been sold as a slave to a self-seeking, pious minister. The fact that Tituba is both a slave and a black makes her particularly vulnerable to suspicion and attack from the obsessed witch hunters in Salem. A sense of foreboding, mounting terror, and hysteria fills this story of great evil done in the name of God.

A different look at the Salem witch trials is provided by Patricia Clapp in *Witches' Children*. The first-person narrator is Mary Warren, a bond servant and one of ten girls who are "possessed." Mary admits to herself that the ravings began as "sport," a way to vent boredom and high spirits, and grew into group hysteria. When she tries to explain, she is not believed and is herself accused. In spite of the grim subject the story moves at a fast and readable pace. A comparison of *Tituba of Salem Village* with *Witches' Children* would provoke much critical thinking by mature readers, especially in considering the two characterizations of Tituba.

During the eighteenth century, colonists pushed farther and farther into the wilderness. Many favorite stories have been set within this background. Jean Fritz has written the poignant story of lonely 10-year-old Ann Hamilton, who was the only girl in the wilderness of early western Pennsylvania. The title of this book, *The Cabin Faced West*, characterizes Ann's father's attitude toward the family's new adventure. They were not to look back to the past, but forward; and so he built the cabin facing west. Someday Ann will have books to read; someday they will have windows in the cabin; and someday there will be a special occasion to use the linen tablecloth and the lavender flowered plates. All the "somedays" seem so very far away to Ann. At last, however, a special occasion does happen. George Washington stops at the Hamilton cabin for dinner. Ann wears ribbons in her hair and sets the table in the way she has longed to do. This final episode is based on fact and really happened to Ann Hamilton, who was the author's great-great-grandmother.

Another lonely girl has been immortalized for children of 7 and 8 by Alice Dalgliesh in her popular book, *The Courage of Sarah Noble*. This is the true and inspiring story of 8-year-old Sarah, who accompanies her father into the wilderness to cook for him while he builds a cabin for their family. Many times Sarah has to remind herself of her mother's final words to her when she left home: "Keep up your courage, Sarah Noble!" Sarah has reason to remember when she hears the wolves howl outside the campfire or when alone one day she is suddenly surrounded by Indian children. The real test of her courage is faced when her father tells her that he must leave her with Tall John, a friendly Indian, while he returns to Massachusetts for the rest of the family. Symbolic of Sarah's courage is the cloak that Sarah's mother had fastened around her just before she left home. When her family are finally reunited in their new home in the wilderness, Sarah is secure in the knowledge that she has "kept up her courage."

The situation in *The Sign of the Beaver* by Elizabeth George Speare is much like that of Sarah Noble's story, as young Matt is left to tend the new cabin in Maine territory while his father goes back to Massachusetts for the rest of the family. Matt eventually learns essential survival skills from Attean, grandson of the chief of the Beaver clan. The story explores their growing friendship, their changing attitudes, and the shifting balance between their two cultures. (See Chapter 12 for a web of discussion and extension ideas on this book.)

Other books, like *The Matchlock Gun* by Walter D. Edmonds, show that the differences between white and Native-American people could not always be bridged. This book, based on the experiences of a Dutch family living in the Hudson Valley in 1756, focuses on the terror as well as the courage of settlers who were victims of fierce Indian raids. This is much more than an exciting adventure story in which a child kills three marauders to protect his baby sister and wounded mother. The characters are very real and true to life. Readers sense the anxiety of the parents when they hear of the Indian raid and can share the fear that seems to fill the silence in the tiny cabin:

There was only the note of the wind in the chimney and the feeling of it on the roof, like a hand pressed down out of darkness. It was easy to think of it passing through the wet woods, rocking the bare branches where only the beech trees had leaves to shake.[11]

This story, which won the Newbery award in 1941, has since been criticized for presenting Native Americans as bloodthirsty savages and for having a child shoot them. Obviously, this account of events is told from the colonists' point of view.

An Indian point of view is given in *Saturnalia*, Paul Fleischman's complex story of life in colonial Boston in 1681. Six years earlier the militia had attacked and nearly wiped out a Narragansett village, bringing back a few of the survivors as servants. Fourteen-year-old William is apprenticed to kindly Mr. Currie, a printer who has the boy taught Greek and Latin and the Bible and treats him as a member of his family. Each night William roams the streets after curfew, searching for his brother by playing an Indian melody on his bone flute. He never finds him, but one night he does find a cousin and uncle, now servants of a cruel eyeglass maker. William goes to see them regularly in order to give them food and to learn of his own Narragansett past. Meanwhile, William's nighttime activities are observed by Mr. Baggot, the tithingman whose grandsons were killed by Indians and who yearns to entrap William as his revenge. When the eyeglass maker is killed, his Indian servants are accused, but William saves them. Then Baggot focuses his accusations on William. The dark side of this novel is lightened by the story of a wig maker's romantic and humorous pursuit of a wealthy widow. Paul Fleischman weaves these many stories of good and evil persons in colonial Boston back and forth like a musical fugue. Only William is a part of all worlds: night and day, servant and family, Indian and Colonial, educated and nonliterate. His is the melody that holds this many-layered novel together.

THE REVOLUTIONARY ERA

One of the best-known stories of the American Revolution for children is *Johnny Tremain* by Esther Forbes. Johnny Tremain is a silversmith's

apprentice, a conceited, cocky young lad who is good at his trade and knows it. The other apprentices are resentful of his overbearing manner and determined to get even with him. Their practical joke has disastrous results, and Johnny's hand is maimed for life. Out of a job and embittered, Johnny joins his new friend Rab and becomes involved in pre-Revolutionary activities. As a dispatch rider for the Committee of Public Safety he meets such men as Paul Revere, John Hancock, and Samuel Adams. Slowly, gradually, Johnny regains his self-confidence and overcomes his bitterness. Rab is killed in the first skirmish of the Revolution, and Johnny is crushed, but not completely. Somehow, this greatest of blows makes him a man of fortitude and courage, a new man of a new nation.

For Johnny Tremain, the decision to join the Patriot cause was clear. In many other books, because the Loyalist tradition and point of view are presented in a more compelling way, the characters are perceived to have a more difficult choice. In *John Treegate's Musket* by Leonard Wibberly, the title character is a solid citizen of Boston who has fought for his king at the Battle of Quebec. Not until he sees hundreds of troops marching through a peaceful countryside to seize two men does he arm himself and join his son Peter to fight the British at the Battle of Bunker Hill. In *Early Thunder* by Jean Fritz, 14-year-old Daniel adopts his father's loyalty to the king. Daniel hates the rowdy Liberty Boys who creep up on Tory porches and distribute their "Liberty Gifts" of garbage or manure, but becomes equally disillusioned by the British attitudes. Daniel's struggle to sort out his loyalties will help children see that issues in war are seldom clear-cut.

My Brother Sam Is Dead by the Colliers tells of conflicting loyalties within a family and the injustices that are always inflicted on the innocent in time of war. Sam is the only member of his Connecticut family who is fighting for the rebel cause. Ironically, it is Sam who is falsely accused of stealing his own cattle and is executed as an example of General Putnam's discipline. No one will believe the real facts of the case, for despite Sam's excellent war record, his family are Tories. This story takes on special poignancy because it

[11]Walter D. Edmonds, *The Matchlock Gun*, illustrated by Paul Lantz (New York: Dodd, Mead, 1941), p. 14.

is told by the younger brother, Tim, who loves and admires Sam.

Some of the same dreams of glory that drew Sam into the Patriot army plague 13-year-old Jonathan in *The Fighting Ground* by Avi. In 1778, near Trenton, Jonathan desperately wants to be in on the "cannons and flags and drums and dress parades. . . . O Lord, he said to himself, make it something *grand!*"[12] Sent to find if the tolling bell at the tavern means bad news, Jonathan agrees to go with a few volunteers to head off a small band of approaching enemy soldiers. Caught up in a real battle and captured by Hessians who seem no worse than the Patriot corporal who enlisted his aid, Jonathan does not know which way to turn. The action takes place in little more than one day, with the text divided into many short segments labeled by the hour and minute. This makes the book look simpler than it is, for although the print is not dense on the page, there are strong emotional demands on the reader.

On Ocracoke, off the North Carolina coast, the islanders have no intention of taking part in the war at all. Then British raiders steal the community pigs and murder the deaf-mute woman who tended them. Angered, the islanders vow to retaliate by donating their two precious barrels of salt to the American army at Valley Forge. Daring boatman Erskin Midgett is chosen to get them there by way of Pamlico Sound and Chesapeake Bay. When he decides to take his son along, the conflict becomes *George Midgett's War* in Sally Edwards's tale of a treacherous journey through poorly charted territory and a special relationship between a man and his son. The Midgetts' story serves as a reminder that some choices in wartime are made on the basis of personal loyalties rather than devotion to a cause.

The title character in Scott O'Dell's *Sarah Bishop* hates war, and with good reason. Her father, a British Loyalist, dies after being tarred and feathered by Patriot sympathizers. Her brother dies on a British prison ship, and Sarah herself is arrested on a false pretense. She escapes and flees to the Connecticut wilderness, where she struggles against the elements instead of sol-

diers. Her biggest battle is with herself, however, as she brings herself to face the world of towns and people once again. This story is based on the experiences of a real Sarah Bishop during the Revolutionary period.

Another little-known story of the American Revolution is that of a spunky young girl named Tempe Wick, who hid her horse in her bedroom for three days to save it from Revolutionary soldiers looting the countryside around their New Jersey camp. Finally, when a soldier demanded to search the house, the feisty Tempe threw him out in the snow. This humorous legend of the Revolutionary War is told by Patricia Lee Gauch in a brief book, *This Time, Tempe Wick?* A fuller characterization of this heroine is given in Ann Rinaldi's novel for older readers, *A Ride into Morning*.

Few stories are available about the role of African Americans during the Revolutionary era. The Collier brothers have featured black characters in several books, however, including a trilogy that deals with the wartime problems of blacks in the northern colonies and their futile hope for a guarantee of liberty under the new government. In *Jump Ship to Freedom* the memory of the late Jack Arabus, who had won his freedom in the courts as a result of his service in the Continental army, serves as inspiration for his son Dan. The boy's first problem is keeping the soldiers' notes earned by Jack to buy his family's freedom away from Captain Ivers and his greedy wife. Even if the notes can be saved, they may be worth nothing under the terms of the new Constitution just being written. Exciting action brings Dan as a messenger to the site of the Constitutional Convention. Because he is bringing important word about the slavery compromise (which will, ironically, set up a fugitive slave law), he gets to meet George Washington, Alexander Hamilton, and other statesmen. He is also threatened by Captain Ivers, but a friendly Congressman intervenes to arrange Dan's freedom. This book has a strong theme in Dan's growing belief in himself and his abilities. The other titles in this trilogy are *War Comes to Willy Freeman* and *Who Is Carrie?*, each featuring a young African-American woman as the central character. In all their books, the Colliers provide detailed authors' notes to explain their background sources. For this series the notes

[12]Avi, *The Fighting Ground* (New York: Lippincott, 1984), p. 9.

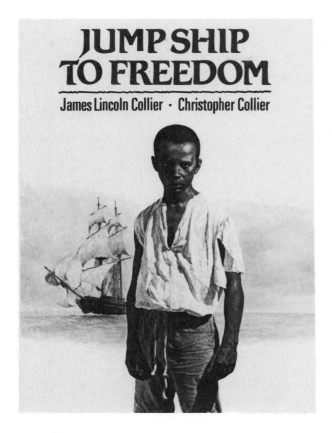

The success of Dan Arabus in winning justice for himself is set against the failure of the Constitutional Convention to abolish slavery.

Jacket illustration by Gordon Crabb for *Jump Ship to Freedom* by James Lincoln Collier and Christopher Collier.

also explain their choice of language, including the liberal use of the term "nigger" in dialogue.

Novels about Revolutionary America offer an intriguing variety of points of view. Individual books will help children feel the intense emotions of the time, but the impact of several read for comparison and contrast will be much greater. Children can also increase their frame of pertinent information about a time period in this way. Knowing more background each time, they will read each succeeding book with greater ease.

NATIVE AMERICANS

Marcia Sewall's glowing pictures and poetic prose describe the life of the Wampanoags, *The People of the Breaking Day*. Her opening sentences suggest the peaceful life of this tribe who lived in southeastern Massachusetts at the time of the landing of the Pilgrims:

> We are Wampanoags, People of the Breaking Day. Nippa'uus, the Sun, on his journey through the sky, warms us first as he rises over the rim of the sea. At his birth each new morning we say, "Thank you, Nippa'uus, for returning to us with your warmth and light and beauty."
>
> But it is Kiehtan, the Great Spirit, who made us all: we, the two-legged who stand tall, and the four-legged; those that swim and those thay fly and the little people who crawl; and flowers and trees and rocks. He made us all, brothers sharing the earth.[13]

In earlier stories Native Americans are often seen as cruel, bloodthirsty savages attacking small groups of helpless settlers. The provocation for the attacks is seldom given. Thus, in Edmonds's story *The Matchlock Gun*, the reader can only guess the Indians' reasons for wounding Edward's mother and burning their cabin. In Rachel Field's *Calico Bush*, the Indians seem equally cruel as they burn the settler's house.

However, in such fine books as Scott O'Dell's *Sing Down the Moon*, and Jamake Highwater's *Legend Days*, the shocking story of the white man's destruction of the Indians' way of life is told from the Native-American perspective.

A story of Indian capture for more mature readers is *Calico Captive* by Elizabeth Speare. Based on real people and events, this is a fictionalized account of the experiences of young Miriam Willard, who had just been to her first dance when she was captured by the Indians. Her sister, brother-in-law, three children, and a neighbor are captured with her, taken to Montreal, and sold as slaves. Their hardships and ordeals are taken from a diary kept by a real "captive" in 1754. Speare tells this story with her usual fine characterizations and attention to authentic detail.

Two stories of whites brought up as Indians lend themselves well to purposes of comparison: *Moccasin Trail* by Eloise McGraw and *The Light in the Forest* by Conrad Richter. In the first book Jim

[13]Marcia Sewall, *The People of the Breaking Day* (New York: Atheneum, 1990), p. 5.

Heath is rescued from a grizzly bear by the Crow Indians and brought up to think and feel like an Indian. Eventually reunited with his younger sister and brothers, Jim begins to long for the sensible Indian ways. Everything that he does seems to be wrong. He steals a horse for Jonnie—the grandest present a Crow Indian can give—and is rebuffed in front of the other settlers and made to return the horse. A loner, Jim decides to leave. Little Daniel is heartbroken and runs away only to be captured by the Umpqua Indians, who keep slaves. Jim rescues him but knows that for his sake and his brother's he must forsake the moccasin trail forever. He symbolically cuts his braids and is at peace with himself and his family at last.

Conrad Richter's book *The Light in the Forest* was written for adults but has been enjoyed by older children. In this story True Son, a white boy reared by an Indian chief, is forced to return to his original home. His love and loyalty for his Indian parents and his rejection of the white man's civilization arouse inevitable conflicts. At last, he runs away and rejoins the Indians. But he betrays the tribe when at the last moment he will not take part in tricking a boatload of whites into an Indian ambush. Instead of calling for help as planned, he sees a small boy who reminds him of his brother, and he shouts a warning. Condemned to die by the Indians, he is rescued by his Indian father who imposes the most severe punishment of all—banishment from the tribe and the forest forever. Forced back to the white man's trail, the boy, who truly felt he was Indian, faces unbearable loneliness:

> Ahead of him ran the rutted road of the whites. It led, he knew, to where men of their own volition constrained themselves with heavy clothing like harness, where men chose to be slaves to their own or another's property and followed empty and desolate lives far from the wild beloved freedom of the Indian.[14]

One of the most popular stories about Indians is Scott O'Dell's Newbery award book, *Island of the Blue Dolphins*. Based on fact, the story concerns Karana, an Indian girl who lived alone on an island off the coast of California for some eigh-

teen years. Following an attack by Aleuts who had come to kill otters, all of Karana's people leave their island home by boat. When Karana realizes her younger brother is left on the island, she jumps overboard and returns to him. Within a few hours the boy is killed by wild dogs, and memories of the tribe are all Karana has left. Despite her despair when she realizes the boat will not return, Karana creates a life for herself. She makes a house and utensils, and fashions weapons, although in so doing she violates a taboo. Eventually she makes friends with the leader of the dog pack, and thereafter enjoys his protection and companionship. When Spanish priests "rescue" Karana, she leaves in sadness. The reader may question whether she will find as much happiness at the mission with human companionship as she had known alone on the island. The question is answered in a sequel, *Zia*, in which Karana's last days are witnessed through the eyes of her niece.

Scott O'Dell's title *Sing Down the Moon* takes on tragic significance when compared to the Southwest Indians' creation myths that tell of "singing up the mountains." O'Dell's book describes the "Long Walk," the disastrous 300-mile forced march of the Navajo from their canyon homes to Fort Sumner. Held as virtual prisoners from 1863 to 1865, more than 1,500 of the Navajos died, and many others lost the will to live. This moving story is told from the point of view of Bright Morning, who somehow maintains her hope for a better future. Tall Boy, the proud and handsome youth who is to become her husband, was once wounded by a Spaniard's bullet, but being held in the American fort causes an even greater injury to his spirit. Only through Bright Morning's urging does he make the effort to escape. The young couple return to a cave in their familiar canyon to begin a new life with the son who is born to them. This is a haunting story told in spare prose that reflects the dignity of the Navajo people.

Sweetgrass by Jan Hudson tells of the daily life of the Blackfoot Indian tribe before the white man's sickness came. Sweetgrass is 15 and longs to marry Eagle Sun, but her father does not believe that his favorite daughter is woman enough to marry. Then the cold prairie winter

[14]Conrad Richter, *The Light in the Forest* (New York: Knopf, 1953), p. 179.

sets in along with smallpox. With the warrior men away, Sweetgrass is one of the few women left to battle the horrible sickness. Her little brother and sister die, but Sweetgrass saves her mother and other brother. With no food to eat, Sweetgrass ignores the tribal taboo on eating fish and kills the fish under the frozen stream to add to their stew. They live. In time her father returns having recovered from the pox himself. He sees what Sweetgrass has done and at last declares her a woman. With the news that Eagle Sun also lived through the illness, Sweetgrass looks to the future with joy and hope.

Jenny of the Tetons by Kristiana Gregory is the fictionalized account of an Englishman named "Beaver Dick" and his Shoshone wife, Jenny. When an Indian attack leaves Carrie Hill wounded and alone, she decides to join Beaver Dick and help care for his family. She is horrified when she finds he is married to a Native American. But gradually she learns to respect this gentle person who carefully tends her wound. Later it is Carrie's responsibility to care for Jenny and her family when they get smallpox. She rides to a neighbor's house through a blizzard to obtain medicine, but it is too late. Jenny and all her children die, leaving only Beaver Dick alive. This is a moving story of changing relationships.

Jamake Highwater brings a strong cultural perspective and gift for vivid language to a powerful novel of the Northern Plains Indians, *Legend Days*, the first book of the Ghost Horse Cycle. The central character, Amana, is a girl who attains adolescence and young adulthood while the buffalo herds dwindle and her people are no longer able to withstand white traders, settlers, soldiers, government, or the hideous smallpox that kills almost everyone in the winter camp. This grim story is infused with the spiritual strength of Amana and her people. The characters' visionary experiences are not set apart from the other events of their lives. This lack of separation between the spiritual and material embodies a Native-American point of view. The aged Crow Woman mourns the breakdown of this relationship between people and their world:

 "... I do not want to see my people fading away day by day. I would rather be free of this bad life. I would rather remember the land as it was when I

was a girl: when each tree told me its secret and the animals gave us power and vision."[15]

Mature readers will also enjoy the highly fictionalized biography of *Ishi, Last of His Tribe* by Theodora Kroeber. Most of the Yahi Indians of California had been killed or driven from their homes by the invading gold-seekers and settlers during the early 1900s. A small band resisted their fate by living in concealment; but everywhere it seemed that Saldu (white people) had come. One by one Ishi's family dies, and, at last, he is the lone survivor of his tribe. Hungry and ill, he allows himself to be found. Haltingly, he tells his story to an anthropologist who takes him to live at the University of California's museum. Here he dwells happily for five years helping to record the language and ways of the Yahi world.

THE AMERICAN FRONTIER

No other period in U.S. history has been more dramatized in films and television than that of the westward movement of the American pioneer. Since civilization grows with a ragged edge, nineteenth-century frontier stories are set in widely scattered locations. Some settlers moved with the wilderness, like Pa Ingalls in what may be the best loved of all American historical fiction, the nine "Little House" books by Laura Ingalls Wilder. These stories describe the growing up of the Ingalls girls and the Wilder boys. In the first book of the series, *Little House in the Big Woods*, Laura is only 6 years old; the last three books—*Little Town on the Prairie*, *These Happy Golden Years*, and *The First Four Years*—tell of Laura's teaching career and her marriage. Based on the author's own life, these books portray the hardships and difficulties of pioneer life in the 1870s and 1880s and describe the fun and excitement that was also a part of daily living in those days. Throughout the stories the warmth and security of family love run like a golden thread that binds the books to the hearts of their readers. There are floods, blizzards, grasshopper plagues, bears and Indians, droughts and the fear of starvation; but there is the wonderful Christmas when

[15]Jamake Highwater, *Legend Days* (New York: Harper & Row, 1984), p. 140.

A tender Christmas scene exemplifies the warmth and simple joy of pioneer living in Garth Williams's cover illustration for *Little House in the Big Woods* by Laura Ingalls Wilder.

Laura receives her rag doll, the new house with real windows, trips to town, and dances. Best of all, there are the long winter evenings of firelight and the clear singing of Pa's fiddle. These mean love and security whether the home is in Wisconsin, the wild Kansas country, as described in *Little House on the Prairie,* in the Minnesota of *On the Banks of Plum Creek,* or *By the Shores of Silver Lake* in Dakota Territory. Children who read these books sense the same feelings of love and family solidarity experienced by Laura in the closing pages of *Little House in the Big Woods:*

🍂 But Laura lay awake a little while, listening to Pa's fiddle softly playing and to the lovely sound of the wind in the Big Woods. She looked at Pa sitting on the bench by the hearth, the firelight gleaming on his brown hair and beard and glistening over the honey-brown fiddle. She looked at Ma, gently rocking and knitting.

She thought to herself, "This is now."

She was glad that the cosy house, and Pa and Ma and the firelight and the music, were now. They could not be forgotten, she thought, because now is now. It can never be a long time ago.[16]

The last book of the series describes *The First Four Years* following Laura's and Manley's marriage in 1885. The manuscript for this story was found among Laura's papers after her death in 1957. Garth Williams illustrated a uniform edition of all the books in the series. His black-and-white pictures capture the excitement and terror of many of the episodes in the books, but they also convey the tenderness, love, amusement, and courage that were necessary requisites to the life of the early settlers.

Another favorite book of pioneer days is *Caddie Woodlawn* by Carol Ryrie Brink. While this story takes place in the Wisconsin wilderness of the 1860s, it is primarily the story of the growing up of tomboy Caddie. She had been a frail baby, and so Caddie's father had persuaded her mother to allow her to be reared more freely than her older sister Clara, who was restricted by the rules of decorum for young ladies. Caddie was free to run about the half-wild Wisconsin frontier with her two brothers. Their escapades and adventures read like a feminine *Tom Sawyer.* Caddie is a self-willed, independent spirit who is assured a memorable place in children's literature. In a second edition of this classic pioneer story, illustrations by Trina Schart Hyman picture Caddie as a spirited young girl.

The Texas frontier has provided a distinctive setting for many exciting stories. One of the best known is Fred Gipson's *Old Yeller,* the story of a boy's integrity and love for his dog on an early Texas homestead. Patricia Beatty's *Wait for Me, Watch for Me, Eula Bee* takes place at the time of

[16]Laura Ingalls Wilder, *Little House in the Big Woods,* illustrated by Garth Williams (New York: Harper & Row, 1953, 1932), p. 238.

the Civil War, when the absence of men who had joined the Confederate army made West Texas homesteads especially vulnerable to Indian attack. Lewallen's mother, brother, and uncle are killed by Comanches, but he and his 3-year-old sister, Eula Bee, with her bouncy red curls that fascinate the warriors, are taken captive. When Lewallen manages at last to escape, he vows to return for his sister. Many months later he makes good his promise, but Eula Bee has forgotten him and has to be carried away, kicking and struggling. Long after they have reached safety, she is won to remembrance by the chance hearing of a song, the popular tune "Lorena," which Lewallen had whistled over and over during their captivity to assure her he was near.

Following the Civil War, Sam White and his family leave the safety and security of their grandparents' white house in Kentucky and head for Dakota Territory. In *The Grasshopper Summer*, Ann Turner details the hardships faced by this determined southern family. After staking their claim, they build a sod house facing south, plant their first crops, and then the grasshoppers came, eating everything green in sight. Sam's younger brother, Bill, said, "They ate up all the pretty things and left all the ugly things."[17] Their neighbors, the Grants, give up and go back home, but the Whites meet the challenge of the harsh land and decide to stay on in their sod house. *Dakota Dugout*, also by Ann Turner, is the perfect picture storybook to read either before or after reading *Grasshopper Summer*. The black-and-white illustrations by Ronald Himler show both the beauty and the ruggedness of living in a sod house sandwiched between the wide prairie and the endless sky.

By the mid-nineteenth century, the far western frontier was in California and Oregon. *Trouble for Lucy* by Carla Stevens uses information from first-person accounts of the Oregon Trail in 1843 to set the scene for each of its brief chapters. Appropriate for 8- and 9-year-old readers, the story focuses on Lucy's efforts to keep her fox terrier puppy from being a nuisance to the oxen and drivers. When he gets lost in a storm and Lucy follows, she and the pup are rescued by friendly Pawnees. Lucy's mother is too busy to scold her, however; she is having a baby in the family's covered wagon, which has been drawn out of the line of march and sits alone on the prairie. There is no pretending here that the pioneers' way was easy, yet the story is more concerned with the universal feelings of childhood than it is with hardship.

The story of a brother and sister who survive an Indian attack on a wagon train is told in Louise Moeri's *Save Queen of Sheba*. King David, 12 years old and named from the Bible, is injured and must struggle to keep going in the hope of finding his parents; the added burden of watching out for his little sister, Queen of Sheba, is almost too much. She is a character to be remembered for her petulance and her dangerously stubborn independence. When she manages to slip away from him, most readers of King David's age have no trouble sympathizing with his temptation to go on without her. This is a taut and suspenseful story of survival that has special intensity because the cast of characters is limited to two.

Kathryn Lasky's *Beyond the Divide* is a dramatic story for mature readers about an Amish father and daughter bound for the California gold rush. The plain ways of Meribah Simon, 14, are thought peculiar by some of her fellow travelers, but she makes many friends among them. The author creates a community of characters who bring very different pasts and problems to the challenging journey they share. Because they do seem like a community, it is all the more shocking that they should decide to abandon Will Simon along the trail when his wagon is disabled and he seems too weak to continue. Angry and disillusioned, Meribah elects to stay with her father. From that point the story hinges on her efforts to save him, and then herself. She is forced to shoot a mountain man who is about to attack her and fights off vultures to get food from the carcass of a deer. With help from a mapmaker who had traveled with the wagon train and from the gentle Indians of Mill Creek who feed her and take her in, Meribah does survive to choose for herself what sort of life she wants.

Another vivid story for older readers is *Prairie Songs* by Pam Conrad. It contrasts two points of view of homesteading in the new lands, that of

---

[17]Ann Turner, *The Grasshopper Summer* (New York: Macmillan, 1989), p. 134.

the Downing family who had settled in a "soddy" and that of the beautiful, cultured wife of the new doctor in Howard County, Nebraska, who has come to live in the next soddy. The story is told by young Louisa Downing and reflects her wonder at the back-East world of wealth and learning that Mrs. Emmeline Berryman represents. But when the doctor's wife loses her premature baby after a long and difficult labor, Louisa is shocked by the gradual changes in her behavior. Always distraught, Mrs. Berryman is terrified out of all reason one winter day by the visit of two Indians. It is shy little Lester who later finds her where she has fled, sitting in the snow, frozen to death. Louisa's narration is vivid, and her casual acceptance of life in a soddy points up the irony of Mrs. Berryman's inability to cope. The woman Louisa had admired could not match her own mother in strength of spirit or the special kind of beauty that made Louisa feel good inside.

Moving westward and settling the frontier was a major force in the life of many Americans throughout the nineteenth century. Farming the vast mid-American prairies put special demands on families. In a beautifully written short novel by Patricia MacLachlan, motherless Anna and Caleb are delighted when Papa's advertisement for a mail-order bride brings *Sarah, Plain and Tall* to their prairie home. Sarah comes from the coast of Maine, and she brings mementos of the sea she loves, her gray cat Seal, a moon shell for Caleb, and a round sea stone for Anna. She has agreed only to a month's visit, and the children, who quickly learn to love her lively, independent ways, are afraid that they will lose her. On the day that Sarah goes to town for colored pencils to add the blue, gray, and green of the ocean to the picture she has drawn of the prairie, they realize that she will stay. She misses the sea, she tells them, but she would miss them more. The rhythm and lyrical simplicity of the writing are especially effective when read aloud. In a slice-of-life picture book that would make a good companion piece for Sarah's story, MacLachlan tells of her great-grandfather when he went to a one-room schoolhouse on the prairie with his dog, *Three Names*. Alexander Pertzoff's lovely watercolors show the beauty and spaciousness of the wide open prairie.

Readers who have never experienced the vast openness of the American prairie can get a sense of it through Alexander Pertzoff's use of space and color in the illustrations for *Three Names* by Patricia MacLachlan.

Good fun and tongue-in-cheek humor enliven the story of *Mr. Mysterious and Company* by Sid Fleischman. In this book a delightful family of traveling magicians journeys to California in the 1880s in their gaily painted wagon, making one-night stands in many frontier towns. All the children share in the magic show in a fine family story that carries the flavor of life in frontier towns of the West. The same author's equally entertaining *Humbug Mountain* features the family of an itinerant newspaperman. His son Wiley is the deadpan narrator of a wild string of adventures on the Missouri River complete with outlaws, a bogus gold rush, and the discovery of a petrified man. There is an underlying comment about human gullibility and greed in this funny, fast-paced story.

Not all stories of this period take place in the West, however. Although set in the early 1900s, Mary Riskind's *Apple Is My Sign* is less an historical novel than a story of a 10-year-old deaf child learning to live among the hearing with his disability. Harry Berger, called "Apple" because of his family's orchards, is sent to a school for the deaf in Philadelphia. While his whole family is deaf, Harry is the first one to go away, and his early days at the school are difficult and lonely. During the fall, however, Harry discovers many doors open for him, learns a new game called football, and makes new friends. He tells his family that he thinks he'd like to be a teacher, but a family friend signs "Hearing best teacher." His mother, however, reassures Harry: "'I-f you want teach deaf, must try. That's-all. Never know, i-f never try. In head must think can. Brave.'"[18] Riskind conveys the rapidity of signed talk by approximating its actual meanings, eliminating the little words or word endings, as signers do, and spelling out meanings for which there are no signs. Through Harry's story readers may come to realize that opportunities for people with disabilities have changed over the years.

THE CIVIL WAR ERA

The Slavery Issue

The country was involved and concerned with the issue of slavery long before the Civil War. *Nettie's Trip South* by Ann Turner is based on the real diary of the author's great-grandmother. When Nettie is 10 years old she goes with her older brother, a reporter, and her 14-year-old sister on a trip from Albany, New York, to Richmond, Virginia. As Nettie writes to her friend Addie, she remembers all of the things she saw in that prewar city including Tabitha, the black slave in the hotel who had no last name, seeing the slave quarters at a nearby plantation, and visiting a slave auction where two children clasping hands were bought by different masters. Ronald Himler illustrated this moving account of a young girl's horror at her first exposure to slavery.

Many stories of the pre–Civil War period relate to slavery and the activities of the underground railroad, when people faced the moral issue of breaking laws out of their compassion for humankind. F. N. Monjo titled his easy-reading book *The Drinking Gourd*, after the "code song" that the slaves sang. The song was used to point the direction for escape by following the North Star, using the Big Dipper as a guide. The words to the song are included in this short story of how a young mischievous boy helps a family on their way to freedom.

In Marguerite de Angeli's book *Thee, Hannah!*, a young Quaker girl helps a black mother and her child to safety. While Hannah is a Quaker, she does not willingly wear Quaker clothes. She particularly despises her stiff, drab bonnet that does not have flowers and a brightly colored lining like that of her friend Cecily. Yet it is her bonnet that identifies her as a Quaker and one who would be trusted to give aid to a runaway slave. Later, when the slaves are safe and tell Hannah this, Hannah's feelings toward her hated bonnet change.

In *Brady*, Jean Fritz tells the story of a very believable boy who discovers his father is an agent for the underground railway. His parents had not told him of their forbidden activities, for Brady just cannot keep a secret. However, Brady, always curious, discovers the secret for himself. On the very night that had been set to transfer a slave to the next station, his father suffers a broken leg during a fire in the barn. On his own, Brady carries out the plan for moving the slave. When his father hears of his son's resourcefulness, he asks for the family Bible and painstakingly writes the following inscription on the page reserved for significant events in family history: "On this day the barn burned down and Brady Minton did a man's work."[19]

A fugitive slave whom Catherine never meets brings changes to her life in *A Gathering of Days: A New England Girl's Journal, 1830–32* by Joan Blos. She and her friend Cassie agonize over a plea for help slipped into her writing book when she leaves it in the woods. They have heard about slavery and the abolition movement from their teacher, yet their activities are circumscribed by

[18]Mary Riskind, *Apple Is My Sign* (Boston: Houghton Mifflin, 1981), p. 119.

[19]Jean Fritz, *Brady*, illustrated by Lynd Ward (New York: Penguin, 1987), p. 219.

strict but loving families. Finally compassion and a sense of justice outweigh their respect for authority, and they leave food and a quilt where the fugitive will be sure to find them. Much later a packet arrives from Canada with a cryptic message and two bits of lace as a thank you; the runaway is safe and free. Meanwhile Catherine must piece a new quilt to replace the one she had given away. The story requires more of Catherine—she must learn to accept her father's new wife, bear Cassie's death, and take first steps toward a life of her own.

Paul Fleischman tells the moving story of Georgina Lott's life in *The Borning Room*. In one of the episodes of that book she recalls hiding a runaway slave in the barn loft. Later when her mother is giving birth and they cannot get the midwife, Georgina goes out to the barn and brings in Cora to help her mother. When her father comes home that night, he drives Cora by moonlight to the home of Mr. Reedy, a Quaker. Georgina's mother says:

> 🍂 It's been a day of deliverance, . . . Cora brought Zeb here out of the womb. And we helped deliver her from slavery. . . . We must continue with that work, Georgina.[20]

A runaway slave is also a part of the many-layered story of *Lyddie* by Katherine Paterson. When her mother abandoned their farm, she hired 13-year-old Lyddie out to a hotel for fifty cents a week. Finally, when the mistress goes away for several days, the cook gives Lyddie permission to go back to the farm for a day. When Lyddie arrives at their old house, she finds the Quakers next door have hidden a runaway slave there. At first Lyddie, who is desperate for money to pay off the mortgage, thinks about the one hundred dollar reward for turning in a slave. But the more she talks with Ezekial, she knows she could never turn him in. In fact she gives him all the money she has and wishes him a safe journey. He in turn hopes she will find her freedom. This is something Lyddie thinks about frequently as she realizes she is no more than a slave at the hotel where she works and later at the textile mill.

[20]Paul Fleischman, *The Borning Room* (New York: HarperCollins, 1991), p. 33.

Jessie Bollier is a 13-year-old white boy who is shanghaied in New Orleans and made to join the crew of a slave ship. In this grim story by Paula Fox, Jessie is forced to play his fife and "dance the slaves" so their muscles will remain strong and they will bring a higher price on the slave market. Jessie, *The Slave Dancer*, is young, innocent, and still capable of feeling shock. Everyone else on board the ship is so hardened as to be indifferent to human suffering. And this is the real message of the story, the utter degradation that eventually engulfs everyone connected with slavery—from the captain to the black Portuguese broker to the depraved Ben Stout and even to Jessie himself. For at one point, Jessie is surprised to find himself hating the blacks; he is so sick of the sight, smell, and sound of their suffering that he wishes they did not exist. In one of the most compelling and symbolic scenes in the book Jessie is forced into the hold of the ship to look for his fife. Here he must touch, literally step on, the black bodies, so crowded together that there is no room to walk. Jessie's descent into that hold somehow represents the descent of the whole of humankind.

Virginia Hamilton has written the complex story of *Anthony Burns: The Defeat and Triumph of a Fugitive Slave*. Born a slave in Virginia, Anthony Burns was 20 when he escaped to Boston. For a few short months he lived as a free man until his former owner came to Boston and invoked the Fugitive Slave Act and demanded him back. Thousands of abolitionists rioted and Richard Dana defended him without charge. Yet it was to no avail. Burns was sent back to Virginia, where he was shackled and imprisoned in a tiny room for the next four months. Finally news of his whereabouts reached two ministers in Boston who raised money for his purchase. He was freed and sent to Canada where he became a minister. He died when he was only 28 years old from the dreadful treatment he had received while in jail. Students in middle school interested in pursuing the meaning of the Fugitive Slave Law could do no better than read this compelling story of the last slave ever seized on Massachusetts soil.

Patricia Beatty's *Jayhawker* is the story of Lije Tulley, a Kansas 12-year-old who joins his family's abolitionist activities. Lije rides in his dead father's place in raids to free slaves across the border in Missouri. As war begins, he becomes a spy to serve the cause, posing as a Southern supporter while working on a Missouri farm. Courage, loneliness, and conflicting loyalties are highlighted in this well-crafted story with a dramatic conclusion.

The Civil War

There are many fine stories for children about the Civil War itself. Most of these describe the war in terms of human issues and suffering, rather than political issues. Two books focus on very different adventures of young drummer boys in the Civil War. *Charley Skedaddle*, written by Patricia Beatty, tells the story of 13-year-old Charley Quinn, a tough kid from the New York Bowery who, after his older brother is killed at Gettysburg, enlists in the Union army as a drummer boy. But when the horrors of war become a reality and he sees his best friend killed, Charley is terrified. He "skedaddles" away from the Union army and from the Confederates who would take him prisoner. Hiding in the Blue Ridge Mountains, he meets Granny Bent, a "wise woman" who is midwife and healer for the mountain folk. Charley lives with her and proves he is no coward on the day he kills a panther and saves Granny Bent's life. Charley's gradual change from a boy filled with bravado to one who shows real bravery is made very believable in this fast-paced story.

Ransom Powell is not as lucky as Charley Skedaddle, for two years after joining the 10th West Virginia Regiment of the Union army, he is captured with eighteen others and sent to Andersonville Prison. Well loved by his company for his humor, helpfulness, and his red cap, Powell beat the taps for every member of his group. G. Clifton Wisler has told Ransom Powell's story in *Red Cap*, based on authentic records and other men's reminiscences. This is the only Civil War story for children that details the horrors of the Andersonville Prison.

In *Thunder at Gettysburg*, Patricia Lee Gauch tells the story of Tillie Pierce, a little girl caught in the midst of battle. She had gone out to a farm for safety and to help a neighbor with her children. The farm was right by Little Round Top, where for three days the battle roared around them. Tillie carried water and helped with the wounded. Black-and-white drawings by Stephen Gammell picture the horror that surrounded Tillie.

The high drama of the three-day battle of Gettysburg is also the focus of *The Slopes of War* by N. A. Perez. Buck Summerhill returns to Gettysburg, his home town, as a soldier in the Army of the Potomac and loses his leg in the fight for Little Round Top. His sister Bekah cares for a wounded Union officer, Captain Waite, upstairs in the family's home while injured Rebels are taken into the parlor. She is delighted when her favorite cousin Custis, a Virginian, slips away from the Rebel camp during the night to visit her, but he is killed the next day on Culp's Hill. Custis's brother Mason is one of the few Confederates to survive Pickett's famous, futile charge on the last day of the battle. Bekah's 12-year-old brother Leander sees enough of this fighting and its terrible aftermath to convince him that war is not the glorious thing he had anticipated. As Captain Waite tells him, "'. . . that's what war is all about, Leander . . . an accumulation of *little* deaths that piles up into enormous grief.'"[21] (See the box "Recurring Themes in Historical Fiction" for books about other times that carry a similar message.) This book is packed with authentic information about real officers and battle strategies, as well as several threads of fictional story line.

The effect of the war on a frontier family in Illinois has been told by Irene Hunt in the fine historical novel *Across Five Aprils*. Jethro Creighton is only 9 years old at the outbreak of the war that at first seemed so exciting and wonderful. But one by one Jethro's brothers, cousins, and his beloved schoolteacher enlist in the Northern army. His favorite brother, Bill, after a long struggle with his conscience, joins the South. As the war continues, Jethro learns that it is not glorious and exciting, but heartbreaking and disruptive to all kinds of relationships. Although the many letters used to carry the action of the story to different places and provide historical detail make difficult reading, this is a beautifully written, thought-provoking book.

[21]N. A. Perez, *The Slopes of War* (Houghton Mifflin, 1984), p. 138.

Rifles for Watie by Harold Keith tells of the life of a Union soldier and spy engaged in fighting the western campaign of the Civil War. Jefferson Davis Bussey, a young farm boy from Kansas, joins the Union forces, becomes a scout, and quite accidentally a member of Stand Watie's Cherokee Rebels. Jeff is probably one of the few soldiers in the West to see the Civil War from both sides. This vibrant novel is rich in detail, with fine characterizations.

In the story of 12-year-old Hannalee Reed from Roswell, Georgia, *Turn Homeward, Hannalee* by Patricia Beatty, Hannalee, her little brother Jem, and hundreds of other young millworkers are branded as traitors for making cloth and rope for the Confederacy. They are sent north to work in mills in Kentucky and Indiana or hired out as servants to northern families. Hannalee has a harsh employer and misses Jem, who has been taken to work on a farm. She runs away, disguises herself as a boy, finds her brother, and together they make their way home to burned-out Roswell.

There is great pride and family feeling built into Hannalee's character. Although she learns that there are good Yankees and bad Yankees, her loyalties are firmly in the South. This book emphasizes the point that few southerners were slaveholders, and it forces readers to consider the war's effects on the common people of the South—a good balance for the many books that present northerners' views. The sequel to this story is *Be Ever Hopeful, Hannalee*, which tells of the family's struggle to survive the aftermath of the war. While continuing the story of spunky Hannalee, Patricia Beatty details the rebuilding of Atlanta by poor whites and poor blacks. Like all of Beatty's books, these two stories were meticulously researched and include long informative author's notes.

Shades of Gray by Carolyn Reeder is also a story about the aftermath of the Civil War. Twelve-year-old Will Page blames the Yankees for the loss of his entire family. He is sent to live with his aunt and uncle out in the Virginia Piedmont area.

RESOURCES FOR TEACHING

◆ RECURRING THEMES IN HISTORICAL FICTION ◆

THEME	TITLE/AUTHOR	SETTING
The clash of cultures	*The Faraway Lurs*, Behn	Prehistoric Denmark
	The Sign of the Beaver, Speare	Maine Territory, 1760s
	Year of Impossible Goodbyes, Choi	North Korea, 1940s
The human cost of war	*My Brother Sam Is Dead*, Collier and Collier	American Revolution
	The Slopes of War, Perez	U.S. Civil War
	After the Dancing Days, Rostkowski	World War I
	The Eternal Spring of Mr. Ito, Garrigue	Canada, World War I
In quest of freedom	*The Dancing Bear*, Dickinson	Byzantium, sixth century
	Jump Ship to Freedom, Collier and Collier	United States, 1780s
	North to Freedom, Holm	Europe, 1940s
	The Clay Marble, Ho	Cambodia, 1980s
Overcoming handicaps	*A Way of His Own*, Dyer	Prehistoric America
	The Stronghold, Hunter	Early Scotland (Orkney Islands)
	Door in the Wall, de Angeli	Medieval England
	Apple Is My Sign, Riskind	United States, early 1900s

He can endure living in the country, but he finds it hard to accept the hospitality of his uncle, who had refused to fight the Yankees because he did not believe in war. It is even more difficult for Will to hang on to his resentment because his uncle is so fair and kind and can do everything well. Gradually Will begins to understand the courage that it took for his uncle to stand up for his beliefs. When his uncle shelters a wounded Yankee on his way home to Pennsylvania, Will learns that there were good men fighting on both sides of the war. Well plotted, this is an exciting story that will make readers think of the many "shades of gray" which surround all prejudices.

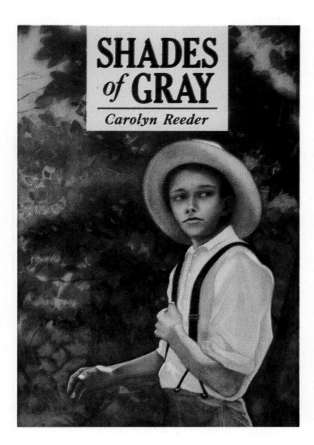

The troubled expression and watchful eyes of Will Page hint at the complexity of his emotions in Carolyn Reeder's *Shades of Gray,* set just after the Civil War.

Cover art by Robin Moore.

INTO THE TWENTIETH CENTURY

Immigrants

Immigrants who came to North America in the nineteenth and early twentieth centuries had many different origins and various destinations. Still, they shared common dreams of a better life and faced similar difficulties in making a place for themselves in a new country.

The problems of the MacDonald children in Margaret Anderson's *The Journey of the Shadow Bairns* are compounded by the death of both father and mother before the family has a chance to set sail from Glasgow. Elspeth, 13, is determined not to be separated from 4-year-old Robbie. Knowing her father's plans for homesteading in western Canada, Elspeth contrives to get herself and her brother past the authorities and on board ship. She makes up the game "shadow bairns" (shadow children) to encourage Robbie to be quiet and keep out of sight of the immigration officials. Together they manage the voyage and the long train trip across Canada. When they reach Saskatchewan Territory, Elspeth falls ill, her money is stolen, and Robbie disappears. It is many weeks before she finds him and a permanent home for them both. This story highlights the uncertainties and misinformation that immigrants had to deal with, but its most memorable images are of Elspeth, resourceful and determined, and Robbie, clinging to his toy Pig-Bear.

If it weren't for the references to the Polish language and Roman Catholic faith, *First Farm in the Valley: Anna's Story* might almost be mistaken for another book about Laura Ingalls and her family. Instead, this is a story by Anne Pellowski based on the 1870s childhood of her great-aunt, the daughter of a Polish immigrant in Wisconsin. The chapters are short episodes geared to the satisfactions of younger elementary children. Anna, just ready to start school, is a spunky heroine who dares to climb the roofbeam of a house to get a bag of nails or brave a hailstorm to bring home the sheep. There is a strong sense of family and of community with neighbors who keep the traditions of Poland alive in the New World. Other books by Pellowski deal with succeeding generations of this extended family.

In story and pictures, *Immigrant Girl* by Brett Harvey tells what it was like to live in a Jewish family in the Lower East Side of New York in 1910. Becky and her large family of nine move from the country in Russia to squeeze into only three rooms above a grocery store. Illustrations by Deborah Kogan Ray depict the crowded conditions, the sweatshop where Becky's Aunt Sonia makes shirtwaists, and the large union meeting at Cooper Square where her aunt speaks out for a strike. Everyone helps each other and they send money for her mother's other sister to come over. Despite their struggles, they maintain the Jewish Sabbath and holidays, the very reason they came to this country.

Immigrant Girl would make a fine introduction to Judie Angell's *One-Way to Ansonia*, which traces seven years in the life of a Russian Jewish immigrant family on New York's Lower East Side. At the center is Rose, who is plump, musically talented, brash, and eager for education despite the scoffing of friends and family. She has been sent out to work for pay since the age of 8 and has chosen herself a husband at 14 to avoid an arranged marriage. Still, Rose is determined to believe that there are other ways to live. It is sheer strength of spirit that takes her out of her close-knit, tradition-bound neighborhood at last, to buy a one-way ticket for an unknown Connecticut town where she hopes to make an easier life for herself, her husband, and their infant son.

Laurence Yep's *The Star Fisher* describes the trials of a Chinese-American family who move from Ohio to Clarksburg, West Virginia, in 1927. When they get off the train the first words they hear are "Darn Monkeys." The father, who thinks of himself as a scholar, is proud and stubborn. He moves his family into a converted schoolhouse and attempts to run a new laundry business. The mother, who was the youngest in her family, never learned to cook. They first meet Miss Lucy their landlady when Mama sets fire to the dinner the night of their arrival. With a mixture of humor and real emotion the family realizes they have no customers in this narrow-minded town that cannot accept outsiders. Only when they conquer their pride and allow Miss Lucy to help them by teaching Mama how to make apple pie, do they finally become a part of the community. The Chinese story of "The Star Fisher," which the oldest daughter tells to the youngest, becomes an extended metaphor throughout this fine story of adjustment to a new life.

In Laurence Yep's earlier books, *The Serpent's Children* and *Mountain Light*, the nineteenth-century Chinese refer to America as "the land of the Golden Mountain." Although these stories are set mainly in China, the promise of the California gold fields is part of the theme as well as the plot. *Mountain Light* includes graphic descriptions of the repugnant conditions on an immigrant ship from Hong Kong to San Francisco and the infighting among clans and factions that carried over from China to the New World. Yep's earlier book, *Dragonwings*, gives a more detailed picture of Chinese immigrants in San Francisco after 1900.

African Americans

The history of African Americans from the late 1800s to the middle of the twentieth century is a bitter record of high hopes brought low by prejudice, hatred, and greed. Because novels which explore these situations examine issues that are still sensitive today, critics with a sociological point of view sometimes disagree about the merits of the books. Some question the authenticity or appropriateness of attitudes portrayed for today's children. Others point to the inherent drama of the stories and their intended themes of tolerance and understanding. In the books that follow, memorable characters face the uncertain future common to African Americans in the South during the first half of this century.

One of the most moving stories of this time period is the Newbery award winner *Sounder* by William Armstrong. This is the stark tale of a black sharecropper and his family who endure cruel injustice with dignity and courage. When the father is thrown into jail for stealing a ham for his starving family, his big hunting dog, Sounder, is cruelly wounded by the sheriff. The dog never bays again until years later, when his master returns. As in the story of Odysseus, the dog is the first to recognize the man. Crippled from a dynamite blast in the prison quarry, the father has come home to die. The story would be one of deep despair except for the fact that during the boy's long searches to find where his father is imprisoned, he meets a kind schoolmaster who enlarges his world by educating him and offering some hope for the future. This is a family that has the courage and faith to endure within a setting so inhuman that they seem to be nameless in contrast to their dog. They do not fight back because they cannot fight back—not in the rural South near the end of the nineteenth century.

In Ouida Sebestyen's compelling *Words by Heart,* black Ben Sills has moved his family to an all-white community in the West and taken a job as hired hand to rich Mrs. Chism. The hatred and resentment of her tenant farmer, Mr. Haney, and his son Tater grow as Ben proves himself honest and hard-working, which the Haneys are not. Ben's oldest child, Lena, also proves herself an eager, keen-minded student whose ability to recite Bible verses "by heart" wins a contest at the book's opening. Even though the family begins to settle in and make progress against their neighbor's uneasiness, the animosity of the Haneys remains. Angered when Lena's father is given a fence-mending job his own father had neglected, Tater rides out with a gun and shoots Ben as he works, but is himself nearly killed in a fall from his horse. It is Lena who finds them and loads both into the wagon—her dying father and the injured boy he has struggled to keep alive. This is a stunning act of mercy, in keeping with the characterization of Ben Sills as a man of faith and strength. However, it does perpetuate the stereotype of a minority character serving the dominant race to the ultimate degree of self-sacrifice.

Mildred Taylor, one of the first black authors to win the Newbery award, has written with understanding about the black experience in rural Mississippi during the 1930s. *Roll of Thunder, Hear My Cry* is the story of the Logan family, their pride in the land they have owned since Reconstruction, and their determination not to let injustice go unchallenged. The crucial action in the narrative is the conflict that 9-year-old Cassie observes in the adult world around her: night riders who terrorize the black community; her mother's teaching job gone as a result of her efforts to organize a boycott of the store whose white owners are among those night riders; her father's dramatic part in rescuing a black teenager, T.J., from a lynch mob. The grim nature of the events is offset by the portrayal of the family caught up in them, the warmth of their concern for one another, the strength of their pride, and their courage.

A direct sequel, *Let the Circle Be Unbroken,* follows the tragic trial of T.J. and carries Cassie's family saga into 1935. Cassie continues to be a witness to the victimization of poor sharecroppers, both black and white, the beginnings of unionization, and the first attempts at black voter registration. It is the family that sustains all through these difficult times, made more so by Stacey's running away to find work. The complex social issues and human relationships in this book make it better suited to middle school or junior high school readers. A younger audience could be introduced to the Logan family in Taylor's *Song of the Trees,* which has the format of a short illustrated book.

Another shorter story of the Logan family is *Mississippi Bridge.* In this tale based on a true story told to Mildred Taylor by her father, the black and white community meet briefly at the Wallace store while they wait for the weekly bus. Jeremy Simms, a 10-year-old white boy and would-be friend of the Logan children, watches as the bus splashes through a heavy rainstorm to stop at the store. When it is fully loaded, Jeremy is dismayed to see the bus driver order the black passengers off to make room for the late-arriving white passengers. In the next few minutes the bus skids off the bridge and all are drowned. This story shows how tragedy and prejudice were a daily part of life in rural Mississippi in the 1930s. While somewhat predictable, it would make an excellent book for classroom discussion.

In the prejudiced climate of tidewater North Carolina in the 1930s, children were expected to acquire bigotry as part of their growth into adulthood. At 11 years old, however, Harrison Hawkins, who is white, and Kitty Fisher, who is black (and a boy), can still be best friends. In *Circle of Fire* by William H. Hooks, these two join forces to help a band of Irish tinkers camped on the Hawkins property escape the wrath of the Ku Klux Klan. The theme of the horrors of intolerance is doubled in force by having two sets of victims, the tinkers who are actually harassed and beaten, and the African Americans, whose fate is implied in every threat of the Klan. This story has a dramatic climax that seems real and immediate.

The World in the Twentieth Century

THE WORLD AT WAR

Unfortunately, much of the history of the twentieth century is the story of a world at war. Many books for young people chronicle its horrors. In these stories the common enemy is war itself. While most of them depict people's inhumanity to each other, they also show many individual acts of humanity and extreme courage.

Oddly enough, very few books for children about World War I have been published. *After the Dancing Days* by Margaret I. Rostkowski is a moving story of the aftermath of that war for those who were wounded. Annie's father is a doctor in one of the veterans' hospitals and, despite her mother's disapproval, Annie goes to visit the soldiers with her father. There she meets Andrew, a bitter withdrawn young veteran with a disfigured face. In time, Annie no longer sees his face as horrible and begins to draw him out of his shell. At the end of the summer Andrew is beginning to heal both physically and psychologically and Annie has matured while confronting the ironies of war.

The majority of the war stories are about World War II and the Holocaust. Several picture storybooks might be used to introduce the topic or as companion books to longer stories. *Rose Blanche* by Christophe Gallaz and Roberto Innocenti is the story of a girl of about 10 who observes the actions of the Nazis and one day follows a van out to a concentration camp. Later she visits the camp and slips food to the inmates. While her actions would not have been possible, they symbolize all of the little efforts made by the people who resisted the war in small ways. The very name Rose Blanche was derived from a group of young German citizens who protested the war. They were all killed as is the Rose Blanche in this story. *Let the Celebrations Begin!* by Margaret Wild is the poignant story of a group of Polish women in Belsen who are determined to make toys for the children in the camp to have on the day of their liberation. So out of scraps of materials, rags, but-

tons, and pockets, they secretly make stuffed elephants, owls, and other toys. Based on a reference to a small collection of toys found at the Belsen concentration camp, this is a moving testament to all that is good in humankind.

Both *Hiroshima No Pika* by Toshi Maruki and *My Hiroshima* by Junko Morimoto record in pictures and story the horror of the atomic bomb. All these picture storybooks (see Chapter 5) are for older children and could well serve as an introduction to units on World War II or units on peace.

Escape and Resistance

Some of the most popular war stories are about families that escaped to freedom or endured long years of hiding from the Nazis. *Journey to America* by Sonia Levitin tells of a German-Jewish family who become refugees when Hitler comes to power. Papa goes ahead to the United States, but Mama and the girls must wait in Switzerland. There Mama is an alien and cannot work, and other living arrangements are made for the children. After a difficult separation, all the family is reunited in America. Simple language and the emphasis on family solidarity and mutual love make this story appealing for 8- to 10-year-olds.

Along with its intriguing title, *When Hitler Stole Pink Rabbit* by Judith Kerr also has the validity of solid detail that comes from personal experience. This is the story of another family's escape to Switzerland and their trials in trying to earn a living there, then in France, and finally in England. Again, this is a prewar story taking place in the 1930s. It is a happier account than *Journey to America;* yet as they leave France for England, Anna wonders if they will ever really belong anywhere.

Others made their escape by hiding for the duration of the war. *Anne Frank: The Diary of a Young Girl* is the classic story of hiding from the Nazis. Autobiographical, this is a candid and open account of the changes wrought upon eight people who hid for two years in a secret annex of an office building in Amsterdam and were ultimately found and imprisoned by the Nazis. Anne's diary reveals the thoughts of a sensitive adolescent growing up under extraordinary conditions. No one who lived in the annex survived the war except Anne's father. He returned to their hiding place and found Anne's diary. When it was published, it became an immediate best-seller and was translated into many languages. Its popularity continues today, an appropriate tribute to Anne Frank's amazing spirit.

The Upstairs Room by Johanna Reiss is a moving account of the author's own experiences when she and her sister were hidden by a farm family, the Oostervelds. The girls spent most of the time in an upstairs room so that they wouldn't be seen. The greatest excitement occurs when German soldiers make the Oosterveld house their tempo-rary headquarters. Mostly, however, this is a story of the reactions of all the characters in close con-finement and secrecy—the irritability, tension, and fear. The real delight of the book is the Oosterveld family with their plain-folks values, salty language, and generosity. Annie's story is continued in *The Journey Back*, which shows the aftereffects of war on her family and her difficul-ties with a perfectionist stepmother.

In *Hide and Seek* Ida Vos tells the story of one Jewish family in the Netherlands after the arrival of the German army. Rachel is bewildered by the constant change of laws, the confiscation of the family's bicycles, the yellow stars that must be sewn on coats, the disappearances of friends and relatives. The first day Rachel must wear her yel-low star she feels very self-conscious. As she boards the tram the driver calls out to them:

> ❧ "It really is springtime in my tram now. All these children with yellow daffodils on their coats. I wish I could wear one."[22]

Many people are as kind as the tram driver, but many are not. Rachel and her sister go into hiding sheltered by various "uncles" and "aunts" who are willing to risk their lives to hide the girls. At the end of the story the children are reunited with their parents, but 105 of her parents' family mem-bers have been killed. Over 100,000 Dutch Jews were killed in German concentration camps.

Uri Orlev's story, *The Island on Bird Street*, takes the reader into an almost deserted Polish ghetto where Alex, not yet 12, has an ingenious hiding place high in the ruins of building No. 78. His mother, a Zionist, has disappeared, and his father is taken away by the Germans along with the last workers cleared from the ghetto. But Alex's instructions are to wait for his return at No. 78—for a day, a week, or even a year, if necessary. As the months pass he proves to be a clever and courageous survivor, avoiding detection even when German soldiers come to blast open a secret bunker under the cellar. The story ends as Alex and his father, now a part of the under-ground, are miraculously reunited. The author's confident tone comes from experience; he spent two years in hiding in the Warsaw ghetto as a child.

One of the best survival stories is *The Endless Steppe* by Esther Hautzig. This is the author's own account of growing up in a slave labor camp in Siberia. The Rudomins, a wealthy Jewish fam-ily, lived in Vilna, a city in Poland. The Russians occupy Vilna and confiscate the family business; and then one day they arrest the whole family as "capitalists and therefore enemies of the people." They are shipped in filthy, stiflingly hot cattle cars across the barren flat land that is to be their home for five endless years—Siberia. Despite the poverty and privation, Esther manages to satisfy her adolescent needs and to find hope in a hope-less situation. During the time they were in Siberia, the Nazis had entered Poland and killed all their Jewish relatives and friends; in retrospect they consider themselves supremely lucky to have been deported to "The Endless Steppe." The ending of this story is less grim than that of *Anne Frank: The Diary of a Young Girl*, but both stories are a tribute to the courage of the human spirit.

Frequently refugees were helped to flee or hide from authorities by common folk who did what they could to resist the invaders. Many stories relate the roles that children played in helping these resisters. Two stories of enduring popularity with young readers are Claire Bishop's *Twenty and Ten*, in which French orphans manage to hide ten Jewish children during a Nazi investi-gation, and Marie McSwigan's *Snow Treasure*, which tells how a brave group of Norwegian chil-dren helped to smuggle gold out of the country.

[22]Ida Vos, *Hide and Seek*, translated by Terese Edelstein and Inez Smidt (New York: Houghton Mifflin, 1991), p. 18.

Lois Lowry tells the dramatic story of the Danish Resistance as they successfully smuggled nearly seven thousand Jews across the sea to Sweden. In *Number the Stars*, she details the story of how one family saved the lives of their friends, the Rosens. Perhaps the most exciting scene is when the German soldiers come to the house where Ellen Rosen is staying and pretending to be a member of their family. She still wears her Star of David necklace and Annemarie hisses to her to take it off. She is unable to get it unclasped, so Annemarie yanks it off just before the Nazis enter the room. When they leave:

🍂 Annemarie relaxed the clenched fingers of her right hand, which still clutched Ellen's necklace. She

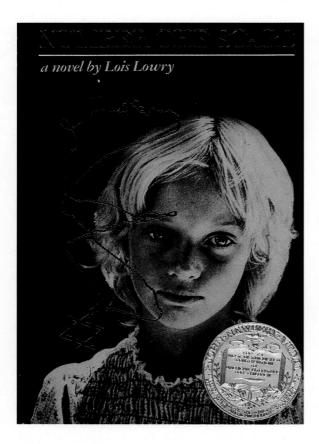

a novel by Lois Lowry

Author Lois Lowry herself took the photograph featured on the cover of her highly acclaimed story of the Danish Resistance, *Number the Stars*.

🍂 🍂 🍂

looked down, and saw that she had imprinted the Star of David into her palm.[23]

Only through the cooperation and extraordinary bravery of the common people were the Danes able to save most of their Jewish population.

Lisa's War by Carol Matas tells of the part the two Jewish young people play in the Danish Resistance. Rather than being saved by others, they are actively involved in the rescue effort. Finally, it becomes too dangerous for them to continue their work and they are persuaded to go to Sweden.

Another story of a dramatic rescue of French Jewish children by a whole town is told in *Waiting for Anya* by Michael Morpurgo. A reclusive widow's farm set high in the hills close to Spain is the perfect escape point for Jewish children, until the German soldiers move in. Benjamin, the widow's son-in-law, is waiting for his own daughter, Anya, to come. In the meantime he escorts the children to the border. When the soldiers start patrolling the borders, some twelve children are hidden at the farm. Finally Benjamin and Jo, a young boy in the village, agree on a plan. The children will be assigned to each family and help move the sheep up to the high pastures. The plan works despite the doubts of one German soldier. However, Benjamin is captured with Leah, the youngest child, who refused to leave him at the border. They are sent to Auschwitz. Ironically, the war is over in a few weeks and Anya comes home at last. This is a moving story of uncommon bravery by the small village of Vichy, France.

Some of the most dramatic stories of young people who lived through the conflict in Europe are autobiographical. However, they employ many of the techniques of fiction, including the creation of dialogue.

In *Touch Wood*, Renée Roth-Hano uses a diary format to record her story of life in occupied France. This Jewish family flees Alsace and lives a precarious existence in Paris until Renée and her sister escape to the shelter of a Catholic women's residence in Normandy. In the end they

[23]Lois Lowry, *Number the Stars* (New York: Houghton Mifflin, 1989), p. 49.

are caught in the middle of crossfire but manage to walk a minefield to safety.

Ilse Koehn's *Mischling, Second Degree* describes her childhood of active participation in the Hitler Youth movement, made ironic by the secret kept even from her at the time: her father's mother was Jewish, and Ilse would have been classified as an enemy of the Third Reich had the fact been known. In Emma Macalik Butterworth's *As the Waltz Was Ending,* an autobiographical account of growing up in Vienna, 8-year-old Emmy auditions for and is accepted by the selective Vienna State Ballet School, but the fairy-tale quality of her life is shattered by the ugliness of politics and the crush of war. Her childhood pains with the *barre* exercises pale beside her adolescent struggles to survive air raids, food shortages, and, finally, kidnap and rape by Russian soldiers. Aranka Siegal's own story of her Hungarian childhood, *Upon the Head of the Goat,* is filled with dread, for the Davidowitz family is Jewish. The final scene is emotionally shattering as Piri, her mother, brother, and two sisters are forced to board a train for a destination with a name that is unfamiliar to them—Auschwitz. Books such as these are really for adolescents, but require maturity of their readers, whatever their age level.

Children in Asia also suffered during the war years. *The House of Sixty Fathers* by Meindert DeJong is an example of a book that does not glorify war; it clearly, vividly tells of the horror of bullets coming in your direction and of the pains of hunger. DeJong's descriptions of Tien Pao's fear, loneliness, and hunger are starkly realistic but couched in terms that even 9- or 10-year-olds can well understand. The Chinese boy and his family flee before the Japanese invasion, but they are separated. Clutching his pet pig, Tien Pao struggles on, not knowing where to go. He finds a U.S. flier who helps him survive. The boy is taken to the barracks and becomes a mascot of the soldiers, his sixty fathers. Although it seems impossible, he continues to believe his parents will be found. In a rather contrived but satisfying ending he does identify his mother from a plane as she is working on the construction of an airfield.

A few Western children, mainly those of missionary parents, were trapped in Asia during World War II. In *The Bombers' Moon* Betty Vander

Els tells the story of Ruth and her little brother Simeon, who must go to an emergency boarding school as the Japanese invaders come closer to their home in China. They endure falling bombs, a terrifying airlift over the Himalayas to India, and one new "home" after another before being reunited with their parents. Unlike many books about World War II, this one has characters who do not grow into adolescence during the story. Thus their natural outlook is not on the political or moral issues of war, but on its immediacy of emotions and images. The author has a gift for expressing the children's own view of their world, including their very real affection for China.

Many authors from England have written about children's experiences there at the time of the bombing raids. Susan Cooper's *Dawn of Fear* and Robert Westall's *The Machine Gunners* are frequently read by young adolescents. One of the best selections for elementary readers is Nina Bawden's *Carrie's War,* about three children who are evacuees living in a Welsh mining town. Nick and Carrie, brother and sister, are sent to live with stern Mr. Evans and his sister, Auntie Lou. The story moves ahead on two levels—the family's feud with Mr. Evans's older sister Dilys and the children's involvement in it. The characters are seen from a child's eye view, with a child's perception of adults. This is a remarkable story that tells much more of the personal wars of living both as children and adults than of the war of bombs and blitzes.

An unusual story that concerns itself with the aftermath of war is *North to Freedom* by Anne Holm. A boy named David is given a chance to escape from the prison camp in eastern Europe where he has lived for most of his twelve years. He has no knowledge of his own background or of the world at large and no feeling about people except that no one can be trusted. Although David is able to read and has learned to speak seven languages from the other prisoners, much of his learning has been without the essential experience that brings meaning. He finds it difficult to relate to the world, avoids people, and makes only tentative gestures toward others. Slowly, his trust in human beings grows, and with it the desire to live and be a part of the world of sunshine, beauty, and color that is in such contrast to the drabness of the prison camp. David's change from an imprisoned creature completely shut off from normal human feelings to a responsive and responsible boy makes for a remarkable story.

Impact of the War in the Americas

While thousands of American families lost sons, fathers, and husbands in World War II, North Americans never endured the physical horror of war in our land. For this reason, perhaps, we have fewer stories about the impact of the war in the West.

Two popular stories tell of the English children who were sent to Canada for the duration of the war. *Searching for Shona* by Margaret Anderson is more about trading identities than it is about the war, but it could not have happened except for the evacuation of the children. In the midst of a crowded train station shy wealthy Marjorie Malcom-Scott sees a girl she knows only casually, Shona. On the spur of the moment, when Marjorie says she'd rather stay in Britain than go to Canada, the girls exchange places with the promise to switch back after the war. The intrigue of who the real Shona is and the rich girl, poor girl exchange captivates children's interest in this story. In another tale, Norah and her younger brother Gavin are sent to live with a rich woman and her sister in Toronto. *The Sky Is Falling* by Kit Pearson details the difficult adjustment of the children, particularly since "Aunt Florence" obviously prefers Gavin to Norah. This well-written story tells a believable tale of the gradual change in relationships between 10-year-old Norah and her sponsor.

The Cay by Theodore Taylor is both a war survival story and one of overcoming prejudice. After the Germans torpedo the freighter on which Phillip and his mother are traveling back home to the United States from wartime Curaçao, Phillip finds himself cast up on a barren little Caribbean Island with an old black man named Timothy. A blow on the head during the wreck has left Phillip blind and completely dependent on Timothy. Both the prejudiced Virginian and the unschooled West Indian are products and prisoners of their backgrounds. Although Phillip gradually begins to understand and trust the wisdom and selflessness

of Timothy, his way of overcoming his prejudice is to make Timothy white in his mind. In return, Timothy forces him to make fish nets, to find his way around the camp, to survive without him. And following the hurricane in which Timothy bears the brunt of the storm while protecting him, Phillip has to live without him, for Timothy dies. Phillip is finally rescued and his sight restored after three operations. This story of a color-conscious white boy and a self-sacrificing man of color does not provide a model for multicultural living today; what it does do is present an exciting account of survival in the Caribbean in 1942, emphasizing human interdependence in time of crisis.

The Summer of My German Soldier by Bette Greene is the story of 12-year-old Patty Bergen, who is Jewish and the awkward elder daughter of a small-town Arkansas department-store owner. Her mother and father fight and are cruel to Patty. Except for the real love of Ruth, the Bergens' African-American cook, Patty lives in a loveless situation. Perhaps this explains her compassion for a handsome, well-educated German prisoner of war named Anton who lives in a prison camp near town and comes to her father's store. Patty begins to think of him as her friend and later, when she sees him running down the railroad tracks, she offers him the safety of her special hideout room over the garage. Only after Anton has gotten away and is captured elsewhere is Patty's role in his escape uncovered. She is arrested and sent to a reform school, clinging to the knowledge that one day she will be free to leave her family and become a "person of value," a term Anton had used.

In *Alan and Naomi* Myron Levoy writes of the aftermath of the Holocaust. At first Alan Silverman does not want to have to make friends with crazy-acting Naomi Kirshenbaum who won't even talk to him. But at the insistence of his parents, he agrees to visit her in her apartment. When he sees her haunted face and hears about her horrifying experiences during the war in France, she becomes a challenge to him. By acting silly with his puppet, he gets her to laugh and speak. Gradually he enjoys the developing friendship. Taunted and teased at school about Naomi and being Jewish, Alan gets into a fight with the school bully. When Naomi sees Alan hit and bleeding, she runs away and hides in the coal pile. Once again she is traumatized and recognizes no one. Alan and his father go to visit her at a nursing home, but it is of no use. Alan cannot reach her. His father assures him that she will be all right in time, but Alan thinks Hitler has destroyed her. The impact of the war had come home.

Citizens of the United States can take no pride in the treatment of Japanese Americans at the beginning of the war against Japan. In *Journey to Topaz*, Yoshiko Uchida has given a fictionalized account of her family's evacuation and internment. Yuki's father, a businessman, is taken away from his family on the very day of Pearl Harbor. It is almost a year before he is paroled. Yuki and her mother and older brother are taken first to a temporary center, a converted racetrack where their "apartment" is a hastily partitioned stall area in one of the stables. The walls have been so sloppily whitewashed that the bodies of cockroaches still cling to the boards. The latrines have no doors, and the mealtime lines are interminable. At the "permanent" camp in Topaz, Utah, Yuki's friend Emi's grandfather is shot by a guard, who sees him looking for arrowheads and thinks he is trying to escape. The author writes the story in a restrained way, with no bitterness. The quiet courage, dignity, and loyalty with which this Japanese family endures their unjust internment makes its own statement to the reader.

Citizens of Japanese descent in Canada were subjected to similar treatment. Sheila Garrigue's *The Eternal Spring of Mr. Ito* helps the reader experience the passionate anti-Japanese feeling along the Pacific Coast even as it demonstrates the blamelessness of those who were shunned, jeered, vandalized, and interned. Sara has come from England to spend the war years with her uncle's family in Vancouver. When her cousin's fiancé is killed in the Japanese attack on Hong Kong, Sara's feelings are torn between grief for the family and sympathy for their loyal Japanese gardener, Mr. Ito. Unable to face the shame of internment, he spends the last days of his life hiding in a cliff-side cave. The ancient bonsai pine that Mr. Ito guards has been in his family for centuries and stands for all that is dignified and

The little known history of the internment of the Japanese in the United States during World War II is sensitively told in *Journey to Topaz* by Yoshiko Uchida.

Illustration by Donald Carrick.

enduring in the Japanese way of life. It would be interesting to discuss with children other objects and actions in the story that have symbolic meaning, such as Uncle Duncan's stoning of the bonsai trees in his own garden.

War Continues

Unfortunately war did not end with World War II but continued with the Korean conflict, Vietnam, and Iraq. Sook Choi writes a poignant story of her childhood in northern Korea in the 1940s in her book, *Year of Impossible Goodbyes*. As the war rages

10-year-old Sookan, her mother, brother, and Aunt Tiger endure the cruelties of the Japanese occupation. Her father is a resistance fighter in Manchuria and her brothers have been taken to Japanese labor camps. When the war is over in 1945, the Koreans hope for a permanent peace, but then the communist Russian troops come. By now Sook Choi and her family have lost everything dear to them. They decide to escape to the Americans at the 38th parallel. Their aunt and her father's nephew stay so as not to arouse suspicion. Their guide double-crosses them, and their mother is stopped at the checkpoint and taken into custody. Sook Choi and her little brother are left all alone. They return to the train station where an elderly porter helps them escape. After a terrifying dash to the barbed wire crossing, the two children finally make it to the Red Cross Center. Later they are reunited with their parents, but their aunt and father's nephew have been executed for their escape. This is a story that emphasizes that all the so-called victors of a war always make the people of a country their victims. Again it relates the uncommon courage of the common people.

The Clay Marble by Minfong Ho tells of 12-year-old Dara and her family, who are among the thousands forced to flee from their villages in war-torn Cambodia during the early 1980s. In the refugee camp, there is peace and plenty of food. Dara makes a new friend, Jantu. For the first time in years, they play and fashion dolls out of clay. Then the shelling and bombing start again, this time in the middle of camp. In the chaos, Dara is separated from her family and from Jantu. Alone, she must find the strength to reunite her family. When she finally finds them her brother wants to enlist in the army instead of going home to help them plant their rice crop. Listening to the propaganda over the loudspeaker, Jantu says:

> 🐛 "They all say the same thing. They seem to think it's a game. . . . They take sides, they switch sides, they play against each other. Who wins, who loses, whose turn it is to kick next—it's like an elaborate soccer game. Except they don't use soccer balls. They use us."[24]

[24]Minfong Ho, *The Clay Marble* (New York: Farrar Straus Giroux, 1991), p. 141.

The author grew up in Thailand and worked as a nutritionist with an international relief organization on the Thai-Cambodian border in 1980. Dara and Jantu's story is every child's story in that refugee camp.

Well-written historical fiction like that reviewed in this chapter may enable children to see the continuity of life and their own places in this vast sweep of history. The power of good historical fiction can give children a feeling for a living past. History can become an extension of their own personal experiences, rather than a sterile subject assigned to be studied in school. Such books can offer children a new perspective by which they come to realize that people make and shape their destinies through the decisions and actions of each individual. The events that are happening today do become the history of tomorrow.

BIOGRAPHY

In children's literature, biography often bridges the gap between historical fiction and informational books. A life story may read like fiction; but, like nonfiction, it will center on facts and events that can be documented. In the past, writers of biography for children have been allowed more freedom in the use of fictional techniques than those who write for adults. As a result, children's biographies over the years have shown a wide range of factual orientations, from strict authenticity to liberal fictionalization. The trend today, however, is clearly toward authenticity.

Authentic biography follows many of the same rules as serious scholarly works written for adults. A book of this type is a well-documented, carefully researched account of a person's life. Only those statements that are actually known to have been made by the subject are included in the conversation. Jean Fritz was one of the first authors to demonstrate that biographies for children could be authentic as well as lively and readable. Her writing helped to set a new standard. Her books about famous figures of the American Revolution, including *And Then What Happened, Paul Revere?* and *Will You Sign Here, John Hancock?*, are based on detailed research. The same is true of her more recent, longer books, such as *Bully for You, Teddy Roosevelt!* No quoted dialogue has been invented, no incidents made up to prove a point. When quotation marks are used, it indicates that, according to record, these actual words were spoken or written. Milton Meltzer's book, *Dorothea Lange: Life Through the Camera*, and Russell Freedman's *The Wright Brothers: How They Invented the Airplane* are other excellent examples of authentic biography.

Fictionalized biography is grounded in thorough research, but lets the author dramatize certain events and personalize the subject rather than present the straight reporting of authentic biography. Fictionalized biography makes use of the narrative rather than the analytical approach. Children come to know the character of the subject as it is presented through actions, deeds, and conversations. In fictionalized biography the author may invent dialogue and even include the unspoken thoughts of the subject. These conversations may be based on actual facts taken from diaries, journals, or other period sources.

F. N. Monjo used the fiction technique of writing from his subject's first-person point of view in *Letters to Horseface: Young Mozart's Travels in Italy*. The author drew on research about Mozart's 1769 tour to "reconstruct" what the young genius might have reported if he had written home to his sister Nannerl (nicknamed "Horseface"). The factual details are essentially true; their presentation in Mozart's voice is imagined. Monjo's endnote says:

> ❦ . . . I think it is fair to say that I have invented very little which had no basis in fact, in the records, and have essentially recast and rephrased many of the recorded thoughts of Leopold Mozart, and of his unbelievably gifted son, Wolfgang.[25]

The same distinction between authentic and fictionalized applies in theory to autobiography. *Self-Portrait: Trina Schart Hyman* by Hyman is an example of authentic autobiography; it features straightforward narrative with many illustrations to document the artist's development. However, most people who write about their own lives for children do so in memoirs told in story form, with recreated conversation.

[25]F. N. Monjo, *Letters to Horseface: Young Mozart's Travels in Italy* (New York: Puffin Books, 1991), p. 89.

Not everyone agrees where to draw the line between fictionalized biography or memoirs and historical fiction. When Jean Fritz wrote about her childhood in China and her much-longed-for trip to the United States in *Homesick: My Own Story*, she found that her "memory came out in lumps" and finally chose not to worry about exact

HOMESICK
M y O w n S t o r y
BY JEAN FRITZ

Illustrated by Margot Tomes

Jean Fritz's story of her own childhood, *Homesick: My Own Story*, brings to life China in the 1920s. The cover by Margot Tomes highlights many significant threads, including the child's perspective, the importance of ships, and the flag as a reminder of national identity.

sequence. She telescoped events of all her childhood into a two-year span:

> . . . but they are all, except in minor details, basically true. The people are real people; the places are dear to me. But most important, the form I have used has given me the freedom to recreate the emotions that I remember so vividly. Strictly speaking, I have to call this book *fiction*, but it does not feel like fiction to me. It is my story, told as truly as I can tell it.[26]

The library cataloging information in the front of the book designates it as fiction, but many readers will think of it as the autobiography of Jean Fritz. The inclusion of a section of family photographs from their days in China strengthens the book's claim to authenticity. Fritz's humor, her depth of feeling, and her vivid portrayal of the turmoil in China during the 1920s make *Homesick* worth reading, regardless of the label that is put on it. Older readers and adults may enjoy a sequel, *China Homecoming*, that is clearly nonfiction.

Biographical fiction consists entirely of imagined conversation and reconstructed action. An example is Robert Lawson's funny *Ben and Me*, the story of Benjamin Franklin as told by his good friend Amos, the mouse who lived in Franklin's old fur cap. The facts of Franklin's life are truly presented, but Amos takes the credit for most of his accomplishments! Lawson used the same tongue-in-cheek pattern for his readable *Mr. Revere and I*, the story of Paul Revere as told by his horse, Scheherazade.

Biography for Today's Child

Publishers of biography for children have been quick to capitalize on trends in the social studies curriculum as well as shifts in children's interests. In the mid-1970s, many biographies about leaders in the American Revolution appeared in connection with the Bicentennial. Likewise, dozens of new books about Christopher Columbus came out in time for the quincentennial observation in 1992. As attention to multicultural education has grown, more stories about women, African

Americans, and other underrepresented groups have also been written.

In the 1980s, new biographies of popular culture celebrities and other contemporary figures outnumbered those of historical subjects as publishers recognized children's tremendous interest in sports and entertainment personalities. Although such books tend to be objective and almost journalistic in their approach, many are superficial in scholarship as well as poorly written. A great number of these and other biographies are published as parts of series, and the result is often life stories tailored to fit certain format specifications rather than explored in all their uniqueness.

In spite of all these cautions we should remember that children's biography, like historical fiction, offers more to choose from today than it did a decade ago. A rekindled interest in the lives of historical figures, the appearance of many autobiographies by children's authors, and the growing use of photographs and picture-book formats have all had significant impact. It is true that many mediocre biographies are still being published, but the number of high-quality books has grown. Biographies have received several prestigious awards in recent years. Russell Freedman won the Newbery Medal in 1988 for *Lincoln: A Photobiography* and a Newbery honor designation in 1992 for *The Wright Brothers: How They Invented the Airplane;* Jean Fritz's *The Great Little Madison* was the first-ever winner of the Orbis Pictus Award for nonfiction; and *Bill Peet: An Autobiography* was named a Caldecott honor book in 1990. Not all good books win awards, of course. Teachers and librarians still need to be able to decide for themselves which biographies are distinctive and deserving of attention.

CRITERIA FOR JUVENILE BIOGRAPHY

The criteria for evaluating biographies for boys and girls differ somewhat from those established for juvenile fiction. They also diverge from generally accepted patterns for adult biography. Children read biography as they read fiction—for the story, or *plot*. Children demand a fast-moving narrative. In biography, events and action become even more exciting because "they really happened." Thus children like biography written

---

[26]Jean Fritz, *Homesick: My Own Story* (New York: Putnam, 1982), Foreword.

as a story with continuity; they do not want just a collection of facts and dates. An encyclopedia gives them facts in a well-organized fashion. Biography, to do more than this, must help them to *know* the person as a living human being.

Choice of Subject

Formerly, most biographies for children were about familiar figures of the past in the United States, particularly those whose lives offered the readiest action material, such as Daniel Boone or Abraham Lincoln. Now the range of subjects is much broader, including artists and intellectuals as well as soldiers and presidents, plus world figures whose presence suggests the widened concerns of our pluralistic society. Biographies of contemporary figures in the sports or entertainment world continue to reflect the influence of the mass media.

For many years biography for children was limited to those subjects whose lives were considered worthy of emulation. This is no longer always true. There are books about people remembered for their misdeeds, like *Traitor: The Case of Benedict Arnold* by Jean Fritz. Such controversial persons as Fidel Castro, Ho Chi Minh, and Lenin have all been subjects of juvenile biographies. As long as the biographies are objective and recognize the various points of view concerning the subjects, these books can serve a useful purpose in presenting a worldview to boys and girls.

Biographies of less-well-known figures or subjects whose accomplishments are highly specialized also have value for children. Marshall Taylor, a champion cyclist at the turn of the century when bicycle racing was a popular sport, was the first black person to ride in integrated races. Mary Scioscia's *Bicycle Rider* tells the story of his first victory, focusing on family values and pride of accomplishment. *El Chino* by Allen Say introduces readers to Bong Way "Billy" Wong, a Chinese American who longed to be a great athlete and found his niche as a bullfighter.

A sense of discovery is added to the satisfaction of a good story where children read about intriguing but little-known lives. Children have a right to read biographies about a wide range of subjects—famous persons, great human beings who were not famous, and even antiheroes.

Accuracy and Authenticity

Accuracy is the hallmark of good biographical writing, whether it is for adults or children. More and more writers of juvenile biography are acknowledging primary sources for their materials either in an introductory note or an appended bibliography. Conscientious authors of well-written children's biographies frequently travel to the locale of the setting in order to get a "feeling" for a place. They visit museums in order to study actual objects that were used by their subjects; they spend hours poring over original letters and documents. Much of this research may not be used in the actual biography, but its effect will be evidenced by the author's true insight into the character of the subject and by the accuracy of the historical detail.

The same kind of careful research should be reflected in the accuracy of the illustrations that convey the time, place, and setting. The dress of the period, the interiors of the houses, the very utensils that are used must be authentic representations. But most difficult of all, perhaps, is the actual portrayal of the subject.

There are many drawings and paintings of most historical figures, but an accurate likeness is problematical, particularly for subjects who lived before the advent of photography. In their book, *Christopher Columbus: The Great Adventure and How We Know About It*, Delno and Jean West point out:

> There are hundreds of paintings, engravings, woodcuts, and statues of Christopher Columbus, but they were all made after he died by people who never saw him.[27]

Several of these competing views are reproduced in their book. They also quote Columbus's son, Ferdinand, who described his father's long face, light eyes, big nose, and red hair so that readers have a basis for reacting to the illustrations.

Photographs provide authentic illustration for many biographical accounts of recent subjects, such as Russell Freedman's highly acclaimed photobiographies and others such as *Jesse Jackson: A Biography* by Patricia McKissack. Photographs play a special role in *Prairie Visions: The Life and*

[27]Delno C. West and Jean M. West, *Christopher Columbus: The Great Adventure and How We Know About It* (New York: Atheneum, 1991), p. 13.

THINKING CRITICALLY ABOUT BIOGRAPHIES

At Hilltonia Middle School in Columbus, Ohio, Richard Roth put his students in groups of four to consider which of two biographies was the better book. Some groups read about Abraham Lincoln, using *Lincoln: A Photobiography* by Russell Freedman and *True Stories About Abraham Lincoln* by Ruth Belov Gross. Other groups read *Bully for You, Teddy Roosevelt!* by Jean Fritz and a second biography of Roosevelt. Still others read two selections about Leonardo da Vinci.

First, students read the books individually and noted their reactions to the cover, the chapter titles, pictures, content (facts, bias, writing style), and usefulness. Groups needed only two copies of each book, since each student could read one title and then trade with a partner. Sharing copies also encouraged students to take good notes, including page numbers for reference.

When the students had read both books, the teacher gave each one a blank chart with space for rating each book on the same items, with the following directions: "Rate the categories for each book from 1 to 10: 10 is excellent, 5, average, and 1, poor. As a group, decide what score each category deserves. Then total the scores and determine which book the group thought best overall." The final step was to work as a group to compose a recommendation of their top book for other students to read.

Although not all the groups chose the book that the teacher (or critics) would have chosen, the students gained valuable experience in exercising their own judgments. The teacher planned this study because he wanted all his students to have the opportunity to take stock of their own responses and share them with classmates. He also knew that his students would participate more fully in discussion if they first had a chance to formulate their ideas and write them down. In retrospect, he reported that this process really did encourage critical thinking. There were meaningful group discussions with healthy disagreements about which book was superior to the other. Moreover, students were able to rethink their own first impressions and make comparisons in the interest of fairness and accuracy. In the whole-class discussion that followed the completion of small group work, the teacher gave students still more to think about by contributing his own perspectives on the books they had read.

As in most middle schools, this teacher has many students and a limited time with them each day. One of the advantages of this biography study was that it gave him new insight into their responses and the factors that contribute to their reading interests. It also confirmed his thinking that it is important for students to work through their own responses as they develop ways to appreciate literature.

Richard Roth
Hilltonia Middle School
Columbus City Schools, Ohio

Times of Solomon Butcher by Pam Conrad. Butcher was a pioneer photographer on the Nebraska prairie; his pictures, reproduced in generous numbers to illustrate the book, describe his work and help to define his character. At the same time they provide authentic details about the time in which he lived. The author shows us that not even photographs are completely trustworthy, however, by describing how Butcher retouched some of his photographs with invented details like a swarm of locusts in a cornfield or a turkey perched on the roof of a soddy.

An authentic biography must be true in every detail. A fictionalized biography must also be true to the factual record, and any invented dialogue or background detail must be plausible and true to the times. Yet the truth of what is included in a biography does not quite answer the entire question of its accuracy. Sometimes what is left out is just as important as what goes in.

Formerly, authors of biographies for children avoided writing about certain aspects in the lives of their subjects. Serious criticism has been leveled at those biographies of Washington and Jefferson that did not include the fact that they owned many slaves. More recent biographies, even those for younger children, do include this information. In the note appended to the end of the biography of Jefferson titled *Grand Papa and Ellen Aroon*, F. N. Monjo points out that Jefferson's will did provide for freeing his personal slaves, but since all of his property (including slaves) was mortgaged and he was in debt, it was not possible to free the majority of them. The book also credits Jefferson with prohibiting slavery in the Northwest Territory and indicates his distress at the fact that his condemnation of slavery was struck from the original draft of the Declaration of Independence.

Certain biographers when writing for younger children may present only a portion of a person's life. In planning their picture book of *Abraham Lincoln*, the D'Aulaires deliberately omitted his assassination and closed the book with the end of the Civil War. The authors' purpose was to present the greatness of the man as he *lived*, for too frequently, they believed, children remember only the manner of Lincoln's death. There is a danger, however, that omissions may oversimplify and thereby distort the truth of a person's life. The critic Jo Carr has argued that it is better not to offer biography to young children at all than to present them with unbalanced portraits distorted by flagrant omissions.[28]

For many years it was thought that children were only interested in reading about the childhoods of great men and women and that the complexities of adult activities would hold no interest for them. For this reason many earlier biographies focused primarily on childhood pranks and legends that suggested future accomplishments, but neglected or rushed through the real achievements of later life. The current emphasis on authentic biography has reversed this trend, since it is much more difficult to find primary source material about a subject's childhood than about his or her adult life. Increasingly, the best authors respect children's right to read honest, objective biographies that tell more of the truth and document their writing with source notes or a bibliography.

Style

The author's language is especially important to biography because it bears the burden of making the subject seem alive and sound real. Documented quotes should be woven smoothly into the narrative. When dialogue is invented, it should have the natural rhythms of speech, regardless of the period it represents, because stilted writing creates an impression of wooden characters.

In today's authentic biography, the author's way with words makes all the difference between a dull and a lively book. The opening paragraph of Jean Fritz's *The Great Little Madison* shows how the writer can choose and present detail in a way that engages the reader:

> James Madison was a small, pale, sickly boy with a weak voice. If he tried to shout, the shout shriveled up in his throat, but of course he was still young. His voice might grow as he did. Or he might never need a big voice.[29]

[28] Jo Carr, "What Do We Do About Bad Biographies?," *Beyond Fact: Nonfiction for Children and Young People* (Chicago: American Library Association, 1982), pp. 119–129.
[29] Jean Fritz, *The Great Little Madison* (New York: Putnam, 1989), p. 7.

The narrator's tone always pervades the presentation, but it is usually a dispassionate point of view that is used for authentic biography. Whatever the form or viewpoint, the background materials should be integrated into the narrative with smoothness and proportion. The judicious use of quotes from letters or journals may support the authenticity of biography, but it should not detract from the absorbing account of the life of the subject. Children enjoy a style that is clear and vigorous. The research must be there, but it should be a natural part of the presentation. Russell Freedman's *Lincoln: A Photobiography* or *The Wright Brothers: How They Invented the Airplane* both provide a masterful demonstration of this kind of clarity.

The choice of narrator, or point of view, is also an important consideration in the style of a biography. Rather than write about the childhood of a famous person, some authors choose to tell the story from the point of view of a child who was close to the adult character. F. N. Monjo was particularly successful in using this approach when writing about Franklin's visit to France with his grandsons in *Poor Richard in France* and in seeing Jefferson through the eyes of his granddaughter in *Grand Papa and Ellen Aroon*. Such a point of view allows the reader to see greatness through the loving eyes of a grandchild. These are joyful, childlike, fictionalized biographies that present authentic facts from a perspective that will capture the imaginations of 7- to 9-year olds.

Characterization

The characterization of the subject of a biography must be true to life, neither adulatory nor demeaning in tone. The reader should have the opportunity to know the person as a real human being with both shortcomings and virtues. In order to emphasize the worthiness of their subjects, juvenile biographers sometimes portray them as too good to be true.

Jean Fritz is one author who manages to create vivid portraits of great figures without according them pseudo-sainthood. She has presented Paul Revere as a busy and sometimes forgetful human being in her humorous yet authentic picture-book biography *And Then What Happened, Paul Revere?* He didn't always meet his deadlines, once pro-

ducing a hymnbook some eighteen months after he had promised it! A dreamer, he even left one page in his "Day Book" simply for doodling. The author does not debunk her character; she simply makes him come alive by admitting his foibles, as well as describing his accomplishments.

Comparing two or more biographies of the same subject is one way of understanding the importance of characterization. Doris Faber's *Eleanor Roosevelt, First Lady of the World* and Maryann Weidt's *Stateswoman to the World: A Story About Eleanor Roosevelt* are similar in length and coverage. Both are generally suitable for grades three to five. While both books emphasize the young Eleanor's growing desire for independence, they provide somewhat different views of the childhood experiences that helped shape her determination and sense of duty.

Jean Fritz's characterization of the famed explorer in *Where Do You Think You're Going, Christopher Columbus?* emphasizes both his courage and his huge pride. The author's sense of irony and her wry humor guard against overdramatizing Columbus's greatness. Alongside the reports of his impressive discoveries are the reminders that he was consistently mistaken about them and fierce in protecting his own personal interests:

> Indeed, Colba [Cuba] *had* to be China, just as this *had* to be the Indies. Columbus had been born to find the Indies. His whole life couldn't be a mistake: God couldn't be wrong. But in case anyone disagreed with him, Christopher Columbus had his entire crew sign an oath, swearing that Colba was part of a continent. The crew was told that if any of them ever denied this, he would have his tongue cut out.[30]

Asking students to describe what kind of person Columbus seems to be at various points during the reading of this book may help them appreciate the complexities of his character.

Biography must not degenerate into mere eulogy; reexamining should not become debunking. The background of subjects' lives, their conversations,

[30]Jean Fritz, *Where Do You Think You're Going, Christopher Columbus?*, illustrated by Margot Tomes (New York: Putnam, 1980), p. 54.

their thoughts, and their actions should be presented as faithfully to the facts as possible. The subject should also be seen in relation to his or her times, for no person can be "read" in isolation.

Theme

Underlying the characterization in all biography—whether it be authentic, fictionalized, or biographical fiction—is the author's interpretation of the subject. No matter how impartial an author may be, a life story cannot be written without some interpretation. The very selection of facts that a biographer chooses may limit the dimensions of the portraiture or highlight certain features. In this context every author walks a thin line between theme and bias. Time usually lends perspective and objectivity, but contemporary biography may tend more toward bias. Teachers and librarians need to help children realize that all biographies have a point of view determined by their authors. Again, a comparison of several biographies of the same person will help children discover this fact.

Frequently in juvenile biography, the theme will be identified in the title as in *Martin Luther King: The Peaceful Warrior* by Ed Clayton or *I'm Nobody! Who Are You? The Story of Emily Dickinson* by Edna Barth. Both these titles contain double meanings and point up the theme of the books. The title of the biography of Dickinson reflects the retiring attitude of the New England poet who in later life became a recluse. It is also, however, the first line of one of Dickinson's well-known poems.

In picture-book biographies, illustrations as well as the story title reveal the theme. Author/illustrator Peter Sis offers an artist's interpretation of Christopher Columbus in *Follow the Dream: The Story of Christopher Columbus*. The artist grew up in Czechoslovakia, a country surrounded by a "wall" known as the Iron Curtain. He relates his background to Columbus's by emphasizing the many forces that walled Columbus in. He describes the ancient maps that showed the known world surrounded by a high wall. One such map is drawn on the book's endpapers; the title page shows a small boy peering out through a small doorway in the wall to the unknown. The wall motif appears consistently

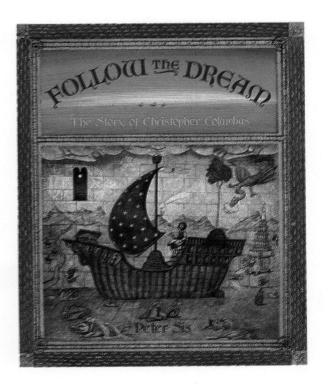

The symbolic wall through which Columbus broke in opening Europeans' vision of a new world is a prominent feature of the cover illustration created by Peter Sis for his book, *Follow the Dream: The Story of Christopher Columbus.*

through the book, always countered by an opening or archway through which Columbus can follow his dream. Although this book ends with the arrival of Columbus in 1492 and says nothing about his character as a leader or his later cruelty to the natives, the theme of breaking down the wall surrounding the old world is a new and fresh insight. A close examination of the last picture and its border, however, suggests that Sis questions the "gift" of civilization to the New World.

There is a danger in oversimplifying and forcing all facts to fit a single mold. An author must not recreate and interpret a life history in terms of one fixed picture, particularly in a biography that covers the full scope of a subject's life. The most common people have several facets to their personalities; the great are likely to be multidimensional. The perceptive biographer concentrates on those items from a full life that helped to mold and form that personality. It is this selection and focus that create the theme of the biography.

Types of Presentation and Coverage

Writers of adult biography are bound by definition to an attempt at recreating the subject's life as fully as possible, with complete detail and careful documentation. Writers of children's biography, however, may use one of several approaches. The resulting types of biography need individual consideration, for each offers to children a different perspective and a different appeal. Keep in mind, however, that a single book may fit into more than one of the following categories.

PICTURE-BOOK BIOGRAPHIES

A biography cast in picture-book form may span the subject's lifetime or a part of it; it may be directed to a very young audience or to a somewhat older one; it may be authentic or fictionalized. Whatever the case, it remains for the pictures to carry a substantial part of the interpretation. Leonard Marcus points out:

> Illustrations, then, contribute more to a picture book biography than occasional picture-equivalents of the

---

GUIDELINES

Evaluating Juvenile Biography

♦ *Choice of Subject:*
Does the subject's life offer interest and meaning for today's child?
Will knowing this historical or contemporary figure help children understand the past or the present?
Can the subject's experiences widen children's views on the possibilities for their own lives?

♦ *Accuracy and Authenticity:*
Do text and illustrations reflect careful research and consistency in presentation?
Does the author provide notes about original source material, a bibliography, or other evidence of documentation?
Are there discrepancies of fact in comparison with other books?
Are there significant omissions that result in a distorted picture of the subject's life?

♦ *Style:*
Are quotations or dialogue used in such a way that the subject is brought to life?
Does the choice of narrator's point of view for a fictionalized biography add to the story?
Is the author's style clear and readable, with background material included naturally?

♦ *Characterization:*
Is the subject presented as a believable multidimensional character, with both strengths and weaknesses?
Does the author avoid both eulogizing and debunking?

♦ *Theme:*
Does the author's interpretation of the subject represent a fair and balanced approach?
Does the author avoid oversimplifying or manipulating the facts to fit the chosen theme?

author's words. They traffic to some degree in unnameable objects, states and feelings. . . . Along with what it tells us about the values, temperament and concerns of a biography's central character, fine illustration also puts us in contact with an individuality—and a form of praise—that is esthetic.[31]

This sense of heightened perception comes with the illustrations by Alice and Martin Provensen for their Caldecott award winner, *The Glorious Flight: Across the Channel with Louis Blériot, July 25, 1909*. Papa carries himself with intrepid grace in his unsuccessful attempts to fly, and the pictures that show him above the channel use contrast and perspective to convey the elation and danger of flight. Many historical and background details appear in the illustrations without being mentioned in the text, inviting speculation, inferences, and discussion. Even the front hardcover binding of this book contains new picture material that will contribute to children's feeling for the time and place.

Joe Lasker's vivid pictures illustrate the military feats of a classic hero, *The Great Alexander the Great*. Since these were real battles which became legendary, it seems appropriate that the art depict both intense human drama and the hovering presence of the mythical gods of Greece. Another book with lively pictures is *The Heroine of the Titanic: A Tale Both True and Otherwise of the Life of Molly Brown* by Joan Blos. Tennessee Dixon's illustrations have a slapdash quality and a cheerful clutter of material possessions that help characterize this controversial turn-of-the-century celebrity. Vivid language and a mixture of narrative and rhyme add appeal to this entertaining biography.

Ingri d'Aulaire and Edgar Parin d'Aulaire were among the first to create beautifully illustrated picture-book biographies for children. As new citizens of this country, they were fascinated with American heroes, including *George Washington*, *Abraham Lincoln*, *Pocahontas*, *Benjamin Franklin*, and *Columbus*. Their charming but idealized pictures made their subjects seem larger than life in some instances.

Jeanette Winter's paintings in *Diego* bring rich color and meaning to the text, which is printed in both English and Spanish. This is a brief book about the life of famous Mexican artist, Diego Rivera. These small pictures construct scenes from his early years that are full of a magical sense of celebrations and play as well as times of turmoil that were reflected in the huge murals he painted as an adult.

The mood or tone of a biography can be quickly established by its pictures. Beginning with the dark watercolor of the march to Selma on the title page of *A Picture Book of Martin Luther King, Jr.* by David Adler, Robert Casilla creates a foreboding mood. Pictures extend the text in this simple biography of the great African-American leader.

Milton Meltzer reminds us that biography is more than the personal history of one person:

> If biography is well done, it is also social history. [As a biographer], I must tell the story of my subject's time and of the people who lived through that time.[32]

This approach usually calls for a complete biography of the subject. In the case of picture-book biographies, it suggests the sharing of several titles with different points of view. Together, they may provide the range of information that sets a subject in context. David Adler's *A Picture Book of Christopher Columbus* portrays a beneficent leader passing out trinkets on the beach at San Salvador and states that he had "found" the New World. Vicki Liestman's *Columbus Day* tries to present a more balanced picture of the accomplishments of Columbus. In her note at the beginning of the book, she mentions the A.D. 1000 landing of Lief Erikson on the coast of North America. She also includes the fact that Columbus forcibly loaded some five hundred natives on ships bound for Spain. To prevent children from getting the impression that Columbus was the only excellent navigator of his time, share Leonard Everett Fisher's distinguished picture-book biography of *Prince Henry, the Navigator*. In this story, the author shows how Prince Henry's school of navigation prepared the way for

---

[31]Leonard S. Marcus, "Life Drawings: Some Notes on Children's Picture Book Biographies," *The Lion and the Unicorn*, vol. 4 (Summer 1980), p. 17.

[32]Milton Meltzer, "Selective Forgetfulness: Christopher Columbus Reconsidered," *The New Advocate*, vol. 5 (Winter 1992), p. 1.

A profusion of color and pattern brings life to the formal figures of Elizabeth's court in Diane Stanley's paintings for *Good Queen Bess* by Diane Stanley and Peter Vennema.

🍃 🍃 🍃

Columbus, for Bartolomeu Dias's trip around Cape Hope, and Vasco da Gama's famous trip to India via the Cape. While Henry himself never sailed on his ships, it was his school that designed the faster caravels and a more accurate compass, improvements that significantly affected all later explorers. Accomplishments like those of Christopher Columbus can only be understood when viewed in the context of their time.

Diane Stanley and Peter Vennema, her husband, have collaborated in writing several complete biographies in picture-book format with exquisitely detailed paintings by Diane Stanley. *Good Queen Bess: The Story of Elizabeth I of England* is an example of their fine work. It tells the story of Elizabeth's life from early childhood to becoming queen at age 25 and on through her rule until her death. Through the paintings and a very readable text, the authors tell of the intrigue, the diplomacy, and the wily tactics that Elizabeth used to steer her country through troubled times. Most importantly they show her many public faces—dancing at court, meeting with villagers,

even in armor on horseback, encouraging her soldiers to do battle prior to the expected Spanish invasion. The defeat of the Spanish Armada brought peace and prosperity to England and a full flowering of art and drama during the Elizabethan age. While no book as brief as this can do full justice to a complex subject, the authors do succeed in portraying Elizabeth's strengths as a leader and in providing an intriguing invitation to further study.

These same authors collaborated in writing *Shaka: King of the Zulus;* Diane Stanley both wrote and illustrated *Peter the Great.* Fay Stanley, the mother of Diane Stanley, wrote *The Last Princess: The Story of Princess Ka'iulani of Hawai'i.* Clear, almost primitive paintings by Diane Stanley help to tell the poignant story of the betrayal of Hawaii by Americans and the sad death of her last princess at age 23.

Several picture-book biographies have been written about Mozart. In Julie Downing's *Mozart Tonight,* the composer rides with his wife in a rented carriage to the opening of his opera, *Don Giovanni.* As he reviews his life with his much-loved Constanza, he confides his hopes that this opera will be a huge success. The illustrations capture the drama of this particular night, conveying the artist's own enthusiasm and love for Mozart's music. In a long note at the end, she tells the reader of the research she did and that the detail and dialogue in the scenes are based on letters written by and about the Mozart family. Catherine Brighton's picture biography, *Mozart: Scenes from the Childhood of the Great Composer,* is told by Nannerl, his talented sister. The two children toured Europe together, giving many concerts, until Nannerl turned 16 and became a teacher of pianoforte. Her brother, however, was already composing and continued to tour with his father. Lisl Weil's *Wolferl: The First Six Years in the Life of Wolfgang Amadeus Mozart, 1756–1762* takes its title from the nickname that Nannerl gave to her little brother. These last two books are partial biographies that do not attempt to go beyond the childhood of this amazing musical genius.

In *The King's Day: Louis XIV of France,* Aliki presents only one day in the life of Louis XIV. Yet a single day in the life of the splendid Sun King reveals much about the man. Louis loved ceremony, and his entire day was planned from the special getting-up ritual called the *Lever* (which lasted for two hours) to the going-to-bed ceremony called the *Coucher*. Sometimes the public was allowed to watch the king as he dined alone on a menu that might include "four soups, a stuffed pheasant, a partridge, a duck, some mutton, sliced ham, three salads, boiled eggs, a dish of pastry, fruit, and compotes."[33] Aliki always includes details that intrigue children, but in so doing provides insight into the way her subjects lived.

In Jean Fritz's *What's the Big Idea, Ben Franklin?*, the droll pictures by Margot Tomes emphasize a particular side of Franklin's character—his ingenuity. Trina Schart Hyman's illustration of Samuel Adams thumbing his nose at the British flag helps set the tone for Fritz's biography, *Why Don't You Get a Horse, Sam Adams?* The same illustrator and author highlight their subject's vanity and penchant for flourishes in *Will You Sign Here, John Hancock?* Tomie de Paola's pictures for *Can't You Make Them Behave, King George?* emphasize Fritz's humor as she helps readers think of the unpopular English monarch in a new way.

A few picture books for older children focus on a subject's work and philosophy rather than his life. Ernest Raboff's series, "Art for Children," presents commentary and full-color reproductions of the work of great artists, along with brief biographical sketches. *Paul Klee, Marc Chagall,* and *Pablo Picasso* are among the subjects.

SIMPLIFIED BIOGRAPHIES

Not all children who have an interest in biographical information are in full command of the skills of reading. Some of these children are beginning readers; some read independently but are not ready for a long or complex text; some are older children with specialized interests but low skill levels. Various kinds of simplified biographies, usually short and with many illustrations, have been published in response to the needs of these children.

Many picture-book biographies, of course, are written in simple language that many primary-grade readers can handle on their own. David

Adler's *A Picture Book of Thomas Jefferson* and *A Picture Book of Benjamin Franklin* provide straightforward accounts of highlights from the lives of these two founding fathers. Companion books are available about George Washington, Abraham Lincoln, and John F. Kennedy as well as several other famous Americans. The advantage of these books is their readability and the support provided by their illustrations. The disadvantage is that in increasing readability, the author had to leave out many of the complexities of character and accomplishment that make these subjects memorable.

Aliki also writes and illustrates easy-vocabulary picture biographies. In *The Story of Johnny Appleseed*, she has captured the humor and simplicity of the legendary pioneer. Similar simplicity is communicated in *A Weed Is a Flower: The Life of George Washington Carver*. Again, Aliki has made meaningful for the youngest reader the inspiring story of a man who was born a slave but lived to become one of the greatest research scientists in the United States. Another picture biography by the same author is *The Many Lives of Benjamin Franklin*.

There are a number of biographies for newly independent readers that are not quite picture books but do have many illustrations as well as limited vocabularies. One of the disadvantages of this kind of writing, however, is that it does frequently sound stilted. Often the sentences are set up line by line for ease of reading, rather than in paragraph form. Unfortunately, this creates a choppy effect. This type of jerky sentence pattern is avoided in Gwenda Blair's *Laura Ingalls Wilder*, "A Beginning Biography" from Putnam. The vocabulary is more demanding than the size of the print would indicate. However, children know the details of this author's life so well from her stories and from television that the material already seems familiar, and this familiarity makes for easy reading. The smooth narrative covers the entire span of Laura's life in sixty-four pages, half of which are taken up by Thomas B. Allen's fine black-and-white drawings.

Few writers can produce a book that is both easy to read and admirable for its style. F. N. Monjo did it in his "I Can Read History Book," *The One Bad Thing About Father*. "Father" is Theodore Roosevelt, and the one bad thing about him, in his son Quentin's eyes, is that he is presi-

[33] Aliki, *The King's Day: Louis XIV of France* (New York: Crowell, 1989), unpaged.

dent of the United States and thus the whole family—including irrepressible sister Alice—must live in the White House.

> 🐦 Some man once asked Father why
> he didn't do something about Alice.
> Father said, "I can do one of two things.
> I can be President of the United States.
> Or I can control Alice.
> I cannot possibly do both."[34]

Many simple biographies are not just for beginning readers but are directed toward an 8- or 9-year-old audience. One account which is simply told but difficult to put down is Ann McGovern's *The Secret Soldier: The Story of Deborah Sampson*. Dressed as a man, Deborah Sampson fought in the American Revolution, managing to escape detection for more than a year. Newly proficient readers will appreciate the detail about Deborah's childhood as well as the format that breaks the text into manageable parts. An even simpler account of Deborah's life, told in lively, direct fashion by Bryna Stevens, is *Deborah Sampson Goes to War*.

The "Crowell Biography" series, with an emphasis on contemporary figures and those from minority populations, is directed to the 7- to 10-year-old age level. Though the books are produced by a variety of authors and illustrators, the formats are uniformly brief and are enhanced by many pictures. Eloise Greenfield has written the story of *Rosa Parks*, the black woman whose refusal to move to the back of a bus in Montgomery, Alabama, triggered events that grew into the civil rights movement. Other books in this fine series include *Cesar Chavez* by Ruth Franchere, *Mary McLeod Bethune* by Eloise Greenfield, and *Malcolm X* by Arnold Adoff.

Another series that aims at the 7- to 10-year-old audience is the Viking "Women of Our Time" series. These biographies are complete in that they cover the subject's life span (up to the time of writing for those women still living). Written by many different authors, they include some fine examples of lively language and thoughtful characterization.

However, each book is similar in length (fifty to sixty pages) with short chapters and several black-and-white drawings. These constraints prevent the authors from examining any subject in great depth or detail, so the format works to simplify the story. *Sandra Day O'Connor: Justice for All* by Beverly Gherman, *Margaret Mead: The World Was Her Family* by Susan Saunders, and *Astrid Lindgren: Storyteller to the World* by Johanna Hurwitz are just a few of the many titles in this series.

Some simplified biographies fall into the high interest–low reading level category, where the most popular subjects seem to be from the sports and entertainment worlds. The text in these books may be very brief and illustrations or photographs may be used very liberally. In short, the books are designed to catch and keep the eye of the reluctant or less able older reader. Unfortunately the writing in some of these books is heavily influenced by the tendency to "hype" a subject. While children do have a great appetite for personal close-ups of celebrities, it is difficult to find books of this type that are written with a sense of perspective and produced with care.

PARTIAL BIOGRAPHIES

One of the liberties allowed juvenile biographers is the freedom to write only part of the story of a subject's life. Authors are able to focus, if they wish, on a time of high drama and let the demands of constructing a good story help set the time frame for the book. David Kherdian deals with only a portion of the life of Veron Dumehjian, his mother, in *The Road from Home: The Story of an Armenian Girl*. What is central to the story is her family's suffering in the massacre and dispersal of Armenians by the Turks. If those events had been related as only a small part of her life experiences, their impact and historical significance might have been dulled. Kherdian also chose to assume his mother's first-person point of view, which adds passion and immediacy to this fictionalized biography.

Some partial biographies do furnish information about the subject's entire life, but focus on a few incidents that are particularly memorable. Other biographies are incomplete for the simple reason that a full treatment of the subject's complex life would make a book too long and unwieldy for

[34]F. N. Monjo, *The One Bad Thing About Father*, illustrated by Rocco Negri (New York: Harper & Row, 1970), p. 38.

young readers. There have been several such biographies of Abraham Lincoln, for instance. Carl Sandburg wrote a partial biography for children titled *Abe Lincoln Grows Up*. It was made from the first twenty-seven chapters of the first volume of the longest and most definitive of biographies of Lincoln for adults, Sandburg's *Abraham Lincoln: The Prairie Years*. For his juvenile biography Sandburg included Lincoln's birth and boyhood until he was 19 and "grown up." In singing prose that begs to be read aloud, the author describes Lincoln's desire for knowledge:

🌿 And some of what he wanted so much, so deep down, seemed to be in books. Maybe in books he would find the answers to dark questions pushing around in the pools of his thoughts, and the drifts of his mind.[35]

Two appealing biographical works about real young people in history serve to provide a limited but interesting view of famous figures who were close to them. Barbara Brenner's *On the Frontier with Mr. Audubon* is technically a partial biography of apprentice painter Joseph Mason. As a young teenager he accompanied John James Audubon on an expedition down the Mississippi River to collect and make life drawings of birds. Mason actually did supply some of the backgrounds for Audubon's *Birds of America* although his name did not appear on the finished paintings. Brenner used Audubon's diary to reconstruct the activities of their trip, then recreated the story as a journal that the apprentice might have kept, focusing on Audubon's obsession with his work.

Harriot Washington was one of several nieces and nephews who became wards of George Washington when their parents died. *Uncle George Washington and Harriot's Guitar* by Miriam Anne Bourne is based on Washington family letters written between 1790 and 1795. It shows Harriot as an obedient, lonely preadolescent at Mount Vernon, caring for two little cousins and longing for an instrument and music lessons. Our perception of "Uncle Washington," who finally provides

the wanted guitar, is enlarged by this firsthand look at his enormous family responsibilities. This is a book that younger middle graders can read for themselves.

Another partial biography of Washington is titled *George Washington Wasn't Always Old*. Author Alice Fleming pulls together what is known of her subject's childhood and young adulthood, up to his appointment as Major Washington of the Virginia militia when he was not quite 21. This book takes the perspective that Washington "wasn't anybody special" when he was a boy because no one knew how famous and important he would become, an idea with great appeal for children.

COMPLETE BIOGRAPHIES

Complete biography spans its subject's lifetime. It may be relatively simple or difficult, authentic or fictionalized. Whatever the case may be, the reader should expect a view that has some depth, some balance, some sense of perspective. Among types of biographies, this category has traditionally been the largest, although in recent years trends have favored other kinds of presentations.

Russell Freedman's *Franklin Delano Roosevelt* is an example of a biography that is complete and authentic. The inherent drama of the subject, the clarity of the writing, and the generous use of photographs all contribute to the book's appeal for readers age 10 and up. This fine biography sketches out Roosevelt's major achievements as a politician and statesman, but its real strength lies in the detailed information it provides about his personal life. Freedman probes the facade of a man who managed to be a very private person in spite of having the very public job of being president of the United States. Students are fascinated by the length to which Roosevelt went in order to camouflage his paralysis. He was hardly ever photographed in a wheelchair, but Freedman does provide one such picture.

Some of Jean Fritz's picture-book biographies could be classified as complete since they deal with the subjects' entire life spans, but she has also written longer books about Benedict Arnold in *Traitor*, Theodore Roosevelt in *Bully for You, Teddy Roosevelt!*, and General Thomas J. Jackson in *Stonewall*. All three deal with complex charac-

[35]Carl Sandburg, *Abe Lincoln Grows Up*, reprinted from *Abraham Lincoln: The Prairie Years*, illustrated by James Daugherty (New York: Harcourt, Brace, 1975), p. 135.

Russell Freedman's choice of photographs for *Franklin Delano Roosevelt* shows many aspects of the subject's life, including his roles as son, husband, and father.

🐛 🐛 🐛

ters in an even-handed way. In *Stonewall*, for instance, Fritz contrasts the general's heroic Civil War battlefield behavior against his personal idiosyncrasies. The man who kept his line "standing like a stone wall" at Manassas prescribed unusual diets for himself (stale bread and lean meat, or lemons to suck) and lived by arbitrary, self-imposed rules for posture, prayer, and every other form of human conduct. Throughout the book the authentic narrative is enlivened by personal observations and quotes from Jackson's contemporaries. Sources for these quotes are listed in a bibliography of nearly forty items. Like her other biographies, *Stonewall* demonstrates the author's high standards for careful scholarship as well as vivid writing.

Among the many complete biographies for children are a few that have been awarded the Newbery Medal. One of these is the story of a little known black pioneer of freedom. *Amos Fortune, Free Man* by Elizabeth Yates is the moving account of a common man who lived simply and greatly. Born free in Africa, he was sold as a slave in North America. In time he purchased his own freedom and that of several others. When he was 80 years old, Amos Fortune purchased

twenty-five acres of land in the shadow of his beloved mountain, Monadnock—meaning "the mountain that stands alone." Like Monadnock, Fortune stood alone, a rock of strength and security for all those he loved.

Children who have a special interest in the arts may be intrigued by another Newbery winner, *I, Juan de Pareja*. Since so little is known about the life of Velázquez and his celebrated black assistant, Elizabeth Borten de Treviño had to invent a great deal of material for her story. The fascination of Juan's life lies in his beginnings as a slave, his secret and remarkable talent for his master's business of painting, and the growth of their relationship from master and slave to equals and friends.

Frequently, biographers choose subjects who are credited with unique achievements, whatever the field. Most authors would be dubious about writing an interesting biography for children about a mathematician, but Jean Lee Latham was challenged. She studied mathematics, astronomy, oceanography, and seamanship. Then she went to Boston and Salem to talk with descendants of Nathaniel Bowditch and to do research on the geographical and maritime backgrounds of her story. The result of all this painstaking preparation was the Newbery award winner *Carry On, Mr. Bowditch*, the amazing story of Nat Bowditch, who had little chance for schooling but mastered the secrets of navigation and wrote a textbook that was used for more than a hundred years.

A more recent Newbery Medal winner is Russell Freedman's *Lincoln: A Photobiography*. One of the great accomplishments of this book is its groundbreaking use of archival photographs, not just to break and decorate the text, but to seriously extend the reader's understanding of the subject. Yet the text stands as an accomplishment in its own right as a comprehensive, insightful, and readable account of a complex person living in a complicated time. It is very difficult to bring fresh perspective, as Freedman has done, to a story that has been so often told.

COLLECTIVE BIOGRAPHIES

Many children looking for biographical information want brief material about specific people or about specific endeavors. Many collective biographies have been published to meet this need. In

---

RESOURCES FOR TEACHING

◆ AUTHOR AUTOBIOGRAPHIES ◆

Ashabranner, Brent. *The Times of My Life: A Memoir.* Dutton, 1990. (Grade 5–up)

Bulla, Clyde. *A Grain of Wheat: A Writer Begins.* Godine, 1985. (Grades 2–6)

Cleary, Beverly. *A Girl from Yamhill: A Memoir.* Morrow, 1988. (Grade 5–up)

Crews, Donald. *Bigmama's.* Greenwillow, 1991. (Grades 1–4)

Dahl, Roald. *Boy: Tales of Childhood.* Farrar, Straus, 1984. (Grade 5–up)

De Paola, Tomie. *The Art Lesson.* Putnam, 1989. (Grades 1–4)

Duncan, Lois. *Chapters: My Growth as a Writer.* Little, Brown, 1982. (Grade 5–up)

Foreman, Michael. *War Boy: A Country Childhood.* Arcade, 1990. (Grades 4–6)

Fritz, Jean. *Homesick: My Own Story,* illustrated by Margot Tomes. Putnam, 1982. (Grade 5–up)

Hyman, Trina Schart. *Self-Portrait: Trina Schart Hyman.* HarperCollins, 1989. (Grades 2–5)

Little, Jean. *Little by Little: A Writer's Childhood.* Penguin, 1988. (Grade 5–up)

Meltzer, Milton. *Starting from Home: A Writer's Beginnings.* Penguin, 1988. (Grade 5–up)

Naylor, Phyllis Reynolds. *How I Came to Be a Writer.* Aladdin, 1987. (Grade 5–up)

Paulsen, Gary. *Woodsong.* Bradbury, 1990. (Grade 5–up)

Peet, Bill. *Bill Peet: An Autobiography.* Houghton Mifflin, 1989. (Grade 3–up)

Stevenson, James. *Higher on the Door.* Greenwillow, 1987. (Grades 2–5)

_____. *When I Was Nine.* Greenwillow, 1986. (Grades 2–5)

---

scope and difficulty they run the gamut—some have one-paragraph sketches of many subjects, others have long essays on just a few. Like other books, collective biographies must be judged on more than title and appearance.

Russell Freedman's *The Wright Brothers: How They Invented the Airplane* is an outstanding biography of two people whose lives and work were so closely intertwined that it would be difficult to choose just one to write about. Using archival photographs as he has done in other books, Freedman reconstructs the engrossing story that led to Kitty Hawk and many years of achievement thereafter. In the process he illuminates the character and commitment of both Wilbur and Orville Wright.

Collective biographies seldom deal with subjects whose stories can be woven together in this way. Most have many brief entries about individuals whose interests or accomplishments are similar. Two such books are *Inspirations: Stories About Women Artists* by Leslie Sills and *Take a Walk in Their Shoes* by Glennette Tilley Turner. This last book introduces fourteen African Americans who played a part in the struggle for racial equality. An unusual feature is the inclusion of brief dramas that can be performed by children to highlight the contribution of each subject. Martin Luther King, Jr., Rosa Parks, Arthur Schomburg, Leontyne Price, Frederick Douglass, and "Satchel" Paige are a few of the prominent African Americans featured in this book.

The "Great Lives" Series offers well-written accounts of achievers in many fields. Doris Faber and Harold Faber are the authors of *Nature and the Environment,* which includes twenty-five biographical sketches spanning almost two centuries. Read individually, each sketch is clear and furnishes the context necessary for understanding its subject. Read as a whole, the book provides excellent perspective on our changing ideas about humans' relationships to their environment. Some of the other titles in this series are *American Government,* also by Doris and Harold Faber; *Exploration* by Milton Lomask; *Sports* by George Sullivan; and *Human Rights* by William Jay Jacobs.

AUTOBIOGRAPHIES AND MEMOIRS

Life stories are often recalled and written down by the subjects themselves, as autobiographies or memoirs. Some children's books based on autobiographical material have been discussed earlier in this chapter as historical fiction. Autobiography has advantages and disadvantages similar to those of informational books of eyewitness history—the warmth and immediacy of personal detail, but a necessarily limited perspective. The criterion of objectivity is reversed here; it is the very subjectivity of this sort of biography that has value. But children do need to be aware of the inherent bias, and they may be encouraged to look to other sources for balance.

Autobiographies by creators of children's books provide an easy introduction to this specialized form of writing. Children who are familiar with books illustrated by Trina Schart Hyman should be able to pick out motifs and characters from them that also appear in *Self-Portrait: Trina Schart Hyman*. The tone of the text, as well as the art, provides clues to character; the writing is sometimes breezy, sometimes intense. The fine photo-biographies in the "Meet the Author" series are written as brief letters to children. Rafe Martin's *A Storyteller's Story*, Cynthia Rylant's *Best Wishes*, and Jane Yolen's *A Letter from Phoenix Farm* show each author at home with their families and pets; clear maps locate where they live. Each author tells something about his or her writing process.

Other popular writers provide longer life stories. In *The Moon and I*, a humorous memoir, Betsy Byars realizes her childhood dream of having a pet snake and reveals much about herself. Some authors focus on their work, explaining the process of writing a book and adding advice for students who dream of writing for publication. *How I Came to Be a Writer* by Phyllis Reynolds Naylor reveals the same wit as her realistic novels.

Chapters: My Growth as a Writer is Lois Duncan's account of her early successes and later development. Roald Dahl in *Boy: Tales of Childhood* recounts stories of his early family life and incidents from his boarding school days, including one that became a scene in one of his own novels.

Beverly Cleary's memoir, *A Girl from Yamhill*, speaks to adults who have read her books, as well as to older students. Careful readers will catch many glimpses of her popular character Ramona Quimby in Cleary's own childhood. The difficult relationship with her mother that she portrays in the book is particularly good for generating discussion.

A few of the memoirs by authors for children are compiled in the box on page 649. Most of the books for primary grades do not give complete coverage but are based on a single autobiographical incident.

Biographies of all types give children a glimpse of other lives, other places, other times. The best of them combine accurate information and fine writing in a context that children enjoy—the story that really happened. Both biography and historical fiction serve to put facts into a frame of human feeling. Children may come to know about historical events or contemporary figures from textbooks, but literature that touches this content will bring them a different quality of knowing—more intimate and more memorable. All children deserve to have such books as part of their experience.

SUGGESTED LEARNING EXPERIENCES

1. Read four or five books about one particular period or place and chart the references to kinds of food, clothing, houses, transportation, language, and so on. Evaluate which books give the most authentic picture.

2. Prepare a decorated portfolio or box of materials of a particular event or period of time to help children build background for selected books of historical fiction. You may want to include copies of newspaper clippings, artifacts, an annotated bibliography, copies of appropriate paperback books, and examples of art, music, and handcrafts. Plan activity cards for children's use and extension of these materials. (See description of jackdaws in Chapter 13.)

3. Work with classmates or middle-grade students in role-playing dramatic confrontations in historical fiction. Some possible choices would be the witch trial of Kit Tyler in *The Witch of Blackbird Pond* by Speare or Sam Meeker's argument with his father about going to war in *My Brother Sam Is Dead* by the Colliers.

4. Collect examples of dialogue and descriptive language from several books of historical fiction. You might want to include something by Patricia Beatty, Paul Fleischman, or Rosemary Sutcliff in this sample. What techniques do the authors use to indicate the setting?

5. Compare the values and attitudes of the heroine of *Lyddie* by Katherine Paterson with those of a young heroine in a contemporary novel, such as Dicey in *Dicey's Song* by Voigt. What are their hopes and expectations? How do they express themselves? How are their priorities different or alike?

6. Compare a picture storybook such as *Rose Blanche* by Christophe Gallaz and Roberto Innocenti, a fantasy such as *The Devil's Arithmetic* by Jane Yolen, and a realistic adventure like *Hide and Seek* by Ida Vos. What does each genre do that is unique? How much information do you receive? Chart the differences and similarities.

7. Look at the selection of biographies in a school library. Make a checklist of how many biographies are about men, how many about women. What people have been the subject of many biographies? Few? One? What contemporary figures are presented in these biographies?

8. Gather several picture-book biographies or simplified biographies with many illustrations. What information appears in the pictures but not the text? How do the illustrations help create focus and characterization?

9. Select several biographies of one subject, such as Christopher Columbus. Make a chart to compare information, omissions, point of view of author, extent of documentation. *Christopher Columbus: The Great Adventure* by Delno and Jean West, *Christopher Columbus: Voyager to the Unknown* by Nancy Smiler Levinson, and *Where Do You Think You're Going, Christopher Columbus?* by Jean Fritz are good possibilities. Read related informational books or historical fiction that would extend the focus, such as *I, Columbus: My Journal—1492* edited by Peter and Connie Roop, *If You Were There in 1492* by Barbara Brenner, or *Pedro's Journal* by Pam Conrad. Consider the ways in which a broader range of information makes you a more discriminating reader.

RELATED READINGS

1. Collier, Christopher. "Johnny and Sam: Old and New Approaches to the American Revolution," *The Horn Book Magazine,* vol. 52 (April 1976), pp. 132–138.

    One of the co-authors of popular novels about the Revolution discusses three historiographic interpretations of that conflict and contends that modern historical fiction should not present historical events in simple or one-sided terms.

2. Fritz, Jean. "The Very Truth," in *Celebrating Children's Books,* ed. by Betsy Hearne and Marilyn Kaye. New York: Lothrop, Lee and Shepard, 1981, pp. 81–86.

    One of the very best writers of juvenile biography addresses the issue of censorship and discusses the necessity for telling all the truth.

3. Haugaard, Erik Christian. "'Before I Was Born': History and the Child," *The Horn Book Magazine,* vol. 55 (October 1979), pp. 514–521.

    The author writes of the relationship between history and truth and makes an eloquent case for the values of history in showing that people always have choices.

4. Hunter, Mollie. "Shoulder the Sky," in *Talent Is Not Enough.* New York: Harper & Row, 1976, pp. 31–56.

    A fine writer reveals her sense of history as human drama while discussing several issues critical to historical fiction, including the portrayal of violence and the relationship of contemporary attitudes to those of the past.

5. Levstik, Linda S. "Research Directions: Mediating Content Through Literary Texts," *Language Arts,* vol. 67 (December 1990), pp. 848–853.

    This article looks at the connection between historical literature and children's ability to think carefully about history's moral and interpretive issues. It is based on a series of studies with children and provides good evidence of the role historical fiction can play in content learning.

6.   *The Lion and the Unicorn,* vol. 4, no. 1 (Summer 1980).
         This entire issue is devoted to Biography for Young People. Of special interest are Elizabeth Segel's article about a biography of Beatrix Potter, Leonard Marcus's comments on picture-book biographies for children, and an interview with Milton Meltzer by Geraldine DeLuca and Roni Natov.

7.   Meltzer, Milton. "Selective Forgetfulness: Christopher Columbus Reconsidered," *The New Advocate,* vol. 5 (Winter 1992), pp. 1–9.
         A writer of fine complete biographies discusses the dark side of the story of Columbus, namely his treatment of the Indians. He quotes letters and Columbus's own journal as documentation. These are included in his biography, *Columbus and the World Around Him* (Franklin Watts, 1990).

8.   Rudman, Masha K., and Rosenberg, Susan P. "Confronting History: Holocaust Books for Children," *The New Advocate,* vol. 4 (Summer 1991), pp. 163–177.
         This practical article discusses several different aspects of Holocaust literature for young people. Specific books are grouped in such categories as "Survivors," "Rescuers," "Group Responsibility," and "Jewish Rescuers and Resistance."

9.   Segel, Elizabeth. "Laura Ingalls Wilder's America: An Unflinching Assessment," *Children's Literature in Education,* no. 25 (Summer 1977), pp. 63–70.
         Segel examines the values portrayed in the Little House series, particularly *Little House on the Prairie,* and points out that Wilder, through the character of Laura, not only presented the attitudes and beliefs of nineteenth-century America but also questioned them.

10. Stanley, Diane. "Picture Book History," *The New Advocate,* vol. 1 (Fall 1988), pp. 209–220.
         The author and illustrator of several picture-book biographies of historical figures describes the difficulties of providing accurate pictures. The background details about *Shaka, King of the Zulus* are interesting to children as well as adults.

11. Zarnowski, Myra. *Learning About Biographies: A Reading-and-Writing Approach for Children.* Urbana, Ill.: National Council of Teachers of English and the National Council on Social Studies, 1990.
         Teachers of upper elementary and middle school students will find many resources here for helping children understand the tasks and responsibilities of a biographer. Discussion of the genre, guides for classroom work, and a bibliography are included.

REFERENCES

HISTORICAL FICTION

Almedingen, E. M. *The Crimson Oak.* Coward McCann, 1983.

Anderson, Joan. *The First Thanksgiving Feast,* photographs by George Ancona. Clarion, 1983.

Anderson, Margaret J. *The Journey of the Shadow Bairns.* Knopf, 1980.

_____. *Searching for Shona.* Knopf, 1989 (1979).

Angell, Judie. *One-Way to Ansonia.* Bradbury, 1985.

Armstrong, William H. *Sounder,* illustrated by James Barkley. Harper, 1969.

Avi (Wortis). *The Fighting Ground.* Lippincott, 1984.

_____. *The True Confessions of Charlotte Doyle.* Orchard, 1990.

Bawden, Nina. *Carrie's War,* illustrated by Colleen Browning. Lippincott, 1973.

Beatty, Patricia. *Be Ever Hopeful, Hannalee.* Morrow, 1988.

_____. *Charley Skedaddle.* Morrow, 1987.

_____. *Jayhawker.* Morrow, 1991.

_____. *Turn Homeward, Hannalee.* Morrow, 1984.

_____. *Wait for Me, Watch for Me, Eula Bee.* Troll, 1986.

Behn, Harry. *The Faraway Lurs.* Putnam, 1982 (1963).

Bishop, Claire Huchet. *Twenty and Ten,* as told by Janet Jolly, illustrated by William Pène du Bois. Viking, 1964.

Blos, Joan W. *A Gathering of Days: A New England Girl's Journal, 1830–32.* Scribner's, 1979.

Brennan, J. H. *Shiva: An Adventure of the Ice Age.* Lippincott, 1989.

Brink, Carol Ryrie. *Caddie Woodlawn,* illustrated by Trina Schart Hyman. Macmillan, 1973.

_____. *Caddie Woodlawn,* illustrated by Kate Seredy. Macmillan, 1936.

Bulla, Clyde Robert. *A Lion to Guard Us,* illustrated by Michele Chessare. Harper Trophy, 1990 (1981).

_____. *The Sword in the Tree,* illustrated by Paul Galdone. Crowell, 1956.

Butterworth, Emma Macalik. *As the Waltz Was Ending.* Four Winds, 1982.

Choi, Sook Nyul. *Year of Impossible Goodbyes*. Houghton, 1991.
Clapp, Patricia. *Constance: A Story of Early Plymouth*. Lothrop, 1968.
_____. *Witches' Children*. Lothrop, 1982.
Collier, James Lincoln, and Christopher Collier. *Jump Ship to Freedom*. Delacorte, 1981.
_____. *My Brother Sam Is Dead*. Four Winds, 1974.
_____. *War Comes to Willy Freeman*. Delacorte, 1983.
_____. *Who Is Carrie?* Delacorte, 1984.
Conrad, Pam. *Pedro's Journal*. Harper, 1991.
_____. *Prairie Songs*, illustrated by Darryl Zudeck. Harper, 1985.
Cooney, Barbara. *Hattie and the Wild Waves*. Viking, 1990.
_____. *Island Boy*. Viking, 1988.
Cooper, Susan. *Dawn of Fear*, illustrated by Margery Gill. Harcourt, 1970.
Dalgliesh, Alice. *The Courage of Sarah Noble*, illustrated by Leonard Weisgard. Scribner's, 1954.
_____. *The Thanksgiving Story*, illustrated by Helen Sewell. Scribner's, 1954.
deAngeli, Marguerite. *The Door in the Wall*. Doubleday, 1949.
_____. *Thee, Hannah!* Doubleday, 1949.
DeJong, Meindert. *The House of Sixty Fathers*, illustrated by Maurice Sendak. Harper, 1956.
Dickinson, Peter. *The Dancing Bear*, illustrated by John Smee. Little, Brown, 1972.
Dionetti, Michelle. *Coal Mine Peaches*, illustrated by Anita Riggio. Orchard, 1991.
Dyer, T. A. *A Way of His Own*. Houghton Mifflin, 1981.
Edmonds, Walter D. *The Matchlock Gun*, illustrated by Paul Lantz. Dodd, Mead, 1941.
Edwards, Sally. *George Midgett's War*. Scribner's, 1985.
Field, Rachel. *Calico Bush*, illustrated by Allen Lewis. Macmillan, 1931.
Fleischman, Paul. *The Borning Room*. Harper, 1991.
_____. *Saturnalia*. Harper, 1990.
Fleischman, Sid. *Humbug Mountain*, illustrated by Eric Von Schmidt. Little, Brown, 1978.
_____. *Mr. Mysterious and Company*, illustrated by Eric Von Schmidt. Little, Brown, 1962.
Forbes, Esther. *Johnny Tremain*, illustrated by Lynd Ward. Houghton Mifflin, 1946.
Fox, Paula. *The Slave Dancer*, illustrated by Eros Keith. Bradbury, 1973.
Frank, Anne. *Anne Frank: The Diary of a Young Girl*, rev. ed., translated by B. M. Mooyart, introduction by Eleanor Roosevelt. Doubleday, 1967.
Fritz, Jean. *Brady*, illustrated by Lynd Ward. Coward McCann, Penguin, 1987 (1960).
_____. *The Cabin Faced West*, illustrated by Feodor Rojankovsky. Coward McCann, 1958.
_____. *Early Thunder*, illustrated by Lynd Ward. Coward McCann, 1967.
Gallaz, Christophe. *Rose Blanche*, illustrated by Roberto Innocenti. Creative Education, 1985.
Garfield, Leon. *Jack Holborn*, illustrated by Anthony Maitland. Pantheon, 1965.
_____. *Smith*, illustrated by Anthony Maitland. Pantheon, 1967.
Garrigue, Sheila. *The Eternal Spring of Mr. Ito*. Bradbury, 1985.
Gauch, Patricia L. *This Time, Tempe Wick?*, illustrated by Margot Tomes. Putnam's, 1974.
_____. *Thunder at Gettysburg*, illustrated by Stephen Gammell. Putnam's, 1990 (1975).
Gipson, Fred. *Old Yeller*, illustrated by Carl Burger. Harper, 1956.
Gray, Elizabeth Janet. *Adam of the Road*, illustrated by Robert Lawson. Viking, 1944.
Greene, Bette. *The Summer of My German Soldier*. Bantam, 1984 (1973).
Gregory, Kristiana. *Jenny of the Tetons*. Harcourt, 1989.
Gross, Virginia T. *The Day It Rained Forever*, illustrated by Ronald Himler. Viking, 1991.
Hahn, Mary Downing. *Stepping on the Cracks*. Clarion, 1991.
Hamilton, Virginia. *Anthony Burns: The Defeat and Triumph of a Fugitive Slave*. Knopf, 1988.
Harvey, Brett. *Immigrant Girl: Beck of Eldridge Street*, illustrated by Deborah K. Ray. Holiday, 1987.
Hautzig, Esther. *The Endless Steppe: Growing Up in Siberia*. Crowell, 1968.
Highwater, Jamake. *Legend Days*. Harper, 1984.
Ho, Minfong. *The Clay Marble*. Farrar, 1991.
Holm, Anne, *North to Freedom*, translated by L. W. Kingsland. Harcourt, 1965.
Hooks, William H. *Circle of Fire*. Atheneum, 1984.
Hudson, Jan. *Sweetgrass*. Philomel, 1989.
Hunt, Irene. *Across Five Aprils*. Follett, 1964.
Hunter, Mollie. *The Stronghold*. Harper, 1974.
_____. *You Never Knew Her as I Did!* Harper, 1981.
Keith, Harold. *Rifles for Watie*. Crowell, 1957.
Kelly, Eric P. *The Trumpeter of Krakow*, rev. ed., illustrated by Janina Domanska. Macmillan, 1966 (1928).

Kerr, Judith. *When Hitler Stole Pink Rabbit*. Coward McCann, 1972.

Koehn, Ilse. *Mischling, Second Degree: My Childhood in Nazi Germany*. Greenwillow, 1977.

Konigsburg, E. L. *A Proud Taste for Scarlet and Miniver*. Atheneum, 1973.

Kroeber, Theodora. *Ishi, Last of His Tribe*, illustrated by Ruth Robbins. Parnassus, 1964.

Kudlinski, Kathleen V. *Hero over Here*, illustrated by Bert Dodson. Viking, 1990.

Lasky, Kathryn. *Beyond the Divide*. Macmillan, 1983.

Levitin, Sonia. *Journey to America*, illustrated by Charles Robinson. Atheneum, 1970.

Levoy, Myron. *Alan and Naomi*. Harper Trophy, 1987 (1977).

Lowry, Lois. *Number the Stars*. Houghton Mifflin, 1989.

McGraw, Eloise Jarvis. *The Golden Goblet*. Viking Penguin, 1986 (1961).

_____. *Mara, Daughter of the Nile*. Viking Penguin, 1985 (1953).

_____. *Moccasin Trail*. Viking Penguin, 1986 (1952).

MacLachlan, Patricia. *Sarah, Plain and Tall*. Harper, 1985.

_____. *Three Names*, illustrated by Alexander Pertzoff. Harper, 1991.

McSwigan, Marie. *Snow Treasure*, illustrated by Mary Reardon. Dutton, 1942.

Maruki, Toshi. *Hiroshima No Pika*. Lothrop, 1980.

Matas, Carol. *Lisa's War*. Scribner's, 1987.

Moeri, Louise. *Save Queen of Sheba*. Dutton, 1981.

Monjo, F. N. *The Drinking Gourd*, illustrated by Fred Brenner. Harper, 1970.

Morimoto, Junko. *My Hiroshima*. Viking, 1987.

Morpurgo, Michael. *Waiting for Anya*. Viking, 1990.

Morrow, Honoré. *On to Oregon!* Beech Tree, 1991 (1946).

O'Dell, Scott. *Island of the Blue Dolphins*. Houghton Mifflin, 1960. (Reissued)

_____. *Sarah Bishop*. Houghton Mifflin, 1980.

_____. *Sing Down the Moon*. Houghton Mifflin, 1970.

_____. *Zia*, illustrated by Ted Lewin. Houghton Mifflin, 1976.

Orlev, Uri. *The Island on Bird Street*, translated from the Hebrew by Hillel Halkin. Houghton Mifflin, 1984.

Paterson, Katherine. *Lyddie*. Dutton, 1991.

Pearson, Kit. *The Sky Is Falling*. Viking, 1989.

Pellowski, Anne. *First Farm in the Valley: Anna's Story*, illustrated by Wendy Watson. Philomel, 1982.

Perez, N. A. *The Slopes of War*. Houghton Mifflin, 1984.

Petry, Ann. *Tituba of Salem Village*. Crowell, 1964.

Pryor, Bonnie. *The House on Maple Street*, illustrated by Beth Peck. Morrow, 1987.

_____. *Seth of the Lion People*. Morrow, 1988.

Reeder, Carolyn. *Shades of Gray*. Macmillan, 1989.

Reiss, Johanna. *The Journey Back*. Crowell, 1976.

_____. *The Upstairs Room*. Crowell, 1972.

Richter, Conrad. *The Light in the Forest*. Knopf, 1953.

Rinaldi, Ann. *A Ride into Morning*. Harcourt, 1991.

Riskind, Mary. *Apple Is My Sign*. Houghton Mifflin, 1981.

Rostkowski, Margaret I. *After the Dancing Days*. Harper, 1986.

Roth-Hano, Renée. *Touch Wood: A Girlhood in Occupied France*. Viking Puffin, 1989.

Sebestyen, Ouida. *Words by Heart*. Little, Brown, 1979.

Siegal, Aranka. *Upon the Head of the Goat: A Childhood in Hungary, 1939–1944*. Farrar, Straus, 1981.

Sewall, Marcia. *The People of the Breaking Day*. Atheneum, 1990.

_____. *The Pilgrims of Plimoth*. Atheneum, 1986.

Speare, Elizabeth George. *The Bronze Bow*. Houghton Mifflin, 1961.

_____. *Calico Captive*, illustrated by W. T. Mars. Houghton Mifflin, 1957.

_____. *The Sign of the Beaver*. Houghton Mifflin, 1983.

_____. *The Witch of Blackbird Pond*. Houghton Mifflin, 1958.

Steele, William O. *The Buffalo Knife*, illustrated by Paul Galdone. Harcourt, 1952.

_____. *Flaming Arrows*, illustrated by Paul Galdone. Harcourt, 1957.

_____. *Winter Danger*, illustrated by Paul Galdone. Harcourt, 1954.

Stevens, Carla. *Trouble for Lucy*, illustrated by Ronald Himler. Clarion, 1979.

Stolz, Mary. *Bartholomew Fair*. Greenwillow, 1990.

Sutcliff, Rosemary. *The Eagle of the Ninth*, illustrated by C. W. Hodges. Walck, 1954.

_____. *Flame-Colored Taffeta*. Farrar, 1986.

_____. *The Lantern Bearers*, illustrated by Charles Keeping. Walck, 1959.

_____. *The Shining Company*. Farrar, Straus, 1990.

_____. *The Silver Branch*, illustrated by Charles Keeping. Walck, 1959.

_____. *Sun Horse, Moon Horse*. Dutton, 1978.

Taylor, Mildred. *Let the Circle Be Unbroken*. Dial, 1981.

_____. *Mississippi Bridge*, illustrated by Max Ginsburg. Dial, 1990.

_____. *Roll of Thunder, Hear My Cry*, illustrated by Jerry Pinkney. Dial, 1976.

_____. *Song of the Trees*, illustrated by Jerry Pinkney. Dial, 1975.

Taylor, Theodore. *The Cay*. Doubleday, 1989 (1969).

Turner, Ann. *Dakota Dugout*, illustrated by Ronald Himler. Macmillan, 1985.

_____. *Grasshopper Summer*. Macmillan, 1989.

_____. *Nettie's Trip South*, illustrated by Ronald Himler. Macmillan, 1987.

_____. *Time of the Bison*, illustrated by Beth Peck. Macmillan, 1987.

Uchida, Yoshiko. *Journey to Topaz*, illustrated by Donald Carrick. Scribner's, 1971.

Vander Els, Betty. *The Bombers' Moon*. Farrar, Straus, 1985.

Vos, Ida. *Hide and Seek*, translated by Terese Edelstein and Inez Smidt. Houghton Mifflin, 1991.

Westall, Robert. *The Machine Gunners*. Greenwillow, 1976.

Wibberley, Leonard. *John Treegate's Musket*. Farrar, Straus, 1959.

Wild, Margaret. *Let the Celebrations Begin!* illustrated by Julie Vivas. Orchard, 1991.

Wilder, Laura Ingalls. *The First Four Years*, illustrated by Garth Williams. Harper, 1971.

_____. *By the Shores of Silver Lake*, illustrated by Garth Williams. Harper, 1953 (1939).

_____. *Little House in the Big Woods*, illustrated by Garth Williams. Harper, 1953 (1932).

_____. *Farmer Boy*, illustrated by Garth Williams. Harper, 1953 (1933).

_____. *Little House on the Prairie*, illustrated by Garth Williams. Harper, 1953 (1935).

_____. *Little Town on the Prairie*, illustrated by Garth Williams. Harper, 1953 (1941).

_____. *The Long Winter*, illustrated by Garth Williams. Harper, 1953 (1940).

_____. *On the Banks of Plum Creek*, illustrated by Garth Williams. Harper, 1953 (1937).

_____. *These Happy Golden Years*, illustrated by Garth Williams. Harper, 1953 (1943).

Wisler, G. Clifton. *Red Cap*. Dutton, 1991.

Yep, Laurence. *Dragonwings*. Harper, 1977.

_____. *Mountain Light*. Harper, 1985.

_____. *The Star Fisher*. Morrow, 1991.

_____. *The Serpent's Children*. Harper, 1984.

Yolen, Jane. *The Devil's Arithmetic*. Viking Penguin, 1990.

BIOGRAPHY

Adler, David A. *A Picture Book of Benjamin Franklin*, illustrated by John and Alexandra Wallner. Holiday, 1990.

_____. *A Picture Book of Christopher Columbus*, illustrated by John and Alexandra Wallner. Holiday, 1991.

_____. *A Picture Book of Martin Luther King, Jr.*, illustrated by Robert Casilla. Holiday, 1989.

_____. *A Picture Book of Thomas Jefferson*, illustrated by John and Alexandra Wallner. Holiday, 1990.

Adoff, Arnold. *Malcolm X*, illustrated by John Wilson. Harper Trophy, 1988 (1970).

Aliki. *The King's Day: Louis XIV of France*. Crowell, 1989.

_____. *The Many Lives of Benjamin Franklin*. Little Simon, 1988 (1977).

_____. *The Story of Johnny Appleseed*. Prentice Hall, 1987 (1963).

_____. *A Weed Is a Flower: The Life of George Washington Carver*. Little Simon, 1988 (1965).

d'Aulaire, Ingri, and Edgar Parin d'Aulaire. *Abraham Lincoln*. Rev. ed. Doubleday, 1957.

_____. *Benjamin Franklin*. Zephyr, 1987 (1950)

_____. *Columbus*. Zephyr, 1987 (1955).

_____. *George Washington*. Doubleday, 1936.

_____. *Pocahontas*. Doubleday, 1985 (1949).

Barth, Edna. *I'm Nobody! Who Are You? The Story of Emily Dickinson*, illustrated by Richard Cuffari. Clarion, 1979.

Blair, Gwenda. *Laura Ingalls Wilder*, illustrated by Thomas B. Allen. Putnam's, 1981.

Blos, Joan. *The Heroine of the Titanic: A Tale Both True and Otherwise of the Life of Molly Brown*, illustrated by Tennessee Dixon. Morrow, 1991.

Bourne, Miriam Anne. *Uncle George Washington and Harriot's Guitar*, illustrated by Elise Primavera. Coward, 1983.

Brenner, Barbara. *If You Were There in 1492*. Bradbury, 1991.

————. *On the Frontier with Mr. Audubon*. Coward, 1977.

Brighton, Catherine. *Mozart: Scenes from the Childhood of the Great Composer*. Doubleday, 1990.

Byars, Betsy. *The Moon and I*. Messner, 1991.

Clayton, Ed. *Martin Luther King: The Peaceful Warrior*, illustrated by David Hodges. Minstrel, 1986 (1968).

Cleary, Beverly. *A Girl from Yamhill: A Memoir*. Morrow, 1988.

Conrad, Pam. *Prairie Visions: The Life and Times of Solomon Butcher*. HarperCollins, 1991.

Dahl, Roald. *Boy: Tales of Childhood*. Farrar, Straus, 1984.

de Treviño, Elizabeth Borten. *I, Juan de Pareja*. Sunburst, 1987 (1965).

Downing, Julie. *Mozart Tonight*. Bradbury, 1991.

Duncan, Lois. *Chapters: My Growth as a Writer*. Little, Brown, 1982.

Faber, Doris. *Eleanor Roosevelt, First Lady of the World*, illustrated by Donna Ruff. Viking, 1985.

Faber, Doris, and Harold Faber. *American Government: Great Lives*. Scribner's, 1988.

————. *Nature and the Environment: Great Lives*. Scribner's, 1991.

Fisher, Leonard Everett. *Prince Henry, the Navigator*. Macmillan, 1990.

Fleming, Alice. *George Washington Wasn't Always Old*, illustrated by Bert Dodson. Simon & Schuster, 1991.

Foreman, Michael. *War Boy: A Country Childhood*. Arcade, 1990.

Franchere, Ruth. *Cesar Chavez*, illustrated by Earl Thollander. Harper Trophy, 1988 (1970).

Freedman, Russell. *Franklin Delano Roosevelt*. Clarion, 1990.

————. *Lincoln: A Photobiography*. Clarion, 1987.

————. *The Wright Brothers: How They Invented the Airplane*. Holiday, 1991.

Fritz, Jean. *And Then What Happened, Paul Revere?* illustrated by Margot Tomes. Coward, 1973.

————. *Bully for You, Teddy Roosevelt!* illustrated by Mike Wimmer. Putnam's, 1991.

————. *Can't You Make Them Behave, King George?* illustrated by Tomie de Paola. Coward, 1982.

————. *China Homecoming*. Putnam's, 1985.

————. *The Great Little Madison*. Putnam's, 1989.

————. *Homesick: My Own Story*, illustrated by Margot Tomes. Putnam's, 1982.

————. *Stonewall*, illustrated by Stephen Gammell. Putnam's, 1979.

————. *Traitor: The Case of Benedict Arnold*. Putnam's, 1981.

————. *What's the Big Idea, Ben Franklin?* illustrated by Margot Tomes. Coward, 1982.

————. *Where Do You Think You're Going, Christopher Columbus?* illustrated by Margot Tomes. Putnam's, 1980.

————. *Why Don't You Get a Horse, Sam Adams?* illustrated by Trina Schart Hyman. Coward, 1982.

————. *Will You Sign Here, John Hancock?* illustrated by Trina Schart Hyman. Coward, 1982.

Gherman, Beverly. *Sandra Day O'Connor: Justice for All*, illustrated by Robert Masheris. Viking, 1991.

Greenfield, Eloise. *Mary McLeod Bethune*, illustrated by Jerry Pinkney. Crowell, 1977.

————. *Rosa Parks*, illustrated by Eric Marlow. Crowell, 1973.

Gross, Ruth Belov. *True Stories about Abraham Lincoln*, illustrated by Jill Kastner. Lothrop, 1989.

Hurwitz, Johanna. *Astrid Lindgren: Storyteller to the World*, illustrated by Michael Dooling. Viking, 1989.

Hyman, Trina Schart. *Self-Portrait: Trina Schart Hyman*. HarperCollins, 1989 (1981).

Jacobs, William Jay. *Great Lives: Human Rights*. Scribner's, 1990.

Kherdian, David. *The Road from Home: The Story of an Armenian Girl*. Greenwillow, 1979.

Latham, Jean Lee. *Carry On, Mr. Bowditch*, illustrated by John O'Hara Cosgrave II. Houghton, 1955.

Lasker, Joe. *The Great Alexander the Great*. Puffin, 1990 (1983).

Lawson, Robert. *Ben and Me*. Little, Brown, 1951 (1939).

————. *Mr. Revere and I*. Little, Brown, 1953.

Levinson, Nancy Smiler. *Christopher Columbus: Voyager to the Unknown*. Lodestar/Dutton, 1990.

Liestman, Vicki. *Columbus Day*, illustrated by Rick Hanson. Carolrhoda, 1991.

Lomask, William. *Great Lives: Exploration*. Scribner's, 1988.

McGovern, Ann. *The Secret Soldier: The Story of Deborah Sampson*, illustrated by Ann Grifalconi. Four Winds, 1987 (1975).

McKissack, Patricia C. *Jesse Jackson: A Biography*. Scholastic, 1989.

Martin, Rafe. *A Storyteller's Story*, photos by Jill Krementz. Richard C. Owen, 1992.

Meltzer, Milton. *Dorothea Lange: Life Through the Camera*, illustrated by Donna Diamond, photos by Dorothea Lange. Viking, 1985.

Monjo, F. N. *Grand Papa and Ellen Aroon*, illustrated by Richard Cuffari. Dell, 1990 (1974).

————. *Letters to Horseface: Young Mozart's Travels in Italy*, illustrated by Don Bolognese and Elaine Raphael. Puffin, 1991 (1975).

_____. *The One Bad Thing About Father*, illustrated by Rocco Negri. Harper, 1987 (1970).

_____. *Poor Richard in France*, illustrated by Brinton Turkle. Dell, 1990 (1973).

Naylor, Phyllis Reynolds. *How I Came to Be a Writer*. Aladdin, 1987 (1978).

Peet, Bill. *Bill Peet: An Autobiography*. Houghton, 1989.

Provensen, Alice, and Martin Provensen. *The Glorious Flight: Across the Channel with Louis Blériot, July 25, 1909*. Viking, 1983.

Raboff, Ernest. *Marc Chagall*. Lippincott, 1988 (1968).

_____. *Pablo Picasso*. Lippincott, 1988 (1968).

_____. *Paul Klee*. Lippincott, 1988 (1968).

Roop, Peter, and Connie Roop, editors. *I, Columbus: My Journal—1492–3*, illustrated by Peter E. Hanson. Walker, 1990.

Rylant, Cynthia. *Best Wishes*, photos by Carlo Ontal. Richard C. Owen, 1992.

Sandburg, Carl. *Abe Lincoln Grows Up*, illustrated by James Daugherty. Harcourt, 1975 (1926).

Saunders, Susan. *Margaret Mead: The World Was Her Family*, illustrated by Ted Lewin. Viking, 1988.

Say, Allen. *El Chino*. Houghton, 1990.

Scioscia, Mary. *Bicycle Rider*, illustrated by Ed Young. Harper, 1983.

Sills, Leslie. *Inspirations: Stories About Women Artists*, illustrated by Ann Fay. Albert Whitman, 1989.

Sis, Peter. *Follow the Dream: The Story of Christopher Columbus*. Knopf, 1991.

Stanley, Diane. *Peter the Great*. Four Winds, 1986.

Stanley, Diane, and Peter Vennema. *Good Queen Bess: The Story of Elizabeth I of England*, illustrated by Diane Stanley. Four Winds, 1990.

_____. *Shaka: King of the Zulus*, illustrated by Diane Stanley. Morrow, 1988.

Stanley, Fay. *The Last Princess: The Story of Princess Ka'iulani of Hawai'i*, illustrated by Diane Stanley. Four Winds, 1991.

Stevens, Bryna. *Deborah Sampson Goes to War*, illustrated by Florence Hill. Carolrhoda, 1984.

Sullivan, George. *Great Lives: Sports*. Scribner's, 1988.

Turner, Glennette Tilley. *Take a Walk in Their Shoes*, illustrated by Elton C. Fax. Cobblehill/Dutton, 1989.

Weidt, Maryann N. *Stateswoman to the World: A Story About Eleanor Roosevelt*, illustrated by Lydia M. Anderson. Carolrhoda, 1991.

Weil, Lisl. *Wolferl: The First Six Years in the Life of Wolfgang Amadeus Mozart, 1756–1762*. Holiday, 1991.

West, Delno, and Jean West. *Christopher Columbus: The Great Adventure and How We Know About It*. Atheneum, 1991.

Winter, Jeanette. *Diego*, text by Jonah Winter, translation by Amy Prince. Knopf, 1991.

Yates, Elizabeth. *Amos Fortune, Free Man*, illustrated by Nora S. Unwin. Dutton, 1967 (1950).

Yolen, Jane. *A Letter from Phoenix Farm*, photos by Jason Stemple. Richard C. Owen, 1992.

Chapter Eleven
Informational Books

We know a 6-year-old who loves to go to the school library because there he can choose any book he wants. At story time he listens eagerly to picture storybooks and other fiction, but the books he chooses to check out, to keep for a time and to pore over at home, are informational. His favorites are about airplanes, rockets, space travel, and complex machinery. He often chooses books far above his level of understanding (once it was an encyclopedia of space facts so big that he could barely carry it by himself). Part of his fun is looking at the illustrations over and over again, but he also wants an adult to "read" these difficult books to him. In this case he means reading the picture captions and talking through main ideas or intriguing details in response to his many questions. He joins in the reading by looking for words he knows or can figure out in the boldface headings or diagram labels.

We call attention to this common scenario because it demonstrates so much about the special role of nonfiction literature in children's lives. The audience for informational books is broad, including young children as well as older students. Adult ideas about appropriate age levels are often less important than a child's desire to know about a particular topic. A reader's approach to an informational book may be different from the first-to-last-page process that fiction demands. In this type of reading, illustration plays a vital part by focusing interest and clarifying or extending information. Most of all, our example shows how informational literature can provide powerful motivation to read and to enjoy experiences with books. Children are curious about the world and how it works, and they develop passionate attachments to the right book at the right time. They deserve teachers and librarians who can help them discover this particular kind of satisfaction in reading.

TRENDS IN INFORMATIONAL BOOKS

New worlds and new interests lie waiting for children between the covers of informational books. The secrets of science photography, mummies, and making maple sugar have all been revealed in attractive and inviting formats. For proof, have a look at Vicki Cobb's *Natural Wonders: Stories Science Photos Tell*, Patricia Lauber's *Tales Mummies Tell*, and Kathryn Lasky's *Sugaring Time*. Informational books also offer children new perspectives on more familiar topics. *A Dentist's Tools* by Kenny DeSantis demystifies the technology of the regular checkup. *How It Feels to Fight for Your Life* by Jill Krementz offers the thoughts and feelings of children faced with serious illness. Some informational books, like *Chameleons: Dragons in the Trees* by James Martin and Art Wolfe, have tremendous eye appeal and invite browsing. Others are designed to reward sustained attention, like James Cross Giblin's explanation of the unraveling of an ancient mystery in *The Riddle of the Rosetta Stone*. Informational books for children are more numerous, more various, and more appealing than ever. Only recently have they

A male chameleon displays his colors in response to his own threatening image in a mirror in this visually exciting photograph by Art Wolfe.

From *Chameleons: Dragons in the Trees* by James Martin.

begun to receive the critical recognition and classroom attention that they have long deserved. We begin here by looking briefly at some of these changes and the trends that characterize informational books for today's child.

In many ways current trends in informational books mirror recent changes in the larger world of children's books. The following overview covers the more obvious developments of recent years.

Increased Quantity and Quality

More and more trade book publishers are producing informational books—and more attractive ones—than ever before. New companies and new imprints have been created to keep up with the demand generated by more teachers using literature in the classroom and more people buying books in retail stores. Crestwood House, for instance, is a recently established affiliate of Macmillan Publishing Company. Its purpose is to produce high-interest books on a wide range of popular topics to entice reluctant readers. Clear writing and abundant photographs in series such as "Top Dog" make the books popular with a wide range of students. Some publishers' catalogs, which previously offered nonfiction only rarely, now show many new titles on a regular basis. Frequently these titles are edited, designed, and produced with the same care that was once reserved for picture books. Cynthia Rylant's *Appalachia: The Voices of Sleeping Birds*, with its distinguished paintings by Barry Moser, is one example. The result is a stunning array of informational books from which teachers, librarians, and children of all ages can choose.

New Focus on the Very Young

Part of the increased production of informational books can be attributed to growing awareness of a new market. In keeping with the recent emphasis on the importance of early childhood education, there is a new focus on the preschool and early primary audience for informational books. Concept books and identification books that provide the names of objects have long been a popular type of informational picture book for young children (see Chapter 4). Recently, however,

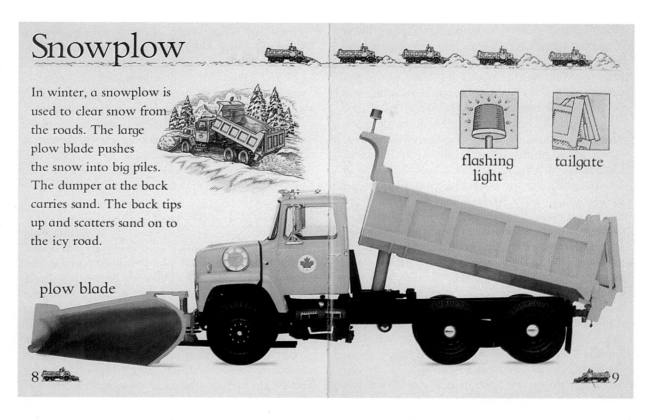

Snowplow

In winter, a snowplow is used to clear snow from the roads. The large plow blade pushes the snow into big piles. The dumper at the back carries sand. The back tips up and scatters sand on to the icy road.

plow blade

flashing light

tailgate

8

9

Informational books for preschoolers need clear illustrations and carefully placed print as in this example from the "Eye-Openers" Series produced by Dorling Kindersley Limited of London.

From *Trucks*. Photo by Stephen Oliver, illustrations by Jane Craddock-Watson and Dave Hopkins.

many types of informational formats have been offered for the very young. Books in the "See How They Grow" series (published by Lodestar) use clear photos and minimal text to show how baby animals change in the first few weeks of life. *Trucks*, by Stephen Oliver and others, a book in the "Eye-Openers" series (published in the United States by Aladdin) focuses on naming and identification but adds information about each truck and close-up drawings of significant details. Both series are printed on extra heavy stock to allow for hard wear by preschoolers. Both also originate in England and share some of the visual characteristics of the popular "Eyewitness Books" series for older readers and their simpler counterparts, "Eyewitness Juniors" (published by Knopf).

The photo essay is another format sometimes directed now to a very young audience, as in Ron Hirschi's gentle commentaries on seasons and the wild in *Spring, Summer, Fall*, and *Winter*. Even experiment books, usually the province of older students, may be appropriate for younger classes if they are as simple and inviting as Neil Ardley's *The Science Book of Electricity*. Although informational series for young children account for many of the new titles, some authors and illustrators do produce fine informational picture books that are one of a kind. Byron Barton's *I Want to Be an Astronaut* and *Bones, Bones, Dinosaur Bones* fit this category.

Growing Importance of Illustration

Another feature of informational books that has changed in recent years is the increased reliance on illustration, especially photography. In our media-conscious society, both children and adults have become more visually oriented, more likely to expect pictures in magazines, newspapers, and other print materials. At the same time, technological improvements in making and reproducing pictures have made it possible to satisfy the demand for color, close-ups, and novel perspectives.

Informational books for all ages often sell themselves, and their topic, on the basis of sophisticated photography or ingenious illustration. A picture postscript in Bianca Lavies's *Wasps at Home* shows how the author/photographer lay on her back "camera in hand and strobe lights at the ready" to photograph paper wasps in their nest through a glass enclosure at her studio window. David Macaulay's collection of explanations titled *The Way Things Work* would probably not have been a bestseller without the drawings, which entertain through humorous touches without distorting important information. Some books simply would not exist without their illustrations because the books are about the pictures. For instance, Patricia Lauber's *Seeing Earth from Space* is about satellite photography, or remote sensing. Although this is an exceptionally well-written book, it would be almost impossible to understand without seeing the vivid color reproductions of the images as they are discussed.

Unconventional Formats and Approaches

A related trend in informational books today is enthusiasm for unconventional approaches, including experimental formats and combinations of fact and fiction. Pop-ups and lift-the-flap books are part of this trend. Tony Potter's *Trucks*, of the "See How It Works" Series, features a see-through plastic page that lets the reader lift a truck's cab to see the location of the engine and transmission. The text of Sheila Hamanaka's distinguished book, *The Journey: Japanese Americans, Racism, and Renewal,* is organized around a mural painted by the author; each segment of text accompanies and describes one or two details of the larger painting.

Other books that look like conventional picture books may be innovative in the ways they deliver information, often using a fictitious story as the vehicle or at least borrowing from the techniques of fiction. *The Magic School Bus Lost in the Solar System* and other books in this series by Joanna Cole and Bruce Degen could be classified as fantasy picture books, with their miniaturized school bus and impossible field trips led by the intrepid teacher, Ms. Frizzle. Student dialogue is presented in speech balloons borrowed from the comics and a wisecracking tone reminiscent of television situation comedy. Yet the books are clearly designed to present information, both in the details of the bus's journey and in the student "reports" displayed as insets in almost every illustration.

Specialized Topics

During the last decade, more informational books have been published about highly specialized topics. While there have always been specialized books (see p. 686), today there are more and more books that reflect very specific interests. They may report personalized perspectives, give detailed information about a narrowly defined topic, or cut across subject matter in a new way. For instance, *What Neat Feet!* by Hana Machotka looks at only one feature of animal anatomy. Primary readers are invited to identify the feet of seven different animals from one clue and a close-up photo. The next page presents a full picture of the animal and a description of the way this foot helps the animal get along in its natural environment. There are books about such special topics as adjectives (Ruth Heller's *Many Luscious Lollipops*), remote prehistoric villages (*Skara Brae* by Olivier Dunrea), and special zoos for insects (*Insect Zoo* by Susan Meyers). Although students may not identify these topics as something they want or need to read about, the books frequently serve to create the interest.

Recognition and Awards

Many of the trends we have looked at here indicate that informational books are innovative and creative. They carry the unique perspective of individual authors and of artists free to experiment with formats and media. It is not surprising, then, that informational books for children are finally being recognized for their aesthetic qualities as literature. In the past, nonfiction books have not earned their fair share of critical attention and recognition. In 1981, author Betty Bacon pointed out that nonfiction books had won the Newbery Medal only six times in fifty-eight years, and those winners were from history or biography, in which the chronological narrative form is very much like fiction.[1] This is quite a contrast to literature for adults, where authors like John McPhee and Tracy Kidder regularly win critical acclaim for their work, and nonfiction frequently dominates the bestseller lists.

Three books of nonfiction have recently been recognized by the Newbery award committee. Russell Freedman's *Lincoln: A Photobiography* won the Newbery Medal in 1988 and his book *The Wright Brothers* was an honor winner in 1992; Patricia Lauber's *Volcano: The Eruption and Healing of Mt. St. Helens* was an honor book in 1987. The Boston Globe-Horn Book Awards have included a nonfiction category for many years. Some of the recent winners in this category have been Peggy Thomson's *Auks, Rocks, and the Odd Dinosaur: Inside Stories from the Smithsonian Museum*, Marcia Sewall's *Pilgrims of Plimoth*, and Virginia Hamilton's *Anthony Burns: The Defeat and Triumph of a Fugitive Slave*.

In 1990 the National Council of Teachers of English established the Orbis Pictus Award for Outstanding Nonfiction for Children. Its name commemorates what is thought to be the first book of facts produced for children, dating back to the seventeenth century. The first two winners of this new award were biographies. In general, biography continues to win more awards than other types of nonfiction, but now at least there are opportunities for all kinds of informational books to receive the acclaim they deserve.

CRITERIA FOR EVALUATING INFORMATIONAL BOOKS

One critic who has given close attention to informational books for children is Jo Carr.[2] Teachers

and librarians who want to choose the very best books available can be guided by her view that a nonfiction writer is first a teacher, then an artist, and should be concerned with feeling as well as thinking, passion as well as clarity. Specific criteria can be used to help identify this level of achievement. Being familiar with these criteria and with the types of books in which information is presented will make it easier to choose the best books at the right time.

In considering the following points, we do not assume that their order of presentation is necessarily their order of importance. Accuracy is discussed first because it *is* of primary importance. No one wants inaccurate information no matter how well it is presented. Beyond accuracy, however, the individual reviewer must judge the relative value of the various criteria in terms of particular books. Sometimes a book's strengths in one or two categories may far outweigh its weakness in others (see box on p. 678).

Accuracy and Authenticity

QUALIFICATIONS OF THE AUTHOR

Informational books are written by people who are authorities in their fields, or they are written by writers who study a subject, interview specialists, and compile the data. A few, like naturalist Jean Craighead George, are both specialists and writers. It is always a good idea to check the book's jacket copy, title page, introduction, or "About the Author" page at the back for information about the author's special qualifications, often expressed in terms of professional title or affiliation. Expertise in one field does not necessarily indicate competency in another, however, so we expect a high degree of authenticity only if the author has limited the book to what appears to be his or her specialty.

If a book is written not by an expert in the field but by a "writer," facts can be checked by authorities and the authority cited. For example, the book *Robots: Your High-Tech World* was written by Gloria Skurzynski, a writer better known for fiction than information. However, the acknowledgments name a long list of experts she interviewed and consulted, corporations that provided materials and information, and the Hewlett-Packard

[1]Betty Bacon, "The Art of Nonfiction," *Children's Literature in Education*, vol. 12 (Spring 1981), p. 3.
[2]Jo Carr, "Writing the Literature of Fact," in *Beyond Fact: Nonfiction for Children and Young People* (Chicago: American Library Association, 1982), pp. 3–12.

official who (twice) reviewed and authenticated her manuscript. Photo credits show that the illustrations were furnished by companies and universities on the cutting edge of this technology. The record of sources and research provided here gives assurance that the book is accurate.

A number of authors have earned the reputation of writing dependably good informational books. When in doubt, teachers and librarians are likely to turn first to writers who have proved their integrity with facts—Laurence Pringle, Vicki Cobb, Seymour Simon, Helen Roney Sattler, and Milton Meltzer, among others. But authorship, while it may be a valuable rule of thumb, is a dangerous final criterion. Each book must be evaluated on its own merits.

ACCURACY OF FACTS

Fortunately, many of the errors of fact in children's informational books are minor ones. Children who have access to a variety of books on one topic should be encouraged to notice discrepancies and pursue the correct answer, a valuable exercise in critical reading.

Errors that teachers and children may recognize are less distressing than those that pass for fact because the topic is unfamiliar or highly specialized. Then the reader must depend on a competent reviewer to identify inaccuracies. Ideally, a book with technical information should be reviewed by someone with expertise in that field. *Appraisal: Children's Science Books* is a periodical that offers paired reviews, one by a science professional, one by a teacher or librarian. *Science Books and Films* includes reviews by specialists in the field. *The Horn Book Magazine* singles out science books for special reviewing efforts, although other nonfiction is included. *School Library Journal* often provides helpful criticism. *Social Education* and *Science and Children* magazines also give some attention to appropriate books. Generally speaking, science books are more likely to be challenged by experts than those about history or other topics in the humanities.

BEING UP TO DATE

Some books that are free of error at the time of writing become inaccurate with the passage of time, as new discoveries are made in the sciences or as changes occur in world politics. Books that focus on the past are less likely to be rapidly outdated, although new discoveries in archaeology or new theories in history and anthropology call for a reevaluation of these materials also. On the other hand, books that focus on areas of vigorous research and experimentation, such as viruses and disease or space technology, are quickly outdated. Steven Lindblom made the engaging admission in his 1985 book, *How to Build a Robot*, that anything written about robot technology will be out of date by the time it reaches the reader. It is worth noting, however, that the latest trade books are almost always more up to date than the latest textbooks or encyclopedias.

It is also difficult, but important, to provide children with current information about other countries where national governments are emerging or where future political developments are uncertain. In the 1970s the situation in Southeast Asia changed so rapidly that often only the daily news could provide completely up-to-date information. Eastern Europe and the Soviet Union posed the same dilemma as the 1990s began. Current events that generate an interest in books about a particular country also call attention to the fact that those books may be out of date. Just months after the publication of Laurie Dolphin's record of an Atlanta family's trip to Tbilisi, *Georgia to Georgia: Making Friends in the U.S.S.R.*, violent changes broke apart the Soviet Union. This does not invalidate the personal and cultural information in the book, but it does mean that statements about government, the economy, and peace efforts are not accurate for today.

Books about minority cultures need to include material on contemporary experience, as well as heritage. Too many studies of Native Americans, for example, have dealt only with tribal life when the country was being explored and settled. It is refreshing now to have books like *Pueblo Storyteller* and *Totem Pole*, both by Diane Hoyt-Goldsmith, that show families who take pride in continuing their traditions but are also clearly people of today's world. In the Pueblo book, 10-year-old April learns her Cochiti heritage of bread making, storytelling, and dancing from her grandparents; she also shoots baskets with a friend and plays golf with her grandfather on a public course

**Blue jeans and flannel shirts are among the
contemporary details that demonstrate the
presence of this Cochiti family in today's world.
Pictures such as these help to combat the image of
Native-American people as museum pieces.**

Photo by Lawrence Migdale from *Pueblo Storyteller* by Diane
Hoyt-Goldsmith.

owned and operated by the tribe. Being up to
date is one of the ways that books of this kind can
combat stereotypes.

INCLUDING ALL THE SIGNIFICANT FACTS

Though the material presented in a book may be
current and technically correct, the book cannot
be totally accurate if significant facts are omitted.
Thirty years ago science books that dealt with
animal reproduction frequently glossed over the
specifics of birth or mating. In Robert McClung's
Possum, the process is explained like this: "All
night long the two of them wandered through the
woods together. But at dawn each went his own
way again. Possum's babies were born just twelve
days later."[3] Fortunately, changing social mores
that struck down taboos in children's fiction also
encouraged a new frankness in books of information. For instance, close-up photographs and a
forthright text in *My Puppy Is Born* by Joanna Cole

show the birth and early development of a terrier's litter. *Egg to Chick* by Millicent Selsam pictures the mating of a rooster and a hen.

Human reproduction and sexuality have so often
been distorted by omissions that books with accurate terminology and explicit information are particularly welcome. An attractive book designed for
parents to share with young children is Sara Stein's
Making Babies, which deals head-on with questions
that adults often find difficult to answer. After suggesting an uncomplicated way to explain the
mechanics of intercourse the author says: "It is
sensible and honest to add that, because it feels
nice, people make love together even when they
are not starting a baby."[4] A more recent book that
speaks of conception with comparable candor is
How I Was Born by Marie Wabbes.

The honest presentation of all information necessary for understanding a topic is just as important in historical or cultural accounts as in the
sciences. This may be difficult to achieve because
social issues are complex and writing for a young
audience requires that the author be brief.
Judging whether a book does include all the significant facts can also be difficult, for deciding
what really counts is a matter of interpretation. A.
P. Porter's *Kwanzaa*, a book designed for early
elementary readers, does an admirable job of
explaining in simple terms the purpose and the
symbolism of this seven-day African-American
holiday. The historical context, however, might
be more helpful if it were more complete. How
does Kwanzaa reflect a heritage that predates slavery, or does it? Was the origin of Kwanzaa related
to changes brought about by the civil rights movement? Is Kwanzaa recognized and celebrated by a
large percentage of African Americans? If a book
leaves important questions unanswered, it has not
included all the significant facts.

AVOIDING STEREOTYPES

A book that omits significant facts tells only part
of the truth; a book that presents stereotypes pretends, wrongly, to have told the whole truth. One
very common sort of stereotyping is by omission.
If we never see women or minorities in science
books, for instance, we are left with the incorrect

[3]Robert McClung, *Possum* (New York: Morrow, 1963),
p. 41.

[4]Sara Bonnett Stein, *Making Babies*, photographs by
Doris Pinney (New York: Walker, 1974), p. 38.

impression that all scientists must be male Caucasians. In recent years, fortunately, some authors, illustrators, and publishers have made conscious efforts to represent the great variety of roles that women and minorities play in science and the world of work. Gloria Skurzynski's *Almost the Real Thing*, a book about high-tech simulation techniques, shows African-American astronaut Mae Jemison in training. *Public Defender: Lawyer for the People* by Joan Hewett describes the real-life work of Janice Fukai, a woman of Asian descent. Harlow Rockwell's *My Doctor* was a leader in portraying a woman physician in a book for the very young, and Gail Gibbons has made many similar contributions, including a woman surveyor on the work crew of *New Road!* Byron Barton's *Machines at Work* shows women as well as men operating heavy equipment. Often it is the illustrations that reveal gender or race. This no-fanfare approach helps combat stereotypes because it encourages children to accept the contributions of all as a matter of course.

Books about countries around the world and those that describe life in a minority culture are the most likely to include stereotypes. Children can be taught to watch for sweeping general statements and for unwarranted claims about what "everybody" thinks or does. However, all readers need to realize that it is almost impossible to portray a country or region completely in *all* its diversity of people, terrain, industry, lifestyles, and the like. When the region is large and the book is limited in length, it is good if the author deliberately highlights differences rather than generalizing too freely. John Chiasson's *African Journey* focuses one by one on six specific locations within the mid-section of Africa. This book illuminates contrasts in geographical conditions and resulting variation in lifestyles through distinguished color photographs and a clear, detailed text.

Another way that authors try to avoid stereotyping is by relating the story of one individual within a community. *Pueblo Boy* by Marcia Keegan describes the life of Timmy Roybal, a 10-year-old Pueblo Indian of the San Ildefonso Pueblo near Santa Fe, New Mexico. Like Diane Hoyt-Goldsmith's *Pueblo Storyteller*, this book personalizes a culture by focusing on a particular child's family, school, and community experiences. Readers associate the facts in the book with specific persons and places. Consequently, they will be less likely to assume that this description of Native-American life represents the way *all* people of Native-American heritage live.

USING FACTS TO SUPPORT GENERALIZATIONS

To be distinguishable from stereotype or simple opinion, a proper generalization needs facts for support. Ron Roy begins his book *Move Over, Wheelchairs Coming Through!* in this way:

> Thousands of kids are wheelchair users. These young people are disabled, but in most cases their disabilities have not stopped them from doing the things they want to do.[5]

The entire book is organized to support this point. Seven young wheelchair users were photographed and interviewed; an essay about each one shows their mobility and determination.

Laurence Pringle says in *Living Treasure: Saving Earth's Biodiversity* that bringing "alien" organisms into areas where they are not native is a threat to other species. Several pieces of evidence are offered. For example, thirty-five species of native African fish have been eaten into extinction by Nile perch brought to Lake Victoria in 1960, and plants introduced to the Hawaiian Islands have crowded out more than two hundred native species of vegetation. Critical readers need to be aware of generalizations and judge for themselves if adequate facts are offered for support.

MAKING THE DISTINCTION BETWEEN FACT AND THEORY

Careful writers make careful distinctions between fact and theory; but, even so, children need guidance in learning to recognize the difference. Often the distinction depends on key words or phrases—such as "scientists believe," "so far as we know," or "perhaps." Consider the importance of the simple phrase "may have" in this description of a prehistoric reptile: "Pterodactyls lived near the shores of prehistoric seas and may

[5]Ron Roy, *Move Over, Wheelchairs Coming Through!*, photos by Rosmarie Hausherr (New York: Clarion Books, 1985), p. 1.

have slept hanging from tree branches by their feet, like bats."[6] Some discussion of different kinds of possible evidence might be in order as children are led to see that one half of this statement is presented as fact, the other as theory.

Books about the disappearance of the dinosaurs make good material for helping children sort out the difference between fact and theory because the problem is dramatic and the evidence provides for legitimate disagreement among scientists. Franklyn Branley's *What Happened to the Dinosaurs?* does a particularly good job of helping primary children understand what a theory is.

While it is important to distinguish between fact and theory in all of the sciences, and the social sciences as well, the matter receives most attention in books dealing with evolution and human origins. In some communities this is a very sensitive topic, but it would seem that children everywhere have a right to information about scientists' discoveries and theories regarding our origins. *Traces of Life* by Kathryn Lasky, a book for older readers, presents "the origins of humankind" in terms of particular fossil discoveries and the sometimes differing interpretations that scientists have made of these. In contrast, David Peters's *From the Beginning: The Story of Human Evolution* fails to acknowledge the process by which ideas about evolution have become accepted in the scientific community.

AVOIDING ANTHROPOMORPHISM

In poetry and fiction the assignment of human feelings and behavior to animals, plants, or objects is called *personification*—an accepted literary device that may be used with great effect. In science, however, the same device becomes unacceptable and is known as *anthropomorphism*. Science writer Millicent Selsam addressed the problem of interpreting what animals do in one of her early books on animal behavior:

It is hard to keep remembering that animals live in a different kind of world from our own. They see, hear, smell, and taste things differently. And they do not have human intelligence or emotions, so we must avoid interpreting their behavior in terms of our own feelings and thoughts. For example, it looks to us as though parent birds are devoted to their young in the same way that human parents are devoted to theirs. But only experimental work can show whether this interpretation is true.[7]

Knowing that young children perceive new things in terms of their experiences and feelings, however, writers have often given names to their animal subject or expressed animal behavior in childlike terms. Many books with these anthropomorphic touches are still in print. Newer informational books are doing a much better job of reporting only observable animal behavior in a straightforward way. In *Manatee: On Location*, Kathy Darling uses some of the names that rangers assigned to members of the Crystal River sea-cow herd as she writes about these particular animals, and she makes many comparisons between manatees and humans. This is not anthropomorphism, just good reporting and clear writing.

Closely related to anthropomorphism is another error called *teleological explanation of phenomena*. Briefly, teleology attempts to account for natural phenomena by assigning a humanlike purpose to the plants, animals, or forces involved. Science books should not suggest that leaves turn toward the light in order to bask in the sun or that Mother Nature, capitalized and personified, is at work carving the walls of canyons. While such a description has a certain poetic effect, it also conveys a basically unscientific attitude.

Content and Perspective

PURPOSE

It is futile to try to pass judgment on the content of an informational book without first determining the purpose for which the book was designed. Identifying the scope of the book lets us know what we can reasonably expect. A quick look at Vicki Cobb's *Why Can't You Unscramble an Egg?* reveals a fascinating collection of questions and explanations for browsing, whereas both the title

---

[6]David C. Knight, *"Dinosaurs" That Swam and Flew*, illustrated by Lee J. Ames (Englewood Cliffs, N.J.: Prentice-Hall, 1985), p. 39.

[7]Millicent Selsam, *Animals as Parents*, illustrated by John Kaufmann (New York: Morrow, 1965), p. 16.

and appearance of Helen Sattler's *The New Illustrated Dinosaur Dictionary* indicate a comprehensive treatment of the topic. Titles can be misleading, particularly those that promise to tell "all about" a subject but offer limited coverage instead. At best, titles both indicate the scope of the book's content and pique the reader's curiosity, as do John J. Loeper's *Going to School in 1876* and *Body Noises* by Susan Buxbaum and Rita Gelman. More about the scope and purpose of informational books can be found in the section "Types of Informational Books," later in this chapter.

INTENDED AUDIENCE

Before evaluating content we have to know not just for what the book was intended, but for whom. Book jackets or book reviews often indicate an age range according to reading level or interest. It is difficult to know whether one or both of these factors are reflected in the age recommended. Generally, the reading level of a book is not as important as its content in relation to the reader's actual interest in a subject. Older students and adults may turn to children's informational books for introductory material on an unfamiliar topic. In using informational books, children will read "beyond their abilities" when reading for particular facts. Children will frequently turn to difficult books if they contain many pictures or useful diagrams. At the same time, vocabulary, sentence length, size of type, and the organization of the book are factors to be considered. When children see crowded pages, relatively small type, and few pictures, they may reject a book that contains useful information.

The choice of topic, then, is an important factor in determining whether a book will be suitable for its intended audience. Books for young children most often reflect their basic egocentric concerns and their curiosity about themselves and other living things. It is a mistake to assume that they will not be interested in other subjects, however. Many early primary children enjoy browsing through the widely diverse titles of the "Eyewitness" series, such as Lionel Bender's *Invention* or *Money* by Joe Cribb, even though these books are designed for an older audience. On the other hand, books that look like picture books are frequently aimed at upper grade children. Tuyosi Mori's *Socrates and the Three Little Pigs*, with its engaging illustrations by Mitsumasa Anno and its conventional picture-book size and shape, certainly appears to be a picture book for younger readers. It only takes a page or two, however, to realize that the story deals with the mathematical concept of factorial analysis and that the illustrations soon become diagrams in support of the author's explanation. This is a book for advanced thinkers, whatever their ages.

Examples chosen by an author to clarify concepts are related to the level of cognitive ability needed to get the most out of a book. In *Sarah Morton's Day*, Kate Waters caters to a young child's need to approach historical understanding through concrete details. One double spread of sequenced color photos shows Sarah, the pilgrim girl, getting dressed in her overgarments. First comes the petticoat, then stockings, garters, two more petticoats, a waistcoat, coif, apron, "pocket," and shoes—a clear contrast to sweatsuits and sneakers!

ADEQUATE COVERAGE

Recognizing the purpose of a book and its intended level, the reader has a basis for deciding if the author has said too much about the topic or too little. Stan Hoig's book for older readers, *A Capital for the Nation*, provides 125 pages of information about the history of the Capitol, the White House, and various monuments and memorials in Washington, D.C. The focus is limited but the treatment is detailed. As a matter of fact, it is hard to imagine any young reader being interested in all the background facts and sidelights that are included. For information about present-day Washington, readers might turn to Shirley Climo's simpler *City! Washington, D.C.*, which has color photos, a travelogue flair, and some basic historical information as well. It is worth noting, though, that neither book's title reveals its purpose or scope.

Broader topics, like the history or culture of a nation, might require many pages in order to allow even brief attention to all the significant material. History textbooks have earned particularly harsh criticism for faulty coverage,[8] and good

[8]See Frances FitzGerald, *America Revised* (Boston: Atlantic-Little, Brown, 1979).

trade books help to fill in perspectives that the textbooks omit. A generation ago, Gerald Johnson expressed the need for careful writing in the introduction to his book, *America Is Born:*

> Part of the story is very fine, and other parts are very bad, but they all belong to it, and if you leave out the bad parts you never understand it all.[9]

Authors who fail to acknowledge more than one viewpoint or theory fail to help children learn to examine issues. Even young children should know that authorities do not always agree, though the context may be simple. It is far more common, though, and certainly more necessary, for books about complex issues to deal with varying points of view. Laurence Pringle's *Nuclear Energy: Troubled Past, Uncertain Future* outlines efforts for and against a "second nuclear era" and identifies proponents of both sides. Anything less would have been inadequate coverage of the topic.

DEMONSTRATION OF SCIENTIFIC METHOD

Since we are concerned about *how* as well as *what* children learn, it is important to note what kind of thinking a book encourages, as well as the body of fact it presents. Informational books should illustrate the process of inquiry, the excitement of discovery. Children in the upper elementary grades are fascinated by the dramatic account of Frank and John Craighead's ground-breaking wildlife research in *Operation Grizzly Bear* by Marian Calabro. Laurence Pringle's *Bearman: Exploring the World of Black Bears* provides a similar but less detailed treatment of the work of naturalist Lynn Rogers. Both these books give readers a good idea of problems scientists try to solve and the kind of day-to-day work that is involved.

While these are fine accounts of the scientific method at work, the reader's involvement is still a vicarious one. Some books are designed to give children more direct experience with the skills of inquiry. The series *A First Look at . . .* by Millicent Selsam and Joyce Hunt doesn't have flashy illustrations or an unusual format, but it is particularly good for helping primary-grade chil-

[9]Gerald Johnson (in an introductory letter to Peter), *America Is Born*, illustrated by Leonard Everett Fisher (New York: Morrow, 1959), pp. viii–ix.

The juxtaposition of items in these carefully composed photographs invites comparison and critical thinking.

Photography by Donald Baird from *Dinosaurs Walked Here* by Patricia Lauber.

dren develop the ability to observe and classify. In *A First Look at Leaves*, instead of pointing out that a ginkgo leaf resembles a fan, the authors direct the reader to find the leaf that looks like a fan, a mitten, a needle; clear line drawings of ginkgo, sassafras, and pine appear on the same page. Other books in this series are about fish, mammals, insects, birds, dogs, and caterpillars.

The photographs in Patricia Lauber's *Dinosaurs Walked Here and Other Stories Fossils Tell* are chosen and placed to help children make their own observations about the fossil record. A photo of a present-day horseshoe crab beside the fossil print of its 140-million-year-old ancestor allows readers to conclude that these creatures have scarcely changed over time; a companion picture lets us discover how beavers have shrunk in the past 15,000 years. All Lauber's books demonstrate this commitment to present scientific evidence in such a way that children can confirm some conclusions for themselves.

Experiment books for all ages should avoid the "cookbook" approach that simply tells, step by step, what to do. The best approaches help children in problem solving through the strategies of open-ended questions, models for observation, and suggestions for further study. Sandra Markle's guides for observing ants in *Exploring Autumn* provide simple directions (no pictures needed), ask questions that direct attention to important features like the relation between the size of an ant's burden to its body, and give background information that helps children interpret what they see.

The scientific method applies to the social sciences, too, but there are fewer books in this area designed to help children learn and use the inquiry approach. Jean Fritz has illustrated techniques of historical research in a fictionalized account that children like very much—*George Washington's Breakfast*. The story illustrates the role of perseverance and good luck in problem solving. After young George, who is trying to find out what George Washington customarily ate for breakfast, has asked questions, exhausted library resources, and gone on a futile fact-finding trip to Mt. Vernon, he happens to find the answer in an old book about to be discarded from his own attic. Intermediate children can find out about using primary sources for studying personal history in *The Great Ancestor Hunt* by Lila Perl. *The Riddle of the Rosetta Stone: Key to Ancient Egypt* by James Cross Giblin demonstrates the use of scholarly techniques in history. This book describes more than a hundred years of research in terms of clues that were ultimately used to solve the mystery of the stone's language.

INTERRELATIONSHIPS AND IMPLICATIONS

A list of facts is fine for an almanac, but most informational books are not almanacs. They should be expected to put facts into some sort of perspective. After all, linking facts in one way or another transforms information into knowledge. Gail Hartman provides a spatial perspective for primary children in *As the Crow Flies: A First Book of Maps*. Harvey Stevenson's pictures show animals on their own home ground with appropriate landmarks sketched in on individual maps of each one's territory. At the end of the book a large map shows how all the previous ones fit together. *Nature's Great Balancing Act: In Our Own Backyard* by E. Jaediker Norsgaard focuses on interrelationships. Information about food chains and how populations are kept in balance is accompanied by photographs that illustrate these concepts in a direct way: a stink bug attacks a caterpillar, a bee collects pollen, one praying mantis devours another.

Interrelationships of a different sort are pointed out in Barbara Brenner's *If You Were There in 1492*. This book helps readers see the cultural context in which a major event, the first voyage of Columbus, took place. The author describes the world as it would have been known to ordinary people in Spain in terms of food, clothing, education, books, the arts, crime, ships, and many other aspects. The vivid presentations of the 1492 expulsion of Jews from Spain and the everyday life of the Lucayan people on the island where Columbus would land are especially good for prompting discussion about the relationship of one culture to another.

Intertwining science and technology with modern culture has become crucial, and many recent informational books have taken this issue as a focus. *Going Green: A Kid's Handbook to Saving the Planet* by John Elkington and others is a popular catalog of information about the effect of daily decisions on the environment. Roland Smith's *Sea Otter Rescue: The Aftermath of an Oil Spill* details in words and photographs one small part of the cleanup that followed the 1989 accident of the supertanker *Exxon Valdez* off the coast of Alaska. Although it is a fascinating account, this book does not take the extra step of weighing the multimillion dollar cost of the operation against its overall impact. Even those books not specifically designed to call attention to the related social problems of science and technology ought to acknowledge that such problems do exist. Where the uses of science have serious implications for society, the relationships should be made clear. (See "Stewards of the Earth" in Chapter 12 for more about this issue.)

Style

CLARITY AND DIRECTNESS

It is difficult to list all of the criteria that influence clarity. The use of precise language and specific detail is one important factor. Nothing is vague in Miriam Schlein's description of a vampire bat's dinner in *Billions of Bats*. She names the animals that are likely prey ("a horse, a cow, a donkey, or even a chicken"), describes the approach and the bite ("only about a tenth of an inch long"), and goes on to explain how the bat curves its tongue into a funnel shape and sucks in blood ("for about a half hour"). The language is simple and direct, giving the reader a clear picture of the process.

In earlier decades we could say with some certainty that information presented in the guise of fiction was confusing and ought to be avoided. A few recent books, however, have offered skillful combinations of fact and fiction in which information is clearly presented. One of these is Joe Lasker's *A Tournament of Knights*. The fictional frame for this story in picture-book format provides names, feelings, and family connections for two jousting knights. Still, the center of interest is the book's information about the tournament itself—how it was organized, what weapons and armor were required, and how the assembled lords and ladies responded as per custom to the action. The story element in books like this can help children understand facts that might otherwise seem too distant. On the other hand, not every author is this successful in making the combination; some fail to do a very good job of entertaining or of informing. Each book must be judged on its own merits.

LEVEL OF DIFFICULTY

Although vocabulary does have to be within the child's range, books for primary-grade children need not be restricted to a narrow list of words. New terms can be explained in context. In *Follow the Water from Brook to Ocean*, Arthur Dorros provides a two-paragraph description of the effects of moving water before introducing the word *erosion*. He also gives helpful context through examples and illustrations for the words *meanders* and *reservoir*.

Context does not serve to explain everything, however; a writer aware of the background of the intended audience takes pains to make new words clear. When a writer does not make that effort, it can pose enormous difficulties for the reader. Consider the background that a child would need to visualize this description of New Zealand in a book that is now, mercifully, out of print:

> Gorse and broom cover the weathered hills in the south but toward the west coast sounds, or Findland, alternating hills and mountains rise beyond canyons, carved by rapidly flowing rivers, until heavy forest is reached.[10]

In the unlikely event that a child knew about "gorse," "broom," "sounds," and "weathering," he or she would still be put off by the length and complexity of the sentence. Too many ideas and concepts are compressed into a brief space; this kind of density makes very difficult reading.

Words that look unpronounceable are another stumbling block for most children. A glossary is helpful, but youngsters who are intent on a book's content may not take time to look in the back. In *Dinosaurs Down Under: And Other Fossils from Australia*, Caroline Arnold shows one way to solve the problem. She provides pronunciation guides in parentheses for daunting words like *Rhoetosaurus, Hypsilophodon*, and the giant goanna lizard, ". . . *Megalania* (meg-a-LANE-ee-a), which means 'the great ripper,' after its method of killing prey."[11] Chances are good that the nickname will help young readers remember this particular specimen.

READER INVOLVEMENT

Authors use many different techniques to engage readers' attention and help them stay involved with a book's subject matter. In the "Just for a Day" nature books, which cross the line into fiction, Joanne Ryder invites readers to become the creatures she writes about. In *Winter Whale*, for instance, the text describes a humpback whale's movements as if the child were experiencing them:

> As you swim, you stretch
> your long, long flippers,
> bending, moving, turning them
> so you can slide

---

[10]Edna Kaula, *The Land and People of New Zealand* (Philadelphia: Lippincott, 1964), p. 15.
[11]Caroline Arnold, *Dinosaurs Down Under: And Other Fossils from Australia*, photographs by Richard Hewett (New York: Clarion, 1990), p. 29.

right
and left
and even upside down.[12]

Nonfiction authors also use direct address, that is, sentences which speak to the reader as "you." Sometimes an author asks direct questions to claim a bond of communication with the reader. Paul Showers hooks the primary audience for *How Many Teeth?* with a variety of rhymes interspersed throughout the text to ask "How many teeth have you?"

Children may be more quickly drawn into an informational book by a sense of immediacy in the writing. The use of present tense sometimes serves this purpose. *Chimney Sweeps* by James Giblin begins with a present-tense account of a modern chimney sweep at work. Parts of the book are cast in past tense to present facts about chimneys and sweeps, but the author returns to present tense and second person to describe a typical day in the life of a "climbing boy" in 1800. He invites the reader to participate:

> Then imagine that you are one of three climbing boys working for a master sweep. You are eleven years old and have been cleaning chimneys ever since you were six, when your parents sold you to the master.
>
> It is 4:30 in the morning when the master comes down into the cellar to wake you.[13]

Children reward the author's efforts with this book by becoming deeply involved in the unusual topic.

VIVID LANGUAGE

The writer of informational books uses the same techniques as the writer of fiction to bring a book to life, although the words must be accurate as well as attractive. Imagery is used to appeal to the senses, frequently to sight, as in Kathryn Lasky's lyrical *Sugaring Time:*

> Fog swirls through the valley and up into the meadow, covering the hills and mountaintops beyond. Everything is milky white. Snow-covered

earth and sky melt together. Pines appear rootless, like ghost trees, their pointy tops wrapped in mist.[14]

Metaphorical language, since it is based on comparison, can be used to contribute to clarity in nonfiction. Carol Carrick's *Octopus* helps the reader visualize that creature's underwater existence through similes: ". . . the octopus floated down over the lobster like a sinister parachute. . . ." and ". . . she crept spider-like over the bottom of the sea."[15] Older readers appreciate the vivid comparisons in *Predator!* by Bruce Brooks. In describing killer whales after a large prey, Brooks says:

> ". . . two of them will taunt a large baleen whale by cruising alongside one to a side, nipping and nudging and poking, like two hoods in stock cars hassling a stern old gent riding in a Cadillac between them."[16]

This book's frequent references to sports and to the contemporary scene present the world of nature in an unusually appealing way, especially for young adolescents.

One of the effects of style is cadence. Authors can create suspense or excitement by quickening the pace of their sentences. Karla Kuskin's style underscores the repetitious pattern of historical events in *Jerusalem, Shining Still.* Her prose has a chantlike rhythm in some sections:

> You may remember that after the Babylonians came from Babylon, the Greeks came. Then came the Romans, those worshippers of gods and omens. Then the Persians came in troops, the Moslems followed, groups and groups.[17]

While children will probably not be able to describe an author's style, they will certainly respond to it. They know that a well-written informational book somehow does not sound the same as an encyclopedia essay, and they enjoy the difference.

---

[12]Joanne Ryder, *Winter Whale,* illustrated by Michael Rothman (New York: Morrow, 1991), unpaged.
[13]James Cross Giblin, *Chimney Sweeps,* illustrated by Margot Tomes (New York: Crowell, 1982), p. 17.

[14]Kathryn Lasky, *Sugaring Time,* photographs by Christopher G. Knight (New York: Macmillan, 1983), unpaged.
[15]Carol Carrick, *Octopus,* illustrated by Donald Carrick (New York: Clarion, 1978), unpaged.
[16]Bruce Brooks, *Predator!* (New York: Farrar, Straus, 1991), p. 23.
[17]Karla Kuskin, *Jerusalem, Shining Still,* illustrated by David Frampton (New York: Harper & Row, 1987), p. 17.

Organization

STRUCTURE

Even though a book is vividly written, accurate, and in command of its topic, children do not find it very useful unless it also furnishes a clear arrangement of information. Every author must choose a structure or organizing principle as a basis for presenting facts. Sometimes an author uses a very obvious principle such as the sequence of the alphabet to organize a collection of facts. For instance, Tim Arnold's *Natural History from A to Z: A Terrestrial Sampler* covers an unusually wide-ranging selection of plants and animals that allows him to introduce older readers to important principles of biology. In this book, as in others, the alphabet device provides little attention to the relationship among facts, although it makes a good format for browsing and is easily understood by children.

Ann McGovern effectively uses the relatively loose structure of questions and answers in her book *. . . If You Lived with the Sioux Indians.* Recognizing what kinds of things children want to know, the author provides answers for: "Where would you sleep?" "Were grownups strict?" "Was there time for fun?" Also included are more conventional questions about hunting and ceremonies. The question-and-answer approach has become more widely used in recent years. For very young children, questions and pictured answers can change a concept book into an engaging guessing game. Margaret Miller's *Whose Shoe?* repeats the title question nine times for nine different shoes; turn the page and discover a word or phrase of identification plus two photographs of that shoe in use. One of the many question books for older readers is *Why Do Volcanoes Erupt?* by Philip Whitfield with the Natural History Museum. This book presents interesting detail about many earth science topics, but the loose structure makes this volume more appropriate for browsing than for reference.

Another structure closely related to questions and answers is the true-false approach that states common myths or misconceptions and then offers corrected or updated information. *Lies (People Believe) About Animals* by Susan Sussman and Robert James dispels the notions that bats are blind, porcupines can shoot their quills, and opossums sleep hanging upside down, among others.

One of the best of these books is Patricia Lauber's *The News About Dinosaurs*, with its meticulous but not too technical updates on the latest scientific interpretations of information about the dinosaurs. Children can use this book to check for distortions and misinformation in volumes with older copyright dates, a good application of critical reading and thinking skills.

A common and sensible arrangement for many books, especially about history or biological processes, is based on chronology. *The President's Cabinet and How It Grew* by Nancy Winslow Parker indicates a chronological approach by its title. The cover also promises a light touch with its lineup of cabinet-rank characters dressed to fit their responsibilities. *Cactus Hotel* by Brenda Guiberson and Megan Lloyd reveals both history and science in its account of the 200-year growth of a giant saguaro cactus.

Regardless of its topic, a general survey type of book should have a system of headings that help the reader get an overview of the content, unless the book is very brief and has pictures that serve as graphic guides for skimming. The longer the book and the more complex its topic, the greater the need for manageable divisions. In John Roberson's comprehensive *Japan: From Shogun to Sony, 1543–1984*, the chapter titles ("A Closed World," "The Gates Forced Open") help to indicate the organization. Within chapters, extra space between paragraphs indicates changes in the direction of the discussion. Subheadings, however, are more helpful as indicators of structure, especially for less practiced readers.

REFERENCE AIDS

With the exception of certain simple and special types, factual books should offer help at both front and back for the reader who needs to locate information quickly. Since it is important for children to develop reference skills early, a table of contents and an index should not be omitted from books for primary-grade readers. *Construction Giants* by Ross Olney has a relatively simple text in spite of the difficulty of some of the words necessary in describing the machines. The table of contents clearly lists five major headings (one is a foreword); the index is clearly set in a typeface as large as the text, with plenty of leading (space) between the lines. The heading "credits" on the index page, however, may require some explanation. The title "Photo Credits" would have been clearer to the intended readers of this book.

An index will be truly useful only if it is complete and has necessary cross references. It is difficult to think of all the possible words children might use to look up a topic or to answer a question, yet writers should consider as many possibilities as would seem reasonable. Lila Perl's *From Top Hats to Baseball Caps, from Bustles to Blue Jeans: Why We Dress the Way We Do* provides the kind of cross references that readers may need. "Blue jeans," "denims," "jeans," and "Levi's" are separate index entries that all lead to the same section of the book; "high-heeled shoes" are listed under the contemporary variant "heels."

Other helpful additions to a book are glossaries, bibliographies, suggestions for further reading, and informational appendixes. Picture glossaries are on the increase with the growing number of informational picture books. Nancy Winslow Parker and Joan Richards Wright include illustrated glossaries that summarize growth patterns and add detail about anatomy in their joint productions, *Bugs* and *Frogs, Toads, Lizards, and Salamanders.* Either book would be good for demonstrating to children the use of reference aids because both have touches of humor that add appeal as well as a full range of devices for locating and extending information. The endpapers serve as a picture glossary for *Books and Libraries* by Jack Knowlton; illustrator Harriett Barton has furnished a brightly colored chart to explain "Melvil Dewey's Decimal System."

If children are to understand the method of inquiry, they need to learn that a writer uses many sources of information. James Giblin's bibliography for *From Hand to Mouth: Or, How We Invented Knives, Forks, Spoons, and Chopsticks & the Table Manners to Go with Them* lists thirty-nine entries dating from 1927 through the 1980s. Suggestions for further reading by children are most helpful if separated from the adult's more technical resources (Giblin uses an asterisk). While many recent informational books include bibliographies, annotated entries are still unfortunately the exception rather than the rule.

Appendixes are used to extend information in lists, charts, or tabulations of data that would

With the increase in picture-book formats, more and more books are providing illustrated reference aids. This cover hints at the picture glossary inside.

Illustration by Nancy Winslow Parker from *Frogs, Toads, Lizards, and Salamanders* by Nancy Winslow Parker and Joan Richards Wright.

🐸 🐸 🐸

seem cumbersome within the text itself. *Commodore Perry in the Land of the Shogun,* Rhoda Blumberg's award-winning account of the opening of Japanese harbors to American ships, seems all the more credible because of the documents and lists presented in the appendixes. Having read that lavish gifts were exchanged during the negotiations, children can discover in Appendix C that the emperor was offered more than thirty items, including two telegraph sets, a copper lifeboat, champagne, tea, muskets, swords, and two mailbags with padlocks.

Illustrations and Format

CLARIFICATION AND EXTENSION OF TEXT

In our visually oriented culture, readers of all ages demand that a book's illustrations make it more interesting and attractive. In an informational book, the illustrations must do that, and much more. One of their basic functions is to clarify and extend the text. *Saturn: The Spectacular Planet* by Franklyn Branley would not be so spectacular without the photographs taken by Voyager 1 and Voyager 2, but it also has drawings and diagrams that help make complicated ideas about gravitation and planetary movement more understandable. Cutaway views and clear labeling are other good features of the pictures in this book.

The more abstract the topic, the more important it is that pictures help children "see" explanations. Latitude, longitude, and other mapping concepts, for instance, are often hard for children to grasp, so it is especially important that they be illustrated clearly, as Harriet Barton has done for Jack Knowlton's introductory book, *Maps and Globes.* These big, bright pictures use color to focus attention on the equator, contour lines, and other specific aspects of simplified maps.

Illustrations are especially important in clarifying size relationships. The beautiful paintings by Kenneth Lilly for *Large as Life Animals* by Joanna Cole have special impact because each figure is exactly the size of the animal it represents. Children could measure the pictures to compare the size of the tiny elf owl with the fruit bat or the giant toad. Not many topics lend themselves to life-size portrayals, of course, and that makes it important for artists to find other ways to be clear. Photographs and drawings often show magnified parts or wholes, and in many instances some information about actual size is needed. When the reader has no frame of reference for the size of an object, comparison with something familiar is most effective. If it weren't for the human hands holding the "Brazilian Princess" topaz pictured in *Earth Alive!* by Sandra Markle, most readers would fail to appreciate its tremendous size.

While in many books the illustrations add detail and extend the information of the text, in others the illustrations themselves provide the bulk of the information, or become the subject of the text. In Vicki Cobb's *For Your Own Protection: Stories Science Photos Tell,* the subtitle confirms this approach. In addition to thermograms of a child's hands, this book shows a balloon popping in a photo made with a stroboscope, a scanning electron micrograph of plaque bacteria magnified 31,000 times, and other remarkable pictures. The

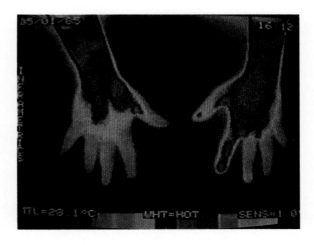

Unfamiliar types of pictures like this thermogram of a child's hands pique the reader's curiosity and invite attention to the text.

From *For Your Own Protection: Stories Science Photos Tell* by Vicki Cobb.

text functions here to clarify and extend the pictures rather than the other way around. When illustrations are this important to a book, they need to have substantive content, high-quality reproduction, and a logical presentation or layout. For other good examples of this effective presentation, look at Seymour Simon's books about the planets or Patricia Lauber's *Volcano: The Eruption and Healing of Mt. St. Helen's.*

SUITABILITY OF MEDIA

Illustrations in any medium can be clear and accurate, but one medium may be more suitable than another for a given purpose. Three-dimensional illustrations are used for clarity and interest in some books of information. People of all ages are fascinated by the paper engineering in *The Human Body* by Jonathan Miller, designed by David Pelham. This goes beyond the entertainment value of a pop-up book; its movable parts reveal more about anatomy than flat pictures can possibly do. For instance, one double spread of the torso allows the reader to flip back the muscular diaphragm, spread the rib cage to reveal the lungs, and open the lungs to study their connection to the heart. Alice and Martin Provensen also use three-dimensional, movable pictures for their book *Leonardo da*

Vinci, to celebrate as well as to demonstrate the inventiveness of this great artist and scholar.

Diagrams and drawings have an impact of their own and also have many uses especially appropriate to science books. Diagrams can reduce technological processes to their essentials or show astronomical relationships that represent distances too great to be photographed. Diagrams are also fine for giving directions, and they can be charming as well as clear. This is true of Byron Barton's work for Seymour Simon's popular *The Paper Airplane Book*, where scenes are interspersed with how-to drawings to enliven the text.

Sometimes the perception of a graphic artist is vital to the purpose of a book. *Cathedral: The Story of Its Construction* is a venture in architecture, engineering, and aesthetics that relies on the author's fine pen-and-ink drawings for its effect. David Macaulay pictures his creation at various stages during the building; his choice of views puts the reader into the action with stunning contrasts of massive proportions and minute detail. A similar format and the same standard of excellence can be found in Macaulay's *City, Castle, Pyramid, Underground,* and *Mill.* Junko Morimoto's first-person account of a terrifying historical event, *My Hiroshima*, communicates part of its message about the scope of atomic destruction through the use of space and color in her paintings. In Leonard Everett Fisher's *The Great Wall of China*, his heavy black-and-white acrylics underscore the grim nature of the story.

In spite of the range of media available for informational books, the medium of choice is now clearly photography. Photographs help establish credibility for real-life stories like *Mom Can't See Me* by Sally Hobart Alexander, an account of living in a family with a blind but very active mother. Photographs reveal the natural world in its astonishing variety, recording minute detail in an instant. The photos by Art Wolfe for James Martin's *Chameleons: Dragons in the Trees* reveal marvels of skin textures, colors, and patterns that would be difficult to reproduce with complete accuracy in a painting (see p. 660).

Photographs in informational books furnish more than technical accuracy, however. Photographers can be artists as well as recorders of information. Ken Robbins uses hand-tinted photographs in *Bridges*, a brief overview of types,

On a clear, moonless night, you can often see a hazy band of pale light stretching across the sky. This luminous band, called the Milky Way, is made up of millions and millions of stars. These stars are so far away from Earth that the tiny points of light blend into one another and you see only a faintly glowing ribbon of light.

The photographs used in Seymour Simon's *Galaxies* provide a sense of beauty as well as accurate information.

and in *A Flower Grows*, showing the sequence of stages from brown bulb to green stem to pink amaryllis blooms to dying flowers and fat seedpods. Sometimes artistry results not from a single photographer's work but from the careful choice of pictures to accompany an informational text. The photographs that illustrate Seymour Simon's many books come from a variety of sources, but their effect can be breathtaking. In *Icebergs and Glaciers*, a hugely magnified single snowflake and a blue ice crystal face each other on opposite pages as the book begins. The spectacular astronomical photographs used in *Galaxies* serve to evoke a sense of wonder as well as interest in the topic.

CAPTIONS

Children need to be able to look at an illustration and know what they are seeing, and that requires wise use of captions and labels. Many writers use the text itself, if it is brief, to explain the pictures, eliminating the need for additional captions. The words of Patricia Lauber and the photographs of

Jerome Wexler are combined in this way for *Seeds: Pop Stick Glide*, a handsome book that explains how plant life spreads. The arrangement of the text on the page and occasional references like "As you can see . . ." or "In this photo, . . ." help readers get maximum information from the illustrations as well as from the writing.

Sometimes it is helpful to have labels or other text printed within the illustration itself. In *Maps: Getting from Here to There* by Harvey Weiss, many drawings and diagrams include labels and arrows to show specifically where terms like "a south latitude" or "an east longitude" are represented on the globe. Explanation within the pictures also helps to identify contour lines and the features of a marine chart. Only occasionally does Weiss use a conventional caption to refer to an entire illustration. However an author chooses to use captions, they should be clear.

FORMAT

The total look of a book is its *format*, involving type size, leading, margins, placement of text and pictures, and arrangement of front and back matter—these include title and copyright pages in the front and indexes, bibliographies, and other aids at the back. *Mummies Made in Egypt* by Aliki incorporates hieroglyphic writing on the dedication and half-title pages, and many of the illustrations are arranged like the friezes that decorated the tombs of antiquity. This author frequently arranges sequences of pictures on the page in a comic strip or storyboard variation. In *How a Book Is Made*, this format allows different levels of information to serve different audiences. Simplified information about bookmaking is provided in a large-type, continuous narrative above and below the illustration frames. These illustrations show the people involved in making a book as well-dressed cats who make comments about the process in speech balloons. In some of the pictures, however, interior captions and detailed drawings give quite technical information. This particular book is a good choice for primary classes preparing for an author visit.

There are no absolute rules for format; the look of a book should be responsive to its purpose and its content. The broad coverage of topic intended in the "Eyewitness" series published by Knopf makes the busy layout of its pages seem rich

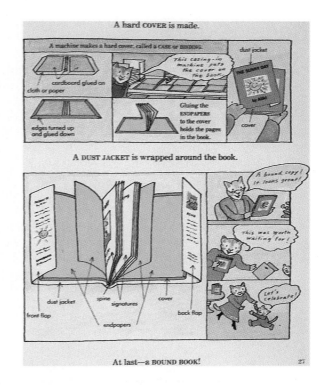

Notice how the page arrangement, illustrations, and speech balloons allow Aliki to present different levels of information in *How a Book Is Made*.

rather than crowded. Jennifer Owings Dewey takes on limited territory in *Animal Architecture;* the wide margins and carefully placed pencil drawings create a slightly formal but very attractive look.

Even a book that is sparingly illustrated may be notable for its overall design. Spacious margins and tastefully ornamented headings can make a long text seem less forbidding. The format of an informational book is an asset if it contributes to clarity or if it makes the book more appealing to its audience.

TYPES OF INFORMATIONAL BOOKS

Anyone who chooses informational books for children soon notices several subgenres or recognizable types with common characteristics. Knowing

GUIDELINES

Evaluating
Informational Books

♦ **Accuracy and Authenticity:**

Is the author qualified to write about this topic? Has the manuscript been checked by authorities in the field?

Are the facts accurate according to other sources?

Is the information up to date?

Are all the significant facts included?

Do text and illustrations reveal diversity and avoid stereotypes?

Are generalizations supported by facts?

Is there a clear distinction between fact and theory?

Do text and illustrations omit anthropomorphism and teleological explanations?

♦ **Content and Perspective:**

For what purpose was the book designed?

Is the book within the comprehension and interest range of its intended audience?

Is the subject adequately covered? Are different viewpoints presented?

Does the book lead to an understanding of the scientific method? Does it foster the spirit of inquiry?

Does the book show interrelationships? Do science books indicate related social issues?

♦ **Style**

Is information presented clearly and directly?

Is the text appropriate for the intended audience?

Does the style create the feeling of reader involvement?

Is the language vivid and interesting?

♦ **Organization:**

Is the information structured clearly, with appropriate subheadings?

Does the book have reference aids that are clear and easy to use, such as table of contents, index, bibliography, glossary, appendix?

♦ **Illustrations and Format:**

Do illustrations clarify and extend the text or speak plainly for themselves?

Are size relationships made clear?

Are media suitable to the purposes for which they are used?

Are illustrations explained by captions or labels where needed?

Does the total format contribute to the clarity and attractiveness of the book?

about these types helps the teacher and librarian provide balanced and rich resources for learning as they choose particular books for particular purposes.

Concept Books

Concept books explore the characteristics of a class of objects or of an abstract idea. Most of the informational books intended for very young children are of this type. Typically they cover such concepts as size, color, shape, spatial relationships, self, and family. Concept books for this age are discussed at length in Chapter 4. For school-age children, concept books begin with what is already familiar and move toward the unfamiliar, some by showing new ways to consider well-known materials, others by furnishing new and different examples or perspectives. Such books are often useful as idea sources for classroom experiences and discussion.

One good book for discussion is Peter Spier's *People*, an oversize picture book that appeals to many different ages as it celebrates the possibilities for variation among the several billion human beings who live on earth. Spier's drawings include many shapes and colors of ears, eyes, and noses; costumes, shelters, and pastimes from around the world; architecture, alphabets, and foods. Although the author emphasizes the uniqueness of individual appearances and preferences, the concept of cultural differences is implicit in the book. Concept books about culture always raise the issue of stereotyping. Help children think about the author's choice of representative images for this book. Primary students might compare Spier's drawings with the photographs of food, transportation, or parents and children around the world in *Bread, Bread, Bread, On the Go*, and *Loving*, all by Ann Morris and Ken Heyman.

A beautiful but difficult book is *The View from the Oak* by Judith and Herbert Kohl. In leisurely, readable prose, the authors examine the concept of *umwelt*, or the world of a living thing as experienced by that creature in terms of its own unique sensory limits. Fascinating bits of information about such diverse animals as wood ticks and oryx antelopes may be gained here, as well as an ethological per-spective. This is the first nonfiction book for children that received the National Book Award.

Informational books for children also deal with concepts related to self. One standard title is Eda LeShan's *What Makes Me Feel This Way?*, which helps children in the upper elementary grades sort out their own experiences and feelings. Jill Krementz has contributed several distinguished books in this category, including *How It Feels When a Parent Dies, How It Feels to Fight for Your Life*, and *How It Feels When Parents Divorce*. All of these are collections of true first-person statements by children from diverse backgrounds and circumstances. Sensitive photo-portraits of the commentators add immediacy by putting a real face with the words. Similar concepts are explored for a younger audience in a series by Fred Rogers, the "Mister Rogers' First Experience Books." *When a Pet Dies, Going to the Hospital*, and *Moving* are three of the many titles in this popular series.

Informational Picture Books

As earlier sections of this chapter show, more and more informational books *look* more and more like picture books—that is, they are lavishly illustrated or published in picture-book format. Only a few of these seem to fit the conventional mold of the picture storybook (see Chapter 5), and many recent titles are anything but conventional in their new ways of combining fact with fiction. Generally these books have a fictional frame with invented characters and a story that is satisfying in its own right. But such a book provides so many facts and understandings about the wider world (places, events, processes) that we consider it a natural choice for sharing information.

One of the first modern picture storybooks, *Pelle's New Suit* by Elsa Beskow, came to this country from Sweden more than sixty years ago. This story shows a little boy getting wool from his pet lamb, then having it carded, spun, dyed, woven, and finally taken to the tailor for a new suit. Compare this classic and *"Charlie Needs a Cloak"* by Tomie de Paola, which also presents, as a story, basic information about making wool into cloth. The saga of Charlie's cloak is enhanced by humor, and the illustrations serve to emphasize the steps in the cloth-making process. De Paola's *The Quicksand Book* combines cartoon-style dialogue with hand-lettered charts and diagrams. Bright, funny pictures show Jungle Boy's haughty rescue of Jungle Girl, his later comeuppance, and an unlikely monkey taking tea. Tomie de Paola was a leader in combining narrative, humor, and attractive pictures to make books that are both good stories and informational resources.

Two beautiful picture books about the medieval period present informational detail and the ambiance of the times even more effectively in their illustrations than in the text. Joe Lasker's *Merry Ever After: The Story of Two Medieval Weddings* contrasts the world of the nobility with that of the peasants by focusing on two typical couples betrothed as children and married as teenagers. Readers must consult the pictures as well as the story to get the full description of the two lifestyles. Aliki's *A Medieval Feast* shows the nobility of a manor house and their serfs preparing for a visit from the king and queen and their large entourage. A flurry of hunting, fishing, and harvesting is followed by scenes in the great kitchen and then the banquet presentation of such foods as a roast peacock reassembled with its feathers and a castle molded of pastry. Both of these picture books are standouts for their glowing, jewel-like colors and the use of decorative symbols and designs from the medieval period.

The Last Dinosaur by Jim Murphy is a surprisingly touching story that speculates about the very last creature of its kind. Drawn from a variety of scientific evidence cited in beginning and endnotes, the story gains emotion from the haunting and sometimes violent paintings by Mark Alan Weatherby. The final, poignant scene in which the female Triceratops sets out across a vast landscape to search for another herd may inspire some readers to continue the story on their own.

The most popular informational picture books of recent years, and some of the most innovative, are the "Magic School Bus" stories by Joanna Cole and Bruce Degen. *The Magic School Bus Inside the Earth* was followed by *The Magic School Bus at the Waterworks*, *The Magic School Bus Inside the Human Body*, and *The Magic School Bus Lost in the Solar System*. All of these fantastic field trips

are presided over by Ms. Frizzle, a memorable teacher, and endured by a group of children who develop recognizable personalities. Characterization, humor, and fantasy allow the creators of these books to approach science from a child's point of view, incorporating feelings ("Yuck," says one student participating in the digestive tract tour) as well as facts. Moreover, they bring all the information home, both literally and figuratively, to the classroom as each book ends.

Another innovative picture book is *A Country Far Away* by Nigel Gray and Philippe Dupasquier. The text, printed midpage, is made up of short, childlike statements: "Today was an ordinary day. I stayed home. . . . Today we went into town to do some shopping. I thought we

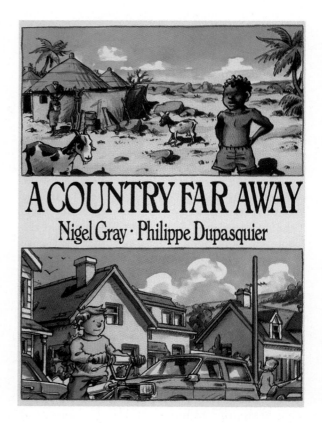

Nigel Gray and Philippe Dupasquier force readers to consider a double view of similar events in a child's life—third world and developed nation— in *A Country Far Away*.

were never going to get there."[18] The illustrations on the top half of each page show an African boy, those on the bottom a Western boy, each living a different version of the same events. Each thinks of the other's homeland as "a country far away." Although there is a loosely organized sequence of events, this is more concept book than storybook. However we choose to classify it, it provides wonderful opportunities for children to consider point of view in relation to culture.

Many informational picture books for older readers tell good stories about places or things, but they do not have the strong human characters that bring warmth to fiction. Books like David Macaulay's *Castle* and William Kurelek's *Lumberjack* are examples of this type. Two volumes by the Swiss artist Jörg Müller, *The Changing City* and *The Changing Countryside*, are really portfolios rather than books. In each, a series of foldout paintings show the many ways in which so-called progress affects the environment. John Goodall's *The Story of an English Village* is a picture book with no text except for a series of decorative labels that identify the changing centuries from the fourteenth to the twentieth. All the pictures represent the same village crossroads and a particular house with alternating exterior and interior scenes plus half-page inserts to show different activities within that setting. Goodall has produced several books using this format, including *The Story of a Castle* and *The Story of a Farm*. These wordless sociology books are particularly good resources for discussion with older children who have some prior knowledge of history.

Photographic Essays

With the increased use of photography in children's books today, the photo essay is an increasingly popular form. However, only some of the books that use photographs can be called photographic essays. Although the books by Dorothy Hinshaw Patent about various animal species (*Gray Wolf, Red Wolf*, for instance) depend on photographs by William Muñoz on almost every page,

they are not photographic essays. The essay relies on the camera in different ways: to particularize general information, to document emotion, to assure the reader of truth in an essentially journalistic fashion.

Sensitivity and vitality in George Ancona's photographs make *Handtalk: An ABC of Finger Spelling and Sign Language* by Remy Charlip and Mary Beth Miller more than a specialized ABC book. Inspired by the language of the deaf, this is a unique volume about communication, made memorable by the expressive photo demonstrations of the language in action. *Handtalk Birthday*, *Handtalk Zoo*, and *Handtalk School*, all authored or co-authored by Mary Beth Miller, continue this documentation of life in the language of the deaf.

In *Koko's Kitten* by Francine Patterson, the photographs by Ronald Cohn serve to assure the reader of truth, for the story of this lowland gorilla who learned sign language and grieved for the death of a pet cat might be dismissed as fiction by a careless reader. These full-color photos also document the emotion of the story as they show the huge primate cuddling her tiny pet and later signing her distress. The arrival of a new kitten some months later provides a happy ending. *Koko's Story* tells more about this intriguing experiment.

Numerous photographic essays present to children a glimpse of life in other lands. Two recent books set in Russia are examples. *On Their Toes: A Russian Ballet School* by Ann Morris and Ken Heyman is an eloquent description of a culture within a culture. Readers believe what the author says about the rigor of the young Soviets' training because they can see it. They will also believe the statement that the young dancers ". . . prefer dancing to anything else in the world"[19] because that message is confirmed in the photos' joyful faces. *Friendship Across Arctic Waters* by Claire Murphy and Charles Mason is a photojournalistic account of the visit of eleven Cub Scouts from Nome, Alaska, to a counterpart group of Young Pioneers across the Bering Strait in Provideniya. The mix of landscapes, action shots, and revealing close-ups of the participants is similar to that

[18]Nigel Gray, *A Country Far Away*, illustrated by Philippe Dupasquier (New York: Orchard Books, 1989), unpaged.

[19]Ann Morris, *On Their Toes: A Russian Ballet School*, illustrated by Ken Heyman (New York: Atheneum, 1991), unpaged.

found in feature magazines. The difference, of course, is the focus on children's activities and details of special interest to them, like visiting a school and shopping for toys.

Adult activities are also of interest to children, especially when they are personalized in terms of single individuals. *Trucker,* written and photographed by Hope Wurmfeld, lets young people see what it is like to drive a big rig. Driver Phil Marcum is making a long haul from Florida to Windsor, Ontario, and then home to Oneida, Tennessee—but not quite in time for his daughters' basketball game. It is the specificity of accounts like this that provide lasting impact. Another fine example is George Ancona's *Riverkeeper.* This description of the work of one man, John Cronin of the Hudson River Fishermen's Association, allows the author to bring a fresh perspective to the timely topic of efforts against pollution.

Identification Books

In its simplest form an identification book is a naming book, and this may well be the first sort of book that a very young child sees. *Tool Book* by Gail Gibbons shows simple drawings of common tools in bright colors, with appropriate labels. A phrase or two describes the common function of all those displayed on a double spread. This is information for the youngest child. But just as children grow in their ability to discriminate and classify, so do identification books become more detailed, precise, and complex. It is hard to imagine any book more thorough or more technically correct than Helen Roney Sattler's updated volume, *The New Illustrated Dinosaur Dictionary.* Students who want to match dinosaur names with further description find plenty of help in this book. Not every book that provides help in naming and classifying the world can be categorized simply as an identification book. For instance, Jan Adkins's *Moving Heavy Things* discusses the concept of mechanical advantage in practical terms, and in so doing identifies several different kinds of knots, jacks, levers, and other tools. The use of labeled diagrams and drawings makes it easier to use the book for identification purposes.

When a child brings a stone or a leaf to school and asks, "What kind is it?" the teacher or librar-ian has a built-in opportunity to introduce books to help that child discover the answer. Millicent Selsam and Joyce Hunt have written a series that is useful in teaching younger children how to examine a specimen and pick out the features that will be important in making an identification. Harriet Springer's line drawings show basic shapes and textures but eliminate the confusion of variable detail. *A First Look at Insects* and *A First Look at Seashells* are two of the many titles in this outstanding process-oriented series.

Life-Cycle Books

A fascination with animals is one of the most general and durable of children's interests, beginning very early and often continuing through adolescence into adulthood. There is always an audience for factual books that describe how animals live, with an emphasis on the inherent story element. These books cover all or some part of the cycle of life, from the birth of one animal to the birth of its progeny or the events of one year in the animal's life or the development of one animal throughout its lifetime.

Life-cycle books for young children are usually published in picture-book format, and the best are notable for both illustration and text. Susan Bonners's *A Penguin Year* has striking illustrations of black-and-white with blue shadings that emphasize the cold of the Antarctic. The narrative follows a pair of Adélie penguins from their winter home on an ice floe to the mainland rookery where they mate and take turns warming their eggs in a stony nest. Efforts to protect and bring food to the new chicks consume the summer, with its dangers from skua gulls and quick snowstorms. When autumn arrives (in March), the pair leave their young, now able to fend for themselves, and return to the open sea. Although the author has assigned the descriptive names "Scarred-wing" and "Brush-tail" to the parent penguins, this is a straightforward scientific account. Helen Cowcher's *Antarctica,* with its glowing illustrations, makes a good companion to this book.

In Barbara Juster Esbensen's *Great Northern Diver: The Loon,* artist Mary Barrett Brown uses double-spread pages and the book's horizontal shape to emphasize the sweep of northern lakes where the loons live from April to September.

The background figure of the wolf in this well-designed illustration helps the reader remember that the loon's call can mimic its mournful howl.

Illustrations by Mary Barrett Brown from *Great Northern Diver: The Loon* by Barbara Juster Esbensen.

The choice of setting dictates the part of the loons' life cycle that will be shown. One pair of birds is the focus, but they are given no names.

While an animal subject can sometimes be given a name, it may not be given powers of speech or human emotions. Even so, an accounting of authentic behavior often produces the effect of characterization; thus children frequently read these books as "stories" rather than as references. Holling C. Holling's beautifully illustrated classics *Minn of the Mississippi* and *Pagoo*, which trace the life histories of a turtle and a crawfish, are unique survival stories. The longer life-cycle stories are often stories of survival against the elements and enemies in the environment. The early books by John and Jean George, such as *Vison the Mink* and *Vulpes the Red Fox* (now out of print), remain outstanding examples of this type. Very few books of this sort are published today.

Experiment and Activity Books

To some children the word *science* is synonymous with *experiment*, and certainly experience is basic

to scientific understandings. Many basic informational books suggest a few activities to clarify concepts; in contrast, experiment books take the activities themselves as content. The appearance of the supplementary experiment or activity, frequently as a final note in a book, is quite common today. For instance, Gail Gibbons includes numbered and illustrated directions for a project on raising bean plants at the end of her book for primary readers, *From Seed to Plant*. However, new books dedicated just to experiments have gone through a period of short supply.

For very young children, experiments and directions for simple observation are usually presented in a picture-book context with illustrations that show interest and enjoyment as well as proper procedure. Seymour Simon's *Soap Bubble Magic*, illustrated by Stella Ormai, is a book of this kind. Simon's directions encourage children to watch carefully and think about what happens:

> Dip the loop into the soapy water.
> Slowly wave the loop through the air.
> What happens?
>   Quickly wave the loop through the air.
> What happens now?
> Does moving fast make more bubbles
> than moving slowly?
> Which way makes bigger bubbles?[20]

Many experiment books for older children also focus on one subject or one material. *The Science Book of Air* and others by Neil Ardley are appropriate for grades one to four. These books, British imports, are among the first to take advantage of full-color photography and high-artistry layouts in a book of directed experiments. Bernie Zubrowski's books, including *Balloons: Building and Experimenting with Inflatable Toys* and *Wheels at Work*, are produced in conjunction with the Boston Children's Museum and emphasize children discovering their own results. Another outstanding book that provides experiments to help students understand one topic is Irwin Math's *Wires and Watts: Understanding and Using Electricity*.

Some of the most engaging books of science experiments are those by Vicki Cobb. An inter-

[20]Seymour Simon, *Soap Bubble Magic*, illustrated by Stella Ormai (New York: Lothrop, 1985), pp. 14–15.

esting approach to chemistry is found in *Science Experiments You Can Eat*, a book that is fun for children old enough to handle various cooking procedures safely. Bits of the history of technology accompany the experiments in *The Secret Life of School Supplies*, which explores the properties and processes necessary to make ink, paper, chalk, glue, crayons, erasers, and other common classroom items. *The Secret Life of Cosmetics* follows the same format with a topic that may attract students who would not usually pick up a book of chemistry experiments. *Chemically Active! Experiments You Can Do at Home* is arranged so that one experiment leads directly to the next. All these books by Cobb are designed with a commentary to link the experiments so that they can be read straight through for information as well as used to guide the actual procedures.

Some books that suggest experiments also include experiences of other kinds, along with collections of interesting facts, anecdotes, or other material. These books that encourage children to explore a topic through a broad range of activities have gained popularity in recent years. *Good for Me! All About Food in 32 Bites* by Marilyn Burns is a compilation of facts, learning activities, experiments, and questions that may lead to further investigation. This is one of many titles from the "Brown Paper School Books" series, which consistently uses this format.

Sandra Markle's *Exploring Winter* includes simple experiments, such as putting one hand in hot water, the other in cold, then noticing which one feels colder when placed in lukewarm water. This book also has charts of good and poor heat conductors, riddles about insulation, recipes for bird food, directions for a winter scavenger hunt, weather myths, suggestions on melting snow to examine it for pollutants, and dozens of other ideas. Three additional volumes with ideas for *Exploring Summer*, *Exploring Spring*, and *Exploring Autumn* furnish activities and experiments for every season.

Books like this make good browsing and are a source of possible projects for individual study or for activities that might be tried and discussed in class. Teachers as well as students appreciate the variety and creativity of the ideas. However, it is important to remember that activity books are not designed for reference. There is seldom an index, and headings may have more entertainment value than clarity. For easy access to specific information, other types of books are required.

Documents and Journals

A small but important contribution to literature for children in recent years has been the publication of books based on original documents and journals. Julius Lester's extraordinary *To Be a Slave*, a Newbery honor book in 1969, provides reproduction of primary sources as a background for the study of African-American history. The author combines the verbatim testimony of former slaves with his own strong commentary:

> To be a slave was to be a human being under conditions in which that humanity was denied. They were not slaves. They were people. Their condition was slavery.[21]

A more recent work that focuses on a broader sweep of history is *Now Is Your Time! The African-American Struggle for Freedom* by Walter Dean Myers. Period photographs and reproductions of lists and documents are an important part of this compelling book.

Firsthand accounts are also the base for Jim Murphy's *The Boys' War: Confederate and Union Soldiers Talk About the Civil War*. On both sides, many soldiers were underage boys who had gone off to war looking for something more adventuresome than routine farm chores. The author quotes a Wisconsin boy who wrote of his experiences at Shiloh:

> "I want to say, as we lay there and the shells were flying over us, my thoughts went back to my home, and I thought what a foolish boy I was to run away and get into such a mess as I was in. I would have been glad to have seen my father coming after me."[22]

Books like this lend authenticity to the picture of conflict that students get in historical fiction such as Patricia Beatty's *Charley Skedaddle*.

[21] Julius Lester, *To Be a Slave*, illustrated by Tom Feelings (New York: Dial, 1968), p. 28.
[22] Jim Murphy, *The Boys' War* (New York: Clarion, 1990), p. 33.

The message attributed to Chief Seattle of the Suquamish tribe on the occasion of a treaty signing in the 1850s became a document famous for its eloquence and its plea for environmental awareness. Susan Jeffers adapts and interprets his words in *Brother Eagle, Sister Sky,* an oversize picture book. Much critical discussion has centered on Jeffers's selection and adaptation of the original and on her use of visual images that represent many Native-American peoples, not just the Suquamish.

Oral history has become increasingly important as a way to document the details of everyday life in the recent past. Alvin Schwartz's *When I Grew Up Long Ago: Older People Talk About the Days When They Were Young* is like having a conversation with several articulate great-grandparents at once. The interview material has been edited and arranged so that different people's recollections about a single topic like school or work can be presented together.

Russell Freedman frequently uses photographs from archival sources to document his historical books as well as his biographies. *Immigrant Kids* includes reproductions of photos of passengers on the steerage deck of an immigrant liner in 1893, street scenes from New York City's Lower East Side in 1898, school scenes, and many views of children at work. *Children of the Wild West* furnishes photographs from a time and place where cameras were scarce. Children interested in the westward movement in the United States can study the pictures as well as the text of this book for information. Photos of families with their covered wagons clearly show modes of dress and meager possessions. Log cabins, sod houses, and schoolrooms can be compared and described. The pictures of Native-American children in tribal dress and at government boarding schools are particularly interesting.

Laura Ingalls Wilder fans will be interested in a book called *West from Home: Letters of Laura Ingalls Wilder, San Francisco 1915.* The letters were written to the author's husband while she was visiting her daughter Rose and attending the 1915 Panama Pacific International Exposition. The firsthand detail provides personal insights, as well as a measure of the country during that year. There is similar documentary value in Wilder's *The First Four Years,* a journal-like account discov-

The use of archival photos lends authenticity and immediacy to historical information.

From *Immigrant Kids* by Russell Freedman.

ered as a handwritten manuscript among the author's posthumous papers. In this book, which tells of the first years of the Wilders' married life on a claim that had to be made into a farm, the reader can see the problems, attitudes, and some of the philosophies of another time. Information without benefit of an intermediary is the unique contribution of documentary literature.

A much older journal has been excerpted and edited by Peter and Connie Roop to help elementary students form some understanding of the complexities of the man Columbus and his discoveries. *I, Columbus: My Journal—1492–3,* shares simple selections from the log of the explorer's first voyage. Usually shelved with biography for the insights it provides into personality, this stands also among the intriguing documents of history.

Survey Books

The purpose of a survey book is to give an overall view of a substantial topic and to furnish a representative sampling of facts, principles, or issues. Such a book emphasizes balance and breadth of coverage, rather than depth.

The Book of Eagles by Helen Roney Sattler offers a chapter of general introduction plus others on eagles as hunters, courting and nesting habits, baby eagles, and relationship with humans. Additional information is presented in list form and an extensive picture glossary. A child looking for in-depth information on a specific genus like the bald eagle, however, might need to go on to other sources. The survey book furnishes an authoritative introduction to a topic but not necessarily all the information a student could want.

A few books attempt to give children a survey of the important people, places, and events in the history of the world. Hendrik Van Loon's *The Story of Mankind* was the first book to interpret world history to children in an interesting and informational fashion. This book, a pioneer in the field and the winner of the first Newbery award in 1922, is now available in a revised edition.

Historical surveys today are more likely to adopt a particular perspective, an "angle" on history that makes wide-ranging content more manageable. Italian artist Piero Ventura in his book *Great Painters* chronicles much of the history of art through reference to the lives and words of more than seventy painters. Ventura's own illustrations add liveliness and humor to this fairly extensive overview. The appended information on styles, periods, and biographical data for the artists is a ready reference source. A similarly successful book for older readers is Suzanne Jurmain's *Once upon a Horse: A History of Horses—and How They Shaped Our History*. Horse lovers and history browsers alike will find many leads to follow in this lively narrative.

Survey books are available at many different levels of complexity and reading difficulty. A teacher or librarian may need to help children skim to find those that are most appropriate for their use.

Specialized Books

Specialized books are designed to give specific information about a relatively limited topic. These books satisfy particular interests; they are more likely to be used intensively than extensively, on a onetime basis rather than as a frequent reference. For example, Caroline Arnold's *Saving the Peregrine Falcon* describes the work of California scientists attempting to preserve this species by retrieving and caring for eggs that have become too thin-shelled to survive under ordinary conditions in the wild. This will be useful information for children studying endangered species.

Many specialized books provide extensions of content areas that are frequently part of the elementary social studies curriculum. *The First Thanksgiving Feast* by Joan Anderson dispels myths about that event which are common to many classrooms. George Ancona's photographs record a reenactment of the early celebration by staff members at Plimouth Plantation in Massachusetts, a living history museum. Costumes and period details have been carefully recreated in this and other titles by the same collaborative team, including *Pioneer Children of Appalachia* and *A Williamsburg Household*. John Loeper's *Going to School in 1876* gives detailed information about an intriguing specific aspect of nineteenth-century history. Upper elementary children studying the Native-American tribes of the Southwest can gain a historical perspective from Stephen Trimble's *The Village of Blue Stone*, which recreates life in an ancient Anasazi village.

Teachers and librarians have noted that specialized books today are more specialized than ever, covering narrow topics and unique interests. These books may be of high quality and of great appeal to children, but they may not be discovered on the library shelf unless they are introduced. Readers do not deliberately seek a book on a topic that they do not know exists. For that reason, an adult may need to point out Suzanne Haldane's *Helping Hands: How Monkeys Assist People Who Are Disabled,* the fascinating account of a program in which capuchin monkeys are trained to perform crucial tasks for quadriplegics.

Many specialized books are geared to the personal interests of children. *What Has Ten Legs and Eats Corn Flakes?* by Ron Roy is about acquiring and caring for three small pets that would be reasonably easy to keep in close quarters. This book has good advice for classroom pet keeping as well as for apartment dwellers or others with limited space. There are books about playing soccer, collecting stamps, losing weight, learning ballet. Whatever the child's interest, it is likely that a specialized book can be found to extend it.

Craft and How-To Books

A fascinating array of craft and activity books give directions for making and doing. Pride of accomplishment is emphasized in Harlow Rockwell's *I Did It,* a just-right combination of easy words and simple directions for primary-grade children. The six activities range in difficulty from making grocery-bag masks to baking bread. Another book geared to younger children is Marc Brown's *Your First Garden Book,* with directions for windowsill, backyard, and sidewalk gardens, plus bright pictures full of good humor.

Cookbooks for children ought to have sparkling, clear directions and adequate warnings about the safe use of tools and equipment. *The Fun of Cooking* by Jill Krementz offers clearly written directions followed by sequential photos of children preparing the recipes they have themselves recommended. Safety tips are outlined in the front of the book opposite the contents page, and reminders are added at appropriate points within the instructions for each recipe. A popular character who has inspired a cookbook is Peter Rabbit. The illustrations in Arnold Dobrin's *Peter Rabbit's Natural Foods Cookbook* are from the original Beatrix Potter books, complementing the theme of simple goodness from nutritional recipes. Two other literature-based recipe collections are Barbara Walker's *The Little House Cookbook: Frontier Foods from Laura Ingalls Wilder's Classic Stories* and *The Louisa May Alcott Cookbook,* compiled by Gretchen Anderson, which furnishes period recipes for foods mentioned in Alcott's *Little Women* and *Little Men.* Children may be surprised to learn that the author of the Alcott

cookbook conceived the idea and tested the recipes when she was only 9 years old.

Clear directions are usually clearer if appropriately illustrated. *Painting Faces* by Suzanne Haldane shows children applying face paint according to different traditions around the globe. Some of the color photographs are sequentially arranged, so that would-be face painters can easily see what areas of paint should be applied first, as well as what the finished product should look like. Line drawings make appropriate pictures to demonstrate the steps of *How to Make Pop-Ups* by Joan Irvine. This book has a high success rate with students; they are able to make quite com-

The engaging photographs of painted faces in this book serve two purposes—to make children want to try face painting for themselves and to give them a guide for the finished product.

From *Painting Faces* by Suzanne Haldane.

plex-looking paper designs in three dimensions with a minimum of adult help.

Some craft books deal so specifically with approaches and techniques common to the activity-centered classroom that it is likely they will be used as much by teachers as by individual children. The Parents' Nursery School book *Kids Are Natural Cooks: Child-Tested Recipes for Home and School Using Natural Foods* is an example. With recipes planned for variation and experimentation, young children are encouraged to work with adults in growing sprouts, grinding peanuts, making vegetable soup, and other experiences. Helen Roney Sattler's *Recipes for Art and Craft Materials* will prove indispensable to teachers. Included are a variety of basic substances that children can make for their own use—such as paste, modeling and casting compounds, papier-mâché, inks, and dried-flower preservatives. See "Making Things" in Chapter 13 for ways to incorporate cookbooks and craft books with other literature.

USING LITERATURE ACROSS THE CURRICULUM

One of the important components of a literature program (see Chapters 12 and 13) is using literature across the curriculum. If children are to become real readers, they should meet good books not only at reading time, but also as they study history, science, the arts—all subject areas. Outstanding informational books, those that might fit author John McPhee's term "the literature of fact," are the most obvious places to begin in choosing titles to use in the content areas.

Informational Books in the Classroom

FUNCTIONS OF INFORMATIONAL BOOKS

As in any genre, the best informational books should be appreciated for their artistry. Good writing, fine illustration, and high-quality bookmaking all have intrinsic aesthetic value. And, like fiction, informational books can provide satisfaction and delight for interested readers. Informational books are a bit different, however. They also fulfill special teaching functions that

need to be considered in planning classroom materials and activities.

Serve as Curriculum Content Resources

The information in trade books is a major content resource for the curriculum. Elementary school textbooks are frequently overgeneralized or oversimplified in the attempt to keep them reasonably short and readable. A selection of informational books can provide the depth and richness of detail not possible in textbook coverage of the same topic. The latest informational books are also likely to be more up-to-date than textbooks, since the process of producing and choosing textbooks may take many months or even years. The adopted series then may not be revised, or replaced, for quite some time. However, new trade books on popular or timely topics appear every year.

Many teachers would use an up-to-date informational book like *Voyager to the Planets* by Necia Apfel to supplement the science textbook. Others might completely bypass the textbook and assemble many books about space and the solar system (probably including such titles as Seymour Simon's *Neptune* and Patricia Lauber's *Journey to the Planets*) to provide information much richer than the text could offer.

Develop Critical Thinking

The availability of several informational books on a single topic is important for teachers to consider because it presents ready-made opportunities to encourage critical reading. When children's information all comes from one source, they are likely to accept the author's selection and interpretation of facts without question. Two or more books provide a built-in comparison. Dorothy Hinshaw Patent's *Yellowstone Fires: Flames and Rebirth* and Patricia Lauber's *Summer of Fire: Yellowstone 1988* are both fine books. Although there are striking similarities, there are differences in coverage and emphasis. Readers need to consider which author provides more information about the forests' recovery. Which book provides better background on the region and its geography? What attitudes about the Park Service burn policy do the authors seem to favor? Encouraging children to ask themselves questions like these helps them make practical and critical judgments about what they are reading.

Using informational books leads to varied opportunities for teaching critical reading in context rather than with skill sheets or sterile exercises. One sixth-grade teacher who had talked with her students about the characteristics of good informational books found them complaining about the quality of some of the titles in the school library. This grew into a project in which all the students participated, comparing and scoring library books about common sixth-grade research topics. One outcome, in addition to the children's increased awareness, was a "wish list" asking the librarian to purchase additional books about castles, endangered wildlife, and other subjects.

At the prereading level, children can compare books read aloud by the teacher, look critically at the illustrations, and decide which ones give them needed information. A kindergarten teacher who shared several books about tools with her children asked them to decide which book's pictures did the best job of showing how the tools worked. To check their judgment, they took turns at the classroom workbench, under adult supervision, trying out the tools.

Most teachers or librarians who encourage the critical comparison of books find that helping children construct a chart of similarities and differences is an aid to clear thinking. The most challenging part is developing good categories. The teacher may start with basic identifying information (title, author, illustrator) and draw descriptive categories from discussion with the children. Questions such as "What did you notice first about this book?" or "Were the same things important in both books?" can be used as a start. Eight-year-olds comparing *The Milk Makers* by Gail Gibbons and *Cows in the Parlor* by Cynthia McFarland might notice that the Gibbons book has paintings whereas the McFarland book has photographs. The Gibbons book includes diagrams of a cow's stomachs, but the other doesn't. The book by McFarland focuses on Jersey cows and one particular farm; the other shows Holsteins in a more generalized setting. Gibbons also includes extra information about how milk is processed and distributed. A very simple type of chart would display the two book titles at the top of a long sheet of paper, with various points of information ("Cows are milked twice a day," "Cows have four stomachs," etc.) listed down the side. Children would then check under the appropriate titles to indicate whether those points were included in each book. In more complete charts, students may supply descriptive detail about content, illustrations, or format, or they may quote brief examples of text. If the teacher

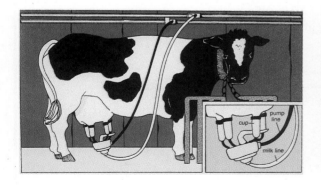 

Compare the information value of these two illustrations of a cow hooked to a milking machine. Which shows the milking hookup more clearly? Which presents a better picture of the whole apparatus?

Illustration by Gail Gibbons from *The Milk Makers*. Photograph by Cynthia McFarland from *Cows in the Parlor*.

HELPING CHILDREN EVALUATE INFORMATIONAL BOOKS

When Rebecca Thomas, a school librarian in Shaker Heights, Ohio, introduced *Storms* by Seymour Simon to a group of fourth graders, she covered up most of the front jacket. With only the title visible, she asked them to think what might be included in a book about storms. Their first response was to name the kinds of storms they knew—thunderstorms, snowstorms, tornadoes, and hurricanes. They also suggested other topics that could be in such a book: winds, thunder and lightning, the damage storms can cause, and how scientists know about storms. They decided that a book about storms should be illustrated with high-quality photographs that really picture storms and their actions.

With the librarian's help, they then began to develop some questions they would use to decide if the book was a good one:

Does the book cover the subject?
How good are the pictures?
Who will be able to understand the book?
How much actual information is included?
Does it set information straight (correct mistaken ideas)?

By the time this brief discussion was finished, the children were eager to see if Seymour Simon's book met their expectations, and of course they registered immediate approval when she showed them the front jacket. As she read aloud, she encouraged students to note if their questions had been answered. She stopped frequently so they could discuss particular pictures and the clarity of the writing based on their "Who will be able to understand the book?" question.

These students used the criteria they had developed in question form to measure not only the success of *Storms* but also of other titles on the same topic as they completed a classroom unit on weather. The librarian's introduction engaged the children's interest in one book as it set the stage for their reading of other nonfiction titles. Helping children focus on the possibilities and the strengths of specific books encourages them to develop understandings about genre and the broader world of literature.

Rebecca Thomas, Librarian
Fernway School
Shaker Heights, Ohio

directs a few chart-making experiences first, children then find it easier to do other comparisons independently or with a small group.

Provide Guides for Children's Reporting

Children who have searched for information on a topic need to synthesize and report their discoveries. Although they will need to have some experience with conventional, straightforward summaries, they can also borrow other forms of reporting from informational books. An ABC book is one way of collecting miscellaneous information about a place or a historical period. Jonathan Hunt's *Illuminations*, with its glowing pictures and manuscript decorations, is one model that has special appeal for older students. Other possibilities are question-and-answer formats, guided

The beauty of Jonathan Hunt's *Illuminations* helps convince older students that making an ABC book is a good way to share information.

❦   ❦   ❦

tours, diaries, and life stories of plants, animals, or machines. Not only is this usually more fun than reports, it often encourages more of the kind of thinking the teacher is trying to promote. For example, studying a natural environment should help children see the interdependence of living things. Interdependence is the focus that Jean George has taken in her nature story *One Day in the Alpine Tundra*. This huge concept is manageable because all the action is focused on one day's time. Birds and animals prey on one another, a storm arises, and a falling boulder causes a chain reaction of changes on the face of the tundra. Children using this frame to write their own "One Day in the Rain Forest" or "One Day on the Beach" would need to sift through all their information and decide what things might really happen during the course of twenty-four hours and how each event would affect others. More about reports based on the structures and formats of children's books, with examples of student work, is included in Chapter 13.

Suggest Areas and Methods of Study

Authors of fine informational books approach their material in interesting ways that may be easily adapted for the classroom. Although it's more usual to find good books that support a lesson, it's also possible for a good book to suggest a lesson. *Tiger Lilies and Other Beastly Plants* by Elizabeth Ring combines science and language study as it examines plants named for their similarity to certain features of animals. A one-page description faces an illustration showing the plant and the animal together for tiger lilies, elephant's ears, skunk cabbage, snake gourd, and several others.

Jim Arnosky's *A Kettle of Hawks* explains in words and watercolors the names used to identify wildlife groups, including a cloud of tadpoles and a gaggle of geese. These attractive books remind us that there is much to be learned about naming in nature study. Either book could be the catalyst for a broad study of names and naming including myths, culture, and geography as well as science and language. Or it could be the basis for a single interesting session.

Middle school teachers can discover a new twist for social studies projects in Catherine Noren's *The Way We Looked: The Magic and*

Meaning of Family Photographs. This book suggests how to look at old portraits and snapshots as a source for inferences about relationships, lifestyles, and levels of prosperity. (How close do people stand? How formal are the poses? In what condition are the subject's clothes and shoes?) Lila Perl's *The Great Ancestor Hunt* offers good suggestions for collecting family folklore at holiday get-togethers as well as tips for using public records. Family tree projects can be confusing for children of blended families, so the focus here on a direct-ancestry chart makes the purpose clearer.

For young children, concept books often lead to ideas for good classification activities. One kindergarten teacher was inspired by the categories used by Joan Rahn in *Holes*, such as "Holes That Hold Things" and "Holes That Let Some Things Go Through But Not Others." She listed each category on chart paper, then divided her class into teams to search the classroom for examples to complete the chart.

CHOOSING INFORMATIONAL BOOKS FOR THE CLASSROOM

Children do not find the most exciting informational books by chance. Some of these books need to be singled out for prominent attention in the school library, but generally the books we most want children to discover should be brought directly to the classroom and made readily available for browsing, reference, and in-depth study. This requires an investment of time by the teacher for tracking down and selecting titles. Unfortunately, textbooks and curriculum materials give few hints about children's books available in their topic areas. Librarians can direct teachers to standard reference sources and bibliographies, but it is also important for the teacher to watch for new books with particular potential for the classroom.

Two annual book lists prepared by content-area specialists in cooperation with the Children's Book Council identify the best of the new books for the sciences and for social studies. The "Outstanding Science Trade Books for Children" list is published each year in *Science and Children* magazine; "Notable Children's Trade Books in the Field of Social Studies" appears annually in *Social Education*. Another source that many teach-

ers find helpful is *The Kobrin Letter*,[23] a newsletter published ten times a year. Each issue reviews new informational books alongside older ones on several topics—books about train travel, for instance, or wild cats or dealing with divorce. *Book Links*, a periodical of the American Library Association, is geared to those who want to make connections among all kinds of books for units or theme studies. Lists that mix fiction and nonfiction appear alongside short feature articles in this helpful resource (see Appendix B).

Choosing books to serve the purposes of both teachers and children is just as important as selecting for quality. Much of the planning and selecting should be done before beginning a study, although children will raise questions and develop interests along the way that require new resources.

Defining some subtopics for a major study makes it easier to find appropriate books. One group of primary teachers who planned together for a science-focused unit study of water made a list that included the following content areas:

Bodies of water
    freshwater rivers and ponds
    saltwater seas and oceans
Water transportation
Water formations
    the water cycle
    fog/mist, rain, snow
Water creatures
    fish, birds, mammals, amphibians
Children's experiences with water
    playing in snow, watering seeds
    making soup, taking a bath

Books for information gathering and for support of the observations and investigations planned in each area were then assembled so that children could begin their study with rich resources.

This kind of preplanning, especially at the upper grade levels, eliminates the frustrations of children who are asked to research a topic only to find that books are not available to answer their questions. Cooperation and communication between the teacher and the librarian are essen-

[23] *The Kobrin Letter,* Beverly Kobrin, Editor, 732N Greer Road, Palo Alto, CA 94303.

tial in order to make the right books accessible at the right time.

Regardless of the topic to be studied, teachers may need to consider common purposes and functions of informational books so that their choices will represent a wide range of possibilities. The following checklist can be used as a reminder:

♦ Books to attract attention to the topic
♦ Books for browsing and exploring content
♦ Books with read-aloud possibilities
♦ Books for independent reading at varying levels of difficulty
♦ Basic reference books
♦ Books with enough information for in-depth study
♦ Books with a limited focus for very specific interests
♦ Books to guide activities and experiments
♦ Books that can be readily compared
♦ Books that introduce new perspectives or connections
♦ Books to accommodate new and extended interests

A selection of quality informational books representing these categories supports children's growth in reading and appreciation for good writing as well as their development of understandings within the content area.

Integrating Fact and Fiction

Using literature across the curriculum may begin with informational books, but it certainly does not have to end there. Many picture books, poems, traditional stories, novels, and biographies are natural choices for extending children's interest or knowledge base in a subject area. However, literature should never be distorted to fulfill the purposes of an informational lesson. One student participant from a university read Taro Yashima's *Crow Boy* to a class of 9- and 10-year-olds. When she finished the book she told the children that the story took place in Japan and asked them if they knew where Japan was. There was a mad dash for the globe to see who could be the first to locate Japan. Then the participant went on to ask what Japan was, finally eliciting the answer she wanted—"an island." Next she asked what appeared to be a very unrelated question: "Why did Chibi have a rice ball wrapped in a radish leaf for his lunch instead of a hamburger?" The children were baffled. Finally, the participant gave

RESOURCES FOR TEACHING

♦ FACT AND FICTION: BOOKS TO USE TOGETHER ♦

EGGS (GRADES K–2)

Chickens Aren't the Only Ones, Heller	Informational
A Chick Hatches, Cole	Informational
The Talking Eggs, San Souci	Traditional
The Bad Egg: The True Story of Humpty Dumpty, Hayes	Traditional
Chicken Man, Edwards	Picture Book
Bread and Jam for Frances, Hoban	Picture Book

WET WEATHER (GRADES 1–3)

Flash, Crash, Rumble and Roll, Branley	Informational
Storms, Simon	Informational
Llama and the Great Flood, Alexander	Traditional
Peter Spier's Rain, Spier	Picture Book
Come a Tide, Lyon	Picture Book

◆ FACT AND FICTION: BOOKS TO USE TOGETHER (CONTINUED) ◆

BUGS (GRADES 2–3)

Bugs, Parker and Wright	Informational
Monarch Butterfly, Gibbons	Informational
Joyful Noise, Fleischman	Poetry
When the Woods Hum, Ryder	Picture Book
James and the Giant Peach, Dahl	Fantasy

NATIVE AMERICANS ON THE PLAINS (GRADES 3–5)

. . . If You Lived with the Sioux Indians, McGovern	Informational
Indian Chiefs, Freedman	Informational
Iktomi and the Boulder, Goble	Traditional
Dancing with the Indians, Medearis	Picture Book

ONCE UPON THE PRAIRIE (Grades 3–6)

Children of the Wild West, Freedman	Informational
Prairie Visions, Conrad	Biography
Dakota Dugout, Turner	Picture Book
Three Names, MacLachlan	Picture Book
My Prairie Christmas, Harvey	Picture Book
Sarah, Plain and Tall, MacLachlan	Fiction
Prairie Songs, Conrad	Fiction
My Daniel, Conrad	Fiction

SLAVERY AND FREEDOM (GRADES 4–6)

Escape from Slavery, Rappaport	Informational
To Be a Slave, Lester	Informational
Lincoln: A Photobiography, Freedman	Biography
Frederick Douglass: The Black Lion, McKissack	Biography
Nettie's Trip South, Turner	Picture Book
The House of Dies Drear, Hamilton	Fiction
Jayhawker, Beatty	Fiction
Shades of Gray, Reeder	Fiction

CHINA (GRADES 5–7)

City Kids in China, Thomson	Informational
A Young Painter, Zhensun and Low	Biography
The Spring of Butterflies, He Liyi	Traditional
Chinese Mother Goose Rhymes, Wyndham	Traditional
The China Year, Neville	Fiction
Year of the Panda, Schlein	Fiction
The Great Wall of China, Fisher	Informational

them a brief but erroneous geography lesson in which she told them that since Japan was an island it was very wet and flat so the Japanese people could only raise rice, not beef for hamburgers! The student's university supervisor finally stepped in to save the day by helping the children talk about Chibi's loneliness and the artist's use of space and visual symbols.

Scholar Louise Rosenblatt[24] warns against this way of "using" literature, saying that teachers have a responsibility not to confuse children about the predominant stance or attitude appropriate for a particular reading purpose. The purpose we most want to encourage for works of fiction is reading for pleasure and insight (what Rosenblatt calls "aesthetic" reading), not the carrying away of factual information ("efferent" reading), which is a secondary purpose.

Literature across the curriculum does not mean forcing connections between fact and fiction, as the student in our example attempted to do. Nor does it mean reading a nature poem for literal information about a bird's habitat or using sentences from a favorite story as the basis for language drill or diagramming sentences. It does mean recognizing that some pieces of literature have a strong background of fact and provide a unique human perspective on historical, scientific, and technological subjects.

Water Sky by Jean Craighead George, for instance, encompasses a thorough knowledge of whales and whaling within an imaginative story about a Boston teenager and his Inuit hosts in Barrow, Alaska. Through its description of the whaling camp and the young visitor's contributions to its work, both good and bad, the book offers a commentary on humanity, cultural difference, and the relationship of civilization and the natural world. *Number the Stars* by Lois Lowry tells the suspenseful story of a Danish child in World War II who plays a part in helping a Jewish friend and her parents escape from the Nazis. This story incorporates a great deal of background information on the Danish resistance movement and the character of Denmark and its people. Even a slim picture book like *Watch the Stars Come Out* by Riki Levinson has a base of historical information in the illustrations by Diane Goode, which show an immigrant ship, the Statue of Liberty, and street scenes on New York's Lower East Side.

Students would not use these books to gather facts in their research on whales, World War II, or immigrants. Even so, they are important books for children who are studying these topics to discover. Fiction gives a perspective that allows us to know facts in another way. It is especially important for children to confirm what they are learning from informational sources by meeting similar ideas in the more human frame of literature.

Pulling together fiction and nonfiction selections that work well together is an ongoing process for most teachers. A record of titles should be kept so that these books can be shelved or displayed together when appropriate. A few sample groupings are shown in the accompanying box.

Combining fact and fiction resources on a large scale can lead to the creation of an integrated theme unit encompassing learning in all subjects. The focus topic may be taken from the sciences (color, for example), from history or social studies (colonial life or houses), or from language and the arts (signs and symbols), but it must be broad enough to allow students to develop in many skill areas as they work through a wide range of interrelated content, using trade books and other materials. Textbooks are used as reference resources, if at all. This challenging but satisfying way of teaching requires a thorough knowledge of children's literature.

Fine informational books and related books of fiction are important to the curriculum whether they serve as the major resource or as supplements to formal instructional materials. Enthusiastic teachers who have learned to recognize the best and to choose wisely for a variety of purposes will put children in touch with an exciting and satisfying way to learn.

[24]Louise Rosenblatt, "Literature—S.O.S.!" *Language Arts*, vol. 68 (October 1991) pp. 444–448.

SUGGESTED LEARNING EXPERIENCES

1. Talk to a group of children to find what special interests or hobbies they have. Make a survey of nonfiction to see what informational books might enrich these interests. Plan a display of some of these books for a classroom or library interest center.
2. Select several informational books on one topic—such as ecology, the solar system, or China. Evaluate them, using the criteria in this chapter. Plan activity cards or questions that would interest children in the books and help them use the books more effectively.
3. Working with one child or a small group of children, select a craft or activity book that seems suited to their age level. Watch carefully as children follow the directions given. What difficulties do they have? What questions do they ask? Could you make the directions clearer, safer, or more imaginative?
4. Working with a small group of your peers, locate informational books published within a single year. Review and discuss these to select one or more "award winners." What criteria would you use? What categories would you establish? What issues arise as you discuss what makes a high-quality book?
5. Work with a group of children in writing an informational book modeled after one of the documentary accounts or a photo essay using their own snapshots. What kinds of research and choices are involved in following the form?
6. Choose one informational book with potential for interconnections in many subject areas, such as Aliki's *Mummies Made in Egypt*. Plan questions and activities; choose other literature to help children explore some of the related topics such as building the pyramids, writing with hieroglyphics, using preservatives, or the art of ancient Egypt.
7. Develop and use with children a learning activity that will encourage critical reading of informational books. Focus on identifying authors' points of view, comparing authenticity of sources, verifying facts, and the like.
8. Begin a file of book combinations that could be used in science, social studies, the arts, or language study. Consider the different perspectives that children will draw from each.

RELATED READINGS

1. "Aspects of Children's Informational Books," John Donovan, guest ed. *Wilson Library Bulletin*, vol. 49, no. 2 (October 1974), pp. 145–177.

    Almost the entire issue of this well-known periodical is devoted to an analysis of children's informational books. Zena Sutherland's excellent article, "Information Pleases—Sometimes," gives criteria for evaluating informational books and takes issue with some of Margery Fisher's criteria in *Matters of Fact*. Olivia Coolidge describes the process of writing authentic biography in her article, "My Struggle with Facts." In an essay, "To Each Generation Its Own Rabbits," Dennis Flanagan, editor of *Scientific American*, shows how *Watership Down* by Richard Adams embraces the two worlds of science and literature. Other articles relevant to this chapter are included in this fine special issue.
2. Carr, Jo, compiler. *Beyond Fact: Nonfiction for Children and Young People*. Chicago: American Library Association, 1982.

    This excellent collection of articles is headlined by a section called "Nonfiction Writing: Books as Instruments of Intelligence," which includes the title piece "Beyond Fact" by Milton Meltzer and a thought-provoking comparison of several books on one topic, "Out in Space" by Denise Wilms. Other sections cover science, history, biography, and controversial books. Lead articles by Carr for each section raise many discussion-worthy points. Appendixes list nonfiction winners of book awards and professional books and journals.

3. Cleaver, Betty P., Barbara Chatton, and Shirley Vittum Morrison. *Creating Connections: Books, Kits, and Games for Children*. Chicago: Garland, 1986.

    This resource guide emphasizes the integration of materials across the curriculum, including the connections to be made between fact and fiction. Six topics of study—Appalachia, bodies, cities, monsters, oceans, and sound—are outlined in detail, with an annotated list of books, kits, and games.

4. Fisher, Margery. *Matters of Fact: Aspects of Non-fiction for Children*. New York: Crowell, 1972.

    This authoritative book by an English author provides criteria for judging and selecting nonfiction books for children. The first chapter describes the various types of informational books; the following chapters take an in-depth look at books about particular themes—such as bread, cowboys, honeybees, and atoms. Three chapters are devoted to an analysis of biographies about Bach, Helen Keller, and Abraham Lincoln. This work has become a standard in the field.

5. Giblin, James Cross. "The Rise and Fall and Rise of Juvenile Nonfiction, 1961–1988." *School Library Journal*, vol. 48 (October 1988), pp. 27–31.

    A distinguished editor and author of informational books provides a firsthand account of nearly three decades of trends and changes in nonfiction for children.

6. Graves, Donald H. *Investigate Nonfiction*. Portsmouth, N.H.: Heinemann, 1989.

    Through its insights into children's efforts to create nonfiction, this slim volume provides new ways of thinking about and teaching about the genre.

7. "Informational Books for Children," Geraldine DeLuca and Roni Natov, eds. *The Lion and the Unicorn*, vol. 6 (1982).

    This theme-centered issue features Patricia Lauber's thoughts on "What Makes an Appealing and Readable Science Book?" and two interviews with science writers Seymour Simon and Anne Ophelia Dowden. This last piece is one of the few to offer insight into the process of illustrating a science book. Other articles and reviews of professional books are also of interest.

8. Kobrin, Beverly. *Eyeopeners! How to Choose and Use Children's Books about Real People, Places, and Things*. New York: Viking, 1988.

    Enthusiastic and practical, this review of more than five hundred nonfiction books offers teaching tips for "parents, grandparents, and other educators." The emphasis on linking specific books and activities and an easy-to-read format combine to make a handy classroom reference.

9. "Nonfiction, Language Learning, and Language Teaching," William H. Teale, ed. *Language Arts*, vol. 68, no. 6 (October 1991).

    This themed issue has articles by Louise Rosenblatt on stances toward fiction and nonfiction in the classroom; by Christine Pappas on young children's readings of informational text; and by Lynne Putnam on dramatizing nonfiction. Evelyn Freeman writes about informational books as models for student reports, and Sylvia Vardell explains the selection criteria for the Orbis Pictus Award.

10. Pappas, Christine C., Barbara Z. Kiefer, and Linda S. Levstik. *An Integrated Language Perspective in the Elementary School: Theory into Action*. White Plains, N.Y.: Longman, 1990.

    The approaches described in this comprehensive text show literature as one of the aspects of language to be integrated throughout the content areas. The specific examples of teaching strategies and of solving problems of classroom logistics are especially helpful.

REFERENCES

INFORMATIONAL BOOKS

Adkins, Jan. *Moving Heavy Things*. Houghton Mifflin, 1980.
Alexander, Sally Hobart. *Mom Can't See Me*, photographs by George Ancona. Macmillan, 1990.
Aliki (Brandenberg). *How a Book Is Made*. Crowell, 1986.

————. *A Medieval Feast*. Crowell, 1983.

————. *Mummies Made in Egypt*. Crowell, 1979.

Ancona, George. *Riverkeeper*. Macmillan, 1990.

Ancona, George, and Mary Beth Miller. *Handtalk Zoo*, photographs by George Ancona. Four Winds, 1989.

Anderson, Gretchen. *The Louisa May Alcott Cookbook*, illustrated by Karen Milone. Little, Brown, 1985.

Anderson, Joan. *The First Thanksgiving Feast*, photographs by George Ancona. Clarion, 1984.

————. *Pioneer Children of Appalachia*, photographs by George Ancona. Clarion, 1986.

————. *A Williamsburg Household*, photographs by George Ancona. Clarion, 1988.

Apfel, Necia H. *Voyager to the Planets*. Clarion, 1991.

Ardley, Neil. *The Science Book of Air*. Gulliver/Harcourt, 1991.

————. *The Science Book of Electricity*. Gulliver/Harcourt, 1991.

Arnold, Caroline. *Dinosaurs Down Under: And Other Fossils from Australia*, photographs by Richard Hewett. Clarion, 1990.

————. *Saving the Peregrine Falcon*, photographs by Richard Hewett. Carolrhoda, 1985.

Arnold, Tim. *Natural History from A to Z: A Terrestrial Sampler*. McElderry, 1991.

Arnosky, Jim. *A Kettle of Hawks*. Lothrop, 1990 (1979).

Barton, Byron. *Bones, Bones, Dinosaur Bones*. HarperCollins, 1990.

————. *I Want to Be an Astronaut*. Crowell, 1988.

————. *Machines at Work*. Crowell, 1987.

Bender, Lionel. *Invention* ("Eyewitness" series). Knopf, 1991.

Blumberg, Rhoda. *Commodore Perry in the Land of the Shogun*. Lothrop, 1985.

Bonners, Susan. *A Penguin Year*. Delacorte, 1981.

Branley, Franklyn. *Flash, Crash, Rumble and Roll*, illustrated by Barbara and Ed Emberley. Rev. ed. Crowell, 1985.

————. *Saturn: The Spectacular Planet*, illustrated by Leonard Kessler. Crowell, 1983.

————. *What Happened to the Dinosaurs?*, illustrated by Marc Simont. Crowell, 1989.

Brenner, Barbara. *If You Were There in 1492*. Bradbury, 1991.

Brooks, Bruce. *Predator!* Farrar, 1991.

Brown, Marc. *Your First Garden Book*. Little, Brown, 1981.

Burns, Marilyn. *Good for Me! All About Food in 32 Bites*. Little, Brown, 1978.

Buxbaum, Susan, and Rita Gelman. *Body Noises*, illustrated by Angie Lloyd. Knopf, 1983.

Calabro, Marian. *Operation Grizzly Bear*. Four Winds, 1989.

Carrick, Carol. *Octopus*, illustrated by Donald Carrick. Clarion, 1978.

Charlip, Remy, and Mary Beth Miller. *Handtalk: An ABC of Finger Spelling and Sign Language*, photographs by George Ancona. Four Winds, 1980.

————. *Handtalk Birthday: A Number and Story Book in Sign Language*, photographs by George Ancona. Four Winds, 1987.

Chiasson, John. *African Journey*. Bradbury, 1987.

Climo, Shirley. *City! Washington, D.C.*, photographs by George Ancona. Macmillan, 1991.

Cobb, Vicki. *Chemically Active! Experiments You Can Do at Home*, illustrated by Theo Cobb. Lippincott, 1985.

————. *For Your Own Protection: Stories Science Photos Tell*. Lothrop, 1989.

————. *Natural Wonders: Stories Science Photos Tell*. Lothrop, 1990.

————. *Science Experiments You Can Eat*, illustrated by Peter Lippman. Lippincott, 1972.

————. *The Secret Life of Cosmetics*, illustrated by Theo Cobb. Lippincott, 1985.

————. *The Secret Life of School Supplies*, illustrated by Bill Morrison. Lippincott, 1981.

————. *Why Can't You Unscramble an Egg? and Other Not Such Dumb Questions About Matter*, illustrated by Ted Enik. Lodestar, 1990.

Cole, Joanna. *A Chick Hatches*. Morrow, 1976.

————. *Large as Life Animals: In Beautiful Life-Size Paintings*, illustrated by Kenneth Lilly. Knopf, 1990.

————. *The Magic School Bus at the Waterworks*, illustrated by Bruce Degen. Scholastic, 1988.

————. *The Magic School Bus Inside the Earth*, illustrated by Bruce Degen. Scholastic, 1987.

————. *The Magic School Bus Inside the Human Body*, illustrated by Bruce Degen. Scholastic, 1989.

————. *The Magic School Bus Lost in the Solar System*, illustrated by Bruce Degen. Scholastic Hardcover, 1990.

————. *My Puppy Is Born*, photographs by Margaret Miller. Mulberry, 1991.

Cowcher, Helen. *Antarctica*. Soundprints, 1990.

Cribb, Joe. *Money* ("Eyewitness" series). Knopf, 1990.

Darling, Kathy. *Manatee: On Location*, photographs by Tara Darling. Lothrop, 1991.

de Paola, Tomie. *"Charlie Needs a Cloak."* Simon & Schuster, 1974.

_____. *The Quicksand Book*. Holiday, 1977.

DeSantis, Kenny. *A Dentist's Tools*, photos by Patricia Agre. Putnam's, 1988.

Dewey, Jennifer Owings. *Animal Architecture*. Orchard, 1991.

Dobrin, Arnold. *Peter Rabbit's Natural Foods Cookbook*. Warne, 1977.

Dolphin, Laurie. *Georgia to Georgia: Making Friends in the U.S.S.R.*, photographs by E. Alan McGee. Tambourine, 1991.

Dorros, Arthur. *Follow the Water from Brook to Ocean*. HarperCollins, 1991.

Dunrae, Olivier. *Skara Brae: The Story of a Prehistoric Village*. Holiday, 1986.

Elkington, John, et al. *Going Green: A Kid's Handbook to Saving the Planet*, illustrated by Tony Ross. Viking, 1990.

Esbensen, Barbara Juster. *Great Northern Diver: The Loon*, illustrated by Mary Barrett Brown. Little, Brown, 1990.

Fisher, Leonard Everett. *The Great Wall of China*. Macmillan, 1986.

Freedman, Russell. *Children of the Wild West*. Clarion, 1983.

_____. *Immigrant Kids*. Dutton, 1980.

_____. *Indian Chiefs*. Holiday, 1987.

Fritz, Jean. *George Washington's Breakfast*, illustrated by Paul Galdone. Coward McCann, 1969.

George, Jean Craighead. *One Day in the Alpine Tundra*, illustrated by Walter Gaffney Kessell. Crowell, 1984.

George, John, and Jean George. *Vison the Mink*. Dutton, 1949.

_____. *Vulpes the Red Fox*. Dutton, 1948.

Gibbons, Gail. *From Seed to Plant*. Holiday, 1991.

_____. *The Milk Makers*. Macmillan, 1985.

_____. *Monarch Butterfly*. Holiday, 1989.

_____. *Tool Book*. Holiday, 1982.

Giblin, James Cross. *Chimney Sweeps: Yesterday and Today*, illustrated by Margot Tomes. Crowell, 1982.

_____. *From Hand to Mouth: Or, How We Invented Knives, Forks, Spoons, and Chopsticks & the Table Manners to Go with Them*. Crowell, 1987.

_____. *The Riddle of the Rosetta Stone: Key to Ancient Egypt*. Crowell, 1990.

Goodall, John S. *The Story of a Castle*. McElderry, 1986.

_____. *The Story of a Farm*. McElderry, 1989.

_____. *The Story of an English Village*. McElderry, 1977.

Gray, Nigel. *A Country Far Away*, illustrated by Philippe Dupasquier. Orchard, 1989.

Guiberson, Brenda Z. *Cactus Hotel*, illustrated by Megan Lloyd. Holt, 1991.

Haldane, Suzanne. *Helping Hands: How Monkeys Assist People Who Are Disabled*. Dutton, 1991.

_____. *Painting Faces*. Dutton, 1988.

Hamanaka, Sheila. *The Journey: Japanese Americans, Racism, and Renewal*, book design by Steve Frederick. Orchard, 1990.

Hartman, Gail. *As the Crow Flies: A First Book of Maps*, illustrated by Harvey Stevenson. Bradbury, 1991.

Heller, Ruth. *Chickens Aren't the Only Ones*. Grosset & Dunlap, 1981.

_____. *Many Luscious Lollipops: A Book About Adjectives*. Grosset & Dunlap, 1989.

Hewett, Joan. *Public Defender: Lawyer for the People*. Photographs by Richard Hewett. Lodestar, 1991.

Hirschi, Ron. *Fall*, photographs by Thomas D. Mangelsen. Cobblehill/Dutton, 1991.

_____. *Spring*, photographs by Tomas D. Mangelsen. Cobblehill/Dutton, 1990.

_____. *Summer*, photographs by Thomas D. Mangelsen. Cobblehill/Dutton, 1991.

_____. *Winter*, photographs by Thomas D. Mangelsen. Cobblehill/Dutton, 1990.

Hoig, Stan. *A Capital for the Nation*. Cobblehill/Dutton, 1991.

Holling, Holling C. *Minn of the Mississippi*. Houghton Mifflin, 1951.

_____. *Pagoo*. Houghton Mifflin, 1957.

Hoyt-Goldsmith, Diane. *Pueblo Storyteller*, photographs by Lawrence Migdale. Holiday, 1991.

_____. *Totem Pole*, photographs by Lawrence Migdale. Holiday, 1990.

Hunt, Jonathan. *Illuminations*. Bradbury, 1989.

Irvine, Joan. *How to Make Pop-Ups*, illustrated by Barbara Reid. Morrow, 1988.

Jeffers, Susan. *Brother Eagle, Sister Sky: A Message from Chief Seattle*. Dial, 1991.

Johnson, Gerald. *America Is Born*, illustrated by Leonard Everett Fisher. Morrow, 1959.

Jurmain, Suzanne. *Once upon a Horse: A History of Horses—and How They Shaped Our History*. Lothrop, 1989.

Keegan, Marcia. *Pueblo Boy: Growing Up in Two Worlds*. Cobblehill/Dutton, 1991.

Knight, David C. *"Dinosaurs" That Swam and Flew*, illustrated by Lee J. Ames. Simon & Schuster, 1985.

Knowlton, Jack. *Books and Libraries*, illustrated by Harriett Barton. HarperCollins, 1991.

————. *Maps and Globes*, illustrated by Harriett Barton. Crowell, 1985.

Kohl, Judith, and Herbert Kohl. *The View from the Oak*, illustrated by Roger Bayless. Little, 1988.

Krementz, Jill. *The Fun of Cooking*. Knopf, 1985.

————. *How It Feels When a Parent Dies*. Knopf, 1988.

————. *How It Feels When Parents Divorce*. Knopf, 1984.

————. *How It Feels to Fight for Your Life*. Joy Street, 1989.

Kurelek, William. *Lumberjack*. Houghton Mifflin, 1974.

Kuskin, Karla. *Jerusalem, Shining Still*, illustrated by David Frampton. Harper, 1987.

Lasker, Joe. *Merry Ever After: The Story of Two Medieval Weddings*. Viking, 1976.

————. *A Tournament of Knights*. Crowell, 1986.

Lasky, Kathryn. *Sugaring Time*, photographs by Christopher G. Knight. Macmillan, 1983.

————. *Traces of Life: The Origins of Humankind*, illustrated by Whitney Powell. Morrow, 1989.

Lauber, Patricia. *Dinosaurs Walked Here and Other Stories Fossils Tell*. Bradbury, 1987.

————. *Journey to the Planets*. 3rd rev. ed. Crown, 1990.

————. *The News About Dinosaurs*. Bradbury, 1989.

————. *Seeds: Pop Stick Glide*, photos by Jerome Wexler. Crown, 1981.

————. *Seeing Earth from Space*. Orchard, 1990.

————. *Summer of Fire: Yellowstone 1988*. Orchard, 1991.

————. *Tales Mummies Tell*. Crowell, 1985.

————. *Volcano: The Eruption and Healing of Mt. St. Helens*. Bradbury, 1986.

Lavies, Bianca. *Wasps at Home*. Dutton, 1991.

LeShan, Eda. *What Makes Me Feel This Way?* Macmillan, 1972.

Lester, Julius. *To Be a Slave*, illustrated by Tom Feelings. Dial, 1968.

Lindblom, Steven. *How to Build a Robot*. Crowell, 1985.

Loeper, John J. *Going to School in 1876*. Atheneum, 1984.

Macaulay, David. *Castle*. Houghton Mifflin, 1977.

————. *Cathedral: The Story of Its Construction*. Houghton Mifflin, 1973.

————. *City: A Story of Roman Planning and Construction*. Houghton Mifflin, 1974.

————. *Mill*. Houghton Mifflin, 1983

————. *Pyramid*. Houghton Mifflin, 1975.

————. *Underground*. Houghton Mifflin, 1976.

————. *The Way Things Work*. Houghton Mifflin, 1988.

McFarland, Cynthia. *Cows in the Parlor: A Visit to a Dairy Farm*. Atheneum, 1990.

McGovern, Ann. . . . *If You Lived with the Sioux Indians*. Scholastic, 1976.

Machotka, Hana. *What Neat Feet!* Morrow, 1991.

Markle, Sandra. *Earth Alive!* Lothrop, 1991.

————. *Exploring Autumn: A Season of Science Activities, Puzzles, and Games*. Atheneum, 1991.

————. *Exploring Spring*. Atheneum, 1990.

————. *Exploring Summer*. Atheneum, 1987.

————. *Exploring Winter*. Atheneum, 1984.

Martin, James. *Chameleons: Dragons in the Trees*, photographs by Art Wolfe. Crown, 1991.

Math, Irwin. *Wires and Watts: Understanding and Using Electricity*, illustrated by Hal Keith. Scribner's, 1988.

Meyers, Susan. *Insect Zoo*, photographs by Richard Hewett. Lodestar, 1991.

Miller, Jonathan. *The Human Body*, designed by David Pelham. Viking, 1983.

Miller, Margaret. *Whose Shoe?* Greenwillow, 1991.

Miller, Mary Beth, and George Ancona. *Handtalk School*, photographs by George Ancona. Four Winds, 1991.

Mori, Tuyosi. *Socrates and the Three Little Pigs*, illustrated by Mitsumasa Anno. Putnam's, 1986.

Morimoto, Junko. *My Hiroshima*. Viking, 1987.

Morris, Ann. *Bread, Bread, Bread*, photographs by Ken Heyman. Lothrop, 1989.

————. *Loving*, photographs by Ken Heyman. Lothrop, 1990.

————. *On the Go*, photographs by Ken Heyman. Lothrop, 1990.

————. *On Their Toes: A Russian Ballet School*, photographs by Ken Heyman. Atheneum, 1991.

Müller, Jörg. *The Changing City*. Atheneum, 1977.

————. *The Changing Countryside*. Atheneum, 1977.

Murphy, Claire Rudolf. *Friendship Across Arctic Waters*. Photographs by Charles Mason. Lodestar, 1991.

Murphy, Jim. *The Boys' War: Confederate and Union Soldiers Talk About the Civil War*. Clarion, 1990.

———. *The Last Dinosaur*, illustrated by Mark Alan Weatherby. Scholastic, 1988.

Myers, Walter Dean. *Now Is Your Time! The African-American Struggle for Freedom*. HarperCollins, 1991.

Noren, Catherine. *The Way We Looked: The Magic and Meaning of Family Photographs*. Dutton, 1983.

Norsgaard, E. Jaediker. *Nature's Great Balancing Act: In Our Own Backyard*. Photographs by Campbell Norsgaard. Cobblehill/Dutton, 1990.

Oliver, Steven, Jane Craddock-Watson, and Dave Hopkins (illustrators). *Trucks* ("Eye-Openers" series). Aladdin, 1991.

Olney, Ross. *Construction Giants*. Atheneum, 1984.

Parents' Nursery School. *Kids Are Natural Cooks: Child-tested Recipes for Home and School Using Natural Foods*, illustrated by Lady McCrady. Houghton Mifflin, 1974.

Parker, Nancy Winslow. *The President's Cabinet and How It Grew*. HarperCollins, 1991.

Parker, Nancy Winslow, and Joan Richards Wright. *Bugs*, illustrated by Nancy Winslow Parker. Greenwillow, 1987.

———. *Frogs, Toads, Lizards, and Salamanders*, illustrated by Nancy Winslow Parker. Greenwillow, 1990.

Patent, Dorothy Hinshaw. *Gray Wolf, Red Wolf*, photographs by William Muñoz. Clarion, 1990.

———. *Yellowstone Fires: Flames and Rebirth*, photographs by William Muñoz and others. Holiday, 1990.

Patterson, Francine. *Koko's Kitten*, photographs by Ronald Cohn. Scholastic Hardcover, 1985.

———. *Koko's Story*, photographs by Ronald Cohn. Scholastic Hardcover, 1987.

Perl, Lila. *From Top Hats to Baseball Caps, from Bustles to Blue Jeans: Why We Dress the Way We Do*, illustrated by Leslie Evans. Clarion, 1990.

———. *The Great Ancestor Hunt: The Fun of Finding Out Who You Are*. Clarion, 1989.

Peters, David. *From the Beginning: The Story of Human Evolution*. Morrow, 1991.

Porter, A. P. *Kwanzaa*, illustrated by Janice Lee Porter. Carolrhoda, 1991.

Potter, Tony. *Trucks* ("See How It Works" series), illustrated by Robin Lawrie. Aladdin, 1989.

Pringle, Laurence. *Bearman: Exploring the World of Black Bears*, photographs by Lynn Rogers. Scribner's, 1989.

———. *Living Treasure: Saving Earth's Threatened Biodiversity*, illustrated by Irene Brady. Morrow, 1991.

———. *Nuclear Energy: Troubled Past, Uncertain Future*. Macmillan, 1989.

Rahn, Joan Elma. *Holes*. Houghton Mifflin, 1984.

Rappaport, Doreen. *Escape from Slavery: Five Journeys to Freedom*, illustrated by Charles Lilly. Harper, 1991.

Ring, Elizabeth. *Tiger Lilies and Other Beastly Plants*, illustrated by Barbara Bash. Walker, 1984.

Robbins, Ken. *Bridges*. Dial, 1991.

———. *A Flower Grows*. Dial, 1990.

Roberson, John R. *Japan: From Shogun to Sony 1543–1984*. Atheneum, 1985.

Rockwell, Harlow. *I Did It*. Macmillan, 1974.

———. *My Doctor*. Macmillan, 1973.

Rogers, Fred. *Going to the Hospital*, photos by Jim Judkis. Putnam, 1988.

———. *Moving*. Putnam, 1987.

———. *When a Pet Dies*, photos by Jim Judkis. Putnam, 1988.

Roop, Peter, and Connie Roop, editors. *I, Columbus: My Journal—1492–3*, illustrated by Peter E. Hanson. Walker, 1990.

Roy, Ron. *Move Over, Wheelchairs Coming Through!*, photographs by Rosmarie Hausherr. Clarion, 1985.

———. *What Has Ten Legs and Eats Corn Flakes?*, illustrated by Lynn Cherry. Clarion, 1982.

Rylant, Cynthia. *Appalachia: The Voices of Sleeping Birds*, illustrated by Barry Moser. Harcourt, 1991.

Sattler, Helen Roney. *The Book of Eagles*, illustrated by Jean Day Zallinger. Lothrop, 1989.

———. *The New Illustrated Dinosaur Dictionary*, illustrated by Joyce Powzyk. Lothrop, 1990.

———. *Recipes for Art and Craft Materials*. Lothrop, 1987 (1973).

Schlein, Miriam. *Billions of Bats*, illustrated by Walter Kessel. Lippincott, 1982.

Schwartz, Alvin, collector and ed. *When I Grew Up Long Ago: Older People Talk About the Days When They Were Young*, illustrated by Harold Berson. Lippincott, 1978.

Selsam, Millicent. *Egg to Chick*, illustrated by Barbara Wolff. Harper Trophy, 1987.

Selsam, Millicent, and Joyce Hunt. *A First Look at Insects*, illustrated by Harriet Springer. Walker, 1974.

———. *A First Look at Leaves*, illustrated by Harriet Springer. Walker, 1972.

———. *A First Look at Seashells*, illustrated by Harriet Springer. Walker, 1983.

Sewall, Marcia. *The Pilgrims of Plimoth*. Atheneum, 1986.

Showers, Paul. *How Many Teeth?*, illustrated by True Kelley. HarperCollins, 1991.

Simon, Seymour. *Galaxies*. Morrow, 1988.

———. *Icebergs and Glaciers*. Morrow, 1987.

———. *Neptune*. Morrow, 1991.

———. *The Paper Airplane Book*, illustrated by Byron Barton. Viking, 1971.

———. *Soap Bubble Magic*, illustrated by Stella Ormai. Lothrop, 1985.

———. *Storms*. Morrow, 1989.

Skurzynski, Gloria. *Almost the Real Thing: Simulation in Your High-Tech World*. Bradbury, 1991.

———. *Robots: Your High-Tech World*. Bradbury, 1990.

Smith, Roland. *Sea Otter Rescue: The Aftermath of an Oil Spill*. Cobblehill/Dutton, 1990.

Spier, Peter. *People*. Doubleday, 1980.

Stein, Sara Bonnett. *Making Babies*, photographs by Doris Pinney. Walker, 1974.

Sussman, Susan, and Robert James. *Lies (People Believe) About Animals*, photographs by Fred Leavitt. Albert Whitman, 1987.

Thomson, Peggy. *Auks, Rocks, and the Odd Dinosaur: Inside Stories from the Smithsonian*. Crowell, 1985.

———. *City Kids in China*. Photographs by Paul S. Conklin. HarperCollins, 1991.

Trimble, Stephen. *The Village of Blue Stone*, illustrated by Jennifer Owings Dewey and Deborah Reade. Macmillan, 1990.

Van Loon, Hendrik W. *The Story of Mankind*. Rev. ed. Liveright, 1985 (1921).

Ventura, Piero. *Great Painters*. Putnam, 1984.

Wabbes, Marie. *How I Was Born*. Tambourine, 1991.

Walker, Barbara M. *The Little House Cookbook: Frontier Foods from Laura Ingalls Wilder's Classic Stories*, illustrated by Garth Williams. Harper, 1979.

Waters, Kate. *Sarah Morton's Day: A Day in the Life of a Pilgrim Girl*. Photographs by Russ Kendall. Scholastic, 1989.

Weiss, Harvey. *Maps: Getting from Here to There*. Houghton Mifflin, 1991.

Whitfield, Philip, Dr., with the Natural History Museum. *Why Do Volcanoes Erupt?* Viking, 1990.

Wilder, Laura Ingalls. *The First Four Years*, illustrated by Garth Williams. Harper, 1971.

———. *West from Home: Letters of Laura Ingalls Wilder, San Francisco 1915*. Roger McBride, ed. Harper, 1974.

Wurmfeld, Hope Herman. *Trucker*. Macmillan, 1990.

Zubrowski, Bernie. *Balloons: Building and Experimenting with Inflatable Toys*, illustrated by Roy Doty. Morrow, 1990.

———. *Wheels at Work*, illustrated by Roy Doty. Morrow, 1986.

OTHER REFERENCES

Alexander, Ellen. *Llama and the Great Flood: A Folktale from Peru*. Crowell, 1989.

Beatty, Patricia. *Charley Skedaddle*. Morrow, 1987.

———. *Jayhawker*. Morrow, 1991.

Beskow, Elsa. *Pelle's New Suit*. Harper, 1929.

Conrad, Pam. *My Daniel*. Harper, 1989.

———. *Prairie Songs*, illustrated by Darryl Zudeck. Harper, 1985.

———. *Prairie Visions: The Life of Solomon Butcher*. HarperCollins, 1991.

Dahl, Roald. *James and the Giant Peach*, illustrated by Nancy Burkert. Knopf, 1962.

Edwards, Michelle. *Chicken Man*. Lothrop, 1991.

Fleischman, Paul. *Joyful Noise: Poems for Two Voices*, illustrated by Eric Beddows. Harper, 1988.

Freedman, Russell. *Lincoln: A Photobiography*. Clarion, 1987.

———. *The Wright Brothers*. Holiday, 1991.

George, Jean Craighead. *Water Sky*. Harper, 1987.

Goble, Paul. *Iktomi and the Boulder*. Orchard, 1988.

Hamilton, Virginia. *Anthony Burns: The Defeat and Triumph of a Fugitive Slave*. Knopf, 1988.

———. *The House of Dies Drear*, illustrated by Eros Keith. Macmillan, 1968.

Harvey, Brett. *My Prairie Christmas*, illustrated by Deborah Kogan Ray. Holiday, 1990.

Hayes, Sarah. *The Bad Egg: The True Story of Humpty Dumpty*, illustrated by Charlotte Voake. Joy Street, 1987.

He Liyi. *The Spring of Butterflies and Other Chinese Folktales*. Lothrop, 1986.

Hoban, Russell. *Bread and Jam for Frances*, illustrated by Lillian Hoban. Harper, 1964.

Levinson, Riki. *Watch the Stars Come Out*, illustrated by Diane Goode. Dutton, 1985.

Lowry, Lois. *Number the Stars*. Houghton Mifflin, 1989.

Lyon, George Ella. *Come a Tide*, illustrated by Stephen Gammell. Orchard, 1990.

McKissack, Patricia, and Fredrick McKissack. *Frederick Douglass: The Black Lion*. Children's Press, 1987.

MacLachlan, Patricia. *Sarah, Plain and Tall*. Harper, 1985.

_____. *Three Names*, illustrated by Alexander Pertzoff. Harper, 1991.

Medearis, Angela Shelf. *Dancing with the Indians*, illustrated by Samuel Byrd. Holiday, 1991.

Neville, Emily Cheney. *The China Year*. Harper, 1991.

Provensen, Alice, and Martin Provensen. *Leonardo da Vinci: The Artist, Inventor, Scientist in Three-Dimensional Movable Pictures*. Viking, 1984.

Reeder, Carolyn. *Shades of Gray*. Macmillan, 1989.

Ryder, Joanne. *When the Woods Hum*, illustrated by Catherine Stock. Morrow, 1991.

_____. *Winter Whale*, illustrated by Michael Rothman. Morrow, 1991.

San Souci, Robert D. *The Talking Eggs*, illustrated by Jerry Pinkney. Dial, 1989.

Schlein, Miriam. *The Year of the Panda*, illustrated by Kam Mak. Crowell, 1990.

Spier, Peter. *Peter Spier's Rain*. Doubleday, 1982.

Turner, Ann. *Dakota Dugout*, illustrated by Ronald Himler. Macmillan, 1985.

_____. *Nettie's Trip South*, illustrated by Ronald Himler. Macmillan, 1987.

Wyndham, Robert. *Chinese Mother Goose Rhymes*, illustrated by Ed Young. Philomel, 1989.

Yashima, Taro. *Crow Boy*. Viking, 1955.

Zhensun, Zheng, and Alice Low. *A Young Painter: The Life and Paintings of Wang Yani, China's Extraordinary Young Painter*. Scholastic, 1991.

Part Three

Developing a Literature Program

Chapter Twelve
Planning the Literature Program

PURPOSES OF THE LITERATURE PROGRAM
DISCOVERING DELIGHT IN BOOKS
LINKING LITERATURE TO LIFE
DEVELOPING LITERARY AWARENESS

GENRES OF LITERATURE
ELEMENTS OF LITERATURE
THE PLACE OF CLASSICS
KNOWING AUTHORS AND ILLUSTRATORS

DEVELOPING APPRECIATION

DIFFERENT PLANS FOR LITERATURE PROGRAMS
LITERATURE WITH A BASAL READING PROGRAM
LITERATURE PROGRAMS USING REAL BOOKS
LITERATURE AND WHOLE LANGUAGE
MAKING THE TRANSITION

PROVIDING FOR A LITERATURE PROGRAM
CREATING THE CLASSROOM LEARNING ENVIRONMENT

AN ENTHUSIASTIC TEACHER
THE CLASSROOM BOOK COLLECTION
CREATING A CLASSROOM READING CENTER
DISPLAY TECHNIQUES

SHARING LITERATURE WITH CHILDREN
READING TO CHILDREN

SELECTING BOOKS TO READ ALOUD
TECHNIQUES FOR READING ALOUD

RESOURCES FOR TEACHING: GUIDELINES FOR READING ALOUD

STORYTELLING

SELECTING STORIES TO TELL
GUIDELINES FOR TELLING STORIES
FELTBOARD STORIES

RESOURCES FOR TEACHING: SUGGESTED STORIES FOR THE FELTBOARD

BOOK TALKS

PROVIDING TIME TO READ BOOKS
SUSTAINED SILENT READING (SSR)

TALKING ABOUT BOOKS WITH CHILDREN
CONVERSATIONS
GUIDED DISCUSSION
WORKING IN SMALL GROUPS

LITERATURE AND THE WRITING PROGRAM
ESTABLISHING THE WRITING CENTER
HELPING CHILDREN WRITE ABOUT BOOKS
HELPING CHILDREN BECOME AUTHORS

GUIDING IN-DEPTH STUDY OF BOOKS
GUIDING DISCUSSIONS

ASKING GOOD QUESTIONS
CHILDREN'S QUESTIONS
GRAPHIC ORGANIZERS
MAKING AND USING GUIDES

WEBBING CURRICULUM POSSIBILITIES

A FRAMEWORK FOR WEBBING
STUDYING ONE BOOK: *THE SIGN OF THE BEAVER* BY ELIZABETH GEORGE SPEARE
STUDYING ONE GENRE: FOLKTALES
STUDYING A SINGLE AUTHOR OR ILLUSTRATOR: PAT HUTCHINS
STUDYING A THEME: STEWARDS OF THE EARTH: ECOLOGY

THE SCHOOL AND THE COMMUNITY
THE WHOLE-SCHOOL PROGRAM

TEACHING FEATURE: A WHOLE-SCHOOL STUDY OF ONE BOOK
PLANNING AUTHOR/ILLUSTRATOR VISITS
THE SCHOOL LIBRARY MEDIA CENTER
THE LIBRARY MEDIA SPECIALIST
WORKING WITH PARENTS AND THE COMMUNITY
WORKING WITH THE PUBLIC LIBRARY

SUGGESTED LEARNING EXPERIENCES
RELATED READINGS
REFERENCES

Students in a fifth- and sixth-grade class unanimously agreed that *The Pinballs* by Betsy Byars was their favorite book. Their teacher then asked them to discuss *The Pinballs*, telling what it was that made them like it so much. Part of their discussion follows:

> Lenny says, "This is the best book I've ever read. I'd like to know Harvey because I'd like to cheer him up." He decides that "He shows real courage because he has two broken legs." Barb adds, "All the kids do because they have to go to a foster home." "So does Thomas J. because the twins are going to die and he has to go to the hospital to see them," says Will.
>
> Jack talks about Carlie, saying, "She's really funny because she's so rude." The teacher suggests that a book that is "basically serious can have funny elements." Tom says, "You know that Carlie is really tough."
>
> Then Tom goes on to explain the title by saying, "Carlie thinks they're pinballs because they are always being thrown around like pinballs."

By April of that year eighteen of the class had read *The Pinballs*. They also were reading other Betsy Byars books; thirteen had read *The Summer of the Swans*, eight *Goodbye, Chicken Little*.[1]

Individual children had read many books (from 24 to 122 over the year), yet they singled out *The Pinballs* as their favorite. While it is still difficult for them to articulate why they like the story, they have moved beyond the usual circular kind of statement, "I liked it because it was good." They are beginning to recognize the importance of character development and readily identify with Carlie and Harvey. Lenny, who was not a particularly good reader and had read few books, empathizes with Harvey to the point of wanting to comfort him. Suburban children, they have extended their horizons to imagine the courage it would require to live in a foster home away from your family and to have to visit the dying in the hospital. Tom attempts a rough statement of the meaning of the title without any prompting.

In this class, book discussions occurred every day during the last 15 minutes of an hour-long period for sustained silent reading. The children readily supported each other in their selection of books and in their evaluations in a way that we have referred to as a "community of readers." It is obvious from their discussion that they were gaining a greater sense of form and were beginning to see more in books than just story.

---

[1] Based on children's comments recorded by Susan Hepler in "Patterns of Response to Literature: A One-Year Study of a Fifth and Sixth Grade Classroom," unpublished Ph.D. dissertation, Ohio State University, 1982.

It takes time for reading and literature to grow in a classroom. The children in this classroom had for the most part been exposed to good literature throughout their school attendance. The teacher had been working on a literature-based reading program over a period of several years. Her major goal was to develop children who could read and who loved reading. From this base she added a growing appreciation for and understanding of good literature.

PURPOSES OF THE LITERATURE PROGRAM

Each school staff will want to develop its own literature program in terms of the background and abilities of the children it serves. Teachers need to know their children and the potential of their material and have an understanding of the structure of literature; then they will be free to make the right match between child and book. This chapter can suggest guidelines and give examples, but it cannot prescribe *the* literature program that would work with all children.

Three middle-grade students delight in finding all of the *Changes* shown in Anthony Browne's surrealistic picture storybook.

Idyllwild Elementary School, Idyllwild, California. Photo by Larry Rose.

Discovering Delight in Books

One of the major purposes of any literature program is to provide children with the opportunity to experience literature, to enter into and become involved in a book. The title of *Hooked on Books* by Daniel N. Fader and Elton McNeil comes close to describing this goal. A literature program must get children excited about reading, turned on to books, tuned into literature.

What if the goal of all reading programs was not only to teach children to learn to read but to help them learn to love reading, to discover joy in reading? Their every activity, every assignment would have to pass the test—"Will this increase children's desire to read? Will it make them want to continue reading?" Story has always motivated children to want to learn to read. Real books are far more interesting than selections from books.

One of the best ways to interest children in books is to surround them with many of the finest. Give them time to read and a teacher who regularly reads to them. Expose them to a wide variety of literature—prose and poetry, realism and fantasy, contemporary and historical fiction, fiction and nonfiction. Provide time for children to talk about books, to share them with others, and to interpret them through various creative activities. Let them see that adults enjoy books too. One 6-year-old and his teacher were reading Arnold Lobel's *Frog and Toad Are Friends* together. When they came to the part where Toad is experiencing his "sad time of day" (waiting for the mail that he never receives), the teacher burst out laughing. The 6-year-old looked up at her and said: "I didn't know grownups liked books!" If children are to like books they must be with adults who enjoy them.

The first step in any literature program is to discover delight in books. This should be the major purpose of the literature program in the elementary school and should not be hurried or bypassed. Delight in books only comes about through long and loving experiences with them.

Linking Literature to Life

As children search for meaning in books, they naturally link what they are reading to their own lives. Kindergarten children listen to *Ira Sleeps Over* by Bernard Waber and talk about their own bears and the decisions they had to make about taking them on vacations or overnights. One 6-year-old when listening to the story of "The Little Red Hen" linked his experience of watching his mom bake cookies with that of the little red hen watching her cake bake. He lifted his head and sniffed, saying, "Just smell that delicious smell!"

When children become engrossed in a book they are usually trying on different roles, living the experience. When asked why Jean George's *My Side of the Mountain* was his favorite book, one student replied, "I just always thought I could do what Sam Gribley did." He then went on to make a comparison chart between what he considered to be Sam's qualities and his own. His list showed good understanding of Sam's character and excellent self-understanding.

Books illuminate children's own perceptions of their lives and provide a window through which they can observe, or try on, so to speak, the lives of others. Michelle Landsberg maintains:

> Books let us see how other people grow towards conclusions and solve dilemmas. More than that they make us *feel* every step of the way; it's as though we could live a dozen lives simultaneously, and draw on the wealth of all of them to help shape our own selves.[2]

One of the major purposes of using real books for a reading program is to help children connect literature with their own lives. As teachers and librarians, we want to encourage children to discover personal meaning in books in order to better understand their lives and to extend their perceptions of other lives.

Developing Literary Awareness

Children in the elementary school can't help but develop some literary awareness. However, knowledge about literature should be secondary to children's wide experiencing of literature. Too frequently, we have substituted the study of liter-ary criticism for the experience of literature itself. Attention to content should precede consideration of form. However, some literary understanding increases children's enjoyment of books. Some 7- and 8-year olds are excited to discover the different variants of "Cinderella," for example. They enjoy comparing the various beginnings and endings of folktales and like to write their own. Obviously, some of this delight has been derived from knowledge of folklore. Teachers need to know something of the structure of literature in order to provide children with a frame of reference to direct their insights. Children, however, should be led to discover these literary elements gradually, and only as these elements help children to understand the meaning of the story or poem. Knowledge of the structure of a discipline frees a teacher in his approach to teaching. Knowing literature, he may tune in to where the children are and extend their thinking and understandings. The teacher does not have to rely on the questions in a literary reader; she is free to ask questions directly related to the needs of the children in the class.

GENRES OF LITERATURE

During the time children are in elementary school they develop some understanding about types of literature or various genres. The primary child can usually differentiate between prose and poetry, between fiction and nonfiction, between realism and fantasy. Young children will not use those words, nor is it important for them to do so. They probably will tell you that Eric Carle's *The Very Busy Spider* "tells a story," while Claudia Schnieper's book *Amazing Spiders* with its close-up photos by Max Meier "tells you real facts about spiders." This represents a beginning step in the development of a useful classification system. Later as children begin to use the library, they learn that nonfiction includes informational books and biography. They discover that poetry and traditional literature—including folktales, legends, and myths—have their own classifications.

Children do not need to learn all these classifications. An understanding of the various types of literature develops as teachers and librarians introduce a variety of books to children. When children have had free access to the school library

[2]Michelle Landsberg, *Reading for the Love of It* (New York: Prentice Hall, 1987), p. 127.

media center for six or seven years, they discover the various types of books and their classifications. A framework for thinking about literature develops gradually as children consider what kinds of stories they particularly like or what kinds of information they need for a particular purpose. Such knowledge is also useful when children begin evaluating books. Then they discover, for example, that the characters in fairy tales are usually flat, two-dimensional characters because they represent goodness (the fairy godmother) or wickedness (the stepmother). These are seen in sharp relief to the characters in realistic fiction, who grow and change and are a mixture of good and bad. Again, this kind of understanding is developed over a period of time with much experiencing of a wide range of literature.

ELEMENTS OF LITERATURE

Knowledge of the components of literature—such as the traditional constants of plot, characterization, theme, style, setting, and point of view of the author—comes about gradually. Some children are intrigued with knowing about such literary devices as symbols, metaphors, imagery, use of flashbacks, and point of view. Such knowledge can be forced and taught superficially without children really understanding the relationship between the use of the device and the author's meaning. Or, if teachers are aware of these well-known components, they can be taught at the so-called teachable moment.

For example, one group of fifth graders puzzled over who was telling E. L. Konigsburg's story *From the Mixed-Up Files of Mrs. Basil E. Frankweiler*. At first the children thought Claudia was telling this story of her flight to the Metropolitan Museum of Art in New York City with her brother, Jamie. But when they came to the last paragraph of the first chapter, they stopped. Who was the "I" in the sentence with the parentheses?

🍃 And in the course of those miles Claudia stopped regretting bringing Jamie along. In fact when they emerged from the train at Grand Central into the underworld of cement and steel that leads to the terminal, Claudia felt that having Jamie there was important. (Ah, how well I know those feelings of hot and hollow that come from the dimly lit concrete ramp.) And his money and radio were not

the only reasons. Manhattan called for the courage of at least two Kincaids.[3]

This sent them back to the introductory letter by Mrs. Basil E. Frankweiler, but they still didn't know how she was able to tell Claudia and Jamie's story as if she were with them. Only when they reached the final chapter, did they understand the reason E. L. Konigsburg had told the story from Mrs. Frankweiler's point of view. They then had an interesting discussion of what difference it had made in the book. Finally, one student said, "It helped to create the mystery"; another one said, "She gave Claudia the chance to be different." These children learned about point of view in the process of reading this story. More importantly they understood why the author used this particular literary device. Discussion of literary form should only be introduced where it leads to a richer understanding of a book, and then only after children have had time to respond to it personally.

THE PLACE OF CLASSICS

Some literature programs recommend a sequence of particular books for study at each age level. However, we believe that there is no one book, or twenty books, or one hundred books that should be read by all children. It would be unfortunate if children missed certain special books but none should be required of all. Knowledge of certain literary classics of childhood—such as *Alice's Adventures in Wonderland* or *The Wind in the Willows* is enriching but not absolutely essential to one's development. What is important is that we give children rich experiencing of literature at various stages of development.

Knowledge of time-tested works of prose, and poetry—such as Mother Goose rhymes, fables, myths, and Bible stories—does provide a background for understanding many literary allusions. "Don't count your chicks before they hatch," "a matter of sour grapes," "dog in the manger," "Midas touch," "Herculean task," and "a coat of many colors" are all examples of often-used expressions derived from literature. However, the

[3]E. L. Konigsburg, *From the Mixed-Up Files of Mrs. Basil E. Frankweiler*, (New York: Atheneum, 1968), p. 27.

reason they continue to be used is that their meanings still have significance for us today. Teachers who know literature share appropriate literary classics with children because they are still *good stories*, not because they are the source of literary allusions. If children are not ready to "connect" with these stories then such stories have little meaning for them and are therefore inappropriate.

KNOWING AUTHORS AND ILLUSTRATORS

Study of the works of particular authors has traditionally been more characteristic of literature at the secondary level than the elementary school. Still, even young children enjoy knowing something about authors and illustrators as they read their books. Teachers and librarians should tell children the name of the author and illustrator of a book as they introduce it. They may ask children if they know any other books that this particular person has illustrated or written. Some children delight in being able to recognize the artwork of Tomie de Paola or Leo Lionni or Chris Van Allsburg. Recognizing the style of an artist's work should be encouraged. Middle-grade children frequently discover favorite authors. They want another book by Lois Lowry, another Gary Paulsen, or another Daniel Pinkwater. They may be reading series books, and so they ask for another one of the "Narnia" series (C. S. Lewis), the "Prydain" series (Lloyd Alexander), or the "Little House" books (Laura Ingalls Wilder). Some children develop special interests in sports stories or mysteries. These are all ways that children categorize books. They show that children are developing a framework for literature, a way of thinking about books.

Knowledge about particular books, authors, and the craft of writing will come about as children find increasing satisfaction in a range and diversity of works. Such knowledge should not be the primary focus of the literature program. It will occur as a natural result of real experiencing of books.

Developing Appreciation

The long-term goal of a literature program is the development of a lifetime pattern of preference for reading quality literature. James Britton maintained that in a quality reading/literature program "a student should read *more books* with satisfaction . . . [and] he should read books with *more satisfaction*."[4] This emphasis on both wide reading and in-depth reading is characteristic of a literature program that develops fluency and appreciation.

We have seen that even kindergarten children can identify the styles of various artists and can recognize different purposes for different genres of literature. Gradually, as children are introduced to more books on their own, they become interested in ways the author and/or illustrator create meaning. This is particularly true as children begin to write and publish their own stories.

All good readers go through a stage when they read series books or easy nondemanding books by the same author. Such wide reading usually produces fluent readers, who read one book after another without much thought. In order to develop appreciation for the better written book, teachers can suggest children compare the humor of Daniel Pinkwater's *The Magic Moscow* with the humor in Sid Fleischman's *The Whipping Boy*. One fifth-grade teacher read aloud Paula Fox's *One-Eyed Cat* to her class. Then she asked a group of girls who had read Judy Blume's *Blubber* to talk about the two books. They realized that the one-dimensional characters in Blume's book never change, never have doubts about the many cruel ways they are teasing Linda Fischer, and show no remorse. But Ned in *One-Eyed Cat* is filled with guilt and has no one to share it with. For eight months, he carries his burden and then finally tells his mother. The girls understood the difference between showing how a cruel action makes a person feel and just describing the cruelty. Children need to discuss books, compare books, and then talk about what they have learned from reading them. Such in-depth reading develops critical appreciative readers.

If children are exposed to the fine writing of authors such as Paula Fox, Paul Fleischman, Katherine Paterson, and Mollie Hunter and given time to discuss such books as *One-Eyed Cat*, *Saturnalia*, *Jacob Have I Loved*, or *A Sound of*

[4]James Britton, "The Nature of the Reader's Satisfaction," in *The Cool Web: The Pattern of Children's Reading* by Margaret Meek, Aidan Warlow, and Griselda Barton (New York: Atheneum, 1978), p. 110.

Chariots, they will be better able to recognize shallow, one-dimensional stories. Once students have knowledge of a repertoire of fine books that they have responded to in a variety of ways, they will begin to become more discriminating readers.

Most parents and some teachers are so relieved their children are reading that they are reluctant to suggest they could be reading more challenging books. If teachers consistently nurture children's enjoyment of literature by reading aloud exciting, well-selected books, if they give children time to read and discuss books in literature groups, their appreciation for quality literature will grow. One major goal of the literature program should be this development of discriminating critical readers (see Chapter 1).

DIFFERENT PLANS FOR LITERATURE PROGRAMS

The growth of literature-based reading programs has been phenomenal in the past ten years. In 1989, Bernice Cullinan[5] reported her findings from a national survey of state department reading and language arts directors which revealed that some twenty-three states had programs in which literature was central to the success of the program. These programs included the California Reading Initiative, in which teachers were encouraged to draw from a long list of recommended trade books for their reading programs, and the Comprehensive Literacy Initiative for Children in Arizona.

No single reason can be given for the expanded role of trade books in the schools; rather, the accumulated weight of evidence of many studies, insights from professional educators, and the success of many teachers who are making literature central to the curriculum seem to be reason enough. Some specific reasons are as follows:

♦ Research on narrative as a primary act of the mind suggests the importance of story in a child's life.

[5]Bernice Cullinan, "Latching on to Literature: Reading Initiations Take Hold," *School Library Journal,* vol. 35 (April 1989), pp. 27–31.

♦ Children are meaning makers. They learn to speak in order to communicate. No one demands whole paragraphs or articulated sentences from a 2-year-old. We help scaffold their language. If we accept children as emergent readers in the same way we accept their beginning language, they will become readers.
♦ Research linking reading aloud to the development of children's own reading skills suggests they are learning to read naturally as they listen to stories they love.
♦ Frank Smith's statement that we learn to read by reading implies children should have many opportunities to read books of their own choosing.
♦ Previous basal readers emphasized skills over enjoyment. All children had to go through the same sequenced material.
♦ Children are not reading outside of schools, so it becomes imperative that we give them more time to read and enjoy books inside of school.
♦ Some teachers have always used real books in their reading programs. These teachers are enthusiastic advocates of their literature-based reading program.
♦ The number of books, particularly the number of predictable books for the very young (see Chapter 4), has increased dramatically.
♦ Good paperback books are available for literature groups. No longer is it necessary to buy a basic text for each child when so many books are available.

Literature with a Basal Reading Program

It should come as no surprise that textbook publishing companies quickly aligned themselves with the new interest in literature and produced basal readers using selections from children's books. These are advertised as "literature-based reading programs," when in reality, they are the old basal readers with new content, but the same workbooks, teachers' manuals, ditto sheets, and end-of-the-unit tests. The emphasis is still placed on teaching reading skills and the greatest amount of time is devoted to filling in the blanks in the workbooks rather than actually reading. Since the texts are drawn from literature (although frequently abridged), the content is more interesting than the "Dick and Jane" type of basal reader. However, children are given no choice of what to read and frequently little time to discuss their response to the stories. Despite the advertisements heralding this "new" approach, it is well to remember that the McGuffey readers, the old Elson readers, and some of the basal readers of the 1960s also included literature selections.

The two aspects of a literature program that most teachers do find time to incorporate into their basal reading programs are a read-aloud time and a sustained silent reading time. Teachers usually have a Sustained Silent Reading (SSR) period every day. The purpose of such a period is to provide children time to read self-selected books in an atmosphere in which everyone is reading and enjoying the process, including the teacher. SSR time also provides children with an opportunity to practice their reading and develop fluency. Since they usually only read one story a day in their basal readers, they need this time to read widely. This extensive or wide reading for enjoyment develops fluency.

To be successful, an SSR period requires a quantity of interesting, exciting books for children to read. Where basal readers take a large share of the funds for materials, teachers have had to find various ingenious ways to obtain books. Some of these include borrowing many books from the school library to initiate a classroom library, borrowing particular books from public libraries for certain children, involving parents or the PTA in setting up a book fair, the profits of which go for classroom libraries, and initiating the idea of a child giving the class a "birthday book" with a name plate in it, rather than a school birthday party. Teachers who know books have also been successful in obtaining some good ones at discount bookstores and secondhand bookstores. Another successful way to obtain books is to participate in book clubs. (See listing at end of Appendix C.) As children sign up for particular books, the teacher may receive bonus books for the classroom library.

Time is a constant problem in many classrooms, particularly when teachers meet with three to four reading groups a day. While the teacher works with these children, the rest of the class is assigned workbook pages and worksheets. In Anderson's report to the nation on reading practices, he maintains that 70 percent of students' reading instructional time is spent on these activities and that classroom research suggests the amount of time devoted to workbook-worksheet activities is unrelated to year-to-year gains in reading proficiency.[6] He maintains that students should do more reading and writing during this time. Some teachers have been successful in substituting some of the literature extension activities suggested in Chapter 13—having children write their own stories and create their own books rather than filling in worksheets.

Some teachers are trying innovative ways to provide more time for children to read real books. For example, some teachers eliminate sections or stories in the basals or have the children read them more quickly in order to complete them earlier in the year. The children can then begin to read sets of paperback trade books. Other teachers alternate paperbacks with the basal readers. Some teachers feel more comfortable in letting the best readers read trade books independently while keeping the slower readers in the basals. An alternate plan, and one the authors endorse, is to give the least able readers many easy real stories to generate enjoyment and fluency. One fifth-grade teacher let her lowest reading group read the paperback of *Stone Fox* by John Gardiner. They became so enthusiastic about their reading time that every other group wanted to read paperbacks, too.

Textbooks are used in social studies, science, mathematics, health, and language arts. While some teachers try to relate their read-aloud book to social studies or science, there is little time to share the fine informational books that would support the use of literature across the curriculum.

The use of the school library is usually directly related to the school curriculum. In textbook-oriented classrooms, there is less reliance on other resource books. Time in the library may be

[6]Richard C. Anderson, et al., *Becoming a Nation of Readers* (Washington: National Institute of Education, 1984).

limited to a scheduled half hour per week for children to select and check out books. Older children frequently receive lessons on the use of the library and reference tools during their library time. This limits the time when the librarian might read stories and poems or talk with children about exciting books. In some instances librarians are expected to meet with forty to fifty classes per week, sometimes in two or more schools, give grades to children on library skills, and order materials! Other librarians have been more successful in seeing their major role as interesting children in books and promoting wide reading.

Evaluation of children's progress in a basal reading program is usually determined by the level of book they can read successfully and their performance on the publishers' tests that accompany the basals. Some teachers do try to keep a record of the titles and number of books read by each child during SSR time. Unfortunately, a few teachers still make a chart of the number of books read by each child and reward the child reading the greatest number of books. Whole schools attempt to promote reading with read-a-thons, book week activities, or book character days.

Literature Programs Using Real Books

Increasingly schools are moving to a literature program in which trade books are used for all aspects of reading. We used to be able to refer to this type of program as a literature-based program. However, publishers of basal readers have usurped the term, so in some places a literature-based reading program means using basal readers with literature content. In a *true* literature-based program classrooms are flooded with books. Basal readers and workbooks are not used. Funds usually appropriated for the purchase of basal readers and workbooks are used for obtaining large classroom libraries of 400 to 500 books. There are books in an attractive reading corner, sets of paperback books for in-depth study, and a changing collection of books obtained from the school library and public libraries on whatever unit focus is in progress. Books are displayed along with children's work. Children's interpretations of books, book surveys, and big books are seen throughout the room. Few commercial charts or pictures are seen, only quantities of children's work with captions, labels, or writing on it.

Knowing the research on the importance of reading aloud in developing concepts about print, a sense of story, prediction of plot, and understanding of characters, teachers read aloud to primary children three and four times a day. They frequently reread favorite stories until children almost know them by heart. Parent aides are encouraged to read aloud to small groups of children. Frequently, teachers establish a "buddy system" when older children may read with one or two younger ones.

Rather than work on worksheets or workbook activities, children do a variety of things. Some may be seen reading from the big books, others may be reading individually with the teacher, while still others may be busy reading or writing stories of their own or writing in their literature response journals. Many of the literature extension activities described in Chapter 13 are done during this worktime. Quiet talk about books flows as children create murals or map the action of a story.

An SSR or independent reading time is provided every day. Frequently, however, children read quietly in pairs. Time for discussion of books almost always follows these periods.

The in-depth study of the books of one author, a genre of books, or one book begins as early as the kindergarten. With older children sets of such paperbacks as *The Whipping Boy* by Sid Fleischman, *The Island of the Blue Dolphins* by Scott O'Dell, *Strider* by Beverly Cleary, and *A Wrinkle in Time* by Madeleine L'Engle are used for literature study. While all children are involved in groups of in-depth reading, the groups are not formed on the basis of ability but of interest in the book.

Reading and writing across the curriculum are characteristic of this integrated program. Children do research in informational books on the particular class unit. Library skills are learned in the process of using many books and reference books for children's projects. The library is open all day long for children to use as they research particular topics. Parent assistants may help children in one part of the room to find their materials if the librarian is reading a story or working with others.

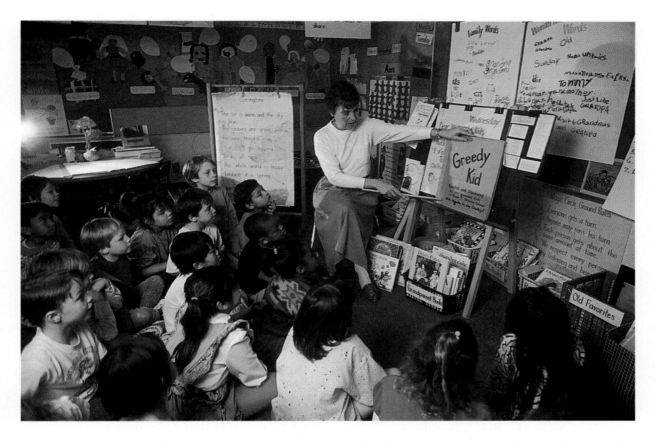

Teacher and children share the reading of the alternative text they created, "Greedy Kid," following the pattern of *Greedy Cat* by Joy Cowley.

Mission School, Redlands Public Schools, Redlands, California. Nancy Anderson, teacher. Photo by Larry Rose.

Teachers and children keep records of children's reading. Each child has a portfolio containing samples of his or her story writing, artwork, and research reports from the beginning of school. These are shared with parents during individual conference times. Book reports are not required, since children are sharing books in a variety of ways. Teachers know what children are reading because they are reading and reacting to their reading journals each week (see Chapter 13). All children know what others are reading because they discuss their books every day. Children frequently recommend books to others, as they know each other's reading interests. These children become a community of readers as they discuss and recommend particular titles. Books are an essential part of their lives.

Literature and Whole Language

The term *whole language* is used by Kenneth Goodman to describe integrated curriculums where the emphasis is placed on learning language (including reading and writing) by using it for a variety of real and functional purposes. The whole-language movement believes that you learn to read and write while you read and write to learn.[7]

In a whole-language program, children not only learn to read from real books as just described, but they use real books across the curriculum for all their studies. Units and projects that cut across

[7]Kenneth Goodman, *What's Whole in Whole Language?* (Portsmouth, N.H.: Heinemann, 1986).

traditional subject-matter areas may be chosen by a class or a small group of children to study. For example, over the period of a year, one second/third grade class studied "Fairy Tales," "Plumbing and Water Sources," and "Immigration to the United States." They also had mini-units on "Books by Pat Hutchins," "Grandparents," and "Dinosaurs."

All of these focus units cut across information usually studied in social studies, science, and, in some instances, math. The theme of immigration connected to the history of their ancestors and the fact that, except for Native Americans, all of us came from somewhere. Books on immigration, Ellis Island, and many books about grandparents were read. Using information found in the many dinosaur books, children measured and marked out the size of a dinosaur on the playground. They discussed the various theories related to the disappearance of dinosaurs. Children had a choice in selecting the focus units, helped plan how to find information from various sources, and what they would do with each one.

In their study of fairy tales the children read many books. During their SSR time or recreational reading, some of them chose to read such easy folk tales as "The Three Bears," "The Three Pigs," *The Great Big Enormous Turnip* by Alexei Tolstoy, and *The Fat Cat* by Jack Kent. For in-depth reading, different groups met and read all the Cinderella stories and the many stories about magic pots. These were then compared and charts were made. They learned library research skills in the process of investigating their topics, not in isolated drills. No worksheets or workbooks were used. Rather children wrote in their response journals, did purposeful reading, and created their own books and group projects.

Whole-language instruction and literature-based reading programs that use real books offer a challenge to teachers. They require an in-depth knowledge of children and children's literature. Only when a teacher knows the potential of a child and a book and is willing to trust the interaction between the two, does learning really occur.

Making the Transition

It is not easy to go from reliance on basal readers and teachers' guides with their careful plans for each lesson to letting children choose their own books, allowing them to respond in a variety of ways, and helping them plan meaningful activities.

Most teachers in the classroom today had basal readers in their own early schooling. Their teacher-training program may have helped them think of other ways of teaching reading or it may have reinforced their reliance on basal readers. No doubt their student teaching was with a teacher who used basal readers. So it is little wonder that when teachers first try to use real books they tend to use them like basal readers. They divide children into ability groups and then select what they think are appropriate titles for each group. They buy teachers' guides for these books that provide comprehension questions, and workbook-like exercises and even black-line masters to duplicate and give to the whole class. Although a few guides do present the strengths of the books and suggest appropriate learning activities (from which teachers may choose), most of them are merely making basal readers out of some of our best children's literature. Such basalization of fine books will never develop a love of reading—in fact, it may kill it altogether.

Teachers who wish to initiate the use of real books in their reading programs may want to visit another school where such a program has already been successfully introduced. They will want to read many professional books describing the process and to attend professional meetings where they can talk with teachers who are involved in such a program. It also helps if several teachers in a school support each other in making the change and obtain the support of the administration and parents.

The first task will be to obtain many books for the classroom and read them—every one of them! A teacher may want to start gradually as has been suggested and use real books with a few reading groups. One possible disadvantage of this approach is that if basal reading groups and literature groups function at the same time, it is easy to treat both groups alike. A better plan would be to obtain four or five sets of paperback titles; give a brief book talk on each title and let children look at the books to select what they want to read. Then let children read the books they have selected according to interest groups rather than ability groups.

Record your observations of how children seem to be doing and your reactions to the approach. Share these with your fellow teachers. When a group of teachers[8] who had used real books in their reading programs for over five years were asked, "How have you changed in your teaching?" every one of them said they had become more relaxed about their teaching. At first they wrote questions and planned activities for each book. Later, when they saw children were reading more than they ever had read before, were interpreting books with real insight, and were doing just as well in the testing program, they withdrew their questions and trusted the interaction between the books and the children. Their observations appear to be substantiated by the research on such programs.[9]

PROVIDING FOR A LITERATURE PROGRAM

Creating the Classroom Learning Environment

It is possible to visit any classroom and tell something about the quality of education just by observing what appears to be honored there. If books are honored, they are easily accessible and displayed attractively throughout the classroom. Their covers face outward so children can see them, for example. Each classroom has a comfortable reading corner or loft that provides an inviting quiet place to read. A good classroom collection of books provides children with real reading choices. Children's interpretations of books, both written and artistic, are displayed on bulletin boards. Attractive murals of favorite storybook characters or houses from fairy tales or something about an author might be featured. When you visit, write down what appears to be the most important aspects of this classroom: basal readers or trade books; workbooks or children's own writ-

ing; commercial art from teacher stores or children's own artistic interpretations and written work. Are children's seats arranged in ways to encourage talk or in straight rows to discourage it? Are there interesting centers in the room such as a writing center or science center that suggest a variety of activities? Can you tell what topic or subject or book the class is working with just by looking at the displays? Each classroom can be as revealing and individual as a teacher's own fingerprints.

AN ENTHUSIASTIC TEACHER

The most important aspect of the classroom environment is the teacher. He or she creates the climate of the classroom and arranges the learning environment. If the teacher loves books, shares them with children, provides time for children to read and a place for them to read, children will become enthusiastic readers. The teacher who reads to the children every day, talks about books and characters in books as if they were good friends, and knows poems and stories to tell is serving the class as an adult model of a person

Each classroom should have an inviting reading corner or a loft that provides a comfortable quiet place for reading.

Dhahran Hills Elementary School, Dhahran, Saudi Arabia. Photo by Roy Wilson, teacher.

[8]Children's Literature, '91, Conference, Ohio State University, Columbus, Ohio, January 24–26, 1991.
[9]Michael O. Tunnell and James S. Jacobs, "Using Real Books: Research Findings on Literature-Based Reading Instruction," *The Reading Teacher*, vol. 42 (March 1989), pp. 470–477.

who enjoys books. One teacher regularly used to read a new children's book while her class was reading. She would keep the book in an old beat-up briefcase that she delighted in carrying. A kind of game she played with her 7- and 8-year-old students was to keep the book hidden from them. Their delight was to find out what book she was reading, so they could read the same one. Of course they always found out, which was what she had in mind in the first place. Walk into any classroom and you can tell if the teacher really respects books. You can look at the teacher's desk or ask the children what books their teacher is reading to them. You can see what provisions have been made to have books in the classroom; you can look at the quality of the books and talk to children about which ones they have read. Enthusiasm for books is contagious; if the teacher has it, so will the children.

The Classroom Book Collection

If we want children to become readers we will want to surround them with books of all kinds. We know that wide reading is directly related to accessibility; the more books available and the more time for reading, the more children will read and the better readers they will become.

Books should be a natural part of the classroom environment. There should be no argument about whether to have a classroom collection of books or a library media center; both are necessary. Children should have immediate access to books whenever they need them.

The books in the classroom collection will vary from those in the library media center. Many classrooms have an extensive paperback collection (400 to 500 titles). Frequently, there are five or six copies of the same title, so several children can read the same book and have an in-depth discussion of it.

The classroom teacher will also want to provide for a changing collection of books depending on the themes or units the children are studying. The librarian may provide a rolling cart of materials that will enhance children's study of bugs or folktales or the Civil War or explorers. It is important that teachers are thoroughly acquainted with the content of these books so they can help their students use them. If the library media center does not have particular books that the children or the teacher need, they may be obtained from local public libraries or from a bookmobile. Some state libraries will send boxes of books to teachers in communities that are not serviced by public libraries. An increasing number of teachers are demanding and receiving their share of monies allocated for instructional materials. Teachers using real books as the heart of their curriculum should receive the same amount of money as those using basal readers, workbooks, social studies, science, and other textbooks. We admire the number of teachers who spend their own money to buy tradebooks for their classrooms, but at the same time, we question the practice. Do coaches buy the footballs, art teachers the paints and colored paper? Real books are essential to the making of a fluent reader and should be an unquestioned item of every school budget.

Creating a Classroom Reading Center

Most teachers create an inviting reading area where children may go to read. This area should be somewhat secluded and outside the general traffic pattern. It is usually marked off with shelves where trade books are attractively displayed. A rug provides quiet and comfort. Many centers have beanbag chairs, pillows, a rocking chair, and sometimes a comfortable couch for reading. In order to mark off a reading area, one teacher of 8- and 9-year-olds clipped paperback books to clothespins and hung these by strings suspended from the ceiling. Another group of 7- and 8-year olds made a quilt of textile crayon squares depicting their favorite stories. This then became a brightly colored divider for their reading center. Some schools have constructed sturdy lofts in classrooms for the reading area.

Children develop more interest in books when they share in the planning of a reading center. One group of 8-year-olds utilized an unused cloak room for their reading center. With the aid of the teacher and custodian they built and painted bookshelves. Others designed unbleached muslin curtains that were decorated with crayon drawings of their favorite characters from books. A mother provided a hooked rug and a rocking chair to complete the homey aspect of this reading center. Another school changed a storage closet that was between three rooms into a small primary-grade book center. Good lighting, carpeting, and some bookcases made this a quiet, comfortable place for children from several classrooms to meet and share books together.

Inventive teachers and children enjoy planning for and creating their own attractive reading areas.

DISPLAY TECHNIQUES

Teachers will want to feature particular books by displaying them on top of bookshelves or on the

Second and third graders chose their favorite books to illustrate with fabric paints. Their teacher then put their squares together to make a colorful quilt that was used to create a private reading area.

Highland Park Elementary School, South-Western City Schools, Grove City, Ohio. Pam Kessen, teacher.

shelves with their covers facing outward. Old, shabby-looking books placed so one can read only the titles on the spines do not capture the attention of children. We will never forget the first-grade classroom that had some fifty trade books up on shelves so high that no child could possibly reach them. Books should be constantly and freely available in the classroom.

Department stores feature what they want to sell by arranging interesting displays; teachers could do the same. It takes very little time to collect five or six good Halloween stories and poetry books and place them with a pumpkin on a table that has been covered with a piece of orange or black cloth. All the books by one author or illustrator could be exhibited together, along with a picture of the writer or artist. Children might decide on a "book of the week," which could have a special place of honor. One group of 8- and 9-year-olds moves their favorite books to the windowsills for display. One fifth-grade classroom has books in three places, the reading area, a table of books concerned with whatever focus unit they are studying, and a special place for books they have written and bound themselves. To be effective, displays should be changed frequently.

Trade books should be an integral part of the total environment of the room. For example, Jan Feder's informational book on *The Life of a Hamster* might be displayed along with Alan Baker's *Benjamin's Portrait*, a delightful story of a hamster, alongside the cage of the classroom's hamster. Millicent Selsam's book, *A First Look at Leaves*, could accompany a chart of leaves pressed and laminated. If the teacher is reading aloud Jean George's *Julie of the Wolves*, she might display a soapstone sculpture or George's nonfiction book *The Wounded Wolf*, or traditional Eskimo tales such as James Houston's *The Falcon Bow, an Arctic Legend* or Dale DeArmond's beautiful story of *The Seal Oil Lamp*, or *Toughboy and Sister* by Kirkpatrick Hill, another realistic story. Such book cycles help children make connections with books from other genres about a similar topic. After teachers model this kind of display children can be encouraged to find books that will go with the read-aloud book or their show-and-tell artifacts.

Whenever possible, teachers should try to involve children in the process of selecting, obtaining, and arranging books for the reading center. Children may review new books and share in their selection. Excitement mounts as they unpack boxes of books, whether they come from the library or directly from the publisher. They may help with book arrangement and display. One group of three kindergarten children carefully rearranged the books on display in their room into the following categories:

♦ ABC Books and Mother Goose Rhymes
♦ Books by Pat Hutchins
♦ Fat Books
♦ Little Books
♦ Books with Pretty Front Covers

The teacher was using the first group of books with the class. The second group represented their ongoing study of the work of one illustrator. The last three categories were obviously theirs, but the process of rearranging the books forced them to look at each one, to discuss it and come to some tentative conclusion about its size or content. Besides their own childlike categories, they learned that books could be classified by type (genre) and author.

In a fifth- and sixth-grade classroom, children decided to display all the books in which the main characters showed courage of some kind or other. This resulted in much discussion about not only physical courage but also the psychological courage required of the characters in Betsy Byars's book, *The Pinballs* and Katherine Paterson's *The Great Gilly Hopkins* and her historical fiction of the mill girls in *Lyddie*.

SHARING LITERATURE WITH CHILDREN

From the time of the earliest primitive fire circle to the Middle Ages—when minnesingers and troubadours sang their ballads—to the modern age of television, people have found delight in hearing stories and poems. Since literature serves many educational purposes in addition to entertainment and enjoyment, teachers should place a high priority on sharing literature with children. Boys and girls of all ages should have the opportunity to hear good literature every day.

Reading to Children

One of the best ways to interest children in books is to read to them frequently from the time they are able to listen. Preschoolers and kindergarten children should have an opportunity to listen to stories three or four times a day. Parent volunteers, high school students, college participants— all can be encouraged to read to small groups of children throughout the day. Children should have a chance to hear their favorite stories over and over again at a listening center. The child from a book-loving family may have heard over a thousand bedtime stories before she ever comes to kindergarten; some children may never have heard one.

One excellent teacher of kindergarten and first-grade children commented on the importance of sharing books with her children.

> I read to my children a lot—a whole lot! I'll read anywhere from one to three stories at a time. Sometimes I'll reread a favorite story twice. And I read four to five times a day. I read to the whole group, to small groups of four or five children and to individual children. While I'm reading to the groups

A teacher shares her enthusiasm for books with one or two children as well as the class.

Idyllwild Elementary School, Idyllwild, California. Sharon Schmidt, teacher. Photo by Larry Rose.

It is essential that teachers continue to read aloud to older children. This is the time to introduce books they might miss and get them hooked on reading.

Mission School, Redlands Public Schools, Redlands, California. Joan Schleicher, teacher. Photo by Larry Rose.

I'll encourage them to join in on the refrains. With individuals I may point to words, talk about what a word is. Sometimes I'll frame a word with my hands or put it on the board. I put songs, poems and refrains on chart paper so children will try to read them by themselves. And I'll read stories over and over again, just the way children hear bedtime stories. It is not unusual for me to read a book twenty times in one month![10]

Teachers accept the idea of reading a story at least twice a day to the primary-grade child. Increasingly, the daily story time is advocated by almost all authorities in reading. The research done by Cohen, Durkin, Clark, Thorndike, and Wells reported in Chapter 4 emphasizes the importance of reading aloud to all children not only for enjoyment but also for their growth in reading skills. Reading to children improves children's reading. Rereading favorite stories is as important as the initial reading.

Unfortunately, the practice of a daily story time is not as common in the middle grades as in the

[10]Interview with Kristen Kerstetter in *The Best of the WEB, 1976–1982*, Susan Hepler, ed. (Columbus: The Reading Center, College of Education, Ohio State University, 1982), pp. 2–3.

primary grades. Yet, we know that it is just as essential. Reading comprehension is improved as students listen to and discuss events, characters, and motivation. They learn to predict what will happen in such exciting tales as Hunter's *A Stranger Came Ashore*. Their vocabulary increases as they hear fine texts such as Donald Hall's *Ox-Cart Man* or Jane Yolen's poetic text for *Owl Moon*. Older students can discuss homelessness and prejudice as they hear the larger-than-life story of *Maniac Magee* by Jerry Spinelli or they can add to their knowledge of the presidency of *Lincoln* in Russell Freedman's remarkable photo-biography. Teachers can take advantage of this time to introduce various genres such as fantasy, biography, or poetry, which students might not be reading on their own.

Primarily, however, the read-aloud time will cause children to want to read. Once a child has heard a good book read aloud, he or she can hardly wait to savor it again. Reading aloud thus generates further interest in books. Good oral reading should develop a taste for fine literature.

SELECTING BOOKS TO READ ALOUD

Teachers and librarians will want to select books to read aloud in terms of the children's interests and background in literature and the quality of writing. Usually, teachers will not select books that children in the group are reading avidly on their own. This is the time to stretch their imaginations, to extend interests, and to develop appreciation of fine writing. If children have not had much experience in listening to stories, begin where they are. Appreciation for literature appears to be developmental and sequential. Six and 7-year-olds who have had little exposure to literature still need to hear many traditional fairy tales, including "Hansel and Gretel," "Sleeping Beauty," and *The Crane Wife* by Sumiko Yagawa. They delight in such favorite picture storybooks as *Harry the Dirty Dog* by Gene Zion, *Sylvester and the Magic Pebble* by William Steig, or Patricia C. McKissack's *Flossie & the Fox*. Other children of the same age who have had much exposure to literature may demand longer chapter books like *Ramona Forever* by Beverly Cleary, *James and the Giant Peach* by Roald Dahl, or *Rip-Roaring Russell* by Johanna Hurwitz.

In the writers' experience, children tend to enjoy fantasies if they are read aloud. The subtle humor of A. A. Milne's *Winnie-the-Pooh* may be completely lost when the child is reading alone; but, when shared by an appreciative teacher-reader, the awkward but well-meaning "Pooh of Very Little Brain" and the dismal Eeyore become well-loved personages to 7- and 8-year-olds. The mysterious snow-shrouded pictures of *The Polar Express* by Chris Van Allsburg intrigue children of this age. They can discuss the ending of this story and ponder the question of the sound of the Christmas bell. After hearing John Steptoe's *Mufaro's Beautiful Daughters*, children could look for other "generous person/ greedy person" stories (see Chapter 6).

Picture storybooks are no longer just for "little kids." There is a real place for sharing some of the beautiful picture books with older children as well as younger ones. *Dawn* by Uri Shulevitz creates the same feeling visually as one of Emily Dickinson's clear, rarefied poems. It is a literary experience for all ages, but particularly for anyone who has felt "at oneness" with the world before the sunrise. Older students particularly enjoy Chris Van Allsburg's mysterious *The Stranger* or David Macaulay's puzzling four stories in one in *Black and White*.

The teacher should strive for balance in what is read aloud to children. Children tend to like what they know. Introducing a variety of types of books will broaden their base of appreciation. If 11- and 12-year-olds are all reading contemporary fiction, the teacher might read Brian Jacques's powerful fantasy of the fight to save the ancient stone abbey of *Redwall*, or introduce them to Katherine Paterson's indomitable *Lyddie*, who struggles against the unbearable working conditions of factory girls in the Lowell, Massachusetts mills of the 1840s. The finely honed writing of Patricia MacLachlan's *Sarah, Plain and Tall*, the story of a mail-order bride and the family who longed for a new mother, could be shared with children as young as third grade and as old as fifth. Most of these books are too good for children to miss and should be read aloud to them.

Primary-grade teachers will read many books to their children, certainly a minimum of three to four a day. Middle-grade teachers may present parts of many books to their students during book talks or as teasers to interest children in reading the books. But how many entire books will a teacher read in the course of one school year? An educated guess might be that starting with 8-year-olds—when teachers begin to read longer, continuous stories to boys and girls—an average of some six to ten books are read aloud during the year. This means that for the next four years, when children are reaching the peak of their interest in reading, they may hear no more than forty or so books read by their teachers! Today when there are more than 73,000 children's books in print, read-aloud choices must be selected with care in terms of their relevance for students and the quality of their writing. A suggested list of books to read aloud is included on the endpapers of this book to serve as a beginning guide to selection. Notice that the age groups overlap deliberately. There is no such thing as a book for 5-year-olds or 10-year-olds. Very popular books such as those by Dr. Seuss or poems by Shel Silverstein do not appear on our read-aloud lists, since children will have read them on their own. Only a teacher who knows the children, their interests, and their background of experience can *truly* select appropriate books for a particular class.

We note with concern the increasing number of teachers who want to read such complex stories as *Tuck Everlasting* by Natalie Babbitt, *A Wrinkle in Time* by Madeleine L'Engle, or *The Pinballs* by Betsy Byars to 6- and 7-year-olds. While children this age may become involved in the plots of these well-written stories, they will certainly miss much of the deeper meanings reflected in their themes, such as the burden of immortality, the overcoming of evil with love, or the courage of children surviving family rejection and cruelty. Read at the appropriate developmental levels, these books could provide the basis for serious in-depth discussion and study. The period for reading children's literature appears to have decreased as more and more 12- and 13-year-olds begin to read bestsellers and other books written for adults. The inappropriate selection of books for reading aloud by both parents and teachers may contribute to this erosion of childhood.

There is a difference, however, between what parents may choose for family reading and what is appropriate for classroom sharing. Parents have the advantage of knowing all the books that children have enjoyed at home. In a family sharing *Charlotte's Web*, the 5-year-old enjoys the humor of these talking barnyard animals while an 8-year-old may weep at Charlotte's death. The closeness of a family unit helps all members to find enjoyment in a read-aloud story regardless of age level. The teacher, on the other hand, has to consider children's background in literature or lack of background as he or she selects appropriate books to capture their attention.

A read-aloud program should be planned. What books are too good to miss? These should be included in the overall plan. Teachers should keep a record of the books that they have shared with the children they teach and a brief notation of the reaction of the class to each title.

This enables teachers to see what kind of balance is being achieved and what the particular favorites of the class are. Such a record provides the children's future teachers with information on the likes and dislikes of the class and their exposure to literature. It also might prevent the situation that was discovered by a survey of one school in which every teacher in the school, with the exception of the kindergarten and the second-grade teachers, had read *Charlotte's Web* aloud to the class! *Charlotte's Web* is a great book, but not for every class. Perhaps teachers in a school need to agree on what is the most appropriate time for reading particular favorites. Teachers and librarians should be encouraged to try reading new books to children, instead of always reading the same ones. But some self-indulgence should be allowed every teacher who truly loves a particular book, for that enthusiasm can't help but rub off on children.

TECHNIQUES FOR READING ALOUD

Effective oral reading is an important factor in capturing children's interest. Some teachers can

RESOURCES FOR TEACHING

♦ GUIDELINES FOR READING ALOUD ♦

1. Select a story appropriate to the developmental age of the children and their previous exposure to literature.
2. Determine whether you will share the book with the whole class, a small group, or an individual child.
3. Select books that will stretch children's imagination, extend their interests, and expose them to fine art and writing.
4. Read a variety of types of books to capture the interests of all.
5. Remember that favorite stories should be reread at the primary level.
6. Plan to read aloud several times a day.
7. Select a story that you like so you can communicate your enthusiasm.
8. Choose a story or chapter that can be read in one session.
9. Read the book first so you are familiar with the content.
10. Seat the children close to you so all can see the pictures.
11. Hold the book so children can see the pictures at their eye level.
12. Communicate the mood and meaning of the story and characters with your voice.
13. Introduce books in various ways:
    Through a display
    By a brief discussion about the author or illustrator
    By asking children to predict what the story will be about through looking at the cover and interpreting the title
    By linking the theme, author, or illustrator to other books children know
14. Encourage older children to discuss the progress of the story or predict the outcome at the end of the chapter.
15. Help children to link the story with their own experiences or other literature.
16. Keep a list of the books read aloud to the whole class that can be passed on to the next teachers.

make almost any story sound exciting; others plod dully through. The storyteller's voice, timing, and intonation patterns should communicate the meanings and mood of the story. Conversation should be read naturally, and volume varied with the content of the story. Humor, mystery, and disgust, can all be communicated through the tone of the reader's voice. Effective reading suggests that the teacher should be familiar with the story. Certainly his or her enthusiasm for the book will be communicated. It is good for children to see teachers moved by a story. One teacher of our acquaintance says he has never yet been able to finish *Where the Red Fern Grows* by Wilson Rawls without shedding a tear. Others find White's *Charlotte's Web* or Paterson's *Bridge to Terabithia* equally hard to finish. Literature should communicate feelings, real feelings. A well-read story can move us to tears or laughter.

The guidelines for reading aloud in the previous box may prove useful. Check the list before selecting and reading a story to a whole class.

Storytelling

A 5-year-old said to his teacher: "Tell the story from your face." His preference for the story *told* by the teacher or librarian instead of the story read directly from the book is echoed by boys and girls everywhere. The art of storytelling is frequently neglected in the elementary school today. There are so many beautiful books to share with children, we rationalize, and our harried life allows little time for learning stories. Yet children should not be denied the opportunity to hear well-told stories. Through storytelling, the teacher helps transmit the literary heritage.

Storytelling provides for intimate contact and rapport with the children. No book separates the teacher from the audience. The story may be modified to fit group needs. A difficult word or phrase can be explained in context. For example, in telling the story of *The Three Wishes* by Paul Galdone, you could quickly explain that "black pudding" is another word for sausage before continuing the story. Stories can be personalized for very young children by substituting their names for those of the characters. Such a phrase as "and, David, if you had been there you would have

seen the biggest Billy Goat Gruff. . . " will redirect the child whose interest has wandered. The pace of the story can be adapted to the children's interests and age levels.

SELECTING STORIES TO TELL

Stories that are to be told should be selected with care. Stories worth the telling have special characteristics that include a quick beginning, action, a definite climax, natural dialogue, and a satisfying conclusion. It is best to select stories with only three or four speaking characters. Such folktales as "The Three Billy Goats Gruff," "The Little Red Hen," and "Cinderella" are particular favorites of younger children. The repetitive pattern of these tales makes them easy to tell. Originally passed down from generation to generation by word of mouth, these tales were polished and embellished with each retelling. *Gone Is Gone* by Wanda Gág, *The Mousewife* by Rumer Godden, and "The Ogre Who Built a Bridge" a Japanese version of Rumpelstiltskin found in Yoshiko Uchida's collection, *The Sea of Gold*, all exemplify other favorite tales to tell.

Ashley Bryan's wonderful retelling of a West Indian pourquoi story, *The Cat's Purr*, begs to be told to 6-, 7-, and 8-year-olds. The sound effects of the animals, the rich use of language, and the drama of rat stealing cat's drum all make this an exciting tale. The admonition "Remember now, don't rap it or beat it or tap it or poke it. Just stroke it gently. And don't let anyone else play it," sets the stage for the action and would have to be memorized to maintain the flavor of the story. However, the whole story would not have to be memorized, just the refrains. Children this age also enjoy some of the tall tales about American folk heroes such as Paul Bunyan, Pecos Bill, and John Henry. Incidents from biographies and chapters from longer books may be told as a way of interesting children in reading them.

A literary story that is known for its rich language and fine illustrations like Rudyard Kipling's *The Elephant's Child* is better read aloud than told. Besides, the pictures form an integral part of this literary picture book and need to be shared with children. It is best to select a story for telling that sounds like a "told tale" and can stand alone without pictures.

Two first graders enjoy reading books together in the school library.

Wickcliffe Alternative School, Upper Arlington, Ohio. Photo by Diane Driessen, librarian.

GUIDELINES FOR TELLING STORIES

From the time of the early minstrels, storytelling has been considered an art. For this reason many teachers have been afraid to attempt it. However, the classroom teacher is an artist in working with children and should have no fear in telling stories to them. Enjoyment of the tale and knowledge of children will help to convey enthusiasm and appreciation for the story.

If the teacher knows and enjoys the story, techniques will come naturally. The story, however, should be carefully prepared. The teacher needs to be thoroughly familiar with its plot, characters, and the flavor of its language; but it need not be memorized. In fact, memorization often results in a stilted, artificial presentation. Also there is the added danger of being completely confused when a line is forgotten. The storyteller should first visualize the setting; imagine the appearance of the characters, their age and costume; and plan an introduction that will set the mood of the story. It may be wise to learn the pattern of some introductions, such as, "Once there was, and once there wasn't. . . ." If there are repeated chants or refrains, these should be memorized. Outline the sequence of events, including major incidents, the climax, and conclusion. Master the structure of a story by reading it from beginning to end several times. Experienced storytellers allow two to three weeks to make a story their own. They learn the story as a whole, not in parts, and practice telling it to themselves, their family, in fact, anyone who will listen.

The good storyteller does not call attention to himself but to the story. He should use a pleasant, low-pitched voice with enough volume to be heard easily. Gestures, if used at all, should be natural for the storyteller and appropriate to the action of the story. The storyteller is not an actor but the channel through which the story is told. Many storytellers believe sound effects should be omitted. If the lion roars, the narrator should not attempt an imitation of a roar, but the idea can be conveyed as the word "roared" is given a deeper tone and increased volume. The *r* sound may be exaggerated so the lion "rrroarred." Writers and such well-known storytellers as Bob Barton and Augusta Baker suggest variations in pitch, tone, and volume of voice in accordance with the mood of the story to make it more effective. Well-timed pauses may help listeners anticipate a climax. No amount of study of these techniques will substitute for actual practice. With experience comes assurance and a willingness to experiment. Tape recordings can be made to evaluate storytelling skills. A very brave storyteller may be willing to have her presentation videotaped for group critiquing.[11]

FELTBOARD STORIES

Storytelling may be varied by using a flannelboard, feltboard, or magnetic board. To tell a feltboard story, the scenery or characters of a story may be made of flannel, felt, or paper. As the story is told, the figures are placed in the proper positions on the board. If the figures are made of paper, strips of flannel attached to the reverse side will cause them to adhere to the feltboard. Small magnets or magnetic sheets with adhesive backing may be cut and applied directly to the

[11]For further assistance see Caroline Feller Bauer's *Handbook for Storytellers* (Chicago: American Library Association, 1977).

back of characters for use with a magnetic board. Gluing felt to the inside of an artist's cardboard portfolio and trimming it with tape is an easy way to make a feltboard. Feltboards and magnetic boards may also be purchased.

Some tales are more suitable for feltboard presentation than others. The stories should be simple and have few characters. Not every incident or scene in the story needs to be included. Detailed settings are too difficult to recreate. While some rapid changes can be portrayed on a feltboard, most physical action is better dramatized. The cumulative tale, or one in which elements are added, is usually quite appropriate for a felt-story presentation. For example, in what better way could Wanda Gág's *Nothing at All* complete his metamorphosis from a round ball to the shape of a dog, to a live dog with spots, tongue, ears, and tail that wags? Three versions of the Jewish folktale *Could Anything Be Worse?*, as retold by Marilyn Hirsh, as *It's Too Noisy!* by Joanna Cole, and as *It Could Always Be Worse* by Margot Zemach, lend themselves well to telling on a feltboard. This is the tale of the man who complains that his house is too small and so he goes to the rabbi to ask for advice. The rabbi suggests he invite the chickens into the house, then the cow, then his wife's relatives, and so on. When the man can no longer stand it, the rabbi suggests he take them out one by one. Then both the man and his wife appreciate all the room they now have in their house! This story can be easily shown by making a simple outline of the house, adding all the animals, and then taking them out again!

RESOURCES FOR TEACHING

♦ SUGGESTED STORIES FOR THE FELTBOARD ♦

Brett, Jan. *The Mitten*. Putnam's, 1989.

Cole, Joanna. *It's Too Noisy*, illustrated by Kate Duke. Crowell, 1989.

Duvoisin, Roger. *Petunia*. Knopf, 1950.

Freeman, Don. *Dandelion*. Viking, 1964.

Gág, Wanda. *Nothing at All*. Coward McCann, 1928.

Galdone, Paul. *The Gingerbread Boy*. Clarion, 1983.

Ginsburg, Mirra. *Mushroom in the Rain*, illustrated by José Aruego and Ariane Dewey. Macmillan, 1974.

Greenblat, Rodney A. *Uncle Wizzmo's New Used Car*. Harper, 1990.

Hirsh, Marilyn. *Could Anything Be Worse?* Holiday, 1974.

Hogrogian, Nonny. *One Fine Day*. Macmillan, 1971.

Kent, Jack. *The Fat Cat: A Danish Folktale*. Scholastic, 1972.

Lionni, Leo. *Frederick*. Pantheon, 1967.

_____. *Little Blue and Little Yellow*. Astor-Honor, 1959.

McDonald, Megan. *Is This a House for a Hermit Crab?*, illustrated by S. O. Schindler. Orchard, 1990.

Morgan, Pierr. *The Turnip*. Philomel, 1990.

Oppenheim, Joanne. *You Can't Catch Me!*, illustrated by Andrew Shachar. Houghton Mifflin, 1986.

Shaw, Charles G. *It Looked Like Spilt Milk*. Harper, 1947.

Tresselt, Alvin. *The Mitten*, illustrated by Yaroslava. Lothrop, 1964.

Turkle, Brinton. *Do Not Open*. Dutton, 1981.

Waber, Bernard. *"You Look Ridiculous," Said the Rhinoceros to the Hippopotamus*. Houghton Mifflin, 1966.

Williams, Linda. *The Little Old Lady Who Was Not Afraid of Anything*, illustrated by Megan Lloyd. Crowell, 1986.

Wood, Audrey. *The Napping House*, illustrated by Don Wood. Harcourt, 1984.

Zemach, Margot. *It Could Always Be Worse*. Farrar, Straus, 1976.

_____. *The Three Wishes: An Old Story*. Farrar, Straus, 1986.

Zion, Gene. *Harry the Dirty Dog*, illustrated by Margaret Bloy Graham. Harper, 1956.

One of the advantages of using a feltboard is that the figures can be arranged in sequence and thus serve as cues for the story. It is essential to *tell* the feltboard story. If the teller tries to read it and manipulate the figures, he is helplessly lost in a tangle of pages and felt characters. While telling a feltboard story, remember to look at the children rather than the board.

The feltboard story is an attention-getting device. Children are intrigued to see what will appear next. As soon as the storyteller is finished, children like to retell the story again in their own words. This is an excellent language experience and should be encouraged. Children also like to make and tell their own stories.

Try to keep all the pieces of a feltboard story together in a plastic bag clearly marked with the title of the story. If possible, also put a paperback copy of the book or story in the bag to keep the memory of it fresh and to share with the children after the story has been told. If teachers or librarians make just two feltboard stories a year, they will soon build a collection of tales to share. These are fun to make and even more fun to share with an enthusiastic audience. Storytellers have their own favorites, but the ones we list in the accompanying box seem particularly well suited for a feltboard presentation.

In *Osa's Pride* by Ann Grifalconi, the African grandmother tells Osa a story using a story cloth. After hearing this tale, children could glue felt characters on their own story cloth. The Hmong peoples from Laos also use a story cloth. Nancy Hom adapted this technique to create handsome pictures for Blia Xiong's *Nine-in-One Grr! Grr!* a folktale in which Tiger is tricked into forgetting her all-important song by Bird. (See Storytelling Aids in Chapter 13 for other suggestions.)

BOOK TALKS

Librarians and teachers frequently make use of a book talk as a way of introducing books to children. The primary purpose of a book talk is to interest children in reading the book themselves. Rather than reveal the whole story, the book talk tells just enough about the book to entice others to read it. A book talk may be about one title; it may be about several unrelated books that would have wide appeal; or it may revolve around several books with a similar theme, such as "getting along in the family" or "courage" or "survival stories."

The book talk should begin with recounting an amusing episode or with telling about an exciting moment in the book. The narrator might want to assume the role of a character in a book, such as Julie in *Julie of the Wolves* by Jean George, and tell of her experience of being lost without food or a compass on the North Slope of Alaska. The speaker should stop before the crisis is over or the mystery solved. Details should be specific. It is better to let the story stand on its own than to characterize it as a "terribly funny" story or the "most exciting" book you've ever read. Enthusiasm for the book will convey the speaker's opinion of it. This is one reason why book talks should be given only about stories the speaker genuinely likes. Children will then come to trust this evaluation. It is best if the book is on hand as it is discussed, so that the children can check it out as soon as the book is finished.

A good book talk takes time to prepare, yet it is well worth the preparation if children are drawn into reading the book. Some teachers and librarians find it is helpful to tape their book talks in order to listen to and evaluate them. Children who missed the talk might be encouraged to listen to the tape. A list of the books included in the book talk can be made available to children following the talk, so they can remember the names of the titles. Remember, the effectiveness of a book talk is judged by the number of children who want to read the books after they have been introduced.

PROVIDING TIME TO READ BOOKS

One of the primary purposes of giving book talks, telling stories, and reading aloud to children is to motivate them to read. A major goal of every school should be to develop children who not only can read but who *do* read—who love reading and will become lifetime readers.

Unfortunately, schools spend so much of their time teaching the skills of literacy that they fail to develop truly literate persons who read widely and thoughtfully on many diverse subjects. The report of the Commission on Reading titled *Becoming a Nation of Readers* showed how little time students spend in reading both in school and out of school. According to this report, a typical primary class has only 7 or 8 minutes per day for silent reading; middle graders averaged only 15 minutes. In a study of fifth graders' out-of-school reading, 50 percent of the children read books for an average of 4 minutes per day or less, in contrast to the 130 minutes per day spent watching TV. "For the majority of the children, reading from books occupied 1 percent of their free time or less."[12]

To become fluent readers, children need to practice reading from real books that capture their interest and imagination. No one could become a competent swimmer or tennis player by practicing 4 minutes a day. Schools have little influence on the out-of-school life of their students, but they do control the curriculum in school. If we want children to become readers, we must reorder our priorities and provide time for children to just read books of their own choosing every day.

Sustained Silent Reading (SSR)

Recognizing this need, many teachers have initiated a sustained silent reading (SSR) time. The name is somewhat formidable, suggesting more pain than pleasure. Teachers have used other names such as "Recreational Reading," "Free Reading," or even the acronym D.E.A.R. (Drop Everything and Read) used by the teacher in *Ramona Quimby, Age 8* by Beverly Cleary.

One primary teacher called it O.T.T.E.R. Time—"*O*ur *T*ime *T*o *E*njoy *R*eading." This certainly comes closer to the goal of such a program than the ominous-sounding Sustained Silent Reading. Whatever the name, however, this is a time when everyone in the class (in some instances, the entire school) reads, including the teacher. SSR times have been successfully established in kindergarten through middle schools. Usually, one time period is lengthened gradually from 10 minutes a day to 20 to 30 and, in some fifth- and sixth-grade clases, 45 minutes per day.

Third and fourth graders enjoy reading their books during SSR, or recreational reading time.
Mission School, Redlands Public Schools, Redlands, California. Joan Schleicher, teacher. Photo by Larry Rose.

Some teachers allow children to read in pairs, recognizing the social nature of reading.

In classrooms that use real books for teaching reading and studying themes which cut across the curriculum, children are reading and writing throughout the day. Teachers still have a special time each day for children to read the books they have chosen to read for enjoyment. A classroom collection of books supplemented by library books is essential to the organization of this kind of program.

A discouraging note comes from a survey conducted by Patricia Lyons[13] of 1,500 California teachers (K–6) regarding their implementation of the California Integrated Language Arts Curriculum. Ninety-nine percent of these teachers reported reading aloud to their students, but only 79.7 percent had a regular period for sustained silent reading. The shocking information revealed that their average classroom library contained only 191 books, 127 of which had been personally purchased by the teacher. The average

---

[12]Richard C. Anderson, et al., *Becoming a Nation of Readers* (Washington, D.C.: National Institute of Education, 1984), p.77.

[13]Write Patricia Lyons, Professor of Education at California State University, Chico, CA 95929 for a copy of "Implementing a Literature-Based Integrated Language Arts Curriculum: A Survey of K–6 Teachers Throughout California," 1991.

time devoted to sustained silent reading was only 15.7 minutes a day. Children can hardly become engrossed in reading a full-length novel in 15 minutes. And if thirty-five children must select their books from fewer than two hundred titles, there is little choice indeed.

TALKING ABOUT BOOKS WITH CHILDREN

Conversations

Equally important as time for wide reading is time to talk about books children are reading. When adults discuss books, we have good conversations about the ones we like, but we seldom quiz each other about character development, themes, or setting of the story. As teachers, we want to show this same respect for children as they share their thoughts about books.

A good time for informal talk about books is after children have had time to read by themselves. In pairs, small groups, or as a class, children may be invited to tell something about a book, show a picture and tell what is happening, read an interesting or powerful paragraph, and so forth. In discussions such as this, teachers can learn much about what children are reading and how they talk about books. Margaret Meek observes this about talk in the classroom:

> Left to comment on their own, without the stimulus of a question, children often choose to talk about quite other aspects of a tale than those that preoccupy their elders. . . . They create a tissue of collaborative understandings for each other in a way that no single question from an adult makes possible.[14]

Maryann Eeds and Deborah Wells showed how well fifth and sixth graders explored the meaning of novels they were reading through nondirective response groups.[15] The literature discussion groups met two days a week, 30 minutes a day, for four to five weeks. The leaders were undergraduate education students who were instructed to let meaning emerge from the group rather than solicit it. The results of this study showed that the groups collaborated and built meaning which was deeper and richer than what they attained in their solitary reading. The authors concluded that "Talk helps to confirm, extend, and modify individual interpretations and creates a better understanding of the text."

Teachers do not abdicate any direct teaching about books by holding back questions. Rather, as they listen carefully to children's responses, they can identify teaching possibilities, plan future conversations, or make use of a teachable moment to make a point. When the teacher is an active participant rather than the leader of a group, children more readily collaborate to fill their own gaps in understanding and make meaning together.

Guided Discussion

More structured discussion may occur with the books a teacher chooses to read aloud or to read with small groups. When a teacher introduces the

Children need time to share their books, talk about favorites, and become a "community of readers."
Mission School, Redlands Public Schools, Redlands, California. Joan Schleicher, teacher. Photo by Larry Rose.

[14]Margaret Meek, "What Counts as Evidence in Theories of Children's Literature?" *Theory into Practice*, Vol. 21, no. 4 (1982), p. 289.
[15]Maryann Eeds and Deborah Wells, "Grand Conversations: An Exploration of Meaning Construction in Literature Study Groups," *Research in the Teaching of English*, vol. 23, no. 1 (1989), pp. 4–29.

A Stranger Came Ashore

NEW VOCABULARY	CHARACTERS and CHARACTERISTICS	FOLKLORE	PREDICTIONS
SELKIE FOLK	FINN LEARSON— Big eyes, Strange little smile, he is tall. The best Dancer, stormy twins	SELKIES— Turn into morals, (humans) They lose skin Sea (girls with golden under when one try to escape he drowns them and takes there golden hair.	1) Finn is a selkie and Elspeth going to take —c.c.
SHETLAND ISLANDS			2) Selkie turns in to Old Da v.B
BLACK NESS			
VOE	THE HENDERSONS:		
CROFT	PETER— father, he yelled when the poor boy came.		3) Good Selkie will take Elspeth and take her c.c
KOLLIE	JANET— mother		
SHETLAND BEDS		TROWS— They're magic, they're invisible, They take revenge.	4) There was a selkie and is going to take Elspeth down to drown. Finn no take then golden hair
HAAF			
SIXAREEN	ELSPETH: sister has golden hair, might die.		
BUT END			
BEN END			
TROW	ROBBIE— brother super smart, afraid of trows, wants to hold a selkies	LIC STRAW—	5) S.B. Sea Back Elspeth will drown Finn Selkie B.R
FEATHERING			
LICK STRAW			
Shingle	OLD DA— grandfather likes to tell storys he died		6) Nicol will believe Robbie and catch Finn
Peat			

In order to help fifth graders with the Scottish vocabulary and folklore of Mollie Hunter's *A Stranger Came Ashore,* the teacher made this chart and encouraged children to add to it as she finished reading aloud each chapter.

Linda Charles, teacher. Highland Park Elementary School, South-Western City Schools, Grove City, Ohio.

❦ ❦ ❦

story, he may invite children to recognize the author or illustrator, to notice the dedication, or to speculate on the book's content as they look at the cover. As he reads a chapter book, he asks what might happen next or why a character acts as she does. He may introduce Mollie Hunter's *A Stranger Came Ashore* by reading Mordicai Gerstein's *The Seal Mother* or Jane Yolen's *Greyling* and discussing Selkie lore with the class. He may pause at a chapter's end and ask children how Hunter makes the reader feel that something dreadful is about to happen. He may ask what clues suggest that Finn Learson is not who he pretends to be. He may introduce the term *foreshadowing* and ask them to listen for other examples as he reads. (See the discussion on "Asking Good Questions" that appears later in this chapter.) At first the teacher calls attention to aspects such as a well-written passage, an apt chapter heading, or a key moment when a character faces a choice. Later, children will begin noticing the kinds of things the teacher has brought out in these discussions. In this way a teacher models reader behaviors that mature readers practice.

Working in Small Groups

Six or seven children may form a group to discuss a particular title or topic. In a literature-based reading program, children frequently form groups to discuss a novel. They decide with the teacher's help how much they will read prior to the next discussion. They may be encouraged to write down any questions they have, copy a favorite quote, or note anything in their response journals they would like to bring to the next meeting.

After the teacher read the description of Yarl Corbie in Hunter's *A Stranger Came Ashore,* an 11-year-old drew his interpretation of this mysterious Scottish schoolmaster who looked like a raven.

Barbara Friedberg, teacher. Martin Luther King, Jr., Laboratory School, Evanston, Illinois Public Schools.

(See "Writing About Books with Children" that appears later in this chapter.) Teachers may ask open-ended questions such as "What are you thinking about as you are reading this book?" or focus on a previously raised question such as "What survival problems has Brian faced and overcome in the chapters we have read so far?" (Gary Paulsen's *Hatchet*).

Small groups may also be formed on the spur of the moment. As she looked for patterns in fifth and sixth graders' reading records, a teacher noted

A class decided to make animals of various shapes and colors similar to the collage style Lois Ehlert used for *Color Zoo.*

Emerson and Central College Elementary Schools, Westerville, Ohio. Lisa Dapoz, Joan Fusco, and Jean Sperling, teachers. Photo by Connie Compton.

that a group of girls had been reading animal stories. She assembled them at a round table and asked them to discuss titles and patterns in this type of story. They said:

Usually someone is finding an animal or getting them at the time. They never have them to start with. Usually the animal gets hurt in a lot of stories.

The main characters won't accept what their parents say and they're usually very defensive about their animal. Like someone will say "Why don't you get rid of them or kill them?" and they'll say "Not on your life."[16]

Another teacher of kindergartners noticed that four children had chosen books to look at which were illustrated in brilliant collage by Lois Ehlert. She gathered them around her chair to tell her about the pictures. She asked them if they could tell a Lois Ehlert picture from one somebody else had made. One child offered to make a picture "like Lois Ehlert" and created a small collage of bright-colored paper.

In classrooms such as these, where children talk about books, they are free to discover what they think.[17] They may recall or rehearse plots of stories, they may explain, clarify or define meanings for themselves, and they are certainly learning to behave the way readers do.

LITERATURE AND THE WRITING PROGRAM

While literature has made a tremendous impact on reading programs, so too has the new approach to writing. Few teachers would consider teaching reading without including writing, since learning in one area means learning in the other. Literature informs both processes. As children become authors, they look at professional authors to see how a book works and sounds. They borrow and improvise on the language, patterns, and format of published books.[18] Young children rewrite their favorite stories (see Chapter 4), particularly when they can use invented spellings and do not have to produce a "correct" copy.

[16]Hepler, "Patterns in Response to Literature," p. 217.
[17]Susan Hepler, "Talking Our Way to Literacy in the Classroom Community," in *Stories and Readers: New Perspectives on Literature in the Elementary School*, edited by Charles Temple and Patrick Collins (Norwood, Mass.: Christopher-Gordon, 1991), pp. 67–85.
[18]See Frederick R. Burton, "Writing What They Read: Reflections on Literature and Child Writers," in *Stories to Grow On*, edited by Julie M. Jensen (Portsmouth, N.H.: Heinemann, 1989), pp. 97–105.

Writing and reading go on all day in a classroom where language arts and reading are intertwined and literature is at the heart of the curriculum.

Establishing the Writing Center

Just as children need ready access to books to read, so too should they have readily available writing materials. Teachers may vary in what they wish to include in their writing center and where it is located, but it should be obvious and easily approached by several children.

Usually the writing center contains the following items:

Paper
All kinds and sizes, lined and unlined; computer second sheets or yellow lined paper for rough drafts; blank books; books of different shapes (4-inch squares, long skinny, fat, tall, or accordion folds).

Writing Instruments
Pencils; crayons; markers; ballpoint pens.

Writing Supplies
Wallpaper for book covers; construction paper; scissors; glue; white correction fluid; 3-hole puncher; stapler; staple remover; Post-it notes; tape.

Storage Folders
Larger for primary work; manila folders.

Some teachers find it helpful to tie the stapler, scissors, and other large items to a table at the center so they remain there. Teachers also need to decide where children should keep their writing folders. After a child's work has been finished and "published," it may be shared by the child and displayed near the class bookshelf, on the windowsill in a special box, or clothespinned to a line in the reading center.

Ideas for writing may come from the child's own life and from the classroom curriculum. They may also be inspired by books. Teachers can read aloud and then display individual books that serve as springboards or provocative formats for children's writing. Margaret Wise Brown's *The Important Book*, Jack Kent's *The Fat Cat*, Pierr Morgan's *The Turnip*, or Vera B. Williams's *Three Days on a River in a Red Canoe* could serve as possible models for children to use. (See Chapter 13, "Writing from Children's Books" for a discussion

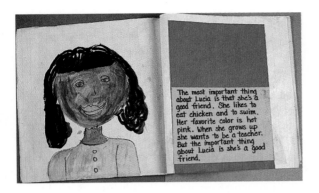

A fifth-grade class tried to capture the important characteristics of each other in interviews. Then they painted pictures and wrote biographical sketches following the pattern of *The Important Book* by Margaret Wise Brown, illustrated by Leonard Weisgard.

Esther L. Walter Elementary School, Anaheim Public Schools. Janine Batzle, teacher.

of many ways children may use literature as starting places for their writing.)

Helping Children Write About Books

In most schools children are no longer required to write book reports, a particularly inert kind of writing. However, many teachers ask children to write about their reading in other ways. This writing resembles talk, in that a child shares ideas and someone responds to those ideas. Teachers find this is a time-saving idea and can set aside a weekly or biweekly time to react in writing to children's written responses. Some teachers demonstrate supportive responses and let pairs of children react to each other's written work as well. There are various ways a teacher can help children write about their reading.

A *reading log* is a simple record of the title and author of each book a child has read. Needless to say, this is a burden for young children, but it is a source of pride for second graders and older children who like to recall their reading and measure their progress. Teachers may give children 6 x 8 cards and let them fill one side. Then the teacher and children can use these records for generalizing as they talk together about a child's reading.

If a child takes her most recent card to the library, librarians may better help her find a book by seeing what she has enjoyed so far.

In a *response journal* children record their comments as they read a novel. Children respond freely as they think about their reading and write about the things that concern or interest them. A *double entry draft* is a two-sided journal entry in which the reader copies or paraphrases a quote from the book on the left half of the paper. On the right, the reader comments on the quote. Teachers react to both of these journals and engage in a written dialogue with the reader (thereby creating a *dialogue journal*). Whatever we call it, children's written responses to the books they read provide teachers with another window into understanding how readers teach themselves to read.

When children write about their reading, they follow certain patterns such as retelling, questioning particular words, clarifying meanings, reacting with like or dislike to a particular part of the story, relating a part of the story to their own lives, or otherwise reflecting. One teacher of fifth graders asked her class to write a weekly reaction to their reading. Kevin, after weeks of writing two or three sentences about his reading, suddenly wrote a long entry based on his discovery of patterns in the books of Mitsumasa Anno. A partial section read:

> In the Anno books besides putting fairy tale characters in, he puts things like Beethoven playing the piano and Shakespeare making a play. A boy climbs on a fence and there is a lady taking a bath. They also have clocks with four hands and a couple of his books have optical illusions like children throwing rings on top of a church steeple. *Anno's Italy* is the funniest of the bunch. The only one I haven't read is *Anno's Alphabet*. (They are all by Mitsumasa Anno. He has a foreign name I think.) [Writes his teacher: He is Japanese.] They are really good, really funny, and have super illustrations.
>
> Kevin Carpenter
> Barrington Road School
> Upper Arlington, Ohio
> Lois Monaghan, teacher

The teacher's comments shared his enthusiasm. While this seems like such a small piece of what a teacher does, it sets the teacher up as someone who is interested in what children think about their reading. And it gives a teacher a valuable chance to rejoice, advise, suggest, connect, question, and gently value the efforts children make to become readers.

Writing about books in the same way every day becomes tedious. Teachers may want to vary the way children can respond. A single dialogue journal may be kept by a group reading the same book. Children can take turns responding. Children may ask their own questions and consider which ones are more interesting to write about. (See the section on "Children's Questions" that appears later in this chapter.)

Teachers may also ask children to address in their journals a particular question about their wide reading or about a class study book. They might write a journal entry from the point of view of a character in the book they are reading, for instance. During the group reading of a novel, a teacher might ask children to write about some issue prior to a class discussion as a way of rehearsing an idea. A small group who has just read Chapter 5 of *On My Honor* by Marion Dane Bauer, for instance, could write about whether Joel could have prevented Tony's drowning. After finishing this novel, children might discuss how and why the main character changed in the story, or what the story makes them think about. They might consider how this book is like others they have read, thus making links between books.

What teachers need to avoid, however, is overusing written responses, or using a journal as a place in which children answer numbers of questions posed by the teacher. The primary power of journals is that the child owns the ideas, not the teacher. The child is director of the reading, and the child reflects on matters of interest to herself. One teacher who compared assigned questions and free-response journals noted, "The thoughtfulness and engagement engendered by the journals resulted in richer, more complete, elaborate responses than I had received when I assigned questions."[19]

Helping Children Become Authors

The more children read and hear stories, the more they want to write their own books. Teachers need some understanding of the writing process, or writing workshop, if they wish to help children develop their abilities. Once a child has completed a rough draft, she may request a *writing conference*. During this time a teacher and child might discuss the child's opinion of the piece of writing. Certain parts might be read aloud. If a child suggests changes or additions, the teacher might help the child by listening to the child further. Then the child can put the writing in her folder or revise it in preparation for a group sharing.[20]

Some teachers establish an *author's chair*, a special place for children or teachers to sit and share writing as a group. Children sign up for the author's chair, read their stories, and ask the listeners for comments. In this way, children hear the reactions and comments of their immediate audience. Maria, a first grader, sat in the author's chair, and her puzzled teacher noted that it wasn't sharing time yet. Maria explained that she was pretend sharing. "I'm thinking; if I get to share this piece with the kids, what will they ask me?"[21] This first grader has already begun to think about what impact she wants her writing to have on her audience, an important step in revision.

When a child is satisfied that a written piece is the best it can be, it is ready to be *published*. Publishing includes making a final draft and displaying it attractively, whether it is the explanation of the graphed results of a class survey or a modern folktale in bound-book form. Older children often want to put their compositions in the computer for a word-processed copy. Some children may wish to make cloth-covered books of their work. (See Chapter 13, "Making Books.") Some schools use parents to set up an in-school publishing program complete with a laminator

[19]J. E. Wollmann-Bonilla, "Reading Journals: Invitations to Participate in Literature," *The Reading Teacher*, vol. 43, no. 2 (November 1989), p. 119.

[20]Thomas Newkirk and Nancie Atwell, eds., *Understanding Writing*, 2nd ed. (Portsmouth, N.H.: Heinemann, 1988), p. 163.
[21]Lucy McCormick Calkins, *The Art of Teaching Writing* (Portsmouth, N.H.: Heinemann, 1986), pp. 20–21.

and spiral-binding machines.[22] Whatever methods and whatever the final product, what is important is that publishing makes a child's work into a work of art. It honors children's thinking, gives real reasons for revision and careful presentation, creates a wider audience for children's work, and values the process of writing.

GUIDING IN-DEPTH STUDY OF BOOKS

Guiding Discussions

If children are to have an opportunity to read and discuss widely, this activity should be balanced with a time for studying books deeply. Teachers can plan in-depth studies of a single book; books by an author or illustrator; a part of a genre, such as dragon folktales or historical fiction that portrays the colonial period; or a theme which cuts across the curriculum but begins with a subject area such as science. The preparation of questions, activities, and guides all work together to help teachers develop curriculum from literature.

ASKING GOOD QUESTIONS

Children need guidance in thinking more widely and deeply about what they read. But teacher questions often follow the pattern of initiation/response/evaluation in a typical classroom. That is, a teacher asks a usually narrow question ("Is this story true?"), a child answers ("No"), and the teacher evaluates the child's answer ("Right. It's just a story") before moving to her next question.[23] Questions like these do nothing to engage children's minds but serve the teacher as a superficial means of evaluating whether a child has "understood" the story. However, in this chapter we have already seen many ways teachers, without resorting to inquisi-

tion, use open-ended questions or activities that encourage children to reveal their understandings.

People who discuss questions use different terms. They differentiate between closed and open questions, lower and higher level questions, questions that lead the reader into or out of the book, questions that lead to convergent or divergent thought, or chains of questions which march up a hierarchical set of steps. Good questions ought to arise from a reader's observation of a book's power and strength. But when teachers generate questions from a set of questioning schemas, the connection between the book and the reader may get lost rather than enhanced.

Christenbury and Kelly examined the research on questions and formed these conclusions:

1. Questioning schemas are helpful guidelines rather than rules by which we write questions;
2. It is better to follow a student lead before proceeding to a teacher question;
3. Teachers should be flexible and be prepared to jettison questions if the discussion is progressing fruitfully;
4. Divergent questions elicit better, more complex responses, especially among lower ability students.[24]

Good discussion questions should improve the quality of the reader's experience with a book. Often, however, a prepared teacher only needs to offer children the opportunity and they will notice all that a teacher intended to bring out. Rosemary Wells's picture book, *Noisy Nora*, is a mouse story of sibling rivalry, and most young children will recognize the ways a jealous Nora tries to get her family's attention. Children who are asked a very general question, "What did you like about this story?", would probably talk about Nora's creative misbehavior and its results. A child might surmise why Nora was so noisy. This might lead to a discussion of ways a child could communicate effec-

[22]See "Setting Up an In-School Publishing Process," in *Invitations: Changing as Teachers and Learners* by Regie Routman (Portsmouth, N.H.: Heinemann, 1991), pp. 263–275.
[23]Courtney Cazden, *Classroom Discourse: The Language of Teaching and Learning* (Portsmouth, N.H.: Heinemann, 1988), p. 55.

[24]A summary of the research on questioning is given in the ERIC report *Questioning: A Path to Critical Thinking* by Leila Christenbury and Patricia P. Kelly (Urbana, Ill.: ERIC Clearinghouse on Reading and Communication Skills and the National Council of Teachers of English, 1983).

tively to parents who seemingly favor one sibling. Children would probably notice the language of "a monumental crash" and would be able to "translate" the words because of picture and text clues. A prepared teacher will have in mind the strengths of the story and be ready with some questions. However, children often discuss all that the teacher had planned to discuss if the teacher merely sets up the group and participates as a discussant rather than leading the group with questions.

Discussions of picture books must give time to the illustrations as well. Most children are familiar with *Where the Wild Things Are* by Maurice Sendak. They understand that Max is in control of the wild things and that the story is a dream adventure. A teacher who asks, "What did Max find in his room? What did it mean?" would let them talk about the symbolic hot meal which proves that Max's mother still loves him. Sometimes children recognize on their own how the illustrations work. If not, a teacher might ask, "What do you see in the first pictures that you see elsewhere in the story?" calling attention to a toy, tent, drawing, and other items which foreshadow Max's adventure. "How do the pictures change?" lets children notice how the pictures grow larger and smaller as Max gets into and out of his dream adventure. Good questions ought to help children see the total story in a new way.

A teacher may set up a question before children begin a story. Julia Redfern in Eleanor Cameron's *Julia and the Hand of God* is destined to be a writer. But readers don't know this until well into the book. A teacher might ask children, "What qualities might a good writer possess?" and generate a list. When the children discover that Julia is a writer, they might discuss what qualities she possesses, such as observational skills, sensitivity, creative mischief, and brooding about history, which will no doubt help Julia's writing powers develop.

Thoughtful questions that provoke good discussions are initially difficult to develop. Teachers need to practice in preparing ones that will open up discussion, enable children to go back to the book for evidence, and help them relate the ideas in books to their own lives. Commercial guides purport to help teachers in this endeavor, but teachers need to examine whether the questions are worth asking. (See "Making and Using Guides" that

appears later in this chapter.) Often lists of generic questions are presented that may be applied to any book. However, these lists tend to ignore the particular power of an individual title as well as the nature of an authentic discussion, and the generic questions may not engage the reader sufficiently to merit their use.

CHILDREN'S QUESTIONS

Children derive real value from developing their own questions for a book. One teacher who regularly uses children's literature as the content of her reading program frequently asks children to write questions when they have finished reading a book. Then she compiles all their questions, and they see if they can answer them in a discussion.

One group of third and fourth graders read their own paperback copies of *Abel's Island* by William Steig. They were encouraged to write questions in the margins of their books and underline favorite passages or particularly descriptive ones in order to make the book theirs through their responses. When they finished the book, they wrote questions to be used in an imaginary interview with Abel by reporters of the "The Mossville News." Their questions were compiled and given to "the reporters" as suggestions for their interview. Some of their questions follow:

QUESTIONS FROM "THE REPORTERS OF
THE MOSSVILLE NEWS" TO ABEL

1. Why did you go after Amanda's scarf in a raging storm?
2. In the beginning, how did you try to get back?
3. How did you feel after you realized you were unable to get back?
4. How long did you live on the island?
5. What did you learn on the island?
6. How will your life in Mossville be different now because of your experience on the island?

QUESTIONS FOR AMANDA AFTER ABEL'S
RETURN HOME

1. What did you do while Abel was missing?
2. How will your life be different now that Abel has returned?

Third and fourth graders
Martin Luther King, Jr., Laboratory School
Evanston, Illinois, Public Schools
Ellen Esrick, teacher

After the children interviewed Abel, the group discussed the questions themselves. One questioning technique this teacher always uses is to develop one or two questions that cannot be answered in the book. The last question for Abel and the two devised for Amanda require children to continue the story in their imagination.

Two teachers showed fourth graders how to create open-ended discussion questions. Then children worked in groups of four to develop their own questions for C. S. Lewis's *The Lion, the Witch, and the Wardrobe.* Each group then chose one of their best questions, some of which were:

1. Why do you think Lucy went with Mr. Tumnus?
2. How do you think the queen felt when she took Edmund? Describe.
3. Why do you think time stopped while Lucy was in the wardrobe?[25]

The teachers reported that children were enthusiastic about this activity and the questions were all discussion generators. This is not time wasted. When children become question makers, they also become question answerers. Good readers continually and unconsciously ask hard questions as they read: Why do people do what they do? What do I think they should do? What's going to happen next and why do I predict that? What does this part mean? How did I know that? What does this story mean to me? How did the author do it? If a teacher encourages children to ask worthwhile questions, she helps them internalize the unconscious question-raising behaviors of good readers.

GRAPHIC ORGANIZERS

A graphic organizer is a visual representation of an idea. For example, in Pat Hutchins's *Rosie's Walk*, an unsuspecting hen takes a walk through a farmyard followed by a fox who meets disaster each time he tries to catch Rosie. A circular map of the action would be a graphic organizer causing children to sequence the plot and discover that Rosie ends her journey in the same place where she began it.

Semantic maps, attribute webs, or word webs

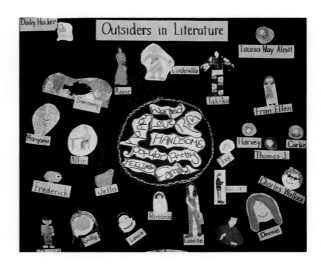

Fifth and sixth graders made a kind of sociogram of literature identifying the "outsiders" in various stories such as Charles Wallace, Gilly, and Carlie. Personality traits that would make you an "insider" were written in the inner circle.

Ridgemont Elementary School, Mt. Victory, Ohio. Sheryl Reed and Peggy Harrison, teachers.

often are used to help children group similar words or ideas into categories following a brainstorming session. In these graphic organizers, a word or idea is placed at the center of a chart with spokes radiating toward related words, attributes, or other examples. One group listed "Outsiders in Literature" at the center of a semantic map and drew lines out to the various characters from novels who seem different from their peers. At the chart's center were clustered words describing insiders. Semantic maps are useful ways to categorize information of what a group knows. Sixth graders who are about to begin Russell Freedman's *Lincoln: A Photobiography* might brainstorm what they already know about him. Facts are then grouped and categorized on a chart, perhaps as "Early years," "What he looked like," "Famous speeches," "His family," "Assassination," and so forth. Word webs or semantic maps are also useful synthesizing aids for children to organize material from a variety of books and sources prior to writing a report. The

[25]Regie Routman, *Invitations: Changing as Teachers and Learners K–12* (Portsmouth, N.H.: Heinemann, 1991), pp. 121–122.

thematic curriculum webs that end this chapter are examples of a kind of semantic mapping.

Venn diagrams consisting of two or more intersecting circles have been used to represent, for instance, the comparison of different versions of a folktale. A more spacious graphic organizer for comparing two things, however, may be a single list of similarities at the top of a chart and a dividing line underneath so that differences may be listed side by side.

Comparison charts have been used as tools for organizing talk and thought, too. One teacher asked a group of children who had read many novels by Betsy Byars to discuss how they are similar. Midway through the conversation children had raised such points as "The parents are never around," "The main character is usually about our age," and "Some big problem is always there." The teacher then helped children generate a chart with the titles of Byars's books, such as *The Night Swimmers*, *Cracker Jackson*, and *The Pinballs* placed top to bottom on the left of a large sheet of paper. Across the top of the chart, the children generated categories: Where the parents are, About the Main Character, Big Problem, Who helps and how, and other categories. Now that the conversation was well under way, the graphic organizer helped children focus and continue the discussion while they filled in the grid they had created on the chart. Later, other Byars books were added, such as *The Summer of the Swans* and *The House of Wings*, which children also read to see how they fit the pattern. This activity actually helped children analyze particular stories, synthesize several stories, and evaluate later readings. From the chart, they were able to generalize about the books by one author, a sophisticated skill for 10- and 11-year-olds.

Many commercial guides suggest all sorts of formats for graphic organizers. Circles, double-pointed arrows, steps and ladders, and lines and slashes purport to show how a plot line or a character develops, the interaction between characters, the relationship between episodes in the story, and so forth. But teachers should be wary of letting the graphic organizer overcome or direct the instruction. Younger children, especially, may better appreciate a story by making drama or art extensions rather than by manipulating words.

Kindergartners/first graders illustrated this chart about various cumulative stories and songs. In the process they learned the sequences of each tale and the name for this type of story or verse. Later the chart helped them to retell the stories in the proper sequence.

Highland Park Elementary School, South-Western City Schools, Grove City, Ohio. Kristen Kerstetter, teacher.

They might better see the cumulative pattern of Audrey Wood's *The Napping House* if they recreate the action in a drama with a stack of stuffed toys and a bed from the play corner rather than construct a chart of stacked words from the "wakeful flea" down to the "cozy bed." In fact, a strip of child-drawn pictures of what accumulates could easily be hung alongside another strip representing a different cumulative story, such as Jan Brett's *The Mitten*. Primary children would be less teacher-dependent in these drama or art extensions as well.

Graphic organizers can generate talk and thinking. Some researchers believe that these specific kinds of extensions help reader comprehension whereas others maintain that less structure-oriented extensions also improve comprehension. However, with the use of graphic organizers also comes the danger of reducing the total power of a book to a series of "Causes = Effect," or "Problem," "Goal," "Event 1, 2, 3," and "Climax" statements. *Charlotte's Web* by E. B. White does not deserve to be treated this way. Graphic organizers also call attention to a structural aspect of a story while ignoring the richness of both the book and children's responses. The reduction of some stories to a structure chart, such as folktales or highly patterned stories, may be a useful tool for would-be writers who have had much experience with stories. But too heavy a reliance on the extension of literature through graphic organizers may subtly tell novice readers that their responses should be channeled in some way rather than expressed—richly, variously, and widely.

MAKING AND USING GUIDES

Many series of commercial guides have been published in response to the increased interest in using literature to teach reading and language arts. Teachers may purchase simple or complex guides. Some include questions for each chapter of a novel; others merely suggest that readers discuss the problem of the novel and the main character's goal. Some have fill-ins, vocabulary study, blank pages for reader responses, and diagrams to copy and complete. Some guides are longer than the picture book whose study they are guiding. Some cost more than a five-book set of the paperback the guide is concerned with. Do teachers need commercial guides?

A good guide can save a teacher time in generating ideas. A guide may be a repository of useful discussion questions, suggestions for activities that send an enthusiastic reader back into the book or out into the world, and a list of other books which might relate to the book under study. Ideally, a good guide causes a reader to say, "I hadn't thought of that!" or to consider a book's depth without abandoning a love of the book. But there is often so much dross in a commercial guide that teachers may have to search longer for the useful nugget than it would take them to consider their

After hearing the story *Galimoto*, the name given to the toys that African children make of wire, students decided to make their own.

George Mason Elementary School, Alexandria City Schools, Alexandria, Virginia. Joanne Larkin, teacher. Photo by Jacki Vawter.

own ideas. Teachers can glean some useful ideas from commercial guides. Especially good suggestions might be jotted down on 6 x 8 cards and filed by book title. But good learning experience and a more time- and money-saving way for a group of teachers to have guides is to make them.[26]

The guide for Karen Lynn Williams's *Galimoto* suggests a modest and useful format for teachers who want to organize ideas, remember what works, and save the money they would otherwise spend on guides to use in purchasing class sets of paperbacks. Valuable outcomes of writing guides are that teachers get better at phrasing open-ended questions, they match books with a specific school district's curriculum, they learn to evaluate a book for classroom possibilities, they collaborate, and they begin to see what helps readers move ahead and what gets in their way.

Webbing Curriculum Possibilities

One way to begin planning curriculum is to make a web of the many possibilities inherent as a class studies a book, a genre, an author, or a theme. A

[26]Susan Hepler, "A Guide for the Teacher Guides: Doing It Yourself," *The New Advocate*, vol. 4, no. 3 (Summer 1988), pp. 186–195.

A Framework for Webbing Book, Theme, Genre, Unit

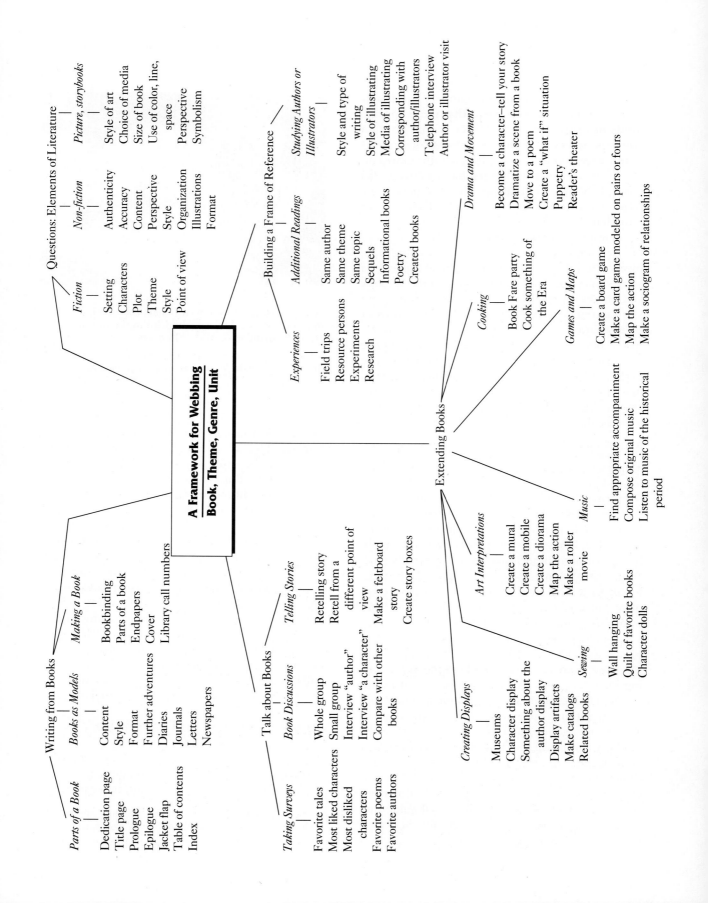

Questions: Elements of Literature

Fiction
- Setting
- Characters
- Plot
- Theme
- Style
- Point of view

Non-fiction
- Authenticity
- Accuracy
- Content
- Perspective
- Style
- Organization
- Illustrations
- Format

Picture, storybooks
- Style of art
- Choice of media
- Size of book
- Use of color, line, space
- Perspective
- Symbolism

Writing from Books

Parts of a Book
- Dedication page
- Title page
- Prologue
- Epilogue
- Jacket flap
- Table of contents
- Index

Books as Models
- Content
- Style
- Format
- Further adventures
- Diaries
- Journals
- Letters
- Newspapers

Making a Book
- Bookbinding
- Parts of a book
- Endpapers
- Cover
- Library call numbers

Building a Frame of Reference

Experiences
- Field trips
- Resource persons
- Experiments
- Research

Additional Readings
- Same author
- Same theme
- Same topic
- Sequels
- Informational books
- Poetry
- Created books

Studying Authors or Illustrators
- Style and type of writing
- Style of illustrating
- Media of illustrating
- Corresponding with author/illustrators
- Telephone interview
- Author or illustrator visit

Talk about Books

Taking Surveys
- Favorite tales
- Most liked characters
- Most disliked characters
- Favorite poems
- Favorite authors

Book Discussions
- Whole group
- Small group
- Interview "author"
- Interview "a character"
- Compare with other books

Telling Stories
- Retelling story
- Retell from a different point of view
- Make a feltboard story
- Create story boxes

Extending Books

Creating Displays
- Museums
- Character display
- Something about the author display
- Display artifacts
- Make catalogs
- Related books

Sewing
- Wall hanging
- Quilt of favorite books
- Character dolls

Art Interpretations
- Create a mural
- Create a mobile
- Create a diorama
- Map the action
- Make a roller movie

Music
- Find appropriate accompaniment
- Compose original music
- Listen to music of the historical period

Cooking
- Book Fare party
- Cook something of the Era

Games and Maps
- Create a board game
- Make a card game modeled on pairs or fours
- Map the action
- Make a sociogram of relationships

Drama and Movement
- Become a character—tell your story
- Dramatize a scene from a book
- Move to a poem
- Create a "what if" situation
- Puppetry
- Reader's theater

A GUIDE FOR *GALIMOTO*

by Karen Lynn Williams, illustrated by Catherine Stock. Lothrop, 1990.

<u>Summary:</u> Kondi, a resourceful boy from Malawi, finds many ways to get enough wire to make an intricate wire toy.

<u>Before Reading:</u> What can you tell about the story from the front and back cover and from the title page? (Save front note for later.)

<u>Possible Questions:</u>

1. What do you like about this story?

2. What words could describe Kondi? What in the story made you think of those words? (Possible word web?)

3. Read the front note and jacket copy. Look at the pages before the story begins. What has the artist shown us? What else do you notice about the artist's work?

4. By reading the pictures, what do you notice about life in this village? Find Malawi on the map; what do you notice?

5. In what ways is Kondi's life like a child's life in our area?

<u>Ideas for Activities</u>

♦ Collect wires for several days. Make galimotos. Tell where or how you got a special piece of wire. Be sure toys are three dimensional and not flat.

♦ Write your own directions, or as Kondi might write them, for making a galimoto.

♦ Draw and write or tell about a time when you made something all by yourself.

♦ Make a list of what we think we know about life in Malawi after reading this book. Find out something more about Malawi.

Related Books: *Steven Caney's Toy Book;* and *Tops* (Zubrowski) are useful for making things. Books about other modern African children: *A Country Far Away* (Gray); "Jafta" series (Lewin); *The Day of Ahmed's Secret* (Heide); *Osa's Pride* (Grifalconi); *Not So Fast, Songololo* (Daly); *At the Crossroads* (Isadora).

---

web is a way of brainstorming and outlining over a period of time. The goal is to get as many ideas and books committed to paper as possible before you shape their use in the classroom.

The chart A Framework for Webbing is really a web on the process of webbing. For this reason, it does not contain any specific titles of books, only general activities for children to do that might help you in your planning. For example, you could place any title of a book, a genre, a topic, or an author/illustrator that the class wants to study in the center of this web and quickly see if there are ideas you could use. Webs are based on the strengths of the books and/or topics and the needs of your students. No two webs are alike.

A FRAMEWORK FOR WEBBING

Each web that follows is an example of a particular kind of web. *The Sign of the Beaver* Web shows the possibilities inherent in this fine book. The Folktales Web shows the many different ways primary children can explore traditional tales; the Pat Hutchins Web points out the way a primary class might study one author/illustrator. The Stewards of the Earth Web details an ecology unit to use across grade levels, but particularly with fifth or sixth graders.

A web is usually just a beginning plan. Once you have thought of the many possibilities, you need to choose the ones that would be the most useful to try in your class. If your primary students have not done surveys, then you might decide to highlight that particular activity. If you like the idea of putting them in small groups to compare different versions or variants of a tale, you might choose that section. Then you can plan a tentative time line: How to begin the unit? What books will you use to introduce the topic?

What activities will get the children intrigued to learn more? Then begin.

STUDYING ONE BOOK: *THE SIGN OF THE BEAVER* BY ELIZABETH GEORGE SPEARE[27]

There is more to the study of a book than just developing questions. The web on *The Sign of the Beaver* shows the many possibilities for study and extensions inherent in this book. One group of third and fourth graders made this book the focus of their curriculum work for some eight weeks. Several children built a fragile but authentic model of Matt's cabin filled with all the provisions he had obtained in anticipation of his family's return. You could lift off the roof of this model cabin and see the cradle Matt had made for the expected baby, the drying ears of corn, the new wooden bowls, the snowshoes propped against the wall. Many details mentioned in the book were reflected in this three-dimensional translation of the story. Another group was equally successful in creating a model of the Abenaki Indian village.

Much writing took place in relationship to this book. Four children created an illustrated catalog of the items Matt used in the story. A table of contents listed four categories: Clothing, Personal Possessions, Hunting Tools, Gifts. Each page pictured an object and description of how it related to the story. For example, in the section on gifts, a picture of snowshoes had this description:

> The snowshoes set Matt free.
> He was happy. For the first time since
> Attean and Attean's Family left.
> Attean's Grandfather gave Matt the
> snowshoes.

Under a picture of a cradle appeared this written description:

> Before whiteness came Matt made a
> cradle for his new baby brother or
> sister. It was made of wood and it
> rocked. The cradle even had a
> headboard.

> Third and fourth graders
> Barrington Road School
> Upper Arlington, Ohio
> Marlene Harbert, teacher

[27]References for each of the four webs are presented together at the end of the chapter references.

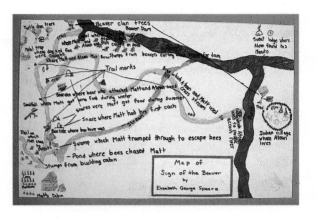

One of the projects that grew out of an in-depth study of *The Sign of the Beaver* was this imaginary map of the places in the story.

Barrington Road School, Upper Arlington, Ohio. Marlene Harbert, teacher.

The cover of this catalog had a picture of Matt's log cabin on the front, and the back symbolically represented the friendship of Matt and Attean by showing two hands clasping, one white for Matt, the other the darker tan of the Abenaki Indian boy, Attean. The book was dedicated to the author, Elizabeth Speare, and a prologue gave a brief summary of the story.

Children also created maps of this story and wrote descriptions of how they made their model canoes, the cabin, and Indian village. One boy assumed Matt's point of view and reflected on being left alone after the Abenakis had gone.

ALL ALONE AGAIN

I must have been all around the forest today searching for a sign that the Indians would come back, just something . . . a sign. But as I searched my thoughts were discouraged. I had just passed all of my memories—everything it seemed, a mark in the underbrush from the dead bear exactly where it fell. I walked to the village or what it used to be. The once busy city was now reduced to a circle of crushed brush and a number of smaller circles in the grass. Also scattered around were chips of birch bark. I sat down in the circle where Saknis's teepee was. There was a pile of black sticks in the center of the teepee, crumbling to ashes. I walked sadly away

Kindergarten children retold and illustrated their favorite fairy tales. Notice Rapunzel's long yellow braids hanging out the window and the title of "The Three Bears" story with its picture of three porridge bowls.

Martin Luther King, Jr., Laboratory School, Evanston Public Schools, Evanston, Illinois. Esther Weiss, teacher.

🍎 🍎 🍎

from the village remains. Then I realized I was missing the Indians even more than my own family. I wondered if my parents would come back and if they didn't what would I do? Right then I started to wish I had gone with the Indians. Sadly I walked back to the cabin.

I heard my dog yelping at the door. He sure didn't know the predicament we were in. Then I thought of Robinson Crusoe. In my own way I was a Robinson Crusoe except my Friday left. I was alone, but if someone can survive alone I can. I have been taught by the Indians, masters of the forest. The air froze around me and snow began to fall. I feared for myself. I wondered how I would reach my traps for food, how I would live in this snow with my worn moccasins and short pants. But my overpowering wonder was—how would I survive?

Jamie Parson, grade 4
Barrington Road School
Upper Arlington, Ohio
Marlene Harbert, teacher

It is obvious that these 8- and 9-year-olds gained much personal satisfaction and knowledge from their in-depth study of this book.

STUDYING ONE GENRE: FOLKTALES

The web on folktales suggests the rich possibilities inherent in a study of one genre of literature. It would also be possible to focus on a smaller

aspect of a genre, such as pourquoi stories or African folktales as well. This particular web was designed with kindergarten through second-grade classrooms in mind. A study of more complex tales or myths could be done with slightly older children. Other genres, such as fantasy, biography, or poetry, would also make a rich unit study. Smaller units such as futuristic fantasy, biographies of twentieth-century people, or narrative poems, would focus even more deeply on a particular aspect of a genre.

This web provides for a serious look at the types of folktales and certain motifs found in tales that would appeal to young children, such as trickery, transformations, and magic pot stories. Before starting such a study, it might be wise to find out what background of experience children have had with these tales. No longer can teachers assume children will know these traditional stories—many do not.

One kindergarten/first-grade group began their study of folktales with reading all the "three" stories in which three animals are the major characters. They then made their own "Book of Threes" with prints of the three bears, three pigs, and three Billy Goats Gruff. The characters were cut out of plastic foam trays and then painted and printed on brown paper. Another group made

Kindergarten children illustrated their favorite fairy-tale characters and the one they disliked the most. They gave reasons for their choices.

Martin Luther King, Jr., Laboratory School, Evanston Public Schools, Evanston, Illinois. Deborah Kaplan, teacher.

🍎 🍎 🍎

Value of Stories

What does this book have to say about the importance of stories and storytelling?

How might Matt tell his story when he is a grandfather?

What books does Matt's family own? Can you find any parallels between *The Sign of the Beaver* and *Robinson Crusoe* (Defoe)?

What stories did Attean's family tell?

What traditional tales might they have known? Read folktales of the Northeastern Indians: *The Talking Stone* (deWit);
North American Legends (Haviland);
The Winter Wife (Crompton);
How Summer Came to Canada (Toye).

Survival

What survival skills did Matt develop? Which did he learn by observation?

Without the Indians, what might have happened to Matt?

Read other stories of survival:
My Side of the Mountain (George);
The Talking Earth (George);
Toughboy and Sister (Hill);
Hatchet (Paulsen).

How does the predicament of the main character in any of these books compare to Matt's?

Try out some of Matt's survival skills. What did he cook? What were common foods in colonial times?

Make johnnycake.
The Heritage Sampler (Hoople)
Slumps, Grunts and Snickerdoodles (Perl)

THEMES

Changing Relationships

Trace the development of friendship between Matt and Attean. What events or passages from the story show a change in ideas about each other's culture?

Think about Matt and Attean as teacher and student. How did Matt become a better teacher? How would you teach someone to read?
What did Attean teach Matt? How did he conduct the lessons?

Discuss the changes in the balance between the Beaver clan's existence and the coming of white settlers.

What other changes do you see in characters' attitudes toward one another?

Growing Up

How does Attean mark his preparation for manhood? What tests must he pass?

What does Matt do that shows he is a man? Which of his actions earns the respect of Attean's people?

Keep a journal for Matt that shows his feelings about passing events.

Freedom

Who is more free, Matt or Attean?

As winter sets in, Matt's snowshoes "set him free." What other things gave him more freedom?

Signs and Symbols

What makes *The Sign of the Beaver* a good title?
How many examples of signs and symbols can you find in the book? Which are Abenaki signs? Signs of the white man? Animal signs?

MOTIFS

Gifts and Exchanges

What gifts are given in this story by Matt? By the Abenaki Indians? Think of some that are not material things.

What gifts would you have to share with a friend like Matt or Attean?

What gifts did Matt make for his family? What does that show you about how he felt?

Animals

How are animals important to this story?
Make a chart picturing the animals. Describe their role in the story's events; explain what that shows about setting, character, or theme.

BOOK CONNECTIONS

Other Books by Speare

Calico Captive
Compare portrayal of Native-American characters
    with Attean and family.
The Witch of Blackbird Pond
The Bronze Bow

**Clash of White and Native-American
Cultures in Colonial Times**

The Double Life of Pocahontas (Fritz)
The Light in the Forest (Richter)
Saturnalia (P. Fleischman)

The Sign of the Beaver

by Elizabeth George Speare

A Web of Possiblities

SETTING

Map the trip that Matt's father made from Maine to
    Massachusetts and back.
Make a time line showing events during Matt's long
    wait. How many ways could you represent time
    passing?
Make an illustrated catalog of items that would have been
    familiar to Matt but are not common today. Consider
    tools, household items, clothing, see *Colonial Living*
    (Tunis).Arrange a display of artifacts (or make your own
    reproduction) of colonial life or the Northeast Native
    Americans.
Build a model of Matt's cabin, or Attean's village.
    Compare and discuss–what differences in life styles are
    dictated by shelter and its surroundings?

STYLE AND TECHNIQUE

Pace of Plot

How long are the chapters?
What kinds of things happen as the
    chapters end?
How do "cliff-hangers" help to keep
    the reader interested?

Predictions

What does the cover make you think the
    book will be about?
Read and predict from chapter endings
    what might happen in the following
    chapter.
Make up your own chapter titles.

Foreshadowing

What bits of warning does the author give that there
    might be trouble from a bear? That something
    might happen to Matt's father's gun?
Can you find early clues for other events?

Use of Language

Notice descriptions that are comparisons (simile and metaphor).
    Compile a list, and suggest others of your own.
    Why would the author say that the gun was smooth as a silk
    dress rather than shiny as a no-wax floor?
How does the author make Attean's speech different from
    Matt's? What problems do you think an author has in deciding
    how people might have talked more than 200 years ago?
Write a story about Matt's family. How might they have felt
    about being separated from Matt?

Based on *The WEB: Wonderfully Exciting Books*, Charlotte Huck and Janet Hickman, eds.
Columbus: The Ohio State University, vol. 8, no. 2 (Winter 1984).

FOLKTALES

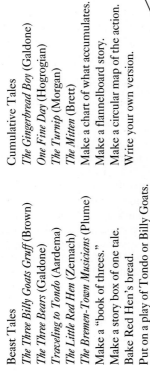

COMPARING VERSIONS AND VARIANTS

Henny Penny (Butler)
Henny Penny (Galdone)
Chicken Little (Kellogg)

The Story of the Three Little Pigs (Jacobs/Cauley)
The True Story of the 3 Little Pigs As Told by A. Wolf (Sciezsca)

Little Red Riding Hood (Grimm/Hyman)
Lon Po Po (Young)

List similarities and differences for each pair.
Compare wolf illustrations.
Write another story from the wolf's point of view.

Yeh-Shen (Louie)
The Egyptian Cinderella (Climo)
Cinderella (Perrault/LeCain)
Compare the three stories.
Write a "found" ad and make a picture for a girl who owns the shoe.
How many years separate these versions?
Why do you think they are so similar?

Prince Cinders (Cole)
Sidney Rella and the Glass Sneaker (Myers)
Write a modern version Cinderella.

TYPES OF TALES

Beast Tales
The Three Billy Goats Gruff (Brown)
The Three Bears (Galdone)
Traveling to Tondo (Aardema)
The Little Red Hen (Zemach)
The Bremen-Town Musicians (Plume)
Make a "book of threes."
Make a story box of one tale.
Bake Red Hen's bread.
Put on a play of Tondo or Billy Goats.
Make paperbag puppets and retell a story.

Cumulative Tales
The Gingerbread Boy (Galdone)
One Fine Day (Hogrogian)
The Turnip (Morgan)
The Mitten (Brett)
Make a chart of what accumulates.
Make a flannelboard story.
Make a circular map of the action.
Write your own version.

Pourquoi or "Why" Tales
The Cat's Purr (Bryan)
How Summer Came to Canada (Toye)
Make a collage picture.
The Great Race (Goble)
The Village of Round and Square Houses (Grifalconi)
Write your own nature "why" tale.

Wonder Tales
Ali Baba and the Forty Thieves (McVitty)
Momotaro, the Peach Boy (Shute)
Tam Lin (Cooper)
Snow White (Grimm)
Baba Yaga (Kimmel)
Puss in Boots (Perrault)
Make a catalog of magical objects.
Make a wanted poster for a villain.
Make a chart of transformations from/to.

MOTIFS

Transformations
The Crane Wife (Yagawa)
The Princess and the Frog (Isadora)
The Story of Jumping Mouse (Steptoe)
The Little Snowgirl (Croll)
List real-life transformations (ice/water; jello; caterpillar/butterfly).
Group by what causes transformation (love, disloyalty, magic, etc.).
Retell from transformed one's point of view.

Trickery
The Boy of the Three-Year Nap (Snyder)
Puss in Boots (Perrault)
Wiley and the Hairy Man (Bang)
Fin M'Coul (De Paola)
The Tales of Uncle Remus (Lester)
Write the tricky plans for a character.
Make a "bad guy" out of stuffed construction paper.
Interview the trickster for television.

ACTIONS

Folktale Party
Dress as a character from a tale.
Invite others.
Serve folktale fare:
  Gingerbread cookies
  Strega Nona's pasta (De Paola)
  Stone Soup (Stewig)
  Fin M'Coul's soda bread
  Snow White's unpoisoned apples
Conduct tours of the Folktale Museum.

Surveys
Favorite folktale character
Best-illustrated version of one story
Most disliked character
Parent's best-remembered tale
Favorite folktale food

Pulling it Together
Make a mural of houses from folktales (Gretel's witch's candy house; Baba Yaga's stilted house).

Assemble a museum of things important to folktales (Princess's pea; Hansel's chicken bone; Wiley's rope; Beauty's rose), and write labels for each one.

Make a "Photograph Album"; draw snapshots of action from a tale.

Locate these tales on a wall map of the world and place a label and string to the country of origin. What do you notice?

One day into the kitchen came two young ladies dressed in stylish clothes. One said, "Where is our mother? We are Muffy and Buffy."

The other girl said, "You must be Kelly, who works in the kitchen."

Older children wrote a modern version of "Cinderella" titled "Kitchen Kelly."
Edison Elementary School
Grandview Heights, Ohio
Mike Weddle, teacher

"before" and "after" pictures for their "Book of Transformations." One page showed the ugly duckling and then the swan, another pictured a pumpkin and mice changed into Cinderella's coach and horses.

They also compared various versions of "Little Red Riding Hood" and "The Three Little Pigs," looking for the scariest wolf picture. The traditional story of *Henny Penny* by Stephen Butler was contrasted with Steven Kellogg's very funny modern variant titled *Chicken Little*. A simple chart helped them see similarities and differences in two versions of *The Three Little Pigs*. They discussed both text and illustrations and then took a survey, placing a picture of themselves on the chart below the title of their choice. They also conducted home surveys to determine the favorite folktale of their parents. Instead of worksheets, they drew pictures of their favorite characters in folktales and their most disliked characters.

The teacher and children developed charts on special folktale words. The one titled "The Land

of Once Upon a Time" contained such words as golden eggs, mirror, poison apple, and a royal pea. Children illustrated these words with their own cutout pictures. Another chart listed "Good Guys and Bad Guys." Little Red Riding Hood, the cobbler and his wife, and the woodman were listed as "good guys"; the wolf and the troll had the distinction of being "bad guys." Around the room were quotations and refrains from folktales, such as "Not by the hair of my chinny chin chin" and "Who's been tasting my porridge?" and "Fee Fi Fo Fum, I smell the blood of an Englishman." The captions read "Who Said It?"

The children created their own story—"The Runaway Pizza"—based on the story of *The Gingerbread Boy*. Their teacher copied it in a big book, which they illustrated and then read many times.

Not only did children learn about folktales in this study, but the unit gave them a real reason for reading, writing, dramatizing, taking surveys, baking, and making various art projects. The children learned that folktales had been told for many years and that even their parents and grandparents knew some of them. They discovered certain patterns in the stories like the use of three, and they learned what to expect from such characters as the wily fox or wolf, the youngest, and the princess. Most importantly, they found out that books were a source of pleasure and that learning to read was fun.

Older children wrote and illustrated their own version of a well-known folktale after studying this genre. "Kitchen Kelly," a modern Cinderella story, told of Kelly who has to live above and work in her stepmother's restaurant after her father remarries. When she wins five hundred dollars and the services of a limousine from a contest on her favorite radio station, she goes to a dance but loses her locket. A young man who has fallen in love with her is able to find her when the picture in the locket he finds matches one Kelly kept in her purse.

STUDYING A SINGLE AUTHOR OR ILLUSTRATOR: PAT HUTCHINS

A classroom study of a single author or illustrator gives children a chance to know one creator of books in depth. Begin by visiting the school and

Titch
Do a class survey on position in the family.
Discuss some of the problems about being the oldest, the middle, the youngest. Make a comparison chart.
Plant Titch's seeds and chart their growth.
Begin a Pat Hutchins's Museum of Real Things, e.g., pinwheel hammer.
Make a *Titch* big book. Put in speech balloons.

Tidy Titch
Display or write about hand-me-down toys or clothes.
List ways Titch can clean his room.

You'll Soon Grow into Them, Titch
Make a list of everything that is growing in this story.
Raid the lost and found box at school for clothes. Dress up in clothes that are too big and too small.

Happy Birthday, Sam
Go around the school and identify things that are too high for you.
Have a party for the characters in Pat Hutchins's stories. Dress up as a character. Write invitations and recipes.
Make a birthday graph of children in the class.
Make a list of useful birthday presents.

Don't Forget the Bacon
Make a list of what you might buy at the supermarket.
Make a story map.
Add items to the museum.
Read other stories about growing up.

GROWING–UP STORIES

TRIPS

Rosie's Walk
Make a story map. Write the fox's thoughts in speech balloons.
View the movie, *Rosie's Walk*. Watch it forward and backward.
Changes, Changes
Using building blocks, have the children build the same things as in the story.
Don't Forget the Bacon
1 Hunter
The Surprise Party
Where's the Baby?
The Tale of Thomas Mead
Take a walk through the school or around your neighborhood. Identify other environmental print Thomas Mead may not be able to read.
Make story maps of the books.
List other trip stories, such as *Round Trip*, *The Trek* (Jonas).
Create your own "trip" stories. Illustrate them.
Take a survey and make a bar graph to find out which trip story is the favorite.

COUNTING BOOKS AND TELLING TIME

1 Hunter
Compare with other counting books. Talk about what makes this one fun.
Compare *1 Hunter* with *Clocks and More Clocks*. How are the hunter and Mr. Higgins alike? (Both are dumb adults!)
Have children create their own counting books, using items from the classroom or holiday counting book (Halloween–1 witch, 2 ghosts . . .).
The Doorbell Rang
With the arrival of each visitor, figure out how many cookies they will have.
Find stories with recipes, like *Country Bear's Good Neighbor* (Brimmer), and *Peter Rabbit's Natural Food Cookbook* (Dobrin).
Create your own recipe.
Select a cookie recipe and make it.
Clocks and More Clocks
Discuss "what was wrong" with Mr. Higgins's clock.
Did Mr. Higgins ever know?
Put clocks in different places in the school. Check them with a "wonderful watch."
Make your own clocks.

SURPRISE STORIES

What Game Shall We Play?
The Surprise Party
The Silver Christmas Tree
The Doorbell Rang
Where's the Baby?
Clocks and More Clocks
One-Eyed Jake!
Plan a surprise party for another room, principal, or parents.

Bake surprise cupcakes with candy in the middle. Make surprise sandwiches. Write the recipes.
Write invitations to your surprise party.
Plan surprise activities, such as "Pass It On" or reading these titles. Make surprise gifts for each other.

Read other stories with surprise endings, e.g.,
The Gingerbread Boy (Galdone)
Just Like Everyone Else (Kuskin)
A Dark, Dark Tale (Brown)
The Piggy Book (Browne)
Night Noises (Fox).
Write and illustrate your own surprise story.

Pat Hutchins
A Web of Possibilities

MONSTER STORIES

The Very Worst Monster
Make a comparison chart. List the things Billy had to do to be the "best" worst monster and compare with the things children have to do to be the "best."
Tell what Billy might do at school to be the "best" student.
Where's the Baby?
Make a story map.
Make a *Where's the Baby?* lift-up flap book [similar to *Where's Spot?* (Hill)].
Create the Monster family. Make large stuffed characters. Write speech balloons.
Write a Lost Ad poster.
List the things baby monster can do in *Where's the Baby?* that he couldn't do in *The Very Worst Monster*.
Read *Leo, the Late Bloomer* (Kraus). Have children list things they can do now that they couldn't do last year.
Find and read other monster books.

PLAYING WITH LANGUAGE

Don't Forget the Bacon
Make a list of what you might pick up in the classroom. Illustrate.
Give the list to one child to act out while others chant the names.
The Surprise Party
Create your own message and play "Pass It On" by whispering it in the children's ears.
Look at the way Hutchins creates textured fur and feathers in these books, *The Silver Christmas Tree, Rosie's Walk, Good-Night Owl!,* and *What Game Shall We Play?*
Make large Pat Hutchins's type animals and birds.

Good-Night Owl!
Have the children make the sounds as you read.
Make a giant tree on mural paper. Ask the children to make birds and animals to place on the tree. Make speech balloons.
Develop an alternative text for a nocturnal animal at the zoo (oppossum). How might other animals disturb his rest?
Make a felt story. Turn off the lights for darkness.
Link to *Owl at Home* (Lobel), *Owl Moon* (Yolen), and *The Owl and the Woodpecker* (Wildsmith).
What Game Shall We Play?
Who knew what game the animals were playing?
Is owl going to be able to find the animals?
Let several children pantomime playing a game and have the others guess its name.

From *The WEB: Wonderfully Exciting Books*, Charlotte Huck and Janet Hickman, eds. Columbus: The Ohio State University (Summer 1988).

public library to gather many books by the selected author. After reading and rereading the books, divide them into categories and decide how the books are connected (e.g., by theme, by continuing adventures of a character, by illustrative technique, and so forth). Then think of the author's or illustrator's strengths and decide what ideas you wish children to discover. Next, make a web of possibilities. Cards on which to record specific discussion questions of a particular core book will help you organize discussions and events. Plan a time line of activities. Write to the publicity department of the publisher(s) of the author or illustrator and ask if they have any material to send you. (See Appendix C, "Publishers' Addresses.") Check book jacket flaps and ask the librarian to help you find out something else about the author. (See Appendix B, "Information About Authors and Illustrators.") Then, the study is ready to begin.

With this much preparation time up front, several teachers from a single building may wish to work together in planning and gathering material which may be kept in a central resource file in the library media center or in the reading teacher's area. Sometimes a telephone interview may be arranged and children may ask previously raised questions. (See "Planning for Author/Illustrator Visits" later in this chapter.)

STUDYING A THEME: STEWARDS OF THE EARTH: ECOLOGY

A thematic unit such as one based on ecology contains many possibilities. With a theme as large as "Stewards of the Earth," it is possible for a whole school to embark on a study of ecology. The accompanying web begins to focus on what aspects of the earth are endangered, why this is so, and what people are doing about it. Some books feature the action of individuals; others show how groups of people form to improve a small part of our ecosystem. Both points are worth making in a study of this magnitude: think globally but act locally; one person can make a difference.

Certain authors are well known for their activist stands on saving the earth. Jean Craighead George, in her novels as well as her nonfiction titles, always addresses interdependence among the living things on the planet. Ron Hirschi, Gail Gibbons, Laurence Pringle, and Helen Roney Sattler are only a few of the many authors of non-

fiction who have raised concerns about the environment. Teachers of middle school children might start with futuristic science fiction such as those titles listed in "Possible Futures?" and raise the question: How did humankind become what it is depicted as being in this imagined future? Teachers of fifth or sixth graders might anchor this study with a core novel such as Jean George's *The Talking Earth*, Miriam Schlein's narrative of Chinese and American efforts to save the endangered panda in *The Year of the Panda*, Susan Sharpe's fictional account of a boy's discovery of who is dumping toxic waste in the Chesapeake Bay told in *Waterman's Boy*, or Caroline MacDonald's fine futuristic story of *The Lake at the End of the World*. Other classes might start with endangered birds, creatures of the sea, the way places change and why, or observances of nature.[28]

In the accompanying web, activities that begin a topic are suggested as useful overarching concerns developed within the section which follows. Other activities may follow a particular book or culminate that section's content. There are many community resources that should be tapped in a study such as this: classroom visits by park rangers and city planners, field trips to preserves or recycling centers, and archives such as the newspaper or interviews with a longtime resident. Books are not the only way to bring the world to the classroom.

Developing a concern for the environment is a lasting topic, and there will always be new problems, new books, and new ways to approach it in the classroom. Even primary children can become interested in the preservation of the earth's natural diversity and interdependence.

THE SCHOOL AND THE COMMUNITY

The Whole-School Program

Children learn what they live. Increasingly, educators are concerned that the quality of living in a

[28]See Patti Sinclair, *E for Environment: An Annotated Bibliography of Children's Books with Environmental Themes* (New York: Bowker, 1992). See also Alicia Eames and Daryl Grabarek, "Dreaming Our World." *Book Links*, vol. 1: no. 2 (September 1991), 54–58.

Sixth graders enjoy reading with their kindergarten and first grade buddies.
Mission School, Redlands Public Schools, Redlands, California. Nancy Anderson, teacher.

school be equal to the quality of learning in that school. The physical environment of the school provides the context of that learning, but it is only one aspect of it. What teachers really believe in and want for their students will usually be taught.

All teachers and librarians must have a strong commitment to literature. Few children discover books by themselves; in most instances, a parent, teacher, or librarian has served as the catalyst for bringing books and children together. As children grow up seeing significant adults as readers, they become readers. Find a teacher who is enthusiastic about children's books and you will find a class of children who enjoy reading. Invariably, the teacher who reads, who knows books, and who shares this enthusiasm with students will inspire a love of reading. Many schools have made the development of readers their top priority. As a total school faculty they have met and planned certain activities to promote children's interest in reading.

Buddy reading involves students from older grades reading with partners in the kindergarten or first grade. Younger children proudly share a book that they can read with their buddies, and the older children then read a book to their partners. Younger children look forward to their buddy time (usually, once a week) while the older students take a special interest in the progress of their special child. Buddy reading requires the cooperation between teachers to establish a time and routine. Older students must be taught how to select appropriate books to read aloud and the importance of being supportive of the younger readers' efforts to read or tell a story. Teachers who have tried such programs speak of their value for both sets of readers.

One school planned a whole-school unit on traditional literature. Children from kindergarten through sixth grade studied fairy tales, traditional folktales, fables, and the myths. They created a

DEVELOPING RESPECT AND A SENSE OF WONDER

What kinds of experience fill us with wonder?

Pretend you are a person in one of these stories. Tell or write about your moment of wonder.

Dawn (Shulevitz)
Salt Hands (Aragon)
Lady and the Spider (McNulty)
Owl Moon (Yolen)
   Find examples of language that evoke senses.

I Wonder if I'll See a Whale (Weller)
Whales' Song (Sheldon)
The Way to Start a Day (Baylor)
   Make up your own way to greet a day.
   Write a story of how your perfect day in nature mightbegin.

Heartland; Mojave; Sierra (Siebert)
The Other Way to Listen (Baylor)
For adults:
Sense of Wonder (Carson)

CARING FOR THE BIRDS

What birds are endangered? Why?

How can people help birds? Why should we?

Bird Watch (Yolen)
The Book of Eagles (Sattler)
Hawk, I'm Your Brother (Baylor)
The Mountain Bluebird (Hirschi)
Saving the Peregrine Falcon (Arnold)
Where Do Birds Live? (Hirschi)

Make a tree on which drawings of local birds are placed.

Let different people count birds at different sites. How many birds can you count in a half hour?

Which site has the fewest/most birds? Why?

Find feathers. Determine whether they are wing, pin, down, or some other kind of feather. Mount your collection.

Make a feeding station. Observe what comes there.

Pigeons (Schlein)
How have pigeons helped humankind?
Follow a pigeon. Try to describe its movements.
Debate: Are pigeons "rats with wings"?

The After-Christmas Tree (Tyler)
Make tree to feed birds.

Stewards of the Earth Ecology

CARING FOR THE ANIMALS

Which animals are endangered? Why?

What animals are now extinct? Why?

Aardvarks Disembark (Jonas)
Professor Noah's Spaceship (Wildsmith)
And Then There Was One: The Mysteries of Extinction (Facklam)
Hey! Get Off Our Train (Burningham)
Winter Harvest (Aragon)

The Year of the Panda (Schlein)
Sterling: The Rescue of a Baby Harbor Seal (White)
The Vanishing Manatee (Clark)
Saving Our Wildlife (Pringle)
The Crocodile and the Crane (Cutchins)

Make a chart of endangered animals; tell why each is endangered; find out what people are doing to help save this animal.

CAN ANIMALS AND HUMANS COMMUNICATE?

How do people communicate with animals? Why is this exciting?

What good is it to communicate with other species?

Koko's Kitten (Patterson)
Dolphin Adventure (Grover)

Observe a family pet or other animal for several days. Write an informational booklet on how this animal communicates. What do noises mean? Body movements? Expressions?

POSSIBLE FUTURES?

Just a Dream (Van Allsburg)
The Lake at the End of the World (MacDonald)
Z for Zachariah (O'Brien)
When the Tripods Came (Christopher)
The Monster Garden (Alcock)

Eva (Dickinson)

How does each author see our future? What kind of world are humans inhabiting? What has disappeared? Why?

SAVING THE FORESTS

What kinds of actions damage forests?
The Lorax (Seuss)
Summer of Fire: Yellowstone, 1988 (Lauber)
Locate rain forest areas on a map.
List individual actions that might help save trees.
Make a mural of a rain forest from canopy to forest floor. Show typical animals found in each zone.

One Day in the Tropical Rainforest (George)
The Great Kapok Tree (Cherry)
Rain Forest (Cowcher)
Where the Forest Meets the Sea (Baker)
Rain Forest Secrets (Dorros)
Make a collage of articles that come from rain forests. What is yet to be discovered in rain forests?
Find out what kinds of paper can be recycled. Start a recycling spot for school waste paper.

CLEANING UP AFTER OURSELVES

Sea Otter Rescue (Smith)
Wump World (Peet)
The World That Jack Built (Brown)
Global Warming (Pringle)
The ABC of Ecology (Milgrim)
Wastes (Miller)
Too Much Garbage (Lauber)
Throwing Things Away (Pringle)
Toxic Waste: Clean-up or Cover Up? (Weiss)

Form a playground or neighborhood trash pickup. Survey the trash to discover patterns. What is the major source of trash? Who is responsible? How might you begin an anti-litter campaign.
Make a "life-cycle" map of a piece of trash. Show where a soda can or cigarette butt starts out and where it might end up. Write about your map.

TAKING ACTION

How can individual people help? How do groups help?
Living Treasure: Saving the Earth's Threatened Biodiversity (Pringle)
The Man Who Planted Trees (Giono)
Miss Rumphius (Cooney)
Make Like a Tree and Leave (Danziger)
Going Green: A Kids' Handbook to Saving the Planet (Elkington)
Greening the City Streets (Huff)
Fifty Simple Things You Can Do to Save the Earth (Earthworks)

Take a field trip to a trash-burning power plant; a recycling center. Report what you have found using a "Magic School Bus" format.
Interview city council members to find out what long-range plans they have for areas such as landfills, recycling, creation of parks, protection of water, etc.
Plant something and watch it grow.
Beautify the grounds and entrance of your school. Take care of the plants.

PROTECTING THE WATER

What endangers our water? How can we help?
The Magic School Bus at the Waterworks (Cole)
Waterman's Boy (Sharpe)
Write a news account of the capture of the polluters.

The King's Fountain (Alexander)
Night Ghosts and Hermits (Stolz)
What are the consequences of water pollution?

THEN AND NOW: CHANGES

Make a "then" and "now" chart for one book.
Pretend you are older and looking back on a special place. Write about your memories and feelings for this place that has changed.
Debate: Is change good or bad?
Toddlecreek Post Office (Shulevitz)
New Providence: A Changing City Scape (Von Tscharner)
Story of an English Village (Goodall)
Make a picture of a place as it is now. Put half a page over this picture showing how it used to look.

The Little House (Burton)
The Changing Countryside (Müller)
The Changing City (Müller)
Shaker Lane (Provensens)
Window (Baker)
Heron Street (Turner)
My Place (Wheatley)
Find old photographs of your city or neighborhood. Find out what has changed since those pictures were taken.
Invite a longtime resident to the classroom to talk about changes he or she has seen in the place where you live.

INTERCONNECTIONS

Who Really Killed Cock Robin? (George)
Who did?
Make a chart of causes and effects.
Big Friend, Little Friend (Sussman)
The Apartment House Tree (Killion)
Stephen and the Green Turtle (Cromic)
The Wounded Wolf (George)
What are symbiotic relationships?
Can you name other connected groups?
How do members depend on each other?

The Talking Earth (George)
The Earth Is Sore (Amon)
Brother Eagle, Sister Sky (Jeffers)
What Native-American ideas about the earth are expressed? Do you agree?
All God's Critters Got a Place in the Choir (Staines)
Sing the song. Think about the metaphor.

A WHOLE-SCHOOL STUDY OF ONE BOOK

The Martin Luther King, Jr., Laboratory School in the Evanston, Illinois, Public Schools frequently has whole-school focus units where the children from kindergarten through grade eight study one particular subject. This year they decided that all children would hear the same book and then discuss it. *The Lemming Condition* by Alan Arkin was read aloud by all elementary teachers and the homeroom teachers in the sixth, seventh, and eighth grades.

Prior to the reading, a group of teachers met to do some background research on the myth and reality of the lemming condition. For example, the science teacher prepared an information sheet on lemmings, their geographical distribution, what they eat, how long they live, and the so-called lemming run. The teachers formulated a guide with possible questions like these:

♦ Have you ever felt like a lemming?
♦ When you plan to do something, do you like to work alone or do what everyone else does?
♦ What advice did the old lemming give to Bubber?
♦ If Bubber didn't follow the crowd, he would lose his family and friends. What did it take for him to act alone?
♦ What heroes do you know who stood by their values and did something that was not popular? (Rosa Parks, Gandhi, Martin Luther King, Jr.)

Forty-two adults in the building including the administrators, secretaries, and nurse each agreed to work with a group of about twelve K–8 students for a one-hour discussion of the book. Back in their own classrooms following these discussions, each child created his or her own unique and recognizable picture of a lemming. These were cut out and placed on a very large mural in the school foyer.

The children loved meeting together to discuss a book that had different meanings for each of them. They listened to the little ones' interpretations and encouraged them to speak. Most of their responses were centered on the idea of peer group pressure to do something they did not want to do. The youngest students focused on feelings of loneliness and being left out when they weren't invited to parties, for example.

The bonding together of a K–8 population sharing one book created cohesive and enthusiastic groups. The staff all agreed that it was an experience they wanted to repeat.

Martin Luther King, Jr., Laboratory School, Evanston, Illinois. Vikki Proctor, Ellen Esrick, Ronna Pritikin, coordinating teachers.

Fairy Tale Museum with such objects as "the very pea which disturbed the princess's sleep" and the golden ball that the Frog Prince retrieved for the spoiled princess. A Fairy Tale Newspaper included interviews with Cinderella and the Pied Piper; classified lost and found ads including an ad for a found glass slipper; a society column; and a sports page describing the race of the Hare and Tortoise. Older children created their own mythological characters and stories. Different groups dramatized such traditional tales as "The Three Billy Goats Gruff" and "Little Red Riding Hood." This whole-school emphasis created a unity among the children and an appreciation for their traditional literary heritage.

Another school offered many different minicourses in literature during Book Week. Children met and made puppets in one course, created a flannel story in another. Many children wrote their own stories in one course. Then, in another, they were introduced to the use of collage, marbleized papers, and ink prints made from plastic foam meat trays. Another course offered bookbinding so that children ended the week with their own bound and illustrated books. Different teachers volunteered to offer the various courses at different times. Some gave minicourses on particular genres of books, like folktales or poetry. Others offered drama and choral speaking. In this particular school, children have an opportunity to do these things frequently. However, the minicourses given near the beginning of school focused attention on bookmaking and provided children with skills they used throughout the year.

No literature program can be successful without the support of the principal. More and more principals and curriculum coordinators are taking time to read aloud to children. One curriculum coordinator[29] makes it a point to read aloud in one

[29]James Mitchell, "Sound Bytes, Hamburgers and Billy Joel: Celebrating the Year of the Lifetime Reader," *Reading Today*, vol. 9 (August/September 1991), p. 29.

Children are delighted to meet "real live" author/illustrator Tomie de Paola, particularly when they have read his books and prepared for his visit.

Columbus School for Girls, Columbus, Ohio. Marilyn Parker, teacher/librarian.

A welcome sign and a large stuffed Strega Nona and Big Anthony hang from the class ceiling to greet Tomie de Paola.

Highland Park Elementary School, Southwestern City Schools, Grove City, Ohio. Pam Kesson, teacher. Photo by Barbara Peterson.

of the classrooms in his school district every day. Children look forward to his coming and he anticipates their response to his choice of books. Another principal has developed a two-tiered reading program called The Principal's Reading Club. Children from kindergarten through second grade make appointments to read with the principal for 15 minutes from a book of their choice. Students in grades three to six select a book from a provided list and after three weeks return to discuss it with the principal. The participants receive a reading certificate, button, and pencil that has "I Read to the Principal" on it. More importantly, children see the principal as someone interested in them and their reading, and it's a wonderful way for the principal to get to know children and their reading abilities and preferences.

Planning Author/Illustrator Visits

The prospect of having a real live author come for a school visit is exciting and motivates students to read his or her books in anticipation of meeting the author. However, it takes good planning to use a visit to full advantage and make it a learning experience for all students. Sometimes a school may be fortunate enough to have a local author or illustrator who will volunteer to come and talk about his or her books. However, more and more schools budget money to pay for such a visit.

The usual procedure for contacting an author or illustrator is to call the person in charge of promotion for his or her publisher and ask about availability, fees, travel arrangements, and so on. Sometimes it is possible to arrange a visit in conjunction with another previously scheduled appearance in your area. This usually cuts down on the major travel expenses, although the author's fee must be paid.

Planning must begin with teachers and children several months before the visit. There is no point in hosting an author or illustrator unless all the children who will be meeting him or her know the books. With authors of books for middle graders this means obtaining many copies of their books, arranging for in-depth discussions of the books, perhaps showing films or filmstrips about the author. It might be wise to keep a running list of questions to ask the author as children are becoming acquainted with the books.

A parent helped children make Strega Nona's famous pasta.

Highland Park Elementary School, South-Western City Schools, Grove City, Ohio. Photo by Barbara Peterson.

Several schools got together and invited Tomie de Paola to visit them when he was going to be at a conference in their area. His books were displayed in the learning center and in many of the classrooms. The children made murals of their favorite books, cooked pasta with a parent, and even wove a cloak for *"Charlie Needs a Cloak"*. First graders made a list of their expectations of Tomie de Paola based on their knowledge of his books—what he would look like, what he would be like. Children thus became acquainted with all the books of one artist and had a chance to talk to him about his life and work.

As Marilyn Parker says in describing a visit by Madeleine L'Engle in an article in *The WEB*, ". . . the actual event of an author's visit should be something like the tip of an iceberg—the most visible part of something much broader and deeper."[30] It is the preparation for the visit that provides the real learning experiences. As children focus on the work of one author or illustrator and have an opportunity to meet him or her, they have their first-time glimpse into the literary world.

The School Library Media Center

Every school needs a trained librarian and a school library media center. While the name has changed over the years to reflect the inclusion of such nonprint materials as films, videos, tapes, slides, computers, and software as well as books, the purpose of the center is to provide the best services and materials to facilitate learning for children.

The library media center should be open all day every day to serve students in its unique way. Flexible scheduling of story hours or lessons on library research may be directed by the librarian in a special area, leaving the rest of the resources free for others to use. Children can learn without the constant presence of a teacher or librarian. A trained aide can help children find relevant books, films, videos, and records. Parents have

served most effectively as volunteers in the school media center. Children increase in their ability to do independent study by using a variety of sources. An abundance of materials should be readily and freely available.

Increasingly, new school library media centers have become the focal point of many schools, with classrooms radiating out from them. The space should be as flexible and fluid as possible to allow for growth and change. The environment should encourage free access to materials at all times. Children flow in and out, doing projects, finding resources, making their own books, producing films. As the library media center becomes more closely identified with the total instructional program, it becomes more integrated into the total school environment.

The Library Media Specialist

The library media specialist[31] plays a very important role in the quality of learning and living that takes place in the library media center, the school, and the community. Serving as a full-time contributing faculty member, the librarian works with children, teachers, parents, and volunteer and professional aides. Specialized training provides background knowledge of children's books and all media for instruction, library media procedures, knowledge of children's development and behavior, understanding of various teaching methods, and knowledge of school curriculum needs and organization. Increasingly, the library media specialist is called on to give leadership not only in providing the materials for instruction but in shaping the curriculum itself. The library media program should be an integral part of the total school program. Working with teachers, the media specialist needs to be responsive to the curricular and instructional needs of the school. What units of study are the teachers planning to initiate this year? Books, films, and tapes on this

[30]Marilyn Parker in *The Best of the WEB, 1976–1982,* Susan Hepler, ed. (Columbus: The Reading Center, College of Education, Ohio State University, 1982), p. 69.

[31]The terms *library media specialist* and *librarian* are used interchangeably to denote the person who is responsible for directing the school library media program. It is assumed that such a director would have had training as a school librarian and a media specialist and in many instances would also have a teaching certificate.

subject should be gathered together for the teachers' and children's use. Bibliographies of print and nonprint materials based on units of work should be developed cooperatively with teachers. Book lists and curriculum resources should be shared. The function of the school library media center is to provide an information-rich environment where teachers and students become effective users of print and non-print materials.

In one school, the fifth grade was studying the rather abstract theme of famous "crossings." The children and teacher had webbed possibilities, and then the teacher had made an appointment with the librarian. The two of them filled a rolling cart full of books, films and videos on such subjects as Columbus, the Pilgrims, the slave trade, crossing the Western Divide, Hannibal crossing the Alps. There were many more topics, but the abstract concept allowed the children to study many time periods and many famous events. Students chose what aspect of the topic they wished to study and then met in their study groups. The librarian worked with each group to find appropriate materials. The children used the card catalogue and the table of contents and index of each book to see what topics were covered. They checked the dates of publications and looked at the qualifications of the authors. All of these research skills were taught in the context of a study in which the children wanted to obtain information, rather than an isolated library skills lesson.

Teachers and library media specialists become partners as they work together to help students learn to use information, to be critical of what they read and see, to make judgments about what is authentic and accurate, and to discover meaning. As students share their findings, they learn to question, compare, and combine information. Only such educated students can become contributing citizens to a democratic society.

Working with Parents and the Community

Parent volunteers can be a particularly rich resource for teachers and librarians. Sometimes these volunteers can be parents of students, sometimes they might be volunteers from a senior-citizen center. One kindergarten/first grade teacher has "grandmothers" from a senior-citizen center who come once a week for the whole morning. They read stories to small groups of children, even individuals. They help make big books that the teacher uses. Whatever is needed, there is an extra pair of hands to do it.

Parents can also serve as resource persons depending upon their background of experience. One parent, who is an Egyptologist, became a tremendous source for third-grade children who were studying mummies. In preparation for this parent's visit, the teacher read aloud *Mummies Made in Egypt,* by Aliki, and the children prepared questions to ask him. He brought Egyptian artifacts and pictures to share with them. Another group of first-grade students were studying about families. They wanted to interview the oldest member of their family about his or her childhood. One grandfather was invited to the class and children learned how to conduct an interview with him. Wherever possible teachers should draw on the expertise of the community.

Students can also reciprocate by contributing to the community themselves. Junior-high school students in the Bronx so loved Katherine Paterson's book, *Bridge to Terabithia,* that they wanted to share it with others. A literature group went out to the local senior citizens's residence and read it aloud to these new friends. Those seniors were invited to keep reading logs and join in the book discussions.[32]

In one school the parents and children created the Book Nook, a tiny paperback bookstore literally made from a broom closet. They decorated it with Maurice Sendak posters and a charming hanging lamp and even turned the old sink into a "trading pot" where children could place a "used" paperback and exchange it for another. The whole school takes justifiable pride in this paperback bookstore. In another school the parents made a large wooden case on wheels that can be opened to create a bookstore anywhere in the building. Closed, it can be pushed flat against a

[32]Shelley Harwayne, "Reading and Writing for Real-World Reasons" in Kenneth S. Goodman, Lois Bridges Bird and Yetta M. Goodman, *The Whole Language Catalog* (Santa Rosa, Calif.: American School Publishers, 1991), p. 337.

wall. Parents will need help in getting such bookstores started and assuming responsibility for their operation. The librarian, a teacher who knows books, parents, and one or two children could serve as the selection committee to order new books. If teachers and parents support the store in the beginning, it will sustain itself once children know its regular hours and can find the books they want to buy and read.

During Book Week one school had someone scheduled to read aloud every hour of the day in the library. The librarian helped the mayor, the police officer, the superintendent, and others select appropriate books for their story time. Different grades were scheduled to hear stories every day that week.

With good planning the community can be a wonderful resource for schools. The more a community participates, the more the people in that community will begin to take ownership and pride in their schools.

Working with the Public Library

The school librarian should work closely with the children's librarian of the public library. At the beginning of the year, she might send her or him a list of the possible study units the school will be undertaking. It is not fair to suddenly deluge the public librarian with requests for books about building houses when she had no warning that the entire third grade would study this topic that year.

Most public librarians are very helpful to teachers who want to supplement their classroom library with particular books. In turn, teachers must see to it that these books are handled carefully and returned to the library on time.

Many public libraries are serving their community in unique ways. Realizing the importance of reading aloud to young children, they have a story hour three and four times a week. These are scheduled at various times convenient for working parents. Many libraries hold "pajama" story hours at 8 P.M. on nights when they are open. All the children come in their PJs, hear several stories, and go home to bed.

Increasingly public libraries are giving outreach service to the many children who do not come to the library. Some librarians are holding story hours in soup kitchens for the homeless children; others are going to churches and day schools and holding story hours for the unserved children of the community whose parents never bring them to the library.

Some visionary public librarians are sending a welcome kit to each newborn infant in the community. These kits, funded by a local business, include a brief pamphlet on the importance of reading aloud to the young child. A recommended list of books is part of the kit along with the notation that all titles are available in the library. Two books are included such as *Goodnight Moon* by Margaret Wise Brown and *Clap Hands* by Helen Oxenbury (see Chapter 4). Along with the books are coupons for two more that may be obtained at the library. These foward-looking librarians know how important it is to read to babies and to develop the library habit early. They know that the future of libraries depends on the development of library users; these are apt to be the very youngsters who learned to love the library at an early age.

When teachers, librarians, and parents concentrate on plans to foster a love of reading in each child, communities become caring, literate places to live. Only when every child has a library card and uses it, when every preschool group hears stories three and four times a day, when all teachers read aloud, when children have substantial time to read books of their own choosing, when all schools have trained librarians and information-rich media centers, only then will we begin to develop a nation of readers.

SUGGESTED LEARNING EXPERIENCES

1. Spend a day in an elementary school. Focus on the environment for learning, the physical environment, the intellectual climate, the emotional climate. Describe the quality of living and learning in the school. Support your descriptions with careful observations.

2. Visit an elementary school and focus on the provisions for a literature program. Does the teacher read to the children? What is read? What are the children reading? What books are available for them to read? How often are these books changed?
3. Spend a day in a school library media center. What does the librarian do? Is she caught up in meeting schedules or does the center have flexible scheduling?
4. Draw a floor plan of a classroom you would hope to have as a teacher. Plan the reading areas and list what you would have in them.
5. Visit the children's rooms of several different libraries and compare what you see. What books are children reading, taking home? May they check out nonprint materials? Talk with children's librarians. What innovative practices have they initiated? What plans for the future do they have?
6. Using the framework for webbing, choose a book, genre, or unit to web for a particular age level. If possible work out some of the planned activities with children.
7. Plan an in-depth study of a book using the types of questions described in the chapter.
8. Examine literature readers, sample kits of literature, and published units on literature. Note the purposes, content, plans of organization, and activities. Analyze the types of questions that have been prepared.
9. Look at several state and local curriculum guides for the elementary school and see what suggestions they give for teaching literature. Literature may be included in the guides for reading or language arts.

RELATED READINGS

1. American Association of School Librarians and Association for Educational Communications and Technology. *Information Power: Guidelines for School Library Media Programs.* Chicago: American Library Association and Association for Educational Communications and Technology, 1988.

    Written jointly by two committees from AASL and AECT, this book sets forth guidelines for developing school library programs. Rather than state quantitative standards of numbers of items, the book suggests guidelines based on "high service programs" identified in a national survey.
2. Atwell, Nancie. *In the Middle: Writing, Reading, and Learning with Adolescents.* Portsmouth, N.H.: Heinemann, 1987.

    A breakthrough book on ways to help middle school students find joy in writing and reading. Much attention is given to dialogue journals, both what students write and how the teacher responds. Reading workshop and mini-lessons are described in this useful book for all teachers.
3. Barton, Bob, and David Booth. *Stories in the Classroom.* Portsmouth, N.H.: Heinemann, 1990.

    Two well-known Canadian educators talk about the importance of story in a child's life and how we can help engage a child in "storying." Discusses ways to share stories and ways to encourage children to respond and to tell their own.
4. Goodman, Kenneth S., Lois Bridges Bird, and Yetta M. Goodman. *The Whole Language Catalog.* New York: American School Publishers, a Macmillan/McGraw-Hill Company, 1991.

    There is something for everyone in this 400-plus page oversize book concerning the theory and practice of whole language. Contributors are professional educators from around the world, teachers, parents, and children. Includes a history of the whole-language movement that documents such early precursors as progressive education, language experience approach, and British primary education.
5. Graves, Donald H. *A Researcher Learns to Write: Selected Articles and Monographs.* Portsmouth, N.H.: Heinemann, 1984.

    A well-known American researcher candidly tells of his growth in understanding the writing process. Graves reports findings from his Ford study and his National Institute of Education report

on ways to work with students to develop writing. One article gives the origin and purpose of "the author's chair" in the classroom.

6. Green, Ellin. *Books, Babies, and Libraries: Serving Infants, Toddlers, Their Parents, and Caregivers* Chicago: American Library Association, 1991.

    Green, who is project director and consultant for the New York Public Library's early childhood program, has written a book to prepare librarians to work effectively with infants and toddlers as well as adults.

7. Hancock, Joelie, and Susan Hill, eds. *Literature-Based Reading Programs at Work*. Portsmouth, N.H.: Heinemann, 1988.

    Twelve teachers and librarians from Australia and New Zealand describe how they made the change from basal reading programs to literature-based ones. The first section presents articles on setting up a literature-based reading program; the second section deals with special-focus programs such as big books, poetry, and biography.

8. Hansen, Jane. *When Writers Read*. Portsmouth, N.H.: Heinemann, 1987.

    One of the most sensible and clearly written books on the relationship between reading and writing. Drawing on her research in the classroom, Hansen explores how a response approach can be used in both writing and reading.

9. Pappas, Christine C., Barbara Z. Kiefer, and Linda S. Levstik. *An Integrated Language Perspective in the Elementary School*. White Plains, N.Y.: Longman, 1990.

    An excellent text that provides integrated language theory and a wealth of examples from the classroom. Eight detailed units for grades K–6 are featured along with webs to show their development. Chapters on observation and assessment techniques are also included. Literature is shown as central to the curriculum.

10. Peterson, Ralph, and Maryann Eeds. *Grand Conversations: Literature Groups in Action*. New York: Scholastic, 1990.

    A fine discussion of teaching with real books. Both theoretical and practical, the book differentiates between *extensive*, or wide reading where children just read for enjoyment and *intensive* reading, where students read and study a book in depth. Highly recommended for any teachers involved in a literature-based reading program.

11. Routman, Regie. *Transitions: From Literature to Literacy*. Portsmouth, N.H.: Heinemann, 1988.

    A very popular book with teachers, this details Routman's growth as a whole-language primary teacher. Her honesty and practical help are appreciated by teachers in transition themselves. Details of her reading-writing program, including many examples of children's work, are given.

12. Smith, Frank. *Joining the Literacy Club*. Portsmouth, N.H.: Heinemann, 1988.

    These enlightening and thought-provoking essays by Smith discuss what it means to be a reader, a writer, and a critical thinker. No one has done more than Frank Smith to cut across old ways of thinking and clearly state new approaches.

REFERENCES

Alexander, Lloyd. The "Prydain" series.
_____. *The Black Cauldron*. Holt, 1986.
_____. *The Book of Three*. Holt, 1964.
_____. *The Castle of Llyr*. Holt, 1966.
_____. *The High King*. Holt, 1968.
_____. *Taran Wanderer*. Holt, 1967.

Aliki. *Mummies Made in Egypt*. Harper, 1985.

Anno, Mitsumasa. *Anno's Alphabet: An Adventure in Imagination*. Harper, 1975.

_____. *Anno's Italy*. Philomel, 1984.

_____. *Anno's Journey*. Philomel, 1981.

Arkin, Alan. *The Lemming Condition*, illustrated by Joan Sandin. Harper, 1976.

Babbitt, Natalie. *Tuck Everlasting*. Farrar, Straus, 1975.

Baker, Alan. *Benjamin's Portrait*. Lothrop, 1987.

Bauer, Marion Dane. *On My Honor*. Clarion, 1986.

Blume, Judy. *Blubber*. Bradbury, 1974.

Brett, Jan. *The Mitten*. Putnam, 1989.

Brown, Margaret Wise. *Goodnight Moon*, illustrated by Clement Hurd. Harper, 1947.

_____. *The Important Book*, illustrated by Leonard Weisgard. Harper, 1949.

Bryan, Ashley. *The Cat's Purr*. Atheneum, 1985.

Byars, Betsy. *Cracker Jackson*. Viking, 1985.

_____. *Goodbye, Chicken Little*. Harper, 1979.

_____. *The House of Wings*. Viking, 1972.

_____. *The Night Swimmers*. Delacorte, 1980.

_____. *The Pinballs*. Harper, 1977.

_____. *The Summer of the Swans*. Viking, 1970.

Butler, Stephen. *Henny Penny*. Tambourine, 1991.

Cameron, Eleanor. *Julia and the Hand of God*, illustrated by Gail Owens. Dutton, 1977.

Caney, Steven. *Steven Caney's Toy Book*. Workman, 1972.

Carle, Eric. *The Very Busy Spider*. Philomel, 1984.

Carroll, Lewis, pseud. (Charles L. Dodgson). *Alice's Adventures in Wonderland*, illustrated by John Tenniel. Macmillan, 1963 (1865 and 1872).

Cleary, Beverly, *Ramona Forever*, illustrated by Alan Tiegreen. Morrow, 1984.

_____. *Ramona Quimby, Age 8*, illustrated by Alan Tiegreen. Morrow, 1981.

_____. *Strider*, illustrated by Paul O. Zelinsky. Morrow, 1991.

Dahl, Roald. *James and the Giant Peach*, illustrated by Nancy Ekholm Burkert. Knopf, 1961.

Daly, Niki. *Not So Fast, Songololo*. McElderry, 1986.

DeArmond, Dale. *The Seal Oil Lamp*. Sierra Club/Little, Brown, 1988.

de Paola, Tomie. *"Charlie Needs a Cloak."* Prentice-Hall, 1974.

_____. *Strega Nona*. Prentice-Hall, 1975.

Ehlert, Lois. *Color Farm*. Lippincott, 1990.

_____. *Color Zoo*. Lippincott, 1989.

Feder, Jan. *The Life of a Hamster*. Children's Press, 1982.

Fleischman, Paul. *Saturnalia*. Harper, 1990.

Fleischman, Sid. *The Whipping Boy*, illustrated by Peter Sis. Greenwillow, 1986.

Flournoy, Valerie. *The Patchwork Quilt*, illustrated by Jerry Pinkney. Dial, 1985.

Fox, Paula. *One-Eyed Cat*. Bradbury, 1984.

Freedman, Russell. *Lincoln: A Photobiography*. Clarion, 1987.

Gág, Wanda. *Gone Is Gone*. Putnam, 1960.

_____. *Nothing at All*. Putnam, 1941.

Galdone, Paul. *The Little Red Hen*. Clarion, 1973.

_____. *The Gingerbread Boy*. Clarion, 1975.

_____. *The Three Wishes*. McGraw-Hill, 1961.

Gardiner, John. *Stone Fox*, illustrated by Marcia Sewall. Harper, 1980.

George, Jean Craighead. *Julie of the Wolves*. Harper, 1972.

_____. *My Side of the Mountain*. Dutton, 1975.

_____. *The Wounded Wolf*, illustrated by John Schoenherr. Harper, 1978.

Gerstein, Mordicai. *The Seal Mother*. Dial, 1986.

Godden, Rumer. *The Mousewife*, illustrated by Heidi Holder. Viking, 1982.

Grahame, Kenneth. *The Wind in the Willows*, illustrated by E. H. Shepard. Scribner, 1940 (1908).

Gray, Nigel. *A Country Far Away*, illustrated by Philippe Dupasquier. Orchard, 1989.

Grifalconi, Ann. *Osa's Pride*. Little, Brown, 1990.

Hall, Donald. *Ox-Cart Man*, illustrated by Barbara Cooney. Viking, 1979.

Heide, Florence Parry, and Judith Heide Gilliland. *The Day of Ahmed's Secret*, illustrated by Ted Lewin. Lothrop, 1990.

Hill, Kirkpatrick. *Toughboy and Sister*. McElderry, 1990.

Hirsh, Marilyn. *Could Anything Be Worse?* Holiday, 1974.

Houston, James. *The Falcon Bow, An Arctic Legend.* McElderry, 1986.

Hunter, Mollie. *A Sound of Chariots.* Harper, 1972.

_____. *A Stranger Came Ashore.* Harper, 1975.

Hurwitz, Johanna. *Rip-Roaring Russell,* illustrated by Lillian Hoban. Morrow, 1983.

Hutchins, Pat. *Rosie's Walk.* Macmillan, 1968.

Hyman, Trina Schart. *Little Red Riding Hood.* Holiday, 1983.

Isadora, Rachel. *At the Crossroads.* Greenwillow, 1991.

Jacques, Brian. *Redwall.* Philomel, 1986.

Kellogg, Steven. *Chicken Little.* Morrow, 1985.

Kent, Jack. *The Fat Cat: A Danish Folktale.* Parents, 1971.

Kipling, Rudyard. *The Elephant's Child,* illustrated by Lorinda Bryan Cauley. Harcourt Brace, 1983.

Konigsburg, E. L. *From the Mixed-Up Files of Mrs. Basil E. Frankweiler.* Atheneum, 1967.

L'Engle, Madeleine. *A Wrinkle in Time.* Farrar, Straus, 1962.

Lewin, Hugh. *Jafta,* illustrated by Lisa Kopper. Carolrhoda, 1983.

_____. *Jafta and the Wedding,* illustrated by Lisa Kopper. Carolrhoda, 1989.

_____. *Jafta: The Journey,* illustrated by Lisa Kopper. Carolrhoda, 1984.

_____. *Jafta: The Town,* illustrated by Lisa Kopper. Carolrhoda, 1984.

_____. *Jafta's Father,* illustrated by Lisa Kopper. Carolrhoda, 1983.

_____. *Jafta's Mother,* illustrated by Lisa Kopper. Carolrhoda, 1983.

Lewis, C. S. The "Narnia" series.

_____. *The Horse and His Boy,* illustrated by Pauline Baynes. Macmillan, 1962.

_____. *The Last Battle,* illustrated by Pauline Baynes. Macmillan, 1964.

_____. *The Lion, the Witch and the Wardrobe,* illustrated by Pauline Baynes. Macmillan, 1950.

_____. *The Magician's Nephew,* illustrated by Pauline Baynes. Macmillan, 1964.

_____. *Prince Caspian, the Return to Narnia,* illustrated by Pauline Baynes. Macmillan, 1964.

_____. *The Silver Chair,* illustrated by Pauline Baynes. Macmillan, 1962.

_____. *The Voyage of the "Dawn Treader,"* illustrated by Pauline Baynes. Macmillan, 1962.

Lobel, Arnold. *Frog and Toad Are Friends.* Harper, 1970.

Macaulay, David. *Black and White.* Houghton Mifflin, 1990.

McKissack, Patricia C. *Flossie & the Fox,* illustrated by Rachel Isadora. Dial, 1986.

MacLachlan, Patricia. *Sarah, Plain and Tall.* Harper, 1985.

Milne, A. A. *Winnie-the-Pooh,* illustrated by Ernest H. Shepard. Dutton, 1926.

Morgan, Pierr. *The Turnip.* Philomel, 1990.

O'Dell, Scott. *Island of the Blue Dolphins,* illustrated by Ted Lewin. Houghton Mifflin, 1990 (1960).

Oxenbury, Helen. *Clap Hands.* Macmillan, 1987.

Paterson, Katherine. *Bridge to Terabithia,* illustrated by Donna Diamond. Crowell, 1977.

_____. *The Great Gilly Hopkins.* Crowell, 1978.

_____. *Jacob Have I Loved.* Crowell, 1980.

_____. *Lyddie.* Lodestar/Dutton, 1991.

Paulsen, Gary. *Hatchet.* Bradbury, 1987.

Pinkwater, Daniel. *The Magic Moscow.* Macmillan, 1980.

Rawls, Wilson. *Where the Red Fern Grows.* Doubleday, 1961.

Schnieper, Claudia. *Amazing Spiders,* photos by Max Meier. Carolrhoda, 1987.

Selsam, Millicent E., and Joyce Hunt. *A First Look at Leaves,* illustrated by Harriett Springer, Walker, 1972.

Sendak, Maurice. *Where the Wild Things Are.* Harper, 1963.

Shulevitz, Uri. *Dawn.* Farrar, Straus, 1974.

Spinelli, Jerry. *Maniac Magee.* Little, Brown, 1990.

Steig, William. *Abel's Island.* Farrar, Straus, 1976.

_____. *Amos & Boris.* Farrar, Straus, 1971.

_____. *Sylvester and the Magic Pebble.* Simon & Schuster, 1969

Steptoe, John. *Mufaro's Beautiful Daughters: An African Tale.* Lothrop, 1987.

Tolstoy, Alexei. *The Great Big Enormous Turnip,* illustrated by Helen Oxenbury. Watts, 1968.

Uchida, Yoshiko. *The Sea of Gold,* illustrated by Marianne Yamaguchi. Creative Arts, 1988. (paper)

Van Allsburg, Chris. *The Polar Express.* Houghton Mifflin, 1985.

_____. *The Stranger.* Houghton Mifflin, 1986.

Waber, Bernard. *Ira Sleeps Over.* Houghton Mifflin, 1975.

Wells, Rosemary. *Noisy Nora.* Dial, 1973.

White, E. B. *Charlotte's Web*. Harper, 1952.
Wilder, Laura Ingalls. The "Little House" series, illustrated by Garth Williams. Harper, 1953.
_____. *By the Shores of Silver Lake* (1939).
_____. *Little House in the Big Woods* (1932).
_____. *Little House on the Prairie* (1935).
_____. *Little Town on the Prairie* (1941).
_____. *The Long Winter* (1940).
_____. *On the Banks of Plum Creek* (1937).
_____. *These Happy Golden Years* (1943).
Williams, Karen Lynn. *Galimoto*, illustrated by Catherine Stock. Lothrop, 1990.
Williams, Vera B. *Three Days on a River in a Red Canoe*. Greenwillow, 1981.
Woods, Audrey. *The Napping House*, illustrated by Don Wood. Harcourt, 1984.
Xiong, Blia. *Nine-in-One Grr! Grr!*, adapted by Cathy Spagnoli, illustrated by Nancy Horn. Children's Book Press, 1989.
Yagawa, Sumiko. *The Crane Wife*, translated by Katherine Paterson, illustrated by Suekichi Akaba. Morrow, 1981.
Yolen, Jane. *Greyling*, illustrated by David Ray. Philomel, 1991.
_____. *Owl Moon*, illustrated by John Schoenherr, Philomel, 1987.
Zemach, Margot. *It Could Always Be Worse*. Scholastic, 1979.
Zion, Gene. *Harry the Dirty Dog*, illustrated by Margaret Graham. Harper, 1956.
Zubrowski, Bernie. *Tops: Building and Experimenting with Spinning Toys*, illustrated by Roy Doty. Morrow, 1989.

REFERENCES FOR THE SIGN OF THE BEAVER WEB

Crompton, Anne Eliot. *The Winter Wife*, illustrated by Robert Andrew Parker. Little, Brown, 1975.
Defoe, Daniel. *Robinson Crusoe*, edited by Angus Ross. Penguin, 1966.
Fleischman, Paul. *Saturnalia*. Harper, 1990.
Fritz, Jean. *The Double Life of Pocahontas*, illustrated by Ed Young. Putnam, 1983.
George, Jean. *My Side of the Mountain*. Dutton, 1975.
_____. *The Talking Earth*. Harper, 1983.
Haviland, Virginia, ed. *North American Legends*. Putnam, 1979.
Hill, Kirkpatrick. *Toughboy and Sister*. McElderry, 1990.
Hoople, Cheryl. *The Heritage Sampler: A Book of Colonial Arts and Crafts*. Dial, 1975.
Paulsen, Gary. *Hatchet*. Bradbury, 1987.
Perl, Lila. *Slumps, Grunts and Snickerdoodles: What Colonial America Ate and Why*, illustrated by Richard Cuffari. Clarion, 1979.
Richter, Conrad. *The Light in the Forest*, illustrated by Warren Chappell. Knopf, 1966.
Speare, Elizabeth George. *The Bronze Bow*. Houghton Mifflin, 1961.
_____. *Calico Captive*. Houghton Mifflin, 1957.
_____. *The Sign of the Beaver*. Houghton Mifflin, 1983
_____. *The Witch of Blackbird Pond*. Houghton Mifflin, 1958.
Toye, William. *How Summer Came to Canada*, illustrated by Elizabeth Cleaver. Oxford, 1988.
Tunis, Edwin. *Colonial Living*. Crowell, 1976.

REFERENCES FOR THE FOLKTALES WEB

Aardema, Verna. *Traveling to Tondo*, illustrated by Will Hillenbrand. Knopf, 1991.
Bang, Molly. *Wiley and the Hairy Man*. Macmillan, 1976.
Brett, Jan. *Beauty and the Beast*, retold and illustrated by Jan Brett. Clarion, 1989.
_____. *The Mitten*. Putnam's, 1989.
Brown, Marcia. *The Three Billy Goats Gruff*. Harcourt, 1957.
Bryan, Ashley. *The Cat's Purr*. Atheneum, 1985.
Butler, Stephen. *Henny Penny*. Tambourine, 1991.
Climo, Shirley. *The Egyptian Cinderella*, illustrated by Ruth Heller. Crowell, 1989.
Cole, Babbette. *Prince Cinders*. Putnam, 1988.

Cooper, Susan. *Tam Lin*, illustrated by Warwick Hutton. McElderry/Macmillan, 1991.
Croll, Carolyn. *The Little Snowgirl*. Putnam's, 1989.
de Paola, Tomie. *Strega Nona*. Prentice-Hall, 1975.
_____. *Fin M'Coul, The Giant of Knockmany Hill*. Holiday, 1981.
Galdone, Paul. *The Gingerbread Boy*. Seabury, 1975.
_____. *The Three Bears*. Scholastic, 1973.
_____. *Henny Penny*. Clarion, 1984.
Gerstein, Mordicai. *The Seal Mother*. Dial, 1986.
Goble, Paul. *The Great Race*. Bradbury, 1985.
Grifalconi, Ann. *The Village of Round and Square Houses*. Little, Brown, 1986.
Grimm Brothers. *Little Red Riding Hood*, illustrated by Trina Schart Hyman. Holiday, 1983.
_____. *Snow White*, translated by Paul Heins, illustrated by Trina Schart Hyman. Little, Brown, 1974.
Haley, Gail. *Jack and the Bean Tree*. Crown, 1986.
Hogrogian, Nonny. *One Fine Day*. Macmillan, 1971.
Isadora, Rachel. *The Princess and the Frog*. Greenwillow, 1989.
Jacobs, Joseph. *The Story of the Three Little Pigs*, illustrated by Lorinda Bryan Cauley. Putnam, 1980.
Johnston, Tony. *Badger and the Magic Fan*, illustrated by Tomie de Paola. Putnam, 1990.
Kellogg, Steven. *Chicken Little*. Morrow, 1985.
Kimmel, Eric. *Baba Yaga*, illustrated by Megan Lloyd. Holiday, 1991.
Lester, Julius. *The Tales of Uncle Remus: The Adventures of Brer Rabbit*, illustrated by Jerry Pinkney. Dial, 1987.
Louie, Ai-Ling. *Yeh-Shen*, illustrated by Ed Young. Philomel, 1982.
McVitty, Walter. *Ali Baba and the Forty Thieves*, illustrated by Margaret Early. Abrams, 1989.
Marshall, James. *Hansel and Gretel*. Dial, 1990.
Mayer, Marianna. *Aladdin and the Enchanted Lamp*, illustrated by Gerald MacDermott. Macmillan, 1985.
Morgan, Pierr. *The Turnip*. Philomel, 1990.
Mosel, Arlene. *The Funny Little Woman*, illustrated by Blair Lent. Dutton, 1972.
Myers, Bernice. *Sidney Rella and the Glass Sneaker*. Macmillan, 1985.
Perrault, Charles. *Cinderella*, illustrated by Errol Le Cain. Bradbury, 1972.
_____. *Puss in Boots*, illustrated by Fred Marcellino. Farrar, 1990.
Plume, Ilse. *The Bremen-Town Musicians*. Doubleday, 1980.
Scieszka, Jon. *The True Story of the Three Little Pigs by A. Wolf*, illustrated by Lane Smith. Viking, 1989.
Shute, Linda. *Momotaro, the Peach Boy*. Lothrop, 1986.
Snyder, Dianne. *The Boy of the Three-Year Nap*, illustrated by Allen Say. Houghton Mifflin, 1988.
Steptoe, John. *The Story of Jumping Mouse*. Lothrop, 1984.
Stewig, John. *Stone Soup*, illustrated by Margot Tomes. Holiday, 1991.
Toye, William. *How Summer Came to Canada*, illustrated by Elizabeth Cleaver. Oxford, 1988.
Yagawa, Sumiko. *The Crane Wife*, translated by Katherine Paterson, illustrated by Suekichi Akaba. Morrow, 1981.
Young, Ed. *Lon Po Po*. Philomel, 1989.
Zemach, Margot, *The Little Red Hen*. Farrar, Straus, 1983.

REFERENCES FOR THE PAT HUTCHINS WEB

Brimmer, Larry D. *Country Bear's Good Neighbor*, illustrated by Ruth T. Councell. Orchard, 1988.
Brown, Ruth. *A Dark, Dark Tale*. Dial, 1981.
Browne, Anthony. *Piggybook*. Knopf, 1986.
Dobrin, Arnold. *Peter Rabbit's Natural Foods Cookbook*, illustrated by Beatrix Potter. Warne, 1977.
Fox, Mem. *Night Noises*, illustrated by Terry Denton. Harcourt, 1989.
Galdone, Paul. *The Gingerbread Boy*. Clarion, 1983.
Hill, Eric. *Where's Spot?* Putnam, 1980.
Hutchins, Pat. *Changes Changes*. Macmillan, 1971.
_____. *Clocks and More Clocks*. Macmillan, 1970.
_____. *Don't Forget the Bacon!* Puffin, 1976.
_____. *The Doorbell Rang*. Greenwillow, 1986.
_____. *Good-Night, Owl!* Macmillan, 1972.

_____. *Happy Birthday, Sam*. Greenwillow, 1978.

_____. *1 Hunter*. Greenwillow, 1982.

_____. *One-Eyed Jake!* Greenwillow, 1979.

_____. *Rosie's Walk*. Macmillan, 1968.

_____. *The Silver Christmas Tree*. Macmillan, 1974.

_____. *The Surprise Party*. Macmillan, 1969.

_____. *The Tale of Thomas Mead*. Macmillan, 1980.

_____. *Tidy Titch*. Greenwillow, 1991.

_____. *Titch*. Macmillan, 1971.

_____. *The Very Worst Monster*. Greenwillow, 1985.

_____. *What Game Shall We Play?* Greenwillow, 1990.

_____. *Where's the Baby?* Greenwillow, 1988.

_____. *You'll Soon Grow into Them, Titch*. Greenwillow, 1983.

Jonas, Ann. *Round Trip*. Greenwillow, 1983.

_____. *The Trek*. Greenwillow, 1985.

Kraus, Robert. *Leo, The Late Bloomer*, illustrated by José Aruego. Crowell, 1971.

Kuskin, Karla. *Just Like Everyone Else*. Harper, 1982.

Lobel, Arnold. *Owl at Home*. Harper, 1975.

Wildsmith, Brian. *The Owl and the Woodpecker*. Watts, 1972.

Yolen, Jane. *Owl Moon*, illustrated by John Schoenherr. Philomel, 1987.

REFERENCES FOR STEWARDS OF THE EARTH WEB

Alcock, Vivien. *The Monster Garden*. Delacorte, 1988.

Alexander, Lloyd. *The King's Fountain*, illustrated by Ezra Jack Keats. Dutton, 1989.

Amon, Aline. *The Earth Is Sore: Native Americans on Nature*. Atheneum, 1981.

Aragon, Jane. *Salt Hands*, illustrated by Ted Rand. Dutton, 1989.

_____. *Winter Harvest*, illustrated by Leslie Baker. Little, 1989.

Arnold, Caroline. *Saving the Peregrine Falcon*, photographs by Richard R. Hewett. Carolrhoda, 1985.

Baker, Jeannie. *Where the Forest Meets the Sea*. Greenwillow, 1988.

_____. *Window*. Greenwillow, 1991.

Baylor, Byrd. *Hawk, I'm Your Brother*, illustrated by Peter Parnall. Macmillan, 1976.

_____. *The Other Way to Listen*, illustrated by Peter Parnall. Macmillan, 1978.

_____. *The Way to Start a Day*, illustrated by Peter Parnall. Macmillan, 1978.

Brown, Ruth. *The World That Jack Built*. Dutton, 1991.

Burningham, John. *Hey! Get Off Our Train*. Crown, 1990.

Burton, Virginia Lee. *The Little House*. Houghton Mifflin, 1942.

Carson, Rachel. *Sense of Wonder*, photographs by Charles Pratt and others. Harper, 1956.

Cherry, Lynne. *The Great Kapok Tree: A Tale of the Amazon Rain Forest*. Harcourt, 1990.

Christopher, John. *When the Tripods Came*. Dutton, 1988.

Clark, Margaret Goff. *The Vanishing Manatee*. Cobblehill, 1990.

Cole, Johanna. *The Magic School Bus at the Waterworks*, illustrated by Bruce Degen. Scholastic, 1986.

Cooney, Barbara. *Miss Rumphius*. Penguin, 1982.

Cowcher, Helen. *Rain Forest*. Farrar, 1988.

Cromic, William J. *Steven and the Green Turtle*, illustrated by Tom Eaton. Harper, 1970.

Cutchins, Judy, and Ginny Johnston. *The Crocodile and the Crane*. Morrow, 1986.

Danziger, Paula. *Make Like a Tree and Leave*. Delacorte, 1990.

Dickinson, Peter. *Eva*. Delacorte, 1989.

Dorros, Arthur. *Rain Forest Secrets*. Scholastic, 1990.

Earthworks. *50 Simple Things You Can Do to Save the Earth*. Andrews & McNeel, 1991.

Elkington, John, et al. *Going Green: A Kid's Handbook for Saving the Planet*, illustrated by Tony Ross. Viking, 1990.

Facklam, Margery. *And Then There Was One: The Mysteries of Extinction*, illustrated by Pamela Johnson. Sierra Club/Little, Brown, 1990.

George, Jean Craighead. *One Day in the Tropical Rainforest*, illustrated by Gary Allen. HarperCollins, 1990.

_____. *The Talking Earth*. Harper, 1983.

_____. *The Wounded Wolf*, illustrated by John Schoenherr. Harper, 1978.

_____. *Who Really Killed Cock Robin?: An Ecological Mystery*. Harper, 1991 (1971).

Giono, Jean. *The Man Who Planted Trees*, illustrated by Michael McCurdy. Chelsea Green, 1985.

Goodall, John. *The Story of a Farm*. Macmillan, 1989.

_____. *The Story of a Main Street*. Macmillan, 1987.

_____. *The Story of an English Village*. Macmillan, 1979.

Grover, Wayne. *Dolphin Adventure: True Story*, illustrated by Jim Fowler. Greenwillow, 1990.

Hirschi, Ron. *The Mountain Bluebird*, photographs by Galen Burrell. Cobblehill, 1989.

_____. *Where Do Birds Live?*, photographs by Galen Burrell. Walker, 1987.

Huff, Barbara. *Greening the City Streets: The Story of Community Gardens*, photographs by Peter Ziebel. Clarion, 1990.

Jeffers, Susan. *Brother Eagle, Sister Sky: A Message from Chief Seattle*. Dial, 1991.

Jonas, Ann. *Aardvarks Disembark*. Greenwillow, 1990.

Killion, Bette. *The Apartment House Tree*, illustrated by Mary Szilagyi. Harper, 1989.

Lauber, Patricia. *Summer of Fire: Yellowstone, 1988*. Orchard, 1990.

_____. *Too Much Garbage*, illustrated by Vic May. Garrard, 1974.

MacDonald, Caroline. *The Lake at the End of the World*. Dial, 1989.

McNulty, Faith. *The Lady and the Spider*, illustrated by Bob Marstall. Harper, 1986.

Milgrom, Harry. *The ABC of Ecology*, illustrated by Donald Crews. Macmillan, 1972.

Miller, Christina, and Louise A. Berry. *Wastes*. Watts, 1986.

Müller, Jörg. *The Changing City*. Atheneum, 1977.

_____. *The Changing Countryside*. Atheneum, 1977.

O'Brien, Robert C. *Z for Zachariah*. Macmillan, 1987 (1975).

Patterson, Francine. *Koko's Kitten*, photographs by Ronald H. Cohn. Scholastic, 1985.

Peet, Bill. *Wump World*. Houghton Mifflin, 1974.

Pringle, Laurence. *Global Warming*. Arcade, 1990.

_____. *Living Treasure: Saving the Earth's Threatened Biodiversity*. Morrow, 1991.

_____. *Saving Our Wildlife*. Enslow, 1990.

_____. *Throwing Things Away: From Middens to Resource Recovery*. Crowell, 1986.

Provensen, Alice, and Martin Provensen. *Shaker Lane*. Penguin, 1988.

Sattler, Helen Roney. *The Book of Eagles*, illustrated by Jean Day Zallinger. Lothrop, 1989.

Schlein, Miriam. *Pigeons*. Photographs by Margaret Miller. Crowell, 1989.

_____. *The Year of the Panda*, illustrated by Kam Mak. Crowell, 1990.

Seuss, Dr. (Theodor S. Geisel). *The Lorax*. Random, 1981.

Sharpe, Susan. *Waterman's Boy*. Bradbury, 1990.

Sheldon, Dyan. *Whales' Song*, illustrated by Gary Blythe. Dial, 1991.

Shulevitz, Uri. *Dawn*. Farrar, Straus, 1974.

_____. *Toddlecreek Post Office*. Farrar, Straus, 1990.

Siebert, Diane. *Heartland*, illustrated by Wendell Minor. Crowell, 1989.

_____. *Mojave*, illustrated by Wendell Minor. Crowell, 1988.

_____. *Sierra*, illustrated by Wendell Minor. Crowell, 1991.

Smith, Roland. *Sea Otter Rescue: The Aftermath of an Oil Spill*. Cobblehill, 1990.

Staines, Bill. *All God's Critters Got a Place in the Choir*, illustrated by Margot Zemach. Dutton, 1989.

Stolz, Mary. *Night Ghosts and Hermits: Nocturnal Life on the Seashore*, illustrated by Susan Gallagher. Harcourt, 1985.

Sussman, Susan, and Robert James. *Big Friend, Little Friend: A Book About Symbiosis*. Houghton Mifflin, 1989.

Turner, Ann. *Heron Street*, illustrated by Lisa Desimini. Harper, 1989.

Tyler, Linda Wagner. *The After-Christmas Tree*, illustrated by Susan Davis. Viking, 1990.

Van Allsburg, Chris. *Just a Dream*. Houghton Mifflin, 1990.

Von Tscharner, Renata, and Ronald L. Fleming. *New Providence: A Changing Cityscape*, illustrated by Dennis Orloff. Harcourt, 1987.

Weiss, Malcolm. *Toxic Waste: Clean-Up or Cover Up?* Watts, 1984.

Weller, Frances. *I Wonder If I'll See a Whale*, illustrated by Ted Lewin. Philomel, 1991.

Wheatley, Nadia. *My Place*, illustrated by Donna Rawlings. Australia in Print, 1990.

White, Sandra Verrill, and Michael Filisky. *Sterling: The Rescue of a Baby Harbor Seal*. Crown, 1989.

Wildsmith, Brian. *Professor Noah's Spaceship*. Oxford, 1980.

Yolen, Jane. *Bird Watch*, illustrated by Ted Lewin. Philomel, 1990.

_____. *Owl Moon*, illustrated by John Schoenherr. Putnam, 1987.

Chapter Thirteen

Extending and Evaluating Children's Understandings of Literature

As part of an all-school theme on Africa, three first-grade teachers immersed children in experiences with literature about the life of African peoples.[1] Children heard and read many stories with African settings. Maps, books, pictures, and things from Africa began to fill the rooms. After hearing Ann Grifalconi's *The Village of Round and Square Houses*, one class discussed "how and why stories" and some children replicated this Cameroon village. The school guidance counselor visited each classroom and read aloud Grifalconi's sequel, *Osa's Pride*, and children compared "good" pride with "bad" pride giving examples from their own lives.

Others read Joyce Arkhurst's *The Adventures of Spider*, Gail Haley's *A Story, a Story*, and Gerald McDermott's *Anansi the Spider*, all about the trickster of West African lore. Some made attribute charts of Anansi's character ("*Trickey* becauls he made the tar baby"; "*Proud* wen his suns helpt him"); others compared two versions of a similar Anansi story in their response logs. Others read John Steptoe's *Mufaro's Beautiful Daughters* and made puppets for a drama of this folktale from Zimbabwe.

They heard Karen Williams's story of *Galimoto*, located the setting of Malawi on their map of Africa, discussed the boy Kondi's skills in bargaining and building, and then made their own wire cars and toys from pipe cleaners. These were labeled and displayed on a table along with the book. Children enjoyed reading Hugh Lewin's South African story of *Jafta* and made a class book of American expressions following the similes using African animals found in the book: "When I'm happy, I purr like a lion cub." One teacher shared Muriel Feelings's *Moja Means One* and some children made a wall display depicting East African numbers.

[1]This description is based on work accomplished under the direction of Virginia Mears, Joanne Larkin, and Mary Jane McIlwain, all first-grade teachers at George Mason Elementary School in Alexandria, Virginia.

A parent who had been to countries in West Africa brought in slides of large buildings and city life, which surprised some children who thought that most Africans lived in huts in small villages. The parent wore African dress, showed African sculpture and textiles, and passed around money from various African countries, which children located on the map. The children shared their knowledge with the parent as well.

The art teacher displayed pictures from Diane Stanley's *Shaka, King of the Zulus* and Shirley Glubok's *The Art of Africa*. Children then made highly patterned miniature Zulu shields. One class made three murals of animals found in the main regions of Africa: the grasslands or plains, the jungle or rain forests, and the desert. To do this, they had to do research in nonfiction, go back to illustrations in the class collection of books, and draw on other sources. Following this three-week study, children's work was displayed along with work from the rest of the school and parents were invited to celebrate a "Cultural Diversity Night."

What did these teachers do? These first-grade teachers organized the classroom environment so that 6- and 7-year-olds could work with books and ideas in ways that were meaningful to them. They planned multiple experiences so that children could choose; they planned opportunities for children to return to books; they worked closely with the librarian and shared ideas with each other; they informed special area teachers of their plans so that music or art could be worked into this thematic study; and they honored children's work by displaying it attractively and letting parents in on the wonderful results.

ACTIVE LEARNING IN THE CLASSROOM

When children work with books in ways that are meaningful to them—through talk, making things, writing, or drama and music—many things happen. Children have greater satisfaction with and clarify personal meanings about what they have read. These activities allow many books to be visible in the classroom. A child's work with a book can dramatically influence another child's willingness to read it. Children working on projects use various skills, exercise more choices, develop planning abilities, and experiment with a variety of learning experiences.

Teachers who know the children in their classes well recognize the diversity of learning styles this sort of active learning accommodates. They know that many options should be open to children so that seldom do all children do the same thing with the same book. They plan those diverse activities that enhance children's delight in books, make them want to continue reading more and better books, and cause them to think both more widely and more specifically about what they have read. The activities in this chapter are planned to increase children's enjoyment and understanding of books.

EXPLORING LITERATURE THROUGH ART AND MEDIA

Flat Pictures and Collage

Too often children are given a box of crayons and a small space at the top of some lined newsprint paper and told to "make a picture" of the story.

A fourth grader made a stunning collage of *Anansi the Spider* using colored tissue paper, yarn, and felt.

Martin Luther King, Jr., Laboratory School, Evanston Public Schools, Evanston, Illinois. Barbara Friedberg, teacher.

❦ ❦ ❦

How much better it is to work with children who are "filled to overflowing" with knowledge about a book or theme. How much more lively might flat artwork be if the teacher provided many materials from which to choose instead of the usual crayons and thin newsprint. Chalk, paints, markers, colored tissue papers, yarn, steel wool, cotton, material scraps, wires—anything that might be useful in depicting characters and scenes should be readily accessible. Teachers might provide more interesting paper such as wallpaper samples, construction paper, hand-painted papers, the "second sheets" of computer paper, and remainders from printers. Then when children are asked to make pictures of their favorite part of a story, of a character doing something in the book they have read, or illustrations for their own stories, the results are more exciting.

The teacher's role is to design a rich environment for creativity by providing materials, challenging children's thinking, and honoring children's work. Teachers can help children think about their stories or poems by asking such focusing questions as:

♦ What would be the most appropriate material for you to use for your picture?
♦ What colors do you see when you think of this story?
♦ How will you portray the main character? How old is he or she? What does he or she wear?
♦ Where does the story take place? When? How could you show this in your picture?

In follow-up discussions when children show their work to the class, teachers may encourage them to talk about choices and reactions with such questions as:

♦ Why did you choose to illustrate this scene or characters?
♦ Why did you choose those particular materials?
♦ How did you make that part of your picture?
♦ Did you discover anything in making this picture?
♦ How does this help us see the book?

In this way, children are encouraged to reflect on or appreciate their own work and that of oth-

ers. In addition, the teacher gains valuable insight into their thinking.

Some stories suggest children create new visual forms. One teacher gave second graders ink and straws with which to blow a monster shape that could have come out of the magic bottle in Brinton Turkle's *Do Not Open*. Third graders who read stories with nighttime settings, such as Jane Yolen's *Owl Moon*, Donald Crews's *Light*, Bill Martin, Jr. and John Archambault's *The Ghost-Eye Tree*, made their own crayon-resist pictures by covering crayon drawings with black watercolor wash to produce eerie effects for their own nighttime stories.

Many illustrators' styles invite children to explore a particular medium. Collage artists, for instance, incorporate interesting commercial and hand-painted papers, twigs and leaves, and other textures in their work. Jeannie Baker in *Window* uses carefully pieced textiles to create the clothes of the characters who observe a quarter century of changes from their Australian window. David Wisniewski works with an X-Acto knife to produce the finely cut paper for his intricate layered illustrations of the Icelandic tale of *Elfwyn's Saga*. Lois Ehlert cuts intricate shapes from her own hand-painted papers to create the birds and flowers in *Feathers for Lunch*. Molly Bang in *The Paper Crane*, Ezra Jack Keats, Elizabeth Cleaver, Susan Roth, Eric Carle, and Leo Lionni have also worked with collage to illustrate their stories. Children who see the surprising kinds of materials that are used in collages will return to their own artwork with new ideas.

Murals

Murals provide children with opportunities to work and plan together. These collaborative efforts need planning, and teachers may suggest that children make preliminary drawings or sketches before beginning. Lightly chalked areas on the final mural paper help children visualize the overall picture. An easier form of mural is one that is assembled from children's artwork cut and pasted to a background. Older children may also discuss how variation in size and shading, or overlapping, creates the illusion of depth.

Murals may be organized around events in one story, a synthesis of children's favorite characters,

Seven-year-olds create a collage mural of the book, _Hi, Cat_ by Ezra Jack Keats. Notice the rich use of material and their attention to the way the illustrator made his pictures.

Barrington Road School, Upper Arlington Public Schools, Ohio. Marlene Harbert, teacher.

or a topic or theme of study. One fourth-grade class made individual collage representations of houses from favorite folktales that were later glued in place along a winding road. Baba Yaga's chicken-footed house from Russian folktales stood between the witch's house from "Hansel and Gretel" and the giant's castle from "Puss in Boots." A written explanation for each house accompanied the mural.

By providing a variety of materials for collage and some organizing assistance, a teacher can help children successfully create eye-catching murals. Backgrounds may be quickly filled in with printing, using sponges dipped in paint for leaves and bushes or potato-printed tree shapes. It is important, both for a writing opportunity and for the many people who will view it, to complete the display of a mural with an explanation of its story or the way it was made.

Media Exploration

A teacher can also make use of a child's desire to replicate an illustrator's way of working by encouraging children to explore various media. Kindergarten children saved their finger painting pictures, cut them up, and used them to create their own story illustrated in the collage style of Eric Carle's trio of bug stories, _The Very Hungry Caterpillar, The Very Busy Spider,_ and _The Very Quiet Cricket._ (See Teaching Feature, Chapter 4.) After seeing Leo Lionni's _Swimmy,_ a group of primary children used lace paper doilies and watercolors to make prints creating similar underwater effects. Older children used dampened rice paper, ink, and watercolor to try to capture the look of traditional Japanese artwork used by Susan Bonners in _Panda_ and by Suekichi Akaba in the illustrations for _The Crane Wife_ by Sumiko Yagawa. These children were answering for themselves the question "How did the illustrator make the pictures?"

Techniques that easily translate to the elementary classroom include scratchboard, marbleized paper, and many varieties of painting. Brian Pinkney's stunning scratchboard illustrations for Burton Albert's _Where Does the Trail Lead?_ portray a young African-American boy exploring an island. Pinkney also uses scratchboard techniques to illustrate William H. Hooks's retelling of _The Ballad of Belle Dorcas,_ a conjure tale from the Carolinas. Barbara Cooney features scratchboard

Following their teacher's reading aloud of *Redwall* by Brian Jacques, a group of fourth and fifth graders made a triptych of the Redwall Abbey, celebrating the heroic events in the life of Matthias, the apprentice mouse.

Highland Park Elementary School, South-Western City Schools, Grove City, Ohio. Rhonda L. Dailey-Dickinson, teacher. Photo by Regina Weilbacher.

illustrations for *The Little Juggler* and *Chanticleer and the Fox* (Geoffrey Chaucer).[2] Though schools may buy commercially prepared scratchboard, similar results may be achieved by crayoning heavily on shiny-surfaced cardboard; then covering the crayon with India ink dabbed on with a cotton ball; then scratching designs or illustrations through the ink with pin or scissor points after the ink has thoroughly dried. Since this process is tedious, the technique is more suited for older children. A simpler "crayon resist" can be done by applying watercolor over a crayon drawing. It is easy to put several drops of food coloring in water and let children paint over crayon drawings to create sky, forest, or other background.

Marbleized paper has frequently been used in endpapers of well-made books. Fine examples of the art may be seen in Nonny Hogrogian's endpa-

pers and illustrations for the Grimm tales, *The Glass Mountain* and *The Devil with the Three Golden Hairs*. Ezra Jack Keats often featured marbleized paper in his books that are illustrated in collage. In a filmed interview (Weston Woods), Keats demonstrated how he made this special paper for the backgrounds of such books as *Dreams* and *In a Spring Garden*, edited by Richard Lewis. Children can create marbleized paper, using any paper and one of several kinds of color. Fill disposable or old baking pans with water and drop the color on the water surface. Oil-based paint (which may be thinned slightly with turpentine) or acrylic paint works well. Some types of poster paint and India ink also give good results. Place a piece of paper face down on the water and floating color, being careful not to trap air bubbles between paper and water. Gently lift the paper and hang it to dry. Colored chalk poses fewer cleanup problems for younger children. Chalk may be grated over the water with a small piece of window screen or an old sieve. Results must be sprayed with fixative when dry. Marbleized paper may be cut and used in collage or in the making of books as endpapers and covers (see Making Books).

Various printing techniques are often used in children's books. Ed Emberley uses thumbprints and fine lines in *Ed Emberley's Great Thumbprint Drawing Book*. Artists known for their woodcuts or linoleum cuts include Evaline Ness in *Sam, Bangs and Moonshine*, Ashley Wolff in *A Year of Birds* and *The Bells of London*, and Keizaburo Tejima in *Owl Lake* and *Fox's Dream*. Blair Lent used cardboard cuts for the illustrations in three stories: Margaret Hodges's *The Wave*, his own *John Tabor's Ride*, and Ernest Small's *Baba Yaga*. The first two titles are out of print but many libraries still have them. In this printing process, the printing plate is built by gluing pieces of cardboard to a heavy backing. Ink is worked into or rolled onto the plate and a print is taken or "pulled" off the plate.

While woodcuts and linoleum block prints are seldom practical or safe for elementary children, similar effects may be achieved with printing plates made from plastic foam trays that grocery stores use to package meat or produce. Lines can be incised on the plate with dull pencils or ballpoint pens and excess foam cut away. Grease

[2]A recipe for preparing scratchboard, including the undercoating over which ink may be brushed, can be found in Helen Roney Sattler's *Recipes for Art and Craft Materials*, illustrated by Marti Shohet (New York: Lothrop, Lee & Shepard, 1987), p. 133.

should be washed from the foam tray before water-based printing ink is rolled on. It takes time to create these pictures, but children find it very satisfying to work in the same media as an illustrator. Often art teachers are happy to be enlisted by the classroom teacher in helping children explore a particular technique or artist's work.

Each year fewer picture books are created with patterned and decorated endpapers, but occasionally teachers and children discover exceptions. Jonathan Allen's endpapers, repeated half circles containing the absurdly sharkish boy Norvin, are a perfect introduction to Margaret Mahy's preposterous tale of *The Great White Man-Eating Shark*. Stephen Butler creates small frames around three repeating images: a perky hen, an oak leaf, and an acorn for the endpapers in his *Henny Penny*. Young

children could create such a geometric pattern either by drawing or printing repeated images. A plate may be made from a cut potato, an image incised on a foam tray, or some other printing medium. A reliable plate that will withstand repeated use may be made from pieces of bicycle inner tubes. Apply rubber cement both to a wood block and to the rubber shapes, arrange on the wood block, and print as with any other block. While this technique takes some careful planning, this plate could then be used to print endpapers for any number of books.

Endpapers say something about the story, its characters, a particular motif, or a specific aspect of setting. Taro Yashima's endpapers for *Crow Boy* depict a butterfly and a blossom, symbols of the main character's growth. Edda Reinl's endpa-

The repetition of three images, a perky hen, an acorn, and an oak leaf, make an interesting pattern for the endpapers of *Henny Penny* by Stephen Butler. Children could try symbolizing their stories and make simple designs cut out of vegetables or plastic foam trays to print endpapers.

pers for *The Three Little Pigs* depict rollicking pigs in the front and their three houses in back. Kathy Jakobsen's endpaper paintings for Reeve Lindbergh's poem of *Johnny Appleseed* depict a map of the region where John Chapman wandered. If a teacher always comments on the endpapers and invites children to speculate on their meaning for the story, children will soon be eager to create their own endpapers when they make a published book.

Illustrators Leo and Diane Dillon inform the reader on the copyright page in *Why Mosquitoes Buzz in People's Ears* by Verna Aardema that they applied watercolors with an airbrush. A stencil print allows children to blend colors for a "finger airbrush" technique. A figure is cut from a piece of heavy paper, leaving the figure (positive) and the figure's shape (negative). The edges of either one are heavily chalked and the figure or shape is laid on a clean piece of paper. By holding the chalked paper stationary and gently brushing the chalk dust off onto the clean paper, an image shape or its outline is formed. Using different colors of chalk creates surprising shadows and shadings. Even primary children enjoy imitating with this technique the trailing, fading smoke Donald Crews creates with an airbrush for *Freight Train*.

Eye-catching displays may be assembled when children's efforts at working in the manner of a well-known illustrator are mounted carefully and placed alongside the book that inspired the work. Explanations written by children help clarify for parents and other classroom observers how the work was created. (See Chapter 5 for other examples of media use.)

Displays, Dioramas, and Museums

Displays naturally attract children. While locked glass cases may be appropriate for some materials, it is the inviting hands-on aspect of a table display that entices readers to investigate books and things they might otherwise not discover. Before beginning a study of the beach with kindergartners and first graders a teacher displayed a child's bathing suit, sand, a souvenir T-shirt from a nearby beach, and some sand toys along with such books as Megan McDonald's *Is This a House for a Hermit Crab?*, Douglas Florian's *A Beach Day*, Gail

Gibbons's *Beacons of Light: Lighthouse*, and Rebecca Jones's *Down at the Bottom of the Deep Dark Sea*. The teacher read these stories aloud and children talked about the books and their own beach experiences. Writing topics and research ideas were proposed. Some children brought in seashells and driftwood to add to the display table. As they talked about the shells and attempted to group them, the teacher added Alex Arthur's "Eyewitness" science book *Shell* to the table. Children began to take the books back to their work spaces, and share information with each other. Soon, the display of books, items, and children's projects and writings spread over two tables and a bulletin board as children became engaged with the topic. Such a display obviously was a catalyst for getting children to talk about and pursue a topic, and the display grew as children's thinking developed.

A diorama, another kind of display, is a three-dimensional scene often including objects and figures. Using cardboard boxes or shoeboxes turned on their sides, children can create a memorable scene from a book. Fifth and sixth graders might depict Billie Wind and her animal companions as they floated by a Calusa mound in the Everglades in Jean Craighead George's *The Talking Earth*. Using a description of the Clock family's household described by Mary Norton in *The Borrowers*, a child might "borrow" similar materials to furnish a diorama. A larger box partitioned in half allows a child to contrast two events or settings. For instance, Virginia Lee Burton's *The Little House* could be depicted first in its pastoral setting and next in the city that grew up around it. Older readers might contrast what was important to the beautiful and musically talented Caroline with what was important to the practical and sea-loving Louise in Katherine Paterson's *Jacob Have I Loved*.

Children should be encouraged to make every part of the diorama. Real items such as sheet music or fishing hooks may be appropriate in symbolizing Caroline and Louise's differences. But commercial figurines tend to cheapen a display and lessen the involvement of the child. If a teacher emphasizes the importance of accurate details, children must return to the book to check descriptions and facts. Teachers should also ask children to write about their diorama—how it was made, what it shows, and which book it is from. Then, observers can appreciate the details and the child has real authority and real purpose in writing.

A museum is a labeled collection of objects an author included in a story. For a museum based on Arnold Lobel's *Frog and Toad Together*, second graders gathered the string Toad used to tie the box of cookies, a feather dropped by a bird who ate the cookies, Toad's list, and a flower from Toad's garden. These and other items were labeled and explained. One group of 7-year-olds made papier-mâché whales, facsimile supplies that accompanied Amos, and models of the good ship *Rodent* as described in William Steig's humorous fable *Amos & Boris*. Sixth graders displayed their museum items on posterboard and presented their artwork to the class, explaining why each item pictured was important to the story. The boy who spoke about Robert Cormier's *The Chocolate War* used the pictures to remind him of characters, symbols, themes, plot, and his feelings about the story because he had

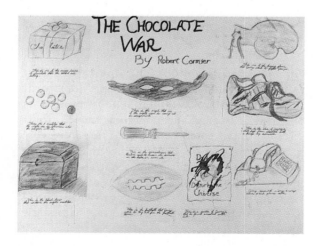

A sixth grader drew objects that could be placed in a museum for *The Chocolate War*. He interested his classmates in Robert Cormier's book by discussing the significance of each object to the plot.

Michael Reukauf, grade 6. George Mason Elementary School, Alexandria City Public Schools, Alexandria, Virginia. Susan Steinberg, teacher.

considered and rehearsed all of this while choosing items for his display. (For other examples, see "Artifacts and Collections.")

Displays, dioramas, and museums have the power to make a book seem more real to readers. In the process of making scenes or visualizing parts of a story, children explore settings, rediscover the author's use of descriptive language, and often are better able to generalize about and discuss a story. These collections and the books from which they are taken then become highly visible to children and further invite them to keep reading.

Story Retelling Aids

Children love to retell stories to each other, and aids help them recall parts of the story or focus on the sequence of events. One skillful kindergarten teacher discovered the power of a story box to turn children into storytellers:

> *October 20:* I sat in front of the class and introduced the cast of characters for Galdone's *The Little Red Hen*. These were all stuffed animal toys and I used an invisible seed, some tall grasses, a tiny bag of white flour, and a loaf of bread for props. At the end of my puppet show I boxed up the cast and props and labelled the box "The Little Red Hen." I put it in the reading corner for anyone who wanted to tell that story. Throughout the morning small groups of children made time to check it all out. Some just fingered the plush toys, examined the bag of flour, and smelled the loaf of unsliced bread. But Allison organized Jamie, Jeffrey, Viviana, and Joey each to be an animal while she spoke the part of the hen. This play was for themselves, not demanding or even needing an audience; the children were unaware of observers. The box is a great idea; there seems to be great ceremony in unpacking and packing up the kit.[3]

Out of the dress-up clothes, one kindergarten teacher gathered men's boots, pants, a shirt, gloves, and a hat that children manipulated as they retold Linda Williams's *The Little Old Lady Who Was Not Afraid of Anything*. A cardboard

[3]Jinx Bohstedt, "Old Tales for Young Tellers," *Outlook*, no. 33 (Fall 1979), p. 34.

pumpkin took the place of a real one, and this collection was boxed and kept in the play corner for the month of October.

A simple retelling aid is a *flip book*. The teacher may cut pictures from two paperbacks of the same story, laminate them on tagboard, and punch a hole in one corner. In this way, the pages may be kept together on a large key ring. Children unclip and arrange the pictures as they retell the story. Child-made flip books are usually shorter and depict the highlights of a story with the child's own drawings.

Feltboards provide another chance for children to practice telling stories more easily. (See Chapter 12, "Feltboard Stories," for how to introduce the subject to children.) Once children have seen a teacher tell Joanna Cole's *It's Too Noisy!* or Margot Zemach's *It Could Always Be Worse*, they are eager to place the animals within a house shape as they tell their own version of the gradually overcrowded house and its effect on a man and his family. When children make their own figures (cutout drawings backed with flannel or felt), they may need to be reminded to make figures big, show only key people or things, and practice the story before telling it to a larger audience. Children should collaborate to help each other clarify the project. Silhouettes placed on an overhead projector create yet another kind of board story. Where color is important, such as in Leo Lionni's *Little Blue and Little Yellow*, tinted acetate unmounted or mounted behind a cutout shape may be used.

A fourth story retelling aid is a child-made *map of the action* or a *time line* of the events of the story. Older children frequently use this kind of linear thinking to produce board games (see Games). On a large sheet of paper or posterboard, important events in the story are pictured in the order in which they happen. Seven- and 8-year-olds can map the action of Ron Roy's *Three Ducks Went Wandering* so that the ducks encounter the bull, the foxes, the hawk, and the snake before returning home to their mother. Other books in which the main character completes a circular journey include many folktales as well as Pat Hutchins's *Rosie's Walk*, Maurice Sendak's *Where the Wild Things Are*, Beatrix Potter's *The Tale of Peter Rabbit*, and *If You Give a Mouse a Cookie* by Laura Joffe Numeroff.

A *roller box movie* is a fifth retelling aid. Each child draws a different important scene, the pictures are arranged sequentially, taped together, and then mounted on rollers. As his picture passes on the "screen," the child tells his part of the story. Needless to say, roller movies require children to talk through what scenes need to appear, who should present what, and so on. Pictures should be reinforced with masking tape on the back before they are attached to each

First-grade children are hard at work mapping the action of "The Story of the Three Little Pigs."
Columbus Public Schools, Columbus, Ohio. Connie Compton, teacher.

other. The strip of pictures is then attached and rolled onto two fat dowel rods. The rods are inserted on either side of a decorated box or carton and the movie is scrolled past the audience.

To make a more compact roller movie, children may mark off spaces on adding machine tape and pull the story tape across a stage made from a smaller box or slits cut in cardboard or an envelope. Many stories lend themselves to this roller technique. When longer books and chapter books are rendered in this way, small groups of children can practice the skills of synopsis and summary as they negotiate what to depict.

Using story retelling aids is a special help to young children and students who have heard few stories read aloud. By practicing storytelling, children develop a sense of how stories are supposed to sound and how stories work. The teacher may introduce and demonstrate any of these aids, but it is in the making of their own projects that children utilize the widest variety of skills. They learn to return to the story for information and confirmation, to extract important points, to sequence events, to become sensitive to the language of the storyteller, and to "sound like a book."

Filmstrips and Videos

Children enjoy making new filmstrips from old ones that have been dipped in a small pan of bleach to remove old emulsion. The blank filmstrip is then washed under clear water, dried with a soft cloth, and left to dry overnight. Children can then draw their own pictures right on the filmstrip, using every four sprocket holes as guides for one frame. Captions may be interspersed between pictures; planning sheets help children discuss options before they begin. Allow for a "leader" at the beginning and the end of stories. Temporary colors may be made from nonpermanent felt-tip markers and, in some cases, pen and pencil. Plastic spray will make them permanent. Acrylic inks, paints, and permanent marker pens may also be used, but if spilled they cannot be removed. Filmstrips have the advantage of being compact and easy to handle; they are always in sequence, and the form seems to fascinate children.

Movie making is not an easy task, but video cameras have given more children a chance to experience this art. Choosing what scenes to portray and critiquing the performances give children a chance to look back at a story for important clues to characters' emotions and moods before they take on the roles. Yvonne Anderson's informative book *How to Make Your Own Animated Movies and Videotapes* describes her work with children aged 5 to 18 in creating films. In *Making Your Own Movies*, Harry Helfman gives hints on how to operate a simple, inexpensive movie camera and presents some basic techniques for shooting a film. A description of panning a picture is given, along with ways to vary the length of the shot. Considering the time involved in making movies, teachers may want to work with someone knowledgeable in the field.

MAKING THINGS

Sewing

Even very young children are intrigued with stitchery. Once they have mastered a few simple stitches such as the running stitch or the hem stitch, they are able to sew together outlines of characters from books such as David McPhail's *Pig Pig Grows Up* or Tomie de Paola's *Big Anthony and the Magic Ring*. These may be stuffed with newspapers for a large character gallery display. Eve Rice's *Peter's Pockets* presents enterprising Mama who sews six pockets on Peter's pocketless pants and saves the day. Primary children could sew a cloth pocket shape on a construction paper pair of pants or decorate a pair of pants in the dress-up corner as Mama did.

A running stitch produces an outline that could be used to emphasize children's burlap drawings. The old-fashioned look of this technique seems particularly well suited to extending books with American historical settings, such as Reeve Lindbergh's *Johnny Appleseed*, Donald Hall's *Ox-cart Man*, or Jean Fritz's *The Cabin Faced West*.

Quilt making has long been a way to conserve materials, save the past, and share the making of things. While we often identify quilts with pioneer women, quilts and the art of stitchery appear

RESOURCES FOR TEACHING

♦ BOOKS ABOUT QUILTS AND STITCHERY ♦

Bang, Molly. *Dawn*. Morrow, 1983. (Literary folktale; Gr. 1–3)

Coerr, Eleanor. *The Josefina Story Quilt*, illustrated by Bruce Degen. HarperCollins, 1986. (Pioneer; Gr. K–3)

Dorros, Arthur. *Tonight Is Carnaval*, illustrated with *arpilleras* sewn by the Club de Madres Virgen del Carmen of Lima, Peru. Dutton, 1991. (Peru; Gr. 1–3)

Ernst, Lisa Campbell. *Sam Johnson and the Blue Ribbon Quilt*. Lothrop, 1983. (Pioneer; Gr. K–3)

Flournoy, Valerie. *The Patchwork Quilt*, illustrated by Jerry Pinkney. Dial, 1985. (Contemporary African American; Gr. 1–3)

Grifalconi, Ann. *Osa's Pride*. Little, Brown, 1990. (African/Cameroon; Gr. 1–4)

Kinsey-Warnock, Natalie. *The Canada Geese Quilt*, illustrated by Leslie W. Bowman. Cobblehill, 1989. (Contemporary Fiction; Gr. 3–6)

Mills, Lauren. *The Rag Coat*. Little, Brown, 1991. (Appalachian; Gr. 1–4)

Paul, Ann Whitford. *Eight Hands Round: A Patchwork Alphabet*. HarperCollins, 1991. (Nonfiction; Gr. 2–6)

Polacco, Patricia. *The Keeping Quilt*. Simon & Schuster, 1988. (Jewish/Family History; Gr. 1–4)

Ringgold, Faith. *Tar Beach*. Crown, 1991. (African American/Family History; Gr. 2–5)

Roth, Susan L., and Phang, Ruth. *Patchwork Tales*. Atheneum, 1984. (Family History; Gr. 1–3)

---

in many settings.[4] The stories listed in the box, "Books About Quilts and Stitchery," suggest that children could make small quilts with patterns and materials significant to them. Quilted squares might be displayed with writing that explains the material choice, the pattern choice, or other features. While a bound quilt of squares made by a whole class is a stunning presentation, children do not then get to keep their creations.

In place of stitchery many teachers let children design quilt blocks drawn on paper with special crayons that transfer when the child's drawing is reversed and ironed onto fabric. Other products such as "liquid embroidery" may be applied directly onto the cloth. Press-on interfacing may be used to fix materials to wall hangings or banners and children may then sew on felt, buttons, lace, beads, or other material. Quilts, banners, and hangings that reflect a theme the class has studied, such as favorite books, Mother Goose

rhymes, "Pioneers," or "things from the beach," make a unifying end project. Children will then also be able to use the books they have studied for sources of artistic inspiration.

Crafts and Construction

Making things by crafts and construction satisfies a child's natural inclination to be doing something actively. Second or third graders read books that feature dragons, such as Kenneth Grahame's *The Reluctant Dragon*, Jane Yolen's *Dove Isabeau*, Jay Williams's *Everyone Knows What a Dragon Looks Like*, Margaret Leaf's *Eyes of the Dragon*, and Margaret Hodges's *Saint George and the Dragon*. They then constructed their own versions of dragons using such items as egg cartons for spiky spines, juice cans for stocky legs, and spools on a string for a whiplike tail. Books with monsters in them, such as Joan Aiken's *The Moon's Revenge*, Harve Zemach's *The Judge*, or Steven Kellogg's *The Mysterious Tadpole* also inspire children to construct. Once again, if small groups of children collaborate on making a monster or dragon they gain valuable language experience in planning, discussion, negotiation, justification, and explication.

[4]See Mary Lou Burket's article, "Quilts," in *Book Links*, May 1991, for an informative annotated bibliography of picture books, fiction, and nonfiction in which quilts play a significant role.

QUILT MAKING HELPS STUDENTS REVIEW
THEIR STUDY OF MEXICO

A second-grade teacher who planned a short thematic unit on Mexico decided to make a quilt top as a culminating activity. The teacher had provided many experiences for the children to consider as she helped them choose appropriate images. She had read aloud such books as Verna Aardema's *Borreguita and the Coyote* with illustrations by Petra Mathers and Harriet Rohmer's story of *Uncle Nacho's Hat* with illustrations by Veg Reisberg. From these, children chose a howling coyote and a sombrero. A third-grade expert on pyramids had visited the classroom to share parts of Leonard Everett Fisher's *Pyramid of the Sun–Pyramid of the Moon*. Children made clay pots and noted some of the clay figures in Betsy James's *The Dream Stair*. So clay pots, stepped architecture, and cactus decorated some squares. The rich colors of both Elisa Kleven's collage illustrations for *Abuela* by Arthur Dorros as well as Richard Jesse Watson's vibrant paintings of *The Dream Stair* by Betsy James encouraged children to work in bright and surprising colors.

They decided that the center square should be the Mexican flag and map of the country. Children had read Jonah and Jeanette Winter's *Diego*, a picture-book biography of artist Diego Rivera. They were struck by the vivid patterned borders of geometric shapes, leaves, flowers, and animals that framed Jeanette Winter's pictures. So the 7-year-olds decided to frame their individual quilt squares with borders.

Each child produced a rough draft that was reviewed by others before he or she began to work on the cotton-and-polyester-blend fabric. Since the supply of fabric markers was small, only a few children could work on their squares at one time. This helped children resist the urge to copy. The teacher taped the fabric square to the table so the child could work without moving the square. Light pencil lines marked the edges of each child's borders so that the frame wouldn't wobble.

When the twenty squares were completed, the teacher asked children how they wanted to arrange them. They decided on three rows and laid out the squares only to discover that two were left over. After much discussion, one child suggested four rows of five squares, which satisfied everyone. Then children discussed whether the arrangement was visually pleasing. Some changed their squares to be by a friend's square; others moved their squares to create better color balance.

A parent volunteered to stitch the twenty squares together with sashing and alternating squares of bright turquoise and magenta print fabric and finished the quilt. It hung in the library media center as a reminder to children of their study of Mexico. But to the teacher, the quilt was a reminder of her classroom community and of all of the activities that had been forerunners of this marvelous piece of work.

Marci El-Baba, second-grade teacher. George Mason Elementary School, and Rosalind Smith Daniels, quilter, Alexandria, Virginia.

Many books that invite extension feature interesting houses. Older children have assembled a cement-block house from Robert C. O'Brien's *Mrs. Frisby and the Rats of NIMH*, a bark-surrounded house in the manner of the one Sam Gribley built in *My Side of the Mountain* by Jean George, or Baba Yaga's chicken-legged hut of Russian folktale fame. A group of second and third graders created a table on which were displayed three-dimensional houses of folktale characters from around the world. Children's written explanations of the constructions accompanied the display.

Often making things helps child readers authenticate a book character's experience. Just as 7-year-old Ramona enjoyed making the "longest picture in the world" and old-fashioned tin-can stilts in *Ramona and Her Father* by Beverly Cleary, second graders are eager to replicate Ramona's pleasure by making their own stilts or pictures. Older children have created a memorial of paper-folded cranes to commemorate their reading of *Sadako and the Thousand Paper Cranes* by Eleanor Coerr.

Barbara Reid models plasticine clay for her illustrations in Edith Chase's *The New Baby Calf* and Joanne Oppenheim's *Have You Seen Birds?*. While young children use clay as a modeling tool, older children are better able to plan and execute small pictures with this medium.[5]

Figures for dioramas and table displays may be made from plasticine or other modeling compounds. In *Recipes for Art and Craft Materials*, Helen Roney Sattler presents numerous recipes for paints, inks, glues, papier-mâché, and other craft materials, including twenty-one recipes for modeling compounds. Here is one that might be used to shape flat character ornaments:

Creative Play Clay

In a saucepan, mix 1 cup baking soda with 1/2 cup cornstarch. Add 2/3 cup warm water. Stir until smooth and cook until mixture looks like mashed potatoes. Pour onto surface to cool. Clay may then be modeled or rolled out into sheets and cut.

Food coloring may be kneaded into the dough or finished work may be painted. This dough hardens quickly so children should have a plan or cardboard pattern before they begin. Dip finished work in varnish or spray with fixative to prevent cracking.[6]

Cooking

Teachers recognize the values of cooking in the classroom—the math concepts used in doubling a recipe, the reading skills involved in following directions, the social skills of working cooperatively, not to mention children's satisfaction in making something for others to enjoy. Cooking that starts from a book can enrich children's experiences with literature.[7]

Several collections of recipes reflect a literary genre, such as Carol MacGregor's *The Fairy Tale Cookbook* or Anne Rockwell's *The Mother Goose Cookie-Candy Book*. Karen Greene's health-conscious *Once upon a Recipe* alludes to many well-known children's books with recipes such as "Princess Peas," "Curiouser and Curiouser Casserole," "Mowgli's Tiger Milk," and "Curious George Slush." Kate MacDonald's *The Anne of Green Gables Cookbook* emphasizes Anne's favorite, sweets, and each recipe is also accompanied by a quote and illustration. *The Wild, Wild Cookbook* by Jean Craighead George tells readers how to prepare wild food as Sam Gribley did in *My Side of the Mountain*.

Several cookbooks would augment older children's reading of historical fiction. Barbara Walker's *The Little House Cookbook* features recipes for preparing all of the food that appears in the Laura Ingalls Wilder books. Quotes, historical notes, and Garth Williams's illustrations enliven the pages. In her collections of historical recipes, *Hunter's Stew and Hangtown Fry: What Pioneer America Ate and Why* and *Slumps, Grunts, and Snickerdoodles: What Colonial America Ate and*

---

[5]See *Playing with Plasticine* by Barbara Reid (New York: William Morrow, 1989) for ideas on how to use this medium with children.

[6]Recipe is modified from "Creative Play Clay," in *Recipes for Art and Craft Material* by Helen Roney Sattler, illustrated by Marti Shohet (New York: Lothrop, Lee & Shepard, 1987), p. 38.

[7]For other ideas, see Jo Osborne, "A Cook's Tour of Children's Cookbooks," *School Library Journal* (February 1986), pp. 28–29.

Why, Lila Perl explains how geography, history, and economics influenced what people ate. While historically authentic, the recipes in these collections use modern ingredients so teachers will not need to find a source for raccoon or skunk meat. Any of these books are useful as supplements to American history social studies as well.

Some books, such as Tomie de Paola's *The Popcorn Book* and *Pancakes for Breakfast* or Benjamin Darling's *Valerie and the Silver Pear* include recipes at the end of the text. Making a *Thunder Cake* with her Russian grandmother helps a little girl be brave during a thunderstorm in Patricia Polacco's story. Children would enjoy making their own cake after reading this story. Other books merely suggest to the imaginative reader a possible cooking extension. Young children have made their own sandwiches or soup after hearing Russell Hoban's *Bread and Jam for Frances* and Maurice Sendak's *Chicken Soup with Rice*.

Older students enjoy literary "Book Fares" in which each person brings to the potluck something suggested by a book. Gurgi's "munchings and crunchings" from Alexander's Prydain series, Carlie's Famous Mayonnaise Cake from Byars's *The Pinballs*, tea made from an herb that Mary Call Luther might have gathered in the Cleavers' *Where the Lilies Bloom*, and Meg's liverwurst and cream cheese sandwiches from L'Engle's Time Trilogy were some of the offerings at one party. A teacher searched through cookbooks to find the recipe for the real Turkish Delight, Edmund's undoing in *The Lion, the Witch and the Wardrobe* by Lewis. She and the children were surprised to discover authentic Turkish Delight is not the familiar white taffy but a gelatin-based candy.

Cooking things with children based on stories they have read makes books memorable. Cooking gives children a reason to return to a story to check information and a chance to make the book character's experiences a part of their own. Children who follow a recipe practice valuable skills such as following directions, measuring, and doubling a recipe. Teachers can encourage authentic writing experiences as well by suggesting children explain how something was made, the cooking problems they faced and how they overcame them, and where the idea for the recipe came from and how it was significant to the characters in the story.

Games

Games provide another means of extending children's knowledge of books and authors. In planning games, children return to books—attending to the sequence of events, learning to evaluate these events in terms of progress or setbacks for the characters, and reinterpreting aspects of the story. In creating games, children become problem solvers as they fit their literary knowledge into the pattern of the game or design new game patterns to fit their book choices. In the construction and playing of games, children satisfy a natural inclination to play with something of their own making. Games bring teachers and children together in the mutual enjoyment of books.

Often picture books suggest games children can repeat in their own play. For instance, *The Surprise Party* by Pat Hutchins shows what happens to Rabbit's message, "I'm having a party tomorrow," as it is whispered from animal to animal. Children have delighted in playing this "telephone game" in a circle after hearing this story. *Uncle Elephant* by Arnold Lobel shows his nephew how to pass the time on a trip by counting houses, trees, or telephone poles. This game may save a long class bus trip for tired first graders. The unnamed boy in Margarette S. Reid's *The Button Box* plays games with his grandmother's collections of buttons such as sorting them into categories, imagining who used them, and lining them up in patterns. Kindergartners would invent many of these same games if given a large box of buttons to play with. They might list different ways of classifying, such as color, size, and shape. They might discover buttons similar to the one Toad lost and the many his friends found in Arnold Lobel's story of "A Lost Button" from *Frog and Toad Are Friends*.

A game that heightens third- and fourth-grade children's observational and descriptive powers is played in Byrd Baylor's *Guess Who My Favorite Person Is*. Two players tell what their favorite things are but must be very explicit. Says the child, "In this game you can't just say it's blue. You have to say what *kind* of blue." Her partner specifies the blue on a lizard's belly, "the sudden kind of blue you see just for a second sometime." Children might enjoy adding their own favorites in this game which ends, in the book at least, when both characters choose the same favorite time of day, "now."

Guessing games are fun for everyone. "Who Am I?" begins a riddle game: "I drive a very small motorcycle by saying Pb-bb-bb. Who am I?" (Ralph, the mouse in Beverly Cleary's *The Mouse and the Motorcycle*). "Twenty Questions" demands astute guessing by increasingly narrowing the field of possibilities. Older children quickly learn to ask selective questions like "Is it a fairy tale?" or "Does it take place in modern times?" before jumping to book titles or characters. Only *yes* or *no* questions may be asked. Crossword puzzles, if made by children, are also ways to get children to explore the various aspects of a book. Word searches, even ones made by children, do little to send a reader back to a book and seem more like time-killing workbook exercises.

Children can be encouraged to construct *board games* or table games based on a single title or many titles. The basic game pattern of several players moving along a path toward a goal is familiar to most children. Players move forward by selecting a question card and answering correctly, by following directions on the board or the card, or by rolling dice or spinning a wheel. The game may be made more interesting by the addition of chance cards or choices of routes to the goal. Part of the fun of game making is choosing the game model, designing the playing pieces, deciding on spinners, cards, or dice for movement, and constructing the playing board.

Fourth graders read Chris Van Allsburg's *Jumanji* and made their own version of the game which, once started, must be finished. Another group of students created a game from Thomas Rockwell's *How to Eat Fried Worms*. A pot of plastic worms provided penalties for landing on certain squares and the player who reached the finish with the fewest number of worms won the game. Other children created a game and rules based on the plot of *Big Anthony and the Magic Ring* by Tomie de Paola. It is helpful if game players know the book, so that clues, rewards, and penalties will be understood. However, after playing

Children created a board game and the rules based on the plot of *Big Anthony and the Magic Ring* by Tomie de Paola.
Highland Park Elementary School, South-Western City Schools, Grove City, Ohio.

the game, children unfamiliar with the book are often motivated to read it.

Younger children may have difficulty creating an entire game from a book, but they can make *maps of the action of a story*. Six- and 7-year-olds might construct an overview of the forest setting from *One Fine Day* by Nonny Hogrogian. On a path trailing through the forest, they could depict the various encounters of the fox. *Rosie's Walk* by Pat Hutchins could be pictured on a map of the barnyard. The "Puddle Trouble" that a boy and his dog get into in Cynthia Rylant's *Henry and Mudge in Puddle Trouble* could be mounted around a large brown puddle shape. Maps of the action work best when a character journeys or is involved in a sequence of acts.

Games and action maps are fine projects for small groups of children to make. Children's writing opportunities from maps include explanations of the map, what it shows, and how it was made. Games, of course, need written directions for playing and, if they are displayed, a description of the source of the game or an explanation of how and by whom it was made.

Card games based on the pair pattern of Old Maid or the fours pattern of Go Fish allow children to classify book titles, synthesize information across titles, or extract similar information from individual titles. Pairs of Mother Goose characters ("Bo Peep and her sheep; "Jack Horner and a Plum"), an author or illustrator and a book title are all possibilities for card games. Using folktales, children might make groups of four cards starting with these categories: magical objects, magical people, tales from a particular country, flying things, famous witches, giants, and so forth. Older children might pick a category such as survival stories and include four categories across thirteen titles for a full deck. Categories might include who survives, the book title and author, and two key items or elements from the story. "Brian" in "*Hatchet* by Gary Paulsen," "a hatchet," and "a moose" would be one example.

Blank cards can be purchased from printers' trimmings and from other sources. The backs of cards may be stamped to unify a deck. Children practice many skills in constructing their own games such as categorizing their reading, recalling facts across a genre, making what they know fit a new pattern or synthesizing, and following through on a complicated set of plans. It is important for teachers to remember that the purpose of making and playing the games is to stimulate children's thinking and willingness to read, not to hasten mastery of isolated details from literature.

SINGING AND MOVEMENT IN THE CLASSROOM

Picture-Book Editions of Single Songs

Among the many values of songbooks in the classroom is their use as predictable and familiar reading material (see Chapter 4). In recent years, there have been numerous fine picture-book interpretations of such well-known songs as *Skip to My Lou*, *The Lady with the Alligator Purse*, and *There's a Hole in the Bucket*, all illustrated by Nadine Bernard Westcott. Music is included in each of Westcott's books. Maryann Kovalski's rollicking version of *The Wheels on the Bus* tells an entirely different story from the one depicted in Sylvie Kantorovitz Wickstrom's French-Canadian setting for the same titled song. Other musically derived picture books for young children feature familiar counting songs such as Mordicai Gerstein's alternating half

and whole pages for *Roll Over!* and John Langstaff's *Over in the Meadow*. Merle Peek also illustrated *Roll Over! A Counting Song* and the very popular song *Mary Wore Her Red Dress and Henry Wore His Green Sneakers*. To children who already know the song, the text of these books presents easy and enjoyable reading.

Songs that follow a cumulative pattern challenge singers to remember the order in which events occur. Children would enjoy comparing four versions of *Old Macdonald Had a Farm* to see how illustrators make a song their own. Glen Rounds creates new verses including one for a skunk, Carol Jones uses die-cut holes through which peeks the animal subject of the next verse. Lorinda Cauley and Tracey Campbell Pearson add busy scenes to their versions. Aliki's *Hush, Little Baby*, and Nadine Westcott's *The Old Lady Who Swallowed a Fly* are good candidates for feltboard or box movie storytelling aids. If children help to create these, they are less likely to get lost in the song.

Another strongly patterned song, John Langstaff's *Oh, A-Hunting We Will Go*, includes such new child-created verses as "We'll catch a bear/And put him in underwear." Children can add their own new verses to this pattern after they enjoy reading what other children have done.

Many familiar folksongs have been researched and presented in authentic historic detail by such illustrators as Robert Quackenbush, Peter Spier, Tomie de Paola, and Aliki. Quackenbush's *There'll Be a Hot Time in the Old Town Tonight* appropriately features the Great Chicago Fire of 1871. Spier presents *The Star-Spangled Banner* and *The Erie Canal* with historical background so that the songs almost become an informational book, too. These various editions are a good way to make American history come alive as children are introduced to many folksongs that are a part of the American folk tradition. De Paola's version of Sara Josepha Hale's *Mary Had a Little Lamb* is framed by an interesting discussion of the disputed authorship of this childhood song and its first appearance in McGuffey's reader in 1830. Aliki's illustrations for *Hush, Little Baby* and *Go Tell Aunt Rhody* reflect early American art in quilt-patterned endpapers and the paint-on-boards method of early limner painters.

In addition to the classroom extensions suggested, children may enjoy making their own book versions of other traditional songs like "Home on the Range," "Where Have All the Flowers Gone," or "Old Dan Tucker." Scott R. Sanders has invented details and told his own stories for twenty folksongs in *Hear the Wind Blow: American Folk Songs Retold*. Some of these long and often funny stories would inspire fifth and sixth graders' imaginations.

Matching Music and Literature

The process of identifying appropriate music to accompany prose and poetry selections helps children appreciate mood and tone in both literature and music. Second graders discussed the kind of music that could accompany the action of Maurice Sendak's *Where the Wild Things Are*. They recognized and created music with increasing tempo and volume, followed by a quiet conclusion of the story. Older children might enjoy reading one of Jack Prelutsky's *Nightmares* poems to music of their own choosing. A teacher might let children listen to Edvard Grieg's "In the Hall of the Mountain King" or Richard Wagner's "Valkyries' Ride" and ask children which of Prelutsky's poems best suit these pieces.

Many themes or subjects featured in literature have counterparts in music. For instance, the quiet awakening of the day in *Dawn* by Uri Shulevitz might be compared to the "Sunrise" movement from the *Grand Canyon Suite* by Ferde Grofé or to Cat Stevens's rendition of Eleanor Farjeon's poem "Morning Has Broken." Teachers can encourage older students to develop their sensitivity to recurring themes in art by juxtaposing literature and music. Other suggestions are given in Chapter 8, "Poetry."

Composing Music

Poetry may be set to music as children create melody and identify the rhythmical elements. One group of talented 7-year-olds composed music to accompany ther own sad tale of a princess who was captured during a battle and taken from her palace. Her knight-in-arms wandered the lonely countryside in search of her, while the poor princess grieved for him in her prison tower. The children made up a musical theme for each of the main characters, which they repeated during the various movements of their composition. The story was first told to their classmates and then the song was played on the autoharp and glockenspiel. Older students composed a three-movement rhythmic symphony for Ged in Ursula K. Le Guin's *A Wizard of Earthsea*. A recorder repeated Ged's theme in appropriate places in this percussion piece. When literature provides the inspiration for children's musical compositions, children's appreciation for both literature and music will be enriched.

Movement and Literature

Increasing attention has been given to children's control of their own body movements. The relationship between thought and movement has received much attention, particularly in England. Basic rhythmical movements might be introduced through Mother Goose rhymes. For example, children could walk to "Tommy Snooks and Bessie Brooks," gallop to "Ride a Cock Horse," jump to "Jack Be Nimble," and run to "Wee Willie Winkie." Nursery rhymes could also motivate dramatic action with such verses as "Hickory Dickory Dock," "Three Blind Mice," and "Jack and Jill."

A favorite poem for young children to move to is "Holding Hands" by Lenore M. Link, which describes the slow ponderous way that elephants walk. By way of contrast, Evelyn Beyer's poem "Jump or Jiggle" details the walk of frogs, caterpillars, worms, bugs, rabbits, and horses. It provides a wonderful opportunity for children to develop diverse movements. Both poems may be found in Jack Prelutsky's collection called *Read-Aloud Rhymes for the Very Young*. In a longer poem illustrated as a picture book by Jerry Pinkney, Jean Marzollo asks children to *Pretend You're a Cat*. Pinkney's watercolors portray twelve animals, and on the facing page, children pretending to walk, wiggle, or jump like a particular animal. Children also enjoy making the hand motions and sounds for *We're Going on a Bear Hunt* by Michael Rosen, as the adventurous family goes through a river, "Splash, splosh."

As children learn basic movements, they can use them in different areas of space, at different levels, and at different tempos. Swinging, bending, stretching, twisting, bouncing, and shaking are the kinds of body movements that may be made by standing tall, at a middle position, or by stooping low. For example, "A Swing Song" by William Allingham could be interpreted by swinging, pushing motions that vary in speed according to the words in the poem. Other poetry that suggests movement includes "Stop, Go" by Dorothy Baruch, "The African Dance" by Langston Hughes, and "The Potatoes' Dance" by Vachel Lindsay. All of these poems may be found in *Favorite Poems Old and New* by Helen Ferris.

Children who have had this kind of experience are ready to create rhythmical interpretations of a longer story. *May I Bring a Friend?* by Beatrice Schenk de Regniers, *Where the Wild Things Are* by Maurice Sendak, or *Koala Lou* by Mem Fox are examples of stories that lend themselves to rhythmical interpretations.

CONNECTING LITERATURE AND LIFE

Artifacts and Collections

Items or artifacts mentioned in books often seem strange to children even if explained in context. A child who read that Ma Ingalls cooked prairie dinners in a spider might be puzzled until she could see this three-legged pan in a reference such as *Colonial Living* by Edwin Tunis. Hefting a modern-day cast-iron replica would give a child a sense of the endurance of these utensils. A child who read Mollie Hunter's *The Third Eye* might be surprised to see that a corn dolly that villagers made is not braided from corn as we know it but is instead a wheat weaving. Each object, although a small part of the story, nonetheless connects reader experience with a part of the real world.

A class collection may involve children in assembling book-related materials on a larger scale. Second graders studying pioneers, for example, made and collected items that pioneers may have taken west with them: a wooden spoon, a cornhusk doll, a flour sack, or a wagon wheel. As

the teacher read aloud *Trouble for Lucy* by Carla Stevens, children added to the display their facsimile of the wagon master's log, a bouquet of wildflowers gathered by those who walked beside the moving wagons, and a "letter" from Marcus Whitman detailing his experiences with the wagon train. Labels were made for each article as it joined the display.

Collections can be created across books, as well. While a "Book Fare" represents a collection of food from many books (see "Cooking"), a collection from realistic fiction might include large items such as Orp's basketball from Suzy Kline's *Orp Goes to the Hoop* and Tony's bicycle from Marion Dane Bauer's *On My Honor*. It might also include smaller items such as a Mars Bar from Jerry Spinelli's *Maniac Magee* or a piece of Alison's jewelry from Robin Kline's *Hating Alison Ashley*. A folktale museum made by older students included a pea slept on by the princess, a chicken bone Hansel used to fool the witch, and a feather left behind by the Crane Wife. Explanatory labels need to be written for each display. If the displays are shared enthusiastically with other classes, some children will surely find books they want to read.

Maps and Time Lines

Often authors of books with historical settings include a geographical map to help the reader locate the story setting. In *Araminta's Paint Box* by Karen Ackerman, a map shows two routes, one which a pioneer girl took to California and the second, the route her paint box took after she lost it. Other stories make sufficient reference to actual places so that children may infer a story location by carefully comparing the story and a contemporary map. One group of fourth graders found on a road map the probable route Ann Hamilton took in the 1780s when she walked across Pennsylvania in Jean Fritz's *The Cabin Faced West*. The movement of the Wilder family in the "Little House" books of Laura Ingalls Wilder may be followed on a map. Many fictional and biographical accounts of immigrants may be traced on world maps.

As with many of the previous activities or projects in this chapter, maps, too, can help children look across a genre. The sources of folktales might be identified on a world map. The domains of tall tale heroes and monsters might be located on a U.S. map. African folktales, fiction, and non-fiction might be located on a map of Africa as a way of differentiating features and regions of the continent. Children need many encounters with maps and their working parts (key, symbols, scale, direction) before they become skilled users of all that a map can reveal.

Older children often enjoy making detailed maps of imaginary "countries of the mind" such as Lloyd Alexander's *The Remarkable Journey of Prince Jen* or his Prydain in *The Book of Three*. Ursula K. Le Guin's archipelagos frequented by *A Wizard of Earthsea*, or Brian Jacques's Mossflower Woods surrounding *Redwall*. While fantasy provides ample opportunities for children to design their own maps imaginatively, other genres of books may be mapped as well.

The concept of time is difficult for children to grasp until sometime near the end of the concrete operational stage of thinking or the beginning of formal operations (ages 11 to 12). Prior to this period, time lines may help students organize events in a person's life as represented in a book. Time lines also allow children to represent a synthesis of events in several books. A time line from Jean Fritz's *And Then What Happened, Paul Revere?* might include the date of his birth, the date Paul took over his father's business, the summer spent in the army, his famous ride, and his death in 1818. Events in the lives of Revere's contemporaries, such as Benjamin Franklin or George Washington, might be more easily compared if they were placed on a time line of the same scale as Revere's.

Placing book events in the world's time challenges even sophisticated readers to select relevant events in both the book and human history. A three-strand time line allows children to separate groups or types of events from others. While *Friedrich*, Hans Peter Richter's story of a Jewish boy caught in pre–World War II Germany, contains a "chronology" of dates in a reference at the back of the book, students might represent selected governmental decrees on one stratum of a time line. A second stratum might represent the number of Jews living in the Third Reich accord-

ing to yearly censuses. A third stratum might list important events in Friedrich's life. In this way children could see more clearly the political events against which Friedrich's tragic life was played out.

In making time lines, children need to agree on a scale so that events may be clearly shown by year or by decade, for instance. Time lines may be made of string from which events and years are hung. If children make time lines on a long roll of paper, entries may be written on cards or Post-it notes and placed temporarily along the line. In this way, corrections or realignments may be made easily.

Jackdaws

The term *jackdaw* comes from the British name for a relative of the crow that picks up brightly colored objects and carries them off to its nest. Commercially prepared jackdaw collections are sometimes available from museums and historical sites. These collections, based on an historical event or period, often include facsimile copies of diaries, letters, newspaper articles, advertisements, and other evidence from the time.

Teachers of elementary school children have modified this concept to suit activities and discussion with younger children. These teacher-made collections assemble resource materials which the teacher and children can handle in discussion, in display, or in actual construction and use. A jackdaw for Yoshiko Uchida's *Journey to Topaz*, for example, might include maps of the western United States on which children could locate the camps in which this Japanese-American family was imprisoned in World War II. The jackdaw might also include photocopies of newspaper headlines of the time, relevant articles from then contemporary magazines such as *Time* and *Colliers*, a facsimile copy of one of the exclusion orders families were handed, and information about the author. Articles and documents that could accompany Laurence Yep's *Dragonwings* include reproductions of photographs of turn-of-the-century San Francisco's Chinatown, photographs of contemporary newspaper accounts of Chinese-built airplanes, a kite like the one Moon Shadow flew, and some green

♦ MAKING A JACKDAW ♦

Though each book may suggest specific items or references to assemble, this list points to general considerations and suggests some ways of representing information.

- ♦ Recipes from the book's time (a typical dinner; a menu for a celebration)
- ♦ Price lists of commonly purchased goods then and now (milk, shoes, a dozen eggs, a car)
- ♦ A time line of the book's events
- ♦ A time line of the period surrounding the book's events
- ♦ A map, actual or imagined, of the setting
- ♦ A letter, diary, log, or news article that could have been written by or about a book character
- ♦ A photocopy of an actual book-related news article or document
- ♦ Artwork from the period (painting, architecture, sculpture)
- ♦ Songs, music, or dances from the book's setting (sheet music or words, tapes)
- ♦ Clothes of characters of the period (paper dolls, catalog format, collage)
- ♦ Something about the author of the book[8]
- ♦ A list of other fiction; other nonfiction references.

tea. Often sources for the factual material on which an historical fiction title is based are given in an author's note. Some jackdaws may then include copies of these actual source materials or may be created as "facsimiles" by children. All materials can be placed in an appropriately decorated portfolio or box.

Teacher-made jackdaws may have a list of contents so that inventory is simple. Suggested uses for the parts of the jackdaw and a bibliography of related literature save time if teachers share jackdaws among themselves.

Part of the challenge and fun of making a jackdaw is locating the material. One teacher gave fifth graders a chance to make jackdaws based on historical fiction. After extensive research from a variety of sources each group assembled five items from a list similar to "Making a Jackdaw."

Helping children make connections between literature and their own experiences is an important teacher role. However, teachers need to recognize when enough is enough. After a six-week study of Laura Ingalls Wilder's *Farmer Boy*, one fifth grader said, "I hate this book." If teachers' first priority is to foster children's love of reading, they will be less likely to overburden children with factual inquiry. Teachers who appreciate the child's desire to know as a prior condition of learning can appreciate Louise Rosenblatt's crite-

rion for the usefulness of background information: "[I]t will have value only when the student feels the need of it and when it is assimilated into the student's experience of particular literary works."[9]

EXTENDING LITERATURE THROUGH DRAMA

Forms of Drama

Books become more real to children as they identify with the characters through creative drama. Young children begin this identification with others through *dramatic play*. A 5-year-old engaged in impromptu play may become an airplane zooming to the airport built of blocks; another assumes the role of mother in the playhouse. Sometimes children of this age will play a very familiar story without adult direction. For example, "The Three Billy Goats Gruff" and "The Three Bears" are often favorites. Dramatic play represents this free response of children as they interpret experience.

[8]See Appendix B, "Information About Authors and Illustrators," for sources.
[9]Louise Rosenblatt, *Literature as Exploration* (New York: Noble and Noble, 1976), p. 123.

Pantomime is a useful form in beginning creative drama. In preparation for acting out Leo Lionni's story *Frederick*, a group of 6-, 7-, and 8-year-olds pantomimed the role of the mice. They scurried and scuttled about the room, busily gathering their winter supplies. Later, the role of Frederick was added, and again all the rest of the children played at being mice. Only after the children had thought about their roles as mice was dialogue included. Children may also pantomime small portions of a scene in order to understand and feel a character more deeply. For example, a group of 9-year-olds pretended they were the evil witch from "Snow White." They pantomimed waking up in the morning and then standing before a mirror to ask the well-known question "Who is the fairest in the land?" Pantomime can be an essential step in the development of believable creative drama with children.

Moving from pantomime to the extemporaneous dialogue of creative drama is an easy transition. *Creative drama* is structured and cooperatively planned playmaking. It is usually developed from a simple story, folktale, or poem or from scenes from a long book. It goes beyond dramatic play or simple improvisation in that it has a form with a beginning, middle, and end. The dialogue is always created by the players, whether the content is taken from a story, poem, or chapter of a book. Children can help decide what characters are essential to the story, what scenes need to be played, and where. For example, some stories such as "Goldilocks and the Three Bears," "The Three Little Pigs," or *Caps for Sale* by Esphyr Slobodkina can be played all around the room. The bears' house can be in one corner, the forest in another. The pigs' houses can be set up in three different areas. In *Caps for Sale*, the peddler can take his long walk around the room prior to sitting down in the shade of a tree to take his nap.

Children play out the story as if they "believe" in the roles they assume. The teacher's major concern is with the process and values for the children involved. While occasionally a play developed creatively may be shared with another classroom, the value of creative drama lies in the *process of playing* and does not require an audience. A more formal production may grow out of creative dramatics, but then its primary purpose

Kindergarten children made missing posters of Goldilocks, giving her name, picture, age, and birthday as part of their improvisation of this well-loved story.

Emerson Elementary School, Westerville, Ohio. Lisa Dapoz, teacher.

becomes entertainment, not expression. For such a production children plan more elaborate settings, acquire props, and wear costumes. Although the lines may become "finalized" as the scenes are rehearsed, they are neither written nor memorized.

Formal plays requiring memorization of written scripts have no place in the elementary school. When children are limited by preplanned dialogue, there is little or no opportunity for them to think through the reactions of the characters to the situation. Creativity is further limited when elementary school children attempt to write scripts. Usually their writing skill is not equal to the task of natural dialogue. Also, the time required to compose scripts often becomes so frustratingly long that interest in the play is killed.

Improvisation takes children beyond the story to the creation of a new situation. For example, in one kindergarten, children heard several versions of "Goldilocks and the Three Bears." The teacher assumed the role of a neighbor reporting that Goldilocks's mother was very concerned because her daughter hadn't come home. The children said they knew where she was and then retold the story. The next day, the teacher became a detective and said she had been hired by Goldilocks's mother because the child still hadn't returned home. In the role of detectives, the children brainstormed what information they would need to create missing person posters for the lost girl: name, picture, age, and birthday. The children paired up to make their posters. At their third meeting, the children created a map of the forest on which they placed imaginary clues such as an apple with a bite out of it, or a trail of pebbles, which Goldilocks could have left. The teacher provided a letter saying, "I am looking for a block parent" and a willing parent played the role, saying yes, indeed, Goldilocks had come to her house tired and hungry. But she knew her own phone number so her mother had come for her and that all was well. The next day, there was a thank-you note from Goldilocks to the detectives. The teacher reported that the children extended their play through this drama for weeks.[10]

Improvisation had allowed these children to imagine the story beyond the story and play it out. Improvisation can be used in all curricular areas. It could involve a meeting between Columbus and a native spokesperson, each reacting to the other, for instance. Dorothy Heathcote,[11] a British educator, has been most successful in using improvisation to help children expand their understanding of life experiences, to recreate the past, or to imagine the future. She frequently "frames" a situation, suggesting, for example, that children who are in the midst of studying pioneer life have just been given a large sum of money to establish an outdoor museum devoted to portraying life in a frontier village. The children then must plan what they will exhibit, how to make it authentic, where to obtain artifacts, and so forth. This invariably sends them

back to books to find answers to the questions they have posed.

Values of Creative Drama

The many values of creative drama suggest its significance for the elementary school curriculum. The child broadens living and learning experiences by playing the roles of people in the past, in other places, and in different situations. In creating plays children obtain information and utilize their understandings from social studies and science classes. Language skills are developed through this form of creative expression. Tensions may be released and emotional and social adjustments can be fostered through creative dramatics. For example, the child who consistently seeks attention through show-off behavior may gain attention legitimately in creative drama. The child who identifies with characters who are alone or scorned gains new insights and understandings of human behavior and becomes more sensitive to the needs of others. Since there is no written script in creative drama, the players are forced to think on their feet and draw on their inner resources. Children develop skills for democratic living through cooperative planning of action and characterization. They learn to accept and give criticism in the informal evaluation period, which should follow each playing, an important aspect of learning. The greatest value of creative drama lies in the process of doing it, the experience itself. Finally, interpretation of literature through drama brings children joy and zest in learning and living, while broadening their understandings of both literature and life.

Dramatizing Stories

The first step in dramatizing narratives is the selection of a good story to read or tell to children. Many teachers and librarians have their favorite stories for dramatizing. However, we suggest some titles here as particularly good starters.

Very young children of 3 through 5 will become involved in dramatic play, but they usually do not have the sustained attention to act out a complete story. They may play a part of a favorite folktale (for example, "The Three Billy Goats Gruff"

[10]Jean Sperling, "And She Jumped out of the Window Never to Be Seen Again," *Literacy Matters*, Ohio State University, Martha L. King Language and Literacy Center, vol. 1, no. 1 (Winter 1989), pp. 4–8.
[11]For a greater picture of this educator's influence, see Liz Johnson and Cecily O'Neill, eds., *Dorothy Heathcote: Collected Writings on Education and Drama.* (Portsmouth, N.H.: Heinemann, 1984).

crossing the bridge), but they seldom will complete a whole story. And no one should expect them to do so.

Primary-grade children enjoy playing simple stories such as *The Turnip* by Pierr Morgan, the funny tale of *Nine-in-One Grr! Grr!* by Blia Xiong, or *Tricky Tortoise* by Mwenye Hadithi and Adrienne Kennaway. The teacher or librarian might read aloud *The Turnip* while six children pantomime being the old man, the old woman, the little granddaughter, the dog, the calico cat, and the mouse. Stopping at appropriate points when the old man calls to his wife for help allows the designated child to create the dialogue.

Folktales are also a rich source of dramatization. They are usually short, have plenty of action, a quick plot, and interesting characters. A favorite is *Stone Soup* by Marcia Brown. This is the story of three jovial French soldiers who trick an entire village into providing them with the ingredients for soup, which the soldiers claim to have made from three large stones. The story naturally divides into three parts—the first scene with the soldiers approaching the village; the making of the soup, with the villagers' help of course; and the last scene when the soldiers leave. Children can decide which scenes they want to play first. Usually they like to play the part where the stone soup is made. With some preliminary discussion of the characters of the soldiers and the villagers, the children may decide who will provide certain ingredients for the soup. Discourage them from

A group of 7-year olds dances "The Wild Rumpus" after hearing Sendak's *Where the Wild Things Are*.
West Lafayette Public Schools, Indiana, Nancy Sawrey, teacher.

actually bringing carrots or barley; instead, ask them to describe their contributions so others can almost smell and taste them. If the action lags, the teacher may enter the play and add a particularly nice morsel of beef, for example, telling how she just happened to have found one piece stored in the cellar. The playing may stop at an agreed-upon signal such as: "I never thought I'd live to see the day when you could make soup out of stones," and the soldiers' reply: "It's all in knowing how!" Following the evaluation period in which the teacher points out some of the good features of the playing (for example, "I liked the way George showed us he was an old man by the way he leaned on his cane" or "How could you tell Ann was cutting carrots?"), the teacher can ask children to tell what they noticed about individual interpretations. Additions to the playing can be discussed and the play then repeated with another group.

Other folktales that children enjoy dramatizing include *The Three Wishes* by Paul Galdone. This is the well-known story of the couple who were granted three wishes. While dreaming and planning how they will use their wishes, the husband foolishly wastes one of his. His wife becomes so angry at him that she wishes a link of sausage will stick to the end of his nose. After much pulling and struggling, they have to use their last wish to correct the second wish, and all their wishes are used up! This can be a lively story, and children love to play it.

Stories from myths, such as "Pandora's Box" or "King Midas' Touch," are fine material for 9- to 11-year-olds to dramatize. Middle-grade children also enjoy presenting parts of books to each other in the form of debates, interviews, or discussions. A group of sixth graders debated one of the issues raised in Alexander Key's science-fiction novel, *The Forgotten Door:* "Resolved: The boy Jon should be turned over to the military intelligence." Three children on either side raised important issues of individual rights and national security in the course of the dialogue. Another group of students in roles of various characters gave advice to an empty chair representing Winnie Foster in Natalie Babbitt's *Tuck Everlasting.* They voiced advantages and disadvantages of Winnie's living forever if she chose to

drink water from a magic spring. Teachers can help children focus on important and complex issues that characters face in literature by providing these opportunities to explore ideas. This exploration is often a precursor of children's developing ability to discover themes in literature or factors which influence characters to change.

Readers' Theater

Teachers who are hesitant to try drama in their classroom might well begin with readers' theater, which involves a group of children in reading a play, a story, or a poem. Children are assigned to read particular parts. After reading through their parts silently, children read the text orally. Most basal readers include at least one play.

Children thoroughly enjoy participating in readers' theater and while they do not create the dialogue as they do in improvisation or drama, they do interact with each other in a kind of play form. The story provides the script, which makes it easy to try in the classroom.

In adapting a story for readers' theater teachers must edit the text to omit "he said" and "she replied." A child narrator needs to read the connecting prose between dialogue. Adrian Klein[12] suggests the following guidelines for editing and marking a prose story for readers' theater:

1. Cut the part of the line that repeats who said it . . . "said Dick." Put the character's name at the beginning of the line with a colon after the name.
2. Add a narrator when a line is necessary to the plot but is not in dialogue form.
3. Change a plot line when appropriate, then add a narrator or two.
4. Cut a line that is not necessary in the story.
5. Change a line when appropriate, then assign it to a character as if it were a line of dialogue.
6. Cut the part of the line that can be done on stage by mime or gesture and make that part

[12]Adrian F. Klein, "Teacher and Student-Centered Procedures for Developing Readers' Theatre Scripts with Prose and Poetry," in *Reading: Blending Theory into Practice Conference Proceedings* (Bakersfield: California State University, 1990).

into a stage direction . . . picked up the clock box becomes (picking up the clock box).

7. Cut the part of the line about the character that they can express for themselves and make that part into a stage direction . . . giggles becomes (giggles).

The most effective readers' theater selections contain a lot of dialogue. Folktales are easily adapted for primary children. Some good choices would be Stephen Butler's *Henny Penny,* Paul Galdone's *The Little Red Hen,* or Joanne Oppenheim's *You Can't Catch Me!,* a tale similar to "The Gingerbread Boy." At first the teacher might read the narrator's part and let children take the different roles. When children become more capable readers and have had practice with readers' theater, they can take over the role of narrator.

Older students may use just a chapter of a story for readers' theater. The first chapter of Katherine Paterson's *The Great Gilly Hopkins,* where Gilly is being driven to her fourth foster home by the social worker, makes a wonderful scene for readers' theater. The third chapter of *Sarah, Plain and Tall* by Patricia MacLachlan can be adapted for readers' theater. This is where Caleb and Anna are waiting for the arrival of Sarah. Her actual arrival and her giving the children her gifts from the sea could be included as a second part.

Readers' theater also works for some poetry. Poems that include conversation such as Karla Kuskin's "Where Have You Been, Dear?" or "The Question" found in her collection, *Dogs & Dragons, Trees & Dreams* have been successfully interpreted in this way. Children reading Mollie Hunter's *The Mermaid Summer* might also wish to read "Overheard on a Saltmarsh," the conversation between a nymph and a goblin about a necklace of green glass beads. This is in Isabel Wilner's book, *The Poetry Troupe,* which includes many poems for choral reading and readers' theater.

Puppetry

Many children will lose themselves in the characterization of a puppet while hidden behind a puppet stage, although they may hesitate to express ideas and feelings in front of the class. Through puppetry, children learn to project their voices and develop facility in varying voice quality to portray different characters. For example, a rather quiet, shy child may use a booming voice as he becomes the giant in "Jack and the Beanstalk." Puppetry also facilitates the development of skills in arts and crafts. Problems of stage construction, backdrops for scenery, and the modeling of characters provide opportunities for the development of creative thinking. A well-played puppet show extends children's appreciation and interpretation of stories and make literature a more memorable experience for them.

Beginning in kindergarten with the construction of paper-bag or simple stick figures, children can gain pleasure from their involvement with puppetry. Materials and types of puppets will range from the simple to the complex, depending on age and the child. Paul Fleischman's story *Shadow Play* shows how one man in a circus sideshow creates the story of "Beauty and the Beast" from shadow puppets. The children in the audience are invited backstage to see the actors and are surprised to discover how a homely man has given them such joy. Fleischman has told the story of "Beauty and the Beast" twice, once in the play and again in the story of the love the children feel for the homely puppeteer. After hearing this story and seeing the pictures by Eric Beddows, children might want to try making a shadow puppet play.

The teaching techniques used in creative drama should be followed, as puppet plays are created cooperatively by children and teachers. It is highly recommended that children "play out" stories before using their puppets. Written scripts are not necessary and may prove very limiting. Playing the story creatively allows the child to identify with the characters before becoming involved with the creation and mechanical manipulation of the puppet.

SELECTING STORIES

The techniques of puppetry are most appropriate for certain stories. For example, a group of 7-year-olds presented a puppet show based on Rudyard Kipling's *The Elephant's Child.* At the appropriate moment the crocodile pulled the elephant's short stocking nose into the familiar elongated trunk. Such action would be nearly impossible for live actors to portray. Another group of 10-year-olds used marionettes to capture the hilarious action of the laughing-gas birthday party described in P.L. Travers's *Mary Poppins*. Again, this scene would be difficult to portray in any other dramatic form. Other stories that lend themselves to interpretation through puppetry are *The Amazing Bone* by William Steig, *The Fat Cat* by Jack Kent, *The Gingerbread Boy* by Paul Galdone, *Rosie's Walk* by Pat Hutchins, *Frederick* and *Alexander and the Wind-Up Mouse* both by Leo Lionni.

CONSTRUCTING PUPPETS AND STAGES

Numerous books are available that tell children how to make puppets, marionettes, and stages. Young children enjoy making simple cardboard figures that can be stapled to sticks or to tongue depressors. Paper bags stuffed with old stockings or newspaper may be tied to represent a puppet head and body. Ears, hair, aprons, and so on, may be attached to create animals or people. By placing a hand in a sock or paper bag, the child can make the puppet appear to talk by moving fingers and thumb.

A very simple puppet may be created by using a Ping-Pong ball for a head and a plain handkerchief. The index finger can be inserted in a hole in the ball; the handkerchief is then slit and slipped over the puppeteer's hand. Two rubber bands secure the handkerchief to the thumb and second finger, thereby making the arms of the puppet. Puppets that are somewhat more complex to construct may have heads of papier-mâché, potatoes, plastic foam balls, or other materials. Cloth bodies can be cut and sewn by the children. Cardboard cylinders and small boxes can be used to create animal puppets. Yarn, fuzzy cloth, or old mittens make good cover materials for animals.

Finger puppets can easily be made with bodies of finger-sized cylinders stapled at the top. Faces may be glued to the cylinder top or painted on the cylinder itself. These simple puppets make fine storytelling aids for younger children. A stage can be made by turning a table on its side. The puppeteer sits or kneels behind the tabletop. Another simple stage can be created by hanging curtains so they cover the lower and upper parts of a doorway. A table, cardboard, or side of a large box can also be placed in a doorway. This type of stage is particularly good because children waiting their turns at the side of the stage are hidden from view. Older children can construct a framework for more durable puppet stages. Permanent stages that can be moved from room to room should be available in the school and can often be made by parent volunteers. Screens or hinged wings may be placed at the side of such a puppet stage. Cloth, paper, or old window shades can be painted for background material. The educational values of planning and creating a puppet show far outweigh the time and effort required to produce it.

WRITING FROM CHILDREN'S BOOKS

Children's written work should grow out of their own rich experiences, whether with people, places, and things, research and observation, or literature. Children's writing about books may take many forms (see Chapter 12, "Literature and the Writing Program"). Nearly all of the activities in this chapter are accompanied by writing suggestions for introducing the work, describing how something is made, explaining how something works, and so forth.

While real possibilities for writing are all around us in the classroom, it is literature that gives children a sense of how the written word sounds and looks. Frank Smith suggests that the role of literature in the writing program is central:

Reading seems to me to be the essential fundamental source of knowledge about writing, from the conventions of transcription to the subtle differences of register and discourse structures in various genres.[13]

When children have a chance to become writers themselves, they begin to notice how other authors work. While literature suggests the many forms which stories, information, or poetry may take, it is only as children experiment with the

[13]Frank Smith, *Writing and the Writer* (New York: Holt, Rinehart and Winston, 1982), p. 177.

model that they begin to develop a sensitivity to the conventions of the form. This awareness in turn allows them to bring a wider frame of reference to the reading and writing that follow.

Children in elementary classrooms should have an opportunity to experience a variety of well-written fiction, poetry, and nonfiction. At the same time they can be encouraged to develop an appreciation of language and form through writing. In this way, children develop a diverse writing repertoire, a sensitivity to language, and an increasing control over the power of words.

Developing Sensitivity to Language

Children's appreciation of the writing of others increases as they listen to many fine stories, read widely themselves, and have many opportunities to create their own stories and poems. Skill in descriptive writing may be developed by helping children to become aware of the power of words in conveying sensory images. After a story has been finished, the teacher and children may reread and relish particularly enjoyable words, phrases, or paragraphs.

Children's use of sensory language in their writing requires many firsthand experiences of touching and feeling and savoring textures, sounds, colors, shapes, rhythms, and patterns. Literature, too, can sharpen sensitivity to nature, people, and relationships. Rich sensory imagery helps children "see" the world around them in new perspectives.

William Steig's love of words is evident as he describes Pearl the pig as she enjoys a spring day in *The Amazing Bone:*

❧ She sat on the ground in the forest between school and home, and spring was so bright and beautiful, the warm air touched her so tenderly, she could almost feel herself changing into a flower. Her light dress felt like petals.

"I love everything," she heard herself say.[14]

In George Ella Lyon's *Come a Tide*, the family stands on a bridge and watches parts of the neighbor's gardens, livestock, and household wash away as a spring storm makes the creek rise.

When they return to their Kentucky holler, "Soggy furniture and mud-mapped rugs made mountains in front of each house." Lyon describes the noises, sights, and smells as people see their possessions emerging from the muck. When someone asks "What do we do now?" it is Grandma who says, "If it was me, I'd make friends with a shovel." By asking primary children to notice how Steig describes a soft breeze or how Lyon's choice of "mud-mapped" and Grandma's pithy statement create pictures in our minds, teachers help children appreciate the ways authors work.[15]

Children would need to have many more experiences with literature and language before they could appreciate the way Natalie Babbitt recreates an oppressively still August day full of foreboding:

❧ The first week of August stands at the very top of the summer, the top of the live-long year, like the highest seat of a ferris wheel when it pauses in its turning. The weeks that come before are only a climb from balmy spring, and those that follow a drop to the chill of autumn, but the first week in August is motionless, and hot. It is curiously silent, too, with blank white dawns and glaring noons, and sunsets smeared with too much color. Often at night there is lightning, but it quivers all alone. There is no thunder, no relieving rain. These are strange and breathless days, the dog days, when people are led to do things they are sure to be sorry for after.[16]

A child's interest in words begins in the cradle and proceeds into adulthood. A 3-year-old memorizes and repeatedly chants "Crash and clang!/ Bash and bang! And up in the road the jazz-man sprang!" simply because he loves the way Eleanor Farjeon's words sound.[17] Older children read to each other the outrageous descriptions and wordplay of such Daniel Pinkwater titles as *Borgel* or *The Hoboken Chicken Emergency.*

Teachers can support children's natural fascination with words, wordplay, and word usage in many ways. A teacher of first graders read aloud

[14]William Steig, *The Amazing Bone* (New York: Farrar, Straus & Giroux, 1976), unpaged.

[15]George Ella Lyon, *Come a Tide*, illustrated by Steven Gammell (New York: Orchard Books, 1990), unpaged.
[16]Natalie Babbitt, *Tuck Everlasting* (New York: Farrar, Straus & Giroux, 1975), p.3.
[17]Eleanor Farjeon, "Jazz-Man," in *Noisy Poems*, collected by Jill Bennett, illustrated by Nick Sharratt (New York: Oxford University Press, 1987), unpaged.

Charlotte Zolotow's *Say It!* and children discussed what the mother and little girl saw on their fall walk.

> When I asked if there were any words or phrases that they especially liked, several children mentioned *splendiferous*. We then talked about what it meant. After such responses as "wonderful" and "beautiful," Meredith suggested that it was made up of two words, *splendid* and *terrific*, and by putting them together, they were better than when they were alone. The class then discussed what they thought would be a splendiferous day. Their ideas included sunny, warm, bright, fun, time to play, and time to be free.
>
> On one or two occasions after this discussion a child commented that it was a splendiferous day.[18]

Another teacher read aloud and discussed William Steig's *Amos & Boris* with third graders. Then the children wrote diary entries as if they were Amos the mouse or Boris the whale. A typical entry on that first day was:

> Dear Diary,
>
> It was Tuesday two days after I saved Amos. We are just starting to be getting acquainted. Amos told me all about land, how I wish I could live on land. I wish we could meet sometime again.
>
> by Boris

A participant-observer in the classroom then shared favorite expressions he had copied from the book. They included:

> He loved to hear the surf sounds . . . the bursting breakers, the backwashes with rolling pebbles.
>
> In a few minutes Boris was already in the water, with waves washing at him, and he was feeling the wonderful wetness.
>
> "Amos, help me," said the mountain of a whale to the mote of a mouse.[19]

The next day children wrote a second diary entry. The contrast between their first writing and the second shows the influence of simply calling attention to Steig's rich use of language:

[18]Joetta M. Beaver, "*Say It!* Over and Over," *Language Arts*, vol. 59 (February 1982), p. 144.
[19]William Steig, *Amos & Boris* (New York: Farrar, Straus, & Giroux 1971), unpaged.

> Dear Diary:
>
> Well it's Tuesday and Amos built a ladder down the great tunnel, well, at least that's what Amos calls it. It really is my spout.
>
> One day we had a feast. We had a fat juicy lobster, some plump juicy sea cucumbers, some meaty clams, and some sand-breaded fish. After that we were so full and tired we talked and talked and finally we went to sleep happy.
>
> Well, Bye. Boris

Barrington Road School, grade 3
Upper Arlington, Ohio
Carolyn Fahrbach, teacher
Roy Wilson, Ohio State University participant-observer

All of the children showed a richer use of language in their second entries. Children seemed to use the first day of writing to master the diary form and to practice taking another point of view. The second day, however, they were ready to consider using language more succinctly and colorfully.

Certain books invite readers to play with language. Kindergartners were eager to make their own two-word rhymes after hearing such examples as "Tan man," "Pink drink," and "Stuck truck" from Bruce McMillan's *One Sun: A Book of Terse Verse*. After reading Mary Ann Hoberman's *A House Is a House for Me*, first graders listed other possibilities for houses including "Arms are houses for hugs" and "Buns are houses for hamburgers." Books such as Jim Arnosky's *A Kettle of Hawks* and Brian Wildsmith's *Birds* call attention to collective nouns.

Idioms, similes, and figurative language contribute color to the language. A group of 7-year-olds who were studying the human body traced a classmate and wrote on this poster the idioms of the human body they collected, such as "broken-hearted," "down in the mouth," and "a green thumb." Marvin Terban explores idioms in two books, *In a Pickle* and *Mad as a Wet Hen*. Other of his titles examine palindromes, homonyms, and double words such as *superduper*. Tom Birdseye's *Airmail to the Moon* is full of the colloquial expressions of Ora Mae Cotton as she describes losing her tooth: she was "popcorn-in-the-pan excited" when it fell out, but when she thought somebody stole it, she vowed if she caught them to "open up a can of gotcha and send 'em airmail to the moon!" Teachers who expose children to the curious and colorful ways the English language conveys meanings will see children's writing change as they notice the use of colorful language in the books they read.

One fourth-grade teacher asked children to find interesting expressions from Sid Fleischman's *The Midnight Horse*. They made a chart that called attention to Fleischman's masterful word play:

THE BOOK SAYS	WE MIGHT SAY
A face as rough as moldy cheese	He had bad complexion, sort of greenish
His eyes were drawn to a billfold like a compass needle to true north.	He couldn't take his eyes off the billfold
A crying girl's eyes brightened like sudden blue sky when she saw the blacksmith.[20]	She liked him and stopped crying. It was like the sun was shining

Children who have had experiences that sensitize them to figurative language and rich descriptive writing are much more likely to recognize the way fine writers such as Katherine Paterson, Russell Freedman, Virginia Hamilton, Bruce Brooks, or Nina Bawden use words.

Single Books as Springboards

Stories with strong organizational patterns often free children from being overwhelmed by the complete set of writers' problems—what to write about, how to begin, organize, sustain an idea, and end. Teachers who invite children to borrow patterns from literature often help especially reluctant writers simply to get started while they challenge more able writers to go beyond what an author has created.

In Rodney A. Greenblat's *Uncle Wizzmo's New Used Car*, a used-car lot sells outlandish cars such as the "Fluffy," which looks like a bunny on wheels. This spurred one 6-year-old to design three cars and the advertising to sell them. Using this same

book, a group of second graders designed their own mural of a used-car lot, drew cars, and wrote descriptions of what their cars could do.

Daniel Pinkwater's *Tooth-Gnasher Superflash* is another remarkable car that can change its shape and fly, but it still "can't do half the things our good old Thunderclap-Eight could do," states the new owner. Children might describe just what was remarkable about that good old car. Pinkwater's primitive felt-tip marker drawings perfectly suit the silly nature of the story.

After hearing the story of *Uncle Wizzmo's New Used Car* by Rodney A. Greenblat, a 6-year-old drew pictures and wrote about other inventive car possibilities such as a "Weather Mobile," "A Cat Mobile," and a "Mountain Car."

[20]Sid Fleischman, *The Midnight Horse*, illustrated by Peter Sis (New York: Greenwillow, 1990), pp. 4, 12.

Judith Viorst's *Alexander and the Terrible, Horrible, No Good, Very Bad Day* has long been a favorite of children from first grade through middle school. Older children especially are masterful portrayers of all that can go wrong in one day. Charlotte Zolotow's ironic *Someday* inspires children to consider the future both seriously and humorously with such ideas as "Someday . . . my brother will introduce me to his friends and say 'This is my sister,' instead of 'Here's the family creep.'" Margaret Wise Brown's *The Important Book* describes what is essential and important about things such as a flower. Young children have written their own definitions of the essence of certain things after hearing this read aloud; older children in fifth grade interviewed each other and wrote descriptions of what they thought was significant about each other. Each illustrated essay was bound in the class's "Important Book" (see p. 733). Joan Blos's *Martin's Hats* is a boy's adventure as he puts on and doffs many different hats. What adventures might Martin or another child have if they tried on a different set of hats? What adventure could a kindergartener tell about after selecting a hat from the dress-up corner? While younger elementary students are able to work with these books, older readers often have a more complete understanding of the sophistication of these titles.

The Mysteries of Harris Burdick by Chris Van Allsburg are fourteen drawings supposedly left with a publisher. Each drawing is accompanied by a tantalizing title and caption. "It was a perfect lift-off" shows "The House on Main Street" levitating; a sleeping "Archie Smith, Boy Wonder," is approached by small circles of light asking "Is he the one?" Children would have a challenging time finishing what the illustrator has started here.

Byrd Baylor's *Everybody Needs a Rock* gives the reader serious rules to consider in selecting favorite rocks. Children have added their own rules for rock selection, and others might follow the pattern, creating rules for selecting a special tree or shell. Children delight in marking their own special days after reading Baylor's *I'm in Charge of Celebrations*. A group of 9-year-olds listened to Baylor's *Your Own Best Secret Place* and talked about the many kinds of secret places people have. After the class discussion one boy's version of "My Own Best Secret Place" described how he got to the place, what it felt like to be there, and how it looked.

Sometimes a particular book suggests a unique writing experience. When a group of fourth

A third- and fourth-grade group heard Byrd Baylor's story *I'm in Charge of Celebrations*. They then wrote about and illustrated their special days to remember.

Mangere Bridge School, Auckland, New Zealand. Colleen Fleming, teacher.

My own best Secret place

To get to my secret place you have to go down the basement steps turn right go in the door on the south wall turn left go up the ladder Crawl in the big hole in the wall and there is my Secret place. It feels good to be in my Secret place becaus the cool air wash's away all my troubles into the back of my head. I have a nice soft carpet that I sit on so the hard tough rocks on the floor don't irritate me. When I go in my Secret place I turn on my light and read a book with my troubles tucked in the back of my head.

Barrington Road School, Upper Arlington, Ohio. Marlene Harbert, teacher.

❦ ❦ ❦

graders finished reading Sid Fleischman's *The Whipping Boy*, they wrote about other practical jokes that Prince Brat could play on his father, the king. One child devised this scheme:

> Prince Brat would get a mouse and put it in the royal soup. First he would hide the mouse in his pocket. Then he would go up to the royal cook and say, "May I smell the soup?" The cook would back away so the prince could smell the soup and slip the mouse into the soup. Then when the soup was served, one unlucky person would get a dead mouse in his or her soup.

Nathaniel Jencks, grade 4
Martin Luther King, Jr., Laboratory School
Evanston, Illinois
Barbara Friedberg, teacher

Tightly patterned or highly formatted stories make it easier for teachers to plan writing extensions. But the example of asking children to invent another of Prince Brat's pranks shows how an alert teacher can plan a writing experience that lets children enter into the mind of a character while at the same time calls attention to a humorous and child-appealing aspect of a story.

Experimenting with Literary Patterns

As children become familiar with many types of literature—folktales, fables, myths, or poetry, for instance—they are able to experiment with these forms in their own writing. A teacher should support writers by exposing children extensively to a well-defined part of a genre, such as alphabet books, pourquoi or wish stories, creation myths, haiku or concrete poetry before asking children to write their own works.

MAKING ALPHABET BOOKS

One teacher of fifth-grade language arts gave her students fifty alphabet books and asked them to decide which ones were easier, which more difficult, and why. On the second day, they categorized the collection on four large wall charts (see Chapter 4, "Alphabet Books"). The 10-year-olds were surprised to see such challenging titles as Jonathan Hunt's medieval informational book, *Illuminations*, and Susan Purviance's alliterative *Alphabet Annie Announces an All-American Album*. When the teacher asked children to make their own 26-letter alphabet books, the results were diverse. There were ABC books of sports, foods, animals, favorite hobbies such as fishing, riddle, lift-the-flap, and hidden picture ABCs, and alliterative stories. The class was so proud of its work that they held an author party at which children shared their work with parents.

Another class of older children read Brian Jacques's *Redwall*, a fantasy set in a medieval fortress defended by mice. They used an alphabet format and extracted events and things from

Fifth graders looked at about fifty ABC books before making their own. Their personal creations varied from an "ABC Book on Sports" to this one titled "An Occupied Alphabet" showing various occupations.
Allison Fraser, grade 5. George Mason Elementary School, Alexandria City Public Schools, Alexandria, Virginia. Susan Steinberg, teacher.

the book to create their own "A Is for Abbey" book. The annotation for an illuminated *E* read:

> E: Evil is a main part of *Redwall*. Cluny, his hoarde, King Bull Sparra, and Asmodeus are all evil. Cluny's thoughts are filled with evil. Here is an example to show Cluny's evil: "'Get out of my way, you sniveling little wretch!' he yelled, shoving Friar Hugo away from him."

> Grade 4–5
> Highland Park Elementary School
> Grove City, Ohio
> Rhonda L. Dailey-Dickinson, teacher

Alphabet books are handy organizers of information from a thematic study. Teachers might use this as a whole-class project on a topic such as ecology, especially if children are encouraged to write a paragraph of information to go with "R is for rain forest," for example.

FOOLING WITH FOLKTALES, FABLES, AND MYTHS

Children's literature offers many examples of how authors and illustrators reinterpret traditional literature for new audiences.[21] Some illustrators modify the sense of a well-known tale by preserving the story but changing the setting. Roberto Innocenti took Charles Perrault's *Cinderella* and

[21]Susan Hepler, "Fooling with Folktales: Updates, Spin-offs, and Roundups," *School Library Journal*, vol. 36, no. 3 (March 1990), pp. 153–154.

elegantly placed it in post–World War I Britain. Anthony Browne updated the Grimms' *Hansel and Gretel* by changing the setting to a bleak present-day city. Other illustrators take a basic tale and modify it with humorous comments or broadly drawn details. James Marshall in *Goldilocks and the Three Bears* and *Red Riding Hood* includes irreverent asides and humor in the pictures. Tony Ross in *Jack and the Beanstalk* depicts the giant's wife serving the giant a whale for dinner.

But many more authors and illustrators take a well-known folktale and change the point of view, mix up the characters, alter the theme, or tell what happened next. Jon Scieszka's *The Frog Prince Continued* is a sequel in which a dissatisfied prince seeks witches from other folktales who can change him back into a frog. His *The True Story of the 3 Little Pigs by A. Wolf* shifts the story to the wolf's point of view. Babette Cole's *Prince Cinders* and Bernice Myers's *Sidney Rella and the Glass Sneaker* present familiar patterns in new stories each with a modern boy protagonist. Jane Yolen's *Sleeping Ugly* plays with our expectations about folktales by giving the ugly but kind girl the prince and leaving the beautiful princess asleep to be used as a hat rack. Other authors who write modern folktales, such as William Steig, Mwenye Hadithi, Brian Wildsmith, and Rudyard Kipling, are discussed in Chapter 5, "Modern Folktale Style."

Children who have been steeped in traditional literature can write wonderful parodies and sophisticated takeoffs. A bookstore[22] staged a "True Story Contest" and invited children in fifth through eighth grades to "explore how much a folktale can change depending on who is doing the telling." In one seventh grader's story, Little White Hooded Wolf is given a special basket of "bones and gristles" to take to her sick grandmother. Her wolf mother warns her to be careful of "that spoiled brat Samantha who will take away your bones and gristles and grind your head into head cheese." A sixth grader's story of "Jack and the Beanstalk" was told from the point of view of

the giant's wife who says she came "from the ancient race of Cyclopes. We traveled across the world of Greek mythology and I was one of the few who strayed into Fantasy, a land above the clouds." It begins:

The Bean Plant Boy

One day I was roasting bears for my ill-tempered husband's dinner. He had a cold and was sleepy that day. I, on the other hand, was brim full of high spirits and mischievous thoughts.

I was just trying to think of some prank to play on him, when I heard the quiet scuffling of a boy. (Boys are nasty creatures and very greedy. We used to catch them on sticky paper littered with tiny gold pieces.)

> Johanna Robinson, Grade 6
> Leonia Middle School, New Jersey
> Eileen Gigon, teacher

A sixth-grade class studied numerous Greek myths and discussed their characteristics. One boy's story perfectly captures aspects of myth such as a crisp beginning, few characters, the explanation of the origins of an animal, and the often deadly and arbitrary action of the gods:

Princess Skunkina and Olfactor

Olfactor, the goddess of scent, was the sweetest smelling immortal around. She was the goddess who gave everything its scent. Olfactor was very nice and sweet when it came to mortals.

Princess Skunkina, known as the one with white hair, was very jealous of Olfactor because she thought she smelled better than Olfactor.

Princess Skunkina assembled the town and made an announcement. "I am the new goddess of scent. I am the sweetest smelling person alive. You will now worship me, not Olfactor, who smells like a herd of cows in comparison to me."

Of course, Olfactor was enraged. She was so angry she decided she'd pay Princess Skunkina a little visit herself. (She rarely visited mortals.) Olfactor flew down from the heavens and spotted the one with white hair in her garden of trees. Olfactor came up to the princess and cast a spell upon her. "You thought you smelled better than me. I'll see to it that you never dethrone a god or goddess again. . . . Olfactor watched as she was dying and took pity over her. She decided to let her live but not as a

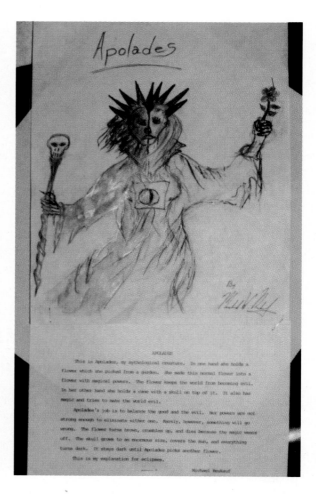

After studying myths, sixth graders created stories and illustrations describing their own mythological creatures and their particular powers.
George Mason Elementary School, Alexandria City Public Schools, Alexandria, Virginia. Susan Steinberg, teacher.

mortal, but a putrid-smelling animal with her beautiful white hair in a stripe down her back.

Michael Polson, Grade 6
George Mason Elementary School
Alexandria, Virginia
Susan Steinberg, teacher

Fables also represent a discrete and highly patterned genre of literature that children can experiment with. Children ought to have many experiences with the original fables by Aesop and La Fontaine before trying their own hands. One

child heard his teacher read Arnold Lobel's *Fables* aloud in September. Then he read it himself and over the next five weeks produced a total of seven fables. Here's one example:

A BULL STORY

One day a bull feeling both strong and mean came down into the valley. To his surprise, there was another bull down there looking as strong and mean as he. They challenged each other to a fight. They killed each other and neither of them carried on a happy life.

Moral: You can't win against an equally equipped opponent.[23]

Working from the moral back to the story, one group of 12-year-olds decided to create other modern versions of fables. They thought of appropriate stories for such well-known morals as "Beauty is only skin deep" and "Don't cry wolf unless you mean it." (See "Fables," Chapter 6, for stories suggesting other morals.)

The box "Fooling with Traditional Literature" contains selections from the many examples a teacher might use to start children thinking. But

nothing is a substitute for exposing children to many examples of traditional literature before asking them to fool with these traditional literary patterns.

EXPERIMENTING WITH POETRY

Poetry provides many opportunities for children's writing. A group of 7- and 8-year-olds studied *The Comic Adventures of Old Mother Hubbard and Her Dog*, illustrated by Tomie de Paola. They created additional verses such as "She went to the orchard to get him a cherry. / But when she got back, he was being scary." And "She went to the hen house to get him an egg./ But when she got back, he was holding his leg." After reading *The Book of Pigericks* by Lobel, a small group of fourth graders wrote their own "Bugericks." See suggestions for other ways to encourage children's writing with poetry in Chapter 8.

---

[23]Fredrick R. Burton, "The Reading-Writing Connection: A One-Year Teacher-as-Researcher Study of Third–Fourth Grade Writers and Their Literary Experiences," unpublished Ph.D. dissertation, Ohio State University, 1985, p. 166.

RESOURCES FOR TEACHING

◆ FOOLING WITH TRADITIONAL LITERATURE ◆

Ahlberg, Janet, and Allen Ahlberg. *The Jolly Postman or Other People's Letters*. Little, Brown, 1986. (Letters from one folktale character to another; Gr. 1–up)

Briggs, Raymond *Jim and the Beanstalk*. Coward, 1970. (Sequel; Gr. 1–4)

Brooke, William J. *A Telling of the Tales: Five Stories*, illustrated by Richard Egielski. Harper, 1990 (Five folktales written as short stories; Gr. 4–up)

Calmenson, Stephanie. *The Principal's New Clothes*, illustrated by Denise Brunkus. Scholastic, 1989. (New version of "The Emperor's New Clothes" in contemporary setting; Gr. 1–4)

Cole, Babette, *Prince Cinders*. Putnam, 1987. (Male character; Gr. 1–4)

Cole, Brock. *The Giant's Toe*. Farrar, 1986. (New version of "Jack and the Beanstalk" with additional characters; Gr. 1–4)

French, Fiona. *Snow White in New York*. Oxford University Press, 1988. (1920s setting; Gr. 4–up)

Hayes, Sara Henderson. "The Builders," in *Reflections on a Gift of a Watermelon Pickle* by Stephen Dunning, et al. Scott Foresman, 1966. (A poem from the smug oldest pig's point of view in "The Three Little Pigs"; Gr. 3–up)[24]

Heide, Florence Parry and Sylvia Worth Van Clief. *Fables You Shouldn't Pay Any Attention To*, illustrated by Victoria Chess. Dell, 1991 (1978). (New morality in an old form; Gr. 2–up)

Lobel, Arnold. *Fables*. Harper, 1980. (Fresh morals in new stories; Gr. 2–up)

Myers, Bernice. *Sidney Rella and the Glass Sneaker*. Macmillan, 1985. (Male character in contemporary setting; Gr. 1–3)

Pomerantz, Charlotte. *Whiff, Sniff, Nibble, and Chew: The Gingerbread Boy Retold*, illustrated by Monica Incisa. Greenwillow, 1984. (Reworked story with additional cookie; Gr. K–3)

Scieszka, Jon. *The Frog Prince Continued*, illustrated by Steve Johnson. Viking, 1991. (Sequel with a surprise ending; Gr. 1–up)

---

[24]See "Folktales" in the box "Poetry and Prose Connections," Chapter 8, for other folktale connections.

Extending Forms of Writing

While it is true that most children usually start by writing stories, they should be given many opportunities to write in other forms as well. Writing a character's diary or journal lets a child assume that character's point of view. Reporting a book's events in newspaper-article format allows a child to reshape events in the story. Children can develop practical writing skills as they write directions for a literature-based game or describe how they made a diorama. All levels of writing may spring from a child's involvement with literature, and teachers need to help children discover writing opportunities. Once again we suggest that children need experiences with a form before they are able to take it on in their own writing. Children who have never looked beyond the comic section of the newspaper should not be asked to write folktale characters, "Letters to Ann Landers," or entries for the "obituaries" column without prior experience with the form of today's newspapers!

DIARIES AND LETTERS

Once children can assume another point of view, they are able to retell a story in the first person. Authors use letters, journals, and first-person narratives to allow a character to reveal thoughts directly to the reader. Older children are more able developmentally to take on another person's point of view. The books they read often assist in this because many popular stories are written as first-person narratives. Authors such as Barbara Park in *Skinnybones,* Walter Dean Myers in *The Mouse Rap,* Phyllis Reynolds Naylor in *Shiloh* or

The Agony of Alice, and Judy Blume in *Are You There, God? It's Me, Margaret* tell their stories from the main character's point of view. Thus readers see through the eyes of another person as they are immersed in the book. Teachers help children take another point of view when they ask them to write about a book as if they were the main character telling a part of his or her story (see "Helping Children Write About Books," Chapter 12).

Other authors reveal a character's thoughts by having the character write diary entries or letters. Libby in Zilpha Keatley Snyder's *Libby on Wednesday* is part of a young authors group and keeps a journal; Sam Gribley's journal reveals the story of *My Side of the Mountain* by Jean George; Henri who spends a year in another culture in Emily Cheney Neville's *The China Year* writes letters to her teachers and friends back in New York. Fourth grader *Anastasia Krupnik* in Lois Lowry's novel keeps modifying her list of "Things I love/Things I hate" as her feelings and thoughts change. Children are quick to notice these narrative conventions if teachers help them.

Primary children are intrigued with William Joyce's *George Shrinks.* The picture book's text is a letter from George's parents telling him what chores he should do while they are out. But George dreams and awakes to find that he is extremely tiny. The pictures reveal the creative ways the now miniature boy takes out the garbage or washes the dishes. It would be interesting for younger children to retell this story from George's point of view simply by using the pictures. Some might make a copy of the parents' letter to George as concrete evidence of "where the words came from."

Several other books use letters to tell the story. Janet and Allan Ahlberg's *The Jolly Postman* includes envelopes containing removable letters to and from various folktale characters that are delivered by a postman. Teachers can supply a variety of envelopes, writing stock, and stamps, and invite children to write a letter as if they were a folktale or picture storybook character.

Vera B. Williams challenges readers to infer the story of *Stringbean's Trip to the Shining Sea* from the backs of the two dozen postcards the boy sends to his family in Kansas. A second-grade teacher asked children to translate this idea to their current topic of study. Children imagined they were visiting the rain forest and wrote a postcard to their parents telling what they had seen there. Some designed clever stamps, as Williams had done in her book.

Judith Caseley's touching *Dear Annie* features some of the letters exchanged between Annie, her mother, and grandfather from the time she is a baby to the time when she shares all eighty-six of them for her grade school show-and-tell. After hearing Caseley's story, children might write their own letters to a treasured older relative or display the letters they have received. Because of their warmth, humor, or innovative formats, books such as these are powerful catalysts to children's writing.

Children may create diaries and letters for book characters who never kept them, such as second graders created for *Amos & Boris*. In Katherine Paterson's *Lyddie*, the story of a New England mill girl, what might Lyddie have confided to her diary? In Mary Downing Hahn's ghost story of *Wait Till Helen Comes*, suppose Molly kept a journal of the strange events leading up to her stepsister's dangerous friendship. How would entries show her gradual change from skepticism to alarm to action?

Imaginary correspondence between characters in one book require children to maintain two points of view. First graders compared different versions of "Stone Soup" and settled on Tony Ross's *Stone Soup*, a takeoff in which a wolf is bested by a chicken. Children discussed what Mr. Wolf would do with the stone after he stole it; they agreed he would probably be frustrated because the stone didn't work. So they wrote in the person of Mr. Wolf:

> Dear Mrs. Hen,
>
> I tried making the soup and it tasted terrible. Could you be my cook? I promise not to eat you.[25]

[25]Reported by Peggy Compton Moberly in "Children's Choices Makes Students Avid Readers," *CBC Features*, vol. 44, no. 2 (July/December 1991).

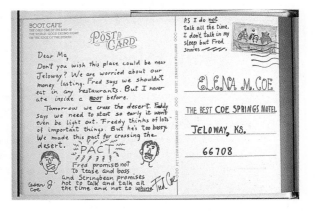

Vera Williams tells of *Stringbean's Trip to the Shining Sea* only through the use of postcards. Students could collect postcards on a trip or make them and tell their own stories.

Illustrations by Jennifer Williams and Vera B. Williams.

FAIRY TALE REVIEW

Gingerbread Man Escapes From Oven

Last Friday at 3:00 p.m a gingerbread man escaped from an oven. As he ran down the road, people who happened to be passing by joined in the chase. It was a long chase because everybody but the gingerbread man was getting tired.

Finally at 3:30 p.m the gingerbread man reached the river where he met a fox. The gingerbread man was last seen being taken across the river by the fox. He was wearing a button coat when last seen. If you have seen him, please notify the local authorities.

Gingerbread man when last seen

Bean Stalks Go Crazy

Two years ago, Jack cut down a bean stalk. Now the bean stalk has grown back and more stalks are sprouting.

The farmers love it because it has so many beans. The stalks have even lifted a few houses off the ground.

A wild bean stalk growing like crazy

Wolf Blows Down Pig's House

Yesterday, after the three little pigs went grocery shopping, the wolf came over and tried to blow down the pig's house. After many attempts, the wolf succeded. Minutes later, the wolf collapsed from loss of breath. When the pigs returned, they called an ambulance and "Hines Lumber and Brick Co." The pigs did not press charges; instead, they made the wolf pay for their new house. The wolf was treated and released from the hospital.

Fourth and fifth graders created a fairy-tale newspaper to sum up their study of these stories.
Martin Luther King, Jr., Laboratory School, Evanston, Illinois Public Schools. Ellen Esrick, reading teacher.

Another primary group decided to write letters between Mother Goose characters. This is the one Little Boy Blue received:

Dear Little Boy Blue:

Never sleep on the job again! The sheep and the cows are eating all the grass and the corn. If you sleep again, you're FIRED!

Sincerely, your boss, the farmer

Barbara Friedberg, teacher
Martin Luther King, Jr., Laboratory School,
Evanston, Illinois

In Carolyn Reeder's *Shades of Gray*, 12-year-old Will Page is forced to move to rural Virginia to live with his uncle, a conscientious objector in the Civil War. Children might write the letters Will never wrote to the friendly doctor who offered to adopt him. Or, they might write Will's journal as he wrestles with the problems presented by the hard realities of rural life in Virginia following the war.

Letters written and sent to authors and illustrators can be encouraged rather than assigned if a child or groups of children have read and are enthusiastic about books by that author. Authors appreciate the inclusion of self-addressed, stamped envelopes, or stamps, and they appreciate a child's candor and individuality above a "canned letter" copied from the chalkboard. Requests for pictures or biographical information should be addressed to publishers; letters to authors or illustrators should be addressed to them in care of the publisher. (See Appendix C for publishers' addresses.)

The box "Books That Serve as Writing Models" (see p. 808) suggests stories teachers might share as examples and incentives for children's own writing efforts.

NEWSPAPERS AND NEWSCASTING

By putting themselves in the role of reporters from newspapers or television news, children can "cover" the events in a book. An interview with Abel after his year-long stay on *Abel's Island* by William Steig might include his advice on how to survive. A series of news accounts of *The Pushcart War* by Jean Merrill could present amusing battles between the mighty trucks and the puny pushcarts in New York City. Fourth graders created a Camazotz newspaper

as part of their activities while the teacher read aloud *A Wrinkle in Time* by Madeleine L'Engle. Their work reflected an awareness of what life might be like on a planet where all persons were required to behave similarly.

As a way of looking across or back on what children know in literature, teachers may help children organize a group newspaper. Sections could include news stories, editorials, announcements, a fashion or society page, sports, lost and found, letters to the editor, advice, obituaries, and so forth. Content could be drawn from a particular genre, such as realistic fiction or folktales. One folktale newspaper, for instance, featured an advertisement for "Big Anthony's Carry-Out Pasta: All You Can Eat!," a breaking-and-entering report at the home of the Three Bears, and a review of society doings at Cinderella's ball. It takes time to develop a successful newspaper, as children must sift through what they have read to recall specific events. If column headings are posted around the classroom, ideas may be noted and children can paste up their rough drafts of articles for reading by the rest of the "newspaper staff." Parents, teacher aides, or high school typing students may often be persuaded to help with typing if the newspapers are to be duplicated for each student.

Expository Writing

DIRECTIONS, EXPLANATIONS, AND SURVEYS

Nearly all of the literature extensions in this chapter have accompanying writing possibilities. Children who write directions for designing and printing from plastic foam trays need to write procedures concisely if others are going to understand the process. Directions for a literary game give children an opportunity to write with clarity and precision. If others can play the game by following what the game maker has written, then the directions have succeeded.

Explanations and descriptions help others understand what children have created or accomplished. If students' work is displayed for a wider audience, as in school corridors, lunchrooms, or the library, then children understand the necessity for informative writing to speak clearly for them in their absence. In addition, displays provide a natural encouragement for children to

◆ BOOKS THAT SERVE AS WRITING MODELS ◆

Ahlberg, Janet, and Allan Ahlberg. *The Jolly Postman, or Other People's Letters*. Little, Brown, 1986. (Letters between folktale characters; Gr. 1–up)

Blos, Joan. *A Gathering of Days: A New England Girl's Journal, 1830–1832*. Scribner's, 1979. (Historical fiction in journal; Gr. 5–up)

Byars, Betsy. *The Burning Questions of Bingo Brown*. Viking Penguin, 1988. (Journal of interesting questions; Gr. 5–8)

Caseley, Judith. *Dear Annie*. Greenwillow, 1991. (Letters between a girl and her grandfather; Gr. 1–4)

Cleary, Beverly. *Dear Mr. Henshaw*. Morrow, 1983. (Story told in letters and journal entries; Gr. 5–7)

_____. *Strider*. Morrow, 1991. (Journal entries; Gr. 6–up)

DuPasquier, Philippe. *Dear Daddy* . . . . Bradbury, 1985. (Letters; Gr. 1–3)

Frank, Anne. *Anne Frank: The Diary of a Young Girl*. Doubleday, 1952. (Historical World War II diary; Gr. 5–up)

George, Jean Craighead. *My Side of the Mountain*. Dutton, 1959. (Diary; Gr. 4–7)

Heinrich, Bernd. *An Owl in the House: A Naturalist's Diary*, adapted by Alice Calaprice. Joy Street, 1990.

Jones, Rebecca. *Germy Blows* the Bugle. Arcade, 1990. (School newspaper; Gr. 5–7)

Joyce, William. *George Shrinks*. Harper, 1985. (Letter; Gr. 1–3)

Kidd, Diana. *Onion Tears*, illustrated by Lucy Montgomery. Orchard, 1991. (Story partially revealed in letters; Gr. 3–6)

Little, Jean. *Hey World, Here I Am!*, illustrated by Sue Truesdell. Harper, 1989. (Poetry and journal entries from *Kate*, also a character of Little's books; Gr. 4–7.)

Lowry, Lois. *Anastasia Krupnik*. Houghton Mifflin, 1971. (List maker and poet; Gr. 4–6)

Neville, Emily Cheney. *The China Year*. Harper, 1990. (Letter writer; Gr. 5–8)

O'Brien, Robert C. *Z for Zachariah*. Atheneum, 1975. (Novel in diary form; Gr. 5–up)

Snyder, Zilpha Keatley. *Libby on Wednesday*. Delacorte, 1990. (Writing group; Gr. 5–up)

Williams, Vera B. *Stringbean's Trip to the Shining Sea*, illustrated by Vera B. Williams and Jennifer Williams. Greenwillow, 1988. (Story in postcard form; Gr. 2–up)

_____. *Three Days on a River in a Red Canoe*. Greenwillow, 1981. (Journal in words and pictures; Gr. 2–5)

revise and recopy, if necessary, for this public writing. Teachers can help children write longer and more complete descriptions by asking such questions as How did you do this? What materials did you use? What part of the book is this based on? Why did you choose it? One such discussion produced the writing shown here from two second-grade boys.

A group of first graders responded to *The Biggest House in the World* by Leo Lionni through a variety of media and math activities. They took surveys of children's preferences for color, kind, and size of house (one, two, or three stories). Their concept of the word "house" was enlarged to include the "houses" of a snail and turtle (shells).

A bulletin board displayed the results of these extensions from a single book.

Literary surveys give children experiences with the representation of findings in graphs. One group of 11- and 12-year-olds surveyed each other on such topics as "Which Judy Blume books have you read?," "How many books did you read in March?," and "Have you read any books from these series: Baby-sitters Club, Nancy Drew, the Hardy Boys?" Data were presented in pie and bar graphs, averages, and percentiles in a variety of interesting displays.

Other surveys have been made of how frequently and how long each teacher reads aloud to the class or where and when children like to read.

We made a diorama of Nantucket Harbor.
We started with a cardboard box. Then we cut out some houses and then we made the whale and glued the whale on at an angle then we painted the whale black. We were going to make the under ground city but it was to hard to make.
We had trouble on the whale we kept making the whale smaller. And we had trouble on the dock And sky and clouds because it was very hard. The windows on the houses were hard to. We painted the clouds 4 times.

Second graders wrote this candid explanation for their diorama constructed after reading Blair Lent's *John Tabor's Ride*.

Dustin DeStefano and Jason Bump, Highland Park Elementary School, Grove City, Ohio. Patty Driggs, teacher.

❦ ❦ ❦

Children doing survey research will learn much about conducting and organizing the results of a survey. In addition, a teacher learns more about a reading profile of the class from these surveys. Teachers may help children state questions clearly so that answers can be categorized and counted. Discussing ways of representing information, such as bar or circle graphs, keys and use of symbols, will help children create more visually interesting survey charts.

NONFICTION'S INFLUENCE ON REPORT WRITING

Contemporary nonfiction provides numerous examples of how information may be presented in interesting, challenging, humorous, or beautiful fashion. Teachers who help children discover format in information writing help avoid the stilted school writing that begins with "my report is on" and proceeds through copied encyclopedia phrases. Seymour Simon's *Animal Fact/Animal*

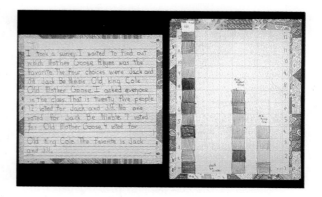

Third graders conducted a survey of the children's favorite Mother Goose rhymes. They then wrote about how they had made the survey and graphed the results.

Columbus Public Schools, Columbus, Ohio. Arlene Stuck, teacher.

❦ ❦ ❦

Fable is organized as a guessing game. Statements about animals, such as "porcupines shoot their quills," are followed on the next page with a paragraph beginning: "Fable: Porcupines cannot really shoot their quills." Diane DeGroat's illustrations are varied from humorous, to close-up, to straightforward. The useful "if" series, such as *If You Lived at the Time of the San Francisco Earthquake* by Ellen Levine, is organized in question-and-answer format. Children can arrange some part of nearly any topical report into a true/false, question-and-answer, or guessing-game format.

In their "Magic School Bus" series, Joanna Cole and Bruce Degen have hit on an ideal format for conveying information. For example, in *The Magic School Bus Inside the Earth*, children take a field trip through the earth's crust; illustrations feature conversation balloons, both serious and comic, in which they discuss what they are seeing. Text advances the story while sidebars of the children's three-hole notebook reports fill readers in on "The Earth's Crust by John" or "What Is Soil by Florrie." Third graders who had been to a city trash-burning power plant created a mural of their trip using this field-trip format.

Children should be exposed to many examples of close-ups, labeled line drawings, processes

✳ Book Making ✳

① Plan your story and illustrations carefully in a "dummy" or practice book. Decide what size your book should be. Then cut paper for pages that is twice the width and the same height as the size you want. Cut half as many pieces as pages you need. Remember to allow for the title pages. Cut two pieces of the same or another color or kind of paper for the end papers. Fold the paper to form pages, placing the end papers on the outside. Complete your pages so that they are just the way you want them!

② Fold the completed pages evenly and either hand or machine stitch up the center.

③ Place the open pages on the material that you will use for the cover. Cut the material to a size approximately two inches larger on all sides than the open pages. Press the fabric flat with the iron.

④ Cut two pieces of cardboard, each just slightly larger than a single book page. These will form the support for the cover.

⑤ Cut four large pieces of Dry Mounting Tissue. Make two pieces the size of the cardboard and two pieces the size of a single page. Also, cut several small strips of Dry Mounting Tissue approximately 2"x ½".

⑥ Place the cover material on a flat surface face down. Position the Dry Mounting Tissue (cardboard size) on the material. Now place the cardboard pieces on top. Leave a space between the cardboard pieces to allow for the pages and for the book to open and close.

⑦ With an iron, set on low, carefully press the cardboard. This will mount the material to the cardboard.

⑧ Place the small pieces of Dry Mounting Tissue between the cardboard and the material and use the iron again to adhere the two. Begin with the corners. Then fold the top, bottom and sides until your book cover is completed!

⑨ Place the two remaining pieces of Dry Mounting Tissue on the cardboard side of the book cover. Position the sewn pages in the middle. Press the first and last pages down to form end papers. Use the iron to mount the pages to the cover.

Bookbinding directions written by Marilyn Parker, Columbus School for Girls, Ohio.

🐛 🐛 🐛

explained in box-and-arrow arrangements or time lines, and picture captions in such visually stunning books as the "Eyewitness" series titles on *Amazing Birds* or *Amazing Poisonous Animals* by Alexandra Parson. Peter Spier's *Tin Lizzie* and Bernd Heinrich's *An Owl in the House: A Naturalist's Diary* are two examples of treatment of a life cycle, the first of a car and the second of an owl. Children could recast studies of objects or animals in these formats.

Photo essays are wonderful ways to capture children's progress through a project. In *The Secretive Timber Rattlesnake* Bianca Lavies docu-ments the behaviors of this snake with magnificent photographs while informative captions and paragraphs further inform the reader. Ron and Nancy Goor's *Insect Metamorphosis: From Egg to Adult* portrays the stages of insect development. Children who are creating a play from a folktale, making stuffed paper figures for a puppet show, or raising chicks in the classroom could develop a photo essay of the process and the finished product or end point as a way of remembering it.

Teachers who encourage children to notice format and form in nonfiction and use it in their own reports do much to help children become literate.

Understanding the conventions by which information is conveyed, whether it is maps, time lines, charts, photographs, captions, surveys, or graphs, is a part of any literate person's skills.

Making Books

Nothing motivates children to write as much as the opportunity to create, bind, and illustrate a book of their own. Teachers need to learn how to bind books themselves before attempting to teach children. Materials for bookbinding should be made constantly available so that children can make books as the need arises. Most bookmaking materials can be readily purchased, but parents may contribute leftover fabric pieces for book covers to ease classroom budgets.

Since bookbinding involves time and some expense, it should be reserved for the "publication" of carefully planned, written, and illustrated books. Children should look at the way beautiful books are made, the various media used, the carefully designed endpapers or title pages, the placement of the words, and so forth, before they complete their own work. Marbleized paper or colored paper may be bound into the book as endpapers or children may stamp their own repeated patterns to symbolize the story. Many children enjoy planning dedications and jacket copy for their books as well. As children create their own books, they learn much about the care and design that have gone into the books they read.

Before binding a book, children can be encouraged to sketch a "dummy" or practice book. There, illustrations are roughed out and lines are drawn where text will be written or typed. In *Her Book* by Janet Wolf, the book's dummy is incorporated into the final product as endpapers, and children may wish to compare Wolf's dummy with the more detailed final illustrations as they work on their own books. Aliki's *How a Book Is Made* gives children an excellent overview of the creation and publication of a children's book. *How to Make Pop-Ups* by Joan Irvine suggests ways children can incorporate three-dimensional artwork into their books.

Materials for bookmaking include paper for pages, paper for endpapers, a threaded needle, cover material (such as cotton fabric, wallpaper, or Contac paper), and cardboard. In addition, an iron and dry-mount tissue (available from photographic supply houses) or white glue and water are needed.

EVALUATION AND ASSESSMENT

Assessment and evaluation of children's growth in any area of learning must be consistent with the goals and purposes of the program. As teachers move toward literature-based reading programs that use real books, it makes little sense to evaluate children with tests that are geared to basal readers and hours of workbook practice of filling in blanks, multiple choice, and short-answer questions. What these end-of-the-unit tests evaluate is such a narrow part of the whole process we know as reading that the essential character of one child's reading is lost. Timed multiple-choice tests following the reading of short paragraphs hardly define what a child has learned as a result of all he or she encounters in the course of reading many books. Information gained by these tests does little to help the classroom teacher plan programs that lead students to become more satisfied, more widely adept readers. Evaluation of children's reading should begin with some knowledge of where individual children are starting; observation and evidence of the child's understandings and abilities as revealed by discussion, classroom interactions, solicited and unsolicited responses to books; and evidence of changes, or growth, in that child's knowledge, appreciation, understandings, and abilities in reading. Needless to say, this method of assessment demands that a teacher constantly sharpen observational skills, develop some means of record keeping, and be able to recognize important signs of insight and growth in the learners he or she teaches.

Determining Children's Literacy Background

Begin where children are. This maxim applies to literature as well as any other area. In planning a literature program, a staff or teacher must first consider what the children's previous experiences with literature have been. Has the child been fortunate enough to have come from a home where reading is valued, where there are many books? Has a child been read to regularly? Or is school the child's first introduction to books? What have previous teachers read aloud to these children? What common experiences, such as author or illustrator studies or thematic groupings in literature, have these children had?

STUDENT INTERVIEWS

Teachers should consider beginning the year with an informal interview with each child. Here are some possible questions:

> What are your favorite stories?
> What kinds of stories do you like?
> Who reads with you at home? When?
> Do you have some favorite authors or
> illustrators? Who?
> How do you feel about reading?
> Why do people read and write?
> Are there any TV programs you always
> watch? What are they?
> When do you usually watch TV?

Teachers can develop brief questionnaires and fill them in as they talk with a child or they can tape children's conversations, which frees them to follow up on some of the child's answers.

Older children could meet in groups and discuss some of their favorite books, authors and illustrators, TV programs, and afterschool activities. These discussions could also be taped as sources for the teacher. The point of these initial interviews is to determine where children are in their literary habits and understandings.

Appreciation for literature seems to be developmental. If children have not had the opportunity to laugh at the antics of *Harry the Dirty Dog* by Gene Zion when they are 5 or 6, they need the experience at 7 or 8. If they have not met "Mother Goose" before they come to school, then early primary grades need to supply this cornerstone of literature. We need research on the sequential stages of appreciating literature, but we have some evidence to show that children must go through the "picture storybook stage," the "nonsense verse stage," even the "series book stage" if they are to become active, involved readers. Knowing where to start, then, is the value of finding what children's exposure to literature has been.

ASSESSING CHILDREN'S READING ABILITIES

One of a teacher's concerns when changing from a basal-driven reading program to one using trade books is, How will I know if children are learning the skills of reading? By learning how to give a variety of informal tests, teachers can learn more about children's reading abilities than they ever learned from standardized tests or publishers' tests.

Concepts of Print Test

Marie Clay developed a simple "concepts of print"[26] test that can be done with any trade book or with the specially developed little books, *Sand* and *Stones*.[27] The child is given a book to read with the teacher, who observes such book handling behaviors as: Does the child know where to begin to read? Does he understand the directionality of print? Does she show a knowledge of one-to-one correspondence of words the teacher reads aloud with words on the page? This takes very little time but does tell the teacher what the young child already knows about book handling and reading print.

Text Approximations

Another easy method for determining young children's growing ability as emergent readers is to ask them to "read" or pretend to read a picture storybook. The teacher reads an unfamiliar story to a child three times (usually over three consecutive days). Each time the child is then invited to "read" the story while the teacher tapes the retelling. The tapes are then transcribed and the child's approximations are compared with the actual text. At first, the child usually tells the story almost entirely from the pictures. By the third retelling, he or she will be using some of the words in the text and including more of the story's details. This is time consuming but it alerts a teacher to the way a

---

[26]See Marie Clay, *The Early Detection of Reading Difficulties*, 3rd ed. (Portsmouth, N.H.: Heinemann, 1985).
[27]Marie Clay, *Sand* and *Stones: Concepts About Print.* (Portsmouth, N.H.: Heinemann, n.d.).

child learns "book language." Kindergarten and first-grade teachers will see the value of giving children many opportunities to pretend to read big books or to read with a partner as a way of strengthening their sense of how stories work.

Running Record

Marie Clay also devised the *running record,*[28] which is a way of recording a child's reading of a text including his self-corrections, omissions, substitutions, accuracy, and error rate. This is a most useful technique for primary teachers to record easily how well a child is reading, what strategies he is using when he encounters new words, his strengths, and the areas where he needs help. All primary teachers in New Zealand know how to give a running record. This, of course, frees them to use any book with a child.

Reading Recovery[29] teachers record their children's reading with a running record every day. In

[28]See Marie Clay, *The Early Detection of Reading Difficulties.*
[29]For an overview of this program, see Gay Su Pinnell, Mary D. Fried, and Rose Mary Estice, "Reading Recovery: Learning How to Make a Difference," *The Reading Teacher,* vol. 43, no. 4 (January 1990), pp. 282–295.

A teacher listens attentively as a first grader reads "The Three Billy Goats Gruff." She is taking a running record of his oral reading.

Columbus Public Schools, Columbus, Ohio. Connie Compton, teacher.

🐛 🐛 🐛

this country there are workshops on how to give, record, and analyze a running record. Often, a reading recovery teacher will train other primary teachers on a staff. Usually a teacher can learn to give a running record in two 3-hour workshops.

Modified Miscue Analysis

The *miscue analysis*[30] was originally developed by Kenneth Goodman in the same year Marie Clay produced the *running record.* The *modified miscue analysis*[31] was further developed by Yetta Goodman and others in an effort to make it easier for teachers to administer. A miscue analysis, like a running record, enables a teacher to gain insight into the child's reading strategies and determine if she is using all three cuing systems: graphic, syntactic, and semantic cues. Again it takes time to learn how to give a miscue analysis, but it is well worth the effort. A running record is best used with first and second graders; a miscue analysis is very useful for third-grade children and up. Both approaches help a teacher to see into the reading process the child is using and can be applied to any piece of text. Both are more congruent with the instruction of reading using real books than the usual standardized texts or end-of-the-unit tests of the basals. And both approaches sharpen a teacher's observational powers.

Record Keeping

As a school year begins, it is important to have some record-keeping systems already in place that are simple and consume as little completion time as possible. In this way, information from the very first days of school may be compared as a child progresses, and the teacher will be better able to plan future curriculum.

ONGOING OBSERVATIONS

One of the best kinds of assessment of children's growth are the notes teachers write as they

[30]Kenneth Goodman, ed., *Miscue Analysis: Applications to Reading Instruction* (Urbana, Ill.: Eric Clearing House, 1973).
[31]Yetta Goodman, Dorothy Watson, and Carolyn Burke, *Reading Miscue Inventory: Alternative Procedures* (New York: Richard C. Owen, 1987).

observe children reading. Many teachers keep a tablet of Post-it notes or sheets of gummed labels on their desk or in other parts of the room where reading is likely to occur. As they observe something significant about a child, they can quickly jot it down. Later, the piece of paper can be transferred to a notebook under the child's name or into the child's individual folder. For example, two 7-year-olds loved Patricia Thomas's *"Stand Back," Said the Elephant, "I'm Going to Sneeze!"* Their teacher asked them if it reminded them of another book. Kelly immediately remembered *The Big Sneeze* by Ruth Brown. The children had made comparison charts of variants of folktales, so the teacher suggested that they might want to compare these two books. She gave them a pad of Post-it notes and a large sheet of paper. Then she stood back to see how the girls would proceed. This is the teacher's observation of how they worked together:

April 6

Cindy and Kelly decided to compare *The Big Sneeze* with *Stand Back Said the Elephant.* Kelly took charge and made two categories:

Alike/Different

BIG SNEEZE—sneeze
STAND BACK—sneeze   Poetry

As I watched them, C. said quietly, "You know, we need more sections to describe them." "Like what?" said K. C. replied, "Well, one is just the story of a sneeze while the other one is how a mouse stopped the sneeze but then the elephant laughed and it was a disaster. *Its plot is more complicated.*" The girls changed their categories to Story; Characters; Kind of writing; and Funny things that happened.

The teacher's record shows that while Kelly was quick to begin, Cindy's more thoughtful comments helped to shape the comparison.

A kindergarten teacher recorded when Jamie wrote his first complete sentence. Another teacher recorded a child's written definition of a story as "a mindfull of life." A fifth-grade teacher recorded one girl's generalizations about the many animal stories she had read during the year. A sixth-grade teacher noted the first time one boy uncharacteristically read for twenty minutes without looking up from his book.

Each day becomes more exciting as the teacher looks for and records typical moments and peak experiences in a child's reading life. These anecdotes make parent conferences rich with positive comments and evidence of growth that the parent recognizes as real. Each observation should be dated so that a teacher can see the ongoing growth of a student over the course of the school year.

FOLDERS

Most teachers want children to keep their work together. In a classroom where the room is divided into work areas, generally each child has a writing folder or a work folder, and perhaps a reading log or response journal (see Chapter 12). Since teachers look at and respond to these, they must be easily accessible to both children and the teacher. Clearly designated boxes, shelves, or bookcases should be reserved for whatever record-keeping folders the classroom encompasses.

ASSESSMENT PORTFOLIOS

At designated times in the year, teachers may ask children to go through their writing and art folders to select their best examples to include in their assessment portfolio. A portfolio of this sort is a year-long collection of a child's work that may be used in various ways by the teacher and child. A child can select from a month of writings the one that should go in the file, for instance. A teacher might honor a child's work by suggesting that it would be a fine addition to her special portfolio. If a student has worked cooperatively with another child to produce a research report, for example, copies can be made and placed in each child's portfolio. Photographs as well as written work might be included in the collection. As teachers and children confer about the work in the portfolio, the teacher can ask each child why he or she chose this work and record the child's reasons on a Post-it note. Together they can build criteria for what constitutes good work. In this way, children know what is expected of them because they have helped to establish the standards.

The assessment portfolio belongs to the child. If he leaves the school, he should be allowed to take it with him. It goes home with him at the end of the year. In the meantime, however, it should be shared with his parents at conference time at least twice during the year. Parents and teachers who compare a child's work in the fall with his work in the winter will see their child's progress in a way that no grades on a paper can record. If teachers must give grades, at least they have the evidence (in the portfolio as well as in other records) to show parents what that grade is based on. Children might also include a list of their reading choices for the year.

Some schools maintain permanent records of a child's work which accompany that child through elementary school. This folder of photocopied work comprises a wonderful record that children are proud to note when, as sixth graders, they compare their primary writing samples with ones done later in school.

Conferences

STUDENT CONFERENCES

Talking with individual children in a conference takes time. Yet in them children frequently reveal their growing edges. Teachers will want to have frequent conferences with children about their reading. It helps if a child brings her reading log or response journal and a current book she is reading to such a conference. Teachers can chat with a child about patterns in her reading selections as evidenced by the log. They can recommend another book that fits the pattern, or suggest a sequel or another book by the child's favorite author. They may ask the child to read aloud from his current SSR book or from a title his small group is reading together. It is helpful to remember that a book conversation with a child may be simply a recounting of plot. Teachers can assist children's thinking by asking such questions as "Could there be any other bridges in Katherine Paterson's *Bridge to Terabithia?*" "Now that you've read three books by Gary Paulsen, how could you recognize one he wrote even if you couldn't see the author and title?" "Since you've read so many mysteries, can you say what makes a book a good mystery?"

Teachers like to have frequent conferences with children about their reading.

Mission School, Redlands Public Schools, Redlands, California. Myrian Trementozzi, teacher.

In many classrooms, children never have a chance to talk alone with the teacher except in disciplinary situations. Conferences can be exceptionally rewarding to both participants.

PARENT CONFERENCES

Most schools establish time for parent conferences several times a year. Then teachers share the work the child has accomplished or is presently working on. Emphasis should always be placed on what the child knows and is learning. For example, parents of young children who are using developmental spelling may be concerned that words are incorrectly spelled. By reading what the child has written and pointing out what she knows about letters and sounds, a teacher can help a parent appreciate what is taking place in the child's learning processes. A kindergarten child drew a detailed picture of "Rapunzel" in her tower with the witch and bats flying around. On the opposite page she wrote:

RPNZL
RPNZL
LT DN
U HR.

This is easy to read and the parent can be assured that all emergent writers begin with consonant sounds. The teacher can even share Marie Clay's book *What Did I Write?*[32] to show other patterns emergent writers develop on their way to becoming experienced writers. Older children's writing and projects can be shared with an emphasis on the message of the writing as well as mechanics. By comparing pieces of work written in September with those written in later months, parents can see a child's growing competency with all aspects of writing. Parents want to see their children succeed. Conferences that emphasize and document growth with writing samples, research and art projects, examples of the kinds of books a child selects, and what the child chooses to notice about those books are very satisfying to both parents and teachers.

Evaluating Children's Literary Understandings

Evaluation of a child's understandings must be seen in light of developmental patterns, as we discussed in Chapter 2. In addition, the teacher must consider a child's understandings as revealed in discussion with the group, in creating products such as murals or imaginary diaries discussed previously, and in some linear sort of way. What did the child start with? What does she know now? What will the child remember long after this moment has passed?

Though the following list of understandings is by no means exhaustive, it may suggest how teachers might look at what children know following a study, for example, of the books of Ezra Jack Keats. Do they notice that

- Many books feature a character named Peter. Other characters overlap, too.
- Stories are set in the city, in apartment buildings, in the street.
- Illustrations are often collage, using materials, newspaper, wallpaper, marbleized paper, and some paint.

[32]Marie M. Clay, *What Did I Write?* (Portsmouth, N.H.: Heinemann, 1975).

- There are some ideas here. "Giving up things that you've outgrown is part of growing up" from *Peter's Chair;* "There are many things to do outside when it snows, but you can't save snowballs!" from *The Snowy Day.*

In addition, would children be able to pick out a Keats illustration from ones by Vera B. Williams or Pat Hutchins? Would they remember Keats's name? Insights such as these would not be easily revealed in a multiple-choice test. But, as children discussed their choices for materials they used in making a picture "Like Ezra Jack Keats did," a teacher would see what children had noticed and remembered. When children went to the media center, a teacher might observe whether they asked the librarian for Keats's books by title, or by author. Later a teacher might hear a child say about another book, "That's just like *Peter's Chair.* She gave her little sister something she had outgrown."

Third graders who studied folktales might be expected to recognize

- Some common tales.
- Typical characters and settings.
- Typical traits of characters.
- That there are formal beginnings, endings, refrains, and other characteristics of folktale language.
- Basic themes such as "Good is always rewarded" or "Little but honest wins over big," although they may not be able to state them succinctly.
- That popular tales such as "Cinderella" exist in many versions and variants.
- Some commonly recurring patterns, or motifs, such as magical objects, trickery, or wishes are in many tales.

Later in fourth or fifth grade, when they hear such tales as Sid Fleischman's *The Whipping Boy* or Mollie Hunter's *The Mermaid Summer,* can they recognize the folktale elements in these more complex tales?

After older children have read Caroline MacDonald's *The Lake at the End of the World* or Robert C. O'Brien's *Z for Zachariah* and studied some of the informational books from the

Stewards of the Earth web (see Chapter 12), can they extrapolate a logical future for the world based on their knowledge? Those who predict the world's ecological death could debate their viewpoint with those who predict a continuation of life either on earth or on another planet. Again, the teacher would be looking for the facts on which the children based their imagined futures.

Children's products also reveal understandings and growth. Did the "story map" of "The Gingerbread Boy" include all the important inci-

dents? Could the child maintain Amos's point of view in his diary from *Amos & Boris* by William Steig. Did the child's version of *The Way to Start a Day* suggest a sensitivity to Byrd Baylor's use and arrangement of words? How did the student's two-part diorama reflect the contrasting settings of seashore and prairie in Patricia MacLachlan's *Sarah, Plain and Tall?* What teachers choose to evaluate depends on what they are hoping to have children understand after reading a book or pursuing a thematic study. It is helpful to list

GUIDELINES

Evaluating Growth of Children

1. Does the child love one book, many books, reading in general?
2. Does the child become easily involved or easily distracted in reading a book?
3. Does the child predict, question, and confirm his way through a book?
4. Does the child prefer one genre, author, or illustrator over others? Is she aware of her preference? Can she recognize characteristics of genre, author, or illustrator?
5. Is the child a flexible reader who reads easily in several genres, who reads often and quickly?
6. Can the child select books that satisfy him? Is he open to suggestions from other readers?
7. What kinds of understanding and awareness do the child's products reveal?
8. Does the child visualize, identify with, become involved with, or understand the motives of characters?
9. Does the child visualize settings?
10. What connections does the child make between a particular book and others by the same illustrator or author? Of the same genre? With the same theme? What patterns does she see?
11. What kind of thematic statements does the child make? Can he see a book title as a metaphor for a larger idea?
12. What connections does the child make between literature and life?
13. What questions does the child's reading raise for her?
14. What literary elements such as prologues, unique dedications, interesting chapter titles, language use, or narrative style does the child notice?
15. How are these reading patterns changing as the school years progress?
16. Is the child voluntarily reading more at school? At home?
17. Is the child responding to a greater range and complexity of work?

some goals and understandings, based on the evaluative criteria for a particular genre or the particular strengths and content of the theme, before evaluating children's literary understandings.

Evaluating Children's Growth

Throughout this text, we have suggested that children's learning accrues, reorganizes, and reformulates based on their own growth both as children and as readers. While observation and evaluation are daily tasks for teachers, it is the long-range goal of creating enthusiastic, versatile, and skillful readers that should be the teacher's focus. By becoming documenters of children's encounters with literature, we become better observers. Observations of change, then, provide us with clues to a child's growth. The preceding guide, "Evaluating Growth of Children," provides a beginning set of questions to guide observations. The most important questions we can ask are often not the easiest to answer. What is a child building? What kind of framework is the child creating based on his experiences? How is this sense of literature changing?

Evaluating the Literature Program

It is as easy to identify a school in which literature is an integral part of the curriculum as it is to recognize a home where books are loved and valued. Since we have not recommended any body of content that all children must learn, but rather have suggested that each school should plan its own literature program to include certain categories of experiences with literature, the "Guidelines: Evaluating a Literature Program" could serve in two ways. First, it suggests to schools in the planning stages of a literature program what experiences ought to be offered to children. Second, it suggests evaluative criteria for assessing a literature program already in place in an elementary or middle school.

Developing Lifetime Readers

The first goal of all literature programs should be to develop lifetime readers. Since we know children are reading less and less in their free time at home, the school becomes their last best hope not only for learning how to read but also for *becoming readers*. Everything we do with books in schools should be measured against these criteria: Will this help children enjoy books? Will this help children become lifetime readers?

We know that children's reading for pleasure drops off when they are faced with added homework and demands of middle school and high school. But if children have learned to love reading before that time, they will continue to read and increase their reading once they leave college. If they have not discovered the joys of reading before high school, they probably will never do so.

One 12-year-old wrote to her former fifth-grade teacher two years after moving away to tell her of a wonderful book she had just read. Here is her letter:

Dear Mrs. Woolard:

I just finished the book *A Ring of Endless Light* and I was so excited about it that I just had to write and tell you about it. (It's by Madeleine L'Engle.) She writes with such description that sometimes the book made me smile, and when the characters were hurt or sad, I was also. On page 308 I wanted to scream along with the characters.

This is by far the *best* book I have ever read. I discovered it at just the right time; it made me enjoy life more. The book really made me think about life, death, happiness, sadness, self-pity, and what kind of person I want to be. If you have not read this book, I suggest you do. Here are some of my favorite passages from the book (she quotes several). I have a lot more passages that I like but these two were my favorites. I have no other news, bye, Love,

Amber[33]

There is no doubt that Amber will be a lifetime reader, discovering just the right book at "just the right time." And because all readers want to share their love of a fine book, Amber will continue to do this. Here, she chose to share her reactions with her former fifth-grade teacher, who loves books and shared her enthusiasm with her students.

[33]Written to Linda Woolard, Miller Elementary School, Newark, Ohio. Reproduced with permission of Linda Woolard and Amber Bewernitz.

GUIDELINES

Evaluating a Literature Program

Availability of Books and Other Media

1. Is there a school library media center in each elementary school building? Does it meet American Library Association standards for books and other media?
2. Is there a professionally trained librarian and adequate support staff in each building?
3. Does every classroom contain several hundred paperbacks and a changing collection of hardbacks?
4. Are reference books easily accessible to each classroom?
5. May children purchase books in a school-run paperback bookstore?
6. Do teachers encourage children to order books through various school book clubs?
7. May children take books home?
8. Are children made aware of the programs of the public library?

Time for Literature

9. Do all children have time to read books of their own choosing every day?
10. Do all teachers read to the children once or twice a day?
11. Do children have time to discuss their books with an interested adult or with other children every day?
12. Are children allowed time to interpret books through art, drama, music, or writing?
13. Do children seem attentive and involved as they listen to stories? Do they ask to have favorites reread?
14. Is literature a part of all areas, across the curriculum?

Motivating Interest

15. Do teachers show their enthusiasm for books by sharing new ones with children, reading parts of their favorite ones, discussing them, and so on?
16. Do classroom and library displays call attention to particular books?
17. Are children encouraged to set up book displays in the media center, the halls, and their classrooms?
18. Does the media specialist plan special events—such as story hours, book talks, sharing films, working with book clubs?
19. Do teachers and librarians work with parents to stimulate children's reading?
20. Are special bibliographies prepared by the librarians or groups of children on topics of special interest—such as mysteries, animal stories, science fiction, fantasy, and so on?
21. Are opportunities planned for contacts with authors and illustrators to kindle interest and enthusiasm for reading?

GUIDELINES

Balance in the Curriculum

22. Do teachers and librarians try to introduce children to a wide variety of genres and to different authors when reading aloud?
23. Do teachers share poetry as frequently as prose?
24. Do children read both fiction and nonfiction?
25. Are children exposed to new books and contemporary poems as frequently as some of the old favorites of both prose and poetry?
26. Do children have a balance of wide reading experiences with small-group, in-depth discussion of books?

Evaluating Growth of Children

27. Do children keep reading logs or records of their free reading?
28. Do older students (grade three and up) keep a response journal of their reading?
29. Do teachers record examples of children's growth and understanding of literature as revealed in their play, talk, art, or writing?
30. Do students and teachers together create an assessment portfolio with samples of children's best work?
31. Are children allowed to respond to books in a variety of ways (art, drama, writing), rather than by required book reports?
32. Is depth of understanding emphasized, rather than the number of books read?
33. Are children responding to a greater range and complexity of work?
34. What percentage of the children can be described as active readers? Has this percentage increased?
35. Are some children beginning to see literature as a source of life-long pleasure?

Evaluating the Professional Growth of Teachers

36. Are teachers increasing their knowledge of children's literature?
37. What percentage of the staff has taken a course in children's literature in the past five years?
38. Are some staff meetings devoted to ways of improving the use of literature in the curriculum?
39. Do teachers attend professional meetings that feature programs on children's literature?
40. Are in-service programs in literature made available on a regular basis?
41. Are in-service programs, such as administering the running record or the miscue analysis, given regularly?

GUIDELINES

42. Are such professional journals as *The New Advocate, The Horn Book Magazine, Book Links,* and *School Library Journal* available to teachers and librarians?
43. Are professional books on children's literature available?
44. Have the teachers and librarians had a share in planning their literature programs?
45. Do teachers feel responsible not only for teaching children to read but also for helping children find joy in reading?

A fourth-grade girl chose to reflect on her reading for a 4–H speech contest. Here is the speech she delivered:

> I know what you're thinking. You're thinking: Uh-oh, another fourth grader about to give another dull speech about another stupid subject that's so boring that you won't be able to stay awake for another five minutes.
>
> And, ordinarily, that's what happens. And I'm a pretty ordinary kid. I'm in fourth grade; I have blond hair. I weigh about 68 pounds; I'm about four and a half feet tall. I have a hamster and two hermit crabs that I'm crazy about and I have a brother I'm not so crazy about. But am I ordinary? You decide while you listen to some of the experiences I've had.
>
> For instance, one time I moved to the beach because my dad was fired. My sisters and I found out that our cousin had a boyfriend her parents didn't know about. My mom and dad were going through some hard times. I found out that my mom was going to have a baby. But, in the end, it turned out all right. Am I ordinary?
>
> Another experience I had was when I moved into a boxcar with three other kids to hide from our grandfather. We found stuff to cook with and eat on in a junk pile. The oldest kid in our group got a job. After living like this for awhile, we met our grandfather and found out that he was actually very nice. Am I ordinary?
>
> Another time I got a plastic Indian from my best friend and a cupboard from my brother. That night I put my Indian in the cupboard and the next morning I heard rapping sounds coming from the cupboard. It was the Indian! The cupboard had turned the Indian into a real human being! I found out that the cupboard turned any plastic object into the real thing. I turned a few other objects real. Do I still sound ordinary?
>
> How would an ordinary kid like me have these experiences? Easy . . . I read. I love to read. I had these experiences in the books *The Jellyfish Season* [Hahn], *The Boxcar Children* [Warner], and *The Indian in the Cupboard* [Banks]. You're probably thinking, she just read them. But when I'm sitting in front of the fire with my dog on my lap and reading those books, I really am having those experiences. So I guess you were right. I am a pretty ordinary kid, but reading gives me extraordinary experiences. And I suggest it to you, if you are tired of being ordinary.

Susan Komoroske, grade 4
George Mason Elementary School
Alexandria City Public Schools, Virginia
Susan Steinberg, teacher

It lies within the power of every teacher and librarian to give children a rich experience with literature, to share our enthusiasms for fine books, and to develop readers like Amber and Susan who will find a lifetime of pleasure in the reading of good books.

SUGGESTED LEARNING EXPERIENCES

1. Select a book or poem and extend it through one of the activities suggested in this chapter. Work alone or with others. Bring your finished product to class and suggest what value this activity might have for children. What seem to be the advantages of working with others? Of working alone

2. Write something to go with your activity in question 1. Mount and display your work and writing. What value would this have for children? What other types of writing could you have done after your activity was completed?

3. Write your own version of one of the ideas in "Writing from Books." What observations can you make about your own writing processes? How does this inform your teaching?

4. Ask at least five children to keep a log of titles and authors of books they have read in a month. What do you observe? What does this suggest to you about these children? About next steps as a teacher?

5. Give a literature inventory to a group of children and draw some conclusions about their previous exposure to literature. Plan what you think might be a rich literature program for them.

6. In a small group, choose a book and list scenes or opportunities for drama—interviews, debates, imaginary conversations, and so forth. Which possibilities seem to have the greatest potential for depth? Why?

7. Try an activity suggested in this chapter with children. Evaluate the children's understandings and your role in their learning. What next steps might you take?

8. Working in a small group, choose a chapter book or a picture book and suggest a variety of activities that would extend children's understanding and appreciation of the book. Be prepared to explain how each activity might extend children's thinking or enjoyment.

9. Using the "Guide for Evaluating a Literature Program," visit an elementary school and evaluate its program. Certain members of the class could be responsible for finding the answers to different sections of the guide. Combine your findings in a report and make recommendations concerning the literature program of that school.

RELATED READINGS

1. Bauer, Caroline Feller. *Read for the Fun of It: Active Programming with Books for Children,* illustrated by L. G. Bredeson. New York: H. W. Wilson, 1992.
    A lively book that encourages activities which promote joy in reading. The author offers advice on reading aloud and ideas for programs, puppetry, and games. She provides many lists of books on such special topics as dogs, stones, dinosaurs, and trees.

2. *Book Links.* American Library Association, 50 East Huron Street, Chicago, IL 60611
    Published six times a year and edited by Barbara Elleman, this invaluable magazine features insider looks at how authors and illustrators work, extended and annotated bibliographies dealing with a particular theme, book strategies, and classroom connections. Essential to a school library media center's teacher resources.

3. Cullinan, Bernice E., ed. *Children's Literature in the Reading Program.* Newark, N.J.: International Reading Association, 1987.
    Articles by various authors discuss aspects of school reading programs that incorporate children's literature. Numerous boxed teaching ideas are succinct, practical, and classroom tested.

4. Griffiths, Clyve. *Books You Can Count On: Linking Mathematics and Literature.* Portsmouth, N.H.: Heinemann, 1988.
    First published in Australia, this book provides many links with mathematical thinking without distorting the essence of a book. One chapter is devoted to activities based on individual books; others are devoted to counting books and activities based on measuring, classifying, and spatial relationships.

5. Johnson, Terry D., and Daphne Louis. *Literacy Through Literature*. Portsmouth, N.H.: Heinemann, 1987.

   The first chapter provides underlying assumptions about the importance of literature in literacy; the remainder of the book gives practical suggestions on how to make story maps, literary letters, literary sociograms, and newspapers. Drama, readers' theater, and mime are also included.

6. McCaslin, Nellie. *Creative Drama in the Classroom*, 5th ed. New York: Longman, 1990.

   A well-known drama specialist provides both the theory and practical help teachers need to initiate a drama program. She includes many suggestions for dramatizing stories and poems, a long section on puppets, and a new one on masks and their importance in drama. A fine revision of a respected book.

7. Moss, Joy. *Focus on Literature: A Context for Literacy Learning*. Katonah, N.Y.: Richard C. Owen, 1990.

   Using twelve focuses such as "Baba Yaga Tales," "Horse Tales," or a novel, Moss shows how teachers may help children see patterns among books and relate literature to life. Theory, a narrative of events, and children's dialogue are blended in this helpful book.

8. Raines, Shirley C., and Robert J. Canady. *Story Stretchers*. Mt. Ranier, Md.: Gryphon House, 1989.

   Activities (discussion, sand table, dress-up corner, cooking, etc.) suitable for preschool through the early primary grades are suggested for ninety different recent and classic picture books.

9. Routman, Regie. *Invitations: Changing as Teachers and Learners K–12*. Portsmouth, N.H.: Heinemann, 1991.

   An extensive compendium of ways to organize and manage a whole-language, literature-based reading and writing program. Journal writing, planning guides, teaching strategies, mini-lessons, evaluation, publishing, and a host of other topics are discussed and illuminated with classroom examples. Helpful bibliographies, both of children's books and of professional references, further extend teachers' thinking.

10. Swartz, Larry. *Dramathemes: A Practical Guide for Teaching Drama*. Portsmouth, N.H.: Heinemann, 1988.

    A Canadian teacher shares many practical suggestions for drama based on thematic exploration of children's literature. The book includes such drama suggestions for using nursery rhymes or Chris Van Allsburg's *The Mysteries of Harris Burdick* and improvising from Deborah Nourse Lattimore's Aztec myth, *The Flame of Peace*.

11. Tierney, Robert, Mark A. Carter, and Laura E. Desai. *Portfolio Assessment in the Reading-Writing Classroom*. Norwood, Mass.: Christopher-Gordon, 1991.

    A lucid and thorough discussion of the theory and use of portfolios of children's work in the classroom. Examples using elementary and high school students' portfolios, self-assessment by students, and the use of portfolios in parent conferences are included.

12. Watson-Ellam, Linda. *Start with a Story: Literature and Learning in Your Classroom*. Portsmouth, N.H.: Heinemann, 1991.

    Written by a Canadian professor who works extensively with teachers, this useful book contains strategies and activities to help make literature come alive in the classroom with drama, music, art, writing, and bookmaking.

13. *The WEB*, Ohio State University, Martha L. King Center for Language, Literature and Reading, Rm. 200 Ramseyer Hall, 29 West Woodruff, Columbus, OH 43210.

    Three yearly issues review books and suggest ways they can be used in the classroom. Each issue features a curriculum web of books and teaching suggestions for a particular topic such as "Dinosaurs and Digs" or "The Wild West," single books, a single author, or a particular theme. Issues alternate focus between primary and older elementary classrooms.

REFERENCES

Aardema, Verna. *Borreguita and the Coyote*, illustrated by Petra Mathers. Knopf, 1991.
_____. *Why Mosquitoes Buzz in People's Ears*, illustrated by Leo and Diane Dillon. Dial, 1975.
Ackerman, Karen. *Araminta's Paint Box*, illustrated by Betsy Lewin. Atheneum, 1990.
Ahlberg, Janet, and Allan Ahlberg. *The Jolly Postman; Or Other People's Letters*. Little, Brown, 1986.
Aiken, Joan. *The Moon's Revenge*, illustrated by Alan Lee. Knopf, 1987.
Albert, Burton. *Where Does the Trail Lead?*, illustrated by Brian Pinkney. Simon & Schuster, 1991.
Alexander, Lloyd. *The Book of Three*. Holt, 1964.
_____. *The Remarkable Journey of Prince Jen*. Dutton, 1991.
Aliki. *Go Tell Aunt Rhody*. Macmillan, 1986.
_____. *How a Book Is Made*. Crowell, 1986.
_____. *Hush, Little Baby*. Prentice-Hall, 1968.
Anderson, Yvonne. *How to Make Your Own Animated Movies and Videotapes*. Little, Brown, 1991.
Arkhurst, Joyce. *The Adventures of Spider: West African Folk Tales*, illustrated by Jerry Pinkney. Little, Brown, 1964.
Arnosky, Jim. *A Kettle of Hawks and Other Wildlife Groups*. Lothrop, 1990.
Arthur, Alex. *Shell*, photographs by Andreas Einsiedel. Knopf, 1989.
Babbitt, Natalie. *Tuck Everlasting*. Farrar, 1975.
Baker, Jeannie. *Window*. Greenwillow, 1991.
Bang, Molly. *The Paper Crane*. Greenwillow, 1985.
Banks, Lynne Reid. *The Indian in the Cupboard*, illustrated by Brock Cole. Doubleday, 1985.
Bauer, Marion Dane. *On My Honor*. Houghton Mifflin, 1986.
Baylor, Byrd. *Everybody Needs a Rock*, illustrated by Peter Parnall. Scribner, 1974.
_____. *I'm in Charge of Celebrations*, illustrated by Peter Parnall. Scribner, 1986.
_____. *The Way to Start a Day*, illustrated by Peter Parnall. Scribner, 1978.
_____. *Your Own Best Secret Place*, illustrated by Peter Parnall. Scribner, 1979.
Bennett, Jill. *Noisy Poems*, illustrated by Nick Sharratt. Oxford, 1987.
Birdseye, Tom. *Airmail to the Moon*, illustrated by Stephen Gammell. Holiday, 1988.
Blos, Joan. *Martin's Hats*, illustrated by Marc Simont. Morrow, 1984.
Blume, Judy. *Are You There, God? It's Me, Margaret*. Bradbury, 1970.
Bonners, Susan. *Panda*. Delacorte, 1978.
Brown, Marcia. *Stone Soup*. Scribner, 1947.
Brown, Margaret Wise. *The Important Book*, illustrated by Leonard Weisgard. Harper, 1949.
Brown, Ruth. *The Big Sneeze*. Lothrop, 1985.
Burton, Virginia Lee. *The Little House*. Houghton Mifflin, 1942.
Butler, Stephen. *Henny Penny*. Tambourine, 1991.
Byars, Betsy. *The Pinballs*. Harper, 1977.
Carle, Eric. *The Very Busy Spider*. Philomel, 1984.
_____. *The Very Hungry Caterpillar*. Putnam, 1989 (1969).
_____. *The Very Quiet Cricket*. Philomel, 1990.
Caseley, Judith. *Dear Annie*. Greenwillow, 1991.
Cauley, Lorinda Bryan. *Old Macdonald Had a Farm*. Putnam, 1989.
Chase, Edith. *The New Baby Calf*, illustrated by Barbara Reid. Scholastic, 1986.
Chaucer, Geoffrey. *Chanticleer and the Fox*, illustrated by Barbara Cooney. Crowell, 1982 (1958).
Cleary, Beverly. *Dear Mr. Henshaw*. Morrow, 1983.
_____. *The Mouse and the Motorcycle*, illustrated by Louis Darling. Morrow, 1965.
_____. *Ramona and Her Father*, illustrated by Alan Tiegreen. Morrow, 1977.
Cleaver, Vera, and Bill Cleaver. *Where the Lilies Bloom*. Harper, 1969.
Coerr, Eleanor. *Sadako and the Thousand Paper Cranes*, illustrated by Ronald Himler. Putnam, 1977.
Cole, Babette. *Prince Cinders*. Putnam, 1987.
Cole, Joanna. *It's Too Noisy!*, illustrated by Kate Duke. Crowell, 1989.
_____. *The Magic School Bus Inside the Earth*, illustrated by Bruce Degen. Scholastic, 1987.
Cooney, Barbara. *The Little Juggler*. Hastings, 1961.
Cormier, Robert. *The Chocolate War*. Pantheon, 1974.
Crews, Donald. *Freight Train*. Greenwillow, 1978.
_____. *Light*. Greenwillow, 1981.
Darling, Benjamin. *Valerie and the Silver Pear*, illustrated by Dan Lane. Four Winds, 1992.

de Paola, Tomie. *Big Anthony and the Magic Ring*. Harcourt, 1979.

_____. *The Comic Adventures of Old Mother Hubbard and Her Dog*. Harcourt, 1981.

_____. *Pancakes for Breakfast*. Harcourt, 1978.

_____. *The Popcorn Book*. Holiday, 1978.

De Regniers, Beatrice Schenk. *May I Bring A Friend?*, illustrated by Beni Montresor. Atheneum, 1964.

Dorros, Arthur. *Abuela*, illustrated by Elisa Kleven. Dutton, 1991.

Ehlert, Lois. *Feathers for Lunch*. Harcourt, 1990.

Emberley, Ed. *Ed Emberley's Great Thumbprint Drawing Book*. Little, Brown, 1977.

Feelings, Muriel. *Moja Means One: A Swahili Counting Book*, illustrated by Tom Feelings. Dial, 1971.

Ferris, Helen, compiler. *Favorite Poems Old and New*, illustrated by Leonard Weisgard. Doubleday, 1957.

Fisher, Leonard Everett. *Pyramid of the Sun-Pyramid of the Moon*. Macmillan, 1988.

Fleischman, Paul. *Shadow Play*, illustrated by Eric Beddows. Harper, 1990.

Fleischman, Sid. *The Midnight Horse*, illustrated by Peter Sis. Greenwillow, 1990.

_____. *The Whipping Boy*, illustrated by Peter Sis. Greenwillow, 1986.

Florian, Doug. *A Beach Day*. Greenwillow, 1990.

Fox, Mem. *Koala Lou*, illustrated by Pamela Lofts. Harcourt, 1989.

Fritz, Jean. *And Then What Happened, Paul Revere?*, illustrated by Margot Tomes. Putnam, 1973.

_____. *The Cabin Faced West*. Putnam, 1958.

Galdone, Paul. *The Gingerbread Boy*. Clarion, 1975.

_____. *The Little Red Hen*. Houghton Mifflin, 1979 (1973).

_____. *The Three Wishes*. McGraw-Hill, 1961.

George, Jean Craighead. *My Side of the Mountain*. Dutton, 1988 (1959).

_____. *The Talking Earth*. Harper, 1983.

_____. *The Wild, Wild Cookbook*, illustrated by Walter Kessell. Crowell, 1982.

Gerstein, Mordicai. *Roll Over!* Crown, 1984.

Gibbons, Gail. *Beacons of Light: Lighthouse*. Morrow, 1990.

Glubok, Shirley. *The Art of Africa*. Harper, 1965.

Goor, Ron, and Nancy Goor. *Insect Metamorphosis: From Egg to Adult*. Atheneum, 1990.

Grahame, Kenneth. *The Reluctant Dragon*, illustrated by Ernest Shepard. Holiday, 1953 (1938).

Greenblat, Rodney A. *Uncle Wizzmo's New Used Car*. Harper, 1990.

Greene, Karen. *Once upon a Recipe*. New Hope Press, 1987.

Grifalconi, Ann. *Osa's Pride*. Little, Brown, 1990.

_____. *The Village of Round and Square Houses*. Little, Brown, 1986.

Grimm Brothers. *The Devil with Three Golden Hairs*, illustrated by Nonny Hogrogian. Knopf, 1983.

_____. *The Glass Mountain*, illustrated by Nonny Hogrogian. Knopf, 1985.

_____. *Hansel and Gretel*, illustrated by Anthony Browne. Knopf, 1988 (1981).

Hadithi, Mwenye. *Tricky Tortoise*, illustrated by Adrienne Kennaway. Little, Brown, 1988.

Hahn, Mary Downing. *The Jellyfish Season*. Clarion, 1985.

_____. *Wait Till Helen Comes*. Houghton Mifflin, 1986.

Hale, Sara Josepha. *Mary Had a Little Lamb*, illustrated by Tomie de Paola. Holiday, 1984.

Haley, Gail. *A Story, a Story*. Macmillan, 1970.

Hall, Donald. *Ox-cart Man*, illustrated by Barbara Cooney. Viking, 1979.

Heinrich, Bernd. *An Owl in the House: A Naturalist's Diary*, adapted by Alice Calaprice. Joy Street, 1990.

Helfman, Harry. *Making Your Own Movies*. Morrow, 1970.

Hoban, Russell. *Bread and Jam for Frances*, illustrated by Lillian Hoban. Harper, 1974.

Hoberman, Mary Ann. *A House Is a House for Me*, illustrated by Betty Fraser. Penguin, 1982.

Hodges, Margaret. *Saint George and the Dragon*, illustrated by Trina Schart Hyman. Little, Brown, 1984.

_____. *The Wave*, illustrated by Blair Lent. Houghton Mifflin, 1964.

Hogrogian, Nonny. *One Fine Day*. Macmillan, 1971.

Hooks, William H. *The Ballad of Belle Dorcas*, illustrated by Brian Pinkney. Knopf, 1990.

Hunt, Jonathan. *Illuminations*. Bradbury, 1989.

Hunter, Mollie. *The Mermaid Summer*. Harper, 1988.

_____. *The Third Eye*. Harper, 1979.

Hutchins, Pat. *Rosie's Walk*. Macmillan, 1968.

_____. *The Surprise Party*. Macmillan, 1969.

Irvine, Joan. *How to Make Pop-ups*, illustrated by Barbara Reid. Morrow, 1987.

Jacques, Brian. *Redwall*, illustrated by Gary Chalk. Philomel, 1986.

James, Betsy. *The Dream Stair,* illustrated by Richard Jesse Watson. Harper, 1990.

Jones, Carol. *Old Macdonald Had a Farm*. Houghton Mifflin, 1989.

Jones, Rebecca C. *Down at the Bottom of the Deep Dark Sea*, illustrated by Virginia Wright-Frierson. Bradbury, 1991.

Joyce, William. *George Shrinks*. Harper, 1985.

Keats, Ezra Jack. *Peter's Chair*, Harper, 1967.

———. *The Snowy Day*. Viking, 1962.

Kellogg, Steven. *The Mysterious Tadpole*. Dial, 1977.

Kent, Jack. *The Fat Cat: A Danish Folktale*. Scholastic, 1972.

Key, Alexander. *The Forgotten Door*. Scholastic, 1986 (1965).

Kipling, Rudyard. *The Elephant's Child*, illustrated by Lorinda Bryan Cauley. Harcourt, 1988.

Kline, Robin. *Hating Alison Ashley*. Penguin, 1987.

Kline, Suzy. *Orp Goes to the Hoop*. Putnam, 1991.

Kovalski, Maryann. *The Wheels on the Bus*. Little, Brown, 1987.

Kuskin, Karla. *Dogs & Dragons, Trees & Dreams*. Harper, 1980.

Langstaff, John. *Oh, a-Hunting We Will Go*, illustrated by Nancy Winslow Parker. McElderry, 1974.

———. *Over in the Meadow*, illustrated by Feodor Rojankovsky. Harcourt, 1957.

Lattimore, Deborah Nourse. *The Flame of Peace: A Tale of the Aztecs*. Harper, 1987.

Lavies, Bianca. *The Secretive Timber Rattlesnake*. Dutton, 1990.

Leaf, Margaret. *Eyes of the Dragon*, illustrated by Ed Young. Lothrop, 1987.

Le Guin, Ursula K. *A Wizard of Earthsea*, illustrated by Ruth Robbins. Parnassus, 1968.

L'Engle, Madeleine. *A Ring of Endless Light*. Farrar, 1980.

———. *A Wrinkle in Time*. Farrar, 1962.

Lent, Blair. *John Tabor's Ride*. Little, Brown, 1966.

Levine, Ellen. *If You Lived at the Time of the Great San Francisco Earthquake*, illustrated by Richard Williams. Scholastic, 1987.

Lewin, Hugh. *Jafta*, illustrated by Lisa Kopper. Carolrhoda, 1983.

Lewis, C. S. *The Lion, the Witch and the Wardrobe*, illustrated by Pauline Baynes. Macmillan, 1968.

Lewis, Richard. *Dreams*, illustrated by Ezra Jack Keats. Macmillan, 1974.

———. *In a Spring Garden*, illustrated by Ezra Jack Keats. Dial, 1978.

Lionni, Leo. *Alexander and the Wind-up Mouse*. Pantheon, 1969.

———. *The Biggest House in the World*. Pantheon, 1968.

———. *Frederick*. Pantheon, 1966.

———. *Little Blue and Little Yellow*. Astor-Honor, 1959.

———. *Swimmy*. Pantheon, 1963.

Lindbergh, Reeve. *Johnny Appleseed*, illustrated by Kathy Jakobsen. Little, Brown, 1990.

Lobel, Arnold. *Fables*. Harper, 1980.

———. *Frog and Toad Are Friends*. Harper, 1970.

———. *Frog and Toad Together*. Harper, 1972.

———. *The Book of Pigericks*. Harper, 1983.

———. *Uncle Elephant*. Harper, 1981.

Lowry, Lois. *Anastasia Krupnik*. Houghton Mifflin, 1981.

Lyon, George Ella. *Come a Tide*, illustrated by Stephen Gammell. Orchard, 1990.

McDermott, Gerald. *Anansi the Spider: A Tale from the Ashanti*. Henry Holt, 1972.

MacDonald, Caroline. *The Lake at the End of the World*. Dial, 1989.

MacDonald, Kate. *The Anne of Green Gables Cookbook*, illustrated by Barbara DiLella. Oxford, 1987.

McDonald, Megan. *Is This a House for a Hermit Crab?*, illustrated by S. D. Schindler. Orchard, 1990.

MacGregor, Carol. *The Fairy Tale Cookbook*, illustrated by Debby L. Carter. Macmillan, 1982.

MacLachlan, Patricia. *Sarah, Plain and Tall*. Harper, 1985.

McMillan, Bruce. *One Sun: A Book of Terse Verse*. Holiday, 1990.

McPhail, David. *Pig Pig Grows Up*. Dutton, 1980.

Mahy, Margaret. *The Great White Man-Eating Shark*, illustrated by Jonathan Allen. Dial, 1990.

Marshall, James. *Goldilocks and the Three Bears*. Dial, 1988.

———. *Red Riding Hood*. Dial, 1987.

Martin, Bill, Jr., and John Archambault. *The Ghost-Eye Tree*, illustrated by Ted Rand. Holt, 1985.

Marzollo, Jean. *Pretend You're a Cat*, illustrated by Jerry Pinkney. Dial, 1990.

Merrill, Jean. *The Pushcart War*. Addison-Wesley, 1964.

Morgan, Pierr. *The Turnip*. Philomel, 1990.

Myers, Bernice. *Sidney Rella and the Glass Sneaker*. Macmillan, 1985.

Myers, Walter Dean. *The Mouse Rap*. Harper, 1990.

Naylor, Phyllis Reynolds. *The Agony of Alice*. Atheneum, 1985.

_____. *Shiloh*. Atheneum, 1991.

Ness, Evaline. *Sam, Bangs and Moonshine*. Holt, 1966.

Neville, Emily Cheney. *The China Year*. Harper, 1990.

Norton, Mary. *The Borrowers*, illustrated by Beth and Jo Krush. Harcourt, 1965.

Numeroff, Laura Joffe. *If You Give a Mouse a Cookie*, illustrated by Felicia Bond. Harper, 1985.

O'Brien, Robert C. *Mrs. Frisby and the Rats of NIMH*, illustrated by Zena Bernstein. Atheneum, 1971.

_____. *Z for Zachariah*. Atheneum, 1975.

Oppenheim, Joanne. *Have You Seen Birds?*, illustrated by Barbara Reid. Scholastic, 1986.

_____. *You Can't Catch Me!* illustrated by Andrew Shachat. Houghton Mifflin, 1986.

Park, Barbara. *Skinnybones*. Knopf, 1982.

Parson, Alexandra. *Amazing Birds*, illustrated by Jerry Young. Knopf, 1990.

_____. *Amazing Poisonous Animals*, illustrated by Jerry Young. Knopf, 1990.

Paterson, Katherine. *Bridge to Terabithia*, illustrated by Donna Diamond. Crowell, 1977.

_____. *The Great Gilly Hopkins*. Crowell, 1978.

_____. *Jacob Have I Loved*. Crowell, 1980.

_____. *Lyddie*. Dutton, 1991.

Pearson, Tracey Campbell. *Old Macdonald Had a Farm*. Dial, 1984.

Peek, Merle. *Mary Wore Her Red Dress and Henry Wore His Green Sneakers*. Ticknor & Fields, 1985.

_____. *Roll Over! A Counting Song*. Houghton Mifflin, 1981.

Perl, Lila. *Hunter's Stew and Hangtown Fry: What Pioneer America Ate and Why*, illustrated by Richard Cuffari. Houghton Mifflin, 1979.

_____. *Slumps, Grunts, and Snickerdoodles: What Colonial America Ate and Why*, illustrated by Richard Cuffari. Houghton Mifflin, 1979.

Perrault, Charles. *Cinderella*, illustrated by Roberto Innocenti. Creative Education, 1983.

Pinkwater, Daniel. *Borgel*. Macmillan, 1990.

_____. *The Hoboken Chicken Emergency*. Prentice-Hall, 1977.

_____. *Tooth-Gnasher Superflash*. Macmillan, 1990.

Polacco, Patricia. *Thunder Cake*. Philomel, 1990.

Potter, Beatrix. *The Tale of Peter Rabbit*. Frederick Warne, 1972 (1902).

Prelutsky, Jack. *Nightmares: Poems to Trouble Your Sleep*, illustrated by Arnold Lobel. Greenwillow, 1976.

_____, ed. *Read-Aloud Rhymes for the Very Young*, illustrated by Marc Simont. Knopf, 1986.

Purviance, Susan, and Marcia O'Shell. *Alphabet Annie Announces an All-American Album*, illustrated by Ruth Brunner-Strosser. Houghton Mifflin, 1988.

Quackenbush, Robert. *There'll Be a Hot Time in the Old Town Tonight*. Harper, 1988 (1974).

Reeder, Carolyn. *Shades of Gray*. Macmillan, 1989.

Reid, Barbara. *Playing with Plasticine*. Morrow, 1989.

Reid, Margarette S. *The Button Box*, illustrated by Sarah Chamberlain. Dutton, 1990.

Reinl, Edda. *The Three Little Pigs*. Picture Book, 1983.

Rice, Eve. *Peter's Pockets*, illustrated by Nancy Winslow Parker. Greenwillow, 1989.

Richter, Hans Peter. *Friedrich*. Holt, 1970.

Rockwell, Anne. *The Mother Goose Cookie-Candy Book*. Random, 1983.

Rockwell, Thomas. *How to Eat Fried Worms*. Franklin Watts, 1973.

Rohmer, Harriet. *Uncle Nacho's Hat*, illustrated by Veg Relsberg. Children's Book Press, 1989.

Rosen, Michael. *We're Going on a Bear Hunt*, illustrated by Helen Oxenbury. Macmillan, 1989.

Ross, Tony. *Jack and the Beanstalk*. Delacorte, 1980.

_____. *Stone Soup*. Dial, 1987.

Rounds, Glen. *Old Macdonald Had a Farm*. Holiday, 1989.

Roy, Ron. *Three Ducks Went Wandering*, illustrated by Paul Galdone. Houghton Mifflin, 1979.

Rylant, Cynthia. *Henry and Mudge in Puddle Trouble*, illustrated by Suçie Stevenson. Bradbury, 1987.

Sanders, Scott R. *Hear the Wind Blow: American Folk Songs Retold*, illustrated by Ponder Goembel. Bradbury, 1985.

Sattler, Helen Roney. *Recipes for Art and Craft Materials*, illustrated by Marti Shohet. Lothrop, 1987.

Scieszka, Jon. *The Frog Prince Continued*, illustrated by Steve Johnson. Viking, 1991.

_____. *The True Story of the 3 Little Pigs by A. Wolf*, illustrated by Lane Smith. Penguin, 1989.

Sendak, Maurice. *Chicken Soup with Rice*. Harper, 1962.

_____. *Where the Wild Things Are*. Harper, 1963.

Shulevitz, Uri. *Dawn*. Farrar, Straus, 1974.

Simon, Seymour. *Animal Fact/Animal Fable*, illustrated by Diane DeGroat. Crown, 1979.

Slobodkina, Esphyr. *Caps for Sale*. Harper, 1947.

Small, Ernest. *Baba Yaga*, illustrated by Blair Lent. Houghton Mifflin, 1966.

Snyder, Zilpha Keatley. *Libby on Wednesday*. Delacorte, 1990.

Spier, Peter. *The Erie Canal*. Doubleday, 1970.

_____. *The Star-Spangled Banner*. Doubleday, 1973.

_____. *Tin Lizzie*. Doubleday, 1978.

Spinelli, Jerry. *Maniac Magee*. Little, Brown, 1990.

Stanley, Diane, and Peter Vennema. *Shaka, King of the Zulus*, illustrated by Diane Stanley. Morrow, 1988.

Steig, William. *Abel's Island*. Farrar, 1976.

_____. *The Amazing Bone*. Farrar, 1976.

_____. *Amos & Boris*. Farrar, 1971.

Steptoe, John. *Mufaro's Beautiful Daughters: An African Tale*. Lothrop, 1987.

Stevens, Carla. *Trouble for Lucy*, illustrated by Ronald Himler. Clarion, 1979.

Tejima, Keizaburo. *Fox's Dream*. Putnam, 1987.

_____. *Owl Lake*. Putnam, 1987.

Terban, Marvin. *In a Pickle and Other Funny Idioms*, illustrated by Giulio Maestro. Clarion, 1983.

_____. *Mad as a Wet Hen and Other Funny Idioms*, illustrated by Giulio Maestro. Clarion, 1987.

_____. *Superdupers: Really Fun Real Words*, illustrated by Giulio Maestro. Clarion, 1989.

Thomas, Patricia. *"Stand Back," Said the Elephant, "I'm Going to Sneeze!"*, illustrated by Wallace Tripp. Lothrop, 1990.

Travers, P. L. *Mary Poppins*, illustrated by Mary Shepard. Harcourt, 1981.

Tunis, Edwin. *Colonial Living*. Harper, 1976.

Turkle, Brinton. *Do Not Open*. Dutton, 1981.

Uchida, Yoshiko. *Journey to Topaz*, illustrated by Donald Carrick. Creative Arts Books, 1985 (1971).

Van Allsburg, Chris. *Jumanji*. Houghton Mifflin, 1981.

_____. *The Mysteries of Harris Burdick*. Houghton Mifflin, 1984.

Viorst, Judith. *Alexander and the Terrible, Horrible, No Good, Very Bad Day*, illustrated by Ray Cruz. Atheneum, 1972.

Walker, Barbara. *The Little House Cookbook*, illustrated by Garth Williams. Harper, 1979.

Warner, Gertrude Chandler. *The Boxcar Children #1* Whitman, 1990 (1924).

Westcott, Nadine Bernard. *I Know an Old Lady Who Swallowed a Fly*. Little, Brown, 1980.

_____. *The Lady with the Alligator Purse*. Little, Brown, 1988.

_____. *Skip to My Lou*. Little, Brown, 1989.

_____. *There's a Hole in the Bucket*. Little, Brown, 1990.

Wickstrom, Sylvie Kantorovitz. *The Wheels on the Bus*. Crown, 1988.

Wilder, Laura Ingalls. *Farmer Boy*, illustrated by Garth Williams. Harper, 1973.

Wildsmith, Brian. *Birds*. Oxford, 1980.

Williams, Jay. *Everyone Knows What a Dragon Looks Like*, illustrated by Mercer Mayer. Macmillan, 1976.

Williams, Karen Lynn. *Galimoto*, illustrated by Catherine Stock, Lothrop, 1990.

Williams, Linda. *The Little Old Lady Who Was Not Afraid of Anything*, illustrated by Megan Lloyd. Harper, 1986.

Williams, Vera B. *Stringbean's Trip to the Shining Sea*, illustrated by Vera B. Williams and Jennifer Williams. Greenwillow, 1988.

Wilner, Isabel. *The Poetry Troupe*. Scribner, 1977.

Winter, Jonah. *Diego*, illustrated by Jeanette Winter. Knopf, 1991.

Wisniewski, David. *Elfwyn's Saga*. Lothrop, 1990.

Wolf, Janet. *Her Book*. Harper, 1982.

Wolff, Ashley. *The Bells of London*. Putnam, 1984.

_____. *A Year of Birds*. Putnam, 1984.

Xiong, Blia. *Nine-In-One Grr! Grr!*, adapted by Cathy Spagnoli, illustrated by Nancy Hom. Children's Book Press, 1989.

Yagawa, Sumiko. *The Crane Wife*, translated by Katherine Paterson, illustrated by Suekichi Akaba. Morrow, 1981.

Yashima, Taro. *Crow Boy*. Viking, 1955.

Yep, Laurence. *Dragonwings*. Harper, 1977.

Yolen, Jane. *Dove Isabeau*, illustrated by Dennis Nolan. Harcourt, 1979.

_____. *Owl Moon*, illustrated by John Schoenherr. Philomel, 1987.

_____. *Sleeping Ugly*, illustrated by Diane Stanley. Putnam, 1981.

Zemach, Harve. *The Judge*, illustrated by Margot Zemach. Farrar, 1969.

Zemach, Margot. *It Could Always Be Worse*. Farrar, 1977.

Zion, Gene. *Harry the Dirty Dog.* Harper, 1956.
Zolotow, Charlotte. *Say It!*, illustrated by James Stevenson. Greenwillow, 1980.
_____. *Someday*, illustrated by Arnold Lobel. Harper, 1965.

APPENDIX A

Children's Book Awards

The John Newbery Medal is named in honor of John Newbery, a British publisher and bookseller of the eighteenth century. He has frequently been called the father of children's literature, since he was the first to conceive the idea of publishing books expressly for children.

The award is presented each year to "the author of the most distinguished contribution to American literature for children." To be eligible for the award, the author must be an American citizen or a permanent resident of the United States. The selection of the winner is made by a committee of the Association for Library Service to Children (ALSC) of the American Library Association. There are now fifteen members on this committee. The winning author is presented with a bronze medal designed by René Paul Chambellan and donated by Frederick G. Melcher. The announcement is made in January. Later, at the summer conference of the American Library Association, a banquet is given in honor of the award winners.

The following list of books includes the award winners (capitalized and listed first) and the Honor Books for each year. The date on the left indicates the year in which the award was conferred. All books were necessarily published the preceding year.

1922   THE STORY OF MANKIND by Hendrik Van Loon. Boni & Liveright.
The Great Quest by Charles Boardman Hawes. Little, Brown.
Cedric the Forester by Bernard G. Marshall. Appleton.
The Old Tobacco Shop by William Bowen. Macmillan.
The Golden Fleece by Padraic Colum. Macmillan.
Windy Hill by Cornelia Meigs. Macmillan.

1923   THE VOYAGES OF DOCTOR DOLITTLE by Hugh Lofting. Stokes.
[No record of the runners-up.]

1924   THE DARK FRIGATE by Charles Boardman Hawes. Little, Brown.
[No record of the runners-up.]

1925   TALES FROM SILVER LANDS by Charles J. Finger. Illustrated by Paul Honoré. Doubleday.
Nicholas by Anne Carroll Moore. Putnam.
Dream Coach by Anne and Dillwyn Parrish. Macmillan.

1926   SHEN OF THE SEA by Arthur Bowie Chrisman. Illustrated by Else Hasselriis. Dutton.
The Voyagers by Padraic Colum. Macmillan.

1927   SMOKY, THE COWHORSE by Will James. Scribner.
[No record of the runners-up.]

1928   GAY NECK by Dhan Gopal Mukerji. Illustrated by Boris Artzybasheff. Dutton.
The Wonder-Smith and His Son by Ella Young. Longmans, Green.
Downright Dencey by Caroline Dale Snedeker. Doubleday.

1929   TRUMPETER OF KRAKOW by Eric P. Kelly. Illustrated by Angela Pruszynska. Macmillan.
The Pigtail of Ah Lee Ben Loo by John Bennett. Longmans, Green.
Millions of Cats by Wanda Gág. Coward-McCann.
The Boy Who Was by Grace T. Hallock. Dutton.
Clearing Weather by Cornelia Meigs. Little, Brown.
The Runaway Papoose by Grace P. Moon. Doubleday.
Tod of the Fens by Eleanor Whitney. Macmillan.

1930   HITTY, HER FIRST HUNDRED YEARS by Rachel Field. Illustrated by Dorothy P. Lathrop. Macmillan.
Pran of Albania by Elizabeth C. Miller. Doubleday.
The Jumping-Off Place by Marian Hurd McNeely. Longmans, Green.
A Daughter of the Seine by Jeanette Eaton. Harper.

1931   THE CAT WHO WENT TO HEAVEN by Elizabeth Coatsworth. Illustrated by Lynd Ward. Macmillan.
Floating Island by Anne Parrish. Harper.
The Dark Star of Itza by Alida Malkus. Harcourt.
Queer Person by Ralph Hubbard. Doubleday.
Mountains Are Free by Julia Davis Adams. Dutton.
Spice and the Devil's Cave by Agnes D. Hewes. Knopf.
Meggy McIntosh by Elizabeth Janet Gray. Doubleday.

1932   WATERLESS MOUNTAIN by Laura Adams Armer. Illustrated by Sidney Armer and the author. Longmans, Green.
The Fairy Circus by Dorothy Lathrop. Macmillan.
Calico Bush by Rachel Field. Macmillan.
Boy of the South Seas by Eunice Tietjens. Coward-McCann.
Out of the Flame by Eloise Lounsbery. Longmans, Green.
Jane's Island by Marjorie Hill Alee. Houghton Mifflin.
Truce of the Wolf by Mary Gould Davis. Harcourt.

1933   YOUNG FU OF THE UPPER YANGTZE by Elizabeth Foreman Lewis. Illustrated by Kurt Wiese. Winston.
Swift Rivers by Cornelia Meigs. Little.
The Railroad to Freedom by Hildegarde Swift. Harcourt.
Children of the Soil by Nora Burglon. Doubleday.

1934   INVINCIBLE LOUISA by Cornelia Meigs. Little, Brown.
Forgotten Daughter by Caroline Dale Snedeker. Doubleday.

Swords of Steel by Elsie Singmaster. Houghton Mifflin.
ABC Bunny by Wanda Gág. Coward McCann.
Winged Girl of Knossos by Erick Berry. Appleton.
New Land by Sarah L. Schmidt. McBride.
Apprentices of Florence by Anne Kyle. Houghton Mifflin.

1935 DOBRY by Monica Shannon. Illustrated by Atanas Katchamakoff. Viking.
The Pageant of Chinese History by Elizabeth Seeger. Longmans, Green.
Davy Crockett by Constance Rourke, Harcourt.
A Day on Skates by Hilda Van Stockum. Harper.

1936 CADDIE WOODLAWN by Carol Ryrie Brink. Illustrated by Kate Seredy. Macmillan.
Honk the Moose by Phil Stong. Dodd, Mead.
The Good Master by Kate Seredy. Viking.
Young Walter Scott Elizabeth Janet Gray. Viking.
All Sail Set by Armstrong Sperry. Winston.

1937 ROLLER SKATES by Ruth Sawyer. Illustrated by Valenti Angelo. Viking.
Phoebe Fairchild: Her Book by Lois Lenski. Stokes.
Whistler's Van by Idwal Jones. Viking.
The Golden Basket by Ludwig Bemelmans. Viking.
Winterbound by Margery Bianco. Viking.
Audubon by Constance Rourke. Harcourt.
The Codfish Musket by Agnes D. Hewes. Doubleday.

1938 THE WHITE STAG by Kate Seredy. Viking.
Bright Island by Mabel L. Robinson. Random House.
Pecos Bill by James Cloyd Bowman. Whitman.
On the Banks of Plum Creek by Laura Ingalls Wilder. Harper.

1939 THIMBLE SUMMER by Elizabeth Enright. Farrar & Rinehart.
Leader by Destiny by Jeanette Eaton. Harcourt.
Penn by Elizabeth Janet Gray. Viking.
Nino by Valenti Angelo. Viking.
"Hello, the Boat!" by Phyllis Crawford. Holt.
Mr. Popper's Penguins by Richard and Florence Atwater. Little, Brown.

1940 DANIEL BOONE by James H. Daugherty. Viking.
The Singing Tree by Kate Seredy. Viking.
Runner of the Mountain Tops by Mabel L. Robinson. Random House.
By the Shores of Silver Lake by Laura Ingalls Wilder. Harper.
Boy with a Pack by Stephen W. Meader. Harcourt.

1941 CALL IT COURAGE by Armstrong Sperry. Macmillan.
Blue Willow by Doris Gates. Viking.
Young Mac of Fort Vancouver by Mary Jane Carr. Crowell.
The Long Winter by Laura Ingalls Wilder. Harper.
Nansen by Anna Gertrude Hall. Viking.

1942 THE MATCHLOCK GUN by Walter D. Edmonds. Illustrated by Paul Lantz. Dodd, Mead.
Little Town on the Prairie by Laura Ingalls Wilder. Harper.
George Washington's World by Genevieve Foster. Scribner.
Indian Captive by Lois Lenski. Stokes.
Down Ryton Water by E. R. Gaggin. Viking.

1943 ADAM OF THE ROAD by Elizabeth Janet Gray. Illustrated by Robert Lawson. Viking.
The Middle Moffat by Eleanor Estes. Harcourt.
"Have You Seen Tom Thumb?" by Mabel Leigh Hunt. Stokes.

1944 JOHNNY TREMAIN by Esther Forbes. Illustrated by Lynd Ward. Houghton Mifflin.
These Happy Golden Years by Laura Ingalls Wilder. Harper.
Fog Magic by Julia L. Sauer. Viking.
Rufus M. by Eleanor Estes. Harcourt.
Mountain Born by Elizabeth Yates. Coward McCann.

1945 RABBIT HILL by Robert Lawson. Viking.
The Hundred Dresses by Eleanor Estes. Harcourt.
The Silver Pencil by Alice Dalgliesh. Scribner.
Abraham Lincoln's World by Genevieve Foster. Scribner.
Lone Journey by Jeanette Eaton. Harcourt.

1946 STRAWBERRY GIRL by Lois Lenski. Lippincott.
Justin Morgan Had a Horse by Marguerite Henry. Wilcox & Follett.
The Moved-Outers by Florence Crannell Means. Houghton Mifflin.
Bhimsa, the Dancing Bear by Christine Weston. Scribner.
New Found World by Katherine B. Shippen. Viking.

1947 MISS HICKORY by Carolyn Sherwin Bailey. Illustrated by Ruth Gannett. Viking.
The Wonderful Year by Nancy Barnes. Messner.
Big Tree by Mary Buff and Conrad Buff. Viking.
The Heavenly Tenants by William Maxwell. Harper.
The Avion My Uncle Flew by Cyrus Fisher. Appleton.
The Hidden Treasure of Glaston by Eleanore M. Jewett. Viking.

1948 THE TWENTY-ONE BALLOONS by William Pène du Bois. Viking.
Pancakes-Paris by Claire Huchet Bishop. Viking.
Li Lun, Lad of Courage by Carolyn Treffinger. Abingdon-Cokesbury.
The Quaint and Curious Quest of Johnny Longfoot by Catherine Besterman. Bobbs-Merrill.
The Cow-Tail Switch by Harold Courlander and George Herzog. Holt.
Misty of Chincoteague by Marguerite Henry. Rand McNally.

1949 KING OF THE WIND by Marguerite Henry. Illustrated by Wesley Dennis. Rand McNally.
Seabird by Holling Clancy Holling. Houghton Mifflin.
Daughter of the Mountains by Louise Rankin. Viking.
My Father's Dragon by Ruth S. Gannett. Random House.
Story of the Negro by Arna Bontemps. Knopf.

1950 THE DOOR IN THE WALL by Marguerite de Angeli. Doubleday.
Tree of Freedom by Rebecca Caudill. Viking.
Blue Cat of Castle Town by Catherine Coblentz. Longmans, Green.
Kildee House by Rutherford Montgomery. Doubleday.

George Washington by Genevieve Foster. Scribner.
Song of the Pines by Walter Havighurst and Marion Havighurst. Winston.

1951 AMOS FORTUNE, FREE MAN by Elizabeth Yates. Illustrated by Nora Unwin. Aladdin.
Better Known as Johnny Appleseed by Mabel Leigh Hunt. Lippincott.
Gandhi, Fighter without a Sword by Jeanette Eaton. Morrow.
Abraham Lincoln, Friend of the People by Clara I. Judson. Wilcox & Follett.
The Story of Appleby Capple by Anne Parrish. Harper.

1952 GINGER PYE by Eleanor Estes. Harcourt.
Americans before Columbus by Elizabeth Chesley Baity. Viking.
Minn of the Mississippi by Holling Clancy Holling. Houghton Mifflin.
The Defender by Nicholas Kalashnikoff. Scribner.
The Light at Tern Rock by Julia L. Sauer. Viking.
The Apple and the Arrow by Mary Buff. Houghton Mifflin.

1953 SECRET OF THE ANDES by Ann Nolan Clark. Illustrated by Jean Charlot. Viking.
Charlotte's Web by E. B. White. Harper.
Moccasin Trail by Eloise J. McGraw. Coward-McCann.
Red Sails for Capri by Ann Weil. Viking.
The Bears on Hemlock Mountain by Alice Dalgliesh. Scribner.
Birthdays of Freedom by Genevieve Foster. Scribner.

1954 AND NOW MIGUEL by Joseph Krumgold. Illustrated by Jean Charlot. Crowell.
All Alone by Clarie Huchet Bishop. Viking.
Shadrach by Meindert DeJong. Harper.
Hurry Home, Candy by Meindert DeJong. Harper.
Theodore Roosevelt, Fighting Patriot by Clara I. Judson. Follett.
Magic Maize by Mary Buff. Houghton Mifflin.

1955 THE WHEEL ON THE SCHOOL by Meindert DeJong. Illustrated by Maurice Sendak. Harper.
The Courage of Sarah Noble by Alice Dalgliesh. Scribner.
Banner in the Sky by James Ramsey Ullman. Lippincott.

1956 CARRY ON, MR. BOWDITCH by Jean Lee Latham. Houghton Mifflin.
The Golden Name Day by Jennie D. Lindquist. Harper.
The Secret River by Marjorie Kinnan Rawlings. Scribner.
Men, Microscopes and Living Things by Katherine B. Shippen. Viking.

1957 MIRACLES ON MAPLE HILL by Virginia Sorensen. Illustrated by Beth Krush and Joe Krush. Harcourt.
Old Yeller by Fred Gipson. Harper.
The House of Sixty Fathers by Meindert DeJong. Harper.
Mr. Justice Holmes by Clara I. Judson. Follett.
The Corn Grows Ripe by Dorothy Rhoads. Viking.
The Black Fox of Lorne by Marguerite de Angeli. Doubleday.

1958 RIFLES FOR WATIE by Harold Keith. Illustrated by Peter Burchard. Crowell.
The Horsecatcher by Mari Sandoz. Westminster.
Gone-away Lake by Elizabeth Enright. Harcourt.

The Great Wheel by Robert Lawson. Viking.
Tom Paine, Freedom's Apostle by Leo Gurko. Crowell.

1959 THE WITCH OF BLACKBIRD POND by Elizabeth George Speare. Houghton Mifflin.
The Family under the Bridge by Natalie S. Carlson. Harper.
Along Came a Dog by Meindert DeJong. Harper.
Chucaro by Francis Kalnay. Harcourt.
The Perilous Road by William O. Steele. Harcourt.

1960 ONION JOHN by Joseph Krumgold. Illustrated by Symeon Shimin. Crowell.
My Side of the Mountain by Jean George. Dutton.
America Is Born by Gerald Johnson. Morrow.
The Gammage Cup by Carol Kendall. Harcourt.

1961 ISLAND OF THE BLUE DOLPHINS by Scott O'Dell. Houghton Mifflin.
America Moves Forward by Gerald Johnson. Morrow.
Old Ramon by Jack Schaefer. Houghton Mifflin.
The Cricket in Times Square by George Selden. Farrar.

1962 THE BRONZE BOW by Elizabeth George Speare. Houghton Mifflin.
Frontier Living by Edwin Tunis. World Publishing.
The Golden Goblet by Eloise J. McGraw. Coward-McCann.
Belling the Tiger by Mary Stolz. Harper & Row.

1963 A WRINKLE IN TIME by Madeleine L'Engle. Farrar.
Thistle and Thyme by Sorche Nic Leodhas. Holt, Rinehart and Winston.
Men of Athens by Olivia Coolidge. Houghton Mifflin.

1964 IT'S LIKE THIS, CAT by Emily Neville. Illustrated by Emil Weiss, Harper & Row.
Rascal by Sterling North. Dutton.
The Loner by Ester Wier. McKay.

1965 SHADOW OF A BULL by Maia Wojciechowska. Illustrated by Alvin Smith. Atheneum.
Across Five Aprils by Irene Hunt. Follett.

1966 I, JUAN DE PAREJA by Elizabeth Borten de Treviño. Farrar, Straus.
The Black Cauldron by Lloyd Alexander. Holt, Rinehart and Winston.
The Animal Family by Randall Jarrell. Pantheon.
The Noonday Friends by Mary Stolz. Harper & Row.

1967 UP A ROAD SLOWLY by Irene Hunt. Follett.
The King's Fifth by Scott O'Dell. Houghton Mifflin.
Zlateh the Goat and Other Stories by Isaac Bashevis Singer. Harper & Row.
The Jazz Man by Mary Hays Weik. Atheneum.

1968 FROM THE MIXED-UP FILES OF MRS. BASIL E. FRANKWEILER by E. L. Konigsburg. Atheneum.
Jennifer, Hecate, Macbeth, William McKinley, and Me, Elizabeth by E. L. Konigsburg. Atheneum.
The Black Pearl by Scott O'Dell. Houghton Mifflin.
The Fearsome Inn by Isaac Bashevis Singer. Scribner.
The Egypt Game by Zilpha Keatley Snyder. Atheneum.

1969 THE HIGH KING by Lloyd Alexander. Holt, Rinehart and Winston.
To Be a Slave by Julius Lester. Dial.
When Shlemiel Went to Warsaw and Other Stories by Isaac Bashevis Singer. Farrar, Straus.

1970 SOUNDER by William H. Armstrong. Harper & Row.
Our Eddie by Sulamith Ish-Kishor. Pantheon.
The Many Ways of Seeing: An Introduction to the Pleasures of Art by Janet Gaylord Moore. World.
Journey Outside by Mary Q. Steele. Viking.

1971 SUMMER OF THE SWANS by Betsy Byars. Viking.
Kneeknock Rise by Natalie Babbitt. Farrar, Straus.
Enchantress from the Stars by Sylvia Louise Engdahl. Atheneum.
Sing Down the Moon by Scott O'Dell. Houghton Mifflin.

1972 MRS. FRISBY AND THE RATS OF NIMH by Robert C. O'Brien. Atheneum.
Incident at Hawk's Hill by Allan W. Eckert. Little, Brown.
The Planet of Junior Brown by Virginia Hamilton. Macmillan.
The Tombs of Atuan by Ursula K. LeGuin. Atheneum.
Annie and the Old One by Miska Miles. Atlantic-Little, Brown.
The Headless Cupid by Zilpha Keatley Snyder. Atheneum.

1973 JULIE OF THE WOLVES by Jean Craighead George. Harper & Row.
Frog and Toad Together by Arnold Lobel. Harper & Row.
The Upstairs Room by Johanna Reiss. Crowell.
The Witches of Worm by Zilpha Keatley Snyder. Atheneum.

1974 THE SLAVE DANCER by Paula Fox. Bradbury.
The Dark Is Rising by Susan Cooper. Atheneum.

1975 M. C. HIGGINS THE GREAT by Virginia Hamilton. Macmillan.
My Brother Sam Is Dead by James Collier and Christopher Collier. Four Winds.
Philip Hall Likes Me. I Reckon Maybe. by Bette Greene. Dial.
The Perilous Gard by Elizabeth Pope. Houghton Mifflin.
Figgs & Phantoms by Ellen Raskin. Dutton.

1976 THE GREY KING by Susan Cooper. Atheneum.
Dragonwings by Laurence Yep. Harper & Row.
The Hundred Penny Box by Sharon Mathis. Viking.

1977 ROLL OF THUNDER, HEAR MY CRY by Mildred D. Taylor. Dial.
Abel's Island by William Steig. Farrar, Straus.
A String in the Harp by Nancy Bond. Atheneum.

1978 BRIDGE TO TERABITHIA by Katherine Paterson. Crowell.
Anpao: An American Indian Odyssey by Jamake Highwater. Lippincott.
Ramona and Her Father by Beverly Cleary. Morrow.

1979 THE WESTING GAME by Ellen Raskin. Dutton.
The Great Gilly Hopkins by Katherine Paterson. Crowell.

1980 A GATHERING OF DAYS: A NEW ENGLAND GIRL'S JOURNAL, 1830–32 by Joan W. Blos. Scribner.
The Road from Home: The Story of an Armenian Girl by David Kherdian. Greenwillow.

1981 JACOB HAVE I LOVED by Katherine Paterson. Crowell.
The Fledgling by Jane Langton. Harper & Row.

Ring of Endless Light by Madeleine L'Engle. Farrar, Straus.

1982 A VISIT TO WILLIAM BLAKE'S INN: POEMS FOR INNOCENT AND EXPERIENCED TRAVELERS by Nancy Willard. Illustrated by Alice and Martin Provensen. Harcourt Brace Jovanovich.
Ramona Quimby, Age 8 by Beverly Cleary. Morrow.
Upon the Head of the Goat: A Childhood in Hungary, 1939–1944 by Aranka Siegal. Farrar, Straus.

1983 DICEY'S SONG by Cynthia Voigt. Atheneum.
The Blue Sword by Robin McKinley. Greenwillow.
Doctor De Soto by William Steig. Farrar, Straus.
Graven Images by Paul Fleischman. Harper & Row.
Homesick: My Own Story by Jean Fritz. Putnam.
Sweet Whispers, Brother Rush by Virginia Hamilton. Philomel.

1984 DEAR MR. HENSHAW by Beverly Cleary. Morrow.
The Wish-Giver by Bill Brittain. Harper & Row.
A Solitary Blue by Cynthia Voigt. Atheneum.
The Sign of the Beaver by Elizabeth George Speare. Houghton Mifflin.
Sugaring Time by Kathryn Lasky. Photographs by Christopher Knight. Macmillan.

1985 THE HERO AND THE CROWN by Robin McKinley. Greenwillow.
The Moves Make the Man by Bruce Brooks. Harper & Row.
One-Eyed Cat by Paula Fox. Bradbury.
Like Jake and Me by Mavis Jukes. Illustrated by Lloyd Bloom. Knopf.

1986 SARAH, PLAIN AND TALL by Patricia MacLachlan. Harper & Row.
Commodore Perry in the Land of the Shogun by Rhoda Blumberg. Lothrop.
Dogsong by Gary Paulsen. Bradbury.

1987 THE WHIPPING BOY by Sid Fleischman. Greenwillow.
A Fine White Dust by Cynthia Rylant. Bradbury.
On My Honor by Marion Dane Bauer. Clarion.
Volcano by Patricia Lauber. Bradbury.

1988 LINCOLN: A PHOTOBIOGRAPHY by Russell Freedman. Clarion.
After the Rain by Norma Fox Mazer. Morrow.
Hatchet by Gary Paulsen. Bradbury.

1989 JOYFUL NOISE: POEMS FOR TWO VOICES by Paul Fleischman. Harper & Row.
In the Beginning: Creation Stories from Around the World by Virginia Hamilton. Harcourt.
Scorpions by Walter Dean Myers. Harper & Row.

1990 NUMBER THE STARS by Lois Lowry. Houghton Mifflin.
Afternoon of the Elves by Janet Taylor Lisle. Orchard.
Shabanu: Daughter of the Wind by Suzanne Fisher Staples. Knopf.
The Winter Room by Gary Paulsen. Orchard.

1991 MANIAC MAGEE by Jerry Spinelli. Little, Brown.
The True Confessions of Charlotte Doyle by Avi. Orchard.

1992 SHILOH by Phyllis Reynolds Naylor. Atheneum.
Nothing but the Truth by Avi. Orchard.
The Wright Brothers by Russell Freedman. Holiday.

The Caldecott Medal is named in honor of Randolph Caldecott, a prominent English illustrator of children's books during the nineteenth century. This award is presented each year by an awards committee of the Association for Library Service to Children (ALSC) of The American Library Association. It is given to "the artist of the most distinguished American picture book for children." The following list of books includes the award winners and Honor Books for each year. If the illustrator's name is not cited, it means the author illustrated the book.

1938 ANIMALS OF THE BIBLE, A Picture Book. Text selected from the King James Bible by Helen Dean Fish. Illustrated by Dorothy O. Lathrop. Stokes.
Seven Simeons by Boris Artzybasheff. Viking.
Four and Twenty Blackbirds compiled by Helen Dean Fish. Illustrated by Robert Lawson. Stokes.

1939 MEI LI by Thomas Handforth. Doubleday.
The Forest Pool by Laura Adams Armer. Longmans, Green.
Wee Gillis by Munro Leaf. Illustrated by Robert Lawson. Viking.
Snow White and the Seven Dwarfs translated and illustrated by Wanda Gág. Coward-McCann.
Barkis by Clare Turlay Newberry. Harper.
Andy and the Lion by James Daugherty. Viking.

1940 ABRAHAM LINCOLN by Ingri d'Aulaire and Edgar Parin d'Aulaire. Doubleday.
Cock-a-Doodle-Doo by Berta Hader and Elmer Hader. Macmillan.
Madeline by Ludwig Bemelmans. Simon and Schuster.
The Ageless Story by Lauren Ford. Dodd, Mead.

1941 THEY WERE STRONG AND GOOD by Robert Lawson. Viking.
April's Kittens by Clare Turlay Newberry. Harper.

1942 MAKE WAY FOR DUCKLINGS by Robert McCloskey. Viking.
An American ABC by Maud Petersham and Miska Petersham. Macmillan.
In My Mother's House by Ann Nolan Clark. Illustrated by Velino Herrera. Viking.
Paddle-to-the-Sea by Holling Clancy Holling. Houghton Mifflin.
Nothing at All by Wanda Gág. Coward McCann.

1943 THE LITTLE HOUSE by Virginia Lee Burton. Houghton Mifflin.
Dash and Dart by Mary Buff and Conrad Buff. Viking.
Marshmallow by Clare Turlay Newberry. Harper.

1944 MANY MOONS by James Thurber. Illustrated by Louis Slobodkin. Harcourt.
Small Rain. Text arranged from the Bible by Jessie Orton Jones. Illustrated by Elizabeth Orton Jones. Viking.
Pierre Pidgeon by Lee Kingman. Illustrated by Arnold Edwin Bare. Houghton Mifflin.

Good-Luck Horse by Chih-Yi Chan. Illustrated by Plato Chan. Whittlesey.
Mighty Hunter by Berta Hader and Elmer Hader. Macmillan.
A Child's Good Night Book by Margaret Wise Brown. Illustrated by Jean Charlot. W. R. Scott.

1945 PRAYER FOR A CHILD by Rachel Field. Pictures by Elizabeth Orton Jones. Macmillan.
Mother Goose. Compiled and illustrated by Tasha Tudor. Oxford.
In the Forest by Marie Hall Ets. Viking.
Yonie Wondernose by Marguerite de Angeli. Doubleday.
The Christmas Anna Angel by Ruth Sawyer. Illustrated by Kate Seredy. Viking.

1946 THE ROOSTER CROWS by Maud Petersham and Miska Petersham. Macmillan.
Little Lost Lamb by Margaret Wise Brown. Illustrated by Leonard Weisgard. Doubleday.
Sing Mother Goose. Music by Opal Wheeler. Illustrated by Marjorie Torrey. Dutton.
My Mother Is the Most Beautiful Woman in the World by Becky Reyher. Illustrated by Ruth C. Gannett. Lothrop.
You Can Write Chinese by Kurt Wiese. Viking.

1947 THE LITTLE ISLAND by Golden MacDonald. Illustrated by Leonard Weisgard. Doubleday.
Rain Drop Splash by Alvin R. Tresselt. Illustrated by Leonard Weisgard. Lothrop.
Boats on the River by Marjorie Flack. Illustrated by Jay Hyde Barnum. Viking.
Timothy Turtle by Al Graham. Illustrated by Tony Palazzo. Robert Welch.
Pedro, Angel of Olvera Street by Leo Politi. Scribner.
Sing in Praise by Opal Wheeler. Illustrated by Marjorie Torrey. Dutton.

1948 WHITE SNOW, BRIGHT SNOW by Alvin Tresselt. Illustrated by Roger Duvoisin. Lothrop.
Stone Soup. Told and illustrated by Marcia Brown. Scribner.
McElligot's Pool by Theodor S. Geisel (Dr. Seuss). Random House.
Bambino the Clown by George Schreiber. Viking.
Roger and the Fox by Lavinia R. Davis. Illustrated by Hildegard Woodward. Doubleday.
Song of Robin Hood. Anne Malcolmson, ed. Illustrated by Virginia Lee Burton. Houghton Mifflin.

1949 THE BIG SNOW by Berta Hader and Elmer Hader. Macmillan.
Blueberries for Sal by Robert McCloskey. Viking.
All Around the Town by Phyllis McGinley. Illustrated by Helen Stone. Lippincott.
Juanita by Leo Politi. Scribner.
Fish in the Air by Kurt Wiese. Viking.

1950 SONG OF THE SWALLOWS by Leo Politi. Scribner.
America's Ethan Allen by Stewart Holbrook. Illustrated by Lynd Ward. Houghton Mifflin.
The Wild Birthday Cake by Lavinia R. Davis. Illustrated by Hildegard Woodward. Doubleday.

Happy Day by Ruth Krauss. Illustrated by Marc Simont. Harper.

Henry-Fisherman by Marcia Brown. Scribner.

Bartholomew and the Oobleck by Theodor S. Geisel (Dr. Seuss). Random House.

1951   THE EGG TREE by Katherine Milhous. Scribner.

Dick Whittington and His Cat told and illustrated by Marcia Brown. Scribner.

The Two Reds by Will (William Lipkind). Illustrated by Nicolas (Mordvinoff). Harcourt.

If I Ran the Zoo by Theodor S. Geisel (Dr. Seuss). Random House.

T-Bone the Baby-Sitter by Clare Turlay Newberry. Harper.

The Most Wonderful Doll in the World by Phyllis McGinley. Illustrated by Helen Stone. Lippincott.

1952   FINDERS KEEPERS by Will (William Lipkind). Illustrated by Nicolas (Mordvinoff). Harcourt.

Mr. T. W. Anthony Woo by Marie Hall Ets. Viking.

Skipper John's Cook by Marcia Brown. Scribner.

All Falling Down by Gene Zion. Illustrated by Margaret Bloy Graham. Harper.

Bear Party by William Pène du Bois. Viking.

Feather Mountain by Elizabeth Olds. Houghton Mifflin.

1953   THE BIGGEST BEAR by Lynd Ward. Houghton Mifflin.

Puss in Boots. Told and illustrated by Marcia Brown. Scribner.

One Morning in Maine by Robert McCloskey. Viking.

Ape in a Cape by Fritz Eichenberg. Harcourt.

The Storm Book by Charlotte Zolotow. Illustrated by Margaret Bloy Graham. Harper.

Five Little Monkeys by Juliet Kepes. Houghton Mifflin.

1954   MADELINE'S RESCUE by Ludwig Bemelmans. Viking.

Journey Cake, Ho! by Ruth Sawyer. Illustrated by Robert McCloskey. Viking.

When Will the World Be Mine? by Miriam Schlein. Illustrated by Jean Charlot. W. R. Scott.

The Steadfast Tin Soldier translated by M. R. James. Adapted from Hans Christian Andersen. Illustrated by Marcia Brown. Scribner.

A Very Special House by Ruth Krauss. Illustrated by Maurice Sendak. Harper.

Green Eyes by Abe Birnbaum. Capitol.

1955   CINDERELLA by Charles Perrault. Illustrated by Marcia Brown. Harper.

Book of Nursery and Mother Goose Rhymes. Compiled and illustrated by Marguerite de Angeli. Doubleday.

Wheel on the Chimney by Margaret Wise Brown. Illustrated by Tibor Gergely. Lippincott.

1956   FROG WENT A-COURTIN' by John Langstaff. Illustrated by Feodor Rojankovsky. Harcourt.

Play with Me by Marie Hall Ets. Viking.

Crow Boy by Taro Yashima. Viking.

1957   A TREE IS NICE by Janice May Udry. Illustrated by Marc Simont. Harper.

Mr. Penny's Race Horse by Marie Hall Ets. Viking.

1 Is One by Tasha Tudor. Oxford.

Anatole by Eve Titus. Illustrated by Paul Galdone. Whittlesey.

Gillespie and the Guards by Benjamin Elkin. Illustrated by James Daugherty. Viking.

Lion by William Pène du Bois. Viking.

1958   TIME OF WONDER by Robert McCloskey. Viking.

Fly High, Fly Low by Don Freeman. Viking.

Anatole and the Cat by Eve Titus. Illustrated by Paul Galdone. Whittlesey.

1959   CHANTICLEER AND THE FOX. Edited and illustrated by Barbara Cooney. Crowell.

The House That Jack Built by Antonio Frasconi. Crowell.

What Do You Say, Dear? by Sesyle Joslin. Illustrated by Maurice Sendak. W. R. Scott.

Umbrella by Taro Yashima. Viking.

1960   NINE DAYS TO CHRISTMAS by Marie Hall Ets and Aurora Labastida. Viking.

Houses from the Sea by Alice E. Goudey. Illustrated by Adrienne Adams. Scribner.

The Moon Jumpers by Janice May Udry. Illustrated by Maurice Sendak. Harper.

1961   BABOUSHKA AND THE THREE KINGS by Ruth Robbins. Illustrated by Nicolas Sidjakov. Parnassus.

Inch by Inch by Leo Lionni. Obolensky.

1962   ONCE A MOUSE by Marcia Brown. Scribner.

The Fox Went Out on a Chilly Night by Peter Spier. Doubleday.

Little Bear's Visit by Else Minarik. Illustrated by Maurice Sendak. Harper.

The Day We Saw the Sun Come Up by Alice Goudey. Illustrated by Adrienne Adams. Scribner.

1963   THE SNOWY DAY by Ezra Jack Keats. Viking.

The Sun Is a Golden Earring by Natalia Belting. Illustrated by Bernarda Bryson. Holt, Rinehart and Winston.

Mr. Rabbit and the Lovely Present by Charlotte Zolotow. Illustrated by Maurice Sendak. Harper & Row.

1964   WHERE THE WILD THINGS ARE by Maurice Sendak. Harper & Row.

Swimmy by Leo Lionni. Pantheon.

All in the Morning Early by Sorche Nic Leodhas. Illustrated by Evaline Ness. Holt, Rinehart and Winston.

Mother Goose and Nursery Rhymes by Philip Reed. Atheneum.

1965   MAY I BRING A FRIEND? by Beatrice Schenk de Regniers. Illustrated by Beni Montresor. Atheneum.

Rain Makes Applesauce by Julian Scheer. Illustrated by Marvin Bileck. Holiday.

The Wave by Margaret Hodges. Illustrated by Blair Lent. Houghton Mifflin.

A Pocketful of Cricket by Rebecca Caudill. Illustrated by Evaline Ness. Holt, Rinehart and Winston.

1966   ALWAYS ROOM FOR ONE MORE by Sorche Nic Leodhas. Illustrated by Nonny Hogrogian. Holt, Rinehart and Winston.

Hide and Seek Fog by Alvin Tresselt. Illustrated by Roger Duvoisin. Lothrop.

Just Me by Marie Hall Ets. Viking.

Tom Tit Tot. Joseph Jacobs, ed. Illustrated by Evaline Ness. Scribner.

1967 SAM, BANGS AND MOONSHINE by Evaline Ness. Holt, Rinehart and Winston.
One Wide River to Cross by Barbara Emberley. Illustrated by Ed Emberley. Prentice-Hall.

1968 DRUMMER HOFF by Barbara Emberley. Illustrated by Ed Emberley. Prentice-Hall.
Frederick by Leo Lionni. Pantheon.
Seashore Story by Taro Yashima. Viking.
The Emperor and the Kite by Jane Yolen. Illustrated by Ed Young. World Publishing.

1969 THE FOOL OF THE WORLD AND THE FLYING SHIP by Arthur Ransome. Illustrated by Uri Shulevitz. Farrar, Straus.
Why the Sun and the Moon Live in the Sky by Elphinstone Dayrell. Illustrated by Blair Lent. Houghton Mifflin.

1970 SYLVESTER AND THE MAGIC PEBBLE by William Steig. Windmill/Simon and Schuster.
Goggles by Ezra Jack Keats. Macmillan.
Alexander and the Wind-up Mouse by Leo Lionni. Pantheon.
Pop Corn and Ma Goodness by Edna Mitchell Preston. Illustrated by Robert Andrew Parker. Viking.
Thy Friend, Obadiah by Brinton Turkle. Viking.
The Judge by Harve Zemach. Illustrated by Margot Zemach. Farrar, Straus.

1971 A STORY, A STORY by Gail E. Haley, Atheneum.
The Angry Moon by William Sleator. Illustrated by Blair Lent. Atlantic-Little, Brown.
Frog and Toad Are Friends by Arnold Lobel. Harper & Row.
In the Night Kitchen by Maurice Sendak. Harper & Row.

1972 ONE FINE DAY by Nonny Hogrogian. Macmillan.
If All the Seas Were One Sea by Janina Domanska. Macmillan.
Moja Means One: Swahili Counting Book by Muriel Feelings. Illustrated by Tom Feelings. Dial.
Hildilid's Night by Cheli Duran Ryan. Illustrated by Arnold Lobel. Macmillan.

1973 THE FUNNY LITTLE WOMAN by Arlene Mosel. Illustrated by Blair Lent. Dutton.
Hosie's Alphabet by Hosea Baskin, Tobias Baskin, and Lisa Baskin. Illustrated by Leonard Baskin. Viking.
When Clay Sings by Byrd Baylor. Illustrated by Tom Bahti. Scribner.
Snow-White and the Seven Dwarfs by the Brothers Grimm, translated by Randall Jarrell. Illustrated by Nancy Ekholm Burkert. Farrar, Straus.
Anansi the Spider by Gerald McDermott. Holt, Rinehart and Winston.

1974 DUFFY AND THE DEVIL by Harve Zemach. Illustrated by Margot Zemach. Farrar, Straus.
The Three Jovial Huntsmen by Susan Jeffers. Bradbury.
Cathedral by David Macaulay. Houghton Mifflin.

1975 ARROW TO THE SUN. Adapted and illustrated by Gerald McDermott. Viking.
Jambo Means Hello: Swahili Alphabet Book by Muriel Feelings. Illustrated by Tom Feelings. Dial.

1976 WHY MOSQUITOES BUZZ IN PEOPLE'S EARS by Verna Aardema. Illustrated by Leo and Diane Dillon. Dial.

The Desert Is Theirs by Byrd Baylor. Illustrated by Peter Parnell. Scribner.
Strega Nona retold and illustrated by Tomie de Paola.

1977 ASHANTI TO ZULU: AFRICAN TRADITIONS by Margaret Musgrove. Illustrated by Leo and Diane Dillon. Dial.
The Amazing Bone by William Steig. Farrar, Straus.
The Contest by Nonny Hogrogian. Greenwillow.
Fish for Supper by M. B. Goffstein. Dial.
The Golem by Beverly Brodsky McDermott. Lippincott.
Hawk, I'm Your Brother by Byrd Baylor. Illustrated by Peter Parnall. Scribner.

1978 NOAH'S ARK by Peter Spier. Doubleday.
Castle by David Macaulay. Houghton Mifflin.
It Could Always Be Worse by Margot Zemach. Farrar, Straus.

1979 THE GIRL WHO LOVED WILD HORSES by Paul Goble. Bradbury.
Freight Train by Donald Crews. Greenwillow.
The Way to Start a Day by Byrd Baylor. llustrated by Peter Parnall. Scribner's.

1980 OX-CART MAN by Donald Hall. Illustrated by Barbara Cooney. Viking.
Ben's Trumpet by Rachel Isadora. Greenwillow.
The Treasure by Uri Shulevitz. Farrar Straus.
The Garden of Abdul Gasazi by Chris Van Allsburg. Houghton Mifflin.

1981 FABLES by Arnold Lobel. Harper & Row.
The Bremen-Town Musicians by Ilse Plume. Doubleday.
The Grey Lady and the Strawberry Snatcher by Molly Bang. Four Winds.
Mice Twice by Joseph Low. Atheneum.
Truck by Donald Crews. Greenwillow.

1982 JUMANJI by Chris Van Allsburg. Houghton Mifflin.
A Visit to William Blake's Inn: Poems for Innocent and Experienced Travelers by Nancy Willard. Illustrated by Alice and Martin Provensen. Harcourt Brace Jovanovich.
Where the Buffaloes Began by Olaf Baker. Illustrated by Stephen Gammell. Warne.
On Market Street by Arnold Lobel. Illustrated by Anita Lobel. Greenwillow.
Outside Over There by Maurice Sendak. Harper & Row.

1983 SHADOW by Blaise Cendrars. Illustrated by Marcia Brown. Scribner.
When I Was Young in the Mountains by Cynthia Rylant. Illustrated by Diane Goode. Dutton.
A Chair for My Mother by Vera B. Williams. Morrow.

1984 THE GLORIOUS FLIGHT: ACROSS THE CHANNEL WITH LOUIS BLERIOT, JULY 25, 1909 by Alice and Martin Provensen. Viking.
Ten, Nine, Eight by Molly Bang. Greenwillow.
Little Red Riding Hood by Trina Schart Hyman. Holiday.

1985 SAINT GEORGE AND THE DRAGON adapted by Margaret Hodges. Illustrated by Trina Schart Hyman. Little, Brown.
Hansel and Gretel by Rika Lesser. Illustrated by Paul O. Zelinsky. Dodd.
The Story of Jumping Mouse by John Steptoe. Lothrop.

Have You Seen My Duckling? by Nancy Tafuri. Greenwillow.

1986　POLAR EXPRESS by Chris Van Allsburg. Houghton Mifflin.
The Relatives Came by Cynthia Rylant. Illustrated by Stephen Gammell. Bradbury.
King Bidgood's in the Bathtub by Audrey Wood. Illustrated by Don Wood. Harcourt Brace Jovanovich.

1987　HEY AL by Arthur Yorinks. Illustrated by Richard Egielski. Farrar, Straus.
Alphabatics by Suse MacDonald. Bradbury.
Rumpelstiltskin by Paul O. Zelinsky. Dutton.
The Village of Round and Square Houses by Ann Grifalconi. Little, Brown.

1988　OWL MOON by Jane Yolen. Illustrated by John Schoenherr. Philomel.
Mufaro's Beautiful Daughters: An African Story. Adapted and illustrated by John Steptoe. Lothrop.

1989　SONG AND DANCE MAN by Karen Ackerman. Illustrated by Stephen Gammell. Knopf.
The Boy of the Three-Year Nap by Dianne Stanley. Illustrated by Allen Say. Houghton Mifflin.
Free Fall by David Wiesner. Lothrop.
Goldilocks and the Three Bears. Adapted and illustrated by James Marshall. Dial.
Mirandy and Brother Wind by Patricia McKissack. Illustrated by Jerry Pinkney. Knopf.

1990　LON PO PO: A RED RIDING HOOD STORY FROM CHINA. Adapted and illustrated by Ed Young. Philomel.
Bill Peet: An Autobiography by Bill Peet. Houghton Mifflin.
Color Zoo by Lois Ehlert. Lippincott.
Herschel and the Hanukkah Goblins by Eric Kimmel. Illustrated by Trina Schart Hyman. Holiday.
The Talking Eggs by Robert D. San Souci. Illustrated by Jerry Pinkney. Dial.

1991　BLACK AND WHITE by David Macaulay. Houghton Mifflin.
Puss in Boots by Charles Perrault. Translated by Malcolm Arthur. Illustrated by Fred Marcellino. Farrar, Straus.
"More More More," Said the Baby by Vera B. Williams. Greenwillow.

1992　TUESDAY by David Wiesner. Clarion.
Tar Beach by Faith Ringgold. Crown.

The Batchelder Award, established in 1966, is given by the Association of Library Service to Children (ALSC) of the American Library Association to the publisher of the most outstanding book of the year, first published in another country, and published in translation in the United States. In 1990, honor books were added to this award. The original country of publication is given in parentheses.

1968　THE LITTLE MAN by Erich Kastner, translated by James Kirkup, illustrated by Rick Schreiter. Knopf. (Germany)

1969　DON'T TAKE TEDDY by Babbis Friis-Baastad, translated by Lise Somme McKinnon. Scribner. (Norway)

1970　WILDCAT UNDER GLASS by Alki Zei, translated by Edward Fenton. Holt. (Greece)

1971　IN THE LAND OF UR by Hans Baumann, translated by Stella Humphries. Pantheon. (Germany)

1972　FRIEDRICH by Hans Peter Richter, translated by Edite Kroll. Holt. (Germany)

1973　PULGA by S. R. Van Iterson, translated by Alison and Alexander Gode. Morrow. (Netherlands)

1974　PETROS' WAR by Alki Zei, translated by Edward Fenton. Dutton. (Greece)

1975　AN OLD TALE CARVED OUT OF STONE by A. Linevsky, translated by Maria Polushkin. Crown. (Russia)

1976　THE CAT AND MOUSE WHO SHARED A HOUSE by Ruth Hurlimann, translated by Anthea Bell, illustrated by the author. Walck. (Germany)

1977　THE LEOPARD by Cecil Bødker, translated by Gunnar Poulsen. Atheneum. (Denmark)

1978　KONRAD by Christine Nostlinger, illustrated by Carol Nicklaus. Watts. (Germany)

1979　RABBIT ISLAND by Jörg Steiner, translated by Ann Conrad Lammers, illustrated by Jörg Müller. Harcourt. (Germany)

1980　THE SOUND OF THE DRAGON'S FEET by Alki Zei, translated by Edward Fenton. Dutton. (Greece)

1981　THE WINTER WHEN TIME WAS FROZEN by Els Pelgrom, translated by Maryka and Rafael Rudnik. Morrow. (Netherlands)

1982　THE BATTLE HORSE by Harry Kullman, translated by George Blecher and Lone Thygesen-Blecher. Bradbury. (Sweden)

1983　HIROSHIMA NO PIKA by Toshi Maruki. Lothrop. (Japan)

1984　RONIA, THE ROBBER'S DAUGHTER by Astrid Lindgren, translated by Patricia Crampton. Viking. (Sweden)

1985　THE ISLAND ON BIRD STREET by Uri Orlev, translated by Hillel Halkin. Houghton Mifflin. (Israel)

1986　ROSE BLANCHE by Christophe Gallaz and Roberto Innocenti, translated by Martha Coventry and Richard Graglia. Creative Education. (Italy)

1987　NO HERO FOR THE KAISER by Rudolf Frank, translated by Patricia Crampton. Lothrop. (Germany)

1988　IF YOU DIDN'T HAVE ME by Ulf Nilsson, translated by Lone Thygesen-Blecher and George Blecher, illustrated by Eva Eriksson. McElderry. (Sweden)

1989　CRUTCHES by Peter Härtling, translated by Elizabeth D. Crawford. Lothrop. (Germany)

1990　BUSTER'S WORLD by Bjarne Reuter, translated by Anthea Bell. Dutton. (Denmark)

1991　TWO LONG AND ONE SHORT by Nina Ring Aamundsen. Houghton Mifflin. (Norway)

1992　THE MAN FROM THE OTHER SIDE by Uri Orlev. Houghton Mifflin. (Israel)

The Laura Ingalls Wilder Award is given to an author or illustrator whose books (published in the United States) have made a substantial and lasting contribution to literature for children. Established in 1954, this medal was given every five years through 1980. As of 1983, it is given every three years by the Association of Library Service to Children (ALSC) of the American Library Association.

1954   Laura Ingalls Wilder
1960   Clara Ingram Judson
1965   Ruth Sawyer
1970   E. B. White
1975   Beverly Cleary
1980   Theodor S. Geisel (Dr. Seuss)
1983   Maurice Sendak
1986   Jean Fritz
1989   Elizabeth George Speare
1992   Marcia Brown

The Hans Christian Andersen Prize, the first international children's book award, was established in 1956 by the International Board on Books for Young People. Given every two years, the award was expanded in 1966 to honor an illustrator as well as an author. A committee composed of members from different countries judges the selections recommended by the board or library associations in each country. The following have won the Hans Christian Andersen Prize:

1956   Eleanor Farjeon for THE LITTLE BOOKROOM. Oxford (Walck).
1958   Astrid Lindgren for RASMUS PA LUFFEN. Rabén and Sjögren (Viking; titled RASMUS AND THE VAGABOND).
1960   Eric Kästner. Germany.
1962   Meindert DeJong. United States.
1964   René Guillot. France.
1966   Tove Jansson (author). Finland.
       Alois Carigiet (illustrator). Switzerland.
1968   James Krüss (author). Germany.
       Jose Maria Sanchez-Silva (author). Spain.
       Jiri Trnka (illustrator). Czechoslovakia.
1970   Gianni Rodari (author). Italy.
       Maurice Sendak (illustrator). United States.
1972   Scott O'Dell (author). United States.
       Ib Spang Olsen (illustrator). Denmark.
1974   Maria Gripe (author). Sweden.
       Farshid Mesghali (illustrator). Iran.

1976   Cecil Bødker (author). Denmark.
       Tatjana Mawrina (illustrator). U.S.S.R.
1978   Paula Fox (author). United States.
       Svend Otto (illustrator). Denmark.
1980   Bohumil Ríha (author). Czechoslovakia.
       Suekichi Akaba (illustrator). Japan.
1982   Lygia Bojunga Nunes (author). Brazil.
       Zibigniew Rychlicki (illustrator). Poland.
1984   Christine Nostlinger (author). Austria.
       Mitsumasa Anno (illustrator). Japan
1986   Patricia Wrightson (author). Australia.
       Robert Ingpen (illustrator). Australia.
1988   Annie M. G. Schmidt (author). Netherlands.
       Dusan Kallay (illustrator). Yugoslavia.
1990   Tormod Haugen (author). Norway.
       Lisbeth Zwerger (illustrator). Austria.
1992   Virginia Hamilton (author). United States.
       Kvĕta Pacovská (illustrator). Czechoslovakia.

GENERAL AWARDS

BOSTON GLOBE-HORN BOOK AWARDS

The Horn Book Magazine, 14 Beacon Street, Boston, MA 02108. Currently given for outstanding fiction or poetry, outstanding nonfiction, and outstanding illustration.

GOLDEN KITE AWARD

Presented annually by the Society of Children's Book Writers to members whose books of fiction, nonfiction, and picture illustration best exhibit excellence and genuinely appeal to interests and concerns of children.

INTERNATIONAL READING ASSOCIATION CHILDREN'S BOOK AWARD

International Reading Association, 800 Barksdale Rd., Newark, DE 19711. Annual award for first or second book to an author from any country who shows unusual promise in the children's book field. Since 1987, the award has been presented to both a picture book and a novel.

NEW YORK TIMES CHOICE OF BEST ILLUSTRATED CHILDREN'S BOOKS OF THE YEAR

The New York Times, 229 W. 43rd St., New York, NY 10036. Books selected for excellence in illustration by panel of judges.

AWARDS BASED ON SPECIAL CONTENT

JANE ADDAMS BOOK AWARD

Jane Addams Peace Association, 777 United Nations Pl., New York, NY 10017. For a book with literary merit stressing themes of dignity, equality, peace, and social justice.

ASSOCIATION OF JEWISH LIBRARIES AWARDS

National Foundation for Jewish Culture, 122 E. 42nd St., Room 1512, New York, NY 10168. Given to one or two titles which have made the most outstanding contribution to the field of Jewish literature for children and young people. The Sydney Taylor Body of Work Award, established in 1981, is given for an author's body of work.

CATHOLIC BOOK AWARDS

Catholic Press Association of the United States and Canada, 119 N. Park Ave., Rockville Centre, NY 11570. Honors selected in five categories and awarded to books with sound Christian and psychological values.

CHILD STUDY CHILDREN'S BOOK COMMITTEE AT BANK STREET COLLEGE AWARD

Bank Street College of Education, 610 W. 112th St., New York, NY 10025. For distinguished book for children or young people that deals honestly and courageously with problems in the world.

CHRISTOPHER AWARDS

The Christophers, 12 E. 48th St., New York, NY 10017. Given to works of artistic excellence affirming the highest values of the human spirit.

EVA L. GORDON AWARD FOR CHILDREN'S SCIENCE LITERATURE

Helen Ross Russell, Chairman of Publications Committee, ANNS, 44 College Dr., Jersey City, NJ, 07305. Given by the American Nature Study Society to the body of work by an author or illustrator whose science trade books are accurate, inviting, and timely.

JEFFERSON CUP AWARD

Children's and Young Adult Roundtable of the Virginia Library Association, P.O. Box 298, Alexandria, VA 22313. Presented for a distinguished book in American history, historical fiction, or biography.

EZRA JACK KEATS AWARDS

Given biennially to a promising new artist and a promising writer. The recipients receive a monetary award and a medallion from the Ezra Jack Keats Foundation.

CORETTA SCOTT KING AWARDS

Social Responsibilities Round Table of the American Library Association, 50 E. Huron St., Chicago, IL 60611. Given to a black author and black illustrator for outstanding inspirational and educational contributions to literature for children.

NATIONAL COUNCIL OF TEACHERS OF ENGLISH AWARD FOR EXCELLENCE IN POETRY FOR CHILDREN

National Council of Teachers of English, 1111 Kenyon Rd., Urbana, IL 61801. Given formerly annually and presently every three years to a living American poet for total body of work for children ages 3–13.

NATIONAL JEWISH BOOK AWARDS

JWB Jewish Book Council, 15 E. 26th St., New York, NY 10010. Various awards are given for work or body of work which makes a contribution to Jewish juvenile literature.

NEW YORK ACADEMY OF SCIENCES CHILDREN'S SCIENCE BOOK AWARDS

The New York Academy of Sciences, 2 E. 63rd St., New York, NY 10021. For books of high quality in the field of science for children; three awards are given: Younger Children, Older Children, and the Montroll Award for a book that provides unusual historical data or background on a scientific subject.

SCOTT O'DELL AWARD FOR HISTORICAL FICTION

Zena Sutherland, 1418 E. 57th Street, Chicago, IL 60637. Honors a distinguished work of historical fiction set in the New World.

ORBIS PICTUS AWARD FOR OUTSTANDING NONFICTION FOR CHILDREN

Presented annually by the National Council of Teachers of English to the outstanding nonfiction book of the previous year.

PHOENIX AWARD

Given to author of a book published for children twenty years before which has not received a major children's book award. Sponsored by the Children's Literature Association.

EDGAR ALLAN POE AWARDS

Mystery Writers of America, 1950 Fifth Ave., New York, NY 10011. For best juvenile mystery.

WASHINGTON POST/CHILDREN'S BOOK GUILD NONFICTION AWARD

Washington Post, 1150 15th St., NW, Washington, DC 20071. Given to an author or illustrator for a body of work in juvenile informational books.

WESTERN WRITERS OF AMERICA SPUR AWARD

The Western Writers of America, Inc., 508 Senter Pl., Selah, WA 98942. For best western juvenile in two categories, fiction and nonfiction.

CARTER G. WOODSON BOOK AWARD

National Council for the Social Studies, 3501 Newark St., NW, Washington, DC 20016. Presented to outstanding social science books for young readers which treat sensitively and accurately topics related to ethnic minorities.

LASTING CONTRIBUTIONS OR SERVICE TO CHILDREN'S LITERATURE

ARBUTHNOT AWARD

The International Reading Association, 800 Barksdale Rd., Newark, DE 19714. Named after May Hill Arbuthnot, an authority on literature for children, this award is given annually to an outstanding teacher of children's literature.

ARBUTHNOT HONOR LECTURE

The Association of Library Service to Children (ALSC) of the American Library Association, 50 E. Huron St., Chicago, IL 60611. This free public lecture is presented annually by a distinguished author, critic, librarian, historian, or teacher of children's literature. Both the lecturer and site for the lecture are chosen by an ALSC committee.

GROLIER FOUNDATION AWARD

American Library Association Awards Committee, 50 E. Huron St., Chicago, IL 60611. Given to a librarian in a community or school who has made an unusual contribution to the stimulation and guidance of reading by children and young people.

LANDAU AWARD

Salt Lake County Library System, 2197 E. 7000 S. Salt Lake City, UT 84121. Cosponsored by the Department of Education of the University of Utah and Salt Lake County Library System. The award is given biennially to a teacher of children's literature who has most inspired students to pursue a knowledge of the field.

LUCILE MICHEELS PANNELL AWARD

Awards in the "general" store category and in "children's specialty bookstore category" are presented annually by the Women's National Book Association to the owners of two bookstores whose innovative programs encourage children's reading.

REGINA MEDAL

Catholic Library Association, 461 West Lancaster Ave., Haverford, PA 19041. For "continued distinguished contribution to children's literature."

UNIVERSITY OF SOUTHERN MISSISSIPPI CHILDREN'S COLLECTION MEDALLION

University of Southern Mississippi Book Festival, USM Library, Hattiesburg, MS 39401. For writer or illustrator who has made an "outstanding contribution to the field of children's literature."

For more information about these and other awards, including complete lists of the prizewinners, see *Children's Books: Awards & Prizes*, published and revised periodically by The Children's Book Council, 568 Broadway, New York NY 10012. Beginning in 1990, each year's *Books in Print* also publishes a listing of the current winners of various prizes.

APPENDIX B

Book Selection Aids*

Compiled by Barbara Chatton, University of Wyoming, Laramie

I. COMPREHENSIVE LISTS AND DIRECTORIES

1. *Children's Books in Print.* R.R. Bowker, 245 W. 17th St., New York, NY 10011. Annual. $124.95.

    A comprehensive listing of children's books currently in print. Includes titles for grades K–12. Titles are arranged alphabetically by author, title, and illustrator. A list of publisher addresses is provided. Also includes children's book awards for the previous ten years.

2. *Children's Media Market Place*, 3rd ed. Delores Blythe Jones. Neal-Schuman Publishers, 23 Leonard St., New York, NY 10013. 1988. 397 pp. $45.00, paper.

    An annotated list of publishers of books and producers and distributors of nonprint materials indexed by format, subject, and special interest. Includes a directory of wholesalers, bookstores, book clubs, and children's television sources.

3. *Educational Media and Technology Yearbook.* Libraries Unlimited, P.O. Box 263, Littleton, CO 80160. Annual. $50.00.

    Includes articles, surveys, and research on various aspects of media administration, creation, and use. Lists organizations, foundations, and funding agencies for media as well as information on graduate programs. Includes an annotated mediography of basic resources for library media specialists.

4. *The Elementary School Paperback Collection.* John T. Gillespie. American Library Association, 50 E. Huron St., Chicago, IL 60611. 1985. 306 pp. $17.50.

    Includes 3,800 titles for preschool through sixth grade, arranged by popular interest categories, with descriptions including age level and a brief summary.

5. *Fiction, Folklore, Fantasy and Poetry for Children, 1876–1985.* R.R. Bowker, 245 W. 17th St., New York, NY 10011. 1986. 2 vols. 2,563 pp. $495.00.

    Contains 133,000 entries compiled from a variety of sources and indexed by author, title, illustrator, and awards.

6. *Guide to Reference Books for School Media Centers*, 3rd ed. Christine Gehret Wynar. Libraries Unlimited, P.O. Box 263, Littleton, CO 80160. 1986. 407 pp. $36.00.

    Includes annotations and evaluations for 2,000 useful reference tools for school media centers. Materials are arranged in order by subject. Also includes a list of sources and selection aids for print and nonprint materials.

7. *Magazines for Children.* Donald R. Stoll, ed. International Reading Association, 800 Barksdale Rd., P.O. Box 8139, Newark, DE 19714-8139. 1989. 48 pp. $5.25, paper.

    Lists more than 125 magazines for infants through teenagers. Includes age and subject indexes.

8. *Magazines for Children: A Guide for Parents, Teachers, and Librarians*, 2nd ed. Selma K. Richardson. American Library Association, 50 E. Huron St., Chicago, IL 60611. 1990. 225 pp. $19.95, paper.

    An annotated list of magazines designed especially for children ages 2 to 14, which includes descriptions of the publications, age levels of users, and evaluative comments. Complements *Periodicals for School Media Programs.*

9. *Magazines for Young People*, 2nd ed. Bill Katz and Kinda Sternberg Katz. R.R. Bowker, 245 W. 17th St., New York, NY 10011. 1991. 250 pp. $49.95.

    Evaluates over 1,000 magazines, journals, and newsletters for children and teachers in 60 subject areas.

10. *Reference Books for Children.* Carolyn Sue Peterson and Ann D. Fenton. Scarecrow Press, 52 Liberty St., Box 4167, Metuchen, NJ 08840. 1981. 273 pp. $19.50.

    Contains about 900 annotated entries over a broad range of curriculum areas, collection needs, interests, and reading levels of children. Books are classified by subject. Annotations provide some guidance in making selections for school collections.

11. *Subject Guide to Children's Books in Print.* R.R. Bowker, 245 W. 17th St., New York, NY 10011. Annual. $124.95.

    A companion volume to *Children's Books in Print.* Arranges all children's titles currently in print using over 6,000 subject headings. Particularly useful for finding and ordering titles on specific subjects; however, titles are not annotated.

II. GENERAL SELECTION AIDS

1. *Adventuring with Books: A Booklist for Pre-K–Grade 6*, 9th ed. Mary Jett-Simpson, ed. National Council of Teachers of English, 1111 Kenyon Rd., Urbana, IL 61601. 1989. 550 pp. $16.50, paper.

    Annotates about 1,800 children's titles published from 1984 to 1988. Annotations include summary, age, and interest levels. Contents are arranged by genre, broad subject, and theme. Author, title, and subject indexes.

2. *Award-Winning Books for Children and Young Adults.* Betty L. Criscoe. Scarecrow Press, 52 Liberty St., Box 4167, Metuchen, NJ 08840. Annual. $37.50.

    Lists books that won awards during the previous year. Includes descriptions of the awards, criteria used for selection, plot synopses of winners, grade levels, and genres.

3. *Best Books for Children: Pre-school Through Grade 6*, 4th ed. John T. Gillespie and Corinne J. Naden. R.R. Bowker, 245 W. 17th St., New York, NY 10011. 1990. 950 pp. $44.95.

   An annotated listing of 11,299 books that are selected to satisfy recreational, curricular needs, and interests of elementary schoolchildren. Books are arranged by broad age groups that are subdivided by types of books. Contains author, title, and illustrator as well as subject indexes.

4. *The Best in Children's Books: The University of Chicago Guide to Children's Literature, 1985–1990*. Zena Sutherland, Betsy Hearne, and Roger Sutton, eds. University of Chicago Press, Chicago, IL 60637. 1986. 522 pp. $37.50.

   A selection of reviews that originally appeared in the *Bulletin of the Center for Children's Books*. Earlier editions cover 1966 to 1978, 1979–1984. Reviews are arranged in order by author and are indexed by title, subject, and type of literature.

5. *Beyond Fact: Nonfiction for Children and Young People*. Jo Carr. American Library Association, 50 E. Huron St., Chicago, IL 60611. 1982. 236 pp. $59.30.

   Contains articles on and brief lists of high-quality nonfiction for young people.

6. *Bibliography of Books for Children*. Helen Shelton, ed. Association for Childhood Education International, 11141 Georgia Ave., Suite 200, Wheaton, MD 20902. 1989. 112 pp. $11.00.

   Lists the best books reviewed by the Association for Childhood Education over the previous two years. Books are evaluated for readability and absence of sexism and racism. Entries are annotated and grouped by age levels. Indexed and cross-referenced.

7. *Children's Catalog*, 16th ed. H. W. Wilson Co., 950 University Ave., Bronx, NY 10452. 1991. 1,346 pp. $90.00

   A classified (Dewey Decimal System) catalog of about 6,000 recent "best" children's books including publishing information, grade level, and a brief summary of each title. Also includes alphabetical author, title, subject, and analytical indexes. Contains a list of publishers with addresses. New edition is issued every five years, with annual supplements in other years.

8. *Choosing Books for Children*. Betsy Hearne. Delacorte Press, 1 Dag Hammerskjold Plaza, 245 E. 47th St. New York, NY 10017. 1989. 250 pp. $16.95.

   Contains general selection advice for parents, teachers, and librarians, combined with bibliographies.

9. *Collected Perspectives: Choosing and Using Books for the Classroom*. Hughes Moir, et al., eds. Christopher-Gordon Publishers, 480 Washington St., Norwood, MA 02062. 1990. 280 pp. $32.95.

   Contains over 500 reviews of literature published in the past five years, taken from reviews appearing in *Perspectives*.

10. *The Elementary School Library Collection*, 17th ed. Lois Winkel, ed. Brodart Co., 500 Arch St., Williamsport, PA 17705. 1990. 1,150 pp. $99.95.

    A basic bibliography of materials, both print and nonprint, for elementary school media center collections. Materials are interfiled and arranged by subject classification (Dewey Decimal System). All entries include bibliographic information, age level, and a brief annotation. Contains author, title, and subject indexes.

11. *Exciting, Funny, Scary, Short, Different, and Sad Books Kids Like about Animals, Science, Sports, Families, Songs, and Other Things*. Frances Laverne Carroll and Mary Meacham. American Library Association, 50 E. Huron St., Chicago, IL 60611. 1984. 192 pp. $10.00, paper.

    An annotated bibliography of titles through 1982 that focuses on subjects and books which have been popular with children in second through fifth grade.

12. *Eyeopeners!: How to Choose and Use Children's Books About Real People, Places, and Things*. Beverly Kobrin. Penguin, 40 West 23rd St., New York, NY 10010. 1988. 317 pp. $7.95, paper.

    Over 500 nonfiction titles are arranged in subject categories and annotated with brief summaries and ideas for classroom use. Indexed by author, illustrator, title, and subject.

13. *Fiction for Youth: A Guide to Recommended Books*, 2nd ed. Lillian L. Shapiro. Neal-Schuman Publishers, 23 Leonard St., New York, NY 10013. 1985. 264 pp. $29.95.

    Provides a core collection of titles designed to encourage reading by young people who can read but don't choose to do so.

14. *The Horn Book Guide to Children's and Young Adult Books*. Horn Book, Inc. 14 Beacon St., Boston, MA 02108. Semiannual.

    Provides short reviews of children's and young adult books published in the United States during the prior publishing season with references to longer reviews in *Horn Book Magazine*. Books are given a numerical evaluation from one to six.

15. *Let's Read Together: Books for Family Enjoyment*, 4th ed. Association for Library Service to Children, American Library Association, 50 E. Huron St., Chicago, IL 60611. 1981. 124 pp. $5.00, paper.

    Annotated list of books for children from preschool through age 15. Arranged in categories of interest and age level. Books are particularly suitable for reading aloud, but list is useful for helping parents to select books for their children.

16. *A Multimedia Approach to Children's Literature*, 3rd ed. Mary Alice Hunt, ed. American Library Association, 50 E. Huron St., Chicago, IL 60611. 1983. 182 pp. $16.50, paper.

    Annotated listings of over 500 books followed by annotated listings of media productions based on the books. Many have been used with children and include their responses. Includes lists of related readings, selection aids, and publishers' addresses.

17. *New York Times Parents' Guide to the Best Books for Children*. Eden Ross Lipson. Times Books/Random House, 201 East 50th St., New York, NY 10022. 1988. 421 pp. $12.95.

Indexes books by age appropriateness, listening level, author, title, illustrator, and subject. Books are arranged in broad categories such as wordless books, picture storybooks, and so on.

18. *Opening Doors for Preschool Children and Their Parents*, 2nd ed. Preschool Services and Parent Education Committee, Association for Library Service to Children, American Library Association, 50 E. Huron St., Chicago, IL 60611. 1981. 98 pp. $6.00, paper.

An annotated list divided into three sections: "Books and nonprint materials for parents and adults working with preschool children"; "Books for preschool children"; and "Nonprint materials for preschool children."

19. *A Parent's Guide to Children's Reading*, 5th ed. Nancy Larrick. Westminster/John Knox. 100 Witherspoon St., Louisville, KY 40202-1396. 1983. 284 pp. $12.95.

A handbook for parents suggesting appropriate titles for children's reading at each stage of their development. Contains chapters on television, language development, how reading is taught, poetry, and paperbacks.

20. *Tried and True: 500 Nonfiction Books Children Want to Read*. George Wilson and Joyce Moss. R. R. Bowker, 245 W. 17th St., New York, NY 10011. 1992. 300 pp. $34.95.

Lists popular titles arranged by grade level, then by books to be read for pleasure and books to be read for research.

21. *Your Reading: A Booklist for Junior High and Middle School Students*. James E. Davis and Hazel K. Davis, eds. National Council of Teachers of English, 1111 Kenyon Rd., Urbana, IL 61801. 1988. 494 pp. $13.95.

An annotated list of over 2,000 books for grades 5–9, arranged in broad subject categories. Includes author and title indexes.

III. BOOKLISTS FOR VARIOUS LEVELS OF READERS

1. *The Best: High/Low Books for Reluctant Readers*. Marianne Laino Pilla. Libraries Unlimited, P.O. Box 263, Littleton, CO 80160. 1990. 100 pp. $12.50, paper.

Includes books of high literary quality for reluctant readers in grades 3–12. Has brief annotations, reading and interest levels, and popular subject headings.

2. *Beyond Picture Books: A Guide to First Readers*. Barbara Barstow and Judith Riggle. R. R. Bowker, 245 W. 17th St., New York, NY 10011. 1989. 354 pp. $39.95.

Annotates 1,600 first readers for ages 4 to 7, with a plot summary, brief evaluation, and bibliographic information. Indexes by title, illustrator, readability, series, and subject.

3. *Books for Children to Read Alone: A Guide for Parents and Librarians*. George Wilson and Joyce Moss. R. R. Bowker, 245 W. 17th St., New York, NY 10011. 1988. 184 pp. $39.95.

Lists books in which concepts and language structures are accessible to beginning readers in the first through third grades. Includes subject index.

4. *Books for the Gifted Child*. Volume 1, Barbara Holland Baskin and Karen H. Harris. 1980. 263 pp. $29.95; Volume 2, Paula Hauser and Gail Nelson. 1988. 244 pp. $39.95. R. R. Bowker, 245 W. 17th St., New York, NY 10011.

Each volume critically annotates about 150 titles that would be useful in working with gifted children, ages preschool through 12. They are arranged in alphabetical order with bibliographic information and reading level included. Several chapters on the gifted are included in the book.

5. *Choices: A Core Collection for Young Reluctant Readers*, Vol. 2. Julie Cummins and Blair Cummins, eds. John Gordon Burke, Publisher, P.O. Box 1492, Evanston, IL 60204-1492. 1990. 544 pp. $45.00.

Annotates 275 books for second through sixth graders reading below grade level, published between 1983 and 1988, with plot summary, interest level, and reading level. Contains author and subject indexes.

6. *Easy Reading: Book Series and Periodicals for Less Able Readers*, 2nd ed. Randall Ryder, et al. International Reading Association, 8000 Barksdale Rd., P.O. Box 8139, Newark, DE 19714-8139. 1989. 96 pp. $8.75, paper.

An annotated list reviews 44 book series and 15 periodicals for fourth- through twelfth-grade readers who have difficulty with materials generally written for their age level.

7. *Exploring Books with Gifted Children*. Nancy Polette and Marjorie Hamlin. Libraries Unlimited, P.O. Box 263, Littleton, CO 80160. 1980. 214 pp. $19.00.

Provides suggested units with activities and lists of books for four primary elements of literature (style, theme, character, setting). Books that stress these elements, or can be used to motivate thinking about them, are included in the lists.

8. *Picture Books for Gifted Programs*. Nancy Polette. Scarecrow Press, 52 Liberty St., Box 4167, Metuchen, NJ 08840. 1981. 228 pp. $15.00.

Annotated lists of books that encourage growth of communication and thinking skills for all ages, as well as ideas for their use in classrooms and libraries.

9. *Primary Plots*. Rebecca L. Thomas. R. R. Bowker, 245 W. 17th St., New York, NY 10011. 1989. 392 pp. $39.95.

Provides plot summaries for 150 books organized in eight chapters. Each featured title includes bibliographic information, suggested use and reading level, thematic material, book talk material and activities, audiovisual adaptations, related titles, and information about the author and illustrator. Includes subject index.

IV. BOOKLISTS AND INDEXES FOR PARTICULAR SUBJECTS

A. Picture Books and Concept Books

1. *A to Zoo: Subject Access to Children's Picture Books*, 3rd ed. Carolyn W. Lima. R. R. Bowker, 245 W. 17th St., New York, NY 10011. 1989. 939 pp. $44.95.

Provides subject access to over 8,000 picture books through 600 subject headings with cross references and full bibliographic citations. Most titles are useful for children from preschool through second grade. Includes author, illustrator, and title lists.

2. *Alphabet: A Handbook of ABC Books and Activities for the Elementary Classroom.* Scarecrow Press, 52 Liberty St., Box 4167, Metuchen, NJ 08840. 1984. 220 pp. $17.50.

Reviews over 200 alphabet books and provides about 80 activities to use with children from preschool to grade six.

3. *Alphabet Books as a Key to Language Patterns: An Annotated Action Bibliography.* Patricia L. Roberts. Shoe String Press, P.O. Box 4327, 925 Sherman Ave., Hamden, CT 06514. 1987. 263 pp. $27.50.

Lists over 500 alphabet books that can be used in aiding language development under categories such as alliteration, rhymes and verses, and wordless books.

4. *Counting Books Are More Than Numbers: An Annotated Action Bibliography.* Patricia L. Roberts. Shoe String Press, P.O. Box 4327, 925 Sherman Ave., Hamden, CT 06514. 1989. 264 pp. $32.50.

Describes 350 books for preschool through second grades that can be used to encourage early understanding of mathematical concepts.

5. *Picture Books for Children*, 3rd ed. Patricia Jean Cianciolo. American Library Association, 50 E. Huron St., Chicago, IL 60611. 1990. 243 pp. $25.00, paper.

An annotated listing of picture books divided into major subject areas such as "Me and My Family" or "The Imaginative World." Annotations include descriptions of media, age levels, and brief synopses of plot. Material is largely new to this edition, so older editions remain useful.

6. *Wordless/Almost Wordless Picture Books: A Guide.* Virginia H. Richey and Katharyn Tuten-Pucket. Libraries Unlimited, P.O. Box 263, Littleton, CO 80160. 1991. 125 pp. $17.50.

Lists books with a brief annotation. Includes thematic and subject indexes.

B. Folklore and Storytelling and Reading Aloud

7. *Books Kids Will Sit Still For: The Complete Read-Aloud Guide*, 2nd ed. Judy Freeman. R. R. Bowker, 245 W. 17th St., New York, NY 10011. 1990. 660 pp. $34.95.

Lists over 2,000 titles recommended for reading aloud including plot summaries, extension ideas, and related titles.

8. *For Reading Out Loud! A Guide to Sharing Books with Children.* Margaret Mary Kimmel and Elizabeth Segel. Dell Publishing, 666 Fifth Ave., New York, NY 10103. 1988. 240 pp. $16.95, paper.

Contains suggestions for reading aloud effectively to elementary and middle school students and an annotated list of good titles.

9. *Index to Fairy Tales, 1949–1972: Including Folklore, Legends, and Myths in Collections.* Norma Olin Ireland. 1973. 741 pp. $39.50.
Index to Fairy Tales, Myths and Legends, 2nd rev. ed. Mary H. Eastman, ed. 1926. 610 pp. $20.00.
Index to Fairy Tales, Myths and Legends. Supplement 1. Mary H. Eastman, ed. 1937. 566 pp. $20.00.
Index to Fairy Tales, Myths and Legends. Supplement 2. Mary H. Eastman, ed. 1952. 370 pp. $20.00.
Index to Fairy Tales, 1973–1977: Including Folklore, Legends and Myths in Collections. Norma O. Ireland, comp. 1985. 259 pp. $26.00.
All published by Scarecrow Press, 52 Liberty St., Box 4167, Metuchen, NJ 08840.

Indexes a broad number of collections of folk tales and other folk literature by author, compiler, subject of tale (including characters, countries, and so on), and titles of tale. Various editions cover different collections so that the total coverage is quite broad.

10. *The New Read-Aloud Handbook*, rev. ed. Jim Trelease. Penguin Books, 40 W. 23rd St., New York, NY 10010. 1989. 352 pp. $9.95, paper.

Contains a rationale for reading aloud, tips for good presentations, and an annotated list of books recommended for reading aloud.

11. *Stories: A List of Stories to Tell and Read Aloud*, 7th ed. Marilyn B. Iarusso, ed. New York Public Library Publications Office, Fifth Ave. & 42nd St., New York, NY 10018. 1987. 120 pp. $6.00.

Suggests proven stories to tell and read aloud to children. Includes poetry. Entries are briefly annotated.

12. *The Story Vine: A Sourcebook of Unusual and Easy-to-Tell Stories from Around the World.* Anne Pellowski. Macmillan, 866 Third Ave., New York, NY 10022. 1984. 160 pp. $14.95. $7.95, paper.

A collection of stories that can be highlighted with simple props such as string figures, picture drawings, musical instruments, or concrete objects.

13. *Storyteller's Sourcebook.* Margaret Read MacDonald, ed. Gale Research, 835 Penobscot Bldg., Detroit, MI 48226-4094. 1982. 840 pp. $95.00.

Provides access to folk tales and folk literature in 700 collections. Tales are indexed by subject, motif, and title. Index is particularly useful in locating variants of tales.

14. *Storytelling: A Selected Annotated Bibligraphy.* Ellin Greene and George Shannon. Garland, 136 Madison Ave., New York, NY 10016. 1986. 183 pp. $27.00.

Provides bibliographies of stories, telling techniques, stories for different settings, and lists of tellers.

15. *Storytelling Folklore Sourcebook.* Norma J. Livo and Sandra A. Rietz. Libraries Unlimited, P.O. Box 263, Littleton, CO 80160. 1991, 400 pp. $34.00.

A sourcebook of folk tales, legends, songs, poetry, and aphorisms.

16. *The Storytime Sourcebook: A Compendium of Ideas and Resources for Storytellers.* Carolyn M. Cullum. Neal-Schuman Publishers, 23 Leonard St., New York, NY 10013. 1990. 175 pp. $24.95.

Arranged by themes, lists plans for story hour programs including books, films, filmstrips, videocassettes, and toys. Includes activities. For 3- to 7-year-olds. Print and nonprint indexes.

C. Historical Fiction, History, and Biography

17. *American History for Children and Young Adults: An Annotated Bibligraphic Index.* Vandelia VanMeter. Libraries Unlimited, P.O. Box 263, Littleton, CO 80160. 1990. 324 pp. $32.50.

    Books reviewed between 1980 and 1988 are arranged by time periods, subdivided by subject. Indexed by grade level.

18. *Index to Collective Biographies for Young Readers,* 4th ed. Karen Breen, ed. R. R. Bowker, 245 W. 17th St., New York, NY 10011. 1988. 494 pp. $44.95.

    Indexes biographies in collections by individuals' names and by subject. Biographies are suitable for elementary school through junior high school.

19. Reading for Young People Series:
    The Great Plains. Mildred Laughlin. 1985. 168 pp. $12.00, paper.
    Kentucky, Tennessee, West Virginia. Barbara Martins. 1985. 157 pp. $12.00, paper.
    The Middle Atlantic. Arabelle Pennypacker. 1980. 164 pp. $11.00, paper.
    The Midwest. Dorothy Hinman and Ruth Zimmerman. 1979. 250 pp. $11.00, paper.
    The Mississippi Delta. Cora Matheny Dorsett. 1983. 157 pp. $15.00, paper.
    New England. Elfrieda B. McCauley. 1985. 168 pp. $17.50, paper.
    The Northwest. Mary Meachum. 1981. 152 pp. $11.00, paper.
    The Rocky Mountains. Mildred Laughlin. 1980. 192 pp. $11.00, paper.
    The Southeast. Dorothy Heald. 1980. 174 pp. $11.00, paper.
    The Southwest. Dorothy Heald. 1980. 176 pp. $11.00, paper.
    The Upper Midwest. Marion Fuller Archer. 1981. 142 pp. $11.00, paper.
    All published by the American Library Association, 50 E. Huron St., Chicago, IL 60611.

    A series of annotated bibliographies of fiction and nonfiction for primary grades through grade ten that describe and annotate books covering the history and life of various American regions.

20. *Peoples of the American West: Historical Perspectives Through Children's Literature.* Mary Hurlbut Cordier. Scarecrow, 52 Liberty St., P.O. Box 4167, Metuchen, NJ 08840. 1989. 230 pp. $22.50.

    Contains an analysis of historical fiction of the West as a genre and an annotated list of 100 books separated into grades K–3 and 4–9.

21. *Reference Guide to Historical Fiction for Children and Young Adults.* Lynda G. Adamson. Greenwood Dr., 88 Post

Rd., W., P.O. Box 5007, Westport, CT 06881. 1987. 401 pp. $49.95.

    Authors, titles, main characters, and historical events are listed in dictionary format with longer entries under authors that describe their works. Appendices list books by periods and events and by readability level.

22. *World History for Children and Young Adults.* Vandelia VanMeter. Libraries Unlimited, P.O. Box 263, Littleton, CO 80160. 1991. 425 pp. $29.50.

    Lists and annotates books about world history by time period and subject. Includes fiction and nonfiction.

D. Cultural and Sexual Identity

23. *American Indian Reference Books for Children and Young Adults.* Barbara J. Kuipers. Libraries Unlimited, P.O. Box 263, Littleton, CO 80160. 1990. 200 pp. $32.50.

    Lists over 200 nonfiction sources of material on Native Americans for grades three to twelve. Includes strengths and weaknesses of each book as well as curriculum uses. A section of the book deals with general selection criteria to use for these subjects.

24. *American Indian Stereotypes in the World of Children: A Reader and Bibliography.* Arlene B. Hirschfelder. Scarecrow Press, 52 Liberty St., Box 4167, Metuchen, NJ 08840. 1982. 312 pp. $22.50.

    Contains selected articles about attitudes toward Native Americans and images of them in children's trade and textbooks. Includes an annotated bibliography of articles about images of Native Americans and a short list of articles, books, and current materials that convey a more positive image.

25. *Basic Collection of Children's Books in Spanish.* Isabel Schon. Scarecrow, 52 Liberty St., Box 4167, Metuchen, NJ 08840. 1986. 230 pp. $17.50.

    More than 500 titles for preschool through grade six are arranged in Dewey order, with access through author, title, and subject indexes. A list of Spanish language distributors is included.

26. *Bilingual Books in Spanish and English for Children.* Doris Cruger Dale. Libraries Unlimited, P.O. Box 263, Littleton, CO 80160. 1985. 163 pp. $23.50.

    Annotated entries provide evaluations of 254 bilingual books for preschool and elementary school children published and distributed in the United States since the 1930s. Most have been published since 1970. Includes some out-of-print titles.

27. *The Black American in Books for Children: Readings in Racism,* 2nd ed. Donnarae MacCann and Gloria Woodward. 1985. 310 pp. $27.50.
    Cultural Conformity in Books for Children: Further Readings in Racism. 1977. 215 pp. $20.00. Scarecrow, 52 Liberty St., Box 4167, Metuchen, NJ 08840.

    Collections of articles in which the issue of racism in children's books is considered from a variety of points of view. Includes many citations to books of both good and poor quality that reflect positive and negative values.

28. *The Black Experience in Children's Books.* Barbara Rollock, selector. New York Public Library Publications Office, Fifth Ave. & 42nd St., New York, NY 10018. 1989. 112 pp. $5.00.

An annotated list that presents titles about the black experience in the United States as well as in other areas of the world. Criteria for selection and inclusion in the list are determined.

29. *Books in Spanish for Children and Young Adults: An Annotated Guide.* Series III. Isabel Schon. Scarecrow, 52 Liberty St., P.O. Box 4167, Metuchen, NJ 08840. 1985. 108 pp. $16.50.

Contains listings of books for preschool through high school students that have been published since 1982. Books represent diverse Hispanic cultures including Mexico, Central and South America, and Spain.

30. *Children's Books of International Interest*, 3rd ed. Barbara Elleman, ed. American Library Association, 50 E. Huron St., Chicago, IL 60611. 1985. 112 pp. $7.50, paper.

Annotates 350 titles that deal with universal themes in other cultural settings.

31. *Girls Are People Too!: A Bibliography of Nontraditional Female Roles in Children's Books.* Joan E. Newman. Scarecrow Press, 52 Liberty St., Box 4167, Metuchen, NJ 08840. 1982. 203 pp. $17.50.

A list of 500 books with nontraditional females as characters. Most are fiction, although some nonfiction is included. Arranged by fiction, nonfiction, then by age range (preschool through grade 4–9), then by minority groups and handicapped.

32. *A Guide to Non-Sexist Children's Books: Volume II, 1976–1985.* Denise Wilms and Ilene Cooper, eds. Academy Publisher, 213 W. Institute Pl., Chicago, IL 60610. 1987. 240 pp. $17.95. $8.95, paper.

Lists over 600 books in sections by grade level up through twelfth grade, which are then subdivided into fiction and nonfiction. Indexes by author, title, fiction, and nonfiction subjects. Volume I, which covered books up to 1976, is also available.

33. *Hey Miss! You Got a Book for Me? A Model Multi-Cultural Resource Collection*, 2nd ed. Joanna F. Chambers. Austin Bilingual Language Editions, P.O. Box 3864, Austin, TX 78764. 1981. 91 pp. $12.95, paper.

A listing of 350 good multicultural and bilingual books and audiovisual materials. Includes mainly Spanish language with some materials in Chinese, French, Greek, and Vietnamese.

34. *A Hispanic Heritage: A Guide to Juvenile Books About Hispanic Peoples and Cultures*, Series III. Isabel Schon. Scarecrow Press, 52 Liberty St., Box 4167, Metuchen, NJ 08840. 1988. 158 pp. $17.50.

An annotated subject bibliography of works about the people, history, culture, and politics in the Hispanic countries as well as works about Hispanic people in the United States. The author indicates in the annotations

the passages in which cultural bias and stereotyping may appear. Covers grades K–12. Volumes I (1980) and II (1985) are also available.

35. *Literature by and about the American Indian: An Annotated Bibliography*, 2nd ed. Anna Lee Stensland. National Council of Teachers of English, 1111 Kenyon Rd., Urbana, IL 61601. 1979. 382 pp. $12.50, paper.

Identifies over 775 books published since 1973 including a section of books for elementary school children. Annotations describe and critique content of books. Essays discuss stereotypes, the themes of American Indian literature, difficulties of selecting literature that accurately depicts Native-American life, and so on.

36. *Our Family, Our Friends, Our World: An Annotated Guide to Significant Multicultural Books for Children and Teenagers.* Lyn Miller-Lachman. R. R. Bowker, 245 W. 17th St., New York, NY 10011. 1992. 400 pp. $39.95

Annotated lists of fiction and nonfiction about ethnic and cultural minority groups in the United States and Canada, and about cultures in various parts of the world.

37. *Reading Ladders for Human Relations*, 6th ed. Eileen Tway, ed. National Council of Teachers of English and American Council of Education, 1 DuPont Circle, Washington, DC 20036. 1981. 398 pp. $14.25.

Annotated list of titles arranged according to five basic themes: "Growing into Self"; "Relating to Wide Individual Differences"; "Interacting in Groups"; "Appreciating Different Cultures"; and "Coping in a Changing World." Covers ages preschool through high school, with books arranged in order of reading difficulty. All books are recommended titles.

38. *Selecting Materials for and About Hispanic and East Asian Children and Young People.* Patricia F. Beilke and Frank J. Sciara. Library Professional Publications/Shoe String Press, P.O. Box 4327, 925 Sherman Ave., Hamden, CT 06514. 1986. 178 pp. $26.00.

Includes bibliographies of materials as well as providing criteria for evaluation and suggestions for professional growth in understanding other cultures.

39. *Shadow and Substance: Afro-American Experience in Contemporary Children's Fiction.* Rudine Sims. National Council of Teachers of English, 1111 Kenyon Road, Urbana, IL 61801. 1982. 112 pp. $8.95, paper.

Annotations of 150 children's books published from 1965 to 1979 that present images of Afro-American children. Examines historical context, distortions, and social conscience as expressed in these books as well as providing some guidelines for teachers and librarians on how to make better informed selections. Includes bibliographies and a reference list.

E. Other Social Issues

40. *The Aging Adult in Children's Books and Nonprint Media: An Annotated Bibliography.* Catherine Townsend Horner.

Scarecrow Press, 52 Liberty St., Box 4167, Metuchen, NJ 08840. 1982. 266 pp. $22.50.

A comprehensive list of fiction and nonprint materials about the aging adult. Lists of fiction, arranged according to age levels, include books about relationships, concerns, and activities of older people in relation to children as well as books about illness and death. Nonprint materials are largely factual in approach. No nonfiction book titles are included.

41. *The Bookfinder, Volume 3: When Kids Need Books: Annotations of Books Published 1979–1982.* Sharon Spredemann Dreyer. American Guidance Service. Publishers' Building, Circle Pines, MN 55014-1796. 1985. 519 pp. $64.95. $29.95, paper.

This is the third volume of the Bookfinder series. Subject, author, and titles indexes are provided on the top half of the publication and lengthy reviews that include subject cross references, age levels, and specific information about the content of the book are on the bottom half. Both fiction and nonfiction are included. The books focus on problems children may experience, feelings, and relationships.

42. *Books to Help Children to Cope with Separation and Loss,* Vol. 3. Joanne E. Bernstein and Masha K. Rudman, comp. R. R. Bowker, 245 W. 17th St., New York, NY 10011. 1988. 532 pp. $44.95.

Includes several chapters on bibliotherapy plus annotated lists of titles in such categories as death, divorce, adoption, and foster children, and loss of mental or physical functions. About 600 books are arranged by topic with an annotation evaluation and recommendations for use with children. Age level from 3 to 16; interest, and reading level are included in each annotation.

43. *Drugs: A Multimedia Sourcebook for Young Adults.* Sharon Ashenbrenner and Charles and Sari Feldman. Neal-Schuman Publishers, 23 Leonard St., New York, NY 10013. 1980. 200 pp. $27.95.

Contains annotations for fiction and nonfiction as well as nonprint materials about drugs of all kinds. Guidelines for selection are carefully laid out. Also includes appendix that contains professional reading, a list of publishers, and an author, title, and subject index.

44. *Portraying the Disabled: A Guide to Juvenile Fiction.* Debra Robertson. R. R. Bowker, 245 W. 17th St., New York, NY 10011. 1991. 500 pp. $39.95.

Updates *Notes from a Different Drummer* and *More Notes from a Different Drummer,* books which provide annotated lists of titles that portray the disabled. Includes titles that promote better understanding and acceptance of the disabled.

45. *Portraying the Disabled: A Guide to Juvenile Non-Fiction.* Joan Brest Friedberg, June B. Mullins, and Adelaide Weir Sukiennik. R. R. Bowker, 245 W. 17th St., New York, NY 10011. 1991. 363 pp. $34.95.

Updates *Accept Me as I Am,* listing over 350 titles about the disabled. Includes introductory essays about the portrayal of disabilities in literature for children.

F. Curriculum Areas and Genres of Literature

46. *Anatomy of Wonder: A Critical Guide to Science Fiction.* Neil Barron, ed. R. R. Bowker, 245 W. 17th St., New York, NY 10011. 1987. 874 pp. $39.95.

Includes a chapter that annotates 180 titles for children and young adults, as well as 2,400 additional titles which would appeal to readers of the genre.

47. *Best Science Books and A-V Materials for Children: Selected and Annotated.* S. M. O'Connell, V. J. Montenegro, & K. Wolff, eds. American Association for the Advancement of Science, 1333 H. Street NW, 8th Floor, Washington, DC 20005. 1988. 350 pp. $20.00.

An annotated list of high-quality trade books, filmstrips, films, and videos in the sciences that were published or produced between 1982 and 1988.

48. *Careers in Fact and Fiction: A Selective, Annotated List of Books for Career Backgrounds.* June Klein Bienstock and Ruth Bienstock Anolick. American Library Association, 50 East Huron St., Chicago, IL 60611. 1985. 165 pp. $18.95.

Annotates 1,000 works of fiction, nonfiction, and biography that discuss careers. Oriented to a high school audience but useful for upper elementary.

49. *Celebrations: Read-Aloud Holiday and Theme Book Programs.* Caroline Feller Bauer. H. W. Wilson, 950 University Ave., Bronx, NY 10452. 1985. 301 pp. $35.00.

Includes readings and plans for holiday activities for both well-known and Bauer's invented holiday occasions.

50. *Children's Mathematics Books: A Critical Bibliography.* Margaret Matthias and Diane Thiessen. American Library Association, 50 E. Huron St., Chicago, IL 60611. 1979. 68 pp. $6.00, paper.

Reviews almost 200 books suitable for elementary schoolchildren. Books are arranged in six major areas: Counting, Geometry, Measurement, Number Concepts, Time, and Miscellaneous. Annotations describe contents and indicate when activities are included in the text. Grade levels and ratings of quality are included for each title.

51. *E for Environment: An Annotated Bibliography of Children's Books with Environmental Themes.* Patti Sinclair. R. R. Bowker, 245 W. 17th St., New York, NY 10011. 1992. 400 pp. $39.95.

Lists 500 books that focus on environmental themes such as endangered species, pollution, recycling, and so on.

52. *Energy: A Multi-Media Guide for Children and Young Adults.* Judith H. Higgins. Neal-Schuman Publishers, 23 Leonard St., New York, NY 10013. 1979. 195 pp. $27.95.

A list of both print and nonprint materials from a variety of sources including commercials, government, and trade materials for students in grades K–12. Annotations are critical, pointing out flaws in production, accuracy, or usefulness. Materials are arranged in groups by subject and then subdivided into print and nonprint formats.

53. *Fantasy Literature for Children and Young Adults: An Annotated Bibliography*, 3rd. ed. Ruth Nadelman Lynn. R. R. Bowker, 245 W. 17th St., New York, NY 10011. 1988. 771 pp. $44.95.

Annotates about 3,300 fantasy novels for 8- to 17-year-olds in ten chapters arranged by topics. Includes specific subject indexes.

54. *Fun for Kids: An Index to Children's Craft Books.* Marion F. Gallivan. Scarecrow Press, 52 Liberty St., Box 4167, Metuchen, NJ 08840. 1981. 340 pp. $22.50.

An index to several hundred craft books commonly purchased for library collections. Specific craft or art activities are listed with references to books in which plans and directions for the activity can be located.

55. *Health, Illness and Disability: A Guide to Books for Children and Young Adults.* Pat Azarnoff. R. R. Bowker Co., 245 W. 17th St., New York, NY 10011. 1983. 259 pp. $34.95.

An annotated list of over 1,000 books about health issues and problems.

56. *Index to Children's Songs: A Title, First Line, and Subject Index.* Carolyn Sue Peterson and Ann D. Fento. H. W. Wilson Company, 950 University Ave., Bronx, NY 10452. 1979. 318 pp. $33.00.

Indexes over 5,000 songs in 298 children's songbooks, both single titles and collections. Songs are indexed by title and first line as well as by 1,000 subject headings and cross-references.

57. *Index to Poetry for Children and Young People, 1976–1981.* John E. Brewton, et al. 1983. 350 pp. $38.00.
Index to Poetry for Children and Young People, 1970–1975. John E. Brewton, G. Meredith Blackburn, comps. 1978. 471 pp. $38.00.
Index to Poetry for Children and Young People, 1964–1969. John E. Brewton, et al., 1972. 574 pp. $38.00.
Index to Children's Poetry. John E. Brewton and Sara W. Brewton, eds., 1942. $30.00.
First Supplement, 1954. $18.00.
Second Supplement, 1965, $18.00.
All five books published by the H. W. Wilson Co., 950 University Ave., Bronx, New York 10452.

Each volume indexes collections of poetry by author, title, first line, and subject. Different collections are indexed in each volume. Classifies poems under a wide variety of subjects, making for easy access to poems by their topics.

58. *The Literature of Delight: A Critical Guide to Humorous Books for Children.* Kimberly Olson Fakih. R. R. Bowker, 245 W. 17th St., New York, NY 10011. 1992. 350pp. $39.95.

Lists 1,000 fiction and nonfiction books with humorous presentations. Chapters include books of nonsense, books of satire and parody, poetry, and so on.

59. *The Museum of Science & Industry Basic List of Children's Science Books.* Bernice Richter and Duane Wenzel. American Library Association. 50 E. Huron St., Chicago, IL 60611. 1988. 180 pp. $11.95, paper.

An annotated listing of 1,400 science trade books for K–12 done in conjunction with the Chicago Museum of Science and Industry. Updates earlier volumes that cover 1973–1984 and 1983–1986.

60. *Poetry Anthologies for Children and Young People.* Marycile E. Olexer. American Library Association, 50 E. Huron St., Chicago, IL 60611. 1985. 288 pp. $40.00.

Lists subject anthologies and collections of poetry by individual poets, giving bibliographic information, a summary and critique, and age range. Books are suitable for preschool through ninth grade. Includes author, title, and subject indexes.

61. *Science and Technology in Fact and Fiction: A Guide to Children's Books.* DayAnn M. Kennedy, Stella S. Spangler, and Mary Ann Vanderwerf. R. R. Bowker, 245 W. 17th St., New York, NY 10011. 1990. 331 pp. $35.00.

Includes summaries and evaluations for 350 books of both fiction and nonfiction for preschool and elementary students. Indexed by author, title, illustrator, subject, and readability.

62. *Science Books for Children: Selections from Booklist, 1976–1983.* Selected by Denise Murcko Wilms. American Library Association, 50 E. Huron Street, Chicago, IL 60611. 1985. 192 pp. $15.00, paper.

A selection of reviews of science books from *Booklist* are arranged in Dewey classification order with author/title and subject indexes.

V. INFORMATION ABOUT AUTHORS AND ILLUSTRATORS

1. *Behind the Covers: Interviews with Authors and Illustrators of Books for Children and Young Adults.* Jim Roginski. Libraries Unlimited, P.O. Box 263, Littleton, CO 80160. 1985. 249 pp. $23.50.

Interviews 22 authors and illustrators about their work.

2. *Bookpeople: A First Album.* 1990. 175 pp. $17.00, paper.
Bookpeople: A Second Album. 1990. 200 pp. $18.00, paper.
Sharron L. McElmeel. Libraries Unlimited, P.O. Box 263, Littleton, CO 80160.

A First Album introduces 41 authors and illustrators of picture books. *A Second Album* introduces authors of intermediate books (grades 3–9). Brief biographies with highlights of life and career and selected bibliographies.

3. *The Illustrator's Notebook.* Lee Kingman, ed. Horn Book, 14 Beacon St., Boston, MA 02108. 1978. 168 pp. $28.95.

Contains excerpts from articles by artists and illustrators that have appeared in *The Horn Book Magazine.* Articles discuss philosophy of illustration, history, illustration's place in the arts, and their experiences with various techniques of illustration.

4. *Books by African-American Authors and Illustrators for Children and Young Adults.* Helen E. Williams. American Library Association, 50 E. Huron St., Chicago, IL 60611. 1991. 270 pp. $39.00.

Presents a comprehensive listing of works by African Americans. Clear, concise annotations are given in three sections divided by reading/interest level: Pre-K–4, 5–8, 9+. Also includes profiles and critical discussion of 53 African-American authors and illustrators.

5. *Illustrators of Children's Books 1744–1945*. Bertha E. Mahony, Louise Payson Latimer, and Beulah Formsbee, eds. 1947. 527 pp. $35.95.
Illustrators of Children's Books 1946–1956. Bertha Mahony Miller, Ruth Hill Viguers, and Marcia Dalphin, eds. 1958. 229 pp. $30.95.
Illustrators of Children's Books 1957–1966. Lee Kingman, Joanna Foster, and Ruth Giles Lontoft, eds. 1968. 295 pp. $30.95.
Illustrators of Children's Books 1967–1976. Lee Kingman, Grace Allen Hogarth, and Harriet Quimby, eds. 1978. 290 pp. $35.95.
All published by Horn Book, 14 Beacon St., Boston, MA 02108.
All four volumes contain brief biographical and career sketches of artists and illustrators for children who were actively at work in this field during the period included in each volume. Articles discuss techniques, philosophy, and trends in illustration during the period. Bibliographies are included for each illustrator as well as selected bibliographies covering art and illustration of the period. Volume 4 contains cumulative index.

6. *The Junior Book of Authors*, 2nd rev. ed. Stanley J. Kunitz and Howard Haycraft, eds. 1951. 309 pp. $30.00.
More Junior Authors. Muriel Fuller, ed. 1969. 235 pp. $25.00.
Third Book of Junior Authors and Illustrators. Doris de Montreville and Donna Hill, eds. 1972. 320 pp. $30.00.
Fourth Book of Junior Authors and Illustrators. Doris de Montreville and Elizabeth D. Crawford. 1978. 370 pp. $35.00.
Fifth Book of Junior Authors and Illustrators. Sally Holmes Holtze, ed. 1983. 357 pp. $38.00.
All published by H. W. Wilson Company, 950 University Ave., Bronx, NY 10452.
Provides readable biographies of popular authors for young people that include, generally, a biographical statement by the author or illustrator, a photograph, a brief biography, and a list of that person's works.

7. *The Marble in the Water: Essays on Contemporary Writers of Fiction for Children and Young Adults*. David Rees. Horn Book, 14 Beacon St., Boston, MA 02108. 1980. 224 pp. $9.95, paper.
Includes essays on 18 British and American authors including Beverly Cleary, Paula Fox, Judy Blume, Paul Zindel, and others.

8. *Newbery Medal Books: 1922–1955*. Bertha Mahony Miller and Elinor Whitney Field, eds. 1955. 458 pp. $22.95.
Caldecott Medal Books: 1938–1957. Bertha Mahony Miller and Elinor Whitney Fields, eds. 1957. 239 pp. $22.95.
Newbery and Caldecott Medal Books: 1956–1965. Lee Kingman, ed. 1965. 300 pp. $22.95.
Newbery and Caldecott Medal Books: 1966–1975. Lee Kingman, ed. 1975. 321 pp. $22.95.
All published by Horn Book, 14 Beacon St., Boston, MA 02108.

Each volume contains biographical sketches and texts of the award winners' acceptance speeches as well as general observations of trends in the awards.

9. *Pipers at the Gates of Dawn: The Wisdom of Children's Literature*. Jonathan Cott. Random House, 201 East 50th St., New York, NY 10022. 1983. $19.45.
Seven essays on authors and illustrators for children that focus both on biographical information and on how these creators fit into the world of literature. Includes essays on Dr. Seuss, Maurice Sendak, William Steig, Astrid Lindgren, Achebe, P. L. Travers, and the Opies.

10. *A Sense of Story: Essays on Contemporary Writers for Children*. John Rowe Townsend. Horn Book, 14 Beacon St., Boston, MA 02108. 1973. 216 pp. $6.95.
Includes essays on 19 English language authors for children including brief biographies, notes on their books, critical remarks, and lists of their books. Essays reflect the critical position of the author.

11. *Something About the Author*. Anne Commaire. Gale Research, 835 Penobscot Bldg., Detroit, MI 48226-4094. There are 61 volumes currently in print, added to periodically. $70.00/volume.
Clear and sizable essays on contemporary authors and illustrators. Updating allows more recent authors to be included. Contain photographs as well as reproductions from works of the illustrators. Suitable for middle-grade children to use for gathering biographical information.

12. *A Sounding of Storytellers: New and Revised Essays on Contemporary Writers for Children*. John Rowe Townsend. Harper & Row, 10 E. 53rd St., New York, NY 10022. 1979. 218 pp. $15.25.
Townsend reevaluates seven of the authors included in his earlier "A Sense of Story," including the new ground they have covered in more recent works. Several American authors are included in the new selections, including Vera and Bill Cleaver, Virginia Hamilton, E. L. Konigsburg.

VI. PERIODICALS

1. *Appraisal: Science Books for Young People*. Children's Science Book Review Committee, 36 Cummington St., Boston University, Boston, MA 02215. Quarterly. $24.00.
Each issue contains reviews of about 75 children's and young adult science and technology books. Gives age levels and ratings of quality.

2. *Book Links*. American Library Association, 50 E. Huron St., Chicago, IL 60611. Six times/year. $14.95.
Edited by Barbara Elleman, this publication connects books, libraries, and classrooms. Special features include "book strategies" or guides for teaching a particular book, interviews with author/illustrators to discover their personal story behind the book, book themes, poetry, and "Just for Fun," books for children to read and enjoy.

3. *Book Review Digest*. H. W. Wilson Co., 950 University Ave., Bronx, NY 10452. Ten times/year. Service basis rates quoted on request.

Evaluates about 4,000 adult and children's books per year. For those books included, provides citations from several reiveys that have appeared in other review periodicals.

4. *Bookbird: Literature for Children and Young People.* Lucia Binder. Knud-Egil Hauberg-Tychsen, Mayerhofgasse 6, A-1040, Vienna, Austria. Quarterly. $18.00.

    An international periodical on literature for children issued by the IBBY contains papers, lists of prizewinning books, and lists of translated titles. Forty-five countries contribute. Reviews and articles in English and summation of major articles in Spanish.

5. *Booklist.* American Library Association, 50 E. Huron St., Chicago, IL 60611. Twice/month. $60.00.

    Reviews both adult and children's titles, including both print and nonprint materials. Reviews are annotated and graded by age levels and grades. Includes reviews of new selection tools. Often contains subject lists of good books in particular fields. Lists prizewinning books annually.

6. *Book World.* c/o *Washington Post,* 1150 15th St., NW, Washington, DC 20071. Weekly. $10.00

    A weekly supplement to the *Post* and several other newspapers. Reviews children's books regularly. Issues large special children's book editions in fall and spring.

7. *The Bulletin of the Center for Children's Books.* University of Illinois Press, 54 E. Gregory Dr., Champaign, IL 61820. 11 issues. $29.00.

    Reviews about 75 current children's books in each issue with negative as well as favorable reviews. Each entry is graded. Annotations stress curricular use, values, and literary merit.

8. *CBC Features.* Children's Book Council, 568 Broadway, New York, NY 10012. A one-time $35.00 charge for placement on a mailing list. Twice/year.

    A newsletter about children's books, including information about special events, free and inexpensive materials from publishers, and lists of prizewinners, as well as discussion of new books.

9. *CM: Canadian Materials for Schools and Libraries.* Canadian Library Association, 200 Elgin St., Ste. 602, Ottawa, Ontario K2P115. Bimonthly. $30.00

    Reviews English language materials written by Canadians or published in Canada. Evaluates books, films, filmstrips, games, and periodicals.

10. *Canadian Children's Literature.* CC Press, P.O. Box 335, Guelph, Ontario. NIH 6K5, Canada. Quarterly. $16.00.

    Literary analysis, criticism, and reviews of Canadian children's literature. A thematic approach for each issue. Predominantly written in English, but some articles are in French or French and English.

11. *Childhood Education.* Association for Childhood Education International. 3615 Wisconsin Ave., NW, Washington, DC 20016. Five times/year. $45.00.

    Includes a column on children's books that contains annotated reviews on about 25 books.

12. *Children's Literature in Education.* c/o Agathon Press, 111 8th Ave., New York, NY 10011. Quarterly. $32.00.

    Publishes longer articles on English and American children's literature including criticism, history, and biographical essays.

13. *Cricket Magazine.* Marianne Carus. Carus Corp., 315 Fifth St., Peru, IL 61354. Monthly. $22.50.

    A literary magazine for children of elementary school age. Includes new stories and poems by well-known children's authors as well as excerpts and serializations of older pieces of literature. Includes children's reviews of books, interviews with authors, and children's writing.

14. *Five Owls.* Five Owls, 2004 Sheridan Ave., S., Minneapolis, MN 55405. Bimonthly. $18.00.

    Each issue provides an article on a theme or topic and bibliographies that enhance or support it. Includes a signed review section.

15. *Horn Book Magazine.* Horn Book, Inc. 14 Beacon St., Boston, MA 02108. Bimonthly. $36.00.

    Includes detailed reviews of children's books judged by the editorial staff to be the best in children's literature. Contains articles about the literature, interviews with authors, and text of important speeches in the field of literature (Newbery and Caldecott Acceptance speeches are published in the August issue each year). October issue gives a list of the outstanding books of the previous year.

16. *Interracial Books for Children Bulletin.* Council on Interracial Books for Children, Inc. 1841 Broadway, New York, NY 10023. Eight times/year. $24.00.

    Articles and review focus on issues of racism, sexism, handicapism, and other issues in children's literature. Attempts to establish guidelines and criteria for evaluation of children's materials.

17. *Journal of Youth Services in Libraries.* Association for Library Services to Children and Young Adult Services Division, American Library Association, 50 E. Huron St., Chicago, IL 60611. Quarterly. $35.00.

    Formerly *Top of the News.* Provides articles on issues in children's literature and children's librarianship, international news, texts of speeches, and lists of upcoming events of interest in the field. Articles are often annotated bibliographies on subjects of current interest.

18. *Language Arts.* National Council of Teachers of English, 1111 Kenyon Rd., Urbana, IL 61801. Monthly, September to May. $40.00.

    "Books for Children" section features regular reviews of new books. Several issues focus on literature and reading, containing articles on authors, using literature in the classroom, and so on.

19. *The Lion and the Unicorn.* Department of English, Brooklyn College, Brooklyn, NY 11210. Annual. $7.95.

    Presents articles of literary criticism, book reviews, and interviews with authors of children's literature.

Each issue presents a particular theme or genre around which articles are centered.

20. *The New Advocate.* Christopher-Gordon, 480 Washington St., Norwood, MA 02062. Quarterly. $27.00.

   Includes articles about authors and illustrators, literary qualities, and classroom uses of children's literature as well as selected book reviews.

21. *The New York Times Book Review.* New York Times Co., 229 W. 43rd St., New York, NY 10036. Weekly. $26.00.

   Weekly column entitled "For Younger Readers" reviews a few children's books. Two issues in fall and spring are devoted to children's books exclusively. Before Christmas, a list of outstanding books is included.

22. *Perspectives.*Christopher-Gordon Publishers, Inc., 480 Washington St., Norwood, MA 02062. Five times/year. $24.95.

   Each issue contains around 100 reviews of current titles with teaching suggestions and related titles. Also includes columns on topics such as poetry, multicultural classrooms, writing, and reading aloud.

23. *Phaedrus: An International Annual of Children's Literature Research.* Fairleigh Dickinson University, 285 Madison Ave., Madison, NJ 07940. $32.00.

   Articles emphasize research and theoretical aspects of children's literature.

24. *Publisher's Weekly.* R. R. Bowker, 245 W. 17th St., New York, NY 10011. Weekly. $84.00.

   Twice a year, in spring and fall, a "Children's Book Number" is published that includes new titles from all major publishers, as well as reviews. Negative reviews are included. Does occasionally include feature articles on children's books and publishing for children.

25. *School Library Journal.* R. R. Bowker, Box 13706, Philadelphia, PA 19101. Monthly. $63.00.

   Reviews most children's books using as reviewers librarians, teachers, and critics from around the country. Includes both positive and negative reviews. Categorizes reviews by age levels. Also includes feature articles on children's literature, children's library services, technology, and nonprint materials. December issue includes a "Best Books" section.

26. *School Library Media Quarterly.* American Association of School Librarians. American Library Association, 50 E. Huron St., Chicago, IL 60611. Quarterly. $35.00.

   Official journal of AASL. Includes articles on book evaluations, censorship, library services, standards of service, and so on.

27. *Science Books and Films.* Amercian Association for the Advancement of Science. 1333 H St., NW, Washington, DC 20005. Quarterly. $28.00.

   Reviews trade, test, and reference books for students in all grades in both pure and applied sciences. Includes nonprint materials. Indicates level of expertise required to use a piece of material. Books are reviewed by specialists in the field.

28. *Science and Children,* National Science Teachers Association, 1201 16th St., NW, Washington, DC. Eight times/year. $37.00.

   Includes a monthly column that reviews books and nonprint materials.

29. *Signal: Approaches to Children's Books.* Thimble Press, Lockwood Station Road, South Woodchester, Glos. GL5 5EQ England. Three times/year. $14.50.

   Articles of criticism on history of children's literature and on theory and practice of classroom usage. Literature considered is largely British.

30. *The WEB: Wonderfully Exciting Books.* The Ohio State University, The Reading Center, 200 Ramseyer Hall, Columbus, OH 43210. Three times/year. $10.00

   Devoted to helping teachers incorporate children's literature into the curriculum through reviews that emphasize classroom use and through a "web of possibilities" for a major thematic area which is included in each issue. Reviews are written by practicing teachers and librarians.

31. *Wilson Library Bulletin.* The H. W. Wilson Co., 950 University Ave., Bronx, NY 10452. Monthly, September to June. $38.00.

   Includes discussions and reviews of all types of books and materials. Features a monthly column of reviews of children's books, plus articles about authors, a list of awards, and so on. The October issue is devoted to children's books.

APPENDIX C

Publishers' Addresses*

ABRAMS, 100 Fifth Avenue, New York, NY 10010.

ADDISON-WESLEY, 1 Jacob Way, Reading, MA 01867.

ALADDIN BOOKS, see Macmillan.

ARCADE PUBLISHING, 141 Fifth Avenue, New York, NY 10010.

ASTOR-HONOR, 48 East 43rd Street, New York, NY 10017.

ATHENEUM PUBLISHERS, see Macmillan.

ATLANTIC MONTHLY PRESS, 19 Union Square West, New York, NY 10013.

AVON BOOKS, 105 Madison Avenue, New York, NY 10016.

BANTAM BOOKS, 666 Fifth Avenue, New York, NY 10103.

BLACK BUTTERFLY CHILDREN'S BOOKS, see Writers and Readers Publishing.

BOYDS MILL PRESS, 910 Church Street, Honesdale, PA 18431.

BRADBURY PRESS, see Macmillan.

CAMELOT, see Avon.

CANDLEWICK PRESS, 2067 Massachusetts Avenue, Cambridge, MA 02140.

CAROLRHODA BOOKS, INC., 241 First Avenue North, Minneapolis, MN 55401.

CHILDREN'S BOOK PRESS, 1461 North Avenue, San Francisco, CA 94122.

CLARION BOOKS, 215 Park Avenue, New York, NY 10003.

COBBLEHILL BOOKS, see Dutton.

COLLIER, see Macmillan.

CREATIVE ARTS BOOKS, 833 Bancroft Way, Berkeley, CA 94710.

CRESTWOOD HOUSE, see Dutton.

THOMAS Y. CROWELL, see HarperCollins.

CROWN PUBLISHERS, 225 Park Avenue South, New York, NY 10003.

DELACORTE PRESS, 666 Fifth Avenue, New York, NY 10013.

DELL PUBLISHING, see Delacorte.

DIAL, see Penguin USA.

DISNEY PUBLICATIONS, 114 Fifth Avenue, New York, NY 10011.

DOUBLEDAY, 666 Fifth Avenue, New York, NY 10103.

DOVER PUBLICATIONS, INC., 180 Varick Street, New York, NY 10014.

DUTTON CHILDREN'S BOOKS, see Penguin USA.

FARRAR, STRAUS & GIROUX, INC., 19 Union Square West, New York, NY 10003.

FOUR WINDS PRESS, see Macmillan.

DAVID R. GODINE, PUBLISHERS, INC., 300 Massachusetts Avenue, Boston, MA 02115.

GOLDEN PRESS, see Western.

GREEN TIGER PRESS, 435 E. Carmel Street, San Marcos, CA 92069.

GREENWILLOW BOOKS, 1350 Avenue of the Americas, New York, NY 10019.

GROSSET & DUNLAP, INC., 200 Madison Avenue, New York, NY 10016.

GULLIVER BOOKS, see Harcourt Brace Jovanovich.

HARCOURT BRACE JOVANOVICH, INC., 1250 Sixth Avenue, San Diego, CA 92101.

HARPERCOLLINS CHILDREN'S BOOKS, 10 East 53rd Street, New York, NY 10022.

HARPER TROPHY PAPERBACKS, see HarperCollins.

HENRY HOLT AND COMPANY, INC., 115 West 18th Street, New York, NY 10011.

HOLIDAY HOUSE, 425 Madison Avenue, New York, NY 10017.

HOUGHTON MIFFLIN, 2 Park Street, Boston, MA 02108.

HYPERION BOOKS, see Little, Brown.

THE JEWISH PUBLICATION SOCIETY, 60 East 42nd Street, Suite 1339, New York, NY 10165.

JOY STREET BOOKS, see Little, Brown.

ALFRED A. KNOPF, 225 Park Avenue South, New York, NY 10003.

LERNER PUBLICATIONS COMPANY, 241 First Avenue North, Minneapolis, MN 55401.

LIPPINCOTT JUNIOR BOOKS, see HarperCollins.

LITTLE, BROWN & CO., 34 Beacon Street, Boston, MA 02108.

LODESTAR BOOKS, see Dutton.

LOTHROP, LEE & SHEPARD BOOKS, 1350 Avenue of the Americas, New York, NY 10019.

MARGARET K. McELDERRY BOOKS, see Macmillan.

MACMILLAN PUBLISHING CO., 866 Third Avenue, New York, NY 10022.

MORROW JUNIOR BOOKS, 1350 Avenue of the Americas, New York, NY 10019.

MULBERRY BOOKS, see Morrow.

NATIONAL GEOGRAPHIC PRESS, 1145 17th Street NW, Washington, DC 20036.

NORTH-SOUTH BOOKS, 1133 Broadway, Suite 1016, New York, NY 10010.

ORCHARD BOOKS, see Franklin Watts.

OXFORD UNIVERSITY PRESS, 200 Madison Avenue, New York, NY 10016.

PANTHEON, 201 East 50th Street, New York, NY 10022.

PARENTS MAGAZINE PRESS, 685 Third Avenue, New York, NY 10017.

PARNASSUS PRESS, see Houghton Mifflin.

PENGUIN USA, 375 Hudson Street, New York, NY 10014.

PHILOMEL BOOKS, see Putnam.

PICTURE BOOK STUDIO, 10 Central Street, Saxonville, MA 01701.

*Note: Publishers' addresses may change. For complete and up-to-date information, see the current edition of *Literary Market Place* or *Children's Books in Print*.

PLEASANT COMPANY, 8400 Fairway Place, P.O. Box 998, Middleton, WI 53562.

PRENTICE-HALL, 115 Columbus Circle, New York, NY 10023.

PUFFIN BOOKS, see Penguin USA.

G. P. PUTNAM'S SONS, 200 Madison Avenue, New York, NY 10016.

RAND MCNALLY, P.O. Box 7600, Chicago, IL 60680.

RANDOM HOUSE, 225 Park Avenue South, New York, NY 10003.

SCHOLASTIC INC., 730 Broadway, New York, NY 10003.

CHARLES SCRIBNER'S SONS, see Macmillan.

SIMON AND SCHUSTER BOOKS FOR YOUNG READERS, 1230 Avenue of the Americas, New York, NY 10020.

STEWARD, TABORI & CHANG, INC., 575 Broadway, New York, NY 10012.

TAMBOURINE BOOKS, see Morrow.

TROLL ASSOCIATES, 100 Corporate Drive, Mahwah, NJ 07430.

VIKING, see Penguin USA.

WALKER & CO., 720 Fifth Avenue, New York, NY 10019.

FREDERICK WARNE & CO., INC., see Penguin USA.

FRANKLIN WATTS, INC., 387 Park Avenue South, New York, NY 10016.

WESTERN PUBLISHING CO., INC., 8550 Third Avenue, New York, NY 10022.

WRITERS AND READERS PUBLISHING INC., P.O. Box 461, Village Station, New York, NY 10014.

PAPERBACK BOOK CLUB ADDRESSES

THE TRUMPET BOOK CLUBS
Bantam Doubleday Dell
666 Fifth Avenue
New York, NY 10103

THE SCHOLASTIC BOOK CLUBS
(Firefly—Preschool–K; See Saw—K–1; Lucky—Gr. 2–3; Arrow—Gr.4–6)
Scholastic, Inc.
730 Broadway
New York, NY 10003

THE TROLL BOOK CLUBS
Troll Associates, Inc.
100 Corporate Drive
Mahwah, NJ 07430

ACKNOWLEDGMENTS

FOR ILLUSTRATIONS ARRANGED BY PAGE NUMBER IN THE TEXT:

From *The Big Book for Peace*, edited by Ann Durell and Marilyn Sachs, copyright © 1990 by Dutton Children's Books. Illustration by Leo and Diane Dillon © 1989. Reprinted by permission of Leo and Diane Dillon. p. 10.

From *True Confessions of Charlotte Doyle* by Avi. Illustration © 1990 by Ruth E. Murray. Reprinted with permission of the publisher, Orchard Books, New York. p. 22.

Illustration from *Frog and Toad Are Friends* by Arnold Lobel. Copyright © 1970 by Arnold Lobel. Selection reprinted by permission of HarperCollins Publishers. p. 24.

From *Ramona and Her Father* by Beverly Cleary, illustrated by Alan Tiegreen. Copyright 1975, 1977 by Beverly Cleary. Reprinted by permission of William Morrow & Co., Inc./Publishers, New York. p. 25.

From *Winnie the Pooh* by A. A. Milne, illustrated by E. H. Shepard. Copyright 1926 by E. p. Dutton, renewed 1954 by A. A. Milne. Used by permission of Dutton Children's Books, a division of Penguin Books USA Inc. p. 25.

Illustration from *Little House in the Big Woods* by Laura Ingalls Wilder. Pictures copyright © 1953 by Garth Williams, renewed 1981 by Garth Williams. Selection reprinted by permission of HarperCollins Publishers. p. 26.

Title page illustration from *Jerusalem, Shining Still* by Karla Kuskin. Illustration copyright © 1987 by David Frampton. Selection reprinted by permission of HarperCollins Publishers. p. 31.

From *Ox-Cart Man* by Donald Hall, illustrated by Barbara Cooney. Copyright © 1979 by Barbara Cooney Porter for illustrations. Used by permission of Viking Penguin, a division of Penguin Books USA Inc. p. 37.

Illustration from *In the Night Kitchen* by Maurice Sendak. Copyright © 1970 by Maurice Sendak. Selection reprinted by permission of HarperCollins Publishers. p. 44.

From *Fish Is Fish* by Leo Lionni. Copyright © 1970 by Leo Lionni. Reprinted by permission of Pantheon Books, a division of Random House, Inc. p. 64.

From *Piggybook* by Anthony Browne. Copyright © 1986 by Anthony Browne. Reprinted by permission of Alfred A. Knopf, Inc. p. 68.

Illustration from *Let's Be Enemies* by Janice M. Udry. Illustrations copyright © 1961 by Maurice Sendak. Selection reprinted by permission by HarperCollins Publishers. p. 107.

From *Alice's Adventure in Wonderland* by Lewis Carroll, illustrated by Anthony Browne. Illustrations copyright © 1988 by Anthony Browne. Reprinted by permission of Alfred A. Knopf, Inc. p. 126.

From *Mother Goose*, illustrated by Arthur Rackham, published by Penguin USA. p. 129.

From *Joan of Arc* by Maurice Boutet de Monvel, English translation by Gerald Gottlieb. Copyright © 1980 by Gerald Gottlieb. Used by permission of Viking Penguin, a division of Penguin Books USA Inc. p. 132.

Illustration from *The Tale of Jemima Puddleduck* by Beatrix Potter. Copyright © 1908, 1987 by Frederick Warne & Co. Reprinted by permission of Frederick Warne & Co. p. 134.

Illustration by Wanda Gag from *Millions of Cats* by Wanda Gag, copyright 1928 by Coward-McCann, Inc., copyright renewed © 1956 by Robert Janssen. Reprinted by permission of Coward-McCann, Inc. p. 135.

Reprinted with permission of Charles Scribner's Sons, an imprint of Macmillan Publishing Company from *Stone Soup* written and illustrated by Marcia Brown. Copyright 1947 Marcia Brown, 1975 Marcia Brown. p. 140.

Illustration from *Stevie* by John Steptoe. Copyright © 1969 by John L. Steptoe. Selection reprinted by permission of HarperCollins Publishers. p. 150.

Illustration from *Toddlecreek Post Office* by Uri Shulevitz. Copyright © 1990 by Uri Shulevitz. Reproduced by permission of Farrar, Straus and Giroux, Inc. p. 240.

Illustrations from WHERE THE WILD THINGS ARE by Maurice Sendak. Copyright © 1963 by Maurice Sendak. Selection reprinted by permission of HarperCollins Publishers. p. 242.

From *Just Plain Fancy* by Patricia Polacco. Copyright © 1990 by Patricia Polacco. Used by permission of Bantam Books, a division of Bantam Doubleday Dell Publishing Group, Inc. p. 243.

Illustrations and text from *Black and White* by David Macaulay. Copyright © 1980 by David Macaulay. Reprinted by permission of Houghton Mifflin Company. All rights reserved. p. 244.

Illustration by Ashley Wolff reprinted by permission of G. P. Putnam's Sons from *A Year of Birds*, copyright © 1984 by Ashley Wolff. p. 245.

Where Does the Trail Lead? by Burton Albert, illustrated by Brian Pinkney. Illustration copyright © 1991 by Brian Pinkney. Reprinted by permission of the publisher, Simon & Schuster Books For Young Reader, New York, NY. p. 246.

From *The Snowy Day* by Ezra Jack Keats. Copyright © 1962 by Ezra Jack Keats, renewed © 1990 by Martin Pope. Used by permission of Viking Penguin, a division of Penguin Books USA Inc. p. 247.

From *The Ghost-Eye Tree* by Bill Martin, Jr. and John Archambault. Illustrations © 1988 by Ted Rand. Reprinted by permission of Henry Holt and Company, Inc. p. 248.

Illustration by Robert J. Blake reprinted by permission of Philomel Books from *Riptide* by Frances Ward Weller, illustrations copyright © 1990 by Robert J. Blake. p. 249.

Cover illustration from *Osa's Pride* by Ann Grifalconi. Copyright © 1990 by Ann Grifalconi. Reprinted by permission of Little, Brown and Company. p. 250.

Jumanji by Chris Van Allsburg. Copyright © 1981 by Chris Van Allsburg. Reprinted by permission of Houghton Mifflin Company. All rights reserved. p. 250.

Illustration from *The Napping House*, text copyright © 1984 by Audrey Wood, illustrations copyright © 1984 by Don Wood, reproduced by permission of Harcourt Brace Jovanovich, Inc. p. 253.

Illustration by John Schoenherr reprinted by permission of Philomel Books from *Owl Moon* by Jane Yolen, illustrations copyright © 1987 by John Schoenherr. p. 253.

Illustration from *The Big Concrete Lorry* by Shirley Hughes. Copyright © 1989 by Shirley Hughes. Reprinted by permission of Lothrop, Lee & Shepard Books, a division of William Morrow & Co., Inc. *The Big Concrete Lorry* © 1989 Shirley Hughes. Published in the UK by Walker Books Limited. p. 254.

Illustration from *Say It* by Charlotte Zolotow, illustrated by James Stevenson. Text copyright © 1980 by Charlotte Zolotow. Illustration copyright © 1980 by James Stevenson. Reprinted by permission of Greenwillow Books, a division of William Morrow & Company, Inc. p. 255.

Illustration from *A Chair for My Mother* by Vera Williams. Copyright © 1982 by Vera B. Williams. Reprinted by permission of Greenwillow Books, a division of William Morrow & Company, Inc. p. 255.

Illustration from *Wilfrid Gordon McDonald Partridge*. Illustrations copyright © 1984 Julie Vivas. Reprinted by permission of Kane/Miller Book Publishers and Omnibus Books. p. 256.

From *Changes* by Anthony Browne. Copyright © 1990 by Anthony Browne. Reprinted by permission of Alfred A. Knopf, Inc. *Changes* © 1990 Anthony Browne. Published in the UK by Walker Books Limited. p. 257.

Illustration from *The Chalk Doll* by Charlotte Pomerantz. Illustrations copyright © 1989 by Frané Lessac. Selection reprinted by permission of HarperCollins Publishers. p. 258.

Excerpt and illustration from *The Three Billy Goats Gruff* by P. C. Asbjørnsen and J. E. Moe, illustrations copyright © 1957 and renewed 1985 by Marcia Brown, reproduced by permission of Harcourt Brace Jovanovich, Inc. p. 317.

From *Strega Nona* by Tomie de Paola. Copyright © 1975. Used by permission of the publisher, Prentice Hall, a Division of Simon and Schuster, Englewood Cliffs, NJ. p. 322.

Illustration from *Princess Furball* by Charlotte Huck, illustrated by Anita Lobel. Text copyright © 1989 by Charlotte Huck. Illustrations copyright © 1989 by Anita Lobel. Reprinted by permission of Greenwillow Books, a division of William Morrow & Co., Inc. p. 332.

Illustration by Ed Young reprinted by permission of Philomel Books from *Yeh-Shen: A Cinderella Story from China* by Ai-Ling Louie, illustrations copyright © 1982 by Ed Young. p. 332.

Illustration by Fred Marcellino from *Puss in Boots* by Charles Perrault. Copyright © 1990 by Fred Marcellino. Reproduced by permission of Farrar, Straus and Giroux, Inc. p. 336.

Illustration from *The Mitten*, text and illustrations copyright © 1989 by Jan Brett. Reprinted by permission of G. P. Putnam's Sons. p. 338.

Illustration by Ed Young reprinted by permission of Philomel Books from *Lon Po Po: A Red-Riding Hood Story from China*, copyright © 1989 by Ed Young. p. 342.

Illustration from *Mufaro's Beautiful Daughters* by John Steptoe. Copyright © 1987 by John Steptoe. Reprinted by permission of Lothrop, Lee & Shepard Books, a division of William Morrow & Company, Inc., with the approval of the Estate of John Steptoe. p. 347.

From *Iktomi and the Ducks*. Copyright © 1990 by Paul Goble. Reprinted with permission of the publisher, Orchard Books. p. 352.

Illustration from *Jump! The Adventures of Brer Rabbit* by Van Dyke Parks and Malcolm Jones, illustrated by Barry Moser, text copyright © 1986 by Van Dyke Parks and Malcolm Jones, illustrations copyright © 1986 by Pennyroyal Press, reproduced by permission of Harcourt Brace Jovanovich, Inc. p. 357.

From *The Talking Eggs* by Robert D. San Souci, pictures by Jerry Pinkney. Copyright © 1989 by Jerry Pinkney for pictures. Used by permission of Dial Books for Young Readers, a division of Penguin Books USA Inc. p. 358.

Illustration from *The Legend of Johnny Appleseed* by Reeve Lindbergh, with paintings by Kathy Jakobsen. Illustrations copyright © 1990 by Kathy Jakobsen. Reprinted by permission of Little, Brown and Company. p. 361.

Reprinted with permission of Macmillan Publishing Company from *Doctor Coyote* by John Bierhorst. Illustrations by Wendy Watson. Illustrations copyright © 1987 Wendy Watson. p. 364.

Illustration from *The Arrow and the Lamp: The Story of Psyche* retold by Margaret Hodges, with illustrations by Donna Diamond. Text Copyright © 1989 by Margaret Hodges. Illustrations copyright © 1989 by Donna Diamond. Reprinted by permission of Little, Brown and Company. p. 368.

Illustration from *Saint George and the Dragon* retold by Margaret Hodges with illustrations by Trina Schart Hyman. Illustrations copyright © 1984 by Trina Schart Hyman. Reprinted by permission of Little, Brown and Company. p. 374.

Illustration copyright © 1987 by Charles Mikolaycak. All rights reserved. Reprinted from *Exodus* by Miriam Chaikin by permission of Holiday House. p. 377.

Illustration by Alan Lee, from *Merlin Dreams* by Peter Dickinson. Copyright © 1988 by Peter Dickinson, illustration copyright © 1988 by Alan Lee. Used by permission of Dell Books, a division of Bantam Doubleday Dell Publishing Group, Inc. and Victor Gollancz Ltd. p. 396.

Illustration from *Dove Isabeau*, text copyright © 1989 by Jane Yolen, illustrations copyright © 1989 by Dennis Nolan, reproduced by permission of Harcourt Brace Jovanovich, Inc. p. 399.

Illustration from *Charlotte's Web* by E. B. White. Illustrations copyright renewed © 1980 by Garth Williams. Selection reprinted by permission of HarperCollins Publishers. p. 403.

Jacket illustration by Troy Howell, reprinted by permission of Philomel Books from *Mossflower* by Brian Jacques, jacket illustration copyright © 1988 by Troy Howell. p. 407.

Illustration from *The Borrowers* by Mary Norton, illustrated by Beth and Joe Krush, copyright 1953 by Mary Norton and renewed 1981 by Mary Norton, Beth Krush, and Joe Krush, reproduced by permission of Harcourt Brace Jovanovich, Inc. p. 413.

From *Knights of the Kitchen Table* by Jon Scieszka, illustrated by Lane Smith. Copyright © 1991 by Lane Smith for illustrations. Used by permission of Viking Penguin, a division of Penguin Books USA Inc. p. 415.

Illustration from *The Midnight Horse* by Sid Fleischman, illustrated by Peter Sis. Text copyright Sid Fleischman, Inc. Illustrations copyright © 1990 by Peter Sis. Reprinted by permission of Greenwillow Books, a division of William Morrow & Company, Inc. p. 417.

Illustration from *Tam Lin*, text copyright © 1990 by Jane Yolen, illustrations copyright © 1990 by Charles Mikolaycak, reproduced by permission of Harcourt Brace Jovanovich, Inc. p. 418.

Jacket illustration, copyright © 1982 by Leo and Diane Dillon. Reprinted by permission of Philomel Books from *Sweet Whispers, Brother Rush* by Virginia Hamilton. p. 421.

A Wizard of Earthsea by Ursula K. LeGuin. Illustrations copyright © 1968 by Ruth Robbins. Text copyright © 1968 by the Inter-Vivos Trust for the LeGuin Children. Reprinted by permission of Houghton Mifflin Company. All rights reserved. p. 434.

Illustration by Lloyd Bloom from *The Green Book* by Jill Paton Walsh. Copyright © 1982 by Lloyd Bloom. Reproduced by permission of Farrar, Straus and Giroux, Inc. p. 436.

From *A Handful of Time* by Kathleen Pearson. Cover illustration by Laura Fernandez copyright © 1987. Reprinted by permission of Laura Fernandez. p. 424.

"Rope Rhyme" illustration from *Honey, I Love* by Eloise Greenfield, illustrated by Diane and Leo Dillon. Illustrations copyright © 1978 by Diane and Leo Dillon. Selection reprinted by permission of HarperCollins Publishers. p. 456.

Illustration from "Galoshes," copyright © 1988 by Marcia Brown. Reprinted from *Sing a Song of Popcorn*, by permission of Scholastic, Inc. p. 457.

"Woodpecker" illustration by Ted Lewin reprinted by permission of Philomel Books from *Bird Watch* by Jane Yolen, illustrations copyright © 1990 by Ted Lewin. p. 459.

Illustration from *Sierra* by Diane Siebert. Illustrations copyright © 1991 by Wendell Minor. Selection reprinted by permission of HarperCollins Publishers. p. 461.

Positive and negative ink illustrations by Charles Keeping for *The Highwayman* by Alfred Noyes. Illustrations copyright © 1981 by Charles Keeping. Reproduced by permission of Oxford University Press. p. 466.

From *In a Spring Garden* by Richard Lewis, editor, pictures by Ezra Jack Keats. Copyright © 1965 by Ezra Jack Keats for pictures. Used by permission of Dial Books for Young Readers, a division of Penguin Books USA Inc. p. 468.

From *A Hippopotamusn't* by J. Patrick Lewis, pictures by Victoria Chess. Copyright © 1990 by Victoria Chess for pictures. Used by permission of Dial Books for Young Readers, a divison of Penguin Books USA Inc. p. 471.

Cover illustration from *Something Big Has Been Here* by Jack Prelutsky, illustrated by James Stevenson. Copyright © 1990 by James Stevenson. Reprinted by permission of Greenwillow Books, a division of William Morrow & Company, Inc. p. 472.

Illustration by Ted Rand reprinted by permission of G. P. Putnam's Sons, from *My Shadow* by Robert Louis Stevenson, illustrations copyright © 1990 by Ted Rand. p. 473.

"How Elegant the Elephant" illustration from *A Fine Fat Pig and Other Animal Poems* by Mary Ann Hoberman. Art copyright © 1991 by Malcah Zeldis. Selection reprinted by permission of HarperCollins Publishers. p. 475.

Illustration from *Black Is Brown Is Tan* by Arnold Adoff. Copyright © 1973 by Emily Arnold McCully. Selection reprinted by permission of HarperCollins Publishers. p. 477.

From *Turtle in July*. Illustration by Jerry Pinkney. Reprinted with permission of Macmillan Publishing Company from *Turtle in July* by Marilyn Singer. Illustrations copyright © 1989 by Jerry Pinkney. p. 479.

Illustration by Tomie de Paola reprinted by permission of G. P. Putnam's Sons from *Tomie de Paola's Book of Poems*, illustrations copyright © 1988 by Tomie de Paola. p. 482.

Illustration by Ed Young reprinted by permission of Philomel Books from *Cats Are Cats* by Nancy Larrick, illustrations copyright © 1988 by Ed Young. p. 486.

Illustration copyright © 1989 by Stephen Gammell. All rights reserved. Reprinted from *Dancing Teepees: Poems of American Indian Youth*, edited by Virginia Driving Hawk Sneve, by permission of Holiday House. p. 493.

From *The Most Beautiful Place in the World* by Ann Cameron, illustrated by Thomas B. Allen. Illustrations copyright © 1988 by Thomas B. Allen. Reprinted by permission of Alfred A. Knopf, Inc. p. 529.

From *The Stories Julian Tells* by Ann Cameron, illustrated by Ann Strugnell. Illustrations copyright © 1981 by Ann Strugnell. Reprinted by permission of Alfred A. Knopf, Inc. p. 534.

Cover illustration by Diane de Groat from *Anastasia at This Address* by Lois Lowry. Copyright © 1991 by Lois Lowry. Reprinted by permission of Houghton Mifflin Company. All rights reserved. p. 535.

Cover illustration from *My Daniel* by Pam Conrad, cover art by Darryl S. Zudek. Jacket copyright © 1989 by Darryl S. Zudek. Selection reprinted by permission of HarperCollins Publishers. p. 538.

Jacket art, copyright © 1990 by Jerry Pinkney. Reprinted by permission of Philomel Books from *Cousins* by Virginia Hamilton. p. 539.

Cover illustration and text from *The Pinballs* by Betsy Byars. Copyright © 1977 by Betsy Byars. Selection reprinted by permission of HarperCollins Publishers. p. 542.

Illustration by Donna Diamond from *Bridge to Terabithia* by Katherine Paterson. Copyright © 1977 by Katherine Paterson. Selection reprinted by permission of HarperCollins Publishers. p. 546.

Illustration from *Julie of the Wolves* by Jean Craighead George. Illustrations copyright © 1972 by John Schoenherr. Selection reprinted by permission of HarperCollins Publishers. p. 554.

Frozen Fire by James Houston. Reprinted with permission of Margaret K. McElderry Books, an imprint of Macmillan Publishing Company from *Frozen Fire* written and illustrated by James Houston. Copyright © 1977 James Houston. *Frozen Fire: A Tale of Courage*, by James Houston, A Margaret K. McElderry Book, Atheneum, © 1977. p. 555.

Jacket art, copyright © 1990 by Stephen Marchesi. Reprinted by permission of Philomel Books from *Risk 'n Roses* by Jan Slepian. p. 560.

Saying Good-bye to Grandma by Jane Resh Thomas. Illustrations copyright © 1988 by Marcia Sewall. Reprinted by permission of Clarion Books, a Houghton Mifflin Company imprint. All rights reserved. p. 564.

Illustration from *Journey to Jo'Burg* by Beverley Naidoo. Illustration copyright © 1986 by Eric Velasquez. Selection reprinted by permission of HarperCollins Publishers. p. 574.

Illustration from *Stone Fox* by John Reynolds Gardiner. Illustrations copyright © 1980 by Marcia Sewall. Selection reprinted by permission of HarperCollins Publishers. p. 582.

Illustration from *Ramona Quimby Age 8* by Beverly Cleary illustrated by Alan Tiegreen. Copyright © 1981 by Beverly Cleary. Reprinted by permission of Morrow Junior Books, a division of William Morrow & Company, Inc. p. 585.

From *Hattie and the Wild Waves* by Barbara Cooney. Copyright © 1990 by Barbara Cooney. Used by permission of Viking Penguin, a division of Penguin Books USA Inc. p. 600.

From *Lyddie* by Katherine Paterson, jacket illustration by Debbi Chabrian. Copyright © 1991 by Katherine Paterson. Used by permission of Lodestar Books, an affiliate of Dutton Children's Books, a division of Penguin USA Inc. p. 604.

Text and illustration from page 27 of *How a Book Is Made* by Aliki. Copyright © 1986 by Aliki Brandenberg. Selection reprinted by permission of HarperCollins Publishers. p. 677.

From *A Country Far Away*. Text copyright © 1988 by Nigel Gray. Illustration copyright © 1988 by Philippe Dupasquier. Reprinted with permission of the publisher, Orchard Books. p. 680.

Illustration from *Great Northern Diver: The Loon* by Barbara Juster Esbensen, with illustrations by Mary Barrett Brown. Text copyright © 1990 by Barbara Juster Esbensen. Illustrations copyright © 1990 by Mary Barrett Brown. Reprinted by permission of Little, Brown and Company. p. 683.

Photograph from *Immigrant Kids* by Russell Freedman. Reprinted courtesy of the National Park Service. p. 685.

From *Painting Faces* by Suzanne Haldane. Copyright © 1988 by Suzanne Haldane. Used by permission of Dutton Children's Books, a division of Penguin Books USA Inc. p. 687.

Reprinted with permission of Macmillan Publishing Company from *The Milk Makers* by Gail Gibbons. Copyright © 1985 Gail Gibbons. p. 689.

Reprinted with permission of Atheneum Publishers, an imprint of Macmillan Publishing Company from *Cows in the Parlor* by Cynthia McFarland. Photographs copyright © 1990 Cynthia McFarland. p. 689.

Reprinted with permission of Bradbury Press, an affiliate of Macmillan, Inc. from *Illuminations* by Jonathan Hunt. Copyright © 1989 Jonathan Hunt. p. 691.

Illustration (end papers) from *Henny Penny* by Stephen Butler. Copyright © 1991 by Stephen Butler. Reprinted by permission of Tambourine Books, a division of William Morrow & Company, Inc. p. 774.

Boot Cafe postcard and reverse side of Boot Cafe postcard from *Stringbean's Trip to the Shining Sea* by Vera B. Williams, illustrated by Jennifer Williams and Vera B. Williams. Copyright © 1988 by Vera B. Williams and Jennifer Williams. Reprinted by permission of Greenwillow Books, a division of William Morrow & Company, Inc. p. 805.

FOR POETRY ARRANGED BY PAGE NUMBER IN THE TEXT:

Excerpt from *Dragon Kites and Dragonflies*, copyright © 1986 by Demi, reprinted by permission of Harcourt Brace Jovanovich, Inc. p. 191.

Excerpt from *Alison's Zinnias* by Anita Lobel. Copyright © 1990 by Anita Lobel. By permission of Greenwillow Books, a division of William Morrow & Company, Inc. p. 197.

From *Johnny Appleseed* by Reeve Lindbergh. Copyright 1990 by Reeve Lindbergh. By permission of Little, Brown and Company. p. 359.

Excerpt from "Poetry" from Eleanor Farejon's *Poems for Children*. Originally appeared in *Sing for Your Supper*. Copyright © 1938 by Eleanor Farejon, renewed 1966 by Gervase Farejon. Reprinted by permission of HarperCollins Publishers. p. 452.

Excerpt from "I, Says the Poem" is from *A Sky Full of Poems*. Copyright © 1964, 1970, 1973 by Eve Merriam. Reprinted by permission of Marian Reiner for the author. p. 452.

"Cat Kisses" by Bobbie Katz from *Tomie de Paola's Book of Poems* edited by Tomie de Paola. Copyright © 1974 by Bobbi Katz. Used with permission of Bobbie Katz. p. 453.

"Satellite, Satellite" from *Jamboree: Rhymes for All Times*. Copyright © 1962, 1964, 1966, 1973, 1984 by Eve Merriam. All rights reserved. Reprinted by permission of Marian Reiner for the author. p. 453.

"My Key" by Elizabeth A. Smith from *Through Our Eyes* by Lee Bennett Hopkins. Reprinted by permission of Elizabeth A. Smith. p. 454.

"In the Middle" by Myra Cohn Livingston. Reprinted with permission of Margaret K. McElderry Books, an imprint of Macmillan Publishing Company from *There Was a Place and Other Poems* by Myra Cohn Livingston. Copyright © 1988 by Myra Cohn Livingston. p. 454.

"Hello and Goodby" from *Yellow Butter Purple Jelly Red Jam Black Bread*. Reprinted by permission of Gina Macoby Literary Agency. Copyright © 1981 by Mary Ann Hoberman. p. 455.

"Wind Song" from *I Feel the Same Way* by Lilian Moore. Copyright © 1967 by Lilian Moore. Reprinted by permission of Marian Reiner for the author. p. 455.

"Rope Rhyme" from *Honey, I Love* by Eloise Greenfield. Text copyright © 1978 by Eloise Greenfield. Selection reprinted by permission of HarperCollins Publishers. p. 456.

"Galoshes," from *Stories to Begin On* by Rhoda W. Bacmeister. Copyright 1940 by E. P. Dutton, renewed © 1968 by Rhoda W. Bacmeister. Used by permission of Dutton's Children's Books, a division of Penguin Books USA Inc. p. 457.

"The Pickety Fence" from *One at a Time* by David McCord. Copyright 1929, 1952, 1961, 1962 by David McCord. By permission of Little, Brown and Company. p. 457.

"First Snow" by Marie Louise Allen from *Surprises* by Lee Bennett Hopkins. Text copyright © 1984 by Lee Bennett Hopkins. Reprinted by permission of HarperCollins Publishers. p. 458.

"Woodpecker" by Jane Yolen reprinted by permission of Philomel Books from *Birdwatch* by Jane Yolen, text copyright © 1990 by Jane Yolen. p. 459.

Lines from "Mud" by Polly Chase Boyden from *Child Life Magazine*. Copyright 1930, 1958 by Rand McNally & Co.

"Peach" from *Knock at a Star: A Child's Introduction to Poetry* by X. J. Kennedy and Dorothy M. Kennedy. Published by Little, Brown and Company, 1982. p. 459.

"Flying Uptown Backwards" from *The Forgetful Wishing Well*. Reprinted with permission of Margaret K. McElderry Books, an imprint of Macmillan Publishing Company from *The Forgetful Wishing Well* by X. J. Kennedy. Copyright © 1985 by X. J. Kennedy. p. 460.

"library" from *Small Poems Again* by Valerie Worth. Copyright © 1975, 1986 by Valerie Worth. Reprinted by permission of Farrar, Straus & Giroux, Inc. p. 460.

"Steam Shovel" from *Upper Pastures: Poems* by Charles Malam. Copyright 1930, © 1958 by Charles Malam. Reprinted by permission of Henry Holt and Company, Inc. p. 461.

"Sierra" from *Sierra* by Diane Siebert. Text copyright © 1991 by Diane Siebert. Reprinted by permission of HarperCollins Publishers. p. 461.

"Fueled" from *Serve Me a Slice of Moon*, copyright © 1965 by Marcie Hans, reprinted by permission of Harcourt Brace Jovanovich, Inc. p. 462.

"The Sidewalk Racer or, On the Skateboard" from *The Sidewalk Racer and Other Poems of Sports and Motion* by Lillian Morrison. Copyright © 1965, 1967, 1968, 1977 by Lillian Morrison. Reprinted by permission of Marian Reiner for the author. p. 462.

"Listening to Grown Ups Quarreling" from *The Marriage Wig*, copyright © 1968 by Ruth Whitman, reprinted by permission of Harcourt Brace Jovanovich, Inc. p. 462.

"Windy Nights" by Robert Louis Stevenson from *Sing a Song of Popcorn*, edited by Beatrice Schenk de Regniers, et al. p. 465.

"I'm a Lean Dog, Keen Dog" from *Song to Save a Soul* by Irene Rutherford McLeod. Copyright 1915 by Chatto & Windus. Used by permission of Viking Penguin, a division of Penguin Books, USA Inc. p. 466.

"Write Me a Verse" from *One at a Time* by David McCord. Copyright 1929, 1952, 1961, 1962 by David McCord. *First appeared in *The Saturday Review*. By permission of Little, Brown and Company. p. 466.

Pig limericks from *The Book of Pigericks* by Arnold Lobel. Copyright © 1983 by Arnold Lobel. Reprinted by permission of HarperCollins Publishers. p. 466.

"chairs" from *Small Poems* by Valerie Worth. Copyright © 1972 by Valerie Worth. Reprinted by permission of Farrar, Straus & Giroux, Inc. p. 467.

"An Old Silent Pond" from *Cricket Songs: Japanese Haiku* translated by Harry Behn. © 1964 by Harry Behn. All rights reserved. Reprinted by permission of Marian Reiner. p. 467.

"Windshield Wiper" from *Out Loud*. Copyright © 1973 by Eve Merriam. All rights reserved by Eve Merriam. Reprinted by permission of Marian Reiner for the author. p. 468.

"Tom Tigercat" by J. Patrick Lewis, from *A Hippopotamusn't* by J. Patrick Lewis. Copyright © 1987, 1990 by J. Patrick Lewis. Used by permission of Dial Books for Young Readers, a division of Penguin Books USA Inc. p. 471.

"See I Can Do It" by Dorothy Aldis. Reprinted by permission of The Putnam Publishing Group from *All Together* by Dorothy Aldis. Copyright © 1925 by Dorothy Aldis. p. 474.

"How Elegant the Elephant" from *A Fine Fat Pig and Other Poems* by Mary Ann Hoberman. Text copyright © 1991 by Mary Ann Hoberman. Reprinted by permission of HarperCollins Publishers. p. 475.

Excerpt from "Quarter Past Seven" from *Dogs & Dragons, Trees & Dreams: A Collection of Poems* by Karla Kuskin. Copyright © 1980 by Karla Kuskin. Reprinted by permission of HarperCollins Publishers. p. 475.

"The Question" from *Dogs & Dragons, Trees & Dreams: A Collection of Poems* by Karla Kuskin. Copyright © 1980 by Karla Kuskin. Reprinted by permission of HarperCollins Publishers. p. 475.

Text of "Black is brown is tan" from *Black Is Brown Is Tan* by Arnold Adoff. Reprinted by permission of HarperCollins Publishers. p. 476.

"Pussy Willows" by Aileen Fisher from *Read Aloud Rhymes for the Very Young*. Reprinted by permission of author. p. 478.

"Turtle in July" reprinted with permission of Macmillan Publishing Company from *Turtle in July* by Marilyn Singer. Copyright © 1989 by Marilyn Singer. pp. 478–479.

"This Is My Rock" from *One at a Time* by David McCord. Copyright 1929, 1952, 1961, 1962 by David McCord. *First appeared in the *The Saturday Review*. By permission of Little, Brown and Company. p. 480.

"Secret Door" by Myra Cohn Livingston from *Worlds I Know and Other Poems*. Reprinted with permission of Margaret K. McElderry Books, an imprint of Macmillan Publishing Company from *Worlds I Know and Other Poems* by Myra Cohn Livingston. Copyright © 1985 by Myra Cohn Livingston. pp. 480–481.

Excerpted from "Alligator on the Escalator" in *Catch a Little Rhyme* by Eve Merriam. Copyright © 1966 by Eve Merriam. Reprinted by permission of Marian Reiner for the author. p. 482.

"Farewell My Younger Brother" reproduced by permission of the Smithsonian Institution Press from page 24 of *Fifth Annual Report of the Bureau of American Ethnology 1883-1884*. p. 493.

"After English Class" from *Hey World, Here I Am*. Copyright © 1986 by Jean Little. Reprinted by permission of Kids Can Press Ltd., Toronto, Canada. Available in the U.S. from HarperCollins Publishers. pp. 497–498.

Line from "Spring" by Marjorie Frost Fraser. Reprinted by permission of the author. p. 505.

"Things" from *Honey, I Love* by Eloise Greenfield. Copyright © 1978 by Eloise Greenfield. Reprinted by permission of HarperCollins Publishers. p. 507.

"the drum" from *Spin a Soft Black Song* by Nikki Giovanni. Copyright © 1971 by Nikki Giovanni. Reprinted by permission of Farrar, Straus & Giroux, Inc. p. 508.

Reprinted with permission from Amy A. McLure with Peggy Harrison and Sheryl Reed: *Sunrises and Songs: Reading and Writing Poetry in an Elementary Classroom* (Heinemann Educational Books, Inc., Portsmouth, NH, 1990). pp. 508–509.

"Street Song" from *The Way Things Are and Other Poems* by Myra Cohn Livingston. Copyright © 1974 by Myra Cohn Livingston. Reprinted by permission of Marian Reiner for the author. p. 515.

"The Grobbles" from *The Snopp on the Sidewalk and Other Poems*. by Jack Prelutsky. Copyright © 1986, 1977 by Jack Prelutsky. By permission of Greenwillow Books, a division of William Morrow & Company, Inc., New York. pp. 515–516.

"Water Striders" from *Joyful Noise* by Paul Fleischmann. Copyright © 1988 by Paul Fleischmann. Reprinted by permission of HarperCollins Publishers. p. 516.

From *Winter Whale* by Joanne Ryder. Copyright 1991 by Joanne Ryder. By permission of Morrow Junior Books, a division of William Morrow & Company, Inc., New York. pp. 671–672.

SUBJECT INDEX

AUTHOR, ILLUSTRATOR, TITLE INDEX